# BRITISH HISTORY
## 1945–1987

**For Robert**

*Multas per gentes et multa per aequora uectus*
*advenio has miseras, frater, ad inferias,*
*ut te postremo donarem munere mortis*
*et mutam necquiquam alloquerer cinerem.*
*quandoquidem fortuna mihi tete abstulit ipsum,*
*heu miser indigne frater adempte mihi,*
*nunc tamen interea haec, prisco quae more parentum*
*tradita sunt tristi munere ad inferias,*
*accipe fraterno multum manantia fletu,*
*atque in perpetuum, frater aue atque uale.*

# BRITISH HISTORY
# 1945–1987

## An Annotated Bibliography

PETER CATTERALL

Published for the
Institute of Contemporary British History
by Basil Blackwell

Copyright © Institute of Contemporary British History, 1990

First published 1990
First published in USA 1991

Basil Blackwell Ltd
108 Cowley Road, Oxford OX4 1JF, UK

Basil Blackwell, Inc.
3 Cambridge Center
Cambridge, Massachusetts 02142, USA

*British Library Cataloguing in Publication Data*

Catterall, Peter
  British history 1945–1987: an annotated bibliography.
  1. Great Britain. 1901– —Bibliographies
  I. Title
  016.941085

  ISBN 0–631–17049–9

*Library of Congress Cataloging in Publication Data*

Catterall, Peter, 1961–
  British history, 1945–1987: an annotated bibliography / Peter Catterall.
    880 p.
  "First published 1990"—T.p. verso.
  Includes index.
  ISBN 0–631–17049–9 (hardback)
  1. Great Britain—History—1945– —Bibliography. I. Title.
Z2020.3.C37  1991
[DA592]
016.941085—dc20                    90–44366
                                          CIP

Typeset in 8/9pt Times by Institute of Contemporary British History
Printed in Great Britain by Alden Press, Oxford

# PREFACE

My thoughts on the literature on post-war Britain have already been distilled into an an article referenced elsewhere in this work (see entry 62). My aim here therefore is not to discuss the themes, debates and quality of this literature, or to draw attention to those areas which have been relatively neglected, but to set forth methods of researching it and organizing it into this bibliography.

It might be assumed, in view of the considerable reluctance to teach the history of post-war Britain that remains in schools and universities, that the literature on the period is limited and inadequate. The objective in researching this bibliography, as well as demonstrating the areas where further research is required, has been to establish the range and quality of the material available. In the process the bibliography provides that essential teaching tool, a detailed guide to the literature. If this helps to encourage the teaching of recent British history and thus to provide a greater general awareness of the roots of the concerns, policies, and political, economic and social characteristics of contemporary Britain then it will have made a considerable contribution to furthering the mission of the Institute of Contemporary British History.

As the following pages demonstrate there is an abundance of work which can be used as the basis for teaching material. I am still prepared to concede that the number of reasonable historical, as opposed to political science, textbooks on the post-war period remains limited, though I am aware that a number of significant new studies will shortly be appearing or are already in press. However, of the material on which good historical studies and reassessments of the post-war period could be based there is no lack.

Historians have perhaps only in recent years began to pay serious attention to the post-war years, partly in response to the steady accumulation of accessible material for the early part of the period in the Public Record Office under the thirty year rule. However, much work of merit has already been done by their colleagues in other academic departments. The detailed case studies of village and town life and communities that were a feature of sociological endeavour in the early post-war years will, for instance, retain their value as source material. In fact there is a great range of books which help to illuminate some aspect of post-war history or are of some use as sources for students of this period; as the bibliographer learns only too well as he contemplates the daunting task of trying to produce as near a comprehensive bibliography as possible. In some fields this is a prohibitively extensive task. For instance, there are so many individual histories of institutions such as schools, hospitals or churches that it has been impossible to attempt to note all these in the bibliography.

There have also been a large and growing number of articles and theses on all aspects of post-war British history. The expansion of higher education over the period, the proliferation of academic departments concerned with politics, social administration, industrial relations or other specialized subjects, and the accompanying rise in the number of academic journals of all types, including historical, have all played a part in this process. One of the tasks of this bibliography is to draw the attention of the historian and the more general reader to the many articles of interest which have appeared in the growing number of specialist academic journals which have flourished since the Second World War, and which might otherwise easily be overlooked by researchers. Where appropriate I have also noted official publications, serial publications, oral archives, specialist bibliographies and databases.

The classification of the literature for the purposes of this bibliography has been, in a few places, constrained by a dearth of material. Whereas for some subjects the literature has been so rich and varied as to require a considerable number of sub-categories, in others it has been necessary to lump together works under more general headings. At these points I have tried to draw attention to gaps in the literature on post-war British history. These gaps have meant that it has not everywhere been possible to provide a rough guide to developments in post-war Britain through the accumulation of policy, as presented in official publications, and through their treatment in the secondary literature. Generally, however, I have been able, in classifying the material, to cover and reflect as far as possible the themes, issues and characteristics of the period.

In doing so I have retained separate classifications for Scotland, Wales and Northern Ireland. This is not the result of any particular animosity towards the union. It is in part because it seemed appropriate to retain this feature of the method of classification for material on British history of earlier periods used in the Royal Historical Society's bibliographical series which has served, to some extent, as a model for this work. More importantly it seemed expedient in the light of the fact that there is a substantial literature which refers specifically to Wales, Scotland or Northern Ireland. It would be artificial not to reflect this in the classification of the material. I have followed this rule not only for the literature on subjects such as sectarian conflict in Northern Ireland, but also for biographies, autobiographies and memoirs. The main exceptions to the rule are in the fields of political, military, colonial and diplomatic biographies. Thus, for instance, whereas biographies of Scottish sportsmen, artists, literary figures and scientists have been placed in the section on Scotland, I have deemed it more appropriate to put all the biographies of politicians active in the major parties, military commanders, colonial and diplomatic officials, whatever their national origin, in consolidated sections. Nationalist and (in Northern Ireland) Unionist politicians however are covered in their respective national sections under the relevant category on Plaid Cmyru, the Scottish Nationalist Party, the Ulster Unionists or the SDLP.

The only other exception to this rule is that nationalism, where it has been examined as a general feature of British politics or as a problem for the British state, rather than specifically in the context of the particular strains found in Scotland, Wales and Ireland or elsewhere, has been dealt with in the Political History section under the heading Nationalism and Devolution [273–81].

The bibliography includes a large amount of material on nationalism in the colonial empire in the post-war years as well as on nationalism in the British Isles. The aim in this section on the empire and the Commonwealth has been to provide an extensive guide to the nature of the literature on the demission of power, both generally and area by area, and, where appropriate, on the continuation of Commonwealth relations. The section is therefore selective in the sense that it concentrates on material which reflects on British policy or in some other way is relevant to the study of British history, leaving out material which deals exclusively with the domestic circumstances of the countries concerned. Accordingly recent books on Australian or New Zealand foreign policy which incorporate some reflections on continuing relations with Britain are included below. Those which do not have a British dimension have been left out. This also explains the pattern of selection of Commonwealth and colonial biographies and memoirs. It has been considered relevant to include studies of Jan Christian Smuts, H F Verwoerd, Siaka Stevens or Sir Robert Menzies because the works on these Commonwealth figures also contain valuable reflections on British policy in their respective countries and, in Siaka Stevens' case, and in many other cases as well, on British policy in the colonial empire. Figures of undoubted importance in their own country's history who however had comparatively weak links with Britain or were much less affected by British policy, such as Gough Whitlam or Indira Gandhi have however been excluded.

Inevitably in a large and complex bibliography of this kind the classifying of some material is a delicate decision. Where necessary therefore I have included short notes at the head of a particular section drawing attention to the location of other literature of relevance to those interested in each particular subject. I have also used these notes, where necessary, to point to neglected areas or deficiencies in the literature. There are also, where necessary, cross-references which present the relevant entry numbers within square brackets.

In organizing the material in each section the principle followed has been to proceed from the general to the particular. Thus both generally and within each section and sub-section the reference material and general literature is followed by more specialized works examining shorter periods (arranged in chronological order), particular or local aspects of the subject and by biographies and similar sources. Biographies, business and institutional histories and other material of this kind have been listed in alphabetical order within each category. A chronological arrangement has also been used where appropriate. For instance the studies of the various spy scandals of the post-war period have been detailed according to the order in which the events they refer to took place.

The work on the bibliography began in April 1988 as a research project funded by the Leverhulme Trust, without whose support this book would have been impossible. It was decided then that the bibliography should encompass the literature on events and developments in British history between the general election that brought Labour to power in 1945, and the general election of 1987. The second date was not chosen because it was seen as a significant date in itself, or because it could be argued that it marked the end of post-war British history in the way that the 1945 election could be said to have marked its commencement, but simply as a convenient *terminus ad quem*. As far as possible I have tried to include those books and articles of relevance to this period published up to the end of 1989 (and have also managed to incorporate a few of the more important books published in 1990). The bibliography also includes British theses, and some American theses, accepted for higher degrees up to the end of 1989.

The bulk of the research for this book has been carried out in the various sections of the British Library. I am particularly indebted to Richard Cheffins of the Official Publications Library for his assistance in tracking down government publications and conquering the vagaries of the British Library catalogue. Alice Prochaska and her staff at the Institute of Historical Research's library have also been unfailingly helpful. David Blake and Jolanta Uhlar at the Institute of Commonwealth Studies provided invaluable assistance in researching the imperial and Commonwealth sections of the bibliography. I have also spent long hours in the University of London Library, the British Library of Political and Economic Science at the London School of Economics, and Queen Mary and Westfield College Library. A number of more specialist libraries have also proved most helpful, including the Office of Population, Censuses and Surveys Library, the Royal Institute of Public Administration Library, the Institute of Education Library, Dr Williams' Library, Friends' House Library and the London School of Hygiene and Tropical Medicine Library. In addition, as my wife knows only too well, it was impossible to enter a bookshop during the last two years without browsing along the shelves looking for gems on post-war history I may somehow have missed elsewhere and so, to innumerable bookshops, I also owe my thanks.

I would also like to thank John Barnes and Peter Hennessy, who have not only provided much needed support during the lengthy task of researching and writing the bibliography but have guided me to valuable material and afforded me access to their private libraries. I must also thank numerous colleagues who have given me the benefit of their detailed knowledge of particular areas in the field of post-war history.

I have also benefited greatly from the support and encouragement of Anthony Seldon and Stephanie Maggin at the Institute of Contemporary British History. Special thanks must indeed go to Stephanie and to Virginia Preston for typesetting the book, and to Katrin Barlow and Peter Kinsella of Oryx Systems and Caroline Bundy, Alyn Shipton, Veronica Yuill and Jeff Borer of Basil Blackwell and to Kathy Lang for their assistance with this and other aspects of the work. I must also thank Udo Kords for his invaluable assistance in the final stage of the research for the project. My wife Christine has not only suffered with good humour having to share her husband and home with the bibliography for the last two years but has given me all the assistance she could to finish it as soon as possible along the way. I would like to thank her for her love, support and help.

Working on a bibliography such as this schools a researcher to appreciate the value of a succinct and informative preface. I hope I have managed in this Preface to match the best examples I came across in my research. Needless to say I take full responsibility for any remaining errors and all the omissions in the ensuing work.

# LIST OF CHAPTERS

# CONTENTS

# CONTENTS

# 1 GENERAL

## A. BIBLIOGRAPHIES AND OTHER REFERENCE BOOKS

### (1) Library Guides and Catalogues

**1**  Ellen M Codlin *Aslib Directory of Information Sources in the United Kingdom* 2v, 5th ed, Aslib 1984. This is the principal directory of library resources in the UK. It is especially useful for specialist libraries, giving details of holdings, publications and addresses. Volume I covers libraries in the science, technology and commerce fields; volume II those interested in social sciences, medicine and the humanities. Libraries are listed alphabetically rather than by subject area.

**2**  Jack Burkett *Library and Information Networks in the United Kingdom* 5th ed, Aslib 1979. A useful review of information sources and databases in the UK. Jack Burkett *Library and Information Networks in Western Europe* Aslib 1983, gives similar if briefer coverage of European sources, especially those carrying information on the various European bodies to which Britain belongs.

**3**  Stephen Roberts, Alan Cooper and Lesley Gilder *Research Libraries and Collections in the United Kingdom. A Selective Inventory and Guide* Clive Bingley 1978.

**4**  R T Atkins (ed) *Guide to Government Departments and Other Libraries* 28th ed, British Library, Science Reference and Information Service 1988. The coverage in this annotated biennial publication is much wider than just government departments. It is worth consulting in conjunction with [1], not least because of its arrangement by subject.

**5**  H M Levine and D B Owen *An American Guide to British Social Science Abstracts* Scarecrow Press 1976, gives details of holdings and access to over 200 British libraries for those interested in the social sciences field. It should also be noted that the Library Association publish a series of regional guides to library resources, which are periodically updated.

**6**  R Collison *Published Library Catalogues: An Introduction to Their Contents and Use* Mansell 1973. A good guide.

**7**  *The British Library General Catalogue of Printed Books to 1975* 360v Clive Bingley/K G Saur 1979–87. There were flaws in the production of this work. The archaic organization also takes more than a little getting used to. It is nevertheless very useful, particularly for chasing up biographies, which are usually helpfully listed under the subject's name. A six volume supplement was published by K G Saur in 1987–8. Material received since 1975 is available on microfiche. The various subject indexes of the British Library should also be consulted: *Subject Index of Modern Books Acquired 1946–1950* 4v, Trustees of the British Museum 1961, *1951–1955* 6v, British Library 1974, *1956–1960* 6v, Trustees of the British Museum 1965, *1961–1970* 12v, British Library 1982, *1971–1975* 14v and 1 supplement, British Library 1986, *The British Library General Subject Catalogue 1975–1985* 75v, K G Saur 1986. These tend to be somewhat inconsistent in format, quirky in their subject headings, and rather less comprehensive than they are supposed to be. They cannot be treated as a definitive guide to what was published on a given subject in a given period. As general reference works they are however most useful. The sections on England, Scotland, Wales and Northern Ireland are well worth consulting.

**8**  *The National Union Catalog Pre-1956 Imprints: A Cumulative Author List Representing Library of Congress Printed Cards and Titles Reported and Other American Libraries: Compiled and Edited with the Co-operation of the Library of Congress and the National Union Catalog Sub-Committee of the Resources and Technical Services Division, American Library Association* 754v, Mansell 1968–81. Continued by *The National Union Catalog . . . 1958–1962* 54v, Rowman and Littlefield, New York 1963, *The National Union Catalog . . . Motion Pictures and Filmstrips 1963–1967* 2v, J W Edwards, Ann Arbor, Michigan 1969, *The National Union Catalog . . . Author List 1963–1967* 67v, J W Edwards, Ann Arbor, Michigan 1969, *The National Union Catalog . . . Motion Pictures and Filmstrips*

*1968–1972* 4v, J W Edwards, Ann Arbor, Michigan 1973, *The National Union Catalog . . . Author List 1968–1972* 119v, J W Edwards, Ann Arbor, Michigan 1973, *The National Union Catalog . . . Films 1973–1977* 7v, Rowman and Littlefield, Totowa, New Jersey 1978, *The National Union Catalog . . . Author List 1973–1977* 135v, Rowman and Littlefield, Totowa, New Jersey 1978. Since then the catalog has been continuously updated and published by the Library of Congress, Washington DC, more recently on microfiche.

**9** *Library of Congress Catalog: A Cumulative List of Works Represented by Library of Congress Printed Cards: Books: Subjects 1950–1954* 20v, J W Edwards, Ann Arbor, Michigan 1955. Continued by volumes on *1955–1959* 22v, Pageant Books, Paterson, New Jersey 1960, *1960–1964* 25v, J W Edwards, Ann Arbor, Michigan 1965, *1965–1969* 42v, J W Edwards, Ann Arbor, Michigan 1970, *1970–1974* 100v, Rowman and Littlefield, Totowa, New Jersey 1976. This series has been updated quarterly with annual and multi–annual cumulations. More recent material is available on microfiche.

**10** *A London Bibliography of the Social Sciences* 4v, London School of Economics 1931–. Periodically updated. This is effectively the catalogue of the British Library of Political and Economic Science at the London School of Economics. It has been published by Mansell since volume 6 and is now updated annually.

**11** Department of the Environment/Department of Transport Library *Library Bulletin* The Library 1972–. Formerly *Monthly Index to Periodicals* it now appears twice monthly with an annual cumulation. This covers material on subjects such as planning, building, transport and urban affairs. There is a *Monthly Supplement* on recent legislation, circulars and standards. *Library Digest* contains abstracts.

### (2) Guides to Reference Material and Data

**12** A J Walford *Guide to Reference Material* 3v, 4th ed, Library Association 1980–7. The most comprehensive of its kind. Volume I covers science and technology; volume II, social and historical sciences, philosophy and religion; and volume III, generalia, language, literature and the arts.

**13** Gavin L Higgens *Printed Reference Material* 2nd ed, Library Association 1984. Well annotated and indexed if less comprehensive than [1].

**14** Eugene P Sheehy (ed) *Guide to Reference Books* 10th ed, American Library Association 1986. Well organized and annotated, but with less emphasis on Britain.

**15** Lois A Harzfeld *Periodical Indexes in the Social Sciences and Humanities: A Subject Guide* Scarecrow Press 1978. An annotated classified guide to serial bibliographies, abstracts and indexes.

**16** Peter J Taylor *Information Guides: A Survey of Subject Guides to Sources of Information Produced by Library and Information Services in the United Kingdom* British Library 1978. A bibliography of over 500 reference guides. J Stephens *Inventory of Abstracting and Indexing Services Produced in the United Kingdom* 2nd ed, British Library 1983, is a guide to reference producing bodies rather than to reference material.

**17** Ronald Staveley and Mary Piggott (eds) *Government Information and the Research Worker* 2nd rev ed, Library Association 1965, is a guide to government data resources and facilities. So is A F Comfort and C Loveless *Guide to Government Data: A Survey of Unpublished Social Science Material in Libraries of Government Departments in London* Macmillan 1974. See also *Guide to Government and Other Libraries and Research Bureaux* HMSO 1975.

### (3) Historical Reference Books

**18** David Edgeworth Butler and Gareth Butler *British Political Facts 1900–1985* Macmillan 1986. An indispensable reference work furnishing a wealth of information on subjects such as twentieth century government, parliament, elections, defence, the legal system, trade unions, social conditions and religion. Chris Cook and John Stevenson *The Longman Handbook of Modern British History 1714–1987* 2nd ed, Longman 1988, is more of a textbook.

**19** Geoffrey Foote *A Chronology of Post-War British Politics* Croom Helm 1988. A detailed chronology going up to the date of the 1987 general election.

**20** Richard Rose and Ian McAllister *United Kingdom Facts* Macmillan 1982. This concentrates on Scotland, Wales and Northern Ireland from 1945–79.

**21** Frank Edward Huggett *A Dictionary of British History 1815–1973* Blackwell 1974.

**22** E B Fryde, D E Greenway and I Roy (eds) *Handbook of British Chronology* 3rd ed, Royal Historical Society 1986. Useful quick reference for lists of officers of state, nobility and bishops.

## (4) Guides to Sources

**23** Anthony Seldon (ed) *Contemporary History: Practice and Method* Blackwell 1988. Focusing on the postwar era this looks at sources such as oral history, the media, books and journals, opinion polls, public records, private papers and parliamentary information.

**24** Janet Foster and Julia Sheppard *British Archives* 2nd ed, Macmillan 1988. A well annotated guide to archives and their holdings.

**25** Robert B Downs *British and Irish Library Resources: A Bibliographical Guide* Mansell 1981. An unannotated guide to bibliographical material detailing and highlighting the library collections of the British Isles. It concentrates on archive holdings.

**26** Historical Manuscripts Commission *Accessions to Repositories and Reports Added to the National Register of Archives* HMSO 1954–. 1923–1953: this was published by the Institute of Historical Research in their *Bulletin*. 1953–1956: it appeared as part of the *Bulletin* of the National Register of Archives. Since then it has been a separate publication. A few of the entries concern the post-war era. Unfortunately the list only indexes repositories not subject matter. Periodic subject indexes do however make good this deficiency.

**27** *Archives* 1948–. Journal of the British Record Association. Articles about archives and archive collections. See also *Journal of the Society of Archivists* 1972–.

**28** Historical Manuscripts Commission *Record Repositories in Great Britain: A Geographical Directory* 8th ed, HMSO 1987.

**29** Richard Storey and Alistair Tough (comp) *Consolidated Guide to the Modern Records Centre* University of Warwick Occasional Publication No. 14 1986. A rare published guide to an archive collection. Its holdings are mainly twentieth century, and its particular strengths are trade union and pressure group records. This provides an annotated guide to the material held.

**30** Chris Cook *Sources in British Political History 1900–1951* 6v, Macmillan 1975–85. Volume 1 is a guide to the archives of selected organizations and societies, volume 2 a guide to the private papers of selected public servants, volumes 3 and 4 are guides to the papers of MPs, volume 5 (with Jeffrey Weeks) is a guide to the papers of selected eminent and influential people, whilst volume 6 is the first consolidated supplement. The entries, which are alphabetically arranged, go into considerable detail, although subsequent events, such as the demise of the Beaverbrook Library, has rendered some of the information out of date. The work on this series meanwhile continues. It might be argued now that its scope could usefully be extended beyond 1951. See also Cameron Hazlehurst and Christine Woodland *A Guide to the Papers of British Cabinet Ministers 1900–1951* Royal Historical Society 1974.

## (5) General Bibliographies

**31** *British National Bibliography* Council of the British National Bibliography 1950–74, British Library Bibliographical Services 1975–. Effectively limited to books published in the UK. Published weekly with monthly and annual consolidations. Also available is the databank BLAISE, supplied by the British Library bibliographical services division. Unfortunately it is not as comprehensive as it is supposed to be. However many titles that do not appear in *BNB* are covered by *British Books in Print: The Reference Catalogue of Current Literature* Whitaker 1965– (annual 1967–). This was published irregularly as *The Reference Catalogue of Current Literature* 1874–1961. It records all books announced as in print by publishers, excluding most government publications. The weekly listing in *The Bookseller* should also be consulted.

**32** *Books in English* British Library 1971– Published on microfiche six times a year, with annual cumulation. Covers books published in English worldwide, compiled from the holdings of the British Library and the Library of Congress.

**33** *Whitaker's Cumulative Book List* Whitaker 1924– (quarterly). Lists under author-title and broad subject categories books printed and reprinted in Britain. For more up to date information see *Whitaker's Books of the Month and Books to Come* Whitaker 1970–.

**34** Theodore Besterman *A World Bibliography of Bibliographies and of Bibliographical Catalogues, Calendars, Abstracts, Digests, Indexes and the Like* 5v, 4th ed, Societas Bibliographica 1965–6, is dated and of limited value, as is the update by Alice F Toomey (comp) *A World Bibliography of Bibliographies 1964–1974* 2v, Rowman and Littlefield, Totowa, New Jersey 1977.

**35** *Bibliographical Index: A Cumulative Bibliography of Bibliographies* H W Wilson, New York 1937–. Thrice yearly with cumulations. Includes not only books and pamphlets but also bibliographies appearing in articles in some of the 2,600 periodicals scanned. Arranged by subject.

**36** N Roberts (ed) *Use of Social Science Literature* Butterworths 1977. A useful source book, this is a guide to the nature and uses of the literature on subjects such as politics, education, planning, public administration and criminology. It gives details on important sources, journals, official publications, bibliographies, abstracts and major titles. Emphasis is on British material.

**37** Richard A Gray (comp) *Serial Bibliographies in the Humanities and Social Sciences* Pierion Press 1969. Useful guide to bibliographies. Classified according to the Dewey system and unannotated.

## (6) Indexes of Periodicals and Theses

**38** *British Humanities Index* Library Association 1962–. Succeeded *Subject Index to Periodicals* 1918–61. Indexes periodicals and the quality press. Appears quarterly with annual cumulations. The material is arranged alphabetically by subject. It is well organized and easy to use.

**39** *Public Affairs Information Service Bulletin* Public Affairs Information Service, New York 1915–. An indexing service covering over 1,000 English language periodicals, as well as books, pamphlets and reports. International in character it concentrates on public issues and public policy and is listed by subject. It appears twice monthly with cumulations and an annual bound volume. See also Ruth Matteson Blackmore (ed) *Cumulative Subject Index to the Public Affairs Information Service Bulletin 1915–74* Carrollton Press 1977. There is also (telephone: New York (212) 869 6186) the on-line database PAIS INTERNATIONAL.

**40** K I Macdonald *The Essex Reference Index: British Journals of Politics and Sociology 1950–1973* Macmillan 1975. Lists every article and research note in the major British political and social science periodicals of the period.

**41** *Recently Published Articles* American Historical Association 1976–. Twice and later three times a year. Unannotated and not strong on the post-war period.

**42** *Index to Theses Accepted for Higher Degrees in the Universities of Great Britain and Ireland* Aslib 1953–. Covers theses accepted 1950–. In the earlier volumes it is not always easy to tell when the thesis was accepted. The series has however gradually become more comprehensive and detailed. CNAA Theses were incorporated in 1967–8. Abstracts began to appear on fiche in 1976 and since 1985 have been incorporated in the text.

**43** *Dissertation Abstracts International* Xerox University Microfilms (later University Microfilms International), Ann Arbor, Michigan 1938–. Formerly *Dissertation Abstracts*. Monthly compilation of short abstracts of American and Canadian theses. Copies of all theses abstracted are available from University

Microfilms International. However this listing is not comprehensive. *American Doctoral Dissertations* H W Wilson, New York 1934– (previously *Index to American Doctoral Dissertations* and before that *Doctoral Dissertations Accepted by American Universities*), is much fuller, but is not abstracted or microfilmed. It also covers both American and Canadian theses.

**44** P M Jacob *History Theses 1901–70: Historical Research for Higher Degrees in the Universities of the United Kingdom* Institute of Historical Research, University of London 1976. Continued by Joyce M Horn *History Theses 1971–80* 1984, and by annual supplements which also detail post-graduate work in progress.

**45** *Comprehensive Dissertations Index 1861–1972: Volume 28: History* Xerox University Microfilms 1973. Alphabetical listing of American history theses. The print quality is poor. There are no abstracts and, more seriously, no index. However the continuation by Warren F Kuehl *Dissertations in History 1970– June 1980: An Index to Dissertations Completed in History Departments of United States and Canadian Universities* ABC–Clio 1985 is both indexed and much better organized and therefore far more useful.

## (7) Historical Bibliographies

**46** Alfred F Havighurst *Modern England 1901–1984* 2nd ed, Cambridge University Press 1987. Short, largely unannotated bibliography under general subject headings.

**47** Charles Loch Mowat *British History Since 1926: A Select Bibliography* Historical Association 1960.

**48** John Westergaard, Anne Weyman and Paul Wiles (eds) *Modern British Society: A Bibliography* 2nd ed, Pinter 1977. This is probably the most comprehensive, if unannotated, guide to the literature on Britain's social and political structure in recent years.

**49** W H Chaloner and R C Richardson *Bibliography of British Economic and Social History* 2nd ed, Manchester University Press 1984. Covering 1066–1970, this is of limited value for the post-war period.

**50** Joan C Lancaster *Bibliography of Historical Works Issued in the United Kingdom 1946–56* Institute of Historical Research, University of London 1957. Similar bibliographies for *1957–60* (1962), *1961–65* (1967), and *1966–70* (1972), were compiled by William Kellaway, and for *1971–1975* (1977) by Rosemary Taylor. These were the result of the lists of British historical publications presented to the annual conference of British and American historians. They are unannotated and include only books. The Institute of Historical Research still draws up catalogues for the annual conference but these have not been published in recent years.

**51**   D J Munro (ed) *Writings on British History 1946–1948* Institute of Historical Research, University of London 1973. Continued by D J Munro (ed) *1949–1951* (1975), J M Sims (ed) *1952–1954* (1975), J M Sims and P M Jacobs (eds) *1955–1957* (1977), Heather J Creaton (ed) *1958–1959* (1977), Charles H E Philpin and Heather J Creaton (eds) *1960–1961* (1978), Heather J Creaton (ed) *1962–1964* (1979), *1965–1966* (1981), *1967–1968* (1982), *1969–1970* (1984), *1971–1972* (1985), and *1973–1974,* (1986). Each volume covers material published on British history in the years specified in the title. It is selective on recent and especially post-war history, and also unannotated. However it does cite some interesting near contemporary articles in economics journals and foreign language material.

**52**   Royal Historical Society *Annual Bibliography of British and Irish History* Harvester 1976–. Appearing annually this covers the years 1975–, and follows on from [51]. The speed of production prohibits comprehensiveness. It is also of inconsistent quality. However, it is easy to use and contains some material on the post-war period.

**53**   *Annual Bibliography of Historical Literature* Historical Association 1911–. This addresses the literature in the form of bibliographical essays. A selective, critical analysis of important books and articles. The quality of coverage varies considerably from year to year. The section on twentieth century British history, if small, is nevertheless generally quite useful.

**54**   *English Historical Review* carries an annual list of articles on British history. See also [570].

**55**   *Economic History Review* annually publishes a list of recent works on British and Irish economic and social history.

**56**   *International Bibliography of Historical Sciences* Armand Colin 1935–. Annual. From 1980 onwards (i.e. writings published in 1976–7) it has been published by K G Saur. It is published with UNESCO under an international committee of historical science. It is well indexed but unannotated. The typeface is also very irritating.

**57**   *International Bibliography of Political Science* UNESCO 1954–. Annual. Now published by Tavistock. Covers work published 1952–. Prepared by the International Political Science Association. It is unannotated but well indexed and the coverage of the UK is quite good.

**58**   *International Bibliography of Sociology* UNESCO 1950–. Annual. Similar to [56, 57]. Published by Tavistock since 1961.

**59**   Bruce Stevenson *Reader's Guide to Great Britain* National Book League 1977. Unannotated, books only bibliography. Covers all periods but ranges widely.

**60**   Peter R Lewis *The Literature of the Social Sciences* Library Association 1960. Introductory guide and survey. Useful for serial publications and periodicals, though now rather dated.

**61**   *British Reports, Translations and Theses* British Library Lending Division 1981–. This succeeds the *BLLD Announcements Bulletin*. It is a guide to 'grey literature' – semi-published material such as reports, theses and translations – which can otherwise be difficult to locate. It is well classified but unannotated, and contains a considerable amount of information of value.

**62**   Peter Catterall 'The State of the Literature on Post-War British History' in Tony Gorst, Lewis Johnman and W Scott Lucas (eds) *Postwar Britain 1945–64: Themes and Perspectives* Pinter 1989 pp 221–41. A historiographical examination of the quality of the literature on post-war British history, the main themes and debates, and the areas which remain either neglected or inadequately covered.

## (8) Abstracts

**63**   *Historical Abstracts* ABC-Clio 1955–. Annual. From 1971 onwards divided into two parts, the second of which focuses on 1914–. International in character. There is however good coverage on Great Britain and her empire. It has become gradually more comprehensive over the years. Only a select few books are listed, and they are never abstracted. This is however by far the best guide to historical articles. It is also available as a database.

**64**   *International Political Science Abstracts* International Political Science Association 1973–. Published by Blackwell 1951–72. Prepared by the International Political Science Association it appears six times a year. It carries about 5,000 abstracts per year in English and French of articles appearing in some 650 periodicals.

**65**   *Human Resources Abstracts* Sage 1965–. Published quarterly with an annual and far from detailed index, it carries about 1,000 abstracts a year. Despite an American bias there are a few items on Britain. The emphasis is towards politics and administration.

**66** *Sociological Abstracts* Sociological Abstracts Inc. 1953–. This now appears five times a year. Its usefulness is unfortunately greatly reduced by the inadequacy of its index.

## (9) Databases and Banks

**67** J L Hall and M J Brown *Online Bibliographical Databases: A Directory and Sourcebook* 3rd ed, Aslib 1983. International survey of databases. Most databases remain North American and science-oriented.

**68** *Inventory of Bibliographical Databases Produced in the UK* British Library 1976.

**69** RIPALIS. The Royal Institute of Public Administration's database is especially strong on recent political and administrative issues. It also now forms the basis of the constant stream of typescript bibliographies on public administration and related topics issued by the Institute to interested members. It is only available to members of the Institute. Contact the Royal Institute of Public Administration, 3 Birdcage Walk, London SW1H 9JH (telephone: 071 222 2248).

**70** The ESRC Data Archive at the University of Essex, Wivenhoe Park, Colchester CO4 3SQ, has databanks established since 1967 on political and sociological material such as census returns, opinion poll surveys, labour statistics, social and economic behaviour, information on rural areas and other similar forms of data. These are derived from government, academic and commercial sources. The Archive has in recent years become increasingly multi-disciplinary. Its material is usually disseminated by the distribution of magnetic tapes. Certain facilities, such as the Central Statistical Office macroeconomic database, and the British Social Attitudes database (see [159]) are however available on-line, as are the Archive's many bibliographical databases. For further information contact the ESRC Data Archive at the University (telephone: 0206 872 103).

**71** ACOMPLINE. This database, established in 1974, has survived the demise of its original sponsor, the Greater London Coucil. It covers subjects such as urban affairs, social policy, housing, planning and transport. The monthly *Urban Abstracts* London Research Centre (formerly the London Research Unit), is derived from the ACOMPLINE database. For further details contact London Research Centre, Research Library, Parliament House, Black Prince Road, London SE1 7SJ (telephone: 071 735 4250).

**72** URBALINE. Another database originally set up by the GLC. This focuses more on issues such as public order, environment, health or the emergency services.

Various publications, such as *Daily Intelligence Bulletin*, or the fortnightly *Financial Digest, Local Economic Development Bulletin* and *Planning News*, are derived from this database. The contact address and telephone number is the same as for [71].

**73** The Central Statistical Office runs a databank service, details of which are available from the Databank Manager, Central Statistical Office, Room 52/4, Government Buildings, Great George Street, London SW1P 3AQ (telephone: 071 270 6386).

## (10) Guides to Periodicals and Newspapers

**74** *Catalogue of the Newspaper Library at Colindale* 8v, British Museum Publications 1975. Colindale is part of the British Library and has the most extensive holdings of British newspapers in the world.

**75** *Benn's Media Directory* 2v, Benn 1978–. Previously *Newspaper Press Directory*, published by Mitchell up until 1948, and by Benn 1949–1978. Volume I covers the UK and volume II is international. Appearing annually volume I gives details of the UK newspaper and periodical press, publishers, agencies, services and other media organizations.

**76** *Willing's Press Guide* British Media Publications, originally published by Willing in 1890. Annual alphabetical listing of UK and some foreign newspapers and periodicals. Gives details such as frequency, and average circulation.

**77** *Ulrich's International Periodicals Directory* 2v, Bowker 1932–. Well organized and indexed guide to world periodicals. The most recent editions now include its sister publication *Irregular Serials and Annuals: An International Directory* Bowker 1967–1987 in a three volume set. The quarterly update, *The Bowker International Serials Update*, has recently been re-titled *Ulrich's Update*.

**78** *The Serials Directory: An International Reference Book* 3v, 2nd ed, EBSCO Publishing, Birmingham, Alabama 1987. This aims to be the most comprehensive guide. It has quarterly update for subscribers.

**79** James D Stewart (ed) *British Union Catalogue of Periodicals: A Record of the Periodicals of the World, from the Seventeenth Century to the Present Day, in British Libraries* 4v, Butterworths Scientific 1955. The supplement to 1960 was published in 1962. This was succeeded by Kenneth I Porter and C J Koster (ed) *New Periodical Titles 1960–1968* 1970, J Gascoigne *New Periodical Titles 1969–1973* 1976, and by annual supplements 1974–. An alphabetical listing. In 1981– it was re-titled *Serials in the British Library*. This appears quarterly with annual cumulations and is published by British Library Bibliographic Services.

**80** Edna Brown Titus (ed) *Union List of Serials in Libraries in the United States and Canada* 5v, 3rd ed, H W Wilson, New York 1965. A list of titles and library holdings. Continued by *New Serial Titles: A Union List of Serials Commencing Publication After December 31, 1949: 1950–1970 Cumulative* 4v, Bowker 1973; *1971–1975* 2v, Library of Congress 1976; *1976–1980* 2v, Library of Congress 1981; *1981–1985* 6v, Library of Congress 1986; *1986–1987* 4v, Library of Congress 1988. It is updated quarterly.

**81** David P Woodworth and Christine M Goodair *Current British Periodicals: A Bibliographical Guide* 4th ed, British Library Document Supply Centre 1986. An occasional publication. Arranged by Dewey classification. Gradually becoming more comprehensive with details on all items listed.

**82** A J Walford with Joan M Harvey (ed) *Walford's Guide to Current British Periodicals in the Humanities and Social Sciences* Library Association 1985. An annotated, well indexed guide to all sorts of material, including general periodicals. It is organized by Dewey classification.

**83** *Technical and Specialised Periodicals Published in Britain: A Selected List* Central Office of Information 1972. A well annotated, classified guide.

**84** E H Boehm, Barbara H Pope and Marie S Ensign (eds) *Historical Periodicals Directory* 5v, ABC-Clio 1981–86. Volume I covers USA and Canada, volume II Western Europe, volume III Eastern Europe and the USSR, volume IV Latin America and the West Indies, and volume V Australia, New Zealand and the cumulative indexes. Each entry gives details such as issuing body, scope, objects and frequency.

**85** J L Kirby *A Guide to Historical Periodicals in the English Language* Historical Association 1970. There are some significant omissions in this annotated guide. It nevertheless covers a wide range of historical periodicals, including those of a number of local history societies.

**86** *A Union List of Statistical Serials in British Libraries* Library Association 1973. An alphabetical listing detailing library holdings.

**87** Jan Wapsiec *Sociology: An International Bibliography of Serial Literature 1880–1980* Mansell 1983. Unannotated alphabetical listing.

**88** Chauncey D Harris and James D Fellman *International List of Geographical Serials* 3rd ed, Department of Geography Research Paper 193, University of Chicago 1980. This is arranged by country of origin, as is Chauncey D Harris *Annotated World List of Selected Current Geographical Serials* 4th ed, University of Chicago, Department of Geography Research Paper 194, 1980.

**89** *The Official Index to The Times* The Times 1906–56. Continued as *The Times Index* 1957–, published by *The Times* until 1971, by Newspaper Archives Developments until 1982, and by Research Publications since then. At first quarterly and later monthly with annual cumulations. Compiled from the final editions it does not tend to mention stories which only appeared in the early editions. Covers not only *The Times* but also the *Sunday Times* and the various *Times* supplements. This remains of great value despite increasing doubts over the validity of its pretensions to be the paper of record in recent years.

**90** *Monthly Index to the Financial Times* Financial Times Business Information 1981–. Monthly with annual cumulations. An equally valuable index. *The Guardian* has also published an index since 1986.

### (11) Directories

**91** C A P Henderson (ed) *Current British Directories* 10th ed, CBD Research Ltd 1985. An alphabetical guide of over 4,000 entries, providing details of publishers, price and a brief synopsis.

**92** *The Top 2000 Directories and Annuals* Alan Armstrong Associates 1980–. Since 1985 this has been *The Top 3000 Directories and Annuals*. An annual guide to major British directories.

**93** Lindsay Seller *Councils, Committees and Boards: A Handbook of Advisory, Consultative, Executive and Similar Bodies in British Public Life* 6th ed, CBD Research Ltd 1984. A compendious annotated guide.

**94** G P Henderson and S P A Henderson *Directory of British Associations and Associations in Ireland* 9th ed, CBD Research Ltd 1988. Alphabetically arranged details on all sorts of organizations, associations and pressure groups.

### (12) Year Books and Registers

**95** *Annual Register: A Record of World Events* Longman 1974–. This is but the latest incarnation of a publication which has appeared continuously, under various titles and publishers, since the eighteenth century. There is plentiful coverage of events in Britain and good reviews of the work of international institutions and of the politics of other countries, many of which touch on Britain's international role, and the whole work is usefully indexed.

**96** *Whitaker's Almanack* Whitaker 1868–. Less scholarly and discursive than [95], this nevertheless contains a plethora of relevant lists and information. There are also annual surveys on various aspects of British life.

**97** *The Statesman's Year Book* Macmillan 1864–. An annually published one volume encyclopaedia of the world. Useful for the general information it supplies on Britain and the Commonwealth. John Paxton (ed) *The Stateman's Year Book Historical Companion* Macmillan 1988, is similarly informative.

**98** *The Year Book of World Affairs* Stevens 1947–. An annual review of events.

**99** *The Times Yearbook of World Affairs* The Times 1978–. A reference guide and chronology of the year past. This is particularly useful not only as a guide to the way *The Times* reported the year, but also because it gives a fair idea of news stories to be found in the other newspapers and when they appeared.

**100** *Keesings Contemporary Archives* Keesings (and subsequently by Longman) 1931–. Looseleaf diary of world events. Weekly until 1983 and monthly since then. This provides an invaluable digest of news with a full set of cumulative indexes.

**101** *Britain: An Official Handbook* HMSO 1954–. The only yearbook to be specifically concerned with Britain. A survey whose value lies in its breadth rather than its depth. It was not however designed to provide historians with interpretations but interested parties, especially those from beyond these shores, with general information. This perhaps accounts for the somewhat rosy picture of contemporary Britain it tends to present.

**102** *Survey of Current Affairs* HMSO 1971–85. Monthly government survey of British affairs with an annual cumulative index. It succeeded *Survey of British and Commonwealth Affairs* 1967–70, and *Commonwealth Survey* 1953–67, both of which appeared fortnightly. It had sections on government and administration (including a list of recent legislation), external affairs and defence, economic and scientific affairs and society and culture. It also included documents and tables.

**103** *Vacher's Parliamentary Companion: A Reference Book for Parliament, National Organisations and Public Offices* A S Kerwill 1832–. A quarterly handbook to central government and national organizations.

**104** *British Political Yearbook 1947* British Yearbooks 1947. The only issue of this yearbook that appeared, it gives details of legislation, the government, the political parties and the Commonwealth.

**105** Robin Oakley and Peter Rose *The Political Year 1970* Pitman 1970. A subsequent volume was published in 1971. Written by two parliamentary lobby correspondents, the focus is very much on events as perceived in parliament. The calendar style presentation of the parliamentary years 1969–1970 and 1970–1971 is divided up into important themes. These volumes also supply plentiful statistics, especially on parliamentary activity, and lists of major government publications, ministerial statements and other government announcements. W Norris *One From Seven Hundred: A Year in the Life of Parliament* Pergamon 1966, is a somewhat similar record of 1965.

**106** A Bax and S Fairfield (eds) *The Macmillan Guide to the UK 1978–79* Macmillan 1979. Examines administration, industrial development, crime, religion, conservation and so on in each regional administrative area in the kingdom in turn. Includes coverage of the Isle of Man but not the Channel Islands. The lack of an index is a major drawback.

## (13) Collective Biography

**107** *Dictionary of National Biography* Oxford University Press. L G Wickham Legg and E T Williams (eds) the sixth supplement, covering eminent people who died during the years 1941–1950 (1959); E T Williams and Helen M Palmer (eds) the seventh supplement, covering 1951–1960 (1971); E T Williams and C S Nicholls (eds) the eighth supplement, covering 1961–1970 (1981); and Robert Blake and C S Nicholls (eds) the ninth supplement, covering 1971–80. It provides pen portraits, often in considerable detail, of celebrated individuals, usually written by an acquaintance of the biographee. Its scope includes not only famous British people but also important Commonwealth figures too. It should be noted that the references to sources at the end of each biography are often of considerable value. There is also *The Dictionary of National Biography: The Concise Dictionary Part II: 1901–1970* Oxford University Press 1982.

**108** *Who's Who* Adam and Charles Black 1897–. Annually updated collection of the potted biographies of the great and the good. An indispensable reference tool. Entries are supplied, on invitation, by the biographees themselves, which means that they vary greatly in quality and that information is sometimes suppressed. It should also be noted that important figures in certain fields, such as sport, are perhaps relatively under-represented. The coverage is worldwide. Nevertheless the emphasis is on Britain and the vast majority of historically significant British and Commonwealth figures are included. The inclusion of a large number of American and, to a lesser extent, European figures is also of value to the student of modern British history. See also *Who Was Who 1941–1950* (1952), *1951–1960* (1961), *1961–1970* (1972), and *1971–1980* (1981), usefully indexed by *Who Was Who: A Cumulated Index 1897–1980* (1981). These collect the *Who's Who* entries of those who have died during the decade stipulated. The problem that a number of people are dropped from *Who's Who* and therefore do not appear in *Who Was Who* nevertheless remains.

**109** *Vacher's Biographical Guide* A S Kerwill 1987–. A biographical guide to a selection of peers, all MPs and MEPs, with tables showing their personal and political interests.

**110** Harold Oxbury *Great Britons: Twentieth Century Lives* Oxford University Press 1985. A useful biographical dictionary.

**111** *Burke's Peerage and Baronetage* Burke's Peerage 1826–. Now appears irregularly. The other main guide to the British nobility is *Debrett's Peerage and Baronetage* Debrett's Peerage 1769–. This is now re-issued every five years. See also Leslie Gilbert Pine *The New Extinct Peerage 1884–1971, Containing Extinct, Abeyant; Dormant and Suspended Peerages with Genealogies and Arms* Heraldry Today 1972 and Francis L Leeson *A Directory of British Peerages* Society of Genealogists 1984.

**112** *Kelly's Handbook to the Titled, Landed and Official Classes* Kelly's Directories, ceased publication in 1977. Alphabetic survey of Royal Warrant Holders, tables of precedence, MPs, peers and baronets, with short biographical entries.

**113** *Debrett's Handbook* Debrett's Peerage 1982–1986. This biennial publication changed its name to *Distinguished People of Today* in the 1988 edition and it is now intended that it should appear annually. A biographical survey of prominent people in British life, including not just the Royal Family and the nobility but businessmen and industrialists.

**114** Frank C Roberts (comp) *Obituaries from The Times 1951–1960* Newspaper Archive Development 1979. There are also volumes of *Obituaries from The Times 1961–1970* and *1971–1975*. The first two volumes feature about 1,500 obituaries in each and the last about 1,000. Some 60% of these are of eminent British people.

**115** *Current Biography* H W Wilson, New York 1940–. This appears monthly except in December. An American publication which also features a number of British people. The articles on biographees tend to include references and portraits. The annual cumulation, *Current Biography Year Book* has about 500 entries. See also *Current Biography Cumulated Index 1940–1970* (1973).

**116** Joyce M Bellamy and John Saville (eds) *Dictionary of Labour Biography* 8v, Macmillan 1972–. Each volume contains an alphabetically arranged sequence of fairly lengthy biographies of trade unionists, co-operators, MPs and other activists in the Labour Movement drawn from the last 200 years. The biographies include useful bibliographical information. The cumulated index is in the latest volume in the series, volume 8. Jean Maitron (ed) *Dictionnaire Biographique du Mouvement Ouvrier International: Grande Bretagne* Tome 1, Les Editions Ouvrieres, Paris 1979 has shorter entries but includes living people. It is a useful substitute.

**117** *Proceedings of the British Academy* British Academy 1903–. Includes often lengthy and detailed obituaries and memoirs of distinguished people from academic life by their colleagues and peers.

## (14) Guides and Catalogues of Official Publications

**118** Stephen Richard *Directory of British Official Publications: A Guide to Sources* 2nd ed, Mansell 1984. Probably the most complete guide to British official publications. Gives details of the various issuing bodies and the sort of material they publish. Particularly useful for the large and increasing number of such bodies which do not publish through Her Majesty's Stationery Office.

**119** John E Pemberton *British Official Publications* Pergamon 1973. A detailed survey of various types of publications. It also includes a concordance of Command Papers 1833–1972, an alphabetical list of Royal Commissions 1900–72, and a select alphabetical list of important departmental committees and inquiries 1900–72.

**120** Frank Rodgers *A Guide to British Government Publications* H W Wilson, New York 1980. A useful and concise survey.

**121** David Butcher *Official Publications in Britain* Clive Bingley 1983. Aims to provide a concise and up to date introduction to the range of material published by government departments, national bodies, local authorities and through the Stationery Office. See also Catherine Hakim *Secondary Analysis in Social Research:*

*A Guide to Data Sources with Examples* Allen and Unwin 1982.

**122** James G Olle *An Introduction to British Government Publications* 2nd ed, Association of Assistant Librarians 1975. Informative both on the publications and on how to trace them.

**123** *Government Publications: Monthly and Consolidated Lists* HMSO 1936–. Renamed *Government Publications* in 1954, and *Annual Catalogue* in 1985. Issued monthly and annually. A well indexed guide to HMSO publications. Lists House of Commons and Command Papers in numerical order and the generality of publications in alphabetical order according to the issuing body. It also incorporates a list of publications sold but not issued by HMSO. These include not only British publications but those issued by the United Nations or the European Community. K A Mallaber 'The Sale Catalogues of British Government Publications 1836 to 1965' *Journal of Librarianship* 5/2 1973 pp 116–31, charts the development of official publications.

**124** Ruth Matteson Blackmore (comp) *Cumulative Index to the Annual Catalogues of Her Majesty's Stationery Office 1922–1972* 2v, Carrollton Press 1976.

**125** Valerie J Nurcombe (ed) *Whitehall and Westminster* Scoop 1984. Proceedings of a seminar which includes papers on government publications, parliamentary information and bibliographical information about official publications.

**126** *Catalogue of British Official Publications Not Published by HMSO 1980–* Chadwyck-Healey 1981–. The number of official publications not published by HMSO has increased remarkably since the war. The appearance of this series is therefore most useful. The catalogues are issued six times a year with annual cumulations. There has been a steady increase in scope, quality and comprehensiveness. It is arranged in alphabetical order by issuing body and well indexed.

**127** Stephen Richard *British Government Publications: An Index to Chairmen and Authors, Volume III: 1941–1978*, and *Volume IV: 1979–1982* Library Association 1982–1984. In Britain government reports tend to become known by the name of the author or the chairman of the issuing committee. This alphabetical list of chairmen and authors is therefore a means of checking the reports with which their names have become associated. It also supplies a reference, for those reports which were published as Command Papers, of their Command number and the volume and year of the Parliamentary Papers in which they appear. It is however unannotated and unindexed, and therefore of little use on those rare occasions when the chairman or author is not known. A Mary Morgan (ed) *British Government Publications: An Index to Chairman and Authors 1941–1966* Library Association 1969, is however rather more detailed. For the period since 1982 the annual pamphlet, *Index to Chairmen of Committees*, published by HMSO, should be consulted. This is however rather better as a reference guide to the chairmen of the various reports produced by parliamentary select committees than those produced by departmental inquiries or Royal Commissions. These latter can best be found by consulting the index of [123].

**128** Hazel Finnie (comp) *Checklist of British Official Serial Publications* 12th ed, British Library 1987. Alphabetically arranged with an index of issuing bodies. Gives frequency of issue and whether they are still published. There are some annotations.

**129** Percy and Grace Ford *A Guide to Parliamentary Papers* 3rd ed, Blackwell 1972. Parliamentary Bills and Accounts, House of Commons Papers and Command Papers are known collectively as Parliamentary Papers. Most British libraries carry extensive runs of bound volumes of Parliamentary Papers. Each set of Parliamentary Papers covers one parliamentary session and is indexed for that session. Since the late 1970s these have been bound in numerical order. The Fords' Guide is the standard aid to their location and use.

**130** *General Index to Parliamentary Papers 1900–1949* HMSO 1960. Continued by *General Alphabetical Index for 1950 to 1958–9* (1963), and *General Alphabetical Index for 1959–1969* (1975). All of these are arranged by subject. These were succeeded by sessional indexes covering each parliamentary year. The publication of these is however increasingly in arrears of the parliamentary year to which they refer. For recent years it is therefore best to consult the relevant sections of [123]. A monthly index on microfiche, supplied by Chadwyck-Healey, is now available for recent material.

**131** Percy and Grace Ford *A Breviate of Parliamentary Papers 1940–54: War and Reconstruction* Blackwell 1961. This provides full summaries of most of the reports of the period, together with details of the nature of the evidence collected and the resulting recommendations. The only important exclusions are those papers dealing with Commonwealth, defence or ecclesiastical affairs. See also Percy and Grace Ford and Diana Marshallsay *Select List of British Parliamentary Papers 1955–1964* Irish University Press, Dublin 1970. This is similar but less detailed. The series is completed by Diana Marshallsay and J H Smith (eds) *Ford List of British Parliamentary Papers 1965–1974, Together with Specialist Commentaries* KTO Press 1979.

**132** Frank Rodgers *Serial Publications in the British Parliamentary Papers 1900–1968: A Bibliography* Library Association 1971. A useful guide to the various regular series of reports in the Parliamentary Papers.

**133** Edward Di Roma and Joseph A Rosenthal (comps) *A Numerical Finding List of British Command Papers Published 1832–1961/2* New York Public Library, New York 1967. A numerical finding list without details. Continued by Elizabeth A McBride (comp) *British Command Papers: A Numerical Finding List 1962/63–1976/77* General Libraries, Emory University, Atlanta, Georgia 1982. Since the 1976/77 parliamentary session a growing tendency to bind Parliamentary Papers in numerical rather than alphabetical order has effectively obviated further need for such reference guides.

### (15) Legislation

**134** *Public General Acts and Measures* HMSO 1945–. The annual publication of the texts of all public acts and Church Assembly (later General Synod) Measures to receive the Royal Assent in a given year. This increasingly appears in multi-volume form.

**135** *Statutes in Force* HMSO 1972–. A looseleaf, well indexed arrangement, in chronological order, of all public acts in force. There are extensive notes. The acts are published separately and arranged alphabetically. This publication omits local acts, acts relating wholly to territory outside the UK, and certain Northern Ireland acts. *Current Law Statutes Annotated* Sweet and Maxwell/Stevens 1948– is a useful guide to statutes and church assembly measures.

**136** *Index to the Statutes Covering the Legislation in Force on 31st December 1985* 2v, HMSO 1987. A regularly updated publication. Does not cover limited, local or personal acts. It is complemented by *Chronological Table of the Statutes* 2v, HMSO 1987, part I of which covers 1235–1950; part II covering 1951– 31st December 1985.

**137** *The Statutory Rules and Orders and Statutory Instruments Revised to December 31 1948* 25v, 3rd ed, HMSO 1949–1952. Excluding those relating to the Irish Republic and Northern Ireland this covers all statutory instruments which were then in force. See also *Statutory Rules and Orders 1945–* HMSO 1946–. This gives the text of all statutory instruments for the year in question other than those of a local, personal or temporary nature. It also includes what has come to be known as the classified list of local instruments, and tables of the effects of the legislation.

**138** *Table of Government Orders Covering the General Instruments to 31 December 1986* HMSO 1988. A regularly updated table, it lists general statutory instruments in chronological order and indicates whether or not they remain in force. Updated by the monthly *List of Statutory Instruments* 1900– and annual cumulations.

**139** *Index to Government Orders in Force on 31st December 1985* 2v, HMSO 1987. Similar to [136] in character, it is also updated regularly.

**140** *Index to Local and Personal Acts and Special Orders and Special Procedure Orders 1801–1947* HMSO 1949. Continued by *Supplementary Index to Local and Personal Acts 1948–1966* HMSO 1967. Local Acts are annually listed and indexed in *Local and Personal Acts* HMSO 1800–.

**141** The Law Commission and the Scottish Law Commission *Chronological Table of Local Legislation Part II: Local and Personal Acts 1909–1973, Private Acts 1539–1973* HMSO 1985.

### (16) General Statistics

**142** W F Mander (gen ed) *Review of United Kingdom Statistical Sources* 25v–, Heinemann 1974–. These volumes are intended eventually to constitute a comprehensive guide to the nature, reliability and use of a whole range of statistical sources when the series is eventually finished. Each volume focuses on a different type of statistics. Volume 1 looks at statistics on personal social services; volume 2 at those on health and social security; volume 3 at housing; volume 4 at leisure and tourism; volume 5 at general sources of statistics; volume 6 at wealth and personal income; volume 7 at road transport; volume 8 at land use and town and country planning; volume 9 at health surveys; volume 10 at inland waterways and civil aviation; volume 11 at coal, gas and electricity; volume 12 at construction; volume 13 at wages and earnings; volume 14 at railways and sea transport; volume 15 at crime; volume 16 at the iron and steel and shipbuilding industries; volume 17 at weather and water; volume 18 at posts and telecommunications; volume 19 at intellectual property rights; volume 20 at religion; volume 21 at finance; volume 22 at printing and publishing; volume 23 at agriculture; volume 24 at local government; and volume 25 at family planning. This will eventually supersede M G Kendall (ed) *The Sources and Nature of the Statistics of the United Kingdom* 2v, Oliver and Boyd 1952–1957, Joan M Harvey *Sources of Statistics* 2nd ed, Clive Bingley 1971 and Bernard Edwards *Sources of Social Statistics* Heinemann 1974. In the meantime however all works remain of value.

**143** *Economic Statistics Collections: A Directory of Research Resources in the United Kingdom for Business: Industry and Public Affairs* Library Association 1970.

**144** Central Statistical Office *Guide to Official Statistics* HMSO 1976–. The successor to *List of Principal Statistical Series and Publications*. Generally published biennially. A well annotated, well organized and well indexed guide to statistics on almost all conceivable aspects of British life. The extensive bibliography which lists a whole range of serial publications – many of them not published by HMSO – is also most useful, not least because of the frequent changes of name to which official statistical series seem subject. This largely supersedes R Maurice *Statistics: Publications of UK Government Departments and International Organisations* HMSO 1975, and Kathleen G Pickett *Sources of Official Data* Longmans 1974. A useful commentary on the nature, uses, abuses and pitfalls of official statistics is Martin Slattery *Official Statistics* Tavistock 1986.

**145** David Mort and Leona Siddall *Sources of Unofficial UK Statistics* Gower 1985. A useful descriptive guide to the statistics produced by a whole range of bodies such as nationalized industries, professional institutions, banks, academic bodies, trade unions, chambers of commerce and so on. It is unfortunately arranged alphabetically by issuing body rather than by subject. The index does however help to make up for this.

**146** Michael Healey (ed) *Urban and Industrial Resources: The Changing UK Database* Geo Books 1983. This supplies information both on economic and regional statistics and on relevant UK databases.

**147** Brian R Mitchell *British Historical Statistics* Cambridge University Press 1988. The principal reference guide with statistics ranging from the twelfth century to the start of the 1980s. Supersedes Brian R Mitchell and H G Jones *Second Abstract of British Historical Statistics* Cambridge University Press 1981. Brian R Mitchell *European Historical Statistics 1750–1975* 2nd rev ed, Macmillan 1981, remains useful because of the comparative material it provides.

**148** *Annual Abstract of Statistics* HMSO 1948–. This replaced *Statistical Abstract of the United Kingdom* 1856–. Updated by *Monthly Abstract of Statistics*. A wealth of general statistical information. For general regional statistics see *Regional Trends* HMSO 1981–. This was formerly known as *Regional Statistics* 1975–1980, and as *Abstract of Regional Statistics* 1965–1974.

**149** Central Statistical Office *Facts in Focus* 5th ed, Penguin 1980. This uses diagrams, charts and statistical tables to examine all aspects of British life. It has been replaced more recently by the annual publication *Key Data* HMSO.

### (17) Atlases

**150** *The Ordnance Survey Atlas of Great Britain* Ordnance Survey/ Country Life Books 1983. This includes maps not just on physical, geological and climatic conditions, but also on historical, economic and social geography. Oliver Mason (comp) *Bartholomew Gazetteer of Britain* Bartholomew 1977, also has a range of thematic maps. D P Bickmore and M A Shaw *The Atlas of Britain and Northern Ireland* Clarendon 1963 remains of value. It features a large range of thematic maps, including some on unusual subjects not dealt with in more recent atlases. There is also much useful information, in *The 'Reader's Digest' Complete Atlas of the British Isles* Reader's Digest Association 1966.

**151** Stephen Fothergill and Jill Vincent *The State of the Nation* Heinemann Education 1985. An atlas concentrating on social, economic and political conditions in the 1980s. Terry Osman *The Facts of Everyday Life* Faber 1985 is an atlas of wealth, housing, income, population, voting, employment, pollution, education, health and crime in contemporary Britain.

**152** *Ordnance Survey Map Catalogue* Ordnance Survey 1979. Lists Ordnance Survey maps of all types. See also J B Harley *Ordnance Survey Maps: A Descriptive Manual* Ordnance Survey 1975. The section (pp 122–75) on the British Isles in C B Muriel Lock *Modern Maps and Atlases: An Outline Guide to Twentieth Century Production* Clive Bingley 1969, which is partly bibliographical and partly a history of British cartography in the twentieth century, is also worth consulting.

**153** J B Harley *Ordnance Survey Maps: A Descriptive Manual* Ordnance Survey 1975. The definitive work of reference to Ordnance Survey maps. A guide to the types of maps produced and the organization of the Ordnance Survey, which also gives some historical information.

**154** *Business Atlas of Great Britain* Gower 1974. This uses statistical information (up to 1972) and maps to supply general information on economic development, industry, commerce, services and consumer patterns. See also *Business in Britain: A Philip Management Planning Atlas* Philip 1975. This maps economic and, to a lesser extent, administrative activity in Britain.

**155** *Road Atlas Britain* Bartholomew 1943–. Updated annually.

**156** *Planning Maps of England and Wales* 2v, Department of the Environment 1975. A loose-leaf collection of 143 maps designed to assist local planning departments. These indicate amongst other things, patterns of administration, housing tenure, population, agriculture and rural life, education, employment, pollution, industry, land use, cultural facilities, trade and commerce and communications. They are largely based on census information and incorporate explanatory texts. The loose-leaf *Atlas of the Environment: England and Wales* 1976–, is a useful continuation.

**157** Malcolm Falkus and John Gillingham (eds) *Historical Atlas of Britain* Continuum, New York 1981. This provides maps with text of Britain's political, social, economic, and imperial development up to the 1970s. See also Rex Pope (ed) *Atlas of British Social and Economic History* Routledge 1989 and G S P Freeman-Grenville *Atlas of British History* Rex Collings 1979.

### (18) Surveys and Opinion Polls

Opinion polls first appeared in Britain in the 1930s. These surveys and the questionnaire sampling techniques that they have encouraged are principally used to analyse social attitudes and shifts in political opinions. Other literature relevant to this section is therefore to be found in those on electoral history and on social surveys.

**158** George H Gallup (ed) *The Gallup International Public Opinion Polls: Great Britain 1937–1975* 2v, Random House 1976. Basically a chronological series of the questions and results. The first volume covers 1937–64, and the second 1965–75. In the process it illustrates the growing complexity of opinion poll surveys. Gordon Heald and Robert J Whybrow *The Gallup Survey of Britain* Croom Helm 1986, similarly uses Gallup material to chart changes in public opinions and attitudes in the 1980s. See also Robert J Whybrow *Britain Speaks Out 1937–1987: A Social History as seen through Gallup Data* Macmillan 1989. Gallup's monthly *Gallup Political Index* Social Surveys (Gallup Poll) Ltd 1960–, meanwhile regularly charts shifts in political and social attitudes. Also useful to refer to in this respect is *Political Social Economic Review* NOP Market Research 1975–. This was formerly *NOP Political Bulletin* National Opinion Polls 1963–1975. It appears every two months, though there are special editions at the time of general elections. Like Gallup this gives poll trend data, summaries of recent reports, and details of methodology, as does *British Public Opinion* MORI. This first appeared, irregularly, in the late 1970s, but has only been routinely published since 1983, being issued ten times a year. To get a full picture of the state of public opinion all three of these need to be consulted.

**159** *British Social Attitudes* Gower 1984–. An annual series surveying public attitudes to political and economic issues, social policy and welfare, education, social and moral values and so on. For details of the database kept at the University of Essex from which this is derived see [70]. A similar study is Mark Abrams, David Gerard and Noel Timms (eds) *Values and Social Change in Britain* Macmillan 1985. Both this and the comparative study, Stephen D Harding and David Phillips with Michael Fogarty *Contrasting Values in Western Europe: Unity, Diversity and Change* Macmillan 1986, are studies conducted for the European Value System Study Group.

**160** Angus Calder and Dorothy Sheridan (eds) *Speak for Yourself: A Mass Observation Anthology 1937–1949* Cape 1984. Mass Observation, founded in the late 1930s, sought to apply anthropological research techniques developed in the study of primitive cultures to the analysis of British society. This book collects extracts from the fascinating results of their research gleaned from the still under-used archive at the University of Sussex.

### (19) Pictures, Photographs, Film, Video and Sound Archives

**161** Graham P Cornish *Archival Collections of Non-Book Material* 2nd ed, British Library Information Guide 3, British Library 1986. Gives details of film and video, sound, photographic, portrait, and mixed media archive collections.

**162** John Wall (comp) *Directory of British Photographic Collections* Heinemann 1977. A well organized and well indexed directory, this lists public, commercial, private and specialist collections giving details of main subject areas, leading photographers and availability. This supersedes G W A Nunn (ed) *British Sources of Photographs and Pictures* Cassell 1952. See also *Classified Index to the Library of Aerial Photographs* Aerofilms Ltd and Hunting Aerosurveys Ltd 1954. An international, well annotated reference guide is Hilary and Mary Evans *Picture Researcher's Handbook: An International Guide to Picture Sources and How to Use Them* 4th ed, Van Nostrand International 1989. There is also the less detailed David N Bradshaw and Catherine Hahn *World Photography Sources* Directories, New York 1982.

**163** Richard Ormond and Malcolm Rogers (eds) *Dictionary of British Portraiture Volume IV: The Twentieth Century: Historical Figures Born Before 1900* Batsford/National Portrait Gallery 1981. The first comprehensive handbook of portraits of famous British men and women. It includes details of where to find the portraits. *20th Century Portraits* National Portrait Gallery 1978, is a useful exhibition catalogue. *Complete Illustrated Catalogue 1876–1979* National Portrait Gallery 1981, is more of an outline guide to the Gallery's holdings.

**164** Elizabeth Oliver (ed) *Researcher's Guide to British Film and Television Collections* 2nd ed, British Universities Film and Video Council 1985. The guide is arranged according to the different types of archives. Each entry gives contacts, history, holdings, component details, cataloging and access details. It also includes an annotated chronological guide to relevant acts and official reports and an annotated bibliography and list of periodicals.

**165** Frances Thorpe (ed) *A Directory of British Film and Television Libraries* Slade Film History Register 1975. A survey of the main existing sources of film, especially those useful for the study of history and sociology. It also includes useful articles on the collections and on methods of work. On the value of film to the historian see Nicholas Pronay, Betty R Smith and Tom Hastie *The Use of Film in History* Historical Association 1972. An early attempt to draw attention to this invaluable source which remains useful is Sir Arthur Elton 'The Film as Source Material for History' *Aslib Proceedings* 7/4 1955 pp 207–39. Paul Smith (ed) *The Historian and Film* Cambridge University Press 1976, not only includes reflections on the value of film to the historian but historical essays on the development of newsreel and the cinema.

**166** James Ballantyne (ed) *Researcher's Guide to British Newsreels* British Universities Film and Video Council 1983. A second volume was published in 1988. These provide details of archives and holdings and information about the nature of newsreels. They also include chronologically arranged abstracts of material written about newsreels.

**167** *Post-War British History: A Select List of Videos and Films Available in the UK* British Universities Film and Video Council/Institute of Contemporary British History 1988. Over 500 well annotated entries arranged by subject headings. Designed most successfully as a guide to teaching material. The Politics Association Resources Bank, 5 Parsonage Road, Heaton Moor, Stockport SK4 4JS (telephone: 061 442 7042), includes much of this type of material. Many of its video and audio tapes on various aspects of recent political history moreover feature MPs, trade unionists or local government leaders who were active in the movements or events they are describing.

**168** Anne McNulty and Hilary Troop *Directory of British Oral History Collections Vol I* Oral History Society 1981. A useful guide to 231 assorted collections. Many of these are of particular value to the local historian. Largely supersedes L Foreman (comp) *Archive*

*Sound Collections: An Interim Directory of Institutional Collections of Sound Recordings in Great Britain Holding Material Other than that Currently Commercially Available* College of Librarianship, Aberystwyth 1974. *Oral History* 1972–, also carries news of oral history archives and of work in progress.

**169** Anthony Seldon and Joanna Pappworth *By Word of Mouth: Elite Oral History* Methuen 1983. A very useful discussion of the value of oral history in a field in which it is still rather frowned on. It analyses the uses and problems of this historical source, drawing on the experiences of many other historians. There is also guidance for the novice oral historian. Also very useful are the details of various oral archives it provides. Oral history has however so far thrived more in the study of the lives of ordinary people and of local communities, with much of this work tending to focus more on the turn of the century than the post-war period. An equally valuable discussion of the uses of oral history in this rather different field is George Ewart Evans *Where Beards Wag All: The Relevance Of the Oral Tradition* Faber 1977. See also David Henige *Oral Historiography* Longman 1982.

**170** The National Sound Archive, 29 Exhibition Road, London SW7 2AS. Formerly known as the British Institute of Recorded Sound until 1983, when it became part of the British Library and took its present title. It contains a vast range of material, including oral history collections, particularly to do with literature, the theatre, the record and broadcasting industries. Tape recordings of parliamentary sessions are also deposited after seven years. It is also linked with the National Life Story Collection which has initiated a number of oral history projects.

**171** BBC Sound Archives Library, Room 532, Broadcasting House, London W1A 1AA. A major sound archive with a vast array of material. An access fee is charged. See also *Catalogue of Recorded Talks and Speeches* 3V, BBC Sound Archives 1966–7. This catalogues alphabetically by speaker and then chronologically talks, speeches and interviews available from the sound archives. It includes short summaries of contents.

**172** Open University Media Library, Walton Hall, Milton Keynes, MK7 6AA. An archive of contemporary political interviews with politicians, civil servants, trade unionists and journalists. There are similar archives at Nuffield College, Oxford, which was started in the 1960s, and at the Sociology Department, University of Essex, Wivenhoe Park, Colchester CO4 3SQ. There is however as yet nothing approaching an oral equivalent of the Public Record Office, or even of the substantial elite oral history collections that have been assembled in the USA. The British Oral Archive of Political and

Administrative History at the London School of Economics and Political Science, Houghton St, London WC2A 2AE has not become as grand as its title. There are full transcripts of a number of useful interviews. However, lack of funding has prevented the development of the archive in recent years. The Institute of Contemporary British History, 34 Tavistock Square, London WC1H 9EZ, has a number of tapes and transcripts of interviews with eminent politicians and civil servants and hopes to develop its holdings into the sort of substantial collection that Britain so far lacks. It also conducts a number of recorded witness seminars, edited transcripts of which appear in the Institute's quarterly journal the *Contemporary Record*. There is also a certain amount of relevant material in the main American oral archives. A number of tapes of interviews with British diplomats are held in the John Foster Dulles Oral History Project at Princeton University Library, Princeton, New Jersey. Some similar material is held in the Harry S Truman Oral History Project at the Harry S Truman Library, Independence, Missouri. In every case it is advisable that those who wish to consult oral collections of this kind should first contact the archive concerned.

## B. GENERAL HISTORY

### (1) Collections of Documents

**173** Richard Brown and Christopher Daniels *Twentieth Century Britain: Documents and Debates* Macmillan 1982. A school textbook. The relevant sections are on the Attlee government, the Conservative governments 1951–64, and the process of decolonization. Documentary collections such as this can be valuable aids in teaching this as yet rather neglected period. However the last volume of the series of edited collections of *British Historical Documents* does not go beyond 1914. Clearly much work remains to be done in this area.

### (2) General Histories

This section includes works that combine social and economic history. General historical works which are principally concerned with politics, society or economics however appear in this bibliography under the general political, social or economic history headings. A number of the works which appear in these sections should nevertheless be consulted in conjunction with those that appear below.

**174** Trevor O Lloyd *Empire to Welfare State: English History 1906–1985* Oxford University Press 1986. Despite the fact that the archives remain largely unopened and the continuing reluctance to teach post-war history

a considerable number of standard histories and text books have already been written on the period. General studies of twentieth century history which, if less extensive in their treatment of the post-war period, otherwise equal Lloyd in value are William M Medlicott *Contemporary England 1914–1964: With Epilogue 1964–1974* Longman 1976, and Arthur John Brereton Marwick *Britain in our Century: Images and Controversies* Thames and Hudson 1984. Medlicott is strong on foreign policy whilst Marwick is outstanding on social history, and very well illustrated. Also of value is his *Britain in the Century of Total War: War, Peace and Social Change 1900–1967* The Bodley Head 1968. Other well regarded histories of twentieth century Britain include Alfred F Havighurst *Britain in Transition: The Twentieth Century* 4th ed, University of Chicago Press 1985, which ends with the 1983 general election, and David Thomson *England in the Twentieth Century* 2nd ed, Penguin 1981. Also of value, particularly on social developments, is Bentley Brinkerhoff Gilbert *Britain Since 1918* 2nd ed, Batsford 1980. Henry Pelling *Modern Britain 1885–1955* Nelson 1960 is elegant, but has limited coverage of the post-war period. This is also true of S R Brett *British History 1901–1961* John Murray 1966.

**175** Lesley M Smith (ed) *The Making of Britain: Echoes of Greatness* Macmillan Education 1988. A well illustrated and stimulating collection of essays that sets out to challenge conventional notions about Britain's decline. It approaches this task by considering a number of important historical themes such as decolonization, the Welfare State, changing social aspirations or immigration. Angus Stewart (ed) *Contemporary Britain* Routledge and Kegan Paul 1983 reviews major trends of recent years, particularly in the fields of economic and social policy. William B Gwyn and Richard Rose (eds) *Britain: Progress and Decline* Macmillan 1980, covers a number of important themes well. Perhaps particularly useful is Gwyn's article on 'Jeremiahs and Pragmatists: Perceptions of British Decline'. Another useful collection of essays is Henry R Winkler (ed) *Twentieth Century Britain* New Viewpoints 1976.

**176** C J Bartlett *A History of Post-War Britain 1945–74* Longman 1977. The standard, if somewhat pedestrian, general history of post-war Britain. It also includes an extensive bibliography. Peter Calvocoressi *The British Experience 1945–1975* The Bodley Head 1978 is a livelier, if rather less comprehensive account. See also L A Monk *Britain 1945–1970* Bell 1976, Peter Lane *A History of Post-War Britain* Macdonald 1971 and Alfred Victor Brown *A History of Britain 1939–1968* Pergamon 1970.

**177** John Denis Hey *Britain in Context* Blackwell 1979, analyses post-war Britain in international context.

Extensive use is made of a whole range of economic and social statistics.

**178** Pauline Gregg *The Welfare State: An Economic and Social History of Great Britain from 1945 to the Present Day* Harrap 1967. The standard account of economic and social changes in post-war Britain. The development of the Welfare State is simply one of the themes considered. It also contains a wealth of rather uncritically presented information. See also Jim Roberts and Ken Rowe *Making the Present: A Social and Economic History of Britain 1918–1972* Hutchinson 1975, Walford Johnson, John Whyman and George Wykes *A Short Economic and Social History of Twentieth Century Britain* 2nd ed, Allen and Unwin 1968, and R W Breach and R M Hartwell *British Economy and Society 1870–1970* Oxford University Press 1972.

**179** P J Madgwick, D Steeds and L J Williams *Britain Since 1945* Hutchinson 1982. The only textbook which confines itself exclusively to the post-war period. Although perhaps focusing over much on policy-making, thus reflecting the fact that thus far it is in politics rather than history courses that post-war history is more likely to be encountered, this is a well written textbook incorporating documents and exercises. Jack B Watson *Success in British History Since 1914* John Murray 1983, is an admirable textbook which gives good coverage of the post-war period. W Robson *20th Century Britain* 2nd ed, Oxford University Press 1983, is a well illustrated introduction to the subject which goes up to 1980. It is however rather better on the earlier period. Lewis Charles Bernard Seaman *Post-Victorian Britain 1902–1951* Methuen 1966, is an excellent text book. It however unfortunately ventures no further into the post-war era than too many school and university courses. Other text books and textbook-like works which cover some, at least, of the post-war years are Herbert L Peacock *A History of Modern Britain 1815 to 1975* 4th ed, Heinemann Educational 1980, Denis Richards and J W Hunt *An Illustrated History of Modern Britain 1783–1980* 3rd ed, Longman 1983, Peter Teed *Britain 1906–1960: A Welfare State* 2nd ed, Hutchinson Education 1967, R W Breach *A History of Our Own Times: Britain 1900–1964* Pergamon 1964, and Ernest Edwin Reynold and Norman Henry Brasher *Britain in the Twentieth Century 1900–1964* Cambridge University Press 1966.

**180** John F Naylor (ed) *Britain 1919–1970* Quadrangle Books, Chicago 1971. A collection of articles that first appeared in the *New York Times Magazine*, presenting contemporary American views of developments in Britain over this period. French perspectives on twentieth century British history are offered in Roland Marx *La Grande Bretagne Contemporaine 1890–1973* Colin, Paris 1973 and Marc Casati *Le Royaume-Uni de 1914 à nos jours* Société d'Edition d'Enseignement Supérieur, Paris 1967.

## (3) Photographic Histories

**181** James Cameron *et al Memory Lane: A Photographic Album of Daily Life in Britain 1930–1953* Dent 1980. The photographs are largely left to speak for themselves. This is continued by B Green *Yesterday – A Photographic Album of Daily Life in Britain 1953–1970* Dent 1982.

**182** Leslie Gardiner *The Changing Face of Britain from the Air* Michael Joseph 1988. This uses aerial photography to provide a visual comparison between Britain before the Second World War and Britain in the 1980s. In the process it illustrates changes such as the encroachment of the town on the countryside, the transformation of industrial landscapes and the eroding coastline. It does this by providing contrasting photographs of the same scene in the 1930s and the 1980s with text detailing the changes that have taken place. For an earlier aerial view see Cyril E Murrell *From the Pilot's Seat: An Airman's View of England and Wales* Chapman and Hall 1950.

## (4) General Histories of Particular Periods

**183** T E B Howarth *Prospect and Reality: Great Britain 1945–1955* Collins 1985. A good study of Britain's difficult adjustment to post-war problems such as declining international status, reconstruction, and balance of payments crises. Michael Nevin *The Age of Illusions: The Political Economy of Britain 1968–1982* Gollancz 1983, tackles the equally painful process, in more recent years, of adjusting to, and attempting to arrest, relative economic decline, nationalist tensions and imperial withdrawal.

**184** Paul Addison *The Road to 1945: British Politics and the Second World War* Cape 1975. An important book which traces both changes in the political mood of the country during the course of the war and the development in wartime of the planning and policies which form the background to the activities of the 1945–51 Labour government. His *Now the War is Over: A Social History of Britain 1945–51* Cape/BBC 1985 is the book of a TV series which traced the same political and social themes up to Churchill's victory in the 1951 general election. It is a well illustrated and comprehensive account. Together these two books form the most considerable analysis of politics and society in the 1940s. Michael Sissons and Philip French (eds) *The Age of Austerity 1945–1951* Hodder and Stoughton 1963 is a well regarded collection of articles on themes such as the Festival of Britain or the setting up of the National

Health Service that has retained its value. Alan Jenkins *The Forties* Heinemann 1977 is a well illustrated coffee table book. A Davies *Where Did the Forties Go? . . . A Popular History* Pluto 1984, focuses on popular expectations of change fuelled by the war, and argues that these hopes were never fully realised. A Ross *The Forties: A Period Piece* Weidenfeld and Nicolson 1951, is an early example of a retrospective on the decade that has just passed.

**185**  Douglas Sutherland *Portrait of a Decade: London Life 1945–1955* Harrap 1988. Semi-autobiographical account of London society in the first post-war decade by the then gossip columnist on the London *Standard.* Anecdotal portraits of the famous and infamous characters of these years.

**186**  Vernon Bogdanor and Robert Skidelsky (eds) *The Age of Illusion 1951–1964* Macmillan 1970. A follow-up to Sissons and French [184], which however does not quite match the original in quality. On the other hand whereas that focused very much on the Attlee government this collection of essays covers a lot more ground. It analyses, for instance, the growth of affluence and the related appearance of youth cultures, such as the Teddy Boys, as well as the record of the Conservative governments in power in this period. An interesting impression of the decade by one of the literary figures who rose to prominence in these years is Colin MacInnes *English, Half English: A Polyphoto of the Fifties* Penguin 1966. Peter Lewis *The 50s* Heinemann 1978, is a coffee table book with a bias to social history. See also John M Montgomery *The Fifties* Allen and Unwin 1965.

**187**  Christopher Booker *The Neophiliacs: A Study of the Revolution in English Life in the Fifties and Sixties* Collins 1969. An influential study of the love of the new and the emphasis on modernity in this period in politics, the Arts and culture. Another interpretative study, focusing on the 1960s, is Bernard Levin *The Pendulum Years: Britain and the Sixties* Cape 1970. Brian Masters *The Swinging Sixties* Constable 1985, focuses on the music, the styles, the changes in social attitudes and the increasing permissiveness of these years. Francis Wheen *The Sixties: A Fresh Look at the Decade of Change* Century 1982, is a lavishly illustrated coffee table book which not only reflects all these developments but also the changes in attitudes to money and work that affluence induced. Trevor Fisher *The 1960s* Batsford 1988 is a scrapbook of the decade. Geoffrey Moorhouse *Britain in the Sixties: The Other England* Penguin 1964, offers an antidote to the metropolitan bias that can be detected in some of these works. It provides distilled contemporary reflections on visits to the West Country, the West Midlands, the Black Country, the North East and Lancashire and Yorkshire.

**188**  Phillip Whitehead *The Writing on The Wall: Britain in the Seventies* Michael Joseph/Channel 4 1985. An excellent television history of this difficult decade, making considerable use of interviews. This account finishes with the 1981 urban riots. Norman Shrapnel *The Seventies: Britain's Inward March* Constable 1980 is a witty and irreverent survey of the increasing insularity and lack of national confidence brought about by loss of empire, economic crisis, industrial tensions, or terrorism. Christopher Booker *The Seventies: Portrait of a Decade* Allen Lane 1980 is not as good as his work on the 1950s and 1960s [187]. Ronald Allison *The Country Life Book of Britain in the Seventies* Book Club Associates 1980 is a chronologically arranged, lavishly illustrated coffee table book.

**189**  Dennis Kavanagh and Anthony Seldon (eds) *The Thatcher Effect: A Decade of Change* Oxford University Press 1989. A good collection of essays examining the policies, political impact and the effect on British society of ten years of Thatcher government. Each essay examines change in a different sphere of British life in the 1980s. Britain in the 1980s is also analysed in Peter Riddell *The Thatcher Decade* Blackwell 1989.

## (5) General Studies of British Decline

Michael Shanks' book [198], was one of the first to draw attention to Britain's relative economic decline. This economic weakness is also the background to Britain's declining ability to maintain her imperial commitments in the post-war years. Since the 1960s managing and reversing this problem has been one of the principal objects of governments. At the same time it has encouraged a steadily growing body of literature which attempts to analyse the causes of this national decline. Much of this literature can be found in the section which is specifically concerned with economic decline as well as in the section below. It should be noted that the causes of this decline remain very much a matter of historiographical controversy.

**190**  Gerry M Smith *Britain in Decline? A Select Bibliography* Headland Press 1979. The references are mainly drawn from the 1970s. There are some annotations. The useful introduction discusses most of the theories that have been put forward to explain decline.

**191**  Alan Sked *Britain's Decline: Problems and Perspectives* Blackwell 1987. A good short introduction to the nature of the problem and the historiographical debates that surround it.

**192**  Samuel H Beer *Britain Against Itself: The Political Contradiction of Collectivism* Faber 1983. A thought provoking analysis of the factors undermining pros-

17

perity and stability in Britain and the difficulties involved in managing these problems in recent years.

**193** Andrew Gamble *Britain in Decline* 2nd ed, Macmillan 1985. This is particularly good on the effect perceptions of decline have had on British politics in recent years. In the second edition he also assesses the attempts of the Thatcher Government to tackle this decline. A useful collection of commentaries on his arguments is Andrew Gamble *et al* 'Symposium: The Decline of Britain' *Contemporary Record* 2/5 1989 pp 18–23. Joel Krieger *Thatcher, Reagan and the Politics of Decline* Polity 1986 is a critique of how the problem of decline has been handled by the closely associated right-wing governments on either side of the Atlantic in the 1980s. Another analysis of the problems of managing a political and economic system weakened by relative economic decline is Bob Jessop *The Political Economy of Post-War Britain* Polity 1987. This puts forward the view that economic decline is the result of what he sees as Britain's flawed political structure. A similar view is expressed in Max Nicholson *The System: The Misgovernment of Modern Britain* Hodder and Stoughton 1967. See also Anthony Wright 'British Decline: Political or Economic?' *Parliamentary Affairs* 40 1987 pp 41–56. John Pitcairn Mackintosh 'Britain's Malaise – Political or Economic?' *Scottish Bankers Magazine* March 1978 pp 7–27, however rejects the argument that the political system is the root cause of Britain's low growth rate. He instead blames low productivity and emphasizes the need to encourage competition and competitiveness. For another view of the nature and possible solutions of the problem see Roy Jenkins 'What's Wrong and What Could be Set Right: Reflections After 29 Years in Parliament' *Encounter* February 1978 pp 11–17.

**194** Henk Overbeek *Global Capitalism and National Decline: The Thatcher Decade in Perspective* Unwin Hyman 1989. This examines the attempts of the Thatcher government to respond to and reverse economic decline in the context of a long historical perspective.

**195** Isaac Kramnick (ed) *Is Britain Dying? Perspectives on the Current Crisis* Cornell University Press 1979. This examines not just Britain's economic problems but also the rise of nationalism and Britain's international decline.

**196** Keith Robbins *The Eclipse of a Great Power: Modern Britain 1870–1975* Longman 1983. An ideal text book and an interesting if not very analytical account, this is particularly good on Britain's international decline. Another book with similar emphases and strengths is Robert Blake *The Decline of Power 1915–1964* Granada 1986. Roy Sherwood *Superpower Britain* Willingham Press 1989 is a short analysis of Britain's failure to maintain great power status focusing on its

inability to maintain technological leads in strategic fields such as the aerospace industries, missile technology or nuclear power.

**197** Richard Clutterbuck *Britain in Agony: The Growth of Political Violence* Faber 1978. A good analysis of growing political violence in the 1960s and 1970s, particularly in industrial relations, but also in the context of Northern Ireland and racial tension. It includes a useful chronology.

**198** Michael Shanks *The Stagnant Society: A Warning* Penguin 1961. An influential argument which in some ways started the whole debate about the nature and causes of Britain's decline. It thus had considerable political impact. Britain's social structure and class divisions were strongly indicted. These arguments were further developed in the revised edition published in 1972. See also Arthur Koestler (ed) *Suicide of a Nation? An Enquiry into the State of Britain Today* Hutchinson 1963. D E Bland and K W Watkins *Can Britain Survive?* Michael Joseph 1971 provide an analysis of the evolution and effects of decline on British government and society. Another influential, and more recent, response to Britain's decline is Ralph Dahrendorf *On Britain* BBC 1982, the published version of his BBC Reith Lectures.

**199** Patrick Hutber (ed) *What's Wrong With Britain?* Sphere/*Sunday Telegraph* 1978. A symposium of 15 conservative thinkers drawn from Britain and abroad on the nature and causes of the British malaise. R E Tyrell (ed) *The Future That Doesn't Work: Social Democracy's Failure in Britain* Doubleday 1977 is another example of conservative thinking. It provoked a retort from Bernard Nossiter, *Britain: A Future That Works* Deutsch 1978.

**200** D Bell 'The Future That Never Was' *Public Interest* Spring 1978 pp 35–73, critically reviews much of the most important literature on Britain's decline. Paul Warwick 'Did Britain Change? An Enquiry into the Causes of National Decline' *Journal of Contemporary History* 20/1 1985 pp 99–133, analyses the economic basis of Britain's twentieth century decline and doubts whether, given the slow rate at which social attitudes change, any of the various remedies tried, such as technological revolution, joining the European Community, trade union reform or monetarism will actually succeed in turning the tide.

## (6) Interpretative Studies and Analyses of the State of Contemporary Britain

**201** Anthony Sampson *The Anatomy of Britain* Hodder and Stoughton 1962. An influential dissection of contemporary politics and society in an historical context. Strong on narrative if sometimes a little misleading in detail. This has been revised or updated successively by *Anatomy of Britain Today* 1965, *The New Anatomy of Britain* 1971, and *The Changing Anatomy of Britain* 1982.

**202** George Douglas Howard Cole *The Post-War Condition of Britain* Routledge and Kegan Paul 1956. A wide ranging survey with tables and text on the contemporary social and economic condition of Britain. See also A M Carr-Saunders, D Caradog Jones and C A Moser *A Survey of Social Conditions in England and Wales* Oxford University Press 1958.

**203** Hugh Thomas (ed) *The Establishment: A Symposium* Anthony Blond 1959. An influential set of polemics. Thomas Balogh's essay on the Civil Service was particularly important [398]. Also interesting is the essay on shady deals in the City. The pieces on public schools, the army, parliament and the BBC are more lightweight.

**204** Barbara Wootton *Contemporary Britain* Allen and Unwin 1971. An incisive and comprehensive statement on the condition of the nation. It is particularly good on social issues. T Noble *Modern Britain, Structure and Change* Batsford 1975 is also excellent on social developments.

**205** Raphael Samuel (ed) *Patriotism: The Making and Unmaking of the British National Identity* 3v, Routledge 1989. A collection of interpretations written by *History Workshop* writers. Volume I deals with history and politics, volume II with minorities and outsiders and volume III with national fictions.

**206** Keith Hutchinson *The Decline and Fall of British Capitalism* 2nd impression, Archon Books, Hamden, Connecticut 1966. First published in 1951. This traces the overthrow of laissez-faire in the late nineteenth century, and the rise of Socialism from the 1880s onwards ending with the election of the Attlee government and the creation of the Welfare State. A book of its time. However no-one has yet tried to re-examine this theme from the very different perspective of the 1980s.

**207** Gregor McLennan, David Held and Stuart Hall (eds) *State and Society in Contemporary Britain* Polity 1984. Marxist perspectives on the state and state policy since 1945. These essays examine subjects such as family policy, health care, science and technology policy or economic planning and management.

**208** Drew Middleton *The British* Secker and Warburg 1957. An American commentary on Britain and British society since 1945. Peter Bromhead *Life in Modern Britain* Longman 1962, is a very informative if not always totally reliable textbook. See also J D Scott *Life in Britain* Eyre and Spottiswoode 1956.

## (7) Collected Journalism: Accounts and Impressions

**209** James McMillan *The Way It Happened 1935–1950: Based on the Files of Express Newspapers* Kimber 1980. An edited collection of newspaper reports. Continued in *The Way It Changed 1950–1975* 1987. Paul Tabori (ed) *Twenty Tremendous Years* Express Books 1961, presents the period as reported in the *Daily Express*. See also *125 Years in Words and Pictures, As Described in Contemporary Reports in the Daily Telegraph 1855–1980* Daily Telegraph 1980 and David Ayerst (ed) *The Guardian Omnibus: An Anthology of 150 Years of Guardian Writing* Collins 1973. *The Times: The Churchill Years 1874–1965* Heinemann 1965, is a similar work drawing on the files of *The Times*. Robert Allen and John Frost *Daily Mirror* Stephens 1981 is a selection of photographs, front pages and cartoons from eighty years of the *Daily Mirror*.

**210** Robert Kee *1945: The World We Fought For* Hamilton 1985. A compilation of newspaper reports from the year the Second World War ended.

**211** James Landsdale Hodson *Thunder in the Heavens* Wingate 1950. Sub-titled, 'being some account of what I have seen and what people have said to me in England and elsewhere between 3rd April 1947 and 29th March 1949'. The diaries of a journalist. Very useful in conveying the feel of the immediate post-war period. See also his *The Way Things Are* Gollancz 1947, which covers May 1945 to January 1947. The reflections of the American correspondent Howard K Smith *The State of Europe* Cresset 1950, are also useful for British domestic history in the late 1940s.

**212** Kingsley Martin *Critic's London Diary* Secker and Warburg 1960. A collection of his pieces from the *New Statesman* 1931–56 (Martin was editor of this journal from 1931–60) which usefully convey an influential journalist's responses to social and political developments.

**213** Graham Turner *The North Country* Eyre and Spottiswoode 1967 is a journalist's impressionistic survey of life in Northern England. It provides a useful travelogue. He particularly visited the towns of Wigan, Prestbury, Manchester, Oldham, Blackpool, Liverpool, Hull and Bradford.

**214** Robert Chesshyre *Return of a Native Reporter* Penguin 1987. A thought provoking and critical journalist's report on Britain in the 1980s. This looks very much at the views and experiences of ordinary people as well as at the state of British institutions. Another well drawn portrait, also from a critical standpoint, of the character and social fabric of Britain in the 1980s is David Selbourne *Left Behind: Journeys into British Politics* Cape 1987. This is a sort of political *English Journey* through places like Hyde, Wolverhampton, Sheffield, Bradford, Liverpool, and Birmingham, reflecting on issues like the 1984–5 Miners' Strike, disillusionment with the Labour Party, race relations, or local politics. An earlier journey is D Meadows *Living Like This: Britain in the Seventies* Arrow 1975. Ian Jack *Before the Oil Ran Out: Britain 1977–86* Secker and Warburg 1987, is a collection of articles which reflect on political and social developments in Britain in these years. See also Terry Coleman *Thatcher's Britain* Bantam Press 1987 and Margaret Jones *Thatcher's Kingdom: A View of Britain in the Eighties* Collins 1984.

### (8) Cartoons

**215** Martin Walker *Daily Sketches: A Cartoon History of British Twentieth Century Politics* Muller 1978. A book in which the cartoons support the text rather than vice versa. This is less true of the exhibition catalogue of the work of four of Britain's greatest political cartoonists *Beaverbrook's England 1940–1965: An Exhibition of Cartoon Originals by Michael Cummings, David Low, Vicky and Sidney 'George' Strube* Centre for the study of Cartoons and Caricatures, University of Kent 1981. Cartoons are of course a useful historical source, presenting, commenting on and encapsulating the issues of the day. The Centre for the Study of Cartoons and Caricatures, University of Kent, Canterbury, Kent CT2 7NZ is performing a considerable service in creating an archive of this source material.

**216** Edward Lucie-Smith (ed) *The Essential Osbert Lancaster* Barrie and Jenkins 1988. Selections from his pocket cartoons in the *Daily Express*.

**217** Colin Seymour-Ure and Jim Schoff (ed) *David Low* Secker and Warburg 1985. Low was perhaps past his best by the post-war period. He nevertheless remained one of the greatest of cartoonists. This volume collects, annotates and interprets over 250 of his cartoons. David Low *Low Visibility: A Cartoon History 1945–53* Collins 1953, and David Low *The Fearful Fifties* The Bodley Head 1960, are two collections of his post-war material.

**218** James Cameron *Vicky. A Memorial Volume* Allen Lane 1967. A tribute volume which introduces and comments on some of the cartoonist's best work. See also the collection of cartoons from 1945–52; Vicky (Victor Weisz) *Stabs in the Back* Reinhardt 1952. *A Selection of Evening Standard Cartoons by Vicky*

Beaverbrook Newspapers was published in 1960, 1962 and 1964.

**219** Michael Cummings *The Uproarious Years* Macgibbon and Kee 1954. Another classified collection covering his work from 1961 onwards is *On the Point of My Pen: The Best of Cummings* Milestone Publications 1985. Frank Whitford *Trog: Forty Graphic Years* Fourth Estate 1987 is a collection from another celebrated cartoonist. Marc (Mark Boxer) published three collections of his cartoons before his recent untimely death. These are *The Times We Live In* Cape 1978, *Marc Time: The Best of Marc* Hodder and Stoughton 1984, and *People Like Us* Hodder and Stoughton 1986. See also the collected work of *The Guardian's* satirical cartoonist, Bryan McAllister *Little Boxes: A Selection of Bryan McAllister's Cartoons from The Guardian* Guardian 1977, and *Look No Feet: The Best of Bryan McAllister Cartoons from the Guardian* Gollancz 1987. A number of cartoonists annually publish collections of their newspaper cartoons. Of those that do some items of use may be found in R A Jackson *Jak On Parade* Express Books 1967–, and Carl Giles *Sunday Express and Daily Express Cartoons* Daily Express 1947–.

### (9) Historical Geography

**220** R J Johnston and J C Doornkamp (eds) *The Changing Geography of the United Kingdom* Methuen 1982. Collected papers on changing land use, agriculture, energy, water supply, transport, industrial structure, the growth of service industries, the changing landscape, social geography, pollution and political geography since 1945. Another useful analysis of the geography of Britain's economic and social structure is John R Short and Andrew Kirby (eds) *The Human Geography of Contemporary Britain* Macmillan 1984. Human and political geography since 1945 is examined in Ray Hudson and Allan Williams *The United Kingdom* Harper and Row 1986. Political geography in the 1970s and 1980s is examined in John Mohan (ed) *The Political Geography of Contemporary Britain* Macmillan 1989. W E Marsden *The Changing Geography of Britain* Oliver and Boyd 1978 is a textbook describing the climate, the water supply, the agriculture and the spatial structure of energy, transport, tourism, industry, population and cities in modern Britain. J Wreford Watson and J B Sissons (eds) *The British Isles: A Systematic Geography* Nelson 1964 and G H Dury *The British Isles: A Systematic and Regional Geography* Heinemann 1961 is now outdated.

**221** B E Coates and E M Rawstron *Regional Variations in Britain* Batsford 1971. The human, particularly social, geography of Britain between 1945 and the 1960s is here analysed in its regional context, copiously supported by statistics and maps. The section on employment is particularly useful. A more recent work which similarly adopts a regional approach to the changing geography of Britain and also tends to focus on social geography is J B Goddard and A G Champion (eds) *The Urban and Regional Transformation of Britain* Methuen 1983.

## (10) Interviews and Biographical Memoirs

**222**  *New Statesman Profiles* Readers Union/Phoenix House 1958. A selection of the pen portraits of distinguished individuals that then regularly appeared in *New Statesman*. It includes profiles of Lord Goddard, Victor Gollancz, Gilbert Harding, Edith Sitwell, Canon Hewlett Johnson, Sir William Haley, Stephen Spender, J D Bernal, Cyril Connolly, Peter Ustinov, R A Butler, Clement Attlee, Robert Boothby, Arthur Koestler, Konrad Adenauer, Jawaharlal Nehru, Edith Summerskill, Sir Malcolm Sargent, Violet Bonham Carter, Sir Kenneth Clark, Krishna Menon, John Boyd-Orr, Bertrand Russell, Malcolm Muggeridge, Harold Macmillan, J B S Haldane, Randolph Churchill, Sydney Silverman, W H Auden, Lord Hailsham, Charles Waterhouse, Duncan Sandys, and Lord Salisbury. Sebastian Haffner (comp) *A Book of British Profiles* Heinemann 1954 is a series of short studies compiled from *The Observer*. It includes articles on Ernest Bevin, John Scott Lidgett, Canon Hewlett Johnson, Margot Fonteyn, J B Priestley, Clement Attlee, Augustus John, Sir Gordon Richards, George Russell, Jacob Epstein, Sir Gladwyn Jebb, Hugh Gaitskell, Aneurin Bevan, Herbert Morrison, Sir Gerald Barry, Sir Thomas Beecham, Viscount Montgomery of Alamein, Henry Moore, Sir Ben Lockspeiser, Sir Winston Churchill, Charles van der Byl, R A Butler, Charlie Chaplin, Oliver Lyttleton, the Duke of Edinburgh, Sir Max Beerbohm, Bishop Barnes of Birmingham and Lord Salisbury.

**223**  Roy Jenkins *Gallery of 20th Century Portraits* David and Charles 1988. Sketches of many of the distinguished British political figures and world statesmen Lord Jenkins has encountered or admired in a lifetime in politics, including Clement Attlee, Tony Benn, Ernest Bevin, George Brown, R A Butler, James Callaghan, Barbara Castle, Tony Crosland, Hugh Dalton, Anthony Eden, Presidents Truman, Eisenhower, Kennedy, and Johnson, Hugh Gaitskell, John Maynard Keynes, Harold Macmillan, Jean Monnet, Lord Soames, Herbert Morrison and Helmut Schmidt.

**224**  Michael Foot *Loyalties and Loners* Collins 1986. Pen portraits of contemporaries such as Jennie Lee, Barbara Castle, Hugh Gaitskell, George Thomas, George Brown, David Owen, Frank Cousins, Tony Benn, John Strachey, Fenner Brockway, Sir Winston Churchill, Enoch Powell, George Orwell, James Cameron, Arthur Koestler and Sir Harold Nicolson.

**225**  Woodrow Wyatt *Distinguished for Talent: Some Men of Influence and Enterprise* Hutchinson 1958. Biographical sketches of figures from the art world (Henry Moore and Sir Philip Hindry), literary figures (John Osbourne), media men (Lord Beaverbrook, Hugh Cudlipp, Valentine Parnell, Sir Ian Jacob, Sir Michael Balcon, and Sir Allen Lane), educationalists (Sir Eric James), scientists (Sir John Cockcroft), trade union leaders (W J Carron and Frank Cousins), industrialists (Harry Ferguson, Sir Alexander Fleck, Sir Simon Marks and John Moores) and politicians (Clement Attlee, Aneurin Bevan, Hugh Gaitskell and Sir Winston Churchill). Alan Watkins *Brief Lives with Some Memoirs* Hamilton 1982, is a similar collection of eminent figures of more recent vintage. It includes profiles of Kingsley Amis, Lord Beaverbrook, Lord Bradwell, Tony Crosland, Richard Crossman, Michael Foot, Sir Ian Gilmour, Denis Healey, Richard Ingrams, Roy Jenkins, Paul Johnson, Sir John Junor, Sir Osbert Lancaster, Iain MacLeod, Hugh Massingham, Malcolm Muggeridge, Anthony Powell, George Moore, Norman St John Stevas, David Steel and A J P Taylor.

**226**  Joan Bakewell (ed) *Face to Face with John Freeman* BBC 1989. This presents an edited selection of Freeman's television interviews from the 1950s and early 1960s. Those interviewed include Lord Birkett, Bertrand Russell, Edith Sitwell, Henry Moore, Stirling Moss, Evelyn Waugh, Gilbert Harding, Lord Reith, Victor Gollancz, Adam Faith and Albert Finney.

**227**  Kenneth Tynan *Profiles* Nick Hern 1989. The profiles collected from the pen of the celebrated critic include those of Charles Laughton, Noel Coward, Alec Guinness, John Gielgud, Graham Greene, the Crazy Gang, C S Lewis, Cyril Connolly, Edith Evans, George Bernard Shaw, Laurence Olivier, Eric Morecambe, Ralph Richardson and Tom Stoppard.

**228**  Richard Austen Butler *The Art of Memory: Friends in Perspective* Hodder and Stoughton 1982. Reminiscences of contemporaries such as Aneurin Bevan, Ernest Bevin, Lord Halifax, Sir Henry 'Chips' Channon, Jawaharlal Nehru, Iain Macleod and Sir Walter Monckton.

**229**  Philip Cunliffe-Lister, The Earl of Swinton with James Margach *Sixty Years of Power: Some Memories of the Men Who Wielded It* Hutchinson 1966. Personal reminiscences of Clement Attlee, Sir Winston Churchill, Sir Anthony Eden, Harold Macmillan, Sir Alec Douglas-Home, various Commonwealth Premiers, Chiefs of Staff, and Cabinet colleagues.

**230** Richard Crossman *The Charm of Politics and Other Essays in Political Criticism* Hamilton 1958. A collection of essays and biographical studies. It includes reflections on Leo Amery, Sir Winston Churchill, the Truman doctrine, Chaim Weizmann, Eamonn de Valera, Konrad Adenauer, Sir Anthony Eden, Lord Halifax, R A Butler, Clement Attlee, Ernest Bevin, Ivor Bulmer-Thomas, E H Carr, Arnold Toynbee, Malcolm Muggeridge, Michael Oakshott, John Strachey, J F C Fuller, Sir John Glubb, Liddell Hart, Klaus Fuchs and Lord Southwood.

**231** A L Rowse *Memories and Glimpses* Methuen 1986. Personal recollections of figures such as Bertrand Russell, John Maynard Keynes, Sir Winston Churchill, Agatha Christie, Lord Beaverbrook, W H Auden, Ernest Bevin, Clement Attlee, Rebecca West, Evelyn Waugh, C S Lewis, Sir John Betjeman and G M Trevelyan. Further profiles of Lord Halifax, Lord Berners, Lord David Cecil, Sir Maurice Bowra, Sir John Beazley, Sir Arthur Bryant, Daphne du Maurier, Sir Harold Acton and Graham Greene appear in his *Friends and Contemporaries* Methuen 1989.

**232** Malcolm MacDonald *Titans and Others* Collins 1972. Rather banal portraits of some of the great men he knew in government and the Colonial Service. The most useful are the studies of Eamonn de Valera, Sir Winston Churchill, Jawaharlal Nehru, and Jomo Kenyatta.

**233** Kenneth Harris *Conversations* Hodder and Stoughton 1967. Collected interviews with Lord Citrine, R A Butler, Ted Dexter, Geoffrey Fisher, George Brown, Sir Hugh Greene, Sir John Hunt, Cecil King, Scobie Breasley, Lord Mountbatten, Lord Cole, Sir Harold Nicolson, the Duke of Edinburgh, Sir Gordon Richards, Edward Heath and Harold Wilson. A further collection, *Kenneth Harris Talking To* Weidenfeld and Nicolson 1971 features interviews with Barbara Castle, Baroness Jane van Lawick-Goodall, Roy Jenkins, the Duke of Norfolk, Sir Laurence Olivier, Lester Piggott, Bertrand Russell, the Duchess of Windsor and Ernest Woodroffe.

**234** Terry Coleman *The Scented Brawl* Elm Tree Books 1978. A selection of interviews first published in *The Guardian*. The political interviews are particularly useful. Interviewees include Sir Anthony Eden, Harold Wilson, Sir Alec Douglas-Home, R A Butler, Lord Brookeborough, Margaret Thatcher, Vanessa Redgrave, Sir John Betjeman, Sir John Gielgud and Sir Ralph Richardson, Lord Olivier, Daphne Du Maurier, Archbishop Donald Coggan, Yehudi Menuhin, David Hockney, Lord Snowden, and Iain Moncrieffe. His subsequent *Movers and Shakers: Conversations with Uncommon Men* Deutsch 1987 features interviews with, amongst others, Denis Healey, Douglas Hurd, Kenneth Baker, Tony Benn, Nigel Lawson, David Owen, Michael Heseltine, John Biffen, Neil Kinnock, John Wakeham, Lord Carrington, John Nott, Enoch Powell, James Callaghan, Edward Heath, Manny Shinwell, Lord Eccles, the Duke of Edinburgh, Germaine Greer, Michael Caine and Frankie Howerd.

**235** Susan Barnes *Behind the Image* Cape 1974. Biographical sketches, mainly of political and literary figures, such as David Irving, Lord Eccles, Lord Longford, R A Butler, Sir John Betjeman, Lord Hailsham, Kenneth Tynan, Lord Melchett, Lord Boothby, Jack Jones and Jeremy Thorpe. Further profiles of Michael Heseltine, Lord Carrington, Paul Johnson, Nigel Lawson, Glenys Kinnock, Garret Fitzgerald, David Steel and A N Wilson are included in her (written as Susan Crosland) *Looking Out, Looking In: Profiles of Others and Myself* Weidenfeld and Nicolson 1987.

**236** John Mortimer *In Character* Allen Lane 1983. Conversations with Lord Denning, Archbishop Runcie, Tony Benn, Enoch Powell, Malcolm Muggeridge, Lord Olivier, Arthur Scargill, Graham Greene, James Anderton, Cardinal Hume, David Hockney, E P Thompson, Sir John Gielgud, Ken Livingstone, R A Butler, Eric Morecambe, Roy Jenkins, Mick Jagger, Catherine Cookson, Frederick Forsyth, Shirley Conran, Denis Healey and Michael Foot.

**237** Diana Mosley *Loved Ones: Pen Portraits* Sidgwick and Jackson 1985. Extensive biographical studies of Violet Hammersley, Evelyn Waugh, Professor Derek Jackson, Lord Berners and Sir Oswald Mosley. Her comments on her husband are especially useful.

**238** Roy Jenkins *Nine Men Of Power* Hamilton 1974. This includes short biographies of John Maynard Keynes, Ernest Bevin, Sir Stafford Cripps, Lord Halifax and Hugh Gaitskell.

**239** Dean Acheson *Sketches from Life of Men I have Known* Hamilton 1961. This includes analyses of Ernest Bevin and Winston Churchill.

**240** George Mallaby *Each in His Office: Studies of Men in Power* Cooper 1972. These are not studies of specific men but of people whom he knew or admired, both contemporary and historical, grouped in categories such as politicians, public servants, those in the armed forces or schoolmasters and dons.

**241** Sir John Colville *The Churchillians* Weidenfeld and Nicolson 1981. Reminiscences of those surrounding Churchill in his wartime and 1951–5 governments. It includes many illuminating biographical sketches of Churchill, his friends and colleagues and the world statesmen he had to deal with.

# 2 POLITICAL AND CONSTITUTIONAL HISTORY

## A. GENERAL

### (1) Reference Books

The books that appear in the section on General Reference Books should also be consulted.

**242**  Dermot Englefield and Gavin Drewry (eds) *Information Sources in Politics and Political Science: A Survey Worldwide* Butterworths 1984. A good bibliographic introduction to sources and libraries, especially for the UK. There is also a useful section on the European Community. John Palmer *Government and Politics in Britain: A Bibliography* Hansard Society 1960, is now rather outdated. Lawrence Palmer and Ian McAllister *A Bibliography of United Kingdom Politics: Scotland, Wales and Northern Ireland* Centre for the Study of Public Policy, University of Strathclyde 1980, provides a good survey of the literature on politics in the Celtic areas of the UK.

**243**  Eileen Clucas (comp) *Annotated Bibliography for 1987* Department of Political Science, Iowa State University, Ames, Iowa 1988. The latest of a series of annual bibliographies on government and politics in Britain produced for the British Politics Group. A well annotated guide to the literature appearing during the past year.

**244**  *Sage Public Administration Abstracts* Sage 1974–. There are about 1,000 abstracts per year. Quite a few of these relate to Britain. This publication is however very selective and the abstracts vary considerably in quality.

**245**  Martin Minogue (ed) *Documents on Contemporary British Government Vol I: British Government and Constitutional Change* Cambridge University Press 1977. A collection of documents on themes such as parliament, the civil service, devolution, the administration of Scotland, Wales and Northern Ireland or the impact of the European Community. See also G H L Le

May *British Government 1914–1953: Select Documents* Methuen 1955. F W S Craig (ed) *The Most Gracious Speeches to Parliament 1900–1974: Statements of Government Policy and Achievements* Macmillan 1975, is a collection of the royal speeches made at the opening of each parliamentary session. These are analysed in Valentine Herman 'What Governments Say and What Governments Do? An Analysis of Post-War Queen's Speeches' *Parliamentary Affairs* 28 Winter 1974–75 pp 22–30.

**246**  *Campaign Guide* Conservative Central Office 1945–. Published as a primer for Conservative candidates before each general election, these if carefully used, can help the historian to see what was happening during the term of office of a particular administration. The bias, for which allowance must be made, is usually easily detectable. The Labour Party has not consistently issued an equivalent. *Speaker's Handbook* Labour Party, was however published for the 1945 and 1959 general elections. A comparable publication is *The Guardian/Quartet Election Guide 1970–1978*, a series of guides to the backgrounds of the 1970–9 general elections.

**247**  *British Political Sociology Yearbook* Croom Helm 1974–. An irregular publication, each issue having a distinctive theme. The articles are preponderantly but not exclusively on British politics. Ralph Miliband and John Saville (eds) *The Socialist Register* Merlin 1964–, is an annual collection of in-depth essays, written from a Left-Wing perspective, on politics and political history in Britain and elsewhere.

**248**  *Parliamentary Affairs* 1947–. This journal regularly carries articles surveying constitutional developments over the past year and the public legislation passed during the last parliamentary session. *Public Administration* 1923–, regularly features articles on recent administrative developments. Mohinder Singh and R N Sharma *Cumulative Index to Public Administration: Journal of the Royal Institute of Public Administration 1923–1977* Concept Publishing Company, Delhi 1979 features author, title and subject indexes of this useful journal.

## (2) Political Histories

It is also worth consulting, in conjunction with the works that appear below, the sections of general histories and of general social histories.

**249** Alan Sked and Chris Cook *Post-War Britain: A Political History* 2nd ed, Penguin 1984. The best general survey of post-war political history, culminating in a lengthy assessment of Mrs Thatcher's first term of office. See also David Childs *Britain Since 1945: A Political History* 2nd ed, Methuen 1982. Alan Thompson *The Day Before Yesterday: An Illustrated History of Britain From Attlee to Macmillan* Sidgwick and Jackson 1971, is the valuable by-product of the first major attempt to tackle contemporary British history on television. It is therefore of historiographical as well as historical interest. The Thames TV series on which it was based made good use of oral sources to enliven its analysis of the Attlee government, Churchill's peacetime administration, Macmillan's premiership and Suez. Frank Stacey *The Government of Modern Britain* Oxford University Press 1968 is a political history of the years 1945–67, to which the well regarded *British Government 1966 to 1975: Years of Reform* Oxford University Press 1975 is the sequel. These volumes constitute an interesting account by a committed advocate of open government. Also worth consulting is Francis Boyd *British Politics in Transition 1945–1963* Pall Mall Press 1964. Mary Proudfoot *British Politics and Government 1951–70: A Study of an Affluent Society* Faber 1974 is a curious book which forsakes normal prose for enumerated paragraph notes. The same period is taken in David Watt 'The Politics of 1951–71' *History Today* 22 1972 pp 3–11. N P Thomas *History of British Politics from the Year 1900* Jenkins 1956 and D C Somervell *British Politics Since 1900* 2nd ed, Dakers 1953 are both now outdated.

**250** F-C Mougel *Vie Politique en Grande Bretagne (1945–1970)* Société d'Edition d'Enseignement Supérieur, Paris 1984.

**251** L J Macfarlane *Issues in British Politics Since 1945* 3rd ed, Longman 1986. A textbook guide to post-war British politics. See also his *British Politics 1918–64* Pergamon 1965. Patrick Cosgrave *From Triumph to Division: British Politics 1945–87* Constable 1987 provides a short overview and interpretation of post-war British politics.

**252** Chris Cook and John Ramsden (eds) *Trends in British Politics Since 1945* Macmillan 1978. A exploration of the important themes in post-war politics. See also Dennis Kavanagh and Richard Rose (eds) *New Trends in British Politics* Sage 1977. Henry Drucker, Patrick Dunleavy, Andrew Gamble and Gillian Peele (eds) *Developments in British Politics* revised ed, Macmillan 1984 is more of a political science textbook, which however focuses more on political trends and events in the 1970s and early 1980s than on the structure and nature of government. Its successor, Henry Drucker, Patrick Dunleavy, Andrew Gamble and Gillian Peele (eds) *Developments in British Politics 2* revised ed, Macmillan 1988, is a highly regarded survey of more recent developments and issues, revised to take account of the 1987 general election. A similar examination of political issues in the 1980s is Lynton Robins (ed) *Updating British Politics* Longman 1985.

**253** Peter Hennessy and Anthony Seldon (eds) *Ruling Performance: British Governments from Attlee to Thatcher* Blackwell 1987. A government by government survey of post-war British political and administrative history. It is excellent, not only as a guide to each post-war government and as an overview of the politics of the period, but also for the detailed chronologies and bibliographies on each administration.

**254** Samuel H Beer *Modern British Politics: A Study of Parties and Pressure Groups in the Collectivist Age* 3rd ed, Faber 1982. The latest edition of a very influential interpretation first published in 1965, surveying political developments since the 1870s. Its most important themes are the links between ideology and policy-making and the activities of pressure groups.

**255** Keith Middlemas *Power, Competition and the State: Vol I: Britain in Search of Balance 1940–61* Macmillan 1986. This develops the themes explored in his *Politics in Industrial Society: The Experience of the British System Since 1911* Deutsch 1979, which argues that the emergence and institutional growth of central bodies representing management and labour in the first half of the twentieth century, together with the reliance placed on them during the two world wars was responsible for an enlargement and fundamental alteration of the political system. This is therefore a history of the political economy of Britain in the immediate post-war years in the context of this concept of corporate bias. Two further volumes are planned to examine firstly the management of crisis in the 1960s and 1970s and secondly the attitudes of corporate institutions and government departments since 1940 and their influence on the development of the modern British state. W H Greenleaf *The British Political Tradition* 3v, Methuen 1983–7 is another highly regarded interpretation of modern political developments. Volume I is on The Rise of Collectivism, Volume II covers The Ideological Heritage of modern politics whilst Volume III, A Much Governed Nation examines administrative developments.

**256** Richard Rose *Do Parties Make a Difference?* Macmillan 1980. This argues that, contrary to the beliefs of those who contend that one of Britain's problems in the post-war era has been the switches of policy resulting from adversarial politics, changes of government have had relatively little effect on its nature and activities.

**257** David McKie and Chris Cook (eds) *The Decade of Disillusion: British Politics in the Sixties* Macmillan 1972. Essays exploring the hopes and failures of the 1960s. Trevor Smith *Anti-Politics: Consensus, Reform and Protest in Britain* Knight 1972 focuses particularly on administrative and constitutional reform and the rise of protest politics in the 1960s. Robert Rhodes James *Ambitions and Realities: British Politics 1964–70* Weidenfeld and Nicolson 1972 is most useful for the Conservatives in opposition, Powellism and the 1970 general election.

**258** J Denis Derbyshire and Ian Derbyshire *Politics in Britain from Callaghan to Thatcher* Chambers 1988. This puts the years 1976–87 in the context of the whole post-war period. Most of the book consists of a good analysis of the Thatcher government. A more interpretative study is Stuart Hall *Thatcherism and the Crisis of the Left: The Hard Road to Renewal* Verso 1988. This both provides an analysis of the politics and objectives of the Thatcher government and examines the impact of this government on the Labour Party and the Left in the 1980s. John Rentoul *Me and Mine: The Triumph of the New Individualism* Unwin Hyman 1988, is a critique of the emphasis on individualism in the 1980s, encouraged by the Thatcher government, and an assessment of the prospects of a return to collectivist politics.

## (3) Studies of Politics and Government

**259** Herbert Morrison *Government and Parliament. A Study from the Inside* 2nd ed, Oxford University Press 1959. A valuable interpretation drawing on a wealth of personal experience. Ian Gilmour *The Body Politic* Hutchinson 1969 is a personal analysis of and an insight into Britain's political structure. Harold Wilson *The Governments of Britain* Weidenfeld and Nicolson/Michael Joseph 1976, is an anecdotal guide to modern British government which similarly uses personal insights to good effect. The autobiographical element in all these books by practising politicians also makes them a lot livelier than most political science textbooks. A similarly valuable work by a civil servant and former head of the Treasury is Sir Douglas Wass *Government and the Governed* Routledge and Kegan Paul 1984. This reflects on the efficiency and responsiveness of government and finds shortcomings in the organization of the cabinet, parliament and Civil Service.

**260** R M Punnett *British Government and Politics* 4th ed, Gower 1987. One of the most highly regarded political textbooks. Detailed and informative, it still suffers from the bloodless nature of the genre especially in the more peripheral areas. It is best on the traditional concerns of works of this kind, government and parliament, the parties, pressure groups and electoral politics. The main virtue of this over similar works is the excellent bibliography.

**261** Peter Godfrey Richards *Mackintosh's The Government and Politics of Britain* 6th ed, Hutchinson 1984. A number of political science textbooks are regularly updated. They therefore present a series of snapshot impressions of the political structure and the nature of political issues in Britain. Of these this work, originally written by John Pitcairn Mackintosh, is probably the best. Another good example is A H Birch *The British System of Government* 4th ed, Allen and Unwin 1980. See also Richard Rose *Politics in England: Persistence and Change* 4th ed, Faber 1985. An earlier example of this type of work is H Plaskitt and P Jordan *Government of Britain, the Commonwealth Countries and the Dependencies* 8th ed (revised by J A Cross), University Tutorial Press 1963.

**262** A H Hanson *Planning and the Politicians and Other Essays* Routledge and Kegan Paul 1969. This collection of articles includes work on political thought, parliament and administration.

**263** Andre Mathiot *The British Political System* Hogarth Press 1958. Fulsome admiration by a Frenchman of the British political structure. An interesting interpretation marred by some errors and omissions. John Gollan *The British Political System* Lawrence and Wishart 1954, is a more critical Marxist analysis.

**264** Jean Blondel *Voters, Parties and Leaders: The Social Fabric of British Politics* Penguin 1963. An influential study in its day best known for the discussion of voting patterns. A revised edition appeared in 1974.

**265** Richard Rose (ed) *Policy-Making in Government: A Reader in Government* Macmillan 1969. Studies on the process of policy-making, including accounts by politicians involved, and case studies drawn from the 1950s and 1960s. See also Richard Rose (ed) *Studies in British Politics: A Reader in Political Sociology* Macmillan 1966 and Norman Wilson *The British System of Government* Blackwell 1963.

**266** William Thornhill (ed) *The Modernization of British Government* Pitman 1975. Both this and George W Keeton *Government in Action in the United Kingdom* Benn 1970, are useful reflections of the characteristics and problems of government and politics in the 1970s. See also Albert Henry Hanson and Malcolm Walles

*Governing Britain: A Guide-Book to Political Institutions* Fontana 1970 and Michael Rush *Parliamentary Government in Britain* Pitman 1981. Brian C Smith and Jeffrey Stanyer *Administering Britain* Robertson 1976 is a very basic political science textbook of the 1970s.

**267** Philip Norton *The British Polity* Longman 1984. There have been many political science textbooks on the structure and nature of British politics and government published in the 1980s. Norton's analysis includes useful historical perspectives on contemporary institutions and problems. Another good survey of British politics and administration in the 1980s is Martin Burch and Michael Moran (eds) *British Politics. A Reader* Manchester University Press 1987. See also Bill Coxall and Lynton Robins (eds) *Contemporary British Politics: An Introduction* Macmillan 1989, Allan Cochrane and James Anderson (eds) *Politics in Transition* Sage 1989, Martin Burch and Bruce Wood *Public Policy in Britain* Blackwell 1989, Michael Moran *Politics and Society in Britain* 2nd ed, Macmillan 1989, John L Irwin *Modern Britain: An Introduction* 2nd ed, Allen and Unwin 1987, James Cable *Political Institutions and Issues in Britain* Macmillan 1987, J B Greenwood and D J Wilson *Public Administration in Britain* Allen and Unwin 1984, and Hugh Berrington (ed) *Change In British Politics* Cass 1984. James Anderson and Allan Cochrane (eds) *A State of Crisis: The Changing Face of British Politics* Hodder and Stoughton 1989 looks at Britain's international decline and the political problems that have ensued. It includes studies of local politics in Glasgow, Sheffield and Lancaster. A G Jordan and J J Richardson *British Politics and the Policy Process: An Arena Approach* Allen and Unwin 1987, is an attempt to adopt a novel approach to the genre which argues, somewhat contentiously, that parliament is marginal to the political process, and doubts the importance generally attached to adversarial politics. John Dearlove and Peter Saunders *Introduction to British Society: Analysing a Capitalist Democracy* Polity 1984 similarly tries a novel approach, focusing on a notional tension between capitalism and democracy. Caricature and sweeping generalisations however play far too large a part in this analysis, deficiencies which are compounded by the absence of a bibliography or references.

**268** Ian Budge and David McKay (eds) *The New British Political System* 2nd ed, Longman 1985. A highly regarded political science textbook that focuses on the inability of successive governments to cope with economic decline and its consequences. Similar problems are addressed, in the context of post-war political history, in Colin Leys *Politics In England: From Labourism to Thatcherism* revised ed, Verso 1989. A political science textbook that focuses on the problems of managing economic problems and decline since the Second World War. C Hood and M Wright (eds) *Big Government In Hard Times* Robertson 1981 concentrates on the diffi-

culties of government during the financial stringency of the 1970s, and examines in detail the impact of cuts in public spending both on society and politics in general and on the policy areas of defence, education and the social services. Douglas E Ashford *Policy and Politics in Britain: The Limits of Consensus* Blackwell 1981 includes selected documents in a rather more wide ranging survey of the resulting political and policy difficulties. See also Max Beloff and Gillian Peele *The Government of the UK: Political Authority in a Changing Society* 2nd ed, Weidenfeld and Nicolson 1985 and Donley T Studlar and Jerome L Waltman (eds) *Dilemmas of Change in British Politics* Macmillan 1984.

## (4) Studies of Particular Themes

### (a) Political Consensus in Post-War Britain

**269** David Marquand *The Unprincipled Society: New Demands and Old Policies* Cape 1988. The overturning of many of the shibboleths of the post-war settlement by the Thatcher government in their efforts to find alternative approaches which will reverse relative economic decline has encouraged a reappraisal, in recent years, of the nature of that settlement and the causes of its breakdown. The most influential analysis so far is that of David Marquand. The arguments and issues raised are examined in the symposium of articles 'The Decline of Post-War Consensus' *Contemporary Record* 2/3 1988 pp 28–34. Dennis Kavanagh *Thatcherism and British Politics: The End of Consensus?* Oxford University Press 1987 examines the components of the post-war consensus, its collapse, the rise of monetarism and the record of the Thatcher government since 1979. Dennis Kavanagh and Peter Morris *Consensus Politics from Attlee to Thatcher* Blackwell 1989 chronicles the rise and fall of consensus politics. Nicholas Deakin *In Search of the Post-War Consensus* Suntory-Toyota International Centre for Economics and Related Disciplines, London School of Economics and Political Science, University of London 1988 is a pamphlet which explores the notion that there was a post-war consensus. He argues that the height of cross-party political consensus was between 1943–8. John Vaisey *In Breach of Promise: Gaitskell, Macleod, Titmuss, Crosland, Boyle: Five Men Who Shaped a Generation* Weidenfeld and Nicolson 1984, critically examines the consensus period in the context of biographical sketches of some of its leading figures.

**270** Gabriel A Almond and Sidney Verba *The Civic Culture: Political Attitudes and Democracy in Five Nations* Princeton University Press, Princeton, New Jersey 1963. This important cross-national survey, which particularly focused on Britain, played a major role in initiating debate about political culture and political consensus. It is reassessed in Dennis Kavanagh 'Political Culture in Great Britain: The Decline of the Civic Culture' in Gabriel A Almond and Sidney Verba (eds) *The Civic Culture Revisited* Little Brown, Boston, Massachusetts 1980 pp 124–76.

**271** Harold Perkin *The Rise of Professional Society* Routledge 1989. The object of this study is to trace the gradual replacement of a society defined by class to one dominated by professionals in the period since 1880. Perkin argues that the class-based society of the Victorian period was superseded in the industrial crises of the early twentieth century by a informal relationship between professional managers, professional trade unionists and professional politicians and civil servants which prefigured the post-war consensus. This analysis is carried right up to the 1980s. The emphasis on professionalism as an explanatory tool however perhaps obscures other and possibly more important ways in which the notions upon which nineteenth century society rested were weakened in the latter part of that century and the early twentieth century. For instance the experience of high unemployment and industrial decline seriously undermined the assumptions upon which both the nineteenth century Poor Law and political economy rested.

**272** David Butler '1945 1977' in David Butler (ed) *Coalitions in British Politics* Macmillan 1978 pp 95–111.

### (b) Nationalism and Devolution

Nationalism in Ireland has been a divisive issue in British politics since the nineteenth century. Although there were calls for Home Rule in Scotland and Wales in the late nineteenth century nationalist parties were only founded in the inter-war years and remained weak until the 1960s. By-election and then, in 1974, general election success, the recommendations of [273], and, in Scotland, North Sea oil, all fuelled Scottish and Welsh nationalism in the 1970s. The need to maintain parliamentary support meanwhile encouraged the beleaguered Labour governments 1974–9 to address the issue. Referenda were held in 1979 on whether separate assemblies should be set up in Scotland and Wales. Devolution was decisively rejected in Wales. In Scotland less than the necessary 40 per cent of the electorate voted for an assembly. The section below covers general material on nationalism and devolution. The sections on nationalism in Northern Ireland, Scotland and Wales should be consulted for material dealing with this subject in each area.

**273** *Royal Commission on the Constitution 1969–1973* Cmnd 5460, *Parliamentary Papers* xi 1973–74. A Royal Commission chaired by Lord Kilbrandon set up to inquire into constitutional relations between the UK and the Channel Islands and the Isle of Man. It also came to examine the development of Scottish and Welsh nationalism. This report provides a great deal of historical detail. Amongst its most important recommendations was the setting up of separate assemblies for Scotland and Wales. Devolution in the Isle of Man and the Channel Islands is also examined in Political and Economic Planning 'Local Self-Government: The Experience of the UK, the Isle of Man and the Channel Islands' *Planning* 444 1960 pp 231–78.

**274** Anthony Harold Birch *Political Integration and Disintegration Within the British Isles* Allen and Unwin 1977. Another standard account of the growth and character of Irish, Scottish and Welsh nationalism since the late nineteenth century which focuses more particularly on political developments is Vernon Bogdanor *Devolution* Oxford University Press 1979. Henry M Drucker and Gordon Brown *The Politics of Nationalism and Devolution* Longman 1980 is a study of the growth of nationalism since 1945 which concentrates particularly on Scotland. Tom Nairn *The Break-Up of Britain: Crisis and Neo-Nationalism* 2nd ed, Verso 1981 is an analysis of nationalism, including English nationalism, in Britain in recent years in the context of Britain's post-war decline.

**275** William Greenberg *The Flags of the Forgotten* Clifton 1969. An objective study of nationalism and its strengths and weaknesses in Scotland, Wales, the Isle of Man and Cornwall. Sir Reginald Coupland *Welsh and Scottish Nationalism: A Study* Collins 1954 is a good early analysis. Owen Dudley Edwards *et al Celtic Nationalism* Routledge and Kegan Paul 1968 is a series of essays on nationalism in Scotland, Wales and Ireland, some of which were written by leading nationalists.

**276** Peter Madgwick and Richard Rose (eds) *The Territorial Dimension in United Kingdom Politics* Macmillan 1982. Collected essays dealing with the development of nationalism and the organization and making of policy in Scotland, Wales and Northern Ireland. It contains studies of the Scottish and Welsh Offices, the national dimension to regional development policy and of the influence of language issues on policy, as well as analyses of the attitudes of the political parties to nationalism.

**277** Jim Bulpitt *Territory and Power in the United Kingdom* Manchester University Press 1983. A general survey of the difficulties of managing centrifugal tendencies in England as well as Scotland and Wales in a very metropolitan state. For a more policy orientated study see Richard Rose *Understanding the United Kingdom: The Territorial Dimension to Government* Longman 1982.

**278** Ian McAllister 'Party Organisation and Minority Nationalism: A Comparative Study in the United Kingdom' *European Journal of Political Research* 9 1981 pp 237–56. A comparative study of Plaid Cymru, the Scottish National Party and the Northern Irish Social and Democratic Labour Party.

**279** Victor Durkacz *The Decline of the Celtic Languages* John Donald 1983. A general history of the decline and neglect of the Celtic languages, especially focusing on Gaelic and Welsh. Includes studies on the role of religion and education in preserving the languages. It also has a good bibliography.

**280** Michael Hechter *Internal Colonialism: The Celtic Fringe in British National Development 1936–1966* Routledge and Kegan Paul 1975. A misleading account of economic relations between England and the Celtic regions of the British Isles. See the perceptive critique in Birch [274] pp 33–4.

**281** *Democracy and Devolution: Proposals for Scotland and Wales* Cmnd 5732, *Parliamentary Papers* v 1974. The devolution White Paper. This was followed by *Our Changing Democracy: Devolution to Scotland and Wales* Cmnd 6348, *Parliamentary Papers* xiv 1975–76, the White Paper outlining the proposals for Scottish and Welsh assemblies. Cmnd 6585 in the same volume is a supplementary statement. The handling of the devolution issue by the 1974–9 Labour governments is assessed in J Barry Jones and Michael Keating 'The Resolution of Internal Conflict and External Pressures: The Labour Party's Devolution Policy' *Government and Opposition* xvii 1982 pp 279–92. See also their *The British Labour Party as a Centralising Force Centre for the Study of Public Policy* 32, University of Strathclyde 1979. The referenda on the devolution proposals are examined in Denis Balsom and Ian McAllister 'The Scottish and Welsh Devolution Referenda of 1979: Constitutional Change and Political Choice' *Parliamentary Affairs* 32 1979 pp 394–409. On nationalism in the 1970s see also P M Rawkins 'Outsiders as Insiders: The Implications of Minority Nationalism in Scotland and Wales' *Contemporary Politics* 10 1978 pp 519–34.

(c) Patronage, Corruption and Scandals

**282** Peter Godfrey Richards *Patronage in British Government* Allen and Unwin 1963. A useful survey of the various areas of government patronage, if a little out of date. See also Robin S Goldston 'Patronage in British Government' *Parliamentary Affairs* 30 1977 pp 80–96. John Walker *The Queen is Pleased: The Scandal of the Honours System* Secker and Warburg 1987, is a critical examination of the honours system since Lloyd George.

See also Michael de la Noy *The Honours System* Allison and Busby 1985.

**283** Keith Sainsbury 'Patronage and Honours and Parliament' *Parliamentary Affairs* 19 1965–66 pp 346–50 examines the favours bestowed on the 1951 Tory intake in the Commons.

**284** *Royal Commission on the Standards of Conduct in Public Life 1974–1976 Report* Cmnd 6524, *Parliamentary Papers* xiv 1975–76. Chaired by Lord Salmon. Set up to inquire into standards of conduct in local and central government in the wake of the Poulson Affair and the recommendations of the Redcliffe-Maud report [7565].

**285** Alan Doig *Corruption and Misconduct in Contemporary British Politics* Penguin 1984. Studies of corruption in the police, the planning process, local government, the Poulson Affair and so on. P Fennell and P A Thomas 'Corruption in England and Wales: An Historical Analysis' *International Journal of the Sociology of Law* 11/2 1983 pp 167–89 provides an analysis of the law dealing with corruption.

**286** Wilfrid March *The Story of the Lynskey Tribunal* Alvin Redman 1949. The Lynskey Tribunal was an inquiry in late 1948 into a corruption scandal in which a director of the Bank of England and a junior minister were implicated. See also Stanley Wade Baron *The Contact Man: The Story of Sidney Stanley and the Lynskey Tribunal* Secker and Warburg 1966 and Henry Taylor Fowkes Rhodes *The Lynskey Tribunal* Thames Book Publishing Co 1949.

**287** I F Nicolson *The Mystery of Crichel Down* Clarendon 1986. A re-examination of the political scandal in 1954 which led to the resignation of the then Minister of Agriculture, Sir Thomas Dugdale, in the light of the recently released official papers. The official inquiry into the case was published as Sir Andrew Clark *Public Inquiry Ordered by the Minister of Agriculture into the Disposal of Land at Crichel Down* Cmnd 9176, *Parliamentary Papers* xi 1953–54. It inspired one quite well balanced instant history, R Douglas Brown *The Battle of Crichel Down* The Bodley Head 1955, and a number of commentaries, such as C J Harman 'The Real Lesson of Crichel Down' and D N Chester 'The Crichel Down Case' *Public Administration* 32/4 1954 pp 383–7 and 388–401, or K J Scott 'Ministerial Responsibility for Crichel Down' *New Zealand Journal of Public Administration* 17/2 1955 pp 1–22. Perhaps the most influential of these however was J A G Griffith 'The Crichel Down Affair' *Modern Law Review* 18/6 1955 pp 557–70, which helped to establish the standard interpretation of the event – that it the classic example of ministerial responsibility in action, with Dugdale accepting the consequences for the much criticized actions of members of his department. In 'Crichel Down: The Most Famous Farm in British Constitutional History' *Contemporary Record* 1/1 1987 pp 35–40, he however revises that view in the light of the official papers. See also K C Wheare 'Crichel Down Revisited' *Political Studies* 1975 pp 268–86.

**288** Alfred, Lord Denning *Lord Denning's Report* Cmnd 2152, *Parliamentary Papers* xxiv 1962–63. Not many Command Papers sell as well as this report on the Profumo Affair did. It clears the disgraced minister, John Profumo, of any breach of security. The affair is examined in Clive Irving, Ron Hall and Jeremy Wallington *Scandal '63: A Study of the Profumo Affair* Heinemann 1963. The first assignment of the *Sunday Times* insight team was to write this instant history of the sex scandal which brought down Macmillan's War Minister in 1963. See also Wayland Young *The Profumo Affair: Aspects of Conservatism* Penguin 1963 and Iain Crawford *The Profumo Affair: A Crisis in Contemporary Society* White Lodge Books 1963. Christine Keeler *Scandal!* Xanadu 1989 is the autobiography of the girl who had been sleeping both with Profumo and with Captain Ivanov of the Russian Embassy. She has also given her view of the episode in 'Beyond the Profumo Affair' in Christine Keeler and Robert Meadley *Sex Scandals* Xanadu 1985 pp 9–23. Mandy Rice-Davies *The Mandy Report* Confidential Publications 1964 is a short illustrated biography by the other girl involved in scandals surrounding Profumo, Stephen Ward and Perec Rachman. Anthony Summers *Honey Trap: The Secret World of Stephen Ward* Weidenfeld and Nicolson 1987 is a study of Stephen Ward, who was involved both in the Profumo Affair and in the subsequent scandal concerning the slum landlord Perec Rachman. See also Philip Knightley and Caroline Kennedy *An Affair of State: The Profumo Case and the Framing of Stephen Ward* Cape 1987 and Ludovic Kennedy *The Trial of Stephen Ward* Gollancz 1964.

**289** Michael Gillard and M Tomlinson *Nothing to Declare* Calder 1980. A study of the web of corruption from local government up to the House of Commons that developed in the late 1960s and early 1970s around the architect John Poulson. See also Michael Gillard *A Little Pot of Money: The Story of Reginald Maulding and the Real Estate Fund of America* Deutsch 1974.

**290** Sara Keays *A Question of Judgement* Quintessential Press 1985. Her account of the affair that led to Cecil Parkinson's resignation in 1983.

**291** *Fourth Report from the Defence Committee: Westland PLC: The Government's Decision Making* House of Commons Papers 519, *Parliamentary Papers* 1985–86. Chaired by Sir Humphrey Atkins. The parliamentary inquiry into the government's conduct over the Westland Affair, the controversy over the future of the helicopter manufacturer which led to the resignations of Michael Heseltine and Leon Brittan in January 1986. *Third Report from the Defence Committee: The Defence Implications of the Future of Westland PLC* HC Papers 518, 1985–86 is also relevant and was also chaired by Sir Humphrey Atkins. The relevant minutes of evidence are in HC Paper 169, 1985–86 and HC Paper 193, 1985–86. Magnus Linklater and David Leigh *Not With Honour – The Westland Scandal* Sphere 1986, is a good account of the whole affair. See also Dawn Oliver (ed) *Political Aspects of the Westland Affair* Faculty of Laws, University College, University of London Working Papers No.3 1986, Dawn Oliver and Rodney Austin 'Political and Constitutional Aspects of the Westland Affair' *Parliamentary Affairs* 40/1 1987 pp 20–41 and Peter Hennessy 'Constitutional Issues of the Westland Affair' *Journal of Law and Society* 13/3 1986 pp 423–32. Lawrence Freedman 'European Collaboration and the British Government: The Case of Westland and the Bias to Europe' *International Affairs* 63/1 1986–7 pp 1–20 concentrates more on the defence and industrial implications of the affair and concludes, somewhat contentiously, that the eventual link-up of Westland with the American manufacturer Sikorsky was the best possible outcome.

## (d) The Political Elite

**292** W L Guttsman *The British Political Elite* Macgibbon and Kee 1963. The standard sociology of the British political class. This has changed considerably over the post-war years. The Labour Party in parliament has become less working class, the Conservative Party less aristocratic, in character. These changes are examined in Martin Burch and Michael Moran 'The Changing British Political Elite: MPs and Cabinet Ministers' *Parliamentary Affairs* 38 1985 pp 1–15. See also R W Johnson 'The British Political Elite' *European Journal of Sociology* 14 1973 pp 35–77. C Shirley Wilson and T Lupton 'The Social Background and Connections of "Top Decision Makers"' *Manchester School of Economic and Social Studies* 27 1959 pp 30–51 looks more broadly at Civil Service and City elites as well.

## B. HISTORIES OF POST-WAR ADMINISTRATIONS

The slow release of the official documents at the Public Record Office under the thirty year rule has not deterred a number of attempts to write the histories of post-war administrations. The Attlee government and the Thatcher government have excited particular interest; the first because it was the first majority Labour government and because of the extensive changes it brought about, not least through its nationalization programme and social welfare legislation; the second because of its challenge to many of the nostrums of the post-war years. The works listed below are general studies of particular governments. Works on specific policy areas (for instance the books on the foreign policy of the Attlee government) however appear in the literature on social, economic or foreign policy rather than below. The various studies of party discipline whilst in government can be found in the sections on Conservative or Labour Party history. Biographies and memoirs can be found in the section on political biography.

## (1) The Attlee Government 1945–51

**293** Kenneth O Morgan *Labour in Power 1945–51* Oxford University Press 1984. A valuable account which emphasizes the government's achievements. For some themes however it may be better to consult Henry Pelling *The Labour Governments 1945–51* Macmillan 1984. Both books benefit from the release of the official documents. Roger Eatwell *The 1945–51 Labour Governments* Batsford 1979, is a reasonable, short analysis. See also Nina Fishman 'The Labour Governments 1945–51' *Politics and Power* 2 1980 pp 61–78. Of earlier accounts Denis Nowell Pritt *The Labour Government 1945–51* Lawrence and Wishart 1963 is the most interesting. It is an account from the Left by a former Labour MP who sat in parliament as an Independent in 1945–50. Robert Alexander Brady *Crisis in Britain: Plans and Achievements of the Labour Government* Cambridge University Press 1950 is a detailed American analysis. Also worth consulting is Ernest Watkins *The Cautious Revolution* Secker and Warburg 1951. Bertrand de Jouvenal *Problems of Socialist England* Betchworth 1949 surveys the difficulties of the first two years of the Attlee government and presents a critical appraisal of the policies adopted. Geoffrey Wakeford *The Great Labour Mirage: An Indictment of Socialism in Britain* Hale 1969 is a criticism from the Right of the legacy of the Attlee years. A more contemporary Conservative critique is Colm Brogan *Our New Masters* 2nd ed, Hollis and Carter 1948. For other contemporary responses see Donald Munro (ed) *Socialism: The British Way: An Assessment of the Nature and Significance of the Socialist Experiment Carried out in Great Britain by the Labour Government of 1945* Essential Books 1948 and J E D Hall *Labour's First Year* Penguin 1947.

**294** Douglas Jay 'The Attlee Government' *Contemporary Record* 2/4 1988 pp 23–4. A brief memoir by one of Attlee's ministers.

## (2) The Conservative Governments 1951–64

**295** Anthony Seldon *Churchill's Indian Summer: The Conservative Government 1951–55* Hodder and Stoughton 1981. The only general history of the 1951–5 government so far is an exhaustive guide to the government's various spheres of activity which attempts to resurrect this administration's reputation. It includes a great deal of reference material and an extensive bibliography. See also [241].

**296** Richard Lamb *The Failure of the Eden Government* Sidgwick and Jackson 1987. A useful if perhaps hastily written study based on the recently released official papers. T E Utley *Not Guilty: The Conservative Reply* Macgibbon and Kee 1957 is a contemporary defence of the government that also reflects Conservative opinion in the aftermath of Suez. A useful source for the history of the Eden government is William Clark *From Three Worlds: Memoirs* Sidgwick and Jackson 1986. The most important part of this journalist's memoirs relate to his time as Eden's Public Relations Adviser 1955–6. The only study of Eden as Premier 1955–7 is Robert L Johnston 'The Premiership of Sir Anthony Eden: A Study of the Man and the Office' University of California, Berkeley PhD Thesis 1962. However see N Rose 'The Resignation of Anthony Eden' *Historical Journal* 25 1982 pp 911–31. W Scott Lucas 'Suez, the Americans and the Overthrow of Anthony Eden' *LSE Quarterly* Sept 1987 pp 227–54 examines the plotting that went on behind the scenes.

**297** Harold Evans *Downing Street Diaries: The Macmillan Years 1957–63* Hodder and Stoughton 1981. These are the memoirs of Macmillan's Press Secretary. There are also a number of relevant memoirs, not least by Macmillan himself, and biographies of members of the government, which can be found in the section on political biography. There are however as yet no general studies of the Macmillan government, though this deficiency may be remedied when the official documents are fully available in a few years time. The only other work published so far is R M Punnett 'The Structure of the Macmillan Government 1957–63' *Quarterly Review* 302 Jan. 1964 pp 12–23. There have not been any studies of the 1963–4 Home government.

**298** David Butler *et al* 'Symposium: 1961–64: Did the Conservatives lose Direction?' *Contemporary Record* 2/5 1989 pp 26–31. An edited transcript of an Institute of Contemporary British History witness seminar on the decline and fall of the Conservatives. It includes a useful chronology.

**299** *Twelve Wasted Years* Labour Research Department 1963. A revision entitled *Thirteen Wasted Years* appeared the following year in time for the general election. Earlier versions of this critique of the Tory governments of the 1950s were David Ginsberg *Three Wasted Years* Labour Research Department 1954 and the Labour Party's *Speaker's Handbook* for the 1959 election. It continues to shape historiographical perspectives on this period of Tory rule. Labour's claims of stagnation and wasted opportunity and the Conservative counter- claims are examined in John Barnes and Anthony Seldon '1951–64: 13 Wasted Years? Part 1: The Argument' *Contemporary Record* 1/2 1987 pp 19–21.

**300** Arthur Butler '1951–9: The Conservatives in Power' *Political Quarterly* 30 1959 pp 325–35.

## (3) The First Wilson Government 1964–70

**301** Harold Wilson *The Labour Government 1964–1970: A Personal Record* Weidenfeld and Nicolson 1971. An excellent memoir of this government drawing extensively on private and official papers. It is however distinctly short of the introspective insight that would have made it a valuable exercise in autobiography as well. Brian Lapping *The Labour Government 1964–1970* Penguin 1970, is a subject by subject assessment written by a Labour sympathiser. Clive Ponting *Breach of Promise* Hamilton 1989 is useful on the government's relations, particularly their economic relations, with the Americans. Ken Coates *The Crisis of British Socialism: Essays on the Rise of Harold Wilson and the Fall of the Labour Party* Spokesman 1971 is not a history but a collection of essays and polemics reflecting on the policies of the government and the dissatisfaction felt by those on the Left of the party. See also Austen Albu *et al* 'Lessons of the Labour Government' *Political Quarterly* 41/2 1970 pp 141–51.

**302** Peter Shrimsley *The First Hundred Days of Harold Wilson* Weidenfeld and Nicolson 1965, is indicative of the expectations initially raised by this government. Its title and tone bear witness to the prevailing optimism and the tendency to compare the new Labour government with the opening phase of the Kennedy administration in America. Gerard Eyre Noel *The New Britain and Harold Wilson: Interim Report 1966 General Election* Campion Press 1966 is a sympathetic interim account focusing very much on Wilson himself. A more critical interim assessment is J Mahon 'The Record of the Labour Government – October 1964 to March 1968' *Marxism Today* 12 1968 pp 231–44.

**303** Desmond Donnelly *Gadarene '68: The Crimes, Follies and Misfortunes of the Wilson Government* Kimber 1968. A semi- autobiographical diatribe by a former Labour MP who rebelled over the re-nationalization of steel and later resigned the Labour whip.

## (4) The Heath Government 1970–4

**304** Douglas Hurd *An End to Promises: Sketch of a Government 1970–74* Collins 1979. Hurd was Heath's Political Secretary 1970–3. This is a good inside account which is particularly revealing on Heath's relationship with his senior civil servants. Another useful study of this government drawing on personal experience is Jock Bruce-Gardyne *Whatever Happened to the Quiet Revolution? The Story of a Brave Experiment in Government* Knight 1974. Martin Holmes *Political Pressure and Economic Policy: British Government 1970–1974* Butterworths 1982 gives a good account of the government's economic record. Ivor Burton and Gavin Drewry *Legislation and Public Policy: Public Bills in the 1970–74 Parliament* Macmillan 1981 surveys the legislative record of the government. A useful, if brief, study of the demise of the Heath government is Stephen Fay and Hugo Young *The Fall of Heath* Sunday Times Publications 1976. This develops newspaper accounts of the time. The struggle with the unions and the eventual fall of the government has also been the subject of an Institute of Contemporary British History witness seminar, drawing on the memories of surviving witnesses. An edited transcript of this was published as 'Symposium: The Trade Unions and the Fall of the Heath Government' *Contemporary Record* 2/1 1988 pp 36–46. The validity of the generally poor historical perspective on the Heath government is debated in Michael A Young and Martin Holmes 'Controversy: Heath's Government Reassessed' *Contemporary Record* 3/2 1989 pp 24–8. On the fall of Heath see also I Robertson and D Sims *The Decline and Fall of Mr Heath: Essays in Criticism of British Politics* Brynmill Publishing 1974.

## (5) The Labour Governments 1974–9

**305** David Coates *Labour in Power? A Study of the Labour Government 1974–79* Longman 1980. A good narrative focusing on the reasons why Labour failed to achieve its objectives. An account which is particularly strong on the economic difficulties that proved the major problem is Martin Holmes *The Labour Government 1974–1979: Political Aims and Economic Reality* Macmillan 1985.

**306** Bernard Donoughue *Prime Minister: The Conduct of Policy Under Harold Wilson and James Callaghan* Cape 1987. A very useful memoir by the Senior Policy Adviser and Head of the Downing Street Policy Unit 1974–79. An insight into the atmosphere and modus operandi of the 1974–79 governments. Sir Harold Wilson *Final Term: The Labour Government 1974–1976* Weidenfeld and Nicolson/Michael Joseph 1979 is not, however, a very revealing survey of his second period as Prime Minister. It does not bear comparison with his volume on his earlier government [301], reading more like a catalogue of events and showing little perception. Joel Barnett *Inside the Treasury* Deutsch 1982 is in contrast a very good study of a major aspect of this government's record, its economic policy, by the then Chief Secretary of the Treasury, whose responsibilities included oversight of public expenditure. His epilogue features a useful general survey of the government's period of office.

**307** Ken Coates (ed) *What Went Wrong? Explaining the Fall of the Labour Government* Spokesman 1979. A critical review of the domestic policy of the government that is also quite useful for the internal politics and wrangling in the party. See also Ivor Keith Wymer *Labour in Office 1974–76 and the Quest for Socialism* New Horizon 1980.

**308** *Policy and Practice: The Experience of Government* Royal Institute of Public Administration 1980. Reflections on the government by cabinet ministers William Rodgers, Edmund Dell, Merlyn Rees, Tony Benn and Shirley Williams.

**309** Alastair Michie and Simon Hoggart *The Pact: The Inside Story of the Lib-Lab Government 1977–8* Quartet 1978. An instant history of the pact with the Liberals that sustained the government in office in this period. David Steel *A House Divided: The Lib-Lab Pact and the Future of British Politics* Weidenfeld and Nicolson 1980, is the diary of the pact by the then Liberal leader.

### (6) The Thatcher Government 1979–

Mrs Thatcher's government has been subjected to more exhaustive analysis than any other post-war government. This extensive literature has examined not only this government's policy but also its style. There has been discussion of whether the Civil Service has been politicized during this administration and whether the cabinet has been overawed by a domineering Prime Minister. The literature on these points appears in the sections dealing with the Civil Service and the cabinet.

**310** Peter Jenkins *Mrs Thatcher's Revolution: The Ending of the Socialist Era* Cape 1987. The best study yet of the impact of this government. This account skilfully places the Thatcher government both in its historical context and in the context of similar developments elsewhere in the world. It is also very perceptive on cultural and political changes in this period. Another valuable study is Peter Riddell *The Thatcher Government* revised ed, Blackwell 1985. John Cole *The Thatcher Years: A Decade of Revolution in British Politics* BBC Books 1987 is a racy account which also usefully reflects, not least in its sub-title, the contemporary response to the

Thatcher government. Ronald Butt *The Unfinished Task: The Conservative Record in Perspective* Centre for Policy Studies 1986 is a Thatcherite progress report.

**311** Martin Holmes *The First Thatcher Government 1979–1983: Contemporary Conservatism and Economic Change* Wheatsheaf 1985. This is good on the development of economic policy but is perhaps overly enthusiastic. He has followed this with his study of the second term of the Thatcher government *Thatcherism: Scope and Limits 1983–87* Macmillan 1989.

**312** Jock Bruce-Gardyne *Mrs Thatcher's First Administration: The Prophets Confounded* Macmillan 1984. There are a number of studies of the government's first term 1979–83. This is a useful insider narrative of the government's record during this period by the Economic Secretary to the Treasury 1981–3. Another sympathetic account of the first term by a former political adviser to Mrs Thatcher is Patrick Cosgrave *Thatcher: The First Term* The Bodley Head 1985. A critical study of Thatcher's first term is Melanie McFadyean and Margaret Renn *Thatcher's Reign: A Bad Case of the Blues* Chatto and Windus 1984. Hugh Stephenson *Mrs Thatcher's First Year* Jill Norman 1980 is an excellent study of the first year of a government that made more of an immediate impact than most.

**313** Kenneth Minogue and Michael Biddiss (eds) *Thatcherism: Personality and Politics* Macmillan 1987. A useful collection of essays examining the government's characteristics and its performance in certain policy areas. There are some interesting assessments although the section on social policy is inadequate. It was written before the 1987 general election. Various aspects and themes of the government are also well examined in Robert Skidelsky (ed) *Thatcherism* Chatto and Windus 1988. A symposium presenting different views on the record and achievements of the Thatcher government in the aftermath of that election is John Campbell *et al* 'Symposium. The Thatcher Years' *Contemporary Record* 1/3 1987 pp 2–26 and pp 30–1.

**314** Stuart Hall and Martin Jacques (eds) *The Politics of Thatcherism* Lawrence and Wishart 1983. An interpretative study which has done much to popularize the concept of Thatcherism. There is a certain artificiality to this notion of Thatcherism, not least in that it serves to disguise the caution and changes of policy which have often characterized the government. As a stick with which to beat the government it seems to have flattered rather than frightened the Prime Minister. This collection of essays from *Marxism Today* nevertheless argues that Thatcherism is an identifiable form of authoritarian populism. For an update of this view see [258]. Bob Jessop, Kevin Bonnett, Simon Bromley and Tom Ling *Thatcherism: A Tale of Two Nations* Polity 1988 instead contends that its principal characteristic is an emphasis on the concept of the free economy in the strong state. This theme has been most fully expressed in Andrew Gamble *The Free Economy and the Strong State: The Politics of Thatcherism* Macmillan 1988.

**315** Jacques Leruez *Le Thatcherisme: Doctrine et Action* CRNS, Paris 1985. A less balanced foreign assessment of the Thatcher government is the admiring account by the Italian journalist Paolo Filo Della Torre *Viva Britannia: Mrs Thatcher's Britain* Sidgwick and Jackson 1985.

**316** David S Bell (ed) *The Conservative Government 1979–84: An Interim Report* Croom Helm 1985. A collection of essays covering the policy spectrum. Peter M Jackson (ed) *Implementing Policy Initiatives: The Thatcher Government 1979–83* Royal Institute of Public Administration 1985 is a similarly valuable series of case studies covering key policy areas. An earlier set of case studies is Peter M Jackson (ed) *Government Policy Initiatives 1979–80: Some Case Studies in Public Administration* Royal Institute of Public Administration 1981. Lynton Robins (ed) *Political Institutions in Britain Longman* 1988, surveys recent changes in the political and administrative structure of Britain. In the process it examines the impact of the Thatcher government on, for instance, the Civil Service, economic policy or the trade unions.

**317** T Mainwaring and N Sigler (eds) *Breaking the Nation: A Guide to Thatcher's Britain* Pluto/New Socialist 1985. A critical assessment of the effect on living standards, services, employment and local government.

## C. CONSTITUTION

### (1) General Works

**318** Jeffrey Jowell and Dawn Oliver (eds) *The Changing Constitution* Clarendon 1985. A well regarded study of constitutional developments over the post-war years.

**319** J Harvey and Leslie Bather *The British Constitution* 5th ed, Macmillan 1982. A major textbook guide. Another useful textbook is T C Hartley and J A G Griffith *Government and Law: An Introduction to the Working of the Constitution in England* 2nd ed, Weidenfeld and Nicolson 1981. The various editions of these books can be used to obtain an impression of the changing state of the British constitution. Earlier constitutional treatises are Geoffrey Marshall and Graeme Cochrane Moodie *Some Problems of the Constitution* 4th ed, Hutchinson 1967, Sir W Ivor Jennings *The British Constitution* 5th ed, Cambridge University Press 1966, and H R

G Greaves *The British Constitution* 3rd ed, Allen and Unwin 1955.

**320** Ian Harden and Norman Lewis *The Noble Lie: The British Constitution and the Rule of Law* Unwin Hyman 1988. An acclaimed study which argues that British government is far less open, accountable and democratic than is popularly believed.

### (2) Interpretative Works

**321** Harold Laski *Reflections on the Constitution: The House of Commons, the Cabinet, the Civil Service* Manchester University Press 1951. In these lectures delivered shortly before his death Laski analyses the efficiency of each of these as instruments of government and suggests reforms. Leo Amery *Thoughts on the Constitution* Oxford University Press 1947 is a more wideranging survey of the state of the constitution in the immediate post-war era.

**322** G W Keeton *The Passing of Parliament* 2nd ed, Benn 1954. This contends there has been a massive increase in the power of the executive and the rule of law and the sovereignty of parliament has become a polite fiction. A dictatorship, he argues, could be imposed in Britain 'with complete legality.'

**323** Walter Bagehot *The English Constitution* New English Library 1964. A re-issue of the famous nineteenth century constitutional treatise with a useful prefatory essay by Richard Crossman in which he launches one of the earliest attacks on what he sees as the growth of Prime Ministerial government.

**324** Quintin MacGarel Hogg, Lord Hailsham *The Dilemma of Democracy: Diagnosis and Prescription* Collins 1978. This is a far ranging analysis of the constitutional and political problems of the post-war years in which he identifies a movement towards what he describes as elective dictatorship by the executive. He responds by proposing major reforms such as the enactment of a Bill of Rights as a restraint on an overweening power of the executive. See also his 1976 Dimbleby Lecture, which was published as *Elective Dictatorship* BBC 1976.

**325** Timothy Raison *Power and Parliament* Blackwell 1979. An interpretative study by a Conservative MP, particularly focusing on parliamentary change and decentralization of government.

**326** Brian Sedgmore *The Secret Constitution. An Analysis of the Political Establishment* Hodder and Stoughton 1980. Not quite a constitutional treatise. An analysis by a Labour MP drawing on his period as a junior minister 1974–9 and including some vivid examples of clashes between his superior, Tony Benn, and the Civil Service.

### (3) The Constitution in Particular Periods

**327** Philip Norton *The Constitution in Flux* Robertson 1982. This examines the stresses on the constitution in the 1970s.

**328** Cosmo Graham and Tony Prosser (eds) *Waiving the Rules: The Constitution Under Thatcherism* Open University Press 1988. A systematic analysis of the impact of the policy and action of the Thatcher government on the constitution. Tam Dalyell *Misrule: How Mrs Thatcher Mislead Parliament from the Sinking of the Belgrano to the Wright Affair* Hamilton 1987 is a sustained series of accusations of impropriety and mendacity against the Thatcher government by one of its most persistent critics.

### (4) Government Secrecy

The media are the section of British life most affected by government secrecy. Most of the material on this particular aspect of government secrecy does not appear below but in the section on the media's relationship with the government[3543–7].

**329** James Michael *The Politics of Secrecy* Penguin 1982. An important critique of secrecy in central and local government. It includes interesting case studies, historical analysis, and a useful bibliography. Annabelle May and Kathryn Rowan (eds) *Inside Information: British Government and the Media* Constable 1982 is a general guide to government secrecy, especially as it affects media access. It also includes a number of case studies. Richard A Chapman and Michael Hunt (eds) *Open Government* Croom Helm 1987 is a similar study of various types of secrecy in central and local government and of recent developments in this field. David Williams *Not in the Public Interest* Hutchinson 1965 is one of the first surveys of this kind. It is particularly good on the Civil Service position on secrecy.

**330** David Leigh *The Frontiers of Secrecy: Closed Government in Britain* Junction Books 1980. An analysis of secrecy in action covering the post-war period. K G Robertson *Public Secrets: A Study in the Development of Government Secrecy* Macmillan 1982 pp 22–91 deals with the development of government secrecy in Britain. The final section of John F Naylor *A Man and an Institution: Sir Maurice Hankey, the Cabinet Secretariat and the Custody of Cabinet Secrecy* Cambridge University Press 1984 is a history of central government

secrecy since 1938. Judith Cook *The Price of Freedom* New English Library 1985 presents a collection of case stories, concentrating on those who have been affected by government secrecy. See also Rosamund Thomas 'The Secrecy and Freedom of Information Debates in Britain' *Government and Opposition* 17 1982 pp 293–311.

**331** Bernard Porter *Plots and Paranoia: A History of Political Espionage in Britain 1790–1988* Unwin Hyman 1989. A good history of the internal security services. See also Tony Bunyan *The History and Practice of the Political Police in Britain* Julian Friedmann 1976. This looks particularly at the secrecy enforcing agencies, from MI5 to private security firms. It also examines the operation of secrecy, through telephone tapping or counter-revolutionary preparations. This analysis of internal security is updated by State Research *Review of Security and the State* Julian Friedmann 1978– . This annual publication aims to cover all aspects of security and secrecy during the year under review, from law-making to civil defence. Mark Hollingsworth and Richard Norton-Taylor *Blacklist: The Inside Story of Political Vetting* Hogarth Press 1988 examines this rather different aspect of political policing not only in the context of vetting in central government but also in the nuclear industry, defence companies, broadcasting and industrial relations.

**332** Norman S Marsh 'Public Access to Government Held Information in the United Kingdom: Attempts at Reform' in Norman S Marsh (ed) *Public Access to Government Held Information: A Comparative Symposium* Stevens 1987 pp 248–91. A survey of legislation and attempts at legislation since the Public Record Act 1958. This Act was passed in response to the report of the committee chaired by Sir John Grigg, *Committee on Departmental Records: Report* Cmnd 9163, *Parliamentary Papers* xi 1953–54, which reviewed the procedure for the selection, transfer and preservation of documents and recommended a fifty year rule on release of material. This was subsequently reduced to a thirty year rule by the first Wilson government. The 1977 Croham Directive did, until curtailed by the incoming Thatcher government in 1979, set up a discretionary system for the release of documents. Colin Bennett and Peter Hennessy *A Consumer's Guide to Open Goverment: Techniques for Penetrating Whitehall* Outer Circle Policy Unit 1980 is essentially an audit of its effects and a bibliography of the items released.

**333** *Departmental Committee on Section 2 of the Official Secrets Act 1911* Cmnd 5104, *Parliamentary Papers* xxxvii 1971– 72. An inquiry chaired by Lord Franks which recommended that the Act be replaced by an Official Information Act with narrower and more specific categories. William Birtles 'Big Brother Knows Best: The Franks Report on Section 2 of the Official

Secrets Act' *Public Law* Summer 1973 pp 100–22 is a commentary on the report.

**334** David Hooper *Official Secrets: The Use and Abuse of the Act* Secker and Warburg 1987. A history of the Official Secrets Act and its operation since 1911. Jonathan Aitken *Officially Secret* Weidenfeld and Nicolson 1971 is also in a sense a history of the Act. It is however principally an autobiographical account by a journalist who was prosecuted under its provisions. Graham Zellick 'National Security, Official Information and the Law' *Contemporary Review* 249 1986 pp 189–96 surveys the implementation of and attempts to reform the Act since the Franks Report.

**335** *Report of a Committee of Privy Councillors on Ministerial Memoirs* Cmnd 6386 *Parliamentary Papers* xiii 1975–76. An inquiry chaired by Lord Radcliffe prompted by the furore over the publication of Richard Crossman's cabinet diaries which laid down new guidelines for the release of this type of material. Hugo Young *The Crossman Affair* Hamilton/Cape 1976 is a good instant history of the attempt to prevent publication of the Crossman diaries. It includes useful documentary evidence.

**336** *Report of the Committee on Cabinet Document Security* Cmnd 6677, *Parliamentary Papers* 1976–77. A committee chaired by Lord Houghton of Sowerby which led to the tightening up of procedure against cabinet leaks. See also [410–1] on security in the Civil Service.

**337** *Modern Public Records: Selection and Access: Report of a Committee Appointed by the Lord Chancellor* Cmnd 8204, *Parliamentary Papers* 1980–81. A review of selection and access policy chaired by Sir Duncan Wilson. See also *Modern Public Records: The Government Response to the Report of the Wilson Committee* Cmnd 8531, *Parliamentary Papers* 1981–82.

### (5) Civil Liberties

**338** Patricia Hewitt *The Abuse of Power: Civil Liberties in the United Kingdom* Robertson 1982. An analysis which includes plenty of historical detail on the various developments of the post-war years. Barry Cox *Civil Liberties in Britain* Penguin 1975 is a good general guide to the issues. See also I N Stevens and D C M Yardley *The Protection of Liberty* Blackwell 1982. Harry Street *Freedom, the Individual and the Law* 5th ed, Penguin 1982 is more of a legal textbook.

**339** *Report of the Committee on Data Protection* Cmnd 7341, *Parliamentary Papers* 1978–79. Report of the committee chaired by Sir Norman Lindop set up to recommend legislation to protect personal data on computers and to suggest the powers and functions of the Data Protection Authority that was subsequently established.

**340** Mark Lilly *The National Council for Civil Liberties: The First Fifty Years* Macmillan 1984. The official history of this important pressure group. See also R Benewick 'British Pressure Group Politics: The National Council for Civil Liberties' *Annals of the American Academy of Political and Social Science* 1974 pp 145–57. Another important pressure group which is principally concerned with civil liberties, though on a global rather than a national scale, is Amnesty International. Jonathan Power *Amnesty International: The Human Rights Story* Pergamon 1981 is a well illustrated 20th anniversary history of this London-based international pressure group, established in the UK in 1961. See also Egon Larsen *A Flame in Barbed Wire: The Story of Amnesty International* W W Norton, New York 1979.

**341** Peter Thornton *Decade of Decline: Civil Liberties in the Thatcher Years* National Council of Civil Liberties 1989. A critical review of the erosion of civil liberties under the Thatcher government.

### (6) Emergency Powers

**342** David M Bonner *Emergency Powers in Peacetime* Sweet and Maxwell 1985. A legal textbook which deals with these powers in the mainland as well as Northern Ireland. It includes a table of relevant statutes. See also A S Klieman 'Emergency Powers and Liberal Democracy in Britain' *Journal of Commonwealth and Comparative Politics* 16 1978 pp 190–211.

## D. THE MONARCHY

### (1) General

**343** F M Hardie *The Political Influence of the British Monarchy 1868–1952* Batsford 1970. The standard work. A more general history is P Howard *The British Monarchy in the Twentieth Century* Hamilton 1977. Alan Alexander 'British Politics and the Royal Prerogative of Appointments Since 1945' *Parliamentary Affairs* 23 1970 pp 148–57 covers one aspect of the monarchy's political influence. On the monarch as Head of the Commonwealth see [1143].

**344** Andrew Duncan *The Reality of Monarchy* Heinemann 1970. An informative plea for a revived, modern monarchy. It includes lots of information on aspects of the monarchy, such as state visits, which it suggests have little impact on trade. Kingsley Martin *The Crown and* the Establishment Hutchinson 1962 drew attention to its etiquette and called for reform. Sir Charles Petrie *The Modern British Monarchy* Eyre and Spottiswoode 1961 also criticizes the monarchy for being out of date. David Sinclair *Two Georges: The Making of the Modern Monarchy* Hodder and Stoughton 1988 argues that the monarchy lost spiritual and temporal power during the reigns of George V and George VI. He also contends that it is a conservative and anachronistic force arresting dynamism in the British economy and society and calls for a constitutional monarchy modelled on the ideas of Prince Albert. Tom Nairn *The Enchanted Glass: Britain and its Monarchy* Radius 1988 is a similar diagnosis but one which develops more as an argument for the republicanism he sees as a solution than as an historical inquiry. Another critical evaluation of the modern monarchy is Piers Brendon *Our Own Dear Queen* Secker and Warburg 1986. The creation of the ritual and character of the modern monarchy is analysed in David Cannadine 'The Context, Performance and Meaning of Ritual: The British Monarchy and "The Invention of Tradition" c1820–1977' in Eric Hobsbawm and Terence Ranger (eds) *The Invention of Tradition* Cambridge University Press 1983 pp 101–64.

**345**   Dermot Morrah *The Work of the Queen* Kimber 1958. An account of the powers, duties, responsibilities and costs of the monarchy and the Queen's role in both Britain and the Commonwealth. Dorothy Laird *How the Queen Reigns* Hodder and Stoughton 1959 is an account of the monarch's duties and of the Royal Household. See also Randolph Churchill *They Serve the Queen: A New and Authoritative Account of the Royal Household* Hutchinson 1953.

**346**   *Voices out of the Air; The Royal Christmas Broadcasts 1932–1981* Heinemann 1981. Introduced by Tom Fleming. It includes the complete texts of the broadcasts and biographical details on each sovereign. See also *King George VI to his People 1936–51: Selected Broadcasts and Speeches* John Murray 1952.

### (2) The Royal Family

**347**   John Pearson *The Ultimate Family: The Making of the Royal House of Windsor* Michael Joseph 1986. A scholarly acccount of the public image of the Royal Family from the time of George V. It is particularly good in dealing with the transformation of this image in recent years. See also Denis Judd *The House of Windsor* Macdonald and Janes 1973 and Elizabeth Pakenham, Countess of Longford *The Royal House of Windsor* Weidenfeld and Nicolson 1974.

**348**   John W Wheeler-Bennett *King George VI: His Life and Reign* Macmillan 1958. The official biography

based on the Royal Archives. See also Patrick Howarth *George VI: A New Biography* Hutchinson 1987, Denis Judd *King George VI 1895–1952* Michael Joseph 1982, Keith Middlemas *The Life and Times of George VI* Weidenfeld and Nicolson 1974 and Sarah Bradford *King George VI and the House of Windsor* Weidenfeld and Nicolson 1989. Christopher Warwick *King George VI and Queen Elizabeth: A Portrait* Sidgwick and Jackson 1985 focuses on the development of a more personal and relaxed monarchy during the years 1936–52, seeing this as more a result of the personality of the Queen Consort than of the King himself. David Sinclair *Queen and Country: The Life of Elizabeth the Queen Mother* Fontana 1980 is a biography of George VI's consort. See also Anthony Holden *The Queen Mother: A Birthday Tribute* Sphere 1985.

**349**   Robert Lacey *Majesty: Elizabeth II and the House of Windsor* Hutchinson 1977. The best biography. See also Elizabeth Longford *Elizabeth R: A Biography* Weidenfeld and Nicolson 1983. There have been many other works written about the present Queen. Most of these however have little lasting value. This is indeed true of the biographies of most royal figures.

**350**   Denis Judd *Prince Philip: A Biography* Michael Joseph 1980. See also Unity Hall *Philip: The Man Behind the Monarchy* Michael O'Mara Books 1987.

**351**   Christopher Warwick *Princess Margaret* Weidenfeld and Nicolson 1983. The official biography. See also Willi Frischauer *Margaret: Princess Without a Cause* Michael Joseph 1977 and Helen Cathcart *Princess Margaret* W H Allen 1974.

**352**   Peter Lane *Prince Charles: A Study in Development* Hale 1988. A perceptive biography. Another good study is Penny Junor *Charles* Pan 1987. Alan Hamilton *The Real Charles* Collins 1988 is good on the influences on the Prince of Wales. Helen Cathcart *Charles – Man of Destiny* W H Allen 1976 is a more intimate and chatty biography. See also Anthony Holden *Charles: Prince of Wales* Pan 1979.

**353**   J Bryan III and Charles J V Murphy *The Windsor Story* Granada 1979. A good general biography of the Duke and Duchess of Windsor. On the Duke see J P D Balfour *The Windsor Years: The Life of Edward as Prince of Wales, King and Duke of Windsor* Collins 1967. A more scandalous biography is John Parker *King of Fools* Macdonald 1988. The Duchess of Windsor has written her autobiography *The Heart Has Its Reasons: The Memoirs of the Duchess of Windsor* Michael Joseph 1956. There is also a biography by her friend Diana Mosley *The Duchess of Windsor* Sidgwick and Jackson 1980. See also Stephen Birmingham *Duchess: The Story of Wallis Warfield Simpson* Macmillan 1981. For the strained relations between the Windsors and the rest of the Royal Family see Michael Thornton *Royal Feud: The Queen Mother and the Duchess of Windsor* Michael Joseph 1985. Two books which draw on the private papers of the Windsors in dealing with this subject, and which caused something of a stir when published in 1988 are Michael Bloch *The Secret File of the Duke of Windsor* Basham 1988, and Charles Higham *Wallis: Secret Lives of the Duchess of Windsor* Sidgwick and Jackson 1988.

**354** James Pope-Hennessy *Queen Mary 1867–1953* Allen and Unwin 1959. A good biography of George V's consort. See also Anne Edwards *Matriarch: Queen Mary and the House of Windsor* Hodder and Stoughton 1984.

**355** Graham Fisher *Prince Andrew: Boy, Man and Prince* W H Allen 1982. There are other biographies of the Prince. This however is probably the best of a rather syrupy collection.

**356** Helen Cathcart *Anne The Princess Royal: A Princess for Our Times* 2nd ed, W H Allen 1988. Other reasonable biographies are Paul James *Anne: The Working Princess* Piatkus 1987 and Nicholas Courtney *Princess Anne: A Biography* Weidenfeld and Nicolson 1986.

**357** Tim Graham *Diana: H R H Princess of Wales* Michael O'Mara Books 1988. A biography of the world's most photographed woman. See also Penny Junor *Diana: Princess of Wales: A Biography* Sidgwick and Jackson 1982. She and her sister-in-law, the Duchess of York, have had a major effect on the public image of the Royal Family. Andrew Morton *Duchess* Michael O'Mara Books 1988 is the first full biography of the Duchess.

**358** Princess Marie Louise *My Memories of Six Reigns* Evans 1956. An autobiography which casts some light on the Royal Family in the early post-war period.

**359** Princess Alice, Duchess of Gloucester *The Memoirs of Princess Alice, Duchess of Gloucester* Collins 1983. This autobiography is also useful for when her husband was Governor-General of Australia during the war until 1947.

# E. ADMINISTRATION AND CENTRAL GOVERNMENT

## (1) Reference Works

**360** *The Civil Service Year Book* HMSO 1974–. Annual guide to British public services. Superseded the *British Imperial Calendar and Civil Service List 1925–*

*1973*. It gives details not only of central government departments but of museums, galleries, quangos and other centrally funded bodies. It is also very informative on Whitehall. The year book is up-dated quarterly by Her Majesty's Ministers and Senior Staff in Public Departments. See also *Civil Service Statistics* HMSO 1970–, an annual survey of the Civil Service. *Staffs Employed in Government Departments* HMSO 1919–, gives details of the size and employment structure of the Civil Service.

**361** *Public Domain: The Public Services Yearbook* Public Finance Corporation/Peat Marwick, McLintock 1986–. The accent in this yearbook, is broader than [360] including local government services and the National Health Service. A very informative annual survey.

**362** *Public Bodies* HMSO 1986–. An annual guide which succeeds *A Directory of Paid Public Appointments Made by Ministers* HMSO, first published 1976. It lists appointments to about 300 bodies and gives brief information on each body.

## (2) General Works

**363** R G S Brown and D R Steele *The Administrative Process in Britain* 2nd ed, Methuen 1979. An excellent study of the work of central government departments. Andrew Gray and William I Jenkins *Administrative Politics in British Government* Harvester 1985 is a survey of the situation in the 1980s which is particularly useful on the Civil Service. See also R A Chapman and Andrew Dunsire (eds) *Style in Administration: Readings in British Public Administration* Allen and Unwin 1971. W J M Mackenzie and J W Grove *Central Administration in Great Britain* Longmans 1957 is a detailed and factual account that remains of great value for the study of the organization and operation of central government after the Second World War. Edgar Norman Gladden *British Public Service Administration* Staples Press 1961 is a useful general guide to the various areas of central government. See also his *The Essentials of Public Administration* 3rd ed, Staples Press 1964 and B Chapman *British Government Observed* Allen and Unwin 1963.

**364** D N Chester and F M G Willson *The Organisation of British Central Government 1914–1964* 2nd ed, Allen and Unwin 1968. A revised and expanded version of D N Chester (ed) *The Organisation of British Central Government 1914–1956* Allen and Unwin 1957. This survey by a Royal Institute of Public Administration study group looked at the organization and responsibilities of government departments and changes in their structure. It was based on memoranda from the departments concerned. The second edition also includes a useful chronology. A similar study is the Royal Institute of Public Administration symposium *British Government Since 1918* Allen and Unwin 1950. This features essays on parliament, cabinet, central administration, administrative law, quangos and local government. See also Richard A Chapman and J R Greenaway *The Dynamics of Administrative Reform* Croom Helm 1980, a survey which covers developments 1850–1970.

**365** John Michael Lee *Reviewing the Machinery of Government 1942–1952: An Essay on the Anderson Committee and Its Successors* Department of Politics, University of Bristol 1977. A useful short study of the ten year insider review which in the end achieved very little.

**366** Geoffrey K Fry *The Administrative Revolution in Whitehall: A Study of the Politics of Administrative Change in British Central Government Since the 1950s* Croom Helm 1981. A good survey of more recent administrative changes. Aspects of this process are touched on in F M G Willson 'Coping with Administrative Growth: Super-Departments and the Ministerial Cadre 1957–77' in David Butler and A H Halsey (eds) *Policy and Politics: Essays in Honour of Norman Chester* Macmillan 1978 pp 35–50. See also A Doig 'The Machinery of Government and the Governmental Bodies' *Public Administration* 57 1979 pp 309–31.

**367** Christopher Pollitt *Manipulating the Machine: Changing the Pattern of Ministerial Departments 1960–83* Allen and Unwin 1984. A good survey of the major changes in the structure of central government departments of this period. Douglas Pitt and Brian Charles Smith *Government Departments: An Organisational Perspective* Routledge and Kegan Paul 1981 is a rather theoretical analysis with some useful case studies.

**368** *The Reorganisation of Central Government* Cmnd 4506, *Parliamentary Papers* xx 1970–71. The White Paper outlining the super-departments the Heath government went on to create. It also created the policy audit system Programme Analysis and Review (PAR). The history of PAR is surveyed in Andrew Gray and Bill Jenkins 'Policy Analysis in British Central Government: The Experience of PAR' *Public Administration* 60 1982 pp 429–50. Andrew Gray and Bill Jenkins (eds) *Policy Analysis and Evaluation in British Government* Royal Institute of Public Administration 1983 is a symposium on the policy analysis systems, management techniques and corporate planning in both central and local government that succeeded PAR in the 1980s. Christopher Hood, Meg Huby and Andrew Dunsire 'Scale Economies and Iron Laws: Mergers and Demergers in Whitehall 1971–1984' *Public Administration* 63/1 1984 pp 61–78, is an analysis and series of case studies of the reorganization of central government departments since the 1970 White Paper.

**369** Lynton Robins (ed) *Politics and Policy Making in Britain* Longman 1988. A survey of developments of the 1970s and 1980s in a select range of policy areas. Another more comprehensive, if less detailed examination of policy areas is Martin Burch and Bruce Wood *Public Policy in Britain* Robertson 1983.

**370** Jock Bruce-Gardyne and Nigel Lawson *The Power Game: An Examination of Decision-Making in Government* Macmillan 1976. A very useful series of case studies of policy on Concorde (pp 10–37), attempts to join the European Community in 1961–3 and 1967 (pp 38–79), the abolition of Resale Price Maintenance (pp 80–117) and the defence of sterling 1964–7 (pp 118–49). Another series of case studies, in the context of an examination of policy-making in the face of crises, such as the Thalidomide problem, is Brian W Hogwood *From Crisis to Complacency? Shaping Public Policy in Britain* Oxford University Press 1987.

**371** John Brown *Management in Central and Local Government* Pitman 1979. An analysis of the development of management techniques in the wake of the 1968 Fulton [398] and the 1972 Bains [7568] reports.

**372** R A W Rhodes *Beyond Westminster and Whitehall: The Sub-Central Governments of Britain* Unwin Hyman 1988. A pioneering analysis of the vast range of service producing agencies outside London.

## (3) Cabinet

**373** Peter Hennessy *Cabinet* Blackwell 1986. A witty and incisive study of the changing character and the quality of cabinet government since the Second World War. Its principal themes are the increasing overload of cabinet government in the post-war years and the power of the Prime Minister. See also H Daalder *Cabinet Reform in Britain 1914–1963* Oxford University Press 1964.

**374** John Pitcairn Mackintosh *The British Cabinet* 3rd ed, Stevens 1977. A valuable study of the institution over a long historical time span which argues that there has been a drift towards prime ministerial government in recent years. Another useful study drawing on actual experience as a cabinet minister is Patrick Gordon Walker *The Cabinet* 2nd ed, Fontana 1972. Valentine Herman and James E Alt (eds) *Cabinet Studies: A Reader* Macmillan 1975 also includes essays by former cabinet ministers. Another reflection on the cabinet by a senior figure in the 1974–9 Labour government is Edmund Dell 'Some Reflections on Cabinet Government by a Former Practitioner' *Public Administration Bulletin* 32 1980 pp 17–33.

**375** Michael Rush *The Cabinet and Policy Formation* Longman 1984. A textbook guide.

**376** J H Brookshire 'Clement Attlee and Cabinet Reform 1930–1945' *Historical Journal* 24 1981 pp 175–88. Attlee's experience of the second Labour government encouraged him to explore different ways of organizing the pinnacle of government when he came to power in 1945. Developments in the cabinet and the cabinet committees structure are examined in Peter Hennessy and Andrew Arends *Mr Attlee's Engine Room: Cabinet Committee Structure and the Labour Governments 1945–51* Centre for the Study of Public Policy Paper 26, University of Strathclyde 1983. The replacement at cabinet rank of the three service ministers with a single minister of defence in 1946 is discussed in Henry D Jordan 'Foreign Government and Politics: The British Cabinet and the Ministry of Defence' *American Political Science Review* 43 1949 pp 73–82.

**377** R S Milne 'The Experiment with "Coordinating Ministers" in the British Cabinet 1951–3' *Canadian Journal of Economic and Political Science* 1955 pp 365–9. A survey of Churchill's experiment with overlord ministers.

**378** R K Alderman and J A Cross 'Problems of Ministerial Turnover in Two Labour Cabinets' *Political Studies* 29 1981 pp 425–30. A study of structural changes and rapid personnel turnover in 1964–70 and 1974–79.

**379** Arthur Silkin 'The "Agreement to Differ" of 1975 and its Effects on Ministerial Responsibility' *Political Quarterly* 48 1977 pp 65–77. An analysis of the agreement to differ in the Labour cabinet over the 1975 Referendum on membership of the European Community.

**380** Martin Burch 'The British Cabinet: A Residual Executive' *Parliamentary Affairs* 41 1988 pp 34–48. A study of the cabinet in the 1980s and its contemporary constitutional position.

**381** Colin Seymour-Ure 'British "War Cabinets" in Limited Wars: Korea, Suez and the Falklands' *Public Administration* Summer 1984 pp 181–200.

**382** Bryum E Carter *The Office of Prime Minister* Faber 1956. The only study so far specifically to deal with the nature of the office. George W Jones 'The Prime Minister and Parliamentary Questions' *Parliamentary Affairs* 26 1973 pp 260–73 considers one aspect of the Prime Minister's role. Rodney Brazier 'Choosing a Prime Minister' *Public Law* 1982 pp 395–417 discusses the rules and conventions whereby a Prime Minister is chosen.

**383** Anthony King (ed) *The British Prime Minister* 2nd ed, Macmillan 1985. One of the principal controversies in the study of cabinet government in recent years is whether or not the cabinet has been eclipsed during the post-war period by a growth in Prime Ministerial power and patronage. This important theme is fully addressed in this volume of collected articles, as is Prime Ministerial style and the work of the Prime Minister and his or her staff. One of the most influential statements supporting this view that Prime Ministerial power has greatly increased is Richard Crossman *Inside View: Three Lectures on Prime Ministerial Government* Cape 1972. See also Humphrey Berkeley *The Power of the Prime Minister* Allen and Unwin 1967, A H Brown 'Prime Ministerial Power' *Public Law* 1968 pp 28–51 and 96–118 and D J Heasman 'The Prime Minister and the Cabinet' *Parliamentary Affairs* 15 1962 pp 461–84. This view is rejected in George W Jones 'The Prime Minister's Power' *Parliamentary Affairs* 18 1965 pp 167–85. The related issue of Prime Ministerial patronage is examined in R K Alderman 'The Prime Minister and the Appointment of Ministers' *Parliamentary Affairs* 29 1976 pp 101–35. See also R K Alderman and J A Cross 'The Prime Ministers and the Decision to Dissolve' *Parliamentary Affairs* 28 1975 pp 386–404.

**384** Dennis Kavanagh *Margaret Thatcher: A Study in Prime Ministerial Style* Centre for the Study of Public Policy Paper 151, University of Strathclyde 1986. The controversy about Prime Ministerial power which developed in the 1960s has been revived in the 1980s by the premiership of Margaret Thatcher. Kavanagh argues that her premiership has been domineering. Jim Bulpitt 'The Discipline of the New Democracy: Mrs Thatcher's Domestic Statecraft' *Political Studies* 34 1985 pp 19–39, however contends that there is more similarity of style with Churchill and Macmillan than is normally allowed. For other interpretations see Michael Doherty 'Prime Ministerial Power and Ministerial Responsibility in the Thatcher Era' *Parliamentary Affairs* 41 1988 pp 49–67, Martin Burch 'Mrs Thatcher's Approach to Leadership in Government 1979 – June 1983' *Parliamentary Affairs* 36 1983 pp 399–416 and N D S Baldwin 'An Imperial Premiership? Thatcher at 10 Downing Street' *British Politics Group Newsletter* 48 1987 pp 6–10.

**385** D H Elletson *Chequers and the Prime Ministers* Hale 1970. A history of the house given to the nation as a country retreat for the Prime Minister in 1917.

**386** John Hudson 'Prime Ministerial Popularity in the UK 1960–81' *Political Studies* 23 1984 pp 86–97. A study, based on opinion poll data, of movements in public approval of Prime Ministers.

**388** Bruce W Heady *British Cabinet Ministers: The Role of Politicians in Executive Office* Allen and Unwin 1974. A useful study of ministerial roles and responsibilities derived from interviews with former ministers and civil servants. Richard Rose 'The Making of Cabinet Ministers' *British Journal of Political Science* 1/4 1971 pp 393–414 analyses the personnel of the cabinet and the growth of government patronage during the post-war years. F M G Willson 'The Route of Entry of New Members of the British Cabinet 1868–1958' *Political Studies* 7 1959 pp 222–32, updated by 'Entry to the Cabinet 1959–1968' *Political Studies* 17 1970 pp 36–8, also deals with this neglected subject. See also John Bonnar 'The Four Labour Cabinets' *Sociological Review* n.s. 6 1958 pp 37–48. R K Alderman and J A Cross *The Tactics of Resignation: A Study in British Cabinet Government* Routledge and Kegan Paul 1967 is a useful short historical analysis with a valuable appendix on resignations on policy grounds 1900–67. In view of a number of spectacular resignations since 1967 it could now usefully be updated. They have also studied dismissals from the cabinet in their 'The Timing of Cabinet Reshuffles' *Parliamentary Affairs* 40 1987 pp 1–19. On cabinet reshuffles see also their 'Rejuvenating the Cabinet: The Records of Post-War British Prime Ministers Compared' *Political Studies* 34 1986 pp 639–46.

**389** Geoffrey Marshall (ed) *Ministerial Responsibility* Oxford University Press 1989. A collection of readings drawn from various sources to illustrate this concept, many of which deal with events and issues of the post-war period. David L Ellis 'Collective Ministerial Responsibility and Collective Solidarity' *Public Law* 1980 pp 367–95 is a good discussion of these government conventions.

### (4) Junior Ministers

**390** Kevin Theakston *Junior Ministers in British Government* Blackwell 1987. The first comprehensive study of junior ministers drawing on research for his thesis which traced their role in government from 1830 onwards. He examines their careers, their work in parliament, contribution to policy making and role in cabinet committees. See also R K Alderman and J A Cross 'The Parliamentary Private Secretary' *Political Studies* 14 1966 pp 199–208.

### (5) Advisers and Political Staff

**391** Sir Alec Cairncross and Nita Watts *The Economic Section 1939–1961: A Study in Economic Advising* Routledge 1989. A study of the history of the economic section of the Cabinet Office drawing on Sir Alec's personal memories.

**392** Tessa Blackstone and William Plowden *Inside the Think Tank: Advising the Cabinet 1971–1983* Heine-

mann 1988. A history of the Central Policy Review Staff (CPRS) set up to advise the government by Heath and disbanded by Thatcher in 1983. An important study of its successes and failures, its relations with civil servants and with cabinet ministers and its contribution to policy in these years. Peter Hennessy, Susan Morrison and Richard Townsend *Routine Punctuated by Orgies: The Central Policy Review Staff 1970–1983* Centre for the Study of Public Policy Paper 31, University of Strathclyde 1985 is a witty analysis which is particularly good on the setting up of the CPRS. Simon James 'The Central Policy Review Staff 1970–1983' *Political Studies* 34 1986 pp 423–40 is a persuasive examination of its failings. See also M Isserlis 'The Central Policy Review Staff and After' *Policy Studies* 4 1984 pp 22–35. A useful early assessment is Christopher Pollitt 'The Central Policy Review Staff 1970–1974' *Public Administration* 52 1974 pp 375–94.

**393** Nathaniel Meyer Victor Rothschild *Meditations on a Broomstick* Collins 1977. A collection of reminiscences and assorted speeches of uneven value which reflect, in part, on his time as the first and most successful head of the CPRS. A similar selection was published as *Random Variables* Collins 1984.

**394** George W Jones 'The Prime Ministers' Secretaries: Politicians or Administrators?' in J A G Griffith (ed) *From Policy to Administration. Essays in Honour of William A Robson* Allen and Unwin 1976 pp 13–38. A history of political advisers and press officers up to the time of the Heath government. The emergence of these staff as a recognizable element of government was particularly rapid 1964–74. This process is analysed by J G J Lenoski 'The Evolution of Political Staffs to British Cabinet Ministers 1964–1974' Essex MPhil Thesis 1983. See also Rudolf Klein and Janet Lewis 'Advice and Dissent in British Government: The Case of the Special Advisers' *Policy and Politics* 6 1977 pp 1–25. A number of these advisers have also written autobiographical accounts; see [296–7, 304, 306, 715, 778].

### (6) The Home Civil Service

There is more to the Civil Service than Whitehall. In the 1960s and after a number of Civil Service agencies were re-located away from the capital. As this was a facet in regional policy the literature on this process has been included in the section on regional development policy. The works listed below are those which deal with Civil Service structure, departments and personnel. Material on Civil Service trade unions and industrial relations also appears elsewhere in this bibiliography in the sections on trade unions and industrial relations. The Post Office, which was a department of state until 1969, is dealt with in the section on the communications industries.

**395** Peter Hennessy *Whitehall* Secker and Warburg 1989. The most comprehensive historical analysis of Civil Service organization, performance and personnel. It also gives extensive coverage of successive attempts to reform Whitehall, particularly those of Mrs Thatcher. J Delafons 'Working in Whitehall: Changes in Public Administration 1952–1982' *Public Administration* 60 1982 pp 253–72 is an insider account of the changes wrought by a series of important reports and of the growing emphasis on managerial efficiency. Edgar Norman Gladden *Civil Services of the United Kingdom 1855–1970* Cass 1967 is a wide-ranging, if now somewhat outdated survey which also covers the civil services of Northern Ireland, the Isle of Man and the Channel Islands. It also has a useful annotated bibliography. Peter Hennessy *et al* 'Symposium: The Civil Service' *Contemporary Record* 2/2 1988 pp 2–15 includes short pieces on changes under Thatcher, the television programme 'Yes Prime Minister', Tony Benn as Postmaster-General and Civil Service relations with Labour governments.

**396** T A Critchley *The Civil Service Today* Gollancz 1951. A good portrait of the Civil Service in the 1950s. See also Dorothy Johnstone 'Developments in the British Civil Service 1945-1951' *Public Administration* 30 1952 pp 49-59. Frank Dunnill *The Civil Service: Some Human Aspects* Allen and Unwin 1956 concentrates on its personnel. Edward Bridges *Portrait of a Profession: The Civil Service Tradition* Cambridge University Press 1950 is a description of Civil Service work and defence of its generalist traditions by the then Head of the Service. W A Robson (ed) *The Civil Service in Britain and France* Hogarth Press 1956 largely consists of essays on various aspects of the British Civil Service in the 1950s by distinguished civil servants and politicians. Paul Marie Gaudemet *Le Civil Service Britannique: Essai sur le Régime de la Fonction Publique en Grande Bretagne* Armand Colin, Paris 1952 is a useful French study. G A Campbell *The Civil Service in Britain* 2nd ed, Duckworth 1965 is a survey of the Service in the 1960s. C H Sisson *The Spirit of British Administration* 2nd ed, Faber 1966 looks at the Civil Service in the 1960s in comparative context.

**397** *Royal Commission on the Civil Service* Cmnd 9613, *Parliamentary Papers* xi 1955–56. Chaired by Sir Raymond Priestley. The report was largely concerned with pay and conditions. Its effects are considered in Geoffrey K Fry 'Civil Service Salaries in the Post-Priestley Era 1956–1972' *Public Administration* 52 1974 pp 319–33. A further inquiry is Sir John Megaw *Civil Service Pay: Report of an Inquiry* 2v, Cmnd 8590, *Parliamentary Papers* 1981–82.

**398** *Report of the Committee on the Civil Service 1966–1968* Cmnd 3638, *Parliamentary Papers* xviii 1967–68. The report of the committee set up under the chairmanship of Lord Fulton, 'to examine the structure, recruitment and training of the Home Civil Service to make recommendations'. Its establishment reflected dissatisfaction with the structure and performance of the Civil Service first given voice in Thomas Balogh's essay 'The Apotheosis of the Dilettante', first published in 1959 [203]. This essay is reprinted in Hugh Thomas (ed) *Crisis in the Civil Service* Anthony Blond 1968, a collection of essays which reflect the attitudes at the time of the Fulton report. Another influential polemic was Robert Nield *The Administrators* Fabian Society 1964. The Fulton committee, its report and the implementation of its recommendations are reconsidered in the Institute of Contemporary British History witness chaired by Peter Hennessy 'Fulton: 20 Years On' *Contemporary Record* 2/2 1988 pp 44–55. The development of policy planning units, which was one of the consequences of Fulton, is assessed in James Macdonald and Geoffrey K Fry 'Policy Planning Units – Ten Years On' *Public Administration* 58 1980 pp 421–38.

**399** Geoffrey K Fry *The Changing Civil Service* Allen and Unwin 1985. An excellent study of developments in the Civil Service since the Fulton report. It includes a good bibliography. John Garrett *Managing the Civil Service* Heinemann 1980 is a critical appraisal of slow progress in reforming administration and accountability in the wake of the Fulton report. Its author, a management consultant to the Fulton committee, felt by 1980 that the need for reform was greater than ever. Enid Russell-Smith *Modern Bureaucracy: The Home Civil Service* Longman 1975 is an introduction to the post Fulton Civil Service by a former civil servant. See also Richard A Chapman and Dudley Lofts 'The Civil Service after Fulton' *Public Administration Bulletin* 27 1978 pp 41–53 and Sir James Dunnett 'The Civil Service: Seven Years After Fulton' *Public Administration* 54 1976 pp 371–9.

**400** Gavin Drewry and Tony Butcher *The Civil Service Today* Blackwell 1988. A good textbook study focusing on the issues the rise of specialists, new technologies and management techniques in the 1980s. A useful survey of the Civil Service in the 1970s and 1980s is Hugo Young and Anne Sloman *No Minister: An Inquiry into the Civil Service* BBC Books 1982. Clive Ponting *Whitehall: Tragedy and Farce* Hamilton 1985 provides critical insider reflections on Whitehall life, its inefficiencies and the difficulties of reform. Dermot Englefield (ed) *Today's Civil Service: A Guide to its Work with Parliament and Industry* Longman 1985 is partly a source book, especially on the policy of the Department of Trade and Industry. There are a number of useful essays by MPs and businessmen.

**401** *Efficiency and Effectiveness in the Civil Service: Government Observations on the Third Report from the Treasury and Civil Service Committee Session 1981–82*

HC 236 Cmnd 8616, *Parliamentary Papers* 1981–82. Major changes, particularly in management techniques in the Civil Service, have been brought about by the Thatcher government. Appendix 3 of this White Paper is the text of the Financial Management Initiative charter of Sir Derek (later Lord) Rayner which initiated the process. *Developing the FMI Principles: Changes in Process and Culture* Royal Institute of Public Administration 1985 is a symposium reviewing the development and implementation of FMI. Geoffrey K Fry 'The Development of the Thatcher Government's "Grand Strategy" for the Civil Service: A Public Policy Perspective' *Public Administration* 62 1984 pp 322–35 is a broader overview of the changes initiated by the Thatcher government.

**402**  Richard Rose *Ministers and Ministries: A Functional Analysis* Clarendon 1987. A survey of the tensions between elected ministers and permanent ministries over the post-war period with case studies of the Welsh, Scottish and Northern Ireland Offices. R K Alderman and J A Cross 'Ministerial Reshuffles and the Civil Service' *British Journal of Political Science* 9 1979 pp 41–65 also reflects generally on relations between ministers and the Civil Service. R S Barker 'Civil Service Attitudes and the Economic Planning of the Attlee Government' *Journal of Contemporary History* 21 1986 pp 473–86 looks at this relationship in the context of the Attlee government. Attlee's own admiration for Civil Service impartiality is reflected in Clement Richard Attlee 'Civil Service, Ministers, Parliament and the Public' *Political Quarterly* 25 1954 pp 308–15. A more critical Prime Ministerial appraisal of the Civil Service is Edward Heath and Anthony Barker 'Heath on Whitehall Reform' *Parliamentary Affairs* 31 1978 pp 363–90. Nor has the Labour Party usually shared Attlee's view of the Civil Service. W B Gwyn 'The Labour Party and the Threat of Bureaucracy' *Political Studies* 19 1971 pp 383–402 concentrates particularly on the animosity felt by the 1964–70 Labour government towards the Civil Service and the resulting efforts to improve the scrutiny of its operation. F F Ridley 'The British Civil Service and Politics: Principles in Question and Traditions in Flux' *Parliamentary Affairs* 36 1983 pp 28–48 argues that the Civil Service has been politicized by the Thatcher government. For a study of relations with the Civil Service by one of Mrs Thatcher's ministers, Jock Bruce-Gardyne, see [798].

**403**  Leslie Chapman *Your Disobedient Servant: The Continuing Story of Whitehall's Overspending* 2nd ed, Penguin 1979. A survey by a former civil servant of Civil Service waste which helped to fuel calls for more accountability and efficiency. His *Waste Away* Chatto and Windus 1982 casts its nets wider to include inefficiency in nationalized industries and local government.

**404**  Mae Y Keary and Bridget M Howard (comps) *Civil Service Department: Its Organisation and History* 2nd ed, Civil Service Department 1979. The Civil Service Department was set up after the Fulton report and abolished in 1981. This is an outline history. See also Richard A Chapman 'The Rise and Fall of the CSD' *Policy and Politics* 11 1983 pp 41–62. *The Work of CSD 1968–1978* Civil Service Department 1979 is an unannotated bibliography of the reports it produced on the working of the Civil Service. It also features bibliographies on two heads of the Civil Service, Sir William Armstrong and Sir Douglas Allen.

**405**  *Civil Service Commission Annual Report 1855–*. The Civil Service Commission oversees the Administration of the entrance examinations and the conditions of service. The official history is K M Reader *The Civil Service Commission 1855–1975* HMSO 1981. Edgar Anstey 'A 30-Year Follow-Up of the CSSB Procedure, with Lessons for the Future' *Journal of Occupational Psychology* Sept 1977 pp 149–59 is useful for an aspect of recruitment procedure. For a study of the setting up of Civil Service Selection Board see [454]. See also C H Dodd 'Recruitment to the Administrative Class 1960–1964' *Public Administration* 45 1967 pp 55–80 and J F Pickering 'Recruitment to the Administrative Class 1960–64 Part 2' *Public Administration* 45 1967 pp 169–99.

**406**  Geoffrey K Fry *Statesmen in Disguise: The Changing Role of the Administrative Class of the British Home Civil Service 1853–1966* Macmillan 1969. The best history of the administrative class, the cream of the Civil Service. Peter Kellner and Lord Crowther-Hunt *The Civil Servants: An Inquiry into Britain's Ruling Class* Macdonald 1980 is a critical study. Lord Crowther-Hunt was involved in the Fulton report. He sees the upper echelons of the Civil Service as responsible for blocking Fulton proposals, in order to remain a self-perpetuating and under-scrutinized elite. See also his power without accountability charges in 'Ministers and Mandarins' *Parliamentary Affairs* 33 1980 pp 373–99.

**407**  Richard A Chapman *The Higher Civil Service in Britain* Constable 1970. A good sociological study, as is R K Kelsall *Higher Civil Servants in Britain from 1870 to the Present Day* Routledge and Kegan Paul 1955. See also Edgar Anstey 'The Civil Service Administrative Class: A Follow-Up of Post-War Entrants' *Occupational Psychology* Jan 1971 pp 27–43. On the situation in the 1980's see Geoffrey K Fry 'The British Career Civil Service Under Challenge' *Political Studies* 34 1986 pp 533–55. *Top Jobs in Whitehall: Appointments and Promotions in the Senior Civil Service: Report of a RIPA Working Group* Royal Institute of Public Administration 1987 concentrates more on a critical survey of the appointments procedure. It also analyses the charge, which it concludes is groundless, that the Civil Service has been politicized by the Thatcher government.

**408** K Gillender and R Mair 'Generalist Administrators and Professional Engineers: Some Developments Since the Fulton Report' *Public Administration* 58 1980 pp 333–56. One of the key objects of reformers and of the Fulton report was to remove the distinction between the dominant generalists, 'the chap with the first in Greats', and the specialist grades in the Civil Service. This issue is also specifically examined in C Goritsas 'The Specialist and Generalist Controversy, with Special Reference to the Legal Class of the British Civil Service' Warwick MA Thesis 1975. Another study which deal with a particular class in the Civil Service is Marjorie Ogilvy-Webb *The Government Explains: A Study of the Information Services* Allen and Unwin 1965. The recruitment and management of the government's scientific staff is examined in *Review of the Scientific Civil Service (1980): Report of a Working Group of the Management Committee for the Science Group (CSD)* Cmnd 8032, *Parliamentary Papers* 1980–81. On the scientific grades see also Philip Gummett *Scientists in Whitehall* Manchester University Press 1980 and M D Knowles 'The Scientist in the British Civil Service' Manchester MSc Thesis 1979.

**409** Desmond Keeling 'The Development of Central Training in the Civil Service 1963–70' *Public Administration* 49 1971 pp 51–72. A survey up to the establishment of the Civil Service College, in the wake of Fulton, in 1970. For the history of this college all there is so far is K J Shanahan *A Brief History of the Edinburgh Centre of the Civil Service College* Civil Service College 1977. Richard A Chapman 'Administrative Culture and Personnel Management: The British Civil Service in the 1980s' *Teaching Public Administration* 4 1984 pp 1–14 reflects on the low value the Civil Service continues to place on training.

**410** *Report of the Committee on the Political Activities of Civil Servants* Cmnd 7718, *Parliamentary Papers* xii 1948–49. Chaired by Sir J C Masterman. This report extended the right to engage in political activities to all below a certain grade and laid down the basic rules. The report of the committee chaired by Sir Arthur L Armitage, *Political Activities of Civil Servants: Report of the Committee* Cmnd 7057, *Parliamentary Papers* 1977–78, reviewed these rules and recommended the extension of this right. See also Eleanor Bontecou 'The English Policy as to Communists and Fascists in the Civil Service' *Columbia Law Review* 51 1951 pp 564–86.

**411** Mark L Joelson 'The Dismissal of Civil Servants in the Interests of National Security' *Public Law* 1963 pp 51–75. See also David C Jackson 'Individual Rights and National Security' *Modern Law Review* 20 1957 pp 364–80. These offer a legal rather than a historical

treatment of this issue. There is indeed no general historical discussion of civil servants and security or other kinds of leaks. Clive Ponting *The Right to Know* Sphere 1985 is his account of his decision to leak documents relating to the sinking, during the Falklands war, of the *General Belgrano*. This affair and the subsequent prosecution of Ponting under the Official Secrets Act is described in Richard Norton-Taylor *The Ponting Affair* Cecil Woolf 1985. Other similar episodes in the 1980s are examined in Robert Pyper 'Sarah Tisdall, Ian Willmore and the Civil Servant's Right to Leak' *Political Quarterly* 56 1985 pp 72–81.

**412** Gavin Drewry 'Lawyers in the UK Civil Service' *Public Administration* 59 1981 pp 15–46. A history and account of the contemporary situation.

**413** Elizabeth Brimelow 'Women in the Civil Service' *Public Administration* 59 1981 pp 313–36. A history and account of the contemporary position of women in the home civil service.

## (7) Individual Departments

Much literature relevant to this section can also be found in those sections dealing with the various areas of government policy.

**414** Susan Foreman *Loaves and Fishes: An Illustrated History of the Ministry of Agriculture, Fisheries and Food 1889–1989* HMSO 1989. A commemorative history of the development of the Ministry and its work. Sir John Winnifrith *The Ministry of Agriculture, Fisheries and Food* Allen and Unwin 1962 is a history and description of the work of the Ministry by the then Permanent Secretary for the New Whitehall series published by Allen and Unwin for the Royal Institute of Public Administration. These are volumes on the various central government departments. The series is still progressing, albeit slowly. The earlier volumes of the series are now somewhat out of date. There is also a tendency towards a certain Civil Service blandness. This is one of the better ones.

**415** R K Mosley *The Story of the Cabinet Office* Routledge and Kegan Paul 1969. A short study of its history and organization. It includes appendices on the Commonwealth Secretariat and the careers of various Cabinet Secretaries.

**416** Sir James Crombie *Her Majesty's Customs and Excise* Allen and Unwin 1962. Part of the New Whitehall series. See also Peter Gillman with Paul Hamann *The Duty Men: The Inside Story of the Customs* BBC 1987.

**417** Sir Ewen Broadbent *The Military and Government: From Macmillan to Heseltine* Macmillan 1988. A good study of the organization of the Ministry of Defence and the making of policy from the 1950s to the 1980s by a former second Permanent Secretary of the Ministry. Another good account is Franklyn A Johnson *Defence by Ministry: The British Ministry of Defence 1944–74* Duckworth 1980. Michael Howard *The Central Organisation of Defence* Royal United Services Institute 1970 particularly examines the Thorneycroft/Mountbatten reforms of 1963. For the history of the ministry since the 1974 reorganization see Brian Taylor 'Coming of Age: A Study of the Evolution of the Ministry of Defence Headquarters 1974–1982' *Journal of the Royal United Services Institute for Defence Studies* 128 1983 pp 44–51. M J V Bell 'Management Audit in the Ministry of Defence' *Public Administration* 62 1984 pp 311–21 deals with the development of resource management and control since the appointment of a Director-General of Management Audit for the Ministry in 1981. See also [2200–4].

**418** Sir Douglas Allen 'The Department of Economic Affairs' *Political Quarterly* 1967 pp 351–9. Allen was the Permanent Under-Secretary at the Department during its short life in the 1960s.

**419** Sir William Pile *The Department of Education and Science* Allen and Unwin 1979. This volume in the New Whitehall series provides a good historical survey of the post-war period. See also Sir Griffith Williams 'The First Ten Years of the Ministry of Education' *British Journal of Educational Studies* 3 1955 pp 101–14, memoir by former deputy secretary.

**420** Paul Draper *Creation of the DOE: A Study of the Merger of Three Departments to Form the Department of the Environment* HMSO 1977. The Department of the Environment was formed in 1970 from an amalgamation of the Ministries of Housing and Local Government, Public Building and Works, and Transport. This is the official history of how and why it was formed and organized. It includes many documents and useful appendices. James Radcliffe 'The Role of Politicians and Administrators in Departmental Reorganisation: The Case of the Department of the Environment' *Public Administration* 63 1985 pp 201–18 surveys the history of the Department up until the splitting off of the Department of Transport in 1976. See also M J Painter 'Policy Coordination in the Department of the Environment 1970–1976' *Public Administration* 53 1980 pp 135–54.

**420A** *A History of ECGD 1919–1979* Export Credits Guarantee Department 1979. A short history of the department.

**421** Muriel Nissel *People Count – A History of the General Register Office* HMSO 1987. The 150th anniversary history of the Office, which is now known as the Office of Population, Censuses and Surveys.

**422** Sir Patrick Nairne 'Managing the Elephant: Reflections on a Giant Department' *Political Quarterly* 58 1987 pp 243–56. Sir Patrick was Permanent Secretary of the Department of Health and Social Security 1975–81. Maurice Kogan and Mary Henkel *Government and Research: The Rothschild Experiment in a Government Department* Heinemann Education 1983 is a study of the effect of the Rothschild report [3133] on research in the Department. See also [393].

**423** *The Home Office: Perspectives on Policy and Administration. Bicentenary Lectures 1982* Royal Institute of Public Administration 1983. Includes reminiscences by James Callaghan, the Home Secretary 1967–70, and Lord Allen of Abbeydale, the Permanent Secretary 1967–72. There are also reflections on police policy, criminal justice and penal policy, broadcasting policy and civil liberties. The volume from the New Whitehall series, Sir Frank Newsam *The Home Office* Allen and Unwin 1954, provides a good comprehensive survey but is increasingly out of date. The Home Office Research Unit, founded in 1957, is discussed in T S Lodge 'The Founding of the Home Office Research Unit' in Roger Hood (ed) *Crime, Criminology and Public Policy: Essays in Honour of Sir Leon Radzinowicz* Heinemann 1974 pp 11–24. R M Morris 'Home Office Crime Policy Planning: Six Years On' *Howard Journal of Penology and Crime Prevention* 19 1980 pp 135–41 surveys the history of the Crime Policy Planning Unit from its establishment in 1974.

**424** Evelyn Sharp *The Ministry of Housing and Local Government* Allen and Unwin 1969. A good departmental study from the New Whitehall series. The Ministry was absorbed by the new Department of the Environment in 1970 [420].

**425** Sir Fife Clark *The Central Office of Information* Allen and Unwin 1970. Part of the New Whitehall series. This succeeded the wartime Ministry of Information during the Attlee government. The operation of the information services during the Attlee government has attracted particular attention, though unfortunately most of this work remains in the form of unpublished theses. S W Crofts 'Techniques of Information and Persuasion Employed by H M Government 1945–51' Open University PhD Thesis 1984 focuses on the use of propaganda in support of the government's economic planning and its production and recruitment campaigns in the textiles, farming and mining industries. See also his article 'The Attlee Government's Economic Information Propaganda' *Journal of Contemporary History* 21 1986 pp 453–71. A Lawrence 'Propaganda, Planning and the Economy: A Study in Government Public Relations 1945–1949' Leeds MPhil Thesis 1982 deals with a similar theme. The design and art work for this publicity material is examined in J A C Freeman 'British Graphic Design with Special Reference to Government Publicity 1939–51' CNAA MPhil Thesis 1979. Tom Wildy 'Propaganda and Social Policy in Britain 1945–1951: Publicity for the Social Legislation of the Labour Government' Leeds PhD Thesis 1985 focuses on the use of government publicity in order to try and win public support and enthusiasm for the welfare programme of the government. A particular aspect of this is explored in his article 'From the MOI to the COI – Publicity and Propaganda in Britain 1945–1951: The National Health and Insurance Campaigns of 1948' *Historical Journal of Film, Radio and Television* 6 1986 pp 2–17. For another facet of the nature of government publicity in this period see S J Deutsch 'The Ministry of Information and the Treatment of the Dependent Empire in Official Publicity 1939–1947' Oxford MLitt Thesis 1980.

**426**  Sir Alexander Johnston *The Inland Revenue* Allen and Unwin 1965. A rather uninformative volume from the New Whitehall series.

**427**  Sir Godfrey Ince *The Ministry of Labour and National Service* Allen and Unwin 1960. Part of the New Whitehall series. This Ministry later became part of the Department of Employment. See also Eric Wigham '80 Years of Ministering to Industrial Relations' *Department of Employment Gazette* 74 1976 pp 235–41.

**428**  Patrick Polden *Guide to the Records of the Lord Chancellors' Department* HMSO 1988. A guide to the records 1870–1951 which is intended to encourage their use by researchers. It also features some tables and details on the development of the Department.

**429**  *Ordnance Survey Annual Report* HMSO 1857–. W A Seymour (ed) *A History of the Ordnance Survey* Dawson 1980 is a good history of the Ordnance Survey from its eighteenth century foundations to 1978. It has quite full coverage of the post-war period. See also J R S Booth *Public Boundaries and Ordnance Survey 1840–1980* Ordnance Survey 1980. Also relevant is *The History of Retriangulation of Great Britain 1935–1962* HMSO 1967.

**430**  Colin Ulph *150 Not Out: The Story of the Paymaster-General's Office 1836–1986* HM Paymaster-General's Office 1985. A useful short history.

**431**  Sir Geoffrey S King *The Ministry of Pensions and National Insurance* Allen and Unwin 1958. Part of the New Whitehall series. The Ministry later became part of the Department of Health and Social Security.

**432**  Sir H Melville *The Department of Scientific and Industrial Research* Allen and Unwin 1962. Part of the New Whitehall series. This Department was set up dur-ing the First World War. It later became part of the Department of Trade and Industry. See also I M Varcoe 'The DSIR: A Study in the Growth of Organised Science' Oxford DPhil Thesis 1972.

**433**  Hugh Barty-King *Her Majesty's Stationery Office: The Story of the First 200 Years 1786–1986* HMSO 1986. The emphasis in this official history is the more recent period and there is good coverage of the post-war years. It also includes a chronology and a useful bibliography.

**434**  M M Simms 'The Ministry of Technology 1964–70' Manchester MSc. Thesis 1973–4. One of Harold Wilson's innovations it was absorbed by the Department of Trade and Industry created by the Heath government.

**435**  Susan Foreman *Shoes and Ships and Sealing Wax: An Illustrated History of the Board of Trade 1786–1986* HMSO 1986. A glossy history with four short chapters on the post-war period. It includes a chronology as well as useful appendices and bibliography. See also *A Century of Trade Marks: A Commentary on the Work and History of the Trade Marks Registry Which Celebrates Its Centenary in 1976* HMSO 1976, and T E Easterfield 'The Special Research Unit at the Board of Trade 1946–1949' *Journal of Operational Research* 34 1983 pp 565–8. The history of the Department of Trade and Industry from its creation in 1970 is surveyed in Brian W Hogwood 'The Rise and Fall and Rise of the Department of Trade and Industry' in Colin Campbell and B Guy Peters (eds) *Organising Governance, Governing Organisations* University of Pittsburgh Press 1988 pp 209–30.

**436**  Sir Gilmour Jenkins *The Ministry of Transport and Civil Aviation* Allen and Unwin 1959. Part of the New Whitehall series. An informative survey with useful appendices and, very rare for this series, a bibliography. The end of the Ministry in the late 1950s in the reorganization which also saw the demise of the Ministry of Supply is charted in A Dunsire 'The Passing of the Ministry of Transport and Civil Aviation' *Public Law* 1961 pp 150–64.

**437**  Hugh Heclo and Aaron Wildavsky *The Private Government of Public Money* Macmillan 1974. A highly regarded study of the operation of the Treasury. Another useful study is Hugo Young and Anne Sloman *But Chancellor: An Inquiry into the Treasury* BBC Books 1984. Lord Bridges *The Treasury* 2nd ed, Allen and Unwin 1967, the relevant volume from the New Whitehall series, is also quite informative. Henry Roseveare *The Evolution of a British Institution: The Treasury* Allen Lane 1969 is a comprehensive and scholarly history of the Treasury up until the aftermath of the Fulton report. Leo Pliatzky *The Treasury Under Mrs Thatcher* Blackwell 1989 is a good account of Treasury management of the economy and the Civil Service since 1979. Adrian Ham *Treasury Rules: Recurrent Themes in British Economic Policy* Quartet 1981 is principally a contribution to the debate about the role of Treasury policy in Britain's relative economic decline since 1945 by a former Treasury official. Sir Richard Clarke *Public Expenditure, Management and Control: The Development of the Public Expenditure Survey Committee* Macmillan 1978 is a posthumously published study by its principal creator of the important committee whereby the Treasury surveys and and seeks to control the expenditure of the spending departments.

**438** Sir Harold Emmerson *The Ministry of Works* Allen and Unwin 1956. Part of the New Whitehall series.

## (8) Biographies and Memoirs of Civil Servants

**439** Peter Hennessy 'Sir Robert Armstrong: "The Most Public Public Servant Since Cardinal Wolsey"' *Contemporary Record* 1/4 1988 pp 28–31. A sympathetic portrait of the Cabinet Secretary 1979–87 and of the effect on his reputation of the *Spycatcher* affair and of the charges that the Civil Service was being politicized by Mrs Thatcher.

**440** Richard A Chapman *Ethics in the British Civil Service* Routledge 1988. A study of moral standards in the Civil Service in terms of the example set by the career of Sir Edward (later Lord) Bridges, the Head of the Civil Service 1945–56.

**441** For Sir Richard Clarke see [437].

**442** Sir John Colville *The Fringes of Power: 10 Downing Street Diaries 1939–1955* Hodder and Stoughton 1985. The richest detail in these somewhat acerbic diaries is for the wartime period and for March 1952 to July 1954. His acute observations are supplemented by annotated and detailed biographical notes. His *Footprints in Time* Collins 1976 is an excellent collection of assorted memoirs and reminiscences.

**443** S W Roskill *Hankey: Man of Secrets: Vol 3: 1931–63* Collins 1974. The Cabinet Secretary 1916–38, Lord Hankey continued to sit on various quangos and committees in the 1940s and 1950s. He was also a Director of the Suez Canal Company from 1945 onwards, and as such had considerable influence during the 1956 Suez crisis.

**444** Neville Goodman *Wilson Jameson: Architect of National Health* Allen and Unwin 1970. Jameson was the Chief Medical Officer in the Ministry of Health at the time of the Attlee government.

**445** Sir George Mallaby *From My Level* Hutchinson 1965. As Secretary of the Joint Planning Staff of the War Cabinet Secretariat 1942–5 Mallaby attended the Potsdam conference. He was Secretary-General of the Brussels Treaty Defence Organisation (the forerunner of Nato), and the Under-Secretary of the Cabinet Office during the Attlee and Churchill governments. In 1954 he was Secretary of the War Council in Kenya during the Mau Mau emergency, and in 1957 the UK High Commissioner in New Zealand. His last post was as First Civil Service Commissioner 1959–64.

**446** Christopher Hassell *Edward Marsh: Patron of the Arts* Longmans 1959. A biography of a wartime civil servant which has useful reflections on some of his political masters such as Churchill.

**447** Donald MacDougall *Don and Mandarin: Memoirs of an Economist* John Murray 1987. McDougall was Chief Economic Adviser to the National Economic Development Council, to George Brown at the Department of Economic Affairs, to the Treasury and finally to the CBI. See also his 'The Machinery of Economic Government: Some Personal Reflections' in David Butler and A H Halsey (eds) *Policy and Politics: Essays in Honour of Norman Chester* Macmillan 1978 pp 169–81.

**448** Alix Meynell *Public Servant Private Woman: An Autobiography* Gollancz 1988. She rose to be Under-Secretary at the Board of Trade by the time she retired in 1955.

**448A** Sir Anthony Part *The Making of a Mandarin* Deutsch 1990. A polished memoir by a distinguished civil servant whose career began in the Board of Education and culminated as Permanent Secretary of the Department of Trade and Industry and its successor 1970–6.

**449** Leo Pliatsky *Getting and Spending* Blackwell 1982. Highly regarded memoirs. Sir Leo served in the Treasury 1950–77 and rose to be Second Permanent Secretary.

**450** Edwin Plowden *An Industrialist in the Treasury* Deutsch 1989. Excellent memoir of his time as a senior Treasury official in the 1940s and early 1950s. It is useful not only for the economic record of the Attlee government but also for Butler's 'Robot' plan to make sterling freely convertible, a plan Plowden helped to scotch.

**451** John, Lord Redcliffe-Maud *Experience of an Optimist* Hamilton 1981. The only autobiography by a Head of a home Civil Service department. In 1945–52 he was Permanent Secretary at the Ministry of Education. He was Permanent Secretary of the Ministry of Fuel and Power 1952–9. Between 1959–63 he was High Commissioner then Ambassador to South Africa and in charge of the High Commission Territories. In 1966–9 he chaired the Royal Commission on Local Government.

**452** Eric Roll *Crowded Hours* Faber 1985. Roll served in an assortment of posts in the Treasury and the Ministry of Agriculture, Fisheries and Food after the War. He was Deputy Leader of the UK delegation negotiating the terms of entry to the EEC in 1961–3. In 1964–6 he was Under-Secretary of the Department of Economic Affairs. He served on the National Economic Development Council 1971–80 and as a Director of the Bank of England 1968–77.

**453** R W Clark *Tizard* Methuen 1965. Sir Henry Tizard was the Chairman of the Advisory Council on Scientific Policy and of the Defence Research Policy Committee 1946–52.

**454** Richard A Chapman *Leadership in the British Civil Service: A Study of Sir Percival Wakefield and the Creation of the Civil Service Selection Board* Croom Helm 1984. This is as much a study of the creation of CSSB and its influence as a model of personnel recruitment as a biography of Sir Percival.

**455** Sir Cecil Weir *Civilian Assignment* Methuen 1953. Weir was the economic adviser to the Control Commission for Germany 1946–9, Chairman of the Dollar Exports Board 1949–51 and Head of the UK delegation to the High Authority of the European Coal and Steel Community 1952–5.

**456** John Wolfenden *Turning Points: Memoirs* The Bodley Head 1976. An eminent public servant, not in the sense that he worked at Whitehall, but in his service on important committees. The most notable of these was his chairmanship of the 1957 report on homosexual offences and prostitution.

**457** Solly Zuckerman *From Apes to Warlords: An Autobiography 1904–1946* Hamilton 1978. The second volume of autobiography is *Monkeys, Men and Missiles: An Autobiography 1946–1988* Collins 1988. Zuckerman has combined eminence as a zoologist (he was the Secretary of the Zoological Society in 1955) with a career as a defence scientist. He was Chairman of the Defence Research Policy Committee 1960–4, and Chief Scientific Adviser to the Ministry of Defence 1964–71.

### (9) Royal Commissions and Committees of Inquiry

**458** K C Wheare *Government by Committee: An Essay on the British Constitution* Oxford University Press 1955. Still the best general guide to the role of committees in British government it covers Royal Commissions, committees of inquiry, advisory committees, quangos, parliamentary committees and tribunals. See also T J Cartwright *Royal Commissions and Departmental Committees in Britain: A Case Study in Institutional Adaptiveness and Public Participation in Government* Hodder and Stoughton 1975. Martin Bulmer (ed) *Royal Commissions and Departmental Committees of Inquiry: The Lesson of Experience* Royal Institute of Public Administration 1983 is a witness seminar on the work of these inquiries and ways of making them more effective.

**459** Richard A Chapman (ed) *The Role of Commissions in Policy-Making* Allen and Unwin 1973. Case studies of the Fulton, Donovan, Redcliffe-Maud, Seebohm and Plowden reports.

**460** Charles J Hinser *Guide to Decision: The Royal Commission* Bedminister Press 1965. A history of the Royal Commission in the twentieth century with a number of case studies.

**461** Gerald Rhodes *Committees of Inquiry* Allen and Unwin 1975. An excellent study of their operation and influence on policy-making 1959–68. An earlier analysis which includes some case studies is Political and Economic Planning *Advisory Committees in British Government* Allen and Unwin 1960.

**462** R E Wraith and G B Lamb *Public Inquiries as an Instrument of Government* Allen and Unwin 1971. A good study of the development and character of public inquiries, with appendices. A Richardson *Participation Concepts in Social Policy — One London* Routledge and Kegan Paul 1983 analyses the development of public participation in administration as a political issue from the 1960s onwards, particularly in the context of Community Health Councils, tenant participation schemes, or parent governors. On this see also N Boaden *et al Public Participation in Local Services* Longman 1982. A useful bibliography is A Barker *Public Participation in Britain: A Classified Bibliography* Bedford Square Press 1979.

### (10) Quangos

**463** Anthony Barker *Quangos in Britain: Government and the Networks of Public Policy-Making* Macmillan 1982. A political science textbook rather than a history. There are some case studies. It however could be rather more detailed. Philip Holland and Michael Fallon *The Quango Explosion: Public Bodies and Ministerial Patronage* Conservative Political Centre 1978 is a tract which reflects the considerable concern felt by Conservatives and others in the 1970s at the profusion of what was seen as an uncontrollable and unanswerable secondary bureaucracy. This concern and Mrs Thatcher's subsequent attempts to prune back this growth is examined in Philip Holland *The Governance of Quangos* Adam Smith Institute 1981, which also lists those quangos abolished and created 1979–81.

**464** Christopher Hood '"A Tale of Two Quango-cracies": Membership of Commercial Public Boards in Britain 1950–Style and 1980–Style' *Policy and Politics* 11 1983 pp 1–14.

### (11) Government Inspectorates

**465** Gerald Rhodes *Inspectorates in British Government: Law Enforcement and Standards of Efficiency* Allen and Unwin 1981. A good study of a neglected aspect of British government which traces the history of inspectorates dealing with trading standards, factories, mines, schools and pollution from the mid-nineteenth century onwards. This supersedes John S Harris *British Government Inspection: The Local Services and the Central Departments* Stevens 1955.

### F. PARLIAMENT

### (1) Reference Works

**466** Robert U Goehlert and Fenton S Martin *The Parliament of Great Britain: A Bibliography* Lexington Books, Lexington, Massachussetts 1983. An extensive but unannotated bibliography. Strathearn Gordon *Our Parliament* 6th ed, Cassell 1964 is a useful introduction and bibliographical guide to parliament which remains of considerable value. See also H S Cobb *A Handlist of Articles and Other Serial Publications Relating to the History of Parliament* House of Lords Record Office 1973.

**467** *House of Commons Debates* 5th Series Vol 410– Vol 1000 May 1945–13th March 1981, and 6th Series Vol 1–16th March 1981–. Transcripts of the debates and proceedings of the House of Commons. There is general index at the end of the volumes covering each parliamentary session. For the House of Lords see *House of Lords Debates* 5th Series Vol 137– 1st August 1945–.

**468** *House of Commons Weekly Information Bulletin* HMSO 1977–. Produced by the House of Commons library. A guide to papers received by the library, the sittings of the Commons, the work of the Select Committees, and so on. This information has been collated in the Sessional Information Digest since the 1983–84 parliamentary session. There was also a *House of Lords Weekly Information Bulletin* 1977–81. Another refer-

ence guide to the work of parliament is the monthly *The House Magazine* Political Communications Ltd 1976–.

**469** POLIS 1980–. This is an on-line database compiled in the House of Commons library. It is available through a number of the larger British public and university libraries and is a very comprehensive index to all of parliament's proceedings and papers.

**470** J A G Griffith and Michael Ryle with M A J Wheeler-Booth *Parliament: Functions, Practice and Procedures* Sweet and Maxwell 1989. A good general study of the work and organization of parliament. See also Norman William Wilding and Philip Laundy *An Encyclopaedia of Parliament* 4th ed, Cassell 1972. This covers all Commonwealth parliaments, but especially Westminster. It includes plenty of bibliographical information.

**471** C J Boulton (ed) Erskine May's *Treatise on the Law, Privileges, Proceedings and Usage of Parliament* 21st ed, Butterworths 1989. The parliamentary bible. Another useful guide to the procedure and functions of parliament is J A G Griffith and M Fyle *Parliament: Functions, Practices and Procedure* Sweet and Maxwell 1989. See also L A Abraham and S C Hawtrey *A Parliamentary Dictionary* Butterworths 1970.

**472** *Dod's Parliamentary Companion* Dod's 1832–. An annual guide to the personnel of parliament, its procedure and other aspects of its work. See also *Who does What in Parliament* Mitchell and Birt 1970–3.

**473** Maurice F Bond *Guide to the Records of Parliament* HMSO 1971. Annotated and of some value.

### (2) General Works

**474** John Pitcairn Mackintosh (ed) *People and Parliament* Saxon House 1978. A useful collection of essays by MPs and academics. Topics covered include MPs, policy-making, parliament and the public and the press and parliamentary reform. Michael Rush *Parliament and the Public* 2nd ed, Longman 1976 is a textbook on the work of parliament. An earlier textbook which remains of some value is Sir W Ivor Jennings *Parliament* 2nd ed, Cambridge University Press 1957. See also Daniel Norman Chester 'The British Parliament 1959–66' *Parliamentary Affairs* 19 1966 pp 417–45, and Sir Edward Fellowes 'Changes in Parliamentary Life 1918–1961' *Political Quarterly* 36 1965 pp 256–65. Philip Norton *et al* 'Symposium: Parliament' *Contemporary Record* 2/3 1988 pp 2–17 is a collection of articles and reflections on parliament since 1945.

**475** A H Hanson and H V Wiseman *Parliament at Work: A Case- Book of Parliamentary Procedure* Stevens 1962. An unusual textbook on procedure illustrated by post-war examples.

**476** Woodrow Wyatt *Turn Again, Westminster* Deutsch 1973 is a diatribe about the dominance of the political process by the major parties and the executive at the expense of parliament. In the process he provides many useful insights into the state of parliament, the organization of the parties in parliament and the constituencies and on parliamentary careers. Tony Benn *Parliament and Power* Verso 1982 is a similar work which includes some autobiographical reflections.

**477** *The State of the Nation: Parliament* Granada Television 1973. The transcript of a TV inquiry. This looks at the work of ministers and of parliament and features a debate between various eminent MPs on the motion 'Most MPs are too ignorant to do their jobs properly'.

**478** G F M Campion (ed) *Parliament: A Survey* Allen and Unwin 1952. A collection of essays by distinguished parliamentarians and academics reflecting the state of parliament in the 1950s.

**479** Philip Norton (ed) *Parliament in the 1980s* Blackwell 1985. A good analysis of recent changes. See also his *Parliament In Perspective* Hull University Press 1987.

**480** Madeleine R Robinson 'Parliamentary Privilege and Political Morality in Britain 1939–1957' *Political Science Quarterly* 73 1958 pp 179–205. See also D C M Yardley 'The House of Commons and Its Privileges Since the Strauss Affairs' *Parliamentary Affairs* 15 1962 pp 500–10.

**481** David Judge (ed) *The Politics of Parliamentary Reform* Heinemann 1983. Essays dealing with electoral reform as well as reform of parliamentary organization and procedure and the prospects. Hansard Society *Parliamentary Reform 1933–60* 2nd ed, Cassell 1967 is a survey of proposals for the reform of parliament. See also P R Thomas 'The Attitude of the Labour Party to Reform of Parliament, with Particular Reference to the House of Commons 1919–1951' Keele PhD Thesis 1974–5.

### (3) Parliamentary Scrutiny

**482** Dermot Englefield *Whitehall and Westminster: Government Informs Parliament: The Changing Scene* Longman 1985. A survey and reference guide to parliamentary scrutiny of and information about government. The relationship between government and parliament is examined in H V Wiseman (ed) *Parliament and the Executive* Routledge and Kegan Paul 1968.

**483** John Eaves Jr *Emergency Powers and the Parliamentary Watchdog: Parliament and the Executive in Great Britain 1939–1951* Hansard Society 1958 is an excellent study of parliamentary restraint upon an executive whose powers were swollen by the emergency of war.

**484** Daniel Norman Chester and Nona Bowring *Questions in Parliament* Clarendon 1962. A good history of one of the most important means of parliamentary scrutiny. For material on the scrutiny of the government by Commons Select Committees see below.

**485** David Goldsworthy 'Parliamentary Questions on Colonial Affairs: A Retrospective Analysis' *Parliamentary Affairs* 23 1970 pp 140–53.

**486** Andrew Cox and Stephen Kirby *Congress, Parliament and Defence: The Impact of Legislative Reform on Defense Accountability in Britain and America* Macmillan 1987 is a useful comparative study of the monitoring of defence policy by parliament in the 1970s. Unfortunately it does not venture beyond the 1979 reform of the Select Committees. See also Masood Hyder 'Parliament and Defence Affairs' *Public Administration* 55 1977 pp 59–78.

**487** Peter Riddell *Parliament and the Scrutiny of Public Finance* Economist Intelligence Unit 1980. A useful general survey. The scrutiny of economic policy is tackled in British Study of Parliament Group 'Parliament and the Economy in Great Britain' in David Leslie Coombes and Stuart A Walkland (eds) *Parliaments and Economic Affairs in Britain, France, Italy and the Netherlands* Heinemann 1980 pp 25–95. Parliamentary control of public spending is examined in Stuart A Walkland 'Parliamentary Control of Public Expenditure in Britain' in David Leslie Coombes *et al The Power of the Purse: The Role of European Parliaments in Budgetary Decisions* Allen and Unwin 1976 pp 179–97. The same volume also contains David Millar 'Parliamentary Control of Taxation in Britain' pp 198–214.

**488** Peter Godfrey Richards *Parliament and Foreign Affairs* Allen and Unwin 1963. A good study of parliamentary scrutiny.

**489** Stephen Ingle and Philip Tether *Parliament and Health Policy: The Role of MPs 1970–1975* Gower 1981 assesses parliament's influence on the Health Service reorganization of these years and argues that it was minimal.

**490** M Kolinsky 'Parliamentary Scrutiny of European Legislation' *Government and Opposition* 10 1975 pp

46–69. See also Michael Ryan and Paul Isaacson 'Parliament and the European Communities' *Parliamentary Affairs* 28 1975 pp 199–216.

## (4) The Legislative Process

**491** Denis Van Mechelen and Richard Rose *Patterns of Parliamentary Legislation* Gower 1986. A useful study covering the period since the Second World War. S A Walkland *The Legislative Process in Great Britain* Allen and Unwin 1968 is the standard introductory textbook.

**492** John Aneurin Grey Griffith *Parliamentary Scrutiny of Government Bills* Allen and Unwin 1974. An analysis using legislation from the 1967–68 to 1970–71 sessions.

**493** David C Marsh and Melvyn Read *Private Members' Bills* Cambridge University Press 1988. A major study of this type of legislation which includes an analysis of the progress and fate of all Bills of this kind since the 1948/49 parliamentary session. P A Bromhead *Private Members' Bills in the British Parliament* Routledge and Kegan Paul 1956 may still be of some value particularly for the earlier period. See also P Norton 'Private Legislation and the Influence of the Backbench MP' *Parliamentary Affairs* 30 1977 pp 356–62.

**494** Sir William Kent *In on the Act: Memoirs of a Lawmaker* Macmillan 1979. Excellent memoirs of a parliamentary draughtsman. His observations on the ministers he had to deal with are particularly acute. Unfortunately the coverage of the post-war period is relatively limited.

**495** E H Beet 'Parliament and Delegated Legislation 1945–53' *Public Administration* 33 1955 pp 325–32.

## (5) The House of Lords

**496** David Lewis Jones *Writings on the House of Lords 1945–1982* House of Lords Library Bulletin 1983. An unannotated bibliography, a large part of which deals with procedure and reform of the House of Lords since 1911.

**497** Frank Pakenham, Lord Longford *A History of the House of Lords* Collins 1988. A general history which contains quite a lot on the post-war era. P A Bromhead *The House of Lords and Contemporary Politics 1911–1957* Routledge and Kegan Paul 1958 remains of considerable value.

**498** Donald Shell *The House of Lords* Philip Allan 1988. A guide to the House of Lords and its contemporary political role. It particularly deals with its increased prominence since 1979. Another study of increasing vigour in the upper house focusing particularly on the impact of the life peers is N D J Baldwin 'The Contemporary House of Lords: A Study of the Composition and Functions of the House of Lords, with Particular Reference to the Nature and Extent of Its Legislative Activity and a Review of Its Position Within the British Body Politic in the Period 1970–1985' Exeter PhD Thesis 1985. See also his *The House of Lords: A Study in Evolutionary Adaptability* Hull Papers in Politics 33, Politics Department, University of Hull 1983. Simon Winchester *Their Noble Lordships: The Hereditary Peerage Today* Faber 1981 is a journalistic study of the peerage. J C T F Whyte-Melville Skeffington, Viscount Massareene and Ferrard *The Lords* Leslie Frewin 1973 is a lively survey which is particularly useful on Wilson's abortive attempts at reform in the 1960s. See also J R Vincent 'The House of Lords' *Parliamentary Affairs* 19 1965–66 pp 475–85.

**499** Janet P Morgan *The House of Lords and the Labour Government 1964–1970* Oxford University Press 1975. This is a good study of attempts to reform the Lords and of the government's relations with a chamber in which it was vastly outnumbered. See also M A J Wheeler-Booth 'The Attempted Reform of the House of Lords 1964–69' *The Table* 38 1969 pp 85–109. Attempts to reform the procedure of the House are dealt with by Lord Northfield 'Reforming Procedure in the Lords' in David Butler and A H Halsey (eds) *Policy and Politics: Essays in Honour of Norman Chester* Macmillan 1976, and by D R Beamish 'The House of Lords Select Committee on Practice and Procedure 1976–1979' *The Table* 47 1979 pp 37–47. The notion that the Lords have demonstrated a new vitality in the 1980s is critically assessed in Andrew Adonis 'The House of Lords in the 1980s' *Parliamentary Affairs* 41 1988 pp 380–401.

**500** G F Hallett 'The Influence of the House of Lords on Legislation from 1911 to 1949' London MSc(Econ) Thesis 1955–6. A study of the Lords between the Parliament Act 1911 and the further restrictions on the Lords ability to hold up legislation enacted in 1949.

**501** Alan Paterson *The Law Lords* Macmillan 1982. An examination, partly based on interviews, of the dynamics of judicial decision making in the House of Lords, especially over the period 1957–73. Another useful study which examines the procedure, personnel and substance of judicial decision making in the Lords in 1952–68 is Louis Blom-Cooper and Gavin Drewry *Final Appeal: A Study of the House of Lords in Its Judicial Capacity* Clarendon 1972. See also Robert Stevens *Law and Politics: The House of Lords as a Judicial Body 1800–1976* Heinemann 1979. Wolfgang Friedmann 'Judicial Law-Making in England: Some Juris-prudential Reflections on Four Recent Decisions of the House of Lords' in R H Code Holland and G Schwarzenberger (eds) *Law, Justice and Equity: Essays in Tribute to G W Keeton* Pitman 1967 pp 9–25 examines the implications of some celebrated decisions in the Lords in the early 1960s. Decisions in the Lords are also examined in D Robertson 'Judicial Ideology in the House of Lords: A Jurimetric Analysis' *British Journal of Political Science* 12 1982 pp 1–25. T H Smith 'Criminal Appeals in the House of Lords' *Modern Law Review* 47 1984 is a critical analysis of the Lords' handling of criminal cases.

**502** Gavin Drewry and Jenny Brock 'Prelates in Parliament' *Parliamentary Affairs* 24 1970–1 pp 222–50. A useful study of the role and activities of the Bishops in the House.

**503** Bernard R Crick 'The Life Peerages Act' *Parliamentary Affairs* 11 1958 pp 455–65. The 1958 Life Peerages Act has had a major effect on the personnel and vigour of the Lords. Another major development of the post-war years is the ability of peers to resign their peerages. The efforts of Tony Benn to resign his Viscountcy and return to the House of Commons, which led to this, are discussed in C O'Leary 'The Wedgwood Benn Case and the Doctrine of Wilful Perversity' *Political Studies* 13 1965 pp 65–78, P A Bromhead 'Mr Wedgwood Benn, the Peerage and the Constitution' *Public Administration* 14 1962 pp 493–506 and M A J Wheeler-Booth 'The Stansgate Case' *The Table* 30 1961 pp 23–56. The other major development of the post-war years is the increasing number of peeresses in the House. Their impact is examined in Gavin Drewry and J Brock *The Impact of Women on the House of Lords* Centre for the Study of Public Policy 20, University of Strathclyde 1983.

**504** Andrew Roth and Janice Kerbey *Lords on the Board* Parliamentary Profiles 1972. A waspish survey of the business interests of members of the upper house.

**505** R M Punnett 'The 1964 Ministers of the Crown Act and Ministerial Representation in the House of Lords' *The Table* 33 1964 pp 69–80.

**506** Philip Norton 'The Forgotten Whips: Whips in the House of Lords' *The Parliamentarian* 57 1976 pp 86–92.

## (6) The House of Commons

### (a) General

**507** Stuart A Walkland (ed) *The House of Commons in the Twentieth Century* Clarendon 1979. The only general history. Philip Norton *The Commons in Perspective* Robertson 1981 is more of a political science textbook albeit one which contains a wealth of historical information. It also has a useful bibliography.

**508** Anthony King and Anne Sloman *Westminster and Beyond* Macmillan 1973. Transcripts of radio broadcasts with MPs dealing with their surgeries and their relations with their constituents, their relations with the press and the work and organization of the House of Commons. Another study of the trials and tribulations of MPs, this time based on a television series, is Anthony King *British Members of Parliament: A Self Portrait* Macmillan 1974.

**509** Norman Shrapnel *The Performers: Politics as Theatre* Constable 1978 is an anecdotal view of the House and its members by a lobby correspondent of long standing.

**510** D G Hitchener 'The Labour Government and the House of Commons' *Western Political Quarterly* 5 1952 pp 417–44.

**511** A H Hanson and Bernard Crick (eds) *The Commons in Transition* Fontana 1970. Essays on legislation, standing orders, the handling of finance and the public sector, parliamentary questions, the ombudsman, the library, parliament and science, the standing committees, the new committees instituted by Richard Crossman, the select committees and parliamentary reform.

**512** Stuart A Walkland and Michael Ryle (eds) *The Commons in the Seventies* Fontana 1977. A general textbook guide. John E Schwarz 'Exploring a New Role in Policy Making: The British House of Commons in the 1970s' *American Political Science Review* 74 1980 pp 23–37 argues that the Commons became much less docile and easy for government whips to manage in the course of the 1970s. See also Philip Norton 'The Changing Face of the British House of Commons in the 1970s' *Legislative Studies Quarterly* 5 1980 pp 333–57.

**513** Michael Rush and Malcolm Shaw *The House of Commons: Services and Facilities* Allen and Unwin 1974. A comprehensive study of the essential infrastructure that enables the Commons to carry on their work. See also Anthony Barker and Michael Rush *The Member of Parliament and His Information* Allen and Unwin 1970. Updated by Michael Rush (ed) *The House of*

*Commons: Services and Facilities 1972–1982* Policy Studies Institute 1983.

## (b) Officers and Procedure

**514** Philip Marsden *The Officers of the Commons 1363–1978* HMSO 1979. A substantial part of this reference guide deals with post-1945 developments, and particularly with reorganization 1965–78.

**515** Philip Laundy *The Office of Speaker* Cassell 1964. A study of the nature of the office. This enquiry is not confined to Britain. Selwyn Lloyd *Mr Speaker Sir* Cape 1978 is a detailed account of the Speaker's duties and responsibilities in the context of his own period as Speaker 1971–76.

**516** On Sir Brian Horrocks as Black Rod 1949–63 see [3794].

**517** Donald Searing and Chris Game 'Horses for Courses: The Recruitment of Whips in the British House of Commons' *British Journal of Political Science* 7 1977 pp 361–85. A good historical analysis drawing on extensive interviewing. See also F M G Willson 'Some Career Patterns in British Politics: Whips in the House of Commons 1906–1966' *Parliamentary Affairs* 24 1970–71 pp 33–42 and J C Sainty 'Assistant Whips 1922–1964' *Parliamentary History* 4 1985 pp 201–4.

**518** G F M Campion *An Introduction to the Procedure of the House of Commons* 3rd ed, Macmillan 1958. This surveys both the history and the 1950s practice of Commons procedure. See also [470–13]. There is otherwise a lack of published work in this area. Useful theses are K Swinhoe 'A Study of Opinion about the Reform of House of Commons Procedure 1945–68' Leeds PhD Thesis 1970–1 and A P Barker 'Aspects of the Development of House of Commons Procedure in the Twentieth Century' Nottingham MA Thesis 1961–2. Select Committees on procedure are considered by E M Balsom 'The Select Committees on Procedure 1945–65' Oxford BLitt Thesis 1968–9 and W A Proctor 'The House of Commons Select Committee on Procedure 1970–1979' *The Table* 47 1979 pp 13–36. See also Sir Edward Fellowes 'Practice and Procedure in the House of Commons 1919–61' *Journal of the Parliaments of the Commonwealth* 43 1962 pp 105–14.

**519** Gavin Drewry 'The Outsider and House of Commons Reform: Some Evidence from the Crossman Diaries' *Parliamentary Affairs* 31 1978 pp 424–35. Despite his interest Crossman achieved relatively little in his efforts to reform Commons procedure when Leader of the House 1966–68.

## (c) Committees

**520** R L Borthwick 'The Standing Committees of the House of Commons, a Study of Membership, Procedure and Working Between 1945 and 1959' Nottingham PhD Thesis 1968.

**521** Alfred Morris (ed) *The Growth of Parliamentary Scrutiny by Committee: A Symposium* Pergamon 1970. A useful general survey. There were certain important changes in the 1960s. A number of departmental and specialist Select Committees were set up by Richard Crossman when Leader of the House of Commons in 1966–68. The effect of these Committees is studied in British Study of Parliament Group *Specialist Committees in the British Parliament: The Experience of a Decade* Political and Economic Planning 1976. See also E Oram 'Investigative Select Committees in the 1966 House of Commons: The Effects of an Experiment in Parliamentary Reform upon the House of Commons, the Political Parties, the Executive and the Public' Strathclyde PhD Thesis 1974–5, D Liversedge 'Parliament and Administration: Four Specialist Select Committees 1966–1969' Hull MA Thesis 1973–4, Martin Partington 'Parliamentary Committees: Recent Developments' *Parliamentary Affairs* 23 1970 pp 366–79 and Donald Shell 'Specialist Select Committees' *Parliamentary Affairs* 23 1970 pp 380–404.

**522** *First Report from the Select Committee on Procedure 1977–78* HC 588, *Parliamentary Papers* 1978–79. This report led to the establishment of departmental Select Committees in 1979. The best assessment of their establishment and subsequent operation is Gavin Drewry (ed) *The New Select Committees: A Study of the 1979 Reforms* 2nd ed, Oxford University Press 1989. Dermot Englefield (ed) *Commons Select Committees: Catalysts for Progress? Understanding the New Departmental Select Committees 1979–83* Longman 1984 is most useful for its extensive indexes on the subjects examined and the nature of the evidence submitted. Francis Pym *et al* 'Select Committees Symposium' *Contemporary Record* 1/1 1987 pp 15–20 offers the views of civil servants, politicians, journalists and academics on the new system. A similar study is Dilys M Hill (ed) *Parliamentary Select Committees in Action: A Symposium* University of Strathclyde Discussion Papers in Politics 1983. An early analysis of the new Select Committees is Anne Davies *Reformed Select Committees* Outer Circle Policy Unit 1980.

**523** K P Poole 'The Powers of Select Committees of the House of Commons to send for Persons, Papers and Records' *Parliamentary Affairs* 32 1979 pp 268–78.

**524** S E Hope 'Select Committees of the House of Commons and Agriculture 1966–1978' Leicester MA

Thesis 1980. One of Crossman's innovations. See also G T Popham and D Greengrass 'The Role and Function of the Select Committee on Agriculture' *Public Administration* 48 1970 pp 137–51.

525  Gordon Reid *The Politics of Financial Control: The Role of the House of Commons* Hutchinson University Library 1966. A useful general survey of the Public Accounts, Expenditure (formerly Estimates) and Nationalized Industries Select Committees. A more recent, but short, study is Peter Riddell *Parliament and the Scrutiny of Public Finance* Economist Intelligence Unit 1980. Basil Chubb *The Control of Public Expenditure: Financial Committees of the House of Commons* Oxford University Press 1952 studies the Public Accounts Committee and the Estimates Committee.

526  Nevil Johnson *Parliament and Administration: The Estimates Committee 1945–1965* Allen and Unwin 1966. The Estimates Committee examines the estimates of expenditure submitted by government departments. This is a good study of its work which also carries a useful summary of reports and evidence published by the Committee in the period. See also Basil Chubb 'The Select Committee on Estimates 1946–48' *Parliamentary Affairs* 2 1949 pp 284–91. The Estimates Committee later became the Expenditure Committee.

527  Ann Robinson *Parliament and Public Spending: The Expenditure Committee of the House of Commons 1970–76* Heinemann 1978. The Expenditure Committee replaced the Estimates Committee as a result of increasing concern in the 1960s about loss of parliamentary control over government spending. According to Robinson however it did not have much effect. A contrary view is advanced by H L Vaid 'Parliamentary Control of Public Expenditure in Britain: The Influence of the Expenditure Committee 1971–74' London PhD Thesis 1984.

528  David Leslie Coombes *The Member of Parliament and the Administration: The Case of the Select Committee on the Nationalized Industries* Allen and Unwin 1966. A good survey of the first ten years of this important Committee set up in 1956. Another useful study is Albert Henry Hanson *Parliament and Public Ownership* Cassell 1961. Toby Low 'The Select Committee on the Nationalized Industries' *Public Administration* 40 1962 pp 1–15 presents the view of a Tory member of the Committee. Ernest Davies 'Ministerial Control and Parliamentary Responsibility of Nationalized Industries' *Political Quarterly* 21 1950 pp 150–9 and his later article 'The Select Committee on Nationalized Industries' *Political Quarterly* 29 1958 pp 378–88 provides a before and after impression of parliamentary scrutiny of the Nationalized Industries.

529  Vilma Flegman *Called to Account: The Public Accounts Committee of the House of Commons 1965/66 to 1977/78* Gower 1980. This Committee examines accounts of expenditure already made by government departments. P H Hanmer 'The Role of the House of Commons Committee of Public Accounts in Questions of Science and Technology' Manchester MSc Thesis 1979 examines the Public Accounts Committee's scrutiny of expenditure on research and development.

530  Roy Gregory 'The Select Committee of the Parliamentary Commissioner for Administration 1967–1980' *Public Law* 1982 pp 49–87. The Parliamentary Commissioner for Administration (the Ombudsman) was set up in 1967 to investigate complaints of maladministration. The Committee was set up in April 1967 and has had some effect on the Ombudsman, if not on the government.

531  Sheldon Himmelfarb 'Consensus in Committee: The Case of the Select Committee on Race Relations and Immigration' *Parliamentary Affairs* 33 1980 pp 54–66. A study of this committee, established in 1968 and disbanded in 1979, derived from his thesis 'Select Committees and Parliamentary Reform: A Case Study of the Select Committee on Race Relations and Immigration' Oxford DPhil Thesis 1982.

532  Christopher Powell and Arthur Butler (comps) *The Parliamentary and Scientific Committee: The First Forty Years 1939–1979* Croom Helm 1980. This was a unofficial committee of the Houses of Lords and Commons for the scrutiny of science policy. See also S A Walkland 'Science and Parliament: The Origins and Influence of the Parliamentary and Scientific Committee' *Parliamentary Affairs* 17 1963–64 pp 308–20 and 389–402, S A Walkland and Norman J Vig 'Parliament, Science and Technology' *Technology and Society* 4 1967 pp 40–5 and Austen Albu 'The Member of Parliament, the Executive and Scientific Policy' *Minerva* 2 1963–4 pp 1–20. On the Select Committee established by Crossman see Roger Williams 'The Select Committee on Science and Technology: The First Round' *Public Administration* 46 1968 pp 299–313.

533  J H Burns 'The Scottish Committees of the House of Commons 1948–59' *Political Studies* 8 1960 pp 272–96. This analysis is continued by G E Edwards 'The Scottish Grand Committee 1958 to 1970' *Parliamentary Affairs* 25 1971–2 pp 303–25 and P Myers 'The Select Committee on Scottish Affairs' *Parliamentary Affairs* 27 1974 pp 366–79.

534  J Nixon and N Nixon 'The Social Services Committee: A Forum for Policy Review and Policy Reform' *Journal of Social Policy* 12 1983 pp 331–57.

**535** D Starkie 'Reassessing the Impact of Select Committees' *Public Adminstration Bulletin* 41 1983 pp 2–13. This particularly deals with transport policy committees 1970–79.

**536** J Barry Jones and R A Wilford *Parliament and Territoriality: The Committee on Welsh Affairs 1979–1983* University of Wales Press 1986. This was created after the devolution debate to scrutinize the Welsh Office and associated bodies. An assessment of its role and MPs' attitudes towards it. *Parliamentary Affairs* 21 1967–68 pp 264–76.

(d) Parties and Members of Parliament

**537** *Times Guide to the House of Commons* Times Publications 1929–. This has appeared after every general election since 1945. It has become increasingly sophisticated and now includes details of the polls for each constituency listed alphabetically, potted biographies of the candidates, photographs of the successful candidates, analysis, statistics, maps and the text of the election manifestos of all the major parties. *The BBC Guide to Parliament* BBC Books 1979– is a similar but less substantial newcomer.

**538** Robert J Jackson *Rebels and Whips: Dissension and Cohesion in British Political Parties Since 1945* Macmillan 1968. A study of the parties in the Commons, their organization and intra-party dissension. Cross-voting, abstentions and party rebellions are also analysed in Philip Norton (ed) *Dissension in the House of Commons: Intra-Party Dissent in the House of Commons Division Lobbies 1945–1974* Macmillan 1975. This has been updated by [615] and Philip Norton (ed) *Dissension in the House of Commons 1974–1979* Clarendon 1980. See also Edward W Crowe 'Cross- Voting in the House of Commons 1945–1974' *Journal of Politics* 42 1980 pp 487–510 and Philip Norton 'Dissent in Committee: Party Dissent in Commons' Standing Committees 1959–74' *The Parliamentarian* 57 1976 pp 15–25. Despite all this the picture that emerges from Richard Rose *British MPs: A Bite as Well as a Bark?* Centre for the Study of Public Policy 98, University of Strathclyde 1982 is of the enduring strength of party discipline in the Commons.

**539** Philip Norton 'Party Committees in the House of Commons' *Parliamentary Affairs* 36 1983 pp 7–27. A historical review of the development of these policy making committees, with an appendix all the committees of the Conservative and Labour parliamentary parties.

**540** Michael Stenton and Stephen Lees (eds) *Who's Who of British Members of Parliament Vol IV: 1945–1979* Harvester 1981. Short biographical entries on all the MPs of this period. For MPs who entered the House after 1979 see [472] and [537]. J F S Ross *Parliamentary Representation* 2nd ed, Eyre and Spottiswoode 1948 includes an analysis of the composition of the 1945 parliament and a discussion of parliamentary reform. Carol Bunker *Who's Who in Parliament* St Botolph Publishing 1947 is a biographical index of the MPs of the 1945 parliament. See also Charles Maurice Regan *The Members of the 1945 House of Commons: Forty Years On* Strathclyde Papers on Government and Politics 46, Department of Politics, University of Strathclyde 1986. John Cohen and Peter Cooper 'The 1959 House of Commons' *Occupational Psychology* 35 1961 pp 181–212 is a study of the 1959 parliament.

**541** Andrew Roth *Parliamentary Profiles* 4v, Parliamentary Profiles Service Ltd 1984. An interesting interpretation of current political developments introduces these volumes of witty and irreverent thumbnail sketches of MPs. This set of volumes amalgamates Andrew Roth and Janice Kerbey *The MPs Chart* Parliamentary Profiles 1962, 1971, 1976 and 1979, and Andrew Roth *The Business Background of MPs* Parliamentary Profiles 1959, 1963, 1967, 1968, 1972, 1975, and 1981. M Hulke Cassell's *Parliamentary Directory* Cassell 1975 is a similar, if less critical, work. There is now also an official register of MPs' extra-curricular activities, the *Register of Members Interests* HMSO 1975–.

**542** Colin Mellor *The British MP: A Socio-Economic Study of the House of Commons* Saxon House 1978. A detailed analytical study of the personnel of the Commons and the social, educational and economic profiles of the parliamentary parties since 1945. An excellent reference guide. Philip W Buck *Amateurs and Professionals in British Politics 1918–59* University of Chicago Press 1963 is both earlier and less detailed.

**543** Austin Mitchell *Westminster Man* Thames Methuen 1982. A study of MPs by a Labour MP who is still in the House. It contains various references to events since 1945 and especially in the 1970s. A similar and rather more autobiographical work, also by a Labour MP is Frederick Thomas Willey *The Honourable Member* Sheldon Press 1974.

**544** Michael Rush *The Selection of Parliamentary Candidates* Nelson 1969. This and Austin Ranney *Pathways to Parliament: Candidate Selection in Britain* University of Wisconsin Press, Madison, Wisconsin 1965 are both classic studies of the process of getting into parliament covering the period 1950–66 and 1950–64 respectively. Both however could do with updating, particularly in view of changes in recent years in the Labour Party. This problem is not solved by the other works on the subject; P Paterson *The Selectorate* Macgibbon and Kee 1967 and A D R Dickson 'MPs' Readoption Conflicts: Their Causes and Consequences' *Political Studies* 23 1975 pp 62–70. On the selection of women see Jorgen S Rasmussen 'Women's Role in British Politics: Impediments to Parliamentary Candidature' *Parliamentary Affairs* 36 1983 pp 300–15.

**545** Anthony King 'The Rise of the Career Politician in Britain – and its Consequences' *British Journal of Political Science* 11 1981 pp 249–85. A good survey of the rise of the career politician in the Commons since 1945 and its implications. This remains an area where more work could be done.

**546** Lisanne Radice, Elizabeth Vallance and Virginia Willis *Member of Parliament: The Job of a Backbencher* Macmillan 1987. The latest of many general studies of backbenchers. Peter Godfrey Richards' two studies, *Honourable Members: A Study of the British Back-Bencher* Faber 1959 and *The Backbenchers* Faber 1972 are comprehensive surveys. See also J D Stancer 'A Study of Backbench Members of Parliament Between 1945 and 1965' London PhD Thesis 1973 and C M Coates 'The Course of Party Discipline in Parliament and the Constituencies over the Past Thirty Years and Its Effect upon the Worth of the Back-Bencher in British Government' Bristol MA Thesis 1959–60. Dick Leonard and Valentine Herman (eds) *The Backbencher and Parliament* Macmillan 1972 contains useful essays on backbenchers' tactics and behaviour and on private members bills. Ronald Butt *The Power of Parliament* Constable 1969 also concentrates on backbencher activities. A short study is John Pitcairn Mackintosh *The Influence of the Backbencher, Now and a Hundred Years Ago* Manchester Statistical Society 1970. David Judge *Backbench Specialisation in the House of Commons* Heinemann Education 1981 is a rather theoretical analysis of backbench members interests. One of the best ways of analysing these interests is to examine the sponsors and signatures on early day motions. This forms the basic source for the following studies of backbench opinion and interests; Hugh B Berrington (ed) *Backbench Opinion in the House of Commons 1945–55* Pergamon 1974, S E Finer, Hugh B Berrington and B J Bartholomew *Backbench Opinion in the House of Commons 1955–59* Pergamon 1961 and Mark N Franklin and Michael Tappin 'Early Day Motions as Unobtrusive Measures of Backbench Opinion in Britain' *British Journal of Political Science* 7 1977 pp 49–69.

**547** Elizabeth Vallance *Women in the House: A Study of Women Members of Parliament* Athlone Press 1979. The work of women MPs and their impact on the House is analysed in Melanie Phillips *The Divided House: Women at Westminster* Sidgwick and Jackson 1980, Pamela Brookes *Women at Westminster: An Account of Women in the British Parliament 1918–1966* Peter Davies 1967 and Beverley P Stobaugh *Women and Parliament 1918–1970* Exposition Press, Hicksville, New York 1970.

**548** William Dale Muller *The 'Kept Men?' The First Century of Trade Union Representation in the British House of Commons 1874–1975* Harvester 1977. A useful history of trade union sponsored MPs. Trevor Park, Mary Lewis and Paul Lewis 'Trade Unions and the Labour Party: Changes in the Group of Trade Union Sponsored MPs' *Political Studies* 34 1986 pp 306–12 looks at change in this group of MPs between 1951 and 1983.

**549** David W Bebbington 'Baptist Members of Parliament in the Twentieth Century' *Baptist Quarterly* 31 1986 pp 252–87. A sociological survey and biographical index.

**550** J Pentney 'Worms that Turned: The Intra-Party Mobility of British Parliamentary Candidates Since 1945' *Parliamentary Affairs* 30 1977 pp 363–72. A brief examination of a neglected subject.

**551** David Judge 'The Politics of MPs' Pay' *Parliamentary Affairs* 37 1984 pp 59–75. This has been something of a controversial issue at times in the 1980s.

## G. PARTY HISTORY AND POLITICAL BIOGRAPHY

### (1) General

**552** Alan R Ball *British Political Parties: The Emergence of a Modern Party System* 2nd ed, Macmillan 1987. A comprehensive study of the development of the modern party system since the late nineteenth century. It is also a good guide to the literature on the subject. There is not however much of a local dimension to this study. Another good study is S E Finer *The Changing British Party System 1945–1979* American Enterprise Institute 1980. See also Stephen Ingle *The British Party System* 2nd ed, Blackwell 1989. Ivor Bulmer-Thomas *The Growth of the British Party System Vol II: 1924–1964* John Baker 1965 is still worth consulting. S D Bailey (ed) *The British Party System* Hansard Society 1952 is dated. Alan Beattie (ed) *English Party Politics Vol II: The Twentieth Century* Weidenfeld and Nicolson 1970 is a rather basic collection of documents.

**553** Raymond Plant *Ideology in Modern British Politics* Philip Allan 1988. A historical analysis of party ideology and of ideological conflict and consensus between the parties in the post-war years.

**554** Robert T Mackenzie *British Political Parties: The Distribution of Power within the Conservative and Labour Parties* 2nd ed, Heinemann 1963. An important study of the internal policies and organization of the Conservative and Labour parties. Some of his views perhaps now seem debatable. This book nevertheless will remain of value if only because of its influence on the way commentators thought and wrote about political parties.

**555** Richard Rose *The Problem of Party Government* Macmillan 1974. An in-depth analysis of party organization, recruitment, staff, finance, electoral organization, leadership, behaviour in government and and so on. There is some material on the Liberals and the nationalists as well as the main parties. It also has a useful bibliography. See also J D Lees and R Kimber *Political Parties in Modern Britain: An Organisational and Functional Guide* Routledge and Kegan Paul 1972. A textbook guide with useful appendices.

**556** Alan Ryan *et al* 'Symposium: Political Parties' *Contemporary Record* 1/4 1988 pp 17–27. Essays on political ideology, general election manifestos and the extent of intra-party consensus since the Second World War.

**557** Gillian Peele *British Party Politics: Competing for Power in the 1980s* Philip Allan 1988. A comprehensive study of the situation in the 1980s up to and including the 1987 general election.

**558** *Report of the Committee on Financial Aid to Political Parties* Cmnd 6601, *Parliamentary Papers* xiii 1975–76. A committee chaired by Lord Houghton of Sowerby which surveyed the finances of the political parties and recommended that they receive state aid.

**559** Michael Pinto-Duchinsky *British Political Finance 1830–1980* American Enterprise Institute 1981. The standard work. This has been updated by his article 'Trends in British Political Funding 1979–1983' *Parliamentary Affairs* 38 1985 pp 328–49. Keith Ewing *The Funding of Political Parties in Britain* Cambridge University Press 1987 is a legal interpretation which has some useful reflections on the situation in the 1980s. See also R J Johnston 'A Further Look at British Political Finance' *Political Studies* 25 1986 pp 466–73. M Harrison 'Political Finance in Britain' *Journal of Politics* 25 1963 pp 664–85 is also worth consulting.

**560** R J Jackson 'Party Discipline in Great Britain Since 1945' Oxford DPhil Thesis 1965–6.

**561** F W S Craig *Conservative and Labour Party Conference Decisions 1945–1981* Parliamentary Research Services 1982. A reference guide organized under broad subject headings.

**562** F W S Craig *British General Election Manifestos 1900–1974* Political Reference Publications 1975. This contains the text of the general election manifestos of the major parties in this period. For subsequent manifestos see [537].

**563** David Jack Wilson *Power and Party Bureaucracy in Britain: Regional Organisation in the Conservative and Labour Parties* Saxon House 1975. A good study in historical context on an otherwise neglected subject. Party agents have also been neglected, although there is George O Comfort *Professional Politicians: A Study of British Party Agents* Public Affairs Press, Washington D.C. 1958. Robert Frasure and Allan Kornberg 'Constituency Agents and British Politics' *British Journal of Political Science* 5 1975 pp 459–76 has some useful information on the situation in the 1970s.

**564** Zig Layton-Henry 'Political Youth Organisations in Britain: A Comparative Study of the Young Conservatives and the Labour Party Young Socialists' Birmingham PhD Thesis 1972–3. A good study.

**565** Richard Rose 'The Political Ideas of English Party Activists' *American Political Science Review* 56 1962 pp 360–71.

**566** Lord Windlesham *Communication and Political Power* Cape 1966. An examination of political advertising. It largely consists of studies of the Conservative advertising and election campaigns in 1957–9 and 1963–4 and of the propaganda during Labour's internal struggle in 1960–1. There is also a section on public opinion on the Common Market. For more material on this theme see the section on the Advertising Industry [3907–18].

## (2) The Opposition

**567** Robert Malcolm Punnett *Front Bench Opposition: The Role of the Leader of the Opposition, the Shadow Cabinet and Shadow Government in British Politics* Heinemann 1973. The standard interpretation. D R Turner *The Shadow Cabinet in British Politics* Routledge and Kegan Paul 1969 is a short historical account from the 1920s to the 1960s.

## (3) Socialism, the Labour Party and the Labour Movement

A number of other sections, such as those dealing with organizations closely linked with the Labour Party like the trade unions should also be consulted. The literature on Labour Party attitudes and policies, towards the European Community for instance, is to found in those sections which deal specifically with such issues. Material on the party in Scotland, Wales or in local areas is to be found in the sections on Scottish, Welsh and Local History. There is also much of relevance in the section on Political Thought.

## (a) Reference

For the *Dictionary of Labour Biography* see [116].

**568** Harold Smith *The British Labour Movement to 1970: A Bibliography* Mansell 1981. A subject organized bibliography which concentrates on the post-war period. Richard Price *Labour in British Society: An Interpretative History* Croom Helm 1986 is an interpretation of the vast literature on British labour history published since 1960.

**569** Victor F Gilbert (comp) *Labour and Social History Theses: American, British and Irish University Theses and Dissertations in the Field of British and Irish Labour History Presented Between 1900 and 1978* Mansell 1982. An unannotated subject listing.

**570** *Bulletin of the Society for the Study of Labour History* 1960–. This carries a very good annual bibliography which usefully updates [568]. Its coverage is so wide, especially in recent years, as to almost qualify as a general bibliography. There are also annual lists of archive deposits and of British, Irish and American theses. The holdings of one of the most important of Labour archives are detailed in John Saville *The Labour Archive at the University of Hull* Brynmor Jones Library, University of Hull 1989.

**571** *Report of the Annual Conference of the Labour Party* Labour Party 1900–. The annual Conference reports.

**572** Royden Harrison, Gillian B Woolven and Robert Duncan *The Warwick Guide to British Labour Periodicals 1790–1970: A Check List* Harvester 1977. An alphabetically arranged guide which is both well indexed and well annotated.

**573** J F Laidler (ed) *The Labour Party Newspaper Cuttings Collection* John Rylands Library 1983. Details on some 25,000 cuttings published 1909–78 held in the collection at John Rylands Library in Manchester.

**574** *Labour Party Bibliography* Labour Party 1968. A list of party publications and reports listed year by year. It also catalogues lists reports by leading Labour politicians year by year. Finally it lists and dates party periodicals.

**575** A Potts and E R Jones (comp) *Northern Labour History: A Bibliography* Library Association 1981. This is perhaps more of a finding list than a bibliography. It covers the co-operative movement, friendly societies, politics, trade unions, unemployment, working class education and biographies. See also Mike Boddington *Labour History in the West Midlands County: A Bibliography* the author 1982.

**576** *Labour Party* 3 series, Harvester Microfilm 1978. The first series reproduces the National Executive Committee 1900–61. The second is a microfilm of pamphlets and leaflets 1900–52. There is also a microfilm of speeches and press statements 1964–73.

## (b) General

**577** Henry Pelling *A Short History of the Labour Party* 8th ed, Macmillan 1985. A useful general history which ends in 1984. Another good general history is Carl F Brand *The British Labour Party: A Short History* 2nd ed, Hoover Institution Press, Stanford, California 1974. Chris Cook and Ian Taylor (eds) *The Labour Party: An Introduction to its History, Structure and Politics* Longman 1980 is equally useful. James E Cronin and Jonathan Schneer (eds) *Social Conflict and Political Order in Modern Britain* Croom Helm 1982 is a more disparate collection of essays on the Labour Movement, mainly dealing with the twentieth century. See also David Howell *British Social Democracy: Its Development and Decay* 2nd ed, Croom Helm 1980. John Saville *The Labour Movement in Britain: A Commentary* Faber 1988 is a general history of the movement which critically reviews the post-war period, dubbing the years 1951–79 'the wasted years'. Keith Laybourn *The Rise of Labour: The British Labour Party 1890–1979: Problems and Perspectives of Interpretation* Edward Arnold 1988 is a short textbook guide with an epilogue on 1951–79. See also William T Rodgers and Bernard Donoughue *The People in Parliament: An Illustrated History of the Labour Party* Thames and Hudson 1966. M Birdsey *Pictorial History of the Labour Party 1900–75: Among Our Souvenirs* Labour Party 1975 is a record drawing on photographs and documents.

**578** Eric Shaw *Discipline and Discord in the Labour Party: The Politics of Managerial Control in the Labour Party 1951–87* Manchester University Press 1988. An excellent study of the intra-party strife of the post-war period, of the gradual loss of control by the leadership and the organizational changes that accompanied it. An historical critique of the power of the leadership in policy formulation and party organization is Ken Coates *Democracy in the Labour Party* Spokesman 1977. Alan Warde *Consensus and Beyond: The Development of Labour Party Strategy Since the Second World War*

Manchester University Press 1982 is another good study which focuses more upon policy and less on party organization. Paul Whiteley *The Labour Party in Crisis* Methuen 1983 concentrates on ideological, membership and electoral difficulties since the war. Kenneth O Morgan 'Symposium: Labour Since 1945' *Contemporary Record* 1/4 1988 pp 5–16 is a collection of short pieces which includes a useful overview and chronology, Peter Mandelson on the Marketing of Labour in the 1987 election, the fragmentation of the Left since 1964 and a study of Attlee. See also G Loewenberg 'The Transformation of British Labour Party Policy Since 1945' *Journal of Politics* 21 1959 pp 234–57.

**579** Robert Currie *Industrial Politics* Clarendon 1979. A very useful historical examination of the industrial objectives of the trade unions and the Labour Party in the twentieth century. It also looks at industrial relations up to the 1978 Bullock report in this context.

**580** Ralph Miliband *Parliamentary Socialism* Allen and Unwin 1961. An influential interpretation which has continued to affect the views of commentators on the Left. Surveying 1900–60 he argues that Labour and the trade unions have been perennially unable to adopt radical policies or support militant working class action because of their commitment to parliamentary government. This theme is taken up in John Saville [577] which ends with an indictment of the party's behaviour in the 1984–5 miners' strike. James Hinton *Labour and Socialism: A History of the British Labour Movement 1867–1974* Harvester 1983 focuses more on the tension between the labourist tendencies of the trade unions and Socialism. David Coates *The Labour Party and the Struggle for Socialism* Cambridge University Press 1976 argues that Labour has failed as a vehicle for the achievement of Socialism. This theme is explored, rather more optimistically, in the context of Brighton Kemptown constituency Labour Party, in Tom Forester *The Labour Party and the Working Class* Heinemann Education 1976. Trevor Blackwell and Jeremy Seabrook *The Politics of Hope: Britain at the End of the Twentieth Century* Faber 1988 is another attempt to explore what went wrong with Socialism in the post-war years, focusing on the effect of materialism and the loss of vision.

**581** Kenneth O Morgan 'The High and Low Politics of Labour: Keir Hardie to Michael Foot' in Michael Bentley and John Stevenson (eds) *High and Low Politics in Modern Britain: Ten Studies* Clarendon 1983 pp 285–312. An analysis of the tensions between constitutionalism and conscience in the Labour movement.

**582** Herbert Tracey (ed) *The British Labour Party: Its History, Growth, Policy and Leaders* 3v, Caxton Publishing Company 1948. A very useful, informative and comprehensive guide. See also Clement Richard Attlee *The Labour Party in Perspective – And Twelve Years*

*Later* Gollancz 1949, a book which was first published in 1937 and to which some additions have subsequently been made.

**583** Barry Jones and Michael Keating *Labour and the British State* Clarendon 1985. A study of Labour's dilemmas over nationalism, the European Community and constitutional questions in recent years. It is best in its treatment of the devolution issue.

**584** Jonathan Schneer *Labour's Conscience: The Labour Left 1945–51* Unwin Hyman 1988. An important study of Left-Wing criticism of the Attlee government. The inability of the Left to deflect the Attlee government from its policies is discussed in David Rubinstein *Socialism and the Labour Party: The Labour Left and Domestic Policy 1945–1950* ILP Square One Publications 1979. Debate and dissent from the Left in this period are also examined in M Kemp 'The Left and the Debate over Labour Party Policy 1943–50' Cambridge PhD Thesis 1985. It is also touched on in R K Alderman 'Discipline in the Parliamentary Labour Party 1945–51' *Parliamentary Affairs* 18 1964–65 pp 293–305. Mark Jenkins *Bevanism – Labour's High Tide: The Cold War and the Democratic Mass Movement* Spokesman 1979 is an excellent study of the Bevanite movement in the 1940s and 1950s. Its central theme is the development of Bevanism in the context of the Cold War and it is particularly good on relations with the Communist Party. Attitudes to the Soviet Union in this period, as an inspiration or as a source of disillusionment for the Left, as well as a foreign policy problem, are well covered in Bill Jones *The Russia Complex: The British Labour Party and the Soviet Union* Manchester University Press 1977. Another good study of the ideological divisions in Labour over attitudes to Russia in this period is K I Moxham 'The Labour Party and the Soviet Union 1945–51' Cambridge PhD Thesis 1986. See also D A Jones 'The British Labour Party and the Soviet Union 1939–49' Wales PhD Thesis 1976.

**585** Leslie David Stevenson Hunter *The Road to Brighton Pier* Barker 1959. The classic account of infighting in the Labour Party 1951–57. The Labour Party in parliament during this period of opposition is dealt with by M T McNevin 'The Left Wing in the British Labour Party: 1951 to 1955' Oxford BLitt Thesis 1964–5. R K Alderman 'Parliamentary Party Discipline in Opposition: The Parliamentary Labour Party 1951–1964' *Parliamentary Affairs* 21 1968 pp 124–36, J Enoch Powell 'Morality in Politics 1951–1959: Labour in Opposition' *Political Quarterly* 30 1959 pp 336–43, R Hornby 'Parties in Parliament 1959–63: The Labour Party' *Political Quarterly* 34 1963 pp 240–8 and R M Punnett 'The Labour Shadow Cabinet 1955–64' *Parliamentary Affairs* 18 1964–65 pp 61–70.

**586** Stephen Haseler *The Gaitskellites: Revisionism in the British Labour Party 1951–64* Macmillan 1969. A study of the attempts by Labour leader Hugh Gaitskell and others in this period to modernize the party and rid it of old shibboleths. Key struggles were Gaitskell's unsuccessful attempt to get the party to drop Clause IV of the party constitution and his eventually successful fight to retain a commitment to nuclear weapons. A key element in these struggles, the Campaign for Democratic Socialism, is examined in Patrick Seyd 'Factionalism Within the Labour Party – A Case Study of the Campaign for Democratic Socialism' Southampton MPhil Thesis 1967–8. For contemporary comment on the struggle over the nuclear weapons issue see K Hindell and P Williams 'Scarborough and Blackpool: An Analysis of Some Votes at the Labour Party Conferences of 1960 and 1961' *Political Quarterly* 33 1962 pp 306–20, L D Epstein 'Who Makes Party Policy: British Labor 1960–1961' *Midwest Journal of Political Science* 6 1962 pp 165–82 and Roy Jenkins 'British Labour Divided' *Foreign Affairs* 38 1960 pp 487–96. The debate over and policy-making towards the nuclear weapons issue in the party in this period is reassessed in David Cross 'Labour and the Bomb 1952–1964' Lancaster PhD Thesis 1986. The valuable support Gaitskell received from trade union MPs is examined in William Dale Muller 'Trade Union Sponsored Members of Parliament in the Defence Dispute of 1960–1' *Parliamentary Affairs* 23 1970 pp 258–76.

**587** John Richard Piper 'Backbench Rebellion, Party Government and Consensus Politics: The Case of the Parliamentary Labour Party 1966–1970' *Parliamentary Affairs* 27 1974 pp 384–96. A useful collection of essays reflecting the attitudes and policies of the Left in the 1960s is Gerald Kaufman *The Left: A Symposium* Anthony Blond 1966.

**588** Michael Hatfield *The House the Left Built: Inside Labour Policy Making 1970–1975* Gollancz 1978. A well regarded account. W Stallard 'The Labour Party in Opposition and in Government 1970–79: The Effects of the Government-Opposition Cycle upon Intra-Party Stability' Keele PhD Thesis 1984 argues that policy making in opposition had an adverse effect when the party was returned to government in the 1970s. He focuses on attitudes to Europe and industrial relations to illustrate the difference between being in government and being in opposition makes to intra-party conflict. The behaviour of the parliamentary Labour Party during the 1974–79 Labour government is analysed in S P Longstreet 'Rebellion in the Parliamentary Labour Party 1974–1979: A Quantative Analysis' Essex PhD Thesis 1984 and John E Schwartz 'Attempting to Assert the Commons' Power: Labour Members in the House of Commons 1974–1979' *Comparative Politics* 14 1981 pp 17–29.

**589** Paul McCormick *Enemies of Democracy* Temple Smith 1979. A study of Left-Wing entryism in the constituency parties in the Labour Party in the 1970s, particularly in the context of Newham North East. See also his article 'Prentice and the Newham North East Constituency: The Making of Historical Myths' *Political Studies* 29 1981 pp 73–90. Peter Tatchell *The Battle for Bermondsey* Heretic 1983 supplies a rather different perspective on this development in the context of his own unsuccessful attempt to win the 1983 Bermondsey by-election as a Left-Wing Labour candidate. The changes which enabled the Left to gain ground in the constituency parties in this period are examined in Paul McCormick 'The Labour Party: Three Unnoticed Changes' *British Journal of Political Science* 10 1980 pp 381–8.

**590** Michael Crick *The March of Militant* 2nd ed, Faber 1986. A good study of the most celebrated of the entryist organizations of this period. See also Peter Shipley *The Militant Tendency: Trotskyism in the Labour Party* Foreign Affairs Publishing Company 1983.

**591** David and Maurice Kogan *The Battle for the Labour Party* Kogan Page 1982. A study of the rise of the Left within the party in the 1970s and the resulting constitutional, ideological and leadership battles culminating in Tony Benn's challenge for the deputy leadership in 1981. It also examines the rise of the urban Left and the start of the vilification of the Left in the popular press. Michael Cocks *Labour and the Benn Factor* Macdonald 1989 is a prejudiced account which nevertheless contains a number of penetrating insights on Tony Benn and his followers. Stephen Haseler *The Tragedy of Labour* Blackwell 1980 is in a sense a sequel to his work on the Gaitskellites charting and expressing the increasing sense of defeat of those on the social democratic wing of the party in the face of the rise of the Left. For the constitutional battles between Left and Right see also Michael Rustin 'Different Conceptions of Party: Labour's Constitutional Debates' *New Left Review* 126 1981 pp 17–42. Patrick Seyd *The Rise and Fall of the Labour Left* Macmillan 1987 is a thorough account of the rise of the Left, its ideas and limitations and its achievements at national and local level, and of Neil Kinnock's attempts in the 1980s to contain its influence.

**592** Dennis Kavanagh (ed) *The Politics of the Labour Party* Allen and Unwin 1982. A collection of essays placing the recent difficulties and debates in the Labour Party in historical context.

**593** Eric Hobsbawm (ed) *The Forward March of Labour Halted?* Verso 1981. The reprint of a 1978 lecture which provoked considerable furore on the Left by pointing to the gradual disappearance of the traditional working class vote. This theme is developed in his collection of writings *Politics for a Rational Left: Pol-*

*itical Writing 1977–1988* Verso 1989. This is also useful for the in-fighting on the Left in the 1980s and efforts, particularly of the London Left, to build a rainbow coalition of discontented minority groups to replace the party's former stalwarts.

**594** Austin Mitchell *Four Years in the Death of the Labour Party* Methuen 1983. An account of the party's difficulties and internal conflicts during the first term of the Thatcher government 1979–83. Hilary Wainwright *Labour: A Tale of Two Parties* Hogarth Press 1987 is a committed study of Labour's internal conflicts in the 1980s, focusing on the demand of the Left for radical change to the structure of the party and the rise of the urban Left.

**595** Lewis Minkin *The Labour Party Conference: A Study in the Politics of Intra-Party Democracy* Allen Lane 1977. A highly regarded study focusing on 1956–70.

**596** Henry M Drucker 'Leadership Selection in the Labour Party' *Parliamentary Affairs* 29 1976 pp 378–95. See also his articles 'Changes in the Labour Leadership' *Parliamentary Affairs* 34 1981 pp 369–91 and 'Intra-Party Democracy in Action: The Election of the Leader and the Deputy Leader by the Labour Party in 1983' *Parliamentary Affairs* 37 1984 pp 283–300.

**597** Alison Young *The Reselection of MPs* Heinemann Education 1983. One of the bones of contention between Left and Right in the party was the idea that the constituency party should be able to de-select an MP with whom it was not satisfied. This work traces this theme from the 1960s, drawing on case studies of celebrated cases of MPs being de-selected, up until the 1980 conference decision to make the re-selection of MPs mandatory. John Bochel and David Denver 'Candidate Selection in the Labour Party: What the Selectors Seek' *British Journal of Political Science* 13 1983 pp 45–69 is a study of the working of the selection and re-selection procedure in the 1970s and 1980s.

**598** Leon D Epstein 'British Class Consciousness and the Labour Party' *Journal of British Studies* 1 1962 pp 136–50. A response to the 1959 general election in which he draws attention to the decline of the working class element in the party leadership and of class consciousness amongst Labour MPs.

**599** Diane Hayter *The Labour Party: Crisis and Prospects* Fabian Society Tract 451, 1977. This focuses on Labour's declining membership since the early 1950s. As Colin Martin and Dick Martin 'The Decline of Labour Party Membership' *Political Quarterly* 48 1977 pp 459–71 points out by 1977 the inability of constituency parties to finance themselves meant that the party only had 86 full time agents and about half had no youth branches. On these agents see D A R Race 'Political Agents and the Development of Bureaucratisation and Deradicalisation in the British Labour Party' Kent PhD Thesis 1979. Hugh Jenkins *Rank and File* Croom Helm 1980 is a profile of the constituency parties. See also Edward G Janosik *Constituency Labour Parties in Britain* Pall Mall Press 1968 and I Gordon and Paul Whiteley 'Social Class and Political Attitudes: The Case of Labour Councillors' *Political Studies* 27 1979 pp 99–113. Barry Hindess *The Decline of Working Class Politics* Macgibbon and Kee 1973 is a study of party activists based on his doctoral research in Liverpool which has had considerable influence on the debate about declining working class political activity. Zig Layton-Henry has written useful articles on the Young Socialists: 'Labour's Militant Youth' *Political Quarterly* 45 1974 pp 418–25 and 'Labour's Lost Youth' *Journal of Contemporary History* 11 1976 pp 275–308. For other work of relevance see the section on Local Politics.

**600** Andrew J Taylor *The Trade Unions and the Labour Party* Croom Helm 1987. A study of the party's relations with the trade unions since 1970, and of the unions influence on the 1974–79 government. Party relations with the trade unions earlier in the post-war period are competently dealt with by Martin Harrison *Trade Unions and the Labour Party Since 1945* Allen and Unwin 1960. A relatively poor book on the subject is Bill Simpson *Labour: The Unions and the Party: A Study of the Trade Unions and the British Labour Movement* Allen and Unwin 1973. See also B Hennessy 'Trade Unions and the British Labour Party' *American Political Science Review* 49 1955 pp 1050–66. In the 1960s and 1970s attempts to apply incomes policies were a crucial element in Labour party/trade union relations and the section on Incomes Policy should therefore also be consulted. There has been little work as yet on the influence of the unions on grassroots Labour politics, but see Andrew J Taylor 'The Modern Boroughmongers? The Yorkshire Area (NUM) and Grassroots Politics' *Political Studies* 32 1984 pp 385–400.

**601** Patricia Pugh *Educate, Agitate, Organise: 100 Years of Fabian Socialism* Methuen 1984. A useful official history of the Fabian Society. Margaret Cole *The Story of Fabian Socialism* Heinemann 1961 remains of value. Deirdre Terrins and Phillip Whitehead (eds) *A Hundred Years of Fabian Socialism 1884–1984* Fabian Society 1984 is a short well illustrated pamphlet.

**602** Thomas F Carbery *Consumers in Politics: A History and General Review of the Co-operative Party* Manchester University Press 1969. A history and a study of the party's problems in the 1960s with useful documentary appendices. For other material of relevance see the section on the Co-operative Movement.

**603** Lucy Middleton (ed) *Women in the Labour Movement: The British Experience* Croom Helm 1977. A study of women in the party, parliament and the trade unions. See also Sarah Perrigo *Trouble and Strife: Women and the Labour Party* Pluto 1985. Women's participation in a local branch is analysed in Nigel Todd 'Labour Women: A Study of Women in the Bexley Branch of the British Labour Party (1945–1950)' *Journal of Contemporary History* 8 1973 pp 159–73.

**604** M McDermott 'Irish Catholics and the Labour Movement: A Study, With Particular Reference to London 1918 to 1970' Kent MA Thesis 1979. A study of one of the traditionally most important elements in the Labour Party. Little work has however been done on the impact and role of such groups in the post-war era.

### (4) The Conservative Party

The literature on Conservative Party attitudes and policies, towards the European Community for instance, is to found in those sections which deal specifically with such issues. Material on the party in Scotland, Wales or in local areas is to be found in the sections on Scottish, Welsh and Local History. There is also much of relevance in the section on Political Thought.

**605** G D M Block *A Source Book of Conservatism* Conservative Political Centre 1964. A chronologically arranged bibliography, which includes official documents and pamphlets. It also includes six short essays on party history.

**606** *Annual Conference Reports* of the Conservative Party 1948–. From 1978 onwards the party has not published a full report. They do however continue to release the text of major speeches by ministers.

**607** William Pidduck *The Radical Right and Patriotic Movements in Britain: A Bibliographical Guide* Harvester 1978. The introduction to this volume discusses the history of the various Right-Wing groupings covered, most of which are within the Conservative Party. It then proceeds to index, by author, title and chronologically, the publications between 1945 and 1974 of groups such as the Bow Group, the Monday Club or Aims of Industry. A rather fuller range of groups has been covered in the annual updating volumes covering the publications of subsequent years.

**608** Robert Blake *The Conservative Party from Peel to Thatcher* Fontana 1985. The standard textbook history. Another good textbook guide is T F Lindsay and M

Harrington *The Conservative Party 1918–1979* 2nd ed, Macmillan 1979. Zig Layton-Henry (ed) *Conservative Party Politics* Macmillan 1980 is a very useful collection of essays on various aspects of the party, most of which have a strong historical element. See also Sheila Moore *The Conservative Party: The First 150 Years* Country Life 1980.

**609** Andrew Gamble *The Conservative Nation* Routledge and Kegan Paul 1974. A well regarded study of the Conservative Party and Conservatism 1945–70. The changes in the party's social composition and economic policies since the 1960s are analysed in A J Walker 'Crisis and Social Development: The British Conservative Party 1964–1983' London PhD Thesis 1985. A good short interpretation of the party's post-war history is John Ramsden 'From Churchill to Heath' in Lord Butler (ed) *The Conservatives: A History from Their Origins to 1965* Allen and Unwin 1977 pp 405–78. Butler's introduction and epilogue should also be consulted. See also John Ramsden 'Conservatives Since 1945' *Contemporary Record* 2/1 1988 pp 17–22.

**610** Philip Norton and Arthur Aughey *Conservatives and Conservatism* Temple Smith 1981. A good general guide to the nature and practice of Conservatism. It is particularly good on the leadership and on leadership struggles. See also T Russel *The Tory Party: Its Policies, Divisions and Future* Penguin 1978. John Ross *Thatcher and Friends: The Anatomy of the Tory Party* Pluto 1983 is a rather polemical assessment of the modern Conservative Party.

**611** Neill Nugent and Roger King (eds) *The British Right: Conservative and Right Wing Politics in Britain* Saxon House 1977. The second section of this book is on the Conservative Party from Macmillan to Thatcher and is particularly useful on Powellism and on grassroots Conservatism. The third part however deals with the far and Fascist Right. There is a good bibliography, but no index.

**612** J D Hoffman *The Conservative Party in Opposition 1945–51* Macgibbon and Kee 1964. In the immediate aftermath of the war the party had to re-establish and revamp the party machine and reassess its policies in the light of its massive defeat in 1945. An internal record of this process incorporating important documents such as the 1947 Industrial Charter is D Clark *Conservatism 1945–50* Conservative Political Centre 1950. These works have tended to give the impression that the party underwent a major readjustment in these years, a view challenged in John Ramsden '"A Party for Owners or a Party for Earners?" How far did the British Conservative Party Really Change After 1945' *Transactions of the Royal Historical Society* 5th Series 37 1987 pp 49–63, in which he argues that there was more continuity from the inter-war years than had previously been thought.

**613** Randolph Spencer Churchill *The Fight for the Tory Leadership: A Contemporary Chronicle* Heinemann 1964. An account of the controversial process whereby Sir Alec Douglas-Home came to replace Macmillan as leader and Prime Minister in 1963. This book was written with Macmillan's assistance and tended to reflect his point of view. Its version of the events drew a furious response from those who had supported Butler for the leadership, most notably in Iain Macleod's article 'The Tory Leadership' *The Spectator* 17/1/1964 pp 65–7. See also A L Teasdale 'The Conservative Leadership Under Challenge: The Leadership Crisis in the British Conservative Party of 1963–65 and some of the Implications for the Subsequent Development of the Party' Oxford BLitt Thesis 1983. Another aspect of in-fighting in the Conservative Party in the 1960s is dealt with in Jorgen S Rasmussen *The Relations of the Profumo Rebels with Their Local Parties* Institute of Government Research, Tucson, Arizona 1966.

**614** Martin Burch 'The Conservative Party in Opposition 1964–1970: The Effects of Opposition Status upon Certain Major Party Policy Positions' Glasgow PhD Thesis 1975. A good study of the re-making of Conservative Party policy in the 1960s.

**615** Philip Norton *Conservative Dissidents: Dissent Within the Parliamentary Conservative Party 1970–74* Temple Smith 1978. A good study of Conservative behaviour in the House during Ted Heath's fraught government.

**616** *The Right Approach: A Statement of Conservative Aims* Conservative Central Office 1976. This was the main policy document to emerge during the next period of reassessment whilst in opposition in 1974–79. Robert Blake (ed) *Conservatism in an Age of Revolution* Churchill Press 1976 may not have an official imprimatur. It does however have a foreword by Margaret Thatcher and in emphasizing the need to roll back the state it is perhaps nearer to her thinking. For the rise of the New Right in this period see [937]. Robert Behrens *The Conservative Party from Heath to Thatcher: Policies and Politics 1974–1979* Saxon House 1980 is a good study of the party in this period of opposition. On Conservative relations with the trade unions during these years see Robert Behrens '"Blinkers for the Cart-Horse": The Conservative Party and the Trade Unions 1974–8' *Political Quarterly* 49 1978 pp 457–66 and Michael Moran 'The Conservative Party and the Trade Unions Since 1974' *Political Studies* 27 1979 pp 38–53. On Conservative relations with the CBI in this period see Wyn Grant 'Business Interests and the British Conservative Party' *Government and Opposition* 15 1980 pp 143–61.

**617** Michael Pinto-Duchinsky 'Central Office and "Power" in the Conservative Party' *Political Studies* 20 1972 pp 1–16. A useful study of relations between the party leadership and Conservative Central Office. On the role of the Conservative Political Centre see Arthur Aughey *Constituency Attitudes and Policy Formulation: The Role of the Conservative Political Centre* Hull Papers in Politics 7, Department of Politics, University of Hull 1981.

**618** John Ramsden *The Making of Conservative Party Policy: The Conservative Research Department Since 1929* Longman 1980. An excellent study of the main policy making organization in the party. The part the Research Department plays within the party structure and as a nursery for leading Conservatives is analysed in Arnold Beichmann 'The Conservative Research Department: The Care and Feeding of Future British Political Elites' *Journal of British Studies* 13 1974 pp 92–113.

**619** Richard N Kelly *Conservative Party Conferences: The Hidden System* Manchester University Press 1989. An in-depth analysis of the Conservative Party conference season in 1986. See also M J Hyslop 'The Role of the Annual Conference in the Conservative Party' Durham MA Thesis 1973–4.

**620** Philip Goodhart *1922: The Story of the 1922 Committee* Macmillan 1973. A good study of the influential backbench committee. Also of relevance to the study of the parliamentary Conservative Party is J A Cross 'Withdrawal of the Conservative Party Whip' *Parliamentary Affairs* 212 1967–8 pp 166–75.

**621** Michael Pinto-Duchinsky 'The Role of Constituency Associations in the Conservative Party' Oxford DPhil Thesis 1971–72. A useful study. Tensions between central and local party organizations are analysed in the context of local opposition to attempts to encourage working class and trade unionist supporters to play a role in the party in J R Greenwood 'Central Control and Constituency Activity in the Conservative Party: The Organisation of "Labour" and Trade Unionist Support 1918–1970' Reading PhD Thesis 1981. See also Greenwood's article 'Promoting Working Class Candidatures in the Conservative Party: The Limits of Central Office Power' *Parliamentary Affairs* 41 1988 pp 456–68. Zig Layton-Henry 'The Young Conservatives 1945–70' *Journal of Contemporary History* 8 1973 pp 143–58 is a good analysis of the party's youth organization.

**622** Richard Rose 'The Bow Group's Role in British Politics' Western *Political Quarterly* 14 1961 pp 265–78. Apart from this and [607] little work has been done on the various groups within the Conservative Party. However see also Patrick Seyd 'Factionalism Within the

Conservative Party: The Monday Club' *Government and Opposition* 7 1972 pp 464–87.

**623** Philip Tether *Clubs: A Neglected Aspect of Conservative Organisation* Hull Papers in Politics 42, Politics Department, University of Hull 1988. A study of Conservative clubs.

## (5) The Liberal Party

Relatively little work has been done on the Liberal Party. Even the revival of the party in the 1980s, in alliance with the SDP, has yet to attract a substantial literature. The success of the party in recent local government elections has also been neglected. Nor is there any literature on the party in traditional areas of strength such as Scotland, Wales or Cornwall. The dearth of material on the post-war Liberal Party partly reflects the chaotic state of the party records and partly the party's lack of success in the post-war period. The party has not been in government at any point during the post-war years. The nearest it came was during the period of the Lib-Lab Pact 1977–8. The literature on this can be found in the section on the 1974–9 Labour Governments [309]. One of the results of this lack of government experience is that very little has been written on Liberal Party policy. Some relevant material can however be found in the sections on European integration [2103] and on Race Relations [5679]. The section on Political Thought [945–7] should also be consulted.

**624** *Directory of Liberal Party Resolutions 1967–1978* Gladstone Club 1978, with annual supplements. A register of resolutions from the annual assembly. Nothing comparable exists for the period before 1967.

**625** Chris Cook *A Short History of the Liberal Party 1900–88* 3rd ed, Macmillan 1988. A useful general history up until the merger with the SDP to form the Social and Liberal Democrats in March 1988. Vernon Bogdanor (ed) *Liberal Party Politics* Oxford University Press 1983 is a good collection of essays surveying Liberal fortunes since 1931. Arthur Cyr *Liberal Party Politics in Britain* John Calder 1977 provides a great deal of detail on the Liberal Party since 1945. It is however more of a political science rather than an historical analysis. Roy Douglas *History of the Liberal Party 1895–1970* Sidgwick and Jackson 1971 is now rather dated. See also Jorgen Rasmussen *Retrenchment and Revival: A Study of the Contemporary British Liberal Party* Constable 1965 and S J Ingle 'The Policy, Leadership and Organisation of the Liberal Party Since 1945' Sheffield MA (Econ) Thesis 1964–5. John Stevenson 'The Liberal Party Since 1945' *Contemporary Record* 2/3 1988 pp 21–5 is a useful short history and chronology of the party since the war.

**626** S J Ingle 'The Recent Revival of the British Liberal Party: Some Geographical, Social and Political Aspects' *Political Science* 2 1966 pp 39–48. The party's revival in the 1960s.

**627** J Josephs *Inside the Alliance: An Inside Account of the Development and Prospects of the Liberal-SDP Alliance* John Martin 1983. A study of the workings of the alliance forged with the SDP up until the 1983 general election.

**628** M E Burton 'The Making of Liberal Party Policy 1945–80' Reading PhD Thesis 1983. This focuses especially on the making of the manifesto and the making of policy on defence and on Europe.

**629** R M Sommer 'The Organisation of the Liberal Party 1936–1960' London PhD Thesis 1961–2. See also A P Brier 'A Study of Liberal Party Constituency Activity in the Mid-1960s' Exeter PhD Thesis 1967–8 and F Ghiles 'The Young Liberals 1959–1969' Keele MA Thesis 1971–2.

**630** Des Wilson *Battle for Power* Sphere 1987. A lively account of the 1987 election campaign and its aftermath by the Chairman of the Alliance's General Election Campaign Committee. In the process it reveals some of the behind the scenes developments that led to the post-election transformation of centre politics in Britain.

## (6) The Social Democratic Party

**631** Geoffrey Lee Williams and Alan Lee Williams *The Rise of the Social Democratic Party* Macmillan 1988. The most complete study of the short history of the SDP from its origins in 1981 to the 1987 general election. This analysis is developed in their *Labour's Decline and the Social Democrats' Fall* Macmillan 1989. The establishment of the SDP produced a number of instant histories of its birth. Ian Bradley *Breaking the Mould? The Birth and Prospects of the Social Democratic Party* Robertson 1981 examines the dissatisfaction with the policies and constitutional changes in the Labour Party which led to its foundation. N Tracey *The Origins of the Social Democratic Party* Croom Helm 1983 traces the long-term origins of the party back to the 1964–70 Labour government, though it might be argued that it could indeed be taken further back, to Gaitskell's Campaign for Democratic Socialism. Hugh Stephenson *Claret and Chips: The Rise of the SDP* Michael Joseph 1982 concentrates more on the new party's leaders and its organization. It includes useful appendices. On the making of the new party see also the material on Roy Jenkins, David Owen and William Rodgers in the section on Labour Party biographies. P Zentner *Social*

*Democracy in Britain: Must Labour Lose?* John Martin 1982 focuses more on the party's policies. The impact of the new party on the media in 1981–83 is examined in Holli Semetko 'Political Communication and Party Development in Britain' London PhD Thesis 1989. See also [627].

**632** Peter Godfrey Richards 'The SDP in Parliament' *Parliamentary Affairs* 35 1982 pp 136–42. A study conducted at a time when the vast majority of the party's MPs were sitting Labour MPs who had transferred their allegiance to the new party.

**633** Patricia Lee Sykes *Losing from the Inside: The Cost of Conflict in the British Social Democratic Party* Transaction Books 1988. An account of the brief history of the SDP 1981–88 in the context of the fratricidal struggle after the 1987 general election which led to the amalgamation of the bulk of the party into a new party with the Liberals (the Social and Liberal Democrats).

### (7) Minor Parties in General

**634** George Thayer *The British Political Fringe: A Profile* Anthony Blond 1965. A well regarded and comprehensive study which takes into its ambit not only the various extremist parties and the nationalist parties but also a whole range of pressure groups. See also Nicholas Harman 'Minor Political Parties in Britain' *Political Quarterly* 33 1962 pp 268–81. John Tomlinson *Left, Right: The March of Political Extremism in Britain* John Calder 1981 is essentially a reference guide which focuses more narrowly on political extremism. It provides details of funding, leaders and international links. It is rather more thorough on the Right than on the Left.

**635** F W S Craig (ed) *Minor Parties at British Parliamentary Elections 1885–1974* Macmillan 1975. A reference guide to the electoral performance of minor parties.

**636** W S Livingstone 'Minor Parties and Minority MPs 1945–1955' *Western Political Quarterly* 12 1959 pp 1017–37.

### (8) The Communist Party

Some relevant material also appears in the ensuing section on the other parties of the Left.

**637** Alan J Mackenzie 'Communism in Britain: A Bibliography' *Bulletin of the Society for the Study of Labour History* 44 1982 pp 23–41. A very informative guide to the literature. It includes details on relevant periodicals, library holdings, and archives.

**638** Communist Party of Great Britain *Pamphlets 1920–1971 and Continuation* World Microfilms 1971–. Microfilms of party literature.

**639** Henry Pelling *The British Communist Party: A Historical Profile* 2nd ed, A and C Black 1975. The best general history. See also Walter Kendall *The History of the Communist Party of Great Britain* Collins Harvill 1986. Michael Woodhouse and Brian Pearce *Essays on the History of Communism in Britain* New Park Publications 1975 is a useful collection of essays. J R Campbell *Forty Fighting Years: The Communist Record* Communist Party of Great Britain 1960 is a somewhat self-congratulatory party history. Paul- Wolfgang Hermann *Die Communist Party of Great Britain: Untersuchungen zur Geschichtlichen Entwicklung, Organisation, Ideologie und Politik der CPGB von 1920–1970* Verlag Anton Hain, Königstein, West Germany 1976 is a reasonable study but is not available in translation. The first fifty years of the Communist Party are also surveyed in J Gollan 'Fifty Years of the Communist Party' *Marxism Today* 14 1970 pp 289–96 and P Kerrigan 'The Communist Party in the Industrial Struggle: 50th Anniversary of the CPGB' *Marxism Today* 14 1970 pp 375–82. See also R Palme Dutt 'Honour to Whom Honour: Some Reflections on Communist Party History' *Labour Monthly* 41 1959 pp 193–204.

**640** William Gallacher *The Case for Communism* Penguin 1949. An argument for Communism in advance of the 1950 general election by a Communist MP.

**641** Kenneth Newton *The Sociology of British Communism* Penguin 1969. The behaviour and attitudes of Communists is also examined in N Wood 'The Empirical Proletarians: A Note on British Communism' *Political Science Quarterly* 74 1959 pp 256–72. The structure and organization of the party is studied in G W Grainger 'Oligarchy in the British Communist Party' *British Journal of Sociology* 9 1958 pp 143–58.

**642** Margot Heinemann '1956 and the Communist Party' *Socialist Register* 13 1976 pp 43–57. The Soviet invasion of Hungary in 1956, coming in the wake of Khrushchev's denunciation of Stalinism, had a major and detrimental effect on the Communist Party. The impact of Khrushchev's attack on Stalin is examined in John Saville 'The XXth Congress and the British Communist Party' *Socialist Register* 13 1976 pp 1–23.

**643** Lee Pitcairn 'Crisis in British Communism: An Insider's View' *New Left Review* 153 1985 pp 102–20. A look at the splits in the party, the shift of the leadership to the Right and other difficulties of the 1980s. See also Raphael Samuel 'The Lost World of British Communism' *New Left Review* 154 1985 pp 3–53, an anecdotal study of the party's history in the light of the recent split between Stalinists and reformists.

**644** Alan McKinnon 'Communist Party Election Tactics: A Historical Review' *Marxism Today* 24 1980 pp 20–6.

**645** Phil Piratin *Our Flag Stays Red* 2nd ed, Lawrence and Wishart 1978. An account of the growth of the party in the East End up to the 1945 general election. Piratin was the Communist MP for Stepney 1945–50.

### (9) Other Parties of the Left

The Far Left in Britain comprises an assortment of fissiparous groups of Trotskyite, Maoist, orthodox Marxist, or Anarchist tendencies. Some of these are on the fringes of the Labour Party. The literature on Militant Tendency is accordingly to be found in the section on Labour Party history. Material on the student sit-ins and radical activities of the late 1960s and early 1970s is to be found in the section on Student Politics [6620–31] which appears in the section on Education.

**646** John Speirs, Ann Sexsmith and Alastair Everitt *The Left in Britain: A Checklist and Guide* Harvester 1976. A guide with historical notes to 37 Left-Wing political movements and groups active 1904–72 whose publications are also available on Harvester microfilm. It is very well indexed. This has been updated biennially and more recently annually. As the series has progressed some new groups have been added.

**647** *The Far Left: Directory of Organisations and Supporters* Common Cause Publications 1985. Details of the origins, policies and objectives of a variety of Left-Wing parties and pressure groups.

**648** P J Thwaites 'The Independent Labour Party 1938–1950' London PhD Thesis 1976. The ILP had been affiliated to the Labour Party until 1932. In 1945 it retained four MPs. Thereafter however it effectively disappeared as a political force and today the name only survives as the description of a Labour Party publication house. Another independent Left-Wing party with connections with the Labour Party which did not thrive in the post-war era was the Common Wealth Party. Founded during the wartime party truce it soon faded after the war. See D L Prynn 'Common Wealth – a British "Third Party" of the 1940s' *Journal of Contemporary History* 7 1972 pp 169–81.

**649** David Widgery *The Left in Britain 1956–68* Penguin 1976. A useful overview of the Left from the rise of the New Left to the advent of the student politics of the late 1960s. It largely consists of selected documents, memoirs and articles. The New Left which emerged in 1956 was characterized by a kind of humanistic Marxism, and by disaffection from the Communist Party in the wake of the Soviet invasion of Hungary and from the pro-nuclear stance of the Labour leadership. On the rise of the New Left see B A D Bryant 'The New Left in Britain 1956–1968: The Dialectic of Rationality and Participation' London PhD Thesis 1981, C L Bamford 'The Politics of Commitment: The Early New Left in Britain 1956–1962' Edinburgh PhD Thesis 1983, G Hughes 'The New Left in Britain 1956–64' Keele MA Thesis 1973–4 and R Hall 'The Politics of Dissent in the Fifties – The New Left' Manchester MA Thesis 1962–3. An overview of the period by one closely involved is Perry Anderson 'The Left in the Fifties' *New Left Review* 29 1965 pp 3–18. On the decline of the New Left see N Young *An Infantile Disorder? Crisis and Decline of the New Left* Routledge and Kegan Paul 1977.

**650** John Callaghan *The Far Left in British Politics* Blackwell 1987. A good general if not totally comprehensive study which traces the growth and development of the Far Left, including the Labour Left, since 1945. Peter Shipley *Revolutionaries in Modern Britain* The Bodley Head 1976 examines the history of the revolutionary Left, particularly the Communist Party and the various Trotskyite and Maoist factions, since 1956. A more hostile account is Blake Baker *The Far Left: An Exposé of the Extreme Left in Britain* Weidenfeld and Nicolson 1981. Jo Freeman *Social Movements of the Sixties and Seventies* Longman 1983 is an analysis of radical movements and social protest. A critical study of Anti-Semitism in the Far Left is Michael Billig 'Anti-Jewish Themes and the British Far Left' *Patterns of Prejudice* 18 1984 pp 3–15.

**651** Tariq Ali *The Coming British Revolution* Cape 1972. A source rather than a history which reflects on post-war developments on the Left and the rise of Trotskyite groups and student politics, in both of which its author was heavily involved.

**652** R Barltrop *The Monument: Story of the Socialist Party of Great Britain* Pluto 1975. An anecdotal history of an unrevolutionary Marxist Party. It does not really explain the continued existence of this party since its foundation in 1904, nor its tactics and attitudes.

**653** Albert Meltzer *The Anarchists in London 1935–55* Cienfuegos Press 1976. Guy Alfred Aldred *No Traitor's Gait: The Autobiography of Guy A Aldred* 3v, Strickland Press 1955–63, is the memoirs of the prominent Glaswegian Anarchist Guy Aldred who died in 1963.

**654** John Callaghan *British Trotskyism: Theory and Practice* Blackwell 1984. A study covering the post-war years. He is best on the Socialist Workers Party and the mood of the 1960s and relatively weak on Militant, the Workers Revolutionary Party and the 1957 split in the Communist Party. On Trotskyism see also B Reid 'Trotskyism in Britain Today' *Marxism Today* 8 1964 pp

274–83, Sam Bornstein *The War and the International: A History of the Trotskyist Movement in Britain 1937–1949* Socialist Platform 1986 and M R Upham 'The History of British Trotskyism to 1949' Hull PhD Thesis 1981.

**655** Ian Birchall *The Smallest Mass Party in the World: Building the Socialist Workers Party 1951–1979* Socialists Unlimited 1981. A useful pamphlet about the SWP and its history.

**656** Gordon Carr *The Angry Brigade: The Cause and the Case* Gollancz 1973. A study of the Anarchist terrorists of the early 1970s in their social, international and ideological milieu and of their subsequent trial and imprisonment.

**657** Tariq Ali *1968 and After: Inside the Revolution* Blond and Briggs 1978. Much material of relevance on the events of 1968 can also be found elsewhere in the section on student politics. This book, by a leading activist, is however the best introduction to how Britain was affected in that year. See also his useful memoir of this time *Street Fighting Years: An Autobiography of the Sixties* Collins 1987. On the underground newspaper *Oz* see [3593].

## (10) The Green Party

**658** Wolfgang Rudig and Philip D Lowe 'The Withered "Greening" of British Politics: A Study of the Ecology Party' *Political Studies* 34 1986 pp 262–84. An analysis of failure of the Ecology Party, later to become the Green Party, to take off as a similar party has in West Germany.

**659** Jonathon Porritt *Seeing Green: The Politics of Ecology Explained* Blackwell 1985. An explanation of Green politics.

## (11) Parties of the Far Right

**660** Ciaran O'Maolain (comp) *The Radical Right: A World Directory* Longman 1987. This includes a large section on the Far Right in Britain and Ulster. It lists not just parties but also pressure groups, publishers and paramilitary organizations. There is a historical outline on each organization and a description of the evolution of the Far Right. Peter Shipley 'The National Front: Racialism and Neo-Fascism in Britain' *Conflict Studies* 97 1978 pp 1–16 is a useful historical study of these groups since the 1960s which incorporates a list of Racialist and Neo-Fascist organizations in the UK, and a chronology of events 1973–8. On the Far Right see also [607].

**661** Philip Rees *Fascism in Britain* Harvester 1979. Annotated bibliography on Fascist, Pro-Nazi, Right-Wing and Anti-Semitic movements between 1923 and 1977. It is arranged by historical period. There is a special section on Mosley. Michael Billig and Andrew Bell 'Fascist Parties in Post-War Britain' *Sage Race Relations Abstracts* 5/1 1980 pp 1–30 is a historical and bibliographical essay identifying gaps in the literature.

**662** D S Lewis *Illusions of Grandeur: Mosley, Fascism and British Society 1931–1981* Manchester University Press 1987. A well regarded history. Richard Thurlow *Fascism in Britain: A History 1918–1985* Blackwell 1987 is good on the inter-war period but less sure on the post-war years. It may be the best general history but it certainly exaggerates, for instance, the impact of the Anti-Nazi League on the decline of the National Front in the late 1970s. Robert Benewick *The Fascist Movement in Britain* Penguin 1972 is useful on the support for the Far Right. Dennis Eisenberg 'Great Britain' in his *The Re-Emergence of Fascism* Macgibbon and Kee 1967 pp 33–69 is a detailed survey of post-war neo-fascism in Britain.

**663** Ray Hill with Andrew Bell *The Other Face of Terror: Inside Europe's Neo-Nazi Network* Grafton Books 1988. Revelations by Hill, who was formerly prominent in Right-Wing organizations. This account is particularly strong on Britain and provides some insights into the tactics and expectations of the Far Right.

**664** Stan Taylor *The National Front in English Politics* Macmillan 1982. The first clear, well referenced study of the history, politics and practices of the most prominent Far Right Party. Nigel Fielding *The National Front* Routledge and Kegan Paul 1981 is useful in that it is based on interviews and insider accounts. It however suffers from a rather uncritical approach and a number of inaccuracies. Martin Walker *The National Front* Fontana 1977 is useful on the founding, in 1967, of the party through the amalgamation of a number of groups as is Max Hanna 'The National Front and Other Right Wing Organisations' *New Community* 3 1974 pp 49–55. See also Q R H Marsh 'The National Front 1967–77' Bradford MPhil Thesis 1978 and David Edgar 'Racism, Fascism and the Politics of the National Front' *Race and Class* 19 1977 pp 111–32. Michael Billig *Fascists: A Social Psychological View of the National Front* Academic Press 1978 focuses on the history of the National Front's ideology and prejudices. Christopher Temple Husbands *Racial Exclusionism and the City: The Urban Support of the National Front* Allen and Unwin 1983 is the best guide to the nature and pattern of support for the National Front. There have also been a number of studies of their electoral performance, particularly during the 1970s. These can be found in the section on Electoral History.

**665** Terry Jones *British Movement: Nazis on our Streets* Anti-Nazi League 1981. A pamphlet which gives a profile and some details on this party, which split off from the National Front in the 1970s.

**666** D Knight *Beyond the Pale: The Christian Political Fringe* CARAF Publications 1982. A study of racist and Right-Wing Christian groups.

**667** Neill Nugent 'The Anti-Immigrant Groups' *New Community* 5 1976 pp 302–10. An examination of the various anti-immigrant and racist organizations which have appeared in the wake of large scale immigration from the New Commonwealth in the post-war years. On Racism see also the section on Race Relations.

### (12) Political Biographies and Memoirs

Much of value can also be found in the section on Collective Biography. The guides and potted biographies of Members of Parliament provided in some of the works listed in the sections on Parliamentary Parties and Members of Parliament should also be consulted [537, 540–1, 543].

**668** Jeremy Moon 'Post-War British Political Memoirs: A Discussion and Bibliography' *Parliamentary Affairs* 35 1982 pp 221–8.

**669** Lesley Abdela *Women with X Appeal: Women Politicians in Britain Today* Optima 1989. An excellent study and personal insight into women's involvement in all aspects and parts of politics in the 1980s, from the town halls, through parliament, to European politics. It includes biographical studies of some leading women politicians. Ann Kramer *Women and Politics* Wayland Press 1988 should also be consulted.

### (a) Collected Biographies of Prime Ministers

**670** John Pitcairn Mackintosh (ed) *British Prime Ministers in the Twentieth Century Vol 2: Churchill to Callaghan* Weidenfeld and Nicolson 1978. A good collection of biographical essays on post-war Prime Ministers. Another useful set of biographical studies is Lord Longford *Eleven at Number Ten: A Personal View of Prime Ministers 1931–1984* Harrap 1984. Herbert Van Thaal (ed) *The Prime Ministers Vol 2: From Lord John Russell to Edward Heath* Allen and Unwin 1975 is less detailed and variable in quality. See also Lewis Broad *The Path to Power: The Rise to the Premiership from Rosebery to Wilson* Muller 1965. Harold Wilson *A Prime Minister on Prime Ministers* Book Club Associates 1977, including essays on Churchill, Attlee and Macmillan, is not very good but is well illustrated. Diana

Pullein-Thompson *Five at 10: Prime Minister's Consorts Since 1957* Deutsch 1985 is a set of rather slight studies of the wives and husband of recent Prime Ministers.

### (b) Political Diarists

**671** Kenneth Young (ed) *The Diaries of Sir Robert Bruce-Lockhart* 2v, Macmillan 1973–80. The second volume covers 1939–65. This diary is particularly useful for the period 1945–50.

**672** Thomas Jones *A Diary with Letters 1931–1950* Oxford University Press 1954. Jones had been an important figure in the inter-war years. Whilst he retained extensive important contacts his diaries are of less value for the post-war era.

**673** Cecil King *The Cecil King Diary 1965–1970* Cape 1972. This offers a very useful, if exaggerated, version of the influence-peddling and intrigue in the background of the first Wilson government. King was an important newspaper proprietor until the late 1960s, when he was ousted as Chairman of IPC, a group which included the *Daily Mirror* in its fold, and he had extensive contacts with leading figures in the Labour Party and the establishment as well as directorates of the Bank of England and the National Coal Board. See also his *The Cecil King Diary 1970–1974* Cape 1975. His memoirs *Strictly Personal: Some Memoirs of Cecil H King* Weidenfeld and Nicolson 1969, whilst also of considerable value, are more concerned with his life as a newspaper man.

**674** Nigel Nicholson (ed) *Sir Harold Nicolson: Diaries and Letters 1930–62* 3v, Collins 1968. Sir Harold had extensive contacts in both the political and the literary world (he was married to Vita Sackville-West and was a literary figure in his own right). He had been a National Labour MP before and during the war, and was a Labour supporter in the post-war years. His son, Nigel, however was a Conservative MP. These diaries accordingly contain reflections on developments in both the major parties. Stanley Olson (ed) *Harold Nicolson: Diaries and Letters 1930–1964* Collins 1980, which contains a slightly different selection, should also be consulted. See also James Lees-Milne *Sir Harold Nicolson: A Biography 1886–1968* 2v, Chatto and Windus 1980–1.

### (c) Labour Biographies

The following are the biographies and memoirs of Labour politicians, national and local party officials, Socialist activists and intellectuals. Although the number of trade union officials pursuing second careers as La-of trade union officials pursuing second careers as Labour politicians has dwindled away since the war the section on Trade Union Biographies should still be consulted. The trade unions continue to exert considerable influence on the party and to play a large role in its internal politics. See also [548].

**675** Kenneth O Morgan *Labour People: Leaders and Lieutenants: Hardie to Kinnock* Oxford University Press 1987. Post-war figures included in this collection of biographical studies are, Harold Laski, Ellen Wilkinson, Hugh Dalton, Christopher Addison, Jim Griffiths, Clement Attlee, Ernie Bevin, Sir Stafford Cripps, Herbert Morrison, Aneurin Bevan, Hugh Gaitskell, Morgan Phillips, Rita Hinden, Harold Wilson, James Callaghan, Michael Foot, Joe Gormley, Arthur Scargill, Evan Durbin, Douglas Jay, Tony Benn, Denis Healey, Roy Hattersley and Neil Kinnock. Norman Mackenzie, Peter Shore, Brian Abel-Smith, Raymond Williams, Peter Townsend, Richard Hoggart, Nigel Calder, Hugh Thomas, Peter Marris, Mervyn Jones, Paul Johnson and Iris Murdoch explain their socialism in Norman MacKenzie (ed) *Convictions* Macgibbon and Kee 1958.

**676** *Labour's Election Who's Who: Parliamentary Candidates General Election 1959* Labour Party 1959. Potted biographies. A similar one appeared in 1964.

**677** John Thomas Murphy *Labour's Big Three: A Biographical Study of Clement Attlee, Herbert Morrison and Ernest Bevin* The Bodley Head 1948.

**678** Leo Abse *Private Member* Macdonald 1973. A good autobiography. A backbench MP since 1958 Abse was heavily involved in the permissive legislation of the 1960s, particularly the reform of the law relating to homosexuals.

**679** Kenneth and Jane Morgan *Portrait of a Progressive: The Political Career of Christopher, Viscount Addison* Oxford University Press 1980. Addison was Leader of the House of Lords during the Attlee government. See also R J Minney *Viscount Addison: Leader of the Lords* Odhams 1958.

**680** Jack Ashley *Journey into Silence* The Bodley Head 1973. A backbencher since 1966. The title refers to his deafness.

**681** Kenneth Harris *Attlee* Weidenfeld and Nicolson 1982. A good biography drawing on conversations with its subject. Attlee was leader of the party 1935–55, Churchill's deputy as Prime Minister 1940–5 and Prime Minister 1945–51. Trevor Burridge *Clement Attlee: A Political Biography* Cape 1985 is another useful study, though it has been criticized for being too uncritical. Francis Williams *A Prime Minister Remembers* Heinemann 1961 examines Attlee's career in government

1940–51, concentrating on foreign and imperial policy. It is heavily based on Attlee's private papers and his personal recollections as told to the author. Another biography which draws heavily on Attlee's own memories is Denis Pitts and Duncan Crow *Clem Attlee* Panther Record 1967. This consists of transcripts of interviews conducted in 1965. Such works can be used as additional volumes of memoirs to flesh out the dry account which appears in Attlee's own autobiography *As It Happened* Heinemann 1954. Roy Jenkins *Mr Attlee: An Interim Biography* Heinemann 1948 is an early admiring account which remains of some value. Jenkins also introduced and selected a volume of Attlee's Prime Ministerial speeches 1945–7. The speeches in Clement Richard Attlee *Purpose and Policy: Selected Speeches* Hutchinson 1947 are on the Labour Party, the productivity drive, the social services, moral values in life and politics, foreign affairs and the Commonwealth. Geoffrey Dellar (ed) *Attlee as I Knew Him* London Borough of Tower Hamlets, Directorate of Social Service 1983 is a tribute volume which consists of memoirs of Attlee by the great as well as by his former constituents in the East End. D J Heasman '"My Station and Its Duties": The Attlee Version' *Parliamentary Affairs* 21 1967–68 pp 75–84 is useful on Attlee's sense of duty and on his retirement. See also John Saville 'Clement Attlee: An Assessment' *Socialist Register* 20 1983 pp 144–67, William Golant 'Mr Attlee' *History Today* 33 1983 pp 12–7 and J Vernon Jensen 'Clement R Attlee and Twentieth Century Parliamentary Speaking' *Parliamentary Affairs* 23 1969–70 pp 277–85.

**682** For Joel Barnett see [306].

**683** Tony Benn *Out of the Wilderness: Diaries 1963–67* Hutchinson 1987. Tony Benn has been the most conscientious political diarist of the modern era. This, the first volume of his diaries to be edited and published, covers in great detail the period from when he returned to the House of Commons having succeeded in his battle to renounce his peerage to the end of 1967. The second volume *Office Without Power: Diaries 1968–72* Hutchinson 1988 covers the end of the first Wilson government, the 1970 defeat and its aftermath and ends with Benn's period as party Chairman in 1972. The third volume, *Against the Tide: Diaries 1973–1976* Hutchinson 1989 traces the coming to power of the second Wilson government, the battles over industrial strategy until Benn was moved from the Industry portfolio he held in 1974–5 to the Department of Energy and the advent of the Callaghan government. The fourth, *Conflicts of Interest: Diaries 1977–80* Hutchinson 1990, covers the conflicts over Europe and within the government and Labour Party, the period of the Lib-Lab Pact and his concern about nuclear power during these years. All come complete with extensive and informative appendices. A further volume on 1980–84 is promised. So far there are no arrangements to publish his volumes of number of volumes of speeches. Joan Bodington (ed) *Speeches by Tony Benn* Spokesman 1974 contains a useful selection of speeches. Chris Mullins (ed) *Tony Benn: Arguments for Democracy* Cape 1981 is a collection of speeches, lectures and articles from 1979–81. Tony Benn *Fighting Back: Speaking out for Socialism in the Eighties* Hutchinson 1988 collects his main speeches from 1980–8. As a cabinet minister in the Labour governments of 1964–70 and 1974–9, but more particularly as a leading figure on the Left in the 1970s and 1980s, Benn has also attracted a number of biographies. Probably the best of these is Robert Jenkins *Tony Benn: A Political Biography* Writers and Readers Publishing Cooperative 1980. Alan Freeman *The Benn Heresy* Pluto 1982 is a sympathetic study of his life and thought. See also Russell Lewis *Tony Benn: A Critical Biography* Associated Business Press 1978, A Browne *Tony Benn: The Making of a Politician* W H Allen 1983 and Terry Pitt *Tony Benn: A Political Portrait* Hamilton 1977. Also of use is the study of the Benn political dynasty, Sydney Higgins *The Benn Inheritance: A Radical Family* Weidenfeld and Nicolson 1984. Geoff Foote 'Interview with Tony Benn' *Capital and Class* 19 1982 pp 27–41 is an interview from a critical, Marxist perspective. See also [591] and [326].

**684** John Campbell *Nye Bevan and the Mirage of British Socialism* Weidenfeld and Nicolson 1987. A valuable corrective to the overly hagiographic Michael Foot *Aneurin Bevan* 2v, Davis Poynter 1962–73. Jennie Lee *My Life with Nye* Cape 1980 is a good memoir of her marriage to Bevan. For more material on Jennie Lee see [729]. Vincent Brome *Aneurin Bevan* Longmans 1953 remains a useful interim biography. Mark M Krug *Aneurin Bevan: Cautious Rebel* Thomas Yoseloff, New York 1961 is however careless and unsatisfactory. His treatment of Bevan as Minister of Health 1945–51 is adequate. He however shows no appreciation of Bevan's charismatic skills and his popularity with the rank and file nor of the way in which Bevan bestraddled the two halves of the Labour Movement, the moral side and the search for power as a means of putting morality into practice. For the Bevanite movement see [584]. See also [920].

**685** Alan Bullock *Ernest Bevin* 3v, Oxford University Press 1960–85. An excellent and detailed biography. The second volume, covering Bevin as Minister of Labour 1940–5 culminates with an account of the 1945 general election. The third volume deals with Bevin's period as Foreign Secretary 1945–51. The only quibble about this valuable volume is the relative neglect of Bevin's interest in intelligence and the role of intelligence in the development of the Cold War in this period. Both the other biographies are somewhat hagiographical. Mark Stephens *Ernest Bevin – Unskilled Labourer and World Statesman 1881–1951* SPA Books 1985 and Francis Williams *Ernest Bevin: Portrait of a Great Englishman* Hutchinson 1952 are nevertheless useful, informative and concise, if relatively unscholarly works. See also [1969].

**686** Raymond Blackburn *I am an Alcoholic* Allan Wingate 1959. This autobiography is largely concerned with his descent into alcoholism and recovery thanks to the assistance of Alcoholics Anonymous. However he also discusses his period as an MP 1945–51 (Labour 1945–50, Independent 1950–1).

**687** Jack and Bessie Braddock *The Braddocks* Macdonald 1963. Jack Braddock was the leader of the Labour Party in Liverpool and leader of the council 1955–61. His wife was a Liverpool MP 1945–70. Both were on the Left of the party. See also Millie Toole *Mrs Bessie Braddock MP* Hale 1957.

**688** Archibald Fenner Brockway *Towards Tomorrow: The Autobiography of Fenner Brockway* Hart-Davis Macgibbon 1977. The most informative of his several autobiographies as far as the post-war period is concerned. See also his *98 Not Out* Quartet 1986 and *Outside the Right* Allen and Unwin 1963. For his pre-war career see also his *Inside the Left: Thirty Years of Platform, Press, Prison and Parliament* Allen and Unwin 1942. An MP 1929–31 and 1950–64 and a Labour peer thereafter. Brockway was active on the Left and particularly interested in colonial affairs. A sympathetic assessment of his activities in this area is R Fletcher 'The Struggle for Colonial Freedom: Tribute to Fenner Brockway' *Plebs* 60 1968 pp 19–31.

**689** George Brown *In My Way* Gollancz 1971. Not a highly regarded political memoir. His version of events during the 1964–70 government when he was Wilson's deputy also seems unduly favourable.

**690** James Callaghan *Time and Chance* Collins 1987. A rather cautious autobiography by the man who served in Wilson's cabinets throughout 1964–70 and 1974–76 and then succeeded him as Premier 1976–79. It does not cover Callaghan's period as Home Secretary during the start of the Troubles in Ulster, which he has dealt with elsewhere (see [8453]). Peter Kellner and Christopher Hitchens *Callaghan: The Road to Number Ten* Cassell 1976 is a rather brief, journalistic account.

**691** Barbara Castle *The Castle Diaries 1964–70* Weidenfeld and Nicolson 1984. Barbara Castle's cabinet diaries from these years have, because of her ability to take shorthand, an immediacy that eludes the more crafted efforts of Crossman and Benn. Her diary of her period as Social Services Secretary 1974–76 *The Castle Diaries 1974–76* Weidenfeld and Nicolson 1980 is similarly vivid. Wilfrid De'Ath *Barbara Castle: A Portrait from Life* Clifton Books 1970 is a sympathetic portrayal which largely consists of transcripts of interviews with Castle, her friends and colleagues.

**692** L P Carpenter *G D H Cole: An Intellectual Biography* Cambridge University Press 1973. Margaret Cole also wrote a biography of her husband *The Life of G D H Cole* Macmillan 1971. Cole was a Socialist intellectual who as Chichele Professor of Social and Political Theory at Oxford 1944–57 and as Chairman, then President of the Fabian Society 1939–46, 1948–50 and 1952–9 exerted considerable influence on the thinking of the party until his death in 1959. A brief but informative assessment of his career and work is G L Houseman *G D H Cole* Twayne, Boston, Massachussetts 1979. See also [929]. Margaret Cole was also an important figure in her own right. Betty D Vernon *Margaret Cole 1899–1980: A Political Biography* Croom Helm 1986 is a workmanlike, if not very enlightening biography. Margaret I Cole *Growing up into Revolution* Longmans 1949 is of some use for her early life.

**693** Maureen Colquhoun *A Woman in the House* Scan 1980. An account of her time as a Labour MP 1974–9.

**694** For Frank Cousins see [4789].

**695** Aidan Crawley *Leap Before You Look: A Memoir* Collins 1988. A junior minister under Attlee, Crawley later became a Conservative MP. He also had a distinguished career in broadcasting.

**696** Eric Estorick *Stafford Cripps* Hodder and Stoughton 1949. A useful biography of one of the most important ministers in the Attlee government which was written with Cripps' co-operation. The official biography, Colin Cooke *The Life of Richard Stafford Cripps* Hodder and Stoughton 1957 is not as good.

**697** Susan Crosland *Tony Crosland* Cape 1982. A well written memoir by his widow of an important member of the 1964–70 and 1974–9 (until his death in 1977) governments and the leading revisionist thinker in the post-war Labour Party. See also [921–2].

**698** Janet Morgan (ed) *Richard Crossman: The Diaries of a Cabinet Minister* 3v, Hamilton/Cape 1975–77. Volume I, *Minister of Housing 1964–66* 1975; volume II, *Lord President and Leader of the House of Commons 1966–68* 1976; and volume III, *Secretary of State for Social Services 1968–70* 1977. For the furore caused by the impending publication of these volumes see [335]. Crossman believed that these diaries would provide a unique record of how government operated in the 1960s. They have certainly been extensively used by historians, though they are no longer unique. A further volume, Janet Morgan (ed) *The Backbench Diaries of Richard Crossman* Hamilton/Cape 1981, covers the period from 1951 to December 1963. Janet Morgan *et al*

'Symposium: The Crossman Diaries Reconsidered' *Contemporary Record* 1/2 1987 pp 22–30 provides a very useful assessment by historians and by cabinet and civil service colleagues of the value of the diaries and the circumstances in which they were published. Anthony Howard (ed) *The Crossman Diaries: Selections from the Diary of a Cabinet Minister 1964–1970* Cape/Hamilton 1979 is a condensed version of the cabinet diaries which includes, in the introduction, a useful short biography. The only full biography is the sympathetic portrayal presented in Tam Dalyell *Dick Crossman* Weidenfeld and Nicolson 1989. See also [919].

**699** Ben Pimlott *Hugh Dalton* Cape 1985. An excellent biography that claims much for its subject. There is if anything a danger that Dalton's role in the Attlee government and in the shaping of the post-war Labour Party may now be exaggerated because of the superior treatment he has received. For instance, a good biography of his successor as Chancellor of the Exchequer, Sir Stafford Cripps, is made all the more necessary by this book. Pimlott has also edited *The Political Diary of Hugh Dalton 1918–40, 1945–60* Cape 1986 and *The Second World War Diary of Hugh Dalton 1940–45* Cape 1986. These diaries form a major and most revealing source. Dalton's own three volumes of memoirs, *Call Back Yesterday: Memoirs 1887–1931* Muller 1953, *The Fateful Years: Memoirs 1931–1945* Muller 1957, and *High Tide and After: Memoirs 1945–1960* Muller 1962, are heavily based on, but present a very expurgated version of his diary. They nevertheless retain an independent value.

**700** Robert Griffiths *S O Davies: A Socialist Faith* Gwasg Gomer 1983. A useful biography. Griffiths was a South Wales MP 1934–72. His constituency party declined to re-adopt him in 1970 so, standing as an Independent, he defeated the official Labour candidate and continued to sit until his death in 1972.

**701** For Desmond Donnelly see [303].

**702** Tom Driberg *Ruling Passions* Cape 1977. The autobiography of a leading Labour MP from 1942 (Independent until 1945) until 1955 and 1959 to 1974. His *The Best of Both Worlds: A Personal Diary* Phoenix House 1953 is a diary covering his dual career as a politician and as a journalist in the immediate post-war years.

**703** For Alf Dubs see [1078].

**704** Peggy Duff *Left, Left, Left: A Personal Account of Six Protest Campaigns 1945–1965* Alison and Busby 1971. The memoirs of the former business manager of *Tribune* and a veteran of countless protest marches.

705 Frederick, Lord Elwyn-Jones *In My Time: An Autobiography* Weidenfeld and Nicolson 1983. Well written memoirs by a Labour politician who had a lengthy political career culminating in the Lord Chancellorship 1974–79.

706 Jane Ewart-Biggs *Lady in the Lords* Weidenfeld and Nicolson 1988. An account of her career as a Labour peeress since her elevation to the Lords in 1981.

707 For Marcia Faulkender see Marcia Williams [778].

708 Harold Finch *Memoirs of a Bedwellty MP* Sterling Press 1972. He was the MP for Bedwellty 1950–70.

709 Eric George Molyneaux Fletcher *Random Reminiscences* Bishopsgate Press 1986. Fletcher was a Labour MP 1945–70. He was also, as this autobiography reflects, very active in the politics of the Church of England and in particular interests like archaeology.

710 Simon Hoggart and David Leigh *Michael Foot: A Portrait* Hodder and Stoughton 1981. A journalistic biography which appeared in the wake of Foot's election to the Labour leadership in 1980. See also R Blackburn and A Cockburn 'Credo of the Labour Left: Interview with Michael Foot' *New Left Review* 49 1968 pp 19–34,

711 Philip M Williams *Hugh Gaitskell: A Political Biography* Cape 1979. A massive study which is perhaps more a general history of the Labour Party in Gaitskell's time than a biography. Gaitskell was Chancellor of the Exchequer 1950–1 and leader of the party from 1955 until his death in 1963. Williams has also edited *The Diary of Hugh Gaitskell 1945–1956* Cape 1983. This diary was kept to record the inside story of those events which he felt would prove to have been historically significant, and contains little information about his private life. Something of his character and the esteem in which he was held emerges from the very good tribute volume by his colleagues, William T Rodgers (ed) *Hugh Gaitskell 1906–63* Thames and Hudson 1963. See also Geoffrey McDermott *Leader Lost: A Biography of Hugh Gaitskell* Leslie Frewin 1972.

712 Muriel Box *Rebel Advocate: A Biography of Gerald Gardiner* Gollancz 1983. A sympathetic biography of the Lord Chancellor in the 1964–70 government.

713 Maureen Callcott 'The Organisation of Political Support for Labour in the North of England: The Work of Margaret Gibb 1929– 57' *Bulletin of the North East Branch of the Society for the Study of Labour History* 11 1977 pp 47–58. A tribute to an important local activist.

714 James Griffiths *Pages from Memory* Dent 1969. Griffiths was a cabinet minister in 1945–51 and in 1964 became the first Secretary of State for Wales. This is an uncomplicated and not very enlightening autobiography. See also the tribute volume, J Beverley Smith *James Griffiths and His Times* W T Maddock and Co 1978.

715 Joe Haines *Politics of Power* Cape 1977. This memoir of his time as Wilson's Press Secretary in 1969–76 is quite revealing.

716 Roy Hattersley *A Yorkshire Boyhood* Chatto and Windus 1983. Neither this nor his other autobiographical work *Goodbye to Yorkshire* Gollancz 1976, deal directly with the political career of the man who has been Labour's deputy leader since 1983. They however do reflect something of his character.

717 Derek Hatton *Inside Left: The Story So Far* Bloomsbury 1987. A waspish autobiography by the man who rose to notoriety as the Militant deputy leader of Liverpool council in the 1980s.

717A George W Jones and Sir William Hart 'Sir Isaac Hayward 1884–1976' *London Journal* 2 1976 pp 239–49. A biography of the Labour politician who was the leader of the London County Council in 1947–64.

718 Denis Healey *The Time of My Life* Michael Joseph 1989. Healey was Minister of Defence 1964–70 and Chancellor of the Exchequer 1974–79. He was deputy leader of the Labour Party 1983–87. Bruce Read and Geoffrey Williams *Denis Healey and the Politics of Power* Sidgwick and Jackson 1971 is good on Healey's period as Minister of Defence and benefited from the assistance of its subject. Denis Healey *Healey's Eye: A Photographic Memoir* Cape 1980 primarily reflects his interest in photography but also contains some useful autobiographical material.

718A George Hodgkinson *Sent to Coventry* Maxwell 1970. A good memoir by an important local politician in Coventry.

719 Philip Inman *No Going Back* Williams and Norgate 1952. His autobiography. A great hospital administrator he held important posts in the BBC and the Church of England in the 1940s before becoming Lord Privy Seal briefly in 1947 and then moving to be Chairman of the Hotels Executive in the newly established Transport Commission.

720 G G Eastwood *George Isaacs: Printer, Trade Union Leader, Cabinet Minister* Odhams 1952. A sort of workman's cottage to Westminster biography of the Minister of Labour in Attlee's government.

721 Douglas Jay *Change and Fortune: A Political Record* Hutchinson 1980. An excellent political memoir.

Jay was a Treasury minister 1947–51 and President of the Board of Trade 1964–7.

**722** Hugh Jenkins *The Culture Gap: An Experience of Government and the Arts* Marion Boyars 1979. This autobiography is particularly concerned with the politics of the Arts, the Arts Council and Arts funding, and the frustrations he felt as Minister for the Arts 1974–6 and as Jennie Lee's assistant when she was the first Minister for the Arts in the 1960s. It is both committed and detailed.

**723** John Campbell *Roy Jenkins: A Biography* Weidenfeld and Nicolson 1983. A campaign biography of Jenkins as he led the SDP into the 1983 general election written with the assistance of its subject. Before he played a central role in the founding of the SDP, going on to lead the new party 1982–3, Jenkins was a cabinet minister in the 1964–70 and 1974–6 Wilson governments. He was also President of the European Commission 1977–81. Roy Jenkins *European Diary 1977–1981* Collins 1989 records this period. C Branson and D Bence *Roy Jenkins* Moat Hall Books 1982 is an inadequate biography. Anthony Lester (ed) *Essays and Speeches by Roy Jenkins* Collins 1967 collects a selection of Jenkins' writing and some of his speeches both as a backbencher and as a minister. Clive Lindley (ed) *Partnership of Principle: Writings and Speeches on the Making of the Alliance by Roy Jenkins* Secker and Warburg 1985 is a well edited volume of documents and speeches which is very useful for tracing the founding of the SDP, its electoral alliance with the Liberals, and the mood that this attempt to break the mould of British politics initially generated.

**724** Gerald Kaufman *How to be a Minister* Sidgwick and Jackson 1980. Not really an autobiography, this nevertheless has some autobiographical reflections on his time as a junior minister 1974–79. His *My Life in the Silver Screen* Faber 1985, about his love affair with the cinema, also has some autobiographical references.

**725** Robert Kilroy-Silk *Hard Labour: Political Diary* Chatto and Windus 1986. Reflections on his time in the House of Commons 1974–86 and especially on his eventually unsuccessful struggle against Militant in his Merseyside constituency party.

**726** For Evelyn King see [836].

**727** Michael Leapman *Kinnock* Unwin Hyman 1987. An admiring campaign biography for the 1987 general election. It is especially useful on Neil Kinnock's leadership of the Labour Party 1983–7. For earlier biographies that deal more fully with his rise to the leadership see Robert Harris *The Making of Neil Kinnock* Faber 1984 and G M F Drower *Neil Kinnock: The Path to Leadership* Weidenfeld and Nicolson 1984.

**728** Kingsley Martin *Harold Laski (1893–1950): A Biographical Memoir* Gollancz 1953. A good biography of a leading Socialist intellectual and important member of the party's National Executive Committee. G G Eastwood *Harold Laski* Mowbrays 1977 adds little. See also [930].

**729** Jennie Lee *This Great Journey* Macgibbon and Kee 1963. An autobiography covering her life up until the end of the Second World War. Her earlier autobiography *Tomorrow is a New Day* Cresset Press 1939, also casts light on her character. She was an MP 1929–31 and 1945–70. See also the section on her husband, Aneurin Bevan [684].

**730** Ken Livingstone *If Voting Changed Anything They'd Abolish It* Collins 1987. The autobiography of the leader of the Greater London Council from 1981 until its abolition in 1986. It is particularly useful on the struggle with the Thatcher government over the abolition. John Carvel *Citizen Ken* 2nd ed, Hogarth Press 1987 is a good biography updated to cover his election to parliament in 1987. Tariq Ali *Who's Afraid of Margaret Thatcher: In Praise of Socialism* Verso 1984 consists of conversations with Livingstone.

**731** For Megan Lloyd George see [879].

**732** Frank Pakenham, Earl of Longford *Born to Believe* Cape 1953. This first volume of autobiography covers Lord Longford's life up to and including his experiences as a minister in Attlee's government. The second volume, *Five Lives* Hutchinson 1964, covers the years 1951–63. The title refers to his banking career, his work in the House of Lords, his concern for penal reform, his Catholicism and his Socialism in this period. The third volume, *The Grain of Wheat* Collins 1974, covers the period of the 1964–70 government, in which he served as a cabinet minister until 1968. His wife's autobiography, Elizabeth Longford *The Pebbled Shore: The Memoirs of Elizabeth Longford* Weidenfeld and Nicolson 1986 is also of considerable value. There is also a useful biography; Mary Craig *Lord Longford: A Biographical Portrait* Hodder and Stoughton 1978.

**733** John McGovern *Neither Fear Nor Favour* Blandford 1960. McGovern was an MP 1930–1959 (ILP until 1947).

**734** *In Memory of J P Mackintosh 1929–1978* Political Quarterly Publishing 1979. A tribute volume to one of the most important political scientists of the post-war era, who also sat as a Labour MP 1966–78. Henry M Drucker (ed) *John P Mackintosh on Scotland* Longman 1982 focuses on Mackintosh's writing on democracy and devolution (of which he was a supporter) in his native Scotland. It however also includes a chronology and a number of essays on his life and work. See also [931].

**735** Jean Mann *Woman in Parliament* Odhams 1962. She was an MP 1945–59.

**736** Leah Manning *A Life for Education: An Autobiography* Gollancz 1970. She was an MP in 1931 and 1945–50.

**737** Richard Marsh *Off the Rails: An Autobiography* Weidenfeld and Nicolson 1978. Useful for Marsh's part in the re- nationalization of steel in the 1960s as well as for his work as Minister of Power and Minister of Transport under Wilson and as Chairman of British Rail 1971–6.

**738** Ewan Butler *Mason-Mac: The Life of Lieutenant General Sir Noel Mason-Macfarlane* Macmillan 1972. Mason-Macfarlane was a Labour MP 1945–6.

**739** William Knox *James Maxton* Manchester University Press 1987. A good biography of a leading figure in the ILP. Maxton was an ILP MP from 1922 until his death in 1946. See also G Brown *Maxton: A Biography* Mainstream 1986 and John MacNair *James Maxton: The Beloved Rebel* Allen and Unwin 1955. *James Maxton* Independent Labour Party 1947 is a short tribute volume.

**740** For Robert Maxwell see [3684].

**741** Christopher Mayhew *Time to Explain* Hutchinson 1987. An attempt at an explanation of Mayhew's political career. Having been a Labour junior minister he defected to the Liberals in 1974. His *Party Games* Hutchinson 1969 consists principally of autobiographical reflections on the political malaise of the 1960s. His *Britain's Role Tomorrow* Hutchinson 1967, whilst reflecting his interest in foreign affairs, is also largely autobiographical.

**742** Ian Mikardo *Backbencher* Weidenfeld and Nicolson 1988. A good autobiography by a prominent Left-Wing backbencher who sat in the House 1945–87.

**743** Edward Milne *No Shining Armour* Calder 1976. Milne was a Labour MP 1960–74. Ousted in 1974 he nevertheless retained his seat as an Independent Labour MP in the February election, only to lose it in the October. This is a useful piece on in-fighting in the Labour Party.

**744** For Austin Mitchell see [543] and [594].

**745** Bernard Donoughue and G W Jones *Herbert Morrison: Portrait of a Politician* Weidenfeld and Nicolson 1973. A good biography of one of the leading figures of the Attlee government. Herbert Morrison's autobiography, *Herbert Morrison: An Autobiography* Odhams 1960, is not very enlightening but retains some independent value. For his personal life Lady Morrison of Lambeth *Memories of a Marriage* Muller 1977 has a certain limited value.

**746** Harford Montgomery Hyde *Strong for Service: The Life of Lord Nathan of Churt* W H Allen 1968. A Labour peer from 1940, Nathan held a couple of junior posts in the Attlee government. This biography covers both this and his later period as a senior Labour peer well.

**747** David J Whittaker *Fighter for Peace: Philip Noel-Baker 1889–1982* William Sessions 1989. A useful biography. Kenneth Lee 'Philip Noel-Baker: Prophet of Peace and Disarmament' in Leonard S Kenworthy (ed) *Living in the Light: Some Quaker Pioneers of the 20th Century Vol II: In the Wider World* Friends General Conference and Quaker Publications, Kennett Square, Pennsylvania 1985 pp 190–205 is a short study that focuses more on Noel-Baker as a worker for international peace than on his long political career, during which he held cabinet office in the Attlee government.

**748** David Owen *Personally Speaking to Kenneth Harris* Pan 1987. A sort of autobiography derived from a series of interviews. Owen, an MP since 1966, was Foreign Secretary 1977–9. He subsequently played an important part in the founding of the SDP as one of the 'Gang of Four' Labour renegades, the others being Roy Jenkins, Shirley Williams and Bill Rodgers. He became leader of the SDP in 1983. There are also some autobiographical reflections in his *Face the Future* Oxford University Press 1981.

**749** John Parker *Father of the House: Fifty Years in Politics* Routledge and Kegan Paul 1982. A well regarded political memoir. Parker was an MP 1935–83 and the General Secretary of the Fabian Society.

**750** Eric Taylor 'An Interview with Wesley Perrins' *Bulletin of the Society for the Study of Labour History* 21 1970 pp 16– 24. An MP 1945–50 and subsequently a General and Municipal Workers organizer, Perrins makes some useful comments on the post-war parliament and the movement in his native Black Country.

**751** Vera Brittain *Pethick-Lawrence* Allen and Unwin 1963. An MP 1923–31 and 1935–45 Frederick William Pethick- Lawrence was Secretary of State for India and Burma 1945–7. For his earlier career see also his autobiography *Fate has been Kind* Hutchinson 1942.

**752** Morgan Philips Price *My Three Revolutions* Allen and Unwin 1969. Price was an MP 1929–31 and 1935–59. This autobiography is better for the earlier part of his career.

**753** Cliff Prothero *Recount: An Autobiographical Account of Trade Union and Labour Party Activity 1898–1981* Hesketh 1982. Memoirs of a Labour Party organizer and miners' union activist in South Wales.

**754** For Merlyn Rees see [8456].

**755** William T Rodgers *The Politics of Change* Secker and Warburg 1982. Not really an autobiography but a personal statement on contemporary politics with some autobiographical reflections. At the time Rodgers, who was Transport Secretary 1976–9, had just left the Labour Party and was one of the SDP's founding 'Gang of Four'.

**756** For Bertrand Russell see [6693].

**757** Mary Saran *Never Give Up* Oswald Woolf 1976. Memoirs of a Hampstead Socialist. She edited *Socialist Commentary* 1941–50, and was very active in international Socialism and in educational causes.

**758** For Brian Sedgemore see [326].

**759** Emmanuel Shinwell *Conflict Without Malice* Odhams 1955. The best of his autobiographies. See also his *I've Lived Through It All* Gollancz 1973 and *Lead with the Left: My First Ninety-Six Years* Cassell 1981. John Doxat *Shinwell Talking: A Conversational Biography to Celebrate His Hundredth Birthday* Quiller 1984 is derived from interviews. Shinwell was an MP 1922–4, 1928–31 and 1935–70 and a prominent Labour peer thereafter. He was Minister of Fuel and Power 1945–7, Secretary of State for War 1947–50 and Minister of Defence 1950–1.

**760** Peter Shore 'Forty Years a Socialist' *Contemporary Record* 1/2 1987 pp 38–41. An interview. Shore held cabinet posts in the 1964–70 and 1974–9 Labour governments.

**761** Edward Short *Whip to Wilson: The Crucial Years of the Wilson Government* Macdonald 1989. A banal memoir of his time as Chief Whip at a time when the Wilson government had a slender majority of three in the Commons in 1964–6.

**762** John Silkin *Changing Battlefields: The Challenge to the Labour Party* Hamilton 1987. Partly autobiographical and partly a commentary on the current state of the Labour Party. Silkin was a cabinet minister in the 1974–9 governments.

**763** Emrys Hughes *Sydney Silverman* Skilton 1969. Silverman was a Left-Wing backbencher from 1935 until his death in 1968. He was particularly involved in the abolition of the death penalty in the 1960s.

**764** Charles James Simmons *Soap Box Evangelist* Janay Publishing Co 1972. Pacifist, temperance advocate, Labour propagandist and Christian Socialist, Simmons was an MP 1929–31 and 1945–59.

**765** M Thompson and M Gillard *Nothing to Declare* Calder 1980. A biography of T Dan Smith. Smith was the leader of Newcastle City Council. He later served a prison sentence because of his close and corrupt involvement with the architect John Poulson. T Dan Smith *An Autobiography* Oriel Press 1970 covers his career and the policies followed by Newcastle council. See also J Elliott 'Political Leadership in Local Government: T Dan Smith in Newcastle upon Tyne' *Local Government Studies* 5 1975 pp 33–43.

**766** For Lord Snow, a junior minister in 1964–6, see [7293].

**767** Michael Stewart *Life and Labour: An Autobiography* Sidgwick and Jackson 1980. An MP 1945–79 Stewart held various cabinet posts 1964–70.

**768** Michael Newman *John Strachey* Manchester University Press 1989. See also Hugh Thomas *John Strachey* Eyre Methuen 1973. Strachey was an MP 1929–31 and 1945–63. He served as Minister of Food 1946–50.

**769** Edith Clara Summerskill *A Woman's World* Heinemann 1967. Her autobiography. Summerskill was an MP 1938–61 and briefly Minister of National Insurance during the Attlee government. See also her *Letters to My Daughter* Heinemann 1957. This collection of letters to her daughter, Shirley, who also later became a Labour MP, contains a number of useful autobiographical reflections.

**770** Dick Taverne *The Future of the Left: Lincoln and After* Cape 1974. Taverne became MP for Lincoln in 1966 only to be ousted eventually by his Left-Wing constituency party. He then won a triumphal by-election in 1973 only to lose the seat in October 1974. This book is partly autobiographical and partly a commentary on Labour and Centre politics in this period.

**771** Anthony Wright *R H Tawney* Manchester University Press 1987. Richard Tawney, who died in 1962, had a major impact on the development of Socialist thought in the twentieth century. This is a good biography that emphasizes this influence. See also Ross Terrill *R H Tawney and His Times: Socialism as Fellowship* Deutsch 1974, T S Ashton 'Richard Henry Tawney (1880–1962)' *Proceedings of the British Academy* 48 1962 pp 461–82 and [932].

**772** Harry Bernard Taylor *Uphill all the Way* Sidgwick and Jackson 1973. He was an MP 1941–66.

773 George Thomas *Mr Speaker* Century 1985. Unlike the memoir of his predecessor as Speaker, Selwyn Lloyd, this autobiography deals not just with the crises and controversies of his period as Speaker 1976–83 but with the whole of his political career. Ramon Hunston *Order! Order!* Lakeland 1981 is a biography which stresses his Christian Socialism

774 Fred Blackburn *George Tomlinson* Heinemann 1954. A useful biography of the Education Minister 1947–51 who died in 1952.

775 George Wigg *George Wigg* Michael Joseph 1972. An MP 1945–67 Wigg was Paymaster-General 1964–67.

776 Betty D Vernon *Ellen Wilkinson* Croom Helm 1982. Wilkinson was Minister of Education from 1945 until her death in 1947. This is a sympathetic biography.

777 For Frederick Willey see [543].

778 Marcia Williams *Inside Number 10* Weidenfeld and Nicolson 1972. Memoirs of her years as Personal and Political Secretary to Wilson 1964–70. The rather more gossipy sequel, *Downing Street in Perspective* Weidenfeld and Nicolson 1983 covers the years 1970–6.

779 Thomas Williams *Digging for Britain* Hutchinson 1965. A useful autobiography by Attlee's Minister of Agriculture.

780 Sir Harold Wilson *Memoirs: The Making of the Prime Minister 1916–64* Weidenfeld and Nicolson/Michael Joseph 1986. This autobiography is better on the inter-war than the post-war period and is generally considered disappointing. His accounts of the two governments over which he presided in 1964–70 and 1974–6 (see [301, 306]) are also useful, though not strictly speaking autobiographical. There are also an assortment of biographies. Michael Foot *Harold Wilson: A Pictorial Biography* Pergamon 1964 is a good campaign biography. A collection of speeches *Purpose in Politics: Selected Speeches by the Rt. Hon. Harold Wilson* Weidenfeld and Nicolson 1964, was also published at this time. Another collection of speeches from his first term of office as Prime Minister is Harold Wilson *Purpose in Power: Selected Speeches* Weidenfeld and Nicolson 1966. Most of the other biographical material also dates from the 1960s. Dudley Smith *Harold Wilson: A Critical Biography* Hale 1964 is a study by one of his Tory opponents which is useful, not least for his comments on Wilson's success in cementing party unity in the run-up to the 1964 general election. Leslie Smith *Harold Wilson* Fontana 1965, contains some good anecdotes and remains of use not least as an example of the response to Wilson in his heyday, despite its rather adulatory tone. Ernest Kay *Pragmatic Premier: An Inti-mate Portrait of Harold Wilson* Leslie Frewin 1967 goes way over the top in his enthusiasm. More representative of the response to the disappointments of Wilson's first government is Paul Foot *The Politics of Harold Wilson* Penguin 1968, a brilliant Left-Wing attack. A similarly hostile attitude is taken in the only biography published since Wilson resigned as Premier in 1976, Andrew Roth *Sir Harold Wilson: Yorkshire's Walter Mitty* MacDonald and Janes 1977. We shall have to hope that a more balanced assessment of Harold Wilson emerges from the official biography by Philip Ziegler and the other biography in preparation by Ben Pimlott.

781 For Barbara Wootton see [6760].

782 Sir Woodrow Wyatt *The Confessions of an Optimist* Collins 1985. Good memoirs by an acute observer who has combined a lengthy career as a journalist with two periods as a Labour MP 1945–55 and 1959–70. It is particularly useful for his opposition to steel re-nationalization in 1965–6. The period of the Attlee government is also covered in his earlier volume of memoirs *Into the Dangerous World* Weidenfeld and Nicolson 1952.

(d) Conservative Biographies

783 Nigel Fisher *The Tory Leaders: Their Struggle for Power* Weidenfeld and Nicolson 1977. A study of Conservative Party leaders from Churchill to Thatcher. It is especially good on their rise to power.

784 Tom Stacey and Roland St Oswald *Here Come the Tories* Tom Stacey 1970. Biographical studies of the incoming Heath government. A similar, if more hostile, study is Andrew Roth *Heath and the Heathmen* Routledge and Kegan Paul 1972. This however focuses more on Heath himself.

785 Nigel Nicolson *Alex: The Life of Field Marshal Earl Alexander of Tunis* Weidenfeld and Nicolson 1973. The Supreme Allied Commander in the Mediterranean 1944–5 was Governor-General of Canada 1946–52. He was not however a success when despite being a non-politician he was plucked from this post to be Churchill's Minister of Defence 1952–4.

786 Harold Julian Amery *Approach March: A Venture in Autobiography* Hutchinson 1973. This account ends with a description of his and Randolph Churchill's unsuccessful campaign in the two member constituency of Preston in 1945.

787 John Barnes and David Nicholson (eds) *The Empire at Bay: The Leo Amery Diaries Vol II: 1929–1945* Hutchinson 1988. Amery was out of parliament after 1945 but his political significance was not ended. The

editors have included a useful epilogue surveying Amery's life in the post-war years.

**789** Sir John W Wheeler-Bennett *John Anderson, Viscount Waverley* Macmillan 1962. A cabinet minister 1938–45 Anderson continued to be closely involved in the development of the Atomic Bomb programme during the period of the Attlee government, despite the fact he was a member of the Conservative shadow cabinet (whilst at the same time sitting in the Commons as an Independent MP). He however refused office under Churchill when he returned to power in 1951, but nevertheless remained an eminent figure until his death in 1958.

**790** Jonathan Mantle *In for a Penny: The Unauthorized Biography of Jeffrey Archer* Hamilton 1988. An MP 1969–74 Archer lost his seat in the midst of bankruptcy. He subsequently became a bestselling novelist, returning to political life in the 1980s as deputy chairman of the Conservative Party.

**791** David Sinclair *Dynasty: The Astors and Their Times* Dent 1984. A useful study of an eminent Conservative political dynasty. They were also important in the newspaper industry.

**792** For Lord Beaverbrook see [3640].

**793** Humphrey Berkeley *Crossing the Floor* Allen and Unwin 1972. Berkeley was in the Conservative Political Centre 1948–57 and a Conservative MP 1959–66. In 1970 he joined the Labour Party. A useful backbencher memoir.

**794** J Reginald Bevins *The Greasy Pole: A Personal Account of the Realities of British Politics* Hodder and Stoughton 1965. Informative and opinionated memoirs by the former Postmaster- General 1959–64 and Liverpool MP 1950–64.

**795** Robert John Graham Boothby *Boothby: Recollections of a Rebel* Hutchinson 1978. These memoirs of a prominent Conservative MP 1924–58 are as useful for his insights on his contemporaries as they are as autobiography. His *My Yesterday, Your Tomorrow* Hutchinson 1962 also contains autobiographical reflections, as well as his response to the contemporary political situation and some personal recollections of his political and artistic friends.

**796** John Boyd-Carpenter *Memoirs* Sidgwick and Jackson 1980. Good memoirs which include vivid sketches of the Prime Ministers he served under 1951–64 as well as useful discussions of the nature of departmental business.

**797** Charles Edward Lysaught *Brendan Bracken* Allen Lane 1979. A good biography of a many-sided man. An MP until 1952 and a close friend of Churchill, Bracken was also Chairman of the *Financial Times* immediately after the Second World War. Another useful biography is Andrew Boyle *Poor, Dear Brendon* Hutchinson 1974.

**798** Jock Bruce-Gardyne *Ministers and Mandarins: Inside the Whitehall Village* Sidgwick and Jackson 1986. Memoirs of his time as a Treasury minister 1981–3. This is particularly useful on relations with the Civil Service. See also [304, 312].

**799** Richard Austen Butler *The Art of the Possible* Hamilton 1971. A classic political memoir by the man who was omnipresent during the Conservative governments of 1951–64. He was also of importance as the minister responsible for the 1944 Education Act, and for his work, as head of the Conservative Research Department, in revamping party policy after the 1945 defeat. It is however an extremely elliptical book which conceals as well as reveals. The best biography is Anthony Howard *RAB: The Life of R A Butler* Cape 1987. See also Francis Boyd *Richard Austen* Butler Rockliff 1956, Ralph Harris *Politics Without Prejudice: A Political Appreciation of the Right Hon Richard Austen Butler* Staples Press 1956, Patrick Cosgrave *R A Butler: An English Life* Quartet 1981 and Gerald Sparrow *'RAB': Study of a Statesman* Odhams 1965. Mollie Butler *August and Rab: A Memoir* Weidenfeld and Nicolson 1987 is a memoir of her two husbands, the second of whom was R A Butler.

**800** Peter Carrington *Reflect on Things Past: The Memoirs of Lord Carrington* Collins 1988. A well documented and thoughtful memoir. It is useful not only for his time as Minister of Defence 1970–4 and as Foreign Secretary 1979–82, but also for his role in the attempt by the Wilson government in the 1960s to reform the House of Lords. Patrick Cosgrave *Carrington: A Life and a Policy* Dent 1986 is a critical biography which should also be consulted.

**801** Robert Rhodes James (ed) *'Chips': The Diaries of Sir Henry Channon* Weidenfeld and Nicolson 1967. A very entertaining and vivid, if not necessarily totally reliable political diary. Channon was an MP 1935–57.

**802** F W F Smith (the Earl of Birkenhead) *The Prof in Two Worlds: The Official Life of Professor F A Lindemann, Viscount Cherwell* Collins 1961. Cherwell was an Oxford physicist who served Churchill as Paymaster-General 1942–5 and 1951–3. Another good biography is Sir Roy F Harrod *The Prof: A Personal Memoir of Lord Cherwell* Macmillan 1959.

**803** Martin Gilbert *Never Despair: Winston S Churchill 1945– 65* Heinemann 1988. The eighth and final volume of the official biography of Sir Winston Churchill. The first two volumes, written by Randolph Churchill, were published in 1966 and 1967, since when the series has been written by Martin Gilbert. This final volume covers his years in opposition 1945–51, his second Premiership 1951–5, and the years of retirement until his death in 1965. It however makes no attempt to provide a concluding assessment of Sir Winston's life and career: Gilbert did not think that the official biographer should undertake such a task. Henry Pelling *Winston Churchill* Macmillan 1974 is a useful one volume assessment. It is however relatively thin in its treatment of the post-war period. Paul Addison 'Churchill in British Politics 1940–1955' in J M W Bean (ed) *The Political Culture of Modern Britain: Studies in Memory of Stephen Koss* Hamilton 1987 pp 243–61 is a useful study. Lewis Broad *Winston Churchill 1974–1955* Hutchinson 1956 is supplemented by his *Winston Churchill: The Years of Achievement* Sidgwick and Jackson 1964, which deals with the years 1939–64, concentrating on the war years. Another biography is Elizabeth Pakenham *Winston Churchill* Sidgwick and Jackson 1974. Piers Brandon *Winston Churchill: A Brief Life* Secker and Warburg 1984 is an unflattering popular biography. See also A G Harvey 'Winston S Churchill: Theory and Practice in Politics' Exeter MA Thesis 1965–6. C M W Moran *Winston Churchill: The Struggle for Survival 1940–65, Taken from the Diaries of Lord Moran* Constable 1966 has had a major influence on perceptions of Churchill in his declining years. This portrayal by Churchill's physician of a statesman increasingly physically incapable of holding the reins of office, particularly during his 1951–5 administration has however come to be seen as somewhat exaggerated (see [295]). Another interesting memoir is Violet Bonham Carter *Winston Churchill as I Knew Him* Eyre and Spottiswoode/Collins 1965. There are also a number of volumes which collect the assessments and tributes of contemporaries. The best of these is Sir John W Wheeler-Bennett (ed) *Action This Day: Working With Churchill* Macmillan 1968. See also C Eade (ed) *Churchill by His Contemporaries* Hutchinson 1953 and *Churchill by His Contemporaries: An Observer Appreciation* The Observer 1965. Another useful assessment is A J P Taylor *et al Churchill: Four Faces and the Man* Allen Lane 1969. For Churchill's speeches see Robert Rhodes James (ed) *Churchill: Complete Speeches 1897–1963* 8v, Chelsea House 1974. For his post-war speeches see also Randolph Churchill (ed) *The Sinews of Peace: Post-War Speeches* Cassell 1948, *Europe Unite: Speeches 1947 and 1948* Cassell 1951, *In the Balance: Speeches 1949 and 1950* Cassell 1951, *Stemming the Tide: Speeches 1951 and 1952* Cassell 1953 and *The Unwritten Alliance: Speeches 1953 to 1959* Cassell 1961. For Churchill's writings see Frederick Woods (ed) *A Bibliography of the Works of Sir Winston Churchill* 2nd ed, St Pauls Bibliographies 1979. This is a very comprehensive guide. On Churchill as a parliamentarian

see Denis Bardens *Churchill in Parliament* Hale 1967 and Robert Rhodes James 'Churchill as Parliamentarian' *Parliamentary Affairs* 18 1964–65 pp 149–55. A pictorial biography is Mary Soames *A Churchill Family Album: A Personal Anthology* Allen Lane 1982. Also of use are the biographies of his wife. Particularly good is Mary Soames *Clementine Churchill by Her Daughter Mary Soames* Cassell 1979. See also Jack Fishman *My Darling Clementine* 2nd ed, Pan 1964. Kenneth Young *Churchill and Beaverbrook* Eyre and Spottiswoode 1966 is a rather chatty study of his friendship with Lord Beaverbrook based largely on correspondence. For Churchill's political philosophy see [943] and for Churchill as historian see [6724]. See also [1432].

804 For William Clark see [296].

805 Anthony Courtney *Sailor in a Russian Frame* Johnson 1968. An MP 1959–66 Courtney was allegedly the victim of a plot by Russian Intelligence.

806 For Aidan Crawley see [695].

807 Julian Critchley *Westminster Blues* Futura 1986. Witty, semi-autobiographical sketches of parliamentary life. Critchley has been an MP 1959–64 and 1970–.

808 For Edwina Currie see [5462].

809 Douglas Dodds-Parker *Political Eunuch* Springwood Books 1986. An MP 1945–59 and 1964–74 Dodds-Parker held junior office 1953–7.

810 Sir Patrick Donner *Crusade: A Life Against the Calamitous Twentieth Century* Sherwood 1984. Sir Patrick was an MP 1931–55 and was particularly interested in imperial questions.

811 For Sir Alec Douglas-Home see Lord Home [827].

812 David McAdam Eccles *Life and Politics: A Moral Diagnosis* Longmans 1967. An MP 1943–62 Eccles held various cabinet posts 1951–62 and 1970–3. He distinguished himself particularly as Minister of Education 1954–57 and 1959–62. This is not really an autobiography but an analysis of contemporary difficulties from his Christian standpoint. His *Halfway to Faith* Geoffrey Bles 1966 is a similar work.

813 Anthony Eden *The Memoirs of Sir Anthony Eden: Full Circle* Cassell 1960. A good political memoir. This volume of his memoirs covers his period as Foreign Secretary 1951–5 and Prime Minister 1955–7. For a useful discussion of Eden in the light of these memoirs see Martin Wight 'Brutus in Foreign Policy: The Memoirs of Sir Anthony Eden' *International Affairs* 36 1960 pp 299–309. The last few pages of the volume of his memoirs dealing with the Second World War, *The*

*Reckoning* Cassell 1965, are also worth consulting, covering as they do the 1945 caretaker government and the general election defeat. The other volume of memoirs, *Facing the Dictators* Cassell 1962, deals with the 1930s. The two principal biographies present very different pictures of Eden. David Carlton *Anthony Eden: A Biography* Allen Lane 1981 makes good use of American sources. It is however rather over-critical. The official biography, Robert Rhodes James *Anthony Eden* Weidenfeld and Nicolson 1986, perhaps errs too far in the opposite direction in response. Sidney Aster *Eden* Weidenfeld and Nicolson 1976 remains a reasonable biography. Randolph S Churchill *The Rise and Fall of Sir Anthony Eden* Macgibbon and Kee 1959 is a rather journalistic account. For instant biographies which reflect the response at the time he became Prime Minister see also Lewis Broad *Anthony Eden* Hutchinson 1955, Denis Bardens *Portrait of a Statesman* Muller 1955 and William Rees-Mogg *Sir Anthony Eden* Rockliff 1956. For Eden as Prime Minister see [296]. For Eden's speeches see Anthony Eden *Freedom and Order: Selected Speeches 1930–46* Faber 1947. A further collection covering speeches 1946–9 is Anthony Eden *Days for Decision* Faber 1949. See also [1966, 1989, 1995].

**814** For Lord Egremont see John Wyndham [875].

**815** Sir Colin Coote *A Companion of Honour: The Story of Walter Elliot* Collins 1965. The official biography. An important inter-war political figure Elliot remained in the House of Commons 1946–58 as a backbencher and elder statesman.

**816** For Sir Ian Gilmour see [939].

**817** For Harold Evans as Macmillan's Press Secretary see [297].

**818** Quintin MacGarel Hogg, Lord Hailsham *The Door Wherein I Went* Collins 1975. A good autobiography, which is as much a statement of his personal philosophy and Christian faith. His full memoirs are *A Sparrow's Flight: Memoirs* Collins 1990. Hailsham was a significant figure in the 1950s more perhaps because of his role and popularity as chairman of the party 1957–9 than because of the offices he held. In 1963 he was a prime contender for the party leadership. For more on this see the interview, Lord Hailsham 'Prime Ministers and Near Prime Ministers' *Contemporary Record* 1/3 1987 pp 57–8. In 1970–4 and 1979–87 he was Lord Chancellor. See also [935].

**819** Ian Harvey *To Fall Like Lucifer* Sidgwick and Jackson 1971. An MP 1950–8 Harvey resigned because of a scandal over his homosexuality whilst a junior figure in the Foreign Office 1957–8.

**820** G S Harvie-Watt *Most of My Life* Springwood Books 1980. An MP 1931–5 and 1937–59 Harvie-Watt was more interested in his work for Consolidated Gold Fields after 1945 than he was in his political career and so there is little on post-war politics in this memoir.

**821** Margaret Laing *Edward Heath – Prime Minister* Sidgwick and Jackson 1972. The best biography so far. Heath was Prime Minister 1970–4. George Hutchinson *Edward Heath: A Personal and Political Biography* Longmans 1970 was the campaign biography for the 1970 general election. Marion Evans *Ted Heath: A Family Portrait* Kimber 1970 is useful for the background and personal details it supplies. See also [784]. None of these can however be considered satisfactory since none of them traces Heath's career even as far as the fall of his government. It is to be hoped that John Campbell's forthcoming biography will remedy this deficiency.

**822** W Gore Allen *The Reluctant Politician: Derick Heathcoat Amory* Christopher Johnson 1958. A modest biography of the moderate Conservative who was then the new Chancellor of the Exchequer.

**823** Julian Critchley *Heseltine: The Unauthorised Biography* Deutsch 1987. A well regarded and witty biography of Michael Heseltine. Heseltine's own *Where There's a Will* Hutchinson 1987 is partly autobiographical and partly his reflections on current political problems. Heseltine was the Secretary of State for the Environment and then for Defence under Mrs Thatcher, until he walked out of the cabinet over the Westland Affair in 1986. S Platt 'Heseltine' *Roof* May/June 1987 pp 20–3 is an interview which covers many of the issues arising, particularly concerning his period at the Department of the Environment. Heseltine's period as Secretary of State for Defence is assessed in T D Bridge 'Heseltine MOD 83/86: For and Against' *Army Quarterly* 116 1986 pp 5–8.

**824** Lord Hill of Luton *Both Sides of the Hill: The Memoirs of Charles Hill* Heinemann 1964. A good autobiography. This is useful not only for his account of the Tory governments of the 1950s and early 1960s in which he served but also because it covers his earlier career as Secretary of the British Medical Association 1944–50. It is therefore also of value for understanding the politics of the establishment of the National Health Service. On Hill's career in broadcasting see [3793].

**825** J A Cross *Sir Samuel Hoare: A Political Biography* Cape 1977. By 1945 Viscount Templewood, as he had become, was an elder statesman who continued to be of importance in the early post-war period because of his influence on criminal justice policy.

**826** Christopher Hollis *Along the Road to Frome* Harrap 1958. Hollis was MP for Devizes 1945–55.

**827** Sir Alec Douglas-Home, Lord Home *The Way the Wind Blows: An Autobiography* Collins 1976. This is perhaps more of a memoir than a autobiography by the former Prime Minister 1963–4, Foreign Secretary 1960–3 and 1970–4 and Commonwealth Relations Secretary 1955–60. His *Letters to a Grandson* Collins 1983, casts some more light on his attitudes, consisting as it does of reflections, in the form of letters, on twentieth century historical developments and current international problems. The best biography is Kenneth Young *Sir Alec Douglas-Home* Dent 1970. See also John Dickie *The Uncommon Commoner* Pall Mall Press 1964.

**828** Judy Hillman and Peter Clarke *Geoffrey Howe: A Quiet Revolutionary* Weidenfeld and Nicolson 1988. A good biography which emphasizes his contribution, through his past in the Bow Group, to the programme of the Thatcher government, in which he has served as Chancellor of the Exchequer and Foreign Secretary.

**829** David Howell *Blind Victory: A Study in Income, Wealth and Power* Hamilton 1986. Not an autobiography. It docs however contain some autobiographical reflections on the Thatcher government, which he served as Secretary of State for Energy 1979–81 and for Transport 1981–3, as well as a discussion of economic policy.

**830** For Douglas Hurd see [304].

**831** For Lord Ismay see [2321].

**832** Donald McIntosh Johnson *A Doctor Reflects: Miracles and Mirages* Johnson 1975. Good informative memoirs by a Scottish backbencher. See also his earlier memoirs, *Doctor in Parliament* Johnson 1958 and *A Cassandra at Westminster* Johnson 1967. His *On Being an Independent MP* Johnson 1964 deals with his period as an Independent MP in 1964 before he fought and lost his seat as an Independent Conservative in the general election of that year.

**833** Aubrey Jones *Britain's Economy: The Roots of Stagnation* Cambridge University Press 1985. Very useful autobiographical reflections on developments in economic policy during his political life. He was a Minister in the 1950s but this book is probably most useful for his period as the consensual chairman of the National Board for Prices and Incomes 1965–70.

**834** Morrison Halcrow *Keith Joseph: A Single Mind* Macmillan 1989. The first substantive biography of one of the key mentors of Mrs Thatcher who served under her at the Departments of Trade and Industry and of Education. Sir Keith Joseph 'Escaping the Chrysalis of Statism' *Contemporary Record* 1/1 1987 pp 26–31 is an interview which is particularly interesting for Sir Keith's portrayal of himself moving from being an 'unconscious statist' during the Macmillan and Heath governments to radical Conservative. See also [938].

**835** David Maxwell-Fyfe *Political Adventure: The Memoirs of the Earl of Kilmuir* Weidenfeld and Nicolson 1964. Kilmuir was Home Secretary 1951–4 and Lord Chancellor 1954–62. He was also closely involved in the re-building of the party after the 1945 defeat.

**836** Evelyn Mansfield King *Closest Correspondence: The Inside Story of an MP* Book Guild 1989. King was an Labour MP 1945–50. He joined the Conservative Party in 1951 and sat as a Conservative MP in 1964–79.

**837** D R Thorpe *Selwyn Lloyd* Cape 1989. A well researched and skilful biography. Lloyd was Minister of Defence 1955, Foreign Secretary 1955–60, Chancellor of the Exchequer 1960–2, Lord Privy Seal and Leader of the House of Commons 1963–4 and Speaker 1971–6. For his memoirs of the Suez episode see [2411]. For his reflections on his time as Speaker see [515].

**837A** Percy Belgrave 'Laddie' Lucas *Five Up: A Chronicle of Five Lives* Sidgwick and Jackson 1978. Lucas was a Conservative MP 1950–59 and managing director of the Greyhound Racing Association.

**838** Oliver Lyttelton *The Memoirs of Lord Chandos* The Bodley Head 1962. Lyttelton was the Colonial Secretary 1951–4.

**839** Nigel Fisher *Iain Macleod* Deutsch 1973. A very perceptive biography. Macleod was an important figure in the governments of the 1950s and early 1960s. His death shortly after his appointment as Chancellor of the Exchequer in 1970 was a bitter blow to the Heath government.

**840** Harold Macmillan wrote a six volume autobiography. The various volumes are *Winds of Change 1914–1939* Macmillan 1966, *The Blast of War 1939–1945* 1967, *Tides of Fortune 1945–1955* 1969, *Riding the Storm 1955–1959* 1971, *Pointing the Way 1959–1961* 1972 and *At the End of the Day 1961–1963* 1973. These volumes reveal little of Macmillan's personality and, in including footnotes and a chronology, have perhaps as much a flavour of general history as of autobiography. Informative though they are, they are also generally seen as being somewhat pedestrian. Macmillan's diary, if it is ever published should however prove a most valuable source for interpreting the 1951–64 governments and particularly Macmillan's period as Prime Minister 1957–63. The first volume of the official biography, Alastair Horne *Macmillan 1894–1956* Macmillan 1988, reveals much more of Macmillan than Macmillan himself did but relies over much for its evidence on Macmillan's version of events. Horne's second volume *Macmillan 1957–1986: Vol II of the Official Biography* Macmillan 1989 also has some surprising omissions of, for instance, the cabinet meeting at which Macmillan persuaded his reluctant colleagues to back the Concorde project or of the development of the civil nuclear power programme, but is nevertheless generally a good study which captures Macmillan's style well and usefully illuminates the period of the late 1950s and early 1960s which remains swathed in official secrecy. Anthony Sampson *Macmillan: A Study in Ambiguity* Allen Lane 1967 remains a useful biography. Nigel Fisher *Harold Macmillan* Weidenfeld and Nicolson 1982 is however somewhat disappointing, particularly in comparison with [839]. George Hutchinson *The Last Edwardian at Number Ten* Quartet 1980 is useful for Macmillan's Prime Ministerial style and the leadership battle over the succession in 1963. Emrys Hughes *Macmillan: Portrait of a Politician* Allen and Unwin 1962 is poor as biography. As a study by a Labour MP it nevertheless remains of interest as an example of how the opposition saw Macmillan. See also Ruth Dudley Edwards *Harold Macmillan: A Life in Pictures* Macmillan 1983.

**841**   For David Maxwell-Fyfe see Lord Kilmuir [835].

**842**   Reginald Maudling *Memoirs* Sidgwick and Jackson 1978. An important figure in the 1951–64 governments culminating in a period as Chancellor of the Exchequer 1962–4 Maudling was also Home Secretary 1970–2. See also [289].

**842A**   Sir Harold P Mitchell *In My Stride* W and R Chambers 1951. Mitchell was Chairman of the party at the time of the 1945 general election.

**843**   Lord Molson 'Fifty-Four Years of Parliamentary Life' *Contemporary Review* 247 (1435) 1985 pp 74–81. Hugh Molson was an MP 1931–5 and 1939–61 and a junior minister in the 1951–64 governments.

**844**   F W F Smith (the Earl of Birkenhead) *Walter Monckton: The Life of Viscount Monckton of Brenchley* Weidenfeld and Nicolson 1969. A good biography. This is useful not only for Monckton as Churchill's conciliatory Minister of Labour and as Eden's Minister of Defence who resigned over the government's policy on the Suez crisis, but also for the end of British rule in India, and for the 1959 Advisory Commission on Central Africa (see [1704]).

**845**   Sir Henry Morris-Jones *Doctor in the Whips Room* Hale 1955. Morris-Jones was a National Liberal MP 1931–50 (having been elected as a Liberal in 1929).

**846**   Sir Charles Mott-Radclyffe *Foreign Body in the Eye (A Memoir of the Foreign Service)* Cooper 1975. An MP 1942–70 this memoir is most useful for his time as chairman of the Conservative parliamentary party's Foreign Affairs Committee 1951–59.

**847**   Sir Gerald Nabarro *NAB 1: Portrait of a Politician* Maxwell 1969. Nabarro was an MP 1950–64 and from 1966 until his death in 1973. A further volume of avuncular reminiscences is *Exploits of a Politician* Barker 1973.

**848**   Nigel Nicolson *People and Parliament* Weidenfeld and Nicolson 1958. Nicolson was an MP 1952–9. This work is particularly useful for his account of the response of his Bournemouth constituency party to the Suez crisis. He retired in 1959 because of the constituency party's disapproval of his failure to support the government's Suez policy in 1956.

**849**   For Sir Anthony Nutting, the Minister of State at the Foreign Office who resigned over Suez, see [1397, 2400, 2488].

**850**   Sir Charles Ponsonby *Ponsonby Remembers* Alden Press 1965. Ponsonby was an MP 1935–50.

**851**   Patrick Cosgrave *The Lives of Enoch Powell* The Bodley Head 1989. A good biography of a complex figure. It has benefited from the considerable support and assistance of Powell himself. T E Utley *Enoch Powell: The Man and His Thinking* Kimber 1968 remains a good biography. Another reasonable biography is Roy Lewis *Enoch Powell: Principle in Politics* Cassell 1979. A controversial figure, Powell has attracted considerable attention. His highest office was as Minister of Health 1960–3. He has however perhaps been more important as a political figure. In 1968 his warnings about the consequences of mass immigration, the famous 'Rivers of Blood' speech, led an embarrassed Heath to drop him from the Shadow Cabinet but generated considerable popular support in the country. His opposition to Britain's accession to the EEC in 1971–3 also made him a considerable, popular figure far beyond the confines of Westminster in the early 1970s. The Powellite movement of these years is examined in Douglas E Schoen *Powell and the Powellites* Macmillan 1977. Powell as a populist figure is also examined in a scurrilous and witty vein in Andrew Roth *Enoch Powell: Tory Tribune* Macdonald 1972. Another somewhat critical biography, written when Powell had broken with the Conservative Party and become an Ulster Unionist MP 1974–87, is Humphrey Berkeley *The Odyssey of Enoch: A Political Memoir* Hamilton 1978. Paul Foot *The Rise of Enoch Powell* Penguin 1969 is a good critical study written in the wake of the 'Rivers of Blood' speech. Doojen Napal *Enoch Powell: A Study in Personality and Politics Part I* AWAAM Press 1975 is a psychological portrait drawing on Powell's poetry and his earlier career as a distinguished Classicist. It is perhaps overly Freudian, but it does contain some useful reflections on Powell's oratorical skills. Part II never appeared. There are also a number of collections of speeches. These are John Wood (ed) *A Nation Not Afraid: The Thinking of Enoch Powell* Batsford 1965, John Wood (ed) *Enoch Powell: Still to Decide* Batsford 1972 and Richard Ritchie (ed) *Enoch Powell: A Nation or no Nation? Six Years in British Politics* Batsford 1978.

**852** James Prior *A Balance of Power* Hamilton 1986. Short but useful memoirs. Heath's Parliamentary Private Secretary in opposition 1965–70, he went on to serve as Minister of Agriculture, Fisheries and Food 1970–2 and as Lord President of the Council and Leader of the House of Commons 1972–4. He also served under Mrs Thatcher as Secretary of State for Employment 1979–81 and for Northern Ireland 1981–4.

**853** Francis Pym *The Politics of Consent* Hamilton 1984. Pym was Northern Ireland Secretary 1973–4 and served Mrs Thatcher in various posts, culminating in his period as Foreign Secretary 1982–3. This is not really an autobiography but a commentary on contemporary politics. It does however contain some useful reflections, particularly on the Thatcher government.

**854** Peter Rawlinson *A Price Too High* Weidenfeld and Nicolson 1989. Rawlinson served as Solicitor-General 1962–4 and as Attorney-General 1970–4.

**855** Norman St John Stevas *The Two Cities* Faber 1984. Autobiographical fragments mixed in with reflections on post-war Christianity, especially Catholicism, and on contemporary Conservative politics. An MP 1964–87 he was Minister for the Arts 1973–4 and combined this portfolio with the Leadership of the Commons 1979–81.

**856** Sir (James) Arthur Salter *Slave of a Lamp: A Public Servant's Notebook* Weidenfeld and Nicolson 1967. An Independent MP 1937–50 Salter was a Conservative MP and minister 1951–3. See also his *Memoirs of a Public Servant* Faber 1961.

**857** There is a forthcoming official biography of Duncan Sandys, an important minister in the 1951–64 governments, by John Barnes.

**858** Sir John Smyth *Only Enemy* Hutchinson 1959. His autobiography. An MP 1950–66 Smyth held junior office 1951–5. See also his *Milestones* Sidgwick and Jackson 1979.

**859** For Keith Speed see [2269].

**860** James Gray Stuart, Viscount Stuart of Findhorn *Within the Fringe* The Bodley Head 1967. An MP 1923–59 he was Secretary of State for Scotland 1951–7.

**861** J A Cross *Lord Swinton* Oxford University Press 1982. Philip Cunliffe-Lister, the Earl of Swinton, was an important political figure during the inter-war years. He was also Chancellor of the Duchy of Lancaster 1951–2 and Commonwealth Relations Secretary 1952–5. See also [229].

**862** Norman Tebbit *Upwardly Mobile: An Autobiography* Weidenfeld and Nicolson 1988. A somewhat abrasive autobiography. Tebbit was one of Mrs Thatcher's most loyal ministers, serving her at the Departments of Employment 1981–3, Trade and Industry 1983–5, and as Chancellor of the Duchy of Lancaster and Chairman of the Conservative Party 1985–7.

**863** Sir (Luke) William Burke Teeling *Corridors of Frustration* Johnson 1970. A backbench memoir that is most useful for the opposition to the integration of Malta into the UK in the 1950s and the Channel Tunnel project in the late 1960s.

**864** Hugo Young *One of Us: A Biography of Margaret Thatcher* Macmillan 1989. Margaret Thatcher, Prime Minister since 1979 and Education Secretary 1970–4, has been the subject of numerous biographies. This is a lengthy and in-depth biography which focuses particularly on her Premiership. Nicholas Wapshott and George Brock *Thatcher: The Major New Biography* Futura 1983 remains a very useful biography. George Gardiner *Margaret Thatcher: From Childhood to Leadership* Kimber 1975 is a sympathetic study which is especially strong on her background. Penny Junor *Margaret Thatcher: Wife, Mother, Politician* Sidgwick and Jackson 1983 is particularly good on the human interest side. See also Russell Lewis *Margaret Thatcher: A Personal and Political Biography* 2nd ed, Routledge and Kegan Paul 1984. Patrick Cosgrave *Margaret Thatcher: A Tory and Her Party* Hutchinson 1978 is a useful study by one of her (then) policy advisers. Andrew Thomson *Margaret Thatcher: The Woman Within* W H Allen 1989 is an insight by the man who served as her constituency agent for six years. Bruce Arnold *Margaret Thatcher: A Study in Power* Hamilton 1984 on the other hand is a sympathetic but not very inspiring study focusing on her ambition and her conduct of government. Kenneth Harris *Thatcher* Weidenfeld and Nicolson 1988, if less tinged with hagiographical tendencies than several of the other biographies, adds relatively little to our knowledge of Mrs Thatcher. He does however draw attention to the fact that there was little trace of the policies and style that have come to be known as Thatcherism before she became leader of the Conservative Party in 1975. The first major biography from a continental perspective is Egbert Kieser *Margaret Thatcher: Eine Frau verändert ihre Nation* Bechtle, Munich 1989. Hugo Young and Anne Sloman *The Thatcher Phenomenon* BBC Books 1986 is not so much a biography as a most useful series of assessments by her contemporaries. Patricia Murray's sympathetic portrait *Margaret Thatcher: A Profile* 2nd ed, W H Allen 1980, also draws considerably on assessments of Mrs Thatcher by others. It is also quite useful for her attitudes and beliefs. Alistair B Cooke (comp) *Margaret Thatcher: The Revival of Britain: Speeches on Home and European Affairs 1975–1988* Aurum Press 1989 is the best of a number of collections of speeches and other material. Margaret Thatcher *In Defence of Freedom: Speeches on Britain's Relations with the World 1976–1986* Prometheus Books 1987 collects fourteen major speeches on foreign policy, including specific issues such as the Falklands War. See also Margaret Thatcher *Let Our Children Grow Tall: Selected Speeches 1975–1977* Centre for Policy Studies 1977. See also [944].

**865**   Harvey Thomas with Judith Gunn *In the Face of Fear* Marshalls 1985. Autobiography of the man who has been in charge of the party's public relations in the 1980s. He also reflects on his previous work for the international evangelists Billy Graham and Luis Palau.

**866**   Colin Thornton-Kemsley *Through Winds and Tide* Standard Press 1974. He was a Scottish MP 1939–64.

**867**   Peter Walker *The Ascent of Britain* Sidgwick and Jackson 1977. Autobiographical reflections on the current political situation, mostly in the context of his periods as Secretary of State for the Environment and then for Trade and Industry under Heath. Neale Stevenson (ed) *Trust the People: The Selected Essays and Speeches of Peter Walker* Collins 1987 deals particularly with his role in the 1984–5 coal dispute as Energy Secretary. It includes letters and other material as well as speeches. Walker has also served Mrs Thatcher at the Ministry of Agriculture, Fisheries and Food and at the Welsh Office.

**868**   Dennis Walters *Not Always with the Pack* Constable 1989. This autobiography by the Conservative MP and arabist is probably most useful for his memoir of the fight for the Conservative leadership in 1963, when he was Lord Hailsham's personal assistant.

**869**   Harold Arthur Watkinson, Lord Watkinson *Turning Points* Michael Russell 1986. Watkinson was the Minister of Transport and Civil Aviation 1955–9 and Minister of Defence 1959–62. He was also an important businessman, and in 1976–7 he was President of the CBI. His reflections on industrial policy, *Blueprint for Industrial Survival* Allen and Unwin 1976, also contains some autobiographical fragments.

**870**   William Whitelaw *The Whitelaw Memoirs* Aurum Press 1989. A memoir. Very revealing of the man and mildly revealing of the operation of the Thatcher government. Whitelaw was a key figure in both the Heath and Thatcher cabinets and in the latter he played, as Home Secretary but particularly as Lord President of the Council, an important consensual role. See also Bruce Anderson *Whitelaw: On the Right Track* Sidgwick and Jackson 1988.

**871**   David James George Hennessy, Lord Windlesham *Politics in Practice* Cape 1975. Memoirs, especially of the 1970–4 government in which he rose to be Lord Privy Seal and Leader of the House of Lords in 1973–4, and reflections on the implications of developments in Northern Ireland, the media and so on during these years.

**872**   Edward Turnour Winterton, Earl Winterton *Fifty Tumultuous Years* Hutchinson 1955. Winterton was an MP 1904–51. See also his *Orders of the Day* Cassell 1953. A useful biography is A H Brodrick *Near to Greatness: A Life of the 6th Earl Winterton* Hutchinson 1961.

**873**   C M Woodhouse *Something Ventured* Granada 1982. An autobiography. An MP 1959–66 and 1970–4 Woodhouse held junior office 1961–4.

**874**   Frederick J Marquis, Earl of Woolton *The Memoirs of the Rt Hon the Earl of Woolton* Cassell 1959. As Chairman of Conservative Central Office 1946–55 Woolton played an important part in the re-building of the party after the 1945 defeat. He served in Churchill's cabinet 1951–5. Helen Langley 'The Woolton Papers' *Bodleian Library Record* 11 1984 pp 320–37 describes his private papers deposited in the Bodleian Library in Oxford.

**875**   John Wyndham, Lord Egremont *Wyndham and Children First* Macmillan 1968. An excellent political autobiography. It is most useful for his period as Macmillan's private secretary 1957–63.

(e) Liberal Biographies

**876**   John Fowler (ed) *Bannerman: The Memoirs of Lord Bannerman of Kildonan* Impulse Books 1972. John MacDonald Bannerman was a prominent Scottish Liberal in the 1950s and 1960s who was also very active in promoting the Gaelic language and the case for Scottish Home Rule.

**877**   D M Roberts 'Clement Davies and the Liberal Party 1929–56' Wales MA Thesis 1974–6. This is the nearest there is to a biography of Davies. It focuses on the years from his first election to parliament in 1929 until he relinquished the leadership of the party he had held since 1945 in 1956. Graham Jones 'The Clement Davies Papers: A Review' *National Library of Wales*

*Journal* 23 1984 pp 406–21 is a commentary on Davies' papers.

**878**   Joseph Grimond *Memoirs* Heinemann 1979. An MP 1950–83 Jo Grimond led the party 1956–67. He was also caretaker leader in 1976 between the resignation of Jeremy Thorpe and the election of David Steel.

**879**   Emry Price *Megan Lloyd George* Gwynedd Archives Services 1983. The daughter of Lloyd George, she was a Liberal MP 1929–51 and a Labour MP from 1957 until her death in 1966. This is a short illustrated biography.

**880**   Annette Penhaligon *Penhaligon* Bloomsbury 1989. A biography of her husband, David Penhaligon, the MP for Truro 1974–86.

**881**   John Bowle *Viscount Samuel: A Biography* Gollancz 1957. Herbert Samuel was an important figure in the party and in national politics from before the First World War and led the Liberal Party 1931–5. Accordingly there is relatively little on the post-war period in this biography. He did however remain significant and led the party in the Lords 1945–55. Samuel's *Memoirs* Cresset Press 1945 do not touch on the post-war era.

**882**   Cyril Smith *Big Cyril* W H Allen 1977. From 1950 until 1966 he was a member of the Labour Party, quitting whilst Lord Mayor of Rochdale. Since 1972 he has been a Liberal MP. This autobiography contains some useful reflections on Heath's abortive negotiations with the Liberals after the inconclusive February 1974 election.

**883**   David Steel *Against Goliath: David Steel's Story* Weidenfeld and Nicolson 1989. An MP since 1965 Steel was instrumental in getting the 1967 Abortion Act on the statute book. He was leader of the party 1976–88. See also Peter Bartram *David Steel: His Life and Politics* W H Allen 1981. For Steel's diary of the 1977–8 Lib-Lab Pact see [309]. Stuart Mole (ed) *The Decade of Re-Alignment: The Leadership Speeches of David Steel 1976–1985* Hebden Royd 1986 is a collection of Steel's speeches to the Liberal Assembly.

**884**   Lewis Chester *Jeremy Thorpe: A Secret Life* Fontana 1979. Both this and Peter Bessell *Cover-Up: The Jeremy Thorpe Affair* Simons Books 1980 perhaps deal more with the scandal that engulfed Thorpe in 1976 than with his political career, in which he served as an MP 1959–79 and led his party 1967–76. See also John Whale 'The Press and Jeremy Thorpe' *Political Quarterly* 47 1976 pp 408–24.

(f) Independents Biographies

**885**   For Sir John Boyd-Orr see [8362].

**886**   Alan Patrick Herbert *Independent Member* Methuen 1950. A witty memoir of his time as an Independent MP 1935–50. Reginald Pound *A P Herbert: A Biography* Michael Joseph 1976 focuses rather more on Herbert's distinguished literary career.

**887**   Denis Nowell Pritt *The Autobiography of D N Pritt* Lawrence and Wishart 3v, 1965–6. A Labour MP from 1935 until he was expelled from the party in 1940 he continued to sit as an Independent until 1950. In 1949–50 he was the Chairman of the Left-Wing Labour Independent group.

**888**   M D Stocks *Eleanor Rathbone* Gollancz 1949. An MP from 1929 until her death early in 1946, she was most important for her championing of the cause of family allowances.

(g) Communist Biographies

**889**   Nellie Connole *Leaven of Life: The Story of George Henry Fletcher* Lawrence and Wishart 1961. Fletcher was a Communist activist in Sheffield until his death in 1958.

**890**   William Gallacher *Rise Like Lions* Lawrence and Wishart 1951. Gallacher was a Communist MP 1935–50. This volume of his memoirs covers the years 1945–50. Subsequent years are covered in his *The Tyrant's Might is Passing* Lawrence and Wishart 1954 and Nan Green (ed) *The Last Memoirs of William Gallacher* Lawrence and Wishart 1966. Earlier volumes are *Revolt on the Clyde: An Autobiography* Lawrence and Wishart 1936 and *The Rolling of the Thunder* Lawrence and Wishart 1947.

**891**   Jim Garnett 'My Autobiography' *North West Labour History Society Bulletin* 9 1983–84 pp 25–35. The life story of a local party activist.

**892**   Douglas Hyde *I Believed: The Autobiography of a Former British Communist* Heinemann 1951. Much of this is concerned with his post-war disillusion and conversion to Catholicism. Hyde had worked on the party's newspaper the *Daily Worker*.

**893**   Raymond Challinor 'Memories of a Militant' *North East Group for the Study of Labour History Bulletin* 9 1975 pp 34–42. A biography complied from interviews with Jack Parks, a long-time party activist.

**894** John Mahon *Harry Pollitt: A Biography* Lawrence and Wishart 1976. Pollitt was General Secretary 1929–56 and Chairman from then until his death in 1960. This biography by a close colleague is perhaps over-sympathetic and his international activities and connections with the Soviet Union are not well covered. The review essay, Monty Johnstone 'Harry Pollitt: A Review Essay of Mahon's Biography' *Bulletin of the Society for the Study of Labour History* 33 1976 pp 56–61, is well worth consulting. See also the short pamphlet *Harry Pollitt: A Tribute* Communist Party 1960. Pollitt's autobiography *Serving My Time: An Apprenticeship in Politics* Lawrence and Wishart 1940 is of use for his earlier life.

**895** Harry McShane and Joan Smith *No Mean Fighter* Pluto 1978. A useful biography constructed from interviews. McShane was an important person in the party until his resignation in 1953.

**896** Peggy Kahn 'An Interview with Frank Watters' *Bulletin of the Society for the Study of Labour History* 43 1981 pp 54–67. Reminiscences about organizing work in the Scottish and Yorkshire coalfields from the 1950s onwards. In the process he reflects on the growth of the Left in the Yorkshire pits and on the 1960s' dialogue between Communism and Christianity. The footnotes contain full biographical details on all the people mentioned in the interview.

(h) Far Right Biographies

**897** David L Baker 'The Making of a British Fascist: The Case of A K Chesterton' Sheffield PhD Thesis 1982. A good analysis of a complex figure. Chesterton was an important figure in the revival of the British Right and was the first Chairman of the National Front. Baker's article 'A K Chesterton, the Strasser Brothers and the Politics of the National Front' *Patterns of Prejudice* 19/3 1985 pp 23–33 stresses the importance of Chesterton's thought in the National Front's search for greater respectability in the 1980s. *Arthur Kenneth Chesterton MC* privately printed 1973 is a short tribute.

**898** Mary Irene Curzon *In Many Rhythms: An Autobiography* Weidenfeld and Nicolson 1953. This includes some material on the beginning of Mosley's post-war activities.

**899** Nicholas Mosley *Beyond the Pale: Sir Oswald Mosley 1933–1980* Secker and Warburg 1983. A useful biography which traces Mosley's career from the founding of the British Union of Fascists until his death. For Mosley's earlier career see also Nicholas Mosley *Rules of the Game: Sir Oswald and Lady Cynthia Mosley 1896–1933* Secker and Warburg 1982. Most prominent in the 1930s Mosley continued to be involved in Far

Right activities in the post-war period. Robert Skidelsky *Oswald Mosley* 2nd ed, Macmillan 1981 is a good official biography which is unfortunately flawed by a number of sins of omission. Mosley's own autobiography, *My Life* Nelson 1968 is useful for his ideas, background and early life. In this he claims that his ideas remained consistent through all his changes of party in the 1920s and 1930s. The autobiography of his second wife, Diana Mosley *A Life of Contrasts: The Autobiography of Diana Mosley* Hamilton 1977 is also of some value.

## H. POLITICAL THOUGHT

### (1) General

**900** Roger Scruton *A Dictionary of Political Thought* Macmillan 1982.

**901** Rodney Barker *Political Ideas in Modern Britain* Methuen 1978. A study of the development of British political thought in the twentieth century focusing particularly on the role of important individuals.

**902** Fred Inglis *Radical Earnestness and English Social Theory 1880–1980* Robertson 1982. A study which concentrates on the contribution of individual thinkers.

**903** Anthony de Crespigny and Kenneth Minogue (eds) *Contemporary Political Philosophers* Methuen 1976. This includes useful essays on Fredrich von Hayek, Michael Oakeshott and Karl Popper. Bhikhu Parekh *Contemporary Political Thinkers* Robertson 1982 analyses the political thought of, amongst others, Isaiah Berlin, Michael Oakeshott and Karl Popper.

### (2) Treatises

**904** Karl Raimund Popper *The Open Society and Its Enemies* 2v, Routledge and Sons 1945. Volume I, *The Spell of Plato* and volume II, *The High Tide of Prophecy: Hegel, Marx and the Aftermath*, constitute an influential statement of political philosophy. For studies of Popper's thought see T E Burke *The Philosophy of Karl Popper* Manchester University Press 1983, *In Pursuit of the Truth: Essays on the Philosophy of Karl Popper on the Occasion of His 80th Birthday* Harvester 1982 and Anthony O'Hear *Karl Popper* Routledge and Kegan Paul 1980. For Popper's autobiography see [6692].

**905** Friedrich von Hayek *The Road to Serfdom* Routledge and Sons 1944. An important statement of libertarian political philosophy which has had a major influence on New Right thinking in recent years. Sir Geoffrey Howe, Sir Keith Joseph and Margaret Thatcher have all been influenced by it and many on the That-cherite Right are members of the Mont Pelerin Society which promotes Hayekian principles. A symposium on this important book organized by the Institute of Economic Affairs, one of the most influential New-Right bodies, is Norman Berry *et al Hayek's Road to Serfdom Revisited: Essays by Economists, Philosophers and Political Scientists on the Road to Serfdom After Forty Years* Institute of Economic Affairs 1984. Also important is Hayek's *The Constitution of Liberty* Routledge and Kegan Paul 1960. Routledge have now also begun to issue his collected works, the first volume of which is *The Fatal Conceit: The Errors of Socialism* Routledge 1988. An edited collection of Hayek's comments on Keynesianism is Sudha R Shenoy (ed) *A Tiger by the Tail: A 40 Years Running Commentary on Keynesianism by Hayek* Institute of Economic Affairs 1972. On Hayek's thought and significance see also Hannes H Gissurarson *Hayek's Conservative Liberalism* Garland 1987, Eamonn Butler *Hayek: His Contribution to the Political and Economic Thought of Our Time* Temple Smith 1983, Norman P Barry *Hayek's Social and Economic Philosophy* Macmillan 1979 and *Essays on Hayek* Routledge and Kegan Paul 1977. *Hayek: His Life and Thought* Institute of Economic Affairs n.d. is a video of Hayek in conversation with John O'Sullivan.

**906** Michael Oakeshott *Rationalism in Politics and Other Essays* Methuen 1962. Oakeshott was an influential conservative political philosopher. Another major work is his *On Human Conduct* Oxford University Press 1975. Paul Franco *The Political Philosophy of Michael Oakeshott* Yale University Press 1990 and W H Greenleaf *Oakeshott's Philosophical Politics* Longmans 1956 are useful studies of his thought. See also T Madood 'Oakeshott's Conceptions of Philosophy' *History of Political Thought* 1 1980 pp 315–22.

**907** Patrick Gordon Walker *Restatement of Liberty* Hutchinson 1951. A defence of collectivism and a critique of Hayekian libertarianism.

**908** Edward Hallett Carr *The New Society* Macmillan 1951.

**909** Kenneth Minogue *The Liberal Mind* Methuen 1963. A study of the nature of liberalism and liberal thought.

**910** Roger Scruton *The Meaning of Conservatism* 2nd ed, Macmillan 1984. An important statement of conservative philosophy.

## (3) Influential Commentaries

**911** Russell Kirk *The Conservative Mind* Faber 1954. A study of conservative political thought in Britain and America.

**912** H L A Hart *The Concept of Law* Clarendon 1961. An influential analysis. See also John Rawls *A Theory of Justice* Clarendon 1972. These studies of jurisprudence both had considerable influence on British political thought.

**913** Milton Friedman and Rose Friedman *Capitalism and Freedom* University of Chicago Press 1962. An influential American study. Friedman's views have had particular influence on the growth of the New-Right and the interest in monetarism and economic liberalism.

## (4) Political Thought Within the Political Parties

### (a) The Labour Party and the Left

**914** Anthony W Wright (ed) *British Socialism: Socialist Thought from the 1880s to the 1960s* Longman 1983. A good collection of documents. There is also an excellent introduction. See also Frank Bealey (ed) *The Social and Political Thought of the British Labour Party* Weidenfeld and Nicolson 1970 and Tony Benn (ed) *Writings on the Wall: A Radical and Socialist Anthology 1215–1984* Faber 1984.

**915** Geoffrey Foote *The Labour Party's Political Thought: A History* 2nd ed, Croom Helm 1986. The best study. Henry Drucker *Doctrine and Ethos in the Labour Party* Allen and Unwin 1979 claims to be an attempt to get away from the artificiality of too many academic works of this kind, yet it remains very much an academic overview. Incredibly, in view of the fact it purports to analyse the ethos of the Labour Party, it fails to discuss seriously the influence of Christianity or of Ethical Socialism on the party.

**916** Norman Dennis and A H Halsey *English Ethical Socialism: Thomas More to R H Tawney* Clarendon 1988. Ethical Socialism has been criticized in academic circles in recent years, not least by historians of the Labour Movement, as a rather nebulous creed which puts more emphasis on ends rather than means. Ethical Socialism does however at least have clear objectives and inspiring values. This is a thorough and timely study of one of the most important, but recently one of the most neglected strands of Socialist thought.

**917** Perry Anderson *Arguments within English Marxism* New Left Books 1980. A good survey of the main historiographical and philosophical controversies in modern English marxism. The views of one of the most influential of post-war British marxists are expressed in Raymond Williams 'Notes on Marxism in Britain Since 1945' *New Left Review* 100 1976 pp 81–94. See also Michael Merrill 'Raymond Williams and the Theory of English Marxism' *Radical History Review* 19 1978–9 pp 9–31.

**918** Bernard Crick 'Socialist Literature in the 1950s' *Political Quarterly* 31 1960 pp 361–73. See also Willard Wolfe 'Writings on the History of Socialism in Britain Part 2: Since 1950' *British Studies Monitor* 10 1981 pp 18–46.

**919** R H S Crossman (ed) *New Fabian Essays* Turnstile Press 1952. An influential collection of essays.

**920** Aneurin Bevan *In Place of Fear* Heinemann 1952. Views on the nature of power and the possibilities of socialists achieving their programme by a leading figure on the Left of the Labour Party.

**921** Anthony Crosland *The Future of Socialism* Cape 1956. The most important of the revisionist tracts of the 1950s. In it Crosland argued for a change of emphasis and particularly for the dropping of the commitment to nationalization that was enshrined in the party constitution. Socialism, he contended, was about equality rather than public ownership. This book was therefore of considerable influence on the debates in the party at the end of the 1950s. Revisionism in this period is examined in D E H Bryan 'The Development of Revisionist Thought Among British Labour Intellectuals and Politicians 1931–64' Oxford DPhil Thesis 1984, D Howell 'The Restatement of Socialism in the Labour Party 1947–1961' Manchester PhD Thesis 1970–1, G T Popham 'Some Revisions of Socialist Thought in the Labour Party 1951–1961' Leicester PhD Thesis 1963–4 and R J Godfrey 'Labour and Capital: The Development of Social Democratic Revisionist Theory and Policy Within the British Labour Party' Sussex MA Thesis 1976.

**922** Anthony Crosland *The Conservative Enemy: A Programme of Radical Reform for the 1960s* Cape 1962. An analysis of policies which carried on from but did not prove as influential or as important in the long term as [921]. His *Socialism Now* Cape 1974 (edited by Dick Leonard) consists of various essays on the issues raised by the Heath government's difficulties 1970–4 and on the policy problems he himself encountered in office 1964–70. On the influence of Crosland see Anthony Arblaster 'Anthony Crosland: Labour's Last "Revisionist"?' *Political Quarterly* 48 1977 pp 416–28.

**923** Roy Jenkins *The Labour Case* Penguin 1959. A statement of the party's position in advance of the 1959 general election.

**924** Harold Wilson *The Relevance of British Socialism* Weidenfeld and Nicolson 1964. Short statement of the traditions, intellectual and ethical roots and the contemporary state and objectives of Socialist thought in Britain by the then leader of the party.

**925** Perry Anderson *et al Towards Socialism* Fontana 1965. A useful collection of essays from the New Left reflecting contemporary hopes and debates.

**926** Stuart Holland *The Socialist Challenge* Quartet 1975. An important and influential Left-Wing response to the traumas of the 1970s and the problems of national decline. It marks as great a repudiation of the consensus politics of the 1950s and 1960s as the Thatcher government's espousal, inspired by Friedman and von Hayek, of free market economics, and minimal state intervention. Holland however in contrast argued for greater public ownership and expenditure, institutional and administrative reform and withdrawal from Europe.

**927** Ben Pimlott (ed) *Fabian Essays in Socialist Thought* Heinemann 1984.

**928** Austin Mitchell *The Case for Labour* Longman 1983. Statement and documents on Labour's policies and objectives at the time of the 1983 general election.

**929** Anthony W Wright *G D H Cole and Socialist Democracy* Clarendon 1979. A study of Cole's life and thought, with the emphasis on the development of his political ideas. For other material on Cole see [692]. For other influential Socialist thinkers like R H Tawney see the section on Labour Biography.

**930** Herbert Andrew Deane *The Political Ideas of Harold J Laski* Oxford University Press 1955. See also W H Greenleaf 'Laski and British Socialism' *History of Political Thought* 2 1981 pp 573–9. See also [782].

**931** David Marquand (ed) *John P Mackintosh on Parliament and Social Democracy* Longman 1982. A collection of his writings. Mackintosh was very influential on the Social Democratic wing of the party. See also [734].

**932** Rita Hinden (ed) *R H Tawney: The Radical Tradition* Penguin 1966. Collected extracts from Tawney's thought.

(b) The Conservative Party

**933** Frank O'Gorman *British Conservatism: Conservative Thought from Burke to Thatcher* Longman 1986. A well organized and introduced selection of documents on conservative political thought from the late eighteenth century to the 1980s. Philip W Buck (ed) *How Conservatives Think* Penguin 1985 is a selection of writings and speeches. John D Fair and John A Hutcheson Jr 'British Conservatism in the Twentieth Century: An Emerging Ideological Tradition' *Albion* 19 1987 pp 549–78 argues that the Conservative Party has become increasingly ideological in the course of the century in response to the rise of the Labour Party. This is a good historical survey of the development of and influences on Conservative thought. Harvey Glickman 'The Toryism of English Conservatism' *Journal of British Studies* 1 1961 pp 111–43 is a useful study of the historical, philosophical and theological roots of the Conservatism of the Macmillan era. For developments in Conservative thought in the immediate post-war era see J Enoch Powell and Angus Maude *The New Conservatism: An Anthology of Post-War Thought* Conservative Political Centre 1955.

**934**  Richard Kidston Law *Return from Utopia* Faber 1950. A very influential critique of the planned economy. It was thus an important Conservative response to the programme of the Attlee government.

**935**  Quintin MacGarel Hogg, Lord Hailsham *The Case for Conservatism* Penguin 1947. A distinguished statement of Conservative political philosophy. A reformulated and revised edition was published in 1959 as *The Conservative Case* Penguin 1959. For further examples of Hailsham's thought see [324].

**936**  Richard Kidston Law, Lord Coleraine *For Conservatives Only* Tom Stacey 1970.

**937**  Nicholas Bosanquet *After the New Right* Heinemann 1983. A good study of the origins, emergence and emphases of the New Right. The New Right is analysed in terms of its views on nationhood, the duty of the state, the political framework, economic policy, immigration and in terms of its relations with the Conservative Party in J H Dunn 'The New Right in Britain' Reading PhD Thesis 1986. New- Right emphases, influenced by Milton Friedman and Friedrich von Hayek, on free market economics, sound money and minimal state intervention were, by the 1970s, coming to be seen as a way out of Britain's economic malaise and were taken up with alacrity by Mrs Thatcher when she became leader of the Conservative Party in 1975. One of the most influential of the bodies advocating this sort of programme is the Institute of Economic Affairs. Its history and activities are examined in Ralph Harris and Arthur Seldon *Not from Benevolence ... Twenty Years of Economic Dissent* Institute of Economic Affairs 1977 and Arthur Seldon (ed) *The Emerging Consensus ... ? Essays on the Interplay Between Ideas, Interests and Circumstances in the First Twenty- Five Years of the Institute of Economic Affairs* Institute of Economic Affairs 1981. Another important New Right group is the Salisbury Group as-

sociated with the philosopher Roger Scruton and with Peterhouse College, Cambridge. A useful collection of essays from this school of thought is Maurice Cowling (ed) *Conservative Essays* Cassell 1978. See also [910]. Another collection of essays by young new Right thinkers is Arthur Seldon (ed) *The 'New Right' Enlightenment: The Spectre that Haunts the Left* Economic and Literary Books 1985. Martin Durham 'Family, Morality and the New Right' *Parliamentary Affairs* 38 1985 pp 180–91 is a comparison with the Moral Majority movement in America. A critique of the rise and nature of the New Right is Ruth Levitas (ed) *The Ideology of the New Right* Polity 1986.

**938**  Sir Keith Joseph *Reversing the Trend* Barry Rose 1975. A collection of his speeches 1974–75. In these he indicts the policies of all post-war governments, indentifying a 'rachet effect' of increasing state intervention under Labour and Conservative administrations alike which he argued had to be reversed in order to facilitate business success and economic growth. In 1974 he also set up, with Margaret Thatcher, the Centre for Policy Studies which played a major part in developing a New Right influenced programme for the Thatcher government. The need to restrict the activities and influence of the state is also reflected in William Waldegrave *The Binding of Leviathan: Conservatism and the Future* Hamilton 1978. See also Rhodes Boyson *Centre Forward: A Radical Conservative Programme* Temple Smith 1978.

**939**  Sir Ian Gilmour *Inside Right: A Study of Conservatism* Hutchinson 1977. An important critical response to the economic liberalism of the New Right and a defence of his Disraelian 'one nation' Conservatism. In it he berates economic liberalism for its 'starkness and its failure to create a sense of community'. In his *Britain Can Work* Robertson 1983 he further defends his consensual brand of Conservatism against the claims of the New Right that it has failed to reverse and indeed has been partly responsible for Britain's relative economic decline.

**940**  Samuel Brittan *A Restatement of Economic Liberalism* Macmillan 1988. A new edition, in the light of the Thatcher government, of his *Capitalism and the Permissive Society* Macmillan 1973. A discussion of market liberalism and the case for personal freedom.

**941**  Charles Moore and Simon Heffer (eds) *A Tory Seer – The Selected Journalism of T E Utley* Hamilton 1989. A well reviewed collection of the writings of one of the most influential Tory thinkers of the post-war period.

**942**  Timothy Raison *Why Conservative* Penguin 1964. A statement of Conservatism at the time of the 1964 general election. A similar statement incorporating documents, from the time of the 1983 election, is Chris Patten *The Tory Case* Longman 1983.

**943** Martin Gilbert *Churchill's Political Philosophy* Oxford University Press 1981. Churchill's penultimate major speech to the House of Commons on 1st March 1955 concluded with the hope that 'the day may dawn when fair play, love for one's fellow men, respect for justice and freedom will enable tormented generations to march forth serene and triumphant from the hideous epoch in which we have to dwell. Meanwhile never flinch, never weary, never despair.' His genuine concern for the condition of the British people as a whole, regardless of class or party affiliation, was reflected in his determination to form a broadly based government. These qualities are emphasized in this study. See also Paul Addison 'The Political Beliefs of Winston Churchill' *Transactions of the Royal Historical Society* 5th ser. 30 1980 pp 23–47.

**944** Arthur Aughey 'Mrs Thatcher's Political Philosophy' *Parliamentary Affairs* 36 1983 pp 389–98.

(c) The Liberal Party and the Alliance

**945** Robert Eccleshall *British Liberalism: Liberal Thought from the 1640s to the 1980s* Longman 1986. A useful collection of documents.

**946** David Steel *et al Partners in the Nation: A New Vision of Britain 2000* The Bodley Head 1985. Useful essays on Liberal thought and policies by various distinguished Liberal politicians and thinkers.

**947** Roger Fulford *The Liberal Case* Penguin 1959. A statement of Liberal thought and policies at the time of the 1959 general election. A similar study incorporating documents from the time of the 1983 election is Alan Beith *The Case for the Liberal Party and the Alliance* Longman 1983.

## I. ELECTORAL HISTORY

### (1) Reference Works

**948** *Electoral Statistics* Office of Population, Censuses and Surveys 1974–. A useful annual guide to election results and electoral developments.

**949** F W S Craig (ed) *British Electoral Facts 1832–1980* Parliamentary Research Services 1981. The most comprehensive guide to all types of electoral information.

**950** Michael Kinnear *The British Voter: An Atlas and Survey Since 1885* 2nd ed, Batsford 1981. The first part of this very useful electoral atlas consists of election by election maps, commentaries and tables. The second part surveys in considerable detail particular themes in electoral geography such as the distribution of mining or agricultural seats.

**951** F W S Craig (ed) *British Parliamentary Election Results 1918–1949* 2nd ed, Parliamentary Research Services 1977. A well indexed constituency by constituency listing of election results between the seat redistributions of 1918 and 1950. This is continued by F W S Craig (ed) *British Parliamentary Election Results 1950–1973* 2nd ed, 1981, F W S Craig (ed) *British Parliamentary Election Results 1974–1983* 1984 and F W S Craig (ed) *Britain Votes Four: British Parliamentary Election Results 1983–1987* 1987. See also B R Mitchell and K Boehm *British Parliamentary Election Results 1950–1964* Cambridge University Press 1966. This includes a map and a brief indication of the principal industries of each constituency as well as the election results.

**952** F W S Craig (ed) *Boundaries of Parliamentary Constituencies 1885–1972* Political Reference Publications 1972. Maps of the arrangement of seats at the various redistributions. It also gives details of the relationship between local and parliamentary electoral boundaries.

**953** F W S Craig (ed) *Chronology of British Parliamentary By-Election Results 1833–1987* Political Research Services 1987. A chronology and very informative and well indexed guide to by-election results.

**954** Robert Waller *The Almanac of British Politics* Croom Helm 1983 and 1987. This consists largely of social and economic profiles of individual constituencies drawing on the evidence of the 1981 census. See also [1052]. A similar work is Ivor Crewe and Anthony Fox *British Parliamentary Constituencies: A Statistical Compendium* Faber 1984. A J Allen *The English Voter* English Universities Press 1964 is a earlier work which analyses the electoral situation and provides a considerable amount of relevant social and economic information.

**955** A Norman Schonfield *Parliamentary Elections* 2nd ed, Stevens and Sons 1955. A textbook on electoral law. No equivalent seems to have appeared since.

### (2) General Studies

In addition to the works listed below there are also a number of important works which specifically deal with local electoral developments and which are therefore listed in the section on Local Politics.

**956** William L Miller *Electoral Dynamics in Britain Since 1918* Macmillan 1977. A rather statistical analysis of electoral change. Geoffrey Alderman *British Elections: Myth and Reality* Batsford 1978 is a useful textbook and supersedes P G J Pulzer *Political Representation and Elections in Britain* Allen and Unwin 1967. W S Livingston 'British General Elections and the Two Party System 1945–55' *Midwest Journal of Political Science* 3 1959 pp 168–88, Ian Budge 'Strategic Issues and Votes: British General Elections 1950–1979' *Comparative Political Studies* 15 1982 pp 171–96 and John Curtice and Michael Steed 'Electoral Choice and the Production of Government: The Changing Operation of the Electoral System in the United Kingdom Since 1955' *British Journal of Political Science* 12 1982 pp 249–82 are interesting articles on changing patterns of electoral support. Also of use is P W Lewis and G E Skipworth *Some Geographical and Statistical Aspects of the Distribution of Votes in Recent General Elections* Department of Geography Miscellaneous Series 32, University of Hull 1966. Ivor Crewe *et al* 'Symposium: Elections and Voting Patterns' *Contemporary Record* 2/4 1988 pp 2–17 contains valuable reflections on voting patterns, electoral geography and the Labour vote since 1959 as well as material on referenda in British politics and opinion polls.

**957** David Butler *British General Elections Since 1945* Blackwell 1989. An excellent short analysis. David Denver *Elections and Voting Behaviour in Britain* Philip Allan 1989 is a useful textbook.

**958** David Butler *The Electoral System in Britain Since 1918* 2nd ed, Clarendon 1963. There are a number of general studies of this kind which remain of considerable value for the nature and operation of the electoral system in the early post-war years. J F S Ross *Elections and Electors: Studies in Democratic Representation* Eyre and Spottiswoode 1955 is a very informative study of electoral history and the electoral system 1918–51. A H Booth *British Hustings 1924–1950* Muller 1956 concentrates more particularly on studies in each of the various general elections up until that of 1950.

**959** David Butler and Donald Stokes *Political Change in Britain: The Evolution of Electoral Choice* 2nd ed, Macmillan 1974. A revision of the 1969 book which had considerable influence, not least in popularizing the idea of class based voting patterns. It uses age cohorts and regression techniques to analyse patterns of and influences on electoral support. Both its methods and its conclusions should however, notwithstanding its fame, be treated with circumspection. A useful critique, particularly of that part of the second edition which deals with an apparent decline in class based voting in the late 1960s

and early 1970s is Paul R Abramson 'Generational Change and Continuity and British Partisan Choice' *British Journal of Political Science* 6 1976 pp 364–8. In this, focusing on the rise of the middle class Labour voter, he argues that apparent class dealignment can be explained by 'a slight modification of the class structure in which many lower grade non-manual workers are performing routine tasks often associated with manual labour'. A H Birch, R Benewick, Jay G Blumler and A Ewbank 'The Floating Voter and the Liberal View of the Representation' *Political Studies* 17 1969 pp 177–95 on the other hand point out that the whole class based model of voting may be an artefact of the research methods employed. It can also be objected that it works much better for the 1950s, when, significantly, psephology was in its infancy, than for the periods before or after. In a longer perspective the class based voting model appears neither normative nor a sufficient explanation.

**960** R R Alford *Party and Society* Murray 1964. Another useful examination of social effects on voting patterns.

**961** Hilde T Himmelweit, Patrick Humphreys and Marianne Jaeger *How Voters Decide: A Longitudinal Study of Political Attitudes and Voting Extending over Fifteen Years* 2nd ed, Open University Press 1985. A study of electoral choices which followed a particular group of voters from 1970–83.

**962** Ivor Crewe, Bo Sarlvik and James Alt 'Partisan Dealignment in Britain 1964–1974' *British Journal of Political Science* 7 1977 pp 129–90. An influential study of partisan dealignment and increasing voter apathy in the 1960s. A useful criticism of the narrow basis of their argument and their exclusion of third parties from the equation is Anthony Mughan 'Party Identification, Voting Preference and Electoral Outcomes in Britain 1964–74' *British Journal of Political Science* 9 1979 pp 115–28.

**963** Bo Sarlvik and Ivor Crewe *Decade of Dealignment: The Conservative Victory of 1979 and Electoral Trends in the 1970s* Cambridge University Press 1983. A good study which takes their analysis of electoral dealignment into the 1970s. Mark N Franklin *The Decline of Class Voting in Britain: Changes in the Basis of Electoral Choice 1964–1983* Oxford University Press 1985 argues that there has been a decline in voting by class and occupation and a commensurate rise in voting by issues. He is not however very good at explaining how or why this process should have occurred. Robert Waller 'The Decline of Class Voting in Britain?' *Parliamentary History* 6 1987 pp 326–9 suggests that one possible explanation is that the impact of television and the consumer society has increasingly made workers think as consumers rather than as producers. Richard Rose and Ian McAllister *Voters Begin to Choose: From Closed*

*Class to Open Elections in Britain* Sage 1986 certainly identify a decline in voting by occupation and a move from the high partisanship of the early post-war period to the low identification with party which has been characteristic of the more fluid politics of the 1980s. Patrick Dunleavy and Christopher Temple Husbands *British Democracy at the Crossroads: Voting and Party Composition in the 1980s* Allen and Unwin 1985, a study which focuses particularly on certain groups of voters such as women or white-collar workers, also argues that the class based voting model no longer fits. Anthony Heath, Roger Jowell and John Curtice *How Britain Votes* Pergamon 1985 however argue that it is not so much that class sentiment is weakening as that the working class is getting smaller. This is a more satisfactory analysis of the problem in that it more clearly takes regional differences into account. Ian McAllister and Anthony Mughan 'Class, Attitudes and Electoral Politics in Britain 1974–1983' *Comparative Political Studies* 20 1987 pp 47–71 also argue that the continuing importance of class should not be underestimated. See also Harold D Clarke and Marianne C Stewart 'Dealignment of Degree: Partisan Change in Britain 1945–83' *Journal of Politics* 46 1984 pp 689–718.

**964**   R J Johnston, C J Pattie and J G Allsopp *A Nation Dividing: The Electoral Map of Great Britain 1979–1987* Longman 1988. The electorate may no longer be divided on class lines. There has developed however, particularly in the 1980s, a division on territorial lines, with the Labour vote collapsing in the South and the Conservatives losing ground in the North and Scotland. In the process Labour have fallen back on their traditional strongholds whilst in some urban and inner city areas the Tory vote has greatly diminished, developments which suggest that in some ways the 1980s have seen more rather than less class based voting. This is a good study of the changing electoral geography of the 1980s and its implications. As R M Punnett 'Regional Partnership and the Legitimacy of British Governments 1868–1983' *Parliamentary Affairs* 37 1984 pp 141–59 points out the result is that the Thatcher government has a narrower basis of regional support than any other this century. The support for the Thatcher government is examined in Harold D Clarke, Marianne C Stewart and G Zuk 'Politics, Economics and Government Popularity in Britain 1979–83' *Electoral Studies* 5 1986 pp 123–41. Class voting during the period 1979–83 is analysed in David Robertson *Class and the British Electorate* Blackwell 1984. The relationship between class and regional differences in voting is explored in R J Johnston 'Class and the Geography of Voting in England – Towards Measurement and Understanding' *Transactions of the Institute of British Geographers* 10 1985 pp 245–55 and A H Taylor 'Variations in the Relationship Between Class and Voting in England 1950 to 1970' *Tijdschrift voor Economische en Sociale Geografie* 64 1973 pp 164–8.

**965**   Robert Jessop *Traditionalism, Conservatism and British Political Culture* Allen and Unwin 1974. A rather theoretical attempt to elucidate voter attitudes.

**966**   A E Green 'Changing Electoral Practices in England 1885–1984' *Journal of Historical Geography* 11 1985 pp 297–311. A study contrasting changes in Hertfordshire with those in Northumberland.

**967**   Chris Cook and John Ramsden (ed) *By-Elections in British Politics* Macmillan 1973. An excellent historical survey of by-elections since 1918, with in-depth studies of by-elections of particular importance, such as the Orpington by-election of 1962. See also S J Stray 'British Parliamentary By-Elections 1950–1982: An Empirical Investigation' Essex PhD Thesis 1986.

**968**   Anthony Mughan *Party and Participation in British Elections* Pinter 1986. One of the few works to focus on turnout in elections, particularly in the context of by-elections 1950–83. D T Denver and H T G Hands 'Marginality and Turnout in British General Elections' *British Journal of Political Science* 4 1974 pp 17–35 looks at the relationship between turnout and marginal seats in the general elections 1959–70. See also P Fletcher 'An Explanation of Variations in 'Turnout' in Local Elections' *Political Studies* 17 1969 pp 495–502.

**969**   Peter J Taylor and Graham Gudgin 'The Myth of Non-Partisan Cartography: A Study of Electoral Biases in the English Boundary Commission's Redistribution for 1955–1970' *Urban Studies* 13 1976 pp 13–26. An analysis of the effects of the drawing of electoral boundaries. They argue that Labour suffered a negative bias of 5 per cent in the 1955 redistribution. David Butler 'The Redistribution of Seats' *Public Administration* 33 1951 pp 125–47 argues that the previous redistribution, which took effect in 1950, was similarly unfavourable to Labour. See also Peter J Taylor 'Some Implications of the Spatial Organisation of Elections' *Transactions of the Institute of British Geographers* 60 1973 pp 121–36.

**970**   J A S Craik 'The Transformation of Election Campaigning Through the Media in Britain Since 1945' Cambridge PhD Thesis 1983. This focuses particularly on the 1979 general election. Kevin Swaddle 'Hi-Tech Elections: Technology and the Development of Electioneering Since 1945' *Contemporary Record* 2/1 1988 pp 32–5 usefully surveys the growing impact of television, the telephone, and computers on post-war electioneering. R J Johnston *Constituency Campaign Spending and Election Results: Analyses of Post-War Trends in the United Kingdom* Croom Helm 1987. A rather technical (and inconclusive) attempt to relate spending on an election with its outcome, focusing on general elections 1950–83. Anthony Mughan 'Electoral Change in Britain: The Campaign Reassessed' *British Journal of Political Science* 8 1978 pp 245–53 does however demonstrate that the campaign is of increasing importance with more people changing votes during its course.

**971** Vernon Bogdanor *The People and the Party System: The Referendum and Electoral Reform in British Politics* Cambridge University Press 1981. A study of constitutional debates about the value of referenda since the 1890s and of their operation in practice in the 1970s. Philip Goodhart *Referendum* Tom Stacey 1971 is a good study of attitudes towards and the actual use of referenda in Britain or the empire in the twentieth century. Another assessment is S Alderson *Yea or Nay? Referenda in the United Kingdom* Cassell 1975. Jo Grimond and Brian Neve *The Referendum* Rex Collings 1975 is an examination of the place of referenda in British political tradition and the reasons for calling the referendum of 1975.

**972** Martin Harrop and Andrew Shaw *Can Labour Win?* Unwin Hyman 1989. An excellent survey of patterns of post-war Labour voting and the social bases of voting patterns in the context of Labour's third successive electoral defeat in the 1987 general election.

**973** Brian Graetz and Ian McAllister 'Party Leaders and Election Outcomes in Britain 1974–1983' *Comparative Political Studies* 19 1987 pp 484–507. This argues that the personality and impact of the party leaders do not have a decisive effect on election results. There are a number of other studies of particular influences on electoral outcomes. Wilfrid Pickles 'Political Attitudes in the Television Age' *Political Quarterly* 30 1959 pp 54–66 is a practitioner's look at the most important of these, television. Television's impact on certain elections has been examined in considerable detail (see [1007, 1011, 1033, 1043, 1053, 1057, 1065]). J F S Ross 'Women and Parliamentary Elections' *British Journal of Sociology* 4 1953 pp 14–24, J Hills 'Candidates: The Impact of Gender' *Parliamentary Affairs* 34 1981 pp 221–8 and C R Bagley 'Does Candidates' Position on the Ballot Influence Voters' Choice? A Study of the 1959 and 1964 British General Elections' *Parliamentary Affairs* 19 1966 pp 162–74 deal with other influences on voters choice.

**974** William L Miller and Gillian Raab 'The Religious Alignment at English Elections Between 1918 and 1970' *Political Studies* 25 1977 pp 227–51. A rather statistical analysis.

**975** V H Benyon and J E Harrison *The Political Significance of the British Agricultural Vote* Report 134, University of Exeter 1962. See also Richard W Howarth 'The Political Strength of British Agriculture' *Political Studies* 17 1969 pp 458–69 and J Roland Pennock 'The Political Power of British Agriculture' *Political Studies* 7 1959 pp 291–6.

**976** Pippa Norris 'Conservative Attitudes in Recent British Elections: An Emerging Gender Gap' *Political Studies* 34 1986 pp 120–8. A study covering the years 1964–83. This notes that since 1979 the traditional slight inbalance in women's voting in favour of the Conservatives has been reversed. Beatrix Campbell *The Iron Ladies: Why do Women Vote Tory* Virago 1987 is based on a series of interviews.

**977** Mark Abrams and J O'Brien *Political Attitudes and Ageing in Britain* Age Concern 1981. A study of voting behaviour amongst the elderly.

**978** Geoffrey Alderman *The Jewish Vote in Great Britain Since 1945* Centre for the Study of Public Policy 72, University of Strathclyde 1980. A useful short study.

**979** Muhammad Anwar *Race and Politics: Ethnic Minorities in the British Political System* Tavistock 1986. This study focuses on ethnic minorities as voters, though it does also reflect on some of their difficulties as candidates. It concentrates on the 1970s and does not really differentiate the attitudes of the different minorities. Zig Layton-Henry and Donley T Studlar 'The Electoral Participation of Black and Asian Britons: Integration or Alienation?' *Parliamentary Affairs* 38 1985 pp 307–18 is a survey which covers 1960–83. M J Le Lohe *Ethnic Minority Participation in Local Elections* University of Bradford 1984 is a short review of ethnic minority participation as electors and candidates over the previous decade.

**980** John Bonham *The Middle Class Vote* Faber 1954. An analysis of middle class voting in the general elections of 1945–51. On the middle class Labour voter see [981].

**981** C Chamberlain 'The Growth of Support for the Labour Party in Britain' *British Journal of Sociology* 24 1973 pp 474–89. A general study. On specific influences on the Labour vote see Geoffrey Ingham 'Plant Size: Political Attitudes and Behaviour' *Sociological Review* 17 1969 pp 235–50, which argues that large industrial plants produce more solidaristic working class Labour voting, and Frank Bealey and Michael Dyer 'Size of Place and the Labour Vote in Britain 1918–1966' *Western Political Quarterly* 24 1971 pp 84–113. Colin S Rallings 'Two Types of Middle Class Labour Voter' *British Journal of Political Science* 5 1975 pp 107–12 seems to be the only literature specifically on the middle class Labour voter, in contrast to the considerable amount of research that has been done on the working class Tory. This is despite the comparative importance of middle class Labour voters and activists.

**982** Robert T Mackenzie and A Silver *Angels in Marble: Working Class Conservatives in Urban England* Heinemann Education 1968. The class based model of voting led to an interest in the 1960s in working class Conservatives as a group which deviated from the assumed norm. This is the best study of this large group of voters. See also Eric A Nordlinger *The Working Class Tories* Macgibbon and Kee 1967. On Conservative women see [976].

**983** For the support for the Liberal Party and the Alliance see the section on the 1983 general election [1058].

**983A** A D R Dickson 'When Rejects Re-run: A Study in Independency' *Political Quarterly* 46 1975 pp 271–9. A study of how rejected MPs fared running as Independent candidates.

**984** M Harrop, J England and Christopher Temple Husbands 'The Bases of National Front Support' *Political Studies* 28 1980 pp 271–83. See also [664]. Michael Steed 'The National Front Vote' *Parliamentary Affairs* 31 1978 pp 282–93 analyses the National Front's electoral record, especially in the Greater London Council elections.

**985** Donley T Studlar 'Policy Voting in Britain: The Coloured Immigration Vote in the 1964, 1966 and 1970 General Elections' *American Political Science Review* 72 1978 pp 46–64. There are a number of studies of the electoral impact of specific political issues. This study finds that race only made an impact as an issue in the 1970 election when the furore stirred up by Enoch Powell seems to have helped the Conservatives considerably. E G Janosik 'The Nuclear Deterrent as an Issue in British Elections 1964–1966' *Orbis* 10 1966 pp 588–604 addresses another important political issue. This is a subject which perhaps requires more attention, particularly in view of its importance in the elections of the 1980s. Finally Christopher Temple Husbands 'Government Popularity and the Unemployment Issue 1966–1983' *Sociology* 1985 pp 1–18 draws attention to to the difference between the electoral impact of high unemployment in the 1960s and the 1980s.

### (3) Studies of Individual General Elections

#### (a) 1945

**986** R B McCallum and Alison Readman *The British General Election of 1945* Oxford University Press 1947. The first of the very useful series of Nuffield studies on post-war elections. These studies, compiled as close to the event as possible and featuring in-depth analyses of the background to and course of the campaign remain valuable examples of instant history at its best.

**987** William Harrington and Peter Young *The 1945 Revolution* Davis Poynter 1978. This is a detailed study of the background changes in social life and attitudes during the war and on the campaign itself. Another useful reassessment of the election is Henry Pelling 'The 1945 General Election Reconsidered' *Historical Journal* 23 1980 pp 399–414. Trevor Burridge 'A Postscript to Potsdam: The Churchill-Laski Electoral Clash' *Journal of Contemporary History* 12 1977 pp 725–39 reconsiders the effect of Harold Laski, then Chairman of the Labour Party, on the election campaign.

**988** G D H Cole 'Why Britain Went Socialist' *Virginia Quarterly Review* 23 1947 pp 509–20. The major transformation brought about by the 1945 general election, with Churchill defeated, against all expectations and a majority Labour government for the first time, prompted a considerable number of contemporary assessments. Cole and his wife Margaret I Cole 'How Labour Came to Power' *Antioch Review* 6 1946 pp 167–78, argued that the election was the expression of natural tendencies which the Conservatives had managed to keep in check during the inter-war years. For other useful contemporary assessments see Mark Abrams 'The Labour Vote in the General Election' *Pilot Papers* 1/1 1946 pp 7–26 and W Morgan 'The British General Election of 1945' *South Atlantic Quarterly* 45 1946 pp 297–312.

**989** Gary McCulloch 'Labour, the Left and the British General Election of 1945' *Journal of British Studies* 24 1985 pp 465–89. This study emphasizes Labour's success in creating a truly national appeal and incorporating the Left-Wing dissent that had been apparent in the late 1930s and during much of the wartime electoral truce. Another useful study is Jonathan Schneer 'The Labour Left and the General Election of 1945' in J M W Bean (ed) *The Political Culture of Modern Britain: Studies in Memory of Stephen Koss* Hamilton 1987 pp 243–61.

**990** Christopher Harvie 'Labour in Scotland during the Second World War' *Historical Journal* 26 1983 pp 921–44. There are a number of studies of regional variations in Labour's success in 1945. This is an analysis of the party's relatively poor showing in Scotland. David Rolf 'Birmingham Labour and the Background to the 1945 General Election' in Anthony Wright and Richard Shackleton (eds) *Worlds of Labour: Essays in Birmingham Labour* History Department of Extra-Mural Studies, University of Birmingham 1983 pp 127–55 examines the election in Birmingham. Sarah Bussey 'The Labour Victory in Winchester in 1945' *Southern History* 8 1986 pp 144–52 seeks to explain Labour's success in capturing a traditionally Tory seat.

**991** Bentley Brinkerhoff Gilbert 'Third Parties and Voters' Decisions: The Liberals and the General Election of 1945' *Journal of British Studies* 11 1972 pp 131–41. One problem with the 1945 election is the poor performance of the Liberals. Gilbert however argues that enthusiasm for social reform at this time has been exaggerated and that the party's strategy in focusing very much on Beveridge, far from being a good move that inexplicably did not come off, was in fact mistaken. Walter L Arnstein 'The Liberals and the General Election of 1945: A Skeptical Note' *Journal of British Studies* 14 1975 pp 120–6 is a response. For a further comment from Gilbert see *Journal of British Studies* 14 1975 pp 127–8.

## (b) 1950

**992** Herbert G Nicholas *The British General Election of 1950* Macmillan 1951. The Nuffield study (for details see [986]).

**993** Peter Godfrey Richards 'General Election (1950)' *Political Quarterly* 21 1950 pp 114–21. Other contemporary assessments are C F Brand 'The British General Election of 1950' *South Atlantic Quarterly* 50 1951 pp 478–98 and T P Jenkin 'The British General Election of 1950' *Western Political Quarterly* 3 1950 pp 179–89. Opinion polls in this election are examined in Mark Abrams 'Public Opinion Polls and the British General Election' *Public Opinion Quarterly* 14 1950 pp 40–52 and S J Eldersveld 'British Polls and the 1950 General Election' *Public Opinion Quarterly* 15 1951 pp 115–32.

**994** S B Chrimes (ed) *The General Election in Glasgow: February 1950* Jackson and Son 1950. A very detailed study of the course of the election in 15 Glasgow constituencies. Mark Benney *et al How People Vote: A Study of Electoral Behaviour in Greenwich* Routledge and Kegan Paul 1956 is a similarly valuable study of the 1950 election in Greenwich.

**995** K R Cox 'Suburbia and Voting Behavior in the London Metropolitan Area' *Annals of the Association of American Geographers* 58 1968 pp 111–27. A study of voting behaviour in London suburbs in the 1950 and 1951 general elections.

## (c) 1951

**996** David Butler *The British General Election of 1951* Macmillan 1952. The Nuffield study (for details see [986]).

**997** J R Williams 'The British General Election of 1951: Candidates and Parties' *Parliamentary Affairs* 5 1952 pp 480–94. Other contemporary assessments are R B McCallum 'L'election generale dans le perspective historique' *Revue Francaise de Science Politique* 2 1952 pp 303–11, C F Brand 'The British General Election of

1951' *South Atlantic Quarterly* 52 1953 pp 29–53, T P Jenkin 'The British General Election of 1951' *Western Political Quarterly* 5 1952 pp 51–65 and M A Fitzsimmons 'The British Elections' *Review of Politics* 14 1952 pp 102–20.

**998** R S Milne and H C Mackenzie *Straight Fight: A Study of Voting Behaviour in the Constituency of Bristol North-East at the General Election of 1951* Hansard Society 1954. A good study of the course of the campaign, the electors' attitudes and voting behaviour in this constituency. Another local study is P W Campbell, David Donnison and A Potter 'Voting Behaviour in Droylsden in October 1951' *Manchester School of Economics and Social Studies* 20 1952 pp 57–65.

**999** M C Roberts and K W Rumage 'The Spatial Variations in Urban Left-Wing Voting in England and Wales in 1951' *Annals of the Association of American Geographers* 55 1965 pp 161–78.

**1000** E J Cleary and H Pollins 'Liberal Voting at the General Election of 1951' *Sociological Review* n.s. 1 1953 pp 27–41.

## (d) 1955

**1001** David Butler *The British General Election of 1955* Macmillan 1955. The Nuffield study (for details see [986]).

**1002** C F Brand 'The British General Election of 1955' *South Atlantic Quarterly* 55 1956 pp 289–312. Other contemporary assessments include A H Birch, P W Campbell and P G Lucas 'Popular Press in the British General Election of 1955' *Political Studies* 4 1956 pp 297–306 and Harry Pollitt 'The Tory Victory and Labour's Future' *Marxist Quarterly* 2 1955 pp 130–40.

**1003** R S Milne and H C Mackenzie *Marginal Seat: A Study of Voting Behaviour in the Constituency of Bristol North-East at the General Election of 1955* Hansard Society 1958. A sequel to [986]. An excellent case study of the course of the election in a marginal constituency.

## (e) 1959

**1004** David Butler and Richard Rose *The British General Election of 1959* Macmillan 1960. The Nuffield study (for details see [986]).

**1005** Mark Abrams and Richard Rose *Must Labour Lose* Penguin 1960. A famous response to Labour's third successive election defeat. This examination of Labour's electoral problems is based on a random sample of 50

constituencies. They argue that Labour's appeal to the working class is diminishing in an increasing affluent and fluid society. Economic planning meant little in a time of general prosperity and low unemployment. Gaitskell's attempts to respond to these difficulties merely divided the party. Anthony Crosland *Can Labour Win?* Fabian Society 1960 is equally gloomy.

**1006**  C F Brand 'The British General Election of 1959' *South Atlantic Quarterly* 59 1960 pp 521–42. Another contemporary assessment worth consulting is R B McCallum 'Thoughts on the General Election' *Contemporary Review* 196 1959 pp 263–9.

**1007**  Joseph Trenaman and Denis MacQuail *Television and the Political Image: A Study of the Impact of Television on the 1959 General Election* Methuen 1961. The 1959 election was the first in which television made a substantial impact. This is a useful analysis of its impact, largely based on case studies of West Leeds and Pudsey.

(f) 1964

**1008**  David Butler and Anthony King *The British General Election of 1964* Macmillan 1965. The Nuffield study (for details see [986]).

**1009**  Anthony Howard and Richard West *The Making of the Prime Minister* Cape 1965. Modelled on Theodore White's critical and commercial success with his study of the 1960 American Presidential election, *The Making of the President*, this journalistic account is quite useful for the leadership changes in both major parties that preceded the election and on the course of the campaign itself. The authors' connections make it particularly useful for the Labour Party's strategy.

**1010**  Hugh B Berrington 'The General Election of 1964' *Royal Statistical Society Journal* 128 1965 pp 17–66. Other useful contemporary assessments include C F Brand 'The British General Election of 1964' *South Atlantic Quarterly* 64 1965 pp 332–50 and B B Schaffer 'The British General Election of 1964: A Retrospect' *Australian Journal of Politics and History* 11 1965 pp 7–22.

**1011**  Jay G Blumler and Denis MacQuail *Television in Politics: Its Uses and Influence* Faber 1968. A survey of the impact of television on the 1964 election.

**1012**  R A Grant 'The Liberal Voter: A Study of Liberal Voting Behaviour in the 1964 General Election' Strathclyde MSc Thesis 1969–70. On the Liberal campaign and mini-revival in the wake of the 1962 Orpington by-election in 1964 see also J D Lees 'Aspects of Third Party Campaigning in the 1964 General Election' *Parliamentary Affairs* 19 1965–6 pp 83–90.

**1013**  Nicholas Deakin (ed) *Colour and the British Electorate: Six Case Studies* Pall Mall Press 1965. Studies of the impact of the race relations issue and of coloured voters in six selected constituencies. These were Sparkbrook, Brixton, Bradford, Southall, Smethick and Deptford. All had relatively large immigrant communities. There was particular controversy over the campaign in Smethick, it being felt that the successful Conservative candidate, Peter Griffiths, had run a racialist campaign against local immigrant communities. See also D Nandy 'Immigrants and the Election' *Labour Monthly* 46 1964 pp 449–53.

**1014**  Leon D Epstein 'The Nuclear Deterrent and the British General Election of 1964' *Journal of British Studies* 5 1965 pp 139–63. A study of the impact of this particular issue on the campaign and its treatment by all three parties. He argues that the Conservatives gained some ground by treating it as a major issue, but not enough to retain power.

**1015**  A T Holt and J E Turner *Political Parties in Action: The Battle of Baron's Court* Collier-Macmillan 1968. A study of party organizations in a London constituency during the 1964 election and their impact on the eventual result.

(g) 1966

**1016**  David Butler and Anthony King *The British General Election of 1966* Macmillan 1966. The Nuffield study (for details see [986]).

**1017**  *The Daily Telegraph Gallup Analysis of Election '66* Daily Telegraph 1966. An exhaustive statistical comparison of the 1964 and 1966 results.

**1018**  Max Beloff 'Reflections on the British General Election of 1966' *Government and Opposition* 1 1966 pp 529–45. Other contemporary assessments are Peter A Bromhead 'The General Election of 1966' *Parliamentary Affairs* 19 1965–66 pp 332–45, C F Brand 'The British General Election of 1966' *South Atlantic Quarterly* 66 1967 pp 131–47 and Ken Coates 'The British General Election' *International Socialist Journal* 3 1966 pp 196–207.

**1019**  A P Hill 'An Analysis of Voting Patterns for the Liberal Party with Initial Reference to the General Election of 1966' Southampton PhD Thesis 1978. An analysis of the social basis of Liberal support.

**1020** Nicholas Deakin *et al* 'Colour and the 1966 General Election' *Race* 8 1966 pp 17–42. A study of the race relations issue and the ethnic minorities vote in the 1966 election.

**1021** *Attitudes to European Unity and World Institutions in the 1966 General Election: A Survey of Election Addresses* Federal Trust for Education and Research 1966.

(h) 1970

**1022** David Butler and Michael Pinto-Duschinsky *The British General Election of 1970* Macmillan 1971. The Nuffield study (for details see [986]).

**1023** Andrew Alexander and Alan Watkins *The Making of the Prime Minister* Macdonald 1970. An attempt at a sequel to [1009]. It deals with the policy making and the problems of the Wilson government prior to the election reasonably enough but is rather flawed by the fact that it was clearly written with the assumption that Heath was going to be defeated. Instant history is not without its pitfalls.

**1024** C F Brand 'British General Election of 1970' *South Atlantic Quarterly* 70 1971 pp 350–64.

**1025** Richard Rose *The Polls and the 1970 Election* University of Strathclyde 1970. In 1970 the opinion polls almost uniformly, and incorrectly as it turned out predicted a Labour victory. This error prompted a number of immediate investigations. See also P Bluff 'British Opinion Polling Before the 1970 General Election' Strathclyde MSc Thesis 1970–1 and Mark Abrams 'Opinion Polls and the 1970 British General Election' *Public Opinion Quarterly* 34 1970 pp 317–24.

**1026** John B Wood (ed) *Powell and the 1970 Election* Elliot Right Way Books 1970. Studies of the impact of the concern about immigration stirred up since Enoch Powell's 1968 'Rivers of Blood' Speech on the 1970 general election. This factor seems to have helped the Conservatives to some extent. See also Nicholas Deakin and J Bourne 'Powell, the Minorities and the 1970 Election' *Political Quarterly* 41 1970 pp 399–415.

**1027** Roger Scott 'The 1970 General Election in Ulster' *Parliamentary Affairs* 1970–71 pp 16–32. A study of the first general election in Ulster since the beginning of the troubles and the stationing of troops in the province.

(i) February 1974

**1028** David Butler and Dennis Kavanagh *The British General Election of February 1974* Macmillan 1974. The Nuffield study (for details see [986]).

**1029** Howard R Penniman *Britain at the Polls: The Parliamentary Elections of 1974* American Enterprise Institute 1975. A series of essays on various aspects of the campaign and the issues in the general elections of February and October 1974.

**1030** James E Alt, Ivor Crewe and Bo Sarlvik 'Partisanship and Policy Choice: Issue Preference in the British Electorate February 1974' *British Journal of Political Science* 6 1976 pp 273–90. An attempt to examine the fit between voters' attitudes and their partisan choice. In the process they reflect upon declining partisanship.

**1031** Hugh B Berrington and Trevor Bedeman 'The February Election (1974)' *Parliamentary Affairs* 27 1974 pp 317–32.

**1032** R J Johnston 'Campaign Expenditure and the Efficiency of Advertising at the 1974 Elections in England' *Political Studies* 27 1979 pp 114–9.

**1033** Jay G Blumler *et al The Challenge of Election Broadcasting* University of Leeds Press 1978. Critical studies of the coverage of the February 1974 election. See also Trevor Pateman *Television and the February 1974 General Election* British Film Institute 1974.

**1034** William L Miller 'The Religious Alignment in England at the General Elections of 1974' *Parliamentary Affairs* 30 1977 pp 258–68.

**1035** James E Alt, Ivor Crewe and Bo Sarlvik 'Angels in Plastic: The Liberal Surge in 1974' *Political Studies* 25 1977 pp 343–68. A study of the Liberal performance in the two general elections of 1974 and particularly of the nature of the electoral support that lay behind the dramatic improvement achieved. See also P H Lemieux 'Political Issues and Liberal Support in the February 1974 British General Election' *Political Studies* 25 1977 pp 323–42.

**1036** M J Le Lohe 'The National Front and the General Elections of 1974' *New Community* 5 1976 pp 292–301. A study both of the National Front's poor electoral performance in the two general elections of this year and of the nature and quality of its candidates.

**1037** Dean Jaensch 'The Scottish Vote 1974: A Realigning Party System' *Political Studies* 24 1976 pp 306–19. A study in the light of the Scottish Nationalist Party's successes in the two 1974 elections. See also J M Bochel and D T Denver 'Political Communication: Scottish Local Newspapers and the General Election of February 1974' *Scottish Journal of Sociology* 2 1977 pp 11–30.

**1037A**  A H Taylor 'Some Recent Parliamentary Changes and the February 1974 General Election' *Cambria* 1 1974 pp 85–97. A study mainly of the Liberal revival in Wales.

(j) October 1974.

See also the section on the February 1974 general election.

**1038**  David Butler and Dennis Kavanagh *The British General Election of October 1974* Macmillan 1975. The Nuffield study (for details see [986]).

**1039**  Muhammad Anwar 'Asian Participation in the October 1974 General Election' *New Community* 4 1975 pp 376–83. This study, focusing on the Asian communities of Lancashire and Yorkshire, notes a high turnout and a strong bias towards Labour.

**1040**  John Gretton *Teachers in the British General Election of October 1974* Times Newspapers 1974. A short survey.

**1040A**  R J Johnston 'The Electoral Geography of an Election Campaign: Scotland in October 1974' *Scottish Geographical Magazine* 93 1977 pp 98–109.

(k) 1979

**1041**  David Butler and Dennis Kavanagh *The British General Election of 1979* Macmillan 1980. The Nuffield study (for details see [986]). On electioneering in this campaign see also [970].

**1042**  Howard R Penniman (ed) *Britain at the Polls 1979* American Enterprise Institute 1981. A series of useful essays on various aspects of the campaign, movements in electoral support and the issues in 1979.

**1043**  Robert M Worcester and Martin Harrop (eds) *Political Communications: The General Election of 1979* Allen and Unwin 1982. Studies of the role of the media, the pollsters and the advertising industry (most famously in the last case in the context particularly of Saatchi and Saatchi's celebrated contract to handle the Conservative Party's advertising) in the 1979 election. On the opinion polls in 1979 see also Richard Rose *Towards Normality – Public Opinion Polls in the 1979*

*Election* Centre for the Study of Public Policy 42, University of Strathclyde 1979.

**1044**  Austin Mitchell *Can Labour Win Again?* Fabian Society 1979. An assessment by a Labour MP of the reasons for the party's defeat. Ian McAllister and Anthony Mughan 'Attitudes, Issues and Labour Party Decline in England 1974–1979' *Comparative Political Studies* 18 1985 pp 37–57 argue that this defeat was not so much the result of long term decline, loss of working class voters or of the particular issues on which the 1979 campaign was fought, but simply because of a backlash against a government which had struggled with but not manifestly solved difficult economic conditions.

**1045**  Peter G Pulzer 'The British General Election of 1979: Back to the Fifties or on to the Eighties' *Parliamentary Affairs* 32 1979 pp 361–75. Another contemporary comment is Kenneth Watkins 'The British General Election of 1979 and its Aftermath' *Policy Review* 9 1979 pp 103–10.

**1046**  Muhammad Anwar *Votes and Policies: Ethnic Minorities and the General Election 1979* Commission for Racial Equality 1980. Exhaustive survey of registration, turnout, issues and party allegiances making due comparisons with the white community. Another examination of racial issues and ethnic minority participation in the 1979 election is Susan Welch and Donley T Studlar 'The Impact of Race on Political Behaviour in Britain' *British Journal of Political Science* 15 1985 pp 528–39.

**1047**  Jorgen Rasmussen 'The Electoral Costs of Being a Woman in the 1979 British General Election' *Comparative Politics* 15 1983 pp 462–75. A study of the apparent bias against female candidates.

**1048**  Jack Brand and William L Miller *The Labour Party in Scotland in 1979: Advance or Retreat?* Strathclyde Papers on Government and Politics 4, Department of Politics, University of Strathclyde 1983.

(l) 1983

**1049**  David Butler and Dennis Kavanagh *The British General Election of 1983* Macmillan 1984. The Nuffield study (for details see [986]).

**1050**  A Ranney (ed) *Britain at the Polls 1983* Duke University Press, Durham, North Carolina 1985. A series of useful essays on various aspects of the campaign, movements in electoral support and the issues in 1983.

**1051** Ian McAllister and Richard Rose *The Nation-wide Competition for Votes: The 1983 British General Election* Pinter 1984. A study which looks particularly at the regional dimension to the election and the role of regional issues such as local government, devolution and decentralization. It however notes that the electoral system exaggerates regional differences and that socio-economic factors remain the most important in determining voter choice. R J Johnston *The Geography of English Politics: The 1983 General Election* Croom Helm 1985 is a good piece of electoral geography which suggests that local factors may be more important than McAllister and Rose concede. He further explores the electoral geography of 1983 in his articles 'A Note on Housing Tenure and Voting in Britain 1983' *Housing Studies* 2 1987 pp 112–21, in which he identifies housing and housing tenure as important factors in voter behaviour, and 'Places, Campaigns and Votes' *Political Geography Quarterly* 5 1986 pp 105–17, in which he examines the relationship between the amount spent in a constituency and the voting patterns.

**1052** Robert Waller *The Atlas of British Politics* Croom Helm 1985. This maps the 1983 election results against employment profiles, housing patterns, the distribution of ethnic minorities, unemployment, car ownership, education patterns, agriculture and mining. There are also maps which compare the election results with the distribution of Welsh or Gaelic speakers in Wales and Scotland and with the geography of religion in Northern Ireland. For other similar studies see also [954].

**1053** Ivor Crewe and Martin Harrop (eds) *Political Communications: The General Election Campaign of 1983* Cambridge University Press 1986. Studies of the role of the media, the pollsters and the advertising industry in the 1983 campaign.

**1054** William L Miller 'There was no Alternative: The British General Election in 1983' *Parliamentary Affairs* 4 1983 pp 364–84. An explanation of the Conservative landslide which argues that it was not so much that the Conservatives won the election as that the Labour Party were unelectable. A different perspective on Labour's failure is provided in Ken Livingstone and Tariq Ali 'Why Labour Lost' *New Left Review* 140 1983 pp 23–39. Vernon Bogdanor 'Of Lions and Ostriches: The Meaning of Mrs Thatcher's Victory' *Encounter* 61 1983 pp 14–9 analyses the Conservative success in the context of post-war history. See also Jorgen S Rasmussen 'How Remarkable was 1983? An American Perspective on the British General Election' *Parliamentary Affairs* 36 1983 pp 371–88.

**1055** David Sanders, Hugh Ward and David Marsh 'Government Popularity and the Falklands War: A Reassessment' *British Journal of Political Science* 17 1987 pp 281–314. At the time of the 1983 election it was widely accepted that the Falklands victory had significantly boosted the Conservatives' fortunes. This article however calls this belief into question and stresses instead improving economic conditions. For responses to this argument see Helmut Norpoth 'The Falklands War and Government popularity in Britain: Rally Without Consequence or Surge Without Decline?' *Electoral Studies* 6 1987 pp 3–16 and the debates in the *Contemporary Record* 1/3 1987 pp 27–9 and 2/1 1988 pp 28–9.

**1056** Carol Thatcher *Diary of an Election: With Margaret Thatcher on the Campaign Trail* Sidgwick and Jackson 1983. A useful account of Mrs Thatcher's campaign in 1983 written by her journalist daughter. Michael Foot *Another Heart and Other Pulses: The Alternative to the Thatcher Society* Collins 1984 is a rather more analytical account of the campaign and issues of 1983 by the Labour leader. This is particularly useful in that it covers not just the actual campaign trail but the Labour Party's preparations and policy making in advance of the election.

**1057** Barrie Gunter, Michael Svenning and Mallory Wober *Television Coverage of the 1983 General Election: Audiences, Appreciation and Public Opinion* Gower 1986. An in-depth study of the television coverage of and impact on the 1983 election.

**1058** Donley T Studlar and Ian McAllister 'Protest or Service? Alliance Support and the 1983 General Election' *Political Studies* 35 1987 pp 39–60. A study of the nature and firmness of the support for the Liberal/SDP Alliance. R J Johnston 'Cracking the Mould: The Changing Geographical Pattern of Voting in England 1979–1983' *Area* 16 1984 pp 101–8 analyses the geographical distribution of the Alliance vote in 1983.

**1059** Michael Laver 'On Party Policy, Polarisation and the Breaking of Moulds: The 1983 British Party Manifestoes in Context' *Parliamentary Affairs* 37 1984 pp 33–9.

**1060** Elizabeth Vallance 'Women Candidates in the 1983 General Election' *Parliamentary Affairs* 37 1984 pp 301–9. A profile of women candidates and their performance.

**1061** Muhammad Anwar *Ethnic Minorities and the 1983 General Election: A Research Report* Commission for Racial Equality 1984. A short report on both the voting of ethnic minorities and of the role of the racial issue in the election. This seems to have had low priority. Another useful short report is M Fitzgerald *Ethnic Minorities and the 1983 General Election* Runnymede Trust 1984. This also draws attention to the performance of black candidates. Their difficulties are considered in some detail in M J Le Lohe 'Voter Discrimination

Against Asian and Black Candidates in the 1983 General Election' *New Community* 11 1983 pp 101–8. On the voting of the ethnic minorities see also Donley T Studlar 'The Ethnic Vote: Problems of Analysis and Interpretation' *New Community* 11 1983 pp 92–100.

**1062**   P E Cousins 'London Votes 1983: The General Election' *London Review of Public Administration* 16 1984 pp 2–13. A study of the election in London, the impact of local issues and the results. W Harvey Cox 'The 1983 General Election in Northern Ireland: Anatomy and Consequences' *Parliamentary Affairs* 37 1983 pp 40–58 is useful study of the election in Northern Ireland.

(m) 1987

**1063**   David Butler and Dennis Kavanagh *The British General Election of 1987* Macmillan 1988. The Nuffield study (for details see [986]).

**1064**   Eric Magee *Election '87* Longman 1988. A collection of responses, documents and statistics on the 1987 election essentially designed as teaching material.

**1065**   Ivor Crewe and Martin Harrop (eds) *Political Communications: The General Election Campaign of 1987* Cambridge University Press 1989. The third in a regular series which is now establishing itself alongside the Nuffield series. It consists of studies of the role of the media, the pollsters and the advertising industry in the 1983 campaign.

**1066**   Rodney Tyler *Campaign: The Selling of the Prime Minister* Grafton Books 1987. An account of the preparation and execution of the Conservative campaign written with the benefit of some inside information and assistance. It may be doubted however that the campaign had much impact on the result. Pippa Norris 'Four Weeks of Sound and Fury . . . The 1987 British Election Campaign' *Parliamentary Affairs* 40 1987 pp 458–67 points out the professionalism and skill of Labour's campaign certainly seemed to do little to help them.

**1067**   Eric Midwinter and Susan Tester *Polls Apart? Older Voters and the 1987 General Election* Centre for Policy on Ageing 1987. This study looks at the limited political influence of the elderly in this election, reflected in the relative unimportance of issues which closely concern them, at the treatment of these issues during the campaign and at the elderly as voters. It is based on case studies of Milton Keynes, Worthing and Greenwich.

**1068**   *Etholiad Cyffredinol 1987 yng Nghymru: The 1987 General Election in Wales* Welsh Political Archive, National Library of Wales 1988. A good survey of the campaign and results in Wales. This is intended to be the first of a series of such studies.

(4) European Elections

**1069**   F W S Craig and T T Machie (eds) *Europe Votes I* Parliamentary Research Services 1980. A listing of the results of the first direct elections to the European Parliament in 1979. F W S Craig (ed) *Europe Votes II* 1985 gives similar details for the 1984 direct elections.

**1070**   *The Times Guide to the European Parliament* Times Books 1980–. The successive editions have covered the direct elections of 1979 and 1984. These provide the results, biographies of the candidates and MEPs, information on the parliament and its structure and committees and details of the European Commissioners. A rather less comprehensive and informative guide is BBC Political Research Unit *Guide to the European Elections 1984* BBC Data Publications 1984, which largely consists of a series of profiles of the British candidates and constituencies.

**1071**   David Butler and Uwe Kitzinger *The 1975 Referendum* Macmillan 1976. Probably the best of a number of studies of the 1975 Referendum over whether or not Britain should pull out of the European Community. See also Anthony King *Britain Says Yes* American Enterprise Institute, Washington DC 1977 and Philip Goodhart *Full Hearted Consent: The Story of the Referendum Campaign and the Campaign for the Referendum* Davis-Poynter 1976.

**1072**   David Butler and David Marquand *European Elections and British Politics* Longman 1981. A good study of the British experience of the first direct elections to the European Parliament in 1979 providing in-depth analysis of the campaign and the results. Chris Cook and Mary Francis *The First European Elections: A Handbook and Guide* Macmillan 1979 is a useful guide to the background, issues and course of the 1979 elections in Britain. A case study of the election in a particular Euro-constituency is Arthur Aughey, F P Rizzuto and Philip Tether *The European Elections: A Case Study: Humberside 1979* Hull Papers in Politics 13, Politics Department, University of Hull 1979.

**1073**   David Butler and Paul Jowett *Party Strategies in Britain: A Study of the 1984 European Elections* Macmillan 1985. The most detailed study of the background, issues and events of the second direct elections in 1984. See also Derek Hearl 'The United Kingdom' in Juliet Lodge (ed) *Direct Elections to the European Parliament 1984* Macmillan 1986 pp 228–49. A study of television coverage of the elections in the UK is Michael Svenning and Barrie Gunter 'Television Coverage of the 1984

European Parliamentary Election' *Parliamentary Affairs* 39 1984 pp 165–78. Juliet Lodge 'Euro-Elections and the European Parliament: The Dilemma Over Turnout and Powers' *Parliamentary Affairs* 38 1984 pp 40–55 focuses on the low turnout and does not envisage a significant increase in support for or of the powers of the European Parliament in the near future.

## J. PRESSURE GROUPS

Pressure groups as a politically significant set of institutions have received considerable attention from political scientists. The works listed below are general studies of the various types and nature of these groups. There are also a considerable number of studies of particular pressure groups. These studies can be found elsewhere in the sections that most appropriately correspond to their specialized interests. For instance works on the British Medical Association are to be found in the section on the Health Services, whilst those on the Campaign for Nuclear Disarmament are located in the section on Peace and Disarmament Groups which is part of the section on Defence.

**1074** Peter Shipley *Directory of Pressure Groups and Representative Associations* Bowker 1979. This gives details of more than 600 British pressure groups covering social, political, economic and cultural interests.

**1075** A G Jordan and J J Richardson *Government and Pressure Groups in Britain* Clarendon 1987. A useful general guide and textbook with a good bibliography. Pressure groups do seem to have some influence on government and legislation. According to Geoffrey Alderman *Pressure Groups and Government in Great Britain* Longman 1984 they also perform valuable functions at parliamentary level and provide MPs with the information necessary to scrutinize government effectively. This short study covers a very wide range of pressure groups. Another useful general study of pressure groups relations with political parties and with governments is W N Coxall *Political Realities: Parties and Pressure Groups* 2nd ed, Longman 1986. It also includes a number of case studies. Graham Wootton *Pressure Politics in Contemporary Britain* Lexington Books, Lexington, Massachussets 1978 features interesting appendices on pressure group tactics over particular issues such as the abolition of Resale Price Maintenance in 1964. It should however be pointed out that most of the works listed here and in the various entries below are primarily interested in pressure groups as political institutions rather than in their history.

**1076** S E Finer *Anonymous Empire: A Study of the Lobby in Great Britain* Pall Mall Press 1958. A pioneering study which remains of great value, particularly on the workings of pressure groups, their relationship with the executive and their role in a parliamentary democracy. A complimentary and very informative study of pressure group lobbying is J D Stewart *British Pressure Groups: Their Role in Relation to the House of Commons* Oxford University Press 1958. Another useful study of similar vintage is Allen M Potter *Organised Groups in British National Politics* Faber 1961. R T Mackenzie (ed) 'Parties, Pressure Groups and the British Political Process' *Political Quarterly* 29/1 1958 is an entire issue devoted to articles on pressure groups.

**1077** Patrick Rivers *Politics by Pressure* Harrap 1974. This study is particularly good on pressure groups concerned with the environment and with technology. Its main purpose is to show that parliament and pressure groups of concerned individuals are no match for lavishly funded commercial and professional pressure groups.

**1078** Des Wilson *Pressure: The A to Z of Campaigning Britain* Heinemann Education 1984. A guide to lobbying and pressure group tactics by a veteran campaigner. In the process it includes lots of incidental details of campaigns that he has been personally involved in. There are also useful case histories of Shelter, a housing charity set up in the early 1960s, and Clear, the Campaign for Lead Free Air set up in 1982. Charles Miller *Lobbying Government: Understanding and Influencing the Corridors of Power* Blackwell 1987 is a more orthodox manual to the processes of government and how to try and influence them. It also provides an insight into the lobbying techniques of modern professional consultants, a fraternity of which the author is a distinguished member. Alf Dubs *Lobbying: An Insider's Guide to the Parliamentary Process* Pluto 1988 is a useful guide by a former Labour MP. He brings some autobiographical reflections to bear upon the process of parliamentary lobbying.

**1079** Richard Kimber and J J Richardson (eds) *Pressure Groups in Britain: A Reader* Dent 1974. A collection of essays and case studies on pressure group activities and on individual pressure groups. Geoffrey Alderman *et al* 'Symposium: Pressure Groups' *Contemporary Record* 2/1 1988 pp 2–15 is a useful collection of short pieces. Wyn Grant *Pressure Groups: Politics and Democracy in Britain* Philip Allan 1989 is a textbook.

**1080** Brian Frost (ed) *The Tactics of Pressure: A Critical Review of Six British Pressure Groups* Galliard 1975. Studies of pressure groups in the overseas aid lobby, Shelter, the Biafra lobby, the homosexual law reform lobby, the campaign against the third London airport, and the Disablement Income Group.

**1081** Roger King and Neill Nugent (eds) *Respectable Rebels: Middle Class Campaigns in Britain in the 1970s* Hodder and Stoughton 1979. A set of essays discussing middle class pressure groups in the context of the perceived pressures on the middle class of the time. Ratepayers' Associations, concern about public morality, and middle class attitudes to the established parties are amongst the themes touched on. John Garrard *et al* (eds) *The Middle Class in Politics* Saxon House 1978 also features essays on middle class unrest, the middle classes and the Church of England and the survival of the middle class. It also has a good bibliography. On middle class pressure groups in the 1970s see also Brian Elliott *et al* 'Bourgeois Social Movements in Britain: Repertoires and Responses' *Sociological Review* n.s. 30 1982 pp 71–96.

# 3 EXTERNAL RELATIONS

## A. GENERAL

In 1945 Britain emerged victorious from the Second World War. She retained the largest empire in the world. In just over 20 years the vast bulk of that empire had been given its independence and the four ministries which had formerly been required in order to regulate Britain's external affairs had been merged into one. The concerns of membership of the European Community have replaced the burdens of empire. Britain's power has diminished and her interests have been realigned. Because of the complexity, range and changes in Britain's external affairs during the post-war period the literature on this subject is vast. It has therefore been expedient to divide the material on external relations into that which deals with imperial and Commonwealth affairs and that which deals with foreign affairs. The latter includes the literature on Britain's membership of the European Community since 1973; a development which has entailed increasing European influence on domestic politics and policy-making. As a result the vast bulk of the relevant works appear under these various headings rather than immediately below. Most of these general works appear instead in the section on Foreign Affairs. Only subjects which could be held to be relevant both to Commonwealth and to foreign affairs, such as the decline of British power are dealt with in the general section below.

### (1) General

**1082**  David Weigall *Britain and the World 1815–1986: A Dictionary of International Relations* Batsford 1987. A comprehensive reference guide with cross-references, a chronology and annotated maps.

**1083**  Gordon Keith Tull and Peter Bulwer *Britain and the World in the 20th Century* Blandford 1966. See also Maurice Howard Bailey *Britain and World Affairs in the 20th Century* Chambers 1971.

## (2) End of World Power

In a sense all studies of British imperial and foreign policy since 1945 necessarily reflect Britain's declining world status. A number of these however focus particularly on this process and do not fit comfortably into the sections on either Imperial and Commonwealth history or on Foreign Affairs and these are therefore listed below. See also the general sections on Imperial and Foreign Affairs. The section on studies of Britain's decline in the general history section should also be consulted.

**1084**  Roy Douglas *World Crisis and British Decline* Macmillan 1986. A traditional narrative history which treats decline as the almost inevitable outcome of the economic costs of the Second World War, and the emergence of America and the Soviet Union as the world's dominant superpowers. Bernard Porter *Britain, Europe and the World 1850–1986: Delusions of Grandeur* 2nd ed, Unwin Hyman 1987 is perhaps better on contributory domestic developments but also rather too damning. It thus reveals something of the British attitude to national decline as much as its processes.

**1085**  Paul Kennedy *The Realities Behind Diplomacy: Background Influences on British External Policy 1865–1980* Allen and Unwin 1981. A good interpretative study of the pressures on foreign policy. Kennedy is also one of the few historians to point out that the economic weakness so often glibly used by diplomatic and defence historians as the source of Britain's declining status has not been properly explained nor has its relationship with loss of Great Power status. A good historiographical essay which does try to address this problem is B R Tomlinson 'The Contraction of England: National Decline and Loss of Empire' *Journal of Imperial and Commonwealth History* 11 1982 pp 58–72.

**1086**  William Jackson *Withdrawal from Empire: A Military View* Batsford 1986. A good overview of the military and strategic aspects of the decline in British power.

**1087** Nicholas Tarling *The Sun Never Sets: An Historical Essay on Britain and Its Place in the World* Oriental University Press 1986. An interesting short interpretative study of imperial decline and post-colonial adjustment.

**1088** John G Darwin 'The Fear of Falling: British Politics and Imperial Decline Since 1900' *Transactions of the Royal Historical Society* 5th series 36 1986 pp 27–43. This focuses particularly on the smoothness of the transition and loss of empire, particularly in domestic politics on which it made little impact.

**1089** David Dilks (ed) *Retreat from Power: Studies in Britain's Foreign Policy in the Twentieth Century Vol II: After 1939* Macmillan 1981. A set of essays which deal not only with foreign policy but with subjects such as nuclear weapons or the withdrawal from India.

**1090** A P Thornton 'Decolonisation' in his *For the File on Empire* Macmillan 1968 pp 349–74. More a study of Britain's post-war problems than of the process of decolonization as such.

(3) The Commonwealth in British Foreign Policy

**1091** B Vivekanandan *The Shrinking Circle: The Commonwealth in British Foreign Policy 1945–1974* Samaiya Publications, Bombay 1983. In 1945 Foreign Office planners saw Britain as being at the centre of the three circles of Europe, the Commonwealth and the North Atlantic. This examines the gradual shift in Britain's interests towards the first of these over the post-war period. In the process it provides a good general analysis of Britain's post-war external relations and attitudes to events in the Commonwealth. It also features a good bibliography. Robert F Holland 'The Imperial Factor in British Strategies from Attlee to Macmillan 1945–63' *Journal of Imperial and Commonwealth History* 12 1984 pp 165–86 shows how British decolonization and entry into Europe was part of an adjustment to a world dominated by the superpowers.

**1092** H C Allen *The Anglo-American Predicament: The British Commonwealth, the United States and European Unity* Macmillan 1960. An example of the British tendency in this period to think in terms of the three circles. A plea for closer ties to cement this relationship.

**1093** Ritchie Ovendale *The English-Speaking Alliance: Britain, the United States, the Dominions and the Cold War 1945–1951* Allen and Unwin 1985. A good study of relations with the Old Dominions and with America in the immediate aftermath of the war. It covers most of Britain's policy problems at the time, including the need to curb South Africa's expansionist tendencies. The conclusion is that a declining Britain was in this period able to persuade America to assist her to maintain superpower status. There is a good bibliography.

**1094** E J Adams 'Commonwealth Collaboration in Foreign Affairs 1939–1947: The British Perspective' Leeds PhD Thesis 1982. This examines the Commonwealth as an element in British diplomacy during and immediately after the wartime alliance.

## B. THE EMPIRE, THE COMMONWEALTH AND THE MANDATED TERRITORIES: GENERAL

(1) Reference Works

**1095** Arthur R Hewitt *Guide to Resources for Commonwealth Studies in London, Oxford and Cambridge with Bibliographical and Other Information* Athlone Press 1957. This gives details on archives, libraries, papers, official publications, theses, and bibliographies. Unfortunately it is now rather out of date. R Warwick (comp) *A Handbook of Library Holdings of Commonwealth Literature: United Kingdom and Europe* 2nd ed, British Library Lending Division 1977 is the nearest thing to an update. It is a directory of over 70 libraries with substantial Commonwealth holdings.

**1096** *Catalogue of the Colonial Office Library* 15v, G K Hall 1964. There are supplements that cover *1963–1967* 1967, *1968–1971* 2v, 1972 and *May 1971–June 1977* 4v, 1979.

**1097** *Subject Catalogue of the Royal Commonwealth Society* 7v, G K Hall 1971. The first supplement, which was published in 1977, covers additions to the library 1971–6, a list of periodical holdings and information on holdings of photographs and engravings.

**1098** Ann C Thurston and S Rayner *Commonwealth Sources in British Official Records: Colonial and Dominions Office* Commonwealth Archivists Association 1985. An unannotated and unindexed guide which does however give the classmark for documents in the Public Record Office and other national archives. Thurston is soon to publish a comprehensive guide which will act as part of the background material for the British Documents on the End of Empire Project (see [1100]).

**1099** Patricia Pugh 'The Oxford Colonial Records Project' *Journal of the Society of Archivists* 6 1978 pp 78–86. This details the major archive held at Rhodes House in Oxford. Important features of this archive include private papers of former colonial servants and an extensive oral archive of tapes and transcripts of interviews with those who have served as soldiers, businessmen or administrators in the colonial empire.

**1100** The British Documents on the End of Empire Project. The aim of this project, which is being conducted under the auspices of the Institute of Commonwealth Studies in London, is to produce edited volumes of documents covering the process of the demission of empire. It follows on from previous series which have covered the end of empire in India [1248] and Burma [1283]. The first territorial study, covering the end of empire in what was Ceylon and is now Sri Lanka, is expected to appear in 1993/4.

**1101** A N Porter and A J Stockwell *British Imperial Policy and Decolonisation 1938–64* 2v, Macmillan 1987–9. A collection of edited documents and unpublished source material organized by themes. The first volume covers 1838–51 and the second 1951–64.

**1102** Nicholas Mansergh (ed) *Documents and Speeches on British Commonwealth Affairs 1931–1952* 2v, Oxford University Press 1953. Supplemented by his *Documents and Speeches on Commonwealth Affairs 1952–1962* Oxford University Press 1963. A rather different collection of Commonwealth documents is *The Commonwealth at the Summit: Communiques of Commonwealth Heads of Government Meetings 1944–1986* Commonwealth Secretariat 1987.

**1103** J P Halstead and S Porcari *Modern European Imperialism: A Bibliography of Books and Articles 1815–1972 Vol I: General and the British Empire* G K Hall 1974. There is no good recent bibliography of the empire and Commonwealth. This therefore remains of some value as does *Reader's Guide to the Commonwealth* 2nd ed, National Book League/Commonwealth Institute 1971, a listing of some 1000 relevant monographs. See also William S Livingston (ed) *Federalism in the Commonwealth: A Bibliographical Commentary* Cassell 1963 and John E Flint *Books on the British Empire and Commonwealth: A Guide for Students* Oxford University Press 1968. A J Horne *The Commonwealth Today: A Select Bibliography on the Commonwealth and Its Constituent Parts* Library Association 1965 is a useful short bibliography on the modern Commonwealth. Harry Hannam and Patricia M Larby 'Commonwealth Studies' *British Book News* Oct 1985 pp 578–83 is the nearest thing to a recent bibliography.

**1104** Francis Carnell (comp) *The Politics of the New States: A Selected Annotated Bibliography with Special Reference to the Commonwealth* Oxford University Press 1961.

**1105** *Round Table* 1910–. In recent years this quarterly journal has regularly featured an annotated bibliography based on accessions to the Institute of Commonwealth Studies library. The *Journal of Imperial and Commonwealth History* 1972– regularly carries lists of British theses on imperial and Commonwealth subjects.

**1106** Robin W Winks (ed) *The Historiography of the British Empire – Commonwealth: Trends, Interpretations and Resources* Duke University Press, Durham, North Carolina 1966. A series of good bibliographical essays on developments in different areas and in the Commonwealth in general.

**1107** *Commonwealth National Bibliographies: An Annotated Directory* Commonwealth Secretariat 1977. An informative guide organized by country.

**1108** *Commonwealth Year Book* HMSO 1987–. Information on the Commonwealth, Commonwealth countries and on Britain's remaining dependencies. This supersedes *Year Book of the Commonwealth* 1967–86. This in turn replaced the previously separate annual publications of the Colonial and Commonwealth Relations Offices. These were firstly the *Colonial Office List* 1862–1966 (not published during the war or in 1947) which disappeared with the disappearance of the Colonial Office, and secondly the *Commonwealth Relations Office List* 1951–3 and 1955–65, which then became the *Commonwealth Relations Office Year Book* in 1966 and the *Commonwealth Office Year Book* 1967–8, at which point the Commonwealth Office was merged into the Foreign and Commonwealth Office and its yearbook merged into *Year Book of the Commonwealth*.

**1109** Chris Cook and John Paxton *Commonwealth Political Facts* Macmillan 1979. A country by country reference guide covering the twentieth century. It supplies assorted information on the political and constitutional history of each country. See also Robin Bidwell (comp) *Bidwell's Guide to Government Ministers Vol III: The British Enpire and Successor States 1900–72* Cass 1974.

**1110** *Who's Who in the Commonwealth* Melrose 1982 and 1984. Useful for some of the most prominent people in the various parts of the Commonwealth. However [108] remains the best biographical guide for Commonwealth figures. See also [107].

## (2) General

The major themes in post-war imperial and Commonwealth history are the rapid decolonization of the period and the consequent changes in the nature of the Commonwealth. Some of the works listed below encompass both of these themes. Others concentrate either on the decline of empire and the process of decolonization or on the development of the Commonwealth. Until 1947 the British Commonwealth remained a club composed of a few white members. Its membership both expanded and changed dramatically in character as former colonies gained their independence and joined. However it was not until the late 1960s that the distinction between the empire and the Commonwealth effectively disappeared. Therefore an important distinction remained between imperial and Commonwealth history until the 1960s. The flag has been lowered for the last time in a number of places since. There are indeed a few outposts where it still flies. Nevertheless the empire had largely ceased to be by the end of the 1960s. It is the history of a much enlarged and relatively inchoate Commonwealth that is the concern of the works listed below which deal with developments in the 1970s and 1980s.

**1111** Denis Judd and Peter Slinn *The Evolution of the Modern Commonwealth 1902–80* Macmillan 1982. A clear narrative history. Nicholas Mansergh *The Commonwealth Experience Vol II: From British to Multiracial Commonwealth* 2nd ed, Macmillan 1982 is a highly regarded study of these themes which is perhaps particularly good for the process of decolonization. 'Empire to Commonwealth' *Round Table* 240 1970 pp 375–617 is a special diamond jubilee edition presenting many valuable perspectives. Clement Richard Attlee *Empire into Commonwealth* Oxford University Press 1961 is a short study of the changes in the conception and structure of the empire over the previous fifty years. J D B Miller 'The Commonwealth and World Order: The Zimmern Vision and After' in Norman Hillmer and Philip Wigley (eds) *The First British Commonwealth: Essays in Honour of Nicholas Mansergh* Cass 1980 pp 159–74 analyses changing views of the nature of the Commonwealth from 1925 to the 1970s. Paul Knaplund *Britain, Commonwealth and Empire 1901–1955* Hamilton 1956 is a survey of the development of the Commonwealth and the constituent parts of the empire and Commonwealth which remains of some value. See also Don Taylor *The Years of Challenge: The Commonwealth and the British Empire 1945–1958* Hale 1959.

**1112** William David McIntyre *The Commonwealth of Nations: Origins and Impact 1869–1971* Oxford University Press 1977. A very wide ranging and good general survey with a useful bibliography.

**1113** Jack Gallagher *The Decline, Revival and Fall of the British Empire* Cambridge University Press 1982. An important collection of essays on the decline of the empire in India and Africa in the twentieth century. Jan Morris *Farewell the Trumpets: An Imperial Retreat* Faber 1978 is an excellent impressionistic study of the twilight years of the British empire in the twentieth century. Bernard Porter *The Lion's Share: A Short History of British Imperialism 1850–1983* 2nd ed, Longman 1984 surveys the process of imperial decline. A popular history of this process ending with the death of George VI in 1952 is Peter Townsend *The Last Emperor: Decline and Fall of the British Empire* Weidenfeld and Nicolson 1976. Another popular history is Colin Cross *The Fall of the British Empire 1918–1968* Hodder and

Stoughton 1968. The final section of Sir Percival Griffiths *Empire to Commonwealth* Benn 1969 examines, area by area, the demission of empire in the post-war years.

**1114** C E Carrington *The Liquidisation of the British Empire* Harrap 1961. An interesting interpretation. A P Thornton 'The Combined Assault' in his *The Imperial Idea and Its Enemies* Macmillan 1984 is an incisive interpretation of the process of decline in the 1940s and 1950s, particularly in terms of debates in parliament and Conservative attitudes.

**1115** John Strachey *The End of Empire* Gollancz 1959. Reflections on the stresses of empire, the problems caused by Suez and the fragility of the oil empire in the Middle East, the weakness of the sterling balances and so on. Rajani Palme Dutt *The Crisis of Britain and the British Empire* Lawrence and Wishart 1953 is an interesting interpretation of Britain's economic and imperial problems 1945–52.

**1116** John Darwin *Britain and Decolonisation: The Retreat from Empire in the Post-War World* Macmillan 1987. There have been a number of studies which have particularly focused on the process of decolonization. This is a major study surveying the influence of the various factors involved in the process. An interesting interpretative essay on the demission of empire is Donald Anthony Low 'Sequence in the Demission of Power' in his *Lion Rampant: Essays in the Study of British Imperialism* Cass 1973 pp 148–87. Brian Lapping *The End of Empire* Granada 1985 illustrates both the strengths and weaknesses of TV history. On the one hand it is well told and well illustrated. However it concentrates almost exclusively on the areas where the end of empire was violent and therefore made good television. These areas certainly existed but cannot be taken as representative. This book thus presents a rather distorted picture of the demission of empire. The picture of orderly withdrawal in response to Colonial Office policy that emerges in Sir Charles Jefferies *Transfer of Power: Problems of the Passage to Self-Government* Pall Mall Press 1960, an account by a former senior Colonial Office official, can also be seen as somewhat overdrawn. The liberalism of the Colonial Office, as opposed to the Colonial Service (the administrators on the ground rather than in Whitehall) and the importance of the planning of decolonization, particularly during Creech Jones' tenure of the Colonial Office 1946–50, is nevertheless borne out by John Michael Lee *Colonial Development and Good Government: A Study of Ideas Expressed by the British Official Classes in Planning Decolonisation 1939–1964* Clarendon 1967. On the impact of the Second World War on Colonial Office policy see also his [1156]. A criticism of Colonial Office policy is W P Kirkman *Unscrambling an Empire: A Critique* *of British Colonial Policy 1956–1966* Chatto and Windus 1966.

**1117** W H Morris-Jones and Georges Fischer (eds) *Decolonisation and After: The British and French Experience* Cass 1980. There are a number of comparative studies of European decolonization. This is a good set of essays by French and British scholars. Miles Kohler *Decolonisation in Britain and France: The Domestic Consequences of International Relations* Princeton University Press, Princeton, New Jersey 1984 focuses particularly on the impact of the process on domestic politics, in which there were significant differences between the two countries. See also T Smith 'A Comprehensive Study of French and British Decolonisation' *Comparative Studies in Society and History* 30 1978 pp 70–102. R F Holland *European Decolonisation 1918–1981: An Introductory Survey* Macmillan 1985 is a good study which concentrates particularly on the process in the British empire. Another comparative study is Rudolf von Albertini 'Great Britain' in his *Decolonisation: The Administration and Future of the Colonies 1919–1960* Doubleday, New York 1971 pp 33–264.

**1118** Tom Pocock *East and West of Suez: The Retreat From Empire* The Bodley Head 1986. A journalist's impressions of the end of empire in places like Suez, Cyprus, Arabia, and South East Asia.

**1119** Paul B Rich *Race and Empire in British Politics* Cambridge University Press 1985. This traces British thinking on race and racial differences from the end of the nineteenth century to 1960. This is viewed particularly in the context of attitudes to the colonial empire, colonial development and the gradual disappearance of the sense of innate superiority.

**1120** William Roger Louis 'The "Special Relationship" and British Decolonisation: American Anti-Colonialism and the Dissolution of the British Empire' *International Affairs* 61 1985 pp 395–420. He argues that the influence of the disapproval of colonialism of Britain's principal ally on the end of empire was small.

**1121** T G Fraser *Partition in Ireland, India and Palestine: Theory and Practice* Macmillan 1984. A study of partition as a form of crisis management during imperial withdrawal in Ireland in 1921 and Palestine and India in 1947. In all three cases it emerges as a flawed instrument, leaving a legacy of war and communal violence. See also William Roger Louis 'British Imperialism and the Partitions of India and Palestine' in Chris Wrigley (ed) *Warfare, Diplomacy and Politics: Essays in Honour of A J P Taylor* Hamilton 1986 pp 189–209.

**1122** David Goldsworthy *Colonial Issues in British Politics: From 'Colonial Development' to 'The Wind of Change'* Oxford University Press 1971. A good study of the impact of colonial issues on British domestic politics. See also James F Tierney 'Britain and the Commonwealth: Attitudes in Parliament and the Press in the United Kingdom Since 1951' *Political Studies* 6 1958 pp 220–33.

**1123** Hugh Tinker *Men Who Overturned Empires: Fighters, Dreamers and Schemers* Macmillan 1987. Biographical sketches of nationalists involved in the end of the British, Dutch and French empires. The relevant studies are of Mohammad Ali Jinnah, Jawaharlal Nehru, Kwame Nkrumah and Jomo Kenyatta.

**1124** *Race and Power: Studies of Leadership in Five British Dependencies* Bow Group 1956. Studies of British Guiana, the Gold Coast, Kenya, Malaya, and Northern Rhodesia.

**1125** Dan Horowitz 'The British Conservatives and the Racial Issue in the Debate on Decolonisation' *Race* 12 1970 pp 169–87.

**1126** Partha Sarathi Gupta *Imperialism and the British Labour Movement 1914–64* Macmillan 1975. A good historical study of the Labour Movement's attitude to the empire. S J Howe 'Anti- Colonialism in British Politics: The Left and the End of Empire' Oxford DPhil Thesis 1985 analyses the various anti-colonial pressure groups within the party and their critiques of empire 1939–64.

**1127** Sir Alan Burns *In Defence of Colonies* Allen and Unwin 1957. A reasoned defence of Britain's colonial record by one of the most distinguished of Britain's colonial governors. In the process he reflects on anti-colonialism in America and the emerging nations drawing on his experiences as a member of the United Nations Trusteeship Council.

**1128** Rita Hinden (ed) *Fabian Colonial Essays* Allen and Unwin 1945. A set of essays which had considerable impact on the contours of colonial policy as pursued by Creech Jones. See also Arthur Creech Jones (ed) *New Fabian Colonial Essays* Hogarth Press 1959.

**1129** S A H Haqqi *The Colonial Policy of the Labour Government 1945–1951* Muslim University, Aligarh 1961. A study based on his doctoral thesis at London in 1957–58. See also Partha Sarathi Gupta 'Imperialism and the Labour Government of 1945–51' in Jay Winter (ed) *The Working Class in Modern British History: Essays in Honour of Henry Pelling* Cambridge University Press 1983. Co-operation with the other main European colonial power, France, during and after the war is surveyed in John Kent 'Anglo-French Colonial Co-operation 1939–49' *Journal of Imperial and Commonwealth History* 17 1988 pp 55–82.

**1130** John M Mackenzie *Propaganda and Empire: The Manipulation of British Public Opinion 1880–1960* Manchester University Press 1984. A study of the various ways in which the idea of empire was projected and promoted, from the observance of Empire Day to adverts on biscuit tins.

**1131** J D B Miller *Britain and the Old Dominions* Chatto and Windus 1966. A good general history of Britain's relations with the old dominions of Canada, Australia, New Zealand and South Africa, focusing especially on issues and loosening ties 1945–65.

**1132** Nicholas Mansergh *Survey of British Commonwealth Affairs: Problems of Wartime Co-operation and Post-War Change 1939–1952* Oxford University Press 1958. A good survey of developments in the Commonwealth and in its place in world affairs in this period. This is updated by J D B Miller *Survey of Commonwealth Affairs: Problems of Expansion and Attrition 1953–1969* Oxford University Press 1974. The changes in the constitution and nature of the Commonwealth in this period are also reflected in M S Rajan *The Post-War Transformation of the Commonwealth: Reflections on the Asian–African Contribution* Asia Publishing House, Bombay 1963.

**1133** Frederick Madden and D K Fieldhouse (eds) *Oxford and the Idea of Commonwealth: Essays Presented to Sir Edgar Williams* Croom Helm 1982. Essays on the Commonwealth, Oxford's influence on imperial historiography, the university's cultural contacts with Commonwealth countries, and on Margery Perham's influence on colonial administration.

**1134** Nicholas Mansergh *The Commonwealth and the Nations: Studies in British Commonwealth Relations* Royal Institute of International Affairs 1948. A good study of the state of the Commonwealth in the immediate aftermath of the war incorporating his personal impressions of the end of British rule in India. An update is his *The Multi-Racial Commonwealth* Royal Institute of International Affairs 1955 which reports the proceedings of the fifth unofficial Commonwealth Conference in 1954 and surveys developments 1949–54. It includes a useful chronology.

**1135** James Eayrs *The Commonwealth and Suez: A Documentary Survey* Oxford University Press 1964. A useful collection of documents with commentary on the generally hostile reaction of the Commonwealth to the Suez affair in 1956. See also Jitendra Mohan 'Parliamentary Opinions on the Suez Crisis in Australia and New Zealand' *International Studies* 2 1960 pp 60–104 and A W Martin 'R G Menzies and the Suez Crisis' *Australian Historical Studies* 23 1989 pp 163–85.

**1136** Patrick Maitland *Tasks for Giants: An Expanding Commonwealth* Longmans 1957. A good study of the growth of the Commonwealth and its world role in the 1950s. Another able survey of the situation in the 1950s is J D B Miller *The Commonwealth in the World* 3rd ed, Duckworth 1965. Patrick Gordon Walker *The Commonwealth* Secker and Warburg 1962 is a study of the Commonwealth as an institution by a former Commonwealth Relations Secretary (1950–1). So is M Margaret Ball *The 'Open' Commonwealth* Duke University Press, Durham, North Carolina 1971. Sir W Ivor Jennings *The British Commonwealth of Nations* 4th ed, Hutchinson 1961 is a similar but rather dated study. See also T B Millar 'The Image of the British Commonwealth of Nations' London PhD Thesis 1959–60.

**1137** W B Hamilton, Kenneth Robinson and C D W Goodwin (eds) *A Decade of the Commonwealth 1955–1964* Duke University Press, Durham, North Carolina 1966. A useful set of essays on diplomatic, military, economic and non-governmental relations and on general developments in the Commonwealth. A useful survey of Commonwealth affairs in the 1960s is H Victor Wiseman *Britain and the Commonwealth* Allen and Unwin 1965.

**1138** Guy Arnold *Towards Peace and a Multiracial Commonwealth* Chapman and Hall 1964. This argues that Britain was clearly no longer a world power and that she should look to the Commonwealth to retain her world role. The Wilson government were however disillusioned in their attempts to use the Commonwealth in this fashion, a fact pointed out by Michael P O'Neill 'The Changing Concept of the Commonwealth with Special Reference to the Policies of the Labour Government 1964–70' Manchester PhD Thesis 1977.

**1139** Derek Ingram *The Imperfect Commonwealth* Rex Collings 1977. A survey of the stresses and strains in Commonwealth relations in the 1960s and 1970s, reaching a nadir in 1971 over the Heath government's sale of arms to South Africa. It also examines the institutional developments of this period, particularly the creation of the Commonwealth Secretariat in 1965. The strains in the Commonwealth in the 1960s are also examined in Michael P O'Neill 'Militancy and Accommodation: The Influence of the Heads of Government Meeting on the Commonwealth 1960–1969' *Millenium: Journal of International Studies* 12 1983 pp 211–32. On the Commonwealth in this period see also Andrew Walker *The Modern Commonwealth* Longman 1975.

**1140** A J R Groom and P Taylor (eds) *The Commonwealth in the 1980s* Macmillan 1984. Useful essays on attitudes and tensions in the 1980s. A good short study is Dennis Austin *The Commonwealth and Britain* Routledge and Kegan Paul 1988. See also Donald Anthony Low 'Little Britain and Large Commonwealth' *Round*

*Table* 298 1986 pp 109–21. Shridath Ramphal 'The Commonwealth Since Saskatoon' *Round Table* 301 1987 pp 7–17 looks at developments since the 1985 Saskatoon summit, especially in relations with South Africa.

**1141** Simon Winchester *Outposts* Hodder and Stoughton 1985. A guide, with useful historical reflections, to all the remaining bits of empire. It covers British Indian Ocean Territory, Tristan da Cunha, St Helena, Ascension Island, the Falklands, British Antarctic Territory, Bermuda, Gibraltar, Hong Kong, the remaining bits of British territory in the West Indies and the Pitcairn Islands. The conclusion examines the administration of these territories and criticizes the state of British nationality law.

### (3) Constitutional Development in the Empire

**1142** K C Wheare *The Constitutional Structure of the Commonwealth* Clarendon 1960. The best study of the constitutional development of the Commonwealth since the 1931 Statute of Westminster.

**1143** Trevor McDonald *The Queen and the Commonwealth* Methuen 1986. A study of the Queen's role within the Commonwealth of which she is head.

**1144** David B Swinfen *Imperial Appeal: The Debate on the Appeal to the Privy Council 1833–1986* Manchester University Press 1987. One of the last vestiges of the imperial connection is the right of appeal to the Privy Council from the higher courts of Commonwealth countries. A good history on a little considered question.

**1145** Martin Wight *British Colonial Constitutions 1947* Clarendon 1952. This is basically a documentary survey of the constitutions of the various colonies in force at the start of 1947, with a good historical discussion of the various types of constitutions and legislatures in use. The introduction notes important changes since 1947.

**1146** H Victor Wiseman 'The Colonial Executive Council: The Evolution of the Colonial Executive Council into a Responsible Cabinet – with Particular Reference to the Period 1944–1954 and to the Colonial Territories of Sierra Leone, Jamaica, Barbados, Trinidad, Nigeria, Rhodesia and Malaya' Leeds PhD Thesis 1955–6. At the same time local government was also being developed in the colonies, for much the same reasons; to encourage political development and prepare the way for self-government. The importance of this policy can be discerned from the emphasis placed upon it in the official *Journal of African Administration* 1949–61. Rita Hinden (ed) *Local Government and the Col-onies: A Report to the Fabian Colonial Bureau* Allen and Unwin 1950 is a survey of the development of local government in Jamaica, British Guiana, Mauritius, the Gold Coast, Kenya, Tanganyika, Northern Rhodesia, and the Sudan. It however does not go beyond the situation as it stood in 1946–7.

**1147** Kenneth Robinson 'Constitutional Autochthony and the Transfer of Power' in Kenneth Robinson and Frederick Madden (eds) *Essays in Imperial Government Presented to Margery Perham* Blackwell 1963 pp 249–88. A study of the constitutional aspects of the transfer of power and the process of constitution making in various newly independent countries.

### (4) Commonwealth Bodies

**1148** Margaret Doxey *The Commonwealth Secretariat and the Contemporary Commonwealth* Macmillan 1989. A study of the role of the Secretariat. Stephen Chan *The Commonwealth in World Politics: A Study of International Action 1965–1985* Lester Crook 1988 is a short study of the history of the Commonwealth Secretariat. Arnold Smith and C Sanger *Stitches in Time: The Commonwealth in World Politics* Deutsch 1981 is an account of the founding of the Commonwealth Secretariat in 1965, the election of Smith, a Canadian, as first Secretary-General and his ten year tenure of the office. So far all that has appeared on his successor, the Guyanan Sir Shridath Ramphal is his collection of speeches, *One World to Share: Selected Speeches of the Commonwealth Secretary-General 1975–1978* Hutchinson 1979.

**1149** John Chadwick *The Unofficial Commonwealth: The Story of the Commonwealth Foundation 1965–1980* Allen and Unwin 1982. This body was founded to promote links between the professions of the various countries. This is an account of its origins and achievements by its first director.

**1150** Ian Grey *The Parliamentarians: The History of the Commonwealth Parliamentary Association 1911–1985* Gower 1986. See also W H Morris-Jones 'The Commonwealth Parliamentary Association: Influence and Management in the Conduct of Commonwealth Relations' *Parliamentary Affairs* 36 1983 pp 84–95. On the development of the 'Westminster model' parliament in the Commonwealth and the various constitutional experiments followed see Sir Alan Burns (ed) *Parliament as an Export* Allen and Unwin 1966.

**1151** Trevor R Reese *The History of the Royal Commonwealth Society 1868–1968* Oxford University Press 1968. A voluntary society founded as the Royal Empire Society to promote imperial sentiments and interests the

Royal Commonwealth Society continues to seek to promote good relations within the Commonwealth.

## (5) Economic and Educational Co-operation in the Commonwealth

In addition to the works listed below there is a substantial literature on Colonial and Commonwealth development and on British economic aid to these developing countries. This has been incorporated with the rest of the material on British overseas aid and can be found in the section on Foreign Affairs. The material on the 1950 Colombo Plan, which, if in origin an exercise in regional economic co-operation between Britain and Commonwealth members in the Far East and Australasia, became a much wider scheme of regional co-operation, can also be found in this section.

**1152** Guy Arnold *Economic Co-operation in the Commonwealth* Pergamon 1967. A useful study of the patterns of Commonwealth trade and investment. It also presents a picture of the operation of the Sterling area before the devaluation of 1967 ended Sterling's role as a reserve currency.

**1153** *The Commonwealth and Europe* Economist Intelligence Unit 1960. A very informative survey of Commonwealth trade and of the likely impact of Britain's entry into Europe on what was then the largest preferential trading bloc in the world.

**1154** Hugh W Springer and Alastair Niven *The Commonwealth of Universities: The Story of the Association of Commonwealth Universities 1963–1988* Association of Commonwealth Universities 1988. A useful study which carries on from Eric Ashby *Community of Universities* Cambridge University Press 1963. This latter is an informal history of the Association of Universities of the Commonwealth 1913–63. On Britain's planting of universities in the colonies and Commonwealth see Eric Ashby *Universities, British, Indian, African* Weidenfeld and Nicolson 1966. This was an important part of the process of preparing colonies for independence. Another aspect of educational co-operation is dealt with in Terence James Johnson and Marjorie Caygill *Community in the Making: Aspects of Britain's Role in the Development of Professional Education in the Commonwealth* Institute of Commonwealth Studies, University of London 1972.

## (6) The Commonwealth Office, the Colonial Office and the Colonial Service

**1155** Joe Garner *The Commonwealth Office 1925–1968* Heinemann Education 1978. A good history of the

Office up until the merger that created the Foreign and Commonwealth Office by a former senior official. Another useful study is John Arthur Cross *Whitehall and the Commonwealth: British Departmental Organisation for Commonwealth Relations 1900–1966* Routledge and Kegan Paul 1967. See also J D B Miller 'The CRO and Commonwealth Relations' *International Studies* 2 1960–61 pp 42–59.

**1156** Sir Charles Jeffries *The Colonial Office* Allen and Unwin 1956. A survey of the organization and work of the Colonial Office. This study by a former senior official also includes useful appendices and plenty of historical detail. John Michael Lee '"Forward Thinking" and War: The Colonial Office During the 1940s' *Journal of Imperial and Commonwealth History* 6 1977 pp 64–79 is good on structure and planning.

**1157** *Journal of African Administration* HMSO 1949–61. This quarterly journal later became *Journal of Administration Overseas* 1961–80, and then *Public Administration and Development* 1980–. This was the official journal of the Colonial Office. For its impact on the preparation of colonies for self-government see Ronald E Robinson 'The Journal and the Transfer of Power 1947–51' *Journal of Administration Overseas* 13 1974 pp 255–8 and the memoir by its first editor Sir George Cartland 'Retrospect' *Journal of Administration Overseas* 13 1974 pp 269–72.

**1158** Ronald Robinson 'Sir Andrew Cohen: Proconsul of African Nationalism (1909–1968)' in Lewis H Gann and Peter Duignan (eds) *Africa's Proconsuls: European Governors on Africa* Free Press 1978 pp 353–66. This study focuses especially on Cohen's role in planning for self-government in the Colonial Office in the late 1940s.

**1159** Sir Ralph Furse *Aucuparius: Recollections of a Recruiting Officer* Oxford University Press 1962. Furse was Director of Recruitment at the Colonial Office 1931–48 and the adviser on training courses for the Colonial Service 1948–50. Robert Heussler *Yesterdays Rulers: The Making of the British Colonial Office* Oxford University Press 1963 is a study of the system of recruiting and training colonial administrators created by Furse.

**1160** Sir Charles Jeffries *Whitehall and the Colonial Office: An Administrative Memoir 1939–56* Institute of Commonwealth Studies, University of London 1972. Jeffries was a senior Colonial Office official.

**1161** Sir Charles Jeffries *Partners for Progress: Men and Women of the Colonial Service* Harrap 1949. A Colonial Office picture of the nature and objectives of the Colonial Service.

**1162** Sir Charles Jeffries *The Colonial Police* Max Parrish 1952. A description of the police in the colonies and mandated territories. See also D J Clark 'The Colonial Police and Anti- Terrorism: Bengal 1930–1936, Palestine 1937–1947 and Cyprus 1955–1959' Oxford DPhil Thesis 1978.

## (7) Colonial and Imperial Service Biographies and Memoirs

Other memoirs which relate particularly to service in a certain country can be found in the sections on the countries concerned.

**1163** I F Nicolson and Colin A Hughes 'A Provenance of Proconsuls: British Colonial Governors 1900–1960' *Journal of Imperial and Commonwealth History* 4 1976 pp 77–106. A sociology of colonial governors.

**1164** Anthony H M Kirk-Greene 'Administration and Africanisation: An Autobiographical Approach to an Evaluation' *Journal of Administration Overseas* 13 1974 pp 259–68. A useful historiographical discussion. See also his 'Reflections on a Putative History of the Colonial Administrative Service' *Journal of Administration Overseas* 14 1975 pp 39–44 and 'More Memoirs as a Source for a Service History' *Journal of Administration Overseas* 15 1976 pp 235–40.

**1165** David Rooney *Sir Charles Arden-Clarke* Collins 1982. Arden-Clarke served in Basutoland in 1942–6 and was Governor of Sarawak 1946–9 and last Governor of the Gold Coast 1949–57. Charles Arden-Clarke 'Eight Years of Transition in Ghana' *African Affairs* 57 1958 pp 29–37 reviews his years in Ghana.

**1166** Charles Douglas-Home *Evelyn Baring: The Last Proconsul* Collins 1978. A good biography of one of the most important governors of the twilight of empire. Baring was Governor of Southern Rhodesia 1942–4, High Commissioner to South Africa and for the territories of Basutoland, Bechuanaland and Swaziland 1944–51, Governor and Commander-in-Chief of Kenya during the Mau Mau emergency 1952–9 and Chairman of the Commonwealth Development Corporation 1963–72.

**1167** Sir Kenneth Blackburne *Lasting Legacy: A Story of British Colonialism* Johnson 1976. An autobiographical study. Blackburne was Governor of the Leeward Islands 1950–6 and the last Governor-in-Chief of Jamaica 1957–62.

**1168** Sir Alan Burns *Colonial Civil Servant* Allen and Unwin 1949. Burns was Governor of the Gold Coast

1941–7 and the British representative on the United Nations Trusteeship Council 1947–56.

**1169** Sir Bede Clifford *Proconsul* Evans 1964. Clifford was Governor of Trinidad and Tobago 1942–6.

**1170** Sir Hugh Foot *A Start in Freedom* Hodder and Stoughton 1964. Foot was Chief Secretary in Nigeria 1947–51, Governor-General of Jamaica 1951–7 and the last Governor of Cyprus 1957–60. In 1961–2 he was the ambassador to the United Nations and the British representative on the Trusteeship Council.

**1171** Lawrence Grafftey-Smith *Hands to Play* Routledge and Kegan Paul 1975. Memoirs of the Deputy High Commissioner in Pakistan 1947–51. He also served on the International Commission in the Sudan in 1953–6 and has useful reflections on the end of British rule there too.

**1172** Sir Alexander Grantham *Via Ports: From Hong Kong to Hong Kong* Oxford University Press 1965. Grantham was Governor of Fiji and High Commissioner of the Western Pacific 1945–7 and Governor of Hong Kong 1947–57.

**1173** Sir John Gutch *Colonial Servant* privately printed 1987. A short memoir of his service which included years in Palestine 1936–47, the Colonial Office 1947–8, Cyrenaica 1949 and British Guiana 1950–5 culminating with his period as High Comissioner of the Western Pacific 1955–60.

**1174** For Lord Harding see [2320].

**1175** Molly Huggins *Too Much to Tell* Heinemann 1967. The autobiography of the wife of Sir Jack Huggins, who was Governor of Jamaica 1943–51.

**1176** Malcolm Macdonald *People and Places: Random Reminiscences* Collins 1969. Rather unilluminating autobiographical reflections. Having been both Dominions and Colonial Secretary between 1935–40 MacDonald was High Commissioner in Canada 1941–6, Governor-General of Malaya 1946–8, Commander-General for the UK in South East Asia 1948–55, High Commissioner in India 1955–60 and Governor-General of Kenya 1963–4.

**1177** Sir Philip Mitchell *African Afterthoughts* Hutchinson 1955. Mitchell was Governor of Kenya 1944–52, at the time when the Mau Mau crisis was starting. See also R A Frost 'Sir Philip Mitchell: Governor of Kenya' *African Affairs* 78 1979 pp 535–53.

**1178** Richard Peel *Old Sinister: A Memoir of Sir Arthur Richards GCMG, First Baron Milverton of Lagos and Clifton in the City of Bristol 1885–1978* privately printed 1986. A eulogistic memoir of the Governor of Nigeria 1943–7 by Richards' former private secretary.

**1179**  Sir James Robertson *Transition in Africa: From Direct Rule to Independence: A Memoir* Christopher Hurst 1974. A senior official in the Sudan political service 1945–53 Robertson was Governor-General of Nigeria 1955–60.

**1180**  Sir Robert Stanley *King George's Keys: A Record of Experiences in the Overseas Service of the Crown* Johnson 1973. Stanley was Chief Secretary in Northern Rhodesia 1947–52 and High Commissioner for the Western Pacific 1952–5.

**1181**  For Sir Gerald Templer see [2328].

**1182**  Julian Darrell Bates *A Gust of Plumes* Hodder and Stoughton 1972. A biography of Sir Edward Twining, who was Acting Governor of St Lucia 1946, Governor of North Borneo 1946–49 and Governor of Tanganyika 1949–58. Lord Twining 'The Last Nine Years in Tanganyika' *African Affairs* 58 1959 pp 15–24 reviews his years in Tanganyika.

## C. THE EMPIRE AND COMMONWEALTH IN ASIA

### (1) General

**1183**  Mary Doreen Wainwright and Noel Matthews *A Guide to Manuscripts and Documents in the British Isles Relating to the Far East* Oxford University Press 1977. A classified well indexed guide. The locations of material are given. See also R B Smith and A J Stockwell (eds) *British Policy and the Transfer of Power in Asia: Documentary Perspectives: Papers from a Symposium at the India Office Library and Records Division of the British Library September 1985* School of Oriental and African Studies, University of London 1988.

**1184**  Centre for South Asian Studies, University of Cambridge. This research centre includes a large and important oral history archive relating to British colonial history. These include valuable reflections on British rule in South Asia. Particularly useful is the collection of interviews on India, especially with people connected with Gandhi and the Swaraj movement.

**1185**  Stephen N Hay and Margaret H Case (eds) *South East Asian History: A Bibliographical Guide* Praeger, New York 1962. A semi-annotated guide to articles, books and theses. South East Asia is here interpreted rather widely to include Burma, Ceylon, Malaya, North Borneo, and Singapore.

**1186**  F S V Donnison *British Military Administration in the Far East 1943–1946* HMSO 1956. Part of the official history of the Second World War. It includes an account of events in the aftermath of the war and the gradual restoration of civil government in areas which had been occupied by the Japanese. This also reflects on the British efforts to help restore the colonial empires of the French and Dutch in Indo-China and Indonesia as well as their own. Indian troops as well as British were involved in these occupation forces. Their role is examined in Bisheshwar Prasod (General editor) *Official History of the Indian Armed Forces in the Second World War 1939–1945: Post War Occupation Forces, Japan and South East Asia* Combined Inter-Services Historical Section, India and Pakistan, New Delhi 1958. F C Jones, Hugh Borton and B R Pearn *The Far East 1942–1946* Oxford University Press 1955 is a useful survey of events. Peter Dennis *Troubled Days of Peace: Mountbatten and the South East Asia Command 1945–46* Manchester University Press 1987 is a thorough account of the difficulties the British became embroiled in. For the diary of Mountbatten, then the Supreme Allied Commander, South East Asia, see [2285]. Hugh Tinker 'The Contraction of Empire in Asia 1945–48: The Military Dimension' *Journal of Imperial and Commonwealth History* 16 1988 pp 218–33 is a useful survey of the military difficulties posed by over commitment immediately after the war.

### (2) The Indian Sub-Continent

#### (a) General

**1187**  Mary Doreen Wainwright, J Iltis and Donald Anthony Low *Government Archives in South Asia: A Guide to National and State Archives in Ceylon, India and Pakistan* Cambridge University Press 1969. A classified well indexed guide. The locations of material are given. See also M Thatcher (ed) *Cambridge South Asian Archive: Records of the British Period in South Asia Relating to India, Pakistan, Ceylon, Burma, Nepal and Afghanistan held in the Centre of South Asian Studies, University of Cambridge* Mansell 1973.

**1188**  S P Aiyar *The Commonwealth in South Asia* Lalvani, Bombay 1969. A study of the continuing Commonwealth ties in India, Pakistan and Ceylon (Sri Lanka). See also Nicholas Mansergh 'The Commonwealth in Asia' *Pacific Affairs* 3 1950 pp 3–21 and Sir W Ivor Jennings 'Crown and Commonwealth in Asia' *International Affairs* 32 1950 pp 137–47.

## (b) The Indian Empire

### (i) General

**1189** Joan C Lancaster *A Guide to Lists and Catalogues of the India Office Records* Commonwealth Relations Office 1966. A brief guide to the records going up to the independence and partition of British India in 1947. Another useful guide to relevant documents is John Sims (comp) *A List and Index of Parliamentary Papers Relating to India 1908–47* India Office Library and Records 1981.

**1190** A K J Singh (comp) *Gandhi and Civil Disobedience: Documents in the India Office Records 1922–46* India Office Library and Records 1980.

**1191** Patrick Wilson (ed) *Government and Politics of India and Pakistan 1885–1955: A Bibliography of Works in Western Languages* Institute of East Asian Studies, University of California, Berkeley, California 1956. A mostly unannotated bibliography of over 5000 entries classified and arranged chronologically. The vast bulk of the entries are books and pamphlets, not articles or official publications. Also of some use is the relevant volume in the Clio world bibliographical series Brijan K Gupta and Datta S Khorbas (eds) *India* Clio Press 1984.

**1192** C H Philips, H L Singh and B N Pandey *The Evolution of India and Pakistan 1858 to 1947: Select Documents* Oxford University Press 1962. See also K P Bhagat *A Decade of Indo-British Relations 1937–1947* Popular Book Depot, Bombay 1959, a selection of documents on the final decade of British rule in India.

**1193** S N Sadhu *Who Was Who in India 1901–1970* Vivek Publishing House, Bombay 1971.

**1194** Sumit Sarkar *Modern India 1885–1947* Macmillan 1988. An excellent synthesizing history of India from the founding of the Congress party to the attainment of independence. B N Pandey *The Break-Up of British India* Macmillan 1969 is a good overview of developments 1900–47. Christopher Baker, Gordon Johnson and Anil Seal (eds) 'Power, Profit and Politics: Essays in Imperialism, Nationalism and Change in Twentieth Century India' *Modern Asian Studies* 15 1981 pp 355–721 is a whole issue devoted to essays on twentieth century Indian history. It also charts the decline of British power in the Indian ocean.

**1195** L P Mathur *History of the Andamar and Nicobar Islands 1756–1966* Sterling, New Delhi 1968. This history concentrates on the period of British colonial administration 1858–1947. They became part of independent India in 1947.

**1196** Nirad C Chaudhuri *Thy Hand Great Anarch: India 1921–1952* Chatto and Windus 1987. An excellent memoir of India in this period. Durga Das *India: from Curzon to Nehru and After* Collins 1969 is a political history/memoir by a leading Indian journalist covering from 1900 to the 1960s.

**1196A** Trevor Royle *The Last Days of the Raj* Michael Joseph 1989. A good social history of the end of empire in India.

**1197** Brian R Tomlinson *The Political Economy of the Raj 1914–1947: The Economics of Decolonisation* Macmillan 1979. A study which emphasizes the economic rather than the political aspects of the progress towards independence.

**1198** Charles Allen and Michael Moon (eds) *Plain Tales of the Raj: Images of British India in the Twentieth Century* Deutsch 1975. An evocative portrait of the last years of the British Raj, using illustrations and oral evidence. See also Charles Allen *Raj: A Scrapbook of British India 1877–1947* Penguin 1979.

**1199** Bakhshish S Nijjar *Panjab Under the British Rule 1849–1947 Vol III: 1932–1947* K B Publications, New Delhi 1974. This is useful for the planning and effects of the partition in the Punjab and for the reaction of the Sikhs, whose opinion does not seem to have been widely considered, to the whole process.

**1200** Michael Edwardes *The Myth of the Mahatma: Gandhi, the British and the Raj* Constable 1986. A challenge to those who argue the immorality of British rule in India and the sanctity of Gandhi.

**1201** Sir Maurice Gwyer and A Appadorai (eds) *Speeches and Documents on the Indian Constitution 1925–47* 2v, Oxford University Press 1957. These trace the debates over and the process of constitutional development leading up to partition and independence. See also Anil Chandra Banerjee *The Making of the Indian Constitution 1930–47: Vol I: Documents* A Mukharjee, Calcutta 1948.

**1202** Shreegovind Mishra *Constitutional Development and National Movement in India 1919–1947* Janaki Prakashan, Patna 1978. On a particular aspect of constitutional development see M D Rashiduzzaman 'The Central Legislature in British India 1921–47' Durham PhD Thesis 1964–5.

**1203** Hugh R Tinker *Separate and Unequal: India and Indians in the British Commonwealth 1920–1950* Christopher Hurst 1976. A study of the problems of India's position in the Commonwealth and its relationship with other Commonwealth countries. In the end India was to have a major impact on the Commonwealth. India became a republic in 1950. Its subsequent adherence to the Commonwealth set the scene for the major transformation of the Commonwealth in the post-war years from being a small group of white nations owing allegiance to the Crown to the large multi-racial mixture of republics and monarchies of the 1980s. See also J L Kember 'India in the British Commonwealth: The Problem of Diplomatic Representation 1917–47' London PhD Thesis 1976.

**1204** Norman Gerald Barrier *Banned: Controversial Literature and Political Control in British India 1907–1947* Missouri University Press, Columbia, Missouri 1974. A useful study of political censorship and control by the British authorities.

**1205** H A Ewing 'The Indian Civil Service 1919–47' Cambridge PhD Thesis 1980.

**1206** Roland Hunt and John Harrison *The District Officer in India 1930–1947* Scolar Press 1980. A good survey of the work of the district officers making good use of reminiscences. It also covers Burma.

**1207** Mary Ann Lind *The Compassionate Memsahibs: Welfare Activities of British Women in India 1900–1947* Greenwood 1988.

*(ii) Biographies and Memoirs of British Officials and Others*

**1208** John Connell *Auchinleck: A Biography* Cassell 1959. Auchinleck was the Commander-in-Chief in India 1943–7 and a member of the Viceroy's executive council. As such he had an important role in the supervision of the partition.

**1209** Neil B Bonarjee *Under Two Masters* Oxford University Press 1970. A very revealing autobiography. Bonarjee served in the Indian Civil Service both under the Raj and in independent India.

**1210** R C B Bristow *Memories of the British Raj: A Soldier in India* Johnson 1974. This memoir is particularly useful for his reminiscences of his military service in the Punjab in 1947 during the partition of this area between India and Pakistan.

**1211** Alan Campbell-Johnson *Mission with Mountbatten* 2nd ed, Hale 1972. Campbell-Johnson was Mountbatten's Press Attache during his time as Viceroy in 1947 and as first Governor-General of independent India in 1947–8. This account, first published in 1951, records his view of the events of this time. K S Hasan 'Campbell-Johnson's "Mission with Mountbatten"' *Pakistan*

*Horizon* 5 1952 pp 96–109 is a Pakistani critique of what were seen as distortions in his account.

**1212** Richard G Casey *An Australian in India* Hollis and Carter 1947. A record of Casey's period as Governor of Bengal 1944–6. There is some additional information in his *Personal Experience 1939–1946* Constable 1962.

**1213** Sir Conrad Corfield *The Princely India I Knew: From Reading to Mountbatten* Indo-British Historical Society, Madras 1975. Corfield served in India 1921–47. He was the last head of the Indian Political Service. This oversaw the administration of the Indian principalities, which accounted for roughly a third of the total area of India.

**1214** Norval Mitchell *Sir George Cunningham: A Memoir* Blackwood 1968. Cunningham was Governor of the North West Frontier Province 1937–46.

**1215** Patrick Beesley *Very Special Admiral: The Life of Admiral J H Godfrey* C B Hamilton 1980. Godfrey was the Flag Officer commanding the Royal Indian Navy 1943–6. This biography is perhaps most useful for his account of Godfrey's handling of the Royal Indian Navy mutiny of 1946.

**1216** For Lord Ismay, Mountbatten's Chief of Staff Mar–Nov 1947 see [2321].

**1217** For Earl Mountbatten of Burma see [1256 and 2285].

**1218** Sir Stanley Reed *The India I Knew 1897–1947* Odhams 1952. An autobiography by an Indiaphil who edited the *Times of India* 1907–23. It contains a number of reflections on the end of the Indian empire. Reed was a Conservative MP 1938–50.

**1219** Humphrey Trevelyan *The India We Left: Charles Trevelyan 1826–65, Humphrey Trevelyan 1929–47* Macmillan 1972. The second part of this book describes his life as one of the last generation of British officials in India. It presents a good portrait of the last days of the Raj. Trevelyan also had a close association with Nehru, whom he helped to set up the Indian Foreign Service.

**1220** Sir Francis Tuker *While Memory Serves* Cassell 1950. Reminiscences of the last two years of British India. Tuker was GOC Eastern Command, India 1946–7 and thus involved in the military aspects of the transfer of power and the partition.

**1220A** David Walker *Lean, Wind Lean: A Few Times Remembered* Collins 1984. This autobiography is most useful for his reminiscences of the end of British India and his observations of Wavell.

**1221** Sir Penderel Moon (ed) *Wavell: The Viceroy's Journal* Oxford University Press 1973. Wavell was Viceroy of India 1943–7. His period and record as Viceroy is surveyed in a useful epilogue. See also Bernard Fergusson *Wavell: Portrait of a Soldier* Collins 1961.


*(iii) Nationalist Movements*


The Congress Party and Indian Nationalism


**1222** Jagdish Saran Sharma *India's Struggle for Freedom: Select Documents and Sources* 3v, Chand, Delhi 1965. A good guide to documents and sources. B N Pandey (ed) *The Indian Nationalist Movement 1885–1947: Selected Documents* Macmillan 1979 focuses particularly on the nationalist elite in the period 1920–47.


**1223** Jagdish Saran Sharma *Indian National Congress: A Descriptive Bibliography of India's Struggle for Freedom* 2nd ed, Chand, Delhi 1971. An annotated bibliography. It also includes a chronology. Another bibliography of the Congress party is S P Das *Fifty Years of Indian Congress History: A Micro-Index Vol I: 1935–47* S S Publishers, Delhi 1986.


**1224** Tara Chaud *History of the Freedom Movement in India Vol 4* Publications Division, Ministry of Information and Broadcasting, Government of India, New Delhi 1972. This official history commissioned by the Indian government covers the period 1924–47. R C Mujumbar *History of the Freedom Movement in India Vol III* Firma K L Mukhopadhyay, Calcutta 1963 is an unofficial history covering 1919–47.


**1225** B N Pandey (ed) *Concise History of the Indian National Congress 1885–1947* Vikas, New Delhi 1985. Essays surveying the history of Congress from its foundation to the attainment of independence. Another useful collection of essays is Donald Anthony Low (ed) *Congress and the Raj: Facets of the Indian Struggle 1917–1947* Heinemann 1977. See also R C Gupta *Indian Freedom Movement and Thought: Nehru and the Politics of 'Right' Versus 'Left' (1930–1947)* Sterling, New Delhi 1983, a study of Congress politics and especially of the development of Nehru's political thought in the years preceding independence.


**1226** Shashi Bairathi *Communism and Nationalism in India: A Study in Inter-Relationship 1919–1947* Aramika Prakashar, New Delhi 1987. A study of the relationship of the Indian Communist Party to the Nationalist movement. For the contribution to the nationalist movement of another party see Kishan C Mahendru *Congress and the Freedom Struggle: Gandhi and the Congress*

*Socialist Party 1934–48: An Analysis of Their Interaction* A B S Publications, Janandhar City 1986.


Muslim Nationalism


**1227** A M Zaidi (ed) *Evolution of Muslim Political Thought in India Vol Six: Freedom at Last* Chand, New Delhi 1975–9. This collects documents, speeches and proceedings of the All-India Muslim League and other important sources 1943–7. Gulam A Allana *Pakistan Movement: Historic Documents* 2nd ed, Paradise Subscription Agency, Karachi 1968. A useful collection of documents covering the years 1900–47. See also Syed Sharifuddin Pirzada (ed) *Foundations of Pakistan: All-India Muslim League Documents 1906–1947 Vol II: 1924–1947* National Publishing House, Karachi 1970. Latif Ahmed Sherwani (ed) *Pakistan Resolution to Pakistan 1940–1947* National Publishing House, Karachi 1960 includes a number of useful documents that do not appear in the other collections. See also K S Hasan (ed) *Documents on the Foreign Relations of Pakistan: The Transfer of Power* Pakistan Institute of International Affairs, Karachi 1966, which covers the years 1940–8.


**1228** K K Aziz *The Historical Background of Pakistan 1857–1947: An Annotated Digest of Source Material* Pakistan Institute of International Affairs, Karachi 1970. A detailed guide that is far more than a bibliography, for it also lists documents, writings, speeches and miscellaneous sources. Periodical literature is listed by year up until 1964.


**1229** K K Aziz *Britain and Muslim India* Longmans 1963. An analysis of British public opinion on the origin, rise and growth of Muslim nationalism 1858–1947. In this he complains that Britain was indifferent to Muslim problems, ignorant of their wishes and heedless and finally hostile to their demands for partition. Indian historians like Y B Mathur *Growth of Muslim Politics in India* Pragati Publications, Delhi 1979 in contrast indict the British for playing a game of divide and rule and thus frustrating Indian aspirations for a united India. As the background to the tense and often bloody relations between India and Pakistan the partition remains an emotive issue and the literature on the subject continues to be littered with mutual recriminations reflecting different national perspectives. See also Ram Gopal *Indian Muslims: A Political History (1898–1947)* Asia Publishing House, Bombay 1959.


**1230** Moin Shakir *Khilafat to Partition: A Survey of Major Political Trends Among Indian Muslims During 1919–1947* Kalamkar Prakashan, New Delhi 1970. A study of the development of religious and political thought that is of some value.


**1231** Ayesha Jalal *The Sole Spokesman: Jinnah, the Muslim League and the Demand for Pakistan* Cambridge University Press 1985. A good study of the politics of the Muslim League, the demand for partition and the creation of Pakistan. See also Ishtiaq Husain Qureshi *The Struggle for Pakistan* 2nd ed, University of Karachi, Karachi 1969 and Bahadur Lal *The Muslim League: Its History, Activities and Achievements* Agra Book Store, Agra 1954.

**1232**  I A Talbot 'The Growth of the Muslim League in the Punjab 1937–1946' *Journal of Commonwealth and Comparative Politics* 20 1982 pp 5–25. This, Shila Sen *Muslim Politics in Bengal 1937–1947* Imprex India, New Delhi 1976 and Partha Chatterjee 'Bengal Politics and the Muslim Masses 1920–1947' *Journal of Commonwealth and Comparative Politics* 20 1982 pp 25–41 deal with the growth of Muslim nationalism in the two areas affected by the partition.

Other

**1233**  Erland Jansson *India, Pakistan or Pakhtunistan? The Nationalist Movements in the North-West Frontier Province 1937–47* Almqvist and Wiksell, Stockholm 1981. A study of nationalist movements and the underlying social divisions in this region of India. The Pakhtuns (Pathans), wanted independence and opposed the Muslim League and its goal of Pakistan.

*(iv) Nationalist Biographies and Memoirs*

Congress

**1234**  Maulana Abul Kalam Azad *India Wins Freedom: An Autobiographical Narrative Orient* Longmans, Bombay 1959. A disappointing autobiography by a Muslim who was among the most important of the Congress leaders.

**1235**  Alan Ross *The Emissary: G D Birla, Gandhi and Independence* Collins Harvill 1986. Birla played an important part, as an emissary of Gandhi, in the negotiations that led to independence.

**1236**  D G Tendulkar *Mahatma: Life of Mohandas Karamchand Gandhi* 8v, Vithalbhal K Jhaveri and D G Tendulkar, Bombay 1951–64. The final two volumes cover 1945–8. Pyarelal *Mahatma Gandhi: The Last Phase* 2v, Navajivan Publishing House, Ahmedabad 1956–8 is a useful account by the Mahatma's private secretary. B R Nanda *Mahatma Gandhi* Allen and Unwin 1965 is a good one volume biography. So is Judith M Brown *Gandhi: Prisoner of Hope* Yale University Press 1989. Louis Fischer *Life of Mahatma Gandhi* Cape 1951 remains of value. See also Geoffrey Ashe *Gandhi: A Study in Revolution* Heinemann 1968. William L Shirer *Gandhi: A Memoir* Abacus 1981 is an

insightful study by one who had known and revered him as a young American journalist. Nirmal Kumar Bose *My Days with Gandhi* Nishana, Calcutta 1953 is a useful account of 1946–8 by a close associate from those years. Jagdish Saran Sharma *Mahatma Gandhi: A Descriptive Bibliography* Chand, Delhi 1955 is an extensive annotated guide to writings about and by Gandhi. Pyarelal (ed) *Mahatma Gandhi: Correspondence with the Government 1944–47* Navajivan Publishing House, Ahmedabad 1959 collects Gandhi's correspondence with figures such as Wavell, Mountbatten, Pethick-Lawrence, Cripps, Attlee and Jinnah. See also *The Collected Works of Mahatma Gandhi* 90v, Publications Division, Ministry of Information and Broadcasting, Government of India, New Delhi 1958–84.

**1237**  Sudhir Ghosh *Gandhi's Emissary* Cresset Press 1967. These memoirs are most useful for his time as Gandhi's emissary in London to the British government 1945–7.

**1238**  D G Tendulkar *Abdul Ghaffar Khan: Faith is a Battle* Popular Prakashan, Bombay 1967. This reflects on the transfer of power and partition from the point of view of the Khans of Peshawar, North West Province. Its subject was a close associate of Gandhi and an opponent of partition.

**1239**  J B Kripolani *Fateful Year: Being the Speeches and Writings During the Year of Presidentship of Congress* Vora and Co, Bombay 1948. A collection of Kripolani's speeches made during his year as President of Congress in 1947.

**1240**  Sarvepalli Gopal *Jawaharlal Nehru: A Biography* 3v, Cape 1975–84. The official biography. The first volume covers Nehru's life up until independence. The others deal with Nehru as Prime Minister of independent India 1947–64. B N Pandey *Nehru* Macmillan 1976 is the best one volume biography. See also Michael Bracher *Nehru: A Political Biography* Oxford University Press 1959 and Frank Moraes *Jawaharlal Nehru: A Biography* Macmillan 1956. Michael Edwardes *Nehru: A Political Biography* Allen Lane 1971 is a good critical biography, which draws more attention than most of his biographers to Nehru's failings and mistakes. The latest biography, M J Akbar *Nehru* Viking 1988 is in contrast heavily eulogistic. Richard Austen Butler *Jawaharlal Nehru – the Struggle for Independence* Cambridge University Press 1966 is a useful tribute by the Conservative statesman. Nehru's role in the independence movement and his relationship with Gandhi is analysed, especially in the context of his political views, in V T Patil *Nehru and the Freedom Movement* Sterling, New Delhi 1977. Jagdish Saran Sharma *Jawaharlal Nehru: A Descriptive Bibliography* Chand, Delhi 1955 is an annotated guide to writings by and about Nehru. Sarvepalli Gopal (ed) *Selected Works of Jawaharlal Nehru* Jawaharlal Nehru Memorial Fund, New Delhi 1972– contains a number of useful documents. Dorothy Norman (ed) *Nehru: The First Sixty Years Vol 2* The Bodley Head 1965 uses significant passages from Nehru's writings, speeches and interviews to cover the years 1939–50. A collection of speeches is J S Bright (ed) *Jawaharlal Nehru Before and After Independence: A Collection of the Most Important and Soul-Stirring Speeches Delivered During the Most Important and Soul-Stirring Years in Indian History 1922–50* Indian Printing Works, New Delhi 1950.

**1241** D V Tahmankar *Sardar Patel* Allen and Unwin 1970. Another important Congress figure. See also K L Panjabi *The Indomitable Sardar* Bhartiya Vidya Bhavan, Delhi 1962. Some of his correspondence, collected in Durga Das (ed) *Sardar Patel's Correspondence 1945–50* 10v, Navajivan Publishing House, New Delhi 1972–4, is also of considerable value.

**1242** A R H Copley *The Political Career of C Rajagopalachari 1937–54: A Moralist in Politics* Macmillan India, Delhi 1978.

Muslim

**1243** Chaudhri Muhammad Ali *The Emergence of Pakistan* Columbia University Press, New York 1967. His memoirs. He was very close to the Muslim League leaders but not to Mountbatten and is inaccurate in a few places.

**1244** Anis Khurshid (ed) *Quaid-i-Azam Mohammad Ali Jinnah: An Annotated Bibliography* 2v, Quaid-i-Azam Academy, Karachi 1978–9. An exhaustive guide to material on the life of Jinnah, the leader of the Muslim League and first Governor-General of Pakistan. The first volume covers material in western languages, and the second material in eastern languages. Probably the best general biography of Jinnah is Stanley Wolpert *Jinnah of Pakistan* Oxford University Press 1984. Others include Ahmed Saeed *The Green Titan: A Study of Quaid-i-Azam Mohammad Ali Jinnah* Sang-e-Meel, Lahore 1976, S M M Qureshi *Jinnah and the Making of a Nation* Council for Pakistan Studies, Karachi 1969, M H Saiyid *Mohammad Ali Jinnah* 2nd ed, Ashraf, Lahore 1953 and Hector Bolitho *Jinnah: Creator of Pakistan* Murray 1954. A highly regarded collection of essays is Sharif Al Mujahid *Quaid-i-Azam Jinnah: Studies in Interpretation* 2nd ed, Quaid-i-Azam Academy, Karachi 1981. Ahmad Hasan Dani (ed) *World Scholars on Quaid-i-Azam Mohammad Ali Jinnah* Quaid-i-Azam University, Islamabad 1979 contains some interesting articles on the transfer of power and why Jinnah decided to become the first Governor-General of Pakistan. See also Misbah ul Haque Siddiqui and M R Malik (eds) *Essays on Quaid-i-Azam* Shahzad, Karachi 1976. Jamil-ud-din Ahmad *Some Recent Speeches and Writings of Mr Jinnah* Ash-

raf, Lahore 1947 covers Jinnah's speeches and writings 1943–6. *Quaid-i-Azam Mohammad Ali Jinnah: Speeches as Governor-General of Pakistan* Ministry of Information and Broadcasting, Islamabad 1977 is a useful collection of Jinnah's speeches as Governor-General from independence in 1947 until his death in 1948. See also M Rafique Afzal *Selected Speeches and Statements of the Quaid-i-Azam Mohammad Ali Jinnah [1911–34 and 1947–8]* Research Society of Pakistan, University of the Punjab, Lahore 1966. A useful selection of Jinnah's most important correspondence covering the years 1918–48 is Syed Sharifuddin Pirzada (ed) *Quaid-i-Azam Jinnah's Correspondence* 2nd ed, Guild Publishing House, Karachi 1966.

**1245** Choudhry Khaliquzzaman *Pathway to Pakistan* Longmans 1961. An autobiography which includes some useful reflections on the transfer of power and partition.

**1246** Aga Khan *World Enough and Time: The Memoirs of Aga Khan* Cassell 1954. This memoir includes a chapter on the transfer of power and partition.

**1247** Ziauddin Ahmad (ed) *Quaid-i-Millat Liaquat Ali Khan: Leader and Statesman* Oriental Academy, Karachi 1970. Liaquat Ali Khan became the first Prime Minister of Pakistan. See also M Rafique Afzal (ed) *Speeches and Statements of Quaid-i-Millat Liaquat Ali Khan 1941–51* Research Society of Pakistan, University of the Punjab, Lahore 1967.

(c) Withdrawal and Partition

**1248** Nicholas Mansergh (editor in chief) *India: The Transfer of Power 1942–7* 12v, HMSO 1970–83. A massive, well edited collection of documents on the end of British rule in India. The successive volumes are *The Cripps Mission January-April 1942* 1970, *Quit India 30 April–21 September 1942* 1971, *Reassertion of Authority, Gandhi's Fast and the Succession to the Viceroyalty 21 September 1942–12 June 1943* 1971, *The Bengal Famine and the New Viceroyalty 15 June 1943–31 August 1944* 1973, *The Simla Conference: Background and Proceedings 1 September 1944–28 July 1945* 1974, *The Post-War Phase: New Moves by the Labour Government 1 August 1945–22 March 1946* 1976, *The Cabinet Mission 23 March–29 June 1946* 1977, *The Interim Government 3 July–1 November 1946* 1979, *The Fixing of a Time Limit 4 November–22 March 1947* 1980, *The Mountbatten Viceroyalty: Formulation of a Plan 22 March–30 May 1947* 1981, *The Mountbatten Viceroyalty: Announcement and Reception of the 3 June Plan 31 May–7 July 1947* 1982 and *The Mountbatten Viceroyalty: Princes, Partition and Independence 8 July–15 August 1947* 1983.

**1248A** Manmath Nath Das *End of the British Indian Empire: POlitics of 'Divide and Quit': Select Documents March–August 1947* Vidyapuri, Cuttack 1983–.

**1249** V P Menon *The Transfer of Power in India 1939–47* Longmans 1957. This is an authoritative account by an important Indian civil servant who was close both to Mountbatten and Patel.

**1250** R J Moore *Escape from Empire: The Attlee Government and the Indian Problem* Clarendon 1983. A good study of the transfer of power. Leonard Mosley *The Last Days of the British Raj* Weidenfeld and Nicolson 1961 has good style and documentation but is perhaps a little biased towards Mountbatten. E W R Lumby *The Transfer of Power in India 1945–47* Allen and Unwin 1954 is a worthy account. Hugh Tinker *Experiment with Freedom: India and Pakistan 1947* Oxford University Press 1967, whilst providing a good short analysis of the transfer of power seems to overestimate the extent to which it marked the end of the imperial vocation. Michael Edwardes *The Last Years of British India* Cassell 1963 is seen as outrageously biased against the Muslims by Pakistani historians.

**1251** S R Mehrotra *Towards India's Freedom and Partition* Vikas, New Delhi 1977. A useful study. Some of the essays in H N Pandit *Fragments of History: India's Freedom Movement and After* Sterling, New Delhi 1982 illuminate aspects of the transfer of power. Kanji Dwarkadas *Ten Years to Freedom* Popular Prakashan, Bombay 1968 looks at India's move towards independence 1937–47.

**1252** Dewan Ram Parkash *Simla Story* Dewan Publications, Lahore 1945. An instant history of the 1945 Simla Conference. Mubarah Singh Kohli and H S Noor *Story of the Cabinet Mission in India* Free-World Publications 1946 is an instant history of the British Cabinet mission of March to June 1946.

**1253** B C Dutt *Mutiny of the Innocents* Sindhu Publications, Bombay 1971. An account of the mutiny in the Royal Indian Navy in early 1946 by one of the ringleaders. Gangadhar M Adhikari *Strike! The Story of the Strike in the Indian Navy* Peoples Publishing House, Bombay 1946 and *The R I N Strike by a Group of Victimised R I N Ratings* Peoples Publishing House, Bombay 1954 are two short committed accounts of the episode.

**1254** Christopher Bromhead Birdwood, Lord Birdwood *A Continent Decides* Hale 1953. Useful reflections on changes in India and Pakistan between 1944 and 1950. Rajani Palme Dutt *India Today and Tomorrow* Lawrence and Wishart 1953 also reflects, from a Left Wing viewpoint, on India during the period of the end of British rule.

**1255** K Veerathappa *British Conservative Party and Indian Independence 1930–1947* Ashish Publishing House, New Delhi 1976. A useful study of Conservative attitudes to Indian progress towards independence.

**1256** Mannath Nath Das *Partition and the Independence of India: Inside Story of the Mountbatten Days* Vision Books, New Delhi 1982. A narrative of the 145 days of the Mountbatten viceroyalty using the Mountbatten papers. An instant history is Roy Murray *The Last Viceroy* Jarrolds 1948. One of the most readable accounts of this period leading up to the transfer of power is Larry Collins and Dominique Lapierre *Freedom at Midnight* Simon and Shuster, New York 1975. It largely consists of transcripts of interviews with Mountbatten and of reproductions of his documents. A collection of speeches from Mountbatten and others from this period is Louis Mountbatten *Time Only to Look Forward: Speeches of Rear Admiral The Earl Mountbatten of Burma as Viceroy of India and Governor-General of the Dominion of India 1947–48* Nicholas Kaye 1949. For Mountbatten's reflections on this period see his *Reflections on the Transfer of Power and Jawaharlal Nehru* Cambridge University Press 1968 and also his 'Address on the Transitional Period in India' *Asiatic Review* 44 1948 pp 345–55. See also Alan Campbell-Johnson 'Reflections on the Transfer of Power' *Asiatic Review* 48 1952 pp 163–82. Another recollection of this period by someone who served with Mountbatten in India is James Wilson 'Mountbatten: Enigma in India' *Army Quarterly and Defence Journal* 116 1986 pp 339–32. W H Morris-Jones 'Thirty-Six Years Later: The Mixed Legacies of Mounbatten's Transfer of Power' *International Affairs* 59 1983 pp 621–8 assesses the successes and failures of Mountbatten's Viceroyalty.

**1257** W H Morris-Jones 'The Transfer of Power 1947: A View from the Sidelines' *Modern Asian Studies* 16 1982 pp 1–32. A useful review of the actual process of the transfer of power in 1947.

**1258** Francis Watson 'Gandhi and the Viceroys' *History Today* 8 1958 pp 88–97. A study of Gandhi's relations with the viceroys, not least Wavell and Mountbatten in the run up to independence.

**1259** Cyril Henry Philips and Mary Doreen Wainwright (eds) *The Partition of India: Policies and Perspectives 1935–1947* Allen and Unwin 1970. An excellent survey of the debates over and the eventual reality of the partition of India.

**1260** Henry Vincent Hodson *The Great Divide: Britain, India, Pakistan* 2nd ed, Oxford University Press 1985. An account of the partition using Mountbatten's papers and written at his request. To a large extent it reflects Mountbatten's view of the partition and has been criticized on these grounds by both Indian and Pakistani historians. Larry Collins and Dominique Lapierre *Mountbatten and the Partition of India March 22–August 15 1947* Vikas, New Delhi 1982 largely consists of transcripts of interviews with Mountbatten and selections from his private papers.

**1261** Anita Inder Singh *The Origins of the Partition of India 1935–1947* Oxford University Press 1987. A skilful example of the divide and quit thesis of the Congress historian. She has however been criticized for compressing the account of the development of British policy and she certainly shows more readiness to understand Congress' position than those of either the British or the Muslim League.

**1262** Syed Hashim Raza (ed) *Mountbatten and Pakistan* Quaid-i-Azam Academy, Karachi 1982. The British were initially rather reluctant to contemplate partition of India. This volume contains a reasoned statement of the thesis of Pakistani historians that, in the negotiations that led to the agreement to divide India and in the actual division of territory Mountbatten was unduly favourable to the Congress. He is also criticized for wishing to set up a common Governor-Generalship after the two Dominions became independent. Mountbatten's reply to this view is reproduced here and critically analysed. Latif Ahmed Sherwani *The Partition of India and Mountbatten* Council for Pakistan Studies, Karachi 1986 similarly reflects Pakistani grievances over British reluctance to partition and the actual process whereby it took place. Another criticism of Mountbatten's part in the partition is Y Krishnan 'Mountbatten and the Partition of India' *History* 68 1983 pp 22–37. A useful response to this criticism is I A Talbot 'Mountbatten and the Partition of India: A Rejoinder' *History* 69 1984 pp 29–35. Wali Khan *Facts are Facts: The Untold Story of India's Partition* Sangam Books, Hyderabad 1987 is a mistitled polemic.

**1263** Allen Hayes Merriam *Gandhi versus Jinnah: The Debate over the Partition of India* Minerva Associates, Calcutta 1980. An account of the contest between Gandhi and Jinnah over the Muslim claims for partition covering the period 1937–47. See also S K Majumbar *Jinnah and Gandhi* K L Mukhopadhyay, Calcutta 1966. Sandhya Chaudhri *Gandhi and the Partition of India* Sterling, New Delhi 1984 draws attention to the role of the personalities of and the relationships between the various leaders as a factor in the process that led to the partition of India.

**1264** Shahid Hamid *Disastrous Twilight: A Personal View of the Partition of India* Leo Cooper/Secker and Warburg 1986. A good account of the partition based on the diary he kept in 1946–7 when he was the Personal Secretary to Auchinleck, the Commander-in-Chief.

**1265** Kingsley Davies 'India and Pakistan: The Demography of Partition' *Pacific Affairs* 22 1949 pp 254–64. A good study.

**1266** Hugh Tinker 'Incident at Simla May 1947: What the Documents Reveal: A Moment of Truth for the Historians?' *Journal of Commonwealth and Comparative Politics* 20 1982 pp 200–22. A study of the 10 May negotiations and the changes of plan over the transfer of power and partition that it necessitated by comparing the documents to the existing historical record.

**1267** Mian Muhammad Sadullah *et al The Partition of the Punjab 1947: Official Documents* 4v, National Documentation Centre, Lahore 1983. A collection of maps and documents on the actual mechanics of the division of territory in the main area to be partitioned.

**1268** Penderel Moon *Divide and Quit* Chatto and Windus 1961. An account of the 1947 disturbances in the Punjab and their causes. G D Khosla *Stern Reckoning: A Survey of the Events Leading up to and Following the Partition of India* Bhawnani and Sons, New Delhi 1949 is an instant history which mostly deals with violence in the Punjab. See also Hugh Tinker 'Pressure, Persuasion, Decision: Factors in the Partition of the Punjab August 1947' *Journal of Asian Studies* 36 1977 pp 695–704 and Robin Jeffrey 'The Punjab Boundary Force and the Problem of Order August 1947' *Modern Asian Studies* 8 1974 pp 491–520. For the partition in Bengal see 'Divided Bengal: Problems of Nationalism and Identity in the 1947 Partition' *Journal of Commonwealth and Comparative Politics* 19 1981 pp 137–68.

(d) Britain and India Since 1947

**1269** S C Gangal 'India and the Commonwealth' *International Studies* 6 1964–5 pp 333–44. A useful critical survey of the primary and secondary sources.

**1270** R L Gupta *Conflict and Harmony: Indo-British Relations: A New Perspective* Trimurti Publications, New Delhi 1971. A good study of Indo-British relations between Indian independence and India becoming a republic in January 1950.

**1271** R J Moore *Making the New Commonwealth* Clarendon 1987. Britain in 1947 wished to draw India and Pakistan into the Commonwealth for a mixture of strategic, economic and sentimental reasons. This is an excellent study of the process whereby these two Dominions became the first non-white, and India the first republic, territories in the Commonwealth. He also covers in some detail why Burma chose not to join the Commonwealth. Another study which focuses particularly on the British interest in keeping India in the Commonwealth is Anita Inder Singh 'Keeping India in the Commonwealth: British Political and Military Aims 1947–49' *Journal of Contemporary History* 20 1985 pp 469–81. Kamlaksha Bhattacharyya *India and the Commonwealth: A Study in Admission (1929–1949)* Inter-India Publications, New Delhi 1985 is a useful attempt to explain why India chose to join the Commonwealth. Aspects of this decision are further explored in T A Keenleyside 'Nationalist India and the issue of Commonwealth Membership' *Journal of Indian History* 60 1982 pp 227–50, Balaram Singh Pavadya 'The Attitude of the Indian National Congress to Dominion Status 1930–1947' *International Studies* 6 1964–65 pp 285–309, Balaram Singh Pavadya 'Mr Nehru, the Indian National Congress and India's Membership in the Commonwealth' *International Studies* 4 1962–63 pp 298–310 and Michael Bracher 'India's Decision to Remain in the Commonwealth' *Journal of Commonwealth and Comparative Studies* 12 1975 pp 62–90.

**1272** Anita Inder Singh 'Post-Imperial British Attitudes to India: The Military Aspect 1947–51' *Round Table* 296 1985 pp 360–75. There have been a number of studies of Indo-British defence and economic as well as Commonwealth relations in the immediate aftermath of Indian independence. This study traces Britain's gradual disillusionment with the idea of the strategic importance of India and the possibility of the Commonwealth as an independent military force. Another aspect of British thinking in this period was a determination to keep India in the Sterling area if at all possible. For this see B R Tomlinson 'Indo-British Relations in the Post-Colonial Era: The Sterling Balance Negotiations of 1947–1949' *Journal of Imperial and Commonwealth History* 13 1985 pp 142–62 and Anita Inder Singh 'Economic Consequences of India's Position in the Commonwealth: The Official British Thinking in 1949' *Indo-British Review* 11 1984 pp 106–11.

**1273** Larry Collins and Dominique Lapierre *Mountbatten and Independent India 16 August 1947–18 June 1948* Vikas, New Delhi 1984. This uses transcripts of interviews with Mountbatten and documents from his papers to examine his period as first Governor-General of independent India.

**1274** Arun Kumar Banerji *India and Britain 1947–68: The Evolution of Post-Colonial Relations* Minerva Associates, Calcutta 1977. A useful survey of economic, military and Commonwealth relations between the two countries. Maurice and Taya Zinkin *Britain and India: Requiem for Empire* Chatto and Windus 1964 is an impressionistic study of Indo-British relations up to the 1960s.

**1275** S C Gangal *India and the Commonwealth* Agrawala and Co, Agra 1976. A good study of India's

relations with the Commonwealth since independence. It includes useful appendices. Cyriac Maprayil *Nehru and the Commonwealth* Radiant Publishers, New Delhi 1976 is a short study with documents of Nehru's view of and impact on the Commonwealth.

**1276** D P Barooah *Indo-British Relations 1950–60* Sterling, New Delhi 1977. This surveys military and diplomatic tensions and economic and cultural co-operation in a period when Indo-British relations were tested by the Korean war, Suez and the Indian seizure of Goa. M S Rajan 'Stresses and Strains in Indo-British Relations 1954–56' *International Studies* 2 1960 pp 153–89 analyses these relations between the high point of Indo-British diplomatic co-operation at the 1954 Geneva conference over Indo-China and the low point reached over Suez. During these years India both sought to steer a non-aligned course between the superpower blocs locked in Cold War and adopted a critical attitude to continuing British colonialism. British reactions to this are surveyed in Shri Ram Sharma *India's Foreign Policy: The British Interpretation 1947–57* Gyan Mandir, Lucknow 1961 (this is also available as a London PhD Thesis 1958–9).

**1277** Michael Lipton and John Firn *The Erosion of a Relationship: India and Britain Since 1960* Oxford University Press 1975. A detailed study, making extensive use of statistics, of the erosion of diplomatic, military, educational, economic and cultural relations between India and Britain.

**1278** Parimal Kumar Das 'The Reaction of the Commonwealth of Nations' *International Studies* 5 1963–64 pp 64–9. An analysis of Commonwealth reactions to the Sino-Indian border dispute of 1962.

**1279** Nandhini Iyer *India and the Commonwealth: A Critical Appraisal* ABC Publishing House, New Delhi 1983. This focuses particularly on the post-Nehru era after 1964. There have always been important elements in Indian politics hostile to the Commonwealth. He argues that it is now seen as a useful forum and as a means of promoting economic co-operation, but it is not an important plank of Indian policy. On India and the Commonwealth see also S C Gangal *India and the Commonwealth* Agarwala 1970 and S C Gangal 'The Commonwealth and Indo-Pakistani Relations' *International Studies* 15 1976.

## (e) Britain and Pakistan Since 1947

**1280** K K Aziz *The Making of Pakistan* Chatto and Windus 1967. There are a number of studies of the creation and formative phase of Pakistan. This is a useful analysis of the demand for a separate Muslim state and its fruition with the creation of Pakistan. An instant history of the background to and creation of Pakistan and its politics and relations with India 1947–49 is Richard Symonds *The Making of Pakistan* Faber 1950. Ian Stephens *Horned Moon* Chatto and Windus 1953 is also useful for the origins and early years of Pakistan. See also Khalid bin Sayeed *Pakistan: The Formative Phase* 2nd ed, Pakistan Publishing House, Karachi 1968 and M Hasan 'The Transfer of Power in Pakistan and its Consequences' Cambridge PhD Thesis 1966–7. Jamil-ud-din Ahmad *The Final Phase of the Struggle for Pakistan* Publishers United, Lahore 1964 is a committed account of the negotiations that led to the creation of Pakistan from the 1945 Simla conference to independence. Indian interpretations of this process are Sachin Sen *The Birth of Pakistan* General Printers and Publishers, Calcutta 1955 and V V Nagarkar *Genesis of Pakistan* Allied Publishers, New Delhi 1975. The latter is particularly good on why Jinnah accepted so much less than the Muslims were demanding. On Jinnah's role in the creation of Pakistan see also Ahmad Hasan Dani (ed) *Quaid-i-Azam and Pakistan* Quaid-i-Azam University, Islamabad 1981. On Jinnah's decision to become the first Governor-General of Pakistan see Ayesha Jalal 'Inheriting the Raj: Jinnah and the Governor-Generalship Issue' *Journal of Commonwealth and Comparative Studies* 19 1985 pp 29–53.

**1281** Ian Stephens *Pakistan* 3rd ed, Benn 1967. A history up to 1962. It has quite a lot on the partition, the cooling of Anglo-Pakistani relations, the Kashmir dispute as a thorn in British relations with both powers on the sub-continent and the anti-British riots that followed the Suez attack on a fellow Muslim country. On British and Commonwealth relations with Pakistan see also M A Qureshi 'British Relations with Pakistan 1947–62: A Study of British Policy Towards Pakistan' Oxford DPhil Thesis 1967–8.

**1282** M Sohail 'Pakistan's Relations with Britain 1947–51 with Particular Reference to some Problems of Partition' Leeds PhD Thesis 1986. A study of military and economic relations in the immediate post-imperial period. There was a gradual decline in relations, largely because Pakistan feared India and felt that Britain, anxious to remain on good terms with both, was tending to favour India. This is certainly the view of K K Aziz *Britain and Pakistan: A Study of British Attitudes Towards the East Pakistan Crisis of 1971* University of Islamabad Press, Islamabad 1974. This surveys Anglo-Pakistani relations 1947–70 and British attitudes during the secession of East Pakistan (now Bangladesh) in 1971. Commonwealth recognition of this new state led Pakistan to withdraw from the Commonwealth in 1972.

(f) Burma

**1283** Hugh Tinker (ed) *Constitutional Relations Between Britain and Burma: Burma: The Struggle for Independence 1944–1948: Documents from Official and Private Sources* 2v, HMSO 1983–4. Volume I covers the end of the wartime Japanese occupation and the restoration of civil government 1 January 1944 to 31 August 1946. Volume II covers the Burmese general strike and the advance towards independence 31 August 1946 to 4 January 1948. These volumes include not just documents but chronological tables, biographical details and personal narratives of events.

**1284** A Griffin *A Brief Guide to the Sources for the Study of Burma in the India Office Records* India Office Library and Records 1979.

**1285** K T Htar 'Select Bibliography of Books on British Burma 1826–1948' FLA Thesis London 1967. Josef Silverstein 'The Other Side of Burma's Struggle for Independence' *Pacific Affairs* 58 1985 pp 98–108 is a good historiographical article.

**1286** Frank Joseph Shulman *Burma: An Annotated Bibliographical Guide to International Dissertation Research 1898–1985* University Press of America 1986. Despite the difficulty of conducting research in Burma in recent years a substantial amount of work has been done.

**1287** John F Cady *A History of Modern Burma* Cornell University Press 1958. An exhaustive history 1784–1953. It is quite good on the final phase of British rule and Burmese relations with the Commonwealth (which they did not join) after independence. F S V Donnison *Burma* Benn 1970 is a general account of the country which is also quite useful for the end of British rule. See also Dorothy Woodman *The Making of Burma* Cresset Press 1962 and Frank N Trager *Burma from Kingdom to Republic* Praeger, New York 1966.

**1288** Maurice Collis *Last and First in Burma 1941–1948* Faber 1956. A study of the end of British rule in Burma. It has been criticized both for a certain amount of carelessness in handling documents and for being too favourable to the Governor, Sir Reginald Dorman-Smith. Mountbatten, the Supreme Allied Commander South East Asia, later felt that his assent to the early return of Dorman-Smith to Burma led to their secession from the Commonwealth, a view Nicholas Tarling 'Lord Mountbatten and the Return of Civil Government to Burma' *Journal of Imperial and Commonwealth History* 11 1983 pp 197–226 regards as improbable. See also Louis Allen 'Transfer of Power in Burma' *Journal of Imperial and Commonwealth History* 13 1985 pp 185–94.

**1289** John S Furnivall 'Twilight in Burma: Reconquest and Crisis' *Pacific Affairs* 22 1949 pp 3–20 and 155–72. A good summary of the situation in Burma 1945–8 by a British civil servant who remained in Burma after independence.

**1290** Leslie Glass *The Changing of Kings: Memories of Burma 1934–1949* Peter Owen 1985. Light-hearted but evocative memoirs of his time in the Indian civil service in Burma. On Burma in the immediate post-war era see also George Appleton 'Burma Two Years After Liberation' *International Affairs* 23 1947 pp 510–20. Appleton was Archdeacon of Rangoon 1943–6.

**1291** Maung Maung *Aung San of Burma* Martinus Nijhoff, The Hague 1962. A biography of the Burmese nationalist who led the Burmese Independence Army against the British in World War Two and then later led resistance to the Japanese. After the restoration of British rule he took a prominent part in the negotiations that were leading to independence until his assassination in July 1947. There are also useful reflections on the end of British rule in Burma and the Burmese decision to remain outside the Commonwealth in Maung Maung *Burma in the Family of Nations* Djambatan, Amsterdam 1957, Maung Maung *Burma's Constitution* Martinus Nijhoff, The Hague 1959 and Maung Maung *Burma and General Ne Win* Asia Publishing House 1969.

**1292** F Nemenzo 'Revolution and Counter-Revolution: A Study of British Colonial Policy as a Factor in the Growth and Disintegration of National Liberation Movements in Burma and Malaya' Manchester PhD Thesis 1964–5.

**(g) Ceylon (Sri Lanka)**

**1293** Vijaya Sameraweera *Sri Lanka* Clio Press 1987. An annotated bibliography.

**1294** K M de Silva (ed) *History of Ceylon Vol III: From the Beginning of the Nineteenth Century to 1948* University of Ceylon, Colombo 1973. This contains useful articles on the development of nationalism and the constitution under British rule and on the transfer of power. N E Weerasoaria *Ceylon and Her People Vol 4* Lake House Investments Ltd, Colombo 1971 covers the history of Ceylon from the 1870s. Covering a longer time span but also of some use for British relations with Ceylon since 1945 is E F C Ludowyk *The Modern History of Ceylon* Weidenfeld and Nicolson 1966. S A Pakeman *Ceylon* Benn 1964 is a general guide to Ceylon which has some personal reflections on the transfer of power.

**1295** Sir Charles Jeffries *Ceylon – The Path to Independence* Pall Mall Press 1962. On the background to Ceylon's progress to independence see also Sir W Ivor Jennings *Nationalism and Political Development in Ceylon* Institute of Pacific Studies, New York 1950.

**1296** I D S Weerawardeena *Government and Politics in Ceylon 1931–1946* Ceylon Economic Research Association, Colombo 1951. A study of the working of the 1931 Donoughmore constitution up until the appointment of the Soulbury Commission based on his London PhD Thesis.

**1297** *Ceylon: Commission on Constitutional Reform: Report* Cmnd 6677, *Parliamentary Papers* x 1945–46. The report of the Commission chaired by Lord Soulbury. The best study of the Soulbury Commission which framed the constitution for independent Ceylon remains Sir W Ivor Jennings *The Constitution of Ceylon* 3rd ed, Oxford University Press 1953. See also J F Rees 'The Soulbury Commission' *Ceylon Historical Journal* 5 1955–56 pp 23–48.

**1298** Sir Charles Collins *Public Administration in Ceylon* Institute of Pacific Relations, New York 1952. A study of the gradual and successful transition from British rule to independence. The author spent 38 years in the Ceylon civil service. See also W A Wiswa-Warnapala 'Role of the Ceylon Civil Service Before and After Independence' Leeds PhD Thesis 1970.

**1299** S Namasivayan *The Legislatures of Ceylon 1928–1948* Faber 1951. A legal rather than historical account.

**1300** T Y Wright *Ceylon in My Time 1889–1949* Columbo Apothecaries Company Ltd, Columbo 1951. This memoir is quite useful for British life in Ceylon, and his reactions to nationalism and independence.

**1301** Michael Roberts (ed) *Documents of the Ceylon National Congress and Nationalist Politics in Ceylon 1929–1950* 4v, National Archives, Columbo 1978. See also Brian H Farmer 'The Social Basis of Nationalism in Ceylon' *Journal of Asian Studies* 24 1965 pp 431–9.

**1302** W Thalgodapitya *Portraits of Ten Patriots of Sri Lanka* T B S Godamunne and Sons, Kandy 1966. The relevant biographies in this collection are of Sir Paul E Pieris (1874–1957) and D S Senanyake (1884–1952). For Senanyake see also S D Sapramadu (ed) 'D S Senanyake' *Ceylon Historical Journal* 5 1955–56, a whole issue devoted to his life and work.

**1303** Lucy M Jacob *Sri Lanka: From Dominion to Republic, A Study of the Changing Relations with the United Kingdom* National Publishing House, Delhi

1973. This concentrates on economic and military relations between 1948–72.

**1304** Sir Charles Jeffries *'O E G': A Biography of Sir Oliver Ernest Goanetilleke* Pall Mall Press 1969. Goanetilleke was the High Commissioner of Ceylon in the UK 1948–51 and the first Ceylonese Governor-General of Ceylon 1954–62.

**1305** Sir John Kotelawala *An Asian Prime Minister's Story* Harrap 1956. An autobiography which illuminates the smoothness of the transfer of power and the continuing affection for Britain in Ceylon after her imperial departure. Sir John was Prime Minister of Ceylon 1953–6.

### (3) The Indian Ocean

**1306** Julia J Gotthold and Donald W Gotthold *Indian Ocean* Clio Press 1988. An annotated bibliography of the various islands and territories of the Indian ocean. It includes material on the British imperial past in the Maldives, Seychelles and Mauritius and on the British Indian Ocean Territory. Material on all these can be found below. For the Andaman and Nicobar islands see [1195].

#### (a) General

**1307** V K Bhasin *Super Power Rivalry in the Indian Ocean* Chand, Delhi 1981. This reviews the decline of British power and the rise of superpower rivalry in the region. A historical review of British interests in the area is Admiral Terence Lewin 'The Indian Ocean and Beyond: British Interests' *Asian Affairs* 9 1978 pp 247–59. An analysis of Britain's interests and commitments in the region before the 1968 decision to withdraw from East of Suez is Alistair Buchan 'Britain in the Indian Ocean' *International Affairs* 42 1966 pp 184–93.

**1308** *British Islands in the Southern Hemisphere 1945–1951* Cmnd 8230, *Parliamentary Papers* xxvi 1950–51. A useful survey of British islands in the Indian Ocean, the Western Pacific and the Southern Atlantic.

#### (b) British Indian Ocean Territory

**1309** Jooneed Khan 'Diego Garcia: The Militarisation of an Indian Ocean Island' in Robin Cohen (ed) *African Islands and Enclaves* Sage 1983 pp 165–93. A review of the history of the Chagos archipelago, the creation of British Indian Ocean Territory in 1968 as a response to increasing Soviet naval activity in the Indian ocean and the subsequent development of the American base on

Diego Garcia. K S Jawatkar *Diego Garcia in International Diplomacy* Sangam Books 1983 is an Indian critique of the development of this base, which in the process usefully reviews the great power rivalries of the Russians, Americans, British, French and Chinese in the Indian ocean. See also [1141].

**1310** Mauritius Legislative Assembly *Report of the Select Committee on the Excision of the Chagos Archipelago* Government Printer, Port Louis 1983. An inquiry into the excision from Mauritian jurisdiction in the late 1960s of the Chagos archipelago to form the British Indian Ocean Territory. A useful commentary on this report is Joel Larus 'Negotiating Independence? Mauritius and Diego Garcia' *Round Table* 294 1985 pp 132–45.

**1311** Ram Mannick *Diego Garcia: Victim of Imperialism or Mauritian Muddle?* Mauritius Educational Association, Port Louis 1983. A critical evaluation of the development of the base. It is however primarily concerned with the treatment of the islanders displaced by the development of the base and resettled on Mauritius, and the efforts to get compensation from Britain. See also John Madeley *Diego Garcia: A Contrast to the Falklands* Minority Rights Group 1982 and [1929].

#### (c) The Maldives

**1312** Andrew D W Forbes 'Archives and Resources for Maldivian History' *South Asia* 3 1980 pp 70–82.

**1313** Urmila Phadnis and Ela Dutt Luithui *Maldives: Winds of Change in an Atoll State* South Asia Publishers, New Delhi 1985. A pioneering study of the Maldives. They became fully independent in 1965. Close ties with Britain however remained at least until the RAF left Gan in 1976. This useful study also has a good bibliography. See also M Adeney and W K Carr 'The Maldives Republic' in John Ostheimer (ed) *The Politics of the Western Indian Ocean* Praeger, New York 1975 pp 139–59.

#### (d) Mauritius

**1314** Central Office of Information *Mauritius* HMSO 1968. A guide to Mauritian political, economic and social life to coincide with independence. For the excision of the Chagos archipelago to form British Indian Ocean Territory see above [1309–11].

**1315** Moonindra Nath Verma *The Road to Independence* the author, Quatre Bornes 1976. An account which focuses particularly on nationalism in Mauritius. Jay Narain Roy *Mauritius in Transition* the author, Port Louis 1960 contains rather patchy reflections on racial tensions and British divide and rule in the final years of empire.

**1316** Moonindra Nath Verma *Profiles of Great Mauritians* the author, Quatre Bornes 1981. Rather sketchy biographies of important figures in Mauritian politics. The most useful are those of Dr Maurice Cure, Emmanuel Arquetil, Guy Rozemont and Ranganaden Seaneevasen. See also his *Rise and Fall of Three Leaders* the author, Quatre Bornes 1981, which features biographies of Sookdeo Bissoodoyal, Jules Koenig and Abdul Razack Mohamed.

**1317** Seewoosagur Ramgoolam with Anand Mulloo *Our Struggle: 20th Century Mauritius* Vision Books, New Delhi 1982. A semi-autobiographical account of politics and nationalism in Mauritius. Ramgoolam led Mauritius to independence in 1968. He was Chief Minister 1965–8, Prime Minister 1968–82 and Governor-General from 1984 until his death in 1986. See also Moonindra Nath Verma *The Struggle of Dr Ramgoolam* the author, Quatre Bornes 1975. Anand Mulloo (ed) *Our Freedom: Seewoosagur Ramgoolam* Vision Books, New Delhi 1982 is a collection of Ramgoolam's speeches 1935–. Another collection of speeches is K Hazareesingh (ed) *Selected Speeches of Sir Seewoosagur Ramgoolam* Macmillan 1979.

**(e) The Seychelles**

**1318** Central Office of Information *Seychelles* HMSO 1976. A guide to the political, social and economic structure of the islands issued to coincide with their independence.

**1319** Deryck Scarr 'Whisphers of Fancy: With Mr Arthur Creech Jones in Seychelles' *Journal of Imperial and Commonwealth History* 11 1983 pp 322–38. A study of the failure of Colonial Office liberalism in the Seychelles in the immediate aftermath of the war.

**1320** Christopher Lee *Seychelles: Political Castaways* Elm Tree Books 1976. The relevant part of this book is essentially a eulogy of James Mancham, the playboy who led the Seychelles to independence and was then overthrown in a 1977 coup.

**(4) South East Asia**

**(a) General**

**1321** J D Pearson (comp) *A Guide to Manuscripts and Documents in the British Isles Relating to South and South-East Asia Vol I: London* Mansell 1989. An anno-

tated guide to the holdings of a wealth of depositories. See also Mary Doreen Wainwright and Noel Matthews *A Guide to Manuscripts and Documents in the British Isles Relating to the Far East* Oxford University Press 1977, which is an informative guide to collections and their locations.

**1322** Clive J Christie *A Preliminary Survey of British Literature on South East Asia in the Era of Colonial Decline and Decolonisation* Bibliography and Literature Series 3, Centre for South East Asian Studies, University of Hull 1986.

**1323** Peter Lowe *Britain in the Far East 1819 to the Present* Longman 1981. A general history. See also D K Bassett and V T King *Britain and South East Asia* Centre for South East Asian Studies Occasional Paper 13, University of Hull 1986. Also of use is R Fifield *The Diplomacy of Southeast Asia 1945–1958* Harper, New York 1958.

**1324** Charles Allen and Michael Mason (eds) *Tales from the South Seas: Images of the British in South East Asia in the Twentieth Century* Deutsch 1983. An evocative picture of the British as traders and rulers in South East Asia based on oral accounts. See also the survey Saul Rose *Britain and Southeast Asia* Chatto and Windus 1962.

**1325** J E Williams 'Britain's Role in Southeast Asia 1945–55' Wales PhD Thesis 1973.

**1326** *British Dependencies in the Far East 1954–1949* Cmnd 7709, *Parliamentary Papers* xiii 1948–49. A survey of the problems of restoration after Japanese rule, post-war developments and Communist insurgency in Malaya, North Borneo, Sarawak, Brunei and Hong Kong. It includes a useful chronology.

**(b) Malaysia**

Material on the Malayan Emergency 1948–60 and on the Confrontation with Indonesia 1963–66 is in the section on Colonial Wars.

**1327** K G Tregonning (ed) *Malaysian Historical Sources* Department of History, University of Singapore, Singapore 1962. This guide is of some use for the post-war era.

**1328** Robert Heussler (ed) *British Malaya: A Bibliographical and Biographical Compendium* Garland 1981. A very useful annotated bibliography and biographical guide. Ian Brown and Rajeswary Ampalavaner *Malaysia* Clio Press 1981 is another annotated bibliography, but it is not nearly so useful. There is an extensive bibliography in A J Stockwell's historiographical essay, 'The Historiography of Malaysia: Recent Writings in English on the History of the Area Since 1874' *Journal of Imperial and Commonwealth History* 5 1976 pp 82–110. See also W R Roff *Autobiography and Biography in Malay Historical Studies* Insititute of Southeast Asian Studies, University of Singapore 1972 and H R Cheeseman (comp) *Bibliography of Malaya, Being a Classified List of Books Wholly or Partly in English Relating to the Federation of Malaya and Singapore* Longmans 1959.

**1329** J de V Allen, A J Stockwell and L R Wright (eds) *A Collection of Treaties and Other Documents Affecting the States of Malaysia 1761–1963* 2v, Oceana Publications 1981. This collection includes lots of policy documents as well. It is well annotated.

**1330** John Bestin and Robin W Winks (eds) *Malaysia: Selected Historical Readings* KTO Press 1979. A collection of documents and related material. The final section covers the rise of nationalism, the Japanese occupation and the British restoration, the progress to independence in Malaya, North Borneo and Singapore, the Malayan Emergency 1948–60 and the Confrontation with Indonesia 1963–66, the Brunei coup 1962 and so on.

**1331** James P Ongkili *Nation-Building in Malaysia 1946–1974* Oxford University Press 1985. A study of the attempts to create a national consciousness that would transcend Malaya's different ethnic communities from the failed British attempt to introduce a Malayan union in 1946. One aspect of this process was the repeated British post-war attempts to arrange some sort of federation covering the Malay kingdoms and incorporating Singapore as well. This process of political unification down to the secession of Singapore in 1965 from the Federation of Malaysia which had been created in 1963 from an amalgamation of British North Borneo and Singapore with Malaya (which had been independent since 1957) is well told in Mohamed Noordin Sopice *From Malayan Union to Singapore Separation: Political Unification in the Malaysian Region 1945–1965* University of Malaya Press, Kuala Lumpur 1974. Another good study of this process is Badu Simandjuntak *Malayan Federalism 1945–1963: A Study of Federal Problems in a Plural Society* Oxford University Press 1969. See also T H Silcock *Towards a Malayan Nation* Donald Moore, Singapore 1961.

**1332** Tunku Abdul Rahman *Malaysia, the Road to Independence* Pelanduk Publications, Petaling Jaya 1985. Reflections on the progress to independence by Malaya's first Prime Minister. See also Kim Hoong Khong *Merdeka! British Rule and the Struggle for Independence in Malaya 1945–1957* Institute for Social Analysis, Petaling Jaya 1984. For a discussion of different interpretations of the process of the transfer of power in Malaysia see D C Hawkins 'Britain and Malaysia –

Another View – Was the Decision to Withdraw Entirely Voluntary or was Britain Pushed a Little?' *Asian Survey* 9 1969 pp 546–62.

**1333** Mohamed Amin and Malcolm Caldwell (eds) *Malaya: The Making of a Neo-Colony* Spokesman 1977. Essays on developments in Malaya and Singapore 1945–57.

**1334** Richard Clutterbuck *Riot and Revolution in Singapore and Malaya 1945–1963* Faber 1973. This looks at urban riots and inter-communal strife as well as the long drawn out war with Communist insurgents 1948–60.

**1335** Central Office of Information *Malaya: The Making of a Nation* HMSO 1957. A useful pamphlet on politics, the economy, society and culture in newly independent Malaya.

**1336** Victor Purcell *Malaysia* Thames and Hudson 1965. A survey of the law, people, history, economy and government of Malaya, Singapore and North Borneo with the emphasis on the period since 1945. J M Gullick *Malaya* Benn 1963 is a general guide to Malaya by a former member of the Malay Civil Service. A useful collection of essays on contemporary Malaysia is Wang Gungwu (ed) *Malaysia: A Survey* Pall Mall Press 1964. Particularly useful are the essays on the Malayan Communist Party and on Malayan relations with Commonwealth. Norton Ginsburg and Chester F Roberts Jr *Malaya* University of Washington Press, Seattle 1958 is a report on contemporary political and economic developments. Vernon Bartlett *Report from Malaya* Derek Verschoyle 1954 is essentially a travelogue. It usefully conveys the atmosphere in the last years of British Malaya and reflects on the problem of the Emergency, and not least its cost. So does John Slimming *Temiar Jungle: A Malayan Journey* Murray 1958. Another useful travelogue is S K Chattur *Malayan Adventure* Mission Press 1948.

**1337** Robert Heussler *Completing a Stewardship: The Malayan Civil Service 1942–1957* Greenwood 1983. A good history. See also Gerald Hawkins 'The Passing of the MCS' *The Straits Times Annual* 1967 pp 121–6. Stanley Lytle *Public Administration in Malaya* Royal Institute of International Affairs 1953 is a useful short study. Rupert Emerson *Representative Government in Southeast Asia* Harvard University Press, Cambridge, Massachusetts 1955 includes an indictment of British administration in Malaya and also reflects on the rise of nationalism. See also the textbook on the administration of British Malaya, S M Middlebrook and A W Pinnick *How Malaya is Governed* Longmans 1949.

**1338** *Report of the Committee on the Malayanisation of the Government Service* Government Press, Kuala

Lumpur 1954. The Malayanisation of the Civil Service helped to ease the progress towards independence. This process is well examined in Robert O Tilman *Bureaucratic Transition in Malaya* Duke University Press, Durham, North Carolina 1964.

**1339** *The Federation of Malaya and Its Police 1786–1952* Grenier, Ipoh, Perak 1952. A brief official history. It has some material on the police's role in the Emergency.

**1340** C N Parkinson *Templer in Malaya* Donald Moore, Singapore 1954. A short tribute to the highly effective High Commissioner. Sir Gerald Templar was appointed in January 1952 in the wake of the assassination of his predecessor Sir Henry Gurney and played a key role in developing the strategy that won the campaign against the Communist insurgents before his departure in 1954.

**1341** Andrew Gilmour *An Eastern Cadet's Anecdotage* University Education Press, Singapore 1974. There are a number of memoirs by former members of the Malayan Civil Service. Gilmour's autobiography recalls his service between the 1920s and 1950s. See also his *My Role in the Rehabilitation of Singapore 1946–1953* Institute of South East Asian Studies, University of Singapore 1973. This is part of an oral history project that records his recollections of his work in the Secretariat in Singapore in these years. Arthur Locke *The Tigers of Trengganau* Museum Press 1954 is a picture of Malay Civil Service life on the east coast of Malaya after 1945. J D H Neill *Elegant Flower* Murray 1956 is a memoir of the Chinese Protectorate section of the Malay Civil Service by one of its last recruits. It is particularly useful for inter-communal relations in Malaya and in the MCS. Malays had also served in the MCS long before the launch of the Malayanization programme. Datuk Mohd Yussoff Hj. Ahmed *Decades of Change: (Malaysia 1910s–1970s)* Arts Printing Works, Kuala Lumpur 1983 is a useful autobiography by one of these. Another is Mubin Sheppard *Taman Budiman: Memoirs of an Unorthodox Civil Servant* Heinemann, Kuala Lumpur 1979, which recounts Sheppard's service from 1928 onwards.

**1342** Lennox Algernon Mills *Malaya: A Political and Economic Appraisal* Oxford University Press 1958. This survey of the last years of British rule is most useful for its account of the re-establishment of British rule 1945–47. See also Martin Rudner 'The Organisation of the British Military Administration in Malaya 1946–1948' *Journal of Southeast Asian History* 9 1968 pp 95–106.

**1343** A J Stockwell 'British Imperial Policy and Decolonisation in Malaya 1942–1952' *Journal of Imperial and Commonwealth History* 13 1984 pp 68–87. Britain's 1942 defeat at the hands of the Japanese led to new stress on nation building absent in the inter-war years. Only in the 1950s did Britain come to accept that independence might be conceded without first eradicating racial tensions.

**1344** *Malayan Union and Singapore: Summary of Proposed Constitutional Arrangements* Cmnd 6749, *Parliamentary Papers* xix 1945–46. The proposals for the short lived Malayan union. Revised proposals, *Federation of Malaya: Summary of Revised Constitutional Proposals* Cmnd 7171, *Parliamentary Papers* xix 1946–47, were implemented in 1948.

**1345** A J Stockwell *British Policy and Malay Politics During the Malayan Union Experiment 1942–1948* Malaysian Branch of the Royal Asiatic Society, Kuala Lumpur 1979. A good study of British constitutional experiments and Malayan political developments in this important period. The idea of Malayan union was a product of wartime Colonial Office planning. For this see C M Turnbull 'British Planning for Post-War Malaya' *Journal of South East Asian Studies* 5 1974 pp 239–54. Introduced in 1946 it aroused so much opposition it had been dropped by 1948. For this see Yeo Kim Wah 'The Anti-Federation Movement in Malaya 1946–48' *Journal of South East Asian Studies* 4 1973 pp 31–51. Another good analysis of the development and impact of British policy in this period is A K H Lau 'The Politics of Union and Citizenship: The Evolution of British Constitutional Policy Towards Malaya and Singapore 1942–1948' London PhD Thesis 1986. James de V Allen *The Malayan Union* South East Asia Studies, Yale University, New Haven, Connecticut 1967 is a study of its implementation and rapid failure based extensively on interviews. His analysis fails however to pick all the flaws in the scheme, as M R Stenson 'The Malayan Union and the Historians' *Journal of Southeast Asian History* 10 1969 pp 344–54 points out.

**1346** Michael R Stenson *Industrial Conflict in Malaya: Prelude to the Communist Revolt of 1948* Oxford University Press 1970. A good study of the background of social and industrial unrest to the Communist Emergency 1948–60. Cheah Boon Kheng *Red Star Over Malaya: Persistance and Social Conflict During and After the Japanese Occupation of Malaya 1941–46* Singapore University Press, Singapore 1983 deals particularly with social unrest 1945–46, though the relationship between this and the difficulties of re-establishing British rule is not fully explored. An interesting contemporary commentary on the inter-communal and policy problems of the immediate post-war period is Sir Tan Cheng Lock *Malayan Problems from a Chinese Point of View* Tannesco, Singapore 1947.

**1347** Charles Gamba *The Origins of Trade Unionism in Malaya: A Study in Colonial Labour Unrest* Donald Moore, Singapore 1962. A study that is useful both for the relations between the colonial government and the unions from the 1930s and for the labour unrest that forms part of the background to the Emergency.

**1348** William R Roff *The Origins of Malay Nationalism* Yale University Press 1967. A good study of the rise of communal and national feeling amongst Malays in the twentieth century. See also 'Nationalism in Malaya' *Journal of Southeast Asian History* 1 1960 pp 1–99, a whole issue devoted to the subject, and T H Silcock and Ungku A Aziz 'Nationalism in Malaya' in William L Holland (ed) *Asian Nationalism and the West* Macmillan 1953 pp 267–346. See also [1292].

**1349** Cheah Boon Kheng 'The Erosion of Ideological Hegemony and Royal Power and the Rise of Post-War Malay Nationalism 1945–46' *Journal of South East Asian Studies* 19 1988 pp 1–27. This study points to the role of the Malay union proposals in undermining the power and importance of the Malay kingdoms and thus helping to create the conditions which led to the foundation of the first nationalist organization in May 1946. A J Stockwell 'The Formation and First Years of the United Malays National Organisation (UMNO) 1946–1948' *Modern Asian Studies* 11 1977 pp 481–513 charts its history down to the declaration of the Emergency.

**1350** Tunku Abdul Rahman Putra *Political Awakening* 2nd ed, Pelanduk Publications, Petaling Jaya 1987. A rather unrevealing autobiography. Harry Miller *Prince and Premier: A Biography of Tunku Abdul Rahman Putra Al-Haj: First Prime Minister of the Federation of Malaya* Harrap 1959 is an uncritical biography of the UMNO leader who was Prime Minister 1957–70. Mubin Sheppard *Tunku – A Pictorial Biography 1957–1987* Pelanduk Publications, Petaling Jaya 1987 makes use of Rahman's personal reminiscences.

**1351** Ahmad Boestamam *Carving the Path to the Summit* Ohio University Press, Athens, Ohio 1979. Memoirs of a Malay nationalist and radical.

**1352** Kennedy C Tregonning 'Tan Cheng Lock: A Malayan Nationalist' *Journal of South East Asian Studies* 10 1979 pp 25–76. A sympathetic account of the life and career of a dominant figure in the Chinese community in Malaya and his involvement in the events leading to independence in 1957.

**1353** Gene S Hanrahan *The Communist Struggle in Malaya* 2nd ed, University of Malaysia Press, Kuala Lumpur 1971. A history of the Malayan Communist Party including biographical details and documents. Cheah Boon Kheng *The Masked Comrades: A Study of the Communist United Front in Malaya 1945–48* Singapore University Press, Singapore 1979 is an excellent study of the party in the period before the declaration of the Emergency.

**1354** Kennedy C Tregonning *North Borneo* HMSO 1960. Part of the Corona library series of illustrated volumes under the sponsorship of the Colonial Office dealing with the way of life and government of dependent territories. It is not an official guide. Another survey is George L Harris *et al North Borneo, Brunei, Sarawak (British Borneo)* Human Relations Area Files, New Haven, Connecticut 1956, which gives information on the history, geography, government and economy of North Borneo.

**1355** Anwar Sullivan and Cecilia Leong (eds) *Commemorative History of Sabah 1881–1981* Sabah State Government Centenary Publications Committee, Kota Kinabalu 1981. This includes good coverage of administrative, political and economic developments during the British direct rule of this colony 1946–63. See also Cecilia Leong *Sabah: The First 100 Years* Perctakan Nan Yang Muda, Kuala Lumpur 1982 and Kennedy C Tregonning *A History of Modern Sabah (North Borneo 1881–1963)* Oxford University Press 1965. M H Baker *Sabah: The First Ten Years as a Colony 1946–1956* 2nd ed, Malaysia Publishing House, Singapore 1965 surveys progress and development in the colony in the first years since it was taken over by the British North Borneo Company.

**1356** Sir Steven Runciman *The White Rajahs: A History of Sarawak 1841–1946* Cambridge University Press 1960. A somewhat flawed history of Sarawak under the Brooke family. It passed to the Crown in 1946. R H W Reece *The Name of Brooke: The End of White Rajah Rule in Sarawak* Oxford University Press 1982 is a good study of the end of Brooke rule and the anti-cession movement that culminated in the assassination of Governor Stewart in 1949.

**1357** *Report of the Commission of Enquiry, North Borneo and Sarawak 1962* Cmnd 1794, *Parliamentary Papers* xi 1961–62. The Commission chaired by Lord Cobbold which reported in favour of the amalgamation of the two colonies with the Federation of Malaya.

**1358** *Malaysia: Agreement Concluded Between the United Kingdom and Northern Ireland, the Federation of Malaya, North Borneo, Sarawak and Singapore* Cmnd 2094, *Parliamentary Papers* xxxviii 1962–63. The agreement which united the British colonies of Sarawak and Sabah with the Federation of Malaya to form Malaysia. Singapore also joined the Federation in 1963 but left it in 1965.

**1359** T E Smith *The Background to Malaysia* Oxford University Press 1963. A short study. Ronald McKie *Malaysia in Focus* Angus and Robertson 1963 is a reasonable journalistic account. Michael Liefer 'Anglo-American Differences over Malaysia' *World Today* 20 1964 pp 156–67 deals with Anglo-American tensions over the creation of the Federation and the subsequent Confrontation with Indonesia. See also W A Hanna *The Formation of Malaysia* American University Field Staff, New York 1964, Robert O Tilman 'Malaysia: Problems of Federation' *Western Political Quarterly* 16 1963 pp 897–911, R Catley 'Malaysia: The Last Battle for Merger' *Australian Outlook* 21 1967 pp 44–60, H F Armstrong 'The Troubled Birth of Malaysia' *Foreign Affairs* 41 1963 pp 673–93, G P Means 'Malaysia – A New Federation in Southeast Asia' *Pacific Affairs* 36 1963 pp 138–59 and Vishal Singh 'The Struggle for Malaysia' *International Studies* 5 1963–64 pp 221–39. R Stephen Milne and K J Ratnam *Malaysia – New States in a New Nation: Political Development of Sarawak and Sabah in Malaysia* Cass 1974 looks at the incorporation of Sabah and Sarawak and their place in the new state of Malaysia.

**1360** Sir Richard Allen *Malaysia: Prospect and Retrospect: The Impact and Aftermath of Colonial Rule* Oxford University Press 1968. A study which is mostly concerned with charting declining ties with Britain since independence, particularly with the British decision to withdraw East of Suez in 1968.

**1361** Arnold C Brackman *Southeast Asia's Second Front: The Power Struggle in the Malay Archipelago* Pall Mall Press 1966. An account of contemporary developments that has some material on the creation of Malaysia and the Confrontation with Indonesia.

**1362** *Proposed Agreement on External Defence and Mutual Assistance Between the Government of the United Kingdom of Great Britain and Northern Ireland and the Government of the Federation of Malaya* Cmnd 263, *Parliamentary Papers* xxvi 1956–57. The most important aspect of Anglo-Malayan relations after independence was this Anglo-Malayan Defence Agreement. Britain was supported in the defence of Malaya and Singapore by Australia and New Zealand, an arrangement provided for by the *Arrangements for the Employment of Overseas Commonwealth Forces in Emergency Operations in the Federation of Malaya After Independence* Cmnd 264, *Parliamentary Papers* xxvi 1956–57. On the Anglo-Australian discussions which led to Australian military involvement in the Emergency in 1950 see Peter Edwards 'The Australian Commitment to the Malayan Emergency 1948–1950' *Historical Studies* 22 1987 pp 604–16. An excellent study of the resulting unique defence system is Chin Kin Wah *The Defence of Malaysia and Singapore: The Transformation of a Security System 1957–1971* Cambridge University Press 1983. Another useful study is David Hawkins *The Defence of Malaysia and Singapore: From AMDA to ANZUK* Royal United Services Institute for Defence Studies 1972. This system came to an end with Britain's withdrawal East of Suez, to be replaced by a loose five power arrangement. This new agreement, set up in 1971, is examined in T B Millar 'The Five Power Agreement

and Southeast Asian Security' *Pacific Community* 3 1972 pp 341–51. Derek McDougall 'The Wilson Government and the British Defence Commitment in Malaysia and Singapore' *Journal of South East Asian Studies* 4 1973 pp 229–40 analyses the factors that led to Britain's withdrawal. Anglo-Australian co-operation in the defence of Malaysia from 1945 through the Emergency and the Confrontation with Indonesia down to the final withdrawal of British troops in 1976 is surveyed in T B Millar 'Anglo-Australian Partnership in Defence of the Malaysian Area' in A F Madden (ed) *Australia and Britain: Studies in a Changing Relationship* Cass 1980 pp 71–89. A useful study of the impact of Britain's withdrawal on Malayan attitudes is Chandran Jeshurun *Malaysian Defence Policy: A Study in Parliamentary Attitudes 1963–1973* University of Malaya Press, Kuala Lumpur 1980.

**1363** Dato' Abdullah Ahmad *Tengku Abdul Rahman and Malaysia's Foreign Policy 1963–1970* Berita Publishing, Kuala Lumpur 1985. A study, based on a Cambridge MLitt Thesis 1984, written with Rahman's assistance. It includes reflections on the creation of Malaysia, the Confrontation with Indonesia and the decline of Anglo-Malaysian relations after independence. Michael Liefer 'Anglo-Malaysian Alienation' *Round Table* 285 1983 pp 56–63 is a study of the increasingly cool relations after the end of defence co-operation. Roger Kershaw 'Anglo-Malaysian Relations: Old Roles Versus New Rules' *International Affairs* 59 1983 pp 629–44 is a good account of the difficult relations 1980–82 when the Malaysian government introduced a 'Buy British Last' policy.

### (c) Singapore

Singapore became fully independent as part of the Federation of Malaysia in 1963. It withdrew from Malaysia in 1965. The constitutional development of Singapore has been distinctive from that of Malaya. Its ethnic structure is certainly distinctive. A large majority of the population are Chinese. Therefore although much of the literature on Malaysia is also relevant for Singapore (as is the material on the Emergency and the Confrontation in the section on Colonial Wars) there is also a certain amount which relates particularly to Singapore and is accordingly listed below.

**1364** Stella R Quah and Jon S T Quah *Singapore* Clio Press 1988. An annotated, classified bibliography. Edwin Lee 'The Historiography of Singapore' in B K Kapur (ed) *Singapore Studies: Critical Surveys of the Humanities and Social Sciences* Singapore University Press, Singapore 1986 pp 1–32 is a useful bibliographical essay.

**1365** C M Turnbull *A History of Singapore 1819–1975* Oxford University Press 1977. The standard history. It also has a good bibliography. This is also true of the collection of essays celebrating the 150th anniversary of the arrival of Sir Stamford Raffles, the founder of Singapore; Ooi Jin-Bee and Chiang Hai Ding (eds) *Modern Singapore* University of Singapore, Singapore 1969. Noel Barber *The Singapore Story: From Raffles to Lee Kuan Yew* Fontana 1978 is a more popular general history which includes quite good coverage of Anglo-Singaporean relations since independence. See also Alex Josey *Singapore: Its Past, Present and Future* Eastern Universities Press, Singapore 1979. Donald Moore and Joanna Moore *The First 150 Years of Singapore* Donald Moore, Singapore 1969 does not have much on the post-war period.

**1366** Toni Schönenberger *Der britische Rückzug aus Singapore 1945–1976* Atlantis, Zurich 1981. A study of the British military presence and eventual withdrawal from Singapore. It contains an English summary and a useful bibliography. See also the pamphlet C N Parkinson *Britain in the Far East: The Singapore Naval Base* Donald Moore, Singapore 1955.

**1367** Yeo Kim Wah *Political Development in Singapore 1945–1955* University of Singapore, Singapore 1963. See also Thomas J Bellows 'The Singapore Party System' *Journal of Southeast Asian History* 8 1967 pp 122–38, a study of the development of the party system from 1945 to independence. Bellows has also studied the party Lee Kuan Yew has led since he founded it in 1954 in *The People's Action Party of Singapore: Emergence of a Dominant Party System* Yale University Press 1970.

**1368** Alex Josey *David Marshall's Political Interlude* Eastern Universities Press, Singapore 1982. A political history of Singapore 1955–63.

**1369** Oswald Gilmour *With Freedom to Singapore* Benn 1950. Personal comments on the post-war situation.

**1370** A J Stockwell 'Imperial Security and Moslem Militancy, with Special Reference to the Hertogh Riots in Singapore (December 1950)' *Journal of South East Asian Studies* 17 1986 pp 322–35. These riots were significant in that they targeted Europeans rather than, as usual, focusing on Sino-Malay relations.

**1371** Lee Ting Hui *The Communist Organisation in Singapore 1948–66* Singapore University Press, Singapore 1976. This includes material on the Emergency and on urban riots in Singapore.

**1372** Chan Heng Chee *A Sensation of Independence: A Political Biography of David Marshall* Oxford University Press 1984. A good biography of the first Chief Minister of Singapore. David Marshall *Singapore's Struggle for Nationhood 1945–1959* University Education Press, Singapore 1971 is a transcript of a speech in which he reflects on his part in the process.

**1373** Francis Thomas *Memoirs of a Migrant* University Education Press, Singapore 1972. Thomas was a minister in Singapore governments in the 1950s. This is his memoirs of the end of the colonial era.

**1374** James Minchin *No Man is an Island: A Study of Singapore's Lee Kuan Yew* Allen and Unwin 1986. The least prejudiced of the biographies of the man who has been Singapore's Prime Minister since 1959. It is good on personalities but not always good on the background detail. Alex Josey *Lee Kuan Yew* 2nd ed, Times Books 1980 is rather hagiographical. T J S George *Lee Kuan Yew's Singapore* Deutsch 1973 is hostile.

**1375** Alex Josey *Lee Kuan Yew and the Commonwealth* Donald Moore, Singapore 1969. An analysis of Lee Kuan Yew's influence on Commonwealth affairs, especially in the context of the 1969 Commonwealth conference, which he also examines. This is useful not least for its reflections on the British withdrawal East of Suez.

## (d) Brunei

Some material of relevance can also be found in the section on Malaysia.

**1376** Sylvia C Engelen Krausse and Gerald H Krausse *Brunei* Clio Press 1988. An annotated, classified bibliography.

**1377** A V M Horton 'The Development of Brunei During the British Residential Era 1906–1959: A Sultanate Regenerated' Hull PhD Thesis 1985. A useful study ending with the regaining of internal autonomy in Brunei in 1959. See also his *The British Residency in Brunei 1906–1959* Occasional Paper 6, University of Hull 1984.

**1378** B A Hamzah 'Oil and Independence in Brunei: A Perspective' *Southeast Asian Affairs 1981* pp 93–102. A good survey of the growth of nationalism 1956 onwards, the abortive coup of 1962 and the reasons for the long continuation of the British protectorate.

**1379** A J Crosbie 'Brunei in Transition' *Southeast Asian Affairs 1981* pp 75–92. A study of changes in the final days of the British protectorate. Brunei became fully independent 1st January 1984. Roger Kershaw 'Illuminating the Path to Independence: Political Themes in Pelita Brunei in 1983' *Southeast Asian Affairs 1984* pp 67–88 reviews the final year of the protectorate and the continuing British military and political influence in Brunei.

### (e) Hong Kong

**1380** *Hong Kong* Hong Kong Government Services, Hong Kong. An excellent well illustrated annual review. It succeeds *Annual Report on Hong Kong for the Year 1946*– Hong Kong Government, Hong Kong 1947–.

**1381** G B Endacott *Government and People of Hong Kong: A Constitutional History 1841–1962* Oxford University Press 1965. The standard history. For more recent studies of the politics and administration of Hong Kong see N J Miners *Government and Politics of Hong Kong* Oxford University Press 1982 and Peter Harris *Hong Kong: A Study in Bureaucratic Politics* 2nd ed, Heinemann 1980.

**1382** Harold Ingrams *Hong Kong* HMSO 1952. Part of the Corona library series of illustrated volumes under the sponsorship of the Colonial Office dealing with the way of life and government of dependent territories. It is not an official guide. Jan Morris *Hong Kong: Xianggang* Viking 1988 and Nigel Cameron *Hong Kong: The Cultured Pearl* Oxford University Press 1978 are also good impressionistic studies of the Crown Colony. Felix Patrikeeff *Mouldering Pearl* George Philip 1989 conveys something of the atmosphere of Hong Kong in the 1980s as the reversion of the colony to China draws nearer. See also [1141].

**1383** S Y-S Tsang 'Great Britain and Attempts at Constitutional Reform in Hong Kong (1945–1952)' Oxford DPhil Thesis 1986. Discussions on local elected self-government were aborted in 1952 when the Governor declared them inopportune in the light of the Korean war. The fear was that a Kuomingtang victory might have led to a Chinese attempt to seize the colony. See also N J Miners 'Plans for Constitutional Reform in Hong Kong 1946–52' *China Quarterly* 107 1986 pp 463–82.

**1384** David Podmore 'Localisation in the Hong Kong Government Service 1948–1968' *Journal of Commonwealth Political Studies* 9 1971 pp 36–51. A good study of the increasing Sinification of the Hong Kong Civil Service.

**1385** E F Szczepanik *The Economic Growth of Hong Kong* Oxford University Press 1958. A short study.

**1386** Ng Ting Fun 'Hong Kong: A Study of Its Relationships with China and Britain Since 1949' London PhD Thesis 1981. The most important development in recent years has been the 1985 Sino-British agreement

on the future of Hong Kong when the lease on the New Territories runs out in 1997. 'A Draft Agreement Between the Government of the United Kingdom of Great Britain and Northern Ireland and the Government of the People's Republic of China on the Future of Hong Kong' *Asian Journal of Public Administration* 6 1984 pp 193–226 discusses the 1982–4 negotiations that led to the September 1984 draft agreement and the nature of Chinese policy and prints this agreement in full. Peter Harris 'Hong Kong Confronts 1997: An Assessment of the Sino-British Agreement' *Pacific Affairs* 59 1986 pp 45–68 reviews the negotiations and the agreement of 1985.

**1387** Joseph Y S Chang (ed) *Hong Kong in Transition* Oxford University Press 1987. Papers analysing change in various areas, especially in the light of the impending reversion to Chinese rule from 1997. Another useful collection of essays is Joseph Y S Chang (ed) *Hong Kong in the 1980s* Summerson Eastern Publishers Ltd, Hong Kong 1982. Philip Geddes *In the Mouth of the Dragon: Hong Kong Past, Present and Future* Century/TVS 1982 is a popular view of contemporary developments derived from a TV series. See also Ian Kelly *Hong Kong: A Political-Geographical Analysis* Macmillan 1987.

**1388** Austin Coates *Myself a Mandarin: Memories of a Special Magistrate* Muller 1968. Memoirs of service in Hong Kong after the Second World War.

### D. THE MIDDLE EAST

### (1) General

**1389** Mary Doreen Wainwright and Noel Matthews *A Guide to Manuscripts and Documents in the British Isles Relating to the Middle East and North Africa* Oxford University Press 1980. A classified well indexed guide. The locations of material are given. Ian Richard Netton *Middle East Materials in United Kingdom and Irish Libraries: A Directory* Library Association 1983 is an annotated guide to library holdings which is alphabetically arranged.

**1390** T G Fraser (ed) *The Middle East 1914–79* Arnold 1980. A useful collection of documents. See also J C Hurewitz *Diplomacy in the Near and Middle East: A Documentary Record Vol 2: 1944–1956* Van Nostrand, Princeton, New Jersey 1972.

**1391** *The Middle East Journal* 1947–. This regularly contains a bibliography of periodical literature on the Middle East. The section on modern history and politics continues to be worth consulting.

**1392** Jacob Abadi *Britain's Withdrawal from the Middle East 1947–1971: The Economic and Strategic Imperatives* Kingston Press, Princeton, New Jersey 1983. A rather conventional narrative of Britain's retreat in the Middle East from the withdrawal from Palestine to the East of Suez decision and the end of the British presence in the Persian Gulf. Elizabeth Monroe *Britain's Moment in the Middle East 1914–1971* 2nd ed, Chatto and Windus 1981 is a useful general history. So is Ann Williams *Britain and France in the Middle East and North Africa 1914–1967* Macmillan 1968. John Barrett Kelly *Arabia, the Gulf and the West* Weidenfeld and Nicolson 1980 is a good overview of the recent history of the Middle East, especially in the light of the British withdrawal and its consequences, which he deals with in considerable detail. Sir Reader William Bullard *Britain and the Middle East* 2nd ed, Hutchinson 1964 is a general survey by the former (1939–46) ambassador to Iran. It is good on the importance of the oil of the region to Britain. Matthew A Fitzsimons *Empire by Treaty: Britain and the Middle East in the Twentieth Century* University of Notre Dame Press 1964 is an analysis of the complex web of treaties and protectorates whereby Britain maintained her paramountcy in the Middle East and the influences subverting her position. Sir John Bagot Glubb *Britain and the Arabs: A Study of Fifty Years 1908 to 1958* Hodder and Stoughton 1959 is a study by one of the most distinguished Britons to serve in the region. It traces Britain's influence in the area until what he sees as its eclipse with the expulsion of British officers from Jordan (most notably Glubb himself) in 1956 and the Iraqi revolution of 1958 and the increasing activities of other powers, not least the Russians. It also provides useful insights into the Arab mind. John Marlowe *Arab Nationalism and British Imperialism: A Study in Power Politics* Cresset Press 1961 looks particularly at Suez and Iraq. Erskine B Childers *The Road to Suez: A Study of Western-Arab Relations* Macgibbon and Kee 1962 puts the 1956 Suez episode in the context of post-war Western relations and objectives in the Middle East. See also Pierre Rondat *The Changing Patterns of the Middle East 1919–1958* Chatto and Windus 1961 and M V Seton-Williams *Britain and the Arab States: A Survey of Anglo-Arab Relations 1920–1948* Luzac and Co 1948.

**1393** Mordechai Abir *Oil, Power and Politics: Conflict in Arabia, the Red Sea and the Gulf* Cass 1974. A selection of papers mostly concerned with the decline of Britain's influence in the region.

**1394** William Roger Louis *The British Empire in the Middle East 1945–51: Arab Nationalism, the United States and Post-War Imperialism* Oxford University Press 1984. Louis sees British strategy in these years as focused on an attempt to maintain world power status based on hegemony in the strategically and, in view of its oil wealth, economically important Middle East. He does not stress sufficiently the importance of oil or Arab nationalism. This is nevertheless a massive and well documented study which also includes a useful chronology. Another important study is Barry Rubin *The Great Powers in the Middle East 1941–47: The Road to the Cold War* Cass 1980. British policy in the area is also examined in O Zametica 'British Strategic Planning for the Eastern Mediterranean and the Middle East 1944–47' Cambridge PhD Thesis 1986. Jon Kimche *Seven Fallen Pillars: The Middle East 1945–52* 2nd ed, Secker and Warburg 1953 is an Israeli view of the decline of British power in the region in this period. An important factor in this process was the polarizing effect of the creation of the state of Israel in 1948 from the former British mandate of Palestine. See also the short contemporary study G Kirk *Survey of International Affairs: The Middle East 1945–50* Oxford University Press 1954.

**1395** Amikam Nachmani '"It is a Matter of Getting the Mixture Right": Britain's Post-War Relations with America in the Middle East' *Journal of Contemporary History* 18 1983 pp 117–40. A study of mutual suspicion and of the role of America in weakening Britain in the Middle East in the 1940s and 1950s. See also M El-H Maghmoul 'Anglo-American Relations in the Eastern Mediterranean 1945–1958' London MPhil Thesis 1980. A useful memoir by an American diplomat is Bartley C Crum *Behind the Silken Curtain: A Personal Account of Anglo-American Diplomacy in Palestine and the Middle East* Simon and Shuster, New York 1947. There is considerable coverage of Anglo-American conflict over oil exploration and exploitation in Joseph J Malone 'America and the Arabian Peninsula: The First Two Hundred Years' *Middle East Journal* 30 1976 pp 406–24.

**1396** Chatham House Study Group (Chairman: Sir Knox Helm) *British Interests in the Mediterranean and Middle East* Oxford University Press 1958. An assessment of British interests and weaknesses in the region after Suez. An analysis of Britain's weaknesses and critical study of British policy in Cyprus and Suez is Michael Foot and Mervyn Jones *Guilty Men 1957: Suez and Cyprus* Gollancz 1957.

**1397** Anthony Nutting *I Saw for Myself: The Aftermath of Suez* Hollis and Carter 1958. An account of the riots that followed the Suez debacle of 1956 across North Africa and the Middle East.

**1398** David Holden *Farewell to Arabia* Faber 1966. Excellent journalist's impressions of Britain's difficulties in the Arabian peninsula in the wake of Suez.

**1399** P Mangold 'The Role of Force in British Policy Towards the Middle East 1957–66' London PhD Thesis 1972–3.

**1400** J Edelman 'Europe and the Third World: The Role of Britain and France in the Middle East Crisis of 1967' *Columbia Essays in International Affairs* 4 1968 pp 210–31. This includes reflections on Britain's response to the Arab-Israeli Six Day War in 1967.

## (2) General Memoirs of Service in the Middle East

Most of the memoirs of Britons serving in the Middle East deal with their time in a particular country. These do not appear below but are included with the literature on the countries in question.

**1401** Sir Gawain Bell *Shadows on the Sand: The Memoirs of Sir Gawain Bell* Christopher Hurst 1983. This memoir covers his time in the Sudan political service 1931–54 and his service as Political Agent in Kuwait 1955–7.

**1402** Sir (John Edmund) Hugh Boustead *The Wind of Morning: The Autobiography of Hugh Boustead* Chatto and Windus 1971. Boustead was British Agent in the East Aden Protectorate 1949–58, the Development Secretary in Oman 1958–61 and the Political Agent in Abu Dhabi 1961–5.

**1403** Sir Anthony Parsons *They Say the Lion: Britain's Legacy to the Arabs: A Personal Memoir* Cape 1986. Memoirs of his career in the Middle East from his appointment as military attache in Baghdad 1952–4, through service in the Jordan (1959–60), Egypt (1960–1) and Sudan (1964–5) embassies, to his appointment as Political Agent in Bahrain 1965–9. It is thus a very useful record of Britain's role in the Middle East in these difficult years.

**1404** Humphrey Trevelyan *The Middle East in Revolution* Macmillan 1970. Autobiographical reflections on the difficulties the British had in dealing with revolution in Egypt in the 1950s and Iraq from 1958 onwards and during the final period of British rule in Aden until the withdrawal in 1967.

## (3) Egypt

For material on the Suez Crisis of 1956 see also [2397–2414].

**1405** Ragai N Makar *Egypt* Clio Press 1988. An annotated bibliography which contains some material of value.

**1406** Keith M Wilson (ed) *Imperialism and Nationalism in the Middle East: The Anglo-Egyptian Experience*

*1882–1982* Mansell 1983. Eight essays covering Anglo-Egyptian relations dowm to the present day. John Marlowe *Anglo-Egyptian Relations 1800–1956* 2nd ed, Cass 1965 is a good general survey which covers the post-war period well. See also Peter Mansfield *The British in Egypt* Weidenfeld and Nicolson 1971 and the short outline study, Royal Institute of International Affairs *Great Britain and Egypt 1914–51* 2nd ed, Oxford University Press 1954. Derek Hopwood *Egypt: Politics and Society 1945–1984* 2nd ed, Allen and Unwin 1985 is also worth consulting.

**1407** Trefor E Evans (ed) *The Killearn Diaries 1934–1946: The Diplomatic and Personal Record of Lord Killearn, Sir Miles Lampson, High Commissioner and Ambassador to Egypt* Sidgwick and Jackson 1972. Killearn was High Commissioner (1934–6) then Ambassador (1936–46) to Egypt and High Commissioner for the Sudan 1934–46. See also Evans' *Mission to Egypt 1934–46: Lord Killearn High Commissioner and Ambassador* University of Wales Press 1971.

**1408** H J Schonfield *The Suez Canal in Peace and War 1868–1969* revised ed, Vallentine Mitchell 1969. A general history which includes reflections on the Suez Canal Company and the 1956 Suez crisis.

**1409** E Letman 'The Egyptian Question 1942–1947: The Deterioration of Britain's Position in Egypt, Al-Alamein to the UN Debate of 1947' London PhD Thesis 1982. One factor weakening Britain's position was the Egyptian desire to re-negotiate the 1936 treaty. The abortive negotiations of 1946 are examined in H Rahman 'The Anglo-Egyptian Negotiations of 1946 and Britain's Post-Second World War Strategy in the Middle East' London PhD Thesis 1982. See also P L Hanna 'The Anglo-Egyptian Negotiations 1950–2' *Middle Eastern Affairs* 3 1952 pp 213–32. Britain meanwhile relinquished efforts to establish a Middle East Command in Egypt in the face of Russian ambitions in the Middle East, a process examined in Peter L Hahn 'Containment and Egyptian Nationalism: The Unsuccessful Effort to Establish the Middle East Command 1950–53' *Diplomatic History* 11 1987 pp 23–40. The agreement reached in 1954 to withdraw British troops from Egypt is discussed in C B Selak 'The Suez Canal Base Agreement of 1954: Its Background and Implications' *American Journal of International Law* 49 1955 pp 487–505. The progressive withdrawal 1954–6 and the plans for the continued operation and maintenance of the base by a civilian force is considered in Sir Norman Kipping *The Suez Contractors* Kenneth Mason Publications 1969.

**1410** Robert L Tignor 'Decolonisation and Business: The Case of Egypt' *Journal of Modern History* 59 1987 pp 479–505. A good analysis of business anxieties and their attempts to influence imperial policy in Egypt in the post-war era.

**1411**  Gabriel R Warburg 'The Sinai Peninsula Borders 1906–47' *Journal of Contemporary History* 14 1979 pp 677–92. This is useful on the controversy over the Sinai boundary of Egypt in 1946–7 and its effect on Anglo-Egyptian relations.

**1412**  Joel Beinin and Zachary Lockman *Workers on the Nile: Nationalism, Communism, Islam and the Egyptian Working Classes 1882–1954* I B Tauris 1988. A study of the development of the Egyptian labour movement and its effect on Nationalism and Nasserism.

**1413**  Peter Mansfield *Nasser's Egypt* Penguin 1969. A good short history of nationalist Egypt from 1954.

**1414**  Nejla M Abu Izzeddin *Nasser of the Arabs: An Arab Assessment* Third World Centre for Research and Publishing, New York 1981. A sympathetic portrait. This is useful not only for the Suez expedition and the end of British power in Egypt. Nasser, as President of Egypt 1954–70, played a large part in undermining Britain elsewhere in the Middle East. His career is exhaustively examined in Dan Hofstadter (ed) *Egypt and Nasser* 3v, Facts on File, New York 1973. See also *'Abd al-Majid Farid Nasser: A Reassessment* Arab Research Centre 1981, Shirley Graham DuBois *Gamel Abdel Nasser: Son of the Nile: A Biography* Third Press, New York 1972, Peter Mansfield *Nasser* Methuen 1969 and Jean Lacouture *Nasser: A Biography* Secker and Warburg 1973.

### (4) The Sudan

The Sudan was administered as an Anglo-Egyptian condominium from the time of its re-conquest by Kitchener in 1898. It became independent in 1956.

**1415**  L E Forbes 'The Sudan Archive, Durham as a Source for the Study of Modernization in the Sudan' in M W Daly (ed) *Modernization in the Sudan: Essays in Honor of Richard Hill* Lilian Barber Press, New York 1985 pp 161–72. A guide to the archive at Durham University.

**1416**  Abdel Rahman el Nasri (comp) *A Bibliography of the Sudan: 1938–1958* Oxford University Press 1962. Although unannotated this is well organized and indexed and it contains a wealth of useful material, including pamphlets, articles and official publications. M W Daly *Sudan* Clio Press 1983 is an annotated bibliography which is also of some value.

**1417**  Richard Leslie Hill *A Biographical Dictionary of the Sudan* 2nd ed, Cass 1967. An essential reference guide with over 1900 entries.

**1418**  Peter Woodward *Condominium and Sudanese Nationalism* Rex Collings 1979. A good history of the British in the Sudan. It particularly concentrates on the period 1945–56. So does L A Fabunmi *The Sudan in Anglo-Egyptian Relations: A Case Study in Power Politics 1800–1956* Longmans 1960. This study is useful not only for the tensions between the two condomini but also for Britain's legacy in the Sudan. It also has good appendices. Mekki Abbas *The Sudan Question: The Dispute Over the Anglo-Egyptian Condominium 1884–1951* Faber 1952 is also useful for tensions between the two condomini and between the Muslim North and the Christian and Animist South and for developments towards independence. Robert O Collins and Francis M Deng (eds) *The British in the Sudan 1898–1956: The Sweetness and the Sorrow* Macmillan 1984 is a good collection of essays focusing on the men who ruled Anglo-Egyptian Sudan. Nicole Grandin *Le Soudan Nilotique et L'Administration Britannique (1898–1956): Elements d'interpretation Socio-Historique d'une Experience Coloniale* Brill, Leiden 1982 is a somewhat conventional history. See also P M Holt *A Modern History of the Sudan from the Funf Sultanate to the Present Day* Weidenfeld and Nicolson 1961.

**1419**  Muddathir 'Abd Al-Rahman *Imperialism and Nationalism in the Sudan: A Study in Constitutional and Political Development 1898–1956* Clarendon 1969. An important Sudanese history of the Anglo-Egyptian Sudan. One of its objects is to correct what he views as the tendency of British historians to deny that Islam and Arabic costumes were controlled or forbidden in the South by the British authorities. The differences between the North and South, which have led to long periods of civil war since independence, have thus had some effect on the historiography of the British in the Sudan. See also M Sinada 'Constitutional Development in the Sudan 1942–56' Oxford DPhil Thesis 1973 and R C Mayall 'Recent Constitutional Developments in the Sudan' *International Affairs* 28 1952 pp 310–21.

**1420**  K D D Henderson *Sudan Republic* Benn 1965. An excellent study of the Sudan by a former officer of the Sudan Political Service. It is useful for regional differences in the British administration, the end of British rule and relations with Britain since independence. Another good survey of the Sudan, worth consulting for political developments 1947–53, is Sir Harold MacMichael *The Sudan* Benn 1954.

**1421**  H Z Sabry *Sovereignty for Sudan* Ithaca Press 1982. A history of the last years of the condominium, partly based on the author's memories of his service in Khartoum 1949–53. See also J S R Duncan *Sudan's Path to Independence* Blackwood 1957.

**1422**  Robert O Collins *Shadows in the Grass: Britain in the Southern Sudan 1918–1956* Yale University Press

1983. A splendid study of British administration on the upper Nile. It also features a good bibliography. See also Mohamed Omer Beshir *The Southern Sudan: Background to Conflict* Christopher Hurst 1968. A study of the administration in the North of the country is K El-D O Salih 'The British Administration in the Nuba Mountain Region of the Sudan 1900–1956' London PhD Thesis 1982.

**1423** G Bell and B D Dee *Sudan Political Service 1899–1956* Oxonian Press 1958. A history. See also J S R Duncan *The Sudan: A Record of Achievement* Macmillan 1952.

**1424** K D D Henderson *Set Under Authority* Castle Cary Press 1987. A good portrait of the life of the district officer in the Sudan based on his own and his former colleagues' recollections. H C Jackson *Behind the Modern Sudan* Macmillan 1955 is a memoir of the Sudan Political Service. Sir Harold MacMichael *Sudan Political Service 1899–1956* Oxonian Press n.d. is a compilation of biographical information on its members.

**1425** Mohamed Omer Beshir *Educational Development in the Sudan 1898–1956* Clarendon 1969. Educational development played a part in preparing for independence.

**1426** Conrad C Reining *The Zande Scheme: An Anthropological Case Study of Economic Development in Africa* Northwestern University Press 1966. The Zande scheme was a scheme for economic development in the southern Sudan.

**1427** Mohamed Omar Beshir *Revolution and Nationalism in the Sudan* Rex Collings 1974. Another useful study is Gabriel Warbury *Islam, Nationalism and Communism in a Traditional Society: The Case of Sudan* Cass 1978. See also Peter M Holt 'Sudanese Nationalism and Self-Determination' in Walter Lacquer (ed) *The Middle East in Transition* Praeger, New York 1958 pp 166–82 and Saad ed Din Fawzi *The Labour Movement in the Sudan 1946–1955* Oxford University Press 1957.

## (5) Palestine

For the literature on the problems of terrorism and the attempts of the British to develop a counter-insurgency strategy see the section on Colonial Wars.

**1428** Philip Jones (comp) *Britain and Palestine 1914–1948: Archival Sources for the History of the British Mandate* Oxford University Press 1979. A well annotated and organized guide to documents and archives in Britain.

**1429** Neil Caplan *Futile Diplomacy Vol 2: Arab-Zionist Negotiations and the end of the Mandate* Cass 1986. A valuable collection of documents from 1929 onwards. It contains much more Jewish than Arab material, simply because far more Jewish material exists.

**1430** Esther M Snyder *Israel* Clio Press 1985. An annotated bibliography which contains some material of value.

**1431** Nicholas Bethell *The Palestine Triangle: The Struggle Between the British, the Jews and the Arabs 1935–48* Deutsch 1979. A good general history of the final years of the British mandate from the Royal Commission in the mid-1930s to the withdrawal in 1948. A sympathetic portrayal of Britain's entanglement in Palestine from the 1917 Balfour Declaration is Christopher Sykes *Crossroads to Israel: Palestine from Balfour to Bevin* Collins 1965. Arthur Koestler *Promise and Fulfilment: Palestine 1917–1949* Macmillan 1949 is a rather idiosyncratic study. The bulk of the book deals with the period after 1945 and makes use of his own contemporary observations. Esco Foundation for Palestine Inc *Palestine: A Study of Jewish, Arab and British Policies* 2v, Yale University Press, New Haven, Connecticut 1947 mainly deals with inter-war developments. The second volume however has a lengthy and detailed chronology 1945–46. John Marlowe *The Seat of Pilate: An Account of the Palestine Mandate* Cresset Press 1962 and A M Hyamson *Palestine Under the Mandate 1920–1948* Methuen 1950 have been superseded.

**1432** H M Deegan 'British Party Policy – Palestine 1937–1950: A Case Study' Keele PhD Thesis 1984. A study which juxtaposes government and party policy. Labour for instance, having been strongly pro-Zionist in opposition were obliged by the realities of office to adopt a more Arabist policy after 1945. See also Joseph Gorny *The British Labour Movement and Zionism 1917–1948* Cass 1983 and A Sargent 'The British Labour Party and Palestine 1917–1949' Nottingham PhD Thesis 1980. Michael J Cohen *Churchill and the Jews* Cass 1986 is a study of Churchill's attitude from 1900 down to his advocacy of British recognition of Israel in 1949.

**1433** Alan R Taylor *Prelude to Israel: An Analysis of Zionist Diplomacy 1897–1947* Darton, Longman and Todd 1961. This has some reflections on the Zionist success in influencing American policy. See also J M Linthwaite 'Zionism and British Policy in Palestine, with Special Reference to the Period 1914–1947' Nottingham MPhil Thesis 1980.

**1434** A-A Badrud-Din 'The Arab League in Palestine 1944–1949' Oxford BLitt Thesis 1959–60. Though there are a considerable number of studies of Zionism and of Jewish organizations there are not many, partly because of the dearth of material, which are concerned with Arab organizations. Also of some relevance is M K Budeiri 'The Palestine Communist Party: Its Arabisation and the Anglo-Jewish Conflict in Palestine 1929–1948' London PhD Thesis 1977.

**1435** Norman and Helen Bentwich *Mandate Memories 1918–1948* Hogarth Press 1965. The Bentwiches were Anglo-Jewish Zionists. Norman Bentwich had served in the mandate administration before becoming a professor at Jerusalem University. See also Norman Bentwich *My 77 Years: An Account of My Life and Times 1883–1960* Routledge and Kegan Paul 1962.

**1436** William Roger Louis 'Sir Alan Cunningham and the End of British Rule in Palestine' *Journal of Imperial and Commonwealth History* 16 1988 pp 128–47. A sympathetic study of the last British High Commissioner. See also Sir Alan Cunningham 'Palestine: The Last Days of the Mandate' *International Affairs* 24 1948 pp 481–90.

**1437** J L Finegold 'British Economic Policy in Palestine 1920–1948' London PhD Thesis 1979.

**1438** C J Morris '"With Malice Towards None": Publicity Considerations in the Formulation and Conduct of the Labour Government's Policy Towards Palestine 1945–1947' Leeds MPhil Thesis 1989.

**1439** *A Survey of Palestine: Prepared in December 1945 and January 1946 for the Information of the Anglo-American Committee of Inquiry* 2v, Government Printer, Jerusalem 1946. A fairly comprehensive survey compiled to assist the deliberations of the Committee.

**1440** Martin Jones *Failure in Palestine: British and United States Policy After the Second World War* Mansell 1986. A damning study of British policy in Palestine in the final years of the mandate and of the difficulties posed by American pro-Zionism. Ritchie Ovendale *Britain, the United States and the End of the Palestine Mandate 1942–1948* Royal Historical Society 1989 lays stress on the importance of the political pressure American Jews brought to bear on President Truman in the eventual outcome in Palestine. On Anglo-American policy see also M J Haron *Palestine and the Anglo-American Connection 1945–1950* Peter Lang, New York 1986. For the increasing American interest in Palestine see A Ilan 'The Origins and Development of American Intervention in Britain's Palestine Policy 1938–47' Oxford DPhil Thesis 1973–4. On British policy in the post-war period see also Michael Leifer 'Zionism and Palestine in British Opinion and Policy 1945–1949' London PhD Thesis 1959–60.

**1441** William Roger Louis and Robert W Stookey (eds) *The End of the Palestine Mandate* I B Tauris 1986. This presents essays on the British, American, Soviet Jewish and Arab perspectives on the end of the mandate. It also includes an overview and a historiographical essay. On great power interests in Palestine after the Second World War see also Michael J Cohen *Palestine and the Great Powers 1945–8* Princeton University Press 1982.

**1442** Amikam Nachmani *Great Power Discord in Palestine: The Anglo-American Committee of Inquiry into the Problems of European Jewry and Palestine 1945–1946* Cass 1987. This study should be complemented by Allen Howard Podet *The Success and Failure of the Anglo-American Committee of Inquiry 1945–1946: Last Chance in Palestine* Edwin Mellen Press, Lewiston, New York 1986, which makes much more use of American documents. See also L Dinnerstein 'America, Britain and Palestine: The Anglo-American Committee of Enquiry' *Diplomatic History* 6 1982 pp 283–301 and M J Cohen 'The Genesis of the Anglo-American Committee on Palestine, November 1945: A Case Study on the Assertion of American Hegemony' *Historical Journal* 22 1979 pp 185–207. The committee was appointed in response to protests about British restrictions on Jewish immigration to Palestine. Richard Crossman, who became strongly pro-Zionist in the process, wrote a memoir of his service on this Committee, *Palestine Mission: A Personal Record* Hamilton 1947. James G McDonald *My Mission in Israel* Gollancz 1951 is a memoir by an American member of the committee.

**1443** Jon and David Kimche *The Secret Roads: The 'Illegal' Migration of a People 1938–1948* Secker and Warburg 1954. The story of Jewish immigration into Palestine despite British attempts to stop it. See also M J Haron 'Note: United States-British Collaboration on Illegal Immigrants to Palestine 1945–1947' *Jewish Social Studies* 42 1980 pp 177–82.

**1444** Simha Flapan *The Birth of Israel: Myths and Realities* Pantheon 1987. Another study of the factors leading to the creation of the state of Israel in 1948 is Richard Crossman *A Nation Reborn: The Israel of Weizmann, Bevin and Ben-Gurion* Hamilton 1960. Harry Sacher *Israel: The Establishment of a State* Weidenfeld and Nicolson 1952 is an overview of this process which is very critical of Bevin, both in the last days of the mandate and in the course of the 1948 Arab-Israeli War. See also Jacob Coleman Hurewitz *The Struggle for Palestine* W W Norton, New York 1950.

**1445** Ritchie Ovendale 'The Palestine Policy of the British Labour Government 1945–1946' *International Affairs* 55 1979 pp 409–31. See also his 'The Palestine Policy of the British Labour Government 1947: The Decision to Withdraw' *International Affairs* 56 1980 pp 73–93.

**1446** Jon and David Kimche *Both Sides of the Hill: Britain and the Palestine War* Secker and Warburg 1960. A good military history of the first Arab-Israeli war in 1948 which is also useful for British attitudes at the time and on the effect of the war on Britain's position in the Middle East. They see the defeat of the Arabs (including Britain's ally Jordan) as far more a defeat for Britain since it weakened Britain's hold on the Arab world. Another military account of the war is Natenal Lorch *The Edge of the Sword: Israel's War of Independence 1947–1949* Putnam 1961. On Britain and Jordan during the 1948 war see Avi Shlaim *Collusion Across the Jordan: King Abdullah, the Zionist Movement and the Partition of Palestine* Clarendon 1988 and Richard L Jesse 'Great Britain and Abdullah's Plan to Partition Palestine: A Natural Sorting Out' *Middle Eastern Studies* 22 1986 pp 505–21. See also 'Britain and the Arab-Israeli War of 1948' *Journal of Palestine Studies* 16/4 1987 pp 50–76.

**1447** Joseph Heller 'Failure of a Mission: Bernadotte and Palestine 1948' *Journal of Contemporary History* 14 1979 pp 515–34. Count Bernadotte was appointed UN mediator on 20th May 1948 (just after the British withdrawal and the de facto declaration of Israel on 14th May) and assassinated in September by the Stern gang, who suspected he was a British agent planning to hand over Jerusalem to Jordan. See also Mordechai Gazit 'American and British Diplomacy and the Bernadotte Mission' *Historical Journal* 29 1986 pp 677–96 and Cary David Stanger 'A Haunting Legacy: The Assassination of Count Bernadotte' *Middle East Journal* 42 1988 pp 260–72. Pablo de Azcarte y Florez *Mission in Palestine 1948–1952* Middle East Institute, Washington DC 1966 is a memoir by the Spaniard who headed the UN mission in Palestine in this period.

**1448** Ilan Pappe *Britain and the Arab-Israeli Conflict 1948–51* Macmillan 1988. An analysis of Britain's policy towards Israel in the post-mandate era, based as it was on Britain's close alliance with Jordan. This relationship led Britain to contemplate war with Israel on behalf of Jordan in 1955–56. This is explored in Stuart A Cohen 'A Still Stranger Aspect of Suez: British Operational Plans to Attack Israel 1955–1956' *International History Review* 10 1988 pp 261–81.

**1449** Eitan Haber *Menachem Begin: The Legend and the Man* Delacorte Press, New York 1978. Begin was one of the leaders of the Jewish terrorist organizations of the last years of the mandate. He later became Prime Minister of Israel.

**1450** Moshe Dayan *Story of My Life* Weidenfeld and Nicolson 1978. An autobiography which includes reflections on the end of the mandate and the negotiations with the French and British before the Suez episode in 1956.

**1451** Shabtai Teveth *Ben-Gurion: The Burning Ground 1886–1948* Hale 1988. A massive and detailed study of Israel's first Prime Minister. David Ben Gurion *Israel: A Personal History* New English Library 1972 is a good semi-autobiographical account. Maurice Edelman *Ben Gurion: A Political Biography* Hodder and Stoughton 1964 is also useful for Suez. So is Avraham Avi-Hai *Ben Gurion State-Builder: Principles and Pragmatism 1948–1963* Israel Universities Press, Jerusalem 1974. See also Michael Bar-Zohar *The Armed Prophet: A Biography of Ben Gurion* Barker 1967.

**1452** Norman Rose (ed) *Baffy: The Diaries of Blanche Dugdale 1936–1947* Vallentine Mitchell 1973. She was a British Zionist.

**1453** Golda Meir *My Life* Weidenfeld and Nicolson 1975. She was Israel's first Foreign Secretary.

**1454** Norman Rose *Lewis Namier and Zionism* Clarendon 1980. The Anglo-Jewish historian Lewis Namier did much work for Zionism. He however lost influence on Weizmann after his baptism as a Christian.

**1455** Norman Rose *Chaim Weizmann: A Biography* Weidenfeld and Nicolson 1987. Weizmann was an Anglo-Jew who became the first President of Israel. See also Meyer W Weisgal and Joel Carmichael (eds) *Chaim Weizmann: A Biography by Several Hands* Weidenfeld and Nicolson 1962, Chaim Weizmann *Trial and Error: The Autobiography of Chaim Weizmann* Hamilton 1949 and Vera Weizmann *The Impossible Takes Longer: The Memoirs of Vera Weizmann, Wife of Israel's First President, as Told to David Tutaev* Hamilton 1967. For Weizmann's papers see Joseph Heller (ed) *The Letters and Papers of Chaim Weizmann Vol 22 Series A May 1945 to July 1947* Transaction Books 1979 and Barnet Litvinoff (ed) *The Letters and Papers of Chaim Weizmann Series B Vol 2: Papers December 1931 to April 1952* Transaction Books 1984.

## (6) Jordan

Much of the literature in the Palestine section (particularly [1446–8]) is also relevant for Britain's policy towards and concern to maintain good relations with Jordan.

**1456** Ian J Seccombe *Jordan* Clio Press 1984. An annotated bibliography which contains some material of use.

**1457** James Morris *The Hashemite Kings* Faber 1959. An analysis of the relationship between the Hashemite dynasty (which has ruled Jordan since 1921 and ruled Iraq 1921–1958) and Britain 1916–1958.

**1458** P J Vatikiotis *Politics and the Military in Jordan: A Study of the Arab Legion 1921–1957* Cass 1967. A good study of the role of the Legion in the creation of modern Jordan. The contribution of British officers is duly emphasized. Godfrey Lias *Glubb's Legion* Evans Brothers 1956 is a mainly anecdotal account up to the dismissal of Glubb in 1956.

**1459** B Shwadran 'The Kingdom of Jordan: To be or not to be' *Middle East Affairs* 8 1957 pp 206–25 and 270–88. An analysis of Jordan's viability as an independent entity and the weakening of British influence in the wake of the dismissals of 1956.

**1460** Sir John Bagot Glubb *The Changing Scenes of Life: An Autobiography* Quartet 1984. Glubb was the commander of the Arab Legion from 1939 until his dismissal by King Hussein in 1956. This is also useful for the Arab Legion's part in the Arab-Israeli war of 1948. See also Glubb's *A Soldier with the Arabs* Hodder and Stoughton 1957. James Lunt *Glubb Pasha: A Biography* Harvill Press 1984 is an official biography by a former Arab Legion officer.

**1461** Charles Johnston *The Brink of Jordan* Hamilton 1972. Johnston was Ambassador to Jordan 1956–60. This is useful for the end of the Anglo-Jordanian treaty, the response to revolution in the neighbouring Hashemite Kingdom of Iraq in 1958 and the subsequent Operation Fortitude in which British paratroops restored order in Jordan.

**1462** Alec Kirkbride *From the Wings: Amman Memoirs 1947–1951* Cass 1976. A memoir of his time as the British Minister in Jordan.

**1463** Mary C Wilson *King Abdullah, Britain and the Making of Jordan* Cambridge University Press 1987. An in-depth study of a key figure in Middle East politics from the 1920s until his death in 1948. See also P Graves (ed) *Memoirs of King Abdullah of Transjordan* Cape 1950.

**1464** King Hussein of Jordan *Uneasy Lies the Head* Heinemann 1962. An autobiography covering the years from his accession to the throne in 1953 to 1961. See also James Lunt *Hussein of Jordan: A Political Biography* Macmillan 1989.

## (7) Cyprus

Britain administered Cyprus from 1878 (from 1914 as colonial ruler) until independence in 1960. From 1954 the British were engaged in a struggle against the EOKA terrorists demanding 'enosis' (union) with Greece. It instead became an independent republic with a constitution designed to balance and protect the two ethnic communities of the island, the Greeks and the Turks. The history of Cyprus since independence has nevertheless been bedevilled by inter-communal struggles. Its connections with Britain have meanwhile remained close. Britain retains sovereign bases on the island and Cyprus has remained a member of the Commonwealth, the only Commonwealth member in the Middle East.

**1465** Paschalis M Kitromilides and Marios L Evriviades *Cyprus* Clio Press 1982. One of the best volumes in the Clio world bibliographical series. A well annotated bibliography.

**1466** Ludwig Dischler *Die Zypernfrage* Alfred Metzner Verlag, Frankfurt am Main 1960. Despite its title this is almost entirely in English. It largely consists of a documentary record of the British in Cyprus from 1878 to the Zurich/London compromise agreements of 1958–9.

**1467** John Reddaway *Burdened with Cyprus: The British Connection* Weidenfeld and Nicolson 1986. A history of the British connection from 1878 up to the present day. He is critical of Britain's conduct as guarantor power since Cyprus became independent in 1960, and of Britain's failure to intervene during the crises of 1964 and 1974. This book includes useful appendices. John T A Koumoulides (ed) *Cyprus in Transition* Trigraph 1986 features a number of essays on the British connection with the island. These include not only reflections on the British administration in Cyprus but also Lord Carver, as Deputy UN Commander in 1964 and Chief of Defence Staff in 1974, commenting on British policy during these crises. See also Naomi Rosenbaum 'Success in Foreign Policy: The British in Cyprus 1878–1960' *Canadian Journal of Political Science* 13 1970 pp 605–27.

**1468** Nancy Cranshaw *The Cyprus Revolt: An Account of the Struggle for Union with Greece* Allen and Unwin 1978. The best study of Cyprus' post-war history. It includes good appendices and an extensive bibliography. Another well-regarded study is Francois Crouzet *Le Conflit de Chypre 1946–1959* 2v, Etablissements Emile Bruylant, Brussels 1973. See also Charalambos D Marinos *La Tragedie Chypriote* Athens 1964.

**1469** George M Alexander 'British Policy on the Question of Enosis 1945–6' *Kypriakai Spoudai* 43 1979 pp 79–94. A study of the deliberations in the British government at this time on the question of ceding Cyprus to Greece.

**1470** Lord Harding of Petherton 'The Cyprus Problem in Relation to the Middle East' *International Affairs* 34 1958 pp 291–6. An analysis of British policy in Cyprus in the context of British policy in the Middle East.

**1471** Stephen G Xydis 'Towards "Toil and Moil" in Cyprus' *Middle East Journal* 20 1966 pp 1–19. A study of Greek policy towards Cyprus 1945–55. His *Cyprus: Conflict and Conciliation 1954–1958* Ohio State University Press, Columbus, Ohio 1967 and *Cyprus: Reluctant Republic* Mouton, Paris 1973 also focus on later stages of Greek policy and the Greek Cypriot demand for 'enosis'.

**1472** Leontios Lerodiokonos *The Cyprus Question* Almquist and Wiksell, Stockholm 1971. A study which concentrates on 1954–9. *Cyprus: The Dispute and the Settlement* Royal Institute of International Affairs 1959 draws largely on the accounts in the British press and parliament. It includes extracts of documents. Also useful for the policies of the British, Greek and Turkish governments is T S Bahcheli 'Communal Discord and the Stake of Interested Governments in Cyprus 1955–1970' London PhD Thesis 1972–3.

**1473** Lawrence Durrell *Bitter Lemons* E P Dutton 1958. This book reflects the novelist's experiences as Director of Public Relations for the Cyprus government 1953–6.

**1474** Sylvia Foot *Emergency Exit* Chatto and Windus 1960. Impressions and memories of the last two years of British rule by the wife of the last governor, Sir Hugh Foot.

**1475** Michael Harbottle *The Impartial Soldier* Oxford University Press 1970. Memoirs of his time as Chief of Staff to the United Nations peace-keeping force in Cyprus 1966–8. This force, brought in 1964 after intercommunal violence erupted in 1963, was the first UN force Britain had taken part in. This memoir includes reflections on the British part and on the continuing role of the British sovereign bases.

**1476** Agop Garabedjan 'The Struggle for "Enosis" and the Efforts to Achieve Political Unity in Cyprus (1945–1947)' *Etudes Balkaniques* 21 1985 pp 14–27. This looks at Left and Right attitudes to 'enosis' at a time when the Greek civil war (in which the British were involved in combating the Communists) was still raging.

**1477** Spyros Kyprianou *The Cyprus Question: The British Reply to the British National Committee for the Self-Determination of Cyprus* Athens 1956. The case for self-determination made by a future President of Cyprus.

**1478** P N Vanezis *Makarios: Faith and Power* Abelard-Schuman 1971. This is continued by his *Makarios: Pragmatism Versus Idealism* 1974 and *Makarios: Life and Leadership* 1979. Archbishop Makarios, the head of the Orthodox church in Cyprus was one of the leaders of the campaign for 'enosis'. His links with terrorism led to his deportation 1956–7. He later became President of Cyprus from 1960 until his death in 1977. Stanley Mayes *Makarios: A Biography* Macmillan 1981 is a one volume critical biography. See also his *Cyprus and Makarios* Putnam 1960.

**1479** *The Tripartite Conference on the Eastern Mediterranean and Cyprus* Cmnd 9594, *Parliamentary Papers* xli 1955–56. The text of the conference between Britain, Greece and Turkey.

**1480** *Cyprus: Correspondence Exchanged Between the Governor and Archbishop Makarios* Cmnd 9708, *Parliamentary Papers* xxxv 1955–56. The official text of correspondence between the Governor, Sir John Harding and Archbishop Makarios.

**1481** Lord Radcliffe *Constitutional Proposals for Cyprus* Cmnd 42, *Parliamentary Papers* x 1956–57. These suggest self-government with British sovereignty to remain unaffected. The next British initiative was the Macmillan plan for tripartite British, Greek and Turkish control of Cyprus, announced in *Cyprus: Statement of Policy* Cmnd 455, *Parliamentary Papers* xxiv 1957–58. The modified plan produced by NATO, in which all three were members, *Discussion on Cyprus in the North Atlantic Treaty Organisation* Cmnd 566, *Parliamentary Papers* xxx 1958–59 however proved unacceptable to Greece.

**1482** *Conference on Cyprus* Cmnds 679 and 680, *Parliamentary Papers* xxx 1958–59. The text of the Zurich/London agreements which led to the creation of an independent Cyprus in 1960.

**1483** Eric Baker 'The Settlement in Cyprus' *Political Quarterly* 30 1959 pp 244–53. A study of the final phase of the negotiations that led to the agreements. See also Roy P Fairfield 'The Settlement in Cyprus' *Middle East Journal* 13 1959 pp 235–48.

**1484** *Report from the Select Committee on Cyprus Together with the Proceedings of the Committee, Minutes of Evidence and Appendices* HC Paper 331, *Parliamentary Papers* xvii 1975–76. A critical analysis of British policy towards Cyprus, of the failure of the Wilson government to intervene in the crisis in Cyprus in 1974 and of British conduct during that crisis and after.

## (8) Libya

**1485** Richard I Lawless *Libya* Clio Press 1987. An annotated bibliography of some value.

**1486** John Wright *Libya: A Modern History* Croom Helm 1981. There is no history of the British in Libya. This however is quite useful on Britain's relations with King Idris, the British military presence from 1943–69 and the Wilson government's refusal to intervene in the coup shortly after the withdrawal of British troops that overthrew Idris and brought Colonel Gaddafi to power. Wright's *Libya* Benn 1969 is also of considerable value.

**1487** Adrian Pelt *Libyan Independence and the United Nations: A Case of Planned Decolonisation* Yale University Press 1970. A very detailed study of the negotiations in the UN from 1948 onwards which led to the creation of the independence Kingdom of Libya in 1951. It includes many documents in its appendices. Nina Epton *Oasis Kingdom: The Libyan Story* Jarrolds 1952 is an account of a visit shortly before independence which contains a detailed description of the negotiations in the UN. See also Ann Dearden 'Independence for Libya: The Political Problem' *Middle East Journal* 4 1950 pp 395–409.

**1488** Lisa S Anderson 'Religion and Politics in Libya' *Journal of Arab Affairs* 1 1981 pp 53–77. This charts the rise of Islamic nationalism in Libya.

**1489** *On the Evacuation of British Forces* Department of Public Relations, Ministry of Education and National Guidance, Tripoli n.d. (1970?). On the British evacuation in 1969 and the end of the Anglo-Libyan treaty.

### (9) Aden

For the campaign against the terrorists who destroyed the South Arabian Federation the British had attempted to set up and instead created the Communist People's Republic of South Yemen after the Wilson government had decided to cut its losses and withdraw in 1967 see the section on Colonial Wars.

**1490** Jens Plasse and Ulrich Gehre *Die Aden-Grenze in der Südarabienfrage (1900–1967)* C W Leske Verlag, Opladen 1967. Documents and materials (in German).

**1491** G Rex Smith *The Yemens* Clio Press 1984. An annotated bibliography which is quite good on the British presence in Aden.

**1492** Robin Bidwell *The Two Yemens* Longman 1983. A general history of North and South Yemen from the sixteenth century.

**1493** David Ledger *Shifting Sands: The British in South Arabia* Peninsular Press 1983. A very good and vivid history. R J Gavin *Aden Under British Rule 1839–1967* C Hurst 1975 is a general history with good appendices. Also useful is Z H Kour *The History of Aden* Cass 1981.

**1494** Manfred W Wenner *Modern Yemen 1918–1966* John Hopkins University Press, Baltimore, Maryland 1967. A general history up to the end of the civil war between republicans and monarchists in North Yemen. Harold Ingrams *The Yemen: Imams, Rulers and Revolutions* Murray 1963 brings out the impact of events in North Yemen on the Aden protectorate more clearly in this account of the events leading up to the 1962 republican revolution. See also Rupert Hay 'Great Britain's Relations with Yemen and Oman' *Middle East Affairs* 11 1960 pp 142–9. A Yemeni criticism of Britain's support of Oman in the Buraimi oasis dispute and of British policies in Aden at this time is *British Imperialism in Southern Arabia* Arab Information Center, New York 1958.

**1495** Christopher Gandy 'Yemen: The Land of Might-Have-Been' *Asian Affairs* 19 1988 pp 61–8. A good overview and critique of British policy in Southern Arabia from 1945 onwards.

**1496** Sir Bernard Reilly *Aden and the Yemen* HMSO 1960. An official account of the development of the South Arabian Federation and of Britain's relations with the Yemen. It includes useful supporting material.

**1497** Gillian King *Imperial Outpost – Aden: Its Place in British Strategic Policy* Oxford University Press 1964. A criticism of Britain's attempt to create a major military base in Aden in the 1960s.

**1498** K K Pieragostini 'A Decision Making Analysis of Government Policy: A Case Study of British Policy Towards Aden and the South Arabian Federation 1963–1966' London PhD Thesis 1982. A good study drawing extensively on interviewing.

**1499** Tom Little *South Arabia: Arena of Conflict* Pall Mall Press 1968. An account of the South Arabian Federation Britain established in the Aden protectorate down to its replacement by a Marxist republic in 1968. On the rise of radical politics in the final years of British rule see Joseph Kostiner 'Arab Radical Politics: al-Qawniyyun al-'Arab and the Marxists in the Turmoil of South Yemen 1963–1967' *Middle Eastern Studies* 17 1981 pp 454–76 and Hussein Ali and Ken Whittingham 'Notes Towards an Understanding of the Revolution in South Yemen' *Race and Class* 16 1974 pp 83–100.

**1500** Sir Tom Hickinbotham *Aden* Constable 1958. An overview of the situation in the colony and protectorate drawing on memories of service there since the 1930s (1951–6 as governor). At no point does he hint that Britain would have left in less than ten years.

**1501** Charles Hepburn Johnston *The View from Steamer Point: Being an Account of Three Years in Aden* Collins 1964. An account of his time in Aden in 1960–3 when, as Governor then High Commissioner, he presided over the creation of the South Arabian Federation.

**1502** Sir Kennedy Trevaskis *Shades of Amber: A South Arabian Episode* Hutchinson 1968. A study of the collapse of British power in Aden 1951–67. Whilst critical of Colonial Office policy he also acknowledges his mistakes as High Commissioner in Aden 1963–5.

## (10) The Persian Gulf

Britain had developed protective treaty arrangements with the sheikdoms of the Gulf in the days of the Indian empire. In the post-war period the oil wealth of the region ensured that it remained important to Britain. Britain only withdrew from the various states concerned in this section, Bahrain, Kuwait, Qatar, and what is now the United Arab Emirates at the end of 1971 as a result of the decision to withdraw from East of Suez.

**1503** Penelope Tucson *The Records of the British Residency and Agencies in the Persian Gulf* India Office Library and Records 1979. An unannotated guide to records files in the India Office Library.

**1504** *The Persian Gulf Gazette* HMSO Oct 1953–May 1972. The official gazette issued by the British Political Residency in the Gulf.

**1505** P T H Urwin *Bahrain* Clio Press 1984. A bibliography which usefully contains a select and annotated list of publications on the British connection and withdrawal. Other useful bibliographies from the same world bibliographical series are P T H Unwin *Qatar* Clio Press 1982, Frank A Clements *United Arab Emirates* Clio Press 1983, and Frank A Clements *Kuwait* Clio Press 1985.

**1506** S H Al-Sagri 'Britain and the Arab Emirates 1820–1956: A Documentary Study' Kent PhD Thesis 1988.

**1507** John Marlowe *The Persian Gulf in the Twentieth Century* Cresset Press 1962. This has not yet been superseded. British interests and oil are well covered.

**1508** Husain M Abaharna *The Legal Status of the Arabian Gulf States* Manchester University Press 1968. This study is useful for understanding the basis of Britain's position in the Gulf. It covers Britain's treaties with the Trucial States, Bahrain, Qatar, Kuwait and Muscat and the important question of the defining of

boundaries. See also John Barrett Kelly 'The Legal and Historical Basis of the British Position in the Persian Gulf' *St Anthony's Papers* 4 1958 pp 119–60.

**1509** John Barrett Kelly 'The British Position in the Persian Gulf' *World Today* 20 1964 pp 238–49. A study of the Gulf's economic and strategic significance to the British in the 1960s.

**1510** William Luce 'Britain in the Persian Gulf: Mistaken Timing over Aden' *Round Table* 227 1967 pp 277–83. A criticism of the destablizing effects of Britain's withdrawal from Aden.

**1511** Sir Anthony Parsons 'Gulf Withdrawal: Britain's Withdrawal from the Gulf 1965–71' *Contemporary Record* 2/2 1988 pp 41–3. A useful overview drawing on his personal experiences as Political Agent in Bahrain 1965–9. For studies of the reasons behind the withdrawal, announced in 1968, and of the reactions to it in the Gulf and elsewhere see Alvin J Cottrell 'British Withdrawal from the Persian Gulf' *Military Review* 50 1970 pp 14–21, H G Balfour Paul 'Recent Developments in the Persian Gulf' *Royal Central Asian Journal* 56 1969 pp 12–9, Donald Cameron Watt 'The Decision to Withdraw from the Gulf' *Political Quarterly* 39 1968 pp 310–21, Sir William Luce 'Britain's Withdrawal from the Middle East and Persian Gulf' *Royal United Services Institute Journal* 114 1969 pp 4–10 and William D Brewer 'Yesterday and Tomorrow in the Persian Gulf' *Middle East Journal* 23 1969 pp 149–58.

**1512** Rosemarie Said Zohlan *The Origins of the United Arab Emirates: A Political and Social History of the Trucial States* Macmillan 1978. The best general history. Donald Hawley *The Trucial States* Allen and Unwin 1970 is a history of the seven Trucial States from the earliest times. It is quite useful for the British connection. See also Nelson R Beck 'Britain's Withdrawal from the Persian Gulf and the Formation of the United Arab Emirates 1968–1971' *Towson State Journal of International Affairs* 12 1978 pp 77–98.

**1513** H Sirriyyeh 'The Gulf: British Withdrawal and US Policy 1968–1977' Oxford DPhil Thesis 1981. A study of the effect of the British withdrawal on the Gulf states and on American policy in the region. Another study of the process of British withdrawal and its effect on the regional balance of power is M S Agwani *Politics in the Gulf* Vikas, New Delhi 1978. See also Jacob Coleman Hurewitz *The Persian Gulf: Prospects for Stability* Foreign Policy Association, New York 1974 and Denis Wright 'The Changed Balance of Power in the Persian Gulf' *Asian Affairs* 60 1973 pp 255–62. Elizabeth Monroe *The Changing Balance of Power in the Persian Gulf* American Universities Field Staff, New York 1972 is also particularly useful for the interests of other powers, such as the Soviet Union or China, in the region in the wake of the British withdrawal.

**1514** John Whelan (ed) 'UK and the Gulf 1971–1981: A MEED Special Report' *Middle East Economic Digest* Dec 1981. A whole issue on the changed economic and political relations since withdrawal. 'The UK and Arabia: A Commemorative issue to Mark the Visit of HM Queen Elizabeth II' *Middle East Economic Digest* Feb 1979 is another whole issue which concentrates on trade, construction and banking. A study of Britain's diplomatic problems in the region 1970–86, complicated by factors such as the Gulf War between Iran and Iraq, is Peter Savigear 'Political Change in the Gulf: A Dilemma for Britain' *Contemporary Review* 250 1987 pp 10–15.

## (11) Oman

For Britain's involvement in the defence and support of Oman, from the Buraimi oasis dispute of the 1950s to the Dhofar war of 1972–5 see the section on Colonial Wars.

**1515** Frank A Clements *Oman* Clio Press 1981. This includes an extensive annotated bibliography on the British in Oman and British military support for the Sultan.

**1516** Abid A al-Marayati 'The Question of Oman' *Foreign Affairs Reports* 15 1966 pp 99–109. This describes the support of Britain for Oman in disputes with North Yemen in the 1950s and the criticism of British policy in the UN by the Arab League. See also [1494].

**1517** Neil McLeod Innes *Minister in Oman: A Personal Narrative* Oleander Press 1987. Innes was the Foreign Minister of Oman 1953–8.

## (12) Iran

**1518** Reza Navabpour *Iran* Clio Press. An annotated bibliography which contains some material of value on the British in Iran during and immediately after the Second World War and on the dispute over the nationalization of the Anglo-Iranian Oil Company (BP) in the early 1950s.

**1519** L P Elwell-Sutton *Persian Oil: A Study in Power Politics* Lawrence and Wishart 1955. A study of relations between the Anglo-Iranian Oil Company and the Iranian government up to the nationalization crisis of 1951–3.

**1520** Fakhreddin Azimi *Iran: The Crisis of Democracy 1941–1953* I B Tauris 1988. A good general history of Iran from the Anglo-Soviet occupation of 1941 to the restoration of the Shah in 1953. A good study of British policy in Iran in this period is C S Amaratunga 'The British Presence and the Nationalist Challenge: Anglo-Iranian Relations 1941–1953' London PhD Thesis 1986.

**1521** Central Office of Information *Paiforce: The Official History of the Persia and Iraq Command 1941–1946* HMSO 1948.

**1522** William Roger Louis and James A Bill (eds) *Mussaddiq, Iranian Nationalism and Oil* I B Tauris 1988. In 1951 Mussaddiq, the Iranian Prime Minister, nationalized Anglo-Iranian Oil. In 1953 a CIA engineered coup ousted him and restored the Shah. This valuable collection of essays examines the origins of his movement, the nationalization, the coup, the consortium of oil companies that replaced the British monopoly in 1954, the attitudes of Iran, America and Britain in the crisis and its influence on British thinking during the Suez crisis and after. Also useful are A W Ford *The Anglo-Iranian Oil Dispute of 1951–52: A Study of the Role of Law in the Relations of States* Cambridge University Press 1954, S Hodgshon 'Tensions Between Britain and the United States in the Middle East 1945–54, with Special Reference to the Anglo-Iranian Oil Crisis 1951–54' Sussex D Phil Thesis 1977 and H Enayat 'British Public Opinion and the Iranian Oil Crisis from 1951 to 1954' London MSc (Econ) Thesis 1957. See also Benjamin Shwadran 'The Anglo-Iranian Oil Dispute 1948–53' *Middle Eastern Affairs* 5 1954 pp 193–231, L Lockhart 'The Causes of the Anglo-Persian Oil Dispute' *Journal of the Royal Central Asian Society* 40 1953 pp 134–50, H Carrière d'Encausse 'Le Conflit Anglo-Iranien 1951–54' *Revue Française de Science Politique* 15 1965 pp 731–43 and J Frankel 'The Anglo-Iranian Dispute' *Yearbook of World Affairs* 1952 pp 56–74.

**1523** Kermit Roosevelt *Countercoup: The Struggle for the Control of Iran* McGraw-Hill 1979. A narrative of the 1953 coup by the leader of the operation.

## (13) Iraq

For the Hashemite kings of Iraq see the section on the other Hashemite kingdom of Jordan [1457].

**1524** Majid Khadduri *Independent Iraq 1932–58: A Study in Iraqi Politics* 2nd ed, Oxford University Press 1960. Iraq, put under the British mandate after the First World War, became independent in 1932. Ties with Britain however remained close until the revolution of 1958 in which King Feisal and his Prime Minister Nuri As-Said were overthrown and assassinated. Stephen

Hemsley Longrigg *Iraq 1900 to 1950: A Political, Social and Economic History* Oxford University Press 1953 includes some reflections on Britain's continuing influence in the lengthy chapter on post-war Iraq. Pierre Rondot 'L'Expérience Britannique en Iraq (1920–1955)' *L'Afrique et L'Asie* 2nd series 30 1955 pp 3–26 covers Britain's relations with Iraq up to the 1955 Baghdad Pact.

**1525** G T A Al-Shibly 'Iraqi-British Relations – with Special Reference to Inter-Arab Politics 1948–1958' Aberdeen MLitt Thesis 1972–3.

**1526** Caractacus (pseud) *Revolution in Iraq: An Essay in Comparative Political Opinion* Gollancz 1959. This is useful for British attitudes at the time of the 1958 revolution.

**1527** Christopher Bromhead, Lord Birdwood *Nuri As-Said: A Study in Arab Leadership* Cassell 1959. A biography of the Prime Minister of Iraq who was overthrown in 1958. Waldemar J Gallman *Iraq Under General Nuri: My Recollections of Nuri al-Said 1954–1958* Johns Hopkins University Press, Baltimore, Maryland 1964 also comments usefully on British interests in Iraq.

## E. SUB–SAHARAN AFRICA

### (1) General

**1528** Mary Doreen Wainwright and Noel Matthews *A Guide to Manuscripts and Documents in the British Isles Relating to Africa* Oxford University Press 1981. A classified well indexed guide. The locations of material are given. Ilse Sternberg and Patricia M Larby (eds) *African Studies* British Library 1986 is a collection of papers which present a wealth of information on sources in Britain and elsewhere.

**1529** *Journal of African Administration* HMSO 1949–61. A quarterly journal which contains bibliographies, details of recent legislation, policy statements and so on.

**1530** *Current Themes in African Historical Studies: A Selected Bibliographical Guide to Resources for Research in African History* African Bibliographical Center, Washington DC 1964–. A regularly published, but unannotated bibliography. *International African Bibliography: Current Books, Articles and Papers in African Studies* Mansell 1971– is a geographically arranged unannotated annual bibliography. See also John N Paden and Edward W Soja (eds) *The African Experience Vol III A: Bibliography* Northwestern University Press,

Evanston, Illinois 1970, a large and partly annotated bibliography.

**1531** Peter Duignan (ed) *Guide to Research and Reference Works on Sub-Saharan Africa* Hoover Institution Press, Stanford, California 1971. A massive well annotated and indexed bibliography.

**1532** *African Affairs* 1902–. The quarterly issues regularly feature a bibliography of recent books and articles.

**1533** Robert B Shaw and Richard L Sklar *A Bibliography for the Study of African Politics* African Studies Center Occasional Paper 9, University of California, Los Angeles, California 1973. An unannotated and geographically arranged bibliography. It is superior to William John Hanna and Judith Lynne Hanna *Politics in Black Africa: A Selective Bibliography of Relevant Periodical Literature* African Studies Center, Michigan State University, East Lansing, Michigan 1964. This latter is also unannotated.

**1534** Oliver B Pollak and Karen Pollak *Theses and Dissertations on Southern Africa: An International Bibliography* G K Hall, Boston, Massachusetts 1976. An unannotated classified listing.

**1535** Michael Crowder (ed) *The Cambridge History of Africa Vol 8: From c1940 to c1975* Cambridge University Press 1984. A useful general history. See also John D Hargreaves *Decolonisation in Africa* Longman 1988.

**1536** Lewis H Gann and Peter Duignan (eds) *Colonialism in Africa 1870–1960* 5v, Cambridge University Press 1969–75. The various volumes are on different themes. They contain a number of useful essays on British colonialism in Africa. Volume 5 is a bibliography.

**1537** P J M McEwan (ed) *Twentieth Century Africa* Oxford University Press 1968. A book of readings covering Africa by region followed by a section on nationalism in Africa. It includes a chronology.

**1538** Kenneth Kirkwood *Britain and Africa* Chatto and Windus 1965. A rather unanalytical overview of Britain's role in Africa. It seeks to provide a contemporary picture, concentrating on developments since 1945. Much of the book is concerned with Britain's relations in the various regions of Africa, which are examined in turn. See also Maurice Pollet *L'Afrique du Commonwealth* Editions Saint-Paul, Paris 1963.

**1539** Margery Perham *Colonial Sequence 1930 to 1949: A Chronological Commentary upon British Colonial Policy in Africa* Methuen 1967. Continued by *Colonial Sequence 1949 to 1969* 1970. Largely a record of her efforts to influence colonial policy. A chronologically arranged commentary, illustrated by extracts from her writings. It presents a rather sanitized account of the problems and processes of policy making.

**1540** Malcolm Hailey 'Post-War Changes in Africa' *Journal of the Royal Society of Arts* 103 1955 pp 579–90. Reflections by a great Colonial Office administrator.

**1541** Sir Andrew Cohen *British Policy in Changing Africa* Routledge and Kegan Paul 1959. As Assistant Under Secretary at the Colonial Office 1947–51 Cohen had a major influence on the development of post-war colonial policy. His main theme here is the importance of training colonies for independence.

**1542** R J R Rodd *British Military Administration of Occupied Territories in Africa During the Years 1941–7* HMSO 1948. Part of the official history of the Second World War. The main areas of interest are Libya, Ethiopia, Eritrea and Italian Somaliland. There is also some material on military administration in the Middle East and East Africa 1944–6 and in the Dodecanese 1943–7. There is a good chronology, maps and appendices.

**1543** David Killingray and Richard Rathbone (eds) *Africa and the Second World War* Macmillan 1987. This includes quite a few essays on the impact of the war on British colonial Africa.

**1544** R D Pearce *The Turning Point in Africa: British Colonial Policy 1938–48* Cass 1982. A study of Colonial Office planning which he sees as moving, under the influence of the war and of American pressure, from the complacent trusteeship of the inter-war years to a strategy for decolonization. However as he points out in 'The Colonial Office and Planned Decolonisation in Africa' *African Affairs* 83 1984 pp 77–94 there was no blueprint but simply tentative plans for change. See also John Flint 'The Failure of Planned Decolonisation in British Africa' *African Affairs* 82 1983 pp 389–412. On the background and effect of Creech Jones' circular despatch of February 1947 on preparations for self-government see John W Cell 'On the Eve of Decolonisation: The Colonial Office's Plans for the Tranfer of Power in Africa' *Journal of Imperial and Commonwealth History* 8 1980 pp 235–57 and Pearce's response 'The Colonial Office in 1947 and the Transfer of Power: An Addendum to John Cell' *Journal of Imperial and Commonwealth History* 10 1982 pp 211–15. See also the statement of policy by the then Minister of State, the Earl of Listowel 'The Modern Conception of Government in the British Colonies' *Journal of African Administration* 1 1949 pp 99–105.

**1545** Charles Armour 'The BBC and the Development of Broadcasting in British Colonial Africa 1946–1956' *African Affairs* 83 1984 pp 359–402. Broadcasting policy was an element in the process of decolonization.

**1546** Ronald Hyam 'Africa and the Labour Government 1945–1951' *Journal of Imperial and Commonwealth History* 16 1988 pp 148–72. A useful study of the Attlee government's colonial, economic development and strategic policy in Africa.

**1547** A Fenner Brockway *African Journeys* Gollancz 1955. Brockway, a leading figure on the Labour Left, was very active in anti-colonial campaigns.

**1548** George Padmore *Africa: Britain's Third Empire* Dennis Dobson 1949. A critical study of British policy, particularly economic development policy, in Africa after the Second World War by one of the founding fathers of African nationalism. Padmore himself came from Trinidad but his Pan-Africanism had a major influence on a whole generation of nationalist leaders, particularly in Nkrumah's Ghana. A useful biography is James R Hooker *Black Revolutionary: George Padmore's Path from Communism to Pan-Africanism* Pall Mall Press 1967. The Pan-African Movement, of which Padmore was a leading figure, is examined in Peter O Esedebe 'A History of the Pan-African Movement in Britain 1900–1948' London PhD Thesis 1968.

**1549** Dan Horowitz 'Attitudes of British Conservatives Towards Decolonisation in Africa During the Period of the Macmillan Government 1957–63' Oxford DPhil Thesis 1967–8. A study of the response of the party to the important steps in the direction of decolonization taken by the Macmillan government. See also his 'Attitudes of British Conservatives Towards Decolonisation in Africa' *African Affairs* 59 1970 pp 9–26.

**1550** R I Rotberg 'The Federation Movement in British East and Central Africa 1889–1953' *Journal of Commonwealth Political Studies* 2 1963–4 pp 141–60. An examination of how white settlers in Central Africa were able to set up a Federation in 1953 whilst the Colonial Office resisted similar demands for one in East Africa.

**1551** Anthony H M Kirk-Greene *A Biographical Dictionary of the British Colonial Governor Vol I: Africa* Harvester 1980. A very useful reference guide which includes biographical, bibliographical and sociological details. His 'On Governorship and Governors in British Africa' in Lewis H Gann and Peter Duignan (eds) *African Proconsuls: European Governors in Africa* Collier Macmillan 1978 pp 209–64 is a good study on the character, careers, role and work of governors. See also his 'The Progress of Pro-Consuls: Advancement and Migration Among the Colonial Governors of British African Territories 1900–1965' *Journal of Imperial and Commonwealth History* 7 1979 pp 180–212.

**1552** Anthony H M Kirk-Greene (ed) *Africa in the Colonial Period III: The Transfer of Power: The Colonial Administrator in the Age of Decolonisation* Inter-

Faculty Committee for African Studies, University of Oxford 1979. A symposium which includes papers on the role of various levels of the Colonial Service drawing on personal experiences, on Africanization and decolonization and on the role of British constitutional models for colonial political development.

**1553** Charles Allen (ed) *Tales from the Dark Continent: Images of British Colonial Africa in the Twentieth Century* Deutsch/BBC 1979. An evocative portrait of colonial Africa making good use of oral evidence. For the Colonial Service see also Anthony H M Kirk-Greene 'The Thin White Line: The Size of the British Colonial Service in Africa' *African Affairs* 79 1980 pp 25–44 and Pat Holden *Women Administrative Officers in Colonial Africa 1944–1960* Oxford Development Record Project Report 5, Rhodes House Library, Oxford 1985.

**1554** Anthony Clayton *The British Military Presence in East and Central Africa* Oxford Development Records Project 1982. A excellent survey up to independence and beyond based on papers and interviews. It includes a guide to relevant documents at Rhodes House, Oxford.

**1555** Bryan Keith-Lucas 'The Dilemma of Local Government in Africa' in Kenneth Robinson and A Frederick Madden (eds) *Essays in Imperial Government Presented to Margery Perham* Blackwell 1963 pp 193–208. The development of local government was important in training Africans for self-government and was emphasized in Creech Jones' circular despatch in 1947. This is an analysis of successes and failures. See also 'A Survey of the Development of Local Government in the African Territories Since 1947' *Journal of African Administration* 4 1952 pp 1–83.

**1556** Maurice, Lord Hailey *Native Administration in the British African Territories* 5v, HMSO 1950–3. A massive survey. Part I covers Uganda, Kenya and Tanganyika; Part II Zanzibar, Nyasaland and Northern Rhodesia; Part III Nigeria, the Gold Coast, Sierra Leone and the Gambia and Part V the High Commission territories. Part IV is a general survey of the system of native administration.

**1557** Anthony Clayton and David Killingray *Khaki and Blue: The Military Police in British Colonial Africa* Ohio University Press 1989. A very useful study which goes up to the end of empire. See also Clayton's *The Thin Blue Line: Studies in Law Enforcement in Late Colonial Africa* Oxford Development Records Project 1985.

**1558** Godfrey M Brown and Mervyn Hiskett (eds) *Conflict and Harmony in Education in Tropical Africa* Allen and Unwin 1975. The section on Islamic education (pp 91–272) in particular contains references to British education policy in Africa.

**1559** Cyril Ehrlich 'Building and Caretaking: Economic Policy in British Tropical Africa 1890–1960' *Economic History Review* 2nd series, 26 1973 pp 649–67. See also J Forbes Munro *Britain in Tropical Africa 1880–1960: Economic Relationships and Impact* Macmillan 1984.

**1560** Thomas Hodgkin *Nationalism in Colonial Africa* Muller 1956. See also Terence O Ranger 'Connexions Between Primary Resistance Movements and Modern Mass Nationalism in East and Central Africa' *Journal of African History* 9 1968 pp 437–53 and 631–42, Robert I Rotberg 'The Origins of Nationalist Discontent in East and Central Africa' *Journal of Negro History* 48 1963 pp 130–41 and Bernard T Chidzero 'African Nationalism in East and Central Africa' *International Affairs* 36 1960 pp 464–75.

**1561** Yusuf Bangura *Britain and Commonwealth Africa: The Politics of Economic Relations 1951–75* Manchester University Press 1983. A good study of trade, aid, monetary relations and investment. Ali A Mazrui *The Anglo-African Commonwealth: Political Friction and Cultural Fusion* Pergamon 1967 is an erudite and discursive analysis of ties of sentiment, politics and culture. John D Hargreaves *et al Collected Seminar Papers on the Impact of African Issues on the Commonwealth* Institute of Commonwealth Studies, University of London 1969 deals with the impact of issues such as the Biafran war on the Commonwealth. James Mayall 'Britain and Anglophone Africa' in Amadu Sesay (ed) *Africa and Europe: From Partition to Interdependence or Dependence?* Croom Helm 1986 pp 52–74 is a sketchy and glib portrait of relations since independence, concentrating on aid, South Africa and the notion of neo-colonialism. See also the short seminar paper, J K Mwale *Britain and Commonwealth Africa: An Assessment of Britain's Change of Policy Towards Commonwealth Africa 1965–1975* History Department, Malawi University, Zomba 1976.

**1562** Martin Meredith *The First Dance of Freedom: Black Africa in the Post-War Era* Hamilton 1984. A good, if gloomy picture of post-war black Africa with a good bibliography. Evgeny Tarabrin *The New Scramble for Africa* Progress Publishers, Moscow 1974 is a fascinating study of the power without responsibility of post-independence neo-colonialism in Africa; although his concentration on rivalry between France, America and Britain for trade and influence in post-colonial Africa whilst leaving China and the Soviet Union out of the equation does give it a certain artificiality. He also gives less weight to arms as a form of influence than might have been expected. His *The Strategy and Tactics of British Neo-Colonialism* Neuka Publishers, Moscow 1969 is also useful on Britain's continuing influence and the activities of British companies in Africa. He however possibly exaggerates the extent of that influence.

## (2) East Africa

### (a) General

**1563** Thomas P Ofcansky *British East Africa 1856–1963: An Annotated Bibliography* Garland 1986. Over 3000 entries. It has however been criticized for poor classification and some important omissions.

**1564** Donald Anthony Low and Alison Smith (eds) *History of East Africa Vol 3* Clarendon 1976. The standard history. This covers 1945–63 and has a good bibliography. Anthony J Hughes *East Africa: Kenya, Tanzania, Uganda* 2nd ed, Penguin 1969 is useful for political development in the region. See also Kenneth Ingham *A History of the East Africa* 3rd ed, Longmans 1965. Cyril Ehrlich 'Economic and Social Developments Before Independence' in Bethell A Ogot and J A Kiernan (eds) *Zamani: A Survey of East African History* East African Publishing House, Nairobi 1968 pp 334–48 is a rather sketchy study.

**1565** Elspeth Huxley *The Sourcerer's Apprentice: A Journey Through East Africa* Chatto and Windus 1948. A very informative travelogue derived from a journey in 1947. Her *A New Earth: An Experiment in Colonialism* Chatto and Windus 1960 is part travelogue, part analysis of colonial development, especially in agriculture, and part reflections on the Mau Mau emergency.

**1566** *East Africa Royal Commission 1953–55* Cmnd 9475, *Parliamentary Papers* xiii 1955–56. Chaired by Sir Hugh Dow this report was very concerned with the improvement of the agricultural conditions that had contributed to the outbreak of the Mau Mau rebellion.

**1567** E A Brett *Colonialism and Underdevelopment in East Africa* NOK Publishers 1973. A critical study of economic development under colonial rule.

**1568** Ann Beck 'Colonial Policy and Education in British East Africa' *Journal of British Studies* 5 1966 pp 115–38. Education policy was seen as contributing to economic and political development.

**1569** S Nyagah *The Politicalization of Administration in East Africa: A Comparative Analysis of Kenya and Tanzania* Kenya Institute of Administration, Lower Kabete 1968. A well regarded short analysis.

**1570** N J Westcott 'Closer Union and the Future of East Africa 1939–1948: A Case Study of the "Official Mind of Imperialism"' *Journal of Imperial and Commonwealth History* 10 1981 pp 67–88. A study of settler enthusiasms for and Colonial Office attitudes to Federation of the territories in East Africa and why it did not occur. The role of Mau Mau in this is considered in D F Gordon 'Mau Mau and Decolonisation: Kenya and the defeat of Multi-Racialism in East and Central Africa' *Kenya Historical Review* 5 1977 pp 329–48.

**1571** John Lonsdale 'Some Origins of Nationalism in East Africa' *Journal of African History* 9 1968 pp 119–46. This looks at the role of ordinary rural Africans in the origins of nationalist movements.

### (b) Kenya

The literature on the Mau Mau emergency of 1952–6 can be found in the section on Colonial Wars.

**1572** Robert G Gregory, Robert M Macon and Leon P Spencer *A Guide to the Kenya National Archives* Syracuse University Program of East African Studies, Syracuse, New York 1968.

**1573** M F Morris *Government Publications Relating to Kenya and the East African High Commission 1897–1963* EP Microfilm 1976. This collects relevant documents on 134 reels of film.

**1574** John B Webster *et al A Bibliography on Kenya* Syracuse University Program on East African Studies 1967. A comprehensive bibliography. An annotated bibliography of some value is Robert L Collison *Kenya* Clio Press 1982.

**1575** Richard Frost *Race Against Time: Human Relations and Politics in Kenya Before Independence* Rex Collings 1978. A good study of post-war racial tensions and political developments with a good bibliography. Also of some use is David F Gordon *Decolonisation and the State in Kenya* Westview, Boulder, Colorado 1986. Marshall MacPhee *Kenya* Praeger, New York 1968 is a general history, especially from c1920 onwards. George Bennett *Kenya: A Political History: The Colonial Period* Oxford University Press 1963 is a textbook history. See also Bethell A Ogot 'Kenya Under the British 1895 to 1963' in Bethell A Ogot and A Kiernan (eds) *Zamani: A Survey of East African History* East African Publishing House, Nairobi 1968 pp 255–89. Central Office of Information *Kenya* HMSO 1963 is a short informative pamphlet published to accompany independence.

**1576** David Throup *Economic and Social Origins of Mau Mau 1945–53* Heinemann, Nairobi 1987. The best account of the social, economic and political background to the Mau Mau emergency, even if much of his analysis of socio-economic changes does not command universal agreement. It also has a useful bibliography. Bruce J Berman 'Bureaucracy and Incumbent Violence: Colonial Administration and the Origins of the "Mau Mau"

Emergency in Kenya' *British Journal of Political Science* 6 1976 pp 143–72 examines the role of the colonial administration in the origins of the emergency. Mugu Gucaru *Land of Sunshine: Scenes of Life in Kenya Before Mau Mau* Lawrence and Wishart 1958 offers useful reflections on life and politics in Kenya since the war. He indicts the racial and economic dominance of the white settlers as well as the Mau Mau. Also useful is George Delf *Jomo Kenyatta: Towards Truth About 'the Light of Africa'* Greenwood 1961. This contains not just reflections on Kenyatta but also on the influence of British anti-colonialists like Fenner Brockway, the course of British policy and the problem of racial tensions. The relations between settlers and Africans are also brought out in Richard K P Pankhurst *Kenya: The History of Two Nations* Independent Publishing Co 1954. Unfortunately, as with most accounts he focuses almost entirely upon the Kikuyu. D H Rawcliffe *The Struggle for Kenya* Gollancz 1954 is also good for the attitude of the Indian population. A rather more journalistic account of racial tensions and the origins of Mau Mau is Colin Wills *Who Killed Kenya?* Dennis Dobson 1953. S and K Aaronovitch *Crisis in Kenya* Lawrence and Wishart 1947 is a critique of British policy in Kenya at the time and particularly of its development as a military base. Edward Grigg, Lord Altrincham *Kenya's Opportunity: Memories, Hopes and Ideas* Faber 1955 is not only a memoir of his own time as Governor of Kenya 1925–31 but a critique of the policy of his successors, particularly Sir Philip Mitchell (Governor 1944–52).

**1577** George Bennett 'Imperial Paternalism: The Representation of African Interests in the Kenya Legislative Council' in Kenneth Robinson and Frederick Madden (eds) *Essays in Imperial Government Presented to Margery Perham* Blackwell 1963 pp 142– 62. A study of the gradual Africanization of the Kenya government. George Bennett and C G Rosberg *The Kenyatta Election: Kenya 1960–1961* Oxford University Press 1961 is a useful study of an important stage in the transfer of power in Kenya. For the influence of the Mau Mau emergency on this process see B E Kipkorir 'Mau Mau and the Politics of the Transfer of Power in Kenya 1957–1960' *Kenya Historical Review* 5 1977 pp 313–28.

**1578** Gary Wasserman *Politics of Decolonisation: Kenya Europeans and the Land Issue 1960–1965* Cambridge University Press 1976. A key aspect of racial tension was the land issue. This deals with the eventual settlement of the issue. Its role in the origins of the Mau Mau emergency is discussed in Tabitha Kanogo *Squatters and the Roots of Mau Mau* Currey 1987. See also J W Harbison 'Land Reform and Politics in Kenya 1954– 70' *Journal of Modern African Studies* 9 1971 pp 231–51 and M McWilliam 'Economic Policy and the Kenya Settlers 1945–48' in Kenneth Robinson and Frederick Madden (eds) *Essays in Imperial Government Presented to Margery Perham* Blackwell 1963 pp 142–62.

**1579** Paul Mosley *The Settler Economies: Studies in the Economic History of Kenya and Southern Rhodesia* Cambridge University Press 1983. The standard economic history.

**1580** Sir Michael Blundell *So Rough a Wind* Weidenfeld and Nicolson 1964. Memoirs of a settler politician who supported the nationalist cause and was accordingly ostracized by other settler politicians. He was an important figure in the progress towards independence.

**1581** Gerald Wallop, Earl of Portsmouth *A Knot of Roots: An Autobiography* Geoffrey Bles 1965. Recollections of Kenyan politics after the war. It is also of some use for post-war agricultural policy in Britain.

**1582** Eleanor Cole *Random Recollections of a Pioneer Kenya Settler* Baron Publishing 1975. Reflections on settler life 1917–72. So is Elspeth Huxley and Arnold Curtis (ed) *Pioneer's Scrapbook: Reminiscences of Kenya 1890–1968* Evans 1980, mostly from before 1939.

**1583** K David Patterson *The Pokot of Western Kenya 1910– 1963: The Response of a Conservative People to Colonial Rule* Maxwell Graduate School of Citizenship and Public Affairs, Syracuse University, Program of Eastern African Studies Occasional Paper 53 1969. One of the few accounts to focus on the impact of Colonialism on any tribe other than the Kikuyu.

**1584** Bethell A Ogot 'British Administration in the Central Nyanza District of Kenya 1900–1960' *Journal of African History* 4 1963 pp 249–74.

**1585** W R Foran *The Kenya Police 1887–1960* Hale 1962. A useful study not least because of their role in the confronting of Mau Mau.

**1586** B E Kipkorir (ed) *Biographical Essays in Imperialism and Collaboration in Colonial Kenya* Kenya Literature Bureau, Nairobi 1980. Very useful essays on the Kikuyu and Nandi chiefs and indirect rule, the influence of colonial educators like the highly respected headmaster, Carey Francis, and so on. These successfully illuminate the nature of the colonial system in Kenya. On Carey Francis and his influence on education in Kenya see the excellent biography L B Greaves *Carey Francis of Kenya* Rex Collings 1969. Another useful collection of biographies is Kenneth King and Ahmed Salim (eds) *Kenya Historical Biographies* East Africa Publishing House, Nairobi 1971. This includes studies of Molonker ole Sempele, Sir Philip Mitchell, Yona Omolo and Harry Thuku.

**1587** Anthony Clayton and Donald C Savage *Government and Labour in Kenya 1895–1963* Cass 1974. A comprehensive study of the development of trade unions and colonial labour policy. For the trade unions during the Mau Mau years see Makhan Singh *1953–56: Crucial Years of Kenya Trade Unions* Uzima Press, Nairobi 1980. See also S B Stichter 'Workers, Trade Unions and the Mau Mau Rebellion' *Canadian Journal of African Studies* 9 1975 pp 253–75.

**1588** S N Boyonko *Kenya 1945–1963: A Study in African National Movements* Kenya Literature Bureau, Nairobi 1980. This charts the rapid development of nationalism after the war. Bethell A Ogot (ed) *Hadith 4: Politics and Nationalism in Colonial Kenya* East Africa Publishing House 1972 contains useful essays on nationalism, collaboration and Mau Mau.

**1589** John Spencer *The Kenyan African Union* KPI Ltd 1985. A good history from 1919 down to its dissolution in 1953 by the government in the face of the Mau Mau emergency. It also has a good bibliography.

**1590** E R Turton 'Somali Resistance to Colonial Rule and the Resistance Rule and the Development of Somali Political Activity in Kenya 1893–1960' *Journal of African History* 13 1972 pp 119–43. This illustrates the problem of the Somali minority in Northern Kenya.

**1591** John Spencer *James Beauttah: Freedom Fighter* Stellascope Publishing, Nairobi 1983. A biography of a nationalist politician, most active in the inter-war years.

**1592** Bildad Kaggia *Roots of Freedom 1921–1963: Autobiography* East African Publishing House, Nairobi 1975. A trade unionist who was detained 1952–61 during the Mau Mau emergency. A minister for a time under Kenyatta he usefully reflects on the variety of attitudes towards Mau Mau which continue to divide both Kenyan politics and historiography.

**1593** Jeremy Murray-Brown *Kenyatta* Allen and Unwin 1972. A highly regarded biography of the leader of the Kenya African Union who became President of Kenya from independence in 1963 until his death in 1978. Montagu Slater *The Trial of Jomo Kenyatta* 2nd ed, Secker and Warburg 1956 is an in-depth account of his trial on the charge of managing Mau Mau which led to his detention 1952–61. Jomo Kenyatta *Suffering Without Bitterness: The Founding of the Kenya Nation* East African Publishing House, Nairobi 1968 is a biography which also collects Kenyatta's speeches 1963–7. For Kenyatta's speeches at the time of independence see Jomo Kenyatta *Harambee! The Prime Minister's Speeches 1963–1964* Oxford University Press, Nairobi 1964.

**1594** Hyder Kindy *Life and Politics in Mombasa* East African Publishing House, Nairobi 1972. Autobiography of a Muslim from the coastal region who was involved in nationalist politics.

**1595** Jack R Roelker *Mathu of Kenya: A Political Study* Hoover Institution Press, Stanford, California 1976. Mathu was a leading African politician 1944–57. Despite being dropped by the government in 1954 because of his increasingly critical attitude he was too moderate and tainted by collaboration to have influence in independent Kenya, in which he became Kenyatta's private secretary.

**1596** David Goldsworthy *Tom Mboya: The Man Kenya Wanted to Forget* Heinemann 1982. A leading trade unionist and nationalist Mboya was one of the most significant political figures in Kenya in the 1950s and 1960s until his assassination in 1969. See also the autobiographical reflections on Kenya's road to independence, Tom Mboya *Freedom and After* Deutsch 1963.

**1597** J M Nazareth *Brown Man. Black Country: A Peep into Kenya's Freedom Struggle* Tidings Publications, New Delhi 1981. Semi-autobiographical reflections on the Indian community's perceptions of constitutional and political developments on the road to independence.

**1598** Oginga Odinga *Not Yet Uhuru* Heinemann 1967. Odinga was a Luo who became an important nationalist. In this autobiography he regards Mau Mau with more favour than most constitutional nationalists.

**1599** Harry Thuku *An Autobiography* Oxford University Press 1970. Thuku was an important nationalist in the 1920s. This autobiography is most useful for the post-war years for the opposition to Mau Mau which he shared.

(c) Uganda

**1600** Robert L Collison *Uganda* Clio Press 1981. An annotated bibliography of some value.

**1601** Jan J Jorgensen *Uganda: A Modern History* Croom Helm 1981. A good general history. Dan Wadada Nabudere *Imperialism and Revolution in Uganda* Onyx Press 1980 is a Marxist analysis of recent Ugandan history into the 1970s.

**1602** David E Apter *The Political Kingdom in Uganda* Princeton University Press, Princeton, New Jersey 1961. A good study of post-war political developments. M S M Kiwanuka 'Uganda Under the British' in Bethell A Ogot and J A Kiernan (eds) *Zamani: A Survey of East African History* East African Publishing House, Nairobi 1968 pp 312–33 is a good survey of the colonial period from 1890 until the overthrow of the kingdom of Buganda in 1966, four years after independence. Kenneth

Ingham *The Making of Modern Uganda* Allen and Unwin 1958 remains of some use.

**1603** H Ingrams *Uganda* HMSO 1960. A good general survey from the Corona Library series. Central Office of Information *Uganda: The Making of a Nation* HMSO 1962 is a pamphlet guide issued at the time of independence.

**1604** A F Evans 'The Africanisation of the Civil Service in Uganda – A Problem of De-Colonisation' Manchester MA (Econ) Thesis 1964–5. On the declining use of non-official European and Asian advisers by the Protectorate government after the war see G F Engholm 'The Decline of Immigrant Influence on the Uganda Administration 1945–52' *Uganda Journal* 31 1967 pp 73–88.

**1605** Joel D Barkan *et al Uganda District Government and Politics 1947–1967* University of Wisconsin East African Studies Program 1978. On the development of local government in Uganda see C Vickerman 'British Colonial Policy on Local Government in Uganda Since the War' Manchester MA (Econ) Thesis 1964–5. Another constitutional development is covered in G F Engholm 'The Westminster Model in Uganda' *International Journal* 18 1963 pp 463–87.

**1606** Donald Anthony Low *Political Parties in Uganda 1949–62* Athlone Press 1962. A useful short study. See also R Cranford Pratt 'The Growth of Nationalist Parties in Uganda 1952–60' in P J M McEwan (ed) *Twentieth Century Africa* Oxford University Press 1968 pp 222–26 and R Cranford Pratt 'Nationalism in Uganda' *Political Studies* 9 1961 pp 157–78

**1607** Donald Anthony Low *Buganda in Modern History* Weidenfeld and Nicolson 1971. The kingdom of Buganda was a quarter of the protectorate of Uganda and contained half its population. It was ruled indirectly. Donald Anthony Low and R Cranford Pratt *Buganda and British Overrule 1900–1955: Two Studies* Oxford University Press 1960 analyses its relations with the colonial government. Donald Anthony Low *The Mind of Buganda: Documents of the Modern History of an African Kingdom* Heinemann 1971 includes quite a few documents on the post-war era.

**1608** Sir Edward Mutesa, Kabaka of Buganda *Desecration of My Kingdom* Constable 1967. This royal memoir reflects politics in Uganda in the last years of British rule as well as the defeat of the Ganda in their secession struggle in 1966 which led to the Kabaka's exile. On the crisis over the decision of Sir Andrew Cohen, the Governor, to exile the Kabaka in 1953–5 see Paulo Kavuma *Crisis in Buganda 1953–5: The Story of the Exile and Return of the Kabaka Mutesa II* Rex Collings 1979.

(d) Tanganyika

**1609** Colin Darch *Tanzania* Clio Press 1985. This annotated bibliography contains some material of value.

**1610** John Iliffe *A Modern History of Tanganyika* Cambridge University Press 1979. A good history, concentrating on Tanganyika in the twentieth century up to independence in 1961. It also has a good bibliography. R Cranford Pratt *The Critical Phase in Tanzania 1945–1968: Nyerere and the Emergence of a Socialist Strategy* Cambridge University Press 1976 is an excellent study of post-war political and constitutional developments, which also has a good bibliography. Political and constitutional change in the post-war era is also well examined in A G Ross 'Multiracialism and European Politics in Tanganyika 1945–61' London PhD Thesis 1981. This focuses particularly on the transformation from the European domination of Tanganyikan administration in 1945. See also M McLean 'A Comparative Study of Assimilationist and Adoptionist Policies in British Colonial Africa (With Special Reference to the Gold Coast and Tanganyika)' London PhD Thesis 1978. Another useful study of post-war Tanganyika up to the army mutinies in East Africa in 1964 which British troops helped to quell, is Judith Listowel *The Making of Tanganyika* Chatto and Windus 1965. The collection of essays, M H Y Kaniki (ed) *Tanzania Under Colonial Rule* Longman 1980, includes analyses of post-war politics and policies and the end of the colonial era. Hugh W Stephens *The Political Transformation of Tanganyika 1920–67* Praeger, New York 1968 is a largely superseded general history.

**1611** James Clagett Taylor *The Political Development of Tanganyika* Stanford University Press, Stanford, California 1963. Tanganyika was originally a German colony which was administered by Britain as a Trust Territory after the First World War. This study focuses on this aspect of Tanganyikan history and does it rather better than the dull Bernard Thomas Gibson Chidzero *Tanganyika and International Trusteeship* Oxford University Press 1961.

**1612** John Hatch *Tanzania: A Profile* Pall Mall Press 1972. A contemporary portrait which includes some material on British rule, the rise of nationalism and Commonwealth relations. Central Office of Information *Tanganyika: A Story of Progress* HMSO 1961 is a pamphlet guide to Tanganyika issued at the time of independence.

**1613** N J Westcott 'The Impact of the War on Tanganyika 1939–49' Cambridge PhD Thesis 1982. By-products of the war included the rise of nationalism and schemes for economic development, notably the groundnuts scheme.

**1614** Sir Edward Twining 'The Situation in Tanganyika' *African Affairs* 50 1951 pp 297–310.

**1615** William Tordoff *Government and Politics in Tanzania: A Collection of Essays Covering the Period from September 1960 to July 1966* East Africa Publishing House, Nairobi 1967. Covers events such as independence for Tanganyika in 1961 and the 1964 union with Zanzibar after it became independent in 1963 and the 1964 army mutinies which were put down with British assistance.

**1616** John Sidney Richard Cole and William Neil Denison *Tanganyika: The Development of Its Laws and Constitutions* Stevens 1964. A clear survey.

**1617** Robert Heussler *British Tanganyika: An Essay and Documents on District Administration* Duke University Press, Durham, North Carolina 1971. This study goes up to the early 1950s.

**1618** Julian Darrell Bates *A Fly-Switch from the Sultan* Hart-Davis 1961. A memoir of his time as a District Commissioner in Tanganyika.

**1619** Cyril Ehrlich 'Some Aspects of Economic Policy in Tanganyika 1945–60' *Journal of Modern African Studies* 2 1964 pp 265–77. An instant history of the ill-fated and costly groundnut scheme which was set up in 1947 is Alan Wood *The Groundnut Affair* J Lane 1950.

**1620** A J Temu 'The Rise and Triumph of Nationalism' in I N Kimambo and A J Temu (eds) *A History of Tanzania* Heinemann Education 1969 pp 189–213. A study of nationalism in Tanganyika from revolts under German rule up to President Nyerere's Arusha Declaration in 1967. In the process it brings out the importance of rural resistance to colonial economic and particularly agricultural policy in the development of nationalism. On this see L Cliffe 'Nationalism and the Reaction to enforced Agricultural Change in Tanganyika During the Colonial Period' in L Cliffe and J S Saul (eds) *Socialism in Tanzania: An Interdisciplinary Reader Vol I: Politics* East African Publishing House, Nairobi 1972 pp 17–23. See also Isaria N Kimambo *Mbiru: Popular Protest in Colonial Tanzania* East African Publishing House, Nairobi 1971. This examines the revolt of the Pare people against the Mbiru graduated local rate introduced in January 1945 and its consequences, not least in encouraging nationalism, up to 1947.

**1621** David R Smith *The Influence of the Fabian Colonial Bureau on the Independence Movement in Tanganyika* Ohio University Press, Athens, Ohio 1985. A short monograph.

**1622** Gabriel Ruhumbika (ed) *Towards Ujamaa: Twenty Years of TANU Leadership* East African Literature Bureau, Kampala 1974. The Tanganyika African National Union which led Tanganyika to independence was formally proclaimed by Nyerere in 1954. A general history is Ulotu Abubakar Ulotu *Historia ya TANU* East African Literature Bureau, Kampala 1971. See also George Bennett 'An Outline History of TANU' *Makerere Journal* 7 1963 pp 1–18. There are also a number of local studies of the rise of nationalism and TANU. G Andrew Maguire *Towards 'Uhuru' in Tanzania: The Politics of Participation* Cambridge University Press 1969 looks at political development in Sukumoland. See also his 'The Emergence of the Tanganyika African National Union in the Lake Province' in Robert I Rotberg and Ali A Mazrui (eds) *Protest and Power in Black Africa* Oxford University Press 1970 pp 639–70, J J Mbuli *The Tanganyika African Association in Tanga* University of Dar es Salaam, Dar es Salaam 1970 and Dean S McHenry 'A Study of the Rise of TANU and the Demise of British Rule in Kigama Region, Western Tanzania' *The African Review* 3 1973 pp 403–21.

**1623** G R Mutahaba *Portrait of a Nationalist: The Life of Ali Migeyo* East African Publishing House, Nairobi 1969. A short biography based on interviews.

**1624** H A K Mwenegoha *Mwalimu Julius Kambarage Nyerere: A Bio-Bibliography* Foundations Books, Nairobi 1976. Nyerere, the TANU leader was President of Tanganyika (Tanzania from the union with Zanzibar in 1964) 1962–85. William Edgett Smith *Nyerere of Tanzania* Gollancz 1973 is an admiring biography, which does not have much on the pre-independence period but is quite useful for the ups and downs of Britain's relations with Tanzania since independence. John Hatch *Two African Statesmen: Kaunda of Zambia and Nyerere of Tanzania* Secker and Warburg 1976 offers rather better and more rounded biographies of two important figures. See also Julius K Nyerere *Freedom and Unity: Uhuru na Umoja: A Selection from Writings and Speeches 1952–1965* Oxford University Press 1967.

(e) Zanzibar

The Sultanate of Zanzibar received its independence from Britain in 1963. A revolution followed in January 1964, the Sultan was overthrown and a republic proclaimed. Shortly thereafter Zanzibar united with Tanganyika to form Tanzania. Some of the material in the section on Tanganyika is therefore likely to be of use for the study of Zanzibar's history.

**1625** Samuel Ayany *A History of Zanzibar – A Study of Constitutional Development 1934–1964* East African Literature Bureau, Kampala 1970. An informative study

BIBLIOGRAPHIES

up to the union with Tanganyika. See also Ingeborg Aumüller *Dekolonisation und Nation werdung in Sansibar; Prozesse zur Unabhüngigkeit und territorial Integration* Weltforum Verlag, Munich 1980.

**1626** Anthony Clayton *The 1948 Zanzibar General Strike* Research Report 32, Scandinavian Institute of African Studies, Uppsala 1976. A short study of the strike and how it was handled by the colonial administration.

**1627** Central Office of Information *Zanzibar* HMSO 1963. A survey at the time of independence.

**1628** Michael F Lofchie *Zanzibar: Background to Revolution* Oxford University Press 1965. A good study of the background to the 1964 revolution in British colonial policy and the political developments of the late colonial period. See also Anthony Clayton *The Zanzibar Revolution and Its Aftermath* Christopher Hurst 1981.

**1629** John Okello *Revolution in Zanzibar* East African Publishing House, Nairobi 1967. This autobiography by one of the leaders of the 1964 revolution has some reflections on the last years of British rule and on British rule elsewhere in East Africa.

(f) British Somaliland

**1630** Mohamed Khalief Salad (comp) *Somalia: A Bibliographical Survey* Greenwood 1977. A massive unannotated classified bibliography. Mark W DeLancey *et al Somalia* Clio Press 1988 is a select annotated bibliography.

**1631** I M Lewis *A Modern History of Somalia* 2nd ed, Longman 1980. This includes material on the British occupation of Italian Somaliland after the Second World War and the administration of British Somaliland until independence outside the Commonwealth in 1960. It also covers the subsequent amalgamation of the British and Italian enclaves and the fraught nature of Anglo-Somali relations after independence.

**1632** John Drysdale *The Somali Dispute* Pall Mall Press 1964. A good analysis of the background to the greater Somalia dispute. Lack of British support for the Somali claim to the Ogaden and Haud from Ethiopia and to sections of Kenya led to the China's replacement of Britain as the predominate influence on the Somalis and the rupture of Anglo-Somali relations. On this dispute see also Saadia Touval *Somali Nationalism – International Politics and the Drive for Unity in the Horn of Africa* Harvard University Press, Cambridge, Massachusetts 1963. The fact that the British had been responsible for some cessions of territory to Ethiopia and had moved to thwart Somali ambitions in Kenya did not help, as demonstrated in the Somali critique of British administration in the region, *The Somali Peninsula: A New Light on Imperial Motives* Information Service of the Somali Government, Mogadishu 1962.

(3) West Africa

(a) General

**1633** Noel Matthews *Materials for West African History in the Archives of the United Kingdom* Athlone Press 1973. A comprehensive and detailed guide. See also *West African Sources in British Colonial Office Records* Commonwealth Archivists Association 1987.

**1634** James S Coleman 'A Survey of Selected Literature on the Government and Politics of British West Africa' *American Political Science Review* 49 1955 pp 1130–50. This includes some useful information on post-war literature, especially periodicals, newspapers and official publications.

**1635** Sir Frederick Pedler *Main Currents of West African History 1940–1978* Macmillan 1979. A rather pedestrian general history.

**1636** Michael Crowder *West Africa Under Colonial Rule* Hutchinson 1968.

**1637** John D Hargreaves *The End of Colonial Rule in West Africa: Essays in Contemporary History* Macmillan 1979. Succinct overview of the end of British and French rule in the region. This is particularly good on the importance of educational development in the training of African elites for self-government. It also surveys useful archives. Olajide Aluko 'Politics of Decolonisation in British West Africa 1945–1960' in J F A Ajayi and Michael Crowder (eds) *History of West Africa Vol 2* Longman 1974 pp 622–63 concentrates more on economic colonialism and economic dependence.

**1638** C R Nordman 'Prelude to Decolonisation in West Africa: The Development of British Colonial Policy 1938–1947' Oxford DPhil Thesis 1976. The effect of imperial priorities and attempts to maintain Great Power status on policy in this period are examined in John Kent 'The International Dimensions of British West Africa Policy 1939–1949' Aberdeen PhD Thesis 1985. See also J H Bowden 'Development and Control in British Colonial Policy with Reference to Nigeria and the Gold Coast 1935–1948' Birmingham PhD Thesis 1979–80. On the constitutional developments of the post-war period see T Olawale Elias 'Towards Nationhood in Nigeria' *Occasional Papers in Nigerian Affairs* 1955 pp 5–24 and

D C Holland 'Constitutional Experiments in British West Africa' *Current Legal Problems* 6 1953 pp 62–81.

**1639** F H Hilliard *A Short History of Education in British West Africa* Nelson 1957. A history up to the 1950s. Education policy was an important part of preparing for self-government. See also F Borsali 'British Colonial Policy Towards Higher Education in West Africa and the Foundation of the University Institutions 1939–51' Aberdeen PhD Thesis 1983.

**1640** John Flint 'Scandal at the Bristol Hotel: Some Thoughts on Racial Discrimination in Britain and West Africa and Its Relationship to the Planning of Decolonisation 1939–47' *Journal of Imperial and Commonwealth History* 12 1983 pp 74–93. In February 1947 a senior Colonial Office official was barred from the Bristol Hotel in Lagos because he was black. This examines the effects of that incident.

**1641** William Gutteridge 'The Nature of Nationalism in British West Africa' *Western Political Quarterly* 11 1958 pp 574–82. See also Martin L Kilson 'Nationalism and Social Classes in British West Africa' *Journal of Politics* 20 1958 pp 368–87.

**1642** Dennis Austin *West Africa and the Commonwealth* Penguin 1957.

**(b) The Gold Coast (Ghana)**

**1643** David P Henige 'The National Archives of Ghana: A Synopsis of Holdings' *The International Journal of African Historical Studies* 6 1973 pp 475–86.

**1644** G B Kay (ed) *The Political Economy of Colonialism in Ghana: A Collection of Documents and Statistics 1900–1960* Cambridge University Press 1972. This concentrates on economic relations with Britain. G E Metcalfe *Great Britain and Ghana: Documents of Ghana History 1807–1957* Nelson 1964 is broader in scope but is limited after 1940, largely consisting of speeches, debates and reports. These are chronologically arranged.

**1645** Albert F Johnson (comp) *A Bibliography of Ghana 1930–1961* Longmans 1964. This lists over 2600 items on all aspects of Ghana. See also J K Kafe (comp) *Ghana: An Annotated Bibliography of Academic Theses 1920–1970 in the Commonwealth, the Republic of Ireland and the United States of America* G K Hall, Boston, Massachusetts 1973.

**1646** J O Hunwick (ed) *Proceedings of the Seminar on Ghanaian Historiography and Historical Research* Department of History, University of Ghana, Accra 1977. This contains two useful historiographical essays; Margaret Priestley 'Colonial Policy and Administration' pp 167–83, and S K B Asante 'Political and Constitutional Developments in Ghana Since 1945: A Review of the Scope of Research' pp 184–206.

**1647** Florence Mabel Bourret *Ghana – The Road to Independence 1919–1957* 2nd ed, Oxford University Press 1960. A good survey of Ghanaian history up to independence in 1957. This also looks at the development of British Togoland, a mandated territory which became part of independent Ghana. A good short study of post-war Ghana is Dennis Austin *Politics in Ghana 1946–1960* Oxford University Press 1970. J G Amamoo *The New Ghana* Pan 1958 is a descriptive account of 1947–57. G H C Bing *Reap the Whirlwind: An Account of Kwame Nkrumah' Ghana from 1950 to 1966* Macgibbon and Kee 1968 examines Ghana up to the coup which overthrew Nkrumah in 1966. See also C L R James *Nkrumah and Ghana Revolution* Allison and Busby 1977, David E Apter *The Gold Coast in Transition* Princeton University Press, Princeton, New Jersey 1955 and Richard Rathbone 'The Transfer of Power in Ghana 1945–1957' London PhD Thesis 1967–8.

**1648** Michael Dei-Anang *Ghana Resurgent* Waterville Publishing House, Accra 1964. Reflections on independence, Nkrumah and so on. *Ghana: A Survey of the Gold Coast on the Eve of Independence* Royal Institute of International Affairs 1957 is a survey of developments from 1946 onwards and of the Ghanaian administration and economy at the time of independence.

**1649** Adrienne Misrael 'Measuring the War Experience: Ghanaian Soldiers in World War II' *Journal of Modern African Studies* 25 1987 pp 159–68. A study of the influence of wartime service experience on post-war nationalist movements in Ghana.

**1650** Richard Rathbone 'The Government of the Gold Coast after the Second World War' *African Affairs* 67 (268) July 1968 pp 209–18. This looks particularly at the Accra riots of 1948. The official report on these riots, which had a considerable impact on colonial policy, is *Disturbances in the Gold Coast* HMSO 1948. This was chaired by Aiken Watson.

**1651** P B Redmayne *Gold Coast to Ghana* Macmillan 1957. Ghana was the first colony in British Africa to receive independence. The process of transition is examined by the last British governor in Charles Arden-Clarke 'Gold Coast into Ghana: Some Problems of Transition' *International Affairs* 34 1958 pp 49–56.

**1652** E V C De Graft Johnson 'The Evolution of the Executive in the Constitutional Development of the Gold Coast' Leeds PhD Thesis 1958–9. Martin Wight's excellent historical study, *The Gold Coast Legislative*

*Council* Faber 1947, is of limited value for the post-war period.

**1653** *Report of the Select Committee of the Legislative Council on the Africanisation of the Public Service* Government Printer, Accra 1950. This surveys the history of the government service and outlines the plan for Africanization in every department. See also [1610].

**1654** Richard C Crook 'Decolonisation, the Colonial State and Chieftaincy in the Gold Coast' *African Affairs* 85 1986 pp 75–105. In the 1950s Britain abandoned indirect rule through chiefs and instead began to cultivate educated African elites. This examines this process. On British indirect rule in various parts of Ghana see A Cawson 'Local Politics and Indirect Rule in Cape Coast, Ghana 1928–1957' Oxford DPhil Thesis 1975 and M S M Salim 'The Reactions and Attitudes of Africans in Southern Ghana to the British Colonial Policy of Indirect Rule 1925–1951' Edinburgh PhD Thesis 1976. See also R L Stone 'Colonial Administration and Rural Politics in South-Central Ghana 1919–1951' Cambridge PhD Thesis 1974 and A Hannigan 'Local Government in the Gold Coast' *Journal of African Administration* 7 1955 pp 116–23.

**1655** Josephine F Milburn *British Business and Ghanaian Independence* Christopher Hurst 1977. A contribution to the debate on the nature of Third World development. This analyses the role of British business on the development of the Ghanaian economy and its influence on Colonial Office decisions 1907–57. The role of one of the most important companies, the United Africa Company, now part of Unilever, is examined in Paula Jones 'The United Africa Company in the Gold Coast/Ghana 1920 to 1965' London PhD Thesis 1983.

**1656** David A Kimble *A Political History of Ghana – The Rise of Gold Coast Nationalism 1850–1958* Clarendon 1963. See also R Jenkins 'The Role of History and the Historian in the Development of Nationalist Thought and in the Process of Nation- Building in Ghana 1895–1955' Birmingham PhD Thesis 1985, A Adu Boaken 'The Roots of Ghanaian Nationalism' *Journal of African History* 5 1964 pp 127–32, David E Apter 'The Development of Ghana Nationalism' *United Asia* 9 1957 pp 23–30 and K A Jones-Quartey 'Press and Nationalism in Ghana' *United Asia* 9 1957 pp 55–60.

**1657** T Adamafio *By Nkrumah's Side: The Labour and the Wounds* Collins 1982. A personal account 1950–62 by one of Nkrumah's aides.

**1658** L H Ofusu-Appiah *The Life and Times of Dr J B Danquah* Waterville Publishing House, Accra 1974. Danquah was a major figure in the nationalist movement who was gradually eclipsed by Nkrumah after the 1948 Accra riots. He served two terms as a political prisoner

after independence before his death in 1965. His correspondence is also useful for nationalist politics, constitutional development and colonial policy: see H K Akyeampong (ed) *Journey to Independence and After (J B Danquah's Letters) Vol I: 1947–1948* Waterville Publishing House, Accra 1970; *Vol II: 1949–1951* 1971; and *Vol III: 1952–1957* 1972.

**1659** David Rooney *Kwame Nkrumah: A Political Kingdom in the Third World* I B Tauris 1988. Nkrumah organized the first Pan- African Congress in 1945 and led Ghana to independence in 1957. This is a good exploration of his political career and influential ideas (felt far beyond the confines of Ghana) and of the flaws that led to his overthrow in the military coup of 1966. Another good biography is Basil Davidson *Black Star: A View of the Life and Times of Kwame Nkrumah* Allen Lane 1973. Bankhole Timothy *Kwame Nkrumah from Cradle to Grave* Gavin Press 1981 is a critical assessment. Timothy's previous biography, *Kwame Nkrumah: His Rise to Power* 2nd ed, Allen and Unwin 1963 is more eulogistic, reflecting the rather different reaction Nkrumah then evoked, and is perhaps more useful on progress towards independence. See also C L R James *Nkrumah and the African Revolution* Allison and Busby 1977. Kwame Nkrumah *I Speak of Freedom* Heinemann 1961 consists of speeches and autobiographical reflections. See also Kwame Nkrumah *The Autobiography of Kwame Nkrumah* Nelson 1967. Henry L Bretten *The Rise and Fall of Kwame Nkrumah* Pall Mall Press 1966 is an inadequate and misleading biography.

## (c) Nigeria

**1660** C C Aguolu *Nigeria: A Comprehensive Bibliography in the Humanities and Social Sciences 1900–1971* G K Hall, Boston, Massachusetts 1973. A good bibliography of 6,500 entries, many annotated, including theses, official publications and conference papers.

**1661** Michael Crowder *The Story of Nigeria* 4th ed, Faber 1978. The standard history. Okoi Arikpo *The Development of Modern Nigeria* Penguin 1967 is quite useful on post-war changes. I F Nicolson *The Administration of Nigeria 1900–1960: Men, Methods and Myths* Clarendon 1969 is by a former Nigerian official and makes use of his personal insights. See also Frederick Uzoma Anyiam *Men and Matters in Nigerian Politics 1934–1958* John Odwesa, Yaba 1959 and K Onwuka Dike *100 Years of British Rule in Nigeria 1851–1951* Federal Information Service/Nigeria Broadcasting Corporation, Lagos 1956.

**1662** Cornelius Ogu Ejimofor *British Colonial Objectives and Politics in Nigeria* Africana-FEP Publications,

Onitsha 1987. An analysis of the roots of Nigeria's post-independence difficulties in the colonial period.

**1663** G O Okusanya *The Second World War and Politics in Nigeria 1939–1953* Evans 1973. A study of the impact of the war on Nigerian politics and society. C C M Thomas 'Colonial Government Propaganda and Public Relations in Nigeria 1939–51' Cambridge PhD Thesis 1986 examines the constitutional changes that flowed from the war with Nigerians by 1951, under the Macpherson constitution, being admitted for the first time to central political structures. R D Pearce 'Governors, Nationalists and Constitutions in Nigeria 1935–51' *Journal of Imperial and Commonwealth History* 9 1981 pp 289–307 considers colonial policy in this period in the context of rising nationalism.

**1664** Kenneth W J Post and George D Jenkins *The Price of Liberty: Personality and Politics in Colonial Nigeria* Cambridge University Press 1973. A major study of the process of decolonization and the flaws in British constitution-making using the insights of the prominent Nigerian politician, Adegoke Adelabu, of whom it is thus also in a sense a biography. Another account from the viewpoint of a prominent politician is Obafemi Awolowo *Path to Nigerian Freedom* Faber 1966. See also Frederick A Schwartz *Nigeria – The Tribes, the Nation, the Race: The Politics of Independence* MIT Press, Cambridge, Massachusetts 1965. S L Akintola and Tafawa Balewa 'Nigeria Debates Self Government' in Rupert Emerson and Martin Kilson (eds) *The Political Awakening of Africa* Prentice-Hall 1975 pp 65–73 is a reprint of a debate in the Nigerian House of Representatives in 1957 calling for immediate independence.

**1665** Royal Institute of International Affairs *Nigeria: The Political and Economic Background* Oxford University Press 1960. A survey of Nigeria at the time of independence. See also Central Office of Information *Nigeria: The Making of a Nation* HMSO 1960.

**1666** Kalu Ezera *Constitutional Developments in Nigeria: An Annotated Study of Nigeria's Constitution-Making Developments and the Historical and Political Factors that Affected Constitutional Change* 2nd ed, Cambridge University Press 1964. A useful guide to the constitutional evolution that Nigeria gradually underwent, particularly in the post-war era. See also Oleiwole I Odumosu *The Nigerian Constitution: Its History and Development* Sweet and Maxwell 1963 and T Olawale Elias *Nigeria: The Development of its Laws and Constitution* Stevens 1967. C R Niven *How Nigeria is Governed* Longman, Green and Co 1950 analyses the situation after the 1947 Richards Constitution. A useful historical and contemporary analysis of the apex of colonial government is Joan C Wheare *The Nigerian Legislative Council* Faber 1950. See also T N Tamuno *Nigeria and Elective Representation 1923–47* Heinemann 1966.

**1667** Jeremy White *Central Administration in Nigeria 1914–1948: The Problem of Polarity* Cass 1981. An analysis of the centrifugal tendencies in Nigeria up to the shortcomings of the Richards Constitution.

**1668** Anthony H M Kirk-Greene (ed) *The Principles of Native Administration in Nigeria: Select Documents 1900–1947* Oxford University Press 1965. This deals mainly with Northern Nigeria.

**1669** *Report of the Commission Appointed by His Excellency the Governor to Make Recommendations About the Recruitment and Training of Nigerians for Senior Posts in the Government Service of Nigeria* Government Printer Lagos 1948. The Commission chaired by Sir Hugh Foot which outlined the programme of Nigerianization of the government service. Progress is reviewed in Sir Sydney Phillipson and S O Adebo *The Nigerianisation of the Civil Service: A Review of Policy and Machinery* Government Printer, Lagos 1954. This process is analysed in Omorogbe Nwanwane 'The Civil Service in Nigeria: problems and Progress of its Nigerianisation 1940 to the Present Day' London PhD Thesis 1966, G O Olusanya 'The Nigerian Civil Service in the Colonial Era: A Study of Imperial Reactions to Changing Circumstances' in Boniface I Obichere (ed) *Studies in Southern Nigerian History* Cass 1982 pp 175–200 and Taylor Cole 'Bureaucracy in Transition' in Robert O Titmas and Taylor Cole (eds) *The Nigerian Political Scene* Duke University Press, Durham, North Carolina 1962 pp 89–114.

**1670** Ntieyong U Akpan *Epitaph to Indirect Rule: A Discourse on Local Government in Africa* Cassell 1956. A study of the nature and development of local government in Nigeria. See also Philip J Harris *Local Government in Southern Nigeria* Cambridge University Press 1957. The development of local government paved the way for the constitutional developments of the post-war era with which this is largely concerned.

**1671** J F Awojinrin 'British Direct Investment and Economic Development in Nigeria 1955–1972' Keele PhD Thesis 1974–5.

**1672** N J Miners *The Nigerian Army 1956–1966* Methuen 1971. A history from the small British officered colonial force to the popular agent of the 1966 military coup. The army was an important in the transfer of power and Nigerianization. This study could however do with more on the failure of the British to secure a military base at Kano and the breakdown of the 1960–2 defence agreement.

**1673** C S Whitaker *The Politics of Tradition, Continuity and Change in Northern Nigeria 1946–1966* Oxford University Press 1970. A study of political and constitutional development in the Muslim, traditionally ruled North. The useful appendices include a biographical dictionary. See also B J Dudley *Parties and Politics in Northern Nigeria* Cass 1968 and T Olawale Elias 'Towards Nationhood in Nigeria' *Occasional Papers on Nigerian Affairs* 1954 pp 5–20. A sympathetic study of British colonial administration in the area from the establishment of the protectorate in 1900 up to independence in 1960 is Robert Heussler *The British In Northern Nigeria* Oxford University Press 1968.

**1674** O Oyinloye *The Changing Role of the District Officer in Northern Nigeria 1945–1965* Institute of Administration Research Memorandum 3, Ahmadu Bello University, Zaria 1966. A good analysis.

**1675** Helen Callaway *Gender, Culture and Empire: European Women in Colonial Nigeria* Macmillan 1987. An evocative portrait of twentieth century colonial society through the eyes of its female participants. See also Sylvia Leith-Ross *Stepping-Stones: Memoirs of Colonial Nigeria 1907–60* Peter Owen 1983.

**1676** Sir Rex Niven *Nigerian Kaleidoscope: Memoirs of a Colonial Servant* Christopher Hurst 1982. Niven served in Nigeria 1921–61. Stanhope White *Dan Bana* Cassell 1966 is the account of the experiences of a district officer in Northern Nigeria. Another useful memoir is Bryan Sharwood Smith *Recollections of British Administration in the Cameroons and Northern Nigeria 1921–1957: 'But Always as Friends'* Duke University Press, Durham, North Carolina 1969. John Smith *Colonial Cadet in Nigeria* Duke University Press, Durham, North Carolina 1968 is a memoir of his first five years in Northern Nigeria by a member of the last full year of British recruitment to the Nigerian service in 1951. It provides an intimate glimpse into life as a colonial officer.

**1677** Richard L Sklar *Nigerian Political Parties: Power in an Emergent African Nation* Princeton University Press, Princeton, New Jersey 1963. A massive and indispensable study of Nigerian politics before 1960. It also has a good bibliography and appendices. Another highly regarded study is James Smoot Coleman *Nigeria: Background to Nationalism* University of California Press, Berkeley, California 1959. The role of tribalism in the growth of nationalism is considered crucial in Sklar's 'The Contribution of Tribalism to Nationalism in Western Nigeria' *Journal of Human Relations* 8 1960 pp 407–18. The influential movement associated with Nnamdi Azikiwe is considered in G O Olusanya 'The Zikist Movement – A Study in Political Radicalism 1946–50' *Journal of Modern African Studies* 4/3 1966 pp 323–33. The Zikist movement is usefully put into perspective by Mokwugo Okoye *A Letter to Dr Nnamdi Azikiwe: A Dissent Remembered* Fourth Dimension Publishers, Enugu 1979.

**1678** Victor Lapido Akintola *Akintola: The Man and the Legend* Delta Publications, Enugu 1982. A short biography (by his son) of an important nationalist who succeeded Awolowo as Premier of Western Nigeria in 1959.

**1679** Obafemi Awolowo *Awo: The Autobiography of Chief Obafemi Awolowo* Cambridge University Press 1960. A major politician who was Prime Minister of Western Nigeria 1952–59 and remained an important and controversial figure until his death in 1987. The collection, Obafemi Awolowo *Voice of Reason: Selected Speeches Vol I* Fagbamigbe Publications, Ibadan 1981, is also of some use.

**1680** Vincent C Ikeotuonye *Zik of New Africa* P R Macmillan, Ibadan 1961. A biography of Nigeria's first President, Nnamdi Azikiwe. See also Kwatei Jones-Quartey *A Life of Azikiwe* Penguin 1966 and F C Ogbalu *Dr Zik of Africa: Biography and Speeches* African Literature Bureau, Onitsha 1961. Azikiwe's autobiography, *My Odyssey: An Autobiography* Christopher Hurst 1971 really only goes up to the start of his political career in the late 1940s. Also of use is his *Zik: A Selection from the Speeches of Nnamdi Azikiwe* Cambridge University Press 1961.

**1681** Sir Abubakar Tafawa Balewa *Mr Prime Minister* Nigerian National Press, Lagos 1964. Balewa became Nigeria's first Prime Minister in 1957. A collection of speeches dating mainly from the 1940s and early 1950s. Sam Epelle (ed) *Nigeria Speaks: Alhaji Sir Abubakar Tafawa Balewa: Speeches Made Between 1957 and 1964* Longmans of Nigeria, Ikeja 1964 is more useful on the independence period and attitudes to the Commonwealth.

**1682** Sir Ahmadu Bello *My Life* Cambridge University Press 1962. The autobiography of the Sardauna of Sokoto, the first Prime Minister of Northern Nigeria, includes useful reflections on the end of British rule. See also John N Paden *Ahmadu Bello, Sardauna of Sokoto: Values and Leadership in Nigeria* Hodder and Stoughton 1986.

**1683** Akinjide Osuntokun *Power Broker: A Biography of Sir Kashim Ibrahim* Spectrum Books, Ibadan 1987. A biography of a prominent Northern Nigerian politician.

**1684** Alan Feinstein *African Revolutionary: The Life and Times of Nigeria's Aminu Kano* Quadrangle 1973. Biography of a Northern Nigerian radical.

**1685** Chris Offodile *Dr M I Okpara: A Biography* Fourth Dimension Publishers, Enugu 1980. Okpara was an important nationalist who succeeded Azikiwe as Premier of Eastern Nigeria in 1957.

**1686** Dennis C Osadebay *Building a Nation (An Autobiography)* Macmillan Nigeria, Lagos 1978. Useful personal reflections on political and constitutional developments in the twentieth century.

**1687** Olasupo Ojedokun 'Nigeria's Relations with the Commonwealth, with Special Reference to Her Relations with the United Kingdom 1960–1966' London PhD Thesis 1968–9. See also his 'The Anglo-Nigerian Entente and Its Demise 1960–1962' *Journal of Commonwealth Political Studies* 9 1971 pp 210–33 which analyses the brief history of the defence pact and the attempt to build a special relationship.

**1688** C C Aguolu *The Nigerian Civil War 1967–1970: An Annotated Bibliography* G K Hall, Boston, Massachusetts 1973. A useful guide to the literature. Auberon Waugh and Suzanne Gonje *Biafra: Britain's Shame* Michael Joseph 1969 is a critique of the Wilson government's support for the Federal government in Nigeria in the bitter civil war 1966–70 against the attempt to set up the secessionist state of Biafra. Britain's involvement in the frustration of humanitarian aid for the Biafrans is critically examined in D Jacobs *The Brutality of Nations* Alfred A Knopf, New York 1987. For British attitudes see O O Fafawara 'A Comparative Study of British Attitudes and Policy Towards Secessionist Moves in the Congo (1960–63) and in Nigeria (1966–69)' Oxford BLitt Thesis 1977 and George Knapp *Aspects of the Biafran Affair: A Study of British Attitudes and Policy Towards the Nigerian-Biafran Conflict* Britain- Biafra Association 1968. See also W A Ajibola 'The Part Played by Pressure Groups, News Media and Parliament in the Formulation of British Policy Towards Nigeria 1966–1970' Manchester PhD Thesis 1972–3 and Roy Lewis 'Britain and Biafra: A Commonwealth Civil War' *Round Table* 239 1970 pp 241–8.

(d) Sierra Leone

**1689** G J Williams *A Bibliography of Sierra Leone 1925–1967* Africana Publishing Corporation 1971. This unannotated bibliography has over 3,000 items.

**1690** Christopher Fyfe *A History of Sierra Leone* Oxford University Press 1962. The only general history. John F Cartwright *Politics in Sierra Leone 1947–67* University of Toronto Press 1970 covers from the rise of nationalism to the military coup in 1967. See also Martin Kilson *Political Change in a West Africa State: A Study of the Modernization Process in Sierra Leone*

Harvard University Press, Cambridge, Massachussets 1966.

**1691** Roy Lewis *Sierra Leone: A Modern Portrait* HMSO 1954. A good portrayal of Sierra Leone from the Colonial Office Corona Library series. Central Office of Information *Sierra Leone; the Making of a Nation* HMSO 1961 is a general survey issued at the time of independence.

**1692** Siaka Stevens *The Rising Sun: A History of the All Peoples Congress Party of Sierra Leone* the Party Secretariat 1982. A useful history with maps, documents and speeches.

**1693** William Henry Fitzjohn *Ambassador of Christ and Caesar* Daystar Press, Ibadan 1975. Fitzjohn was the Sierra Leone High Commissioner in London in the early 1960s. His memoirs also contain some useful reflections on the end of British rule.

**1694** Siaka Stevens *What Life has Taught Me: The Autobiography of His Excellency Dr Siaka Stevens, President of Sierra Leone* Kensal Press 1984. A useful autobiography by the dominant political figure in Sierra Leone from before independence. It is also quite useful for Anglo-Sierra Leone relations since independence in 1961.

(e) The Gambia

**1695** David P Gamble *Bibliography of the Gambia* Government Printer, Bathurst 1967. This lists over 2,000 items, including official publications. His *The Gambia* Clio Press 1988 is a less extensive, annotated bibliography.

**1696** Harry L Gailey Jr *A History of the Gambia* Routledge and Kegan Paul 1964. A general history. It is quite useful on post-war political developments and has good appendices.

**1697** Berkeley Rice *Enter Gambia: Birth of an Improbable Nation* Angus and Robertson 1966. A journalistic account of the background to the granting of independence in 1965. An official survey on the eve of independence is Central Office of Information *The Gambia* HMSO 1964.

(f) British Cameroons

**1698** Mark W DeLancey and Peter J Schroeder *Cameroon* Clio Press 1986. An annotated bibliography of some value.

**1699**  Victor T LeVine *The Cameroons from Mandate to Independence* University of California Press, Berkeley, California 1964. A former German colony the Cameroons were split into British and French mandates after the First World War. The British section was united with the much larger French one at independence. A study of the plebiscites which led to this reunification is N B Nyamndi 'The International Politics of the British Cameroons Plebiscites 1959–1961' London PhD Thesis 1984. See also Edwin Ardener 'The Nature of the Reunification of Cameroon' in Arthur Hazlewood (ed) *African Integration and Disintegration* Oxford University Press 1967 pp 285–337.

**1700**  Elizabeth Chilver 'Native Administration in the West Central Cameroons 1902–1954' in Kenneth Robinson and Frederick Madden (eds) *Essays in Imperial Government Presented to Margery Perham* Blackwell 1963 pp 91–139.

## (4) Central Africa

### (a) General

**1701**  I M D J Mendoza 'White Settler Ideology, African Nationalism and the "Coloured" Question in Southern Africa: Southern Rhodesia/Zimbabwe, Northern Rhodesia/Zambia and Nyasaland/Malawi 1900–1976' York DPhil Thesis 1979. A general history tracing British activity in the area from the mid-nineteenth century to the end of the Federation is A J Hanna *The Story of the Rhodesias and Nyasaland* 2nd ed, Faber 1965.

### (b) The Central African Federation 1953–63

**1702**  Harry Franklin *Unholy Wedlock: The Failure of the Central African Federation* Allen and Unwin 1963. A hostile account of the attempt to federate the Rhodesias and Nyasaland 1953–63. A rather more sympathetic account is Patrick Keatley *The Politics of Partnership* Penguin 1963. The extent to which the Federation did actually involve racial partnership is examined in T R M Creighton *The Anatomy of Partnership: Southern Rhodesia and the Central African Federation* Faber 1960, E M Clegg *Race and Politics: Partnership in the Federation of Rhodesia and Nyasaland* Oxford University Press 1960 and T M Franck *Race and Nationalism: The Struggle for Power in Rhodesia-Nyasaland* Allen and Unwin 1960.

**1703**  Ronald Hyam 'The Geopolitical Origins of the Central African Federation: Britain, Rhodesia and South Africa 1948–53' *Historical Journal* 29 1986 pp 921–47. Fears of South African designs in the region played a large part in the thinking behind the creation of the Federation.

**1704**  *Report of the Advisory Commission on the Review of the Constitution of Rhodesia and Nyasaland* Cmnds 1148–50, *Parliamentary Papers* xi 1959–60. The Federation was not thoroughly condemned in this report chaired by Viscount Monckton of Brenchley. It did nevertheless contribute to the process that led to its eventual dismantling. Clyde Sanger *Central African Emergency* Heinemann 1960 reflects on the difficulties that led to the calling of the Commission. See also Philip Mason *Year of Decision: Rhodesia and Nyasaland in 1960* Oxford University Press 1960.

**1705**  R A Sowelem *Towards Financial Independence in a Developing Economy* Allen and Unwin 1967. A study of economic relations in the Federation.

**1706**  H B K Sondashi 'The Politics of the Voice: An Examination and Comparison of British Pressure Groups, Capricorn Africa Society, the Africa Bureau and the Movement for Colonial Freedom, Which Sought to Influence Colonial Policies and Events: The Case of Central Africa 1949–1962' York MPhil Thesis 1981.

**1707**  Cuthbert J M Alport *The Sudden Assignment: Being a Record of Service in Central Africa During the Last Controversial Years of the Federation of Rhodesia and Nyasaland 1961–1963* Hodder and Stoughton 1965. Alport's reflections on his time as High Commissioner in Salisbury 1961–3 and on the strains that broke up the Federation.

**1708**  Gil Thomas Llewellin *A Biography of Jay (John Jestyn) The Rt Hon Lord Llewellin of Upton GBE MC TD MA* Barker 1961. A biography of the first Governor-General of the Federation of Rhodesia and Nyasaland.

**1709**  Sir Roy Welensky *Welensky's 4000 Days* Collins 1964. The memoirs of Welensky, the Prime Minister of the Central African Federation 1956–63. See also J R T Wood *The Welensky Papers: A History of the Federation of Rhodesia and Nyasaland* Graham Publications, Durban 1983, D Taylor *The Rhodesian: The Life of Sir Roy Welensky* Museum Press 1955 and Garry Allighan *The Welensky Story* Macdonald 1962.

### (c) Rhodesia (Zimbabwe)

**1710**  Elaine Windrich *The Rhodesia Problem: A Documentary Record 1923–1973* Routledge and Kegan Paul 1975. This covers from the granting of self-government for the white settlers.

**1711** Oliver B Pollak and Karen Pollak *Rhodesia/Zimbabwe: An Annotated Bibliography* G K Hall 1977. There are over 11,000 entries in this classified bibliography. It is especially good on journals. See also their *Rhodesia/Zimbabwe* Clio Press 1979 in the world bibliographical series. This latter is annotated and has a rather better index. M E Doro *Rhodesia/Zimbabwe: A Bibliographical Guide to the Nationalist Period* G K Hall 1984 covers the literature on the period from the unilateral declaration of independence (UDI) in 1965 to the 1980 settlement.

**1712** Anthony Verrier *The Road to Zimbabwe 1890–1980* Cape 1986. This is very critical of the British handling of Rhodesia from the declaration of UDI by the white settlers led by Ian Smith to the 1980 settlement. Britain is indeed seen as the creator of the white settler nationalism of the Rhodesian problem in Martin Loney *Rhodesia: White Racism and Imperial Response* Penguin 1975. See also C Munhamu Utete *The Road to Zimbabwe: The Political Economy of Settler Colonialism, National Liberation and Foreign Intervention* University Press of America, Washington DC 1979 and Henry V Moyan 'British Complicity Policy on Rhodesia 1923 to 1970' *Pan-African Journal* 8 1975 pp 45–74.

**1713** Robert Blake *A History of Rhodesia* Eyre Methuen 1977. A good general history as is Martin Meredith *The Past is Another Country: Rhodesia 1890–1979* Deutsch 1979. The paperback edition of the latter, *The Past is Another Country: UDI to Zimbabwe* Pan 1980 is a meticulous account of the UDI period. Claire Palley *The Constitutional History and Law of Southern Rhodesia 1888–1965, with Special Reference to Imperial Control* Clarendon 1966 is a massive and detailed study. Lewis H Gann *A History of Southern Rhodesia to 1953* Chatto and Windus 1965 examines its history up the formation of the Central African Federation. See also [1579].

**1714** H Holderness *Lost Chance: Southern Rhodesia 1945–1958* Zimbabwe Publishing House, Harare 1984. This study traces the failure of racial partnership and the ends with the beginnings of the rise of white nationalism that led to UDI. The gradual shift of white voters towards the Right is examined in Stephen E C Hintz 'The Political Transformation of Rhodesia' *African Studies Review* 15 1972 pp 173–83. The attitudes that led to UDI are also considered in Ian Henderson 'White Populism in Southern Rhodesia' *Comparative Studies in Society and History* 14 1972 pp 387–99. See also R Fitzhenry 'Social Sources of the Politics of Resistance and Repression in Southern Africa: The Case of Southern Rhodesia 1945–1964' Southampton MPhil Thesis 1970–1.

**1715** John Stonehouse *Prohibited Immigrant* The Bodley Head 1960. A useful account of early white nationalism. Stonehouse was a Labour MP who was deported from the Federation in 1959.

**1716** Colin Leys *European Politics in Southern Rhodesia* Clarendon 1961. A useful study of white politics.

**1717** I Hancock *White Liberals, Moderates and Radicals in Rhodesia 1953–1980* Croom Helm 1984. A good study of the minority of whites who opposed the policies of their fellows.

**1718** B V Mtshali *Rhodesia: Background to Conflict* Leslie Frewin 1967. This looks at the political developments and nationalism, both black and white, that led to the conflict that followed UDI. The influence of nationalism on UDI is analysed in L J MacFarlane 'Justifying Rebellion: Black and White Nationalism in Rhodesia' *Journal of Commonwealth Political Studies* 6 1968 pp 54–79. Nathan Shamayerira *Crisis in Rhodesia* Deutsch 1965 examines black politics in Rhodesia from the 1920s onwards.

**1719** Kenneth Young *Rhodesia and Independence: A Study in British Colonial Policy* 2nd ed, Dent 1969. An analysis of the background to UDI. See also James Barber *Rhodesia: The Road to Rebellion* Oxford University Press 1967, Andrew Skaen *Prelude to Independence* Nasionale Boekhandel, Cape Town 1966 and Margery Perham 'The Rhodesia Crisis: The Background' *International Affairs* 42 1966 pp 1–13. On the legality of UDI see M E Mazzawi 'Rhodesia's UDI and the Law' London PhD Thesis 1971–2.

**1720** Elaine Windrich *Britain and the Politics of Rhodesian Independence* Croom Helm 1978. On Britain's role in and response to the crisis see also Martin W Mason *Responsibility with Power: Britain and Rhodesia Since 1965* Norman Paterson School of International Affairs Occasional Paper 29, Carlton University, Ottawa 1975. On the international attempts to find a solution see Robert Good *UDI: The International Politics of the Rhodesian Rebellion* Faber 1973. The significance of the crisis in Commonwealth affairs is considered in *Journal of Commonwealth Political Studies* 7/2 1969, which is a whole issue devoted to the subject.

**1721** David Martin and Phyllis Johnson *The Struggle for Zimbabwe: The Chimurenga War* Zimbabwe Publishing House, Harare 1981. This concentrates on the nationalist cause in the guerrilla war against white Rhodesia, but it also reflects on Britain's view of the war and on the eventual settlement. Another useful account of the final years of white Rhodesia is David Caute *Under the Skin: The Death of White Rhodesia* Penguin 1982.

**1722** Goswin Baumhogger *The Struggle for Independence: Documents on the Recent Development of Zimbabwe 1975–1980* 7v, Institut für Afrika-Kunde, Hamburg 1984. A detailed study of the negotiations that led to the 1980 settlement is A M Chakaodza 'Zimbabwe: The Politics and Diplomacy of Decolonisation (1974–1980)' London PhD Thesis 1983. A I Astrow 'The Nationalist Movement in Zimbabwe: A Critique, with Special Reference to the Period 1975–1980' Kent PhD Thesis 1982, which portrays Mugabe as a petit bourgeois quisling whose success ensures the future of British neo-colonialism in the region, is of rather more dubious value.

**1723** T H Bingham and S M Gray *Report on the Supply of Petroleum and Petroleum Products to Rhodesia* HMSO 1978. The official report which revealed the extent to which British companies had circumvented the sanctions imposed on Rhodesia after UDI. A journalistic account is Martin Bailey *Oilgate: The Sanctions Scandal* Coronet 1979. Also useful is Lionel Cliffe 'The Racial Implications of Britain's Sanctions Cover-Up' *Sage Race Relations Abstracts* 4 1979 pp 1–8.

**1724** *Southern Rhodesia: Constitutional Conference Held at Lancaster House, London September–December 1979* Cmnd 7802, *Parliamentary Papers* 1979–80. The negotiations, chaired by Lord Carrington, that led to the transition to black majority rule. These negotiations, the brief restoration of British rule under the governorship of Lord Soames that followed and the transfer of power are examined in Harry Wiseman and Alastair M Taylor *From Rhodesia to Zimbabwe: The Politics of Transition* Pergamon 1981. See also W H Morris-Jones and Dennis Austin (eds) *From Rhodesia to Zimbabwe: Behind and Beyond Lancaster House* Cass 1980.

**1725** *Southern Rhodesia Independence Elections 1980: Report of the Election Commissioner Sir John Boynton MC* Cmnd 7935, *Parliamentary Papers* 1979–80. On Smith's election held in 1979 before Lancaster House see Lord Chitnis and Eileen Sudworth *Free and Fair! The 1979 Rhodesian Election* Parliamentary Human Rights Group 1979.

**1726** Ken Flower *An Intelligence Chief on Record: Serving Secretly: Rhodesia into Zimbabwe 1964–1981* Murray 1987. An informative memoir by a man who served both Smith and Mugabe as head of intelligence. It is quite useful for Anglo-Rhodesian contacts during the nationalist period.

**1727** Lewis H Gann and Michael Gelfand *Huggins of Rhodesia: The Man and His Country* Allen and Unwin 1964. A rather uncritical biography of the Prime Minister of Rhodesia 1933–56 and the creator of the Federation.

**1728** David Smith and Colin Simpson *Mugabe* Sphere 1981. The leader of one of the two black organizations that opposed white Rhodesia, Mugabe became Prime Minister of Zimbabwe in 1980. See also Robert Gabriel Mugabe *Our War of Liberation: Speeches, Articles, Interviews 1976–1979* Mambo Press, Gweru 1983.

**1729** Joshua Nkomo *Nkomo: The Story of My Life* Methuen 1984. Nkomo was the other main black nationalist leader in Rhodesia.

**1730** Peter Joyce *Anatomy of a Rebel: Smith of Rhodesia: A Biography* Graham, Salisbury, Rhodesia 1977. Ian Smith, the leader of the white nationalist Rhodesia Front, was Prime Minister of Rhodesia 1964–79.

**1731** David Chanaiwa 'The Premiership of Garfield Todd: Racial Partnership Versus Colonial Interest 1953–1958' *Journal of Southern African Affairs* 1 1976 pp 83–94.

**1732** Sir Robert Tredgold *The Rhodesia that was My Life* Allen and Unwin 1968. An important judge, Tredgold acted as Governor of Southern Rhodesia and as Governor-General of the Central African Federation on many occasions.

**1733** Changatai J M Zvobgo 'Southern Rhodesia Under Edgar Whitehead 1958–1962' *Journal of Southern African Affairs* 2 1977 pp 481–92. Whitehead was the last liberal politician who tried to pursue racial partnership in the face of the rising tide of nationalism amongst the white electorate.

(d) Northern Rhodesia (Zambia)

**1734** W E Rous *A Bibliography of Pre-Independence Zambia: The Social Sciences* G K Hall 1978. An unannotated but extensive bibliography. Anne M Bliss and J A Rigg *Zambia* Clio Press 1984 is an annotated bibliography which contains some material of value.

**1735** Richard Hall *Zambia 1890–1964: The Colonial Period* 2nd ed, Longmans 1976. A good general history. See also Andrew Roberts 'The Political History of Twentieth Century Zambia' in T O Ranger (ed) *Aspects of Central African History* Northwestern University Press, Evanston, Illinois 1968 pp 154–89. Lewis H Gann *A History of Northern Rhodesia: Early Days to 1953* Chatto and Windus 1964 traces its history up to the creation of the Federation.

**1736** J W Davidson *The Northern Rhodesian Legislative Council* Faber 1948. A constitutional and historical study.

**1737** R A Smyth 'The Development of Government Propaganda in Northern Rhodesia up to 1953' London PhD Thesis 1983. An examination of the successfully favourable portrayal of colonial government and Britain to Africans in Zambia 1935–53. On colonial labour policy before the Federation see Ian Henderson 'Labour and Politics in Northern Rhodesia 1900–1953: A Study in the Limits of Colonial Power' Edinburgh PhD Thesis 1973.

**1738** Robert I Rotberg *The Rise of Nationalism in Central Africa: The Making of Malawi and Zambia 1873–1964* Harvard University Press, Cambridge, Massachussets 1966. A good analysis. See also S E Wilmer 'African Opposition to Federation in Northern Rhodesia 1950–3' Oxford BLitt Thesis 1973–4.

**1739** David C Mulford *Zambia – The Politics of Independence 1957–1964* Oxford University Press 1967. A good study of the changes that preceded independence in 1964.

**1740** Richard Hall *The High Price of Principles: Kaunda and the White South* Hodder and Stoughton 1969. Reflections on Zambia's problems in relations with the white regimes that then surrounded it, the problem of sanctions against Rhodesia, relations with Britain and so on.

**1741** Fergus MacPherson *Kenneth Kaunda of Zambia: The Times and the Man* Oxford University Press 1974. Kaunda led Zambia to independence. He has been President of Zambia since 1964. This is a good, sympathetic biography. It traces Kaunda's career up to the end of colonial rule, and includes a useful chronology. For other biographical studies see Richard Hall *Kaunda: Founder of Zambia* Longmans 1965 and [1624]. An autobiography is Kenneth Kaunda *Zambia Shall be Free: An Autobiography* Heinemann 1962. See also Colin Legum (ed) *Zambia: Independence and Beyond: The Speeches of Kenneth Kaunda* Nelson 1966. Kenneth Kaunda *A Humanist in Africa* Longmans 1966 is a collection of letters which reflect Kaunda's attitudes and career.

**1742** Robin Short *African Sunset* Johnson 1973. The memoirs of a former district commissioner in Northern Rhodesia. They are particularly useful for the end of the Federation.

### (e) Nyasaland/Malawi

**1743** Robert B Boeder *Malawi* Clio Press 1979. An annotated bibliography of some value.

**1744** F Debenham *Nyasaland* HMSO 1955. A useful general survey.

**1745** Roderick J Macdonald (ed) *From Nyasaland to Malawi: Studies in Colonial History* East Africa Publishing House, Nairobi 1975. This contains two relevant essays: Peter Dalleo 'Britain's Decolonisation Policy for Africa 1945–64: Nyasaland, a Case in Point' pp 282–306 and Roger Tangri 'From the Politics of Union to Mass Nationalism: The Nyasaland African Congress 1944–59' pp 254–81.

**1746** John McCrachen 'African Politics in Twentieth Century Malawi' in T O Ranger (ed) *Aspects of Central African History* Northwestern University Press, Evanston, Illinois 1968 pp 190–209. On nationalism in Nyasaland see also [1738].

**1747** Griff Jones *Britain and Nyasaland* Allen and Unwin 1964. A critique of British policy during the Federation period by a former administrative officer.

**1748** C A Baker 'The Development of the Civil Service in Malawi from 1891 to 1972' London PhD Thesis 1981.

**1749** Central Office of Information *Malawi* HMSO 1964. A pamphlet describing the country at the time of independence.

**1750** Philip Short *Banda* Routledge and Kegan Paul 1974. A good biography. Hastings Banda led Malawi to independence and has been President ever since.

### (5) South Africa

**1751** D W Kruger (ed) *South African Parties and Policies 1910–1960: A Select Source Book* Bowes and Bowes 1960.

**1752** Reuben Musiker *South Africa* Clio Press 1979. An annotated bibliography of some value.

**1753** T R H Davenport *South Africa: A Modern History* Macmillan 1981. A useful general history. G M Carter *The Politics of Inequality: South Africa Since 1948* Thames and Hudson 1958 studies the imposition of the structure of apartheid since the National party's election victory in 1948. See also D W Kruger *The Making of a Nation: A History of the Union of South Africa 1910–1961* Macmillan 1969 and Hilda Bornstein *The World that was Ours* Heinemann 1967. Alexander Hepple *South Africa: A Political and Economic History* Pall Mall Press 1966 is a critical history.

**1754** James Barber *The Uneasy Relationship: Britain and South Africa* Heinemann 1983. Another good survey of relations is Dennis Austin *Britain and South Africa* Oxford University Press 1966. D J Geldenhuys 'The

Effects of South Africa's Racial Policy on Anglo-South African Relations 1945– 1961' Cambridge PhD Thesis 1977 examines relations up to South Africa's withdrawal from the Commonwealth in 1961. See also H Griffiths 'A Study of British Opinion on the Problems and Policies of the Union of South Africa, from the end of the Second World War Until South Africa's Withdrawal fron the Commonwealth' London MSc Thesis 1962–3.

**1755**  Geoff Berridge *Economic Power in Anglo-South African Diplomacy: Simonstown, Sharpeville and After* Macmillan 1981. A good analysis of the economic ties that bound Britain to one of her oldest Dominions and their effect on the negotiations over the Simonstown naval base in the 1950s and on Britain's efforts to keep South Africa in the Commonwealth after the 1960 Sharpeville massacre. The best study of these economic ties is Ruth First, Jonathan Steele and Christabel Gurney *The South African Connection: Western Investment in Apartheid* Temple Smith 1972. Rosalynde Ainslie and Dorothy Robinson *The Collaborators* Anti-Apartheid Movement 1963 is an exposé of British economic involvement in South Africa. *The British Stake in South Africa* National Assocation of British Manufacturers 1963 is a report chaired by the Conservative MP Sir Gerald Nabarro on the economic advantages derived and opposing the demand for sanctions.

**1756**  James Barber 'BOSS in Britain' *African Affairs* 82 1983 pp 311–28. A study of the operation of the South African secret services in Britain since the 1960s.

**1757**  R H Wagenberg 'Commonwealth Reactions to South Africa's Racial Policy 1948–1961' London PhD Thesis 1965–6. On the negotiations that led to South Africa's withdrawal see J R T Wood 'The Roles of Diefenbaker, Macmillan and Verwoerd in the Withdrawal of South Africa from the Commonwealth' *Journal of Contemporary African Studies* 6 1987 pp 153–82 and J D B Miller 'South Africa's Departure' *Journal of Commonwealth Political Studies* 1 1961–63 pp 56–84. Frank Hayes 'South Africa's Departure from the Commonwealth 1960–1961' *International History Review* 2 1980 pp 453–84 is an analysis of Commonwealth diplomacy on the issue which focuses in particular on Canada's attitudes since 1947 and on Canada's crucial role in the crisis.

**1758**  H M Grayson 'The British Labour Movement and South Africa 1945–1970' York DPhil Thesis 1982. See also C J Sansom 'The British Labour Movement and Southern Africa 1918–1955: Labourism and the Imperial Tradition' Birmingham PhD Thesis 1982, his article 'Anticommunism and Apartheid: The British Trade Union Movement and South Africa 1945–54' *Bulletin of the Society for the Study of Labour History* 46 1983 pp 15–20 and Ritchie Ovendale 'The South African Policy of the British Labour Government 1947–

51' *International Affairs* 59 1982–3 pp 41–58. Anne Darnborough *Labour's Record on Southern Africa* Anti-Apartheid Movement 1967 is an indictment of the failure of the Wilson government to fulfil their promises in opposition.

**1759**  Shaun Johnson 'Between the Devil and the Deep Black Sea? Black Perceptions of British Policy Towards South Africa' *International Relations* 8 1986 pp 443–54. A critical evaluation of policy towards South Africa under Thatcher.

**1760**  W K Hancock *Smuts: The Fields of Force 1919–1950* Cambridge University Press 1968. The masterly second volume of his biography. Smuts was Prime Minister of South Africa until the National Party victory in 1948. He died in 1950. Another good biography is Kenneth Ingham *Jan Christian Smuts: The Conscience of a South African* Weidenfeld and Nicolson 1986. Bernard Friedman *Smuts: A Reappraisal* Allen and Unwin 1975 is an interpretation of his failings. J C Smuts *Jan Christian Smuts* Cassell 1952 is a biography by his son. See also W K Hancock and Jean van der Poel *Selections from the Smuts Papers Vol 7: August 1945–October 1950* Cambridge University Press 1973.

**1761**  Henry Kenny *Architect of Apartheid: H F Verwoerd* Jonathan Ball Publishers, Johannesburg 1980. Verwoerd was the South African Prime Minister who took South Africa out of the Commonwealth. Alexander Hepple *Verwoerd* Penguin 1966 is a critical study. See also Pieter Willem Grobbelaar *This was a Man* Human and Rousseau, Cape Town 1967.

## (6) The High Commission Territories

### (a) General

**1762**  J E Spence 'British Policy Towards the High Commission Territories' *Journal of Modern African Studies* 2 1964 pp 221–46. A general survey of developments in the territories since 1914.

**1763**  G V Doxey *The High Commission Territories and South Africa* Oxford University Press 1963. Britain refused to allow South Africa fulfil her ambition of absorbing these territories. See also Ronald Hyam 'The Politics of Partition in Southern Africa 1908–1961' *Journal of Contemporary History* 8 1973 pp 3–12.

### (b) Basutoland (Lesotho)

**1764**  Shelagh M Willett and David Ambrose *Lesotho* Clio Press 1980. An excellent annotated bibliography.

**1765** A Coates *Basutoland* HMSO 1966. A general survey at the time of independence which is part of the Corona Library series which is perhaps over-favourable in its treatment of British policy and of the South African mining industry. On the process of independence see John E Spence *Lesotho: The Politics of Independence* Oxford University Press 1968.

**(c) Bechuanaland (Botswana)**

**1766** P Mohome and J B Webster *A Bibliography on Bechuanaland* Maxwell Graduate School of Citizenship and Public Affairs, Syracuse University, Syracuse, New York 1966. A listing of over 500 items.

**1767** B A Young *Bechuanaland* HMSO 1966. A good general survey at the time of independence. Part of the Corona Library series.

**1768** Ronald Hyam 'The Political Consequences of Seretse Khama: Britain, the Bangwato and South Africa 1948–52' *Historical Journal* 29 1986 pp 921–47. An account of the crisis caused by his marriage to a white woman and subsequent deprivation of the chieftaincy of the Bangwato by the British.

**1769** Anthony J Dachs *Khama of Botswana* Heinemann 1971. A biography of Seretse Khama, the first President of Botswana 1966–80. See also Sidwell Mhaladi Gabatshwane *Seretse Khama and Botswana* J G Mmusi and S M Gabatshwane, Kenye, Botswana 1966.

**(d) Swaziland**

**1770** C S Wallace *Swaziland: A Bibliography* Department of Bibliography, Librarianship and Typography, University of the Witswaterand, Johannesburg 1967. This lists over 1,100 entries. Balam Nyeko *Swaziland* Clio Press 1981 is an annotated bibliography of some value.

**1771** Dudley Barker *Swaziland* HMSO 1965. A useful general survey from the Corona Library series.

**1772** Balam Nyeko *Interpreting the Colonial period in African History: The Case of Swaziland* History Department, University of Zambia, Lusaka 1982. A short analysis.

**1773** Hilda Kuper *Sobhuza II: Ngwanyama and King of Swaziland: The Story of an Hereditary Monarch and His Kingdom* Duckworth 1978. A highly regarded biography. Sobhuza was king of Swaziland 1921–1982. His kingdom became independent in 1968.

## F. THE CARIBBEAN

### (1) General

**1774** Bernard Naylor, Laurence Hallewell and Colin Steele *Directory of Libraries and Special Collections on Latin America and the West Indies* Athlone Press 1975. A directory of useful collections in the UK. See also Peter Walne (ed) *A Guide to Manuscript Sources for the History of Latin America and the Caribbean in the British Isles* Oxford University Press 1973 and Kenneth E Ingram *Manuscripts Relating to Commonwealth Caribbean Countries in United States and Canadian Repositories* Bowker 1975.

**1775** Kenneth J Grieb (ed) *Research Guide to Central America and the Caribbean* Wisconsin University Press, Madison, Wisconsin 1985. An extensive and detailed guide to source material.

**1776** William Lux *Historical Dictionary of the British Caribbean* Scarecrow Press 1975. A reference guide to essential historical and statistical information.

**1777** *Constitutional Development of the West Indies 1922–1968: A Selection from Major Documents* Caribbean University Press/Bowker 1975. A voluminous collection which also features an extensive bibliography.

**1778** Audrey Roberts (comp) *Bibliography of Commissions of Enquiry and Other Government-Sponsored Reports on the Commonwealth Caribbean 1900–1975* Seminar on the Acquisition of Latin American Library Materials, Madison, Wisconsin 1985.

**1779** Alma Jordan and Barbara Comissiong *The English- Speaking Caribbean: A Bibliography of Bibliographies* G K Hall 1984. A well annotated and classified guide to relevant bibliographies and library catalogues. See also Henry C Chang *A Selected Annotated Bibliography of Caribbean Bibliographies in English* Caribbean Research Institute, College of the Virgin Islands, St Thomas, US Virgin Islands 1975.

**1780** *Current Caribbean Bibliography* Caribbean Commission 1951–. An annual guide to publications in the English, French and Dutch speaking West Indies. The *Bibliography of the English-Speaking Caribbean* 1979– is another annual bibliography and is semi-annotated and well classified.

**1781** Lambros Comitas *The Complete Caribbeana 1900–1975: A Topical Bibliography* University of Washington Press, Seattle, Washington 1977. A massive well organized but unannotated bibliography concentrating on the non-Hispanic Caribbean. Roger Hughes (comp) *The Caribbean: A Basic Annotated Bibliography for Students, Librarians and General Readers* Commonwealth Institute Library Services 1987 is the best introduction to the literature on the Commonwealth Caribbean. Another short bibliography is *The Commonwealth in the Caribbean: An Annotated List* National Book League 1969.

**1782**  Enid M Baa (comp) *Doctoral Dissertations and Selected Theses on Caribbean Topics Accepted by Universities of Canada, United States and Europe from 1778–1968* Bureau of Public Libraries and Museums, Department of Conservation and Cultural Affairs, St Thomas, US Virgin Islands 1969. See also Commonwealth Caribbean Resource Centre (comp) *Theses on the Commonwealth Caribbean 1891–1973* Office of International Education, University of Western Ontario n.d. (1970s?) and David S Zubatsky (comp) *Doctoral Dissertations in History and the Social Sciences in Latin America and the Caribbean Accepted by Universities in the United Kingdom 1920–1972* Institute of Latin American Studies, University of London 1973.

**1783**  Elizabeth Wallace *The British Caribbean from the Decline of Colonialism to the end of Federation* Toronto University Press, Toronto 1977. A good general history of political development in the British West Indies 1900–62. See also W M Macmillan *The Road to Self-Rule: A Study in Colonial Evolution* Praeger, New York 1960. There are useful essays on post-war British economic policy, British Guiana and British Honduras in Sir Harold Mitchell *Europe in the Caribbean: The Policies of Great Britain, France and the Netherlands Towards Their West Indian Territories in the Twentieth Century* Chambers 1963. See also Jesse Harris Proctor 'British West Indies Society and Government in Transition 1920–60' *Social and Economic Studies* 11 1962 pp 273–304 and Ronald Vernon Sires 'Government in the British West Indies: An Historical Outline' *Social and Economic Studies* 6 1957 pp 108–32.

**1784**  *The British Caribbean: A Brief Political and Economic Survey* Royal Institute of International Affairs 1957. A general survey which includes material and statistics on developments in each territory.

**1785**  *British Dependencies in the Caribbean and North Atlantic 1939–1952* Cmnd 8575, *Parliamentary Papers* xxiv 1951–52. A survey which includes Bermuda. It includes a chronology.

**1786**  Harry Luke 'The West Indies Since the Moyne Report' *Geographical Magazine* 22 1949 pp 165–76. The Moyne report was published in 1939.

**1787**  Carl Stone and Henry Page (eds) *The Newer Caribbean: Decolonisation, Democracy and Development* Institute for the Study of Human Issues, Philadel-

phia 1983. Many of these essays are about the process of decolonization and its consequences in the British West Indies. See also Edward A Lang 'Independence and Islands: The Decolonisation of the British Caribbean' *New York University Journal of International Law and Politics* 12 1979 pp 281–312.

**1788**  E W Evans 'A Survey of the Present Constitutional Situation in the British West Indies' in *Developments Towards Self-Government in the Caribbean: A Symposium Held Under the Auspices of the Netherlands Universities Foundation for International Co-operation at The Hague September 1954* W Van Heover, The Hague 1955 pp 23–33. See also P G Singh 'The Development and Working of Local Self-Government in the British Caribbean, with Special Reference to the Period Since 1945' London PhD Thesis 1963–4.

**1789**  E S Jones 'Pressure Group Politics in the West Indies – a Case Study of Colonial Systems: Jamaica, Trinidad and British Guiana' Manchester PhD Thesis 1970–1. On constitutional developments in the Lesser Antilles see C A Hughes 'Politics and Constitution-Making in the Eastern Group of the British West Indies 1922 to the Present Day' London PhD Thesis 1951–2.

**1790**  Hugh Tinker 'British Policy Towards the Separate Indian Identity in the Caribbean 1920–1950' in Bridget Brereton and Winston Deokeran (eds) *East Indians in the Caribbean: Colonialism and the Struggle for Identity* Kraus International 1981 pp 33–48.

**1791**  Charles C Moskos Jr *The Sociology of Political Independence: A Study of Nationalist Attitudes Among West Indian Leaders* Schenkman, Cambridge, Massachusetts 1967. See also Marley Ayearst *The British West Indies: The Search for Self- Government* Allen and Unwin 1960, C L R James *Party Politics in the West Indies* Vedic Enterprises 1962, Rawle Farley *Nationalism and Industrial Development in the British Caribbean* Daily Chronicle, Georgetown, British Guiana 1958 and George T Daniel 'Labor and Nationalism in the British Caribbean' *Annals of the American Academy of Political and Social Science* 310 1957 pp 162–71.

**1792**  Jean F Freymond *Political Integration in the Commonwealth Caribbean: A Survey of Recent Attempts with Special Reference to the Associated States (1967–1974)* Institute Universitaire de Hautes Etudes Internationales, Geneva 1980. The 1967 West Indies Act made a number of Caribbean islands associate states of the United Kingdom. This is a useful study of the reasons behind this development and its subsequent history. It also includes a useful bibliography.

**1793**  Kenneth Blackburne 'Changing Patterns of Caribbean International Relations: Britain and the "British" Caribbean' in Richard Millett and W Marvin Will (eds)

*The Restless Caribbean: Changing Patterns of International Relations* Praeger, New York 1979 pp 204–18. See also Gordon K Lewis 'The Social Legacy of British Colonialism in the Caribbean' *New World Quarterly* 3 1967 pp 13–32.

#### (2) The West Indian Federation 1958–62

**1794** Yvonne Stephenson (comp) *A Bibliography on the West Indian Federation* University of Guyana Library, Georgetown 1972. Another listing is Anne Benewick *A List of Books on West Indian Federation* 2nd ed, West Indian Reference Library, Institute of Jamaica, Kingston 1962.

**1795** Bernard L Foote *The Caribbean Commission: Background of Co-operation in the West Indies* University of South Carolina Press, Columbia, South Carolina 1951. The Caribbean Commission was a pre-Federation organization for co-operation amongst the West Indian islands. See also Frank A Stockdale 'The Work of the Caribbean Commission' *International Affairs* 23 1947 pp 213–20.

**1796** Eric Eustace Williams (ed) 'The Historical Background of the British West Indian Federation: Select Documents' *Caribbean History Review* 3–4 1954 pp 13–69. On the historical background to the Federation see also Jesse Harris Proctor 'The Development of the Idea of Federation of the British Caribbean Territories' *Revista de Historia de America* 30 1955 pp 61–105, Jesse Harris Proctor 'Britain's Pro- Federation Policy in the Caribbean: An Inquiry into Motivation' *Canadian Journal of Economics and Political Science* 22 1956 pp 319–37, Fred D Schneider 'British Policy in West Indian Federation' *World Affairs Quarterly* 30 1959 pp 241–65, Gordon K Lewis 'The British Caribbean Federation: The West Indian Background' *Political Quarterly* 28 1957 pp 49–65, Lloyd E Braithwaite 'Progress Towards Federation 1938–56' *Social and Economic Studies* 6 1957 pp 133–84 and Shridath Ramphal 'The West Indies – Constitutional Background to Federation' *Public Law* 1959 pp 128–51.

**1797** Colin A Hughes 'Experiment Towards Closer Union in the British West Indies' *Journal of Negro History* 43 1958 pp 85–104.

**1798** John Mordecai *The West Indies: The Federal Negotiations* Allen and Unwin 1968. A history of the creation and breakup of the Federation 1958–62. Another general study is Lewis E Bobb 'Federation in the British West Indies' Leicester MA Thesis 1963–4. His article 'The Federal Principle in the British West Indies: An Appraisal of Its Use' *Social and Economic Studies* 15 1966 pp 239–65 sees the constitution of the Feder-

ation as too rigid to contain the centrifugal forces that led to its eventual demise. Another interpretation is F A Barrett 'The Rise and Demise of the Federation of the West Indies' *Canadian Review of Studies in Nationalism* 1 1974 pp 248– 54. David Lowenthal (ed) *West Indian Federation: Perspectives on a New Nation* Columbia University Press, New York 1961 is a contemporary portrait which includes a useful bibliography.

**1799** Hugh W Springer *Reflections on the Failure of the First West Indian Federation* Center for International Affairs, Occasional Papers in International Affairs 4, Harvard University, Cambridge, Massachusetts 1962. See also Samuel J Hurwitz 'The Federation of the West Indies: A Study in Nationalisms' *Journal of British Studies* 6 1966 pp 139–68, Elizabeth Wallace 'The West Indian Federation: Decline and Fall' *International Journal* 17 1962 pp 269–88 and Charles H Archibald 'The Failure of the West Indian Federation' *World Today* 18 1962 pp 233–42. C L R James *Federation: 'We Failed Miserably': How and Why* Vedic Enterprises 1962 is a view from Trinidad on the Federation's failure. The impact of Jamaica's decision to quit the Federation in 1961 is assessed in Garnet H Gordon 'The West Indies Before and After Jamaica's Quit Vote' *Commonwealth Journal* 4 1961 pp 274–9.

#### (3) The Bahamas

**1800** D Gail Saunder *Guide to the Records of the Bahamas* Government Printing Department, Nassau 1973.

**1801** Paul Albery *The Story of the Bahamas* Macmillan 1975. A general history up to the granting of independence to this island group in 1973. Colin A Hughes *Race and Politics in the Bahamas* University of Queensland Press, St Lucia, Queensland 1981 is a political history 1953–77.

**1802** M Holmes-Hanek 'Bahamian Nationalism: The Thirty Years Preceding Independence' Bradford MPhil Thesis 1980.

**1803** Sir Etienne Dupuch *Tribune Story* Benn 1967. This history of an important Bahamian newspaper/autobiography is quite useful on Bahamian politics, the colonial administration and the activities and views of the British governors.

#### (4) British Honduras/Belize

**1804** Ralph Lee Woodward Jr *Belize* Clio Press 1980. An annotated bibliography of some value. See also Clarence Minkel and Ralph Alderman *A Bibliography* *of British Honduras 1900–1970* Latin American Studies Center, Michigan State University, East Lansing, Michigan 1970.

**1805** Cedric H Grant *The Making of Modern Belize: Politics, Society and British Colonialism in Central America* Cambridge University Press 1976. The standard history. See also N Dobson *A History of Belize* Longman 1973. Stephen L Caiyer *British Honduras: Past and Present* Allen and Unwin 1951 and David A G Waddell *British Honduras: An Historical and Contemporary Survey* Oxford University Press 1961 present useful portraits. A R Greg *British Honduras* HMSO 1968 is a general survey from the Corona Library series. William David Setzekorn *Formerly British Honduras: A Profile of the New Nation of Belize* 2nd ed, Ohio University Press 1981 is a survey at the time of independence in 1981. See also Waddell's 'Case Study: British Honduras' in Burton Benedict (ed) *Problems of Smaller Territories* Athlone Press 1967 pp 56–67.

**1806** P K Menon 'The Anglo-Guatemalan Territorial Dispute Over the Colony of Belize (British Honduras)' *Journal of Latin American Studies* 11 1979 pp 343–71. This is a good study of the legality of the Guatemalan claim to Belize and the history of the dispute. Donald Grunewald 'The Anglo-Guatemalan Dispute Over British Honduras' *Caribbean Studies* 5 1965 pp 17–43 traces the history of the dispute up to 1949. See also William J Bianchi *Belize: The Controversy Between Guatemala and Great Britain Over the Territory of British Honduras in Central America* Las Américas Publishing Co, New York 1959. Carlos Garcia Bauer *La Controversia Sobre et Territoria de Belize y el Procedimiento ex aequo et bono* Editorial Universitaria, Guatemala City 1958 is one of the more dispassionate of the many Guatemalan contributions to the extensive literature on the dispute. Miguel Ydígoras Fuentes *Belice, Guatemala, la Gran Bretaña y Centro América* Sánchez and de Guise, Guatemala City 1976 is a strong criticism of British control of Belize by a man who as President of Guatemala 1958–63 pursued a strongly anti-British line.

**1807** *British Honduras: Report of an Inquiry held by Sir Reginald Sharpe QC into Allegations of Contacts Between the People's United Party and Guatemala* Cmnd 9139, *Parliamentary Papers* x 1953–54. This reports casts light on relations between Britain, the PUP, which has dominated Belizean politics since the 1950s, and Guatemala. See also C P Cacho 'British Honduras: A Case of Deviation in Commonwealth Caribbean Decolonisation' *New World Quarterly* 3 1967 pp 33–44, which warns of a Belizean drift towards absorption by Guatemala.

**1808** Assad Shoman *The Birth of the Nationalist Movement in Belize 1950–1954* West Indian University 1973. A good short study. On the background influences

see Peter Ashdown 'Marcus Garvey, the UNIA and the Black Cause in British Honduras 1914– 1949' *Journal of Caribbean History* 15 1981 pp 41–55.

**1809** Tony Thorndike 'Belizean Political Parties: The Independence Crisis and After' *Journal of Commonwealth and Comparative Politics* 21 1983 pp 195–211. A study of the political and racial tensions of the 1970s, the continuing difficulties with Guatemala and the circumstances in which independence was granted.

## (5) Cayman Islands

**1810** Neville Williams *A History of the Cayman Islands* Government of the Cayman Islands, Georgetown, Grand Cayman 1970. A general history. The Cayman Islands remain a British Dependency. See also [1141].

## (6) British Guiana/Guyana

**1811** Frances Chambers *Guyana* Clio Press 1988. An annotated and classified select bibliography.

**1812** Thomas J Spinner *A Political and Social History of Guyana 1945–1983* Westview Press 1986. A good general history, especially in the context of the ethnically bi-polar politics between the Indian and Afro-Caribbean communities that characterize this former colony which received its independence in 1966. Reynold A Burrowes *The Wild Coast: An Account of Politics in Guyana* Schenkman, Cambridge, Massachusetts 1984 examines Guyanan politics 1950–80. Peter Simms *Trouble in Guyana: An Account of People, Personalities as they were in British Guiana* Allen and Unwin 1966 is a useful commentary on some of the events and political developments of the final years of British rule. A general survey from the Corona Library series is M Swan *British Guiana* HMSO 1957.

**1813** F L Kellner 'A Comparative Study of Colonial Development and Racial Division: The Moyne Report and British Guiana 1939 to 1966 and the Spate Report and Fiji 1959 to 1970' Oxford MPhil Thesis 1985. Other studies of British policy are Jonathan Wouk 'British Guiana: A Case Study in British Colonial and Foreign Policy' *Political Scientist* 3 1967 pp 41–59 and Robert D Tomasek 'British Guiana: A Case Study of British Colonial Policy' *Political Science Quarterly* 74 1959 pp 393–411.

**1814** Harold A Lutchman *Some Aspects of the Crown Colony System of Government with Special Reference to Guyana* Critchlow Labour College, Georgetown 1970. On the administrative structure of the colony see also Allan Young *The Approach to Local Self-Government* *in British Guiana* Longmans 1958 and Mohamed Sha-habuddean 'Constitutional Development in Guyana' London PhD Thesis 1970.

**1815**  Ronald Vernon Sires 'British Guiana: The Suspension of the Constitution' *Political Quarterly* 25 1954 pp 554–69. A study of the events leading to the rapid suspension of the new constitution in 1953. The disturbances of the early 1960s are examined in Randolph Rawkins 'What Really Happened in British Guiana' *Journal of Inter-American Studies* 5 1963 pp 140–7.

**1816**  Jacqueline Anne Braveboy-Wagner *The Venezuela-Guyana Dispute: Britain's Colonial Legacy in Latin America* Bowker 1984. A good historical account of the dispute over the border between Venezuela and British Guiana. It includes an extensive bibliography. Another useful study is Betty Jane Kissler 'Venezuela-Guyana Boundary Dispute 1899–1963' Texas PhD Thesis 1971.

**1817**  William Edward Rolison 'British Colonial Policy and the Independence of Guyana' Missouri PhD Thesis 1974.

**1818**  Basil A Ince *Decolonization and Conflict in the United Nations: Guyana's Struggle for Independence* Schenkman, Cambridge, Massachusetts 1974. This includes a discussion of the UN scrutiny of the dispute over the border between British Guiana and Venezuela. See also Colin Henfrey 'Foreign Influence in Guyana: The Struggle for Independence' in Emanuel de Kadt (ed) *Patterns of Foreign Influence in the Caribbean* Oxford University Press 1972 pp 49–81. On the problems involved in Guyana's independence see B A N Collins 'Acceding to Independence: Some Constitutional Problems of a Polyethnic Society (British Guiana)' *Civilizations* 15 1965 pp 376– 403.

**1819**  Andrew Sanders 'British Colonial Policy and the Role of the Amerindians in the Politics of the Nationalist Period in British Guiana' *Social and Economic Studies* 36/3 1987 pp 77–98. A study of the political attitudes of the Amerindians and the effect both on the boundary dispute and on colonial policy.

**1820**  Cheddi Jagan *The West on Trial: My Fight for Guyana's Freedom* Joseph 1966. Jagan was the first Prime Minister of British Guiana 1961–4 and has been leader of the Opposition since. There is no biography of his great rival Forbes Burnham, who ruled Guyana as Prime Minister and President from independence until his death in 1985.

## (7) Jamaica

**1821**  Kenneth E Ingram *Jamaica* Clio Press 1984. An annotated bibliography which contains some material of value. See also *Jamaica: A Selected Bibliography 1900– 1963* Jamaica Library Services 1963.

**1822**  Clinton V Black *History of Jamaica* Collins Educational 1979. A short general history up to independence in 1962. Trevor Munroe *The Politics of Constitutional Decolonisation: Jamaica 1944–1962* Institute of Social and Economic Research, University of the West Indies, Kingston, Jamaica 1972 and Wesley Walton Daley *Political Growth in Jamaica 1938–1968: From Colony to Nationhood* University Microfilms, Ann Arbor, Michigan 1973 are good studies of post-war political development. See also Carl Stone 'Decolonisation and the Caribbean State System – The Case of Jamaica' in Carl Stone and Aggrey Brown (eds) *Perspectives on Jamaica in the Seventies* Jamaica Publishing House, Kingston 1981 pp 3–41.

**1823**  P Abrahams *Jamaica* HMSO 1957. A good general survey from the Corona Library series.

**1824**  Central Office of Information *Jamaica: The Making of a Nation* HMSO 1962 is a pamphlet which provides a general political, social and economic survey of Jamaica at the time of independence.

**1825**  Martin Ira Glassner 'The Foreign Relations of Jamaica and Trinidad and Tobago 1960–1965' *Caribbean Studies* 10 1970 pp 116–53. This includes some reflections on post- independence relations with Britain.

**1826**  Trevor Munroe *The Marxist 'Left' in Jamaica 1940– 1950* Institute of Social and Economic Research, University of the West Indies, Kingston, Jamaica 1977. An examination of the Communist element in the nationalist movement at a crucial point in its development.

**1827**  George E Eaton *Alexander Bustamente and Modern Jamaica* Kingston Publishers, Kingston, Jamaica 1975. A biography of the first Prime Minister of independent Jamaica.

**1828**  Philip Sherlock *Norman Manley* Macmillan 1980. A vivid biography. Manley was Chief Minister 1955–9 and 1959–62. Rex Nettleford 'Manley and the Politics of Jamaica – Towards an Analysis of Political Change in Jamaica 1938–1968' *Social and Economic Studies* 20 1981 pp 1–72 examines his influence on Jamaican politics since he founded the People's National Party in 1938. See also Rex Nettleford (ed) *Norman Washington Manley and the New Jamaica: Selected Speeches and Writings 1938–1968* Longman 1971.

## (8) Leeward Islands

**1829** Edward Cecil Baker *A Guide to Records in the Leeward Islands* Blackwell 1965. A guide to manuscripts, government records, newspapers and other related material.

### (a) Antigua and Barbuda

**1830** Jean A Callender and Audine C Wilkinson 'The Road to Independence: Antigua and Barbuda – A Select Bibliography' *Bulletin of Eastern Caribbean Affairs* 7 1981 pp 50–8.

**1831** Ronald Sanders *Antigua and Barbuda 1966– 1981* Antigua Archives Committee, St Johns, Antigua 1984. A booklet charting Antigua's progress from colony to associate state in 1966 to independence in 1981.

### (b) Montserrat

**1832** Howard A Fergus *History of Alliouayena: A Short History of Montserrat* University Centre, Montserrat 1975. A short general history. Montserrat remains a British dependency. See also [1141].

### (c) St Kitts-Nevis and Anguilla

**1833** Sir Probyn Inniss *Whither Bound St Kitts-Nevis?* the author 1983. A general history from colonization up to the 1980s, published in the year the islands became independent.

**1834** Hugh Wooding (ed) *Report of the Commission of Inquiry Appointed by the Governments of the United Kingdom and St Christopher-Nevis-Anguilla to Examine the Anguilla Problem* HMSO 1970. St Christopher-Nevis-Anguilla became an associated state in 1967. The Anguillans objected to this arrangement and in 1969 the Wilson government felt obliged to send troops in to quell rioting. This problem is also examined in Basil A Ince 'The Diplomacy of New States: The Commonwealth Caribbean and the Case of Anguilla' *South Atlantic Quarterly* 69 1970 pp 382–96, George C Abbot 'Political Disintegration: The Lessons of Anguilla' *Government and Opposition* 6 1971 pp 58–74 and Colin G Clarke 'Political Fragmentation in the Caribbean: The Case of Anguilla' *Canadian Geographer* 15 1971 pp 13–29. Neil Marten *Their's Not to Reason Why: A Study of the Anguillan Operation as Presented to Parliament* Conservative Political Centre 1969 is a critique of the military intervention. Anguilla was formally separated from St Christopher-Nevis in 1980 and remains a British dependency. On Anguilla see also [1141].

## (d) British Virgin Islands

**1835** Isaac Dookhan *A History of the British Virgin Islands 1672–1970* Caribbean Universities Press, Kingston, Jamaica 1975. See also Norwell Harrigan and Pearl Verlack *The British Virgin Islands – A Chronology* BVI Research and Consulting Services Ltd 1970 and [1141].

## (9) Trinidad and Tobago

**1836** Frances Chambers *Trinidad and Tobago* Clio Press 1980. An annotated bibliography which includes some relevant material.

**1837** Bridget Brereton *A History of Modern Trinidad 1783–1962* Heinemann Education 1981. A general history of Trinidad up to independence. See also Eric Eustace Williams *History of the People of Trinidad and Tobago* Deutsch 1964. Henry Iles Woodstock *A History of Tobago* Cass 1971 is a general history of Tobago.

**1838** H Craig *The Legislative Council of Trinidad and Tobago* Faber 1952. A useful historical and constitutional study.

**1839** Ann Spackman 'Constitutional Development in Trinidad and Tobago' *Social and Economic Studies* 14 1965 pp 283–320. A study of development from 1956 to independence in 1962.

**1840** Central Office of Information *Trinida and Tobago: The Making of a Nation* HMSO 1962 is a pamphlet which provides a general political, social and economic survey of Trinidad and Tobago at the time of independence. See also [1825].

**1841** Ivar Oxaal *Black Intellectuals Come to Power: The Rise of Creole Nationalism in Trinidad and Tobago* Schenkman, Cambridge, Massachusetts 1968. This and Selwyn D Ryan *Race and Nationalism in Trinidad and Tobago: A Study of Decolonisation in a Multiracial Society* University of Toronto Press, Toronto 1972 are both stimulating sociological accounts of ethnic politics and nationalism in the final years of colonial rule.

**1842** L D Punch *A Journey to Remember (32 Years in the Civil Service)* Ideal Printery, Port of Spain 1967. A memoir of colonial service in Trinidad and Tobago.

**1843** Khafra Kambon *For Bread, Justice and Freedom: A Political Biography of George Weekes* New Beacon Books 1988. Weekes was the President-General of the Oilfield Workers Trade Union 1962–87. This biography traces his life, and radical politics, from the 1920s. It is also useful on the nationalization of Trinidad's oil.

**1844** Ramesh Deosaran *Eric Williams: The Man, His Ideas and His Politics* Signum, Port of Spain 1981. Williams was the Prime Minister of Trinidad and Tobago 1961–81.

### (10) Windward Islands

**1845** Edward Cecil Baker *A Guide to Records in the Windward Islands* Blackwell 1968. A guide to manuscripts, government records, newspapers and other related material.

### (a) Barbados

**1846** M J Chandler *A Guide to Records in Barbados* Blackwell 1965. A guide to sources such as documents, government records or newspapers.

**1847** Robert B Potter and Graham M S Dann *Barbados* Clio Press 1987. A useful annotated and classified bibliography. *Barbadiana: A List of Works Pertaining to the History of the Island of Barbados* Barbados Public Library, Bridgetown, Barbados 1966 is a classified listing of some 500 items.

**1848** F A Hoyos *Barbados: A History from the Amerindians to Independence* Macmillan 1979. A general history up to independence in 1966. Post-war political history is examined in R L Cheltenham 'Constitutional and Political Developments in Barbados 1946–1966' Manchester PhD Thesis 1966.

**1849** J M Hewitt *Ten Years of Constitutional Development in Barbados* Coles Printery, Bridgetown 1954. A short account of constitutional development 1944–54.

**1850** Gordon K Lewis 'Struggle for Freedom (a Story of Contemporary Barbados)' *New World Quarterly* 3 1966 pp 14–29. On the achievement of independence see Hugh W Springer 'Barbados as a Sovereign State' *Journal of the Royal Society of Arts* 115 1965 pp 283–320 and Jean-Claude Giacottino 'La Barbade Indépendente' *Les Cahiers d'Outre-Mer* 20 1967 pp 209–27.

### (b) Dominica

**1851** Robert A Myers *Dominica* Clio Press 1987. An annotated and classified bibliography. See also J D Shillingford, Jennifer Shillingford and Leona Shillingford *A Bibliography of the Literature on Dominica* Cornell University, New York 1972.

**1852** Cuthbert J Thomas 'From Crown Colony to Associate Statehood: Political Change in Dominica, the Commonwealth West Indies' Massachusetts PhD Thesis 1973. Under the West Indies Act 1967 Dominica and several other West Indian islands ceased to be Crown Colonies and became associate states of the United Kingdom. Dominica became fully independent in 1978.

### (c) Grenada

**1853** George Brizan *Grenada Island of Conflict: From Amerindians to People's Revolution 1498–1979* Zed Books 1984. See also Beverley Steele 'Grenada, an Island State, Its History and Its People' *Caribbean Quarterly* 20 1974 pp 5–43.

**1854** Patrick Emmanuel *Crown Colony Politics in Grenada 1917–1951* Institute of Social and Economic Research, University of the West Indies, Kingston, Jamaica 1978. On political development and social unrest in this period see George Brizon *The Grenadian Peasantry and Social Revolution 1930–1951* Institute of Social and Economic Research, University of the West Indies, Kingston, Jamaica 1979.

**1855** *Independence for Grenada – Myth or Reality? Proceedings of a Conference on the Implications of Independence for Grenada Sponsored by the Institute of International Relations and the Department of Government, University of the West Indies, St Augustine, Trinidad Jan 11–13 1974.* This includes some reflections on the process leading to independence in 1974.

### (d) St Lucia

**1856** Henry H Breen *St Lucia: Historical, Statistical and Descriptive* Cass 1970. A general historical introduction. St Lucia became independent in 1979.

### (e) St Vincent and the Grenadines

**1857** Charles Shepherd *A Historical Account of the Island of St Vincent* Cass 1971. A general history. Ebenezer Duncan *A Brief History of St Vincent with Studies in Citizenship* 3rd ed, St Vincent Reliance Printery, Kingston 1963 is perhaps rather better on post-war political developments. St Vincent became independent in 1979.

## G. AUSTRALASIA AND THE PACIFIC

### (1) General

**1858** Phyllis Mander-Jones (ed) *Manuscripts in the British Isles Relating to Australia, New Zealand and the Pacific* Oxford University Press 1972. A good annotated guide to manuscript collections and their locations.

**1859** William S Livingston and William Roger Louis (eds) *Australia, New Zealand and the Pacific Islands Since the End of the First World War* Australian National University Press, Canberra 1979. A disparate collection of essays. The major theme is the decline of British power and the reorientation of Australia and New Zealand towards their Asian and Pacific neighbours. The rise of nationalism in the Pacific is also examined.

### (2) Australia

This section is designed to include only material which reflects on Australia's changing relationship with Britain. For Australian co-operation in the defence of Malaysia from 1950–76 see the section on Malaysia.

**1860** I Kepars *Australia* Clio Press 1984. An annotated bibliography which however contains little of value on Anglo-Australian relations.

**1861** Neville Meaney *Australia and the World: A Documentary History from the 1870s to the 1970s* Longman Cheshire, Melbourne 1985. This collection is especially useful for Australia's relations with Britain and with America.

**1862** Geoffrey Bolton *The Oxford History of Australia Vol 5: 1942–1986* Oxford University Press 1987. An excellent general history of post-war Australia, charting its declining dependence on Britain. Russell Ward *A Nation for a Continent: The History of Australia 1901–1975* Heinemann Education 1977 focuses on the growth of Australian national consciousness and the resulting changes in attitude to Britain. Charles Wilson *Australia 1788–1988: The Creation of a Nation* Weidenfeld and Nicolson 1987 pursues a similar theme, as indeed do most historians of Australia. Also of use are Frederick Alexander *Australia Since Federation: A Narrative and Critical Guide* Nelson 1967 and Trevor R Reese *Australia in the Twentieth Century: A Short Political Guide* Pall Mall Press 1964.

**1863** J D B Miller (ed) *Australians and British: Social and Political Connections* Methuen 1987. A series of historical essays examining links through immigration, government and law, education, foreign policy, busi-ness, sport and culture. The general theme is the declining importance of all except ties of sentiment. A similar theme emerges in A Frederick Madden and W H Morris-Jones (eds) *Australia and Britain: Studies in a Changing Relationship* Cass 1980. The essays in this volume examine such topics as the defence of Malaysia, the Australian attitude to the Commonwealth, British influence on Australian law and education and changing economic relations. T B Millar (ed) *The Australian Contribution to Britain* Australian Studies Centre, Institute of Commonwealth Studies, University of London 1988 is a study of corresponding Australian influence on Britain in fields such as science, medicine, art, music, the performing arts, the media, or banking and finance. It usefully demonstrates the extent to which the relationship has been one of cross-fertilization. For Australia's continuing political ties to Britain see John Warhurst 'The Australia-Britain Relationship: The Future of Australia's Political Relationship to Britain' *Journal of Commonwealth and Comparative Politics* 24 1986 pp 35–47. On Anglo-Australian diplomatic and military ties see Robert O'Neill *Australia, Britain and International Security: Retrospect and Prospect* Australian Studies Centre, Institute of Commonwealth Studies, University of London 1985.

**1864** Donald J Markwell *The Crown and Australia* Australian Studies Centre, Institute of Commonwealth Studies, University of London 1987. A good short study of the evolution and current state of this constitutional link. It includes a useful bibliography.

**1865** Sir Alan Watt *The Evolution of Australia's Foreign Policy 1938–1965* Cambridge University Press 1967. It was not until 1935 that Australia set up a Department of External Affairs and in 1938 she still only had representation in one non-Commonwealth country. This traces the gradual decline in Australia's diplomatic dependence on Britain up to the Australian involvement in the Vietnam war. See also Bruce Grant *The Crisis of Loyalty: A Study of Australian Foreign Policy* Angus and Robertson 1972.

**1866** P G Richards *Prime Ministers and Diplomats: The Making of Australian Foreign Policy 1901–1949* Oxford University Press 1983. A good study which unfortunately only treats 1945–49 as an epilogue. This period has however been more fully examined in Alan Renouf *Let Justice be Done: The Foreign Policy of Dr H V Evatt* Queensland University Press, St Lucia, Queensland 1983. Evatt was the Australian Minister of External Affairs 1941–9 and Deputy Prime Minister 1946–9.

**1867** Richard G Casey *Friends and Neighbours: Australia and the World* F W Cheshire, Melbourne 1954. A view of Australia's post-war diplomatic interests and ties. It also features a chronology 1950–54. Casey, Minister of External Affairs 1951–60, reaffirms 'Australia is a British community' (p21). Australian external policy in the 1950s is also examined in Sir Alan Watt *Australian Defence Policy 1951–63: Major International Aspects* Department of International Relations, Australian National University, Canberra 1963.

**1868**  T B Millar *Australia's Foreign Policy* Angus and Robertson 1968. A useful study of foreign policy commitments, relations and imperatives in the 1960s. See also his similar *Australia's Defence* 2nd ed, Melbourne University Press, Melbourne 1969 and J Wilkes (ed) *Australia's Defence and Foreign Policy* Angus and Robertson 1964.

**1869**  J D B Miller *The EEC and Australia* Nelson 1976. Britain's entry into the European Community has effected a major transformation in its relations with traditional Commonwealth trading partners like Australia and New Zealand. This study reflects on this in the context of a more general study of Australia's relations with the European Community. The Australian response to Britain's first attempt to join Europe is examined in detail in Harry Gregor Gelber *Australia, Britain and the EEC 1961 to 1963* Oxford University Press 1966. 'Britain in Europe: A Canadian View, An Australian View, A New Zealand View' *Round Table* 209 1962 pp 19–30 reflects the generally antagonistic attitudes in the Old Commonwealth at the time. For other Australian reactions at the time see J D B Miller 'Political Implications of the European Economic Community' *Australian Outlook* 16 1962 pp 229–45 and A L Burns 'Britain and the Common Market: Some Australian Views' *World Today* 18 1962 pp 152–63. On Australian trade policy more generally see John G Crawford with Nancy Anderson and Margery G N Morris (eds) *Australian Trade Policy 1942–1966* Longmans 1968.

**1870**  T B Millar (ed) *Australian Foreign Minister: The Diaries of R G Casey 1951–60* Collins 1972. Casey was Australia's Minister of External Affairs 1951–60. W J Hudson *Casey* Oxford University Press 1986 is a good biography.

**1871**  Paul Hasluck *Sir Robert Menzies* Melbourne University Press, Melbourne 1980. A good biography. Another useful study, by a close acquaintance and senior Australian civil servant, is Sir John Bunting *R G Menzies: A Portrait* Allen and Unwin 1988. Menzies was Prime Minister 1939–41 and 1949–66. He was a great anglophile who sought to keep close ties with Britain and the Commonwealth. This aspect of his life is particularly focused on in Kevin Perkins *Menzies, Last of the Queen's Men* Angus and Robertson 1968. Sir Zelman Cowen *Menzies Remembered* Sir Robert Menzies Centre for Australian Studies, Institute of Commonwealth Studies, University of London 1988 is a short study which is particularly useful for Menzies' attitude

towards Britain and his role in Commonwealth diplomacy. Other biographies are Sir Percy Joske *Sir Robert Menzies 1894–1978 – A New Informal Memoir* Angus and Robertson 1978 and Ronald Seth *Robert Gordon Menzies* Cassell 1960. Sir Robert Gordon Menzies *The Measure of the Years* Cassell 1970 is a collection of assorted memoirs, mostly political. His *Afternoon Light: Some Memories of Men and Events* Cassell 1967 includes assorted memoirs of the war, Churchill and Attlee and the Suez crisis, and reflections on the Commonwealth and the Crown in the Commonwealth.

### (3) New Zealand

For New Zealand's participation in the defence of Malaysia see the section on Malaysia.

**1872**  R F Grover *New Zealand* Clio Press 1980. An annotated and classified bibliography.

**1873**  Ian Wards (ed) *Thirteen Facets: Essays to Celebrate the Silver Jubilee of Queen Elizabeth the Second 1952–1977* Government Printer, Wellington 1977. A collection of essays on aspects of New Zealand history during the reign.

**1874**  Keith Sinclair *A History of New Zealand* 2nd ed, Penguin 1969. The best general history. Michael Turnbull *The Changing Land: A Short History of New Zealand* 2nd ed, Longman 1975 is more of a textbook.

**1875**  Richard Kennaway *New Zealand Foreign Policy 1951–1971* Methuen 1972. This examines New Zealand's relations with Britain and America, defence cooperation in Malaysia and regional relations through bodies such as SEATO. Alister McIntosh *et al New Zealand in World Affairs Vol I* Price Milburn 1977 surveys New Zealand's foreign policy 1930–60. See also Thomas C Larkin (ed) *New Zealand's External Relations* New Zealand Institute of Public Administration 1962.

**1876**  *New Zealand Foreign Policy: Statements and Documents 1943–1957* Government Printer, Wellington 1972. This includes material that reflects New Zealand's changing relationship with Britain.

**1877**  Juliet Lodge *The European Community and New Zealand* Pinter 1982. Britain's entry into the European Community in 1973 has had a major effect on political and economic relations between Britain and New Zealand. This study is largely concerned the continued special access to the UK market of New Zealand's agricultural produce since 1973. For New Zealand's response when Britain first sought to join the Community in 1961–63 see [1869].

## (4) The Pacific

**1878** Roger Hughes (comp) *Oceania: A Basic Annotated Bibliography* Commonwealth Institute 1977. This features some 300 annotated entries on the history, economics and politics of Commonwealth territories in the Pacific. Gerald W Fry and Rufino Mauricio *Pacific Basin and Oceania* Clio Press 1988 is a more broadly based, annotated and classified select bibliography. Diane Dickson and Carol Dossor *World Catalogue of Theses on the Pacific Islands* Australian National University Press, Canberra 1970 is a bibliography of 1,000 entries.

**1879** A Coates *Western Pacific Islands* HMSO 1971. A general survey of politics, economic development and geography in the Solomon Islands, the New Hebrides and the Gilbert and Ellice Islands from the Corona Library series. See also [1308].

**1880** Hartley C Grattan *The Southwest Pacific: A Modern History Vol 2: The Southwest Pacific Since 1900* University of Michigan, Ann Arbor, Michigan 1963.

**1881** H C Brookfield *Colonialism, Development and Independence – The Case of the Melanesian Islands in the South Pacific* Cambridge University Press 1973. A study which deals with post-war developments in, amongst others, the Solomon Islands, the New Hebrides (Vanuatu) and Fiji. An important study.

**1882** Cyril S Belshaw *Island Administration in the South West Pacific* Royal Institute of International Affairs 1950. A historical overview and critique of colonial administration in the New Hebrides and the Solomons by a former administrator of the latter.

### (a) Fiji

**1883** Philip A Snow *A Bibliography of Fiji, Tonga and Rotuma* Australian National University Press, Canberra 1969. A very comprehensive listing of over 10,000 entries.

**1884** Sir Alan Burns *Fiji* HMSO 1963. A good general survey of politics, the economy and society in Fiji from the Corona Library series.

**1885** Oskar Hermann Khristian Spate *The Fijian People: Economic Problems and Prospects: A Report* Government Press, Suva, Fiji 1959. An important policy report for colonial policy in Fiji. See also [1813].

**1886** John Wesley Coulter *The Drama of Fiji: A Contemporary History* Tuttle, Rutland, Vermont 1967. An illustrated general history. G J A Kerr and T A Donnelly

*Fiji in the Pacific: A History and Geography of Fiji* Jacaranda Press, Melbourne 1969 is a textbook history. G K Roth *Fijian Way of Life* 2nd ed, Oxford University Press 1973 includes a useful account of indirect colonial government.

**1887** T P Bayliss-Smith, Richard Bedford, Harold Brookefield and Marc Latham *Islands, Islanders and the World: The Colonial and Post-Colonial Experience of Eastern Fiji* Cambridge University Press 1988. A geographical rather than a historical study this nevertheless contains some material of value.

**1888** Kenneth Bain *Treason at 10: Fiji at the Crossroads* Hodder and Stoughton 1989. A critical examination of the handling by the British and the Commonwealth of the crisis brought about by the 1987 military coup in Fiji.

### (b) The Gilbert and Ellice Islands (Kiribati and Tuvalu) and Nauru

**1889** Barrie Macdonald *Cinderellas of the Empire: Towards a History of Kiribati and Tuvalu* Australian National University Press, Canberra 1982. A painstaking and detailed administrative history and study of the impact of colonialism since the establishment of the Protectorate in 1892. Neglected for most of the twentieth century they were rapidly decolonized in the 1970s, becoming the separate states of Tuvalu (independent in 1978) and Kiribati (independent in 1979). On Kiribati's progress towards independence see 'Issue on Kiribati' *Decolonisation* 15 1979 pp 1–47. See also Alaima Talu *et al Kiribati: Aspects of History* Institute of Pacific Studies, University of the South Pacific, Suva, Fiji 1984.

**1890** Maslyn Williams and Barrie Macdonald *The Phosphaters: A History of the British Phosphate Commissioners and the Christmas Island Phosphate Commission* Melbourne University Press, Melbourne 1985. An excellent detailed history with detailed appendices. The British Phosphate Commission, involving collaboration between Britain, Australia and New Zealand, was established in 1920. Its activities were concentrated on Nauru and Ocean Island (now Banaba). The Christmas Island Commission was established by Australia and New Zealand in 1948. Banaba is now part of Kiribati. Pearl Binder *Treasure Islands: The Trials of the Ocean Islanders* Blond and Briggs 1977 is a detailed history of Banaba which concentrates on the relocation of the Banabans 1,600 miles away in Fiji to facilitate the exploitation of the island's phosphate. It is a good exposé of colonial rapaciousness. On this see also [1929].

**1891** Nancy Viviani *Nauru: Phosphate and Political Progress* Australian National University Press, Canberra 1970. A detailed history. Nauru was an Australian mandated territory after the First World War. The post-war section of this book concentrates on exploitation by the British Phosphate Commission and Nauru's struggle for independence from Australia, which was achieved in 1968. See also Barrie Macdonald *In Pursuit of the Sacred Trust: Trusteeship and Independence in Nauru* New Zealand Institute of International Affairs Occasional Paper 3, Wellington 1988.

(c) New Hebrides (Vanuatu)

**1892** Walter Lini *Beyond Pandemonium: From the New Hebrides to Vanuatu* Asia Pacific Books, Wellington 1980. An account of events by the Anglican priest who led the Anglo-French condominium to independence in 1980 and became the first Prime Minister of Vanuatu. Chris Plant (ed) *New Hebrides: The Road to Independence* Institute of Pacific Studies, University of the South Pacific, Suva, Fiji 1977 is a collection of essays on political development and on the operation of the condominium.

**1893** John Beasant *The Santo Rebellion: An Imperial Reckoning* Heinemann 1984. An account of the rebellion on Espiritu Santo, the largest island in the group, led by Jimmy Stevens, and of its suppression with the aid of first British and French and then Papuan troops. See also Richard Shears *The Coconut War: The Crisis on Espiritu Santo* Cassell 1980.

(d) Pitcairn Island

**1894** Robert Nicolson *The Pitcairners* Angus and Robertson 1966. A general history with a detailed bibliography. See also Ian M Ball *Pitcairn: Children of the Bounty* Gollancz 1973, Harry L Shapiro *The Pitcairn Islanders* revised ed, Simon and Shuster, New York 1968 and David Silverman *Pitcairn Island* World Publishing, New York 1967. Pitcairn remains a British dependency. Joanna Barlow 'Keeping Pitcairn in Touch with the World' *Geographical Magazine* 56 1984 pp 140–7 is useful on Pitcairn in the 1980s. See also [1141].

(e) Western Samoa

**1895** C G R McKay *Samoana: A Personal Story of the Samoan Islands* Reed, Wellington 1968. A personal history of the islands up to independence in 1961. See also C C Marsack *Samoan Medley* Hale 1961.

(f) Solomon Islands

**1896** Charles E Fox *The Story of the Solomons* revised ed, Pacific Publications, Sydney 1975. A short history. The Solomons became independent in 1978. Janet Kent *The Solomon Islands* David and Charles 1972 is a useful survey.

(g) Tonga

**1897** Sione Latukefu *The Tongan Constitution: A Brief History to Celebrate its Centenary* Tonga Traditions Committee Publications, Nuku'alofa 1975. Tonga was under a British protectorate until 1970.

## H. CANADA

**1898** J L Grenatstein and Paul Stevens *Canada Since 1867: A Bibliographical Guide* Hakkert, Toronto 1974.

**1899** Robert Bothwell, Ian Drummond and John English *Canada Since 1945: Power, Politics and Provincialism* University of Toronto Press, Toronto 1981. A reasonable and well illustrated post-war history. See also Michel Horn *Canada: A Political and Social History* 4th ed, Holt, Rinehart and Watson, Toronto 1982. Donald Creighton *The Forked Road: Canada 1939–1957* McClelland and Stewart, Toronto 1976 is an excellent history.

**1900** David B Dewitt and John J Kirton *Canada as a Principal Power: A Study in Foreign Policy and International Relations* Wiley, Toronto 1983. See also C P Stacey *Canada and the Age of Conflict: A History of Canadian External Policies Vol 2* Macmillan, Toronto 1981, which covers the years 1921–48.

**1901** Peter Lyon (ed) *Britain and Canada: Survey of a Changing Relationship* Cass 1976. Essays on economic, diplomatic, military and cultural relations and on Canada's important role in the Commonwealth. J W Holmes *The Better Part of Valour: Essays on Canadian Diplomacy* McClelland and Stewart, Toronto 1970 pp 89–122 examines Canada in the Commonwealth and Anglo-Canadian relations. Peter Nailor 'Canada's External Relations in the 1980s: Britain and Canada – A Strategist's Perspective' *Round Table* 298 1986 pp 123–8 is a rather general dicussion.

**1902** R M Stamp *Kings, Queens and Canadians: A Celebration of Canada's Infatuation with the British Royal Family* Fitzhenry and Whiteside, Markham, Ontario 1987.

**1903** Anthony H M Kirk-Greene 'The Governors-General of Canada 1867–1952: A Collective Profile' *Journal of Canadian Studies* 13 1978 pp 35–57. A typology. For Earl Alexander of Tunis as Governor-General 1946–52 see [785].

**1904** David Dilks 'The Great Dominion: Churchill's Farewell Visits to Canada 1952 and 1954' *Canadian Journal of History/Annales Canadiennes d'Histoire* 23 1988 pp 49–72. This reflects on an important stage in the evolution of Anglo- Canadian relations.

**1905** W B Cunningham (ed) *Canada, the Commonwealth and the Common Market* McGill University Press, Montreal 1962. This symposium presents not just the Canadian reaction to Britain's first attempt to join the European Community but also the perspectives of Britons, Americans, Indians and Ghanaians, as well as that of Jean Monnet, the great architect of European integration. On Canadian views of Britain's application see also [1869].

**1906** Keith G Banting and Richard Simeon *And No One Cheered: Federalism, Democracy and the Constitution Act* Methuen 1983. A symposium on the struggle behind Canada's Constitution Act 1982. In consequence Britain passed the Canada Act 1982 which enabled the Canadians to amend their own constitution without recourse to the British parliament. On the background to this see Roy Romanow, John Whyte and Howard Leeson *Canada Notwithstanding: The Making of the Constitution 1976– 1982* Carswell/Methuen, Toronto 1984. See also Anthony Kershaw 'The Canadian Constitution and the Foreign Affairs Committee of the UK House of Commons 1980 and 1981' *The Parliamentarian* 62 1981 pp 173–92.

**1907** Peter Stursburg *Diefenbaker: Leadership Gained 1956–62* University of Toronto Press, Toronto 1976. This is continued by his *Diefenbaker: Leadership Lost 1962–67* 1976. John George Diefenbaker played an important part in Commonwealth affairs during his years as Canadian Prime Minister 1957–63. These studies are also useful for Canada's changing relations with Britain. Diefenbaker has also written an extensive three volume memoir; *One Canada: Memoirs of the Right Honourable John Diefenbaker Vol I: The Crusading Years 1895–1956* Macmillan, Toronto 1975, *Vol II: The Years of Achievement 1957–1962* 1976 and *Vol III: The Tumultuous Years* 1977.

**1908** J W Pickersgill and D F Foster *The Mackenzie King Record Vol 3: 1945–46* Oxford University Press 1970. This is continued by *Vol 4: 1947–48* 1970. Mackenzie King was Prime Minister of Canada 1921–30 and 1935–48 and as such an important figure in the wartime alliance. These volumes use extensive excerpts from his diaries to give an almost continuous record. They are particularly useful for Anglo- Canadian differences of approach to the onset of the Cold War. For biographies of Mackenzie King see Jack L Granatstein *Mackenzie King: His Life and World* McGraw-Hill 1977 and William Teatero *Mackenzie King: Man of Mission* Personal Library Publishers, Toronto 1979.

**1909** Peter Stursburg *Lester Pearson and the Dream of Unity* Doubleday 1978. The second volume of this biography is *Lester Pearson and the American Dilemma* Doubleday 1980. Useful memoirs on his early career are Lester Bowles Pearson *Memoirs Vol I: 1897–1948: Through Diplomacy to Politics* Gollancz 1973 and *Vol II: 1948–1957: The International Years* Gollancz 1974. Pearson played an important part in re-orientating Canada away from the close relationship with Britain towards a reliance on America during his time as Secretary of State for External Affairs 1948–57 and as Prime Minister 1963–8.

**1910** Maurice A Pope *Soldiers and Politicians: The Memoirs of Lt General Maurice A Pope* University of Toronto Press 1962. This memoir includes quite a lot of reflections on Canada's relations with Britain and the Commonwealth. It is also useful for Pope's role as head of the Canadian Military Mission to the Allied Control Council in Berlin 1945–50.

**1911** Jean Jacques Lefrebvre *Le Très hon Louis-S St Laurent (1882–1973): Jurisconsulte, homme d'Etat, innovateur en politique étrangère* the author, Montreal 1974. St Laurent was Prime Minister of Canada 1948–57.

**1912** George Radwanski *Trudeau* Macmillan of Canada, Toronto 1979. Pierre Trudeau was Prime Minister of Canada 1968–79 and 1980–4.

## I. GIBRALTAR AND MALTA

### (1) Gibraltar

**1913** Graham J Shields *Gibraltar* Clio Press 1987. An annotated and classified select bibliography. Muriel Green *A Gibraltar Bibliography* Institute of Commonwealth Studies, University of London 1980 is a listing of over 900 entries.

**1914** Sir William G F Jackson *The Rock of the Gibraltarians: A History of Gibraltar* Associated University Presses 1988. A general history. George Hills *Rock of Contention: A History of Gibraltar* Hale 1974 is a general history which concentrates on the eighteenth century, though it does go up to 1972. Rather more useful for post-war Gibraltar is John D Stewart *Gibraltar the Keystone* Murray 1967.

**1915** Helen C Magauran *Rock Siege: The Difficulties with Spain 1964–1985* Mediterranean Sun Publishing, Gibraltar 1986. An account of the Anglo-Spanish wrangle over Gibraltar from the imposition of Franco's trade embargo in 1964 to the end of the embargo and the re-opening of the border (closed in 1969) in 1985. It examines the dispute from a Gibraltarian point of view. Howard S Levie *The Status of Gibraltar* Westview Replica 1983 instead tends to sympathize with the Spanish claim to the Rock. The British position on the gathering dispute is set out in *The British White Book on Gibraltar* HMSO 1965. The Spanish government laid out their views in *The Spanish Red Book on Gibraltar* Ministry of Foreign Affairs, Madrid 1965. This is supplemented on, if anything, a more massive scale in *Negotiations on Gibraltar (A New Spanish Red Book)* Ministry of Foreign Affairs, Madrid 1968. All three of these seek to support their case with extensive documentation. The dispute is also examined in Thomas D Lancaster and James L Taulbee 'Britain, Spain and the Gibraltar Question' *Journal of Commonwealth and Comparative Politics* 22 1985 pp 251–66 and J E S Fawchett 'Gibraltar: The Legal Issues' *International Affairs* 43 1967 pp 236–51.

## (2) Malta

**1916** John Richard Thackrah *Malta* Clio Press 1985. An annotated and classified select bibliography.

**1917** *Malta Round Table Conference 1955: Report* Cmnd 9657, *Parliamentary Papers* 1955–56. This conference, under the chairmanship of Lord Kilmuir, was set up in response to the proposal of the Maltese Prime Minister, Dom Mintoff, that there should be closer links between Britain and Malta. The report outlines the difficulties in the path to union but in principle accepted the idea of Maltese representation at Westminster.

**1918** Dennis Austin *Malta and the End of Empire* Cass 1971. A good study of the reasons for the failure of the proposed integration of Malta into the United Kingdom and the events that led to Maltese independence in 1964. See also Edith Dobie *Malta's Road to Independence* University of Oklahoma Press, Norman, Oklahoma 1967 and Dennis Sammut *Too Early for Freedom: The Background to the Independence of Malta 1964* 2nd ed, the author, Valletta 1984. Central Office of Information *Malta* HMSO 1964 is a short survey of politics, the economy and society in Malta at independence.

## J. THE ATLANTIC AND ANTARCTIC

**1919** H R G King *Atlantic Ocean* Clio Press 1985. An annotated and classified select bibliography. For reflections on the conditions in each of the territories listed below see [1141 and 1308].

### (1) British Antarctic Territory

**1920** Peter J Beck *The International Politics of Antarctica* Croom Helm 1985. A good analysis of the various claims to the continent, including British Antarctic Territory. See also his 'Britain's Antarctic Dimension' *International Affairs* 59 1983 pp 429–44 which is especially useful for its discussion of the enhanced importance of Britain's Antarctic policy in the wake of the Falklands War. J D B Miller (ed) *Australia, Britain and Antarctica* Australian Studies Centre, Institute of Commonwealth Studies, University of London 1987 examines British and Australian co-operation, activities and interests in Antarctica.

### (2) Ascension Island

**1921** Duff Hart-Davis *Ascension: The Story of a South Atlantic Island* Constable 1972. As yet this is the only history of this tiny colony. With the need to maintain links with the Falklands it has become much more important since 1982. Between 1945 and 1972 its main occupants were the team of a NASA tracking station.

### (3) Bermuda

**1922** P Heaton *A Bibliography of Bermudiana* Library Association 1971. A listing of some 2,650 entries.

**1923** Terry Tucker *Bermuda Today and Yesterday 1503–1978* 2nd ed, Hale 1978. Bermuda remains a British dependency. See also Selwyn Ryan 'Politics in an Artificial Society: The Case of Bermuda' in Henry Frances (ed) *Ethnicity in the Americas* Mouton, The Hague 1976 pp 159–92.

### (4) The Falklands Dependencies

See also the literature in the section on the Falklands war. Many of the studies of this war contain lengthy analyses of the background to the war. The section on Anglo-Argentine relations is also of relevance.

**1924** *Annual Report of the Falkland Islands and Dependencies 1947–* HMSO 1948–.

**1925** Margaret Patricia Henwood *An Annotated Bibliography of the Falkland Islands and the Falkland Islands Dependencies (as Delimited on 3rd March 1962)* University of Cape Town Libraries, Cape Town 1977. See also Abel Rodolfo Geoghegan 'Bibliografia de las Islas Malvinas: Suplement a la Obra de José Torre Revelo 1954–1975' *Historiografia* 153 1977 pp 31–56.

**1926** Raphael Perl and Everette E Larsen *The Falklands Islands Dispute in International Law and Politics* 2v, Oceana Publications 1983. This largely consists of documents on the territorial claims to the islands from 1498 onwards, including documents on the 1982 war between Britain and Argentina. It also features a chronology and bibliography. See also Enrique Vieyra *An Annotated Legal Chronology of the Malvinas (Falklands) Islands Controversy* Marcos Lerner Editora Cordoba, Cordoba 1985. For the literature on the 1982 war see [2415–35].

**1927** Peter J Beck 'Co-operative Confrontation in the Falklands Islands Dispute: The Anglo-Argentine Search for a Way Forward 1968–1981' *Journal of Inter-American Studies* 24 1982 pp 37–58. A good study of the limited co-operation that preceded the 1982 war.

**1928** C W Guillebaud *Report on an Economic Survey of the Falkland Islands* Government Printer, Port Stanley 1967. This was followed by Edward A A Shackleton *Economic Survey of the Falkland Islands* 2v, HMSO 1976. The first volume of Lord Shackleton's report deals with resources and development potential and the second with strategy and implementation. He discusses its conclusions in 'Prospects of the Falklands Islands' *Geographical Journal* 143 1977 pp 1–13. On the Shackleton report see also José Enrique Grano Valasco 'El Informe Shackleton Sobre las Islas Malvinas' *Revista de Politica Internacional* 153 1977 pp 31–56.

**1929** A J G Knox 'Self-Determination for Small Islanders: Britain's Handling of the Rights of Falklanders, Diego Garcians and Banabans in the Atlantic, Indian and Pacific Oceans' *Canadian Journal of American and Caribbean Studies* 11 1986 pp 71–92. This contrasts Britain's defence of the Falklanders right to self-determination in the 1982 war with the forced migration of the entire population from Banaba in 1946 and from Diego Garcia with the creation of the US military base after 1968.

**1929A** Clive Christie *Nationalism and Internationalism: Britain's Left and Policy towards the Falkland Islands 1982–84* Hull Papers in Politics 37, University of Hull 1985.

## (5) St Helena and Its Dependencies

**1930** Tony Cross *St Helena* David and Charles 1980. A general guide and history. St Helena remains a British dependency. Also of some use is Edward Cannan *A History of the Diocese of St Helena and Its Precursors 1502–1984* Government Printer, Jamestown, St Helena 1985.

**1931** Cledwyn Hughes *Report of an Enquiry into Conditions on the Island of St Helena* Government Printer, Jamestown, St Helena 1958. Reflections on the conditions of the islanders and the conduct of the government of the colony. Not everything in the original report for the Labour party appears here. This edition does however contain the blow-by-blow reply of the St Helena government.

**1932** Peter Munch *Crisis in Utopia: The Story of Tristan da Cunha* Longman 1971. A good historical and sociological study of an isolated community. A more impressionistic study is Allan Crawford *Tristan da Cunha and the Roaring Forties* Charles Skilton/David Philip 1982. Since both include aspects that do not appear in the other they should be treated as complementary. See also George Crabb *The History and Postal History of Tristan da Cunha* the author 1980.

**1933** James P Blair 'Home to Lonely Tristan da Cunha' *National Geographic Magazine* 125 1964 pp 60–81. The islanders were evacuated to England in 1961 after a volcanic eruption. This is an account of their return in 1963.

## K. FOREIGN AFFAIRS

### (1) Reference Works

**1934** *Catalogue of the Foreign Office Library* 8v, G K Hall 1972. Periodic supplements have been issued since.

**1935** *Classified List of Books and Pamphlets Added to the Library* Royal Institute of International Affairs Library 1960–. Originally a fortnightly publication this now appears monthly. Some 600 periodicals are also indexed in *Index to Periodical Articles 1950–1964 in the Library of the Royal Institute of International Affairs* G K Hall, Boston, Massachusetts 1964. Supplements updating this have since appeared. L Adolphus and F L Kent (eds) *Cumulative Index 1922–76 to International Affairs* Learned Information (Europe) 1978 is the index to the Institute's own journal. *Foreign Affairs Bibliography: A Select and Annotated List of Books on International Affairs* Bowker 1933– is a periodical classified guide to books.

**1936** Robert Boardman *Britain and the International System 1945–1973: A Guide to the Literature* Centre for Foreign Policy Studies, Dalhousie University, Halifax, Nova Scotia 1974. An unannotated but well classified guide to relevant books, articles and theses. The index is not very good however and official publications are deliberately excluded.

**1937** *Survey of International Affairs 1924–1963* Royal Institute of International Affairs 1926–1977. A valuable series of surveys of international events and themes in individual years. The decision taken to make the survey of 1963 the last one was made in the light of the changing nature of international affairs and its increasingly complexity. The survey was complemented by *Documents on International Affairs 1928– 1963* Royal Institute of International Affairs 1929–1971. An excellent series of edited collections of documents.

**1938** *Diplomatic Service List* HMSO 1966–. This annual publication contains biographical sketches of important members of the diplomatic corps, information on missions and embassies, details of the structure of the Foreign Office and other similar material. It superseded *The Foreign Office List* and absorbed, in 1966 and 1967 respectively, the lists of the Commonwealth Relations and Colonial Offices.

**1939** Foreign and Commonwealth Office *British and Foreign State Papers* 170v Ridgeway (later HMSO) 1841–1978. These cover the series of state papers from 1812 up to the creation of the Foreign and Commonwealth Office in 1968. They arrange the texts of agreements, treaties, orders in council, parliamentary acts, letters patent and other relevant documents in chronological order and are well indexed.

**1940** Donald Cameron Watt and James Mayall (eds) *Current British Foreign Policy: Documents, Statements and Speeches* Temple Smith 1971–4. These three volumes edit documents and statements of policy in 1970–2. They are well indexed and exhaustive and include a chronological list.

**1941** Foreign Office *Treaty Series* HMSO 1892–. Treaties to which the United Kingdom is a party are published as Command Papers in a special series and bound in with the Parliamentary Papers.

**1942** Clive Parry and Charity Hopkins *An Index of British Treaties 1101–1968* 3v, HMSO 1970. Volume 3 covers 1926–68. It is a chronologically arranged guide to international agreements into which Britain has entered. It has been subsequently continued by supplements, generally covering three years at a time and appearing a few years later. These are arranged by subject, not chronologically. See also J A S Grenville *The Major International Treaties 1914–1973: A History* and Guide with Texts Methuen 1974. This is organized chronologically by region. It includes a useful appendix on Commonwealth defence agreements.

**1943** Rohan Butler and M E Pelly (eds) *Documents on British Policy Overseas: Series 1 Volume 1: The Conference at Potsdam July–August 1945* HMSO 1984. Since 1984 two series of the officially published *Documents on British Policy Overseas* on 1945–50 and 1950–5 respectively have been in progress. All of these to have appeared so far, except where indicated, have been edited by Roger Bullen and M E Pelly. The standard of editing is admirable and the coverage is very full. Other volumes in the first series so far published are *Vol 2: Conferences and Conversations 1945: London, Washington and Moscow* 1985, *Vol 3: Britain and America: Negotiation of the United States Loan 3 August–7 December 1945* 1987, and *Vol 4: Britain and America: Atomic Energy, Bases and Food 12 December 1945–31 July 1946* HMSO 1987. Of the second series, which is concerned with British policy towards Europe, *Vol 1: The Schuman Plan, the Council of Europe and Western European Integration May 1950–Dec 1952* 1986, *Vol 2: The London Conferences: Anglo-American Relations and Cold War Strategy January–June 1950* 1987 and (edited by Roger Bullen) *Vol 3: German Rearmament September–December 1950* 1989 have appeared so far.

## (2) General

The section on general Defence Policy should also be consulted.

**1944** Arthur Cyr *British Foreign Policy and the Atlantic Area: The Technique of Accommodation* Macmillan 1979. A study of Britain's relations with America and Europe since 1945 and gradual accommodation to a reduced world role. Cyr stresses that this adjustment has been successful. Joseph Frankel *British Foreign Policy 1945–1973* Oxford University Press 1975 also concentrates on this process of adjustment and reorientation towards Europe. Michael Liefer (ed) *Constraints and Adjustments in British Foreign Policy* Allen and Unwin 1972 is a collection of essays on policy since 1945 which pursue similar themes. Also useful on Britain's adjustment is Nora Beloff *Transit of Britain: A Report on Britain's Changing Role in the Post-War World* Collins 1973. Frederick Samuel Northedge *Descent from Power: British Foreign Policy 1945–1973* Allen and Unwin 1974 in contrast stresses the decline of power. For other general accounts of foreign policy since 1945 see Christopher Montague Woodhouse *British Foreign Policy Since the Second World War* Hutchinson 1961, P A Reynolds 'British Foreign Policy Since the Second World War' *International Studies* 1 1959 pp 137–53, and Roy Jenkins 'British Foreign Policy Since 1945'

*British Academy Proceedings* 58 1974 pp 153–62. C J Bartlett *British Foreign Policy in the Twentieth Century* Macmillan 1989 is a good textbook study, though better on the pre-1945 period. Also of use are Paul Richardson *Britain, Europe and the Modern World 1918–1968* Cambridge University Press 1970, W N Medlicott *British Foreign Policy Since Versailles 1919–63* Methuen 1968 and M R D Foot *British Foreign Policy Since 1898* Hutchinson 1956.

**1945** Anthony Verrier *Through the Looking Glass: British Foreign Policy in the Age of Illusions* Cape 1983. Case studies of Britain's handling of intervention in Albania 1949, Suez 1956, riots in Kuwait 1961, civil war in Nigeria 1967, Northern Ireland 1972 and the Falklands War 1982.

**1946** William Wallace 'The Management of Foreign Economic Policy in Britain' *International Affairs* 50 1974 pp 251– 67. The impact of a particular economic issue, the 1973 oil crisis, on foreign economic policy is examined in Michael Shackleton 'Oil and the British Foreign Policy Process' *Millenium: Journal of International Studies* 7 1979 pp 137–52.

**1947** Chris Hill 'Public Opinion and British Foreign Policy Since 1945: Research in Progress' *Millenium: Journal of International Studies* 10 1981 pp 53–62. A survey of public attitudes, as reflected in opinion polls and other guides, to foreign policy in the post-war period.

**1948** M R Gordon *Conflict and Consensus in Labour's Foreign Policy 1914–1965* Stanford University Press, Stanford, California 1969. A useful if rather general study of the debates over foreign policy within the party. *The Foreign Policy of the British Labour Party 1920 to Date* Labour Party 1959 is a guide to policy commitments. The attitude of the party's Left is analysed in Eugene Meehan *The British Left Wing and Foreign Policy: A Study of the Influence of Ideology* Rutgers University Press, New Brunswick, New Jersey 1961.

**1949** Ritchie Ovendale (ed) *The Foreign Policy of the British Labour Governments 1945–1951* Leicester University Press 1984. An important collection of essays and assessments. Another excellent collection is Josef Becker and Franz Kipping (eds) *Power in Europe? Great Britain, France, Italy and Germany in a Post-War World 1945–1950* Walter de Gruyter, Berlin 1986. Many of the essays in this latter volume deal with British foreign policy in this period, from the British role in the origins of the Cold War or of Marshall Aid to the British reaction to moves towards the integration of Europe. M A Fitzsimons *The Foreign Policy of the British Labour Government 1945–1951* University of Notre Dame Press, Notre Dame, Indiana 1953 and Elaine Windrich *British Labour's Foreign Policy* Stanford University

Press, Stanford, California 1952 are contemporary American assessments of the Attlee government's handling of foreign policy. Other contemporary assessments are Christopher Mayhew 'British Foreign Policy Since 1945' *International Affairs* 26 1950 pp 477–86, W N Ewer 'The Labour Government's Record in Foreign Policy' *Political Quarterly* 20 1949 pp 112–22, P Gore-Brown 'The Foreign Policy of the Labour Government' *Journal of Politics* 12 1950 pp 371–82 and J L Godfrey 'British Foreign Policy and the Labour Party 1945–7' *South Atlantic Quarterly* 47 1948 pp 137–51. Clement Attlee's internationalist approach to foreign policy is assessed in Raymond Smith and John Zametica 'The Cold Warrior: Clement Attlee Reconsidered 1945–7' *International Affairs* 61 1985 pp 237–52. On the role of Socialism in the policies pursued in this period see P L Aspinwall 'British Socialism and Foreign Policy 1945–1950' Reading MPhil Thesis 1979 and C R Rose 'The Relation of Socialist Principles to British Labour Foreign Policy 1945–1951' Oxford DPhil Thesis 1959. For the attitudes of the Labour Left in this period see E D Shaw 'Socialism and Foreign Policy: The Labour Left and Foreign Affairs 1945–1951' Leeds MPhil Thesis 1973–4 and Jonathan Schneer 'Hopes Deferred or Shattered: The British Labour Left and the Third Force Movement 1945–1949' *Journal of Modern History* 56 1984 pp 197–226. Much material on British policy in this period can also be found in the section on the Cold War.

**1950** M P Blackwell 'The Attitudes Concerning Britain's World Role Held by the Policymakers in the Aftermath of the Second World War (1945–1947)' East Anglia PhD Thesis 1981. An analysis of Britain's continuing commitment to playing a world role that was only to be abandoned, he argues, by force of circumstances, over the ensuing decades.

**1951** John W Young (ed) *The Foreign Policy of Churchill's Peacetime Administration* Leicester University Press 1988. A good collection of essays scrutinising policy at a time when Britain remained an important force in international politics. Anthony Adamthwaite 'Overstretched and Overstrung: Eden, the Foreign Office and the Making of Policy 1951–5' *International Affairs* 64 1988 pp 241–60 is a more critical assessment of the Churchill government's failure to reduce Britain's commitments.

**1952** Donald Duart Maclean *British Foreign Policy: The Years Since Suez 1956–1968* Hodder and Stoughton 1970. A critical assessment of policy from the Suez episode to the final relinquishment of a world role with the 1968 withdrawal from East of Suez. See also M F Camroux 'Consensus and Divergence in British Foreign Policy 1957–1966' Hull MA Thesis 1971–2. Max Beloff *The Future of British Foreign Policy* Secker and Warburg 1969 contains useful reflections on foreign policy problems in the 1960s. Kenneth Younger *Changing Perspectives in British Foreign Policy* Oxford University Press 1964 is an assessment of British interests and objectives in the wake of De Gaulle's veto of Britain's first application to join the European Community. See also R Hilsman and R G Good *Foreign Policy in the Sixties* Oxford University Press 1965.

**1953** Peter Byrd (ed) *British Foreign Policy Under Thatcher* Philip Allan 1988. A collection of essays examining the operation of British policy since 1979 and its impact in various regions. Michael Smith, Steve Smith and Brian White (eds) *British Foreign Policy: Traditions, Change and Transformation* Unwin Hyman 1988 is a collection of variable quality assessing the current influences on, operation and impact of British foreign policy. It includes a good bibliography.

### (3) The Foreign Office and Diplomatic Service

**1954** Geoffrey Moorhouse *The Diplomats: The Foreign Office Today* Cape 1977. An investigation which also covers the External Services of the BBC and the work of the British Council. It also contains much historical detail even though it is not a history as such. Another useful inquiry into the Foreign Office is Simon Jenkins and Anne Sloman *With Respect Ambassador: An Inquiry into the Foreign Office* BBC 1985. The New Whitehall series study of the structure and operation of the Foreign Office is William Strang *The Foreign Office* Allen and Unwin 1955. This is however rather discursive and is of limited value. Robert Boardman and A J R Groom (ed) *The Management of Britain's External Relations* Macmillan 1973 is a useful collection of essays. See also Zara S Steiner *The Foreign Office and Foreign Policy* Cambridge University Press 1970, Donald G Bishop *The Administration of British Foreign Relations* Syracuse University Press, Syracuse, New York 1961 and John Connell *The 'Office': A Study of British Foreign Policy and its Makers 1919–51* Wingate 1958. Only the last two essays, on Foreign Secretaries as diplomats and on the Foreign Office in the future, in Roger Bullen (ed) *The Foreign Office 1782–1982* University Publishers of America 1984 are relevant to post-war historians.

**1955** William Wallace *The Foreign Policy Process in Britain* Allen and Unwin 1976. A good study of the operation of policy. It includes coverage of overseas aid and economic and cultural relations. There are case studies of the pattern of relations with West Germany, Iceland, NATO, Ghana, Ethiopia and the United Nations. David Vital *The Making of British Foreign Policy* Allen and Unwin 1968 is a political science investigation into the making of policy. A good study of the making of policy, which however does not have much material

on the post-war period, is Donald Cameron Watt *Personality and Policies: Studies in the Formulation of British Foreign Policy in the 20th Century* Longmans 1965. Lord Strang 'The Formation and Control of Foreign Policy' *Durham University Journal* n.s. 18 1957 pp 98–108 is the comment of a former Permanent Secretary of the Foreign Office.

**1956** Michael Clarke 'The Foreign Office and its Critics' *Millenium: Journal of International Studies* 7 1979 pp 222–36. This concentrates on criticism of the Foreign Office in the 1970s.

**1957** Yoel Cohen *Media Diplomacy: The Foreign Office in the Mass Communications Age* Cass 1986. A study of the Foreign Office's use of media and the impact of mass media on foreign policy and public opinion. It is good on the Foreign Office's use of leaks but less reliable in its case studies of media management and does not seem to consider the BBC's External Services.

**1958** William Strang *The Diplomatic Career* Deutsch 1962. Comments on the nature, character and qualities required in the diplomatic service.

**1959** *Report of the Review Committee on Overseas Representation 1968–1969* Cmnd 4107, *Parliamentary Papers* xliv 1968–69. The review of the diplomatic service in the wake of the Fulton re-organization of the home Civil Service and the British withdrawal East of Suez. It was chaired by Sir Val Duncan.

**1960** Humphrey Trevelyan *Diplomatic Channels* Macmillan 1973. Reflections on the problems facing British diplomats in the 1970s. See also Sir Geoffrey Jackson *Concorde Diplomacy: The Ambassador's Role in the World Today* Hamilton 1981. Both also contain some autobiographical material.

**1961** D C M Platt *The Cinderella Service: British Consuls Since 1825* Longmans 1971. The only history.

**1962** John B Black *Organising the Propaganda Instrument: The British Experience* Nijhoff, The Hague 1975. Short studies of the overseas information services, the Central Office of Information, the British Council and the BBC external services and comparisons of their operations with comparable bodies in America.

**1963** Lyn Smith 'Covert British Propaganda: The Information Research Department 1947–1977' *Millenium: Journal of International Studies* 9 1980 pp 67–83. A study of the department set up to combat Soviet propaganda which was closed down in 1977.

**1964** *Overseas Information Services: Summary of the Report of the Independent Committee of Inquiry* Cmnd 9138, *Parliamentary Papers* xxxi 1953–54. A report chaired by the Earl of Drogheda which recognized the increasing importance of these services and called for more money to be allocated to them. The full text was not published since it contained confidential information. An account of the working of these services, and also of the British Council and the BBC's External Services by the Secretary of the Drogheda Committee is Sir Robert Marett *Through the Back Door: An Inside View of Britain's Overseas Information Services* Pergamon 1968. This traces their development, making use of autobiographical material, up to the mid-1950s.

**1965** Frances Donaldson *The British Council: The First Fifty Years* Cape 1984. The British Council was founded in 1934 to promote the image and awareness of Britain abroad. It is particularly concerned with cultural and educational exchanges. This history, based on unlimited access to the Council's files and papers is both well told and well illustrated. See also Sir Anthony Parsons 'Vultures and Philistines: British Attitudes to Culture and Cultural Diplomacy' *International Affairs* 51 1984 pp 1–8, D J Eastment 'The Policies and Position of the British Council from the Outbreak of War to 1950' Leeds PhD Thesis 1982 and R R Hawkins 'The British Overseas Information Programme: An Examination of Its Legislative and Executive Origins, Its Growth and Present Administration, with Some Comparisons with Similar Programmes in France, West Germany and the United States of America' London PhD Thesis 1959–60.

## (4) Foreign Office Biography and Memoirs

**1966** Avi Shlaim, Peter Jones and Keith Sainsbury *British Foreign Secretaries Since 1945* David and Charles 1977. A collection of essays on each of the Foreign Secretaries from 1945–74, Ernest Bevin, Herbert Morrison, Sir Anthony Eden, Harold Macmillan, Selwyn Lloyd, Lord Home, R A Butler, Patrick Gordon-Walker, Michael Stewart and George Brown.

**1967** John Zametica (ed) *British Officials and British Foreign Policy 1945–1950* Leicester University Press 1989. Essays on Sir Archibald Clark Kerr (Moscow embassy), Roger Makins (Washington embassy), Frank Roberts (Moscow embassy), Duff Cooper (Paris embassy), Sir Alex Kirkbridge (Palestine policy), Robert Hankey (Northern department), Oliver Franks (Washington embassy), Lord Strang (Permanent Under-Secretary of State), and John Troutbeck (German department).

**1968** Sir John Balfour *Not Too Correct an Aureole: The Recollections of a Diplomat* Michael Russell 1983. Balfour was a Minister in Moscow 1943–5, and in Washington 1945–8 and the Ambassador to Argentina 1948–51 and to Spain 1951–4.

**1969** Sir Roderick Barclay *Bevin and the Foreign Office 1945–1969* the author 1975. This is partly a biography of Bevin and his impact on the Foreign Office and partly an account of Barclay's own career. Barclay was Bevin's private secretary 1949–51. He was Deputy Under Secretary 1953–6 and 1960–3 and Ambassador to Denmark 1956–60 and to Belgium 1963–9. This memoir also contains vignettes of other episodes in which Barclay was involved, such as Heath's negotiations to join Europe 1961–3.

**1970** Sir Reader Bullard *The Camels Must Go: An Autobiography* Faber 1961. This includes reflections on relations with the USSR during and immediately after the war and on the British position in the Middle East and especially Iran in the late 1940s. Bullard was British Minister then Ambassador to Iran 1939–46.

**1971** Sir John Colville *Strange Inheritance* Michael Russell 1986. A life of Victor Cavendish-Bentinck, who was dismissed from the Foreign Office over a divorce case in 1948. See also Patrick Howarth *Intelligence Chief Extraordinary: The Life of the Ninth Duke of Portland* The Bodley Head 1986.

**1972** John Charmley *Duff Cooper: The Authorised Biography* Macmillan 1986. A prominent politician of the inter-war period Duff Cooper was most important in the post-war years as Ambassador to France 1944–7. Also useful is his autobiography *Old Men Forget* Hart-Davis 1954. See also the biography of his wife, Philip Ziegler *Diana Cooper* Hamilton 1981, and their edited correspondence, Artemis Cooper (ed) *A Durable Fire: The Letters of Duff and Diana Cooper 1913–1950* Collins 1983. Diana Cooper's autobiography *Light of Common Day* Michael Russell 1979 (a one volume edition of three autobiographies first published by Hart Davis in 1958–60) may also be worth consulting.

**1973** Piers Dixon *Double Diploma: The Life of Sir Piers Dixon, Don and Diplomat* Hutchinson 1968. A biography by his son largely based on his diaries. Pierson Dixon was Principal Private Secretary to the Foreign Secretary 1943–8, Ambassador to Czechoslovakia 1948–50, Deputy Under-Secretary at the Foreign Office 1950–4, Permanent Representative at the United Nations 1954–60 and Ambassador to France 1960–4.

**1974** Jane Ewart-Biggs *Pay, Pack and Follow: Memoirs* Weidenfeld and Nicolson 1984. Memoirs of the wife of Sir Christopher Ewart-Biggs, who was the British Ambassador to the Irish Republic when he was assassinated by the IRA in 1976.

**1975** Lord Gladwyn *Memoirs of Lord Gladwyn* Weidenfeld and Nicolson 1972. Gladwyn rose to be Deputy Under-Secretary 1949–50, British representative to the UN 1950–4 and Ambassador to France 1954–60.

**1976**  Paul Gore-Booth *With Great Truth and Respect* Constable 1974. Gore-Booth was head of the European Recovery Department 1948–9, Director of British information services in Washington 1949–53, Ambassador to Burma 1953–6, Deputy Under-Secretary (Economic Affairs) 1956–60, High Commissioner in India 1960–5 and Permanent Under-Secretary at the Foreign Office 1965–9.

**1977**  Edward Wood, Earl of Halifax *Fulness of Days* Collins 1957. The final chapter of this memoir deals with his time as Ambassador to Washington 1941–6. A good biography is F W F Smith, Earl of Birkenhead *Halifax: The Life of Lord Halifax* Hamilton 1965.

**1978**  Sir William Hayter *A Double Life* Hamilton 1974. Hayter was an Assistant Under-Secretary in 1948, a minister in Paris in 1949, the Ambassador to the USSR 1953–7 and Deputy Under-Secretary 1953–8. *The Kremlin and the Embassy* Hodder and Stoughton 1966 is a memoir of his time in the USSR.

**1979**  Sir Nicholas Henderson *The Private Office: A Personal View of Five Foreign Secretaries and of Government from the Inside* Weidenfeld and Nicolson 1984. A memoir of his years in the diplomatic service during which he was Ambassador to Poland 1969–72, to West Germany 1972–5, to France 1975–9 and to Washington 1979–82. See also [4419].

**1980**  Richard Hilton *Military Attache in Moscow* Gale and Polden 1949. Reflections on his time in the Moscow embassy 1947–9.

**1981**  Sir David Hunt *On the Spot: An Ambassador Remembers* Peter Davies 1975. Hunt was Private Secretary to Attlee 1950–1 and to Churchill 1951–2 before taking posts in Pakistan, Central Africa, Nigeria, Uganda and Cyprus in a career culminating as Ambassador to Brazil 1969–73.

**1982**  For Sir Geoffrey Jackson see [1960].

**1983**  For Charles Johnson see [1461].

**1984**  Sir David Kelly *The Ruling Few: Or the Human Background to Diplomacy* Hollis and Carter 1952. Kelly was Ambassador to Turkey 1946–49 and the USSR 1949–51.

**1985**  For Lord Killearn see [1407].

**1986**  Sir Ivone Kirkpatrick *The Inner Circle: Memoirs* Macmillan 1959. A rather pedestrian memoir. Kirkpa-

trick was the UK High Commissioner in Germany 1950–3 and the Permanent Under-Secretary 1953–7.

**1987**  Valentine Lawford 'Inside the Foreign Office: Halifax, Eden, Bevin' *Atlantic Monthly* 205 1960 pp 45–54. Lawford served in the Diplomatic Service 1934–50.

**1988**  For Sir Robert Marett see [1964].

**1989**  Geoffrey McDermott *The Eden Legacy and the Decline of British Diplomacy* Frewin 1969. In part an autobiography, in part a critical study of Anthony Eden and in part a series of recommendations.

**1990**  Sir Cecil Parrott *The Serpent and the Nightingale* Faber 1977. A good memoir of a career which culminated as Ambassador to Czechoslovakia 1960–6.

**1991**  Sir Anthony Parsons *The Pride and the Fall: Iran 1974–1979* Cape 1984. A memoir of his time as Ambassador to Iran. See also [1403].

**1992**  Sir Maurice Peterson *Both Sides of the Curtain: An Autobiography* Constable 1950. Peterson was the Ambassador to Turkey 1944–6 and to the USSR 1946–9.

**1993**  Sir George Rendel *The Sword and the Olive: Recollections of Diplomacy and the Foreign Service 1913–54* Murray 1957. Rendel played an important part in the Austrian Treaty Commission of 1940 and the negotiations that led to the Treaty of Brussels 1948. He was the Ambassador to Belgium 1947–50 and the Chairman of the Tripartite Commission on German debts 1951–3.

**1994**  Sir David Scott *Ambassador in Black and White: Thirty Years of Changing Africa* Weidenfeld and Nicolson 1981. Scott served in Egypt 1945–7 and South Africa 1951–3, and was Deputy High Commissioner in Central Africa 1961–3, High Commissioner in Uganda 1967–70 and Ambassador to South Africa 1976–9.

**1995**  Evelyn Shuckburgh *Descent to Suez: Diaries 1951–56* Weidenfeld and Nicolson 1986. An illuminating edited version of his diaries from his time as Principal Private Secretary to Eden 1951–4 and as Under-Secretary in charge of Middle Eastern affairs 1954–6.

**1996**  William Strang *Home and Abroad* Deutsch 1956. Strang was the Permanent Under-Secretary at the Foreign Office 1949–53.

**1997**  Sir Geoffrey Thompson *Front-Line Diplomat* Hutchinson 1959. Thompson had postings in the postwar period in Baghdad, Bangkok and finally Rio.

**1998** Sir Humphrey Trevelyan *Worlds Apart: China 1953–5: Soviet Union 1962–5* Macmillan 1971. A memoir of his time at each embassy, in the latter case as Ambassador. His *Public and Private* Hamilton 1980 reflects more generally on his career but is principally a study of his distinguished family. See also [1219, 1404, 1960].

**1999** Henry Maitland Wilson *Eight Years Overseas 1939–1947* Hutchinson 1950. A brief account of his time as head of the British joint staff mission in Washington 1945–7 is the only point of interest for the post-war period.

### (5) Relations with International Bodies

**2000** Geoffrey Lawrence Goodwin *Britain and the United Nations* Oxford University Press 1957. A study of Britain's role in the setting up of the UN, the impact of the UN on British policy and Britain's reaction to the UN's handling of international crises. See also T B Millar *The Commonwealth and the United Nations* Sydney University Press, Sydney 1967.

**2001** P A Reynolds and E J Hughes (eds) *The Historian as Diplomat: Charles Kingsley Webster and the United Nations 1939–46* Robertson 1976. This study helps to illustrate Britain's role in the creation of the United Nations. E J Hughes 'Winston Churchill and the Formation of the United Nations Organisation' *Journal of Contemporary History* 9 1974 pp 177–94 shows how important the British contribution was, despite as much as because of Churchill.

**2002** G Ferrari-Bravo 'The Development of the International Trusteeship at the United Nations, with Particular Reference to British Reactions 1944–1960' Cambridge PhD Thesis 1976. The UN oversight of trusteeship particularly affected Britain as a major holder of mandated territories.

**2003** E J Johnson 'The British Government's Attitude to United Nations Peacekeeping in the Post-War International System' London PhD Thesis 1985. From 1956–64 Britain regarded the UN's peacekeeping role with suspicion in the light of Suez and its association with decolonization. UN peacekeeping in Cyprus in 1964 was therefore accepted with reluctance. Johnson sees the British experience of this in Cyprus leading to a change in attitude and a much more positive view of the UN's peacekeeping role.

**2004** Max Beloff *New Dimensions in Foreign Policy: A Study in British Administrative Experience 1947–59* Allen and Unwin 1961. An analysis of the effect on British government of international organizations such

as NATO, the Council of Europe or the Western European Union.

**2005** E Farrar 'The British Labour Party and International Organisation: A Study of the Party's Policy Towards the League of Nations, the United Nations and the Western Union' London PhD Thesis 1951–2.

**2006** Geoffrey Howe 'The International Monetary Institutions: The British View' *International Affairs* 58 1982 pp 199–209. By the then Chancellor of the Exchequer.

**2007** Robert D Putnam and Nicholas Bayne *Hanging Together: Co-operation and Conflict in the Seven Power Summits* 2nd ed, Sage 1987. A study of the economic summits of the seven leading industrial powers held regularly since 1975. Bayne, as a Foreign Office official, helped to prepare for several of these.

### (6) Overseas Aid

**2008** *Overseas Development and Aid: A Guide to Sources of Information and Material* Overseas Development Administration 1986.

**2009** *Overseas Development Institute Development Guide: A Directory of Non-Commercial Organisations in Britain Entirely Concerned in Overseas Development and Training* Allen and Unwin 1962–. An irregularly updated guide to some 200 organizations.

**2010** *British Aid Statistics* HMSO 1964–. An annual collection of data on aid from the UK government and UK organizations, on the activities of the Commonwealth Development Corporation, and on overseas manpower financed from the aid programme.

**2011** Jessica Woodroffe and Kathy Jones *British Overseas Aid 1975–1987* Christian Aid 1989. A factsheet largely consisting of tables.

**2012** *British Aid: A Select Bibliography* 5th ed, Ministry of Overseas Development Library 1978. Essentially a guide to holdings, which largely consists of official publications. *Technical Co-operation: A Monthly Bibliography* Overseas Development Administration 1964– is also useful.

**2013** D J Morgan *The Official History of Colonial Development* 5v, Macmillan 1980. A massive study of colonial development aid concentrating on the period from 1945–71. It focuses on Whitehall planning and leaves considerable room for interpretative studies. See also G N Parsons 'Imperial "Partnership": British Colonial Development and Welfare Policy 1938–1950' Oxford MPhil 1985 and *Colonial Development: A Factual Survey of the Origins and History of British Aid to Developing Countries* Overseas Development Institute 1964.

**2014** Vincent Cable *British Interests and Third World Development Overseas* Development Institute, London 1980. A case study of the attitudes of rich countries to overseas development.

**2015** Sir William Rendell *The History of the Commonwealth Development Corporation 1948–1972* Heinemann Education 1976. The main engine of development aid has been the Colonial, from 1963 the Commonwealth Development Corporation. This is a good history by the Corporation's General Manager 1953–73. It was set up by the Overseas Resources Development Act 1948. Since then it has issued an *Annual Report and Statement of Accounts* HMSO 1948–. Another study of the Corporation is C W Dumpleton *The Colonial Development Corporation* Fabian Colonial Bureau 1957. On its early years see Mike Cowen 'Early Years of the Colonial Development Corporation: British State Enterprise Overseas During Late Colonialism' *African Affairs* 83 1984 pp 63–75.

**2016** Charles Stuart (ed) *The Reith Diaries* Collins 1975. The main use of these for the post-war period is for Reith's period as Chairman of the Colonial Development Corporation 1950–9.

**2017** G B Masefield *A History of the Colonial Agricultural Service* Clarendon 1972. A general history of this service which was established in 1935.

**2018** P M P Atkinson 'Aid to Developing Countries as an Issue in Britain's Politics 1945–1972' Oxford BLitt Thesis 1977. See also J Young 'The Evolution of an Aid Lobby in Britain 1962–70' Manchester M.A. (Econ) Thesis 1970–1.

**2019** Sir Percy Spender *Exercises in Diplomacy: The ANZUS Treaty and the Colombo Plan* Sydney University Press, Sydney 1969. One of the most important developments in Commonwealth history in the immediate post-war period was the Colombo Plan in 1950. Sir Percy was the Australian Minister for External Affairs 1949–51 and the leader of the Australian delegation to the Commonwealth meeting in Colombo in 1950 at which he put forward the plan for economic aid to South and South East Asia which subsequently became known as the Colombo Plan. The strategic considerations involved in this plan for economic co-operation and development in South East Asia are examined in Nicholas Tarling 'The United Kingdom and the Origins of the Colombo Plan' *Journal of Commonwealth and Comparative Politics* 24 1986 pp 3–34. The background to it is examined in Tilman Remme 'Britain, the 1947 Asian Relations Conference and Regional Co-operation in South-East Asia' in Tony Gorst, Lewis Johnman and W Scott Lucas (eds) *Postwar Britain 1945–64: Themes and Perspectives* Pinter 1989 pp 109–34. The context was, as he points out, a 1949 cabinet paper in which regional development in the Far East was seen as a way of stemming the tide of Communism, as a sort of Asian Marshall Aid and as a way of ensuring a lasting British presence in a post-colonial South and South East Asia. On the Colombo Plan see also Lalita P Singh *The Colombo Plan: Some Political Aspects* Research School of Pacific Studies, Department of International Relations Working Paper 3, Australian National University, Canberra 1963 and D C Mandeville 'Fifteen Years of the Colombo Plan and the British Contribution to it' *Journal of the Royal Central Asian Society* 53 1966 pp 32–42. L P Goonetilleke and Byung Hak Lee (comps) *The Colombo Plan 1951–1971: 20th Anniversary* Colombo Plan Bureau, Colombo 1971 is a well-illustrated retrospective on its first twenty years.

**2020** Sir Andrew Cohen 'Development in Africa: The Problems of Today' *African Affairs* 67 1968 pp 44–54. A statement of objectives by the then Permanent Secretary at the Ministry of Overseas Development which had been set up by the incoming Labour government in 1964.

**2021** R T Gilbert 'An Evaluation of British Housing Aid Provided by the Ministry of Overseas Development' *Journal of Administration Overseas* 19 1980 pp 73–87. This evaluates progress since 1968.

**2022** M Sutton and A Hewitt 'Taking Stock: Three Years of Conservative Aid Policy' *Overseas Development Institute Review* 1 1983 pp 20–37. This examines the aid policy of the Thatcher government.

**2023** K Freeman *If Any Man Build – The History of the Save the Children Fund* Hodder and Stoughton 1965. A history of the world-wide activities of this charity from its establishment in 1919. See also E Fuller *The Right of the Child* Gollancz 1951.

**2024** M E Adams *Voluntary Service Overseas – The Story of the First Ten Years* Faber 1968. An account of its development from the first party of 18 volunteers to the thousands involved each year by the late 1960s. See also David Wainwright *The Volunteers: The Story of the Overseas Voluntary Service* Macdonald 1965. There is also some useful material in Sir George Shuster's autobiography *Private Work and Public Causes: A Personal Record 1881–1935* D Brown and Sons 1979.

## (7) International Claims and Extradition

**2025**   Richard B Lillich *International Claims: Post-War British Practice* Syracuse University Press, Syracuse, New York 1967. A study of diplomatic protection of citizens or property abroad and the procedure for claiming against the sequestration of British assets. An important study of a neglected area of international relations.

**2026**   V E Hartley Booth *British Extradition Law and Procedure Including Extradition between the United Kingdom and Foreign States, the Commonwealth and Dependent Countries and the Republic of Ireland* 2v, Sifthoff and Noordhoff, Alphen aan den Rijn 1980. The first recent study of this subject. It gives historical details of the development of the law and the relevant statutes and extradition treaties.

## (8) East-West Relations

### (a) The Cold War

In addition to the literature listed below certain other sections should be consulted. Material on Allied policy in occupied Germany, which was of considerable importance in the origins of the Cold War, can be found in the section on British relations with Europe. Material on Marshall Aid, which also contributed to the growing divide in Europe between East and West in the late 1940s, is in the section on Anglo-American Relations. The literature on the origins and creation of NATO is in the section on Defence Policy. For the British military intervention in the Greek civil war which led to the Truman doctrine and which is often seen as a prelude to the Cold War see [2440–1A].

**2027**   Martin McCauley *The Origins of the Cold War* Longman 1983. A collection of documents covering 1941–8.

**2028**   John Lewis Gaddis 'The Emerging Post-Revisionist Synthesis and the Origins of the Cold War' *Diplomatic History* 7 1983 pp 171–90. A general review of Cold War historiography, mainly dealing with the various schools of American thought on the subject. The literature on the European dimension is reviewed in David Reynolds 'The Origins of the Cold War: The European Dimension 1944–1951' *Historical Journal* 28 1985 pp 497–515.

**2029**   Anne Deighton (ed) *Britain and the Cold War* Macmillan 1989. A good collection of essays.

**2030**   Michael Dockrill *The Cold War 1945–1963* Macmillan 1988. A good study focusing on the European experience of the Cold War, in contrast to most of the literature on the subject, which has tended to concentrate on American-Soviet relations. It is only with the release of European, and especially British, documents in recent years that the importance of the European dimension has been re-assessed. Works like Paul Hastings *The Cold War 1945–1969* Benn 1969, D Evan Luard (ed) *The Cold War: A Reappraisal* Thames and Hudson 1964 and D P Fleming *The Cold War and Its Origins 1917–1960* 2v, Doubleday 1961, the work of an American historian, the first volume of which covers 1917–50 with the second covering 1950–60, are thus now somewhat dated.

**2031**   Hugh Thomas *Armed Truce: The Beginnings of the Cold War 1945–1946* Hamilton 1986. A detailed study. An important statement of the revisionist view of the origins of the Cold War, focusing on American-Soviet relations is Daniel Yergin *Shattered Peace: The Origins of the Cold War and the National Security State* Deutsch 1978. Another useful study is John Lewis Gaddis *The United States and the Origins of the Cold War 1941–1947* Columbia University Press, New York 1972. See also Roy Douglas *From War to Cold War 1942–48* Macmillan 1981.

**2032**   Lawrence Aronson and Martin Kitchen *The Origins of the Cold War: A Comparative Perspective: American, British and Canadian Relations with the Soviet Union 1941–48* Macmillan 1988. An important re-focusing of the origins of the Cold War in a wider perspective, rather than just seeing it as a question of American-Soviet relations.

**2033**   Elizabeth Barker *The British Between the Superpowers 1945–50* Macmillan 1983. An account of British disenchantment with the chances of rapprochement with the USSR, alignment with the Americans and consequent abandonment of the third force idea favoured by some Labour politicians. Another good account of British policy in this period is Peter Weiler *British Labour and the Cold War* Stanford University Press, Stanford, California 1988. John Saville *Ernest Bevin and the Cold War 1945–50* Merlin 1984 is a critical appraisal of Bevin's foreign policy, especially in the context of the origins of the Cold War.

**2034**   Victor Rothwell *Britain and the Cold War 1941–47* Cape 1982. Rothwell argues Bevin tried hard to maintain Anglo-Soviet friendship until the failure of the November 1947 foreign ministers conference. This is a view supported in Ray Merrick 'The Russia Committee of the British Foreign Office and the Cold War 1946–47' *Journal of Contemporary History* 20 1985 pp 453–68.

**2035** Terry H Anderson *The United States, Great Britain and the Cold War 1944–1947* Columbia University Press, New York 1981. A study of the role of British influence on American policy in the origins of the Cold War. Harry B Ryan *The Vision of Anglo-America: The US-UK Alliance and the Emerging Cold War 1943–1946* Cambridge University Press 1987 also examines British attempts to influence American policy, particularly in the context of the crises in Greece and Poland and of Churchill's 'Iron Curtain' speech at Fulton, Missouri in 1946. Fraser J Harbutt *The Iron Curtain: Churchill, America and the Origins of the Cold War* Oxford University Press 1986 is an incisive account of events in 1945–46, though it probably exaggerates Churchill's role. Also on Churchill's role see Ritchie Ovendale 'Britain, the USA and the European Cold War 1945–8' *History* 67 1982 pp 217–35.

**2036** Anne and John Tusa *The Berlin Blockade* Hodder and Stoughton 1988. A good account of the first major crisis of the Cold War, the Soviet blockade of Berlin and the Allied airlift to the beleaguered city in 1948–49. See also Eric Morris *Blockade: Berlin and the Cold War* Hamilton 1973, Max Charles *Berlin Blockade* Wingate 1959, W Phillips Davison *The Berlin Blockade: A Study in Cold War Politics* Princeton University Press, Princeton, New Jersey 1958, M B Bell 'Anglo-American Diplomacy and the Problem of the Berlin Blockade' Birmingham PhD Thesis 1981 and Avi Shlaim 'Britain, the Berlin Blockade and the Cold War' *International Affairs* 60 1983– 84 pp 1–14. Daniel F Harrington 'The Berlin Blockade Revisited' *International History Review* 6 1984 pp 88–112 is a re-examination of the crisis and the lessons drawn from it by the West. Dudley Barker in *Berlin Airlift* HMSO 1949 is an official account of the airlift written for the Air Ministry. Robert Rodrigo *Berlin Airlift* Cassell, 1960 is a good account of the operation with detailed appendices.

**2037** *Selected Documents on Germany and the Question of Berlin 1944–1961* Cmnd 1552, *Parliamentary Papers* xxxvii 1961–62. A good collection of documents on the British position on Berlin over this period published in the light of the crisis precipitated by the building of the Berlin Wall and the accompanying Soviet threats.

**2038** B P White 'Britain and East-West Detente 1953–1963' Leicester PhD Thesis 1986. A study of Britain's concept of and role in detente. White argues Britain was an important catalyst of detente, with the determination to maintain a world role and growing concern about nuclear proliferation being the major factors. Some of this argument has been published in his 'Britain and the Rise of Detente' in R Crockett and S Smith (eds) *The Cold War Past and Present* Allen and Unwin 1983 pp 91–109.

(b) Anglo-Soviet Relations

On BBC external broadcasting to the Soviet Union and Eastern Europe see the literature on External Broadcasting [3769–71] in the section on Broadcasting.

**2039** Frederick Samuel Northedge and Audrey Wells *Britain and Soviet Communism: The Impact of a Revolution* Macmillan 1982. This study concentrates on the British view of the Soviet Union. It looks at its impact on British politics, especially on the Labour Movement, and on foreign policy, and at Anglo-Soviet economic relations. See also Duncan Wilson 'Anglo-Soviet Relations: The Effect of Ideas on Reality' *International Affairs* 50 1974 pp 380–93.

**2040** W P Coates and Zelda K Coates *A History of Anglo- Soviet Relations Vol II: 1943–1950* Lawrence and Wishart 1958. A study largely based on parliamentary debates and on British and Russian newspapers.

**2041** Andrei Gromyko *Memories* Century Hutchinson 1989. The memoirs of the long-serving Soviet diplomat are as blandly loyal and bureaucratic as their author. If their publication reflects the effect of perestroika many of the arguments they contain, such as the view that South Korea started the Korean War, do not suggest that it has yet supplanted propaganda as far as Gromyko is concerned. It however contains some interesting points on, for instance, a Soviet proposal for the reunification of Germany in 1952 or on his period as Ambassador to London 1952–3.

**2042** Donald Cameron Watt 'British Military Perceptions of the Soviet Union as a Strategic Threat 1945–1950' in Josef Becker and Franz Knipping (eds) *Power in Europe? Great Britain, France, Italy and Germany in a Postwar World 1945–1950* Walter de Gruyter, Berlin 1986 pp 325–39. On British attitudes in this period see also R Smith 'British Policy Towards the Soviet Union 1945–1947' Liverpool PhD Thesis 1983 and Peter J Boyle 'The British Foreign Office View of Soviet-American Relations 1945–46' *Diplomatic History* 3 1979 pp 307–20.

**2043** Nikolai Tolstoy *Victims of Yalta* Hodder and Stoughton 1977. This book caused considerable controversy. It advances the view that Macmillan was responsible, in the immediate aftermath of the war, for sending thousands of Cossacks and Yugoslavs to Stalin and Tito and certain death. This view is developed in Nikolai Tolstoy *The Minister and the Massacres* Century Hutchinson 1986. See also Nicholas Bethell *The Last Secret: Forcible Repatriation to Russia 1944–7* Deutsch 1974.

**2044** Joan Beaumont 'Trade, Strategy and Foreign Policy in Conflict: The Rolls Royce Affair 1946–1947' *International History Review* 2 1980 pp 602–18. In 1946 Britain sold Rolls Royce engines to the USSR, a modified version of which was later used to deadly effect in Migs in Korea. An account of this blunder at the start of the Cold War.

**2045** Wesley K Wark 'Coming in from the Cold: British Propaganda and Red Army Defectors 1945–1952' *International History Review* 9 1987 pp 48–72.

(c) Other

**2046** S M Max 'Cold War on the Danube: The Belgrade Conference of 1948 and Anglo-American Efforts to Reinternationalize the River' *Diplomatic History* 7 1983 pp 57–77.

**2047** M S Bell 'Britain and East Germany: The Politics of Non- Recognition' Nottingham PhD Thesis 1977–8.

**2048** S M Max *The United States, Great Britain and the Sovietization of Hungary 1945–1948* Columbia University Press, New York 1985. This argues that Hungary's wartime alliance with Germany made the Allies reluctant to do much to save it from Stalin's embrace.

**2049** Beatrice Heuser *Western Containment Policies in the Cold War: The Yugoslav Case 1948–53* Routledge 1989. A good study of American, British and French policy making extensive use of recently released documents. It also covers British operations against Albania.

**2050** Nicholas Bethell *The Great Betrayal: The Untold Story of Kim Philby's Biggest Coup* Hodder and Stoughton 1984. An account of Anglo-American operations against Albania 1949–53. He probably overstates Philby's responsibility for the failure of an operation that seems to have been so badly conceived that it needed little help to turn out disastrously. See also D B Funderburk 'Anglo-Albanian Relations' *Revue des Etudes Sud-Est Européennes* 13 1975 pp 117–23.

## (9) Anglo-American Relations

There is, in addition to the material listed below, a considerable literature on Anglo-American defence co-operation. This can be found in the various categories of the section on Defence Policy. On economic relations see the section on Financial Policy. There are also a number of relevant works listed in the section on Cold War.

**2051** Ian S McDonald (comp) *Anglo-American Relations Since the Second World War* David and Charles 1974. A collection of documents.

**2052** Christopher Grayling and Christopher Langdon *Just Another Star? Anglo-American Relations Since 1945* Harrap 1988. A good history of the ups and downs in the Anglo-American alliance since the war. William Roger Louis and Hedley Bull (eds) *The 'Special Relationship': Anglo-American Relations Since 1945* Clarendon 1986 contains a wide range of essays on all aspects of the Anglo-American relationship. Coral Bell *The Debatable Alliance: An Essay in Anglo-American Relations* Oxford University Press 1964 is a survey of the alliance from the end of the war to the assassination of President Kennedy. David Reynolds 'A "Special Relationship"? America, Britain and the International Order Since World War Two' *International Affairs* 62 1985–6 pp 1–20 is a historiographical and interpretative survey. The tension in British foreign policy over the last twenty years between a transatlantic or a European alignment is examined in his 'Re-thinking Anglo-American Relations' *International Affairs* 65 1988–89 pp 89–111.

**2053** David Dimbleby and David Reynolds *An Ocean Apart* BBC/Hodder and Stoughton 1988. A general history of Anglo- American relations. Based on a television series it is well illustrated and has a good annotated bibliography. It covers cultural as well as diplomatic and military relations. H G Nicholas *The United States and Britain* Chicago University Press 1975 is another general history, the last four chapters of which cover the post-war period. H C Allen *Great Britain and the United States: A History of Anglo-American Relations (1783–1952)* Odhams 1954 also has an extensive and useful section on post-war relations. See also Basil Collier *The Lion and the Eagle: British and Anglo-American Strategy 1900–50* Macdonald 1972. Alastair Buchan 'Mothers and Daughters (or Greeks and Romans)' *Foreign Affairs* 54 1976 pp 645–69 is a general survey focusing on cultural relations.

**2054** Donald Cameron Watt *Succeeding John Bull: America in Britain's Place 1900–1975 – A Study of the Anglo-American Relationship and World Politics in the Context of British and American Foreign Policy-Making in the Twentieth Century* Cambridge University Press 1984. Primarily a study of foreign policy elites rather than of Anglo-American relations. See also Lionel Gelber *America in Britain's Place* Allen and Unwin 1961.

**2055** Kay Halle (ed) *Winston Churchill on America and Britain: A Selection of his Thoughts on Anglo-American Relations* Walker and Co, New York 1970. For Attlee's thoughts on the relationship see Clement Richard Attlee 'Britain and America: Common Aims, Different Opinions' *Foreign Affairs* 32 1954 pp 190–202.

**2056** Basil Collier *Barren Victories: Versailles to Suez (1918–1956)* Cassell 1964. A study of Anglo-American differences and difficulties in the twentieth century.

**2057** Richard E Neustadt *Alliance Politics* Columbia University Press, New York 1970. A study of two mis-adventures in Anglo-American relations, the Suez invasion of 1956 and the British attempt to purchase Skybolt nuclear missiles 1960–2. These episodes are commented on by a former British Ambassador in Washington in Lord Harlech 'Suez Snafu, Skybolt Sabu' *Foreign Policy* 2 1971 pp 38–50. For a more recent critique of Neustadt's model see [2401].

**2058** Robin Edmonds *Setting the Mould: The United States and Britain 1945–1950* Clarendon 1986. A good survey synthesizing recent scholarship. Robert M Hathaway *Ambiguous Partnership: Britain and America 1944–1947* Columbia University Press, New York 1981 examines a crucial period in which Britain's world role passed across the Atlantic. American support at the same time became of great importance to the Foreign Office. The British efforts to ensure this support and to mould American public opinion favourably are examined in Caroline Anstey 'Foreign Office Efforts to Influence American Opinion 1945–1949' London PhD Thesis 1984. See also her 'The Projection of British Socialism: Foreign Office Publicity and American Opinion 1945–50' *Journal of Contemporary History* 19 1984 pp 417–52. Richard A Best Jr *'Co-operation with Like-Minded People': British Influence on American Security Policy 1945–1949* Greenwood 1986 examines and probably exaggerates British influence on American policy in this period. British reactions to American policy in this period are considered in Peter J Boyle 'Britain, America and the Transition from Economic to Military Assistance 1948–51' *Journal of Contemporary History* 22 1987 pp 521–38. See also Peter G Boyle 'The British Foreign Office and America's Foreign Policy 1947–48' *Journal of American Studies* 16 1982 pp 373–89 and Marjorie Bremner 'An Analysis of British Parliamentary Thought Concerning the United States in the Post-War Period' London PhD Thesis 1950–1.

**2059** D J Rimmer 'The Anglo-American Alliance 1939–1947: The Myth of the "Special Relationship"' Exeter MA Thesis 1984. This demonstrates the extent to which the wartime alliance collapsed in 1945 to be succeeded by Anglo-American difficulties in Palestine or over atomic weapons. The alliance with America was only revived by the onset of the Cold War.

**2060** Michael J Hogan *The Marshall Plan: America, Britain and the Reconstruction of Western Europe 1947–52* Cambridge University Press 1987. A good study of the Marshall Aid programme and its positive effects in reviving a Europe that was struggling to recover from the catastrophe of war. He emphasizes its success and takes issue with those revisionist scholars who have sought to demonize or trivialize it in the light of the divisions in Europe to which it might be held to have indirectly contributed. Henry Pelling *Britain and the Marshall Plan* Macmillan 1988 is another good study which makes use of documents hitherto unconsulted. See also Kathleen Burk 'Britain and the Marshall Plan' in Chris Wrigley (ed) *Warfare, Diplomacy and Politics* Hamilton 1986 pp 210–30. The background and planning of the Marshall Plan in February to June 1947 is examined in Joseph Marion Jones *The Fifteen Weeks: An Inside Account of the Genesis of the Marshall Plan* Harcourt, Brace and World Inc, New York 1955. The background to the Plan is also examined in George C Peden 'Economic Aspects of British Perceptions of Power on the Eve of the Cold War' in Josef Becker and Franz Knipping (eds) *Power in Europe? Great Britain, France, Italy and Germany in a Post-War World 1945–1950* Walter de Gruyter, Berlin 1986 pp 237–62 and Scott Newton 'The Sterling Crisis of 1947 and the British Response to the Marshall Plan' *Economic History Review* 2nd series 37 1984 pp 391–408. William C Cromwell 'The Marshall Plan, Britain and the Cold War' *Review of International Studies* 8 1982 pp 233–49 looks at the effect of Marshall Aid on the map of Europe.

**2061** M D Graham 'British Attitudes towards America: An Historical and Empirical Study' London PhD Thesis 1951–2. A study conducted at a time when there was concern about British anti-Americanism. See also T R Fyvel 'Realities Behind British "Anti-Americanism"' *Commentary* 14 1952 pp 555–62.

**2062** Henry L Roberts and Paul A Wilson *Britain and the United States: Problems in Co-operation* Royal Institute of International Affairs 1953. Another contemporary study of Anglo-American relations is Leon D Epstein *Britain – Uneasy Ally* University of Chicago Press 1984. See also M S Rees 'Anglo-American Relations 1953–55: The Institutional and Operational Levels of Compromise' London MPhil Thesis 1976.

**2063** David Nunnerley *President Kennedy and Britain* The Bodley Head 1972. An excellent study of Anglo-American relations 1961–3 based on extensive interviewing. Also of relevance is Richard J Walton *Cold War and Counter-Revolution: The Foreign Policy of John F Kennedy* Viking 1972.

**2064** D F Rahal 'Continuity and Constraint: The Anglo-American "Special Relationship" in its Political and Military Context 1963–1973' London MPhil Thesis 1977.

**2065** Dean Acheson *Present at the Creation* Hamilton 1970. Acheson was Assistant Secretary of State 1941–5, Under Secretary of State 1945–7 and Secretary of State

1949–53. This is a good memoir which necessarily deals extensively with Anglo-American relations.

**2066** James Byrnes *Speaking Frankly* Heinemann 1947. An account of the peace conferences 1945–46 and reflections on foreign policy by the then US Secretary of State (1945–7).

**2067** Michael A Guhin *John Foster Dulles: A Statesman and his Times* Columbia University Press 1972. A perceptive and carefully researched study. He argues that Dulles was a pragmatic statesman rather than the anti-Communist campaigner he somehow contrived to appear. Townsend Hoopes *The Devil and John Foster Dulles* Deutsch 1974 is a critical study of Eisenhower's Secretary of State 1953–9. See also Leonard Mosley *Dulles: A Biography of Eleanor, Allen and John Foster Dulles and Their Family* Hodder and Stoughton 1978 and Richard Goold- Adams *The Time of Power: A Reappraisal of John Foster Dulles* Weidenfeld and Nicolson 1962. See also [2410].

**2068** Dwight D Eisenhower *The White House Years* 2v, Doubleday 1965. Eisenhower's memoirs of his Presidency are *Vol I: Mandate for Change 1953–1956* and *Vol II: Waging Peace 1956–61*. A good biographical study is Stephen Ambrose *Eisenhower: The President Vol II: 1952–1969* Allen and Unwin 1984.

**2069** Walter Millis (ed) *The Forrestal Diaries: The Inner History of the Cold War* Cassell 1952. James Forrestal was US Secretary to the Navy from 1944 until he took the newly created post of Secretary for Defence in 1947. These diaries, covering 1944–9, comment on the international problems of the day and provide some views on Anglo-American relations in the immediate post-war period.

**2070** Arthur Meier Schlesinger Jr *A Thousand Days: John F Kennedy in the White House* Houghton Mifflin 1965. A good account of the Kennedy Presidency 1961–63. See also Frank Pakenham, Lord Longford *Kennedy* Weidenfeld and Nicolson 1976, Ted Sorensen *Kennedy* Hodder and Stoughton 1965 and Pierre Salinger *With Kennedy* Cape 1967.

**2071** Forrest C Pogue *George C Marshall Statesman 1945–59* Viking 1987. This is the fourth and final volume of Pogue's biography. It is a substantial and detailed piece of work. Marshall was Secretary of State 1947–9, in which capacity he was the prime sponsor of the Marshall Plan that bears his name, and Secretary of Defence 1950–1.

**2072** Harry S Truman *Year of Decision 1945* Hodder and Stoughton 1955. His memoirs of his years as President are completed by *Years of Trial and Hope 1946–1953* Hodder and Stoughton 1956. Merle Miller *Plain Speaking: An Oral Biography of Harry S Truman* Gollancz 1974 contains transcripts of conversations. Useful biographies are Harold F Gosnell *Truman's Crises: A Political Biography of Harry S Truman* Greenwood 1980, Roy Jenkins *Truman* Collins 1986 and Robert J Donovan *Tumultuous Years: The Presidency of Harry S Truman 1949–1953* Norton 1982. See also Robert H Ferrell (ed) *Off the Record: The Private Papers of Harry S Truman* Harper and Row, New York 1980.

## (10) Europe

### (a) General

**2073** James Hennessy *Britain and Europe Since 1945: A Bibliographical Guide* Harvester 1973. An author, title and chronological index to British primary source material on Europe and European integration since 1945. It includes historical details on the various organizations listed. This work constitutes a guide to the publisher's microfilm collection of the same title. It is updated by annual supplements.

**2074** Winfried Böttcher, Jürgen Jansen and Friedrich Welsch (eds) *Britische Europaideen 1940–1970: Eine Bibliographie* Droste Verlag, Düsseldorf 1971. An unannotated chronological listing. It principally consists of official publications.

**2075** David Reynolds 'Britain and the New Europe: The Search for Identity Since 1940' *Historical Journal* 31 1988 pp 223–39. A useful historiographical study of British relations with Europe.

**2076** *European Year Book* Martinus Nijhoff, Dordrecht 1955–. An annual guide to pan-European organizations, many of which Britain is a member. It also has an annual bibliography.

**2077A** *Selected Documents Relating to Problems of Security and Cooperation in Europe 1954–1977* HMSO 1977. A collection of Foreign Office documents relating to British policy in Europe.

**2077** Monica Charlot and Jean-Claude Sergeant *Britain and Europe Since 1945* Longman 1986. A good general survey. Elizabeth Barker *Britain in a Divided Europe 1945–70* Weidenfeld and Nicolson 1971 is a detailed analysis of British attempts to deal with major European problems in this period. R D H Seaman *Britain and Western Europe* Arnold 1983 is a textbook guide to Britain's relations with the region since 1919. Britain's policy towards Europe is also surveyed in Michael Fogarty 'Britain and Europe Since 1945' *Review of Politics* 19 1957 pp 90–105 and C M Woodhouse 'Great Britain's European Policy Since the Second World War' *International Journal* 12 1957 pp 300–8.

**2078** F S V Donnison *Civil Affairs and Military Government, North West Europe 1944–1946* HMSO 1961. An exhaustive and detailed study of British military administration in liberated Europe which is part of the official history of the Second World War.

**2079** Alan S Milward *Reconstruction of Western Europe 1945–51* Methuen 1984. A good if somewhat polemical study. It includes a good bibliography.

**2080** Mirjam Kölling *Führungsmacht in Westeuropa? Grossbritanniens Anspruch und Scheitern 1944–1950* Akademie der Wissenschaften der DDR, Berlin 1984. A well regarded study of British policy in Europe in the immediate aftermath of the war. Geoffrey Warner 'Britain and Europe in 1948: the View from the Cabinet' in Josef Becker and Franz Knipping (eds) *Power in Europe? Great Britain, France, Italy and Germany in a Post-War World* Walter de Gruyter, Berlin 1986 pp 27–46 focuses on the effect of the murder of Marasyck and the Communist takeover of Czechoslovakia. The British reaction to the onset of the Cold War in Europe is assessed in Martin Ceadel 'British Political Parties and the European Crisis of the Late 1940s' pp 137–62 and R A C Parker 'British Perceptions of Power: Europe Between the Superpowers' pp 447–60, both of which appear in the same volume.

**2081** Chatham House Study Group *Britain in Western Europe: WEU and the Atlantic Alliance* Royal Institute of International Affairs 1956. A survey of Britain's military and political links with the region 1945–54, focusing on Britain's role in the Western European Union and the NATO alliance.

**2082** Donald Cameron Watt 'Grossbritannien und Europa 1951–1959: Die Jahre konservativer Regierung' *Vierteljahreshefte für Zeitgeschichte* 28 1980 pp 389–409.

**2083** Michael Stewart 'Britain, Europe and the Alliance' *Foreign Affairs* 48 1970 pp 648–59. A contemporary statement on the situation in Europe by a former Foreign Secretary.

**2084** William Wallace *Britain's Bilateral Links Within Western Europe* Routledge and Kegan Paul 1984. A overview of Britain's links with Western Europe in the 1980s, both through the European Community and through normal diplomatic channels.

**(b) Britain and the Occupation of Germany After the Second World War**

**2085** Dennis L Bark and David R Cress *A History of West Germany Vol I: From Shadow to Substance 1945– 1963* Blackwell 1989. An excellent general history. See also Edgar S McInnes (ed) *The Shaping of Post-War Germany* Dent 1960 and Michael Balfour *West Germany: A Contemporary History* Croom Helm 1982.

**2086** Josef Foschepoth and Rolf Steininger (eds) *Die britische Deutschland- und Besatzungspolitik 1945– 1949* Ferdinand Schöningh, Paderborn 1985. Another good collection of essays on British occupation policy is Claus Scharf and Hans- Jurgen Schröder (eds) *Die Deutschlandpolitik Grossbritanniens und die britische Zone 1945–1949* Steiner, Wiesbaden 1979. Michael Leonard Graham Balfour and John Mair *Four Power Control in Germany and Austria 1945–1946* Oxford University Press 1956 surveys the establishment of the occupation zones and administration of the victorious Russians, British, Americans and French in the aftermath of the war. Also of use on occupation policy is H H E Hymans 'Anglo-American Policies in Occupied Germany 1945–1952' London PhD Thesis 1959 and H Schulte 'Die britische Militärpolitik im besetzten Deutschland 1945–1949' *Militärgeschichtliche Mitteilungen* 31 1982 pp 51–75. The local impact of the occupation is examined in H A Balshaw 'The British Occupation of Germany 1945–9 with Special Reference to Hamburg' Oxford DPhil Thesis 1971–2.

**2087** *Welt im Film: A Microfiche Catalogue of the Imperial War Museum's Holdings of Material from the Anglo-American Newsreel Screened in Occupied Germany 1945–1950* Imperial War Museum 1981. A guide to Allied propaganda during the occupation. Anna J Merritt and Richard L Merritt (eds) *Public Opinion in Occupied Germany: The OMGUS Surveys 1945–1949* University of Illinois Press, Champaign, Illinois 1970 is an account of surveys conducted by the Allies to track public opinion in occupied Germany.

**2088** Ann and John Tusa *The Nuremberg Trial* Macmillan 1983. A useful account of the trial of German war criminals that followed the war. See also Robert E Canot *Justice at Nuremberg* Weidenfeld and Nicolson 1983, Werner Maser *Nuremberg* Allen Lane 1979, Airey Neave *Nuremberg* Coronet 1980, Bradley F Smith *Reaching Judgement at Nuremberg* Deutsch 1977, Rebecca West *A Trail of Powder* Macmillan 1955 and August von Knieriem *The Nuremberg Trial* Henry Regnery, Chicago 1959.

**2089** Barbara Marshall 'German Attitudes to British Military Government 1945–47' *Journal of Contemporary History* 15 1980 pp 655–85. A good analysis.

**2090** Nicholas Pronay and Keith Wilson (ed) *The Political Re-Education of Germany and Her Allies* Croom Helm 1985. A good collection of essays, mainly on Germany but also including one essay each on Japan and Italy. It also has a good bibliography. On the British contribution to political development in Germany in the immediate post-war period see Raymond Ebsworth *Restoring Democracy in Germany: The British Contribution* Stevens 1960. See also K Jurgensen 'British Occupation Policy After 1945: The Problems of "Re-Educating Germany"' *History* 68 1983 pp 225–44 and Barbara Marshall 'The Democratisation of Local Politics in the British Zone of Germany: Hannover 1945–47' *Journal of Contemporary History* 21 1986 pp 413–51. For a contemporary analysis see 'Local Government in Bizonia' *Planning* 14 1948 pp 209–28.

**2091** Arthur Hearnden (ed) *The British in Germany: Educational Reconstruction After 1945* Hamilton 1978. Education played an important part in the British occupation policy. Arthur Hearnden *Red Robert: A Life of Robert Birley* Hamilton 1984 is a biography of a important figure in British educational policy who later became headmaster of Eton. Birley comments on this policy in his 'Education in the British Zone of Germany' *International Affairs* 26 1950 pp 32–44. See also Maria Halbritter *Schulreformpolitik in der britischen Zone von 1945 bis 1949* Beltz, Weinheim 1979, Günter Pakschies *Umerziehung in der britischen Zone 1945–1949: Untersuchungen zur britischen Re-education-Politik* Beltz, Weinheim 1979 (the second volume of this was published by Böhlau, Köln 1984), David Phillips (ed) *German Universities after the Surrender: British Occupation Policy and the Control of Higher Education* Department of Educational Studies, University of Oxford 1983, M Cameron 'The Re-Establishment of Compulsory Education in the British Zone of Occupation in Germany 1945–50' Birmingham MEd Thesis 1983–4 and D G Phillips 'The British and University Reform Policy in Germany 1945–49: A Study, with Particular Reference to the Gutachten zur Hochschulreform of 1948' Oxford DPhil Thesis 1983.

**2092** M L G Balfour 'Reforming the German Press 1945–1949' *Journal of European Studies* 3 1973 pp 268–75. Balfour, a British participant in the process is here reviewing Harold Hurwitz *Die Stunde Null der deutschen Presse: Die amerikanische Pressepolitik in Deutschland 1945–1949* Verlag Wissenschaft und Politik, Köln 1972.

**2093** Alec Cairncross *The Price of War: British Policy on German Reparations 1941–1949* Blackwell 1986. The Allies had wanted to exact reparations in kind after the Second World War. This is a study of how, far from receiving reparations, the British, French and American were obliged to feed the zones they occupied by one who was at the time very involved in the formulation of British policy. John Farquharson *The Western Allies and the Politics of Food: Agrarian Management in Post-War Germany* Berg 1985 concentrates on the problems experienced in feeding occupied Germany. He shows that Britain, saddled with the most populous zone and cut off from the food-producing areas in the Russian zone and hampered by her own domestic economic problems, had the greatest difficulties. The process whereby these economic difficulties led to the fusion of the British and American zones by the end of 1947 is examined in Robert W Carden 'Before Bizonia: British Economic Dilemma in Germany 1945–46' *Journal of Contemporary History* 14 1979 pp 535–55. The failure of British land policy is assessed in John Farquharson 'Land Reform in the British Zone 1945–1947' *German History* 6 1988 pp 35–56. Britain's part in the German currency reform of June 1948 is analysed in Ian Turner 'Great Britain and the Post-War German Currency Reform' *Historical Journal* 30 1987 pp 685–708.

**2094** Victor Gollancz *Our Threatened Values* Left Book Club 1946. A plea for better conditions in the British zone in Germany. This was followed by his *In Darkest Germany* Gollancz 1947. Both convey something of the conditions under the British administration at the time. A similar book is A Fenner Brockway *German Diary* Gollancz 1946. John Farquharson '"Emotional but Influential": Victor Gollancz, Richard Stokes and the British Zone of Germany 1945–9' *Journal of Contemporary History* 22 1987 pp 501–19 is a history of the Save Europe Now campaign they launched in late 1945 and a study of their influence on British policy in Germany.

**2095** Henry Faulk *Group Captives: The Re-Education of German Prisoners of War in Britain 1945–8* Chatto and Windus 1977. On German POWs see also Matthew Barry Sullivan *Thresholds of Peace: German Prisoners and the People of Britain 1944–1948* Hamilton 1979. See also A W Mackenzie *The Treatment of Enemy Property in the United Kingdom during and after the Second World War* the author 1982.

**2096** Arthur L Smith Jr *Churchill's German Army: Wartime Strategy and Cold War Politics 1943–1947* Sage 1977. An investigation into why Britain allowed German armies that should have surrendered to the Russians into their zone, permitted the Nazi authorities to function in some areas for weeks after the end of the war and keep German military units active. He concludes that Britain was clearly preparing for the Cold War before the end of the Second World War.

**2097** John H Backer *The Decision to Divide Germany: American Foreign Policy in Transition* Duke University Press, Durham, North Carolina 1978. A study of the background to the division of Germany. In recent years the part played by Britain in this process has been reassessed and emphasized. Anne Deighton 'The "Frozen Front": The Labour Government, the Division of Germany and the Origins of the Cold War 1945–7' *International Affairs* 63 1987 pp 449–65 sees Britain as having played a major part in the events leading to the division of Germany. Josef Foschepoth 'British Interest in the Division of Germany After the Second World War' *Journal of Contemporary History* 21 1986 pp 391–411 argues that Britain began to pursue the idea of separate western and eastern German states from 1946. This apparent turning point in 1946 is explored in Falk Pingel '"Die Russen am Rhein?" Zur Wende der britischen Besatzungspolitik im Frühjahr 1946' *Vierteljahreshefte für Zeitgeschichte* 31 1982 pp 98–116. See also Sean Greenwood 'Bevin, the Ruhr and the Division of Germany: Aug 1945–Dec 1946' *Historical Journal* 29 1986 pp 203–12. Keith Sainsbury 'British Policy and German Unity at the End of the Second World War' *English Historical Review* 94 1979 pp 786–804 argues that Britain may have desired partition but that the outcome was largely shaped by the USA and USSR. The role of the French in the division of Germany is examined in John W Young 'The Foreign Office, the French and the Post-War Division of Germany' *Review of International Studies* 12 1986 pp 223–34.

**2098** George Clare *Berlin Days 1946–1947* Macmillan 1989. A memoir of his service in occupied Berlin.

**2099** John H Backer *Winds of History: The German Years of Lucius DuBignon Clay* Van Nostrand Reinhold 1983. Clay was the deputy military governor 1945–7 and the military governor of the American zone in Germany and the Allied Commander-in-Chief in Europe 1947–9.

(c) Britain and the Integration of Europe 1945–73

**2100** John Paxton (ed) *A Dictionary of the European Communities* 2nd ed, Macmillan 1982. A useful dictionary covering the process of European integration since 1945. See also G and B Parker *Dictionary of the European Communities* Butterworths 1981.

**2101** J Bryan Collester *European Communities: A Guide to Information Sources* Gale, Detroit, Michigan 1979. An annotated and classified bibliography on all aspects of European integration. It is English language only. It also tends to exclude articles and official publications. Karl Kujath *Bibliographie zur europäischen Integration mit Anmerkungen* Europa Union, Bonn 1977 is a major annotated bibliography. Carol Ann Cosgrave *A Reader's Guide to Britain and the European Communities* Chatham House/PEP 1970 is an informative and generally annotated bibliography. It includes many polemics, pamphlets and newspaper articles, as well as more scholarly works.

**2102** Michael Charlton *The Price of Victory* BBC 1983. A good account of British attitudes to European integration up to the rejection of the first application to join the European Community in 1963. Based on a radio series it makes good use of extensive interviewing. See also William Horsfall Carter *Speaking European: The Anglo-Continental Cleavage* Allen and Unwin 1966.

**2103** Stephen Holt 'British Attitudes to the Political Aspects of Membership of the European Communities' in Ghita Ionescu (ed) *The New Politics of European Integration* Macmillan 1972 pp 64–79. On the Labour party's attitude see in the same volume Michael A Wharton 'The Labour Party and Europe 1950–71' pp 80–97.

**2103A** Arthur Aughey *Conservative Party Attitudes Towards the Common Market* Hull Papers in Politics 2, Politics Department, University of Hull 1978. A general study from the 1950s onwards. N Ashford 'The Conservative Party and European Integration 1945–1975' Warwick PhD Thesis 1983 focuses almost as much on the distribution of power within the Conservative party as on the divisions in the party over Europe. A general study of the Liberals more whole-hearted approach is D J Woodhead 'The British Liberal Party and European Integration 1945–64' Manchester MA (Econ) Thesis 1966–7.

**2104** C E Smith 'Britain and the Western European Union 1948–71' Wales MSc (Econ) Thesis 1974–6. The Western European Union was an association of Britain, France, West Germany, Italy, Belgium and Luxemburg to co-ordinate defence, and promote integration and co-operation arising out of the 1948 Brussels Treaty. It was formally established in 1955. It has been largely concerned with military co-ordination since its social and cultural activities were transferred to the Council of Europe in 1960.

**2105** R V Harrison 'Winston Churchill and European Integration' Aberdeen PhD Thesis 1985. This argues that Churchill was of major importance in reviving the European idea and shaping its initial stages after the war. See also C M Edler 'Britain and the Concept of European Union' London PhD Thesis 1956. Efforts to promote British involvement in European integration in the early post-war period are examined in F N Forman 'The European Movement in Great Britain 1945–1954' Sussex DPhil Thesis 1972–3.

**2106** Jean Monnet *Memoirs* Collins 1978. The memoirs of the prime architect of European integration. These are useful both on the initial European desire that Britain should take a lead in the movement and on the European reaction when the British did finally apply to join the Europe that had been created without them.

**2107**  Avi Shlaim *Britain and the Origins of European Unity 1945–51* Reading University Press 1978. A useful general study of British attitudes and policies. John W Young *Britain, France and the Unity of Europe 1945–51* Leicester University Press 1984 looks more generally at the debates about integration in this period and the differences between France and Britain. See also Walter Lipgens *A History of European Integration 1945–1947: The Formation of the European Union* Clarendon 1982. The process whereby France rather than a reluctant and still imperial Britain became the leader of the European movement is particularly examined in R P A Turner 'Two Views of Europe: The British Government's Response to French Proposals for a European Assembly (1948) and for a Coal and Steel Pool (1950)' Newcastle MLitt Thesis 1983. Jan Melissen and Bert Zeeman 'Britain and Western Europe 1945–1951: Opportunities Lost' *International Affairs* 63 1986–7 pp 81–95 is a critique of British policy in this period. On British attitudes and policies see also Geoffrey Warner 'Die britische Labour-Regierung und die Einheit Westeuropas 1948–1951' *Vierteljahrshefte für Zeitgeschichte* 28 1980 pp 310–30, K H Propper 'British Attitudes, from 1945 to 1952, Towards Movements for Closer European Union, with Special Reference to OEEC, the Council of Europe, the European Coal and Steel Community and the EDC' London MSc Thesis 1954–5 and G A B Short 'British Policy Towards European Union 1945–1951' Oxford BLitt Thesis 1960–1. The relationship between economic factors and British policy on European integration is examined in Scott Newton 'Britain, the Dollar Shortage and European Integration 1945–1950' Birmingham PhD Thesis 1981–2. His 'The 1949 Sterling Crisis and British Policy Towards European Integration' *Review of International Studies* 11 1985 pp 169–82 derives from this work. For the Labour Party's attitude in this period see J T Grantham 'The Labour Party and European Unity 1939–1951' Cambridge PhD Thesis 1977.

**2108**  R B Manderson-Jones *The Special Relationship: Anglo-American Relations and Western European Unity 1947–1956* Weidenfeld and Nicolson 1972. This especially focuses on the very different British and American attitudes to European integration. The Americans were far more enthusiatic about a British involvement in schemes such as the European Defence Community mooted in 1950 than were the British themselves. Anglo-American differences over Europe are also examined in R E Jones 'The United States, the United Kingdom and a United Europe: Influences and Events Bearing on the British and American Positions Relative to European Unity 1939–1948 with Special Reference to the Year 1947' Wales MA Thesis 1959–60.

**2109**  Ulrich Sahm 'Britain and Europe 1950' *International Affairs* 43 1967 pp 12–24 with a response from Kenneth Younger pp 24–8. This examines Britain's refusal to take part in the negotiations on the Schuman plan for a European Coal and Steel Community. The standard history of this development is still William Diebold *The Schuman Plan: A Study in Economic Co-operation 1950–1959* Praeger, New York 1959. It also saw Churchill's speech in which he suggested the creation of a Euro pean army. This is examined in G Mai 'Der Churchill-Plan vom August 1950' *Militärgeschichtliche Mitteilungen* 2 1978 pp 137–44. 1950 also saw the French proposal of a European defence community. The history and failure of this proposal between 1950 and 1954 is well analysed in Edward Fursdon *The European Defence Community: A History* Macmillan 1979.

**2110**  Jeremy Moon *European Integration in British Politics 1950–1963: A Study of Issue Change* Gower 1985. A good examination of the gradual change in British attitudes in the decade leading up to the first application to join the European Community. The Churchill government, despite its leader's inte grationist rhetoric, avoided European entanglements. This is examined in John W Young 'Churchill's "No" to Europe: The rejec tion of European Union by Churchill's Post-War Government 1951–1952' *Historical Journal* 28 1985 pp 923–37.

**2111**  Anthony Nutting *Europe Will Not Wait* Hollis and Carter 1960. A discreet account of government attitudes towards European integration in the 1950s by a former Foreign Office minister who very much favoured movement in that direction. See also S M Kennedy 'Anglo-American Relations and Western European Economic Integration 1950–1961: Some Political Considera tions' Oxford MLitt Thesis 1984 and M J Colebrook 'Franco-British Attitudes and European Unity 1949–1961' London MSc Thesis 1964–5. Anthony Morris 'Britain and the European Community' *British Survey* 122 1959 pp 1–25 is a survey of rela tions by a supporter of entry.

**2112**  Robert J Lieber *British Politics and European Unity: Parties, Elites and Pressure Groups* University of California Press, Berkeley, California 1970. A useful study of British reactions to three phases of European negotiations; the 1956–60 attempt to set up a Free Trade Area which led to the creation of EFTA (for which see [4237–40]); and the applications to join the European Community in 1961–3 and 1966–7. See also Robert L Pfaltzgraff Jr *Britain Faces Europe* University Press 1969 and L V Boyd 'The Anglo-American Special Relationship and British-European Integration 1958–1970' University of Pennsylvania PhD Thesis 1971. The transformation of British attitudes in the 1960s is examined in Paul Sharp 'The Rise of the European Community in the Foreign Policy of British Governments 1961–1971' *Millenium: Journal of International Studies* 11 1982 pp 155–71.

**2113** Miriam Camps *Britain and European Community 1955–63* Princeton University Press, Princeton, New Jersey 1964. An exhaustive account of British participation in European negotiations from the Messina conference of 1955 to the end of Britain's first attempt to join the European Community. It remains the best account of this first attempt. Robert L Pfaltzgraff Jr *The British Common Market Decision and Beyond* Foreign Policy Research Institute, University of Pennsylvania, Philadelphia 1962 concentrates more on British attitudes during the negotiations. Nora Beloff *The General Says No: Britain's Exclusion from Europe* Penguin 1963 is useful both for the negotiations and for the reasons behind De Gaulle's veto on the British application in 1963. K Johnson 'The "National Interest" and the Foreign Policy Process: The British Decision on European Membership 1955–61' Cambridge PhD Thesis 1984 focuses on policy making. See also E Liggett 'Organisation for Negotiation: Britain's First Attempt to Enter the EEC 1961–63' Glasgow MLitt Thesis 1971–2. On Conservative attitudes at the time see Ronald Butt 'The Common Market and Conservative Party Politics 1961–1962' *Government and Opposition* 2 1967 pp 372–86. On the effect of agricultural considerations on the negotiations see Richard A Holmes 'The National Farmers' Union and the British Negotiations for Membership in the European Economic Community' *Res Publica* 5 1963 pp 276–87 and Michael Butterwick 'British Agricultural Policy and the EEC' *International Journal of Agrarian Affairs* 4 1964 pp 99–113.

**2114** Douglas Evans *While Britain Slept: The Selling of the Common Market* Gollancz 1975. A polemic anti-European review of the European issue in British politics from the first attempt to join up to the entry into Europe in 1973. The efforts of the opponents of entry in this period are assessed in S W Lennie 'An Unequal Struggle: The Anti-Common Market Lobby 1961–1973' Sheffield MPhil Thesis 1985. Public opinion on the issue is assessed in Roger Jowell and Gerald Hoinville (eds) *Britain into Europe: Public Opinion and the EEC 1961–75* Croom Helm 1976, a short study based on research conducted by Social and Community Planning Research. A good study of the Labour Party's changing attitude to the European Community in the period up to the 1975 Referendum is L J Robins *The Reluctant Party: Labour and the EEC 1961–1975* G W and A Hesketh 1979. See also A J Purves 'Scottish Labour and British Entry: Labour Movement Attitudes to the European Community at Scottish and UK Levels 1960–1977' Edinburgh MPhil Thesis 1978.

**2115** P Gerbet (ed) 'La Candidature de la Grande Bretagne aux Communautés Européenes 1967–68: Les Données du Probleme' *Revue Française de Science Politique* 18 1968 pp 861–1002. A useful collection of essays on the second British attempt to join the European Community. Cynthia W Frey 'Meaning Business: The British Application to Join the Common Market November 1966–October 1967' *Journal of Common Market Studies* 6 1983 pp 197–230 is a good analysis of the decision to apply and the shifts of opinion in the Labour party and the press. See also Kenneth Younger 'Britain and the EEC: The Changed Context for the Second Attempt' *World Today* 23 1967 pp 5–12 and H S Wallace 'The Domestic Policy Making Implications of the Labour Government's Application for Membership of the EEC 1964–70' Manchester PhD Thesis 1974–6. Uwe Kitzinger *The Second Try – Labour and the EEC* Pergamon 1968 is collections of documents illustrating changes of heart in the Labour party on the issue of European integration from 1950 to the Wilson government's application, focusing on the latter. Also of use is M van der Stoël *The British Application for Membership of the European Communities 1963–1968* Western European Union Assembly, Paris 1968, which is a collection of statements on the issue by the govern ments of Britain and the Six.

**2116** Uwe Kitzinger *Diplomacy by Persuasion: How Britain Joined the Common Market* Thames and Hudson 1973. A good study of the negotiations that led to Britain's entry in 1973. It is particularly useful for the parliamentary debates on the issue. See also P S Goodrich 'British Attitudes Towards the EEC October 1971 to February 1974' Manchester PhD Thesis 1974–6.

## (d) The European Community

The European Community should in a sense no longer be treated as a matter for foreign relations. Its influence on British life is increasingly all pervasive. The literature below therefore includes only the main reference works on the Community and other general surveys. Community law, which takes precedence over United Kingdom law, can be found in the section on the Legal System.

**2117** Michael Hopkins (ed) *European Communities Information: Its Uses and Users* Mansell 1985. A good collection on the nature and sources of European information. Another very informative guide is David Overton *Common Market Digest: An Information Guide to the European Communities* Library Association 1983. Stanley A Budd *The EEC: A Guide to the Maze* 2nd ed, Kogan Page 1987 is a good guide to information sources on the workings and policy of the Community. See also Doris Palmer *Sources of Information on the European Communities* Mansell 1979.

**2118** *European Communities Yearbook and Other European Organisations* Editions Delta, Brussels 1977–. An annual guide to the various bodies of the European Community and certain other European organizations.

A good quarterly directory to European institutions is *Vacher's European Companion: A Diplomatic, Political and Commercial Reference Book* A S Kerwill 1972–.

**2119**  *Catalogue of the Publications of the European Communi ty Institutions* Commission of the European Communities, Brus sels 1974–. Since then it has been an annual catalogue. Since 1980 it has been entitled *Publications of the European Commu nities* and published in Luxembourg. There is a parallel series of *Documents: Annual Catalogue*.

**2120**  John Jefferies *A Guide to the Official Publications of the European Communities* 2nd ed, Mansell 1981. A good guide to the various issuing bodies and the types of material they produce.

**2121**  Michael Hopkins (comp) *Policy Formation in the European Communities: A Bibliographical Guide to Community Documentation 1958–1978* Mansell 1981. This indexes and details over 600 important reports, communications and memoranda prepared by or for the European Commission. A useful finding guide is June Neilson (comp) *Reports of the European Communities 1952–1977: An Index to Authors and Chairmen* Mansell 1981.

**2122**  Ray Hudson, David Rhind and Helen Mounsey *An Atlas of EEC Affairs* Methuen 1984. A guide to its history, powers and policies and to the working of the labour market and the economy and the state of social conditions in the Community. It has maps and tables but is, despite its title, mostly text.

**2123**  *European Parliamentary Digest 1973–* New Educational Press 1974–. A annual summary of debates in the European parliament with name and subject indexes.

**2124**  *Official Handbook of the European Parliament* Dod's Parliamentary Companion 1981 and 1984. A biographical guide to the members and officers of the European parliaments elected in 1979 and 1984. It also includes material on Community institutions, such as the European Commission. Another guide, to the parliament elected in 1989, will be published in 1990.

**2125**  Ann Robinson and Caroline Bray (eds) *The Public Image of the European Parliament* Studies in European Politics 10, Policy Studies Institute 1986. An investigation of the parliament's poor public image in Britain. It looks at the power of the parliament, the experiences of a Euro-MP, the poor coverage it receives in the media and the attitudes of the parties.

**(e) Britain and the European Community Since 1973**

**2126**  F E C Gregory *Dilemmas of Government: Britain and the European Community* Robertson 1983. An excellent survey of Britain's first ten years of membership of the European Community. It includes a chronology and a useful bibliography. Other useful surveys are Roy Jenkins (ed) *Britain and the EEC* Macmillan 1982, A M El-Agraa (ed) *Britain Within the European Community* Macmillan 1983, C D Cohen (ed) *The Common Market – Ten Years After* Philip Allan 1983, William Wallace (ed) *Britain in Europe* Heinemann 1980 and K J Twitchett 'Britain and Community Europe 1973–79' *International Relations* 6 1979 pp 698–714.

**2127**  *Britain in the Community 1973–1983: The Impact of Membership* Commission of the European Communities 1982–83. The first of a series of official studies of the economic impact of membership. The others, which assess the effect of membership on the various regions of Britain are *South East England, South West England, West Midlands, East Midlands, East Anglia, Northern England, North West England, Yorkshire and Humberside, Scotland, Wales* and *Northern Ireland in Europe*. Ali M El-Agraa 'Has membership of the European Communities been a Disaster for Britain?' *Applied Economics* 16 1984 pp 299–315 looks at the effects of membership on industry using detailed statistics and defends membership on these grounds.

**2128**  H Lazer 'British Populism: The Labor Party and the Common Market Parliamentary Debate' *Political Science Quarterly* 91 1976 pp 259–77. This examines Labour party attitudes during the debate in the 1970s over whether Britain should withdraw from the Community. Jorgen S Rasmussen and J M McCormick 'The Influence of Ideology on British Labour MPs in Voting on EEC Issues' *Legislative Studies Quarterly* 10 1985 pp 203–21 analyses the influences on Labour voting on twelve contentious EEC issues in the 1974–9 parliament. The rather more positive attitude towards Europe taken in the party in the 1980s, especially after the 1983 defeat, is considered in John Grahl and Paul Teague 'The British Labour Party and the European Community' *Political Quarterly* 59 1988 pp 72–85.

**2129**  R J Dalton and R Duval 'The Political Environment and Foreign Policy Opinions: British Attitudes Towards European Integration 1972–1979' *British Journal of Political Science* 16 1986 pp 113–34. A study of public opinion.

**2130**  Paul Taylor 'The EC Crisis over the Budget and the Agricultural Policy: Britain and Its Partners in the Late 1970s and Early 1980s' *Government and Opposition* 17 1982 pp 397–413. An examination of the long-running battle over the scale of Britain's contributions to the Community Budget and over the operation of the Common Agricultural Policy in Britain.

**2131** Stephen George *The British Government and the European Community Since 1984* University Association for Contemporary European Studies Occasional Paper 4 1987. A short chronological narrative of Britain's role in the Community since the agreement on the Budget in 1984. It examines the extent to which Britain continues to be an awkward partner.

**2132** Hansard Society *The British People: Their Voice in Europe* Saxon House 1977. A study of British representation in the European parliament and British pressure group activity in Europe. The selection of candidates for the European parliament is discussed in M Holland 'Candidates for Europe – The British Experience: An Analysis of the Recruitment and Selection Processes' Exeter PhD Thesis 1982. The only study so far of participation in the European parliament is D A Lowe 'British Conservative Participation in the European Parliament 1973–1979' Birmingham MSocSc Thesis 1979–80.

**2133** For Roy Jenkins as President of the European Commission 1977–81 see [724].

(f) Anglo-French Relations

**2134** Neville Waites (ed) *Troubled Neighbours: Franco-British Relations in the Twentieth Century* Weidenfeld and Nicolson 1971. An invaluable collection of essays. Dorothy Pickles *The Uneasy Entente: French Foreign Policy and Franco-British Misunderstandings* Oxford University Press 1966 is a useful survey of relations since the war. André Guillaume 'British or French Leadership in Europe Since World War II?' *Franco-British Studies* 5 1988 pp 1–16 is a general study which is best on Franco-British relations since 1975.

**2135** André Géraud 'Rise and Fall of the Anglo-French Entente' *Foreign Affairs* 32 1954 pp 374–87. Anglo-French relations since 1904.

**2136** Anton W De Porte *De Gaulle's Foreign Policy 1944–1946* Oxford University Press 1968. A useful study of the foreign policy of De Gaulle's Provisional Government which came to an end with the General's resignation in January 1946. On Anglo-French relations in this period see John W Young 'The Foreign Office and the Departure of General De Gaulle June 1945–January 1946' *Historical Journal* 25 1982 pp 209–16. De Gaulle's resignation ended British efforts to establish a third Anglo-French force between the superpowers and led to a return to the Anglo-American alliance. This is

analysed in Sean Greenwood 'Ernest Bevin, France and "Western Union" August 1945–February 1946' *European History Quarterly* 14 1984 pp 319–38. As he points out in his thesis, 'The Origins of the Treaty of Dunkirk: The British Search for an Anglo-French Alliance 1944–47' London PhD Thesis 1982, the result was that by the time of the 1947 treaty Britain's main concern was not 'Western Union' but to restrict the Communist advance in France. See also Bert Zeeman 'Britain and the Cold War: An Alternative Approach: The Treaty of Dunkirk Example' *European History Quarterly* 16 1986 pp 343–67. On Britain's role in the political restoration in France after the war, of which this was a part see Mirjam Kölling 'Grossbritanniens Westeuropapolitik 1944–1947 und die Stabilisierung der bürgerlichen Herrschaft in Frankreich' *Jahrbuch für Geschichte* 30 1984 pp 117–47.

**2137** Alan Campbell 'Anglo–French Relations a Decade Ago (1)' *International Affairs* 58 1982 pp 237–54. An examination of the Soames affair in 1969 which marked a low point in Anglo-French relations. Poor relations in the late 1960s are also discussed in Thomas Barman 'Britain and France 1967' *International Affairs* 43 1967 pp 29–38. Alan Campbell 'Anglo-French Relations a Decade Ago: A New Assessment (2)' *International Affairs* 58 1982 pp 429–46 discusses the Anglo-French negotiations leading to the meeting between Edward Heath and President Pompidou in May 1971.

**2138** Roger Morgan 'Anglo-French Relations Today' *World Today* 27 1971 pp 285–90. See also Neville Waites 'Britain and France: Towards a Stable Relationship' *World Today* 32 1976 pp 451–8.

**2139** Dan Cook *Charles De Gaulle: A Biography* Secker and Warburg 1984. De Gaulle was the head of the French Provisional Government 1944–6 and the first President of the Fifth Republic 1958–69. See also Jean Lacouture *De Gaulle* Hutchinson 1970. His memoirs are quite revealing. *Salvation* Weidenfeld and Nicolson 1959 is the final volume of his war memoirs, covering the liberation of France and the Provisional Government. His *Memoirs of Hope: Renewal 1958–62, Endeavour 1962* Weidenfeld and Nicolson 1971 are all that he managed to write of his Presidential memoirs before his death in 1970. For De Gaulle's rather prickly views of and relations with the British and Americans see John Newhouse *De Gaulle and the Anglo-Saxons* Viking 1970. See also N P Kestinge 'General De Gaulle's Attitude towards Britain and the British' London MSc Thesis 1962 and David Thomson 'President De Gaulle and the Miséntente Cordiale' *International Journal* 23 1968 pp 211–20.

**2140** Maurice Couve de Murville *Une Politique Etrangere 1958–1969* Plon, Paris 1971. Memoirs of his time as Minister of Foreign Affairs to De Gaulle 1958–68.

## (g) Anglo-West German Relations

**2141** Karl Kaiser and Roger Morgan (eds) *Britain and West Germany: Changing Societies and the Future of Foreign Policy* Oxford University Press 1971. A good series of essays on most aspects of Anglo-German relations. Anglo-German relations over a longer time period are examined in Lothar Kettenacker, M Schlaake and H Seier (eds) *Studien zur Geschichte Englands und deutsch-britischen Beziehungen* Wilhelm Fink, München 1981. This includes, for instance, essays on Adenauer's relations with Britain. See also [2085–99].

**2142** Gustav Schmidt (ed) *Grossbritannien und Europa – Grossbritannien in Europa: Sicherheitsbelange und Wirtschaftsfragen in der britischen Europapolitik nach dem Zweiten Weltkrieg* Studienverlag Dr N Brockmeyer, Bochum 1989. A collection of articles on aspects of British policy towards Europe, particularly Germany, since 1945. Two of the articles are in English.

**2143** Donald Cameron Watt *Britain Looks to Germany: British Opinion and Policy Towards Germany Since 1945* Wolff 1965. This useful study is updated by his 'Britain and Germany: The Last Three Years' *International Journal* 23 1968 pp 560–9. See also Hans von Herwerth and Sir Christopher Steel 'Anglo-German Relations: A German View: A British View' *International Affairs* 39 1963 pp 511–32. On British policy making towards Germany see U Reusch 'Die Londoner Institutionen der britischen Deutschlandpolitik 1943–1958: Eine behördengeschichtliche Untersuchung' *Historisches Jahrbuch* 100 1980 pp 318–443.

**2144** Karl Kaiser and John Roper (eds) *British-German Defence Co-operation: Partners Within the Alliance* Jane's 1988. A good set of essays on the main plank of NATO in Europe.

**2145** Robert W Heywood 'London, Bonn, the Konigswinter Conferences and the Problems of European Integration' *Journal of Contemporary History* 10 1975 pp 131–56. A good study of Anglo-German tensions since the war, starting with the anti-British riots during the occupation that led to the setting up of the Deutsch-Englische Gesellschaft in 1949 in Konigswinter as the most significant of several attempts to improve relations. Christoph von Imhoff *Zwanzig Jahre Königswinter: Deutsch-Englisches Gespräch 1949–1969* Deutsch-Englische Gesellschaft, Düsseldorf 1969 is a history of the Königswinter conferences.

**2146** A Poengen 'Britain and West Germany Since 1973: Bilateral Relations Within a Multilateral Framework' Oxford MPhil Thesis 1985. A study of Anglo-German relations within the European Community.

**2147** M Michel 'German Rearmament as a Factor in Anglo-West German Relations 1949–1955' London PhD Thesis 1963–4. One of the key issues in West European politics in the years immediately after the war was when and if Germany would be allowed to rearm. Another study of British attitudes is J E Davies 'The Attitude of the British Labour Government Towards German Rearmament 1949–51' Wales MSc (Econ) Thesis 1971–2. On the attitude of the Labour party 1950–4 and its effect on the European Defence Community negotiations see Saul Rose 'The Labour Party and German Rearmament: A View from Transport House' *Political Quarterly* 14 1966 pp 133–44.

**2148** Geoffrey McDermott *Berlin: Success of a Mission?* Deutsch 1963. McDermott was sent to Berlin as Minister and Deputy Commandant in the British zone in 1961. He was abruptly recalled in 1962. This is his account of his mission and the scheme he proposed to try and resolve the East-West deadlock in Berlin which led to his recall.

**2149** Hans-Peter Schwarz *Adenauer: der Aufstieg 1876–1952* Deutsche Verlags-Anstalt 1986. The first part of a detailed biography of the West German Chancellor 1949–63. Paul Weymer *Konrad Adenauer* Deutsch 1957 is the authorized biography. Terence Prettie *Konrad Adenauer 1876–1967* Tom Stacey 1972 is not a good biography. Adenauer's own *Memoirs 1945–1953* Weidenfeld and Nicolson 1966 are useful on the post-war reconstruction of West Germany.

## (h) Other

For British involvement in the Greek civil war of the late 1940s see [2440–1A].

**2150** Donald Bittner 'The British Occupation of Iceland 1940–6' *Army Quarterly* 103 1972 pp 81–90. See also [4500].

**2150A** J Eiren *Anglo-Dutch Relations and European Unity 1940–1978* University of Hull 1980. A short paper.

**2151** W Hale and A I Bagis (eds) *Four Centuries of Turco-British Relations: Studies in Diplomatic, Economic and Cultural Affairs* Eothen Press 1984. This includes two essays on Anglo-Turkish relations and trade since the 1920s.

## (11) Britain and the Far East

**2152** J E Williams 'Britain's Role in Southern Asia 1945–1954' Wales PhD Thesis 1973–4. A study from the end of the war to the Geneva conference of 1954 on Indo-China at which Eden played a leading role in ensuring a successful outcome.

### (a) Anglo-Chinese Relations

**2153** Robert Boardman *Britain and the People's Republic of China 1949–1974* Macmillan 1976. A good general account which focuses on the tensions during the early years after the Communist victory in the Chinese civil war in 1949. It is also useful on the role of Hong Kong in the relationship as is D Evan Luard *Britain and China* Chatto and Windus 1962, a study of Anglo-Chinese relations since 1945. J P Jain *China in World Politics: A Study of Sino-British Relations 1949–1975* Robertson 1976 whilst useful has some errors and weaknesses.

**2154** Aron Shai *Britain and China 1941–47: Imperial Momentum* Macmillan 1984. A somewhat disappointing study of Britain's loss of influence in China during and after the war and the anti-British feeling at the time in both the Kuomintang and the Communist party. One of the most important enclaves of Western, not least British, influence in China in this period before the 1949 revolution was Shanghai. A good account of the end of this regime in Shanghai is Noel Barber *The Fall of Shanghai: The Communist Takeover in 1949* Macmillan 1979.

**2155** Brian Porter *Britain and the Rise of Communist China: A Study of British Attitudes 1945–1954* Oxford University Press 1967. A useful study of British attitudes during a time of Anglo-Chinese tension over issues such as the Korean war. For economic relations in this immediate post-war period see G E Mitchell 'China and Britain: Their Commercial and Industrial Relations' *Journal of the Royal Central Asian Society* 49 1952 pp 246–58.

**2156** Edwin W Martin *Divided Counsel: The Anglo-American Response to Communist Victory in China* University of Kentucky Press, Lexington, Kentucky 1986. A scholarly, well researched account which goes up to the 1954 Geneva conference, though it concentrates on the period 1949–51. It supplies a good explanation of the very different British and American responses. Another useful study of these differences is Ritchie Ovendale 'Britain, the United States and the Recognition of Communist China' *Historical Journal* 26 1983 pp 139–58. The importance of considerations of trade and Hong Kong in the British decision to recognise Communist China in January 1950 are analysed in David C Wolf 'To Secure a Convenience: Britain Recognises China 1950' *Journal of Contemporary History* 18 1950 pp 299–326. See also A D Kopkind 'Moral and Political Considerations in the Debate in Britain on Recognition of the Peking Government' London MSc (Econ) Thesis 1960–1.

### (b) Anglo-Japanese Relations

**2157** Ian Nish (ed) *Anglo-Japanese Alienation 1919–52: Papers of the Anglo-Japanese Conference on the History of the Second World War* Cambridge University Press 1982. Parallel chapters, one by a British historian and one by a Japanese, present a commentary on events before, during and after the Second World War.

**2158** Roger Buckley *Occupation Diplomacy: Britain, the United States and Japan 1945–1952* Cambridge University Press 1982. The first study to bring out the British role in the occupation of Japan after the war and the extent of Anglo-American co-operation. It also comments on Britain's already growing concern about Japanese economic strength. Another concern was the speedy restoration of Japanese sovereignty, largely to prevent predominant American influence. Britain's lack of success in this endeavour is analysed in his 'Joining the Club: The Japanese Question and Anglo-American Peace Diplomacy 1950–1951' *Modern Asian Studies* 19 1985 pp 299–319. The Commonwealth role in the occupation is examined in Grant Goodman *et al The British Commonwealth and the Occupation of Japan* Suntory Toyota International Centre for Economics and Related Disciplines, London School of Economics, University of London 1983.

**2159** Arnold C Brackman *The Other Nuremberg: The Untold Story of the Tokyo War Crimes Trials* Collins 1989. See also Richard Minear *Victors' Justice: The Tokyo War Crimes Trials* Princeton University Press, Princeton, New Jersey 1971. The transcripts of the trials are annotated and edited in R John Pritchard and Sonia Zaide (eds) *The Tokyo War Crimes Trial* 3v, Garland 1987.

### (c) Indo-China

**2160** *Documents Relating to British Involvement in the Indo-China Conflict 1945–1965* Cmnd 2834, *Parliamentary Papers* xiv 1965–66. A good collection of documentary extracts with a useful historical introduction.

**2161** J M Rainsbury 'Parliamentary Labour Party Attitudes Towards and Policies in Relation to the Vietnam

Conflict 1945–75' Hull MPhil Thesis 1981. A useful study up to the fall of Saigon in 1975.

**2162** George Rosie *The British in Vietnam: How the Twenty-Five Year War Began* Panther 1970. A critical study of the British role in the reinstatement of French rule in 1945–6 and in the war against Communist guerrillas which had already begun. Peter M Dunn *The First Vietnam War* Christopher Hurst 1985 is an attempt to restore the reputation of General Gracey, the British commander in Vietnam.

**2163** Andrew J Rotter 'The Triangular Path to Vietnam: The United States, Great Britain and Southeast Asia 1945–1950' *International History Review* 6 1984 pp 404–23. Britain's success in drawing the Americans into shoring up the French in Indo-China in this period was seen as a way of protecting Malaya. A D Griffiths 'Britain, the United States and French Indo-China 1946–1954' Manchester MPhil Thesis 1984 is a good study of the changes and differences in Anglo-American attitudes to Indo-China and the threat of Asiatic Communism in this period. See also E V Roberts 'The British Attitude Towards Indo-China 1945–1954' Wales MSc (Econ) Thesis 1969–70.

**2164** James Cable *The Geneva Conference of 1954 on Indo-China* Macmillan 1986. An in-depth account of Britain's last major act of great power-broking and its consequences by a member of the British delegation to the conference. The conference extricated France and successfully prevented the escalation of conflict, even if it did not bring lasting peace to the region.

**2165** Anita Inder Singh 'Containment Through Diplomacy: Britain, India and the Cold War in Indo-China 1954–56' in Ian Nish (ed) *South Asia in International Affairs 1947–56* Suntory Toyota International Centre for Economics and Related Disciplines, London School of Economics, University of London 1987 pp 1–17. This is as much about Britain's over-estimation of India's diplomatic influence as about British policy in Indo-China after Geneva.

**2166** Craig Wilson 'Rhetoric, Reality and Dissent: The Vietnam Policy of the British Labour Government 1964–1970' *Social Science Journal* 23 1986 pp 17–31. This focuses on the split in the Labour Party over the government's non-belligerent support for the Americans in the Vietnam War.

(d) Indonesia

**2167** C W Squire 'Britain and the Transfer of Power in Indonesia 1945–1946' London PhD Thesis 1979. A study of the Anglo-Indian occupation of Indonesia after

the war and the restoration of the Dutch colonial power. S H Drummond 'Britain's Involvement in Indonesia 1945–63' Southampton PhD Thesis 1979 looks at Anglo-Indonesian relations from the end of the war to the start of the Indonesian Confrontation with Malaysia.

(e) Korea

**2168** Chong-Wha Chung and James E Hoare (eds) *Korean-British Relations: Yesterday, Today and Tomorrow* Korean-British Society 1984. Essays celebrating a hundred years of Anglo-Korean relations. See also James E Hoare, Ian Nish and Roger Bullen *Aspects of Anglo-Korean Relations* Suntory Toyota International Centre for Economics and Related Disciplines, London School of Economics, University of London 1984.

### (12) Latin America

(a) General

**2169** Victor Bulmer-Thomas (ed) *Britain and Latin America* Cambridge University Press 1989. Britain was a major investor in and a dominant trading partner of Latin America down to the First World War. The history of the atrophy of such links since and the state of contemporary diplomatic, economic and cultural relations between Britain and Latin America are surveyed in this volume. It also includes an essay examining Britain's attitude towards the drug traffic from South America.

(b) Anglo-Argentine Relations

**2170** P Calvert 'British Relations with Southern Cone States' in Michael A Morris (ed) *Great Power Relations in Argentina, Chile and Antarctica* Macmillan 1988.

**2171** Guillermo A Makin 'Argentine Approaches to the Falklands/Malvinas: Was the Resort to Violence Foreseeable?' *International Affairs* 59 1983 pp 391–404. A useful examination of post-war Anglo-Argentine relations.

**2172** Peter J Beck 'The Anglo-Argentine Dispute over Title to the Falkland Islands: Changing British Perceptions on Sovereignty' *Millenium: Journal of International Studies* 12 1983 pp 6–24. See also his 'Britain, Argentina and Antarctica' *History Today* 37 1987 pp 16–23. The Second World War highlighted the strategic value of the South Atlantic and led to increased conflict between Britain, Argentina and Chile over claims to the Falklands and Antarctic territories. On Anglo-Argentine relations during and immediately after the war see N St

J F Bowen 'Britain, Argentina and the United States 1938–1946: Conflict and Collaboration Within the Atlantic Triangle' Cambridge PhD Thesis 1976.

**2173**   Vincenza R Caracciolo 'Le Falkland-Malvine Alle Nazioni Unite (1960–1983)' *Revista di Studi Politici Internazionali* 51 1984 pp 263–91. This considers the UN's handling of the conflicting claims to the islands.

**2174**   For the Falklands War see [2415–35].

(c) Other

**2175**   John W Young 'Great Britain's Latin American Dilemma: The Foreign Office and the Overthrow of "Communist" Guatemala' *International History Review* 8 1986 pp 573–92. This examines Britain's strong opposition to the CIA overthrow of President Arbenz of Guatemala in 1954.

# 4 DEFENCE

## A. GENERAL

### (1) General Works

**2176** *RUSI and Brassey's Defence Yearbook* Royal United Services Institute/Brassey's 1974–. An annual continuation of a serial publication that first appeared in 1886 as *Brassey's Naval and Shipping Manual*. It has three parts. One is an international strategic review, one an analysis of weapons development during the past year and the last looks at recent literature and includes a chronology.

**2177** *Statement on the Defence Estimates* HMSO 1947/48–. An annual command paper on the cost of Britain's armed forces. The estimates previously appeared separately for each of the three services, and indeed continued to appear as such as Command Papers until 1959–60.

**2178** *Jane's Defence Weekly* Jane's Publishing 1980–. An international guide. Until 1984 it was known as *Jane's Defence Review*.

**2179** Frank Gregory, Mark Imber and John Simpson (eds) *Perspectives upon British Defence Policy 1945–1970* Department of Adult Education, University of Southampton 1980. A good collection of essays on the end of the imperial role, the evolution of defence policy and the economic constraints within which it operates, Polaris and weapons procurement. Another useful collection of essays is John Baylis (ed) *British Defence Policy in a Changing World* Croom Helm 1977. Another collection of essays with a more specialized focus is Margaret Blunden and Owen Greene (ed) *Science and Mythology in the Making of Defence Policy* Brassey's 1989. This includes work on subjects such as the Maginox reactor programme or the concept of nuclear winter.

**2180** Ian Beckett and John Gooch (eds) *Politicians and Defence: Studies in the Formation of British Defence Policy 1845–1970* Manchester University Press 1981. The only relevant essays in this collection are on Duncan Sandys, Defence Secretary 1957–9 and Denis Healey,

Defence Secretary 1964–70. There are also useful chronological appendices and bio-bibliographical information on the various ministers discussed.

**2181** Michael Dockrill *British Defence Policy Since 1945* Blackwell 1989. A useful short history with good appendices and chronology. Some of the other general histories reflect very much, even in their titles, the sense of imperial retreat. See Christopher J Bartlett *The Long Retreat: A Short History of British Defence Policy 1945–1970* Macmillan 1972 and L W Martin *British Defence Policy: The Long Recessional* Adelphi Papers 61, International Institute for Strategic Studies, 1969. R N Rosecrance *Defence of the Realm: British Strategy in the Nuclear Epoch* Columbia University Press, New York 1968 remains a well regarded study of post-war British defence policy. See also J Sabine *British Defence Policy* Allen and Unwin 1969 and William P Snyder *The Politics of British Defence Policy 1945–62* Benn 1965 and G M Dillon 'Britain' in G M Dillon (ed) *Defence Policy Making: A Comparative Analysis* Leicester University Press 1988 pp 9–52.

**2182** Michael Chichester and John Wilkinson *The Uncertain Ally: British Defence Policy 1950–90* Gower 1982. A critical review of policy and options for the future given Britain's limited room for manoeuvre which reappraises the view that Britain has been in continuous decline since 1945. David Hazel and Phil Williams *The British Defence Effort: Foundations and Alternatives* Aberdeen Studies in Defence Economics, University of Aberdeen 1977 is a rather sketchy study of the tensions in British defence policy between interdependence on its allies and independence.

**2183** Malcolm Chalmers *The Cost of Britain's Defence* School of Peace Studies 10, University of Bradford 1983. An analysis of the costs of and spending on defence since 1945.

**2184** John Baylis '"Greenwoodery" and British Defence Policy' *International Affairs* 62 1986 pp 443–57. A discussion of a key historiographical debate. There are two schools of thought on British defence policy since 1945. Some like Baylis hold that reductions have been dictated by economic and financial pressures forcing hasty and piecemeal cutbacks. Others follow David Greenwood in arguing that policy has been as a rational adjustment to changing conditions and needs and that in the process Britain has sensibly reduced her commitments whilst actually improving her fire power.

**2185** Leonard Beaton 'Imperial Defence Without the Empire' *International Journal* 23 1968 pp 531–40. Part of a series of articles examining Britain's post-war defence policy in the light of the 1968 announcement of the withdrawal from East of Suez. The others are L W Martin 'British Maritime Policy in Transition' pp 541–50, T B Millar 'Great Britain's Long Recessional: An Australian View' pp 551–9 and F S Northedge 'Britain's Future in World Affairs' pp 600–10.

**2186** Roy Sherwood *Superpower Britain* Willingham Press 1989. This short work examines British power at the end of the Second World War in the context of British technology, which it argues was the equal of or better than that of either the Americans or the Russians. It also traces Britain's relative technological decline.

**2187** Julian Lewis *Changing Direction: British Military Planning for Post-War Strategic Defence 1942–1947* Sherwood Press 1988. This charts the gradual shift from planning against a resurgence of German or Japanese militarism to facing the Russian threat. It also examines the revolution in strategic thinking brought about by atomic and biological weapons. A key strategic assumption of this period was that there would be no war for ten years. Eric J Grove 'The Post-War "Ten Year Rule" – Myth or Reality' *Journal of the Royal United Services Institute for Defence Studies* 129 1984 pp 48–53 traces the origins of this assumption back to economic necessity.

**2188** Michael Dockrill and John W Young (eds) *British Security Policy 1945–56* Macmillan 1988. A good collection of essays each of which focuses on a particular event or theme of this period, which culminated the Suez operation late in 1956. It thus covers in great depth most of the issues in defence policy in these years. The development of regional defence pacts in this period, such as the Baghdad Pact or SEATO, as a response to Britain's declining ability to defend the empire, and the role of the Commonwealth in this strategy are well examined in the short study, W C B Tunstall *The Commonwealth and Regional Defence* Athlone Press 1959. On SEATO and the problems of imperial strategy in South Asia see Richard Aldrich and Michael Coleman 'Britain and the Strategic Air Offensive Against the Soviet Union: The Question of South Asian Air Bases' *History* 74 1989 pp 400–26. The problems of imperial defence as perceived in the 1950s are also surveyed in A J Stockwell 'Counter-insurgency and Colonial Defence' in Tony Gorst, Lewis Johnman and W Scott Lucas (eds) *Postwar Britain*

*1945–64: Themes and Perspectives* Pinter 1989 pp 135–54. On British defence policy in this period see also H A de Weerd 'Britain's Changing Military Policy' *Foreign Affairs* 34 1955 pp 102–16. On security on the Northern flank of Europe see K E Eriksen 'Great Britain and the Problem of Bases in the Nordic Area 1945–1947' *Scandinavian Journal of History* 7 1982 pp 135–63.

**2189** *Defence: Outline of Future Policy* Cmnd 124, *Parliamentary Papers* xxiii 1956–57. The Sandys White Paper which heralded a major shift of emphasis in Britain's defence policy. In the 1950s there were concerns about the size of the defence budget and its detrimental effect on British industry. By abolishing national service and concentrating on a nuclear deterrent Sandys responded to these economic constraints whilst maintaining Britain's great power status. Martin Navias (ed) 'Defence Turning Point: The Sandys White Paper' *Contemporary Record* 2/4 1988 pp 30–2 is the edited transcript of a witness seminar on the drafting of the White Paper. For a contemporary comment see Noble Frankland 'Britain's Changing Strategic Position' *International Affairs* 33 1957 pp 416–26.

**2190** David Greenwood and David Hazel *The Evolution of Britain's Defence Priorities 1957–76* Aberdeen Studies in Defence Economics 9, University of Aberdeen 1977. A study which focuses on manpower and budgeting and the gradual decline in Britain's defence commitments.

**2191** C Healey 'Labour and Defence 1964–1979: The Struggle for Influence' Salford MSc Thesis 1983. This is as much an attempt to explore the background to the party's internal struggles over defence in the 1980s as a study of the defence policies of the 1964–70 and 1974–79 Labour governments. Mary Kaldor, Dan Smith and Steve Vines (ed) *Democratic Socialism and the Cost of Defence: The Report and Papers of the Labour Party Defence Study Group* Croom Helm 1979 is a very detailed party report and policy document.

**2192** Michael Chichester and John Wilkinson *British Defence: A Blueprint for Reform* Brassey's 1987. A short, critical review of British defence policy since the 1966 Defence Review with recommendations. The 1966 Review, which reduced the carrier force and foreshadowed the withdrawal from East of Suez, is critically discussed by senior retired officers from each service in Sir Peter Gretton, Lord Bourne and Sir Ralph Cochrane 'The Defence White Paper 1966' *Journal of the Royal United Services Institute for Defence Studies* 111 1966 pp 117–23.

**2193** Roy Mason 'Britain's Security Interests' *Survival* 17 1975 pp 217–22. Reflections in the wake of the 1974 Defence Review by the then Defence Secretary.

See also David Greenwood 'The 1974 Defense Review in Perspective' *Survival* 17 1975 pp 223–9.

**2194** E P Thompson *et al Britain and the Bomb: The New Statesman Papers on Destruction and Disarmament* New Statesman 1980. A collections of articles – mostly critical and anti-nuclear in tone – on defence planning, civil defence and Britain's strike capacity.

**2195** David Capitanchik *The Changing Attitude to Defence in Britain* Centrepiece, University of Aberdeen 1982. A useful study of changing public attitudes.

**2196** Dan Smith *The Defence of the Realm in the 1980s* Croom Helm 1980. This discusses policy and problems in the 1970s and outlines future options. The prospects for British defence in the 1980s are discussed in John Baylis (ed) *Alternative Approaches to British Defence Policy* Macmillan 1983 and John Roper (ed) *The Future of British Defence Policy* Gower 1985. John Baylis *British Defence Policy: Striking the Right Balance* Macmillan 1989 contains a wealth of information on British defence policy and its objectives in the 1980s. Britain's strategic problems and interests are set in a global context in Alun Gwynne-Jones, Lord Chalfont *Defence of the Realm* Collins 1987.

**2197** *Statement on the Defence Estimates 1981* 2v, Cmnd 8212, *Parliamentary Papers* 1980–81. The 1981 Defence Review which cut the surface fleet and led to the closure of Chatham and Gibraltar naval dockyards whilst increasing the number of nuclear-powered submarines and Nimrod patrol aircraft. See also the supplementary *The United Kingdom Defence Programme: The Way Forward* Cmnd 8288, *Parliamentary Papers* 1980–81. An aspect of this Review, the decision to purchase Trident missiles to replace Polaris as Britain's nuclear deterrent is discussed by the then Defence Secretary in John Nott 'Decision to Modernise UK's Nuclear Contribution to NATO Strengthens Deterrence' *Atlantic Community Quarterly* 19 1981 pp 339–45. David Greenwood *Reshaping Britain's Defences: An Evaluation of Mr Nott's Way Forward for the United Kingdom* Aberdeen Studies in Defence Economics 19, University of Aberdeen 1981 is a broadly favourable assessment of the Review. Some of the assumptions of the Review are reassessed in the light of the experience of the Falklands War in John Nott *The Falklands Campaign: The Lessons* Cmnd 8758, *Parliamentary Papers* 1982–83. On the implications of the Falklands for defence policy see also Bruce George and Michael Coughlin 'British Defence Policy After the Falklands' *Survival* 24 1982 pp 201–10.

**2198** Dan Smith 'The Political Economy of British Defence Policy' in Martin Shaw (ed) *War, State and Society* Macmillan 1984 pp 194–216. Defence was one of the main planks in the manifesto on which the Con-

servatives were elected in 1979. This analyses the extent to which they have failed to fulfil their objectives. See also S A D'Albertanson 'The Management of British Defence Policy Since 1979' Warwick MA Thesis 1985.

**2199** Trevor Taylor 'Britain's Response to the Strategic Defence Initiative' *International Affairs* 62 1986 pp 217–30. A study of the initial British response to the American proposal of a novel, technically complex and very expensive system of nuclear defence.

## (2) The Organization of Defence

See also the literature on the Ministry of Defence in [417].

**2200** Franklyn A Johnson *Defence by Committee: The British Committee of Imperial Defence 1885–1959* Oxford University Press 1960. A useful history. The last two chapters cover the post-war period.

**2201** John Gooch 'The Chiefs of Staff and the Higher Organisation for Defence in Britain 1904–1984' *Naval War College Review* 39 1986 pp 53–65. A history from the establishment of the Chiefs of Staff in 1904 to the 1984 proposals to remove from them considerable powers.

**2202** Michael D Hobkirk *The Politics of Defence Budgeting: A Study of Organisation and Resource Allocation in the UK and USA* Macmillan 1984. A study which concentrates on the USA.

**2203** Lawrence Freedman *Arms Production in the United Kingdom: Problems and Prospects* Royal Institute of International Affairs 1978. On British arms manufacturers see also J O G Paton *The British Defence Industry* Jordan 1981. A good short contemporary study is Rae Angus *The Organisation of Defence Procurement and Production in the United Kingdom* Aberdeen Studies in Defence Economics 13, University of Aberdeen 1979. On government involvement in defence production during and after the Second World War see P A Winston 'The British Government and Defence Production 1943–50' Cambridge PhD Thesis 1982.

**2204** Frederic S Pearson 'The Question of Control in British Defence Sales Policy' *International Affairs* 59 1983 pp 212–38. A good survey of Britain's international arms business in the 1970s and 1980s. It concludes that there is not much government control of arms sales.

## (3) Civil/Military Relations

See also the literature on the Ministry of Defence in [417].

**2205** John Sweetman (ed) *Sword and Mace: Twentieth Century Civil-Military Relations in Britain* Brassey's 1986. A collection of essays reflecting on aspects such as public opinion and relations with local authorities.

**2206** David Greenwood and John Short *Military Installations and Local Economies: A Case Study: The Moray Air Stations* Aberdeen Studies in Defence Economics 4, University of Aberdeen 1973. A study of the impact of military bases on the local economy. See also John Short, Timothy Stone and David Greenwood *Military Installations and Local Economies: A Case Study: The Clyde Submarine Base* Aberdeen Studies in Defence Economics 5, University of Aberdeen 1974.

## (4) Anglo-American Defence Relations

For Anglo-West German Defence Relations see the section on Anglo-West German Relations.

**2207** John Baylis *Anglo-American Defence Relations 1939–1984* 2nd ed, Macmillan 1984. Defence relations have been one of the most important and fruitful aspects of the post-war 'Special Relationship'. This is an excellent history of Anglo-American defence co-operation. The successful restoration of good defence relations in 1957 in the wake of Suez is examined in G Wyn Rees 'Anglo-American Defence Co-operation' in Tony Gorst, Lewis Johnman and W Scott Lucas (eds) *Postwar Britain 1945–64: Themes and Perspectives* Pinter 1989 pp 203–20.

**2208** Simon Duke *US Defence Bases in the United Kingdom: A Matter for Joint Decision?* Macmillan 1987. A historical study from the arrival of the US Air Force in 1948 to the deployment of Cruise missiles in the 1980s, concentrating on the period 1948–54. It argues that the matter for joint decision formula thrashed out then has subsequently been seriously undermined. On American bases in Britain see also R Jackson *Strike Force: The USAF in Britain Since 1948* Robson 1986.

## (5) The North Atlantic Treaty Organization

**2209** *NATO Facts and Figures* NATO Information Services 1962–. An irregularly published guide to NATO, containing a chronology, statistics and information on its evolution, structure and activities.

**2210** Colin Gordon *The Atlantic Alliance: A Bibliography* Pinter 1978. An unannotated classified bibliography of some 3,000 items arranged in chronological sections. Its value is greatly reduced by the lack of an index. Augustus Norton, Robert A Friedlander, Martin H Greenberg and Donald S Rowe *NATO: A Bibliography and Resource Guide* Garland 1985 is fuller but concentrates much more on American material. It too is unannotated. See also Conference on Atlantic Community, Bruges *The Atlantic Community: An Introductory Bibliography* 2v, Sythoff, Bruges 1962 and *North Atlantic Treaty Organisation: Bibliography* NATO-OTAN 1964.

**2211** William Park *Defending the West: A History of NATO* Wheatsheaf 1986. A history which concentrates on the nuclear issue. It is good on this but his account otherwise suffers from the lack of a political context. On Britain's role in NATO see H de Weerd *British Defence Policy and NATO* Rand 1964. The development of NATO and the issues facing it in the late 1980s are assessed in James R Golden, Daniel J Kaufman, Asa A Clark IV and David H Petraeus (eds) *Nato at Forty: Change, Continuity and Prospects* Westview Press 1989.

**2212** Escott Reid *Time of Fear and Hope: The Making of the North Atlantic Treaty 1947–1949* McClelland and Stewart, Toronto 1977. A useful account of the background to NATO from the Anglo-French Treaty of Dunkirk in 1947. Sir Nicholas Henderson *The Birth of NATO* Weidenfeld and Nicolson 1982 is an account by a member of the seven power working party which drafted the Treaty of the months of diplomatic and political activity which went into the creation of NATO in 1949. Nikolaj Petersen 'Who Pulled Whom and How Much? Britain, the United States and the Making of the North Atlantic Treaty' *Millenium: Journal of International Studies* 11 1982 pp 93–114 is sceptical on the amount of British influence in the creation of NATO. The secret negotiations in March 1948 in Washington between Britain, Canada and the United States which can be seen as a precursor of NATO are examined in Cees Wiebes and Bert Zeeman 'The Pentagon Negotiations March 1948: The Launching of the North Atlantic Treaty' *International Affairs* 59 1983 pp 351–64. See also W M Dobell 'Great Britain and the Search for Security from the Treaty of Dunkirk to the North Atlantic Treaty Organisation' Oxford BLitt Thesis 1956–7. Developments in the wake of another precursor of NATO, the Brussels Pact of 1948, are examined in J N Lane 'Britain and the Brussels Pact 1948–50' Oxford MPhil Thesis 1984 and N C Pickett 'The Search for Western Security: The Creation and Evolution of the North Atlantic Treaty Organisation 1948–1951' Oxford MPhil Thesis 1983.

**2213** Peter Foot *Defence Burden-Sharing in the Atlantic Community 1945–54* Aberdeen Studies in Defence Economics 20, University of Aberdeen 1981. A useful study of differences over paying for the burden of defence between Europeans and Americans in the immediate post-war period in the context of the differences which occurred over the same issue in the 1970s.

**2214** John Baylis 'Britain, the Brussels Pact and the Continental Commitment' *International Affairs* 60 1984 pp 615–29. Another aspect of the post-war British commitment to maintain troops on the European continent is examined in T A Imobighe 'Wartime Influences Affecting Britain's Attitude to a Post-War Continental Commitment' Wales PhD Thesis 1976.

**2215** H Turner 'Britain, the United States and Scandinavian Security Problems 1945–1949' Aberdeen PhD Thesis 1982. A study of Anglo-American attitudes towards Scandinavia in the making of NATO and of why Denmark and Norway but not Sweden joined the organization.

**2216** Hastings Lionel Ismay, Lord Ismay *NATO: The First Five Years 1949–1954* NATO 1954. An assessment by the first Secretary-General, with useful supporting statistics and appendices.

**2217** Robert S Jordan *The NATO International Staff/Secretariat 1952–1957: A Study of International Administration* Oxford University Press 1967. An examination of the development of the Secretariat under Lord Ismay in 1952–57. For Ismay see also [2321].

**2218** Dan Smith *Pressure: How America Runs NATO* Bloomsbury 1989. This is also useful on Anglo-American relations in the 1980s.

### (6) Nuclear Weapons

**2219** John Simpson *The Independent Nuclear State: The United States, Britain and the Military Atom* 2nd ed, Macmillan 1986. A good chronological account of British nuclear defence. It has good appendices. The nuclear special relationship between Britain and America is an important aspect of any history of British nuclear defence. It is well covered in Andrew J Pierre *Nuclear Politics: The British Experience with an Independent Strategic Force 1939–1970* Oxford University Press 1972. Lawrence Freedman *Britain and Nuclear Weapons* Macmillan 1980 is a good account of decision making since the acquisition of the Polaris missiles in the early 1960s. See also his *The Evolution of Nuclear Strategy* Macmillan 1981, which includes a detailed bibliography. Another good study from Polaris up to the decision to buy Trident and allow the siting of American cruise missiles in Britain is G M Dillon *Dependence and Deterrence: Success and Civility in the Anglo-American Special Nuclear Relationship 1962–1982* Gower 1983. The earlier and rather more turbulent period of Anglo-American nuclear diplomacy is well covered in T Botti *The Long Wait: The Forging of the Anglo-American Nuclear Alliance 1945–1958* Greenwood 1987. The title refers to the long wait the British had until the lifting of the provisions of the MacMahon Act and the restoration of the closeness and the sharing of technology that had characterized the wartime alliance. On nuclear decision making see also Scilla McLean 'Britain' in Scilla McLean (ed) *How Nuclear Weapon Decisions Are Made* Macmillan 1986 pp 85–153. See also A J R Groom *British Thinking About Nuclear Weapons* Pinter 1974. The moral dilemmas and objectives in the British possession of nuclear weapons are examined in Roger Ruston *A Say in the End of the World: Morals and British Nuclear Weapons Policy 1941–1987* Oxford University Press 1989. A Russian perspective is presented in V Trukhaerovsky *British Nuclear Policy* Nauka, Moscow 1988.

**2220** Margaret Gowing *Independence and Deterrents: Britain and Atomic Energy 1945–1952* 2v, Macmillan 1974. A excellent official history of the origins of both the British atomic weapons programme and of atomic energy. Ian Clark and Nicholas J Wheeler *The British Origins of Nuclear Strategy 1945–1955* Clarendon 1989 analyses the development of British strategy in this period. The scientific and strategic background to Britain's deterrent is also discussed in Alfred Goldberg 'The Atomic Origins of the British Nuclear Deterrent' *International Affairs* 40 1964 pp 409–29, Alfred Goldberg 'The Military Origins of the British Nuclear Deterrent' *International Affairs* 40 1964 pp 600–18 and Richard Gott 'The Evolution of the Independent British Nuclear Deterrent' *International Affairs* 39 1963 pp 238–52. See also H D Graves 'British Atomic Weapons Development and the Labour Governments 1945–51' Oxford BLitt Thesis 1970–1 and K Hayward 'The British Nuclear Weapons Programme 1945–7' Manchester MA (Econ) Thesis 1971–2.

**2221** James L Gormly 'The Washington Declaration and the "Poor Relation": Anglo-American Atomic Diplomacy 1945–46' *Diplomatic History* 8 1984 pp 125–43. This period saw the end of the wartime atomic relationship between the two powers. The American McMahon Act in 1946 made the passage of classified atomic information to any foreign power, including Britain, illegal and thus deprived Britain of the atomic partnership she felt to be her due. The frustrations that ensued for the British, keen to restore the nuclear relationship, up to their decision to build an independent hydrogen bomb in 1954 are traced in N J Wheeler 'British Nuclear Weapons and Anglo-American Relations 1945–54' *International Affairs* 62 1985–86 pp

71–86 and Francis Duncan 'Atomic Energy and Anglo-American Relations 1946–54' *Orbis* 12 1969 pp 1188–1203.

**2222** *The Report of the Royal Commission into British Nuclear Tests in Australia* 2v, Australian Government Publishing Service, Canberra 1985. The Australian government at the same time issued John L Symonds *A History of British Nuclear Tests in Australia* Australian Government Publishing Service, Canberra 1985. This is an extensive study with a large bibliography. See also his *British Atomic Tests in Australia – Chronology of Events 1950–1968* Australian Government Publishing Service, Canberra 1984. Lorna Arnold *A Very Special Relationship: British Atomic Weapon Trials in Australia* HMSO 1987 is a good study of the trials carried out in the 1950s in the context of Anglo-Australian relations. See also Denys Blakeway and Sue Lloyd-Roberts *Fields of Thunder: Testing Britain's Bomb* Allen and Unwin 1985. The handling of publicity concerning the tests is discussed in Robert Milliken *No Conceivable Injury: The Story of Britain and Australia's Nuclear Cover-Up* Penguin 1986. On access to the tests see also Tim Sharratt 'A Political Inconvenience: Australian Scientists at the British Atomic Weapons Tests 1952–53' *Historical Records of Australian Science* 6 1985 pp 137–52. On the original series of atomic bomb tests on the Monte Bello islands see Peter Bird *Operation Hurricane: A Personal Account of the British Nuclear Tests at Monte Bello 1952* Square One 1987. Wilfrid E Oulton *Christmas Island Cracker: An Account of the Planning and Execution of British Thermo-Nuclear Bomb Tests 1957* Thomas Harmsworth 1987 is a good account of Operation Grapple, the exploding of Britain's first hydrogen bomb in May 1957. Because of the sketchy nature of the records it necessarily relies heavily on oral accounts and his own memories. See also K Glubbard and M Simmons *Operation Grapple: Testing Britain's First H-Bomb* Ian Allan 1985. The effect of these tests in the 1950s and 1960s on UK government personnel is examined in Joan Smith *Cloud of Deceit: The Deadly Legacy of Britain's Atomic Bomb* Faber 1985.

**2223** Stewart Menaul *Countdown: Britain's Strategic Nuclear Forces* Hale 1980. On the V Force bombers which were the backbone of Britain's deterrent from 1958 until they were gradually replaced by Polaris in the 1960s see Andrew Brookes *V-Force: The History of Britain's Airborne Deterrent* Jane's 1982. On this see also R Carey 'The Rise and Demise of the British Airborne Strategic Nuclear Deterrent' Wales MA Thesis 1970–1. Also worth consulting are Neville Brown 'Britain's Strategic Weapons I: The Manned Bomber' *World Today* 20 1964 pp 293–8 and 'Britain's Strategic Weapons II: The Polaris A-3' *World Today* 20 1964 pp 358–64.

**2224** Leon D Epstein 'Britain and the H-Bomb 1955–1958' *Review of Politics* 21 1959 pp 511–29. A study of nuclear politics and policy making from the decision to acquire the H-bomb to the advent of the Campaign for Nuclear Disarmament.

**2225** Peter Nailor *The Nassau Connection* HMSO 1988. An official history of the British acquisition of the Polaris ballistic missile system. The background to the Polaris and the delivery of the first submarines from which the missiles are launched is discussed in I J Galantin 'The Resolution of Polaris' *United States Naval Institute Proceedings* 111 1985 pp 80–8. See also Sir I L M McGeoch 'The British Polaris Project: A Study of the British Naval Ballistic Missile System BNBMS: Its Origins, Procurement and Effect' Edinburgh MPhil Thesis 1975. The state of Britain's nuclear defence in the wake of Macmillan's success in negotiating the British acquisition of Polaris is discussed in Anthony Hartley 'The British Bomb' *Survival* 6 1964 pp 170–81.

**2226** David Greenwood *The Trident Programme* Aberdeen Studies in Defence Economics 22, University of Aberdeen 1982. A critical study of the decision announced in 1980 to replace Polaris with Trident in the context of nuclear decision making since 1962. A more favourable interpretation, placing it in historical and strategic context, is Peter Malone *The British Nuclear Deterrent* Croom Helm 1984. Another useful study of the decision is C J McInnes 'The British Decision to Replace her Polaris Nuclear Deterrent' Wales PhD Thesis 1985. See also Roger Williams 'British Scientists and the Bomb: The Decisions of 1980' *Government and Opposition* 16 1981 pp 267–92 and Hew Strachan 'Britain's Deterrent' *Political Quarterly* 51 1980 pp 424–40.

**2227** Gary Hartcup *Cockcroft and the Atom* Hilger 1984. Sir John Cockcroft was the Director of the Atomic Weapons Research Institute at Harwell.

### (7) Defence Policy East of Suez

**2228** Philip Darby *British Defence Policy East of Suez 1947–68* Oxford University Press 1973. A good study of British defence interests and policy in the East from the independence of India until the withdrawal from East of Suez in the wake of the 1966 Defence Review. On the development of Labour thinking leading up to this decision see T J D Pocock 'The Labour Party and the Decision to Withdraw from East of Suez 1951–68' Southampton MPhil Thesis 1972–3. The decision to withdraw was at the time presented as necessary response to the Wilson government's budgetary difficulties. This assumption is critically examined in David Greenwood's useful analysis of *The Economics of 'the*

*East of Suez Decision'* Aberdeen Studies in Defence Economics 2, University of Aberdeen 1973.

**2229**  R Emery 'Britain and SEATO 1954–1967' Wales MSc (Econ) Thesis 1970–1. The only study of Britain's role in the South East Asian Treaty Organization up to the decision to withdraw from East of Suez.

### (8) Civil Defence

**2230**  *Civil Defence: A Select Bibliography* Derbyshire Library Service 1980. A short list of material on civil defence in the event of a nuclear war.

**2231**  Lawrence J Vale 'Britain' in his *The Limits of Civil Defence in the USA, Switzerland, Britain and the Soviet Union: The Evolution of Policies Since 1945* Macmillan 1987 pp 123–51. A critical assessment of the politics and planning of Britain's civil defence programme. A useful history is G J Crossley 'The Civil Defence Debate in Britain 1957–83' Bradford PhD Thesis 1985.

**2232**  Duncan Campbell *War Plan UK: The Truth About Civil Defence in Britain* Burnett Books 1982. A very informative and well illustrated exposé of the development and contemporary state of Britain's civil defence and a criticism of its inadequacies. It includes an account of the 'Hard Rock' civil defence exercise in 1982. A pamphlet with a rather different message focusing particularly on the 'Brave Defender' exercise in 1985 is Tony Baldry and Jim Spicer *Defence Begins at Home* Conservative Political Centre 1986.

**2233**  A Howe 'No Minister, Councils that Won't Play the Nuclear Free Game' *Sanity* Sept 1984 pp 30–5. This discusses the opposition in the 1980s of anti-nuclear local authorities to involvement in government civil defence planning.

### B. THE SERVICES

### (1) General

**2234**  Robin Higham (ed) *A Guide to the Sources of British Military History* Routledge and Kegan Paul 1972. This features chapters on sources and archive collections with relevant material on such subjects as colonial warfare, defence policy since 1945, or military law. It also has a bibliography.

**2235**  The Imperial War Museum has a department of film archives and a department of sound records, both of which contain material on service life and warfare.

**2236**  Roger Beaumont 'The British Armed Forces Since 1945' in Lewis H Gann (ed) *The Defense of Western Europe* Croom Helm 1987 pp 24–57. A good general study. On the management and organizational structures of the armed forces see J C T Downey *Management in the Armed Forces: An Anatomy of the Military Profession* McGraw-Hill 1977.

**2237**  C B Otley 'Militarism and the Social Affiliations of the British Military Elite' in Jacques Van Doorn (ed) *Armed Forces and Society: Sociological Essays* Mouton, Paris 1968 pp 84–108. A sociological survey of the upper echelons of the British armed forces 1870–1959.

**2238**  R Pope 'The Planning and Implementation of British Demobilisation 1941–46' Open University PhD Thesis 1986. This also covers the demobilization of civilian industry. It argues that although lessons had been learnt from 1919–20 and the process was not as harshly judged as it was then it was in fact little better in 1945–6.

**2239**  Philip Longworth *The Unending Vigil: A History of the Commonwealth War Graves Commission 1917–1984* 2nd ed, Cooper/Secker and Warburg 1985. This body was known as the Imperial War Graves Commission until 1960. This is a good history of its efforts to maintain cemeteries in over 140 countries around the world.

**2240**  Lawrence James *Mutiny in the British and Commonwealth Forces 1797–1956* Buchan and Enright 1987.

**2241**  Doreen Taylor *A Microphone and a Frequency: Forty Years of Forces Broadcasting* Heinemann 1983. A survey of the development of forces broadcasting since 1941 organized by geographical area. See also G Pederick *Battledress Broadcasters: A History of the British Forces Broadcasting Services* British Forces Broadcasting Services 1964.

**2242**  Sir John George Smyth *The Story of the Victoria Cross 1856–1963* Muller 1963. See also his *The Story of the George Cross* Barker 1968.

**2243**  F S Owen 'The Contribution of British Universities to Education in the Armed Forces 1949–1960' Bristol MA (Educ) Thesis 1964–5.

**2244**  Alun Gwynne Jones, Lord Chalfont *The Royal Tournament 1880–1980* Royal Tournament 1980.

## (2) Conscription

**2245** Trevor Royle *The Best Years of Their Lives: The National Service Experience 1945–63* Michael Joseph 1986. An excellent study, particularly of the experiences of national servicemen. It also has a good bibliography. See also Gerald Whiteley 'The British Experience with Peacetime Conscription' *Army Quarterly* 117 1987 pp 318-29 and L J Wallis 'Peacetime Conscription and the British Army' Lancaster MLitt Thesis 1977.

**2246** B S Johnson (ed) *All Bull: The National Servicemen* Quartet 1973. A revealing series of 24 recollections of National Service. A more favourable collection of portraits of contemporary National Service experience is Peter Chambers and Amy Landreth *Called Up: The Personal Experience of Sixteen National Servicemen* Wingate 1955. See also George Forty *Called Up: A National Service Scrapbook* Ian Allan 1980.

**2247** Edmund Ions *A Call to Arms: Interlude with the Military* David and Charles 1972. A sympathetic account of his time as a National Service officer. David Baxter *Two Years To Do* Elek 1959 is a more critical narrative of his National Service.

**2248** Frank Myers 'Conscription and the Politics of Military Strategy in the Attlee Government' *Journal of Strategic Studies* 7 1984 pp 55–73. A study of the thinking behind and the passage of the 1947 National Service Act which introduced peacetime conscription in Britain. See also L V Scott 'The Labour Government and National Service 1945–51' Oxford DPhil Thesis 1983.

**2249** Elliot Feldman *When the Empire Comes Home: Consequences of the Abolition of Military Conscription in Great Britain* Discussion Paper 6, School of Advanced International Studies, John Hopkins University, Baltimore, Maryland 1974. A criticism of the social, political and military consequences of the decision to phase out National Service in 1957 which took effect by 1963.

## (3) Military and Naval Aircraft

**2250** David Oliver *British Combat Aircraft Since 1945* Ian Allan 1985. An enthusiast's book. See also Owen Thetford *Aircraft of the Royal Air Force Since 1918* Putnam 1968, Owen Thetford *British Naval Aircraft Since 1912* Putnam 1977, G P B Naish *Flying in the Royal Navy 1914–64* HMSO 1964, Peter Lewis *The British Fighter Since 1912: Fifty Years of Design and Development* 2nd ed, Putnam 1965 and Peter Lewis *The British Bomber Since 1914: Sixty-Five Years of Change and Development* 3rd ed, Putnam 1980.

**2251** Ray Sturivant *The History of Britain's Military Training Aircraft* Foulis 1987. An enthusiast's book.

**2252** D H Middleton *Test Pilots: The Story of British Test Flying 1903–1984* Willow 1984.

**2253** John Everett-Heath *British Military Helicopters* Arms and Armour 1986.

**2254** John Simpson 'Understanding Weapon Acquisition Processes: A Study of Naval Anti-Submarine Aircraft Procurement in Britain 1945–1955' Southampton PhD Thesis 1976. A study of the policy making and design processes. By the 1970s the cost of development meant that aircraft design was increasing a product of international collaboration. The Anglo-West German-Italian Tornado project is traced in Rae Angus *Collaborative Weapons Acquisition: The MCRA (Tornado)-Panavia Project* Aberdeen Studies in Defence Economics 12, University of Aberdeen 1979.

**2255** Geoffrey Williams, Frank Gregory and John Simpson *Crisis in Procurement: A Case Study of the TSR-2* Royal United Services Institute 1969. The development of the TSR-2 low level bomber was scrapped in April 1965. This examines the history and failings of the project. S Hastings *Murder of the TSR-2* Cassell 1966 is a critique of the decision to terminate the project.

**2256** Robert Jackson *The V-Bombers* Ian Allan 1981. An enthusiast's study of the Valiant, Victor and Vulcan. The main task of these bombers after 1958 was to carry Britain's H-bombs. Until the delivery of Polaris in the 1960s they thus formed Britain's nuclear deterrent. Andrew Gordon *Handley Page Victor* Ian Allan 1988 is an enthusiast's study of every aspect of the Victor's 35 years from the first prototype flight. His *Avro Vulcan* Ian Allan 1985 is an equally useful study from this publisher's series on post-war military aircraft.

**2257** Maurice Allward *Buccaneer* Ian Allan 1981. An enthusiast's history from the series on post-war military aircraft. Maurice Allward *Gloster Javelin* Ian Allan 1983, Chaz Bowyer *Gloster Meteor* Ian Allan 1983 and Philip Birtles *De Havilland Vampire, Venom and Sea Vixen* Ian Allan 1986 are other titles from this series. The development of the delta-wing Avro Vulcan is dealt with in S D Davies 'The History of the Avro Vulcan' *Journal of the Royal Aeronautical Society* 74 1970 pp 350–64.

**2258** Robert Prest *F4 Phantom: A Pilot's Story* Cassell 1979. An autobiographical account of the experience of flying this aircraft by an RAF pilot.

## (4) Weapons

**2259** T L Smith 'Twenty Years of Guided Weapons' *Journal of the Royal Aeronautical Society* 70 1966 pp 583–91. A good account of the development of British guided weapons research. D L Farrar 'The Bloodhound' *Journal of the Royal Aeronautical Society* 63 1959 pp 35–50 is a detailed account of the development of the RAF's Red Duster ground to air missile.

**2260** R M Ogorkiewicz 'Fifty Years of British Tanks' *Royal United Services Institute Journal* 110 1965 pp 254–61.

## (5) Royal Navy

**2261** Ministry of Defence *Author and Subject Catalogues of the Naval Library* 5v, G K Hall 1967. This library contains the world's largest collection of books on the subject.

**2262** *The Navy List* HMSO 1814–. An annual listing of ships, establishments and dockyards. It also has some information on Commonwealth navies.

**2263** J J Colledge *Ships of the Royal Navy: An Historical Index* 2v, David and Charles 1969. An alphabetically arranged glossary. Volume I covers major ships and volume II navy-built trawlers, drifters, tugs and requisitioned ships. Volume I is updated by J J Colledge *Ships of the Royal Navy* Greenhill 1987. The history of the development and role of submarines in the Royal Navy is told in F W Lipscomb *The British Submarine* Conway Maritime Press 1975.

**2264** *Jane's Fighting Ships* Jane's Publishing 1897–. An annual international guide and commentary on navies and naval vessels. On Jane's itself see G H Hurford 'Sixty Years of "Jane's"' *Royal United Services Institute Journal* 103 1958 pp 223–9.

**2265** *Naval Abstracts* Center for Naval Analyses, Arlington, Virginia 1977–. Issued quarterly with an annual cumulative index this provides about 1,000 concise abstracts per year drawn from 275 journals, 48 of which are British.

**2266** Eric Groves *Vanguard to Trident: British Naval Policy Since World War Two* Naval Institute Press, Annapolis, Maryland 1987. A good study of post-war adjustment. It is particularly useful on the financial constraints which have led to a gradual reduction in the size of the Royal Navy. Desmond Wetten *The Decline of British Seapower* Jane's 1982 is a chronological examination 1946–70 with an epilogue on 1970–82. Richard Humble *The Rise and Fall of the British Navy*

Queen Anne Press 1986 is a critical examination of naval policy since the war and a plea for a larger surface fleet instead of nuclear weapons. Another useful study of the Royal Navy since 1945 is A Cecil Hampshire *The Royal Navy: Its Transition to the Nuclear Age* Kimber 1975. A well regarded study of post-war naval policy is William J Crowe Jr 'The Policy Roots of the Modern Royal Navy 1946–63' Princeton University, Princeton, New Jersey, PhD Thesis 1965. Paul Elford Garbutt *Naval Challenge: The Story of Britain's Post-War Fleet* Macdonald 1961 looks more at the ships than at naval policy. See also J E Woods 'The Royal Navy Since World War II' *US Naval Institute Proceedings* 108/3 1982 pp 223–9.

**2267** Paul M Kennedy *The Rise and Fall of British Naval Mastery* 2nd ed, Macmillan 1983. A good thematic interpretation. It does not however deal with the post-war period in great detail.

**2268** Charles Owen *No More Heroes: The Royal Navy in the Twentieth Century: Anatomy of a Legend* Allen and Unwin 1975. See also Brian Betham Schofield *British Sea Power: Naval Policy in the Twentieth Century* Batsford 1967. Anthony Preston (ed) *History of the Royal Navy in the 20th Century* Hamlyn 1987 is a popular illustrated history.

**2269** Keith Speed *Sea Change: The Battle for the Falklands and the Future of Britain's Navy* Ashgrove Press 1982. A criticism of naval policy since the 1960s. Speed focuses particularly on the cuts to the fleet in the 1981 Nott Review which he, as Navy Minister, vehemently opposed until he was sacked by Mrs Thatcher in May 1981. He argues, not implausibly, that his view that Britain needed a larger surface fleet to defend her worldwide interests was vindicated by the 1982 Falklands war. He also reflects on the serious problems posed by the decline in Britain's merchant and fishing fleets. The value of the merchant marine as auxiliaries to the Royal Navy was another of his points that was demonstrated by the experience of the Falklands war.

**2270** J R Hill *British Sea Power in the 1980s* Ian Allan 1985. A short study focusing on ships and weapons.

**2271** Dennis Barker *Ruling the Waves: An Unofficial Portrait of the Navy* Viking 1986. An informative picture of life in the Royal Navy in the 1980s, drawing on extensive interviews. For an earlier survey see Brian Betham Schofield *The Royal Navy Today* Oxford University Press 1960.

**2272** J Lennox Kerr and Wilfred Grenville *The RNVR* Harrap 1957. A useful history of the Royal Naval Volunteer Reserve.

**2273** S W C Pack *Britannia at Dartmouth: The Story of HMS Britannia and the Britannia Royal Naval Col-

*lege* Alvin Redman 1966. This general history goes up to the post-war period. See also David Lewis Summers *HMS Ganges 1866–1966: One Hundred Years of Training Boys for the Royal Navy* HMS Ganges 1966. Another aspect of training is covered in J P Bond 'Objective Training in the Royal Navy: An Evaluation of the System Introduced in 1971' Sussex DPhil Thesis 1979.

**2274** Oscar Grusky 'Career Patterns and Characteristics of British Naval Officers' *British Journal of Sociology* 26 1975 pp 35–51. A sociological study based on research in the 1960s.

**2274A** Ben Warlow *The Purser and his Men: A History of the Supply and Secretariat Branch of the Royal Navy* privately printed 1984. A short illustrated history.

**2275** Gregory Clark *'Doc': 100 Year History of the Sick Berth Branch* HMSO 1984. A history of this branch of the navy from the beginnings of specialist training for sick-berth attendants.

**2276** Ursula Stuart Mason *The Wrens 1917–77: A History of the Women's Royal Naval Service* Educational Explorers 1977. A general history.

**2277** James D Ladd *The Invisible Raiders: The History of the SBS from World War Two to the Present* Arms and Armour Press 1983. A history of the naval special operations service. See also Philip Warner *The SBS – Special Boat Squadron* Sphere 1983.

**2278** W S Hewison *This Great Harbour: Scapa Flow* Orkney Press 1985. Scapa Flow in the Orkneys continued to be used as a naval harbour until 1957. This useful history has a little on post-war naval activity in the area up until the 1970s.

**2279** Henry Trevor Lenton *Warships of the British and Commonwealth Navies* 3rd ed, Ian Allan 1971. This is a guide to the types of ship in service. It was formerly the much briefer *British Warships*, which reached its 7th edition in 1964. John Allan Wingate *HMS Belfast* Profile Publications 1972 is an account of this famous ship's service 1939–71.

**2280** E H H Archibald *The Metal Fighting Ships in the Royal Navy 1860–1970* Blandford 1971. An enthusiast's history as is G M Stephen *British Warship Design Since 1906* Ian Allan 1985. On particular types of ship see Randolph Pears *British Battleships 1892–1957* Putnam 1957, Sydney Leonard Poole *Cruiser: A History of the British Cruiser from 1889 to 1960* Hale 1970, M Cocker *Destroyers of the Royal Navy 1893–1981* Ian Allan 1981, Edgar James March *British Destroyers: A History of Development 1892–1953 Drawn by Admiralty Permission from Official Records and Returns, Ships*

*Covers and Building Plans* Seeley Service 1967 and T D Manning *The British Destroyer* Pitman 1961.

**2281** J A Clements 'Royal Navy Ship-Based Air Defence 1939–1984' *Journal of the Royal United Services Institute for Defence Studies* 129 1984 pp 19–24. A survey of the use of ship based aircraft up to the Falklands war.

**2281A** H A Colgate 'The Royal Navy and Trincomalee: The History of their Connection c1750–1958' *Ceylon Journal of History and Social Studies* 7 1964 pp 1–16.

**2282** Herbert Ellis *Hippocrates RN* Hale 1988. An autobiography of his time as a doctor in the Fleet Air Arm in the 1940s and 1950s. It is also useful on the development of aviation medicine.

**2283** Richard Humble *Fraser of North Cape: The Life of Admiral of the Fleet Lord Fraser (1881–1981)* Routledge and Kegan Paul 1983. Fraser was First Sea Lord 1948–51.

**2283A** Sir Angus Cunninghame Graham *Random Naval Recollections 1905–1951* the author 1979. A memoir of a naval career which culminated with his service as Admiral Superintendent Rosyth 1947–51 and Flag Officer, Scotland 1950–51.

**2284** Oliver Warner *Admiral of the Fleet: The Life of Sir Charles Lambe* Sidgewick and Jackson 1969. Lambe was Commander in Chief in the Far East 1953–4, Second Sea Lord 1955–7, NATO Commander in Chief, Mediterranean 1957–9 and First Sea Lord 1959–60.

**2285** Philip Ziegler *Mountbatten: The Official Biography* Collins 1985. Mountbatten was Supreme Allied Commander, South East Asia 1943–6, last Viceroy of India 1947, Governor- General of India 1947–8, Commander in Chief, Mediterranean 1952–4, First Sea Lord 1954–9 and Chairman of the Chiefs of Staff Committee 1959–65. John Terraine *The Life and Times of Lord Mountbatten* Arrow 1970 is an account based on Mountbatten's television autobiography. Charles Smith *Fifty Years with Mountbatten* Hamlyn 1981 is an account by his butler and valet. Another account by someone who served Moutbatten at close quarters in the 1960s is William Evans *My Mountbatten Years: In the Service of Lord Louis* Headline 1989. Richard Hough *Mountbatten: Hero of our Time* Weidenfeld and Nicolson 1981 is a poor biography. George Edward Baker *Mountbatten of Burma* Cassell 1959 is a short study. See also Sir Ronald Brock 'Mountbatten' in Sir Michael Carver (ed) *The War Lords: Military Commanders of the Twentieth Century* Weidenfeld and Nicolson 1976 pp 357–75. On Mountbatten in South East Asia see Philip Ziegler (ed) *Personal Diary of Admiral The Lord Louis Mountbatten,*

*Supreme Allied Commander, South East Asia 1943–1946* Collins 1988. Another volume of diaries, covering the years 1953–79 is Philip Ziegler (ed) *From Shore to Shore: The Final Volume of Lord Mountbatten's Diaries* Collins 1989. For Mountbatten in India see [1256, 1260]. David Brown 'Mountbatten as First Sea Lord' *Journal of the Royal United Services Institute for Defence Studies* 131 1986 pp 63–8 assesses Mountbatten's achievements in this post.

**2286** George Walter Gillow Simpson *Periscope View: A Professional Autobiography* Macmillan 1972. Simpson was Flag Officer, Germany and Chief British Naval Representative on the Allied Control Commission 1951 and Flag Officer, Submarines 1952–4.

**2287** A Temple Patterson *Tyrwhitt of the Harwich Force: The Life of Admiral of the Fleet Sir Reginald Tyrwhitt* Macdonald and Jane's 1973. Tyrwhitt was Second Sea Lord 1959–61.

### (6) The Army

**2288** Terry Gander *Encylopaedia of the Modern British Army* Patrick Stephens 1980. A very informative guide to the army since 1945.

**2289** *Army List* HMSO 1949–. This was previously published half-yearly. It is now a triennial publication in three parts. The first lists major appointments, establishments and provides regimental and corps lists of serving officers in the Army and the Territorial Army. Part II lists retired officers and Part III, which has restricted circulation, lists active officers.

**2290** A S White (comp) *A Bibliography of Regimental Histories of the British Army* Society for Army Historical Research/The Army Museum Ogilvy Trust 1965. A classified bibliography with some 2,500 briefly annotated entries.

**2291** David Griffin *Encylopaedia of British Army Regiments* Patrick Stephens 1985. This gives brief details of current regiments with tables of lineage. The useful appendices include information on the current brigade and division system. J B M Frederick *Lineage Book of the British Army: Mounted Corps and Infantry 1660–1968* Hope Farm Press 1969 is useful for tracing changes of name. It goes up to the major reorganization of the late 1960s which involved the disbanding of many regiments. See also Arthur Swinson *A Register of the Regiments and Corps of the British Army: The Ancestry of the Regiments and Corps of the Regular Establishment* Archive 1972.

**2292** William Gregory Blaxland *The Regiments Depart: A History of the British Army 1945–1970* Kimber 1971. A useful history focusing on the army's role in imperial retreat. This is studied by area. Good use is made of oral accounts and it is well furnished with maps and appendices.

**2293** Correlli Barnett *Britain and Her Army 1509–1970: A Military, Political and Social Survey* Allen Lane 1970. A more conventional history. Despite the huge period covered it is quite useful on the post-war years. See also B R Newman 'Military Organisations and Social Change, with Particular Reference to the British Army 1962–1975' CNAA PhD Thesis 1976.

**2294** Richard Goold-Adams *et al The British Army in the Nuclear Age* The Army League 1959. A symposium on the needs, structure and deployment of the army in the light of the emphasis on nuclear strategy ushered in by the 1957 White Paper. Also on the army in the 1950s is M C A Henniker *Life in the Army Today* Cassell 1957.

**2295** Dennis Barker *Soldiering On: An Unofficial Portrait of the British Army* Deutsch 1981. An impressionistic description of the army and life in the army. It includes material on tours of duty in Northern Ireland and West Germany. See also Henry Stanhope *The Soldiers: An Anatomy of the British Army* Hamilton 1979.

**2296** J C Garnett 'BAOR and NATO' *International Affairs* 46 1970 pp 670–81. A look at the role of the British Army of the Rhine in NATO strategy. There is as yet no general history of British deployment in Germany.

**2297** Sir John Smyth *Sandhurst: The History of the Royal Military Academy, Woolwich, the Royal Military College, Sandhurst and the Royal Military Academy, Sandhurst 1741–1961* Weidenfeld and Nicolson 1961. See also Hugh Thomas *The Story of Sandhurst* Hutchinson 1961. Developments since are covered in Brian Bond 'Educational Changes at R M A Sandhurst 1966–1983' *Militärhistorisk Tidskrift* 187 1983 pp 33–43. Other aspects of officer training and education are covered in Alun Gwynne Jones 'Training and Doctrine in the British Army Since 1945' in Michael Howard (ed) *The Theory and Practice of War: Essays Presented to Captain B H Liddell Hart* Cassell 1965 pp 311–34 and R S Beresford 'The Development Since 1943 of the Policy for the Non-Specialist Education of Army Officers in Science and Technology' Oxford BLitt Thesis 1969–70.

**2298** C B Otley 'The Social Origins of British Army Officers' *Sociological Review* n.s. 18 1970 pp 213–39. This, in contrast to his 'The Educational Background of British Army Officers' *Sociology* 7 1973 pp 191–209, has little material on the post-war period. See also E S

Turner *Gallant Gentlemen: A Portrait of the British Officer 1600–1956* Michael Joseph 1956 and P E Razzell 'Social Origins of Officers in the Indian and British Home Army 1758–1962' *British Journal of Sociology* 14 1963 pp 248–60.

**2299** Roy Terry *Women in Khaki: The Story of the British Women Soldier* Columbus Books 1988. Published to celebrate the Golden Jubilee of the Women's Royal Army Corps this history was written with their co-operation. Hugh Popham *FANY: The Story of the Women's Transport Services 1907–1984* Cooper/Secker and Warburg 1984 is an official history of the First Aid Nursing Yeomanry, who are now a support service largely concerned with communications, which unfortunately does not have much material on the post-war years.

**2300** Sir John George Smyth *In This Sign Conquer: The Story of the Army Chaplains* Mowbray 1968. The official history of the Army Chaplains Department. It has a small section on the post-war period.

**2301** Kenneth Brookes *Battle Thunder: The Story of Britain's Artillery* Osprey 1973. A history of the Royal Artillery.

**2302** Robin Neillands *By Sea and Land: The Royal Marine Commandos: A History 1942–1982* Weidenfeld and Nicolson 1987. A useful service history up to their involvement in the Falklands war.

**2303** Kenneth Macksey *A History of the Royal Armoured Corps 1914–1975* Newton Publishing 1983.

**2304** Jock Haswell *British Military Intelligence* Weidenfeld and Nicolson 1973. A survey of military intelligence gathering from the time of Wellington to the colonial wars of the post-war era.

**2305** Tony Geraghty *Who Dares Wins: The Story of the Special Air Services 1950–1980* Arms and Armour Press 1980. First formed during the Second World War the SAS was reconstituted for the Malayan Emergency in 1950 as the Malayan Scouts. This regimental history goes up to the Iranian embassy siege in 1980. See also James Ladd *SAS Operations* Hale 1986 and Philip Warner *The Special Air Service* Kimber 1972. William Seymour *British Special Forces* Sidgwick and Jackson 1985 mainly deals with the Second World War but also covers the SAS in the post-war years. Both the SAS and the Parachute Brigade are covered in G G Norton *The Red Devils: The Story of Britain's Airborne Forces* Cooper 1971. This has plenty of information on their post-war combat records. Michael Paul Kennedy *Soldier 'I': SAS* Bloomsbury 1989 is a ghosted autobiography of a member of the regiment who served in Oman, Northern Ireland, the Falklands and the 1980 Iranian embassy siege.

**2305A** K Macksey *The Tanks: History of the Royal Tank Regiment 1945–1975* Arms and Armour 1979. A standard regimental history.

**2306** Julian Thompson *Ready for Anything: The Parachute Regiment at War 1940–1982* Weidenfeld and Nicolson 1989. A good account of this special regiment since its formation giving due weight to its post-war service in conflicts in Palestine, Cyprus, Borneo, Radfan, Aden, Suez and the Falklands.

**2306A** D Wood *Attack Warning Red: The Royal Observer Corps and the Defence of Britain 1925 to 1975* Macdonald and Jane's 1976.

**2307** R C B Anderson *History of the Argyll and Sutherland Highlanders 1st Battalion 1939–1954* Constable 1956. This short regimental history covers operations in the Second World War, Korea, Palestine, Hong Kong and British Guiana. The successful campaign against the disbanding of the regiment in the 1960s is covered in G F Allan 'Pressure Groups and the British Political Process – A Case Study: The "Save the Argylls" Campaign' London PhD Thesis 1974–6. For other histories of Highland regiments see *Historical Records of the Queen's Own Cameron Highlanders Vol 7: 1949–61* Blackwood 1962 and Christopher Sinclair-Stevenson *The Life of a Regiment: The History of the Gordon Highlanders Vol VI: 1945–1970* Cooper 1974.

**2308** Richard Crichton *The Coldstream Guards 1946–1970* Richard Clay 1972. For other Guards regiments see D H Eskine (comp) *The Scots Guards 1919–55* Clowes 1959.

**2309** C N Barclay *History of the 16th/5th: The Queen's Royal Lancers 1925–61* Gale and Polden 1963. For other cavalry regiments see R L V Ffrench Blake *A History of the 17th/21st Lancers 1922–59* Macmillan 1962, J G Pocock *The Spirit of a Regiment: Being the History of the 19th King George V's Own Lancers Vol 6: 1939–48* Gale and Polden 1962, Olivia Fitzroy *Men of Valour: The History of the VII King's Royal Irish Hussars Vol 3: 1927–58* Bates and Son 1961 and D R Guttery *The Queen's Own Worcestershire Hussars 1922–56* Mark and Moody 1958.

**2310** Jack Adams *The South Wales Borderers* Hamilton 1968. A short history with details of actions that the regiment has been involved in. Other relevant regimental histories are C N Barclay *History of the Duke of Wellington's Regiment 1919–52* Clowes 1953, T A Martin *The Essex Regiment 1929–50* Essex Regiment Association 1952, L C Gates (comp) *The History of the Tenth Foot 1919–50* (the Royal Lincolnshire Regiment) Gale and Polden 1955, J J Burke-Gaffeney *The Story of the King's Regiment 1914–48* King's Regiment 1954, C G T Dean *The Loyal Regiment, North Lancashire 1919–53*

Fulwood Barracks 1955, A C Bell *History of the Manchester Regiment Vol 3: First and Second Battalions 1922–48* Sherrett 1954, P K Kemp *The Middlesex Regiment (Duke of Cambridge's Own) 1919–52* Gale and Polden 1956, W J Jervois *History of the Northamptonshire Regiment 1934–48* Northamptonshire Regiment 1953, H D Chaplin *The Queen's Own Royal West Kent Regiment 1920–50* Michael Joseph 1954 (updated by his *The Queen's Own Royal West Kent Regiment 1951–61* Queen's Own Museum Committee 1964), R C G Foster *History of the Queen's Royal Regiment Vol 8: 1924–48* Gale and Polden 1953 (updated by his *History of the Queen's Royal Regiment Vol 9* Gale and Polden 1961), G Blight *History of the Royal Berkshire Regiment (Princess Charlotte of Wales') 1920–47* Staple 1953, D S Daniell *Regimental History: The Royal Hampshire Regiment Vol 3: 1918–54* Gale and Polden 1955, P K Kemp *History of the Royal Norfolk Regiment Vol 3: 1919–51* Royal Norfolk Regiment 1955, J De Courcy *The History of the Welsh Regiment 1919–51* Western Mail 1952, Christopher Bromhead Birdwood, Lord Birdwood *The Worcestershire Regiment 1922–50* Gale and Polden 1952, O F Sheffield *The York and Lancaster Regiment Vol 3: 1919–53* Gale and Polden 1956, A T M Durand and R H W S Hastings *The London Rifle Brigade 1919–50* Gale and Polden 1952, D S Daniell *History of the East Surrey Regiment Vol 4: 1920–52* Benn 1957, R J B Sellar *The Fife and Forfar Yeomanry 1919–56* Blackwood 1960, W E Underhill (ed) *The Royal Leicestershire Regiment, 17th Foot: A History 1928–56* Royal Leicestershire Regiment 1956, Marcus Cunliffe *History of the Royal Warwickshire Regiment 1919–1955* Royal Warwickshire Regiment 1956, C N Barclay *The History of the Sherwood Foresters (Nottinghamshire and Derbyshire Regiment) 1919–57* Clowes 1959, G F Ellenberger *History of the King's Own Yorkshire Light Infantry Vol 6: 1939–48* Gale and Polden 1961, J C Kemp *The History of the Royal Scots Fusiliers 1919–59* House of Grant 1963, Kenneth Whitehead *History of the Somerset Light Infantry (Prince Albert's) 1914–60* Clowes 1961, Eric David Smith *East of Kathmandu: The Story of the 7th Duke of Edinburgh's Own Gurkha Rifles Vol 2: 1948–1973* Cooper 1976, Harold Douglas James and Denis Sheil Small *A Pride of Gurkhas: The 2nd King Edward VII's Own Goorkhas (the Sirmoor Rifles) 1948–1971* Cooper 1975, C R B Knight *Historical Records of the Buffs: Royal East Kent Regiment Vol IV: 1919–48* Medici Society 1951 (updated by William Gregory Blaxland *The Farewell Years: The Final Historical Records of the Buffs: Royal East Kent Regiment 1948–1967* Queen's Own Buffs Office 1967), John Baynes *The History of the Cameronians (Scottish Rifles): The Close of Empire 1948–1968 Vol IV* Cassell 1971, Tim Carew *The Glorious Glosters: A Short History of the Gloucestershire Regiment 1945–1970* Cooper 1970 and Guthrie Moir *The Suffolk Regiment* Cooper 1969.

2311   Howard N Cole *On Wings of Healing: The Story of the Airborne Medical Services 1940–1960* Blackwood 1963. Raised and formed in 1941 it also saw service in Palestine and Suez. R M Adams *Through to 1970: Royal Signals Golden Jubilee* Royal Signals Institution 1970 is a sketchy, if well illustrated history. For other Corps histories see J Piggott *Queen Alexandra's Royal Army Nursing Corps* Cooper 1975 and J Clabby *The History of the Royal Army Veterinary Corps 1919–61* J A Allen 1963.

2312   Howard N Cole *The Story of Catterick Camp 1915–1972* Forces Press 1972. Catterick was the initial port of call for thousands of National Servicemen in the 1940s and 1950s and remains a major training camp.

2313   A V Sellwood *The Saturday Night Soldiers: The Stirring Story of the Territorial Army* Wolfe Publishing 1966.

2314   Oliver Lindsay (ed) *A Guard's General: The Memoirs of Major General Sir Allan Adair* Hamilton 1986. Adair's last service was in the Greek civil war in 1946.

2315   Sir David Fraser *Alanbrooke* Collins 1982. See also Arthur Bryant (ed) *Triumph in the West: The Alanbrooke Diaries* Collins 1959. This includes a few entries for 1946. Lord Alanbrooke was briefly Chief of the Imperial General Staff after the war.

2316   Philip Warner *Auchinleck – The Lonely Soldier* Buchan and Pinright 1981. Auchinleck was the Commander in Chief in India 1943–7.

2317   Michael Carver *Out of Step: The Memoirs of Field Marshal Lord Carver* Hutchinson 1989. Memoirs of a career culminating in his appointment as Chief of the Defence Staff 1973–76, covering service in North Africa, East Africa, the Far East and Cyprus.

2318   Bernard Fergusson *The Trumpet in the Hall 1930–1958* Collins 1970. Memoirs covering the last years in Palestine and the Suez episode.

2319   Sir Richard Gale *Call to Arms* Hutchinson 1968. An autobiography. Gale was GOC Egypt and the Mediterranean 1948–9, Director General of Military Training 1949–52, Commander in Chief, British Army of the Rhine 1952–7 and Deputy Supreme Allied Commander, Europe 1958–60.

2320   Michael Carver *Harding of Petherton: Field Marshal* Weidenfeld and Nicolson 1978. Harding was Commander in Chief of Southern Command 1947–9, of Far East Land Forces 1949–51, of the British Army of the Rhine 1951–2, Chief of the Imperial General Staff 1952–5 and Governor of Cyprus 1955–7.

**2321** Sir Ronald Wingate *Lord Ismay: A Biography* Hutchinson 1970. Ismay was Mountbatten's Chief of Staff in India in 1947, Commonwealth Relations Secretary 1951–2 and first Secretary-General of NATO 1952–7.

**2322** Rowland Ryder *Oliver Leese* Hamilton 1987. Leese was GOC Eastern Command 1945–6.

**2323** Colin Mitchell *Having Been a Soldier* Hamilton 1969. Mitchell served in Palestine, Korea, Cyprus, East Africa, Borneo and Aden. He led the Argylls in the celebrated action at Crater. A memoir written with bitterness over the treatment of his regiment in the 1966 Defence Review.

**2324** Nigel Hamilton *Monty: The Field Marshal 1944–1976* Hamilton 1986. The final volume of the official biography. Montgomery was Commander of the British Army of the Rhine 1945–6, Chief of the Imperial General Staff 1946–8, Chairman of Western Europe Commanders in Chief Committee 1948–51 and Deputy Supreme Allied Commander, Europe 1958–60. See also Bernard Law Montgomery *The Memoirs of Field Marshal, the Viscount Montgomery of Alamein* Collins 1958. Of less value is Alun Gwynne Jones, Lord Chalfont *Montgomery of Alamein* Weidenfeld and Nicolson 1976.

**2325** Sir Harold E Pyman *Call to Arms* Cooper 1971. Pyman was deputy Chief of the Imperial General Staff 1958–61 and Allied Commander in Chief 1961–3.

**2326** Charles Richardson *Flashback: A Soldier's Story* Kimber 1985. This General's memoirs ends with a useful account of the occupation of Berlin 1945–6.

**2327** Ronald Lewin *Slim: The Standardbearer* Hutchinson 1977. A good biography. Slim was the Commander in Chief Allied Land Forces South East Asia 1945–6, Commandant, Imperial Defence College 1946–7, Chief of the Imperial General Staff 1948–52 and Governor-General of Australia 1953–60.

**2328** John Cloake *Templer: Tiger of Malaya: The Life of Field Marshal Sir Gerald Templer* Harrap 1985. A good biography. Templer as High Commissioner in Malaya 1952–4 played a decisive part in the war against Communist insurgents. He was Chief of the Imperial General Staff 1955–8.

**2329** Sir John Smyth *The Will to Live: The Story of Dame Margot Turner DBE, RRC* Cassell 1970. Turner was a celebrated Matron in Chief and Brigadier of Queen Alexandra's Royal Army Nursing Corps.

**2330** Tom Pocock *Fighting General: The Public and Private Campaigns of General Sir Walter Walker* Collins 1973. Walker served in Burma 1944–6, Malaya 1949–59 and Borneo 1962–5 and was GOC Northern Command 1969–72.

**2331** Sir John Smyth *Bolo Whistler: The Life of General Sir Lashmer Whistler* Muller 1967. Whistler served in Palestine 1945–6, India 1947–8 and the Sudan 1948–50. He was GOC West Africa 1951–3 and GOC Western Command 1953–7. In 1957–8 he chaired the Committee on the New Army set up in the wake of the 1957 Defence White Paper.

## (7) Royal Air Force

**2332** *The Air Force List* HMSO 1949–. An annual guide to the establishments and officers of the Royal Air Force.

**2333** Airborne Forces Museum, Aldershot, Hampshire GU11 2DS. This has an oral history collection which includes material on Palestine, Suez and Borneo.

**2334** N A Webber 'A Guide to the Literature on the History of the Royal Air Force 1918–1968' London PhD Thesis 1977. A historiographical examination. See also Ministry of Defence, Adastral Library *Bibliography of the Royal Air Force* Adastral Library 1977. This is a classified bibliography. The Adastral Library also produce mimeographed subject lists for subscribers.

**2335** J J Halley *Royal Air Force Unit Histories* 2v, Air Britain 1969. A collection of potted squadron histories featuring some reference material. In most cases it is sketchy after 1945. Peter Lewis *Squadron Histories: RFC, RNAS and RAF 1912–59* Putnam 1959 combines potted squadron histories with informative appendices.

**2336** James Trevenen *The Royal Air Force: The Past Thirty Years* Macdonald and Jane's 1976. A good study of the post-war RAF. Also useful is J D R Rawlings *The History of the Royal Air Force* Temple Smith 1984. On policy making see Richard Worcester *The Roots of Air Policy* Hodder and Stoughton 1966. Charles Sims *The Royal Air Force: The First Fifty Years* A & C Black 1968 is limited and inadequate in its treatment of the post-war period. See also John W R Taylor and Philip J R Moyes *Pictorial History of the RAF* 3v, Ian Allan 1969, B Harrison *The RAF: A Pictorial History* Hale 1978 and Chaz Bowyer *The History of the RAF* Magna Books 1977. Another pictorial view of the RAF in the 1980s is Jeremy Flack *Today's Royal Air Force in Colour* Batsford 1987.

**2337** Chaz Bowyer *Fighter Command 1936–1963* Dent 1980. See also Peter Wykeham *Fighter Command: A Study in Air Defence 1914–60* Putnam 1960.

**2338** Sir Philip Joubert de la Ferté *Birds and Fishes: The Story of Coastal Command* Hutchinson 1960.

**2339** H R Allen *The Legacy of Lord Trenchard* Cassell 1972. A critique of Trenchard's doctrines, particularly in terms of his emphasis on obliteration bombing. This analysis concentrates on the Second World War but also covers 1945–70. The deficiencies of the V Force bombers, which for a time were the sum of Britain's deterrent, are for instance criticized. A different analysis is Sir John Slessor 'The Place of the Bomber in British Policy' *International Affairs* 29 1953 pp 302–7.

**2340** Air Ministry *The Origins and Development of Operational Research in the Royal Air Force* HMSO 1963.

**2341** Sir David Lee *Eastward: A History of the Royal Air Force in the Far East 1945–1972* HMSO 1984. An official history of operations and bases up until the withdrawal from East of Suez. An equally good official history of the RAF's role in the demission of empire is his *Flight from the Middle East: A History of the Royal Air Force in the Arabian Peninsular and Adjacent Territories 1945–1972* HMSO 1980. On the continuing RAF presence in the Mediterranean see his *Wings in the Sun: A History of the Royal Air Force in the Mediterranean 1945–1986* HMSO 1989. N Shorrick *Lion in the Sky: The Story of Seletar and the Royal Air Force in Singapore* Federal Publications, Singapore 1968 is the official history of the Seletar base at Singapore and its role during the 1948–60 Emergency and the 1962–6 Confrontation with Indonesia.

**2342** Air Training Corps *Twenty-First Birthday 1941–62* HMSO 1962. The ATC train boys who are interested in progressing into the RAF.

**2343** T Hearnshaw 'A History of Technical Training Command in the Royal Air Force 1940–1968' London MPhil Thesis 1971–2.

**2344** J Leslie Hunt *Twenty-One Squadrons: The History of the Royal Auxiliary Air Force 1925–1957* Garnstone Press 1973.

**2344A** E Bishop *The Debt we owe: The Royal Air Force Benevolent Fund 1919–1979* 2nd ed, Allen and Unwin 1979.

**2345** James Beedle *43 Squadron Royal Flying Corps, Royal Air Force: The History of the Fighting Cocks 1916–1966* Beaumont Aviation Literature 1966. For other squadron or station histories see Chaz Bowyer *The Flying Elephants: A History of No. 27 Squadron, Royal Flying Corps, Royal Air Force 1915–1969* Macdonald 1972, Douglas Tidy *I Fear No Man: The Story of No. 74 (Fighter) Squadron Royal Flying Corps and Royal Air Force (The Tigers)* Macdonald 1972, Gordon Kinsey *Seaplanes – Felixstowe: The Story of the Air Station 1913–1964* Dalton 1978, W Fraser *The History of Royal Air Force Manston 1916–1986* 3rd ed RAF Manston 1986 and Gordon Kinsey *Martlesham Heath: The Story of the Royal Air Force Station 1917–1973* Dalton 1975. E B Haslem *The History of Royal Air Force Cranwell* HMSO 1983 is a history of the RAF college and airfield.

**2345A** Neil Cameron *In the Midst of Things: The Autobiography of Lord Cameron of Dalhousie: Marshal of the Royal Air Force* Hodder and Stoughton 1986. The autobiography of a former Chief of the Defence Staff.

**2346** William Sholto Douglas *Years of Command* Collins 1966. The second volume of his autobiography. Douglas was Commander in Chief of the British Air Forces of occupation in Germany 1945–6, and Commander in Chief and Military Governor of the British Zone in Germany 1946–7.

**2347** Prudence Hill *To Know the Sky: The Life of Air Chief Marshal Sir Roderic Hill* Kimber 1962. This biography is useful on the immediate post-war period. Hill retired in 1948.

**2348** Vincent Orange *A Biography of Air Chief Marshal Sir Keith Park* Methuen 1984. Park was Allied Air Commander in Chief in South East Asia in 1945 and retired in 1946.

**2349** Denis Richards *Portal of Hungerford* Heinemann 1977. A good biography. Portal was Chief of Air Staff 1940–5 and Controller, Atomic Energy, Ministry of Supply 1946–51. As such he played an important part in Britain's atomic bomb programme.

**2350** Sir John Cotesworth Slessor *These Remain* Michael Joseph 1969. Slessor was Chief of Air Staff 1950–2.

## (8) Intelligence

A considerable amount of relevant literature can also be found in the section on Government Secrecy [329-37].

**2351** Myron J Smith Jr *The Secret Wars: A Guide to Sources in English Vol II: Intelligence, Propaganda and Psychological Warfare, Covert Operations 1945–1980* Clio Press 1981. An unannotated international bibliography. It is best on American intelligence but is also quite useful for Britain. It includes a useful chronology.

**2352** *Lobster* 1983–. An irregular magazine probing the British intelligence establishment. Issues include for instance a special edition on 'A Who's Who of the

British State – A Guide to Post-War Members of MI5 and MI6'.

2353  J Bloch and Patrick Fitzgerald *British Intelligence and Covert Action: Africa, Middle East and Europe Since 1945* Brandon 1983. The most comprehensive account of the operation of the British intelligence services since the war. A more general history which goes up to the 1960s is Richard Deacon *A History of the British Secret Services* Muller 1969. See also Donald McCormick *A History of the British Secret Service* Taplinger, New York 1970, David Wise and Thomas B Ross 'Great Britain' in their *The Espionage Establishment* Cape 1968 pp 78–131 and Werner F Grunbaum 'The British Security Program 1948–1958' *Western Political Quarterly* 13 1960 pp 264–79. The most scholarly and magisterial, not to mention very funny, history of the British intelligence services, Christopher Andrew *Secret Service: The Making of the British Intelligence Community* Heinemann 1985, unfortunately confines reflections on the post-war years to the epilogue.

2354  Nigel West *The Friends: Britain's Post-War Intelligence Operations* Weidenfeld and Nicolson 1988. A critical study of the failings and bungling of British intelligence operations.

2355  Peter Hennessy and Gail Brownfeld 'Britain's Cold War Security Purge: The Origins of Positive Vetting' *Historical Journal* 25 1982 pp 965–73. A vetting procedure was introduced in 1948. Positive vetting began in 1952. This procedure was introduced partly in order to safeguard atomic secrets.

2356  Anthony Cave Brown *The Secret Servant: The Life of Sir Stewart Menzies, Churchill's Spymaster* Michael Joseph 1987. A massive and eulogistic biography. Menzies remained Chief of the Secret Intelligence Service (MI6) until 1951. This study includes reflections on operations in Iran, the Cold War and the enforced retirement of Philby in 1951, on which point he claims to offer new evidence and a new interpretation.

2357  Richard Deacon *'C': A Biography of Sir Maurice Oldfield, Head of MI6* Macdonald 1985. A good biography of a distinguished service head 1973–8.

2358  A W Cockerill *Sir Percy Sillitoe* W H Allen 1975. This biography has one short chapter on Sillitoe's eight years as Director General of MI5 up until his retirement in 1953. Only the most anodyne comments were left on his period at MI5 by the Home Office vetters in Sir Percy's autobiography, *Cloak and Dagger* Cassell 1955.

2359  Alexander Scotland *The London Cage* Evans 1957. An account of his experiences in intelligence and security work which goes into the post-war period.

2360  Anthony Cavendish *Inside Intelligence* privately printed 1987. A short moderately revealing memoir of service in MI5.

2361  Nigel West *GCHQ: The Secret Wireless War 1900–1986* Weidenfeld and Nicolson 1986. This history is well stocked with anecdotes but lacks a clear narrative. This book is nevertheless a contribution towards remedying one of the deficiencies in the literature on intelligence, which is the lack of material on signals intelligence. It however does little to solve the other major problem, which is the dearth of material on the influence of intelligence on government policy. Also useful is James Bamford *The Puzzle Palace: America's National Security Agency and its Special Relationship with Britain's GCHQ* Sidgwick and Jackson 1982, particularly on the sharing of signals intelligence. The preface is a useful dicussion of the Geoffrey Prime case in 1982. Signals intelligence co-operation, in the light of the UKUSA agreement of 1947, is also examined in Jeffrey T Richelson and Desmond Ball *The Ties that Bind: Intelligence Co-operation in UKUSA Countries – The United Kingdom, the United States of America, Canada, Australia and New Zealand* Allen and Unwin 1985.

2362  Nigel West *A Matter of Trust: MI5 1945–72* Weidenfeld and Nicolson 1982. Also on MI5 see John Bulloch *MI5: The Origin and History of the British Counter-Espionage Service* Barker 1963.

2362A  Tom Bower *The Red Web: MI6 and the KGB Master Group* Aurum Press 1989. An assessment of MI6 activities in the former Baltic states 1945–59, based mainly on interviews, and a limited number of documents.

2363  Patrick Fitzgerald and Mark Leopold *Strangers on the Line: The Secret History of Phone-Tapping* The Bodley Head 1987. A good history of phone-tapping by the counter-espionage services, the Special Branch and other agencies.

2364  Anthony Glees *The Secrets of the Service: British Intelligence and Communist Subversion 1939–51* Cape 1987. A balanced historical survey culminating in the defection of Burgess and Maclean in 1951.

2365  Donald McCormick *The British Connection: Russia's Manipulation of British Individuals and Institutions* Hamilton 1979. A good study of the operation of Russian double-agents and moles in the British system since the war.

2366  John Bulloch *Akin to Treason* Barker 1966. Case studies of treason written from a perspective of extreme dissatisfaction with the existing state of the law. Post-war cases dealt with include the Burgess and Maclean defection to the USSR, Klaus Fuchs and the Vassall case.

**2366A**   Andrew Sinclair *The Red and the Blue: Intelligence, Treason and the Universities* Coronet 1986. A study of the universities as recruiting grounds for agents and for traitors.

**2367**   Norman Moss *Klaus Fuchs, the Man who Stole the Atom Bomb* Grafton Books 1987. Fuchs was arrested in 1950 for passing atomic secrets to the Russians. See also Robert C Williams *Klaus Fuchs: Atom Spy* Harvard University Press 1988 and Harford Montgomery Hyde *The Atom Bomb Spies* Hamilton 1980.

**2368**   John Fisher *Burgess and Maclean: A New Look at the Foreign Office Spies* Hale 1977. Guy Burgess and Donald Maclean were senior members of the Foreign Office who fled to Moscow in May 1951 to escape arrest for passing secrets to the Russians. See also Anthony Purdy and Douglas Sutherland *Burgess and Maclean* Doubleday 1963 and Cyril Connolly *The Missing Diplomats* Queen Anne Press 1952. On Burgess see also the memoir Tom Driberg *Guy Burgess: A Portrait with Background* Weidenfeld and Nicolson 1956. Goronwy Rees *A Chapter of Accidents* Chatto and Windus 1972 is an autobiography which is most useful for his friendship with Burgess. On Maclean see Robert Cecil *A Divided Life: A Biography of Donald Maclean* The Bodley Head 1988. This excellent biography by a close acquaintance sheds new light on Maclean's double career and the disastrous effect his defection had on Anglo-American relations. Also of use is Geoffrey Hoare *The Missing Macleans* Cassell 1955. Peter Hennessy and K Townsend 'The Documentary Spoor of Burgess and Maclean' *Intelligence and National Security* 2 1987 pp 291–301 is a guide to relevant documents in the Public Record Office.

**2369**   Bernard J Hutton *Frogman Spy: The Incredible Case of Commander Crabb* McDowell, Obolensky 1960. Crabb was sent by MI6 to inspect the hull of a Soviet vessel during the goodwill visit of Khrushchev and Bulganin in 1956. His headless body was later washed ashore. See also Kurt D Singer 'The Frogman' in his *Spies for Democracy* Dennison 1960.

**2370**   Gordon Lonsdale *Spy: Twenty Years of Secret Service* Neville Spearman 1965. The Soviet spymaster Konon Molody, who operated under the cover of his alias Gordon Lonsdale, was arrested in January 1961. This is a very flawed account of his undercover activities in Britain. In 1964 he was exchanged for the British businessman Greville Wynne, who had been arrested for spying by the Russians. Wynne's *The Man from Moscow: The Story of Wynne and Penkovsky* Hutchinson 1967 deals mostly with his ordeal after his arrest. The evidence that led to Molody's arrest also led to the

rounding up of the Portland spy ring which had been suppling him with submarine warfare secrets. On this see John Bulloch and Henry Miller *Spy Ring: The Full Story of the Naval Secrets Case* Secker and Warburg 1961.

**2371**   Harford Montgomery Hyde *George Blake Superspy* Constable 1987. See also Edward H Cookridge *George Blake: Double Agent* Hodder and Stoughton 1970 and Edward Spiro *Shadow of a Spy: The Complete Dossier on George Blake* Frewin 1967. Blake was an MI6 officer who was also working for the KGB as a very successful double agent. He was arrested in 1961. Sean Bourke *The Springing of George Blake* Viking 1970 is an account of Blake's escape from prison and flight to Moscow in 1967, in which Bourke played a significant part. His fellow conspirators, the anti-nuclear protestors Michael Randle and Patrick Pottle have also now written their account of the episode, *The Blake Escape* Harrap 1989.

**2372**   *Report of the Tribunal Appointed to Inquire into the Vassall Case* Cmnds 1871 and 2009, *Parliamentary Papers* xxiv 1962–63. Vassall was a homosexual who as Naval Attaché in Moscow had been passing secrets to the Russians. This inquiry chaired by Lord Radcliffe focused on the failing of positive vetting in this case. It concluded that criticism attached in this instance not to the procedure but to the vetters. Cecily I Fairfield *The Vassall Affair* Sunday Telegraph 1963 is a well reported account of the case. See also William J C Vassall *Vassall: The Autobiography of a Spy* Sidgwick and Jackson 1975.

**2373**   Philip Knightley *Philby: The Life and Views of the KGB Masterspy* Deutsch 1988. Philby was retired from the service at the insistence of the CIA in 1951 after the defection of Burgess and Maclean. He was re-employed in 1956 but his cover as a Russian double agent was subsequently blown and he defected in 1963. Harold A R Philby *My Silent War* Macgibbon and Kee 1968 is an unrepentant memoir written after his defection. Hugh Redwald Trevor-Roper *The Philby Affair: Espionage, Treason and Secret Services* Kimber 1968 is an account by a former colleague. See also Eleanor Philby *The Spy I Loved* Hamilton 1968. Other studies are Bruce Page, David Leitch and Philip Knightley *Philby: The Spy who Betrayed a Generation* 2nd ed, Sphere 1977, Patrick Seale and Maureen McConville *Philby: The Long Road to Moscow* Hamilton 1973 and Edward Spiro *The Third Man* Putnam 1968.

**2374**   George Watt *China Spy* Johnson 1972. Watt was arrested in Peking in 1967 at the height of the Cultural Revolution and sentenced to three years for espionage.

**2375**   Andrew Boyle *The Climate of Treason: Five who Spied for Russia* Hutchinson 1973. This is the book which unmasked Anthony Blunt as the so-called 'Fourth Man' who had spied for the Russians whilst serving in British intelligence. On Blunt see also Barrie Penrose and Simon Freeman *Conspiracy of Silence: The Secret Life of Anthony Blunt* Grafton Books 1986, John Costello *Mask of Treachery* Collins 1988 (which also comments on the New Zealander Patrick Costello) and Douglas Sutherland *The Fourth Man* Secker and Warburg 1980.

**2376** Peter Wright *Spycatcher: The Candid Autobiography of a Senior Intelligence Officer* Viking, New York 1987. A book which reflects Wright's obsessions about Soviet penetration of MI5. It can be seen as an attempt to justify his discredited pursuit of Sir Roger Hollis, Director of MI5 1956–65, and also of Prime Minister Harold Wilson. This autobiography is also unreliable in a number of other details. It is perhaps more important for the effect of its publication on the British government and intelligence community than for the story it tells, for much of Wright's case had already appeared by proxy in the writings of Chapman Pincher (see [2377–8]). Malcolm Turnbull *The Spycatcher Trial* Heinemann 1988 is a perceptive account of Whitehall's failed attempts to prevent the publication of the book in Australia by Wright's successful Australian lawyer. It is also perceptive on Wright though the account of the trial itself is rather pedestrian. In the aftermath of this failure the British government brought in an Act amending the 1911 Official Secrets Act in order to prevent further disclosures of this kind.

**2377** Chapman Pincher *Inside Story: A Documentary of the Pursuit of Power* Sidgwick and Jackson 1978. Collected journalism. Although these pieces deal with a variety of topics the principle feature is intelligence. Much of the book is in fact taken up with the story of an MI5 plot against Harold Wilson. David Leigh *The Wilson Plot: The Intelligence Services and the Discrediting of a Prime Minister 1945–1976* Heinemann 1988 is an investigation of this plot.

**2378** Chapman Pincher *Their Trade is Treachery* Sidgwick and Jackson 1981. A controversial book which purported to expose Sir Roger Hollis as a Russian mole. It drew a denial from the Prime Minister in the House of Commons. This and similar claims drawing on the prejudices of Peter Wright (see [2376]) are also pursued in his *Too Secret Too Long* Sidgwick and Jackson 1984.

**2379** Chapman Pincher *The Secret Offensive: Active Measures: A Saga of Deception, Disinformation, Subversion, Terrorism, Sabotage and Assassination* Sidgwick and Jackson 1985. This is essentially about the Russian secret services and their tactics but it contains plenty of reflections on British counter-subversion and counter-espionage tactics.

## (9) Ex-Servicemen

**2380** J Graham Wootton *The Politics of Influence: British Ex-Servicemen, Cabinet Decisions and Cultural Change 1917–1957* Routledge and Kegan Paul 1963. A good study of the political influence of ex-service organizations.

**2381** J Graham Wootton *Official History of the British Legion* Macdonald and Evans 1956. A useful history of the largest and most influential of the ex-service associations. See also Anthony Brown *Red for Remembrance: The British Legion 1921–71* Heinemann 1971.

**2382** P Ryde *Out on a Limb: A Celebration of the British Limbless Ex-Servicemen's Association Golden Jubilee 1932–1982* BLESMA 1982.

## C. WARFARE

## (1) General

**2383** James H Wyllie *The Influence of British Arms: An Analysis of British Military Intervention Since 1956* Allen and Unwin 1984. This provides a series of case studies on British intervention from Suez to the Falklands. It also analyses the contraction of Britain's world military role and her continuing military commitments. See also John Van Wingen and Herbert K Tillema 'British Military Intervention After World War Two: Militance in a Second Rank Power' *Journal of Peace Research* 17 1980 pp 291–303.

**2384** Robert Jackson *Strike from the Sea: A Survey of British Naval Air Operations 1900–69* Barker 1970. See also his *The RAF in Action: From Flanders to the Falklands* Blandford 1985.

## (2) Military Strategists

**2385** Brian Holden Reid *J F C Fuller: Military Thinker* Macmillan 1987. A excellent study of the military thought of Fuller and the evolution of his ideas. Fuller was a pioneer of tank warfare and one of the most important strategists of the twentieth century. See also Anthony John Trythall *'Boney' Fuller: The Intellectual General 1878–1966* Cassell 1977.

**2386** Brian Bond *Liddell Hart: A Study of his Military Thought* Cassell 1977. A good study of the evolution and influence of Liddell Hart's thought. For the post-war development and application of Liddell Hart's thought see Basil H Liddell Hart *Deterrence and Defence* Stevens 1960.

## (3) The Korean War

**2387** Keith Macfarland *The Korean War: An Annotated Bibliography* Garland 1986.

**2388** Max Hastings *The Korean War* Michael Joseph 1987. A general military history which gives good coverage of the British role in the UN forces fighting in Korea 1950–3. Based on a television history it makes extensive and good use of interviews. John Halliday and Bruce Cumings *Korea: The Unknown War* Viking 1988 is another good study which also formed the basis for a television series. Callum A MacDonald *Korea: The War Before Vietnam* Macmillan 1986 concentrates on the American role in the war and its consequences for American strategy. Britain's role in the war and its domestic consequences is examined in Jong-Yil Re 'Britain and the Korean War 1950–1954' Cambridge PhD Thesis 1971–2. Particularly useful on the domestic consequences of the war in Britain is David Rees *Korea: The Limited War* Macmillan 1964. Tim Carew *The Korean War* Cassell 1967 remains good on the conduct and strategy of the war. See also S L A Marshall *The Military History of the Korean War* Franklin Watts, New York 1963. Reginald William Thompson *Cry Korea* Panther 1956 is a war correspondent's account of the conflict.

**2389** James Cotton and Ian Neary (ed) *The Korean War in History* Manchester University Press 1989. A series of studies on various aspects of the war using recently released archives by British, European, American and Korean scholars. Britain's reasons for entering the war are explored in Michael Dockrill 'The Foreign Office, Anglo-American Relations and the Korean War June 1950–June 1951' *International Affairs* 62 1986 pp 459–76.

**2390** Peter Lowe *The Origins of the Korean War* Longman 1986. A well regarded study, as is Bruce Cumings *The Origins of the Korean War* Princeton University Press, Princeton, New Jersey 1981.

**2391** P D Truscott 'The Korean War in British Foreign and Domestic Policy 1950–1952' Oxford DPhil Thesis 1986. A good study of the consequences of the war on the Western Alliance in Europe and the Far East and of the economic and political consequences of Gaitskell's rearmament budget of 1951.

**2392** Jong-Yil Re 'Special Relationship at War: The Anglo-American Relationship During the Korean War' *Journal of Strategic Studies* 7 1984 pp 301–17. A principal British concern was to prevent the escalation of the war. As William Stueck 'The Limits of Influence: British Policy and American Expansion of the War in Korea' *Pacific History Review* 55 1986 pp 65–95 points out that Britain however had little success in this endeavour. The failure of Britain's attempt to call a halt to MacArthur's drive North towards the Chinese border before it provoked Chinese intervention is examined in Peter N Farrar 'Britain's Proposal for a Buffer Zone South of the Yalu in November 1950: Was it a Neglected Opportunity to end the Fighting in Korea' *Journal of Contemporary History* 18 1983 pp 327–51. On the British response to the Chinese intervention in November 1950 and Truman's subsequent comments on the possible use of the atomic bomb see R J Foot 'Anglo-American Relations in the Korean Crisis: The British Effort to Avert an Expanded War December 1950–January 1951' *Diplomatic History* 10 1986 pp 59–73.

**2393** Jeffrey Grey *The Commonwealth Armies and the Korean War: An Alliance Study* Manchester University Press 1988. A good history of the Commonwealth involvement in the war. The various Commonwealth army units in Korea, the bulk of which were British, were formed into a Commonwealth division, the history of which is told in C N Barclay *The First Commonwealth Division: The Story of the British Commonwealth Land Forces in Korea 1950–53* Gale and Polden 1954. See also P Gaston *Thirty-Eighth Parallel: The British in Korea* Hamilton 1976 on the British forces involved in the war.

**2394** Eric Linklater *Our Men in Korea* HMSO 1952. An official account. See also Ashley Cunningham-Boothe and Peter Farrar (eds) *British Forces in the Korean War* British Korean Veterans Association 1988. G I Malcolm *The Argylls in Korea* Nelson 1952 and *The Royal Ulster Rifles in Korea* William Mullan 1952 record regimental tours of duty during the war.

**2395** Anthony Farrar-Hockley *The Edge of the Sword* Muller 1954. This memoir is particularly useful for the Glosters heroic stand in the Battle of the Imjin River 1951.

**2396** Arthur James Barker *Fortune Favours the Brave: The Hook, Korea 1953* Cassell 1974. An account of the last major battle of the war in May 1953 in which the men of the Commonwealth division were heavily involved. D J Hollands *The Dead, the Dying and the Damned* Cassell 1956 is a fictionalized account of service in Korea by one who served as a National Service subaltern in this battle.

## (4) Suez

**2397** Donald Cameron Watt (ed) *Documents on the Suez Crisis 26 July to 6 November 1956* Oxford University Press 1956. A good documentary survey of the background to and the unfolding of the crisis up to the end of hostilities. *The Suez Canal Problem July 26–September 22 1956* US Department of State, Washington DC 1956 provides detailed documentation on the development of the crisis from the American point of view up to the second Suez conference in London in September 1956. On the aftermath see E Lauterpacht (ed) *The Suez Canal Settlement: A Selection of Documents Relating to the Clearance of the Suez Canal and the Settlement of Disputes Between the United Kingdom, France and the United Arab Republic October 1956–March 1959* Stevens 1960.

**2398** Peter Hennessy, Mark Laity and Anthony Gorst 'Suez – What the Papers Say' *Contemporary Record* 1/1 1987 pp 2–13. A resumé of the crisis and a guide to the recently released papers in the Public Record Office. It also includes a useful chronology and a discussion of Whitehall's attempt to suppress Sir Anthony Nutting's account of the crisis [2400]. For a study of the crisis in the light of the recently released papers in the Public Record Office see Anthony Gorst and W Scott Lucas 'Suez 1956: Strategy and the Diplomatic Process' *Journal of Strategic Studies* 11 1988 pp 391–436.

**2399** Hugh Thomas *The Suez Affair* 3rd ed, Weidenfeld and Nicolson 1986. An outstanding account based on extensive interviewing. As the years have taken their toll he has gradually began to reveal his sources. Thanks to the quality of the investigative work that went into this or Paul Johnson's early study, *The Suez War* Macgibbon and Kee 1957, the inner history of the crisis became generally known well before the official papers were released in January 1987. David Carlton *Britain and the Suez Crisis* Blackwell 1988 is the first study to make use of these documents. A good study which includes useful appendices and a chronology, it is interestingly much less damning of Eden than is Carlton's earlier biography [813]. See also the collection of papers, Roger Louis and Roger Owen (eds) *Suez 1956: The Crisis and its Consequences* Oxford University Press 1989. These essays survey the development of the crisis, the perspectives of America and the Commonwealth, the economic situation at the time and the consequences of the episode. Some of the contributors were participants at the time. Anthony Moncrieff (ed) *Suez – Ten Years After* BBC 1967 is an interesting collection of oral accounts based on a radio series. A good study of the background to the crisis is Guy Wint and Peter Calvocoressi *Middle East Crisis* Penguin 1957. See also Wilfrid Byford Jones *Oil on Troubled Waters* Hale 1957, John Connell *The Most Important Country* Cassell 1957 and Michael Adams *Suez and After: Year of Crisis* Beacon Press 1958.

**2400** Sir Anthony Nutting *No End of a Lesson: The Story of Suez* Constable 1967. Nutting resigned as Minister of State at the Foreign Office in protest at Britain's military intervention at Suez on 5th November 1956. This could be seen as a belated resignation statement. It

is also useful on the background of collusion between Britain, France and Israel. Collusion was first broached in the French instant history, Merry and Serge Blomberger *Les Secrets de Suez* Editions des Quatre Fils Aymon, Paris 1957. This is however a rather sensational account to be used with caution. On collusion see also Geoffrey Warner '"Collusion" and the Suez Crisis of 1956' *International Affairs* 55 1979 pp 226–39. Terence Robinson *Crisis: The Inside Story of the Suez Conspiracy* Hutchinson 1965 is an account of the diplomatic intrigues behind the invasion of November 1956.

**2401** Donald Neff *Warriors at Suez: Eisenhower takes America into the Middle East* Simon and Shuster, New York 1981. Essays on the attitudes and roles in the crisis of America, Israel, France and Britain. The relations between Britain and America during the Suez crisis and in Middle Eastern affairs are reassessed in W Scott Lucas 'Neustadt Revisited: A New Look at Suez and the Anglo-American "Alliance"' in Tony Gorst, Lewis Johnman and W Scott Lucas (eds) *Postwar Britain 1945–64: Themes and Perspectives* Pinter 1989 pp 182–202.

**2402** A Thomas *Comment Israel fut Sauvé* A Michel, Paris 1978. This is the most complete French account of the Suez crisis. Georges Assima *La Crise de Suez 1956* L'Age d'Homme, Lausanne 1970 is good French study that also draws on Arab and Soviet sources. It is also good on the consequences of Suez and the adjustment of both France and Britain to the loss of status that followed. Jacques George-Picot *The Real Suez Crisis: The end of a Great Nineteenth Century Work* Harcourt, Brace, Jovanovitch 1978 is an account from the point of view of the Suez Canal Company.

**2403** Mohammed Hassanein Heikel *Cutting the Lion's Tail: Suez Through Egyptian Eyes* Deutsch 1986. An account by Nasser's friend and confidante. This authoritative Egyptian study does not force major reassessment but it does contain interesting revelations and anecdotes. It draws on Nasser's and Egyptian papers. The English translation lacks the appendix of 250 documents of the Arabic original (*Milaffat al-Suways* Al-Ahram Center for Translation and Publishing, New York 1986).

**2404** Roy Fullick and Geoffrey Powell *Suez: The Double War* Hamilton 1979. The best study of the military preparations and operations. It also looks at the Six Day War of 1967 as does Kenneth Love *Suez: The Twice-Fought War* Longman 1970. A J Barker *Suez: The Seven Day War* Faber 1964 is a good account of the campaign and the shortcomings of the British military machine. Another study of the campaign is Geoffrey Blaxland *Objective: Egypt* Muller 1966. The preparations are examined in D A Al-Solami 'British Preparations for the Suez War – 1956' Exeter PhD Thesis 1988.

Robert Jackson *Suez 1956: Operation Musketeer* Ian Allan 1980 is a short popular account.

**2405** 'A Seminar on the Air Aspects of the Suez Campaign – 1956' *Royal Air Force Historical Society Proceedings* 3 1988 pp 9–65. Transcriptions of a series of witness seminars attended by British Air Force officers and civil servants.

**2406** Sir Edwin Herbert *Damage and Casualties in Port Said* Cmnd 47, *Parliamentary Papers* xviii 1956–57. The only inquiry into the Suez episode was this report which focused on the operation and did not enquire into the background planning.

**2407** R R Bowie *Suez 1956* Oxford University Press 1974. A study of the role of international law in the crisis. *International Law and the Middle East Crisis: A Symposium* Tulane Studies in Political Science Vol IV, Tulane University, New Orleans 1957 is a useful study of the UN intervention and the legality of the Anglo-French operation. On this latter point see also E D Briggs 'The Anglo-French Action at Suez 1956: A Study of Opinion Concerning its Compatibility with the United Nations Charter' London PhD Thesis 1959–60.

**2408** Leon D Epstein *British Politics in the Suez Crisis* Pall Mall Press 1964. A good study of the response of politicians and the public to the crisis. See also Russell Braddon *Suez: The Splitting of the Nation* Collins 1973 and Max Beloff 'Suez and British Conscience' *Commentary* 23 1957 pp 309–15.

**2409** Lewis Johnman 'Defending the Pound: The Economics of the Suez Crisis 1956' in Tony Gorst, Lewis Johnman and W Scott Lucas (eds) *Postwar Britain 1945–64: Themes and Perspectives* Pinter 1989 pp 166–81. An important examination of the hitherto largely neglected economic crisis prompted by the Suez adventure.

**2410** Herman Finer *Dulles over Suez: The Theory and Practice of his Diplomacy* Quadrangle Books 1964. An excellent study of the important role played by the American Secretary of State, John Foster Dulles, during the crisis.

**2411** Selwyn Lloyd *Suez 1956: A Personal Account* Cape 1978. The posthumously published memoir of the then British Foreign Secretary. It glosses over the full extent of collusion with the Israelis but nevertheless furnishes some information not available elsewhere. Christian Pineau *1956 Suez* Editions Robert Laffont, Paris 1976 is a useful memoir by the then French Foreign Minister.

**2412** Moshe Dayan *Diary of the Sinai Campaign* Weidenfeld and Nicolson 1966. This is useful both for the Israeli campaign in 1956 and for the negotiations that preceded the operations.

**2413** André Beaufré *The Suez Expedition 1956* Faber 1969. The authoritative account of the French task force commander. Sandy Cavanagh *Airborne to Suez* Kimber 1965 is an account by a medical officer who served with the Parachute regiment in Cyprus and Suez. For other campaign memoirs see D M J Clark *Suez Touchdown* Peter Davies 1964 and Robert Henriques *100 Hours to Suez* Collins 1957.

**2414** David Dilks (ed) *The Diaries of Sir Alexander Cadogan 1938–45* Cassell 1971. This includes a useful epilogue on his time as a governor of the BBC and the problems over the reporting of the Suez crisis, not least because he was a government director of the Suez Canal Company at the time.

## (5) The Falklands War

**2415** *The Falklands War: The Official History* Latin American Newsletters Ltd 1983. This arranges the Argentinian and British official communiqués chronologically and parallel to each other. Flaws and gaps in the official version are commented on in the helpful introduction.

**2416** *The Falklands Campaign: A Digest of Debates in the House of Commons 2 April to 15 June 1982* HMSO 1982. The value of this is reduced by certain omissions, not least of the important session on 22 March after the Argentine seizure of South Georgia.

**2417** 'The South Atlantic Crisis: Bakcground, Consequences, Documentation' *United States Department of State Bulletin* 82/2067 1982 pp 78–90.

**2418** Lawrence Freedman 'Bridgehead Revisited: The Literature of the Falklands' *International Affairs* 59 1983 pp 445–52. A good review article on the copious literature. The Argentinian literature on the war is reviewed in Simon Collier 'The First Falklands War: Argentine Attitudes' *International Affairs* 59 1983 pp 459–64.

**2419** Lawrence Freedman and Virginia Gamba-Stonehouse *Signals of War: The Falklands Conflict of 1982* Faber 1990. The fullest account of the war providing a detailed examination of the process of decision-making on each side written jointly by distinguished British and Argentine authors. Lawrence Freedman *Britain and the Falklands War* Blackwell 1988 is a good overview of the war and the issues that it raised. Max Hastings and Simon Jenkins *The Battle for the Falklands* Michael Joseph 1983 is the best account of the conflict. Another good study of the course of the campaign is Martin Middlebrook *Task Force: The South Atlantic 1982* 2nd ed, Penguin 1987. There are also a large number of instant histories. The most instant of these (and it shows) is Sunday Times Insight Team *The Falklands War: The Full Story* Sphere 1982. Patrick Bishop and John Witherow *The Winter War: The Falklands* Quartet 1982 is a useful account of the conduct of the war and the experiences of the soldiers by a couple of war correspondents. Brian Hanrahan and Robert Fox *'I Counted them all out and I Counted them all back': The Battle for the Falklands* BBC 1982 is a collection of war despatches and retrospective interviews. Robert Fox has also published *Eyewitness Falklands: A Personal Account of the Falklands Campaign* Methuen 1982. Anthony Barrett *Iron Britannia* Allison and Busby 1982 is a critical instant history of Britain's conduct in the crisis. P Calvert *The Falklands Crisis* Pinter 1982 in contrast defends Britain. See also Christopher Dobson, John Miller and Ronald Page *The Falklands Conflict* Coronet 1982.

**2420**  Michael Charlton *The Little Platoon: Diplomacy and the Falklands Dispute* Blackwell 1989. This account based on an acclaimed radio series is particularly useful on the diplomatic efforts to avert the conflict. It draws on interviews with UN, British, American and Argentine figures. See also Philip Windsor 'Diplomatic Dimensions of the Falklands Crisis' *Millenium: Journal of International Studies* 12 1983 pp 88–96. Sir Anthony Parsons 'The Falklands Crisis in the United Nations 31 March–14 June 1982' *International Affairs* 1983 pp 169–78 is an account of the UN's handling of the crisis sparked by the Argentine seizure of South Georgia and the Falklands by the then British ambassador to the UN. The role of the Americans in the crisis is discussed in David Lewis Feldman 'The United States Role in the Malvinas Crisis 1982: Misguidance and Misrepresentation in Argentina's Decision to go to War' *International Studies and World Affairs* 27 1985 pp 1–22. He argues that the lack of clear signals from the Americans encouraged Argentine intransigence and contributed to the failure of negotiations. On pp 23–4 Alexander Haig, the then US Secretary of State, replies. Haig's memoirs, *Caveat* Weidenfeld and Nicolson 1984, are useful but not wholly reliable. British relations with the Americans during the war are discussed in Sir Nicholas Henderson 'America and the Falklands: Case Study in the Behaviour of an Ally' *The Economist* 12/11/1983 pp 49–60. Henderson was the British Ambassador in Washington at the time. On the response of the European Community to the crisis see Geoffrey Edwards 'Europe and the Falklands Islands Crisis 1982' *Journal of Common Market Studies* 22 1983–84 pp 295–313. On the importance of Britain's relations with the Americans and the Europeans in the handling of the crisis see Hugh Macdonald 'Britain and the Falklands War: The Lessons of Interdependence' *Millenium: Journal of International Studies* 12 1983 pp 176–88.

**2421**  Virginia Gamba-Stonehouse *The Falklands/Malvinas War: A Model for North-South Crisis Prevention* Allen and Unwin 1987. The best Argentinian account. Carlos Chubretovich *Las Islas Falkland o Malvinas, su Historia, la Controversia Argentino-Britanica y la guera consiguente* Editorial la Noria, Santiago 1986 is a Chilean account of the background to and course of the war.

**2422**  *Falkland Islands Review: Report of a Committee of Privy Counsellors* Cmnd 8787, *Parliamentary Papers* 1982–83. The committee chaired by Lord Franks. It traces policy towards the islands from 1965 onwards and is particularly detailed on the period 1979–82. Although it is a meticulous guide to British errors of judgement that contributed to the crisis it clears the Thatcher government of blame.

**2423**  G M Dillon *The Falklands, Politics and War* Macmillan 1988. An analysis of the relationship between political judgement, bureaucratic advice and military intelligence in the mismanagement of Britain's Falklands policy. It also discusses policy in the aftermath of war.

**2424**  W Fowler *The Battle for the Falklands: Land Forces* Osprey 1982. In the same series are A English and A Wells *Naval Forces*, and R Braybrook *Air Forces* (also Osprey 1982).

**2425**  David Brown *The Royal Navy and the Falklands War* Cooper 1988. This official history narrates the voyage of the task force and its performance in the war. See also Anthony Preston *Sea Combat off the Falklands: The Lessons that must be Learned* Willow 1982.

**2426**  Jeffrey Ethell and Alfred Price *Air War South Atlantic* Sidgwick and Jackson 1983. A very good account of the battle for command of the air. The role of air power in the campaign is examined in M J Armitage and R A Mason 'The Falklands Campaign' in their *Air Power in the Nuclear Age 1945–82* Macmillan 1983 pp 202–22. The effect of the Argentine failure to use their aircraft carrier is assessed in Gustavo Astaburuaga 'Falklands, la Batalla Aeronaval que no fue' *Revista de Marina* 5 1986 pp 549–60.

**2427**  Valerie Adams 'Logistics Support for the Falklands Campaign' *Journal of the Royal United Services Institute for Defence Studies* 129 1984 pp 43–9. The story of how the problems of maintaining supplies for an unexpected campaign 6,000 miles away were successfully surmounted.

**2428**  Lawrence Freedman 'Intelligence Operations in the Falklands' *Intelligence and National Security* 2 1986 pp 309–35.

**2429** Tam Dalyell *One Man's Falklands . . .* Cecil Woolf 1982. An account of the Falklands crisis in parliament by a Labour MP who was particularly active in raising the question of the British sinking of the Argentine battleship the *General Belgrano* with the loss of over 600 lives. On this controversial episode see Third Report of the House of Commons Foreign Affairs Commit tee *Events of the Weekend of 1st and 2nd May 1982* HC Paper 11, *Parliamentary Papers* 1984–85. The most substan tial, although now to some extent discredited account of the sinking is Desmond Rise and Arthur Gavston *The Sinking of the Belgrano* Secker and Warburg 1984. The debate on this episode has been reassessed in *Report of the Assessors on the Belgra no Inquiry (November 1986)* Belgrano Action Group 1988.

**2430** Jean Carr *Another Story: Women and the Falklands War* Hamilton 1984. A study of the effect of the war on service wives and families and of the compensation for the injured and bereaved.

**2431** Gary W Wynia *Argentina: Illusions and Realities* Holmes and Meier 1986. This is useful on the reasons why Argentina invaded the Falklands. The Argentine experience of the conflict is examined in Martin Middlebrook *The Fight for the 'Malvinas': The Argentine Forces in the Falklands War* Viking 1988. Jimmy Burns *The Land that Lost its Heroes: The Falklands, the Postwar and Alfonsin* Bloomsbury 1987 is an account of Argentina since 1981 by a British journalist based there. It is of some use on Argentina during the war.

**2432** J Woodward and John Moore 'The Falklands Experience' *Journal of the Royal United Services Institute for Defence Studies* 128 1983 pp 25–32. A memoir of the campaign by the sea and land commanders.

**2433** Michael Bilton and Peter Kosminsky *Speaking Out: Untold Stories from the Falklands War* Deutsch 1989. A collection of oral accounts by soldiers, diplomats, politicians and others, British, Argentine and American, derived from an acclaimed television programme.

**2434** Julian Thompson *No Picnic* Secker and Warburg 1985. The best of the campaign memoirs. See also Nick Vaux *March to the South Atlantic* Buchan and Enright 1986. A more critical memoir is John Lawrence and Robert Lawrence *When the Fighting is Over: A Personal Story of the Battle for Tumbledown Mountain and its Aftermath* Bloomsbury 1988. Rick Jolly *The Red and Green Life Machine: Diary of the Falklands Field Hospital* Century 1983 is useful on the atmosphere of the conflict. A valuable corrective to the reminiscences of survivors is David Tinker *A Message from the Falklands* Junction Books 1982. Tinker was killed on *HMS Glamorgan*. This is a collection of letters home. Hugh Tinker 'The Falklands After Three Years' *Round Table*

296 1985 pp 339–44 is the critical reflections on the war of his distinguished father.

**2435** John Smith *74 Days: An Islander's Diary of the Falklands Occupation* Century 1984. A record of the Argentine occupation of the islands.

## (6) Colonial Wars and Counter-Insurgency

### (a) General

**2436** Charles Townsend *Britain's Civil Wars: Counter- Insurgency in the Twentieth Century* Faber 1986. A good series of studies of campaigns in Ireland, the Middle East, Kenya and Malaysia. The majority of British operations since 1945 have been counter-insurgency campaigns against either nationalist or Communist guerrillas. Julian Paget *Counter-Insurgency Campaigning* Faber 1967 mentions some 34 such operations in his study of the problems of this sort of warfare. A similar work is Richard Clutterbuck *Guerrillas and Terrorists* Faber 1977. See also Lawrence James *Imperial Rearguard: Wars of Empire 1919–1985* Brassey's Defence 1988 and M Dewar *Brush Fire Wars: Minor Campaigns of the British Army Since 1945* Hale 1984. Charles Allen *The Savage Wars of Peace* Michael Joseph 1989 is an oral history of these minor wars from the point of view of the soldiers who fought in them.

**2437** J Bowyer Bell *On Revolt: Strategies of National Liberation* Harvard University Press 1976. A general study of revolts against British imperial power, with case studies of Palestine, Malaya, the Gold Coast, Kenya, Egypt, Cyprus, Aden and Northern Ireland. It includes useful reflections on the nature of the British response.

**2438** Frank Kitson *Bunch of Five* Faber 1977. A study of counter-insurgency operations drawing on his experiences in Northern Ireland, Kenya, Malaya, Oman and Cyprus. It is vividly told and heavily autobiographical.

**2439** M J Armitage and R A Mason 'Air Power in Colonial Wars' in their *Air Power in the Nuclear Age 1945–82: Theory and Practice* Macmillan 1983 pp 46–82. A useful study.

### (b) Greece 1941–47

**2440** E D Smith *Victory of a Sort: The British in Greece 1941–46* Hale 1988. A comprehensive account of action in Greece drawing on his own experiences. British policy and involvement in the Greek Civil War against Communist guerrillas after the end of the Second World War is examined in George Martin Alexander *The*

*Prelude to the Truman Doctrine: British Policy in Greece 1944–1947* Clarendon 1982. A more critical analysis of British policy in Greece is H Richter *British Intervention in Greece from Vakiza to Civil War February 1945 to August 1946* Merlin 1985.

**2441** Robert Frazier 'Did Britain Start the Cold War? Bevin and the Truman Doctrine' *Historical Journal* 27 1984 pp 715–27. This argues that the British withdrawal in 1947 and their subsequent replacement by the Americans was not a plot to draw the Americans into the defence of Europe so much as a recognition of an impossible commitment.

**2441A** Eric Leggett *The Corfu Incident* Seeley Service 1974. An account of the incident when two British destroyers were damaged by Albanian mines whilst sailing up the Corfu channel in 1946 and an explanation of why there was so little reaction to this in Britain at the time.

### (c) Palestine

**2442** David A Charters *The British Army and Jewish Insurgency in Palestine 1945–47* Macmillan 1988. The first comprehensive account of the conduct and failings of counter- insurgency operations and intelligence gathering in the last days of the mandate. R D Wilson *Cordon and Search* Gale and Polden 1949 is an account of the operations of the 6th Airborne Division in Palestine.

**2443** J Bowyer Bell *Terror out of Zion: Irgun Zvai Leumi, LEHI and the Palestine Underground 1929–1949* St Martins Press, New York 1977. A good study of Jewish terrorist organizations. On the Irgun see Eli Tavin and Yonah Alexander (eds) *Psychological Warfare and Propaganda: Irgun Documentation* Scholarly Resources, Wilmington, Delaware 1982. Menachem Begin *The Revolt: Story of the Irgun* W H Allen 1951 is an account of the Irgun's operations by one of leading Jewish terrorists. On the activities of the intelligence arm of Hagana, and its role in, for instance, the illegal immigration of Jews to Palestine in 1945–47, see Efraim Dekel *Shai: The Exploits of Hagana Intelligence* Thomas Yoseloff 1959. On the Stern Gang see Y S Brenner 'The "Stern Gang" 1940–1948' *Middle East Studies* 2 1965 pp 2–30.

**2444** Thurston Clarke *By Blood and Fire* Putnam 1981. An account of the blowing up by Jewish terrorists of the mandate offices in the King David Hotel in Jerusalem in 1946.

**2445** Samuel Katz *Days of Fire* W H Allen 1968. A semi- autobiographical study of the struggle for the state of Israel by a former Jewish terrorist. Another terrorist memoir (only available in Hebrew) is Yellin-Mor *Lechumi Herut Yisrael* Shikmana, Jerusalem 1974. See also [1449].

### (d) The Malayan Emergency

**2446** Anthony Short *The Communist Insurrection in Malaya 1948–1960* Muller 1975. A semi-official history, for the Malaysian government, of the war making extensive use of documents and interviews. Harry Miller *Jungle War in Malaya: The Campaign Against Communism 1948–60* Barker 1972 is another good and well illustrated account. Richard Clutterbuck *The Long, Long War: The Emergency in Malaya 1948–1960* Cassell 1967 is particularly good on the military aspects of the campaign. Noel Barber *The War of the Running Dogs: How Malaya Defeated the Communist Guerrillas 1948–60* Collins 1971 is a colourful and occasionally anecdotal account. See also Edgar O'Ballance *Malaya: The Communist Insurgent War 1948–1960* Faber 1966.

**2447** E D Smith *Counter-Insurgency Operations: Malaya and Borneo* Ian Allan 1985. A short but vivid account of tactics in the Emergency and in the Confrontation against Indonesia in 1963–66. The author served in both campaigns. It is well illustrated and has a useful bibliography.

**2448** Robert Thompson *Defeating Communist Insurgency: Experience from Malaya and Vietnam* Macmillan 1978. Reflections on this problem. Thompson served in Malaya and later headed the British advisory mission in South Vietnam.

**2449** Daniel S Challis 'Counter Insurgency Success in Malaya' *Military Review* 67 1987 pp 56–69. This analyses the reasons for the British success in Malaya.

**2450** Harry Miller *Menace in Malaya* Harrap 1954. A survey of the situation in the middle of the Emergency. It is useful on the background to the Emergency and the British tactics. See also Victor Purcell *Malaya: Communist or Free?* Gollancz 1954.

**2451** J B Oldfield *The Green Howards in Malaya (1949–1952): The Story of a Post-War Tour of Duty by a Battalion of the Line* Gale and Polden 1953. For the Gurkhas in the Emergency see A E C Bredin *The Happy Warriors* Blackmore 1961.

**2452** Mark Henniker *Red Shadow over Malaya* Blackwood 1955. Other campaign memoirs are Richard Meirs *Shoot to Kill* Faber 1959, Oliver Crawford *The Door Marked Malaya* Hart-Davis 1958 and Arthur Campbell *Jungle Green* Allen and Unwin 1953.

**2453** Lucian W Pye *Guerrilla Communism in Malaya* Oxford University Press 1956. An uncritical assessment based on interviews with former guerrillas.

### (e) Mau Mau

**2454** Frederick Cooper 'Mau Mau and the Discourses of Decolonisation' *Journal of African History* 29 1988 pp 313–20. A useful historiographical review.

**2455** Fred Madjalany *State of Emergency: The Full Story of Mau Mau* Longmans 1962. This is very useful on the campaign against Mau Mau as is Frank Kitson *Gangs and Counter-Gangs* Barrie and Rockliff 1960. Ladislav Venys *A History of the Mau Mau Movement in Kenya* Charles University, Prague 1970 is a short history with a useful chronology.

**2456** Carl G Rosberg and John Nottingham *The Myth of Mau Mau: Nationalism in Kenya* Praeger, New York 1966. This places Mau Mau in the context of political activity since the 1920s. It rejects the thesis of official accounts that the revolt was the result of tribal savagery, which is seen as essentially a European explanation and propaganda exercise. The principal statement of this official view is F D Corfield *The Origins and Growth of Mau Mau: An Historical Survey* Government Printer, Nairobi 1960. The fullest statement of the official view that Mau Mau was a form of collective psychological disorder akin to devil worship is J C Carothers *The Psychology of Mau Mau* Government Printer, Nairobi 1954. See also Anthony Lavers *Kenya During and After Mau Mau* Government Printer, Nairobi 1957. This sort of view is also expressed in many of the contemporary accounts of the emergency. These accounts, by respected scientists like L S B Leakey, who wrote *Mau Mau and the Kikuyu* Methuen 1954 and *Defeating Mau Mau* Methuen 1954, reiterate similar themes. For other hostile contemporary accounts see Ione Leigh *In the Shadow of Mau Mau* W H Allen 1954 and C T Stoneham 'Mau Mau' Museum Press 1953. A useful response to these views and particularly the arguments advanced by Corfield is *Around Mount Kenya: Comment on Corfield* Makerere Kikuyu Embu and Meru Students Association 1960.

**2457** Robert Buijtenhuijs *Mau Mau: Twenty Years After: The Myth and the Survivors* Mouton, Paris 1973. A good analysis of interpretations and the continuing importance of Mau Mau in Kenyan popular culture, historiography and fiction. David Maughan-Brown *Land, Freedom and Fiction: History and Ideology in Kenya* Zed Books 1983 largely concentrates on the fiction of the revolt.

**2458** Robert Buijtenhuijs *Essays on Mau Mau* African Studies Centre, Leiden 1982. A collection of interpretative essays focusing on the nature of the Mau Mau movement. His *Le Mouvement 'Mau Mau': Une Révolte Paysanne et Anti-Coloniale en Afrique Noire* Mouton, Paris 1971 is a good analysis of the movement's composition. One principal purpose is to explain why the movement was largely confined to the Kikuyu. There is a good bibliography. On the movement itself see Maina wa Kinyatti 'Mau Mau: The Peak of African Political Organisation in Colonial Kenya' *Kenya Historical Review* 5 1977 pp 287–311.

**2459** Robert H Bates 'The Agrarian Origins of Mau Mau: A Structural Account' *Agricultural History* 61 1987 pp 1–28. Bates sees the revolt as a class rebellion not a nationalist one, which was sparked by agricultural change forcing the Kikuyu off the land in the White Highlands. Another aspect of this agrarian discontent is considered in T M J Kanogo 'Rift Valley Squatters and Mau Mau' *Kenya Historical Review* 5 1977 pp 243–52. Mau Mau in the White Highlands is examined in Frank Furedi 'The Social Composition of Mau Mau in the White Highlands' *Journal of Peasant Studies* 1 1978 pp 486–505. For Mau Mau in other areas see M Tamarkin 'Mau Mau in Nakuru' *Kenya Historical Review* 5 1977 pp 225–41. On the participation of tribes other than the Kikuyu in Mau Mau see J T S Kamunchulun 'The Meru Participation in Mau Mau' *Kenya Historical Review* 3 1975 pp 193–216.

**2460** Ali A Mazrui 'Ideology, Theory and Revolution: Lessons from the Mau Mau' *Race and Class* 28 1987 pp 53–81. This challenge to the view that Mau Mau was non-ideological should be treated with caution. It is an example of how Mau Mau has been used by those on the Left to indict the capitalist post-colonial order in Kenya, rather than treat it in a historical fashion.

**2461** Anthony Clayton *Counter-Insurgency in Kenya: A Study of Military Operations Against Mau Mau* Transafrica Publishers, Nairobi 1976. A short account of the campaign and the British security arrangements. On the colonial government's strategy see C J M Alport 'Kenya's Answer to the Mau Mau Challenge' *African Affairs* 53 1954 pp 241–8. William Baldwin *Mau Mau Manhunt* E P Dutton and Co, New York 1957 is a colourful narrative of operations against Mau Mau. The story of the last major event of the campaign, the tracking and capture of the Mau Mau general Dedan Kimathi is vividly told in Ian Henderson and Philip Goodhart *The Hunt for Kimathi* Hamilton 1957. On Kimathi see also Maina wa Kinyatti (ed) *Kenya's Freedom Struggle: The Dedan Kimathi Papers* Zed Books 1987 and Maina wa Kinyatti (ed) *Kimathi's Letters: A Profile of Patriotic Courage* Heinemann Kenya, Nairobi 1987.

**2462** Paul Maina *Six Mau Mau Generals* Gazelle, Nairobi 1977. Uncritical biographies of six Mau Mau leaders. The most thorough biography of a Mau Mau figure is Donald L Barnett and Karari Njama *Mau Mau From Within: The Autobiography of a Mau Mau Leader* Macgibbon and Kee 1966. Njama was a guerrilla leader for two years. This is useful on the organization and oaths of Mau Mau (it even contains a glossary of Mau Mau terms). It also has a good bibliography. Barnett has also published a number of short transcripts of interviews with others involved in the movement. Mohamed Mathu *The Urban Guerrilla* Liberation Support Movement Press, Richmond, British Columbia 1974 and Karigo Muchai *The Hard Core* Liberation Support Movement Press, Richmond, British Columbia 1973 are both of committed activists. Ngugi Kabiro *Man in the Middle* Liberation Support Movement Press, Richmond, British Columbia 1973 focuses on someone on the fringes of the movement.

**2463** Waruhiu Itote *'Mau Mau' General* East African Publishing House 1967. A useful autobiography by the Mau Mau leader who was known as General China. It goes up to the independence negotiations. Another useful autobiography by a Mau Mau leader is J K Murithi with Peter Ndoria *War in the Forest: The Autobiography of a Mau Mau Leader* East African Publishing House, Nairobi 1971.

**2464** Shiraz Durrani *Kimathi: Mau Mau's First Prime Minister of Kenya* Vita Books 1986. Not so much a biography of one of the most important Mau Mau leaders as a polemical tract to be treated with circumspection.

**2465** Josiah M Kariuki *Mau Mau Detainee – The Account by a Kenyan African of his Experiences in Detention Camps 1953–1960* Oxford University Press 1963. See also Ngugi wa Thiong'o *Detained: A Writer's Prison Diary* Heinemann Education 1981.

**2466** Joram Wemweya *Freedom Fighter* East African Publishing House, Nairobi 1971. The autobiography of a Mau Mau fighter.

**(f) The Buraimi Oasis Dispute and the Oman War**

**2467** David Smiley 'Muscat and Oman: Background Events to 1950–1955; the Sultan's Forces; the 1957 Revolt; the Avery Mission; Events from April to November 1958' *Journal of the Royal United Services Institute* 105 1958 pp 29–47. The fullest account of British involvement and military operations in Oman in the 1950s.

**2468** John Barrett Kelly *Eastern Arabian Frontiers* Faber 1964. This traces Saudi pressure on its eastern neighbours during the twentieth century, focusing particularly on the Buraimi Oasis dispute. This strategically important point was seized by the Saudis in 1952. They were driven out in 1955 by Oman and Abu Dhabi with British help. Howard Bushrod Jr 'Buraimi, a Study in Diplomacy by Default' *Reporter* 23/1/1958 pp 13–6 argues the most important factor in the dispute was efforts by American oil companies to increase their concession areas at the expense of the British.

**2469** *The Oman War 1957–1959: A Critical History* Gulf Committee 1975. A study of British intervention in Muscat and Oman in the 1950s in defence of the Sultan against revolutionary insurgents. It also reflects on conflicts between the American backed Saudis and the British sphere of influence and between British and American oil companies.

**2470** A J Deane-Drummond *Operations in Oman* British Army Review 1959. A study of military operations.

**2471** Anthony Shepherd *Arabian Adventure* Collins 1961. An account of service with the Trucial Oman scouts. It includes a detailed description of the role of the scouts in the Buraimi oasis dispute. Other memoirs of military service in Oman in this period are Percy Coriat *Soldier in Oman* Shelton 1960 and David Smiley *Arabian Assignment* Cooper 1975.

**(g) Cyprus**

**2472** *Terrorism in Cyprus: The Captured Documents* HMSO n.d. (1956?). This is the partial publication of documents, photographs and diaries captured by British intelligence in 1956. This material was used to exile Makarios.

**2473** Charles Foley and W I Scobie *The Struggle for Cyprus* Hoover Institution Press, Stanford, California 1975. A study of the guerrilla war 1955–60 which concentrates on EOKA. It is based on numerous interviews. See also Charles Foley *Island in Revolt* Longmans 1961.

**2474** Doras Alastos *Cyprus Guerrilla: Grivas, Makarios and the British* Heinemann 1960. A study of EOKA. It also has a useful documentary appendix.

**2475** Charles Foley (ed) *The Memoirs of General Grivas* Praeger, New York 1965. Grivas was the leader of the EOKA terrorists. George Grivas *Guerrilla Warfare and EOKA's Struggle* Longmans 1964 is his account of the terrorist campaign and the organisation of EOKA. Dudley Barker *Grivas: Portrait of a Terrorist* Cresset Press 1959 is a critical British study. See also W Byford Jones *Grivas and the Story of EOKA* Hale 1959.

**2476** For a memoir of service in Cyprus see [2413].

## (h) Kuwait 1961

**2477** A G Mezerik (ed) *Kuwait-Iraq Dispute 1961* International Review Service, New York 1961. A pamphlet on the Iraqi threat to Kuwait in 1961, the UK response and successful military intervention, and the handling of the dispute in the UN. It includes a chronology.

## (i) The Indonesian Confrontation

**2478** A G Mezerik (ed) *Malaysia-Indonesia Conflict* International Review Service 1965. An analysis of the development of the Confrontation and the roles of Britain, America, the USSR and China. It includes a useful chronology. Douglas Hyde *Confrontation in the East* The Bodley Head 1965 is largely concerned with the politics of the Confrontation, which began as an Indonesian response to the creation of a greater Malaysia with the incorporation of the British colonies of North Borneo and Sarawak in 1963.

**2479** Harold James and Denis Sheil-Small *The Undeclared War: The Story of the Indonesian Confrontation 1962–1966* Cooper 1971. A good account of military operations by British and Commonwealth forces in Borneo in response to the 1962 Brunei revolt and the incursions into Malaysia of Indonesian insurgents. Another useful account is J A C Mackie *Konfrontasi: The Indonesia-Malaysia Dispute 1963–1966* Oxford University Press 1974. See also A Vandenbosch 'Malaysia: Crisis of Confrontation' in his *The Changing Face of Southeast Asia* University of Kentucky Press, Lexington, Kentucky 1966 pp 74–106 and M R Wagstaff 'Britain's Forgotten War – The British Role in the Confrontation of Malaysia by Indonesia' Wales MSc (Econ) Thesis 1969–70. See also [2447].

**2480** P J Craw 'Indonesian Military Incursions into West Malaysia and Singapore Between August 1964 and 30th September 1965' *Journal of the Royal United Services Institute* 111 1966 pp 208–19.

**2481** Peter Dickens *SAS: The Jungle Frontier* Arms and Armour Press 1983. The SAS in Borneo.

## (j) Aden

**2482** Julian Paget *The Last Post: Aden 1964–67* Faber 1969. A good account of the vicious and unsuccessful war against insurgents in which Paget had served.

## (k) The Dhofar War

**2483** J Akehurst *We Won a War: The Campaign in Oman 1965–75* Michael Russell 1982. Akehurst served as a general during the last two years of this conflict against insurgents in Oman. This is a good account of a campaign in which British participation was kept as quiet as possible. Another good account is David C Arkless *The Secret War: Dhofar 1971/1972* Kimber 1988. Britain's role in the war, and its relationship with the previous policy of military withdrawal from the region is considered in John Everett Peterson 'Britain and the Oman War: An Arabian Entanglement' *Asian Affairs* 63 1976 pp 285–98.

**2484** A S Jeapes *SAS: Operation Oman* Kimber 1980. An excellent account of the SAS's role in the Dhofar war.

**2485** R M Burrell 'Rebellion in Dhofar: The Spectre of Vietnam' *New Middle East* Mar/Apr 1972 pp 55–8. This covers the origins of the war and the British intervention to protect western interests. He considers that its proximity to the politically unstable but economically vital Middle East rendered the war of considerably more strategic importance than Vietnam.

**2486** *Dhofar: Britain's Colonial War in the Gulf* Gulf Committee 1972. A critical assessment of Britain's role in the war by the committee set up in London to support the Dhofari rebels.

**2487** Ranulph Fiennes *Where Soldiers Fear to Tread* Hodder and Stoughton 1975. A campaign memoir.

# D. ARMS CONTROL AND DISARMAMENT GROUPS

## (1) Arms Control

**2488** Sir Harold Anthony Nutting *Disarmament: An Outline of the Negotiations* Oxford University Press 1959. A lucid account of attitudes of post-war governments and of progress by a former Foreign Office minister who very much favoured disarmament. On post-war arms control see also J E Davies 'The United Kingdom Approach to the Multilateral Control of Armaments 1945–1964' London PhD Thesis 1971–2.

**2489** J P G Freeman *Britain's Nuclear Arms Control Policy in the Context of Anglo-American Relations 1957–68* Macmillan 1986. This is a useful account, though it possibly exaggerates the role of CND, of the development of British policy in the period leading up to the 1968 Non-Proliferation Treaty. On British attitudes to nuclear proliferation since the British acquired the atomic bomb see John Walker 'British Attitudes to Nuclear Proliferation 1952–1982' Edinburgh PhD Thesis 1986. Frank Barnaby *The NPT: The Main Political Barrier to Nuclear Weapons Proliferation* Stockholm International Peace Research Institute/Taylor and Francis 1980 reviews the Non-Proliferation Treaty in the 1980s and supplies comparative information on Britain's nuclear industry.

**2490** Ronald J Terchek *The Making of the Test-Ban Treaty* Nijhoff, The Hague 1970. Britain played a large part in securing this treaty whereby the three then nuclear powers, America, Britain and the USSR, agreed in 1963 to ban the testing of nuclear devices in the atmosphere, in outer space or under water. The background to this achievement is discussed in Robert A Divine *Blowing in the Wind: The Nuclear Test Ban Debate 1954–1960* Oxford University Press 1978. Sir Michael Wright *Disarm and Verify: An Explanation of the Central Difficulties and of National Policies* Chatto and Windus 1964 is a good memoir by a British delegate to the test ban and disarmament conferences of 1959–63.

**2491** Alun Gwynne-Jones, Lord Chalfont *Disarmament: Nuclear Swords or Unilateral Ploughshares* Papermac 1987. Perspectives by Chalfont, Lord Carver and Bruce Kent of CND.

### (2) Disarmament Groups

### (a) General

**2492** *Peace Research Abstracts* Canadian Peace Research Institute 1964–. A monthly service which provides about 7,500 abstracts per year drawn from 1,000 periodicals. It is classified and indexed, but the index leaves something to be desired.

**2493** Lorna Lloyd and Nicholas A Sims *British Writings on Disarmament from 1914 to 1973: A Bibliography* Pinter 1979. This is largely a list of sources. It contains potted histories on some of the organizations concerned and is generally well annotated.

**2494** James Hinton *Protests and Visions: Peace Politics in Twentieth Century Politics Britain* Hutchinson 1989. A good general history. Richard K Taylor and Nigel Young (eds) *Campaigning for Peace: British Peace Movements in the Twentieth Century* Manchester University Press 1987 is a good series of essays on the various groups within the peace movement and the contribution of Socialists or Christians to it. Opposition to the peace movement is also discussed. Caroline Moorhead *Troublesome People: Enemies of War 1916–1986*

Hamilton 1987 is more a history of twentieth century Pacifism.

### (b) Biography

**2495** Harold Josephson *et al Biographical Dictionary of Modern Peace Leaders* Greenwood 1985. An international dictionary which is nevertheless of considerable use.

**2496** L John Collins *Faith Under Fire* Leslie Frewin 1966. An Anglican clergyman, Collins was one of the early leaders of the Campaign for Nuclear Disarmament. Ian Henderson (ed) *Man of Christian Action: Canon John Collins: The Man and his Work* Lutterworth Press 1976 is an appreciation volume.

**2497** J D B Miller *Norman Angell and the Futility of War: Peace and the Public Mind* Hamilton 1986. Although never a Pacifist Angell was an important anti-war campaigner since before the First World War. The final sections of this biographical study comment on his reactions to nuclear weapons and the value of his ideas in the post-war world.

**2498** Frances Partridge *Everything to Lose: Diaries 1945–1960* Gollancz 1985. The diaries of a Pacifist.

### (c) The Campaign for Nuclear Disarmament and Anti-Nuclear Protest

**2499** Paul Byrne *The Campaign for Nuclear Disarmament* Croom Helm 1988. The fullest history of the movement. John Minman and Philip Bolsover (eds) *The CND Story: The First 25 Years of CND in the Words of the People Involved* Allison and Busby 1983 is a useful oral history. These studies are, as with most studies of CND, overtly sympathetic with their subject. A valuable corrective is Paul Mercier *'Peace' of the Dead: The Truth Behind the Nuclear Disarmers* Policy Research Publications 1986. This is the only critical history of the movement. It has informative appendices and a good bibliography.

**2500** Ruth Brandon *The Burning Question: The Anti-Nuclear Movement Since 1945* Heinemann 1987. A general study which also examines the pre-history of the nuclear movement before the foundation of CND in 1958. On one aspect of anti-nuclear sentiment in that period see Greta Jones 'The Mushroom-Shaped Cloud: British Scientists' Opposition to Nuclear Weapons Policy 1945–1957' *Annals of Science* 43 1986 pp 1–26. This assessment of the significance of scientists' opposition in the light of the later growth of CND argues that they were of underestimated importance.

**2501**  Richard K Taylor *Against the Bomb: The British Peace Movement 1958–1965* Clarendon 1988. The most thorough study of the early years of CND. For contemporary studies of this early phase of CND see Christopher Driver *The Disarmers: A Study in Protest* Hodder and Stoughton 1964, George Clark *Second Wind: A History of CND* Campaign Caravan Workshops 1963 (an internal history) and R A Exley 'The Campaign for Nuclear Disarmament, its Organisation, Personnel and Methods in its First Year' Manchester MA Thesis 1959. Richard Taylor and Colin Pritchard *The Protest Makers: The British Nuclear Disarmament Movement of 1958–1965: Twenty Years On* Pergamon 1980 is a sociological examination based on a survey of 403 former activists. The most celebrated sociological study of CND, Frank Parkin *Middle Class Radicalism: The Social Bases of the British Campaign for Nuclear Disarmament* Manchester University Press 1968, remains of great value. A more recent sociological study of CND is John Mattausch *A Commitment to Campaign: A Sociological Study of CND* Manchester University Press 1989.

**2502**  Philip A G Sabin *The Third World War Scare in Britain: A Critical Analysis* Macmillan 1986. A good analysis of the panic about the risks of a nuclear war in the late 1970s resulting from the decision to deploy Cruise missiles and replace Polaris taken in the light of the Soviet arms build-up.

**2503**  Peter Foot *The Protesters: Doubt, Dissent and British Nuclear Weapons* Aberdeen Centre for Defence Studies, University of Aberdeen 1983. A study of the anti-nuclear movement in the 1980s.

**2504**  Barbara Harford and Sarah Hopkins (eds) *Greenham Common: Women at the Wire* Women's Press 1985. An account of the women's peace camp that grew up in the 1980s around the US Air Force's Cruise missile base at Greenham Common.

(d) Other

**2505**  Peace Pledge Union *Film Van: 21 Years 1961–82* Brotherhood Church 1982. The Peace Pledge Union is a Pacifist body founded in the 1930s. It and the Pacifist cause have been overshadowed by the anti-nuclear cause in the post-war era. This is the only study of any aspect of its activities since 1945.

**2506**  Denis Hayes *Challenge of Conscience: The Story of the Conscientious Objectors 1939–1949* Allen and Unwin 1949. This study looks at the attitudes and treatment of conscientious objectors both during the war and in the peacetime conscription that followed. Debates in the Commons on the issue on 18 November 1946 and 23 July 1953 respectively are abridged and commented on in *The No Conscription Amendment: How the House of Commons Received an Amendment to the Address Against the Extension of Peace-Time Conscription* No Conscription Council 1946 and *Conscientious Objectors: Their Position in 1953* Central Board for Conscientious Objectors 1953.

**2507**  Gertrude Bussey and Margaret Tims *Women's International League for Peace and Freedom 1915–65: A Record of Fifty Years Work* Allen and Unwin 1965.

**2508**  Archibald Kenneth Ingram *Fifty Years of the National Peace Council: A Short History* The Council 1958.

# 5 THE LEGAL SYSTEM

## A. GENERAL

### (1) Reference Works

**2509**  *Halsbury's Laws of England* 4th ed, 56v, Butterworths 1973–87. The most comprehensive guide to the current state of the law. This is updated by the monthly *Current Service* and by annual supplements. The third edition of this legal encyclopaedia (1952–63) remains of historical interest. *The Digest* Butterworths 1970– is a companion series. It is a comprehensive digest of English case law with cumulative annual supplements. It now includes relevant European and selected Scottish, Irish and Commonwealth material.

**2510**  *Halsbury's Statutes of England and Wales* 4th ed, Butterworths 1985–. An exhaustive guide to the state of statute law. It includes tables of statutes and gives the amended text of every public general act and measure with detailed annotation. The fourth edition is planned to run to 50 volumes but is not yet complete. *Current Statutes Service*, which appears six times per year constantly updates volumes both published and planned. There are also annual cumulative supplements to the fourth edition. The third edition (1968–72) and the second edition, which was completed in 1951 remain of value. Both had annual supplements.

**2511**  *Halsbury's Statutory Instruments* 22v, Butterworths 1986–87. A guide to all general and some local statutory instruments. It is impossible to make this volume as comprehensive as [2510] because of the frequent changes to the nature of these instruments. It is kept up to date by a looseleaf service and an annual consolidated index. The looseleaf *Chronological List of Instruments* covers all the instruments listed in the volumes and the service.

**2512**  John S James (ed) *Stroud's Judicial Dictionary of Words and Phrases* 5v, Sweet and Maxwell 1986. A very detailed legal dictionary. John Burke *Jowitt's Dictionary of English Law* 2nd ed, Sweet and Maxwell 1977 is well regarded and more concise. Also worth consulting are P G Osborn *Concise Law Dictionary* 7th ed,

Sweet and Maxwell 1983 and D M Walker *The Oxford Companion to Law* Clarendon 1980.

**2513**  *Current Law* Sweet and Maxwell 1947–. A monthly digest of recent legal developments. *Current Law Year Book* is the annual cumulation. This includes a bibliographical section, notes on bills, legislation and cases. Relevant European and Commonwealth law is also covered.

**2514**  *The Law Reports Consolidated Index* Council of Law Reporting 1951–. This supersedes the *Law Reports Digest*. This is the best general digest, especially of case law.

**2515**  *Weekly Law Reports* Council of Law Reporting 1953–. This aims to report all cases of general interest. It supersedes *Weekly Notes* 1866–1952. This should be supplemented by the annotated and indexed digest *All England Law Reports* Butterworths 1936–. This has monthly and annual cumulative indexes. A three volume consolidated index for 1936–81 is also available.

**2516**  *The Law Reports* Council of Law Reporting 1865–. This appears four times monthly. It aims to produce full, accurate and authoritative reports on appeal court cases, and cases in the Chancery Division, the Family Division (which was the Probate Division until 1972) and the Queen's Bench Division.

**2517**  *The London Gazette* HMSO 1665–. The official channel for communicating to the public changes in the law and official appointments. It appears daily. See also P M Handover *A History of the London Gazette 1665–1965* HMSO 1965.

**2518**  *The Bar List of the United Kingdom* Stevens 1977–. An annual guide to courts, barristers and counsels, the inns of court, the Faculty of Advocates in Scotland and the courts of Northern Ireland. It also has sections on the Channel Islands and the Isle of Man. It succeeded *The Law List* 1841–1976.

**2519**  R G Logan (ed) *Information Sources in Law* Butterworths 1986. A very informative guide to sources.

It contains detailed chapters on sources on all sorts of different aspects of the law.

**2520** A G Chloros (ed) *Bibliographical Guide to the Law of the United Kingdom* 2nd ed, Institute of Advanced Legal Studies, University of London 1973. An extensive classified bibliography which takes in not only all aspects of English and Welsh law but also the law of Northern Ireland, Scotland, the Channel Islands, the Isle of Man, the Commonwealth and the European Community. It is unannotated. However, each section has a lengthy and informative introduction. *Law Books 1876–1981* 4v, Bowker 1981 is a comprehensive listing of books in English. John S James and Leslie F Maxwell (comps) *A Legal Bibliography of the British Commonwealth of Nations Vol 2: English Law from 1801–1954* 2nd ed, Sweet and Maxwell 1957 is a rather poorly organized, unannotated bibliography.

**2521** *Legal Bibliography Index* Louisiana State University, Baton Rouge, Louisiana 1979–. An annual index of about 3,000 entries. It is largely concerned with English and American law. *Index to Legal Periodicals* H W Wilson, New York 1888– has very broad subject classifications which rather limits its usefulness. It is complemented by *Index to Periodical Articles Related to Law* Glanville Publications, Dobbs Ferry, New York 1958–, which covers specialist journals not indexed in the older publication.

**2522** D Campbell *et al Annotated Bibliography on the English Legal Profession and Legal Services 1960–78* Cardiff University College Press 1980.

**2523** LEXIS Butterworths 1980–. An on-line database on case and statute law.

**2524** Jeremy Gibson and Colin Rogers *Coroners' Records in England and Wales* Federation of Family History Societies 1988. A catalogue.

## (2) General Studies

**2525** R J Walker *The English Legal System* 6th ed, Butterworths 1985. A usefully comprehensive textbook. The various editions of these textbooks provide a series of snapshots of legal development which helps to supply the deficiency in modern legal histories. Another useful textbook is A K R Kiralfy *The English Legal System* 7th ed, Sweet and Maxwell 1984. A rather more critical account of the working of the legal system is Michael Zander *Cases and Materials on the English Legal System* 4th Weidenfeld and Nicolson 1984. This includes case studies. See also P F Bailey and S H Smith *The Modern English Legal System* Sweet and Maxwell 1984. R M Jackson *The Machinery of Justice in England* 7th ed,

Cambridge University Press 1977, G P Wilson *Cases and Materials on the English Legal System* Sweet and Maxwell 1973 and Brian Abel-Smith and Robert Stevens *In Search of Justice: Society and the Legal System* Allen Lane 1968 are useful earlier studies.

**2526** Z Bankowski and G Mungham (eds) *Essays in Law and Society* Routledge and Kegan Paul 1980. A series of studies on various aspects of the law. Morris Ginsberg (ed) *Law and Opinion in England in the 20th Century* Stevens 1959 is a collection of essays on trends in legal thought, on legal developments and on related developments in social policy.

**2527** B Roshier and H Teff *Law and Society in England* Tavistock 1980. A critical study of the legal system in the context of its role in society and state in Britain. See also Robert Stevens *Law and Politics 1800–1976* Weidenfeld and Nicolson 1979.

**2528** Michael Zander (ed) *The Law Making Process* 3rd ed, Weidenfeld and Nicolson 1989. An excellent textbook. Christopher Hughes *The British Statute Book* Hutchinson 1957 reflects on the drafting of legislation and the role of statute law in English law.

**2529** Peter Hain *Political Trials in Britain* Allen Lane 1984. A examination of the legal system's handling of cases with political overtones, such as those involving trade unions, the official secrets act or Northern Ireland, and the political pressures on the legal process. It draws on a wide range of cases and some first hand experience.

**2530** *Royal Commission on Legal Services: Final Report* Cmnd 7648, *Parliamentary Papers* 1979–80. A massive and detailed report into the legal profession, legal services, legal aid and sources of legal advice. The Royal Commission was chaired by Sir Henry Benson. Various recommendations for improvement in the service provided by the legal professions or for the development of community law centres are amongst its conclusions. Developments in the legal services, including the growing impact of information technology, are analysed in E Blankenburg (ed) *Innovations in the Legal Services* Gunn and Hain 1980.

**2531** M P Furmston, R Kerridge and B E Sufrin (eds) *The Effect on English Domestic Law of Membership of the European Communities and of Ratification of the European Convention of Human Rights* Nijhoff, The Hague 1983. A good collection of essays on the impact of the growing importance of European law on a whole range of aspects of English law.

## (3) Administrative Law

### (a) General

**2532** Stanley de Smith and Rodney Brazier *Constitutional and Administrative Law* 6th ed, Penguin 1989. An excellent guide to the law and its development. O Hood Phillips and Paul Jackson *O Hood Phillips Constitutional and Administrative Law* 6th ed, Sweet and Maxwell 1978 provides a useful historical introduction to the development of this branch of law. E C S Wade and G Godfrey Phillips *Constitutional and Administrative Law* 10th ed, Longman 1985 is a rather less general but very useful guide. It covers most aspects of administrative law and the various editions provide a picture of developments. Scottish law is also covered in this textbook. T C Hartley and J A G Griffith *Government Law* 2nd ed, Weidenfeld and Nicolson 1981 describes the constitution and powers of government whilst paying particular attention to the political setting. It also features an extensive bibliography. H W R Wade *Administrative Law* 5th ed, Clarendon 1982 and I N Stevens *Constitutional and Administrative Law* Macdonald and Evans 1982 are also good recent textbooks. J A G Griffith and H Street *Principles of Administrative Law* 4th ed, Pitman 1967 and W A Robson *Justice and Administrative Law* 3rd ed, Stevens 1961 are useful on the earlier part of the post-war period.

### (b) Tribunals

**2533** *Report of the Committee on Administrative Tribunals and Enquiries* Cmnd 218, *Parliamentary Papers* viii 1956–57. Administrative tribunals had grown in an *ad hoc* fashion since the 1920s to arbitrate in disputes between government and citizens. This inquiry into their organization arose from a desire to give more form to the system. It was chaired by Oliver Franks.

**2534** *Royal Commission on Tribunals of Inquiry: 1966 Report of the Commission Under the Chairmanship of the Rt Hon Lord Justice Salmon* Cmnd 3121, *Parliamentary Papers* li 1966–67. A review of the working of the Tribunals of Enquiry (Evidence) Act 1921.

**2535** R E Wraith and P G Hutchesson *Administrative Tribunals* Allen and Unwin 1973. A good study of their origins, development, organization and functioning. J A Farmer *Tribunals and Government* Weidenfeld and Nicolson 1974 examines them more in the context of their handling of specific areas of administrative law. See also Robert S W Pollard (ed) *Administrative Tribunals at Work* Royal Institute of Public Administration 1950. There is a case study of tribunals dealing with Selective Employment Tax 1966–73. George William Keeton

*Trial by Tribunal: A Study of the Development and Functioning of the Tribunal of Inquiry* Museum Press 1961 largely consists of case studies, the post-war examples being the Lynskey tribunal 1948, the Bank Rate Leak Tribunal 1957 and the 1959 Waters Tribunal into the conduct of the police. D G T Williams 'The Council on Tribunals: The First Twenty-Five Years' *Public Law* 1984 pp 73–88 examines the history of the statutory advisory body accountable to the Lord Chancellor and the Lord Advocate established in 1958.

**2536** Kathleen Bell *Research Study on Supplementary Benefit Appeal Tribunals* HMSO 1975. This study prompted important changes to the rules governing these tribunals. See also her earlier *Tribunals in the Social Services* Routledge and Kegan Paul 1969.

### (c) The Parliamentary Commissioner for Administration

**2537** Frank Stacey *The British Ombudsman* Clarendon 1971. A study of the campaign for an ombudsman, the drafting and passage of the Parliamentary Commissioner for Administration Bill in 1967 and the first few years of operation. It is based on documents and numerous interviews. The best study of the office and duties of the parliamentary ombudsman is Roy Gregory and Peter Hutchesson *The Parliamentary Ombudsman: A Study in the Control of Administrative Action* Allen and Unwin 1975. The first eleven years of the parliamentary ombudsman is reviewed in I Pugh 'The Ombudsman – Jurisdiction, Powers and Practice' *Public Administration* 56 1978 pp 127–38. A more critical study, particularly of the limited powers of the office, is *Our Fettered Ombudsman* JUSTICE 1977. Limited and inefficient investigative methods, limited powers and lack of reform are also identified in William B Glyn 'The Ombudsman in Britain: A Qualified Success in Government Reform' *Public Administration* 60 1982 pp 177–95. See also his earlier critique 'The British Parliamentary Commissioner for Administration: "Ombudsman or Ombudsmouse"' *Journal of Politics* 35 1973 pp 45–69. On the origins of the ombudsman see also D L Capps 'Britain's Ombudsman: The Politics of Adoption' Glasgow BLitt Thesis 1969–70.

### (4) European Law

**2538** *Encyclopaedia of European Community Law* Sweet and Maxwell 1973–. A looseleaf guide that appears in three sections. The first of these deals with British sources, the second with various treaties and accords and the third with secondary Community law. It is annotated and updated regularly.

**2539**  T C Hartley *The Foundations of European Community* Law Oxford University Press 1981. The most thorough textbook on the subject.

**2540**  Lawrence Collins *European Community Law in the United Kingdom* 3rd ed, Butterworths 1984. A good examination of relations between British and European law now that the latter takes precedence. It also looks at the response of the British courts to Community law and at cases where Britain has been in breach of Community law.

### (5) Other Types of Law

**2541**  A L Chapman and R M Ballard (eds) *Tolley's Company Law* Tolley 1983. A well organized description of the development and current state of the law. Geoffrey Morse *Charlesworth's Company Law* 13th ed, Stevens 1987 is a useful textbook. Also useful is A F Topham and E R H Ivamy *Company Law* 16th ed, Butterworths 1978, which has a supplement on Scottish company law.

**2542**  J A L Sterling and M C L Carpenter *Copyright Law in the United Kingdom and the Rights of Performers, Authors and Composers in Europe* Legal Books 1986. This is quite good on the historical background to the current state of the law.

**2543**  J C Smith and B Hogan *Criminal Law* 5th ed, Butterworths 1983. The best of recent textbooks. Another good and rather less academic textbook is Richard Card *Cross and Jones' Introduction to Criminal Law* 10th ed, Butterworths 1984.

**2544**  H J Wells and Alistair R Brownlie *Drink, Drugs and Driving* 2nd ed, Sweet and Maxwell 1985. A statement of the state of the law and its development. See also P Halnan *Drink Driving: The New Law* Oyez 1984 and B Strachan *The Drinking Driver and the Law* 3rd ed, Shaw 1984.

**2545**  P M Bromley *Family Law* 6th ed, Butterworths 1984. A perhaps less comprehensive but livelier textbook which is better at drawing attention to important developments is S M Cretney *Principles of Family Law* 4th ed, Sweet and Maxwell 1984. Touching on a particular theme in recent developments in family law is J Hall 'The Waning of Parental Rights' *Cambridge Law Journal* 30 1972 pp 248–65.

**2546**  P J Clarke and J W Ellis *The Law Relating to Firearms* Butterworths 1981. A study of the development of the law in both England and Scotland, especially since the 1968 Firearms Act.

**2547**  Allison Morris and Henri Giller *Understanding Juvenile Justice* Croom Helm 1987. A study of the historical background and contemporary situation of the state and administration of the law relating to juveniles.

**2548**  A W B Simpson *A History of the Land Law* 2nd ed, Clarendon 1985.

**2549**  B Gunn *Licensing of Entertainments in England and Wales – Law and Practice* Butterworths 1985.

**2550**  Terence Daintilh and G D M Willoughby *A Manual of United Kingdom Oil and Gas Law* Oyez 1977. A good guide which reflects the historical development of the law. Most of the book consists of relevant documents such as international agreements, EC directives or British legislation.

**2551**  F H Lawson and B Rudden *The Law of Property* 2nd ed, Clarendon 1982. An analysis and functional survey of the law of property as it stood in the early 1980s.

**2552**  Evelyn Ellis *Sex Discrimination Law* Gower 1989. A good textbook including reflections on the application of European law.

**2553**  *Royal Commission on Civil Liability and Compensation for Personal Injury* Cmnd 1054, *Parliamentary Papers* 1977–78. A survey of all types of injuries and the existing levels of compensations by the Commission under Lord Pearson which made various recommendations affecting the law of tort. Glanville Williams and B A Hepple *Foundations of the Law of Tort* 2nd ed, Butterworths 1984 is a good legal textbook on the subject. Recent developments in the law of tort are discussed in A Geal 'The Process of Law Reform in the Law of Tort 1965–1983' Bristol LLM Thesis 1984.

**2554**  George William Keeton *Modern Developments in the Law of Trusts* Northern Ireland Legal Quarterly 1971. A good historical survey of developments, especially since the Trustee Investments Act 1961. On the law on appointment of trustees to administer trusts and wills see F R Crane 'The Law and Literature of Powers of Appointment 1916–1966' in R H Code Holland and G Schwarzenberger (eds) *Law, Justice and Equity: Essays in Tribute to G W Keeton* Pitman 1967 pp 76–86.

### (6) Law Officers

**2555**  John Llewellyn J Edwards *The Law Officers of the Crown: A Study of the Offices of Attorney-General and Solicitor- General of England with an Account of the Office of the Director of Public Prosecutions* Sweet and Maxwell 1964. See also the review by Lord Simon of Glaisdale in *Law Quarterly Review* 81 1965 pp 289–96.

**2556** John Llewellyn J Edwards *The Attorney-General: Politics and the Public Interest* Sweet and Maxwell 1984. A thematic review of the office and its responsibilities 1964–84. It deals in particular with some of the important cases that cropped up in that period.

**2557** Joshua Rozenberg *The Case for the Crown: The Inside Story of the Director of Public Prosecutions* Equation 1987. The development and responsibilities of the office.

## (7) The Legal Professions

**2558** Brian Abel-Smith and R Stevens *Lawyers and the Courts: A Sociological Study of the English Legal System 1750–1965* Heinemann 1968. A yet to be superseded study of the legal professions. Michael Zander *Lawyers and the Public Interest* Weidenfeld and Nicolson 1968 is a critical study of the restrictive practices of the legal professions.

**2559** David Pannick *Judges* Oxford University Press 1987. A useful study of the judiciary. See also Simon Lee *Judging Judges* Faber 1989. The role of judges in court, in their relation with the jury and in the making of case law is discussed with reference to judicial pronouncements by one of the most distinguished of postwar judges in Patrick Devlin *The Judge* Oxford University Press 1979. J A G Griffith *The Politics of the Judiciary* 3rd ed, Fontana 1985 is a critical study of the judiciary in the post-war era. See also K Goldstein-Jackson 'The Social Background of the Judiciary in England and Wales in the Mid-1970s' Southampton MPhil Thesis 1978.

**2560** H Kirk *Portrait of a Profession* Oyez 1976. A portrait, with some historical material, of the solicitor's profession.

**2561** Ken Foster 'The Location of Solicitors' *Modern Law Review* 36 1973 pp 153–66. This demonstrates the unequal geographical distribution of solicitors throughout the country on the basis of the 1971 Law List.

**2562** John Scott *Legibus: A History of Clifford-Turner 1900–1980* King, Thorne and Stace 1980. A well written history of a prominent firm of London solicitors with an international practice. Laurie Dennett *Slaughter and May: A Short History* Granta 1989 is a history of the firm of city solicitors. Judy Slinn *Linklaters and Paines: The First One Hundred and Fifty Years* Longman 1987 is a well regarded history of the city firm. Another history of

a city firm is Judy Slinn *A History of Freshfields* Freshfields 1984.

**2563** *Non-Solicitor Conveyancers – Competence and Consumer Protection* HMSO 1984. This and *Conveyancing Simplifications* HMSO 1985 constitute the two reports by the committee chaired by Julian Ferrand which led to the end of solicitors' monopoly of conveyancing.

## (8) Biography

**2564** R F V Heuston *Lives of the Lord Chancellors* Clarendon 1987. A series of biographies covering the Lord Chancellors who held office between 1940 and 1970. It is particularly weighted in favour of Lord Jowitt, the Lord Chancellor 1945–51, who he feels has been underestimated. The nature and functions of the office are also discussed.

**2565** Iain Adamson *The Old Fox* Muller 1963. A biography of Gilbert Beyfus, a leading barrister whose last case was in 1960, shortly before his death.

**2566** Harford Montgomery Hyde *Norman Birkett: The Life of Lord Birkett of Ulverston* Hamilton 1964. Birkett was a Lord Justice of Appeal 1950–57. See also Dennis Conrad Bardens *Lord Justice Birkett* Hale 1962 and John McConnell *Norman Birkett: Uncommon Advocate* Mayflower 1963.

**2567** Sir Peter Bristow *Judge for Yourself* Kimber 1983. A bland semi-autobiographical account by a former High Court judge. It tells little of the judicial process but reveals rather more of the judicial mind.

**2568** Iain Adamson *A Man of Quality: A Biography of the Hon Judge Cassels* Muller 1964. Cassels retired from the bench in 1958.

**2569** J L Jowell and J P W B McAuslan (eds) *Lord Denning: The Judge and the Law* Sweet and Maxwell 1984. A very useful collection of essays which analyse both Lord Denning as judge and as Master of the Rolls for over twenty years up to his retirement in 1982 and his considerable impact on the development of the law during his distinguished career. Another set of essays concentrating particularly on the latter theme is Peter Robson and Paul Watchman (eds) *Justice, Lord Denning and the Constitution* Gower 1981. Alfred, Lord Denning *The Family Story* Butterworths 1981 is a life story of himself and his five brothers. Rather less autobiographical are his two volumes of reflections on cases and legal questions that arose during his career, *The Discipline of Law* Butterworths 1979 and *The Due Process of Law* Butterworths 1980. All three of these are updated by his

*The Closing Chapter* Butterworths 1983. This is partly autobiography covering the end of his career and partly a series of reports on his last cases which includes more general reflections on public and private law, trade union law and conflict in the courts.

**2570**  Sir Neville Faulks *No Mitigating Circumstances* Kimber 1977. The memoirs of a judge. His *A Law Unto Myself* Kimber 1978 is a further volume.

**2571**  Fenton Bresler *Lord Goddard: A Biography of Rayner Goddard, Lord Chief Justice of England* Harrap 1977. Goddard was Lord Chief Justice 1946–58. Another useful survey of his career is Eric Grimshaw and Glyn Jones *Lord Goddard: His Career and Cases* Allan Wingate 1958. Arthur Henry Smith *Lord Goddard: My Years with the Lord Chief Justice* Weidenfeld and Nicolson 1959 is a memoir by Goddard's clerk.

**2572**  Harford Montgomery Hyde *Sir Patrick Hastings: His Life and Cases* Heinemann 1960. Hastings was a great advocate who retired from the bar in 1948. See also Sir Patrick Hastings *The Autobiography of Sir Patrick Hastings* Heinemann 1948 and Patricia Hastings *The Life of Patrick Hastings* Cresset Press 1959.

**2573**  Stanley Jackson *The Life and Cases of Mr Justice Humphreys: Dramatic Cases of a Famous Judge* Odhams 1951. A life of Travers Humphreys. His last great case was the John Haigh murder trial.

**2574**  John Parris *Under My Wig* Barker 1961. Good memoirs of a barrister in which he reflects on cases, police conduct and Lord Goddard, who once suspended him from the bar for four months.

**2575**  James Pickles *Straight from the Bench: Is Justice Just?* Phoenix House 1987. A forthright commentary on law and life spiced with comments from his career as a somewhat controversial circuit judge. He comments usefully on judicial secrecy and patronage, on plea-bargaining, sentencing and prosecution.

**2576**  Allen Andrews *The Prosecutor: The Life of M P Pugh Prosecuting Solicitor and Agent for the Director of Public Prosecutions* Harrap 1968. Mervyn Pugh was Prosecuting Solicitor in Birmingham 1924–58.

**2577**  Cyril John, Lord Radcliffe *Not in Feather Beds* Hamilton 1968. Radcliffe was a Lord of Appeal in Ordinary 1949–64. He was also involved in many important government inquiries.

**2577A**  Edward Robey *The Jester and the Court* Kimber 1976. A memoir of his music hall father, Sir George Robey, and of his career as a prosecuting barrister, including details of many of his most notable cases,

not least that of the murderer John George Haigh, and as a Metropolitan Stipendary Magistrate.

## B. THE LEGAL PROCESS

For the material on the place of the House of Lords in the judicial process see the section on the House of Lords.

### (1) General

**2578**  *Shaw's Directory of Courts in the United Kingdom* Shaw 1973–. An informative guide.

**2579**  P Archer *The Queen's Courts* Penguin 1956. A survey of the then existing court system.

**2580**  *Royal Commission on Assizes and Quarter Sessions 1966–69* Cmnd 4153, *Parliamentary Papers* xxvii 1968–69. The report of an inquiry chaired by Lord Beeching into the administration of justice outside London. It led to the reconstitution of the high court, the creation of a bench of circuit judges, the rationalization of the system and the ending of long established geographical limitations.

**2581**  J Baldwin and M McConville *Jury Trials* Oxford University Press 1979. A good study which also has a useful bibliography. Nigel Walker (ed) *The British Jury System* Institute of Criminology, University of Cambridge is a short collection of conference papers. The pressures on the jury system in recent years are discussed in H Harman and J A G Griffith *Justice Deserted: The Subversion of the Jury* National Council for Civil Liberties 1980.

### (2) Criminal Justice

The section on Crime should also be consulted.

#### (a) General

**2582**  Mike Fitzgerald and John Muncie *System of Justice: An Introduction to the Criminal Justice System in England and Wales* Blackwell 1983. A good textbook covering all aspects of the criminal justice system. It is particularly useful for a critical assessment of developments in the 1970s and 1980s. P Scraton and P Gordon (eds) *Causes for Concern: British Criminal Justice on Trial?* Penguin 1975 also provides a critical assessment with some case studies.

**2583** J Baldwin and M McConville *Negotiated Justice* Robertson 1977. A growing area of concern in recent years has been the prevalence of plea-bargaining in the criminal justice process. This important study helped to spark off the debate. It argues that plea-bargaining is the norm rather than the exception. It remains the most valuable study. See also their 'Conviction by Consent: A Study of Plea-Bargaining and Inducements to Plead Guilty in England' *Anglo-American Law Review* 7 1978 pp 271–89 and 'Plea-Bargaining and the Court of Appeal' *British Journal of Law and Society* 6 1979 pp 200–18. Plea-bargaining is also discussed in Philip A Thomas 'Plea-Bargaining in England' *Journal of Criminal Law and Criminology* 69 1978 pp 170–8. A related area of concern is examined in J Bell *Policy Arguments in Judicial Decisions* Oxford University Press 1983.

**2584** *Report of the Interdepartmental Committee on the Business of the Criminal Courts* Cmnd 1289, *Parliamentary Papers* xiii 1960–61. An inquiry chaired by Sir G H B Streatfeild which particularly dealt with sentencing policy. The recommendations of the Streatfeild committee and the contemporary concern about sentencing policy are discussed in J E Hall Williams 'Sentencing in Transition: The Streatfeild Report and Beyond' in Tadeusz Grygier, Howard Jones and John C Spencer (eds) *Criminology in Transition: Essays in Honour of Hermann Mannheim* Tavistock 1965 pp 23–42. See also F V Jarvis 'Inquiry Before Sentencing' pp 43–66 in the same volume. Nigel Walker *Sentencing: Theory, Law and Practice* Butterworths 1985 is an excellent general study.

**2585** Advisory Council on the Penal System *Sentences of Imprisonment: A Review of Maximum Penalties* HMSO 1978. A review called in the light of the increasing length of sentences passed since the early 1960s. It was the last major report of the Advisory Council which was abolished in 1979.

**2586** A Askworth *Sentencing and Penal Policy* Weidenfeld and Nicolson 1987. A good account of sentencing practice in the early 1980s. See also David Arthur Thomas *Principles of Sentencing: The Sentencing Policy of the Court of Appeal Criminal Division* 2nd ed, Heinemann 1979. A rare commentary on sentencing policy by a practising judge which makes an early plea for consistent and constructive sentencing is Sir Leo Page *The Young Lag* Faber 1950.

**2587** *Royal Commission on Criminal Procedure Report* Cmnd 8092, *Parliamentary Papers* 1980–81. This recommended sweeping changes in pre-trial procedure and led to the establishment of the Crown Prosecution Service independent of the police under the Police and Criminal Evidence Act 1984. It was chaired by Sir Cyril Phillips. The background to and the recommendations of the Royal Commission are discussed in M McConville and J Baldwin 'Recent Developments in English Criminal Justice and the Royal Commission on Criminal Procedure' *International Journal of the Sociology of Law* 10 1982 pp 287–302. The new prosecution service was outlined in the White Paper, *An Independent Prosecution Service for England and Wales* Cmnd 9074, *Parliamentary Papers* 1983–84. The history of the prosecution service in England and Wales is discussed in the context of this White Paper in S Uglow 'Independent Prosecution' *Journal of Law and Society* 11 1984 pp 233–45. For a survey of the prosecution before the Phillips report see David G T Williams 'Prosecution, Discretion and the Accountability of the Police' in Roger Hood (ed) *Crime, Criminology and Public Policy: Essays in Honour of Sir Leon Radzinowicz* Heinemann 1974 pp 161–96.

**(b) Bail**

**2588** B Harris *Bail* 8th ed, Barry Rose 1982. The various editions of this standard textbook can be used to trace the development of the law relating to bail. This edition analyses the situation in the wake of the 1976 Bail Act and 1980 Magistrates Act.

**(3) Magistrates Courts**

**2589** *Stone's Justices Manual* Shaw (later Butterworths) 1842–. An annual publication, now in three volumes. After a useful preface on recent developments it contains sections on the courts and procedure, the use of evidence, sentencing or the state of the law.

**2590** *Report of the Royal Commission on Justices of the Peace 1946–1948* Cmnd 7463, *Parliamentary Papers* xii 1947–48. The report of a commission chaired by Lord du Parcq. A further inquiry is *Report of the Interdepartmental Committee on Magistrates Courts in London* Cmnd 1606, *Parliamentary Papers* xviii 1961–62, which was chaired by C D Aarvold.

**2591** E Burney *Magistrate, Court and Community* Hutchinson 1979. A good account of the work of the magistrates' courts. P Carlen *Magistrates' Justice* Robertson 1976 is a critical analysis.

**2592** Sir Thomas Skryme *The Changing Image of the Magistracy* 2nd ed, Macmillan 1983. An interesting account of how the position of the magistrate may be changing. A sociological study of the magistracy based on research conducted in the early 1970s is John Baldwin 'The Social Composition of the Magistracy' *British Journal of Criminology* 16 1976 pp 171–4.

**2593** Penny Darbyshire *The Magistrates' Clerk* Barry Rose 1984. See also H Astor 'The Role of the Clerk in Magistrates Courts' Brunel PhD Thesis 1984.

**2594** Roger Tarling and M Wetheritt *Sentencing Practice in Magistrates' Courts* HMSO 1979. A review of the 1970s. Despite the emphasis of the clerks there was little consistency in sentencing policy between the courts. A similar study based on research 1951–4 is Roger Hood *Sentencing in Magistrates: A Study in Variations of Policy* Stevens 1962.

## (4) The Civil Court

**2595** D Casson and I Dennis *Modern Developments in the Law of Civil Procedure* Sweet and Maxwell 1982. A discussion of current problems and issues. See also D Barnard *The Civil Court in Action* 2nd ed, Butterworths 1985.

## (5) The Commercial Court

**2596** Anthony D Colman *The Practice and Procedure of the Commercial Court* Lloyds of London Press 1983. This study traces its development from minor beginnings in the 1950s, through its formal establishment in the Administration of Justice Act 1970 to its various activities as the busiest commercial tribunal in the world in the 1970s.

## (6) Fraud

**2597** *Fraud Trials Committee Report* HMSO 1986. The report of the committee chaired by Lord Roskill set up in 1983 to improve the conduct of fraud trials. It suggested the end of the jury system in fraud trials, to be replaced by a judge assisted by two expert assessors, but had little to suggest in the area of improving investigation.

## (7) The Juvenile Courts

**2598** R Smith *Children and the Courts* Sweet and Maxwell 1979. See also W Cavenagh *The Juvenile Court* Barry Rose 1976. On the background to the Children and Young Persons Act 1969 which to some extent decriminalized these courts see A E Bottoms 'On the Decriminalisation of English Juvenile Courts' in Roger Hood (ed) *Crime, Criminology and Public Policy: Essays in Honour of Sir Leon Radzinowicz* Heinemann 1974 pp 319–46.

## (8) Famous Cases

**2599** Alfred, Lord Denning *Landmarks in the Law* Butterworths 1984. A series of accounts of famous cases including many celebrated actions of the post-war period. One of these was the trial of the wartime traitor William Joyce (Lord Haw Haw). His trial is reported in great detail in John William Hall (ed) *Trial of William Joyce* Hodge 1946.

**2600** David Hooper *Public Scandal, Odium and Contempt: An Investigation of Recent Libel Cases* Secker and Warburg 1984. This is an account of famous libel trials of the 1970s and 1980s. See also Adam Raphael *My Learned Friend* W H Allen 1989.

## (9) Legal Aid

**2601** *Legal Aid Annual Report* HMSO 1950–. The report of the legal aid services created by the 1949 Legal Aid and Advice Act. It is now known as the *Legal Aid Handbook* and is published irregularly. It mostly consists of a survey of relevant legislation and Law Society guidelines though it also contains articles.

**2602** *Committee on Legal Aid and Advice in England and Wales: Report* Cmnd 6641, *Parliamentary Papers* v 1944–45. The report chaired by Lord Rushcliffe that led to the 1949 Act and the setting up of the legal aid system. Various recommendations for improving the system were made in *Report of the Departmental Committee on Legal Aid in Criminal Procedure* Cmnd 2934, *Parliamentary Papers* vi 1965–66, chaired by John Widgery.

**2603** S Pollock *Legal Aid – The First 25 Years* Oyez 1975. An interesting account of the working of the scheme by the former secretary of the legal aid section of the Law Society. A more critical account of its failings is A Paterson *Legal Aid as a Social Service* Cobden Trust 1975.

**2604** Philip Leask 'Law Centres in England and Wales' *Law and Policy* 7 1985 pp 61–76. An analysis of the creation of non-governmental community law centres to provide free legal advice and their struggle to survive. The first of these opened in North Kensington in 1970. Anthea Byles and Pauline Morris *Unmet Need: The Case of the Neighbourhood Law Centre* Routledge and Kegan Paul 1977 assesses its success, work and impact. Another local case study is J Baker *The Neighbourhood Advice Centre: A Community Project in Camden* Routledge and Kegan Paul 1978.

# 6 RELIGION

## A. GENERAL

### (1) Reference Works

**2605** Robert Currie, Alan Gilbert and Lee Horsley *Churches and Churchgoers: Patterns of Church Growth in the British Isles Since 1700* Clarendon 1977. The useful introduction analyses theories of church growth. The bulk of the book consists of very useful sets of church and Sunday School membership statistics (though it should be pointed out that as statistics go religious statistics are amongst the most unreliable). These statistical series go up to 1970 and do not simply cover the mainstream churches.

**2606** *UK Christian Handbook* MARC Europe 1983–. An irregular directory. It contains a wealth of statistics, on other faiths as well as Christianity, and a number of informative articles and constitutes a very thorough guide to the state of religion in Britain. It is a successor to *Protestant Missions Handbook*, which was first published in 1964.

**2607** *A Sociological Year Book of Religion in Britain* SCM Press 1968–75. An annual collection of essays of a historical and sociological nature. The last volume contains a useful bibliography.

**2608** *International Bibliography of the History of Religion 1952–* Brill, Leiden 1954–. This contains about 3,000 unannotated entries per year.

### (2) General

**2609** Terence Thomas (ed) *The British: Their Religious Belief and Practices 1800–1986* Routledge 1988. A good collection of essays covering all the major faiths, popular religion and modern cults. Another valuable collection of essays is Paul Badham (ed) *Religion, State and Society in Modern Britain* Macmillan 1989. David Perman *Change and the Churches: An Anatomy of Religion in Britain* The Bodley Head 1977 is a study of the churches' role in the nation, revivalism and new move-

ments, liturgical change, church finance and morality. Daniel Jenkins *The British: Their Identity and their Religion* SCM Press 1975 is not a history but a perspective on the role of the churches in the community in Scotland, England and Wales. G Stephen Spinks, E L Allen and James Parkes *Religion in Britain Since 1900* Dakers 1952 provides a rather dated perspective on British religion which is nevertheless useful for its coverage of faiths other than Christianity.

**2610** Adrian Hastings *A History of English Christianity 1920–1985* Collins 1986 is the best general history of religion in the twentieth century. It however concentrates on the churches as organizations and becomes somewhat journalistic in its later chapters. R G Worrall *The Making of the Modern Church: Christianity in England Since 1800* SPCK 1988 is a sound introductory text but stronger on the nineteenth than the twentieth century. Edward Norman *Church and Society in England 1770–1970: A Historical Study* Oxford University Press 1976 is written from an Anglican perspective and as a result his handling of Nonconformity in particular leaves a lot to be desired. Daniel Horton Davies *Worship and Religion in England Vol 5: The Ecumenical Century 1900–1965* Oxford University Press 1965, a book which draws particular attention to the importance of ecumenical discussions in twentieth century Christianity, is rather more reliable.

**2611** Rupert E Davies (ed) *The Testing of the Churches 1932–1982: A Symposium* Epworth 1982. A symposium on developments in the Catholic, Anglican, Methodist and other Free Churches focusing particularly on ecumenism. The essays in this volume also offer perspectives on developments in liturgy, theology and comparative religion.

**2612** Michael Argyle *Religious Behaviour* Routledge and Kegan Paul 1958. A good study of religious attitudes and church attendance drawing on surveys over the period 1947–58.

**2613** David Martin *A Sociology of English Religion* SCM Press 1967. A well regarded if somewhat general study. One of the principal debates in the sociology of religion in the 1960s concerned theories of secularization. Bryan R Wilson *Religion in Secular Society: A SociologicalComment* C A Watts 1966 is a once influential statement on this subject. A survey of Anglican and Methodist attitudes at the time of the eventually unsuccessful reunion talks between the two churches in the 1960s is David Clark *Survey of Anglicans and Methodists in Four Towns* Epworth 1965.

**2614** Kenneth Slack *The British Churches Today* 2nd ed, SCM Press 1970 for a state of the churches in the 1960s and 1970s.

**2615** John Dennis Gay *The Geography of Religion in England* Duckworth 1971. A very useful guide to the geographical spread of support for the churches and the historical reasons for this.

**2616** J E A Smith 'The Decline and Rise of Religion in Modern Society: A Cultural Approach' Brunel MPhil Thesis 1981. A novel analysis based on research in Slough which argues that whilst Christianity's institutional decline has continued throughout the twentieth century its cultural significance has been increasing in recent years.

**2617** M Binney and P Burman (eds) *Change and Decay: The Future of Our Churches* Studio Vista 1977. A well illustrated analysis of the reasons for church decline and the loss of buildings. In part it is a lament for the loss of religious and architectural heritage. See also their *cri de coeur* for the preservation of these buildings, *Chapels and Churches: Who Cares?* British Tourist Authority 1977.

**2618** Geoffrey Ahern and Grace Davie *Inner City God: The Nature of Belief in the Inner City* Hodder and Stoughton 1987. A good attempt to analyse religious attitudes, natural religion and residual Christianity in the inner city. It involves case studies of Leeds and Tower Hamlets (in the East End of London).

**2619** David Bebbington *Evangelicalism in Modern Britain: A History from the 1730s to the 1980s* Unwin Hyman 1988. A study from the Methodist revival to the Charismatic movement. Bebbington usefully discusses the causes of the resurgence and relative vitality of evangelicalism since 1945. This evangelical revival is extolled in Christopher Catherwood *Five Evangelical Leaders* Hodder and Stoughton 1984. It includes good biographies of leading evangelicals, including the Anglican John Stott, the Welsh Presbyterian and leader of the international evangelical movement Martyn Lloyd-Jones, James Packer the Anglican evangelical theologian and the American evangelist who has led numerous post-war missions in Britain, Billy Graham.

**2620** S Ranson, A Bryman and B Hinings *Clergy, Ministers and Priests* Routledge and Kegan Paul 1977. A useful sociological study of Anglican, Free Church and Catholic clergy.

**2621** Harold Loukes *Teenage Religion: An Enquiry into Attitudes and Possibilities among British Boys and Girls in Secondary Modern Schools* SCM 1961. A survey of beliefs and attitudes towards religion. *Drift From The Churches: Secondary School Pupil Attitudes Towards Christianity* Christian Education Movement, reveals increasing scepticism amongst pupils.

**2622** Geraint D Fielder *Lord of the Years: Sixty Years of Student Witness: The Story of the Inter-Varsity Fellowship, Universities and Colleges Christian Fellowship 1928–1988* Inter-Varsity Press 1988. A jubilee history of this evangelical student Christian body. See also Douglas Johnson *Contending for the Faith: A History of the Evangelical Movement in the Universities and Colleges* Inter-Varsity Press 1979.

**2623** A D McRae 'The Principles and Practices of Christian Education in the Churches of England and Scotland 1900–1965' St Andrews PhD Thesis 1985. Despite its title this study is not confined to the two established churches. It examines the changing nature of the Sunday Schools, and also the education of adults in the churches.

**2624** William W Simpson 'Jewish-Christian Relations Since the Inception of the Council of Christians and Jews' *Jewish Historical Society of England Transactions* 28 1981–82 pp 89–101. A useful study of a body set up to promote tolerance at a time when the Jews of the Continent were suffering terribly. Since its foundation in 1942 it has also been an important forum of inter-faith dialogue.

**2625** Bryan R Wilson (ed) *Patterns of Sectarianism: Organisation and Ideology in Social and Religious Movements* Heinemann Educational 1967. A useful collection of essays on a disparate group of bodies. These include the Salvation Army, Pentecostalist churches, Brethren, British Israelism and Humanist societies.

**2626** Garth Lean *Frank Buchman: A Life* Constable 1985. Buchman was an American who had a major influence on church life in Britain, especially in the inter-war years, through the Oxford Movement. This movement, which later came to be known as Moral Rearmament, influenced people in most of the mainstream churches. It also had considerable influence in colonial Africa and has been linked with nationalist movements. Anne Wolridge Gordon *Peter Howard: Life and Letters* Hodder and Stoughton 1969 is a biography of a prominent British member of the Moral Rearmament movement. H W Austin and Phyllis Konstam

*Mixed Double* Chatto and Windus 1969 is the autobiography of the pre-war tennis player who became very active in Moral Rearmament in the post-war period.

**2627** John Capon *And Then There was Light . . . The Story of the Nationwide Festival of Light* Lutterworth Press 1972. The Festival of Light arose in 1971 in reponse to the permissiveness of the 1960s. This useful instant history both details the growth of pornography in the 1960s and the history of the Festival.

**2628** Ernest Short (ed) *Post-War Church Building* Hollis and Carter 1947. A study of the problems and needs in building new places of worship and replacing churches damaged in the war.

### (3) Theology and Liturgy

**2629** K W Clements *Lovers of Discord: Twentieth Century Theological Controversies in England* SPCK 1988. A good study of the main debates in English theology. J K Mozley *Some Tendencies in British Theology from the Publication of Lux Mundi to the Present* SPCK 1951 is a more general survey which only just touches on the post-war period.

**2630** Daniel Horton Davies *Varieties of English Preaching* SCM Press 1963.

**2631** J A R Robinson *Honest to God* SCM Press 1963. This statement of radical modernism by the Bishop of Woolwich is the most celebrated theological work of the post-war era. David L Edwards (ed) *The 'Honest to God' Debate: Some Reactions to the Book 'Honest to God'* SCM Press 1963 collects many of the reviews of the book and the reactions of theologians, philosophers and other commentators. It also provides a further chapter on the debate by Robinson. Eric A James (ed) *God's Truth: Essays to Commemorate the Twenty-Fifth Anniversary of the Publication of Honest to God* SCM Press 1988 is a symposium on the book and its impact.

**2632** F P Ferré 'The Linguistic Admissibility of Theology and Theistic Proof in British Discussion 1945–1955' St Andrews PhD Thesis 1958–9.

**2633** B E Foster 'The Impact of the Historical-Critical Method on Modern British Christology' Cambridge PhD Thesis 1984. This studies the debate about the nature of Christ since the Higher Criticism of the New Testament in the late nineteenth century. It has a chapter on post-war conservative and radical theologians in which the inadequate philosophy of both schools of thought are criticized. See also L Watson 'The Christology of G W H Lampe in its Contemporary Setting' Durham MA Thesis 1985. This traces Lampe's progress

from liberal evangelicalism to an open break in 1966 with orthodoxy over the resurrection. For Lampe's theology see also [2738].

**2634** O R Brandon 'Contemporary Evangelism: An Analytical Study of the Problems and Methods of the Modern Preacher' Bristol MA Thesis 1950–1.

**2635** G S Harrison 'The Doctrine of Baptism in the Work of Twentieth Century Theologians: With Special Reference to British Writers in the Period 1925–1960' Oxford BLitt Thesis 1962–3.

**2636** R H Jennings 'Recent Eucharistic Renewal in the Roman, Anglican and Methodist Churches' Durham MA Thesis 1979. A study of liturgical developments marked by the introduction of new service books such as the Anglican *Alternative Service Book* Mowbray 1980, which in many parishes soon came to replace the 1662 *Book of Common Prayer*.

**2637** Alan M G Stevenson *The Rise and Decline of English Modernism* SPCK 1984. A good study of what was until recently one of the principal theological trends of the twentieth century and which continues to be represented by figures such as David Jenkins, Bishop of Durham.

**2638** A R Mather 'The Theology of the Charismatic Movement in Britain from 1964 to the Present Day' Wales PhD Thesis 1983. The Charismatic movement developed in the early 1960s around the idea of baptism in the Holy Spirit. It spawned the House Church movement in the 1970s but also exercised considerable influence on the mainstream churches. See also P D Hocken 'Baptised in the Spirit: The Origins and Early Development of the Charismatic Movement in Great Britain' Birmingham PhD Thesis 1983–4. Thomas A Smail *Reflected Glory: The Spirit in Christ and Christians* Hodder and Stoughton 1975 is an excellent exposition of the theology of the Charismatic movement by the Director of the Fountain Trust, which was set up in 1964 to direct the movement.

### (4) The Churches and Social and Political Questions

**2639** Duncan B Forrester *Christianity and the Future of Welfare* Epworth 1985. A study of the development of Christian thinking on social welfare from the time of the Church of England's Malvern conference in 1941. The most eminent social thinker in the Church at that time was William Temple, who was Archbishop of Canterbury from 1942 until his death in 1944. His influence on Christian social ethics then and since is assessed in A M Suggate *William Temple and Christian Social Ethics Today* T and T Clark 1987.

**2640** Robin Gill *Prophecy and Praxis* Marshall, Morgan and Scott 1981. A study of the difficulties the churches have in speaking prophetically. He argues that on social questions they tend to follow rather than lead public opinion.

**2641** C E Morey 'Social Concern and Twentieth Century British Preaching' Edinburgh PhD Thesis 1978.

**2642** E H Lurkings 'The Origins, Context and Ideology of Industrial Mission 1875–1975' London PhD Thesis 1981. The only study of industrial missions and industrial chaplaincies which goes up to the post-war era.

**2643** J A Borland 'Religion and Politics: A Case Study of Chorley and Salford 1965–74' Wales MA Thesis 1984. An analysis of the relationship between the denominations and the political parties and of the role of religion in politics in these two Lancashire towns. David Sheppard and Derek Worlock *Better Together: Christian Partnership in a Hurt City* Hodder and Stoughton 1988 is an account by, respectively, the Anglican Bishop and the Roman Catholic Archbishop of Liverpool of their efforts to promote reconcilation in a city which was once scarred by sectarianism and has been, for most of the post-war period, just as scarred by economic decline.

**2644** B J Ingyon 'A Study of William Temple as a Christian Socialist and of the Subsequent Development of Christian Socialism to the Present Day' Manchester MA (Theol) Thesis 1979. A study which perhaps rather emphasizes Temple's role in the development of Christian Socialism and his place in Christian Socialist tradition in Britain. Also of use is Stanley Evans' pamphlet *Christian Socialism: A Study Outline and Bibliography* Christian Socialist Movement 1962, published two years after the Christian Socialist Movement was founded from the merger of the Socialist Christian League and the Society of Socialist Clergy. In the 1970s and 1980s a range of bodies have appeared on the Christian Left. These are critically discussed in Rachel Tingle *Another Gospel?* Christian Studies Centre, London 1988.

**2645** P J Gee 'Recent Reappraisals in Christian Ideology: A Sociological Analysis of Four New Christian Periodicals 1957–1970' Oxford DPhil Thesis 1985. A study of the reformulation of Christian ideology in the face of decline in four short lived Christian New Left periodicals.

**2646** *Faith in the City: A Call for Action by Church and Nation: The Report of the Archbishop of Canterbury's Commission on Urban Priority Areas* Church House 1985. This report created a major stir when it came out, being accused of Marxism by members of the Thatcher government. It addressed the problems of the inner cities and made certain recommendations. The prime concern of this commission, chaired by Sir Richard O'Brien, was however to analyse the role, responsibilities and witness of the Church in the inner city areas. The subsequent progress of church action in the inner cities is charted in Michael Le Roy *Churches and Unemployment in the Inner City* Church Action with the Unemployed 1988.

**2647** R Elliott Kendall *Christianity and Race* British Council of Churches 1982. This traces the attitude in the churches since the 1924 publication of *Christianity and the Race Problem* SCM Press and reviews current attitudes. The lack of understanding with which the churches greeted Christian West Indian immigrants and the depths of ignorant prejudice these immigrants faced from their fellow Christians is discussed in Clifford S Hill *West Indian Migrants and the London Churches* Oxford University Press 1963.

**2648** British Council of Churches *The British Nuclear Deterrent: Resolution and Report of the Working Group* SCM Press 1963. A report for the British Council of Churches on the morality of British nuclear weapons. The fullest examination of theology in the nuclear age is Robin Gill *The Cross Against the Bomb* Epworth 1984. In this he points to the inability of the churches to produce unequivocal statements on this issue. Another somewhat critical study of the churches' handling of the nuclear issue is David Martin and Peter Mullen (eds) *Unholy Warfare: The Church and the Bomb* Blackwell 1984. A more deterrence-minded approach to the problem is T E Utley and Edward Norman *Ethics and Nuclear Arms: British Churches and the Peace Movement* Alliance for the Institute of European Defence and Strategic Studies 1983.

**2649** J E McSlarrow 'Church Responses to the Development and Use of Nuclear Energy Technology 1960–1980' St Andrews MPhil Thesis 1981.

**2650** Peter Jones 'Blasphemy Offensiveness and Law' *British Journal of Political Science* 10 1980 pp 129–48. This concentrates on the state of the blasphemy law since it was repealed except as a Common Law offence in 1967 in the light of the successful prosecution of *Gay News* for blasphemy in 1977.

## (5) Ecumenism

**2651** Rupert E Davies *The Church in our Times: An Ecumenical History from a British Perspective* Epworth 1979. A study of the international movement towards church unity with particular respect to developments in

Britain by a keen supporter of the ecumenical movement.

**2652** Robin Gill *Competing Convictions* SCM Press 1989. It has been argued that church competition has been a mark of vigorous church life. This study argues that the strong inter- church rivalry of the nineteenth century has actually contributed to church decline. It is thus a powerful contribution to the debate about the causes of secularization and a major defence of the arguments in favour of ecumenism.

**2653** E G W Bill (ed) *Anglican Initiatives in Christian Unity* SPCK 1967. A collection of essays some of which usefully reflect on the Church of England's ecumenical dialogue with Catholics, Lutherans and Reformed churches.

**2654** Alberic Stacpoole 'Ecumenism on the eve of the Council: Anglican/Roman Catholic Relations' *The Month* 264 1984 pp 300–6, 333–8. A survey of relations 1959–62 before the Second Vatican Council. See also his 'Anglican/Roman Catholic Relations After the Council 1965–1970' *The Month* 267 1985 pp 55–62, 91–8 and John Coventry 'Ecumenism in England Since the Council' *The Month* 236 1975 pp 74–8, 89.

**2655** *Not Strangers but Pilgrims* British Council of Churches/Catholic Truth Society 1987. The statement adopted at the 1987 Swanwick conference which marked an important stage in the development of a dialogue between the Protestant and Catholic churches in Britain.

### (6) Religious Broadcasting

**2656** Kenneth M Wolfe *The Churches and the British Broadcasting Corporation 1922–1956: The Politics of Broadcast Religion* SCM Press 1984. A good study of an important part of the social impact of broadcasting up to the advent of independent television. It draws attention to the difficult relations between the churches and the BBC and the Corporation's gradual downgrading of the importance of religious broadcasting.

**2657** M Dinwiddie *Religion by Radio: Its Place in British Broadcasting* Allen and Unwin 1968. An analysis of the development and influence of religious broadcasting on radio. See also R J E Silvey *Religion on the Air* BBC 1956.

**2658** Michael Svennevig *et al Godwatching: Viewers, Religion and Television* Libbey 1988. A very useful study of attitudes and responses to religious broadcasting. It also features valuable statistics on changing patterns of belief.

**2659** Gerald Priestland *The Unquiet Suitcase: Priestland at Sixty* Deutsch 1988. Reminiscences of a celebrated religious broadcaster (a Quaker). See also his *Something Understood* Arrow 1988.

### (7) Mission

**2660** *International Review of Mission* World Council of Churches, Commission on World Mission and Evangelism 1911–. A guide and commentary on missionary activity.

**2661** S Neill *et al* (eds) *Concise Dictionary of the Christian World Missions* Lutterworth Press 1970. A reasonably comprehensive guide. B L Goddard (ed) *The Encyclopaedia of Modern Christian Missions* Nelson 1967 concentrates on Protestant and especially American missions.

**2662** Max Warren *The Missionary Movement from Britain in Modern History* SCM Press 1965.

**2663** James Moulton Roe *A History of the British and Foreign Bible Society 1905–1954* British and Foreign Bible Society 1965. This society, which pre-eminently translates and distributes Bibles, is now generally known as the Bible Society.

**2664** Leonard Alfred George Strong *Flying Angel: The Story of the Mission to Seamen* Mission to Seamen 1956. The history of another mission to seamen is told in S Pritchard *Fish and Ships: Royal National Mission to Deep Sea Fishermen 1881–1981* Mowbray 1980.

**2665** F E Scott *Dare and Persevere: The Story of One Hundred Years of Evangelism in Syria and Lebanon 1860–1960* Lebanon Evangelical Mission 1960.

**2666** J L Maxwell *Half a Century of Grace: A Jubilee history of the Sudan United Mission* The Mission 1953.

**2667** David M Paton *RO: The Life and Times of Bishop Ronald Hall of Hong Kong* Diocese of Hong Kong and Macao and the Hong Kong Diocesan Association, Hong Kong 1985. A glowing biography of a great Christian and much loved Bishop. Hall was important not only for his role in ecumenism and his vision of a global Christianity in the wake of the destruction of the First World War but also because he became, in the course of the Second World War, the first Anglican bishop to ordain a woman priest.

**2668** Lesslie Newbigin *Unfinished Agenda: An Autobiography* SPCK 1985. A Church of Scotland missionary in India Newbigin was a founder member and Bishop of the Church of South India. He has also been an important figure on the World Council of Churches and in the development of mission in the second half of the twentieth century.

**2669** Roy McKay *John Leonard Wilson* Hodder and Stoughton 1973. Wilson was Bishop of Singapore during and immediately after the Second World War.

**2670** J Rooney 'The History of the Catholic Church in East Malaysia and Brunei 1880–1976' London PhD Thesis 1981.

**2671** Adrian Hastings *Church and Mission in Modern Africa* Burns and Oates 1967. A useful survey. C P Groves *The Planting of Christianity in Africa Vol 4: 1914–1954* Lutterworth Press 1960 is a study which focuses more particularly on Protestant missions.

**2672** A G Blood *The History of the Universities' Mission to Central Africa Vol III: 1933–1957* Universities' Mission to Central Africa 1962. A massive history. Mission was not so important an issue to the churches in the post-war years, though it remains a matter of keen interest and fund-raising activity. One reason is the Africanization of the missionary churches, which is a major theme of this history. It is supplemented by the pamphlet *Supplement to the History of the Universities' Mission to Central Africa 1957–1965* United Society for the Propagation of the Gospel n.d. (1965?), which covers its history up to its merger with the USPG in 1965. Also on mission in Central Africa see S Morrow 'The LMS Mission to Northern Zambia from its origins to 1965' Sussex DPhil Thesis 1985, a study of the work of the London Missionary Society (a body founded by the Congregationalists) in the region.

**2673** Harris W Mobley *The Ghanaian's Image of the Missionary: An Analysis of the Published Critiques of Christian Missionaries by Ghanaians 1897–1965* Brill, Leiden 1970. A useful survey. It includes criticisms of the missions failure to understand nationalism, and of their support for imperialism and reflections on the missionaries' behaviour.

**2674** R H Ozigboh 'The Missions in the Era of Colonialism: A History of the Christian Missions Among the Igbo of Eastern Nigeria 1900–60' Birmingham PhD Thesis 1980. Also on missionary activity in Nigeria see C M Cooke 'The Roman Catholic Mission in Calabar 1903–1960' London PhD Thesis 1977.

### (8) Church Music

**2675** A J Hayden and R F Newton (eds) *British Hymn Writers and Composers: A Check List Giving Their Dates and Places of Birth and Death* Hymn Society of

Great Britain and Ireland 1977. A fairly comprehensive listing.

**2676** H Turner-Evans *A Bibliography of Welsh Hymnology* Arfon/Dwyfor Library 1977.

**2677** R W Wilkinson 'A History of *Hymns Ancient and Modern*' Hull PhD Thesis 1985. A history of the Anglican hymn book 1861–1985. It also reflects to some extent on developments in hymnody.

**2678** John Capon *Sing Emmanuel: The Story of Edwin Shepherd and the London Emmanuel Choir* Words Books 1971. This evangelical choir was established in 1946. Its story is of interest not least because of its role in Billy Graham missions.

### B. CHURCH OF ENGLAND

### (1) Reference Works

**2679** C J Kitching *The Central Records of the Church of England: A Report and Survey Presented to the Pilgrim and Radcliffe Trustees* CIO Publishing 1976. An informative guide.

**2680** *Church of England Year Book* Church House Publishing 1885–. An annual guide and directory to the Anglican communion. The individual dioceses also publish year books.

**2681** *Crockford's Clerical Directory* Church House Publishing 1858–. This largely consists of potted biographies of Anglican clergymen. The prefaces to these irregular publications are often of interest and importance. This is particularly true of the 1987–8 edition. The row over the critical analysis of the state of the church this expressed led to the suicide of its author Dr Gareth Bennett.

**2682** *Church Commissioners for England Annual Report* Church Commissioners 1949–. An annual report on the administration of the property of the church.

**2683** R F Neuss (ed) *Facts and Figures about the Church of England* Church Information Office 1959–65. An annual statistical guide.

**2684** *Historical Magazine of the Protestant Episcopalian Church* 1966–. This features a regular bibliography on the history of the Anglican communion.

## (2) General

**2685** Paul A Welsby *A History of the Church of England 1945–1980* Oxford University Press 1984. The standard history. See also Peter Staples *The Church of England 1961–1980* Research Pamphlet 3, Interuniversitair Instituut voor Missionologie en Oecumenica, Utrecht 1981. Roger Bradhaigh Lloyd *The Church of England 1900–65* SCM Press 1965 is rather journalistic and partisan towards his own Anglo-Catholic party within the Church. See also E R Norman 'The Church During the Past Twenty-Five Years' *Contemporary Review* 230 1977 pp 225–30.

**2686** Kenneth Alfred Thompson *Bureaucracy and Church Reform: The Organisational Response of the Church of England to Social Change 1800–1965* Clarendon 1970. A study of the organizational adjustment to the social changes and population shifts that followed the industrial revolution. Adjustments to the role of the church as the church by law established are examined over a similar time span in D Nicholls *The Church and State in Britain Since 1820* Routledge and Kegan Paul 1969.

**2687** Kenneth H Medhurst and George H Moyser *Church and Politics in a Secular Age: The Case of the Church of England* Clarendon 1988. An excellent investigation of the structure, government and policy-making of the Church of England. It is in a sense a political science treatment of the Church as an organization. Leslie Paul *A Church by Daylight: A Reappraisal of the Church of England and its Future* Chapman 1973 is a history followed by a good discussion of the government, organization, ministry, tasks and objectives of the Church. A similar earlier study is Guy Bedouelle *L'Eglise d'Angleterre et la Société Politique Contemporaine* Librarie Général de Droit et Jurisprudence, Paris 1968. Peter Knight Walker *The Anglican Church Today* Mowbray 1988 is a useful survey of the current state of the Church. Other earlier surveys of the Church which remain of historical interest are Paul Ferris *The Church of England* Penguin 1966, J W C Wand *Anglicanism in History and Today* Weidenfeld and Nicolson 1961, Stephen Neill *Anglicanism* Penguin 1960, Paul A Welsby *How the Church of England Works: Its Structure and Procedure* SPCK 1960 and Guy Mayfield *The Church of England: Its Members and its Business* Oxford University Press 1958.

**2688** Trevor Randall Beeston *The Church of England in Crisis* Davis-Poynter 1973. An examination of the difficulties of the Church in the 1960s.

**2689** Charles Moore, A N Wilson and Gavin Stamp *The Church in Crisis: A Critical Assessment of the Current State of the Church of England* Hodder and Stoughton 1986. A critical survey of the failings of the Church in the 1980s and especially of the central bureaucracy.

**2690** Leslie Francis *Rural Anglicanism* Collins 1985. A study of the problems of the Church of England in rural areas because of declining population and the need for innovations such as the creation of team ministries to spread the available clergy thinly to cover several congregations.

**2691** Eric Kemp 'The Creation of the Synod' in Peter Moore (ed) *The Synod of Westminster: Do We Need It?* SPCK 1986 pp 10–24. This examines the background to the replacement of the Church Assembly by the General Synod as the Church of England's central debating organ in 1970. It appears in a book which is sharply critical of the Synod and which also features articles on the relationship of the Synod with the laity, with the state and with parliament. The Church's relationship with the state and parliament and the political roles of the Bishops and the Synod are examined in George Moyser (ed) *Church and Politics Today: Essays on the Role of the Church of England in Contemporary Politics* T and T Clark 1985. It also assesses the Church's attitude to issues such as nuclear weapons and power, race, education and the economy.

**2692** E Garth Moore and Timothy Briden *Moore's Introduction to English Canon Law* revised ed, Mowbray 1985. A particular aspect of canon law is examined in G H Newson *Faculty Jursidiction of the Church of England* Sweet and Maxwell 1988.

**2693** Barbara Denny *King's Bishop: The Lords Spiritual of London* Alderman Press 1985. A history of the See and of its various bishops up to the present day.

**2694** Mary Walton *A History of the Diocese of Sheffield 1914–1979* Diocesan Board of Finance 1981.

**2695** David L Edwards '101 Years of the Lambeth Conference' *Church Quarterly* 1 1968 pp 21–35. The Lambeth conference is the decennial conference of the entire worldwide Anglican communion.

**2696** Leslie Paul *The Deployment and Payment of the Clergy: A Report* Church Information Office 1964. The Paul report provides an excellent and detailed analysis and remains an indispensable study and source for the Anglican clergy. See also Anthony Russell *The Clerical Profession* SPCK 1980. Robert Towler and A P M Coxon *The Fate of the Anglican Clergy* Macmillan 1979 is a very useful study, principally sociological in design but also reflecting on the changing role and career structures of the clergy, the research for which was largely conducted in the 1960s. See also Paul A Welsby 'Ecclesiastical Appointments 1942–1961' *Prism* 6 1962 pp 21–7.

**2697** D H J Morgan 'The Social and Educational Background of Anglican Bishops – Continuities and Changes' *British Journal of Sociology* 20 1969 pp 295–310. A good study 1860–1960 based on research for his thesis on 'The Social and Educational Backgrounds of English Diocesan Bishops in the Church of England' Hull MA Thesis 1963.

**2698** Jennifer Chapman *The Last Bastion* Methuen 1989. A study of women in the Church of England. See also V N Bellamy 'Participation of Women in the Public Life of the Church from Lambeth Conference 1867–1978' *Historical Magazine of the Protestant Episcopal Church* 51 1982 pp 81–98. Susan Dowell and Linda Hurcombe *Dispossessed Daughters of Eve* SCM Press 1981 is a Christian feminist look at the Church of England and the debate over women's ordination. Alan Aldridge 'In the Absence of a Minister: Structures of Subordination in the Role of the Deaconess in the Church of England' *Sociology* 21 1987 pp 377–92 is a useful study of the role of the deaconess in the Church and on the campaign to allow women to be ordained into the priesthood. It includes a short bibliography. A major concern of the Anglo-Catholic wing of the Church, apart from their theological objections, is that if female ordination is eventually permitted it will have a detrimental effect on movement towards unity with the Catholic Church. On Anglican-Catholic diplomacy on this issue see *Women Priests: Obstacles to Unity? Documents and Correspondence: Rome and Canterbury 1975–1986* Catholic Truth Society 1987.

**2699** Randle Manwaring *From Controversy to Co-existence: Evangelicals in the Church of England 1914–1980* Cambridge University Press 1985. In this period the evangelical party gradually became accepted in the mainstream of the Church. In the process it ceased to be a reform movement in what has become an increasingly pluralist church, a development examined in W H Hopkinson 'Changing Emphases in Self-Identity Amongst Evangelicals in the Church of England 1960–1980' Nottingham MPhil Thesis 1983. It has recently come to be and to regard itself as the most dynamic part of the Church, a self-esteem which is reflected in the title of Michael Saward's *The Anglican Church To-Day: Evangelicals on the Move* Mowbrays 1987. On evangelicals see also Kenneth Hylson-Smith *Evangelicals in the Church of England 1734–1984* T and T Clark 1988. John C King (ed) *Evangelicals Today* Lutterworth 1973 is a useful collection of essays which builds on his short *The Evangelicals* Hodder and Stoughton 1969. The rather different experiences of the Anglo-Catholics at the opposite end of the theological spectrum are reflected in Francis Penhale *The Anglican Church To-day: Catholics in Crisis* Mowbrays 1986. See also William Stuart

Frederick Pickering *Anglo-Catholicism: A Study in Religious Ambiguity* Routledge 1989.

**2700** P F Anson *The Call of the Cloister: Religious Communities and Kindred Bodies in the Anglican Communion* SPCK 1955. A global study with an outline history of each body and a useful bibliography. In the late nineteenth century there was a revival of interest in St Francis which led to the setting up of Anglican orders. Barrie Williams *The Franciscan Revival in the Anglican Communion* Darton, Longman and Todd 1982 mainly covers this movement up to 1945, but it does also look at some post-war developments. See also C P Edmondson 'Modern Developments in Christian Community Living Within the Church of England Since 1945, with Special Reference to St Julian's, Lee Abbey and the Pilsdon Community' Durham MA Thesis 1981.

**2701** M Penelope Hall and Ismene V Howes *The Church in Social Work: A Study of Moral Welfare Work Undertaken by the Church of England* Routledge and Kegan Paul 1965. A specially commissioned survey which examines the historical development, organization and finance and relationship to pastoral work of the Church's social work. Historians may however chafe at the lack of detail in this study.

**2702** S C Little 'The Concept of "Social Responsibility" and its Implementation by the Churches in England' Manchester MEd Thesis 1980. Social responsibility is examined in the context of three organizations, the Church's Board of Social Responsibility 1958–78, the foundation of an Oxford diocesan social responsibility board in 1978 and the first three years of a similar ecumenical body in Milton Keynes.

**2703** W E Rose *Sent from Coventry: A Mission of International Reconciliation* Oswald Woolf 1980. A history of the efforts of the cathedral staff to spread international reconciliation, especially with the German people, in the wake of the bombing of Coventry and the destruction of the mediaeval cathedral in November 1940. On the building of the new cathedral see the account by its architect Sir Basil Urwin Spence *Phoenix at Coventry: The Building of a Cathedral* Collins 1964. The new cathedral was dedicated in 1963. The competition to choose the new building, and the politics and theology of its construction are described in John Thomas *Coventry Cathedral* Unwin Hyman 1987.

**2704** Olive Parker *For the Family's Sake: A History of the Mothers Union 1876–1976* Bailey and Swingen 1976.

**2705** George Moyser 'The Political Organisation of the Middle Class: The Case of the Church of England' in John Gerrard *et al* (eds) *The Middle Class in Politics*

Saxon House 1978 pp 262–91. An examination of the influence of middle class attitudes on the Church.

### (3) Theology, Liturgy and Music

**2706** Alan M G Stephenson *The Rise and Decline of English Modernism* SPCK 1984. A history of Anglican modernist theology, which discounted miracles, the virgin birth and bodily resurrection and emphasized ethics rather than doctrine, since the late nineteenth century. This was at its most influential between the wars but has been somewhat superseded since 1945.

**2707** J L Morgan 'A Sociological Analysis of Some Developments in the Moral Theology of the Church of England Since 1900' Oxford DPhil Thesis 1976.

**2708** P M Hine 'The Anglican Eucharist 1900–1967' Durham MA Thesis 1970–1. See also J M Cassidy 'Eucharistic Litugies of the Church of England 1945–1980' Oxford DPhil Thesis 1981. This examines the liturgy up to the introduction of the *Alternative Service Book* Mowbray 1980. The development of the Parish and People movement from its first conference in 1949 up to 1971 is traced in Peter J Jagger *A History of the Parish and People Movement* Faith Press 1978. This movement played an important part in the development of parish communion and a more liturgical approach to parish life. This history is a valuable corrective to those who argued in the 1970s that it had failed to achieve its objectives. The development of parish communion and alternative liturgies is also examined in D E Netherton 'Modified Rapture: The Church of England and the Parish Communion' London PhD Thesis 1986.

**2709** J Winter 'Music in London Churches 1945–1982' East Anglia PhD Thesis 1984. This particularly examines choral liturgical music.

### (4) Biography

**2710** David L Edwards *Leaders of the Church of England 1828–1978* Hodder and Stoughton 1978. This only has an epilogue on the post-war period.

**2711** Leonard Martin Andrews *Canon's Folly* Michael Joseph 1974. Andrews was a royal chaplain 1936–69.

**2712** Donald Coggan *Cuthbert Bardsley: Bishop, Evangelist, Pastor* Collins 1989. A good biography of an influential evangelical who, as Bishop of Coventry, took a leading role in the building of the new cathedral.

**2713** John Barnes *Ahead of his Age: Bishop Barnes of Birmingham* Collins 1979. Barnes was a politically controversial and theologically radical Bishop of Birmingham 1924–53.

**2714** Frank Russell Barry *Period of my Life* Hodder and Stoughton 1970. Barry was a celebrated liberal theologian and Bishop of Southwell 1941–63. Frank H West *'FRB': A Portrait of Bishop Russell Barry* Grove Books 1980 fills some gaps left by the autobiography.

**2715** R C D Jasper *George Bell, Bishop of Chichester* Oxford University Press 1967. Bell was Bishop of Chichester 1929–58. He was very active in ecumenical affairs and international church contacts and was in 1954 the Honorary President of the World Council of Churches. See also Kenneth Slack *George Bell* SCM Press 1971. J M Rusama 'Moral Issues in the Thought of George K A Bell' Cambridge PhD Thesis 1985 examines his thought drawing on his writings 1917–58.

**2716** John S Peart-Binns *Blunt* Mountain Press 1969. A biography of the Bishop of Bradford 1931–55. Blunt was a high churchman who had a high political profile. Left Wing in sympathies he was denounced as a Communist by Lord Vansittart in the House of Lords in 1950.

**2717** Verily Anderson *The Last of the Eccentrics: A Life of Rosslyn Bruce* Hodder and Stoughton 1972. Bruce was an eminent clergyman who died in 1956.

**2718** Ralph Capenerhurst *Clocking In: Revelations of a Shop Steward Turned Industrial Chaplain* Triangle 1987.

**2719** Margaret Pawley *Donald Coggan: Servant of Christ* SPCK 1987. Coggan was Bishop of Bradford 1956–61, Archbishop of York 1961–74 and Archbishop of Canterbury 1974–80.

**2720** D R Davies *In Search of Myself* Geoffrey Bles 1961. A Left-Wing pacifist and a former Congregationalist minister of extremely liberal theology Davies in the late 1930s and early 1940s became a convert to an orthodoxy influenced by the American theologian, Reinhold Niebuhr, renounced his pacifism and joined the Anglican clergy. He was of some importance, not least as a populariser of Niebuhr's ideas.

**2721** Peter J Jagger *Bishop Henry de Candole: His Life and Times 1895–1971* Faith Press 1975. de Candole was an important figure in the liturgical and the Parish and People movements. He was Bishop of Knaresborough 1949–65.

**2722** S C Carpenter *Duncan-Jones of Chichester* Mowbray 1956. A biography of the Dean of Chichester.

**2723** W E Purcell *Fisher of Lambeth: A Portrait from Life* Hodder and Stoughton 1969. Geoffrey Fisher was Archbishop of Canterbury 1945–61.

**2724** Charles Smyth *Cyril Foster Garbett: Archbishop of York* Hodder and Stoughton 1959. Garbett was Archbishop of York from 1942 until his death in 1955.

**2725** H E Sheen *Canon Peter Green: A Biography of a Great Parish Priest* Hodder and Stoughton 1965. Green was Rector of St Philip's, Salford 1911–50. He had considerable influence on Anglican social thinking in this period and as a regular columnist for the *Manchester Guardian* was one of the most well known of clergymen.

**2726** Kenneth Brill (ed) *John Groser: East End Priest* Mowbrays 1971. Groser was an Anglo-Catholic and Christian Socialist active in local welfare in the East End and the promoting of industrial training of the clergy.

**2727** Sir Kenneth Grubb *Crypts of Power: An Autobiography* Hodder and Stoughton 1971. A layman's autobiography. It is very revealing on ecclesiastical politics, the ecumenical movement and the Church Missionary Society.

**2728** Frank Russell Barry *Mervyn Haigh* SPCK 1964. Haigh was the Bishop of Winchester 1942–52 and the Secretary of the 1948 Lambeth conference.

**2729** John S Peart-Binns *Living with Paradox: John Habgood, Archbishop of York* Darton, Longman and Todd 1987. Hapgood was Bishop of Durham 1973–83 and has been Archbishop of York since 1983.

**2730** A M D Ashley *Joyful Servant: The Ministry of Percy Harthill* Abbey Press 1967. Harthill was Archdeacon and Rector of Stoke 1935–55. He was a Pacifist, an Anglo-Catholic and an important figure in the Church Assembly.

**2731** Deborah Duncan Honoré (ed) *Trevor Huddleston: Essays on his Life and Work* Oxford University Press 1988. Huddleston was Bishop of Stepney 1968–78 and Archbishop of the Indian Ocean 1978–83. He has been President of the Anti-Apartheid Movement since 1981.

**2732** Gordon Hewitt (ed) *Strategist for the Spirit: Leslie Hunter, Bishop of Sheffield 1939–1962* Becket 1985.

**2733** Ted Harrison *The Durham Phenomenon* Darton, Longman and Todd 1985. David Jenkins was enthroned as Bishop of Durham in 1984. This study examines his controversial liberal theology, his high political profile and the response of both media and public. Both his role in encouraging theological debate and as a critic of the Thatcher government are assessed.

**2733A** Alan Dunstan and John S Peart-Binns *Cornish Bishop* Epworth 1977. A biography of Joseph Wellington Hunkin, a liberal churchman who was Bishop of Truro 1935–50.

**2734** Frank Jennings *Men of the Lanes: The Autobiography of the Tramp's Parson* Oldbourne 1958. The appearance in the inter-war years of the tramp preachers remains unstudied. This is the autobiography of a clergyman who essentially devoted himself to this type of work after 1922. It is also useful on the conditions and lifestyles of the homeless.

**2735** Johanna Ernest *The Life of Dorothy Kerin* Dorothy Kerin Trust 1983. A biography of a an Anglican laywoman who devoted her life to a ministry of healing. It includes a chronology and bibliography. See also her *Dorothy Kerin 1889–1963: Her Ministry of Healing* the author 1987. Other biographies are D M Arnold *Dorothy Kerin: Called by Christ to Heal* Hodder and Stoughton 1964, J Davidson Ross *Dorothy: A Portrait* Hodder and Stoughton 1958 and Evelyn Waterfield *My Sister Dorothy Kerin* Mowbray 1964.

**2736** Eric Waldram Kemp *The Life and Letters of Kenneth Escott Kirk, Bishop of Oxford 1937–54* Hodder and Stoughton 1959.

**2737** Robert Hughes *The Red Dean* Churchman 1987. A biography of Canon Hewlett Johnson, the Left Wing clergyman who, as Dean of Canterbury Cathedral 1931–63 was known as 'the Red Dean'.

**2738** C F D Moule (ed) *G W H Lampe* Mowbrays 1982. Lampe was a prominent liberal theologian. See also [2633].

**2739** John S Peart-Binns *Graham Leonard: Bishop of London* Darton, Longman and Todd 1988. A leading Anglo-Catholic and opponent of schemes such as Anglican-Methodist union or the ordination of women Leonard served successively as Bishop of Willesden, Truro and London.

**2740** Joseph McCulloch *My Affair with the Church* Hodder and Stoughton 1976. The memoirs of a leading clergyman who long served as the Rector of St Mary le Bow, Cheapside.

**2741** W R Matthews *Memories and Meanings* Hodder and Stoughton 1969. Matthews was Dean of St Paul's 1934–67. He was also a theologian of note.

**2742** Philip Norris Pare and Donald Bertram Harris *Eric Milner-White 1884–1963: A Memoir* SPCK 1965. Milner-White was Dean of York 1941–63.

**2742A** John Eddison (ed) *Bash: A Study in Spiritual Power* Marshalls 1982. A tribute to the leading evangelical, E J H Nash.

**2743** Edward H Patey *My Liverpool Life* Mowbrays 1983. Patey was Dean of Liverpool Cathedral for 18 years. This autobiography covers the completion of the cathedral, the largest in the world, in 1978, the gradual healing of the city's ancient religious divisions, the 1981 riots and the Orange protesters at the visit of the Pope in 1982.

**2744** J B Phillips *The Price of Success* Hodder and Stoughton 1984. The autobiography of an Anglican priest.

**2745** Jenny Cooke *The Cross Behind Bars: The True Story of Noel Proctor – Prison Chaplain* Kingsway 1983. A biography of the evangelical chaplain of Strangeways Prison in Manchester.

**2746** Jack Putterill *Thaxted Quest for Social Justice: The Autobiography of Father John Putterill Turbulent Priest and Rebel* Precision Press 1977. Putterill succeeded his fellow Anglo-Catholic and enthusiastic Christian Socialist mentor Conrad Noel as Rector of Thaxted. He played an important part in Christian Socialist thought and movements in the Church.

**2747** David Lawrence *Ian Ramsay, Bishop of Durham: A Memoir* Oxford University Press 1973. A short study of one of the most highly regarded of post-war prelates.

**2748** F W Dillstone *Charles Raven: Naturalist, Historian, Theologian* Hodder and Stoughton 1975. One of the most prominent clergymen of the century Raven was theologically liberal and a leading advocate of pacifism. The Regius Professor of Divinity at Cambridge 1932–50 he was also a well regarded biologist.

**2749** John S Peart-Binns *Ambrose Reeves* Gollancz 1973. Reeves was a Christian Socialist priest. He was Rector of Liverpool 1942–9. In 1949 he became Bishop of Johannesburg where he remained until deported by the South African government for his denunciation of apartheid. In the 1960s he served as General Secretary of the Student Christian Movement.

**2750** Eric James *A Life of Bishop John A T Robinson: Scholar, Pastor, Prophet* Collins 1987. A good biography of the controversial theologian who served as Bishop of Woolwich 1959–69.

**2751** Margaret Duggan *Runcie: The Making of an Archbishop* Hodder and Stoughton 1983. Robert Runcie has been Archbishop of Canterbury since 1980. Before that he was Bishop of St Albans 1970–80.

**2752** Ulrich Simon *Sitting in Judgement 1913–1963* SPCK 1978. A good autobiography by a German refugee of Jewish parentage who eventually became the Professor of Christian Literature at King's College, London.

**2753** Nicolas David Stacey *Who Cares?* Blond 1971. A semi-autobiographical account by a clergyman with a strong interest in the social services field into which he has since moved full time. He was Deputy Director of Oxfam 1968–70.

**2754** Mervyn Stockwood *Chanctonbury Ring: An Autobiography* Hodder and Stoughton 1982. Stockwood was Bishop of Southwark 1959–80.

**2754A** Patience Strong *With a Poem in my Pocket: The Autobiography of Patience Strong* Muller 1981. The autobiography of the writer of inspirational verses.

**2755** Henry Sutton *You'll Never Walk Alone* Marshalls 1984. An autobiography which is useful for the politics of the Church Missionary Society and general developments in the Church.

**2756** John S Peart-Binns *Eric Treacy* Ian Allan 1980. Treacy was Bishop of Wakefield 1963–76.

**2757** Alec R Vidler *Scenes from a Clerical Life: An Autobiography* Collins 1977. Vidler was Dean of King's College Cambridge 1956–67.

**2758** Trevor Barnes *Terry Waite: Man with a Mission* Fontana 1987. Terry Waite was Archbishop Runcie's special envoy. Since early 1987 he has been held hostage by Shi'ite fundamentalists in Beirut.

**2759** John S Peart-Binns *Wand of London* Mowbrays 1987. A biography of John William Charles Wand, Bishop of London 1945–55. Wand was also a distinguished scholar. He was on the Anglo-Catholic wing of the Church. His autobiography is *Changeful Page: Autobiography* Hodder and Stoughton 1965.

**2760** Max Warren *Crowded Canvas: Some Experiences of a Life-Time* Hodder and Stoughton 1974. Warren was Vicar of Holy Trinity, Cambridge and later General Secretary of the Church Missionary Society.

**2761** H A Williams *Some Day I'll Find You: An Autobiography* Collins 1982. Williams was a Fellow and theologian at Trinity College, Cambridge 1951–69. Since then he has been a monk in the Community of the

Resurrection at Mirfield. This is a revealing frank autobiography.

**2762** John S Peart-Binns *Defender of the Church of England: The Biography of Ronald Ralph Williams, Bishop of Leicester* Amate Press 1984. Williams was Bishop of Leicester 1953–78.

**2763** Joseph Williamson *Father Joe: The Autobiography of Joseph Williamson of Poplar and Stepney* Hodder and Stoughton 1963. The autobiography of the Vicar of Whitechapel in London's East End. See also his *Friends of Father Joe: Pages from his Diary* Hodder and Stoughton 1965.

**2764** Oliver Tomkins *The Life of Edward Woods* SCM Press 1957. Woods was Bishop of Lichfield from 1937 until his death in 1953.

**2765** Robin Woods *An Autobiography* SCM Press 1986. The autobiography of the son of Edward Woods. This well written memoir is useful on his time as Dean of Windsor and as Bishop of Worcester, his time in industrial mission in Sheffield and on the activities of Bishops in the House of Lords.

## C. THE FREE CHURCHES

### (1) General

**2766** *Year Book of the Free Church Federal Council* Free Church Federal Council 1941–86.

**2767** Leslie Gilbert Pine (ed) *Who's Who in the Free Churches (and Other Denominations)* Shaw 1951.

**2768** *Nonconformist Congregations in Great Britain: A List of Histories and Other Material in Dr Williams' Library* Dr Williams' Library 1974. Dr Williams' Library, Gordon Square, London has the most extensive collection of works and associated material on Nonconformity in the country. This collection includes a large number of the thousands of chapel histories, which whilst often useful to historians, especially local historians, are often rather difficult to trace. This guide to these holdings is somewhat out of date. On the other hand it is the nearest thing to a comprehensive bibliography of histories of British places of worship. A full guide to this sort of material would be extremely useful.

**2769** Paul Sangster *A History of the Free Churches* Heinemann 1983. This is not an entirely satisfactory or comprehensive history of the Free Churches. It does however provide considerable coverage of post-war developments. Christopher Driver *A Future for the Free Churches?* SCM Press 1962 reflects on the situation and problems confronting the Free Churches on the tercentenary of the 1662 Act of Uniformity. See also J T Wilkinson *1662 – And After* Epworth 1962.

**2770** George Thompson Brake *Inside the Free Churches* Epworth 1964. An assessment of the contemporary state and role of the Free Churches. It is a concern to which he returns in his *The English Free Churches: A Struggle for Identity* Robert Odcombe Associates 1989. Both works include some useful reflections on Free Church theology, decline and ecumenism.

**2771** K Rowell *The Fall of Zion: Northern Chapel Architecture and its Future* SAVE Britain's Heritage 1980. A short study of Nonconformist chapel architecture and the demolitions and conversions in the North of the last twenty years. It includes case studies.

**2772** Henry Townsend *The Claims of the Free Churches* Hodder and Stoughton 1949. Townsend was an eminent Baptist minister. He was active in the temperance cause and the Liberation Society (which pressed for the disestablishment of the Church of England). This book reflects his attitudes but should not be taken as representative of those of the Free Churches by this period. It should nevertheless definitely be consulted.

**2773** F W Munson 'The Understanding of Adolescents in some English Free Churches 1939–1955' Leeds MA Thesis 1958–9. This period saw increasing efforts by the churches to cater for young people in the churches, by the creation of youth clubs and other innovations.

**2774** John Peters *Martyn Lloyd-Jones: Preacher* Paternoster 1986. A member of the Presbyterian Church of Wales Lloyd-Jones was the pastor of Westminster Chapel and thus occupied one of the most important Free Church pulpits in London from 1939 to 1968. See also Christopher Catherwood (ed) *Martyn Lloyd-Jones* Highland 1988.

### (2) Baptists

**2775** *The Baptist Union Directory* Baptist Union of Great Britain and Ireland 1862–. An annual directory which also includes some obituaries and biographical information.

**2776** K W Clements (ed) *Baptists in the Twentieth Century* Baptist Historical Society 1983. An excellent collection of essays. Ernest Alexander Payne *The Baptist Union: A Short History* Baptist Union 1959 remains a useful history of the central body to which most (but not, for theological and historical reasons, all) Baptist churches are affiliated.

2777 Kenneth D Brown 'Patterns of Baptist Ministry in the Twentieth Century' *Baptist Quarterly* 33 1989 pp 81–93. An analysis of the ministry 1911–50.

2778 W C Johnson *Encounter in London: The Story of the London Baptist Association 1865–1965* Carey Kingsgate Press 1965.

2779 Ian Sellers (ed) *Our Heritage: The Baptists of Yorkshire, Lancashire and Cheshire 1647–1747–1887–1987* Yorkshire Baptist Association/Lancashire and Cheshire Baptist Association 1988.

2780 K W Bennett *Men in the Service of God: 70 Years of the Baptist Men's Movement* Baptist Men's Movement 1987.

2781 Ernest F Clipsham 'The Baptist Historical Society: Sixty Years Achievement' *Baptist Quarterly* 22 1968 pp 339–51.

2782 Clyde Binfield *People and Pastors: The Biography of a Baptist Church: Queens Road, Coventry* Queen's Road Baptist Church 1984. This chapel history is included because it is both extremely good and because the importance of this particular church and the pastors it attracted were such that this history also reflects on wider Baptist history.

2783 Henry Townsend *Robert Wilson Black* Carey Kingsgate Press 1954. Black was one of the most important, and munificent, Baptist laymen of the twentieth century. This biography tells little of his business life. It is however very useful on his role in the Baptist Union and his activity in the temperance movement and the Liberation Society.

2784 W M S West *To be a Pilgrim: A Memoir of Ernest A Payne* Lutterworth Press 1985. Payne served as General Secretary of the Baptist Union 1951–67 and as its President 1977–78. He was Moderator of the Free Church Federal Council in 1958–59.

2785 J H Y Briggs (ed) *Faith, Heritage and Witness: A Supplement to the Baptist Quarterly Published in Honour of Dr W M S West, President Bristol Baptist College 1971–1987* Baptist Historical Society 1987. A volume of tributes to the memory of W M S West. It concludes with a survey of the Baptists since 1945 by Briggs.

## (3) Congregationalists, Presbyterians, the Churches of Christ and the United Reform Church

2786 *Congregational Year Book* Congregational Union of England and Wales 1846–. An annual guide and directory. It also included obituaries and biographical information. Generally speaking it was the most informative of the Free Church yearbooks. A publication with the same title has continued to appear since the Congregationalists merged with the Presbyterian Church of England in 1972 to form the United Reformed Church. It has been published by the small breakaway fragment of Congregationalism which refused to accept the union, the Congregational Federation.

2787 *Year Book of the Churches of Christ in Great Britain and Ireland* Association of Churches of Christ in Great Britain and Ireland 1846–1981. The Churches of Christ were a small body, with its origins in American Protestantism, that joined the United Reformed Church in the 1980s. David M Thompson *Let Sects and Parties Fall: A Short History of the Association of Churches of Christ in Great Britain and Ireland* Berean Press 1980 is a good, informative history with useful appendices. James Gray *WR: The Man and his Work: A Brief Account of the Life and Work of William Robinson MA BSc DD 1888–1963* Berean Press 1978 is a biography of a leading figure in the Churches of Christ.

2788 *The United Reformed Church Year Book* United Reformed Church 1973–. An annual guide and directory.

2789 J M Ross (comp) *Presbyterian Church of England: Index to the Proceedings of the General Assembly 1921–72* United Reformed Church History Society 1973. A history of the Presbyterian Church of England is being prepared by David Cornick. See also J Johansen-Berg 'An Examination of the Statement of Faith of the Presbyterian Church of England (Approved 1956) and Related Documents, with Special Reference to the Influence of Biblical Criticism upon them and to their Agreement with the Westminster Confession of Faith' Leeds BD Thesis 1965–6.

2790 C B Baxter 'A Study of Organisational Growth and Development of the Congregational, Presbyterian and United Reformed Churches' Brunel PhD Thesis 1981. A study of organizational changes since 1900.

2791 R Tudur Jones *Congregationalism in England 1662–1962* Independent Press 1962. The standard, if rather bland, history. See also Erik Routley *The Story of Congregationalism* Independent Press 1961.

2792 Arthur Macarthur 'The Background to the Formation of the United Reformed Church (Presbyterian and Congregational) in England and Wales in 1972' *Journal of the United Reform Church Historical Society* 4 1987 pp 3–22. A survey of the nine years of negotiations that led to the union in 1972. See also H J Smith 'The Formation of the United Reformed Church: A Theological and Sociological Elucidation' London MPhil Thesis 1978.

**2793** Ian Sellers 'A New Town Story: The United Reformed Churches in the Warrington-Runcorn Complex' *Journal of the United Reformed Church Historical Society* 3 1985 pp 290–306.

**2794** Elaine Kaye *C J Cadoux: Theologian, Scholar and Pacifist* Edinburgh University Press 1988. Cadoux became a pacifist before the First World War. The advent of the Nazis led him to modify but not abandon his pacifism. Both this and his continuing theological liberalism led to conflict with Nathaniel Micklem when both were at Mansfield College, Oxford in the 1930s and 1940s.

**2795** F W Dillstone *C H Dodd: Interpreter of the New Testament* Hodder and Stoughton 1977. A good, scholarly biography of the Congregationalist Biblical theologian, who was Professor of Divinity at Cambridge 1935–49.

**2796** Nathaniel Micklem *The Box and the Puppets* Geoffrey Bles 1957. A good autobiography. Micklem was the Principal and Cadoux the Vice-Principal of Mansfield College, Oxford. A pacifist and theological liberal during the first war he had become a scourge of pacifists and a champion of neo-orthodoxy by the outbreak of the second.

### (4) Methodists

**2797** *Minutes and Yearbook of the Methodist Conference* Methodist Conference Office 1932–. A directory and guide to connexional offices. It also gives some obituaries, some biographical information and some conference decisions.

**2798** The Methodist Archive at the National Sound Archives, 29 Exhibition Road, London SW7. This contains taped interviews with celebrated ministers and laymen and recordings of important occasions or lectures.

**2799** William Leary *Local Methodist Records: A Brief Explanation of Local Methodist Archival Material Deposited in County Record Offices* World Methodist Historical Society 1981. A brief but informative guide to some of the riches that have been deposited in County Record Offices. Unfortunately the Methodist Church stipulates that these voluminous records must remain closed for fifty years unless special permission is obtained, which rather limits research on post-war Methodism.

**2800** Kenneth Benjamin Garlick *Garlick's Methodist Registry 1983* Edsall 1983. This contains a concise history of Methodism, a biographical directory of current ministers and lists of office holders past and present.

**2801** *Proceedings of the Wesley Historical Society* 1893–. This carries an annual unannotated bibliography.

**2802** George Thompson Brake *Policy and Politics in British Methodism 1932–1982* Edsall 1984. A massive survey of Methodist conference decisions and Methodist high politics since the union of 1932.

**2803** Rupert E Davies, A Raymond George, E Gordon Rupp (eds) *A History of the Methodist Church in Great Britain* Vols 3 and 4 Epworth 1983–87. Volume 3 contains some useful essays which cover general and theological developments since 1932. Volume 4 contains a large and classified, if unannotated bibliography.

**2804** Rupert E Davies *Methodism* 2nd ed, Epworth 1985. A guide to the Methodist Church and to Methodist faith and attitudes.

**2805** Robert Currie *Methodism Divided: A Study in the Sociology of Ecumenicalism* Faber 1968. This traces Methodist schisms and reunions since the time of John Wesley. It presents a hostile view of Methodist union in 1932 and the Methodist-Anglican talks of 1965–70. A rather different perspective emerges in John Munsey Turner *Conflict and Reconciliation: Studies in Methodism and Ecumenism in England 1740–1982* Epworth 1985. Some reflections on the dilemmas of an ecumenically-minded Methodist (which he is) in the late twentieth century creep into this collection of essays.

**2806** Bryan S Turner 'Discord in Modern Methodism' *Proceedings of the Wesley Historical Society* 37 1969–70 pp 154–9. This looks at the growth of the Methodist Sacramental Fellowship and the theologically opposed Methodist Revival Fellowship and similar bodies. On the evangelical Methodist Revival Fellowship see also Arthur Skevington Wood *The Kindled Flame: The Witness of the Methodist Revival Fellowship* Headway 1987. This is a short history covering the period 1952–86.

**2807** Bryan S Turner 'The Decline of Methodism: An Analysis of Religious Commitment and Organisation' Leeds PhD Thesis 1969–70. A local study of Methodism's decline in one of its tradition strongholds is K K Harrison 'The Decline of Methodism in Kingston upon Hull in the Twentieth Century' Hull MA Thesis 1973.

**2808** A Raymond George 'The Changing Face of Methodism I: The Methodist Service Book' *Proceedings of the Wesley Historical Society* 41 1977–78 pp 65–72. On recent liturgical change see also David Howard Tripp 'Behind the "Alternative Order"' *Proceedings of the Wesley Historical Society* 43 1981–82 pp 4–8 and Bernard George Holland 'The Background to the 1967 Methodist Service for Infant Baptism' *Church Quarterly* 2 1969–70 pp 43–54.

**2809** George W Dolby 'The Changing Face of Methodism II: The Methodist Church Act 1976' *Proceedings of the Wesley Historical Society* 41 1977–8 pp 97–103.

**2810** J A Thomas 'Liturgy and Architecture 1932–1960: Methodist Influences and Ideas' *Proceedings of the Wesley Historical Society* 40 1976 pp 106–13.

**2811** Arthur Stephen Gregory 'MCMS: The First Five Years' *Methodist Church Music Society Bulletin* 3 1977–82 pp 42–6, 68–72.

**2812** D H Howarth 'Joyful News (1883–1963): Some Reflections' *Proceedings of the Wesley Historical Society* 44 1983 pp 2–15. Joyful News was the newsletter of Cliff College, a basically Methodist centre for the training of evangelists.

**2813** George William Sails *At the Centre: The Story of Methodism's Central Missions* Occasional Papers 15, Methodist Church Home Mission Department 1970. A good account of the oldest central mission in Britain is John Banks *The Story So Far . . . The First 100 Years of the Manchester and Salford Methodist Mission* The Mission/Penwork Ltd 1985. By a former superintendent minister it is most informative on the recent social work of the mission. Philip S Bagwell's history of the West London Mission, *Outcast London: A Christian Response: The West London Mission of the Methodist Church 1887–1987* Epworth 1987 is also good but is rather less informative on the post-war period. This is better covered in [2824].

**2814** Tony Holden *People, Churches and Multi-Racial Projects: An Account of English Methodism's Response to Plural Britain* Methodist Church Division of Social Responsibility 1985. This looks at inter-faith dialogue, anti-racist education, coloured people in the Methodist Church and the Methodist social work with the coloured community.

**2815** Robert Moore *Pitmen, Preachers and Politics: The Effects of Methodism in a Durham Mining Community* Cambridge University Press 1974. A celebrated sociological study of the Dearness valley. It is largely concerned with the period 1870–1926 but it has an epilogue on the 1970s.

**2816** Thomas Shaw *A History of Cornish Methodism* D Bradford Barton 1967. A history of Methodism in one of its strongholds.

**2817** Roy Norman Newell *Methodist Preacher and Statesman: Eric W Baker (1899–1973)* Quantock Prin-

ters 1984. Baker was Secretary of the Methodist Conference 1951–71.

**2818** Evelyn Clifford Urwin *Henry Carter CBE* Epworth 1955. Carter was the Secretary of successive bodies concerned with Methodist social witness from 1911 onwards. A pacifist and ardent temperance campaigner he died in 1951.

**2819** Gordon S Wakefield *Robert Newton Flew 1886–1962* Epworth 1971. A biography of a prominent Methodist theologian.

**2820** Rupert E Davies (ed) *John Scott Lidgett: A Symposium* Epworth 1957. Lidgett, despite his great age, remained an important spokesman for Methodism and the Free Churches, especially on educational matters, up to his death in 1953.

**2821** E Benson Perkins *So Appointed: An Autobiography* Epworth 1964. Benson Perkins was another important figure in Methodist social witness.

**2822** Cyril George Rackett *According to Plan: Sixty Years of Memories, Reflections and Digressions of a Methodist Local Preacher 1926–1986* the author 1986. Memories of lay ministry in the Southampton district of the church.

**2823** Paul Sangster *Doctor Sangster* Epworth 1962. Sangster was the minister at Westminister Central Hall for sixteen years.

**2824** Donald Soper *Calling for Action: An Autobiographical Enquiry* Robson 1984. A good autobiography. Soper was superintendent minister of the West London Mission 1936–78 and is through his open air preaching one of the best known ministers of the century. The President of the Christian Socialist Movement since 1960 his autobiography reflects his political interests and pacifism. See also William Purcell *Portrait of Soper: A Biography of the Reverend the Lord Soper of Kingsway* 2nd ed, Mowbrays 1983 and Douglas Weddell Thompson *Donald Soper: A Biography* Denholm House 1971.

**2825** John Anthony Newton *A Man for all Churches: Marcus Ward 1906–1978* Epworth 1984. The biography of a Methodist very active in ecumenical affairs.

**2826** John Munsey Turner 'Robert Featherstone Wearmouth (1882–1963) Methodist Historian' *Proceedings of the Wesley Historical Society* 43 1982 pp 111–6.

**2827** A Kingsley Weatherhead *Leslie Weatherhead: A Personal Portrait* Hodder and Stoughton 1975. Weatherhead was the minister of the City Temple 1936–60 and thus occupied one of the most important Free

Church pulpits in London. See also Christopher Maitland *Dr Leslie Weatherhead of the City Temple* Cassell 1960.

**2828** G Elizabeth Radford *My Providential Way: A Biography of Francis Brotherton Westbrook* Methodist Church Music Society 1978.

## (5) Salvation Army

**2829** *Salvation Army Year Book* Salvationist Publishing 1906–. An annual directory and guide.

**2830** Bernard Watson *A Hundred Years War: The Salvation Army 1865–1965* Hodder and Stoughton 1965. A centenary history. A G Wiggins *The History of the Salvation Army Vol IV: 1886–1964* Nelson 1964 is an international history. John Coutts *The Salvationists* Mowbrays 1978 is a survey of the Salvation Army and their beliefs and attitudes.

**2831** M K Beard 'The Contribution of the Salvation Army to the Religious and Moral Education of Children and Young People 1865–1965' London MA Thesis 1968–9.

**2832** Catherine Branwell-Booth *Commissioner Catherine* Darton, Longman and Todd 1983. The autobiography of the most celebrated Salvationist of the period. See also Mary Batchelor *Catherine Bramwell-Booth* Lion 1986.

## (6) Quakers

**2833** *Minutes and Proceedings of the London Yearly Meeting of the Society of Friends* London Yearly Meeting 1857–. A very informative annual guide to developments in Quaker thought and the deliberations both of the London Yearly Meeting and of various other Quaker bodies.

**2834** 'Dictionary of Quaker Biography'. A typescript located in Friends House Library, Euston Road, London which features potted biographies on prominent Quakers and information on the location of relevant material.

**2835** John Sykes *The Quakers: A New Look at their Place in Society* Allan Wingate 1958. A short general history as is John Punshon *Portrait in Grey: A Short History of the Quakers* Quaker Home Service 1984.

**2836** E H Milligan *The Past is Prologue: 100 Years of Quaker Overseas Work 1868–1968* Friends Service Council 1968. For Quaker relief work during and immediately after the Second World War see R C Wilson

*Quaker Relief: An Account of the Relief Work of the Society of Friends 1940–48* Allen and Unwin 1952.

**2837** Percy Bartlett *Barrow Cadbury: A Memoir* Bannisdale Press 1960. Biography of a Quaker social reformer 1862–1958.

**2838** Frederick Jenner Tritton *Carl Heath: Apostle of Peace* Friends Home Service Committee 1951.

**2839** John Lampden 'Will Warren: An Instrument of Peace' in Leonard S Kenworthy (ed) *Living in the Light: Some Quaker Pioneers of the 20th Century Vol II: In the Wider World* Friends General Conference and Quaker Publications, Kennett Square, Pennsylvania 1985 pp 236–52. Warren was very active in the peace movement. This volume also contains essays on the scientist Kathleen Lonsdale (pp 129–44) and the Labour politician Philip Noel-Baker (pp 190–205).

## (7) Pentecostalism

This section also encompasses black-led churches most of which are Pentecostalist bodies.

**2840** R D Massey 'British Pentecostalism in the 20th Century: An Historical Introduction and Phenomenological Study' Leicester MA Thesis 1976. Also relevant, although its main focus is on sects derived from a different theological root, is T R Warburton 'A Comparative Study of Minority Religious Groups with Special Reference to Holiness and Related Movements in Britain in the Last 50 Years' London PhD Thesis 1965–6. For a study of one of the oldest established Pentecostalist groups, the Elim Four Square Gospel Church see [2863].

**2841** Andrew Walker *Restoring the Kingdom: The Radical Christianity of the House Church Movement* Hodder and Stoughton 1985. An excellent study of the various restorationist, charismatic and pentecostal groups which have come to be given this generic label. It clearly explains the historical development of these movements, their theology and their relations with the mainline churches. See also Joyce Thurman *New Wineskins: A Study of the House Church Movement* Verlag Peter Lang 1982.

**2841A** John Carter *A Full Life: The Autobiography of a Pentecostal Pioneer* Evangel Press 1979. Carter was a founder member of the Assemblies of God of Great Britain and Ireland in 1924 and served the church as pastor, evangelist, general secretary and Bible College principal.

**2842** M J C Calley *God's People: West Indian Pentecostalist Sects in England* Oxford University Press 1965. The standard account. Gerloff Roswith 'Partnership in Black and White' [Methodist] *Home Mission Occasional Papers* Apr 1977 pp 7–37 examines the history and theology of black-led churches in Britain. In addition to detailing the experiences of some black church leaders he includes an annotated bibliography. The development of these black-led churches is discussed in Clifford S Hill *Black Churches: West Indian and African Sects in Britain* Community and Race Relations Unit of the British Council of Churches 1971.


### (8) Other


**2843** *The General Assembly of Unitarian and Free Christian Churches Year Book* Unitarian Headquarters 1890–. This has had various names. It is now published in two sections. There is a quinquennial handbook and an annual directory.


**2844** *Year Book of the Wesleyan Reform Union* Wesleyan Reform Union 1899–. The annual directory and guide of this offshoot of Methodism.


**2845** Seraphim Newton-Norton *The Time of Silence: A History of the Catholic Apostolic Church 1901–71* 3rd ed, Albury Society Publications 1975.


## D. ROMAN CATHOLIC CHURCH


**2846** *The Catholic Directory of England and Wales* Associated Catholic Newspapers Ltd 1839–. An annual directory.


**2847** *Catholic Archives* Catholic Archives Society 1980–. A guide to recent depositions. This includes details of post-war accessions.


**2848** Michael P Hornsby-Smith *Roman Catholics in England: Studies in Social Structure Since the Second World War* Cambridge University Press 1987. A sociological study of Roman Catholics since 1945. See also John Hickey *Urban Catholics: Urban Catholicism in England and Wales from 1829 to the Present Day* Chapman 1967 and A E C W Spencer 'Demography of Catholicism' *The Month* 236 1975 pp 100–5.


**2849** George Andrew Beck (ed) *The English Catholics 1850–1950: Essays to Commemorate the Centenary of the Restoration of the Hierarchy of England and Wales* Burns Oates 1950. A collection of essays on the Bishops, the orders, education, the Irish, the Catholic press and Catholic literature.

**2849A** J D Crichton, H E Winstone and J R Ainslie *English Catholic Worship: Liturgical Renewal in England Since 1900* Geoffrey Chapman 1979. A history of liturgical change, not least in the aftermath of the Second Vatican Council.


**2850** G B Smith 'Music and the Mass in England Since Vatican II' Southampton MPhil Thesis 1979. A study of developments since the Second Vatican Council in the early 1960s.


**2851** Philip Morgan 'Catholics and the British Churches' *The Month* 264 1984 pp 392–8. An analysis of relations with the British Council of Churches. The unecumenical outlook of the church in 1949 is discussed in Alberic Stacpoole 'Catholic Inflexibility in England' *The Month* 264 1984 pp 158–62 and 198–204.


**2852** F P McHugh 'The Changing Social Role of the Roman Catholic Church in England 1958–1982' Cambridge PhD Thesis 1983. Peter Coman *Catholics and the Welfare State* Longman 1977 examines the Catholic response to the founding of the Welfare State 1940–65 using statements of the hierarchy, Catholic journals and the views of Catholic MPs.


**2853** John Martin Cleary *Catholic Social Action in Britain 1909–59: A History of the Catholic Social Guild* Catholic Social Guild 1961. A history of the body in the Church specifically concerned with social questions.


**2854** A Dummett and M Hollings *Restoring the Streets: Catholics in Multi-Racial Britain* Catholic Committee for Racial Justice 1974. The role of the Catholic Church in racial integration as a church which has long catered particularly for immigrant communities is also considered in Anthony Spencer 'The Catholic Community as a British Melting Pot' *New Community* 11 1973 pp 125–31.


**2855** P R Matthews 'Radical Catholicism and the New Left in Britain in the 1960s' Trinity College, Dublin PhD Thesis 1984–5. A sociological analysis. See also Douglas Hyde 'The New Catholic Left' *The Month* n.s. 36 1966 pp 315–22.


**2856** Peter F Anson *The Religious Orders and Congregations of Great Britain and Ireland* Stanbrook Abbey Press 1949. The only comprehensive guide to be published this century. It includes a brief history of each order and congregation.


**2857** David Milburn *A History of Ushaw College: A Study of the Origins, Foundation and Development of an English Catholic Seminary, with an Epilogue 1908–62* Ushaw Bookshop 1964.

**2858** Michael Clifton *Amigo: Friend of the Poor: Bishop of Southwark 1904–1949* Fowler Wright Books 1987. Peter Amigo was an important figure in the Catholic Church.

**2859** John Carmel Heenan *Not the Whole Truth* Hodder and Stoughton 1971. This is followed by his *A Crown of Thorns: An Autobiography 1951–1963* Hodder and Stoughton 1974. Heenan was Archbishop of Westminster 1963–75. He became a Cardinal in 1965.

**2860** Tony Castle *Basil Hume: A Portrait* Collins 1986. Cardinal Hume has been Archbishop of Westminster since 1975.

**2861** Penelope Fitzgerald *The Knox Brothers: Edmund ('Evoe') 1881–1971, Dillwyn 1883–1943, Wilfrid 1886–1950, Ronald 1888–1957* Macmillan 1977. Only Ronald Knox remained important after 1945. He was a close friend of Macmillan's, a Jesuit and a famous convert to Catholicism from the Anglican church. See also Evelyn Waugh *Ronald Knox* Chapman and Hall 1959.

**2862** Philip Caraman *C C Martindale: A Biography* Longmans 1967. Martindale was a leading Jesuit.

## E. CHRISTIAN AND QUASI–CHRISTIAN GROUPS

**2863** Bryan Ronald Wilson *Sects and Society: A Sociological Study of Three Religious Groups in Britain* Heinemann 1961. A study of the Elim Four Square Gospel Church, Christian Science and the Christadelphians.

**2864** G K Nelson 'The Development of Organisation of the Spiritualist Movement in Britain' London PhD Thesis 1966–7.

**2865** Brian Graham *Clare Cameron: A Human and Spiritual Journey* Werner Shaw 1984. A biography of the English mystic and poet with connections with theosophy and buddhism.

## F. NON–CHRISTIAN RELIGIONS

Some of the literature in the section on Race Relations is of relevance to the history and progress of other faiths in post-war Britain.

### (1) Judaism

**2866** Aubrey Newman *The Board of Deputies of British Jews 1760–1985: A Brief Survey* Vallentine Mitchell 1987. A well-illustrated short history.

**2867** Aubrey Newman *The United Synagogue 1870–1970* Routledge and Kegan Paul 1976. A centenary history of an institution which has served the Jewish community in London. On the Council of Christians and Jews see [2624]. For other material on Judaism since the war see the entries on the Jews in the section on Race Relations [5730–44].

**2868** Immanuel Jakobovits *If Only My People . . . Zionism in My Life* Weidenfeld and Nicolson 1984. Jakobovits was Chief Rabbi of the United Hebrew Congregations of the British Commonwealth 1967–90.

### (2) Islam

**2869** Daniele Jody and Jorgen Nielsen *Muslims in Britain: An Annotated Bibliography 1960–1984* Bibliographies in Ethnic Relations 6, Centre for Research in Ethnic Relations, University of Warwick 1985. This short bibliography covers work published 1960–84.

**2870** M M Ally 'History of Muslims in Britain' Birmingham MA Thesis 1981–2. This covers 1850–1914 and 1945–80. The latter section is however more sociological than historical.

**2871** Muhammed Akram 'Islam and Muslims in Liverpool' Liverpool MPhil Thesis 1980. A history of the Muslim community in Liverpool followed by a survey of the community's practices, rites, education and social relations.

**2872** B Benedict 'Muslim and Buddhist Associations in London' London Ph.D Thesis 1953–4.

### (3) Hinduism

**2873** Richard Burghart (ed) *Hinduism in Great Britain: The Perpetuation of Religion in an Alien Cultural Milieu* Tavistock 1987. Papers on various aspects of the Hindu community. It has some errors and does not sufficiently pursue the extent to which the alien culture has changed the faithfuls' attitude to their religion. It is nevertheless very useful and has an excellent bibliography. Also useful are J Swinney *The Hindus in Britain* Batsford 1988 and Helen Kanitkar and Robert Jackson *Hindus in Britain* Extramural Division Occasional Paper 6, School of Oriental and African Studies, University of London 1982.

**2874** D G Bowen 'The Sathya Sai Baba Community in Bradford: Its Origin and Development, Religious Beliefs and Practices' Leeds PhD Thesis 1986. A study of the development of a Gujurati Hindu sect since 1970.

**2875** Séan Casey 'The Hare Krishna Movement and Hindus in Britain' *New Community* 10 1982 pp 477–86.

### (4) Buddhism

**2876** Ian P Oliver *Buddhism in Britain* Rider 1979. A general study and history. A M Church 'Buddhist Groups in Britain: Adaptation and Development of Traditional Religious Forms Within a Western Environment' Manchester MA Thesis 1982 looks particularly at the development of Buddhist centres from the 1950s onwards. See also G R Kerr 'The Nature of Buddhism in Britain' London MPhil Thesis 1974–6. See also [2872].

### (5) Other

**2877** Arthur Wesley Helweg *Sikhs in England: The Development of a Migrant Community* 2nd ed, Oxford University Press 1986. A good study of the Sikh community and its experiences in Britain. This includes a case study of the community in Gravesend. James Walvin *Passage to Britain* Penguin 1984 is an extensive history of the Sikh community in Britain and of the relative ease with which the Sikhs have been assimilated. This success at assimilation and the nature of Sikh culture are the main focuses of Parminder Bhachu *Twice Migrants: East African Sikh Settlers in Britain* Tavistock 1985.

**2878** Ernest Cashmore *Rastaman: The Rastafarian Movement in England* Allen and Unwin 1979. An in-depth enquiry which looks at Rastafarianism and its attitudes and links with the Ethiopian Orthodox Church. It includes a good bibliography and discography. J Plummer *Movement of Jah People: The Growth of the Rastafarians* Press Gang 1977 is a short sociological study.

**2879** G M Towler Mehta 'Parsees in Britain: The Experiences of a Religious Minority Group' *New Community* 10 1982 pp 243–50.

## F. HUMANISM AND ATHEISM

**2880** Susan Budd *Varieties of Unbelief: Atheists and Agnostics in English Society 1850–1960* Heinemann 1977. The standard work on the subject. Her thesis 'The British Humanist Movement 1860–1966' Oxford DPhil Thesis 1968–9 is also worth consulting.

**2881** Colin B Campbell 'Humanism and the Culture of the Professions: A Study of the Rise of the British Humanist Movement 1954–1963' London PhD Thesis 1967–8. The only publication derived from this doctoral research is his 'The Membership Composition of the British Humanist Association' *Sociological Review* 13 1965 pp 327–37.

## G. THE OCCULT

### (1) Psychical Research

**2882** Renée Haynes *The Society for Psychical Research 1882–1982: A History* Macdonald 1982. A good history of a respectable and sceptical body researching into pyschic phenomena.

### (2) Witchcraft and the Occult

**2883** M Carol 'The 20th Century Witch in England and the United States: An Annotated Bibliography' *Bulletin of Bibliography* 39 1982 pp 69–83.

**2884** Tanya Luhrmann *Persuasions of the Witch's Craft: Ritual, Magic and Witchcraft in Present-Day England* Blackwell 1989. A partly autobiographical investigation into the state of the art in contemporary England. For an earlier study by a committed witch see G B Gardiner *Witchcraft Today* Aquarian Press 1954.

**2885** June Johns *King of the Witches: The World of Alex Sanders* Peter Davies 1969. Sanders was the most prominent witch in Britain of the post-war period. This biographical study also reflects on the growth of witchcraft since the repeal of the Witchcraft Act in 1951. Another autobiography of a prominent witch is Sybil Leek *Diary of a Witch* Leslie Frewin 1975. Julian Symonds *The Great Beast* Rider 1951 is the biography of Aleister Crowley, who died in 1947. Another, sympathetic, portrait by Crowley's former secretary is Israel Regardie *The Eye of the Triangle* Falcon Press 1982.

# 7 ECONOMIC HISTORY

## A. GENERAL

### (1) Reference Works

**2886** *Economic Statistics Collections: A Directory of Research Resources in the United Kingdom for Business, Industry and Public Affairs* Library Association 1970. An informative library guide. K M Bolton *Sources of Information for Business Organisations in the British Isles* Institute of Chartered Accountants of England and Wales 1973 is another library guide. C A Westwick *Sources of British Business Comparative Data* Institute of Chartered Accountants in England and Wales 1980 gives details on the publishing organizations and the frequency of publication.

**2887** Rex Pope and Bernard Hoyle (eds) *British Economic Performance 1880–1980* Croom Helm 1985. A collection of documents and commentaries. See also R W Breach and R M Hartwell (eds) *British Economy and Society 1870–1970: Documents, Descriptions and Statistics* Oxford University Press 1972.

**2888** C H Feinstein *National Income, Expenditure and Output of the United Kingdom 1855–1965* Cambridge University Press 1972. A collection of statistical tables with detailed commentary also covering such areas as capital stock, population, employment and unemployment or prices and wages.

**2889** *Economic Situation Report* Confederation of British Industry 1975–. This monthly survey has become much fuller in recent years. It gives an overview of industrial trends, lists and analyses economic and financial indicators and provides economic forecasts.

**2890** John Fletcher (ed) *Information Sources in Economics* Butterworths 1984. A bibliography and source book focusing on Britain. It gives details on periodicals, databases, official publications, international publications and statistical series.

**2891** *International Bibliography of Economics* Stevens 1952–. An annual unannotated bibliography. *Economic Abstracts* Martinus Nijhoff, The Hague 1953/4– is an companion series of abstracts. It appears twice monthly abstracting both books and articles. The abstracts are given in the language of the original.

**2892** *Journal of Economic Abstracts* 1963–. This quarterly publication gives English language abstracts from periodical articles, usually written by the authors.

**2893** *Economic History Review* has since 1950 carried a regular unannotated bibliography of books and articles on the economic history of Britain and Ireland. At first this was an occasional series but now it appears annually.

**2894** Michael Healey (ed) *Urban and Regional Industrial Research: The Changing UK Data Base* Geobooks 1983. A very informative survey of relevant databases.

### (2) Guides to Statistics

The literature on statistical guides in the section on General Reference Books should also be consulted.

**2895** Bernard Edwards *Sources of Economics and Business Statistics* Heinemann 1972. An informative study. See also F M M Lewes *Statistics of the British Economy* Allen and Unwin 1967. A good earlier guide is E Devons *Introduction to British Economic Statistics* Cambridge University Press 1956. Charles Frederick Carter and Andrew Donald Roy *British Economic Statistics: A Report* Cambridge University Press 1954 is a detailed critical examination with recommendations for improved services.

**2896** *United Kingdom National Accounts: Sources and Methods* HMSO 1985. An essential guide for users of the blue books and *Economic Trends*. It gives details of the conception, definitions, statistical sources, methods of compilation and the reliability of the various statistical series. Another useful guide, especially to the blue books, is Harold Copeman *The National Accounts: A Short Guide* HMSO 1981. An earlier guide which is rather wider in scope is *National Income Statistics: Sources and Methods* HMSO 1956.

## (3) Statistics

**2897** London and Cambridge Economic Service *The British Economy: Key Statistics 1900–1970* Times Newspapers 1975. A collection of tables on various aspects of the economy. For an international comparison see Thelma Liesner *Economic Statistics 1900–1983: United Kingdom, United States of America, France, Germany, Italy and Japan* Facts on File, New York 1985.

**2898** *Economic Trends* HMSO 1953–. A monthly collection of tables and charts providing a broad background to trends in the economy. The *Annual Supplement* 1976–, presents long runs of quarterly figures for all the main series.

**2899** *United Kingdom National Accounts* HMSO 1984–. Before 1984 this was known as *National Income and Expenditure*. It is generally known as the 'Blue Book'. It annually provides detailed estimates of national product, income and expenditure, covering value-added by industry, personal sector, public corporations, central and local government, capital formation and financial accounts.

**2900** *United Kingdom Balance of Payments* HMSO 1959–. This annual is generally known as the 'Pink Book'. It is the basic reference guide for balance of payments statistics, with information on visible trade, invisibles, investment and other capital transactions.

**2901** *British Business* HMSO 1979–. A weekly magazine. Before 1979 it was *Trade and Industry* 1970–79 and before that was the *Board of Trade Journal* 1886–1970. It provides a wide range of statistics and commentaries on current economic developments.

## (4) General Histories

**2902** Sidney Pollard *The Development of the British Economy 1914–80* 3rd ed, Arnold 1983. The standard general study. B W E Alford *British Economic Performance Since 1945* Macmillan 1988 is a good short analysis. A video on the subject by a notable economic adviser is Alan Walters *British Post-War Economic Performance from Attlee to Thatcher* Institute of Economic Affairs 1987. The British economy 1945–80 is examined in J E House (ed) *The UK Space: Resources, Environment and Future* 3rd ed, Weidenfeld and Nicolson 1982. Another useful survey of the post-war economy is J F Wright *Britain in the Age of Economic Management: An Economic History Since 1939* Oxford University Press 1979. Also of use is A J Youngson *Britain's Economic Growth 1920–1966* 2nd ed, Allen and Unwin 1968 and A G Armstrong *Structural Change*

in the British Economy 1948–1968 Chapman and Hall 1974. Charles Feinstein (ed) *The Managed Economy: Essays in British Economic Policy and Performance Since 1929* Oxford University Press 1983 is a good collection of essays which touch on economic management since the war. There is also a chapter by Sir Alec Cairncross on the post-war British economy in Roderick Floud and Donald McCloskey (eds) *The Economic History of Britain Since 1700 Vol 2: 1860 to the 1970s* Cambridge University Press 1981. See also A R Nobay 'Money, Inflation and Economic Activity in the Post-War UK Economy' Southampton PhD Thesis 1974–6.

**2903** G A Phillips and R T Maddock *The Growth of the British Economy 1918–68* Allen and Unwin 1973. A textbook history, as is L J Williams *Britain and the World Economy 1919–70* Collins 1971. Patrick David Henderson *Economic Growth in Britain* Weidenfeld and Nicolson 1966 surveys the performance of the economy 1945–61.

**2904** Frank Walter Paish *Studies in an Inflationary Economy: The United Kingdom 1948–61* Macmillan 1966.

**2905** Lawrence John Williams *Britain and the World Economy 1919–70* Fontana 1971.

**2906** A R Prest and D J Coppock (eds) *The UK Economy: A Manual of Applied Economics* 8th ed, Weidenfeld and Nicolson 1980. A general survey of the British economy. Another rather more elementary introduction to the economy is Maurice Peston *The British Economy: An Elementary Macroeconomic Perspective* Philip Allan 1982. Contemporary developments in the economic geography of Britain are examined in the Open University course textbook, John Allen and Doreen Massey (eds) *Restructuring Britain: The Economy in Question* Sage 1988. K S Reader *The Modern British Economy in Historical Perspective* Longman 1969 is a textbook examining contemporary conditions and the poor growth rate in historical context.

**2907** *National Institute Economic Review* National Institute for Economic and Social Research 1963–. A quarterly independent summary and appraisal of the performance of the British economy, industrial production and prospects.

**2908** E Victor Morgan *The Structure of Property Ownership in Great Britain* Clarendon 1960. A study of property ownership sector by sector supported by good statistics.

**2909** R Lewis *The New Service Economy* Longman 1973. A general outline of the growth of service industries. J N Marshall *et al* 'Understanding the Location and Role of Producer Services in the United Kingdom' *En-*

*vironment and Planning A* 19 1987 pp 575–95 looks at the expansion and locational trends in the service economy in the 1980s.

**2910** Derek H Aldcroft *The British Economy Vol 1: The Years of Turmoil 1920–1951* Harvester 1986. This is the first of a projected three volume series on the British economy in the twentieth century. Most of this volume is concerned with the 1930s and the one chapter on the Attlee government does not really add anything new.

**2911** Alan S Milward *The Economic Effect of the Two World Wars in Britain* Macmillan 1970. There are some reflections on the impact on the post-war economy in this pamphlet.

**2912** G D N Worswick and P H Ady (eds) *The British Economy 1945–50* Oxford University Press 1952. A well-regarded collection of essays that has retained its value.

**2913** G D N Worswick and P H Ady (eds) *The British Economy in the Nineteen Fifties* Oxford University Press 1962. This is another well regarded collection of essays.

**2914** Robert Appleby *Profitability and Productivity in the United Kingdom 1954–1964* British Institute of Management 1968. A discussion of economic problems and disincentives to higher productivity in this period.

**2915** Jack Revell *The National Balance Sheet of the United Kingdom 1957–1961* Cambridge University Press 1967. A survey of British national stocks, assets and expenditure in this period. It contains plentiful statistical data.

**2916** John and Anne-Marie Hackett *The British Economy: Problems and Prospects* Allen and Unwin 1967. This is particularly useful in its analysis of the Wilson government's attempts at economic planning in the 1960s.

**2917** W B Reddaway *Effects of UK Direct Investment Overseas* Cambridge University Press 1967–68. A report for the CBI. The interim report appeared in 1967 and the final report in 1968. It analyses the effect of British investment and subsidiaries overseas on the British economy.

**2918** P J Dawkins and Peter Maunder (eds) *The British Economy in the 1970s* Heinemann Educational 1980. The economic difficulties that followed the massive oil price increases of 1973 are examined in Nick Gardner *Decade of Discontent: The Changing British Economy Since 1973* Blackwell 1987. As a former Chief Economist at the Department of Employment and an adviser

to those struggling to deal with these problems Gardner is particularly strong on economic policy. The impact of North Sea oil on the British economy since it first came on stream in the 1970s is assessed in Fred Atkinson and Stephen Hall *Oil and the British Economy* Croom Helm 1983.

**2919** Harold D Clarke, Marianne C Stewart and Gary Zuk (eds) *Economic Decline and Political Change: Canada, Great Britain and the United States* University of Pittsburgh Press, Pittsburgh, Pennsylvania 1989. A comparative analysis of the political response to the macroeconomic difficulties of the 1970s and 1980s. The coverage on Britain in this volume is limited.

**2920** Alan R Townsend *The Impact of the Recession on Industry, Employment and the Regions 1976–1981* Croom Helm 1983. This examines the industrial and regional distribution of the 1976–81 recession in the context of post-war history and contemporary economic policy. C F Pratten *Destocking in the Recession* Gower 1985 is an analysis of the destocking policies in 1980–81 recession by manufacturers, retailers and distributers which led to the fastest drop in manufacturing output on record.

**2921** Geoffrey Maynard *The Economy Under Thatcher* Blackwell 1988. A useful survey of the performance and management of the economy in the 1980s. The political and academic debate on the extent of economic revival in these years is reflected, albeit in a rather unbalanced way given the editors' sympathies with the Left, in David Coates and John Hillard (eds) *The Economic Revival of Modern Britain: The Debate Between Right and Left* Edward Elgar 1987. Peter Robinson *The Unbalanced Recovery* Philip Allan 1988 argues that the recovery of these years has been unbalanced, leaving behind whole communities and the bulk of the long-term unemployed. He uses a case study of Cleveland to elaborate his argument. DeAnne Julius 'Britain's Changing International Interests: Economic Influences on Foreign Policy Priorities' *International Affairs* 63 1987 pp 375–94 is an interesting assessment of economic success and international trade and investment in the 1980s.

## (5) Economic Decline

**2922** C J F Brown and T D Sherriff *De-Industrialisation in the UK: Background Statistics* National Institute of Economic and Social Research, Discussion Paper 23 1978.

**2923** David Coates and John Hillard (eds) *The Economic Decline of Modern Britain: The Debate Between Right and Left* Wheatsheaf 1986. This collects in one volume all the main arguments and theories of British economic decline. It is however rather weak on that school of thought which associates decline with an anti-industrial culture.

**2924** Bernard Elbaum and William Lazonick (eds) *The Decline of the British Economy* Clarendon 1986. A collection of essays on decline in the cotton, iron and steel, shipbuilding and motor vehicles industries. Technical education, industrial research, finance, regional economic policy and state intervention are also examined. The general thesis is that decline has been caused by fragmented industrial structures and poor industrial relations. The value of such conclusions based on such a narrow sample of industries is not however above question.

**2925** M W Kirby *The Decline of British Economic Power Since 1870* Allen and Unwin 1981. A good analysis of Britain's relative economic decline. Some commentators have been inclined to treat decline as a post-war problem. Relative decline has however been a problem since the late ninteenth century. Indeed Ben Fine and Laurence Harris *The Peculiarities of the British Economy* Lawrence and Wishart 1985 is a Marxist analysis which argues that the roots of the problem lie in the unique history of capitalism in Britain. Another analysis of British economic decline from the late nineteenth century to the monetarist experiments of the Thatcher years is Keith Smith *The British Economic Crisis: Its Past and Future* Penguin 1984. Also useful is the Keynesian analysis, John Eatwell *Whatever Happened to Britain? The Economics of Decline* Oxford University Press 1984. Gordon Wynne Roderick and Michael Stephens (eds) *The British Malaise: Industrial Performance, Education and Training in Britain Today* Falmer Press 1983 examines this decline since 1870 in terms of education and vocational training, the numbers of scientists and engineers, research and development, management and manpower planning and the effect of the trade unions. They particularly indict low investment. On investment see also P N Junankar 'The Relationship Between Investment and Spare Capacity in the United Kingdom' *Economica* 37 1970 pp 277–91.

**2926** Sidney Pollard *The Wasting of the British Economy: British Economic Policy 1945 to the Present* 2nd ed, Croom Helm 1984. An analysis of the causes of decline which particularly focuses on the effects of government policy, especially the defence of exchange rates and balances of payments which he argues were pursued instead of and at the expense of economic growth. The literature on the controversial subject of British economic decline is dominated by books such as this which offer various, sometimes contradictory but always strongly argued theses. A more general and rather less well known study of decline since 1945 is G

Bernard Stafford *The End of Economic Growth? Growth and Decline in the UK Since 1945* Robertson 1981.

**2927** Stephen Black 'Britain: The Politics of Foreign Economic Policy, the Domestic Economy and the Problem of Pluralistic Stagnation' *International Organisation* 31 1977 pp 673–722. This sees slow growth and relative decline as a result of the priority given to maintenance of great power status and commitments in the immediate post-war period, until there was an attempt to move away from this and promote higher growth in the 1960s.

**2928** Scott Newton and Dilwyn Porter *Modernization Frustrated: The Politics of Industrial Decline in Britain Since 1900* Unwin Hyman 1988. This study links low investment to the disproportionate influence of the financial sector in government circles, leading to the pursuit of policies that have favoured the City rather than manufacturing industry.

**2929** Andrew Glyn and Bob Sutcliffe *Workers, British Capitalism and Profits Squeeze* Penguin 1972. An analysis which argues the importance of the defensive strength of the trade unions as a factor in Britain's economic decline, in lowering the return on investment and presenting obstacles in the way of modernization programmes. There is a similar emphasis in Andrew Kilpatrick and Tony Lawson 'On the Nature of Industrial Decline in the UK' *Cambridge Journal of Economics* 4 1980 pp 85–102 and in David Purdy 'British Capitalism Since the War' *Marxism Today* 20 1976 pp 270–7, 310–8. Paul Einzig *Decline and Fall: Britain's Crisis in the Sixties* Macmillan 1969 from a different ideological perspective also indicts the trade unions and the high labour costs in Britain, as well as condemning the high level of public spending. Robert Taylor 'Trade Unions Since 1945: Scapegoats of Economic Decline?' *Contemporary Record* 1/2 1987 pp 7–10 however argues that trade union militancy was not a cause but a consequence of decline.

**2930** Martin J Weiner *English Culture and the Decline of the Industrial Spirit 1850–1980* Cambridge University Press 1981. The classic argument for the importance of an anti-industrial spirit in Britain's economic decline. G C Allen *British Disease – Short Essay on the Nature and Causes of the Nation's Lagging Wealth* Institute of Economic Affairs, Hobart Paper 67 1976 also draws attention to cultural factors such as the class system or civil service attitudes. See also Michael Burrage 'Culture and British Economic Growth' *British Journal of Sociology* 20 1969 pp 117–33.

**2931** Correlli Barnett *The Audit of War: The Illusion and Reality of Britain as a Great Nation* Macmillan 1986. One of the most celebrated studies on the subject of British economic weakness. It draws attention to the flaws in the British economy revealed by the Second World War and the British dependence in a number of areas on American supplies and skills. The British failure to respond to these problems is seen as the root of post-war malaise, a failure which Barnett feels was compounded by a wartime determination instead to build a Welfare State. See also the useful discussion on the themes raised in this book, Corelli Barnett *et al* 'Symposium: Britain's Post-War Decline' *Contemporary Record* 1/2 1987 pp 11–18.

**2932** Michael Stewart *Politics and Economic Policy Since 1964: The Jekyll and Hyde Years* Pergamon 1978. The most influential indictment of the adverse effects on the British economy of adversarial politics. This is approached in a rather different manner in Andrew Gamble and S A Walkland *The British Party System and Economic Policy 1945–1983: Studies in Adversary Politics* Oxford University Press 1984. See also Andrew Glyn and J Harrison *The British Economic Disaster* Pluto 1984. Government policy, as well as structural problems are seen as the cause of poor economic performance since 1966 in 'The performance of the Economy: Past and Future' *Cambridge Economic Policy Review* 7 1981 pp 8–24. The effect of popular expectations of economic policies, and of other aspects of political behaviour on the process of economic decline is assessed in James E Alt *The Politics of Economic Decline: Economic Management and Political Behaviour in Britain Since 1964* Cambridge University Press 1980.

**2933** M R Weale 'The Accounts of the United Kingdom Public Sector 1972–82' *Three Banks Review* 141 1984 pp 18–32. An analysis of the effect of public sector borrowing and expenditure on investment, consumption and ownership of wealth.

**2934** Robert Bacon and Walter Eltis 'Stop-go and Deindustrialisation' *National Westminster Bank Quarterly Review* 1975 pp 31–43. In the 1970s it was argued that the stop-go policies that had been pursued since the 1950s had led to low investment and growth. C Thain 'The Treasury and Britain's Decline' *Political Studies* 32 1984 pp 581–95 however argues that the evidence for this view is inconclusive.

**2935** Robert Bacon and Walter Eltis *Britain's Economic Problem – Too Few Producers* 2nd ed, Macmillan 1978. A influential critique of the size of Britain's service sector.

**2936** G Jones and M Barnes *Britain on Borrowed Time* Penguin 1967. A wide-ranging critique of the weakness of British management, their fear of innovation and their inefficiency. This is highly particularly in the context of their use of manpower. Another criticism of poor management both in business and in other relevant areas such as education is Charles Villiers *Start Again, Britain*

Quartet 1984. The reasons behind the relatively poor performance of British manufacturing industry since 1950 are examined in Karel Williams, John Williams and Dennis Thomas *Why are British Bad at Manufacturing?* Routledge and Kegan Paul 1983. This includes case studies of GEC, British Leyland and the shipbuilding industry. See also D J W Bing and M Stamp 'Is British Management Bad?' *Moorgate and Wall Street* 1975 pp 17–38.

**2937** F Blackaby (ed) *De-Industrialisation* Heinemann 1978. A collection of essays examining the decline in British manufacturing industry. See also Bob Rowthorn and J R Wells *Deindustrialisation and Britain's Changing Role in the World Economy* Cambridge University Press 1984. The geography of industrial contraction and job loss 1945–80 and the regional management of industrial decline is examined in Ron Martin and Bob Rowthorn (eds) *The Geography of De-Industrialisation* Macmillan 1986. The management of industrial decline by governments, trade unions and management is also discussed in Tony Dickson and David Judge (ed) *The Politics of Industrial Closure* Macmillan 1987.

**2938** Stephen Davies and Richard E Caves *Britain's Productivity Gap* Cambridge University Press 1987. An attempt to explain why Britain's productivity was about 60 per cent lower than in America in the 1960s and 1970s. They find under-investment in everything from skills to business administration. The age and obsolescence of British plant as a factor in poor economic performance is investigated in Robert Bacon and Walter Eltis *The Age of US and UK Machinery* National Economic Development Office 1974.

**2939** Keith Pavitt (ed) *Technical Innovation and British Economic Performance* Macmillan 1980. Essays on British deficiencies in both areas, examining poor management, low investment, attitudes to engineering education, policy and innovation in various sectors of industry.

**2940** Sir Nicholas Henderson 'Valedictory Despatch' *The Economist* 2/6/1979 pp 29–40. An analysis of Britain's economic decline on his retirement as Britain's Ambassador to France. Britain's economic performance is compared with that of France and West Germany.

**2941** Political and Economic Planning *Growth in the British Economy: A Study of Economic Problems and Policies in Contemporary Britain* Allen and Unwin 1960. One of the first studies of why Britain's economic growth was relatively slow. Attention is drawn to lack of investment and the low rate of increase in productivity. No evidence of an adverse effect from social services spending was found. This study was followed by a number of others in the 1960s on slow economic growth, the most celebrated of which was Nicholas Kaldor

*Causes of the Slow Rate of Economic Growth in the United Kingdom* Cambridge University Press 1966. Slow growth is examined at both micro- and macro-economic levels in F V Meyer, D C Corner and J E S Parker *Problems of a Mature Economy* Macmillan 1970. A useful comparative study is J-P Azam 'The Slow Economic Growth of the UK Since the Second World War: A Comparison with France' London PhD Thesis 1980. The factors influencing Britain's relatively poor performance are discussed in Leslie Manison 'Some Factors Influencing the United Kingdom's Economic Growth Performance' *IMF Staff Papers* 25 1978 pp 705–38. See also C F Pratten 'The Reasons for the Slow Economic Progress of the British Economy' *Oxford Economic Papers* n.s. 24 1972 pp 180–96 and Charles P Kindleburger 'Foreign Trade and Growth: Lessons from the British Experience Since 1913' *Lloyds Bank Review* 65 1962 pp 16–28.

**2942** Robert C O Matthews, C H Feinstein and I Odling-Smee *British Economic Growth 1856–1973: The Post-War Period in Historical Perspective* Clarendon 1982. An important analysis. Also of considerable value is Derek H Aldcroft *Britain's Economic Growth Failure 1950–1980* Harvester 1983. See also Phyllis Deane and W A Cole *British Economic Growth 1688–1959* Cambridge University Press 1967. Derek H Aldcroft and Peter Fearon (eds) *Economic Growth in Twentieth Century Britain* Macmillan 1969 is a good collection of essays which puts the slow growth of the post-war period into historical context. The growth rate of the post-war years in fact compares favourably with all but that of the inter-war years, a point also made in Robert C O Matthews 'Some Aspects of Post-War Growth in the British Economy in Relation to Historical Experience' *Transactions of the Manchester Statistical Society* 1964 pp 3–25 and D Paige 'Economic Growth – The Last Hundred Years' *National Institute Economic Review* 16 1961 pp 24–49. A discrepancy with growth rates of competitors however became apparent in the 1950s. See also John Knapp and Kenneth Lomax 'Britain's Growth Performance: The Enigma of the 1950s' *Lloyds Bank Review* 74 1964 pp 1–24.

**2943** Wilfrid Beckermann (ed) *Slow Growth in Britain: Causes and Consequences* Clarendon 1979. A valuable collection of papers on the nature of slow growth and its effects on social welfare, the labour market, poverty and the redistribution of wealth.

**2944** Richard E Caves (ed) *Britain's Economic Prospects* Brookings Institution, Washington DC 1968. A gloomy report. Its conclusions are re-assessed and the performance of the British economy since the 1967 devaluation re-evaluated in Sir Alec Cairncross (ed) *Britain's Economic Prospects Reconsidered* Allen and Unwin 1971. Another response to the Brookings report that also focuses on slow growth is E H Phelps Brown 'The Brookings Study of the Poor Performance of the British Economy' *Economica* 36 1969 pp 235–52. A further, similarly gloomy prognostication from the Brookings Institution is R E Caves and L B Krause (eds) *Britain's Industrial Performance* Brookings Institution 1980.

## (6) Inflation

**2945** Maxime MacCafferty (comp) *Inflation in the United Kingdom* Aslib 1977. A bibliography of 473 references, mostly annotated, drawn from books, periodicals and newspapers from the period of high inflation 1974–76.

**2946** Michael Parkin and Michael T Sumner (eds) *Inflation in the United Kingdom* Manchester University Press 1978. A rather technical collection of interpretations. For a more political interpretation see Andrew Gamble and P Walton *Capitalism in Crisis: Inflation and the State* Macmillan 1976. See also W W Daniel *The PEP Survey on Inflation* Political and Economic Planning 1975, Charles Goodhart 'Problems of Monetary Management – The UK Experience' in Anthony S Courakis (ed) *Inflation, Depression and Economic Policy in the West* Alexandrine Publishing 1981 pp 111–36, P J Curwen *Inflation* Macmillan 1976, B Griffiths *Inflation: The Price of Prosperity* Weidenfeld and Nicolson 1976 and K J W Alexander 'The Politics of Inflation' *Political Quarterly* 45 1974 pp 300–9.

**2947** D Ballante, S O Morrell and A Zardkoohi 'Unanticipated Money Growth, Unemployment, Output and the Price Level in the United Kingdom 1946–1977' *Southern Economic Journal* 49 1982 pp 62–76.

**2948** A W Phillips 'The Relationship Between Unemployment and the Rate of Change of Money Wages in the United Kingdom 1861–1957' *Economica* n.s. 25 1958 pp 283–99. The famous Phillips curve essay. This argues that the rate of change of money wage rates can be explained by the level of unemployment and the rate of change in unemployment, except in or immediately after a sufficiently rapid rise in the price of imported goods to offset the tendency for increased productivity to reduce the cost of living. It had considerable effect on British economic policy. Michael Parkin and Michael T Sumner (eds) *Incomes Policy and Inflation* Manchester University Press 1974 is a set of useful if rather technical essays on subjects such as the Phillips curve. A contemporary response is Richard G Lipsey 'The Relations Between Unemployment and the Rate of Change of Money Wage Rates in the United Kingdom 1862–1957: A Further Analysis' *Economica* 27 1960 pp 1–31. See also A G Hines 'Unemployment and the Rate of Change of Money Wage Rates in the United Kingdom 1862–

1957: A Reappraisal' *Review of Economic Statistics* 50 1968 pp 60–7.

**2949** R G D Allen *On the Decline in the Value of Money* Athlone Press 1957. In the late 1950s there was considerable concern about the level of post-war inflation. This charts inflation and its causes since 1938. See also L A Dicks-Mireaux 'The Inter-Relationship Between Cost and Price Changes 1946–1959: A Study of Inflation in Post-War Britain' *Oxford Economic Papers* n.s. 13 1961 pp 267–92, F W Paish 'Inflation in the United Kingdom 1948–1957' *Economica* n.s. 25 1958 pp 94–105, Sir G D A MacDougall 'Inflation in the United Kingdom' *Economic Record* 25 1959 pp 371–88, A T Peacock and W J L Ryan 'Wage Claims and the Pace of Inflation 1948–1951' *Economic Journal* 63 1953 pp 385–92 and Eric Wyn Evans 'Trade Unions and the Post-War Inflation' *Institute of Bankers Journal* 83 1962 pp 295–305.

**2950** I D McAvinchey 'A Study of Wage and Price Movements in the UK Since 1958' Manchester PhD Thesis 1977.

## (7) The Black Economy

**2951** Edward Smithies *The Black Economy in England Since 1914* Gill and Macmillan, Dublin 1984. An analysis of its operation in five towns 1914–70. He particularly examines tax evasion and sentencing policy. S Smith *Britain's Shadow Economy* Oxford University Press 1987 is less of a historical analysis which reflects usefully on the growth of moonlighting and tax evasion.

**2952** K Matthews 'The Debate on the Black Economy: National Income and the Black Economy' *Economic Affairs* 3 1982–83 pp 261–7. This suggests that many of the unemployed may in fact be active in the black economy.

## (8) Local Economic Histories

**2953** Clive Howard Lee *Regional Economic Growth in the United Kingdom Since the 1880s* McGraw-Hill 1981. The relationship between regional growth and regional unemployment is examined in a theoretical context in R J Dixon and A P Thirlwall *Regional Growth and Unemployment in the United Kingdom* Macmillan 1975.

**2954** R Barker *Iron Ore and After – Boom Time, Depression and Survival in a West Cumbrian Town: Cleator Moor 1840–1960* Cleator Moor Local Studies Group 1977.

**2955** Peter Lewis and Philip N Jones *The Humberside Region* David and Charles 1970. A study of the industrial geography of the region.

**2956** J E Martin *Greater London: An Industrial Geography* Bell 1966. A useful study of the region. P Damesick 'The Inner City Economy: In Industrial and Post-Industrial London' *London Journal* 6 1980 pp 23–35 is a study of the decline of manufacturing and the rise of the service sector. Peter Hall *The Industries of London Since 1861* Hutchinson 1962 is an examination of the industry of the region sector by sector.

**2957** John William House *The North East* David and Charles 1969. A study of the industrial geography of the region.

**2958** David M Smith *The North West* David and Charles 1969. A study of the industrial geography of the region. See also E G W Allen 'Post-War Industrial Development in Lancashire and Merseyside' *Transactions of the Manchester Statistical Society* 1963–4 pp 1–29. B L Anderson and P J M Stancy (eds) *Commerce, Industry and Transport: Studies in Economic Change on Merseyside* Liverpool University Press 1983 is a useful collection of essays. The last four essays in this collection deal with regional policy and development, transport, the ports and the recent development of the service sector on Merseyside since 1945.

**2959** Martin Boddy, John Lovering and Keith Bassett *Sunbelt City? A Study of Economic Change in Britain's M4 Growth Corridor* Clarendon 1986. A study of the recent burgeoning of high-technology industries in a belt from Cambridge to Bristol. This study focuses on growth and its effects in Bristol.

**2960** D A Jagger 'Business Failures in North Staffordshire 1974–1984, with Particular Reference to the nature and Causes of Business Failure and the Sources of Assistance Available for Small Businesses' Keele MA Thesis 1985. A local attempt to answer why firms fail. The conclusion is that poor management fails in a crisis. The development of small business advice centres is pointed to as a way of reducing this risk of business failure.

**2961** R G Walton *The History of the Nottingham Chamber of Commerce 1860–1960* Nottingham Chamber of Commerce 1963.

**2962** Ken Spicer *Crisis in the Industrial Heartland: A Study of the West Midlands* Clarendon 1986. A useful study of regional industrial decline. The industrial geography of the region is examined in Peter A Woods *The West Midlands* David and Charles 1976. Decline and job loss in Coventry is discussed in Michael Healey and D Clark 'Industrial Decline in a Local Economy: The Case of Coventry 1974–1982' *Environment and Planning A* 17 1985 pp 1351–67.

**2963**  G H J Daysh (ed) *A Survey of Whitby and the Surrounding Area* Shakespeare Head Press 1958. A study of the industrial geography of the area.

## B. ECONOMIC POLICY

### (1) General

**2964**  Jim Tomlinson *British Macroeconomic Policy Since 1940* Croom Helm 1986. A good survey of the main contours and turning points of post-war economic policy. It adopts a sceptical attitude to the once generally held view that there was a 'Keynesian revolution' in the direction of policy after the war. The contribution of the ideas of Keynes and Beveridge to a post-war consensus on economic policy and the break-up of that consensus is assessed in Tony Cutter, Karel Williams and John Williams *Keynes, Beveridge and Beyond* Routledge and Kegan Paul 1986. Samuel Brittan *Steering the Economy* Penguin 1971 is a good survey of the Treasury's operation and its management of the economy which critically assesses in particular the effect of the stop-go policies of the 1950s. A similar critique emerges in J C R Dow's rather technical *The Management of the British Economy 1945–1970* 2nd ed, Cambridge University Press 1970. Andrew Shonfield *British Economic Policy Since the War* 2nd ed, Penguin 1958 is an interesting and still relevant analysis in which he argues that an excess of traditional colonial and defence commitments were leading to recurrent balance of payments crises which detrimentally affected investment. Of other general studies of post-war economic policy Nicholas Davenport *The Split Society* Gollancz 1964 is a lively if polemical account. See also Lionel Robbins *Aspects of Post-War Economic Policy* Occasional Paper 42, Institute of Economic Affairs 1974 and J Harold Wilson *Post-War Economic Policies in Britain* Fabian Society 1957.

**2965**  Rod Cross *Economic Theory and Policy in the UK: An Outline and Assessment of the Controversies* Robertson 1982. A study of the achievements and failures of policy in the last twenty years in the context of the debates between the main economic schools of thought.

**2966**  Frances Cairncross (ed) *Changing Perceptions of Economic Policy: Essays in Honour of the Seventieth Birthday of Sir Alec Cairncross* Methuen 1981. A collection of essays by the policy makers of two generations. These contain many useful reflections and reminiscences on the contours of British post-war economic policy.

**2967**  C T Sandford, M S Bradbury *et al Case Studies in Economics: Economic Policy* 2nd ed, Macmillan 1977. A series of case studies of economic policy in the European Community, mostly relating to Britain.

**2968**  Sir D Macdougall *Studies in Political Economy Vol 2: International Trade and Domestic Economic Policy* Macmillan 1975. This includes articles on the regulation of the economy, planning, inflation, the impact of the EC, productivity and prices and exports.

**2969**  L S Pressnell *External Economic Policy Since the War Vol 1: The Post-War Financial Settlement* HMSO 1988. The first volume of the official peacetime history. It covers from Lend- Lease in 1941 to the Anglo-Canadian financial settlement in March 1946. An excellent study of an important formative period.

**2970**  Leo Pliatzky *Getting and Spending: Public Expenditure, Employment and Inflation* 2nd ed, Blackwell 1984. A well regarded study of Treasury control, especially of financial and monetary policy, by a former senior Treasury official. He makes good use of his own and his colleagues' recollections. This study is especially useful on the period 1964–80. Edward Bridges *Treasury Control* Athlone Press 1950 is a lecture on the Treasury control of economic policy by a former Permanent Under-Secretary. See also the brief but penetrating study, Samuel H Beer *Treasury Control: The Co-ordination of Financial and Economic Policy in Great Britain* 2nd ed, Oxford University Press 1957.

**2971**  William Keegan and Rupert Pennant-Rea *Who Runs the Economy? Control and Influence in British Economic Policy* Temple Smith 1979. A study of the policy making network in the context of policy since the war. It includes various case studies. See also Wyn Grant and Shiv Nath *The Politics of Economic Policy* Robertson 1984. F W Paish *How the Economy Works* Macmillan 1970 is a collection of essays concentrating on monetary and incomes policy.

**2972**  W A P Manser *Britain in Balance: The Myth of Failure* Longman 1971. A critique of post-war economic policy and especially of the concern about the balance of payments. Another critical study is Norman MacRae *Sunshades in October: An Analysis of the Main Mistakes in British Economic Policy Since the Mid-Nineteen Fifties* Allen and Unwin 1963. This is an attempt to explain why demand-management made Britain less cost-competitive and less export-orientated rather than more so. It also criticizes the pursuit of a balance of payments surplus and horror of inflation, which he sees as having been wrongly diagnosed as demand-led rather than wage-pushed.

**2973** Donald Winch *Economics and Policy: A Historical Study* Hodder and Stoughton 1969. British economic policy 1900–63.

**2974** William Wallace 'The Management of Foreign Economic Policy in Britain' *International Affairs* 50 1974 pp 251–67.

**2975** K Schott 'The Rise of Keynesian Economics: Britain 1940–64' *Economics and Society* 11 1982 pp 292–316. A contribution to the growing historiographical debate of recent years over the extent to which Keynesianism influenced and shaped post-war economic policy. Schott argues that constraints, such as American pressure and the domestic situation prevented it being applied in a radical fashion in Britain. The traditional picture of the debate between Keynes and the Treasury over the management of economic policy between 1919 and his death in 1946 is revised in G C Peden *Keynes, the Treasury and British Economic Policy* Macmillan 1988. According to Alan Booth 'The "Keynesian Revolution" in Economic Policy-Making' *Economic History Review* 36 1983 pp 103–23 the Treasury conversion to Keynesianism was a protracted affair, the major milestone being the acceptance of the management of aggregate demand in 1947 in an attempt to control inflation. This theme is also developed in his 'Simple Keynesianism and Whitehall 1936–47' *Economics and Society* 15 1986 pp 1–22. Neil Rollings 'British Budgetary Policy 1945–1954: A "Keynesian Revolution"?' *Economic History Review* 2nd series 41 1988 pp 283–98 also sees it as a process of gradual conversion. Will Hutton *The Revolution that never was: An Assessment of Keynesian Economics* Longman 1986 however argues that Keynesianism was never properly applied. In the 1970s and 1980s it has ceased to supply even the guiding shibboleths of policy, a process which is assessed in Robert Skidelsky (ed) *The End of the Keynesian Era* Macmillan 1979.

**2976** Alan P Dobson *The Politics of the Anglo-American Economic Special Relationship 1940–1987* Wheatsheaf 1988. The economic side of the special relationship was an important aspect of it until the sterling area ceased to be of significance after the 1967 devaluation. This is good history concentrating on the period to 1967. See also Richard N Gardner *Sterling-Dollar Diplomacy* 2nd ed, McGraw-Hill 1969 and Gardner's later return to his thesis in his article 'Sterling-Dollar Diplomacy in Current Perspectives' *International Affairs* 62 1985–86 pp 21–33. An illuminating memoir of the wartime origins of the economic special relationship is Sir Richard Clarke (edited by Sir Alec Cairncross) *Anglo-American Economic Collaboration in War and Peace 1942–1949* Oxford University Press 1982. Economic relations between the two countries during the war up to the negotiation of the Washington Loan are usefully surveyed in Alan P Dobson *US Wartime Aid to Britain 1940–1946*

Croom Helm 1986. The role of the Marshall Plan in British economic planning and post-war reconstruction is assessed in William C Mallalieu *British Reconstruction and American Policy 1945–1955* Scarecrow 1956. An interesting critical contemporary appraisal of Anglo-American economic relations immediately after the war is offered in Leo S Amery *The Awakening: The Present Crisis and the Way Out* Macdonald 1948. The harsh conditions attached to the 1946 Washington Loans Agreement and its effects are criticized in Amery's *The Washington Loans Agreements* Macdonald 1946.

**2977** Robert Millward 'Price Restraint, Anti-Inflation Policy and Public and Private Industry in the United Kingdom 1949–1973' *Economic Journal* 86 1973 pp 226–42. A study of post-war anti-inflation policy.

**2978** Peter Self *Econocrats and the Policy Process* Macmillan 1975. A study of the role of economists as advisers on economic policy. On p 203 he concludes that historians 'may be surprised at the credence and importance accorded to economists in the 1970s'. On economists as advisers see also D D Henderson 'The use of Economists in British Administration' *Oxford Economic Papers* 13 1961 pp 5–26. The influence of developments in economics on economic policy is assessed in T W Hutchison *Economic and Economic Policy in Britain 1946–1966: Some Aspects of their Interrelations* Allen and Unwin 1968.

**2979** Sir Alec Cairncross (ed) *The Robert Hall Diaries 1947–1953* Unwin Hyman 1989. An economic adviser to the government 1947–61 these diaries cover Hall's years as Director of the Economic Section.

**2980** Anthony Philip Thirlwall *Nicholas Kaldor* Wheatsheaf 1987. A good biography. Kaldor was special adviser to the Chancellor of the Exchequer 1964–8 and 1974–6. He was responsible for the experiment in the 1960s with Selective Employment Tax. Nicholas Kaldor *Collected Economic Essays* 7v, Duckworth 1980 contains a selection of pieces, including several previously unpublished articles. These look at economic policy, value and distribution, applied economics and taxation. Volume 7, on taxation, includes a specially written piece on Selective Employment Tax. *Cambridge Journal of Economics* 13/1 1989 is a whole issue containing a memorial tribute to Kaldor and articles on aspects of his work.

**2981** Sir Roy Harrod *The Life of John Maynard Keynes* Macmillan 1951. The official biography. Keynes' influence on post-war economic policy and thought and his role in the creation of the post-war international financial order was immense. He died Easter 1946 having just returned from negotiating the Washington Loan Agreement. Another good biography is Donald E Moggeridge *Keynes* 2nd ed, Macmillan 1980. See also Charles H Hession *John Maynard Keynes: A Personal Biography of the Man who Revolutionised Capitalism and the Way We Live* Collier Macmillan 1984 and Austin Robinson 'John Maynard Keynes: Economist, Author, Statesman' *Proceedings of the British Academy* 57 1973 pp 197–214. Also available is the video on Keynes' life and work, Mark Blaug *John Maynard Keynes: Life, Ideas, Legacy* Institute of Economic Affairs 1988. Anthony Philip Thirlwall (ed) *Keynes as a Policy Adviser* Macmillan 1982 is a useful set of studies on Keynes' role in government. This includes reflections on the role of economic advisers in policy formation in general. Keynes' influence is also assessed in M Keynes (ed) *Essays on John Maynard Keynes* Cambridge University Press 1975, J C Gilbert *Keynes' Impact on Monetary Economics* Butterworths 1982, S E Harris (ed) *The New Economics: Keynes' Influence on Theory and Public Policy* Dennis Dobson 1947, S E Harris *John Maynard Keynes: Economist and Policy Maker* Scribner 1955 and Donald E Moggridge and Susan Howson 'Keynes on Monetary Policy 1910–46' *Oxford Economic Papers* 26 1976 pp 226–47. On Keynes' political philosophy see A Fitzgibbons *Keynes' Vision: A New Political Economy* Oxford University Press 1988. This is also examined in Roger Middleton 'Keynes's Legacy for Postwar Economic Management' in Tony Gorst, Lewis Johnman and W Scott Lucas (eds) *Postwar Britain 1945–64: Themes and Perspectives* Pinter 1989 pp 22–42, a robust defence of Keynes against his detractors of the 1970s and 1980s. Sir Austin Robinson and Donald E Moggridge (eds) *The Collected Writings of John Maynard Keynes Vol XXIV: Activities 1944–46: The Transition to Peace* Macmillan 1979 collects Keynes' writing from a period covering the financial transition to peacetime and the negotiation of the Washington Loan Agreement. Also useful are *Vol XXVI: Activities 1943–46: Shaping the Post-War World: Bretton Woods and Reparations* Macmillan 1980 and *Vol XXVII: Activities 1940–46: Shaping the Post-War World: Employment and Commodities* Macmillan 1981.

**2982** Sir Frederick Leith-Ross *Money Talks – Fifty Years of International Finance: The Autobiography of Sir Frederick Leith-Ross* Hutchinson 1968. Leith-Ross was Chief Economic Adviser to the government 1932–46.

**2983** Susan Howson (ed) *The Collected Papers of James Meade* 4v, Unwin Hyman 1988. A collection of important papers on economic policy. The first two volumes cover the domestic economy. Volume three contains papers on international economic co-operation, GATT, Bretton Woods and other aspects of the post-war international financial settlement. Volume four contains the diary he kept as Director of the Economic Section of the Cabinet Office between November 1944 and September 1946.

**2984** Sir Alec Cairncross *Years of Recovery: British Economic Policy 1945–51* Methuen 1985. A good assessment of the Attlee government's achievements. Ben W Lewis *British Planning and Nationalisation* Allen and Unwin 1952 is an instant American interpretation of the government's economic programme. The foreign and domestic constraints on economic policy in this period are assessed in E A Brett, S Gilliat and A Pople 'Planned Trade, Labour Party Policy and US Intervention: Successes and Failures of Post-War Reconstruction' *History Workshop* 13 1982 pp 130–42. See also Jim Tomlinson 'Labour's Management of the National Economy 1945–51: Survey and Speculations' *Economics and Society* 18 1989 pp 1–24.

**2985** Peter Browning *The Treasury and Economic Policy 1964–1985* Longman 1986. An authorative narrative account and an assessment of the Treasury and its oversight of particular areas of the economy and of the crises of these years. It includes a useful chronology.

**2986** F Y Blackaby, M J Artis, R W R Price and J H B Tew (eds) *British Economic Policy 1960–74: Demand Management* Cambridge University Press 1978. The best survey of the period. Also useful is C D Cohen *Britain's Economic Policy 1960–69* Butterworths 1971. Wilfrid Beckerman (ed) *The Labour Government's Economic Record 1964–70* Duckworth 1972 is a variable collection of essays, some given to special pleading, on the policy of the Wilson government. N Wulwick 'British National and Regional Economic Policy October 1964–June 1967' Kent PhD Thesis 1981 examines the influence of economic theory on the policy of the Wilson government with respect to the National Plan, selective employment tax, regional policy and other innovations. Derek Lee *Control of the Economy* Heinemann 1974 is a textbook which surveys economic policy 1964–74.

**2987** Ralph Harris and Brendon Sewill *British Economic Policy 1970–1974: Two Views* Occasional Paper 43, Institute of Economic Affairs 1975. This offers differing interpretations of the policies and u-turns of the Heath government. See also M A Wilkes 'The Economic Policies of Edward Heath's Government 1970–4' Oxford MPhil Thesis 1983.

**2988** Michael Nevin *The Age of Illusions: The Political Economy of Britain 1968–1982* Gollancz 1983. This discusses the various expedients and remedies tried in this period to manage and reverse relative economic decline. R W Johnson *The Politics of Recession* Macmillan 1984 is a study of the problems of managing economic decline 1973–83. See also Peter A Hall 'The Political Economy of Britain' in his *Governing the Economy: The Politics of State Intervention in Britain and France* Polity 1986 pp 23–136.

**2989** Samuel Brittan *The Economic Consequences of Democracy* Temple Smith 1977. A collection of his articles critically surveying economic policy 1970–76. These include useful insights into the impact of politics, pressure groups and expectations on the implementation of economic policy.

**2990** David Smith *The Rise and Fall of Monetarism: The Theory and Politics of an Economic Experiment* Penguin 1987. A study of the pursuit of monetarist policies in Britain from the mid-1970s to the mid-1980s. See also Brian Griffiths and Geoffrey E Wood (eds) *Monetarism in the United Kingdom* Macmillan 1984.

**2991** Howard Vane and Terry Caslin (eds) *Current Controversies in Economics* Blackwell 1987. A series of useful analyses on issues that have come to the fore since 1979, such as supply-side economics, the control of inflation, market structure, inequality of income and wealth, privatization or de-industrialization. All these have attached bibliographies. Conservative economic policy since 1979 is usefully surveyed in Grahame Thompson *The Conservatives' Economic Policy* Croom Helm 1986. William Keegan *Mrs Thatcher's Economic Experiment* Allen Lane 1984 is a somewhat polemical but well regarded critique. The performance and policy of Nigel Lawson as Chancellor from 1983 is assessed in William Keegan *Mr Lawson's Gamble* Hodder and Stoughton 1989, a book written and published before Lawson's dramatic 1989 resignation. The economic policy of the Thatcher government is also critically examined in Nicholas Kaldor *The Economic Consequences of Mrs Thatcher: Speeches in the House of Lords* Duckworth 1983. A much more favourable assessment by an insider of economic policy since 1979 is Alan Walters *Britain's Economic Renaissance: Margaret Thatcher's Reforms 1979–1984* Oxford University Press 1986. Walters was economic adviser to the government 1981–3 and has been a part-time adviser since then. The major shift in priorities with the advent of the Thatcher government from the pursuit of objectives such as full unemployment or economic growth to intermediate targets is commented on in Willem H Buiter and Marcus H Miller *The Macroeconomic Consequences of a Change in Regime: The UK Under Mrs Thatcher* Centre for Labour Economics Discussion Paper 179, London School of Economics, University of London 1983.

**2992** A Batkin 'The Impact of Local Authorities on Labour Party Economic Policy' *Local Economics* 2 1987 pp 14–24. An analysis of the influence of local Labour authorities job creation strategies on Labour's economic policy since 1983.

## (2) Financial Policy

### (a) General

**2993** Graham C Hockley *Public Finance: An Introduction* Routledge and Kegan Paul 1970. A very wide-ranging textbook on the British financial system. Sir Herbert Brittain *The British Budgetary System* Allen and Unwin 1959 is a useful clear exposition by a former Treasury official. Ursula K Hicks *British Public Finances: Their Structure and Development 1880–1952* Oxford University Press 1954 is an informative survey which is quite useful for the period 1945–52. See also A R Ilersic *Government Finance and Fiscal Policy in Post-War Britain* Staples 1955. This is particularly concerned with the effect of taxation on the economy and includes case studies of Dalton's cheap money and Butler's dear money experiments.

**2994** J G Stansford 'Monetary Policy, Fiscal Policy and the Level of Economic Activity in the Postwar United Kingdom' Manchester MA (Econ) Thesis 1971–2. A study of the impact of financial policy.

**2995** D Bruce 'A Review of Socialist Financial Policy 1945–1949' *Political Quarterly* 20 1949 pp 301–16.

**2996** Joan Eileen Mitchell *Crisis in Britain 1951* Secker and Warburg 1963. An excellent account of the rearmament budget of 1951 and the political storm it created.

**2997** Phyllis Colvin *The Economic Ideal in British Government: Calculating Costs and Benefits in the 1970s* Manchester University Press 1985. A rather technical analysis.

### (b) Public Expenditure and Its Control

**2998** H Heclo and A Wildavsky *The Private Government of Public Money* 2nd ed, Macmillan 1981. The best interpretation of the interaction between Treasury officials, spending departments and ministers which produces the patterns of public expenditure. It is particularly good on the 1960s and 1970s. A good inside account of this process by a former senior Treasury official is Sir Samuel Goldman *The Developing System of Public Expenditure Management* HMSO 1973. Another inside account is John Diamond *Public Expenditure in Practice* Allen and Unwin 1975. Diamond was Chief Secretary to the Treasury 1964–70. He is excellent on cabinet decision making but much of the rest of his account is banal. P K Else and G P Marshall *The Management of Public Expenditure* Policy Studies Institute 1979 is another useful analysis. Graham Welshe *Planning Public*

*Spending in the UK* Macmillan 1987 is a short account of public expenditure policy 1960–86.

**2999** Malcolm Levitt and Michael Joyce *The Growth and Efficiency of Public Spending* Cambridge University Press 1987. A study of the growth of public expenditure since the 1960s. It includes case studies of spending on the police, health and education. The first major study of the growth of public expenditure, going up to about 1955, is Alan T Peacock and Jack Wiseman *The Growth of Public Expenditure in the United Kingdom* 2nd ed, Allen and Unwin 1967. A rather Right-Wing analysis which reflects the mood of the 1970s that government was overspending and inefficient is David Galloway *The Public Prodigals: The Growth of Government Spending and How to Control It* Temple Smith 1976. See also A E Holmes 'The Growth of Public Expenditure in the United Kingdom Since 1950' *Manchester School of Social and Economic Studies* 36 1968 pp 313–28 and J C Peterson 'The Growth of Government Expenditure in Britain (1960–1976), with Special Reference to the Resource Crowding out Hypothesis' Leeds PhD Thesis 1982.

**3000** *Report of the Committee on Control of Public Expenditure* Cmnd 1432, *Parliamentary Papers* xx 1960–61. The report of the committee chaired by Lord Plowden. This led to some significant changes in budgetary planning, not the least of which being the setting up of the Public Expenditure Survey Committee. The Plowden Report is assessed in a series of articles in *Public Administration* 41 1963 pp 1–50 introduced by Lord Plowden. See also T H Caulcott 'The Control of Public Expenditure' *Public Administration* 40 1962 pp 267–88.

**3001** Sir Richard Clarke (edited by Sir Alec Cairncross) *Public Expenditure Management and Control: The Development of the Public Expenditure Survey Committee* Macmillan 1978. An authoritative account of the development of PESC by one of its chief architects. He concentrates on the early 1960s. This important study includes a short memoir of Clarke by Cairncross. Christopher Pollitt 'The Public Expenditure Survey 1961–72' *Public Administration* 55 1977 pp 127–40 is a short analysis of its origins and operation.

**3002** B L R Smith and D C Hague (eds) *The Dilemma of Accountability in Modern Government: Independence Versus Control* Macmillan 1971. Case studies of the management of expenditure and government contracts in the 1960s.

**3003** John Short 'The Regional Distribution of Public Expenditure in Great Britain 1969/70–1973/74' *Regional Studies* 12 1978 pp 499–510.

**3004** Maurice Wright (ed) *Public Spending Decisions: Growth and Restraint in the 1970s* Allen and Unwin

1980. A good collection of essays tracing the adjustment of central and local government to the end of assumptions about the continuing growth of public spending in the 1970s and the onset of financial stringency. The impact of the cutbacks in public expenditure after 1976 is assessed in Christopher Hood and Maurice Wright (eds) *Big Government, Hard Times* Robertson 1981. Maurice Mullard *The Politics of Public Expenditure* Croom Helm 1987 is a series of case studies covering the period 1970–83.

**3005** P Mountfield 'Recent Developments in the Control of Public Expenditure in the United Kingdom' in A Premchand and J Burkhead (eds) *Comparative International Budgeting and Financing* Transaction Books 1984 pp 109–30. A useful study of the development of expenditure control under the Thatcher government. The innovative Medium Term Financial Strategy brought in by this government is assessed in Colin Thain 'The Education of the Treasury: The Medium Term Financial Strategy 1980–84' *Public Administration* 63 1985 pp 261–85. The Thatcher government also passed the National Audit Act in 1983. The background to this Act and the operation of its provisions is discussed in John Garrett 'Developing State Audit in Britain' *Public Administration* 64 1986 pp 421–33. Controlling public expenditure is a major objective of the Thatcher government. The mechanisms it uses are discussed in S Jenkins 'The "Star Chamber", PESC and the Cabinet' *Political Quarterly* 56 1985 pp 113–21. On the cuts during the government's first term 1979–83 see Vic Duke and Stephen Edgell 'Public Expenditure Cuts in Britain and Consumption Sectoral Cleavages' *International Journal of Urban and Regional Research* 8 1984 pp 177–201. The extent to which the Thatcher government has succeeded in restricting public expenditure and reducing the government's role in the economy is assessed in John Gretton, Anthony Harrison and Danny Beaton 'How far have the Frontiers of the State been rolled back Between 1979 and 1987?' *Public Money* 7 1987 pp 17–25. See also P K Else and G P Marshall 'The Unplanning of Public Expenditure; Recent Problems in Expenditure Planning and the Consequences of Cash Limits' *Public Administration* 59 1981 pp 253–78.

(c) Monetary Policy

(i) General

**3006** *Bank of England Statistical Abstract Vol 1* Bank of England 1971. A collection of statistics on the monetary system. These are mostly 1945–69 but some series only cover the 1960s. The Bank's invaluable *Bank of England Quarterly Bulletin* Bank of England 1960–, which contains informative articles and statistics should also be consulted, as should the *Bank of England Report* Bank of England 1946/47–.

**3007** Forrest Capie and Alan Webber *A Monetary History of the United Kingdom 1870–1982* 2v, Allen and Unwin 1985. Volume one contains data and information on sources and methods and volume two contains analyses. See also the notable monetarist analysis of monetary policy by Milton Friedman and Anna J Schwartz *Monetary Trends in the United States and the United Kingdom: Their Relations to Income, Prices and Interest Rates 1867–1975* University of Chicago Press 1982. This includes a good bibliography.

**3008** Michael J Artis and M K Lewis *The Monetary Mechanism and Monetary Policy in the UK* Philip Allan 1988. An excellent textbook survey of monetary policy in Britain. Artis' earlier *Foundations of British Monetary Policy* Blackwell 1965 is useful on the development of monetary policy and of the Bank of England since the war. Another useful textbook is David T Llewellyn (ed) *The Framework of UK Monetary Policy* Heinemann Education 1982. The breakdown of the financial stability of the 1950s in the ensuing decades is studied in A T K Grant *Economic Uncertainty and Financial Structure: A Study of the Obstacles to Stability* Macmillan 1977. See also K Lyford 'Monetary Policy in Britain Since 1951' London MSc Thesis 1976.

**3009** Charles Goodhart *Monetary Theory and Practice: The UK Experience* Macmillan 1984. A collection of papers dating from his period as special adviser on monetary economics at the Bank of England 1968–82. They reflect on the conduct of monetary policy in this period.

**3010** Douglas Jay *Sterling: Its Use and Misuse: A Plea for Moderation* Sidgwick and Jackson 1985. A criticism of current monetary management which surveys monetary policy over the period since the war.

**3011** R F G Alford 'Indicators of Direct Controls on the United Kingdom Capital Markets 1951–1969' in Maurice Peston and Bernard Corry (eds) *Essays in Honour of Lord Robbins* Weidenfeld and Nicolson 1972 pp 324–55. A guide to the monetary controls operating in the period. See also D Fisher 'The Instruments of Monetary Policy and the Generalised Trade-Off Function for Britain 1955–1968' *Manchester School of Social and Economic Studies* 38 1970 pp 209–22.

**3012** Susan Howson 'Cheap Money and Debt Management in Britain 1932–51' in P L Cottrell and Donald E Moggridge (eds) *Money and Power: Essays in Honour of L S Pressnell* Macmillan 1988 pp 199–226.

**3013** Peter Kenen *British Monetary Policy and the Balance of Payments 1951–57* Harvard University

Press, Cambridge, Massachusetts 1961. See also D E Greenwood 'British Monetary Policy 1951–1956' Liverpool MA Thesis 1958–9.

**3014** Richard Arnold Chapman *Decision Making: A Case Study of the Decision to Raise the Bank Rate in September 1957* Routledge and Kegan Paul 1971. An excellent study.

**3015** *Working of the Monetary System: Report of the Committee* Cmnd 827, *Parliamentary Papers* 1958–59. The report of the committee chaired by Lord Radcliffe appointed to inquire into how best to control the money supply against the background of rising inflation that led to the raising of the Bank Rate in 1957. See also C M Cannon 'A Critical Summary of the Evidence and the Report of the Radcliffe Committee on the Working of the Monetary System 1959 and its Effect upon Policy 1957–62' Birmingham MSocSc Thesis 1962–3.

**3016** David R Groome and Harry G Johnson (eds) *Money in Britain 1959–69* Oxford University Press 1970. Studies of monetary policy and financial institutions in the wake of the Radcliffe Report. On interest rate policy in the 1960s see J D Evans 'An Empirical Study of Flows of Funds in the Determination of Interest Rates in the UK 1963–1970' Stirling MSc Thesis 1972–3.

**3017** David T Llewellyn, G E J Davies, Maximilian B Hall and J G Nellis *The Framework of UK Monetary Policy* Heinemann Education 1982. Another good overview of monetary policy in the 1970s with a useful bibliography is Peter D Spencer *Financial Innovation, Efficiency and Disequilibrium: Problems of Monetary Management in the United Kingdom 1971–1981* Clarendon 1986. See also the informative textbooks by Paul Templeton *A Guide to UK Monetary Policy* Macmillan 1986 and Maximilian B Hall *Monetary Policy Since 1971: Conduct and Performance* Macmillan 1983. The frequent changes in monetary policy in the early part of the 1970s are discussed in David Gowland *Monetary Policy and Credit Control – The UK Experience* Croom Helm 1978. M A Pigato 'Monetary Control in the Context of a Banking System Practising Liability Management: The Case of the United Kingdom 1971–1981' London PhD Thesis 1985 argues that the problems in controlling the money supply and aggregate demand in the 1970s were fundamentally due to a failure to evaluate the importance of bank liability management.

**3018** Michael Moran *The Politics of Banking: The Strange Case of Competition and Credit Control* Macmillan 1984. A study of monetary policy in the context particularly of attempts by the Treasury and the Bank of England in the 1970s to shape the behaviour of the banks, culminating in the 1979 Banking Act.

**3019** D Laidler 'Monetary Policy in Britain: Successes and Shortcomings' *Oxford Review of Economic Policy* 1 1985 pp 35–43. On monetary policy in the 1980s see also J Tobin 'The Monetarist Counter-Revolution: A Reappraisal' *Economic Journal* 91 1981 pp 23–57. This is an article and a discussion of his arguments by prominent economists.

*(ii) The Sterling Area and the Control of the Currency*

**3020** Susan Strange *Sterling and British Policy: A Political Study of an International Currency in Decline* Oxford University Press 1971. An excellent account of the post-war decline of sterling from the standpoint of international relations. F V Meyer *The Functions of Sterling* Croom Helm 1973 is an account of the management of the currency in the twentieth century in an attempt to put the 1971 decision to float the pound in context. It includes a case study of the 1967 devaluation. A good set of studies of various devaluations is Sir Alec Cairncross and Barry Eichengreen *Sterling in Decline: The Devaluations of 1931, 1949 and 1967* Blackwell 1983. Cairncross writes with personal experience of the 1949 and 1967 devaluations.

**3021** Judd Polk *Sterling: Its Meaning in World Finance* Oxford University Press 1956. An American analysis of the management of sterling and the sterling area and its international role. Britain's post-war difficulties with the sterling-dollar balances are discussed in Elliot Zupnick *Britain's Post-War Dollar Problem* Columbia University Press, New York 1957.

**3022** K T H Graves 'The Pound Sterling and the Restoration of Convertibility (1946–1958)' London MPhil Thesis 1972–3.

**3023** A R Conan *The Rationale of the Sterling Area: Texts and Commentary* Macmillan 1961. A survey of its development since 1945 with documents. Conan earlier wrote *The Sterling Area* Macmillan 1952, a detailed study of its operation. Another good study is Jean de Sailly *La Zone Sterling* Armand Colin, Paris 1957. Philip W Bell *The Sterling Area in the Post-War World: Internal Mechanism and Cohesion 1949–1952* Clarendon 1956 is a useful study with a good bibliography. See also R J Whitelaw 'The Sterling Area as a Changing Mechanism of Financing International Payments' London PhD Thesis 1951–2. A R Conan 'Restructuring the Sterling Area' *The Banker* 118 1968 pp 429–36 discusses the restructuring of the sterling area after the devaluation of 1967.

**3024** J M Livingstone 'The Problem of the Blocked Sterling Balances and Their Disposal 1945–1957' London PhD Thesis 1958–9.

**3025** Alastair E Hinds 'Sterling and Imperial Policy 1945–51' *Journal of Imperial and Commonwealth History* 15 1987 pp 148–69. For a study of an important aspect of this see B R Tomlinson 'Indo-British Relations in the Post-Colonial Era: The Sterling Balance Negotiations 1947–49' *Journal of Imperial and Commonwealth History* 13 1985 pp 163–82.

**3026** Frederick Victor Meyer *Britain, the Sterling Area and Europe* Bowes and Bowes 1952. The role of the currency in Britain's attitude to European integration in this period is reassessed in Scott Newton 'Britain, the Sterling Area and European Integration 1945–50' *Journal of Imperial and Commonwealth History* 13 1985 pp 163–82. See also Graham L Rees *Britain and the Post-war European Payments Systems* University of Wales Press 1963.

**3027** Scott Newton 'The Sterling Crisis of 1947 and the British Response to the Marshall Plan' *Economic History Review* 2nd series 37 1984 pp 391–408. A good account of the 1947 convertibility crisis.

**3028** Scott Newton 'The 1949 Sterling Crisis and British Policy Towards European Integration' *Review of International Studies* 11 1985 pp 169–82.

**3029** William Davis *Three Years Hard Labour: The Road to Devaluation* Deutsch 1968. A useful instant history of the Wilson government's defence of the $2.80 parity 1964–67 and the decision to devalue to $2.40 in 1967. The defence of sterling 1964–66 is also well told in another account using inside sources in Henry Brandon *In the Red* Deutsch 1966. The devaluation is discussed in J R Artus 'The 1967 Devaluation of the Pound Sterling' *IMF Staff Papers* 223 1975 pp 595–640. Samuel Brittan *et al* 'Symposium: 1967 Devaluation' *Contemporary Record* 1/4 1988 pp 44–53 is a very informative witness seminar on the decision to devalue. It includes a useful chronology.

**3030** Stephen Fay and Hugo Young *The Day the Pound Nearly Died* Sunday Times Publications 1977. A good account of the 1976 run on the pound and the IMF loan. The background to and course of the 1976 crisis is explored and commented on by leading participants in a witness seminar the transcript of which was published as Kathleen Burk and Samuel Brittan '1976 IMF Crisis' *Contemporary Record* 3/2 1989 pp 39–45.

*(iii) Decimalization*

**3031** *Report of the Committee of Inquiry on Decimal Currency* Cmnd 2145, *Parliamentary Papers* xi 1962–63. The report of the committee chaired by the Earl of

Halsbury. It recommended a decimal system, which was introduced in February 1971.

## (d) Taxation

### (i) General

**3032** *British Tax Encyclopaedia* Sweet and Maxwell 1921–. An annual guide. It is now published in five looseleaf and three bound volumes. The bound volumes provide textbook introductions to the more detailed looseleaf volumes. *Yellow Tax Handbook* Butterworths is an annual guide to the statutes relating to income tax, capital gains tax and corporation tax. *Orange Tax Handbook* Butterworths is an annual guide to capital transfer tax, development land tax (1976–85), stamp duty, value added tax and other assorted taxes and duties.

**3033** Gerry Hart *Dictionary of Taxation* Butterworths 1981. A clear guide. Unfortunately the entries do not detail the development of the various taxes mentioned which undermines the value of this book to the historian.

**3034** *Inland Revenue Statistics* HMSO 1970–. An annual report on the main revenue collecting service.

**3035** Richard Rose and Terence Karran *Taxation by Political Inertia: Financing the Growth of Government in Britain* Unwin Hyman 1988. See also their *Increasing Taxes, Stable Taxes, Both? The Dynamics of the UK Tax Revenues Since 1948* Centre for the Study of Public Policy 116, University of Strathclyde 1983. Their view that parties have not had much effect on the nature of the tax regime is rejected by Oliver Morrissey and Sven Steinmo 'The Influence of Party Competition on Post-War UK Tax Rates' *Policy and Politics* 15 1987 pp 195–206 who argue that frequent changes have both been noticeable and economically detrimental.

**3036** A Dilnot, J Kay and N Morris 'The UK Tax System: Structure and Progressivity 1948–1982' *Scandinavian Journal of Economics* 86 1985 pp 150–65. Another study of the post-war development of the tax structure is C C Hood 'British Tax Structure Development as Administrative Adaptation' *Policy Sciences* 18 1985 pp 3–31.

**3037** Ann Robinson and Cedric Sandford *Tax Policy Making in the United Kingdom: A Study of Rationality, Ideology and Politics* Heinemann Education 1983. A good study of policy making from the 1960s onwards making good use of interviews.

**3038** J A Kay and M A King *The British Tax System* Oxford University Press 1980. The standard textbook

account. Another useful textbook is Simon James and Christopher Nobes *The Economics of Taxation* 3rd ed, Philip Allan 1988.

**3039** Cedric Sandford, Chris Pond and Robert Walker (eds) *Taxation and Social Policy* Heinemann Education 1980. Studies of the raising of revenue for spending on social purposes, such as the capital transfer tax introduced in 1974.

**3040** Paul Mosley 'When is a Policy Instrument not an Instrument? Fiscal Markmanship in Britain 1951–1984' *Journal of Public Policy* 5 1985 pp 69–86.

**3041** *Royal Commission on the Taxation of Profits and Incomes* Cmnd 8761, *Parliamentary Papers* xviii 1952–53. The report of the committee chaired by Cyril John Radcliffe. The committee's second report is Cmnd 9105, *Parliamentary Papers* xix 1953–54 and its final report is Cmnd 9474, *Parliamentary Papers* xxvii 1955–56.

**3042** J Whalley 'The United Kingdom Tax System 1968–70: Some Fixed Point Indications of its Economic Impact' *Economica* 44 1977 pp 1837–58.

**3043** J Whalley 'A General Equilibrium Assessment of the 1973 United Kingdom Tax Reform' *Economica* 42 1975 pp 139–61.

### (ii) Income Tax

**3044** B E V Sabine *A History of Income Tax* Allen and Unwin 1966.

**3045** C M Hoffman 'A Survey of the Income Tax Provisions Relating to Settlements and Transfers of Assets Abroad (1922–1970)' Oxford BLitt Thesis 1970–1.

### (iii) Value Added Tax

**3046** D S Buchanan (comp) *Value Added: The Tax and the Concept* Aslib 1972. A short bibliography. It predates the introduction of VAT in Britain but has some items on the debate about its impending introduction.

**3047** T G S A Wheatcroft and J F Avery Jones *Encyclopaedia of Value Added Tax* Sweet and Maxwell 1973–. A detailed guide to VAT in Britain and the European Community which has been published since its introduction in Britain in 1973.

**3048** Cedric Sandford, M R Godwin, P J W Hardwick and M I Butterworth *Costs and Benefits of VAT* Heinemann Education 1981. The most complete study of its introduction and application in Britain. Dorothy

Johnstone *A Tax Shall Be Charged: Some Aspects of the Introduction of the British Value Added Tax* HMSO 1975 is a good account of the introduction of VAT.

### (iv) Selective Employment Tax

**3049** Robert D Sleeper 'Manpower Redeployment and the Selective Employment Tax' *Bulletin of Oxford University Institute of Economic Statistics* 32 1970 pp 273–99. Selective employment tax was the brainchild of Nicholas Kaldor and was designed to direct labour away from the service sector into productive industry. It was introduced in the 1966 Budget. This article analyses its effects on the labour force. See also his 'SET and the Shake out: A Note on the Productivity Effects of the Selective Employment Tax' *Oxford Economic Papers* 29 1972 pp 197–211.

**3050** A A McLean 'Selective Employment Tax: Impact on Prices and the Balance of Payments' *Scottish Journal of Political Economy* 18 1970 pp 1–17.

**3051** W B Reddaway *et al The Effects of the Selective Employment Tax: First Report on the Distributive Trades* HMSO 1970. This was followed by W B Reddaway *et al Effects of the Selective Employment Tax: Final Report* Cambridge University Press 1973. These reports pointed out SET's flaws and its detrimental effects on the service and construction industries and led to its abolition in 1973. On the effect of SET on the construction and service industries see also D C Corner and C H Fletcher 'Some Effects of Selective Employment Tax on the Construction and Service Industries' *Bulletin of Oxford University Institute of Economic Statistics* 31 1969 pp 47–54. On its effect on manufacturing industry see J G Pellegrini 'The Effects of the Selective Employment Tax on British Manufacturing Industries' London PhD Thesis 1971–2.

### (v) Other Taxes and Duties

**3052** D S Brandon 'The Introduction of Corporation Tax in the United Kingdom 1965–72' Keele LIM Thesis 1978.

**3053** Clifford Joseph *Development Land Tax: A Practical Guide* Oyez 1976. A valuable account of the tax introduced by the Development Land Tax Act 1976 and abolished 1985. Robert W Maas *Development Land Tax* Tolley 1976 is a fuller and more demanding study. David Goy *Development Land Tax* Sweet and Maxwell 1976 is a rather technical legal study.

**3054** Nicholas Oulton 'Effective Protection of British Industry' in W M Carden and Gerhard Fels (eds) *Public Assistance to Industry: Protection and Subsidies in Britain and Germany* Macmillan 1974 pp 46–90. A study of policy towards protective tariffs in the 1960s and 1970s.

**3055** Alan Patrick Herbert *'No Fine on Fun': The Comical History of the Entertainments Duty* Methuen 1957. Entertainments duty was first levied on a variety of cultural and sporting events in 1916. Much of this witty study is devoted to criticism of the failure of post-war Chancellors to abolish it.

**3056** Richard Rose *Charging for Public Services* Centre for the Study of Public Policy 172, University of Strathclyde 1989. This and the companion David Heald *Charging by British Government* Centre for the Study of Public Policy 173, University of Strathclyde 1989 are the first studies into charging and the revenues from charging of government departments.

### (e) Debt Policy

**3057** A R A K Abdel Meguid 'British Government Debt Policy 1939–1952' Birmingham MCom Thesis 1954–5.

**3058** A A M Ahmed 'Management of the British National Debt (1950–1962) with Special Reference to Monetary Policy' St Andrews PhD Thesis 1964–5.

### (3) Economic Planning

**3059** Jacques Leruez *Economic Planning and Politics in Britain* Robertson 1975. An excellent analysis of economic planning 1945–51, 1961–64, 1964–70 and 1970–74. Trevor Smith *The Politics of the Corporate Economy* Robertson 1979 analyses economic planning since 1945, rightly emphasizing the importance of the experience of the inter-war years to the creation of post-war policy and the intellectual debate that led to post-war economic planning. Alan Budd *The Politics of Economic Planning* Fontana 1978 is a short but valuable account of the changing attitudes to economic planning since the 1930s. M E Herberg 'Politics, Planning and Capitalism: National Economic Planning in France and Britain' *Political Studies* 29 1981 pp 497–516 is a useful comparative study. He argues that the fact that France did not have strong trade unions or a dominant financial sector accounts for the greater success of the French at economic planning. He thus contends that it was the power structure that ensured the failings of planning in Britain, and not inherent flaws in the plans. The power structure within which planning operates is also analysed in F H Longstreth 'State Economic Planning in a Capitalist Society: The Political Sociology of Economic Policy in Britain 1940–1979' London PhD Thesis 1983. Trevor Smith 'United Kingdom' in Raymond Smith (ed) *Big Business and the State: Changing Relations in Western Europe* Macmillan 1974 pp 87–104 generally surveys the indifferent success of British economic planning.

**3060** Michael Shanks *Planning and Politics: The British Experience 1960–1976* Allen and Unwin 1977. A good study. The planning exercises of 1961–74 are in the end dismissed as 'charades rather than serious exercises in national growth and survival'.

**3061** Alan Booth 'Corporatism, Capitalism and Depression in Twentieth Century Britain' *British Journal of Sociology* 33 1982 pp 200–23. This argues that a corporatism method of economic management by cooperation between government, industry and unions was tried during periods of national difficulties but dropped during international slumps. On the impact of new technology on tripartism in the National Economic Development Office see J J Richardson 'Tripartism and the New Technology' *Policy and Politics* 10 1982 pp 343–62.

**3062** Keith Middlemas *Industry, Unions and Government: Twenty-One Years of the National Economic Development Office* Macmillan 1983. The official history of NEDO since its establishment in 1961, written with full access to reports and records. NEDO is a tripartite body on which government, employers and unions are represented. See also T C Fraser 'Economic Development Committees: A New Dimension in Government-Industry Relations' *Journal of Management Studies* 4 1967 pp 154–67.

**3063** C T Sandford *National Economic Planning* 2nd ed, Heinemann Educational 1976. A textbook.

**3064** Derek H Aldcroft 'Studies in the Abolition of Economic Controls in Great Britain After the Two World Wars' Manchester PhD Thesis 1961–2. This includes something on the reversion from a command economy under the Attlee government.

**3065** M J Chick 'Economic Planning, Managerial Decision Making and the Role of Fixed Capital Investment in the Economic Recovery of the United Kingdom 1945–1955' London PhD Thesis 1986. A well regarded study.

**3066** Gilbert Walker *Economic Planning by Programme and Control in Great Britain 1945–50* Heinemann 1957. An account of planning under the Attlee government by a former official in the Ministry of Supply. A good study of this is A Chester 'Planning, the Labour Governments and British Economic Policy 1943–51' Bristol PhD Thesis 1983. See also M M Black 'Aspects of National Economic Planning Under the Labour Government' *Journal of Politics* 12 1950 pp 260–

81 and Gilbert Walker 'The Genesis of the British Economic Plan 1945 to 1950' *Journal of Politics* 12 1950 pp 282–9.

**3067** P R Herrington 'The Financing of UK Economic Expansion 1954–1963' Southampton MSc (Econ) Thesis 1965–6.

**3068** Richard Bailey *Managing the British Economy: A Guide to Economic Planning in Britain Since 1962* Hutchinson 1968. An important aspect of planning in these years was the National Plan produced by the Department of Economic Affairs in 1965. On this see M J C Surrey 'The National Plan in Retrospect' *Bulletin of Oxford University Institute of Economic Statistics* 34 1972 pp 249–68. An analysis of the 1965 national plan. See also Wilfrid Beckerman *et al* 'The National Plan: A Discussion Before the Royal Statistical Society . . . November 24 1965' *Journal of the Royal Statistical Society* series A 129 1966 pp 1–24 and N Gould 'The National Plan 1965: The Political Dimension of Economic Planning' Sussex MA Thesis 1975.

## (4) Industrial Policy

### (a) General

**3069** Stephen C Young *An Annotated Bibliography on Relations Between Government and Industry in Britain 1960–1982* 2v, Economic and Social Science Council 1984. A complex and very full bibliography. There is a lengthy introduction and each section is also introduced in detail. The main weakness of this work is the lack of indexes.

**3070** David R Steel 'Government and Industry in Britain' *British Journal of Political Science* 12 1982 pp 449–504. A review article containing an extensive bibliography.

**3071** J W Grove *Government and Industry in Britain* Longmans 1962. Still the best general account of relations between government and industry. A systematic and comprehensive review. Another useful general survey is Merlyn Rees *The Public Sector in the Mixed Economy* Batsford 1973. Allen Skuse *Government Intervention and Industrial Policy* 2nd ed, Heinemann 1972 traces the history of central government intervention in industry from the mid-nineteenth century to Heath's disengagement policy 1970–71.

**3072** John Redwood *Going for Broke . . . Gambling with Taxpayers Money* Blackwell 1984. A critical study of state intervention in industry by the then head of Mrs Thatcher's Policy Unit. It is seen, especially in the context of the rescue of ailing industries, as an expensive way of postponing and making even more traumatic structural changes that will have to come anyway. It contains numerous case studies.

**3073** R P Guttman 'The Evolution of Industrial Policy in the United Kingdom 1964–1978' CNAA PhD Thesis 1980.

**3074** *Politics and Industry – The Great Mismatch* Hansard Society 1979. The report of a committee chaired by Sir Richard Marsh and composed of retired politicians and industrialists. Its main conclusion was that there was a detrimental mismatch in time scales. The problem that the lifetime of government policies rarely accorded with investment time scales was compounded by adversarial politics. For another useful report see *Allies of Adversaries? Perspectives on Government and Industry in Britain* Royal Institute of Public Administration 1981.

**3075** Richard Minns and Jennifer Thornley *State Shareholding: The Role of Local and Regional Authorities* Macmillan 1978. A somewhat theoretical study of the growth of shareholding by these authorities in the 1960s and 1970s. They assess the reasons for and economic impact of this development.

**3076** Arnold A Rogow *The Labour Government and British Industry 1945–51* Blackwell 1955. A good study of the Attlee government's relations with industry and its industrial policy.

**3077** Nigel Harris *Competition and the Corporate State: British Conservatives, the State and Industry 1945–64* Methuen 1972. A study of the gradual replacement of the policy of decontrol by a more interventionist and corporatist policy in the course of the 1950s.

**3078** Stephen Young and A V Lowe *Intervention in the Mixed Economy: The Evolution of British Industrial Policy 1964–72* Croom Helm 1974. A good study which concentrates on intervention in the private sector. Geoffrey Denton 'Financial Assistance to British Industry' in W M Carden and Gerhard Fels (eds) *Public Assistance to Industry: Protection and Subsidies in Britain and Germany* Macmillan 1976 pp 120–64 covers the period 1960–74. Industrial policy in the period up to the Heath u-turn signalled by the 1972 Industry Act is also considered in Edmund Dell *Political Responsibility and Industry* Allen and Unwin 1973. In this he draws on his experiences as a minister 1964–70. He illustrates his argument with case studies of the Industrial Reorganisation Corporation and the Geddes report on the shipbuilding industry. Frank Broadway *State Intervention in British Industry 1964–68* Kaye and Ward 1969 is an unsympathetic Tory analysis of Wilson's industrial policy at the height of Conservative enthusiasm for disen-

gagement from and non-intervention in industry. It does however provide a useful descriptive survey and a sample of their current Conservative thinking.

**3079** Douglas Chalmers Hague and Geoffrey Wilkinson *The IRC: An Experiment in Industrial Intervention: A History of the Industrial Reorganisation Corporation* Allen and Unwin 1983. A good official history. The IRC, set up by the Wilson government, was abolished almost immediately by the Heath government that succeeded it. See also W G McClelland 'The Industrial Reorganisation Corporation 1966/71: An Experimental Prod' *Three Banks Review* 94 1972 pp 23–42 and M E Bealey and G M White 'The Industrial Reorganisation Corporation: A Study of Choice in Public Management' *Public Administration* 51 1973 pp 61–89.

**3080** Michael Hodge *Multinational Corporations and National Governments: A Case Study of the UK's Experience 1964–70* Saxon House 1974. An informative study of the role of multinationals in the British economy and government control of and attitudes towards them. It includes case studies of the motor and computer industries.

**3081** Wyn Grant *The Political Economy of Industrial Policy* Butterworths 1982. An exploration of corporatist policy-making 1972–81. See also S Young 'Industrial Policy in Britain 1972–1977' in J Hayward and O A Narkiewicz (eds) *Planning in Europe* Croom Helm 1978 pp 79–100. On the policies of the 1974–79 Labour governments see David Coates *Capital and State in Britain: The Industrial Policy of the Labour Government 1974–1979* Department of Politics Paper 24, University of Hull 1981 and A P Taylor 'State Intervention in Production in the 1970s: Labour's Industrial Strategy' Birmingham MPhil Thesis 1979–80. David Marsh and Gareth Locksley 'Capital in Britain: Its Structural Power and Influence over Policy' in David Marsh (ed) *Capital and Politics in Western Europe* Cass 1983 pp 36–60 examines the watering down in office of some this government's most radical proposals, especially those which eventually saw light in attenuated form in the 1975 Industry Act.

**3082** *The Regeneration of British Industry* Cmnd 5710, *Parliamentary Papers* vii 1974. The White Paper that led to the setting up of the National Enterprise Board. On this see *National Enterprise Board Annual Report and Accounts* National Enterprise Board 1976–. The National Enterprise Board was created by the 1975 Industry Act to assist the establishment and development of particular industries, extend public ownership and promote industrial democracy. In 1981 it was forced to sell off its investments and merged with the National Research Development Corporation to form the British Technology Group. Its record is assessed in T Pissimissis 'The National Enterprise Board as an Agent of Regeneration of British Industry' Bradford MPhil Thesis 1981. See also Michael Parr 'The National Enterprise Board' *National Westminister Bank Quarterly Review* 1979 pp 51–62.

**3083** R T Harrison and C M Mason 'The Regional Impact of the Small Firms Loan Guarantee Scheme in the United Kingdom' *Regional Studies* 20 1986 pp 535–50. A study of the impact of the Small Businesses Loan Guarantee Scheme set up in 1981. One of the by-products of this attempt to assist small businesses is assessed in E C M McAllister 'Local Enterprise Trusts: A Growth Industry' Strathclyde MSc Thesis 1984.

(b) Nationalization and Privatization

This section only gives the general literature on nationalization, the nationalized industries and privatization. For particular industries the literature in the appropriate section should be consulted.

**3084** *The Nationalised Industries and Public Corporations: A List of Their Annual Reports and Accounts to 1980* Exeter University Library 1981. A useful listing by subject categories. It includes public corporations like the the urban development corporations. Andrew Likierman *The Reports and Accounts of Nationalized Industries: A User's Guide* Civil Service College Handbook 20, HMSO 1979 is short but valuable and informative.

**3085** M B Brown 'Nationalisation in Britain: A Select Review of Recent Literature' *Socialist Register* 1964 pp 242–58.

**3086** Albert Henry Hanson *Nationalisation: A Book of Readings* Allen and Unwin 1963. A collection of documents and other material up to 1960. This is continued by Leonard Tivey (ed) *The Nationalised Industries Since 1960: A Book of Readings* Allen and Unwin 1973.

**3087** Frank Welsh *The Afflicted State: A Survey of Public Enterprise* Century 1983. An informative survey. This covers not only the nationalized industries but the Countryside Commission, the research councils, the British Tourist Authority, the National Health Service, the Ordnance Survey and other public services.

**3088** Tony Prosser *Nationalised Industries and Public Control: Legal, Constitutional and Political Issues* Blackwell 1986. Good reflections on the political control, public accountability of nationalized industries and the regulation of privatized industries. See also J H Smith and T E Chester 'The Distribution of Power in Nationalised Industries' *British Journal of Sociology* 2 1951 pp 275–93.

**3089** Peter J Curwen *Public Enterprise: A Modern Approach* Wheatsheaf 1986. A useful textbook on the history and organization of nationalized industry and the development of the privatization programme under the Thatcher government. It includes a number of case studies of recent examples of deregulation and privatization. For another general survey of the rise and fall of nationalization see Kenneth O Morgan 'The Rise and Fall of Public Ownership in Britain' in J M W Bean (ed) *The Political Culture of Modern Britain: Studies in Memory of Stephen Koss* Hamilton 1987 pp 277–98.

**3090** Reuben Kelf-Cohen *British Nationalisation 1945–1973* Macmillan 1973. A useful history which also takes in the mixed economy since state intervention in the 1960s led to increasing blurring of the distinction between the public and private sectors. Another invaluable account is Leonard Tivey *Nationalisation in British Industry* 2nd ed, Cape 1973. William A Robson *Nationalised Industry and Public Ownership* 2nd ed, Allen and Unwin 1962 is a comprehensive survey with a good bibliography. It succeeds the earlier William A Robson (ed) *Problems of Nationalized Industry* Allen and Unwin 1952, which examines their organization, ministerial control, parliamentary scrutiny, industrial relations and a variety of other themes. Michael Shanks (ed) *The Lessons of Public Enterprise* Cape 1963 is a Fabian Society study of nationalized industry policy and parliamentary control.

**3091** Richard Pryke *Public Enterprise in Practice: The British Experience of Nationalisation over Two Decades* Macgibbon and Kee 1971. A valuable critical study. This is continued by his *The Nationalised Industries: Policies and Performance Since 1968* Robertson 1981.

**3092** George Polyani and Priscilla Polyani *Failing the Nation: The Record of the Nationalised Industries* Fraser-Ansbacher 1974. A short polemic.

**3093** Martyn Sloman *Socialising Public Ownership* Macmillan 1978. A committed account of the philosophy of nationalization since 1900 and the operation of the nationalized industries since 1950. At the time this was a contribution to the debate about industrial democracy stimulated by the Bullock Report. It is particularly concerned with the poor progress towards industrial democracy in the nationalized industries.

**3094** Chris Harlow *Innovation and Productivity Under Nationalisation: The First Thirty Years* Allen and Unwin 1977. A study of technical changes and updating of capital equipment in various nationalized industries.

**3095** Graham L Reid and Kevin Allen *The Nationalised Industries* Penguin 1970. A contemporary survey of the nationalized industries rather than a historical account. See also W Thornhill *The Nationalised Industries* Nelson 1968.

**3096** R Turvey (ed) *Public Enterprise: Selected Readings* Penguin 1968. This includes useful essays on the telephone service, coal, the Post Office and the electricity and water industries.

**3097** David Coombs *State Enterprise: Business or Politics?* Allen and Unwin 1971. A survey of twenty years of experience which argues that excessive political interference has hampered the commercial success of nationalized industries. This argument is developed by way of comparisons with Sweden and Italy.

**3098** Clive Jenkins *Power at the Top: A Critical Survey of the Nationalised Industries* Macgibbon and Kee 1959. A study of the boards as posts of patronage. The type of men appointed is closely analysed. An informative survey.

**3099** Christopher Foster *Politics, Finance and the Role of Economics: An Essay on the Control of Public Enterprise* Allen and Unwin 1971. This study of public control concludes that ministers' powers are limited and ineffective. Bad relations between government and parliament and the nationalized industries are revealed in National Economic Development Office *A Study of UK Nationalised Industries* HMSO 1976. See also J A Sabine 'Ministerial Control of Nationalised Industries' Manchester MA (Econ) Thesis 1961–2. On political control see also [528].

**3100** D A Heald 'Economic and Financial Controls of UK Nationalised Industries' *Economic Journal* 90 1980 pp 243–65. This charts the development of financial controls since 1961 and their effects on pricing and investment. An earlier study of economic control is S Please 'Government Control of the Capital Expenditure of the Nationalised Industries' *Public Administration* 33 1955 pp 31–41.

**3101** Sir Norman Chester *Nationalisation of British Industry 1945–51* HMSO 1975. A massive and authoritative official peacetime history of the nationalization programme of the Attlee government. See also E Eldon Barry *Nationalisation in British*

Politics: The Historical Background Cape 1965 and A W H MacDonald 'The Schemes for Compensation in the Nationalisation Acts' London MSc Thesis 1961–2.

**3102** John Redwood *Public Enterprise in Crisis: The Future of the Nationalised Industries* Blackwell 1980. A case by case study of the performance of the nationalized industries which displays marked sympathies with the case for privatization.

**3103** Karel Williams *et al* 'Accounting for Failure in the Nationalised Industries – Coal, Steel and Cars Since 1970' *Economics and Society* 15 1986 pp 167–219. An analysis of strategic miscalculations in the 1970s.

**3104** *Privatisation: The Facts* 2nd ed, Price Waterhouse 1989. A calendar of events and details on all the public offers for sale.

**3105** John Kay, Colin Mayer and David Thompson (eds) *Privatisation and Regulation: The UK Experience* Clarendon 1986. A good collection of essays on privatization, deregulation and contracting out since 1979. It includes a number of case studies and a substantial bibliography. Cento Veljanovski *Selling the State: Privatisation in Britain* Weidenfeld and Nicolson 1987 presents the privatization of public enterprises under the Thatcher government in a favourable light. Madsen Pirie *Privatisation* Wildwood House 1988 enthusiastically surveys the British trailblazing of privatization in global context. The history of privatization in Britain is also analysed in an international context in *Privatisation: Learning the Lessons from the UK Experience* Price Waterhouse 1989. See also Dennis Swann *The Retreat of the State: Deregulation and Privatisation in the UK and USA* Wheatsheaf 1988, Stephen Young 'The Nature of Privatisation in Britain 1979–85' *West European Politics* 9 1986 pp 235–52 and Heidrun Abromeit 'British Privatisation Policy' *Parliamentary Affairs* 41 1988 pp 68–85.

**3106** *Does Privatisation Work: Lessons from the UK* London Business School 1988. This argues that this change in the nature of ownership does not guarantee greater efficiency or necessarily change the culture of these businesses.

**3107** Andrew Cox 'Privatisation and Public Enterprise in Britain 1979–1985' *Teaching Politics* 15 1986 pp 30–59. A critical study which argues that the engine driving privatization was not economic but a desire by the Thatcher government to reduce the Public Sector Borrowing Requirement. See also B Buckland and E W Davis 'Privatisation Techniques and the PSBR' *Fiscal Studies* 5 1984 pp 44–53.

**3108** Kate Ascher *The Politics of Privatisation: Contracting Out Local Services* Macmillan 1987. A systematic study of the policy of contracting out and its effects on service provision by local authorities and local health authorities. Julian Le Grand and Ray Robinson (eds) *Privatisation and the Welfare State* Allen and Unwin 1984 is a similar study which includes a useful bibliography. See also R Halford 'Contracting out in the Early Eighties' *Local Government Studies* 9 1983 pp 51–7.

(c) Restriction of Monopolies

**3109** Board of Trade *Competition, Monopoly and Restrictive Practices: A Select Bibliography* HMSO 1970. A list of some 1,200 items. It mainly concentrates on official publications and articles published between 1950–67. There are some brief annotations.

**3110** C L Pass and J R Sparkes *Monopoly* 2nd ed, Heinemann 1980. A guide to the development of policy and legislation since the 1948 Monopolies and Restrictive Practices Act. G C Allen *Monopoly and Restrictive Practices* Allen and Unwin 1968 is a useful survey of developments 1948–68. A legal interpretation of the various pieces of legislation is A Hunter *Competition and the Law* Allen and Unwin 1966. An earlier study which only goes up to the 1956 Restrictive Trade Practices Act is Paul H Guénault and J M Jackson *The Control of Monopoly in the United Kingdom* Longmans 1960. See also J Jewkes 'British Monopoly Policy 1944–1956' *Journal of Law and Economics* 1 1958 pp 1–19, J S Wilson 'A Critique of Restrictive Trade Practices Policy in the United Kingdom' Strathclyde MA Thesis 1969–70 and Lo Sum Yee 'The Development of British Anti-Monopoly Policy Since World War II' London MSc Thesis 1959–60.

**3111** C K Rowley *The British Monopolies Commission* Allen and Unwin 1966. This Commission was set up by the 1948 Monopolies and Restrictive Practices Act. This is a study of its history, structure, authority and procedure.

**3112** Robert Stevens and Basil Yamey *The Restrictive Practices Court: A Study of the Judicial Process and Economic Policy* Weidenfeld and Nicolson 1965. This court was set up by the 1956 Restrictive Trade Practices Act.

**3113** *Report of the Committee on Resale Price Maintenance* Cmnd 7696, *Parliamentary Papers* xx 1948–49. The report of this committee, chaired by G H Lloyd Jacob, argued that resale price maintenance should be allowed to continue in restricted form.

**3114** S R Dennison 'Restrictive Practices and the Act of 1956' *Lloyds Bank Review* 59 1961 pp 35–52. See also C Lysaught 'The Definition and Determination of the Public Interest in the Restrictive Trade Practices Act 1956' Cambridge MLitt Thesis 1967–8 and J J Richardson 'The Making of the Restrictive Trade Practices Act 1956 – A Case Study of the Policy Process in Britain' Manchester MA (Econ) Thesis 1965–6. Richardson has also published 'The Making of the Restrictive Trade Practices Act 1956' *Parliamentary Affairs* 20 1967 pp 350–74. The Act is examined in the light of Monopolies Commission reports in J B Heath 'The 1956 Restrictive

Trade Practices Act: Price Agreement and the Public Interest' *Manchester School of Economic and Social Studies* 27 1959 pp 72–103.

**3115** John Frederick Pickering *Resale Price Maintenance in Practice* Allen and Unwin 1966. A study of the enforcement of resale price maintenance, a system whereby retailers agreed not to sell below a minimum price fixed by wholesalers, from 1955 to its abolition in 1964. On its abolition see his 'The Abolition of Resale Price Maintenance in Great Britain' *Oxford Economic Papers* n.s. 26 1974 pp 120–46. See also G Haley 'The Politics of Resale Price Maintenance 1959–1964: A Case Study in the Activities of "Peak" Pressure Groups' Sheffield PhD Thesis 1968–9.

**3116** Ronald Ernest Barker and George Raymond Davies *Books are Different: An Account of the Defence of the Net Book Agreement Before the Restrictive Practices Court in 1962* Macmillan 1966. Under the 1899 Net Book Agreement booksellers are only allowed to sell at the full net price fixed by publishers. This was successfully defended in 1962 and in the face of the abolition of resale price maintenance in 1964. On the background politics see C W Guillebaud 'The Marshall-Macmillan Correspondence over the Net Book System' *Economic Journal* 75 1965 pp 518–38.

(d) Science and Technology

There is also some literature on the parliamentary oversight of science policy which can be found in the section on House of Commons committees.

**3117** Michael Jubb *Guide to the Records Relating to Science and Technology in the British Public Record Office* UNESCO, Paris 1984.

**3118** *Annual Report of the Advisory Council on Scientific Policy* HMSO 1947/48–1963/64. After the 1965 Science and Technology Act this body was replaced by the Council on Science Policy and its reports no longer appeared as Command Papers. Since then it has published reports on an irregular basis.

**3119** *Statistics of Science and Technology* HMSO 1967–70. A short-lived annual series providing a guide to government efforts in the field of research and development.

**3120** *National Research Development Corporation: Annual Report and Accounts* HMSO 1950–. This body was set up to encourage the exploitation of technical innovations and inventions under the 1948 Development of Inventions Act.

**3121** *Annual Review of Government Funded R&D* HMSO 1983–. A useful statistical survey.

**3122** John B Poole and Kay Andrews (eds) *The Government of Science in Britain* Weidenfeld and Nicolson 1972. An introduced collection of documents on science policy in Britain 1875–1970.

**3123** Martin Ince *The Politics of British Science* Wheatsheaf 1986. An overview of science policy. See also M Goldsmith (ed) *UK Science Policy: A Critical Review of Policies for Publicly-Funded Research* Longman 1984. The development of science policy since the war is traced in Norman J Vig 'Policies for Science and Technology in Great Britain: Postwar Development and Reassessment' in T Dixon Long and Christopher Wright (eds) *Science Policies of Industrial Nations* Praeger, New York 1975 pp 62–109. Hilary Rose and Steven Rose *Science and Society* Allen Lane 1969 discusses the relationship between science and government over the last 300 years, and particularly since 1945. Science policy in the 1980s is discussed in Terence Kealey *Science Fiction – and the True Way to Save British Science* Centre for Policy Studies 1989. C Freeman 'Government Policy' in K Pavitt (ed) *Technical Innovation and British Economic Performance* Macmillan 1980 pp 310–25 is a short critical account of the effect of policy.

**3124** B White 'State Intervention in Technology in the Post-War Years: Case Studies in Technology Policy' Aston PhD Thesis 1986. A study of attempts to encourage technological change in private industry 1945–79, with particular reference to the computer, machine tool and textile machinery industries. See also R Williams 'British Technology Policy' *Government and Opposition* 19 1984 pp 30–51.

**3125** Philip J Gummett *Scientists in Whitehall* Manchester University Press 1980. The definitive study of the role of scientists in government. It illustrates departmental research policies and the working of the research council system. The low level of central co-ordination in the 1980s is criticized and the adequacy of government research questioned. See also Michael Gibbons and Philip J Gummett 'Recent Changes in the Administration of Government Research and Development in Britain' *Public Administration* 54 1976 pp 247–66. The relationship between government scientists and Whitehall bureaucrats is discussed in Eric Hutchinson 'Government Laboratories and the Influence of Organised Scientists' *Science Studies* 1 1971 pp 331–56.

**3126** Philip J Gummett 'British Science Policy and the Advisory Council on Science Policy 1947–1964' Manchester PhD Thesis 1973. See also Philip J Gummett and Geoffrey L Price 'An approach to the Central Planning of British Science: The Formation of the Advisory Council on Scientific Policy' *Minerva* 15 1977 pp 119–43.

**3127** S T Keith 'The Role of Government Research Establishments: A Study of the Concept of Public Patronage for Applied Research and Development' Aston PhD Thesis 1982. A detailed historical examination of the development of public laboratories and their recent unplanned decline.

**3128** G E Haigh 'The National Research Development Corporation: An Historical Study' Manchester MSc Thesis 1970–1. The NRDC, set up in 1949, has since been replaced by the British Technology Group. Its role was to encourage the development of British technological breakthroughs and to protect patents. See also S T Keith 'Inventions, Patents and Commercial Development from Governmentally Financed Research in Great Britain: The Origins of the National Research Development Corporation' *Minerva* 19 1981 pp 92–122.

**3129** J F McAllister 'Civil Science Policy in British Industrial Reconstruction 1942–51' Oxford DPhil Thesis 1986.

**3130** *Scientific Manpower – Report of a Committee Appointed by the Lord President of the Council* Cmnd 6824, *Parliamentary Papers* xiv 1945–46. This report of the committee chaired by Sir Alan Barlow recommended the doubling of the output of scientists and engineers from the higher education system within a decade.

**3131** *Committee of Inquiry into the Organisation of Civil Science* Cmnd 2171, *Parliamentary Papers* ix 1963–64. This committee, chaired by Sir Burke Trend, recommended the reorganization of the research councils.

**3132** Norman J Vig *Science and Technology in British Politics* Pergamon 1968. A detailed account of science policy debates 1959–64.

**3133** *A Framework for Government Research and Development* Cmnd 4814, *Parliamentary Papers* xxxv 1971–72. This Command Paper incorporates the Rothschild report on the organization and management of government research and development, the Dainton report on the future of the research council system and a memorandum by the government. The Rothschild report was particularly influential. See the assessment of its effect, Gordon McLachlan *Five Years After: A Review of Health Care Research Management After Rothschild* Oxford University Press 1978.

**3134** Lord Zuckerman 'Scientists, Bureaucrats and Ministers' *Proceedings of the Royal Institute of Great Britain* 56 1984 pp 205–29. An analysis of the deficiencies of the relationship between the government and scientists, especially in the field of defence research, since the establishment of the Advisory Council on Science Policy in 1947.

**3135** Roger Williams 'UK Science and Technology' *Political Quarterly* 59 1988 pp 132–44. A review of science and technology policy in the 1980s.

**3136** Russell Moseley 'Science, Government and Industrial Research: The Origins and Development of the National Physical Laboratory 1900–1975' Sussex PhD Thesis 1976.

**3137** Sir F M Lee *Science and Building: A History of the Building Research Station* HMSO 1971.

**3138** Sir Harrie Massey and M D Robins *A History of British Space Science* Cambridge University Press 1986. Massey was one of the prime movers in British space research until his death in 1983. This is an excellent detailed history of space research, rocket programmes, satellite work, European collaboration through the European Space Agency and other aspects of British space science and policy. James Eberley and Helen Wallace *British Space Policy and International Collaboration* Routledge and Kegan Paul 1987 is a short critical study from the Blue Streak to Hotol of the incoherence and myopia of British space policy.

**3139** Jill Hills *Information Technology and Industrial Policy* Croom Helm 1984. A study, with a good bibliography, of the government response to the growth of information technology and its policy in the areas of computing, telecommunications and microelectronics. Policy in each area since 1964 is analysed and contrasted with policies in competitor countries. British policy emerges as incoherent and complacent, leading to a weak industry and dependency on the United States. A similar warning is given in Kevin Cahill *Trade Wars: The High Technology Scandal of the 1980s* W H Allen 1986. This is an account of the American attempt to keep a stranglehold on the supply of computer technology, and particularly the imposition of American law, with the compliance of the British government, on the British computer industry. Much of the book is also given over to an allegation of CIA involvement in the supplying of the IRA.

**3140** A Caliman 'Biotechnology Policy in Britain: A Study of Political Rhetoric and Industrial Reality' Manchester PhD Thesis 1983. A study of policy and industrial development of this new area of technology 1974–83.

**(e) Regional Policy and Development**

The literature which is specifically concerned with regional policy in Scotland, Wales and Northern Ireland is located elsewhere in the bibliography in the relevant national sections. Since the 1960s an increasingly important aspect of regional policy has been a series of attempts to revitalize the inner cities. Under the Thatcher government this has indeed become the principal theme of regional policy. Much of the literature relevant to this aspect of regional policy can be found in the section on Urban Policy.

**3141** Kevin Allen (gen ed) *Regional Problems and Policies in the European Community: A Bibliography Vol I: Federal Republic of Germany, Italy, United Kingdom* Saxon House 1978. An unannotated bibliography organized by country. F E Ian Hamilton *Regional Economic Analysis in Britaib and the Commonwealth: A Bibliographical Guide* Weidenfeld and Nicolson 1969 is a semi- annotated guide to the literature which contains a number of bibliographical essays. P J M Stoney and A T Paterson *A Bibliography of Studies in Regional Industrial Development* Department of Business Studies, University of Liverpool 1978 concentrates on regional policy in Britain and particularly in the North West. It is an extensive but unannotated bibliography. There was a supplement in 1979.

**3142** D W Parsons *The Political Economy of Regional Policy* Croom Helm 1986. A political history of regional policy since 1934. Gavin McCrone *Regional Policy in Britain* Allen and Unwin 1969 remains a very useful history of regional policy. Duncan Maclennan and John B Parr (eds) *Regional Policy: Past Experience and New Directions* Robertson 1979 is a collection of essays assessing regional policy in its spatial and political framework, especially since 1945. David Keeble *Industrial Location and Planning in the United Kingdom* Methuen 1976 is a good account of the history of planned industrial location in Britain. See also Morgan E C Sant *Industrial Movement and Regional Development: The British Case* Pergamon 1975 and L Needleman and B Scott 'Regional Problems and Location of Industry Policy in Britain' *Urban Studies* 1 1964 pp 153–73. On the effect of town planning on industrial location policy see Anthony Goss *British Industry and Town Planning* Fountain Press 1962. Gerald Manners, David Keeble, Brian Rodgers and Kenneth Warren *Regional Development in Britain* 2nd ed, John Wiley 1980 traces the development and current state of policy and planning for each of the planning regions of Britain. Barry Moore and John Rhodes 'Evaluating the Effects of British Regional Economic Policy' *Economic Journal* 83 1973 pp 87–110 evaluates regional policy 1950–71.

**3143** C M Law *British Regional Development Since World War One* Methuen 1980. A good study of the regional structure of the British economy since 1918 and attempts to remedy regional inbalances through government policy. Also on regional economics see A J Brown *The Framework of Regional Economics in the UK* Cambridge University Press 1972. This considers regional policy in relation to problems of national economic development. See also the consideration of the problems of regional policy since the 1960s in Peter Damesick and Peter Wood (eds) *Regional Problems, Problem Regions and Public Policy in the United Kingdom* Oxford University Press 1987. An informative outline of attempts to remedy the imbalance between the prosperous South East and the rest of the country, and, more recently, to revitalize the inner cities is C R Barclay *Regional Policy and the North-South Divide* House of Commons Library Research Department 1987. See also M Frost and N Spence 'Policy Responses to Urban and Regional Economic Change in Britain' *Geographical Journal* 14 1981 pp 321–49.

**3144** R R Mackay *Planning for Balance: Regional Policy and Regional Employment – The UK Experience* Centre for Urban and Regional Development Studies Discussion Paper 18, University of Newcastle 1978. A rather technical analysis of the impact of regional policy on the distribution of employment and unemployment. See also A A Aiad 'A Study of Some Aspects of Government Policy with Regard to Regional Unemployment in Great Britain 1934–62' Manchester MA (Econ) Thesis 1964–5, A P Thirlwall 'Regional Unemployment and Public Policy in Great Britain 1948 to 1964' Leeds PhD Thesis 1967–8 and D A Shinton 'Post-War Regional Unemployment and Development' Exeter MA Thesis 1965–6.

**3145** David Keeble 'Spatial Policy in Britain: Regional or Urban?' Area 9 1977 pp 3–8. This article points to the shift from regional policy to the regeneration of the inner cities that has occurred in the 1970s and 1980s.

**3146** *Offices: A Bibliography* Location of Offices Bureau 1970. A short unannotated bibliography covering location of offices policy 1957–69. This was an important aspect of regional policy in the 1960s. The best general study of location of offices policy since the beginnings of a policy of dispersal in the 1960s is Gerald Manners and Diana Morris *Office Policy in Britain: A Review* Geo Books 1988. See also John B Goddard *Office Location in Urban and Regional Development* Oxford University Press 1975 and John Rhodes and Arnold Kan *Office Dispersal and Regional Policy* Cambridge University Press 1971. P W Daniels *Spatial Patterns of Office Growth and Location* John Wiley 1979 is a more specialist account. The factors which encouraged the development of location of offices policy are discussed in R L Pinninger 'The Office Problem in Central London 1945–1975' Kent MPhil Thesis 1979. Maurice Wright 'Provincial Office Development' *Urban Studies* 4 1967 pp 218–57 is an informative account of office development outside the South East since 1945, particularly in the context of the attempts under the Control of Office and Industrial Development Act 1965 to encourage office development outside London. See also J S Webe 'Office Decentralisation: An Empirical Study' *Urban Studies* 3 1966 pp 35–55.

**3147** Sir Henry Hardman *Dispersal of Government Work from London: Report* Cmnd 5322, *Parliamentary Papers* vi 1972–73. A review of the possibility of decanting more civil service work from London. This report was concerned not just with the dispersal of routine work, as was the case with the unpublished report by Sir Gilbert Flemming in 1962–63, but also with the decanting of policy makers from London. As E Hammond 'Dispersal of Government Offices: A Survey' *Urban Studies* 4 1967 pp 258–75 points out dispersal was first thought of in the 1930s but only really began in the 1950s. Dispersal under the Wilson government is reviewed in J A Cross 'The Regional Decentralisation of British Government Departments' *Public Administration* 48 1970 pp 423–41.

**3148** R Muller and A Bruce 'Local Government in Pursuit of an Industrial Strategy' *Local Government Studies* 7 1981 pp 3–18. Local government in the 1970s played an increasingly active role in attempting to stimulate local economies. The history of the efforts of one particular local authority from its formation in the 1974 reorganization is traced in D J Storey and J F F Robinson 'Local Authorities and the Attraction of Industry: The Case of Cleveland County Council' *Local Government Studies* 7 1981 pp 21–38. A comparative study of local economic development initiatives is Allan Cochrane and Nevil Johnson *Economic Policy Making by Local Authorities in Britain and West Germany* Allen and Unwin 1981. One aspect of the efforts of local authorities to create local economic regeneration is the spread of innovation centres; a trend discussed in R Leigh and D North 'Innovation Centres: The Policy Options for Local Authorities' *Local Economy* 2 1986 pp 45–67. Local efforts to promote economic development in the 1980s are examined in Peter Totterdill 'Local Economic Strategies as Industrial Policy: A Critical Review of British Developments in the 1980s' *Economics and Society* 18 1989 pp 478–96. This includes a valuable bibliography. Local economic strategy as a way of combatting the high unemployment of the 1980s is analysed in J J Richardson, C B Moore and Jeremy Moon *Local Partnership and the Unemployment Crisis* Unwin Hyman 1989. See also P McKeown 'County Councils and Economic Development in the Early 1980s' *Local Government Studies* 13 1987 pp 37–49.

**3149** Herbert Loebl *Government Factories and the Origins of British Regional Policy 1934–1948: Including a Case Study of North Eastern Trading Estates Ltd* Avebury 1988. An excellent study which is useful both for the origins of regional policy in the 1930s and the over-ambitious factory construction programme of 1945–48.

**3150** W B Shore 'Distribution of Industry Act 1945: A Political and Administrative Study of its Origins and Application' Manchester MA Thesis 1952–3.

**3151** D Jacques 'The State Control of the Location of Industry in Great Britain – Mainly from 1945 to 1950' Cambridge MSc Thesis 1954–5. See also G S Smolias 'Government Policy with Regard to the Location of Industry in Britain Since 1939' Oxford BLitt Thesis 1956–7 and G Llewellyn 'Industry Location Policy in England and Wales Since 1934' Wales MA Thesis 1953–4.

**3152** L Thomson *Industrial Performance and Regional Policy 1952–71* Centre for Urban and Regional Development Studies Discussion Paper 21, University of Newcastle 1978.

**3153** J F Twomey 'Regional Policy and the Inter-Regional Movement of Manufacturing Industry in Great Britain' Lancaster PhD Thesis 1985. This covers developments 1960–7?. See also M B Gahagan 'Regional Economic Planning in Great Britain 1959–72' Manchester MA (Econ) Thesis 1973–4. Regional policy in the 1960s is also discussed in B D Clark 'Industrial Movement to Government Assisted Areas 1958–1963' *Loughborough Journal of Social Studies* 2 1967 pp 5–16, A Clark 'Government Policy and the Spatial Distribution of Investment in Great Britain 1964 to 1969' Cambridge PhD Thesis 1976, C H Fletcher 'Budgetary Policy 1964–1967, with Special Reference to Regional Policy and Regional Development in Great Britain' Exeter MA Thesis 1967–8 and P J Lund and R H Gleed 'The Development Area Share of Manufacturing Industry Investment 1966–1969' *Regional Studies* 13 1979 pp 61–72.

**3154** A E Holmans 'Industrial Development Certificates and Control of the Growth of Employment in South East England' *Urban Studies* 1 1964 pp 138–52. This surveys the growth of industry in the South East and the attempts from 1958 to redirect growth to poorer areas. It concludes that industrial development certificates had had little success in restricting growth in the South East.

**3155** William H Miernyk 'Experience under the British Local Employment Acts of 1960 and 1963' *Industrial Labour Relations Review* 20 1966 pp 30–49. See also A P Thirlwall 'The Local Employment Acts 1960 and 1963: A Progress Report' *Yorkshire Bulletin of Economic and Social Research* 18 1966 pp 49–63.

**3156** *The Intermediate Areas: Report of a Committee under the Chairmanship of Sir Joseph Hunt* Cmnd 3998, *Parliamentary Papers* xxxv 1968–69. This report suggested small business centres, the extension of government training centres outside the designated development areas and land reclamation.

**3157** A G Powell 'Strategies for the English Regions: Ten Years of Evolution' *Town Planning Review* 49 1978 pp 5–13. This surveys regional planning from the mid-1960s. Barry Moore, John Rhodes and P Tyler 'The Impact of Regional Policy in the 1970s' *Centre for Environmental Studies Review* 1 1977 pp 67–77 compares the impact of regional policy 1971–6 with 1960–71. See also J F MacDonald 'Parliamentary Interest in British Regional Policy from 1968 to 1976' Wales MSc (Econ) Thesis 1978.

**3158** David Keeble 'Industrial Decline, Regional Policy and the Urban and Rural Manufacturing Shift in the United Kingdom' *Environment and Planning A* 12 1980 pp 945–62. This notes the marked and consistent shift in manufacturing employment in the 1970s from urban to rural areas.

**3159** H Morison *The Regeneration of Local Economies* Clarendon 1987. A detailed examination of attempts in the 1980s to stimulate local economies. It particularly concentrates on Scotland because of the innovative approach adopted there.

**3160** H W Armstrong 'The Division of Regional Policy Powers in Britain: Some Implications of the 1984 Policy Reforms' *Environment and Planning C: Government and Policy* 4 1986 pp 325–42. The 1984 reforms further weakened the role of central government, which has been gradually reducing since the early 1970s, in the direction of regional policy. In the meantime the European Community, local and regional government have become increasingly important.

**3161** *Enterprise Zone Information: Great Britain* HMSO 1985–. An annual guide to enterprise zone activities. A Catalano *Review of UK Enterprise Zones* CES Ltd 1983 describes and evaluates the Thatcher government's experiment with enterprise zones and briefly describes each in turn. L Ceach, D Mundy and R Stores *The Impact of Local Enterprise Agencies in Great Britain: Operational Lessons and Policy Implications* Centre for Employment Initiatives/Business in the Community 1984 is a favourable review of their performance. S M Butler *Enterprise Zones: Greenlining the Inner Cities* Heinemann 1981 is a useful account of the development of the idea and of the introduction both of enterprise zones and of freeports as ways of regenerating depressed urban economies. On the modifications in the course of implementation and the initial operation of the enterprise zones see S Taylor 'The Politics of the Enterprise Zones' *Public Administration* 59 1981 pp 421–39, K Harrop 'Policy Symbols and Urban Recovery: An Appraisal of Enterprise Zones' *Northern Economic Review* 1 1981 pp 7–10 and Peter J Purton and Clive Douglas 'Enterprise Zones in the United Kingdom: A Successful Experiment?' *Journal of Planning and Environment Law* 1982 pp 412–22. 'Freeports and Enterprise Zones' *Estates Times* 8/8/1985 pp 9–17 reviews progress. A critical note is struck by J Shutt 'Tory Enterprise Zones and the Labour Movement' *Capital and Class* 23 1984 pp 19–44. He argues that they are not innovative, that they are heavily dependent on state support and have created few jobs. Nevertheless many Labour councils have been keen to have enterprise zones in their areas.

**3162**  Board of Trade *The Movement of Manufacturing Industry in the UK 1945–1965: Study of Movement Affecting the North West Region* HMSO 1969. See also E G W Allen *Post-War Industrial Development in Lancashire and Merseyside* Manchester Statistical Society 1964, G Coleman 'The Development of Regional Development Policy in the North West Since 1945' Manchester MA Thesis 1972–3 and J M Penny 'An Evaluation of the Effect of British Regional Policy in the North West' London MPhil Thesis 1977.

**3163**  G Coleman 'Regional Development Policy: The Merseyside Experience 1949–1966' in A D M Phillips and B J Turton (eds) *Environment, Man and Economic Change: Essays Presented to S H Beaver* Longman 1975 pp 336–54. See also P E Lloyd 'Industrial Change in the Merseyside Development Area 1949–1959' *Town Planning Review* 35 1965 pp 285–98. On the efforts of Michael Heseltine as Minister for Merseyside to regenerate the Merseyside economy in the wake of the 1981 Toxteth riots see J Duffy 'Government's Response to Inner City Riots: The Minister for Merseyside and the Task Force' *Parliamentary Affairs* 37 1984 pp 76–96.

**3164**  M E Frost 'The Impact of Regional Policy: A Case Study of Manufacturing Employment in the Northern Region' *Progress in Planning* 4 1975 pp 169–237. A study over the period 1952–68. See also Herbert Loebl 'Government-Financed Factories and the Establishment of Industries by Refugees in the Special Areas of the North of England 1937–1961' Durham MPhil Thesis 1978. The marked improvement in manufacturing employment effected by regional policy in the Northern region in the 1960s and the changing industrial structure of the region is analysed in W Green 'Evaluating the Effects of Government Regional Assistance in the Northern Region 1958–71' Newcastle MA Thesis 1977.

**3165**  Graham Childs and C L W Miney *The Northern Pennine Rural Development Board: A Rural Develop-ment Agency in Theory and Practice* Working Paper 30, Oxford Polytechnic 1977. A study of the brief life of this development board, set up by the Agriculture Act 1967 and dissolved in 1971.

**3166**  R C Scarlett 'Regional Planning and North East England' in John William House (ed) *Northern Geographical Essays. In Honour of G H J Daysh* Oriel Press 1966 pp 25-39. A general study of regional policy in the area. W G Oliver 'The North East Development Council: Its Aims, Resources and Achievements' Durham MA Thesis 1975 is a study of its brief history and limited achievements before it was replaced by the North of England Development Board in 1972. Development policies in Newcastle in the 1970s and 1980s are assessed in Fred Robinson, Colin Wren and John Goddard *Economic Development Policies: An Evaluative Study of the Newcastle Metropolitan Region* Clarendon 1987. Local industrial and urban renewal policies in Cleveland are analysed in D G Etherington 'Local Authority Policies, Industrial Restructuring and the Unemployment Crisis: An Evaluation of the Formation and Impacts of Local Economic Initiatives in Cleveland 1963–1982' Durham MA Thesis 1984.

**3167**  J P Cook 'Decentralisation and Industrial Relocation: A Critical Study of Post-War Planning Policies with Particular Reference to London and Southeast England' London MPhil Thesis 1970–1. The activities of the Greater London Enterprise Board created by the Greater London Council in 1982 are reviewed in Richard Eastall *Restructuring for Labour? Job Creation by the Greater London Enterprise Board* Department of Government, Victoria University of Manchester 1989.

**3168**  Malcolm J Moseley and Morgan E C Sant *Industrial Development in East Anglia* Geobooks 1977. A useful survey of industrial movements, employment change and town development schemes. It seeks to explain why East Anglia, a region of slow industrial development 1851–1951, became the region of fastest economic growth 1951–71.

**3169**  D J Spooner 'Industrial Development in Devon and Cornwall 1939–67' Cambridge PhD Thesis 1971–2.

**3170**  W K Thomas 'Industry and Employment in Metropolitan Kent 1945–1960' London PhD Thesis 1971–2.

**3171**  N M Kay 'The Growth and Development of Industrial Estates within Leeds County Borough 1960–1978' Leeds MPhil Thesis 1980.

**3172**  Ian Barnes and Jill Preston 'The Scunthorpe Enterprise Zone: An Example of Muddled Interventionism' *Public Administration* 63 1985 pp 171–81. An analysis of the enterprise zone which was set up at Scunthorpe in 1983.

## (5) Prices and Incomes Policy

The section on industrial relations policy should also be consulted.

**3173** Russell Jones *Wages and Employment Policy 1936–1985* Allen and Unwin 1985. A Keynesian general history of incomes policy. A history from an unusual perspective is Felix Burdjalov *State Monopoly Incomes Policy: Conception and Practice in the Context of Great Britain* Progress Publishers, Moscow 1976. See also P A Heywood 'The Political Development of Incomes Policy in Britain from 1945–75, with Special Reference to Relations Between Government and the Trade Union Movement' Oxford DPhil Thesis 1983 and R Tarling and F Wilkinson 'The Social Contract: Post-War Incomes Policies and Their Inflationary Impact' *Cambridge Journal of Economics* 1 1977 pp 395–414.

**3174** Barbara Wootton *The Social Foundations of Wage Policy: A Study of Contemporary British Wage and Salary Structure* 2nd ed, Unwin University Books 1962. A study of the basic elements in post-war wages policy. See also K G J C Knowles and D Robinson 'Wage Rounds and Wage Policy' *Bulletin of Oxford University Institute of Economic Statistics* 24 1962 pp 269–329, A D Flanders 'Wage Movements and Wage Policy in Postwar Britain' *Annals of the American Academy of Political and Social Science* 310 1957 pp 87–98 and J R Campbell 'The Development of Incomes Policy in Britain' *Marxism Today* 9 1965 pp 69–75.

**3175** Leo Panitch *Social Democracy and Industrial Militancy: The Labour Party, the Trade Unions and Incomes Policy 1945–1974* Cambridge University Press 1976. A critical study of attitudes to incomes policies, particularly in the period 1964–70. Hugh Armstrong Clegg *How to Run an Incomes Policy and why we made such a mess of the last one* Heinemann 1971 is a review of incomes policy since 1945 and especially of the weaknesses and failings of policy 1964–70 during which time he was a member of the Prices and Incomes Board.

**3176** Brian Bercusson *Fair Wages Resolutions* Mansell 1978. A massive and detailed study of fair wages policy 1891–1976.

**3177** W H Fishbein *Wage Restraint by Consensus: Britain's Search for an Incomes Policy Agreement 1965–79* Routledge and Kegan Paul 1984. A study of the attempts of governments of this period to gain agreement with the trade unions on wage restraint. Incomes policy in this period is also assessed in Lord McCarthy 'The

Politics of Incomes Policy' in David Butler and A H Halsey (eds) *Policy and Politics: Essays in Honour of Norman Chester* Macmillan 1978 pp 182–200. Prices and incomes policy in the 1960s and 1970s as a means of resolving industrial relations problems, high wage demands and inflationary pressures are examined in Colin Crouch *Class Conflict and the Industrial Relations Crisis: Compromise and Corporatism in the Politics of the British State* Heinemann 1977.

**3178** J G Corina 'The British Experiment in Wage Restraint with Special Reference to 1948–1950' Oxford DPhil Thesis 1960–1. On wages policy in the 1940s see also B D Nomvete 'British Wages Policy 1940–1950, a Study of the Decisions of the National Arbitration Tribunal' Manchester MA (Econ) Thesis 1954–5.

**3179** D J Robertson 'The Inadequacy of Recent Wages Policies in Britain' *Scottish Journal of Political Economy* 5 1958 pp 99–113.

**3180** W W Daniel and Neil McIntosh *Incomes Policy and Collective Bargaining at the Workplace* Political and Economic Planning 1973. A study of the effects of the attempts by the Wilson government to influence and regulate collective bargaining 1966–9. See also P M Smith 'Prices and Incomes Policies 1964–70' Manchester MA (Econ) Thesis 1970–1, D W Saunders 'Incomes Policy 1964: A Study of Policy Formulation and Political Interaction' Loughborough MA Thesis 1976–7 and Tony Topham 'The Labour Government's Incomes Policy and the Trade Unions' *Trade Union Register* 1970 pp 116–26.

**3181** Allan Fels *The British Prices and Incomes Board* Cambridge University Press 1972. The National Board of Prices and Incomes was set up in 1965 to review movements of prices and incomes and to encourage the growth of productivity. This is the official history. It also reviews prices and incomes policy 1948–62 and the work of the National Incomes Commission established in 1962. Joan Mitchell *The National Board for Prices and Incomes* Secker and Warburg 1972 is an analysis of its policy, functions and weaknesses by a founder member which traces its history up to its demise in 1971. On the Board's achievements see R J Liddle and W E J McCarthy 'The Impact of the Prices and Incomes Board on the Reform of Collective Bargaining: A Preliminary Survey of Specific Pay References' *British Journal of Industrial Relations* 10 1972 pp 412–39. See also P C Madhuysen 'Wage Decisions of the British National Board for Prices and Incomes 1965–1969' *Journal of Industrial Relations* 13 1971 pp 117–29 and J F Pickering 'The Prices and Incomes Board and Private Sector Prices: A Survey' *Economic Journal* 81 1971 pp 225–41.

**3182** Robin E J Chater, Andrew Dean and Robert F Elliott (eds) *Incomes Policy* Clarendon 1981. A collection of studies on incomes policy in the 1970s.

**3183** L C Hunter 'British Incomes Policy 1972–1974' *Industrial Labor Relations Review* 29 1975 pp 67–84. The impact on and eventual destruction of the Heath government's incomes policies by the miners is discussed in Kevin H Hawkins 'Miners and Incomes Policy 1972–1975' *Industrial Relations Journal* 6 1975 pp 2–22 and Joel D Wolfe 'Corporatism and Union Democracy: The British Miners and Incomes Policy 1973–74' *Comparative Politics* 17 1985 pp 421–36. The effects of Heath's prices and incomes policy on industry are analysed in M S Haque 'The Nature and Effects of the UK Price Controls During Stages 2–4 with Special Reference to Company Profitability and Financial Viability' Manchester PhD Thesis 1977.

**3184** E G Murray 'Trade Unions and Incomes Policies: British Unions and the Social Contract in the 1970s' Warwick PhD Thesis 1985. A study of trade union participation in the voluntary incomes policy known as the Social Contract under the Labour governments of 1974–9 and the developing opposition in the union movement to the policy culminating in its collapse in the 'Winter of Discontent' in 1978–9. It focuses on six unions in the context of TUC decision making. See also J G Boston 'The Theory and Practice of Voluntary Incomes Policies, with Particular Reference to the British Labour Government's Social Contract 1974–79' Oxford DPhil Thesis 1983 and S A Kennett 'Collectivist Politics and its Discontents: The Structure of Trade Unionism in Britain and the Failure of the Social Contract' Oxford MPhil Thesis 1984. Union policy in the earlier post-war period is discussed in R L Bowlby 'Union Policy Toward Minimum Wage Legislation in Postwar Britain' *Industrial Labor Relations Review* 11 1957 pp 72–84.

**3185** I H Lightmann 'Price Controls in the United Kingdom 1973–1978' *Journal of Agricultural Economics* 29 1978 pp 311–8.

### (6) Metrication

**3186** *Metrication Bibliography: Books and Pamphlets* Department of Trade and Industry 1972. This is largely a list of reports.

**3187** *Report of the Committee on Weights and Measures Legislation* Cmnd 8219, *Parliamentary Papers* xx 1950–51. The report of the committee chaired by Edward H Hodgson which urged the need to replace the imperial with the metric system.

**3188** R D Connor *The Weights and Measures of England* HMSO 1987. An excellent general history. The final chapter traces progress towards metrication since the Hodgson Report. Another survey of progress is Ritchie Calder 'Conversion to the Metric System' *Scientific American* 223 1970 pp 17–25.

### (7) British Summer Time

**3189** Alan Patrick Herbert *In the Dark: The Summer Time Story and the Painless Plan* The Bodley Head 1970. British Summer Time, or daylight saving, was introduced in the 1966 British Summer Time Act to assist agriculture and trade. This book is however largely concerned with the effect of the British Standard Time Act 1968 which temporarily introduced daylight saving all year round. Herbert is very critical of this measure.

**3190** O B Pollak 'Efficiency, Preparedness and Conservation: The Daylight Savings Time Movement' *History Today* 31 1981 pp 5–9.

## C. BUSINESS HISTORY

### (1) General

### (a) Reference Works

**3191** Lesley Richmond and Alison Turton *Directory of Corporate Archives* 2nd ed, Business Archives Council 1987. This gives potted histories of each company, details of holdings and access and information on any published material. It is rather fuller than Lesley Richmond and Bridget Stockford *Company Archives: The Survey of 1,000 of the First Registered Companies in England and Wales* Gower 1986. John Armstrong and Stephanie Jones *Business Documents: Their Origins, Sources and Uses in Historical Research* Mansell 1987 is a good guide which contains a wealth of information. C A Jones *Britain and the Dominions: A Guide to Business and Related Records in the United Kingdom and Concerning Australia, Canada, New Zealand and South Africa* G K Hall 1978 is an excellent descriptive guide to the records of British overseas companies. The state of corporate archives is monitored in *Business Archives* 1934–, the quarterly bulletin of the Business Archives Council. This features articles, details of recent deposits, book reviews and a regular bibliography. Business records in one particular area are listed in Joan Lane (comp) *Register of Business Records of Coventry and Related Areas* Department of Politics and History, Lanchester Polytechnic 1977.

**3192** Paul Norkett *Guide to Company Information in Great Britain* Longman 1986. A handbook showing how and where to find information on British companies and how to interpret their results. James Tudor *Macmillan Directory of Business Information Sources* Macmillan 1987 is a useful guide to sources and publications.

**3193** Business Statistics Office *Historical Records of the Census of Production 1907–1970* HMSO 1978. A large collection of statistics covering, among other things, industrial production, imports, capital expenditure, wages costs and prices. These censuses were taken at roughly five year intervals. It is continued by *Annual Census of Production* HMSO 1970–. The Business Statistics Office also publishes an extensive series of *Business Monitors* HMSO 1962–. These provide a detailed up-to-date picture of business trends. Each monitor covers a different type of product. The range of products covered in this way is fairly comprehensive. Most monitors appear on a quarterly basis though there are also some monthly, annual and occasional series. Since 1975 Data Research Group has also been publishing a whole series of information guides to all sorts of UK trades, types of commerce and manufacturing industries.

**3194** Thomas Derdak (ed) *International Directory of Companies Histories* 4v, St James Press 1988–. A guide to the histories of many of the world's leading (including a considerable number of British) corporations, organized alphabetically by industrial sector.

**3195** *Who Owns Whom* Roskill 1958–. This annual publication gives details on over 7,000 parent companies in the United Kingdom and the Republic of Ireland, their structure and the links between them and their subsidiaries and associates. It also lists the foreign parents of certain British companies.

**3196** *The Times 1000: Leading Companies in Britain and Overseas* Times Publishing 1965–. An annual publication. It started out in 1965 as *The Times 300*, progressed rapidly to being *The Times 500* before reaching its current format. It gives details on the capital, profit, turnover and size of labour force of each of the 1,000 largest companies in Britain. It also gives information on the largest banks, building societies, insurance companies and unit and investment trusts as well as details on large companies elsewhere in the world.

**3197** *The Top 2,000: Britain's Privately Owned Companies* Jordans 1988. A statistical guide.

**3198** *Industrial Trends Survey* Federation of British Industry (since 1965 Confederation of British Industry) 1958–. A quarterly survey of business confidence, trends and attitudes compiled from questionnaires circulated to members. The history of the publication and some reflections on its value as a source are given in *25 Years of Ups and Downs* Confederation of British Industry 1983.

**3199** *The Times Review of Industry* 1916–. A monthly survey. See also *Financial Times Annual Survey of Industry* 1954–. *The Hambros Company Guide: A Detailed Guide to Every Company Listed in the Financial Times 1978/9–* Investment Evaluator 1979– is a valuable annual guide to companies and their performance.

**3200** *British Bulletin of Commerce* 1940–1955. A periodical publication which was succeeded by *Histories of Famous Firms* 1956–60. These contain numerous well illustrated potted business histories.

**3201** K D C Vernon (ed) *Information Sources in Management and Business* Butterworths 1984. An excellent descriptive guide to the literature available.

**3202** Stephanie Zarach (ed) *Debrett's Bibliography of Business History* Macmillan 1987. This bibliography is organized by industrial category. It is neither annotated nor comprehensive and it only lists books and pamphlets. It nevertheless remains rather more useful than the poorly indexed, if more comprehensive Francis Goodall (ed) *A Bibliography of British Business Histories* Gower 1987. This latter bibliography is also unannotated. In addition there are a number of regional bibliographies of business histories. The first of these was Joyce M Bellamy (ed) *Yorkshire Business Histories: A Bibliography* Bradford University Press 1970. This is a massive guide which includes articles as well as books. It is well indexed if unannotated. It served as the model for D J Rowe (ed) *Northern Business Histories: A Bibliography* Library Association 1979. This is an alphabetically arranged unannotated bibliography which also lists holdings of business archives and relevant law reports and general histories. See also S Horrocks *Lancashire Business Histories* Joint Committee on the Lancashire Bibliography 1971.

## (b) General Histories and Surveys

For industrial development in particular areas see also the literature which is included with that on regional policy and development in the section on Economic Policy.

**3203** Leslie Hannah *The Rise of the Corporate Economy* 2nd ed, Methuen 1983. A study of the rise of large firms, merger waves and the decline of small businesses in the course of the twentieth century. Graham Turner *Business in Britain* 2nd ed, Penguin 1971 is a detailed study of developments of the post-war era. Drawing on extensive interviewing with the captains of industry he examines the role of government, US multinationals, the banks, business schools and management consultancy in the business world. Using case studies of large companies and nationalized industries and in a survey of the various sectors of the economy he warns of Britain's industrial weakness. The post-war performance of British industry is surveyed in R Wragg and J Robertson 'Britain's Industrial Performance Since the War' *Department of Employment Gazette* 86 1978 pp 512–9. G Gilchrist *Spotlight on British Industry in the Twentieth Century* Wayland 1986 and Margaret Ackrill *Manufacturing Industry Since 1870* Philip Allan 1987 are introductory textbooks.

**3204** R P T Davenport-Hines and Geoffrey Jones (eds) *Enterprise, Management and Innovation in British Business 1914–80* Cass 1988. A good collection of essays on management, growth, marketing, science and technology and privatization.

**3205** G C Allen *British Industries and the Organisation* Longman 1970. A survey of recent developments in British industry, sector by sector. Derek French Channon *The Strategy and Structure of British Enterprise* Macmillan 1973 is a very informative analysis of the development of Britain's top 100 firms 1950–70. Useful earlier general studies of British industry are J H Dunning and C J Thomas *British Industry: Change and Development in the Twentieth Century* Hutchinson 1961 and Ronald S Edwards and Harry Townsend *Business Enterprise: Its Growth and Organisation* Macmillan 1958.

**3206** Peter Pagnamenta and Richard Overy *All Our Working Lives* BBC 1984. A good book derived from an excellent TV series. A survey of changes in the cotton, steel, retailing, shipbuilding, chemicals, coal, farming, cars and electronics industries in the twentieth century it draws attention to the factors that have in too many of these cases led to their decline. Recollections of working conditions and industrial relations are used extensively and to good effect.

**3207** G C Allen *The Structure of Industry in Britain* Longman 1970. A survey of structural changes in British industry in the course of the twentieth century. Kenneth D George 'The Changing Structure of Competitive Industry' *Economic Journal* 80 1972 pp 353–68 is a rather technical account of changes 1924–68. Peter Johnson (ed) *The Structure of British Industry* 2nd ed, Unwin Hyman 1988 is a good survey of recent developments and the current situation across the various sectors of the British economy. It includes essays on agriculture, North Sea oil and gas, retailing, finance and transport as well as the various types of manufacturing industry. There is a large bibliography and many statistical tables. The first study of the structure and state of post-war industry is Duncan Burn (ed) *The Structure of British Industry: A Symposium* 2v, Cambridge University Press 1958. This

is a slightly less comprehensive sector by sector survey. It too provides good bibliographical details.

**3208** Derek Ezra and David Oates *Advice from the Top: Business Strategies of Britain's Corporate Leaders* David and Charles 1989. Advice on running businesses drawing on the experience of and interviews with leading industrialists such as Sir John Cuckney, Sir Austin Pearce, Sir Adam Thomson, Sir Francis Tombs or Sir Adrian Cadbury.

**3209** T Hazledine 'Distribution, Efficiency and Market Power: A Study of the UK Manufacturing Sector 1954–73' Warwick PhD Thesis 1978. William Brian Reddaway and A D Smith 'Progress in British Manufacturing Industries in the Period 1948–54' *Economic Journal* 70 1960 pp 17–37. On industry in the 1970s see George A Luffman and Richard Reed *The Strategy and Performance of British Industry 1970–80* Macmillan 1984.

**3210** P E Hart *Studies in Profit, Business Savings and Investment in the United Kingdom 1920–1962* 2v, Allen and Unwin 1965–68. Volume I is concerned with collection of data on and the effects of the size of the firm on changes in profit. Volume II uses the results to examine trends in key financial variables and economic theories of their behaviour. On investment in industry, especially manufacturing industry, by the government, the City, and from other sources see W A Thomas *The Finance of British Industry 1918–1976* Methuen 1978. This is a useful study, though it could do with more information on the impact of changes in tax regimes and on flows of investment overseas.

**3211** E Shapiro 'Cyclical Fluctuations in Prices and Output in the United Kingdom 1921–1971' *Economic Journal* 86 1976 pp 746–58. See also R J Nicholson 'Capital Stock, Employment and Output in British Industry 1948–64' *Yorkshire Bulletin of Economic and Social Research* 18 1966 pp 65–85 and I Aristidou 'Trends in Capital, Employment and Output in the British Manufacturing Industry 1900–1962' London PhD Thesis 1965–6.

**3212** E Primorac 'A Study of the Division Between Pay and Profits of the Product of British Manufacturing Industry 1924–1958 with Special Reference to Short Run Variations 1948–1958' London PhD Thesis 1965–6.

**3213** R F Guestella 'Total Productivity Changes in British Manufacturing Industry 1948–1964' Edinburgh MSc Thesis 1968–9. See also H Suleiman 'A Survey of the Factors Affecting British Industrial Productivity 1948–61' Sheffield MA (Econ) Thesis 1963–4.

**3214** G Meeks and Geoffrey Whittington 'Giant Companies in the United Kingdom 1948–1969' *Economic Journal* 85 1975 pp 824–43. A comparison with statistics analysing changes in the nature of large industries. See also Geoffrey Whittington 'Changes in the Top 100 Quoted Manufacturing Companies in the United Kingdom 1948 to 1968' *Journal of Industrial Economics* 21 1972 pp 17–34, Geoffrey Whittington 'The Profitability and Size of United Kingdom Companies 1960–74' *Journal of Industrial Economics* 28 1980 pp 335–52 and Alan Armstrong and Aubrey Silberston 'Size of Plant, Size of Enterprise and Concentration in British Manufacturing Industry 1935–1958' *Journal of the Royal Statistical Society series A* 128 1965 pp 395–420.

**3215** John Stopford and Louis Turner *Britain and the Multinationals* John Wiley 1985. A study of the changing impact on the economy and policies of Britain since the 1960s of British and foreign multinationals. See also A D Chandler 'The Growth of the Transnational Industrial Firm in the United States and the United Kingdom: A Comparative Analysis' *Economic History Review* 2nd series 33 1980 pp 396–410. Geoffrey Jones (ed) *British Multinationals: Origins, Management and Performance* Gower 1986 provides overviews of British multinationals and case studies of companies like Dunlop, Vickers, Courtaulds, GKN, Pilkingtons, Cadburys and Glaxo. Michael Hodges *Multinational Corporations and National Government: A Case Study of the UK's Experience 1964–70* Saxon House 1974 is a good survey of the rapid growth of these corporations in the 1960s and their impact on government policy. The impact of foreign multinationals is assessed in Stephen Miller and James Hamill *Foreign Multinationals and the British Economy: Impact and Policy* Croom Helm 1988. The developing spatial distribution of foreign multinationals in Britain is examined in I J Smith 'The Role of Acquisitions in the Spatial Distribution of the Foreign Manufacturing Sector in the United Kingdom' in Michael Taylor and Nigel Thrift (eds) *The Geography of Multinationals* Croom Helm 1982 pp 221–51. The spatial distribution of these is gradually becoming more even according to a paper which looks particularly at foreign multinationals in Liverpool and Manchester, P Dicken and P E Lloyd 'Patterns and Processes of Change in the Spatial Distribution of Foreign-Controlled Manufacturing Employment in the United Kingdom 1963 to 1975' *Environment and Planning A* 12 1980 pp 1405–25. About 60% of these corporations are North American. The small if growing role of the Japanese in Britain is analysed in John H Dunning *Japanese Participation in British Industry* Croom Helm 1986. See also L Turner *Industrial Collaboration with Japan* Routledge and Kegan Paul 1987.

**3215A** R P T Davenport-Hines and Geoffrey Jones (eds) *British Business in Asia Since 1860* Cambridge University Press 1989. After overviews of the performance, political implications and impact on Asia of British businesses this examines British business in the following countries; Iran, Soviet Asia, India, Malaysia and Singapore, China and Japan.

**3216** Donald A Hay and Derek J Morris *Unquoted Companies: Their Contribution to the United Kingdom Economy* Macmillan 1984. Only since 1967 have companies not quoted on the stock exchange been required to file annual reports with Companies House and this has led to a growing awareness of this sector. This important book sheds much light whilst reflecting favourably on the performance of these companies. It is based on a survey and interviews. *Macmillan's Unquoted Companies 1988: Financial Profiles of Britain's Top 10,000 Unquoted Companies* Macmillan 1988 is a useful alphabetically arranged guide to these companies.

**3217** Stephen Aris *The Jews in Business* Cape 1970. An account of Jewish businesses in Britain.

**3218** Stephen Aris *Going Bust: Inside the Bankruptcy Business* Deutsch 1985. A rare look at business failure. It provides a study of procedures and the role of the Official Receiver and the banks. A number of recent cases are examined in considerable detail. The surge in bankruptcies 1976–81 is discussed in G Hall and A W Stark 'Bankruptcy Risk and the Effects of Conservative Policy 1979–81' *International Journal of Industrial Organisation* 4 1986 pp 317–32.

**3219** Chloe Mailer and Peter Musgrave *The History of the Industrial Society 1918–1981* Industrial Society 1987.

(c) Mergers and Concentration

**3220** S J Prais *The Evolution of Giant Firms in Britain: A Study of the Growth of Concentration in Manufacturing Industry in Britain 1909–70* Cambridge University Press 1976. A good study of mergers, acquisitions and concentration in British industry. Sam Aaronovitch and Malcolm C Sawyer *Big Business: Theoretical and Empirical Aspects of Concentration and Mergers in the United Kingdom* Macmillan 1975 is a Marxist analysis of concentration and merger activity in Britain since 1918, focusing particularly on the period since 1955. Merger activity 1919–76 is examined in Leslie Hannah and J A King *Concentration in Modern Industry: Theory, Measurement and the UK Experience* Macmillan 1977. P E Hart and R Clarke *Concentration in British Industry 1935–75: A Study of the Growth, Causes and Effects of Concentration in British Manufacturing Industries* Cambridge University Press 1980 is a rather statistical analysis.

**3221** P E Hart, M A Utton and G Walshe *Mergers and Concentration in British Industry* Cambridge University Press 1973. A good informative study of developments 1954–70. G Walshe *Recent Trends in Monopoly in Great Britain* Cambridge University Press 1973 is a companion volume of case studies. See also M A Utton 'Mergers in Manufacturing Industry in the UK with Special Reference to the Period 1954–70' Reading PhD Thesis 1973–4 and Pramod Verma 'Mergers in British Industry 1949–1966' *Journal of Business Policy* 3 1972 pp 31–9.

**3222** G Meeks *Disappointing Marriage: A Study of the Gains from Merger* Cambridge University Press 1977. A critical study of the objectives and effects of mergers. Meeks finds them generally unjustified and argues for greater regulation. The industrial strategy of merger and acquisition is also criticized in J Constable 'Diversification as a Factor in UK Industrial Strategy' *Long Range Planning* 19 1986 pp 52–60. In this Constable points out that most company diversification in the UK since the 1960s has been by mergers and acquisitions and not by internal development. He suggests that this has led to the neglect of internal development, a neglect which is reflected in Britain's relatively poor economic performance.

**3223** Richard Evely and I M D Little *Concentration in British Industry: An Empirical Study of the Structure of Industrial Production 1935–51* Cambridge University Press 1960. The empirical section in this study is not in fact very large.

**3224** William Davis *Merger Mania* Constable 1970. A good study of the spate of mergers in the 1960s. It includes useful case examples. A symposium on the merger trends and strategies of this period is Ronald Victor Arnfield (ed) *Company Mergers and Acquisitions* University of Strathclyde 1967. They are also discussed in D Kuehn *Takeovers and Theories of the Firm: An Empirical Analysis for the UK 1957–1969* Macmillan 1975.

## (d) Small Businesses

**3225** *Quarterly Survey of Small Businesses in Britain* Small Businesses Research Trust 1984–. This publication logs the recent growth, after many years of decline, of the small business sector and reflects on current problems and opportunities.

**3226** P Ganguly and G Bannock (eds) *UK Small Business Statistics and International Comparisons* Harper and Row 1985.

**3227** *Small Business Bibliography* London Business School 1980. A comprehensive bibliography of publica-

tions since 1970. J L Salond *Small Business: A Bibliography* University of Aston 1969 is a classified bibliography of British and American books, reports, articles, theses and working papers which has since been periodically updated.

**3228** *Small Firms: Report of the Committee of Inquiry into Small Firms* Cmnd 4811, *Parliamentary Papers* ix 1971–72. This committee chaired by J E Bolton was set up by Crosland in 1969 to consider the role of small firms in the economy, the facilities available to help them and their problems. Its report is most informative. Neglected by government and in long term decline the report recognized their value and urged that a small firms division of the Department of Trade and Industry should be set up.

**3229** James Curran, John Stanworth and David Watkins (eds) *The Survival of the Small Firm* 2v, Gower 1986. A disparate collection of essays, some of a rather theoretical nature. Generally though this collection provides an informative picture of the role of small firms in the contemporary economy. Case studies include analyses of industrial relations in small firms, their role in technological developments and small firms policy.

**3230** I H Fazey *The Pathfinder: The Origins of the Enterprise Agency in Britain* Financial Training 1987. These organizations have played a key role in the start up and growth of small businesses in the 1980s. The first was created in St Helens in the face of the recession of the late 1970s and early 1980s.

**3231** David Storey, Kevin Keasey, Robert Watson and Pooran Wynerczyk *The Performance of Small Firms: Profits, Jobs and Failures* Croom Helm 1987. This analysis of the current situation includes much statistical data.

**3232** J Shutt and R Whittington 'Fragmentation Strategies and the Rise of Small Units: Cases from the North West' *Regional Studies* 13 1987 pp 13–23. This argues that much apparent recent growth in small firms is really the result of the fragmentation of larger firms.

## (e) Industrial Organizations

**3233** Deborah G Jenkins *Confederation of British Industry: Predecessor Archives* Swift Printers 1982. This lists the archives of the Federation of British Industry, the Director-General's papers and the Economic Directorate's subject files.

**3234** P Millard and J Drummond (comp) *Trade Associations and Professional Bodies in the United Kingdom* 6th ed, Pergamon 1979. A directory.

**3235**  Stephen Blank *Government and Industry in Britain: The Federation of British Industries in Politics 1945–65* Saxon House 1974. A valuable study which finds little evidence of the Federation influencing political attitudes or decisions. See also S E Finer 'The Federation of British Industry' *Political Studies* 4 1956 pp 61–84. In 1965 the Federation merged with the British Employers Confederation and the National Association of British Manufacturers to form the Confederation of British Industry. The record of the new body 1965–74 is analysed in Wyn Grant and David Marsh *The CBI* Hodder and Stoughton 1977. They see it as weak and lacking a common strategy. Accordingly it had little influence on government which makes them sceptical of the notion of corporatism. This view is developed in Wyn Grant with Jane Sargent *Business and Politics in Britain: An Introduction* Macmillan 1987. This well regarded study is particularly useful on the CBI as a pressure group.

**3236**  Michael Useem *The Inner Circle: Large Corporations and the Rise of Business Political Activity in the US and UK* Oxford University Press 1984. Whilst concentrating on America this covers the resurgence of business political activity under the Thatcher government. It is also useful on the different ethos of American and British businesses. Also useful on business political activity during the Thatcher years is David Willis and Wyn Grant 'The United Kingdom: Still a Company State' in M P C M Schendelen and R J Jackson *The Politicisation of Business in Western Europe* Croom Helm 1987 pp 158–83. This argues that Thatcher's policies have paradoxically led to an increased politicization of business and an increased role for business in government.

**3237**  Sir Norman Kipping *Summing Up* Hutchinson 1972. Kipping was Director-General of the Federation of British Industry 1946–65.

**3238**  Hugh Barty-King *Round Table: The Search of Fellowship 1927–1977* Heinemann 1977. See also John Creasey *Round Table: The First Twenty-Five Years of the Round Table Movement* National Association of Round Tables of Great Britain and Ireland 1953. This organization was established in 1927 as a place where young businessmen could get together and exchange ideas, and rapidly spread across the empire.

**(f) Business and Management**

**3239**  David J Jeremy (ed) *Dictionary of Business Biography: A Biographical Dictionary of Business Leaders Active in the Period 1860–1980* 5v, Butterworths 1984–86. This contains alphabetically arranged in-depth biographies of selected businessmen.

**3240**  *Directory of Directors* 2v annually, Skinner 1880–. This lists directors and companies in separate sections but does not go beyond the barest details in either.

**3241**  John Scott and Catherine Griff *Directors of Industry: The British Corporate Network 1904–76* Polity 1984. A historical and sociological study. On the network of directors in the 1960s see P Stanworth and A Giddens 'The Modern Corporate Economy: Interlocking Directorships in Britain 1960–1970' *Sociological Review* n.s. 23 1975 pp 5–28.

**3242**  David J Jeremy 'Anatomy of the British Business Elite 1860–1980' *Business History* 26 1984 pp 3–23. A sociological analysis based on the material collected for [3239]. See also P Cross 'The British Business Creed: Changing Ideologies and Self-Images of Business Elites and Management in Britain' London PhD Thesis 1976.

**3243**  Roy Lewis and Rosemary Stewart *The Boss: The Life and Times of the British Businessman* Phoenix House 1958.

**3244**  Cyril Sofer *Men in Mid-Career: A Study of British Managers and Technical Specialists* Cambridge University Press 1970.

**3245**  Clive Rassem *Secrets of Success* Sidgwick and Jackson 1988. A series of profiles of the successful entrepreneurs behind new departures like the Body Shop, Datron Instruments or Blue Arrow. It is really a handbook for future entrepreneurs but contains useful material and is an interesting reflection on the growth of emphasis on entrepreneurship during the Thatcher years.

**3245A**  Anthony Gater *et al Thrusters and Sleepers: A Study of Attitudes in Industrial Management: A PEP Report* Allen and Unwin 1965. A very valuable study of management and its failings in British business, focusing on the wool textiles, shipbuilding, electronics, domestic appliances, earthmoving equipment and metal working machine tools industries.

**3246**  Patricia Tisdall *Agents of Change: The Development and Practice of Management Consultancy* Heinemann 1982. A study of the development of management consultancy, particularly since the 1960s. A good history drawing on archives and interviews.

**3247**  Mildred Wheatcroft *The Revolution in British Management Education* Pitman 1970. A study that could usefully be updated. It traces the rapid development of management education in the 1960s and the changing attitude in industry to management training. The histories of the various management institutes are described. See also V Kelly 'The Education of Industrial Supervisors: A Study in Curriculum Development, with

Special Reference to the Tyne-Wear Region 1941–73' Newcastle MEd Thesis 1978.

3248  S P Keeble 'University Education and Business Management from the 1890s to the 1950s: A Reluctant Relationship' London PhD Thesis 1984. Until the 1950s British industry did not look to universities to prepare people for a career in management and neither sought to recruit graduates nor to develop formal business education. Britain's poor growth performance and the increasing complexity of management led to a change in attitudes in the 1950s.

3249  Diedre Gill, Bernard Ungerson and Menab Thakur *Performance Appraisal in Perspective: A Survey of Current Practice* Institute of Personnel Management 1973. An analysis of management appraisal and the rise of assessment centres.

3250  L T Simister and J Turner 'The Development of Systematic Forecasting Procedures in British Industry' *Journal of Business Policy* 1972–73 pp 43–54. A study of one aspect of the effect of management thinking on business procedures in Britain. A more comprehensive analysis of its effect would be extremely useful.

(g) New Technology and Research and Development

3251  *Information Technology Review* Price Waterhouse 1986–. A good annual review with statistics of developments in British industry in the field of high technology.

3252  'Current Bibliography in the History of Technology' *Technology and Culture* 1964–. An international bibliography which is annually updated. It is unannotated. See also *British Technology Index* 1962–. A monthly index to periodical literature. Prior to 1962 consult the *Subject Index to Periodicals*.

3253  *Automation* Bibliography 84, House of Commons Library 1956. A short unannotated listing.

3254  *Microelectronics: An Annotated Bibliography* Department of Industry 1980. A short bibliography of material on the impact of microelectronics on industry and society.

3255  L Grayson (comp) *The Social and Economic Impact of New Technology 1978–84: A Select Bibliography* Technical Communications 1984. A guide to British, American and European literature appearing in this period. An update covering items published 1984–6 has also appeared.

3256  Stephanie Wilson (comp) *Science Parks: A Select Bibliography* Department of Trade and Industry 1984. A 37 item bibliography which selects material illustrating the growth of science parks.

3257  Peter Fairley *British Inventions in the 20th Century* Hart-Davis 1972. See also J Townsend *et al Science and Technology Indicators for the UK: Innovation in Britain Since 1945* Science Policy Research Unit Occasional Paper 16, University of Sussex 1981. On the role of the universities in research and development see Michael Sanderson *The Universities and British Industry 1850–1970* Routledge and Kegan Paul 1975.

3258  Ian Benson and John Lloyd *New Technology and Industrial Change: The Impact of the Scientific-Technical Revolution on Labour and Industry* Kogan Page 1983. A study of the impact, in terms of productivity, of redundancies or of the disappearance of skilled work, of new technology and automation.

3259  Trevor I Williams *A Short History of 20th Century Technology c1900–c1950* Clarendon 1982. An illustrated history.

3260  *Environmental and Industrial Process Technology 1959–1984* Warren Spring Laboratory 1984.

3261  *Technological Innovation in Britain: Report of the Central Advisory Council for Science and Technology* HMSO 1968. The chairman of this body was Sir Solly Zuckerman.

3262  Jim Northcott *Microelectronics in Industry: Promise and Performance* Policy Studies Institute 1986. A study of the use of microelectronics in processes and production throughout industry. It is largely based on the results of a questionnaire sent to some 1,200 representative factories. Together with the earlier studies Jim Northcott and Petra Rogers *Microelectronics in British Industry: The Pattern of Change* Policy Studies Institute 1984 and Jim Northcott and Petra Rogers *Microelectronics in Industry: What's Happening in Britain* Policy Studies Institute 1982 (with the accompanying volume of *Survey Statistics* Policy Studies Institute 1982) this series provides a useful sequence of pictures of the impact of microelectronics in Britain.

3263  Robin Oakey, A T Thwaites and P A Nash *The Regional Distribution of Innovative Manufacturing Establishments in Britain* Centre for Urban and Regional Development Studies, University of Newcastle 1980. A short paper that argues that firms in the South East are more innovative than elsewhere in the country. This analysis is developed in the comparative study, Robin Oakey *High Technology, Small Firms: Innovation and Regional Development in Britain and the United States* Pinter 1984. K Pavitt, M Robson and J Townsend 'The

Size Distribution of Innovating Firms in the UK: 1945–1983' *Journal of Industrial Economics* 35 1987 pp 297–316 analyses the relationship between the size of firm and innovation in the context of 4,000 plus significant innovations developed in the UK 1945–83. They find far more activity in firms with less than 1,000 employees than was expected. The use of research and development by British firms over a longer historical period is examined in S B Saul 'Research and Development in British Industry from the End of the Nineteenth Century to the 1960s' in T C Smout (ed) *The Search for Wealth and Stability: Essays in Economic and Social History Presented to M W Flinn* Macmillan 1979 pp 114–38.

**3264** Carol E Heim 'R and D, Defense and Spatial Divisions of Labor in Twentieth Century Britain' *Journal of Economic History* 47 1987 pp 365–78. This paper argues that research and development has been concentrated near London whilst assembly has been located away from the capital in areas of cheaper labour. She claims that regional policy compounded this, decanting unskilled labour to the regions whilst leaving the decision making in the South East.

**3265** Robert Millward 'The Relationship Between Research and Development Activity and Output and Productivity in British Manufacturing Industry in the Post-War Period' Manchester PhD Thesis 1965–6.

**3266** Jim Northcott *et al Robots in British Industry: Expectations and Experience* Policy Studies Institute 1986.

**3267** M E Leary *High Technology Development in Oxford and Cambridge* Department of Town Planning Working Paper 89, Oxford Polytechnic 1986. Cambridge developed a thriving high technology centre in the 1970s. In Oxford the development was less apparent and more scattered. This paper analyses the reasons behind these differences. An important study on the development of high technology industries in Cambridge is *The Cambridge Phenomenon: The Growth of High Technology Industry in a University Town* Segal Quine and Partners 1985. See also N Carter and C Watts *The Cambridge Science Park* Royal Institute of Chartered Surveyors 1984; a short paper on its development and impact. The background to and reasons for Cambridge's differential success is examined in D E Keeble 'High-Technology Industry and Regional Development in Britain: The Case of the Cambridge Phenomenon' *Environment and Planning C: Government and Policy* 7 1989 pp 153–72.

**3268** Michael J Brehany and Ronald W McQuaid *The M4 Corridor: Patterns and Causes of Growth in High Technology Industry* Department of Geography Geographical Papers 87, University of Reading 1985. The M4 corridor is the other main location of high technol-ogy industries in England. See also their 'HTUK: The Development of the United Kingdom's Major Centre of High Technology Industry' in Michael J Brehany and Ronald W McQuaid (eds) *The Development of High Technology Industries: An International Survey* Croom Helm 1987 pp 297–354. This examines both the locational factors and the number of jobs it has created and its contribution to the national economy.

## (h) Design

**3269** Anthony J Coulson *A Bibliography of Design in Britain 1851–1970* Design Council 1979. A good, if unannotated bibliography. It has a chronology and there are historical comments scattered throughout.

**3270** Fiona McCarthy *A History of British Design 1830–Present* Allen and Unwin 1979. This general history has an extensive section on post-war industrial design, and especially the activities of the Council of Industrial Design. See also her *British Design Since 1880: A Visual History* Lund Humphries 1982. Another general history is S Bayley *In Good Shape: Style in Industrial Products 1900–1960* Design Council 1979.

**3271** Penny Sparke (ed) *Did Britain Make It? British Design in Context 1946–1986* Design Council 1986. A study which puts British design in international context.

**3272** Derek Hudson and Kenneth William Luckhurst *The Royal Society of Arts 1794–1954* Murray 1954. The Royal Society of Arts has traditionally played an important role in the encouragement of good industrial design. This history is supplemented by *The Society's History: A Bibliographical and Tabular Supplement April 1954– April 1975* Royal Society of Arts 1975.

**3273** Michael Farr *Design in British Industry: A Mid-Century Survey* Cambridge University Press 1955. A good survey of the situation in the 1940s and 1950s.

**3274** Jennifer Harris, Sarah Hyde and Greg Smith *1966 and All That: Design and the Consumer in Britain 1960–1969* Trefoil Books 1986. An exhibition catalogue. It largely concentrates on the design of consumer goods. The text reflects on the growing significance of design and packaging in the 1960s, the new trends in retailing and the impact of the consumer boom on design.

**3275** P A Sparke 'Theory and Design in the Age of Pop: Problems in British Design in the 1960s, a Case Study for a Methodology for Design History' CNAA PhD Thesis 1976. On Pop Design see also N S Whiteley 'The History and Theory of Pop Design in Britain' Lancaster PhD Thesis 1982.

**3276** Frederique Huygen *British Design: Images and Reality* Thames and Hudson 1989. A well illustrated, excellent study which concentrates on design in the 1980s but places it firmly in the context of post-war developments.

**3277** Catherine McDermott *Street Style: British Design in the 1980s* Design Council 1987. A survey, largely of fashion, graphic design and interior and product design.

**3278** Noel Carrington *Industrial Design in Britain* Allen and Unwin 1976. Reminiscences which illustrate the history of the Design and Industries Association which was founded in 1915. A more formal history to celebrate its diamond jubilee appears in *Design Action – DIA Yearbook 1975* Design and Industries Association 1975.

**3279** John E Blake 'Growing Pains of a New Profession' *Design* 197 1965 pp 28–35. A history of the Society of Industrial Artists since 1930.

**3280** John Blake and Avril Blake *The Practical Idealists: Twenty Five Years of Designing for Industry* Lund Humphries 1969. A history of the firm of design consultants, Design Research Unit. Another history of a design partnership is *Pentagram Design Partnership Pentagram* Lund Humphries 1972.

**3281** Gordon Russell *Designer's Trade: Autobiography of Gordon Russell* Allen and Unwin 1968. The autobiography of an important industrial designer. Russell was Director of the Council of Industrial Design 1947–59 and founder of the eponymous furniture firm. See also Ken and Kate Baynes *Gordon Russell* Design Council 1980.

**3281A** Fiona MacCarthy *Eye For Industry: Royal Designers for Industry 1936–1986* Lund Humphries 1986.

(i) Exhibitions and Trade Fairs

**3282** Hugh A Auger *Trade Fairs and Exhibitions* Business Publications 1967. A guide to their cost, design and presentation. It includes a list of trade fairs and exhibitions in Britain. Exhibitions and business conferences have since been a major growth area, though this is not yet reflected in the literature. This is despite the fact that such conferences have become an important subsidiary form of income for universities and hotels as well as the inspiration for a number of purpose built venues. 'Trade Fairs and Exhibitions' *Planning* 23 1957 pp 110–39 studies methods of promoting British goods abroad and possible ways of improving exhibition facilities in Britain.

**3283** Mary Benham and Bevis Hillier (eds) *A Tonic to the Nation: Festival of Britain 1951* Thames and Hudson 1976. This catalogue of the 1976 commemorative exhibition contains many reminiscences. One of the Festival's prime movers reflects upon it in Sir Gerald Barry 'The Festival of Britain: Three Cantor Lectures' *Journal of the Royal Society of Arts* 100 1952 pp 667–704. See also his 'The Influence of the Festival of Britain on Design Today' *Journal of the Royal Society of Arts* 109 1961 pp 503–15 and Nikolaus Pevsner 'Ten Years After the Festival' *Design and Industries Yearbook* 1961–62 pp 14–21.

(j) Industrial Migration

**3284** Peter Gripaios 'Industrial Decline in London: An Examination of its Causes' *Urban Studies* 14 1977 pp 181–9. A study of the effect of the decline of the docks and the relocation of industry on South East London. See also D E Keeble 'Industrial Migration from North West London 1940–1964' *Urban Studies* 2 1965 pp 15–32.

## (2) Textiles and Clothing

(a) General

**3285** WORLD TEXTILES 1970–. The specialized textiles information service database. For information contact Shirley Institute, Manchester M20 8RX (telephone 061 445 8141). This covers anything to do with the world textiles industry. The printed version is *World Textile Abstracts*.

**3286** N Kassa 'Adjustment Assistance Policy in the UK Textile and Clothing Industries and LDC Exports of Textile and Clothing Products to the UK Market' Strathclyde MSc Thesis 1986. A study of protection of the UK industry since the 1930s and the impact of imports from the less developed world. Kassa argues that the drop in employment in the industry has not been caused by these imports but by increased productivity and slack demand. The protection of the industry since the 1950s is also discussed in Caroline Miles 'Protection of the British Textile Industry' in W M Carden and Gerhard Fels (eds) *Public Assistance to Industry: Protection and Subsidies in Britain and Germany* Macmillan 1976 pp 184–214.

**3287** Robert L Tignor *Egyptian Textiles and British Capital 1930–1956* American University in Cairo Press, Cairo 1989. An evaluation of the operation in Egypt of certain British textile firms and their response to the gradual British withdrawal from Egypt.

**3288** Caroline Miles *Lancashire Textiles: A Case Study of Industrial Change* Cambridge University Press 1968. A study of the decline of the once powerful Lancashire textile industry and the growing importance of synthetic fibres in an area once dominated by cotton. See also H Lazer 'Politics, Public Policy Formation and the Lancashire Textile Industry 1954–1970' London PhD Thesis 1975.

**3289** John Singleton 'Lancashire's Last Stand: Declining Employment in the British Cotton Industry 1950–1970' *Economic History Review* 2nd series 39 1985 pp 92–107. A good study of the decline of the Lancashire cotton industry. Its decline up to 1950 is charted in William Lazonick 'Industrial Organisation and Technological Change: The Decline of the British Cotton Industry' *Business History Review* 57 1983 pp 195–236. See also K L Wallwork 'The Cotton Industry in North West England 1941–1961' *Geography* 47 1962 pp 241–55.

**3290** R Robson *The Cotton Industry in Britain* Macmillan 1957. An analysis of the contemporary situation with detailed statistics and many references to the historical background.

**3291** R L Holt 'The Changing Industrial Geography of the Cotton Areas of Lancastria 1951–61: A Study of Mill Conversion and Employment' Manchester MA Thesis 1963–4. See also A H Irving 'Changes in the Distribution of Cotton Manufacturing in an Area of South East Lancashire Since 1936' London MSc Thesis 1963–4.

**3292** S P S Pruthi 'A Study of Productivity Problems in the Cotton Industries of the UK (Lancashire) and India (Bombay and Ahmedabad) Since the Second World War' London PhD Thesis 1961–2.

**3293** R G Newbery 'Quality in the Lancashire Cotton Spinning Industry: The Economic, Technological and Managerial Aspects of its Definitions, Establishment and Control, with Particular Reference to the Period 1945–1959' Manchester MA (Econ) Thesis 1963–4.

**3294** W A Wardle 'A History of the British Cotton Growing Association, with Special Reference to its Activities in Africa' Birmingham PhD Thesis 1980. See also W F Tewson *The British Cotton Growing Association: Golden Jubilee 1904–54* The Association 1954. Jack Wiseman and Basil Selig Yamey 'The Raw Cotton Commission 1948–52' *Oxford Economic Papers* n.s. 8 1956 pp 1–34 analyses the centralized buying mechanism set up by the Cotton (Centralized Buying) Act 1947.

**3295** Marguerite Dupree (ed) *Lancashire and Whitehall: The Diary of Sir Raymond Streat* 2v, Manchester University Press 1987. The second volume covers the period 1939–57. Streat was the Secretary of the Manchester Chamber of Commerce between the wars and the Chairman of the Cotton Board 1940–57. This remarkable diary provides a running commentary on the difficulties of the industry and its decline and the efforts of government and the industry itself to stem this decline. The role of the Manchester Chamber of Commerce as a business pressure group and in the reorientation of policy after 1945 is discussed in H J Goodwin 'The Politics of the Manchester Chamber of Commerce 1921 to 1951' Manchester PhD Thesis 1982.

**3296** Pnina Werbner 'From Rags to Riches: Manchester Pakistanis in the Textile Trade' *New Community* 8 1980 pp 84–95. A study of the success of an immigrant community.

**3297** N Moor and P Waddington *From Rags to Ruins: Batley Woollen Textiles and Industrial Change* Community Development Project/Political Economy Collective 1980. A study of the collapse of the woollen industry in Batley and its effects in the light of the government's regional policies. The industry in another part of Yorkshire is discussed in I Hardill 'The Woollen and Worsted Industry of the Huddersfield Area 1954–1970' Wales MA Thesis 1980. This traces its post-war reorganization and the gradually declining employment in the industry.

**3297A** Frederick Arthur Wells *The British Hosiery and Knitwear Industry* revised ed, David and Charles 1972. See also Stanley Chapman 'Mergers and Takeovers in the Post-War Textile Industry: The Experience of Hosiery and Knitwear' *Business History* 30 1988 pp 219–39 and J A Smith 'The Hosiery and Knitwear Industry: A Study in Post-War Industrial Development' Liverpool MA Thesis 1968–9. On the knitting industry see S M Al-Douri 'Some Features of the Development of the UK Knitting Industry During the Post-War Period' Leeds MPhil Thesis 1977. On the hosiery industry see R C Eaglen 'The Economic Effects of Recent Technical Change on the Hosiery Industry, with Special Reference to Leicestershire' Leicester MA Thesis 1966–7.

**3298** D E Varley *A History of the Midlands Counties Lace Manufacturers Association 1915–1958* Lace Productions 1959.

**3299** P R Mountfield, D J Unwin and K Guy 'The Influence of Size, Siting, Age and Physical Characteristics of Factory Premises on the Survival and Death of Footwear Manufacturing Establishments in the East Midlands, UK' *Environment and Planning A* 17 1985 pp 777–94. A study of the otherwise neglected footwear industry in the period 1957–79. See also P R Mountfield 'The Footwear Industry of the East Midlands 5, the Modern Phase: Northamptonshire and Leicestershire Since 1911' *East Midland Geographer* 4 1967 pp 154–75.

**3300** Ken and Kate Baynes (eds) *The Shoe Show: British Shoes Since 1790* Crafts Council 1979. An exhibition catalogue.

## (b) Business Histories

**3301** P Allen *Background to Aristoc 1919–1957* Aristoc Ltd 1957. A short history of the hosiery manufacturers.

**3302** R Redmayne (ed) *Ideals in Industry: Being the Story of Montague Burton Ltd 1900–1950: Golden Jubilee* Montague Burton 1951. A history of the menswear firm.

**3303** Kenneth Hudson *Towards Precision Shoemaking: C and J Clark Limited and the Development of the British Shoe Industry* David and Charles 1968. A short history of the growth of this shoemaking company, much of which deals with the post-war years.

**3303A** Jon Press 'G B Britton and Footwear Manufacturing in Bristol and Kingswood 1870–1973' in Charles E Harvey and Jon Press (eds) *Studies in the Business History of Bristol* Bristol Academic Press 1988 pp 213–38. A history until the takeover of the company by Ward White.

**3304** D C Coleman *Courtaulds: An Economic and Social History Vol 3: Crisis and Change 1940–1965* Clarendon 1980. A good company history. It provides a detailed analysis of company strategy and examines in depth the 1962 ICI takeover bid for Courtaulds. Recent Courtaulds history, particularly in the context of relations with central government, is also the theme of Arthur Knight *Private Enterprise and Public Intervention: The Courtaulds Experience* Allen and Unwin 1974. Knight was a former chairman of the company.

**3305** J Wajcman 'Fakenham Enterprises: The Rise and Fall of a Women's Co-operative' Cambridge PhD Thesis 1980. A historical and sociological analysis of a shoe manufacturing co-operative of the 1970s.

**3306** E R Pafford and J H P Pafford *Employer and Employed: Ford Ayrton and Co Ltd: Silk Spinners with Worker Participation, Leeds and Lwo Bentham 1870–1970* Pasold Research Fund (Pasold Occasional Papers 2) 1974.

**3307** Chris Cornforth *The Garment Co-operative: An Experiment in Industrial Democracy and Business Creation* Open University Co-operative Research Unit 1981. An account of a workers' co-operative.

**3308** Frederick Arthur Wells *Hollins and Viyella: A Study in Business History* David and Charles 1968. This company is now part of Coats Viyella.

**3309** E W Pasold *Ladybird, Ladybird: A Story of Private Enterprise* Manchester University Press 1973. Ladybird specialize in children garments.

**3310** Eric Newby *Something Wholesale: My Life and Times in the Rag Trade* Secker and Warburg 1962. Memoirs of his time as a commercial traveller for the family firm of Lane and Newby 1945–56.

**3311** Jocelyn Morton *Three Generations in a Family Textile Firm* Routledge and Kegan Paul 1971. A history of Morton Sundour Fabrics.

**3312** Warren Tute *The Grey Top Hat: The Story of Moss Bros of Covent Garden* Cassell 1961. A history of the menswear and hire firm.

**3313** Guy Christie *Storeys of Lancaster 1848–1964* Collins 1964. A history of Storey Brothers and Co Ltd.

**3314** Sidney Pollard and R Turner 'Profit-Sharing and Autocracy: The Case of J T and J Taylor of Batley, Woollen Manufacturers 1892–1966' *Business History* 18 1976 pp 4–34. A good history of a firm which helped pioneer profit-sharing. It focuses particularly on industrial relations at the firm down to its demise in 1966.

## (c) Fashion

**3315** Colin McDowell *McDowell's Directory of Twentieth Century Fashion* Muller 1984. An alphabetically arranged guide to international designers and couture houses.

**3316** Georgina Howell (ed) *In Vogue: Six Decades of Fashion* Allen Lane 1975. Twentieth century fashion as reflected in the pages of a leading women's fashion magazine. See also Alison Adburgham '1953–1973 – A Journalist's View' *Costume* 8 1974 pp 4–12.

**3317** B B Baines *Fashion Revivals from the Elizabethan Age to the Present Day* Batsford 1981.

**3318** Julian Robinson *Fashion in the Forties and Fifties* Academy Editions 1976. See also Jane Dorner *Fashion in the Forties and Fifties* Ian Allan 1975.

**3319** Elizabeth Wilson *Through the Looking Glass* BBC Books 1989. A good, well-illustrated history of fashion in the twentieth century. Sandra Barwick *A Century of Style* Allen and Unwin 1984 is a good, well-illustrated history of women's fashion, and especially of the aristocracy. Alan Mansfield and Phillis Cunnington *Handbook of English Costume in the Twentieth Century 1900–1950* Faber 1973 is a well illustrated and organized guide. It however has little on developments in men's styles. There is a good bibliography. Another well illustrated and well regarded study of fashion to the middle of the century is C W Cunnington and Phillis Cunnington *English Women's Clothing in the Present Century* Faber 1952. See also I Brooke *English Costume 1900–50* Methuen 1951.

**3320**  Barbara Bernard *Fashion in the '60s* Academy Editions 1978. See also R T Horowitz 'Fashion in Britain in the 1960s: A Study of Attitudes' Leicester PhD Thesis 1970–1.

**3321**  Rodney Bennett-England *Dress Optional: The Revolution in Menswear* Peter Owen 1967. A study of men's fashions at a time when London was the world centre of fashion. This examines the trade, the designers, manufacturers, models and journalists. Children's fashions are examined in A Guppy *Children's Clothes 1939–1970: The Advent of Fashion* Blandford 1978.

**3322**  Edwin Hardy Amies *Still Here: An Autobiography* Weidenfeld and Nicolson 1984. The autobiography of a celebrated men's fashion designer. See also his earlier autobiography, *Just So Far* Collins 1954.

**3323**  Frances Kennett *et al Norman Hartnell* A Zwemmer 1985. A catalogue of his designs which includes recollections of him and an outline of his career. See also his autobiographical *Silver and Gold* Evans 1955.

**3324**  Mary Quant *Quant by Quant* Cassell 1966. Quant played a major part in the changes in fashion in the 1960s.

**3325**  Jean Dawney *How I Became a Fashion Model* Nelson 1960. Dawney was Britain's top fashion model in the 1950s. Another view of modelling from a leading model of the period is Jean Shrimpton *The Truth about Modelling* W H Allen 1964. One of the leading fashion models of the 1960s and 1970s, Twiggy (her real name was Lesley Hornby), has also written an autobiography, *Twiggy: An Autobiography* Hart-Davis Macgibbon 1975.

### (3) Mining and Quarrying

Certain aspects of British mining activity are not represented below. In the case of tin mining this is the result of the dearth of literature on the subject. In the case of coal mining it is because the literature on this subject appears in the section on Energy.

**3326**  *United Kingdom Mineral Statistics* HMSO 1973–. An annual statistical guide to the British mining industry (in this case including coal mining).

**3327**  J Blunden *The Mineral Resources of Britain* Hutchinson 1975. A good geographical survey.

**3328**  A M Hiron 'An Appraisal of the Marine Sand and Gravel Industry of the United Kingdom' Manchester MSc Thesis 1983. A study of the development of what has become an increasingly important aspect of the British aggregates industry since the 1950s. By 1980 it accounted for 12% of the aggregates market. There is no other literature on the aggregates industry.

**3329**  Peter Stanier 'The Granite Quarrying Industry in Devon and Cornwall: Part Two 1910–1985' *Industrial Archaeology Review* 9 1986 pp 7–23. This traces its steady decline since the 1920s. The mining of lead and barytes in Devon is examined in Christopher J Scmitz 'The Development and Decline of the Devon Barytes Industry 1875–1958' *Report and Transactions of the Devonshire Association for the Advancement of Science, Literature and Art* 109 1977 pp 117–33.

**3330**  Kenneth Hudson *The History of English China Clays: Fifty Years of Pioneering and Growth* David and Charles 1969. A history of the company, now known as ECC.

**3331**  Paul Johnson *Gold Fields: A Centenary Portrait* Weidenfeld and Nicolson 1987. A well illustrated history of the mining and quarrying group, Consolidated Gold Fields.

**3332**  Charles E Harvey *The Rio Tinto Company: An Economic History of a Leading International Mining Concern 1873–1954* Alison Hodge 1981. This contains a little on the post war transformation of the company from one based upon operations in Spain into a multinational. In 1962 a merger with Zinc Corporation led to the formation of RTZ. See also Richard West *River of Tears: The Rise of the Rio Tinto-Zinc Mining Corporation Ltd* Earth Island Ltd 1972.

**3333**  Peter Greenhalgh *West African Diamonds 1919–83: An Economic History* Manchester University Press 1985. A history of diamond mining in colonial territories up to the decline of the mines in the 1970s and 1980s. Another study of diamond mining in an African colony, this time in Tanganyika in the 1940s and 1950s, is John Knight and Heather Stevenson 'The Williamson Diamond Mine, De Beers and the Colonial Office: A Case Study of the Quest for Control' *Journal of Modern African Studies* 24 1986 pp 423–45.

## (4) Metals Industries

### (a) Iron and Steel

**3334** *Annual Report and Accounts of the British Steel Corporation* British Steel Corporation 1972–. In 1967–71 this was published by HMSO as a House of Commons Paper. Before renationalization reports had been published as *Iron and Steel Board Annual Report and Accounts 1953/4–66* and *Iron and Steel Holding and Realisation Agency Annual Report and Accounts 1953/4–66*. Iron and Steel Corporation Annual Report and Accounts 1951–52 are the reports published during the first period of nationalization before the corporation was privatized for the first time by the Churchill government in 1953. BSC also publish *Annual Statistics of the British Steel Corporation* and *Iron and Steel Industry Annual Statistics*.

**3335** *British Independent Steel Producers Annual Report* BISPA 1953–.

**3336** John Vaizey *The History of British Steel* Weidenfeld and Nicolson 1974. A semi-official history of the steel industry from 1918 to the 1960s. It is well illustrated and makes good use of documents. Elizabeth Cottrell *The Giant with Feet of Clay: The British Steel Industry 1945–1981* Centre for Policy Studies 1981 is a critical study of the industry. David Walter Heal *The Steel Industry in Post-War Britain* David and Charles 1974 is a thorough study of the economic geography of the industry in the post-war years. B S Keeling and A E G Wright *The Development of the Modern Steel Industry* Longmans 1964 examines the development of the industry since the 1920s concentrating on its post-war expansion. Also still useful are Duncan Burn *The Steel Industry 1939–59: A Study in Competition and Planning* Cambridge University Press 1961 and J C Carr and W Taplin *History of the British Steel Industry* Blackwell 1962. Doug McEachern *A Class Against Itself: Power and the Nationalisation of the British Steel Industry* Cambridge University Press 1980 is a rather theoretical attempt to provide a political science analysis of decision making in and for the industry 1914–67.

**3337** David E Pitfield 'Regional Economic Policy and the Long- Run: Innovation and Location in the Iron and Steel Industry' *Business History* 16 1974 pp 160–74. Government intervention in the location of the industry is here considered and obliquely condemned.

**3338** George Ross *The Nationalisation of Steel: One Step Forward Two Steps Back?* Macgibbon and Kee 1965. A dating study which nevertheless remains the most competent account of the nationalization of the industry under the Attlee government.

**3339** Kathleen Burk *The First Privatisation: The Politicians, the City and the Denationalisation of Steel* Historians Press 1988. An excellent account of the denationalization carried out in 1953 using the records of the government, the Bank of England and the merchant banks involved. Aspects of the relationship of the government with the privatized industry is examined in J A W Davies 'Aspects of the Relationship Between the Central Government and Research Organisations in the British Iron and Steel Industry 1955–65' Manchester MA (Econ) Thesis 1966–7.

**3340** Keith Ovenden *The Politics of Steel* Macmillan 1978. An exhaustive study of the renationalization of the steel industry 1965–67.

**3341** R A Bryer, T J Brignall and A R Maunders *Accounting for British Steel: A Financial Analysis of the Failure of the British Steel Corporation 1967–80 and Who was to Blame* Gower 1982. An investigation into the difficulties of the renationalized corporation. See also Jeremy John Richardson *Steel Policy in the UK: The Politics of Industrial Decline* Centre for the Study of Public Policy 10, University of Strathclyde 1983.

**3342** Industry and Trade Select Committee *Effects of BSC's Corporate Plan* House of Commons Paper 221, *Parliamentary Papers* 1980–81. A study of the reorganization of the then state-owned company which followed and which prompted a lengthy strike before they could be implemented.

**3343** Heidrun Abromeit *British Steel: An Industry Between the State and Private Sector* Berg 1986. The successful privatization of British Steel in 1986 is analysed in Jonathan Ayles 'Privatisation of the British Steel Corporation' *Fiscal Studies* 9 1988 pp 1–25.

**3344** Stephen Young 'The Implementation of Britain's National Steel Strategy at the Local Level' in Y Meny and V Wright (eds) *The Politics of Steel: Western Europe and the Steel Industry in the Crisis Years 1974–1984* de Gruyter, Berlin 1986 pp 369–415.

**3345** Charles H Wilson *A Man and His Times: A Memoir of Sir Ellis Hunter* Newman Neame 1962. Hunter was President of the British Iron and Steel Federation 1945–53. He was Managing Director 1938–61 and Chairman 1948–61 of the accountancy firm of Dorman, Long and Co Ltd.

**3346** Norman Lee and Peter Stubbs *The History of Dorman Smith 1878–1972* Newman Neame 1972. A history of a steel company.

**3347** *TI Metsec 1931–1981: Steel Components for the World's Industries* Melland 1981. A short history.

**3348** R Peddie *The United Steel Companies Ltd 1918–1968: A History* Nicholls and Co Ltd 1969. An earlier in-depth study of this company which closely examines its performance and development in the run-up to nationalization in 1951 in the light of the accusations of the inefficiency of private companies in the course of the debate over nationalization is P W S Andrews and Elizabeth Brunner *Capital Development in Steel (A Study of the United Steel Companies Ltd)* Blackwell 1951.

**3349** J Austin and M Ford *Steel Town: Dronfield and Wilson Cammell 1873–1983* Scarsdale Publications 1983.

**(b) Other**

**3350** *The History of the British Aluminium Company 1894–1955* the Company 1955. This is now British Alcan Aluminium.

**3351** Frank Stones *The British Ferrous Wire Industry 1882–1962* Northend 1977.

**3352** David Rowe *Lead Manufacturing in Britain: A History* Croom Helm 1983. An official history of Associated Lead Manufacturers Ltd and its predecessor companies. The last chapter deals with the post-war era.

**3353** W E Minchinton *The British Tinplate Industry* Oxford University Press 1957. This history does not really cover the post-war decline of the industry. For the industry's post-war history see P J Weaver 'The Development of the South Wales Tinplate Industry 1945–1970' Wales MSc (Econ) Thesis 1973–4.

**3354** W J Reader *Metal Box: A History* Heinemann 1976. A good company history of the printing and packaging company.

**(5) Pharmaceuticals**

**3355** Heinz Redwood *The Pharmaceutical Industry: Trends, Problems and Achievements* Oldwicks 1988. An earlier exploration of the industry in Britain is William Brackton *The Drug Makers* Eyre Methuen 1972. See also M H Cooper *Prices and Profits in the Pharmaceuticals Industry* Pergamon 1966. The research and development in the industry and the pharmaceutical companies influence on politics, the National Health Service and the doctors is analysed in W Duncan Reekie and Michael H Weber *Profits, Politics and Drugs* Macmillan 1979. On the political influence of the pharmaceuticals industry see also Ronald W Lang *The Politics of Drugs: The British and Canadian Pharmaceutical Industries and Governments* Saxon House 1974.

**3356** Sunday Times Insight Team *Suffer the Children: The Story of Thalidomide* Deutsch 1979. Thalidomide was a drug administered to expectant mothers in the late 1950s and early 1960s. Many of the children born to these mothers had serious deformities at birth. This is a critical account of the testing, development and effects of the drug. The legal and medical aspects of the thalidomide tragedy are examined in H Sjöström and R Nilsson *Thalidomide and the Power of the Drug Companies* Penguin 1972.

**3357** H G Lazell *From Pills to Penicillin: The Beecham Story: Personal Account* Heinemann 1975. A history of the Beecham group.

**3358** C A Bailey *On This Slender Thread a Life May Depend: An Authorised History of Ethnicon Ltd* Ethnicon Ltd 1977.

**3358A** Charles W Robinson *Twentieth Century Druggist: Memoirs* Galen Press 1983. A memoir of his career with Evans Medical until it was taken over by Glaxo, and of his subsequent career with Runcorn Urban Development Corporation.

**3359** Sir Harry Jephcott (comp) *The First Fifty Years* W S Cowell 1969. A history of Glaxo. Another history is currently in progress.

**3360** Judy Slinn *A History of May and Baker* Hobsons 1984. May and Baker is now part of the French Rhône-Poulenc group.

**(6) Chemicals**

**3361** D W F Hardie and J D Pratt *A History of the Modern British Chemical Industry* Pergamon 1966. A survey from the industrial revolution to the present.

**3362** C G Gill 'Employer Organisations in the UK Chemical Industry' *Industrial Relations Journal* 9 1978 pp 37–47.

**3363** Wyn Grant, William Paterson and Colin Whitson *Government and the Chemical Industry: A Comparative Study of Britain and West Germany* Oxford University Press 1989. A well-written comparative study.

**3364** D W Broad *Centennial History of the Liverpool Section, Society of Chemical Industry 1881–1981* Society of Chemical Industry 1981. See also W A Campbell *A Century of Chemistry on Tyneside 1868–1968* Society of Chemical Industry, Newcastle-upon-Tyne Section 1968.

3365 George Copping *A Fascinating Story: The History of OCCA 1918–1968* OCCA 1968. The history of the Oil and Colour Chemists' Association.

3365A W S Keatley *The Fertilizer Manufacturers Association: The Second Fifty Years 1925-1975* Fertilizer Manufacturers Association 1977. The jubilee history of another association is told in S H Bell *The First Half of the Century: A History of the Paint Manufacturers Association 1926–76* Paint Manufacturers Association 1976.

3366 N J Travis and E J Cocks *The Tincal Trail: A History of Borax* Harrap 1984. Borax (Holdings) Ltd merged with Rio Tinto Zinc in 1968.

3367 A E Musson *Enterprise in Soap and Chemicals: Joseph Crosfield and Sons Ltd 1815–1965* Manchester University Press 1965.

3368 W J Reader *Imperial Chemical Industries: A History Vol II: The First Quarter Century 1926–1952* Oxford University Press 1975. The history of the Mond family who played a major part in the early years of the company is told in J Goodman *The Mond Legacy: A Family Saga* Weidenfeld and Nicolson 1982. The last twenty years of the company's history are thoroughly analysed in A M Pettigrew *The Awakening Giant: Continuity and Change in Imperial Chemicals Industries* Blackwell 1985. E F Thurston *Winnington Research Laboratory: The First Fifty Years* Winnington Research Laboratory 1979 is the history of ICI's Alkali Division's research laboratory.

3369 *Documentation of the Ernest Bader Papers* Scott Bader Commonwealth Ltd n.d. ?1982. The Scott Bader Commonwealth is a chemicals firm which was founded by Ernest Bader. It was transformed into a workers' commonwealth in 1951 by Bader. This well annotated guide to his papers is introduced by a brief biography and a short history of the firm. The papers, which mainly date from the period between 1942 and Bader's death in 1982, cover not only the history of the firm but also Bader's many interests, not least his involvements in the Industrial Common Ownership Movement, pacifism and the Society of Friends. Fred H Blum *Work and Community: The Scott Bader Commonwealth and the Quest for a New Social Order* Routledge and Kegan Paul 1968 a study of the firm and the ideals that inspired it. On the firm see also Roger Hadley 'Participation and Common Ownership: A Study in Employee Participation in a Common Ownership Firm' London PhD Thesis 1971. Bader's life and ideals are examined in Susanna Hoe *The Man Who Gave His Company Away: A Biography of Ernest Bader Founder of the Scott-Bader Commonwealth* Heinemann 1978.

3369A G Hetherington *Portrait of a Company: Thermal Syndicate Limited 1906–1981* TSL Thermal Syndicate PLC 1981. A history of the silicon tubing and optical engineering company based in the North East, and of its various overseas subsidiaries.

3370 W J Reader *Fifty Years of Unilever 1930–1980* Heinemann 1980. A good general history of the Anglo-Dutch multinational. See also Charles Henry Wilson *Unilever 1945–1965: Challenge and Response in the Industrial Revolution* Cassell 1968. The overseas operations of the company are examined in D K Fieldhouse *Unilever Overseas: The Anatomy of a Multinational 1895–1965* Croom Helm 1978. He claims that these have promoted development both during the colonial period and since, thus leaping to the defence of multinational companies. His study focuses on Unilever's operations in twelve countries but excludes the activities of the United Africa Company. For this see [1655].

## (7) Ceramics and Glass

3371 P W Gay and R W Smith *The British Pottery Industry* Butterworths 1974. A study of the state of the industry in the post-war period. It provides statistics in abundance. It also surveys the recent performance of various individual firms.

3372 G A Godden *English China* Barrie and Jenkins 1985. A historical account of English Chinaware 1727–1980.

3373 V J M Irvine 'The Domesticware Sector of the British Pottery Industry 1948–67 with Special Reference to Mergers' Keele MA Thesis 1969–70.

3374 R L Smyth 'The British Pottery Industry 1970–1977' *North Staffordshire Journal of Field Studies* 17 1979 pp 65–73.

3375 Lucien Myers *The First 100 Years of the Story of Poole Pottery 1873–1973* Poole Pottery 1973.

3376 Desmond Eyles *Royal Doulton 1815–1965* Hutchinson 1965. See also his *The Doulton Burslem Wares* Barrie and Jenkins/Royal Doulton 1980 which traces the history of the wares, the factory and the production techniques since 1877.

3377 A Kelly *The Story of Wedgwood* Faber 1975. See also G Wills *Wedgwood* Country Life 1980.

3378 T C Barker *The Glassmakers Pilkington: The Rise of an International Company 1826–1976* Weidenfeld and Nicolson 1977. See also his study of Pilkingtons successful development of the float glass process, 'Business Implications of Technical Developments in the Glass Industry 1945–1965: A Case Study' in Barry Supple (ed) *Essays in British Business History* Clarendon 1977 pp 187–206. This development was profitable by 1965 and put Pilkingtons ahead of all its international rivals.

**3379** Alec W Clark *Through a Glass Clearly* Golden Eagle 1980. An account of Beatson, Clark and Co, the Rotherham glass firm.

## (8) Engineering

For government intervention in the offshore engineering industries that have developed since the advent of North Sea oil and gas see the literature on Oil and Gas in the section on Energy.

### (a) General

**3380** Simon Caulkin 'Engineering's Hard Road' *Management Today* Mar 1979 pp 82–9. A study of the decline of the engineering industry and the rise of import penetration, especially in the vital machine tool industry.

**3381** Eric Wigham *The Power to Manage: A History of the Engineering Employers Federation* Macmillan 1973. A history of one of most important, and in industrial relations one of the most intransigent, of the employers federations.

**3382** Peter Davis, Charles Harvey and Jon Press 'Locomotive Building in Bristol in the Age of Steam 1837–1958' in Charles E Harvey and Jon Press (eds) *Studies in the Business History of Bristol* Bristol Academic Press 1988 pp 109–36. A history up to the closure of the works in 1958.

**3383** G A Dummett *From Little Acorns: A History of the APV Company Ltd* Hutchinson Benham 1981.

**3384** K R Day *Alvis: The Story of the Red Triangle* Gentry Books 1981. On Alvis cars see [3423].

**3385** C A Muir *The History of Baker Perkins* Heffer 1968.

**3386** *The Leaf and the Tree 1947–1962: A Story of Expansion* Riverside Works, Norwich 1962. The second volume of the history of the Norwich engineering firm Boulton and Paul.

**3387** R Fulford *The Sixth Decade 1946–1956* privately printed 1956. A history of the British Electrical Traction Company. It is continued by G E Mingay *Fifteen Years On 1956–1971* privately printed 1973.

**3388** Desmond Donnelly *David Brown's: The Story of a Family Business 1860–1960* Collins 1960. Traditionally a shipbuilding firm in the post-war period Brown's diversified, partly through the acquisition of companies such as Aston Martin.

**3389** Martyn Wilson and K Spink *Coles 100 Years: The Growth Story of Europe's Largest Crane Manufacturers 1879–1979* Coles Cranes Ltd 1978.

**3390** L T C Rolt *The Dowty Story* Newman Neame 1962. The history of the Dowty group.

**3391** A D Young *EMB Trams* Light Rail Transit Association 1985. The Electro-Mechanical Brake Company had specialized in brake systems for trams in the inter-war years. In the post-war period it had to go into general engineering.

**3392** Ralph Davis *Twenty One and a Half Bishop Lane: A History of J H Fenner and Co Ltd 1861–1961* Newman Neame 1961. A history of a mechanical and electrical engineering firm.

**3393** A history of GKN is in preparation and the first volume, Edgar Jones *A History of GKN Volume 1: Innovation and Enterprise 1759–1918* Macmillan 1987, has already appeared.

**3394** R A Whitehead *Garratts of Leiston* Marshall 1965.

**3395** J F Clarke *Power on Land and Sea: 160 Years of Industrial Enterprise on Tyneside: A History of R and W Hawthorn Leslie and Co Ltd* Clark Hawthorn Ltd 1979.

**3396** L T C Rolt *A Hunslet Hundred: One Hundred Years of Locomotive Building by the Hunslet Engine Co* Macdonald 1964.

**3397** David Ewart Evans *Lister's: The First Hundred Years* Sutton 1979. A history of R A Lister.

**3398** Tony Eccles *Under New Management* Pan 1981. An account of Kirby Manufacturing Engineering Co-operative. Eccles was an adviser to the co-operative and present at its meetings. He provides a sympathetic evaluation of this experiment of the 1970s and the reasons for its failure and analyses what needs to be done if workers co-operatives are to succeed in future.

**3399** Charles Henry Wilson *Men and Machines: A History of D Napier and Son Engineers Ltd 1808–1958* Weidenfeld and Nicolson 1958.

**3400**  D R Grace and D C Phillips *Ransomes of Ipswich: A History of the Firm and Guide to its Records* Ransomes, Sims and Jeffries 1975. A history of Ransomes, Sims and Jeffries Ltd since its establishment in 1869.

**3400A**  B H Tripp *Renold Chains: A History of the Company and the Rise of the Precise Chain Industry 1879–1955* Allen and Unwin 1956. This history of Renold Ltd is continued by B H Tripp *Renold Ltd 1956–1967* Allen and Unwin 1969.

**3401**  J S Dorlay *The Roneo Story* Roneo Vickers Ltd 1978. A history of Roneo Vickers.

**3401A**  *Turner and Newall Limited: 50 Years 1920–1970* Turner and Newall 1970. A short history.

**3402**  J D Scott *Vickers: A History* Weidenfeld and Nicolson 1963. This is updated by Harold Evans *Vickers Against the Odds 1956–1977* Hodder and Stoughton 1978. In the 1950s Vickers remained very much involved in traditional heavy engineering, such as arms, shipbuilding or aircraft. In the ensuing decades the company adjusted to changing world markets by diversifying and establishing itself as a multinational. On Vickers aircraft see [3478].

**3403**  W J Reader *The Weir Group: A Centenary History* Weidenfeld and Nicolson 1971. A history of a major engineering group. It is quite useful for the post-war period during which this group was obliged to diversify into general engineering and away from its traditional dependence on shipbuilding.

(b) Motors

*(i) General*

**3404**  *The Motor Industry of Great Britain* Society of Motor Manufacturers and Traders 1926–. An annual statistical guide and survey of the state of the industry.

**3405**  Jonathan Wood *Wheels of Fortune: The Rise and Fall of the British Motor Industry* Sidgwick and Jackson 1988. A good study of the post-war difficulties of the industry. In 1950 Britain was the leading motor manufacturer in Europe. By the 1980s Britain was well down the list of European motor producers. Wood argues that the main problem was long term reliance on an insular self-taught leadership who did not appreciate the importance of engineering, but he also looks at the effect of the poor management decisions of the 1970s and of industrial militancy. The poor quality of the management of the industry is also criticized in Wayne Lewchuk *American Technology and the British Vehicle Industry* Cambridge University Press 1987. In this he argues that the British managers did not adapt their attitudes to the needs of the industry and that the defensive mergers of the 1950s only made the situation worse. Graham Turner *The Car Makers* Eyre and Spottiswoode 1963 is another historical account of the industry which also draws attention to its management. He also considers its poor industrial relations and poor workmanship.

**3406**  George Maxcy and Aubrey Silberton *The Motor Industry* Allen and Unwin 1959. A detailed analysis of the state of the industry in the 1950s. See also H G Castle *Britain's Motor Industry* Clerke and Cockeran 1950.

**3407**  Krish Bhaskar *The Future of the UK Motor Industry* Kogan Page 1979. The problems of the industry in the 1970s and the threat from imported cars are well analysed in this study.

**3408**  Peter Dunnett *The Decline of the British Motor Industry: The Effects of Government Policy 1945–1979* Croom Helm 1980. A somewhat superficial examination of the effect of government policies. The inconsistent nature of government policy in the post-war period, making it difficult for companies to plan effectively, is seen as largely responsible for the decline of the industry in M Berg 'Government Policy and its Impact on the Motor Industry' *Long Range Planning* 18 1985 pp 40–7. Stephen Wilks *Industrial Policy and the Motor Industry* Manchester University Press 1984 sees policy as having been essentially reactive and as over-sensitive to the wishes of the City and the need to defend the currency rather than to the needs of the motor industry. He focuses particularly on the decline since the 1960s and supplies a good bibliography.

**3408A**  George A Oliver *Cars and Coachbuilding: One Hundred Years of Road Vehicle Development* Sotheby Parke Bernet 1981. A history of the Institute of British Carriage and Automobile Manfacturers.

**3409**  Roy Church 'The Effects of American Multinationals on the British Motor Industry 1911–83' in Alice Teichova, Maurice Lévy-Laboyer and Helga Nussbaum (eds) *Multinational Enterprise in Industrial Perspective* Cambridge University Press 1986 pp 116–30. A study of the impact of Ford, General Motors and Chrysler on the British industry and their relations with the British government.

**3410**  John Cubbin 'Quality Change and Pricing Behaviour in the United Kingdom Car Industry 1956–1968' *Economica* 42 1975 pp 43–58.

**3411**  A Jennings 'The British Motor Industries' Export Performance in the Post-War Period' Liverpool MA Thesis 1967–8. See also E J B Sieve 'British Motor

Vehicle Exports (An Analysis of the Inter-War Period and Some Post-War Trends)' London PhD Thesis 1951–2.

**3412** M J Healey and P W Roberts *Economic Change and Policy in the West Midlands* Lanchester Polytechnic 1985. A collection of essays attempting to explain the decline of the once prosperous vehicle industry of the West Midlands in recent years. David Thomas and Tom Donnelly *A History of the Motor Vehicle Industry in Coventry* Croom Helm 1985 surveys the rise and decline of the industry since the 1890s. It is better on the earlier period than on the post-war years. On production strategies by management towards organized labour see their 'Trade Unions, Management and the Search for Production in the Coventry Motor Car Industry 1939–75' in Charles Harvey and John Turner (eds) *Labour and Business in Modern Britain* Cass 1989 pp 98–113.

**3413** D G Rhys 'The Structure of the British Commercial Vehicle Industry 1945–66' Birmingham MCom Thesis 1966–7.

**3414** S W Stevens-Stratten *British Lorries 1945–83* Ian Allan 1988. A well-illustrated enthusiasts history, as is Gavin Booth *The British Motor Bus: An Illustrated History* Ian Allan 1973.

**3415** Barbara Mary Dimond Smith *The History of the British Motorcycle Industry 1945–1975* Centre for Urban and Regional Studies Occasional Paper 3, University of Birmingham 1981. A short study. The machines themselves are examined in C J Ayton *The Hamlyn Guide to Postwar British Motorcycles* Hamlyn 1982 and Steve Wilson *British Motor Cycles Since 1950* 2v, Stephens 1982. Roy Bacon *British Motorcycles in the 1960s* Osprey 1988 is a good study of the state of the industry and its vulnerability in the 1960s when the mistakes were made that led to its demise. See also Bob Currie *Great British Motor Cycles of the Sixties* Hamlyn 1981. A factor in its collapse was the impact of Japanese motorcycles, which is analysed in J W E Kelly 'Japanese Impact on the Motor Cycle Market' Bradford MSc Thesis 1973–4. On the industry in Wolverhampton see P Neeld 'Wolverhampton Motorcycles: The Growth and Decline of an Industry' *Transport History* 9 1978 pp 52–9.

**3416** Jeff Clew *Francis Beart – A Single Purpose* Haynes 1978. A biography of a designer of engines for racing motorcycles.

**3417** *The UK Automotive Components Industry* The Economist Intelligence Unit 1988. A detailed study of the contemporary state and structure and of recent innovations in the industry. It also includes profiles of 60 companies.

**3418** C S Williams 'Past, Current and Future Trends in Electric Vehicle Manufacture for Municipalities' *Solid Wastes* 69 1979 pp 268–74. A history of the manufacture and use of electric vehicles in local government since 1911.

**3419** J Wood *Classic Motor Cars* Shire Publications 1985. A short illustrated history of British cars from the 1920s which concentrates on their design. On particular types of car see Graham Robson *The Postwar Touring Car* Haynes 1977 and Martyn Watkins *British Sports Cars Since the War* Batsford 1974. On racing cars see Cyril Posthumus *The British Competition Car* Batsford 1959.

**3420** Bart H Vanderveen *British Cars of the Late Forties 1946–1949* Warne 1974. Illustrations and descriptions of many of the cars of the period. See also Bart H Vanderveen *British Cars of the Early Fifties 1950–1954* Warne 1976, Bart H Vanderveen *British Cars of the Late Fifties 1955–1959* Warne 1975, Michael Allen *British Family Cars of the Fifties* Haynes 1985 and D J Voller *British Cars of the Late Sixties 1965–1969* Warne 1982.

*(ii) Business Histories*

**3421** Alan Thomas and John Aldridge *AEC: 'Builders of London's Buses'* Henry 1979.

**3422** Denis Jenkinson *From Chain Drive to Turbocharger: The AFN Story* Stephens 1984. A history of AFN Ltd, the former motor manufacturer, racer and trader which is now part of Porsche.

**3423** K R Day *The Alvis Car 1920–1966* Day 1966. See also [3384].

**3424** Geoff Courtney *The Power Behind Aston Martin* Oxford Illustrated Press 1978. A popular account of Aston Martin, the luxury and sports car manufacturers. See also Dudley Coram *et al Aston Martin: The Story of a Sports Car: Book Two 1946 to 1957* Motor Racing Publications 1957.

**3425** Robert J Wyatt *The Austin 1905–1952* David and Charles 1981. A study of Austin Cars up to their amalgamation with Morris to form the British Motor Corporation, one of the predecessor organizations of British Leyland.

**3426** *A Pictorial History of BRS: 35 Years of Trucking* Warne 1982.

**3427** Bob Holliday *The Story of BSA Motor Cycles* Stephens 1978. See also Barry Ryerson *The Giants of*

*Small Heath: The History of Birmingham Small Arms* Foulks 1980. Norah Docker *Norah: The Autobiography of Lady Docker* W H Allen 1969 is the autobiography of a society lady whose third husband, Sir Bernard Docker, was the chairman of BSA.

**3428** Walter Owen Bentley *An Illustrated History of the Bentley Car* Allen and Unwin 1984.

**3429** Karel Williams, John Williams and Colin Haslam *The Breakdown of Austin Rover: A Study in the Failure of Business Strategy and Industrial Policy* Berg 1987. An in-depth study of the weaknesses and failings of the Austin Rover group, formerly known as British Leyland, in the 1970s and 1980s. A good history of the British Leyland group and its constituent parts based on access to all but the latest documents and plentiful from the then Chairman, Lord Stokes, is Graham Turner *The Leyland Papers* revised ed, Pan 1973. It concentrates particularly on the period since the merger between Leyland and British Motor Holdings. Pre-dating the difficulties which led to British Leyland's nationalization it is perhaps unduly favourable towards Stokes. The future for the newly nationalized company was mapped out in the report of the committee chaired by Sir Don Ryder, *British Leyland: The Next Decade: An Abridged Version of a Report by a Team of Inquiry* Cmnd 342, *Parliamentary Papers* xiv 1974-75. One consequence of nationalization was the appointment of Sir Michael Edwardes to guide the company back to profitability and cure its seemingly endemic labour problems. Edwardes reflects on his eventually successful efforts in this endeavour in his autobiography *Back from the Brink: An Apocalyptic Experience* Collins 1983. There are also a number of histories of constituent parts of this group (now, as Rover Group, part of British Aerospace) or of certain of its marques. See therefore Graham Robson *The Rover Story: A Century of Success* Stephens 1984, Graham Robson *The Land-Rover: Workhorse of the World* David and Charles 1976, F W McComb *The MG* Shire Publications 1985 Laurence Pomeroy *The Mini Story* Temple Press 1964 and Nick Baldwin *The Illustrated History of Leyland Trucks* Haynes 1986. For Jaguar, a former element in the group, see [3435].

**3430** Stephen Young and Neil Hood *Chrysler UK: A Corporation in Transition* Praeger 1977. The American group Chrysler took over the Rootes group in the 1960s. This is an account of its activities in Britain and the 1975 rescue of the corporation by the Labour government. Relations between the government and the corporation are analysed in S R M Wilks 'Government and the Motor Industry, with Particular Reference to Chrysler (UK) Limited' Manchester PhD Thesis 1980. *Chrysler and the Cabinet: How the Deal was Done* Granada 1976 is a pamphlet based on a TV reconstruction of the Cabinet's handling of the issue and the eventual rescue package.

**3431** Doug Nye *Cooper Cars* Osprey 1983. An affectionate history of the racing car firm which flourished 1946-60 and which developed the Mini Cooper. It includes detailed appendices. See also Arthur Owen *The Racing Coopers* Cassell 1959.

**3432** Ivan Fallon *Dream Maker: The Rise and Fall of John Z De Lorean* Putnam 1983. De Lorean was an American who persuaded the British government to invest substantially in his ill-fated attempt to build luxury cars in Northern Ireland.

**3433** Pat Kennet *Dennis* Stephens 1979. A study of Dennis Brothers, manufacturers of commercial and municipal vehicles, buses and fire engines. See also *An Illustrated History of Dennis Buses and Trucks* Haynes 1987. Shirley Corke 'Dennis of Guildford' *Surrey History* 3 1987 pp 107-14 is a brief history and a guide to the company records.

**3434** David Weguelin *et al The History of English Racing Automobiles Limited* White Mouse 1980. A well illustrated enthusiast's history of the racing car manufacturer 1934-51.

**3435** Philip Porter *Jaguar: History of a Classic Marque* Sidgwick and Jackson 1988. A good illustrated history of the company and the cars that have born its name. It makes good use of the company archives and of interviewing. Another company history is E J B Montagu *Jaguar: A Biography* Cassell 1967. See also A Whyte *Jaguar: The History of a Great British Car* 2nd ed, Stephens 1985, Paul Skilleter *Jaguar Sports Cars* Foulis 1975 and, a study of the company's most celebrated sports car, Chris Harvey *E Type: End of an Era* Oxford Illustrated Press 1977. In view of the lengthy period Jaguar spent as part of British Leyland before being floated off separately in the 1980s much of the literature listed in [3429] should also be consulted.

**3436** Ian Vernon Hardy Smith *Lotus: The First Ten Years* Motor Racing Publications 1958. A study of the development of the racing car and sports car firm.

**3437** Harold Nockolds *Lucas: The First Hundred Years Vol 2: 1939 to Today* David and Charles 1977. A good history of the components manufacturer.

**3438** R J Overy *William Morris, Viscount Nuffield* Europa 1976. A biography of the founder of Morris cars and the Chairman of the company 1919-52. See also P W S Andrews and Elizabeth Brunner *The Life of Lord Nuffield: A Study in Enterprise and Benevolence* Blackwell 1959 and Edward Gillbanks *Lord Nuffield* Cassell 1959.

**3439** Bob Holliday *Norton Story* 2nd ed, Stephens 1981. A history of the motorcycle firm.

**3440** Barry M Jones *The Story of Panther Motor Cycles* Stephens 1983. A well-illustrated history of Phelon and Moore's motor cycles until they ceased production in 1966.

**3441** Gregory Houston Bourden *The Story of the Raleigh Cycle* W H Allen 1975. A history of the bicycle-manufacturing firm and its products.

**3442** Martin Bennett *Rolls Royce: The History of the Car* Oxford Illustrated Press 1974. A popular history of the cars rather than the company, as is George A Oliver *Rolls Royce* Haynes 1988.

**3443** Roy H Bacon *Royal Enfield* Osprey 1982. A history of the firm and its motorcycles. See also Peter Hartley *The Story of Royal Enfield Motor Cycles* Stephens 1981.

**3444** Harry Louis *The Story of Triumph Motor Cycles* 3rd ed, Stephens 1981. On Triumph until 1960 see Ivor Davies *Its a Triumph* Haynes 1980. The government intervention 1973–7 in the ill-fated attempt by a workers co-operative to keep the factory going is critically assessed by Jock Bruce-Gardyne *Meriden: Odyssey of a Lame Duck* Centre for Policy Studies 1978.

**3445** Louis Klemantaski and Michael Frostick *The Vanwall Story* Hamilton 1958. A well-illustrated short history of a famous racing marque. Denis Jenkinson and Cyril Posthumus *Vanwall: The Story of Tony Vandervell and his Racing Cars* Stephens 1975 is a study of the racing car developer and his cars.

**3446** L T Holden 'A History of Vauxhall Motors to 1950: Industry, Development and Local Impact on the Luton Economy' Open University MPhil Thesis 1984. This includes some reflections on the company's success with light trucks and in general in the 1940s and on its relatively smooth labour relations.

**3447** J W E Kelly 'A History of Veloce Limited – Motor Cycle Manufacturers, Hall Green, Birmingham' Bradford PhD Thesis 1979. This study concentrates on the twenty years prior to liquidation in 1971. Rod Burris *Velocette: A Development History of the MSS, Venom, Viper, Thruxton and Scrambler Models* Haynes 1982 is a technical history of these products of Veloce Ltd.

**3448** St J C Nixon *Wolseley: A Sign of the Motor Industry* Foulis 1949. A study of the company and its cars.

**3449** Greg Lanning *et al Making Cars: A History of Car Making in Cowley, by the People who make the Cars* Routledge and Kegan Paul 1985. An oral history of the Morris works in Oxford. Huw Benyon *Working for Ford* Allen Lane 1973, is a social history, also drawing heavily on oral testimony, of another group of car workers. It includes material on the 1969 Ford strike. On another group of car workers see Paul Thompson 'Playing at being Skilled Men: Factory Workers and Pride in Work Skills among Coventry Car Workers' *Social History* 13 1988 pp 45–69.

(c) Aircraft and Aerospace

*(i) General*

**3450** Aubrey Joseph Jackson *British Civil Aircraft Since 1919* Putnam 1973. An alphabetically arranged directory.

**3451** Arthur Reed *Britain's Aircraft Industry: What Went Right? What Went Wrong?* Dent 1973. A general history of the industry since 1945. Government intervention in the industry in the post-war period is examined in Keith Hayward *Government and British Civil Aerospace: A Case Study in Post-War Technology Policy* Manchester University Press 1983. The adverse effects of the 1954 Comet disaster and the transition from turbo-props to jet engines on the British industry in the post-war years, which enabled the Americans to establish a dominance of the industry by the 1960s, are discussed in Peter Fearon 'The Growth of Aviation in Britain' *Journal of Contemporary History* 20 1985 pp 21–40. See also his 'Aviation Past and Present' *Journal of Transport History* n.s. 4 1977–8 pp 47–54.

**3452** R H T Harper 'The Fifth Halford Memorial Lecture' *Journal of the Royal Aeronautical Society* 70 1966 pp. 477–86. A study of the changing structure of aircraft 1939–64. There are also some memories of some value in C L Cowdrey 'A Century of British Aeronautics' *Journal of the Royal Aeronautical Society* 70 1966 pp 433–40.

**3453** Keith Hartley and Peter A Watt 'Profits, Regulation and the UK Aerospace Industry' *Journal of Industrial Economics* 29 1981 pp 413–28. A study of profitability in an industry which, for most of the post-war period, had state-determined profits rates.

**3454** R F Ryder 'An Economic History of the British Aircraft Industry 1908–1948' Southampton MSc (Econ) Thesis 1957–8.

**3455** M C S Dixson 'Parliament and the Aircraft Industry 1951– 65' Oxford DPhil Thesis 1971–2.

**3456** D J Pickup 'The British Aircraft Industry from 1957–1971 and its Relationship to Defence Policy' London MPhil Thesis 1984. A study of the military aircraft industry from the Sandys White Paper to the Rolls Royce crash. It also supplies a brief survey of events since then. Government intervention in the military aircraft industry during the Second World War, when Shorts and Power Jets were nationalized, and in its immediate aftermath, when the Attlee government rejected the idea of nationalizing the entire industry, is analysed in D E H Edgerton 'Technical Innovation, Industrial Capacity and Efficiency: Public Ownership and the British Military Aircraft Industry 1935–1948' *Business History* 26 1984 pp 247–79.

**3457** *Report of the Committee of Inquiry into the Aircraft Industry* Cmnd 2853, *Parliamentary Papers* iv 1965–66. This report of the committee chaired by Lord Plowden called for collaborative projects with European countries in both the civil and military spheres and argued that Britain should take the initiative in setting these up. It also argued that there were better ways to support the Northern Ireland economy than by special support for Shorts.

**3458** G Thomas 'British Aerospace Collaboration with Europe 1959–1974' Sussex MA Thesis 1977.

**3459** Elliot J Feldman *Concorde and Dissent: Exploring High Technology Failures in Britain and France* Cambridge University Press 1985. A good study of the most famous collaborative project, the Anglo-French Concorde. Geoffrey Knight *Concorde: The Inside Story* Weidenfeld and Nicolson 1976 is a memoir of the planning and construction of this supersonic aircraft by the former Vice-Chairman of the British Aircraft Corporation. It was a very costly project which ran far over budget, an aspect which tends to be emphasized in Peter Hall 'The Anglo-French Concorde' in his *Great Planning Disasters* Weidenfeld and Nicolson 1980 pp 87–108, as well as in a series of books which looked at the development of the project; Andrew Wilson *The Concorde Fiasco* Penguin 1973, John Costello and Terry Hughs *The Battle for Concorde* Compton Press 1971 and John Davis *The Concorde Affair* Frewin 1969. See also H W Caswell 'A Study of some of the Technical, Administrative and Political Factors Affecting the Development of the Concorde Aircraft' Manchester MSc Thesis 1973–4 and Annabelle May 'Concorde – Bird of Harmony or Political Albatross?' *International Organisation* 33 1979 pp 481–508.

**3460** Keith Hayward 'Airbus: Twenty Years of European Collaboration' *International Affairs* 64 1987–88 pp 11–26. The European Airbus as a collaborative venture between Britain, France and West Germany to challenge the American dominance of the world civil aircraft market began with an agreement in 1967. The development of the project and the shifts in British attitudes towards it (Britain withdrew in 1969 and only rejoined in 1978) are well charted in this article.

**3461** D W Cairns 'Intergovernmental Co-operation in Science and Technology: The Experience of the European Space Research Organisation and the European Space Vehicle Launcher Development Organisation' Keele PhD Thesis 1977. Aerospace otherwise remains a neglected field.

**3462** P S Johnson 'The Development of the Hovercraft in the United Kingdom' *Three Banks Review* 104 1974 pp 28–45. A study of the development of the hovercraft by Christopher Cockerell and the impact of policy on the nascent industry.

## (d) Business Histories

**3463** D H Middleton *Airspeed: The Company and its Aeroplanes* Terence Dalton 1982. See also Harold Anthony Taylor *Airspeed Aircraft Since 1931* Putnam 1970. This is an extensive, well illustrated and detailed enthusiast's history.

**3464** Oliver Tapper *Armstrong Whitworth Aircraft Since 1913* Putnam 1973.

**3465** A J Jackson *Avro Aircraft Since 1908* Putnam 1965. A good enthusiast's history.

**3466** Charles Gardner *The British Aircraft Corporation: A History* Batsford 1981. A history of the company and its aircraft. J E Murpurgo *Barnes Wallis: A Biography* 2nd ed, Ian Allan 1987 is a life of the man responsible for some of the British technological breakthroughs of the Second World War who served as Chief of Aeronautical Research and Development at the British Aircraft Corporation 1945–71.

**3467** A J Jackson *Blackburn Aircraft Since 1909* Putnam 1968. A good history which is very useful on the development of aircraft such as the Buccaneer, which entered service in 1962. See also *The Blackburn Story 1909–1959* Blackburn Aircraft Ltd 1960.

**3468** C H Barnes *Bristol Aircraft Since 1910* Putnam 1964. A detailed enthusiast's history. See also Geoffrey Green *Bristol Aerospace Since 1910* the author 1985.

**3469** Cecil Martin Sharp and D H Martin *A History of De Havilland* Airlife 1982. A good study of the aircraft made by this company is A J Jackson *De Havilland Aircraft Since 1915* Putnam 1962. See also J K Archer 'De Havilland Aircraft (1908–1960)' *Transport History* 9 1978 pp 60–9. On the ill-fated Comet, which was Britain's first jet-powered passenger aircraft, see D D Dempster *The Tale of the Comet* Wingate 1959. Sir Geoffrey de Havilland *Sky Fever* Hamilton 1961 is a useful autobiography by the founder of the firm. See also the biographical tribute by R M Clarkson 'Geoffrey de Havilland 1882–1965' *Journal of the Royal Aeronautical Society* 71 1967 pp 67–92.

**3470** Harold Anthony Taylor *Fairey Aircraft Since 1915* Putnam 1974. A good enthusiast's history.

**3471** D N James *Gloster Aircraft Since 1917* Putnam 1971. A detailed study.

**3472** C H Barnes *Handley Page Aircraft Since 1907* Putnam 1976.

**3473** Frank K Mason *Hawker Aircraft Since 1920* Putnam 1971. A useful enthusiast's history. See also Bruce Robertson *Sopwith: The Man and his Aircraft* Air Review 1970. A biography of Sir Thomas Sopwith who was founder President of Hawker Siddeley and its Chairman 1935–63.

**3474** D L Brown *Miles Aircraft Since 1925* Putnam 1970.

**3475** John Golley and Bill Gunston *Whittle: The True Story* Airlife 1987. Despite the assistance of its subject this is a somewhat inadequate biography of the inventor of the jet engine and the founder of Power Jets Ltd, which was nationalized during the Second World War. Whittle's own autobiography, Sir Frank Whittle *Jet: The Story of a Pioneer* Power Jets Ltd 1953, remains of value.

**3476** I Lloyd *Rolls Royce: The Years of Endeavour* Macmillan 1978. A good history of the company from 1918. Rolls Royce remains one of the three major engine manufacturers in the world. See also M Donne *Leaders of the Skies: Rolls Royce: The First Seventy Five Years* Muller 1981, R W Harker *The Engines were Rolls Royce: An Informal History of that Famous Company* Collier Macmillan 1979, R W Harker *Rolls Royce from the Wings: Military Aviation 1925–1971* Oxford Illustrated Press 1976 and L J K Setright *Rolls Royce* Foulis 1985. On the crash of the company in 1971 when it was driven into receivership by the cost of developing the RB 211 engines and was rescued and nationalized by the government see M Davis 'Political Factors in the Fall of Rolls Royce' *Canadian Public Administration* 16 1973 pp 206–19.

**3477** C H Barnes *Short Aircraft Since 1900* Putnam 1967. A useful study of the Northern Ireland firm and its aircraft. Shorts were nationalized during the Second World War. See also J M Preston *A Short History: A History of Short Bros Aircraft Activities in Kent 1908–1964* North Kent Books 1978.

**3478** Charles F Andrews *Vickers Aircraft Since 1908* Putnam 1969. A good enthusiast's study. On the Vickers Viscount, the company's most famous post-war passenger aeroplane, see P St John Turner *Handbook of the Vickers Viscount* Ian Allan 1968. For the general histories of the company see [3402].

**3479** Lawrence Freedman 'The Case of Westland and the Bias Towards Europe' *International Affairs* 63 1986–7 pp 1–19. There is no general history of the Westland helicopter manufacturing company. There are however a number of studies, mostly on the politics of the issue, on the Westland Affair. This study examines the way in which the political battle over a link between the ailing company and either the American Sikorsky group or a European consortium in 1985–86 obscured the real issue, the future of Britain's helicopter industry. For studies of the politics of this Affair see [291].

(e) Shipbuilding

**3480** L A Ritchie (comp) *Modern British Shipbuilding: A Guide to Historical Records* Maritime Monographs and Reports 48, National Maritime Museum 1980. An annotated, alphabetically arranged guide to archives and their location.

**3481** B W Hogwood *Government and Shipbuilding: The Politics of Industrial Change* Saxon House 1979. A chronological study of government intervention in the industry from 1959 up to its nationalization in the 1970s.

**3482** Kenneth Cloves Barnaby *The Institute of Naval Architects 1860–1960* Royal Institute of British Architects 1960.

**3483** *Shipbuilding Enquiry Committee Report 1965–1966* Cmnd 2937, *Parliamentary Papers* vii 1965–66. This report of the committee chaired by R M Geddes surveyed the decline and failings of the industry since 1945 and argued the need to reorganize facilities and practices, with a possibility of arranging the industry into geographical groupings.

**3484** Kenneth Cloves Barnaby *100 Years of Specialised Shipbuilding and Engineering: John I Thorneycroft Centenary* Hutchinson 1964.

**3485** Peter Du Cane *An Engineer of Sorts* Nautical Publishing Company 1971. An autobiography by a designer for and later Managing Director of Vospers. It is useful for the design and engineering of the ships as well as the company's history.

**3486** Alastair Borthwick *Yarrow and Company Limited: The First Hundred Years 1865–1965* Yarrow 1965.

## (f) Electrical

**3487** T A B Corley *Domestic Electrical Appliances* Cape 1966. A study of the rise of this industry since 1880, concentrating on the post-war period, and of the factors that encouraged its development.

**3488** Doreen Massey and Richard A Meegan 'The Geography of Industrial Reorganization: The Spatial Effects of the Restructuring of the Electrical Engineering Sector under the Industrial Reorganisation Corporation' *Progress in Planning* 10 1979 pp 155–237. A study of the impact of the IRC on the industry from the late 1960s.

**3489** J H Hatch 'Competition in the British White Goods Industry 1954–1965' Cambridge PhD Thesis 1969–70.

**3490** Jerome Kraus 'The British Electron-Tube and Semi-Conductor Industry 1935–1962' *Technology and Culture* 11 1968 pp 544–61.

**3491** Hugh Barty-King *Light up the World: The Story of the Success of the Dale Electric Group 1935–1985* Dale Electric Group 1985.

**3492** John F Wilson 'The Ferrantis and the Growth of the Electrical Industry 1883–1952' Manchester PhD 1980. Amongst the achievements of Ferranti was the pioneering of computers in the early 1950s.

**3493** Robert Jones and Oliver Marriott *Anatomy of a Merger: A History of GEC, AEI and English Electric* Cape 1970. A good study. GEC took over AEI in 1967 and absorbed English Electric a year later. Also on the mergers between these three firms and the role of government in them is Jill Hills 'The Industrial Reorganisation Corporation: The Case of the AEI/GEC and English Electric/GEC Mergers' *Public Administration* 59 1981 pp 63–83.

**3494** H Miller *Halls of Dartford 1785–1985: Founded in the Industrial Revolution: Pioneer of Refridgeration: Halls of Dartford Celebrate 200 Years of Progress* Hutchinson Benham 1985. Halls moved to concentrate on the manufacture of refridgerators in the twentieth century.

**3495** W J Baker *A History of the Marconi Company* Methuen 1970. A good company history.

**3496** John Rowland *Progress in Power: The Contribution of Charles Merz and his Associates to Sixty Years of Electrical Development* Newman Neame 1961. A history of Merz and McLellan.

**3497** J Dummelow *1899–1949* Metropolitan-Vickers 1949. A history of the Manchester electrical engineering firm Metropolitan-Vickers.

**3498** Derek Martin *Thorn EMI: 50 Years of Radar: 50 Years of Company Involvement with Radar Technology 1936–1986* Thorn EMI Electronics, Radar Division 1986. For a general history of this company see [3893].

## (g) Computers and Information Technology

**3499** Tim Kelly *The British Computer Industry: Crisis and Development* Croom Helm 1987. The high growth rate of the British industry in recent years has not matched that of its competitors and this has been reflected in the increasing foreign ownership of the industry and deteriorating balance of trade. The history and current state of the industry is examined in this useful study which concludes that a new policy towards the industry is necessary if an indigenous industry is to survive. This account is particularly strong on developments in the 1970s and 1980s. For earlier developments see S H Hollindale and G C Toothill *Electronic Computers* Penguin 1965, P Drath 'The Relationship Between Science and Technology, University Research and the Computer Industry 1945–1962' Manchester PhD Thesis 1973 4 and M J Mitchell 'The Evolution of the Electronic Computer' Manchester MSc Thesis 1976.

**3500** Simon H Lavington *A History of Manchester Computers* NCC Publishing 1975. Collaboration between Manchester University and Ferranti produced the world's first commercial computer in 1949. This is a useful history of this and subsequent developments.

**3501** M G Croaken 'The Centralisation of Scientific Computation in Britain 1925–1955' Warwick PhD Thesis 1985. By the 1920s desk calculators and accounting machines were increasingly normal. Computing centres began to emerge. NPL Mathematics Division was especially important as it was set up in 1945 to act as a national computing centre, representing the highpoint of the centralization of computing in Britain.

**3502** Simon H Lavington *Early British Computers: The Story of Vintage Computers and the People Who Built Them* Manchester University Press 1980. Also on the early history of the industry see Martin Campbell-Kelly 'Foundations of Computer Programming in Britain (1945–1955/80)' CNAA PhD Thesis 1980. Campbell-Kelly has also published articles derived from his doctoral research on 'The Development of Computer Programming in Britain 1945 to 1955' *Annals of the History of Computing* 4 1982 pp 121–39 and 'Programming the Pilot ACE: Early Programming Activity at the National Physical Laboratory' *Annals of the His-*

tory of Computing 3 1981 pp 133–62. A fascinating insight into the early history of the British computer industry is offered in M R Williams and Martin Campbell-Kelly (eds) *The Early British Computer Conferences* MIT Press 1989. After an historical introduction this presents the reports of conferences held at Britain's three key computing centres in the early years, at Cambridge in 1949, Manchester in 1951 and the National Physical Laboratory in 1953. John Hendry 'Prolonged Negotiations: The British Fast Computer Project and the Early History of the British Computer Industry' *Business History* 26 1984 pp 280–306 is a critical study of the caution with which the British computer industry developed 1945–50. Poor decision making in the development of the machines, lack of support from government and industry and lack of awareness of the computers commercial potential all combined to ensure that the British industry rapidly fell well behind the Americans.

**3503**   John Hendry 'The Teashop Computer Manufacturer: J Lyons, LEO and the Potential and Limits of High-Tech Diversification' *Business History* 29 1987 pp 73–102. Lyons in the 1940s began to manufacture computers under the brand name LEO.

**3504**   Heidi Gottfried 'The Internationalization of Production: Intra-Core Relations and the State: IBM and the British Computer Industry' *Political Studies* 34 1986 pp 387–405. A study of the impact of the American computer giant IBM on the British industry and of the government reactions, which including the government inspired mergers in the 1960s which led to the creation of ICL.

**3505**   David Keeble and Timothy Kelly 'New Firms and High- Technology Industry in the United Kingdom: The Case of Computer Electronics' in David Keeble and Egbert Wever (eds) *New Firms and Regional Development in Europe* Croom Helm 1986 pp 75–104. A study of the surge of small computer firms in the 1970s.

**3506**   Martin Campbell-Kelly 'Christopher Strachey 1916–1975: A Biographical Note' *Annals of the History of Computing* 7 1985 pp 19–42. Strachey was an important innovator in computer design and programming.

**3507**   Andrew Hodges *Alan Turing: The Enigma of Intelligence* Burnett Books 1983. Turing was a brilliant computer scientist who played an important part in breaking the enigma codes during the war and in the development of the ideas on which post-war computers have been based. See also Sara Turing *Alan M Turing* Heffer 1959.

(h) Construction and Property Development

The section on Housing should also be consulted, particularly for material on house-building policy and related matters. For the impact on Selective Employment Tax in the 1960s see the relevant section in the category on Taxation.

**3508**   *Housing and Construction Statistics* HMSO 1972–. This statistical series replaced *Housing Statistics, Great Britain* HMSO 1966–72 and *Monthly Bulletin of Construction Statistics* HMSO 1966–72. It gives details on matters such as the number of house starts and other construction work. Earlier official statistics on the industry are collected in *Construction and the Related Professions: Statistics Collected by the Ministry of Works 1941–1956* Department of the Environment 1980.

**3509**   *House's Guide to the Regulations, Recommendations and Statutory and Advisory Bodies of the Construction Industry* 9th ed Van Nostrand Reinhold 1985. A directory and guide which in its various editions provides a useful statement on the situation in the industry.

**3510**   P A Harlow *A Decade of Quantity Surveying: Review of the Literature 1970–1979* Institute of Building 1980.

**3511**   Christopher G Powell *An Economic History of the British Building Industry 1815–1979* Methuen 1980. A useful general history. See also E W Cooney 'Innovation in the Post-War British Building Industry: A Historical View' *Construction History* 1 1985 pp 52–9.

**3512**   Patricia M Hillebrandt *Analysis of the British Construction Industry* Macmillan 1988. A comprehensive survey of the industry. A useful earlier analysis is Marion Bowley *The British Building Industry: Four Studies in Response and Resistance to Change* Cambridge University Press 1966.

**3513**   C E Topliss *Demolition* Construction Press 1982. A history of the demolition industry in Britain.

**3514**   C C Knowles and P H Pitt *A History of Building Regulation in London 1189–1972 with an Account of the District Surveyors Association* Architectural Press 1972.

**3515**   Nathan Rosenberg *Economic Planning in the British Building Industry 1945–9* Pennsylvania University Press, Philadelphia, Pennsylvania 1960. An account of the impact of government economic planning on the industry in the period.

**3516**   Will Howie and Mike Chrimes (eds) *Thames Tunnel to Channel Tunnel: 150 Years of Civil Engineers: Selected Papers from the Journal of the Institution of*

*Civil Engineers Published to Celebrate its 150th Anniversary* Telford 1987. A collection of papers on various major civil engineering projects around the world carried out by British engineers.

**3517** Derek Walker (ed) *Great Engineers: The Art of British Engineers 1837–1987* Academy 1988. A collection of essays of variable quality on the work of civil and structural engineers. The main engineers of the post-war period featured are Ove Arup and Sir Owen Williams. It also provides a historical review of inventions, short biographies and a bibliography.

**3518** Valerie White *Balfour Beatty 1909–1984* Balfour Beatty 1984. A useful company history.

**3519** Ray Coad *Laing: The Biography of Sir John W Laing CBE 1879–1978* Hodder and Stoughton 1979. A biography of a major figure in the construction industry who remained active in Laings until late in life.

**3520** Martin Gaskell *Harry Neal Ltd: A Family of Builders* Granta 1989. A business history.

**3521** E C Baker *Preece and Those Who Followed: Consulting Engineers in the Twentieth Century* Reprographic Centre 1980. A history of Preece, Cardew and Rider, consulting engineers.

**3522** J B F Earle *Blacktop: A History of the British Flexible Roads Industry* Blackwell 1974. A history of Tarmac. See also his history of one division of the company, *A Century of Road Materials: The History of the Roadstone Division* Blackwell 1971.

**3523** Alan Jenkins *Built on Teamwork* Heinemann 1980. A history of Taylor Woodrow.

**3524** Valerie White *Wimpey: The First Hundred Years* Wimpey News 1980.

**3525** H Smyth *Property Companies and the Construction Industry in Britain* Cambridge University Press 1985. A study of the property industry 1939–79 and particularly of the property boom of the 1950s and 1960s.

**3526** R Goodchild and R Munton *Development and the Landowner: An Analysis of the British Experience* Allen and Unwin 1985. Case studies of the influences of landowners on the timing scale and pattern of development.

**3527** Andrew Cox 'The Unintended Consequences of Policy Initiatives: A Study of the British Conservative Government's Property Policy in the 1970s' *Environment and Planning C: Government and Policy* 1 1983 pp 347–56. The Conservatives' policy in 1970–4 created an unintended boom in property prices. The government reaction created a crisis in the financial sector causing yet another change in policy. The 1971–3 property boom and its collapse is also examined in C Hyman and S Markowski 'Speculation and Inflation in the Market for House-Building Land in England and Wales' *Environment and Planning A* 12 1980 pp 1119–30. The boom and bust pattern of the 1970s is also analysed in W D Fraser 'A Study of the Commercial Property Investment Market 1970–1977' Strathclyde MSc Thesis 1979. P Ambrose and B Colenutt *The Property Machine* Penguin 1975 takes a critical look at this market. The recovery of the property development industry after the 1973 crash is examined in D A Chippendale 'The Development Industry and the Production of Industrial Property in Britain Since 1973' London MPhil Thesis 1986. This includes a case study of development in Berkshire.

**3528** R S Langton *et al Developments in London 1967–1980: A Special Study* Bernard Thorpe and Partners 1981. This reviews trends in property development and grants of planning permission. It includes statistics and case studies.

**3529** William Joseph Reader *To Have and to Hold: An Account of Frederick Bundet's Life in Business* Hunting Gate Group 1983. An official, well illustrated history of the property development and investment group.

**3530** Christopher Grayling *The Bridgewater Heritage: The Story of Bridgewater Estates* Bridgewater Estates 1983.

**3531** David Clutterbuck and Marion Davies *Clore: The Man and His Millions* Weidenfeld and Nicolson 1987. A biography of Sir Charles Clore the property developer who also had interests in engineering and shipbuilding.

**3532** Hugh Barty-King *Scratch a Surveyor* Heinemann 1975. Memoirs, especially of the firm of Drivers Jonas.

**3533** Nigel Broackes *A Growing Concern: An Autobiography* Weidenfeld and Nicolson 1979. A memoir of his business career at Trafalgar House, the shipping, property and construction group, of which he had been managing director since 1958 and chairman since 1969.

## (9) Media and Communications

### (a) News Media

#### (i) General

**3534** Jeremy Tunstall *The Media in Britain* Constable 1983. A well documented critique of the state of the media. It has an extensive annotated bibliography.

**3535** John Whale *The Politics of the Media* Manchester University Press 1980. A good study of the development of the media and the relations between the media and governments since 1945. James Curran and Jean Seaton *Power Without Responsibility: The Press and Broadcasting in Britain* 4th ed, Methuen 1987 is a highly regarded political analysis of the media, its ownership and power and the controls within which it operates. It also draws attention to the danger of distortion to which the media is always prey, as does James Curran's critical appraisal *Bending Reality: The State of the Media* Pluto 1984. See also Peter Golding, Graham Murdoch and P Schlessinger *Communicating Politics: Mass Communication and the Political Process* Leicester University Press 1986 and Michael Cockerell *et al* 'Symposium: Politics and the Media' *Contemporary Record* 2/5 1989 pp 2–14. Useful earlier studies of the concentration of ownership and the social and political role of the media are Anthony Smith *The Politics of the Media* Macmillan 1972, Colin Seymour-Ure *The Political Impact of Mass Media* Constable 1974 and Raymond Williams *Britain in the Sixties: Communications* Penguin 1962.

**3536** Alistair Hetherington (ed) *News, Newspapers and Television* Macmillan 1985. A study of contemporary editing, especially in the case of the *Daily Mail*, *Daily Mirror*, *Guardian*, *The Times* and TV newsdesks. It includes a case study of the media coverage of the 1984–5 miners' strike. On a particular aspect of news gathering see R K Bird 'The News Interview: Its Historic Origins and Present-Day Expressions' Wales MEd Thesis 1980.

**3537** Rodney Bennett-England (ed) *Inside Journalism* Peter Owen 1967. Studies of subjects such as journalism for the national and provincial press, periodicals, radio and television, journalism training, journalism and the law, editing, types of reporting, cartoons, women in journalism and press organizations.

**3538** James Curran, Anthony Smith and Pauline Wingate (eds) *Impacts and Influences: Essays on Media Power in the Twentieth Century* Methuen 1987. A disparate collection of essays. Topics covered include newsreel, the press barons, the press and the Left-Wing GLC 1981–6, media and gender, the impact of media coverage of events, the influence of magazines on teenage girls and the record industry.

**3539** James Curran, Michael Gurevitch and Janet Woollacott (eds) *Mass Communication and Society* Arnold 1977. Studies of the organization of the media, its place in capitalist society and its role and relations with contemporary culture.

**3540** J Scupham *The Revolution in Communications* Holt, Rineman and Winston 1970. This is mainly concerned with the changing impact of the mass media on society.

**3541** Geoffrey Robertson and Andrew G L Nicol *Media Law: The Rights of Journalists and Broadcasters* Oyez Longman 1984. A comprehensive reference source full of historical reflections. They argue that the legal system is harsh on investigative journalism whilst comparatively lenient on the Sunday paper muck-raker.

**3542** Paul O'Higgins *Censorship in Britain* Nelson 1973. A popular account of wartime press censorship from the Crimean War to Suez.

#### (ii) Government and the Media

In addition to the literature listed below the material on government secrecy and the campaign for freedom of information which appears in the section on the Constitution should obviously be consulted.

**3543** James Margach *The Abuse of Power: The War Between Downing Street and the Media from Lloyd George to Callaghan* W H Allen 1978. An excellent account of the way in which government seeks to control the media's access to information drawing extensively on his own experiences. Ralph Negrine *Politics and the Mass Media in Britain* Routledge 1989 is a study of the role of the media at all levels of political activity down to the relations between pressure groups and the media.

**3544** Michael Cockerell, Peter Hennessy and David Walker *Sources Close to the Prime Minister: Inside the Hidden World of the News Manipulators* Macmillan 1984. A study of the press service of the Prime Minister and the government and an attack on the lobby system.

**3545** Colin Seymour-Ure *The Press, Politics and the Public: An Essay on the Role of the National Press in the British Political System* Methuen 1968. A study of the national press which pays particular attention to the lobby system. John Whale *Journalism and Government* Macmillan 1972 is now a dated textbook.

3546 James Margach *The Anatomy of Power: An Enquiry into the Personality of Leadership* W H Allen 1979. This is not only revealingly autobiographical about one of the most important political journalists of the post-war period but also a good insider history of the Westminster lobby system. He is very critical of the system of unattributable briefings that this involves. The first detailed account of the lobby system and the lobby correspondents published was Jeremy Tunstall *The Westminster Lobby Correspondents: A Sociological Study of National Political Journalism* Routledge and Kegan Paul 1970. See also Arthur Butler 'The History and Practice of Lobby Journalism' *Parliamentary Affairs* 13 1959 pp 54–60.

3547 *Committee of Privy Counsellors Appointed to Inquire into 'D' Notice Matters* Cmnd 3309, *Parliamentary Papers* xlviii 1966–67. 'D' notices are discretionary notices which the government use to ask for a ban on publication and are not mandatory. This particular inquiry arose from an article by Chapman Pincher on telephone-tapping (reproduced here) in the *Daily Express* which was published despite a 'D' notice. The committee, which was chaired by Lord Radcliffe, exonerated the newspaper and Pincher and the process reveals something of the flavour of Fleet Street and government/press relations in the 1960s. The government reposted with *'D' Notice System* Cmnd 3312, *Parliamentary Papers* lviii 1966 67 and continued to fulminate against Pincher for potential damage to the public interest. Peter Hedley *The 'D'-Notice Affair* Michael Joseph 1967 is an instant history of the episode. The history of the system is subjected to witty and perceptive analysis in Alasdair Palmer 'The History of the 'D'-Notice Committee' in Christopher Andrew and David Dilks (eds) *The Missing Dimension: Governments and Intelligence Communities in the Twentieth Century* Macmillan 1984 pp 227–49.

*(iii) Media Handling of Particular Issues*

3548 Jean Seaton and Ben Pimlott (eds) *The Media and British Politics* Avebury 1987. A collection of case studies. Peter Hennessy *What The Papers Never Said* Portcullis 1985 critically examines the quality of the coverage, or lack of it, given by the press on the announcement of the decision to build a British Atomic bomb in 1948, the 1949 Sterling crisis, the cabinet committee on coloured immigration 1950–1 and the development of the Chevaline missile 1967–80.

3549 G B Farnworth 'A Study of Consumer Journalism in British Newspapers up to 1978' Wales MEd Thesis 1983. A study of the development of the media as a consumer watchdog.

3550 Stephen J Chibnall *Law and Order News: An Analysis of Crime Reporting in the British Press* Tavistock 1977. A study of the press' handling of crime and public order, how journalists in this field obtain their information and the handling of them by the police. See also [3562].

3551 Paul Mosley *The British Economy as Represented by the Popular Press* Centre for the Study of Public Policy 105, University of Strathclyde 1982.

3552 A J Woodthorpe 'Education and the National Daily Press 1945–1975' Leeds PhD Thesis 1980.

3553 A C H Smith with Elizabeth Immerci and Trevor Blackwell *Paper Voices: The Popular Press and Social Change* Chatto and Windus 1975. A study of the reporting of elections in the *Daily Mirror* and the *Daily Express* 1945–65.

3554 First Report of the House of Commons Defence Committee *Handling of Press and Public Information During the Falklands Conflict* HC Paper 490, *Parliamentary Papers* 1981–82. The handling of the media and the media's treatment of the war is analysed in R Harris *Gotcha! The Media, the Government and the Falklands War* Faber 1983. The title of this derives from the headline in the *Sun* which greeted the sinking of the *General Belgrano*. Derrick Mercer, Geoff Mungham and Kevin Williams (eds) *The Fog of War: The Media on the Battlefield* Heinemann 1987. A survey sponsored by the Ministry of Defence which provides the fullest survey of government/media relations during the Falklands War. Valerie Adams *The Media and the Falklands Campaign* Macmillan 1986 is a valuable account which includes a chronology and bibliography. It however glosses the role of the Prime Minister's Press Office and the importance of the British media to perceptions of the war in Argentina. David E Morrison and Howard Tumber *Journalists at War: The Dynamics of News Reporting During the Falklands Conflict* Sage 1988 is a good critique of poor quality of the army's information services and of government hostility to the media during the conflict. Glasgow University Media Group *War and Peace News* Open University Press 1985 is a critical study of the media's coverage of the war. Differences in the handling of the war between the Scottish and English press are examined in William L Miller *Testing the Power of a Media Convention: A Comparison of Scots and English Media Treatment of the Falklands Campaign* Centre for the Study of Public Policy 17, University of Strathclyde 1983.

3555 Wayne Parsons *The Power of the Financial Press: Journalism and Economic Opinion in Britain and America* Edward Elgar 1989. A history of financial journalism and its influence since the early nineteenth century.

**3556** M Curtis 'The BBC's Treatment of Foreign Affairs' *BBC Quarterly* 9 1954 pp 150–5.

**3556A** Anna Karpf *Doctoring the Media: The Reporting of Health and Medicine* Routledge 1988. A good study of the relationship between the medical professions and the media.

**3557** Nicholas Jones *Strikes and the Media: Communication and Conflict* Blackwell 1986. Critical reflections by an industrial correspondent on the media's handling of industrial disputes in the 1980s. On the media's handling of such disputes see also David Morley 'Industrial Conflict and the Mass Media' *Sociological Review* 24 1976 pp 245–64 and J D H Downing 'Some Aspects of the Presentation of Industrial Relations and Race Relations in some Major British News Media' London PhD Thesis 1974–5. Glasgow University Media Group *Bad News* Routledge and Kegan Paul 1976 and *More Bad News* Routledge and Kegan Paul 1980 provide critical studies. David Jones, Julian Petley, Mick Power and Lesley Wood *Media Hits the Pits* Campaign for Press and Broadcasting Freedom 1985 alleges a collective and deliberate policy against the NUM during the 1984–5 miners' strike. Also on media treatment of the miners' strike see G Cumberbatch *et al Television News and the Miners' Strike* Broadcasting Research Unit, Aston University 1986.

**3558** Liz Curtis *Ireland: The Propaganda War: The Media and the 'Battle for Hearts and Minds'* Pluto 1984. A polemical accusation of unbalanced reporting of the situation in Northern Ireland. The handling of the situation in Northern Ireland and the ethics of portraying terrorism are discussed in P Schlessinger and Graham Murdoch *Televising Terrorism* Comedia 1986. See also R B Audley 'The Problems of Impartiality: A Case Study of BBC Policy and Practice, and Responses to its Reporting in Relation to the Troubles of Northern Ireland During 1971 and 1972' Queens MSocSc Thesis 1982.

**3559** Peter Bromhead 'Parliament and the Press' *Parliamentary Affairs* 16 1962–63 pp 279–92.

**3560** Peter Hennessy 'The Quality of Political Journalism' *Royal Society of Arts Journal* 135 1987 pp 926–41. An attack upon the quality of political journalism in Britain.

**3561** Richard Clutterbuck *The Media and Political Violence* Macmillan 1981. An examination of the handling by the media of industrial disputes, political demonstrations, the police, terrorism or the siege at the Iranian Embassy in 1980. It includes a number of case studies and an annotated bibliography.

**3562** Paul Hartmann and Christopher Temple Husbands *Racism and the Mass Media: A Study of the Role of the Mass Media in the Formation of White Beliefs and Attitudes in Britain* Davis- Poynter 1974. A more committed analysis is Phil Cohen and Carl Gardner *It Ain't Half Racist Mum: Fighting Racism in the Media* Comedia 1982. This is a collection of articles on racism and the handling of racism in the media. See also Paul Gordon and David Rosenberg *Daily Racism: The Press and Black People in Britain* Runnymede Trust 1989. C Jones *Race and the Media: Thirty Years Misunderstanding* Occasional Paper 1, Commission for Racial Equality 1982 is a brief history of attitudes to immigration and race relations in the media in the post-war period. Chris Searle 'Your Daily Dose: Racism and the *Sun*' *Race and Class* 29 1987 pp 55–71 is an analysis of racism in the newspapers owned by Rupert Murdoch. The tendency to associate street crime with blacks which developed in the 1970s and 1980s is discussed in Brian Gearing 'The Convergence of Race and Crime News' *Sage Race Relations Abstracts* 10 1985 pp 16–32. He however concentrates too much on institutional racism and fails to give sufficient weight to the context of rising crime figures. See also [3557].

**3563** J Halloran, P Elliott and Graham Murdoch *Demonstrations and Communication: A Case Study* Penguin 1970. This argues that the media coverage of the anti-Vietnam war demonstration in Grosvenor Square, London on 27th October 1968 was biased by a concentration on a tiny violent minority. H Tumber *Television and the Riots: A Report* British Film Institute 1982 is a report on the coverage of the inner city riots in the summer of 1981. Nancy Murray 'Reporting the "Riots"' *Sage Race Relations Abstracts* 11 1986 pp 29–34 is an analysis of the media's handling of the 1985 inner city riots.

**3564** Douglas Keay *Royal Pursuit: The Palace, The Press and the People* Severn House 1983. An examination of the relations between the Royal Family and the media.

**3565** Stanley Cohen and Jack Young *The Manufacture of News: Deviance, Social Problems and the Mass Media* Constable 1973. An examination of the media's treatment of social problems and social issues.

**3566** Guillaume Parmentier 'The British Press and the Suez Crisis' *Historical Journal* 23 1980 pp 399–414. An examination of the handling of the Suez crisis. This provoked the response from Ralph Negrine 'The Press and the Suez Crisis: A Myth Re- Examined' *Historical Journal* 25 1982 pp 975–83. See also H Evans 'The Suez Crisis: A Study in Press Performance' Durham MA Thesis 1966. Thomas Matthews *The Sugar Pill: An Essay on Newspapers* Gollancz 1957 is an examination of how the *Daily Mirror* and the *Manchester Guardian* used information for their very different readerships during their common anti-Suez stance.

## (iv) The Press

**3567** *Catalogue of the Newspaper Library* 8v, British Library 1975. The newspaper section of the British Library has the most extensive collection of British newspapers in the world.

**3568** Anthony Smith (ed) *The British Press Since the War* David and Charles 1974. A compendium of documents.

**3569** David Linton and Ray Boston (eds) *The Newspaper Press in Britain: An Annotated Bibliography* Mansell 1987. A poorly organized and indexed bibliography with annotations of variable quality. Its alphabetical arrangement (by author) does not make it easier to use. It does however cover the literature on the national and local, but not the specialist, press in Britain. It also features a chronology. See also Brian Lake *British Newspapers: A History and Guide for Collectors* Sheppard Press 1984 and Frank Atkinson *The English Newspaper Since 1900* Library Association 1960.

**3570** *Journal of Newspaper and Periodical History* 1985–. This regularly carries a feature on sources for newspaper and periodical history and an annual review of work in the field.

**3571** *Who's Who in the Press: A Biographical Guide to British Journalism* Carrick Publishing 1986. A collection of alphabetically arranged potted biographies.

**3572** Stephen Koss *The Rise and Fall of the Political Press in Britain Vol 2: The Twentieth Century* Hamilton 1984. An authoritative analysis of the political influence of the press. Although his narrative goes up to the 1980s it is however rather limited in its coverage of the post-war period and deals almost exclusively with the national press. Francis Williams *Dangerous Estate: The Anatomy of Newspapers* Longmans 1957 is an excellent survey of post-war developments.

**3573** Cyril Bainbridge (ed) *One Hundred Years of Journalism: Social Aspects of the Press* Macmillan 1984. A celebration of the foundation of the National Association of Journalists (chartered as the Institute of Journalists in 1890). Part I appraises the role of the press in modern society and part II is a history of the Institute of Journalists. Another centenary compilation is Andrew Ewart and Vernon Leonard (eds) *100 Years of Fleet Street: As Seen Through the Eyes of the Press Club* Brent Wright Associates 1982. This contains brief contributions on the history of the Press Club, cartoons, war correspondents, press photographs, City news, foreign correspondents and newspapers that have disappeared. See also Denys Ainsworth *A Hundred Years of Us* Manchester Press Club 1970.

**3574** Harry Henry (ed) *Behind the Headline: The Business of the British Press* Associated Business Press 1978. A collection of essays on the finance and technology of the press, including the local and some types of specialized press. On the finance of the national press see also 'Balance Sheet of the Press' *Planning* 21 1955 pp 141–56.

**3575** Simon Jenkins *Newspapers: The Power and the Money* Faber 1979. A historically flavoured account of the nature of newspaper control and the changing character of their proprietors. The advent of new technology and the reaction of the industry is also discussed. His *Market for Glory: Fleet Street Ownership in the Twentieth Century* Faber 1986 is the most thorough analysis of the changing pattern of ownership of the national press in the twentieth century. Piers Brandon *The Life and Death of the Press Barons* Secker and Warburg 1982 is a selective guide to British and American newspaper proprietors from 1830 to the rise of Rupert Murdoch. See also Graham Murdoch and Peter Golding 'The Structure, Ownership and Control of the Press 1914–76' in George Boyle, James Curran and Pauline Wingate (eds) *Newspaper History from the Seventeenth Century to the Present Day* Constable 1978 pp 130–50 and Adriano Bruttini *La Stampa inglese: Monopoli e fusioni 1890–1972* Guanda, Parma 1973. William Ewert Berry, Viscount Camrose *British Newspapers and Their Controllers* Cassell 1947 reviews the ownership and control of every morning, evening and Sunday newspaper then published (including the local press, the news agencies, the press in the Channel Islands and the Isle of Man) and also the ownership of some periodicals. See also 'Ownership of the Press' *Planning* 21 1955 pp 209–24.

**3576** Graham Cleverley *The Fleet Street Disaster: British National Newspapers as a Case Study in Mismanagement* Constable 1976. A critical study of the state of the industry in 1973.

**3577** Tom Bairstow *Fourth-Rate Estate – An Anatomy of Fleet Street* Comedia 1985. A highly critical analysis of the quality of the national press in Britain. James Curran (ed) *The British Press: A Manifesto* Macmillan 1978 is an analysis of Right-Wing bias in the press and the effect of advertising pressure on editorial policy from a committed Left-Wing stance.

**3578** James Edward Gerald *The British Press Under Government Economic Controls* University of Minnesota Press, Minneapolis, Minnesota 1956. A well documented study which argues that the controls on newsprint and advertising 1939–55 had a paradoxically liberating effect on Fleet Street, enabling it to ignore the usual commercial pressures and concentrate on news-gathering.

**3579** W D Bernetson *The Economics of Newspapers and News Agencies* Scottish Academic Press 1973. An essay on the great pruning of the British press in the late 1950s and early 1960s which blames the broadcasters for most of the closures.

**3580** D G H Rowlands 'The Development of the Thomson Foundation Editorial Study Centre 1963–1979' Wales MEd Thesis 1983. The history of a new departure in journalist training until it left Cardiff for London in 1979 and slightly reduced the scale of its activities.

**3581** Cynric Mytton-Davies *Journalist Alone: The Story of the Freelance and the Freelance Section of the Institute of Journalists* Institute of Journalists 1968.

**3582** Charles Vere Wintour *Pressures on the Press: An Editor Looks at Fleet Street* Deutsch 1972. A good analysis of the contemporary situation by the then editor of the *Evening Standard*. It concentrates on the pressures on the press, from the use of D-notices to the defamation laws. A survey by another eminent editor which instead concentrates on the editor's role is Sir Linton Andrews *Problems of an Editor: A Study in Newspaper Trends* Oxford University Press 1962. Another survey of this period which concentrates more on the press as an industry is *National Newspaper Industry: A Survey Conducted for the Federation by the Labour Research Department* Printing and Kindred Trades Federation 1972.

**3583** D Campbell *The British Press: A Look Ahead* Commonwealth Press Union 1978. Thirty-five brief but illuminating contributions on the state of the national and local press in the 1970s. It includes interviews and examples of early enthusiasm for electronic media. The impact of new technology on Fleet Street 1975–9 is assessed in Roderick Martin *New Technology and Industrial Relations in Fleet Street* Clarendon 1981. The passage of Michael Foot's Closed Shop Bill in 1976 and its implications for editorial freedom are critically examined in Nora Beloff *Freedom Under Foot* Temple Smith 1976.

**3584** Henry Porter *Lies, Damned Lies – And Some Exclusives* Chatto and Windus 1984. An arraignment of Fleet Street in the election year 1983, both for errors and falsehoods and for Right-Wing bias. It includes a useful appendix on the people who run Fleet Street. He concludes that the Press Council is inadequate to deal with these powerful men. A similar study is M Hollingsworth *The Press and Political Dissent: A Question of Censorship* Pluto 1986.

**3585** Linda Malvern *The End of the Street* Methuen 1986. An account of the dramatic move of Rupert Murdoch's News International from Fleet Street to Wapping and of the impact of new technology on the press.

**3586** *Royal Commission on the Press 1947–1949* Cmnd 7700, *Parliamentary Papers* xx 1948–49. This Royal Commission, chaired by W D Ross, led to the establishment of the Press Council. This watchdog over the conduct of the press was established in 1954 as the General Council of the Press (the name was changed in 1963). Its annual report, *The Press and the People* 1954–, contains facts and figures, details of cases and articles on developments in the industry as well as press ethics. Herman Philip Levy *The Press Council: History, Procedures and Cases* Macmillan 1967 is a detailed history. See also George McIntosh Murray *The Press and the Public: The Story of the British Press Council* Feffer and Simons 1972. Geoffrey Robertson *People Against the Press: An Inquiry into the Press Council* Quartet 1983 is an examination of the workings of the Council and its failings as a brake on the excesses of journalists. Noel Strange Paul (ed) *Principles for the Press: A Digest of Press Council Decisions 1953–1984* Press Council 1985 is a compilation under 108 headings of decisions on cases heard by the Council. See also [3663].

**3587** *Royal Commission on the Press: Report* Cmnd 1811, *Parliamentary Papers* xxi 1961–62. This Royal Commission, chaired by Lord Shawcross, led to the introduction of lay members of the Press Council.

**3588** *Royal Commission on the Press: Report* Cmnd 6433, *Parliamentary Papers* xli 1975–76 and Cmnd 6810, *Parliamentary Papers* xl 1976–77. The reports of this Royal Commission, chaired by Oliver McGregor, reflect on the poor financial state of the press in the 1970s and the need to introduce new technology and to reduce manpower to save costs. The Royal Commission also stimulated a very useful series of research reports on subjects such as industrial relations in the press, public attitudes to the press and the concentration of ownership.

**3589** Harry Henry *The Dynamics of the British Press 1961–1984: Patterns of Circulations and Cover Prices* Advertising Association 1986. A collection of tables, charts and commentaries. The circulations of the national morning and London evening newspapers are surveyed in John Cunningham 'National Daily Newspapers and Their Circulations in the UK 1908–1978' *Journal of Advertising History* 4 1981 pp 16–18.

**3590** J W Hobson and Harry Henry (eds) *Hulton Readership Survey* Hulton Press 1947–55. An annual guide for advertisers to the readership profiles of newspapers by region, sex, age and social class. Charles Madge and Tom Harrisson (eds) *The Press and its Readers* Art and Technics 1949 is a Mass Observation report. Another useful, if briefer survey of readership profiles is W D McCelland *Readership Profiles of Mass Media* Institute of Practitioners in Advertising 1963.

**3591** Peter A Clark *Sixteen Million Readers: Evening Newspapers in the UK* Holt, Rinehart and Watson 1981. A useful survey and statistical guide. It includes special chapters on London and Glasgow.

**3592** Stanley Harrison *Poor Men's Guardians: A Survey of the Struggle for a Democratic Newspaper Press 1963–1973* Lawrence and Wishart 1974. A study of the Left-Wing press. Harrison has clear preferences in this area and is not very good on the Trotskyite press.

**3593** Jonathon Green *Days in the Life: Voices from the English Underground 1961–1971* Heinemann 1988. A study of the underground press. See also Nigel Fountain *Underground London: The Alternative Press in London 1968–1974* Routledge 1988. One of the most famous of these alternative newspapers was *Oz*. Tony Palmer *The Trials of Oz* Blond and Briggs 1971 is an account of the proceedings against *Oz* and a commentary on the spirit of 1968. John Leonard Noyce (ed) *The Directory of British Alternative Periodicals 1965–1974* 4th ed, Harvester 1979 provides a detailed, alphabetically arranged guide to over 1,200 titles. See also Ruth Sandys *The Underground and Alternative Press in Britain During 1973: A Bibliographical Guide: A Title and Chronological Index to the Underground and Alternative Microform Collection* Harvester 1975. This has since been updated.

**3594** Alvin Sullivan (ed) *British Literary Magazines Vol 4: The Modern Age 1914–1984* Greenwood 1986.

**3595** Tony Grace 'The Trade Union Press in Britain' *Media, Culture and Society* 7 1985 pp 233–56. A useful study.

**3596** David Doughan and Denise Sanchez *Feminist Periodicals 1855–1984: An Annotated Critical Bibliography of British, Irish, Commonwealth and International Titles* Harvester 1988. A very useful guide which annotates 920 items. See also Sarah Oerton 'The Feminist Press in Britain Since 1970' Swansea MA Thesis 1981.

**3597** Cynthia L White *The Women's Periodical Press in Britain 1946–76* HMSO 1977. One of the research papers for the McGregor Royal Commission. See also her *Women's Magazines 1693–1968* Michael Joseph 1970.

**3598** Lewis Chester and Jonathan Felby *The Fall of the House of Beaverbrook* Deutsch 1979. An account of the failing of the Beaverbrook empire 1969–79. It is indispensable for anyone wishing to consult the *Daily Ex-press, Sunday Express* or *Evening Standard* in this period.

**3599** Susan Goldenberg *The Thomson Empire* Methuen 1984. An analysis of the growth of the Canadian based International Thomson Organisation.

**3600** Guy Schofield *The Men that Carry the News: A History of United Newspapers Limited* Cranford Press 1976. This company mainly controlled provincial newspapers in the North and major periodicals such as *Punch*.

**3601** Robert Allen *Voice of Britain: The Inside Story of the Daily Express* Stephens 1983. A popular history from 1900 to the 1980s. See also Trevor Blackwell 'A Study of the Popular Press: Readings in the *Daily Mirror* and the *Daily Express* 1945–1969' Birmingham PhD Thesis 1971–2.

**3602** Rajani Palme Dutt *The Rise and Fall of the Daily Herald* Labour Monthly/Daily Worker 1964. A short account of the history of the Labour movement's journal. See also Huw Richards 'The *Daily Herald* 1912–64' *History Today* 31 1981 pp 12–6.

**3603** Maurice Edelman *The Mirror: A Political History* Hamilton 1966. A somewhat superficial official history. Hugh Cudlipp *Publish and be Damned! The Astonishing Story of the Daily Mirror* Dakers 1953 is a rather autobiographical celebration of fifty years of this popular newspaper. See also [3601].

**3604** Edward Frederick Lawson, Lord Burnham *The Story of the Daily Telegraph* Cassell 1955. A centenary history. See also E F Lawson *Peterborough Court: The Story of the Daily Telegraph* Cassell 1955.

**3605** William Rust *The Story of the Daily Worker* People's Press Printing Society 1949. This history of the Communist Party daily, which was founded in 1930, was completed after Rust's death by Allan Hutt. The *Daily Worker* became the *Morning Star* in 1966.

**3606** David Kynaston *The Financial Times: A Centenary History* Viking 1988. A good history, particularly of its growth after its merger with *Financial News* in 1945.

**3607** David Ayerst *Guardian: Biography of a Newspaper* Collins 1971. A good newspaper history which however has only limited coverage of the post-war years. It ends with an account of the newspaper's critical stance over the Suez Crisis.

**3608** Rajani Palme Dutt 'Three Decades' *Labour Monthly* 33 1951 pp 289–300. A survey of the first thirty years of this Communist Party periodical.

**3609** *Lloyds List 250th Anniversary Special Supplement* Lloyds of London Press 1984. An illustrated history and survey of the newspaper which specializes in news of the insurance and shipbroking world.

**3610** George Glenton and William Pattinson *The Last Chronicle of Bouverie Street* Allen and Unwin 1963. A study of the demise of the *News Chronicle* and its London evening sister the *Star* which captures the sadness and bitterness felt at the merger of the *News Chronicle* with the *Daily Mail* and the *Star* with the *Evening News*. Edward Martell and Ewan Butler *The Murder of the News Chronicle and the Star* Johnson 1960 is an account in the immediate aftermath of the demise of these newspapers. Their view that they were 'killed by trade union restrictive practices' is however too simple to explain such a long drawn out and complex marketing failure.

**3611** Stafford Somerfield *Banner Headlines* Scan Books 1979. A history of the *News of the World* in the context of the author's ten years as its editor.

**3612** Edward Solomon Hyams *The New Statesman: The History of the First Fifty Years 1913–1963* Longmans 1963. A useful history of the radical weekly journal.

**3613** Tom Hopkinson (ed) *Picture Post 1938–50* Penguin 1970. A collection of edited extracts from this very successful and influential magazine which ceased publicaton in 1957. Also of use is Robert Kee (ed) *The Picture Post Album* Barrie and Jenkins 1989.

**3614** Patrick Marnham *The Private Eye Story: The First Twenty-One Years* Deutsch/Private Eye 1982. A good history of the satirical magazine. See also Richard Ingrams (ed) *The Life and Times of Private Eye 1961–1971* Penguin 1971. Ingrams was *Private Eye's* founding editor.

**3615** R G G Price *A History of Punch* Collins 1957. This history is quite informative on the post-war years and goes up to the editorship of Malcolm Muggeridge in the 1950s.

**3616** Peter Allen '*Socialist Worker* – Paper with a Purpose' *Media, Culture and Society* 7 1985 pp 205–32. A study of the weekly newspaper of the Socialist Worker Party.

**3616A** Reginald Pound *The Strand Magazine 1891–1950* Heinemann 1966.

**3617** Roslyn Grose *The Sun-Sensation: Behind the Scenes of Britain's Bestselling Newspaper* Angus Press 1989. A breathlessly uncritical account of the newspaper Rupert Murdoch took over in the 1960s and made into Britain's bestselling tabloid.

**3618** Sir Harold Hobson, Philip Knightley and Leonard Russell *The Pearl of Days: An Intimate Memoir of the Sunday Times* Hamilton 1972. A massive and authoritative history.

**3619** *The History of the Times Vol 4: The 150th Anniversary and Beyond 1921–1948* Macmillan 1952. The official history is continued by Iverach McDonald *Vol 5: Struggles in War and Peace 1939–1966* Macmillan 1984. This includes an appendix by E C Hodgkin which takes the story up to 1982. Philip Howard *We Thundered Out: 200 Years of The Times 1785–1985* Times Books 1985 is a celebratory general history. See also Oliver Woods and James Bishop *The Story of the Times: Bicentenary Edition* revised ed, Michael Joseph 1985. On the 1978–9 management lock-out see [4674].

**3620** Brian MacArthur *Eddie Shah, Today and the Newspaper Revolution* David and Charles 1988. An account of Shah's efforts to break into the national press with the launch of *Today* in 1986 by the first editor of this newspaper. Shah was unsuccessful and *Today* is now part of Rupert Murdoch's collection of titles. Its launch did however hasten the introduction of new technology and working practices to the newspaper industry and its move from its traditional home in Fleet Street to the East End. See also David Goodhart and Patrick Wintour *Eddie Shah and the Newspaper Revolution* Coronet 1986.

**3621** Douglas Hill (ed) *Tribune 40: The First Forty Years of a Socialist Newspaper* Quartet 1977. A celebratory symposium.

**3622** Janice Winship *Femininity and Women's Magazines: A Case Study of Women's Own: 'First in Britain for Women'* Open University Press 1983.

**3623** Jonathan Fenby *The International News Services* Schocken Books 1986. A survey of the four big international news agencies. Another critical and detailed study of these agencies is Oliver Boyd-Barrett *The International News Agencies* Constable 1980. John Ralph Lawrenceson and Lionel Porter *The Price of Truth: The Story of the Reuters Millions* Mainstream 1985 is the history of the Reuters news agency up to its 1984 stock market flotation. George Scott *Reporter Anonymous: The Story of the Press Association* Hutchinson 1968 is an official centenary history of the Press Association. James Maurice Scott *Extel 100: Centenary History of the Exchange Telegraph* Benn 1972 is the history of another press agency. Kelly McParland 'Gemini and the Commonwealth' *Round Table* 300 1986 pp 395–402 surveys the history of the Gemini news agency, founded in 1967, which is especially active in Commonwealth countries.

**3624** H R P Boorman *Your Family Newspaper* Kent Messenger 1968. A jubilee history of the Home and Southern Counties Newspaper Proprietors Federation and their local titles.

**3625** Geoffrey Nulty (ed) *Guardian Country: Being the First 125 Years of Cheshire County Newspapers* Cheshire County Newspapers 1978.

**3626** Gordon Sewell *Echoes of a Century: The Centenary History of Southern Newspapers Ltd 1864–1964* Southern Newspapers 1964. This group had titles in various South Coast towns.

**3627** Charles Alpin (general editor) *Bibliography of British Newspapers*. This will eventually constitute an exhaustive county-by-county listing of titles, places of publication, changes of title and other details. The volumes published so far are Robin K Bluhm (ed) *Wiltshire County* Library Association 1975, Winifrid F Bergess (ed) *Kent County* British Library 1982, Frank W D Manders (ed) *Durham and Northumberland County* British Library 1982, Anne Mellors and Jean Radford (eds) *Derbyshire County* British Library 1986 and Michael Brook (ed) *Nottinghamshire County* British Library 1986.

**3628** David Murphy *The Silent Watchdog: The Press in Local Politics* Constable 1976. Most studies of the local press are celebratory histories of individual titles. The political role and influence of the local press has, with a few honourable exceptions such as this, yet to be subjected to the same scrutiny as that of the national press. However see A J Beith 'The Press and English Local Government' Oxford BLitt Thesis 1968–9. See also Ian Jackson *The Provincial Press and the Community* Manchester University Press 1971. This examines the historical background, content, cultural and political attitudes, ownership and readership profiles of the local press.

**3629** Harvey Cox and David Morgan *City Politics and the Press: Journalists and the Governing of Merseyside* Cambridge University Press 1973. A study more of Merseyside's local press than of its political content and influence, focusing on the 1960s.

**3630** Crispin Aubrey, Charles Landry and David Morley *Here is the Other News: Challenges to the Local Commercial Press* Minority Press Group 1980. This traces the fortunes of community and local radical newspapers and broadsheets in Britain in the 1970s. A similar study, focusing particularly on the five year life of the Liverpool Free Press, is Brian Whitaker *News Ltd: Why you can't read all about it* Minority Press Group 1981.

**3631** James Morgan 'A Free for all Future' *Journalism Studies Review* 7 1982 pp 8–10. One of the most marked trends in the local press in recent years has been the growth of free newspapers. This is surveyed in the context of Northampton in this article.

**3632** A W Jones *The Bedfordshire Times 1845–1969* Bedford County Press 1969. The history of this weekly provincial. Other histories of local newspapers are H R G Whates *The Birmingham Post 1857–1957: A Centenary Retrospect* Birmingham Post and Mail 1957, Peter Drake 'The Town Crier: Birmingham's Labour Weekly 1919–1951' in Anthony Wright and Richard Shackleton (eds) *Worlds of Labour: Essays in Birmingham Labour History* Department of Extramural Studies, University of Birmingham 1983 pp 103–26, Ernest Averis (ed) *Hold the Front Page* Bristol United Press 1984 (a short history of the *Bristol Evening Post*, established in 1932, which also traces the complex fortunes of Bristol's other morning and evening newspapers), *Cambridge Evening News: Inside Story* Cambridge Evening News 1971, Herbert Hughes *Chronicle of Chester: The 200 Years 1775–1975* Macdonald and Janes 1975 (a good history of the weekly *Chester Chronicle*), C G Smith *The Reporter 1856–1966* Gravesend Reporter 1966, G M Denison *The Evening Post: The Story of a Newspaper and a Family* T Bailey Forman 1978 (the centenary history of the independently owned Nottingham *Evening Post*, formerly in association with the morning *Nottingham Guardian*), John Christie-Miller (ed) *The Development of Stockport 1922–1972 and the History of the Stockport Advertiser* Stockport Advertiser 1972, H R P Boorman and Eric Maskell *Tonbridge Free Press Centenary* Tonbridge Free Press 1969, James Mildren *125 Years with the Western Morning News* Bossiney Books 1985 (the history of this Plymouth daily is also examined in C Gill 'The Western Morning News 1860–1985' *Devonshire Association Report and Transactions* 117 1985 pp 195–226) and Ray Seaton *Malcolm Graham: Sixty Years in the News* Wolverhampton Express and Star 1983 (a tribute to the chairman of the group in the form of a history of these two newspapers and of the development of the Midlands News Association).

*(v) Biographies of Journalists, Editors and Proprietors*

**3633** *Who's Who in the Press: A Biographical Guide to British Journalism* Carrick Publishing 1984. A second edition was published in 1986.

**3634** Sir Linton Andrews and H A Taylor *Lords and Laborers of the Press: Men Who Fashioned the Modern British Newspaper* Southern Illinois University Press, Carbondale, Illinois 1970. A collection of biographical studies of, among others, Lord Beaverbrook, Michael Cummings, Lord Thomson, Cecil King and Hugh Cudlipp.

**3635** Sir Linton Andrews *Linton Andrews: The Auto-biography of a Journalist* Benn 1964. Andrews was the editor of the *Yorkshire Post* and the *Leeds Mercury*.

**3636** For the Astor family as newspaper proprietors see [791].

**3637** Noel Barber *The Natives Were Friendly: An Autobiography* 2nd ed, Collins 1985. The autobiography of a widely travelled foreign correspondent who has spent much of his career in the Far East.

**3638** Donald Harvey McLachlan *In the Chair: Bar-rington-Ward of the Times 1927–48* Weidenfeld and Nicolson 1971. An admirable biography of the editor of *The Times* 1941–8 based on Barrington-Ward's diaries.

**3639** Vernon Bartlett *I Know What I Liked* Chatto and Windus 1974.

**3640** A J P Taylor *Beaverbrook* Hamilton 1972. An ebullient if not entirely error-free biography of the great press baron and Tory maverick. Logan Gourley (ed) *The Beaverbrook I Knew* Quartet 1984 collects thirty-three widely differing memoirs of Beaverbrook and a good selection of cartoons. Tom Driberg *Beaverbrook: A Study in Power and Frustration* Weidenfeld and Nicolson 1956 is a close-up and far from flattering portrait. Another critical study by another former Beaverbrook journalist is Alan Wood *The True History of Lord Beaverbrook* Heinemann 1965. The narrative of this ends in 1952 but it does have a brief epilogue. See also Peter Dunsmore Howard *Beaverbrook: A Study of Max the Unknown* Hutchinson 1964. On Beaverbrook's last years see the memoir by his secretary, Colin M Vines *A Little Nut-Brown Man: My Three Years with Lord Beaverbrook* Frewin 1968. Adrian Smith 'Low and Lord Beaverbrook: Cartoonist and Proprietor' *Encounter* 65 1985 pp 7–24 examines his business relationship with the great cartoonist 1919–63. On Beaverbrook's political friendship with Churchill see [803].

**3641** James Cameron *Point of Departure: Experiment in Biography* Barker 1967. The memoirs of a foreign correspondent up to his coverage of the Korean War.

**3642** Christopher Brookes *His Own Man: The Life of Neville Cardus* Methuen 1985. The biography of a celebrated cricket and music correspondent. See also John Twigg 'Neville Cardus: A Review Essay' *British Journal of Sports History* 3 1986 pp 234–48. There are also three volumes of autobiography, *Autobiography* Collins 1947, *Second Innings* Collins 1950 and *Full Score* Cassell 1970.

**3643** Arthur Christiansen *Headlines All My Life* Heinemann 1961. The memoirs of one of the most

successful of editors. He was on Beaverbrook's *Daily Express* 1933–57.

**3644** Anita Leslie *Cousin Randolph: The Life of Randolph Churchill* Hutchinson 1985. A sympathetic biography. Randolph Churchill wrote for both the *Daily Telegraph* and the *Evening Standard*. See also B Roberts *Randolph: A Study of Churchill's Son* Hamilton 1984. Kelf Halle (ed) *Randolph Churchill: The Young Pretender* Heinemann 1974 is a collection of tribute essays.

**3645** Winston S Churchill *Memories and Adventures* Weidenfeld and Nicolson 1989. This memoir is mostly about his career as a foreign correspondent before he entered parliament in 1970. It contains useful reflections on his father Randolph and his grandfather Winston.

**3646** For William Clark see [296].

**3647** Robert Clough *A Public Eye* Hamilton 1981. The discursive memoirs of a leading Newcastle journalist and editor.

**3648** Douglas J Cock *Every Other Inch a Methodist* Epworth 1987. Recollections of a staff reporter on the *Methodist Recorder*.

**3649** Claud Cockburn *Cockburn Sums Up: An Autobiography* Quartet 1981. Cockburn was a considerable journalist and a regular columnist on *Punch*. He also edited the Left-Wing gossip sheet *The Week* 1936–46.

**3650** Robert Connor *Cassandra: Reflections in a Mirror* Cassell 1969. A filial tribute to Sir William Connor, the *Daily Mirror* polemicist who dubbed himself Cassandra.

**3651** Sir Colin Coote *Editorial: The Memoirs of Colin R Coote* Eyre and Spottiswoode 1965. Coote was with *The Times* before moving to the *Daily Telegraph* where he became managing editor.

**3652** Hugh Cudlipp *At Your Peril* Weidenfeld and Nicolson 1962. An autobiographical survey of Fleet Street by this most successful of tabloid journalists. A further volume of memoirs charting his years at the top of the Mirror Group of newspapers is his *Walking on the Water* The Bodley Head 1976. Both of these volumes are also useful for those interested in the history of the Labour Party and its links with the world of journalism. See also [3603].

**3653** Nicholas Davenport *Memoirs of a City Radical* Weidenfeld and Nicolson 1974. Reflections on financial journalism and policy by a close friend of Hugh Dalton.

**3654** Stanley Devon *'Glorious': The Life Story of Stanley Devon* Harrap 1957. An autobiography of the

Kemsley Group's chief photographer illustrated by some of his work.

**3655** Robert Edwards *Goodbye Fleet Street* Cape 1988. Edwards twice edited the *Daily Express* as well as stints editing the *People* and the *Sunday Mirror*. He comments usefully on both Beaverbrook and Maxwell and reflects on the major changes in the industry, and not least in popular journalism, during his career.

**3656** Paul Einzig *In the Centre of Things: The Auto-biography of Paul Einzig* Hutchinson 1960. Einzig was the foreign editor of *Financial News* 1922–45. These memoirs mostly deal with the inter-war period but also usefully reflect on the merger of the *Financial News* with the *Financial Times* in 1945.

**3657** Harold Evans *Good Times, Bad Times* Weiden-feld and Nicolson 1983. Although this opens with an account with his time on the *Northern Echo* 1961–6 it largely deals with his eventful year as editor of *The Times* 1981–2.

**3658** Frank Giles *Sunday Times* Murray 1986. A good autobiography. Giles was the foreign editor of the *Sunday Times* and eventually rose to be editor 1981–3.

**3659** For Malcolm Graham see [3632].

**3660** For Joe Haines see [715] and [3684].

**3661** Dennis Hamilton *Editor in Chief: Fleet Street Memoirs* Hamilton 1989. These trace his career in the press in which he rose from being the assistant to Lord Kemsley shortly after the end of the war to the editorship in chief of *The Times* and the *Sunday Times* in the 1980s.

**3662** Bert Hardy *My Life* Gordon Fraser 1985. An autobiography, mainly in the context of his time on *Picture Post*.

**3663** H W Harris *Life So Far* Cape 1954. Harris was editor of the *Spectator* 1932–43. This autobiography is mainly useful for his account of [3586].

**3664** Louis Heren *Growing Up On The Times* Hamil-ton 1978. Heren joined *The Times* in 1936 and eventually rose to be deputy editor. His memoirs are continued by his *Memories of Times Past* Hamilton 1988 which is a mixture of memoirs and *The Times* history.

**3665** Alistair Hetherington *Guardian Years* Chatto and Windus 1981. Hetherington was editor of *The Guardian* 1956–75 during which time it changed its name (from the *Manchester Guardian* in 1959) and moved to London (in 1961).

**3666** Sir Tom Hopkinson *Of This Our Time: A Jour-nalist's Story 1905–1950* Hutchinson 1982. This auto-biography culminates with his period as editor of *Picture Post* 1940–50 until his resignation over a dispute with the proprietor. His autobiography is continued by *Under the Tropic* Hutchinson 1984.

**3667** Anthony Howard 'Historians at Work' *Contem-porary Record* 1/1 1987 pp 31–4. Reflections on his career in which he has been editor of the *New Statesman* 1972–81 and *The Listener* 1979–81 and deputy editor of *The Observer*.

**3668** Derek Hudson *Writing Between the Lines: An Autobiography* High Hill Books 1965. Reminiscences of his journalistic career.

**3669** E G W Hulton *Conflicts* Neville Spearman 1966. The memoirs of a magazine publisher who sold out to Odhams in 1959. His most famous conflict was with Tom Hopkinson in 1950 which led to the latter's resig-nation from *Picture Post*.

**3670** Brian Inglis *Downstart* Chatto and Windus 1989. An autobiography covering a varied career which in-cluded a spell as editor of *The Spectator*.

**3671** Derek Jameson *Touched by Angels* Ebury Press 1988. His journalist's career, which began in 1944, culminated in stints as managing editor of the *Daily Mirror* 1976–7, editor of the *Daily Express* 1977–9, editor in chief of the *Star* 1978–80 and editor of the *News of the World* 1981–4.

**3672** Frank Johnson *Out of Order* Robson 1982. Witty memoirs and sketches drawn from his years as the parliamentary sketch writer for the *Daily Telegraph* 1972–82.

**3673** For Cecil King see [673].

**3674** Sir Larry Lamb *Sunrise* Macmillan 1989. The autobiography of the man who made *The Sun* Britain's biggest selling paper during his editorships 1969–72 and 1975–81. Lamb also edited the *Daily Express* 1983–6.

**3675** Richard Boston *Osbert* Collins 1989. A good biography of the *Daily Express's* pocket cartoonist, Os-bert Lancaster. There are two volumes of autobiography; Osbert Lancaster *All Done from Memory* Murray 1963 and Osbert Lancaster *With an Eye to the Future* Murray 1967.

**3676** David F Hubback *No Ordinary Press Baron: A Life of Walter Layton* Weidenfeld and Nicolson 1985. Layton was Chairman of *The Economist*, the *News Chronicle* and the *Star* and a director of Reuters, the *Daily News* and Tyne Tees Television.

**3676A** Bernard Levin *Enthusiasms* Cape 1983. The autobiography of *The Times* columnist.

**3677** Sir David Low *Low's Autobiography* Michael Joseph 1956. The autobiography of an outstanding New Zealand cartoonist first introduced to British readers in the *Star* in 1919. He was allowed remarkable latitude by Beaverbrook whilst at the *Evening Standard* 1927–50. For his working relationship with Beaverbrook see [3640]. He later worked on the *Daily Herald* and the *Guardian*.

**3678** René MacColl *Deadline and Dateline* Oldbourne 1955. The autobiography of a long serving foreign correspondent with the *Daily Express*, and earlier with the *Daily Telegraph*.

**3679** Iverach MacDonald *A Man of The Times: Talks and Travels in a Disrupted World* Hamilton 1976. Memoirs of his period on *The Times* which he joined in 1932 and from which he retired as associate editor in 1973.

**3680** Norris McWhirter *Ross: The Story of a Shared Life* Churchill 1976. The McWhirter twins were sports journalists, publishers and, from 1955, the editors of *The Guinness Book of Records*. They were also both active in the Right-Wing pressure group the Freedom Association. Ross McWhirter was murdered by the IRA in 1975.

**3681** James Margach *The Abuse of Power* W H Allen 1978. A revealing autobiography by the doyen of political journalists. It also contains pen portraits of other significant political journalists. See also [3546].

**3682** C H Rolph *Kingsley: The Life, Letters and Diaries of Kingsley Martin* Gollancz 1973. A very readable biography of the editor of the *New Statesman* 1931–60. Kingsley Martin *Portrait and Self-Portrait* Barrie and Jenkins 1969 is the final posthumously published volume of Martin's memoirs and the only one which covers the post-war years.

**3683** For Keith Mason see [4511].

**3684** Joe Haines *Maxwell: The Definitive Biography* Macdonald 1988. This is the nearest to an official biography of the publisher, proprietor of the Mirror Group (since 1984) and erstwhile Labour MP, and presents a deferential view of its subject. Two other biographies that were published in 1988 were subsequently withdrawn for legal reasons.

**3685** Noel Monks *Eyewitness* Muller 1956. The autobiography of a foreign correspondent for the *Daily Express* and *Daily Mail*.

**3686** C G P Moore, Earl of Drogheda *Double Harness: Memoirs* Weidenfeld and Nicolson 1978. Drogheda was managing director of the *Financial Times* 1945–70 and its chairman 1971–5. He was chairman of the Newspaper Publishers Association 1968–70.

**3687** Alan Moorhead *A Late Education: Episodes in a Life* Hamilton 1970. Memoirs of a leading war correspondent for the *Daily Express*.

**3688** Nicolas Barber *Stanley Morison* Macmillan 1972. The first major biography of Morison who for thirty years, especially as a typographer, exercised great influence on *The Times*. He also edited the *Times Literary Supplement* 1945–8. See also John Carter *Stanley Morison* Hart-Davis 1956 and [3888].

**3689** Claud Morris *I Bought a Newspaper* Barker 1963. The autobiography of a Fleet Street journalist who bought and rebuilt the nearly bankrupt *South Wales Voice* and launched his *Voice* magazines for industry in various areas.

**3690** Ian Hunter *Malcolm Muggeridge: A Life* Collins 1980. A biography of the writer, journalist (he edited *Punch* 1953–7) and broadcaster. Malcolm Muggeridge *Chronicles of Wasted Time* 2v, Fontana 1972–5 is two volumes of revealingly opinionated autobiography. See also Malcolm Muggeridge *Like It Was: The Diaries of Malcolm Muggeridge* Collins 1981. Malcolm Muggeridge *Conversion: A Spiritual Journey* Collins 1988 is an account of his conversion to Catholicism in the 1980s.

**3691** Michael Leapman *Barefaced Cheek: The Apotheosis of Rupert Murdoch* Hodder and Stoughton 1983. A biography by a former *Times* journalist full of grudging admiration for the material if not ethical achievements of the Australian who through his News Corporation owns the *Sun*, the *News of the World* and the Times Group of titles. George Munster *A Paper Prince* Viking 1975 is good on Murdoch's Australian origins and his business life. See also Simon Regan *Rupert Murdoch: A Business Biography* Angus and Robertson 1976 and Thomas Kiernan *Citizen Murdoch* Hale 1987.

**3692** Leslie William Needham *Fifty Years of Fleet Street* Michael Joseph 1973. The autobiography of the then recently retired advertising director of Beaverbrook Newspapers.

**3693** Jean Nicol *Meet Me at the Savoy* Museum Press 1955. Memoirs of a radical political journalist.

**3694** John Pilger *Heroes* Cape 1986. The memoirs of the *Daily Mirror* foreign correspondent include useful reflections on Robert Maxwell's takeover of the Mirror

Group and some trenchant criticisms of the rise of international newspaper proprietors.

**3695** Eric Price *Boy in the Bath or How to Work on 13 Newspapers and Survive* Abson Books 1982. Among his various posts was that of editor of the *Western Daily Press*.

**3696** John Pringle *Have Pen Will Travel* Chatto and Windus 1973. Pringle was on *The Times* 1948–52 and later became deputy editor of *The Observer*.

**3697** Henry Proctor *The Street of Disillusion* Wingate 1958. Proctor worked on the *Daily Mirror*, the *Daily Mail* and the *Sunday Pictorial*. The disillusion refers to the effects of needlessly sensational reporting.

**3698** Alan Pryce-Jones *The Bonus of Laughter* Hamilton 1987. A memoir of a career in literary journalism, including twelve years as editor of the *Times Literary Supplement*.

**3699** William Clark *Hugh Redwood: With God in Fleet Street* Hodder and Stoughton 1976. Redwood was a religious broadcaster and the religious editor of the *News Chronicle* until 1953.

**3700** J W Robertson Scott *'We' and Me: Memories of Four Eminent Editors I Worked With, a Discussion by Editors of the Function of Editing, and a Candid Account of the Founding and Editing, for Twenty-One Years, of my Magazine* W H Allen 1956. Robertson Scott was the founder and editor of the *Countryman*. The four editors of the title were all of inter-war vintage.

**3701** Cecil H Rolph *Living Twice: An Autobiography* Gollancz 1974. Rolph (whose real name was Cecil Hewitt) was a journalist and author.

**3702** Jean Rook *Rook's Eye View* Express Books 1978. A survey of her career on the *Sun*, the *Daily Sketch*, the *Daily Mail* and finally the *Daily Express*.

**3703** Clare Sheridan *To the Four Winds* Deutsch 1957. Memoirs of a foreign correspondent.

**3704** For Mary Stott see [5607].

**3704A** For Douglas Sutherland see [185].

**3705** Ernest W Swanton *Sort of a Cricket Person* Collins 1972. Memoirs of the much respected *Daily Telegraph* cricket correspondent. See also his *Follow On* Collins 1977.

**3706** C L Sulzberger *A Long Row of Candles: Memoirs and Diaries 1934–1954* Macdonald 1969. Sulzberger was the *New York Times* correspondent in Europe. His

memoirs contain many useful reflections on developments in Britain in this period.

**3707** Tom Driberg *'Swaff': The Life and Times of Hannen Swaffer* Macdonald 1971. Swaffer was the gossip columnist in the *Daily Herald* for over 30 years. He remained active, if not as influential as during the inter-war period, into the 1950s.

**3708** Norman Thelwell *Wrestling With A Pencil: The Life of a Freelance Artist* Methuen 1985. The autobiography of the cartoonist (especially with *Punch*) and painter of the English rural landscape.

**3709** Roy Thomson, Lord Thomson of Fleet *After I was Sixty: A Chapter of Autobiography* Hamilton 1975. A modest account of how this Canadian came to Britain at the age of 59 and acquired *The Scotsman*, set up Scottish TV, took over the Kemsley Group (including *The Times*) and established himself as publisher, broadcaster and press baron. Russell Braddon *Roy Thomson of Fleet Street and How He Got There* Collins 1965 adds little to this.

**3710** Russell Davies and Liz Ottaway *Vicky* Secker and Warburg 1987. A good biography of the famous cartoonist and creator of Supermac (a skit on Harold Macmillan) with a personal memoir by Michael Foot.

**3711** Edward Ward, Viscount Bangor *I've Lived Like a Lord* Michael Joseph 1970. Memoirs of a foreign correspondent.

**3712** Edward Francis Williams *Nothing So Strange: An Autobiography* Cassell 1970. Williams edited the *Daily Herald* in the 1930s and *Forward* in the 1950s. He was also the press adviser to Attlee when the latter was Prime Minister.

**3712A** For Woodrow Wyatt see [782].


(b) Broadcasting


*(i) General*

Special kinds of broadcasting are covered elsewhere in the bibliography. Thus the material on forces broadcasting appears in the section on Military History and the material on religious broadcasting in that on Religious History. The material on radio and television drama and comedy is to be found in the section on the Dramatic Arts. For the campaigns against sex and violence on broadcast services of the National Viewers' and Listeners' Association led by Mary Whitehouse see the section on the Permissive Society.

**3713** Zabelle Stenton (ed) *The Blue Book of British Broadcasting: A Handbook for Professional Bodies and Students of Broadcasting* 14th ed, Tellex Monitors Ltd 1988. A useful guide, especially to programming and personnel.

**3714** *BBC Annual Report and Handbook* BBC 1928–. This was not published 1953–4. Since 1980 it has been entitled *BBC Handbook*. An annual review of the past year in public service broadcasting.

**3715** Independent Broadcasting Authority *Annual Reports and Accounts* HMSO 1954/55–1971/72. Since 1971–2 this has been published by the IBA. In 1976 this merged with the annual report on the independent television services, *ITV* (1963–75), to become *Television and Radio: IBA Guide to Independent Broadcasting* IBA 1976–.

**3716** Anthony Smith (ed) *British Broadcasting* David and Charles 1974. A collection of documents, speeches, official reports, letters and statutes.

**3717** Barrie Macdonald *Broadcasting in the United Kingdom: A Guide to Information Sources* Mansell 1988. A very informative guide to all the organizations concerned with the making and regulation of broadcasting, their history, objectives and publications. It also features a chronology, a well annotated bibliography, and a guide to relevant holdings in libraries, archives and museums. An indispensable reference work.

**3718** Gavin Higgens (ed) *British Broadcasting 1922–1982: A Selected and Annotated Bibliography* BBC Data Publications 1983. A good, well annotated bibliography covering a wide range of subjects. It updates the earlier BBC bibliography by Joan Houlgate. *Broadcasting: A Select Bibliography* IBA 1980 is a much shorter, though still annotated, bibliography. Robert L Collison *Broadcasting in Britain: A Bibliography* Cambridge University Press 1961 is now superseded.

**3719** Burton Paulu *Television and Radio in the United Kingdom* Macmillan 1981. An examination of the origins of the BBC and IBA, a brief survey of their development and an assessment of their services in 1978–9. See also his earlier *British Broadcasting: Radio and Television in the United Kingdom* Oxford University Press 1957.

**3720** J Scupham *Broadcasting and the Community* C A Watts and Co 1967. A survey of the development of the broadcasting institutions and their broadcasting policy and impact. The public response to broadcasters is surveyed in Barrie Gunter and Michael Svennevig *Attitudes to Broadcasting over the Years* Libbey 1988.

**3721** E G Wedell *Broadcasting and Public Policy* Michael Joseph 1968. This surveys the government of broadcasting, the services provided, the audience and audience research, and the state of industrial relations in the industry. David James George Hennessy, Lord Windlesham *Broadcasting in a Free Society* Blackwell 1980 analyses the relationship between the government and broadcasting from the viewpoint of one who has served in both.

**3722** Joan Bakewell and Nicholas Garnham *The New Priesthood* Allen Lane 1970. A study of broadcasting and its responsibilities from the 1920s to the 1970s based on extensive interviewing with executives, engineers, producers and writers.

**3723** Asa Briggs *History of Broadcasting in the United Kingdom Vol IV: Sound and Vision* Oxford University Press 1979. A massive treatment of developments 1945–55, up to the advent of independent television. It also features a useful bibliography. Keith Geddes *Broadcasting in Britain 1922–1972* HMSO 1972 is a short survey of developments in the first fifty years of broadcasting.

**3724** M Gorham *Broadcasting and Television Since 1900* Dakers 1952. A survey of the development of broadcasting from its inception to the publication of the Beveridge Report.

**3725** R H Coase *British Broadcasting: A Study in Monopoly* Longmans 1950. A study of the nature and effects of the monopoly of broadcasting that the BBC then had.

**3726** Justin Davis Smith 'The Struggle for Control of the Airwaves: The Attlee Governments, the BBC and Industrial Unrest 1945–51' in Tony Gorst, Lewis Johnman and W Scott Lucas (eds) *Postwar Britain 1945–64: Themes and Perspectives* Pinter 1989 pp 53–67. The Attlee government, whilst recognizing the independence of the BBC, was anxious to do all in its power to prevent the unofficial strikes of the period damaging its economic and reconstruction policy. This is a study of the pressure put on the BBC to structure the news so as to encourage a swift return to work and to ensure that the unofficial strikers had no access to the airwaves, and of the resistance the BBC put up.

**3727** *Report of the Broadcasting Committee 1949* Cmnd 8116, *Parliamentary Papers* ix 1950–51. This committee, chaired by Lord Beveridge, made a number of recommendations, including the development of VHF broadcasting, improvements in programming and audience research, greater use in adult education and the introduction of regional broadcasting commissioners and regional news. Perhaps its most important recommendations were however that the existing bar on the discussion on radio or television of a subject due to be debated in parliament within fourteen days should be reconsidered, that broadcasts should be more topical and that greater coverage of election campaigns should be permitted.

**3728** Burton Paulu *British Broadcasting in Transition* Macmillan 1961. A study of the effects of competition in broadcasting 1955–60.

**3729** *Report of the Committee on Broadcasting* Cmnd 1753, *Parliamentary Papers* ix 1961–62. Whilst rejecting calls for a Broadcasting Consumers Council, for subscription television and for Scottish and Welsh BBC's this committee, chaired by Sir Harry Pilkington, recommended local radio, local traffic news, a change in the number of lines on the television screen and the introduction of colour television.

**3730** *Report of the Commission on the Future of Broadcasting* Cmnd 6753, *Parliamentary Papers* 1976–77. The main proposal of this Commission, chaired by Lord Annan, to be taken up was that which led to the establishment of Channel 4. It also supported the idea of a Welsh television channel.

**3731** *Report of the Inquiry into Cable Extension and Broadcasting Policy* Cmnd 8679, *Parliamentary Papers* 1982–83. This committee, chaired by Lord Hunt of Tanworth, made various suggestions for the growth of cable television whilst safeguarding public services. It suggested a franchise system and stipulated that the government, political parties and religious bodies should not be allowed to own cable services. The encouragement of the development of cable and satellite television has been a feature of the broadcasting policy of the Thatcher government. This is reflected in policy documents such as *Direct Broadcasting by Satellite* HMSO 1981 and *The Development of Cable Systems and Services* Cmnd 8866, *Parliamentary Papers* 1982–83.

**3732** Ralph Negrine 'Great Britain: The End of the Public Service Tradition?' in Raymond Kuhn *The Politics of Broadcasting* Croom Helm 1985 pp 15–46. A study of the effect of the Thatcher government's emphasis on competition and encouragement of satellite and cable services, particularly on the BBC.

**3733** Alisdair Clayre *The Impact of Broadcasting or Mrs Buckle's Wall is Singing* Compton Russell 1973. A study of the social impact of broadcasting since the 1920s.

**3734** Asa Briggs *The BBC: The First 50 Years* Oxford University Press 1985. A one volume history of the BBC 1922–72 pending the appearance of the next volume of his mammoth history of broadcasting in Britain. It is not a balanced alternative to his detailed history however and while full of anecdotal reflections lacks an analytical

edge. P Black *The Biggest Aspidistra in the World: A Personal Celebration of Fifty Years of the BBC* BBC 1972 is a fond account of the Corporation's development. See also Colin Reid *Action Stations: A History of Broadcasting House* Robson 1986. *'Radio Times' 50th Anniversary Souvenir 1923–1973* BBC 1973 is a history of the BBC's weekly programme guide and magazine.

**3735** Asa Briggs *Governing the BBC* BBC 1979. A history and study of the constitution of the BBC's Board of Governors 1927–77. It includes a number of case studies of their handling of controversial episodes, such as the BBC coverage of Suez or the satirical programme 'That Was The Week That Was'. Tom Burns *The BBC: Public Institution and Private World* Macmillan 1977 is a partly sociological, partly historical analysis of the BBC as an institution based on research and interviews conducted in 1963 and 1973.

**3736** E D Simon *The BBC from Within* Gollancz 1953. A survey by the former chairman of the BBC governors of the objectives, structure and finance of the Corporation at the time.

**3737** *Report of the Committee on Financing the British Broadcasting Corporation* Cmnd 9824, *Parliamentary Papers* 1985–86. This committee, under the chairmanship of Professor Alan Peacock, was set up to assess alternatives to the licence fee as a means of funding the BBC. An interesting response to and assessment of this report is Richard Collins, Nicholas Garnham and Gareth Locksley *The Economics of Television: The UK Case* Sage 1988.

**3738** Michael Leapman *The Last Days of the Beeb* 2nd ed, Coronet 1987. This analyses the difficulties of the BBC in the 1980s, and particularly its controversy-ridden relations with the government both over the finance of the Corporation and its handling of news reporting.

**3739** Robert Silvey *Who's Listening? The Story of BBC Audience Research* Allen and Unwin 1974. A study of its increasingly sophisticated techniques since it was established in 1936. Silvey was the founder of BBC Audience Research and its director for 32 years. This is very much a personal account. Tim Madge *Beyond the BBC* Macmillan 1988 surveys how the Corporation researches its audience and responds to it, through letters, public meetings and advisory committees as well as through Audience Research.

**3740** Edward Pawley *BBC Engineering 1922–1972* BBC 1972. A lengthy detailed and technical history which includes an extensive bibliography. See also his short review of technical progress, *BBC Sound Broadcasting 1939–1960: A Review of Progress* Institute of Electrical Engineers 1961.

*(ii) Television*

**3741** Eddie Tedder (ed) *Who's Who in Television* 3rd ed, ITV Books 1985. A collection of potted biographies of leading British television personalities.

**3742** A Davis *History of Television Vol 1: The First Forty Years* Severn House/ITV Books 1976. The first of a three volume popular series on the history of television since 1936. The others are A Davis *Here is the News* 1976 and P Fairley *How it Works* 1976.

**3743** Peter Black *The Mirror in the Corner: People's Television* Hutchinson 1972. A history of television and its social impact 1952–70. James D Halloran (ed) *The Effects of Television* Panther 1970 studies the impact of television on society, politics, the arts, advertising, the other media and education. Wilfrid Altman, Denis Thomas and David Sawers *TV: From Monopoly to Competition* Institute of Economic Affairs 1962 is a historical, sociological and economic analysis of the development of television broadcasts.

**3744** Stuart Hood *A Survey of Television* Heinemann 1967. A semi-autobiographical survey of the development of television and its audience.

**3745** M Schulman *The Least Worst Television in the World* Barrie and Jenkins 1973. A critical survey of the British television service.

**3746** R W Burns *British Television: The Formative Years* Peter Peregrinus 1986. A study which concentrates on technological developments.

**3747** Michael Tracey *The Production of Political Television in Britain* Routledge and Kegan Paul 1978. A study of the coverage of politics and current affairs on television and of the relations between the medium and government and politicians. John Whale *The Half-Shut Eye: Television and Politics in Britain and America* Macmillan 1969 is a well regarded study. The delicacy of the BBC's handling of politics and politicians is well expressed in Grace Wyndham Goldie *Facing the Nation: Television and Politics 1936–1976* The Bodley Head 1977. This is a well regarded semi-autobiographical account. See also Anthony Smith 'Britain: The Mysteries of a Modus Vivendi' in Anthony Smith (ed) *Television and Political Life: Studies in Six European Countries* Macmillan 1979 pp 1–40.

**3748** Michael Cockerell *Live from Number 10: The Inside Story of Prime Ministers and Television* Faber 1988. A study of the initial reluctance and then the growing need of Prime Ministers to be able to master the medium. A good study of an important aspect of political television.

**3749** Geoffrey Cox *See It Happen: The Making of ITN* The Bodley Head 1983. The relatively high political content and aggressive style of ITN revolutionized television news reporting and interviewing when it first appeared in the 1950s. This is a semi-autobiographical history from then down to the Falklands War. Michael Tracey *In the Culture of an Eye – Ten Years of Weekend World* Hutchinson 1983, an account of an ITV current affairs programme, is also useful.

**3750** P H Dorté 'The BBC Television Newsreel' *BBC Quarterly* 3 1949 pp 229–34. This first appeared in January 1948. Regular bulletins did not begin until 1955. The development of BBC television news broadcasts was resisted by the newsreel companies, a fact which is commented on in Tom Wildy 'British Television and Official Film 1946–1951' *Historical Journal of Film, Radio and Television* 8 1988 pp 195–202.

**3751** R Shaw 'Television: Freedom and Responsibility' *Blackfriars* 47 1966 pp 453–65. This discusses the set-up of the Clean-Up Television campaign, Mary Whitehouse's National Viewers' and Listeners' Association and other organizations campaigning for the reduction of sex and violence on television.

**3752** G Ross *Television Jubilee: The Story of 25 Years of BBC Television* W H Allen 1961. An anecdotal history 1936–61.

**3753** Bernard Sendall *The History of Independent Television in Britain* 4v, Macmillan 1982–9. Volume I, *Origins and Foundation 1946–62* 1982 surveys the campaign for ITV and its establishment up to the Pilkington Report. Volume II, *Expansion and Change 1958–68* 1983 analyses the development of the network. Volume III (by Jeremy Potter) is *Coming of Age 1968–80* 1989 and Volume IV surveys *The Companies and Their Programmes* 1989. *Twenty-Five Years on ITV 1955–80* ITV Books/Michael Joseph 1980 is a lavishly illustrated guide to programming trends and to the most popular programmes.

**3754** W A Belson *The Impact of Television: Methods and Findings in Programme Research* Crosby Lockwood 1967. A study of the social impact of television.

**3755** H H Wilson *Pressure Groups: The Campaign for Commercial Television* Secker and Warburg 1961. An analysis of the background to the establishment of ITV as a commercial television service in 1955, and particularly of the conflict in the Conservative Party over the introduction and passage of the Independent Television Act. See also W G Fleming 'Group Theory as Applied to the British Governmental Process: A Study of the Origins of ITV' London MSc (Econ) Thesis 1959–60.

**3756** J Tinker *The Television Barons* Quartet 1980. An analysis of the rise of commercial television which particularly focuses on the role of Lew Grade, Sidney Bernstein, Howard Thomas and other executives of the ITV companies. See also Clive Jenkins *Power Behind the Screen: Ownership, Control and Motivation in British Commercial Television* MacGibbon and Kee 1961. On the sharing out of the franchises for the commercial television stations see Asa Briggs and Joanne Spicer *The Franchise Affair: Creating Fortune and Failure in Independent Television* Century 1986 and S Domberger and J Middleton 'Franchising in Practice: The Case of Independent Television in the UK' *Fiscal Studies* 6 1985 pp 17–33.

**3757** Anglia Television *About Anglia* Boydell Press 1974. A history of the company. *Granada: The First Twenty-Five Years* British Film Institute 1981 is a collection of articles, speeches and interviews reflecting the history of the company. Another illustrated company history is Anthony Brown *Tyne Tees Television: The First Twenty Years: A Portrait* Tyne Tees Television Ltd 1978. On the difficulties during the establishment of TV-AM see Michael Leapman *Treachery? The Power Struggle at TV-AM* Allen and Unwin 1984.

**3758** S Lambert *Channel Four: Television with a Difference?* British Film Institute 1982. A study of the background decision making to the establishment of the fourth channel in 1982. It includes informative and detailed appendices.

**3759** Christopher Parsons *True to Nature: Twenty-Five Years of Wildlife Filming with the BBC National History Unit* Stephens 1982. A study of the development of this Bristol based unit since 1957 which looks at BBC natural history film making since 1946.

**3760** J Redmond 'Television Broadcasting 1960–70: BBC 625-Line Services and the Introduction of Colour' *IEE Reviews* 117 1970 pp 1469–88. A review of technical developments.

**3761** BBC Engineering Information Department *CEEFAX: Its History and the Record of its Development by BBC Research Department* BBC 1978. A collection of papers covering the development of this project 1974–77. So far this is the only study of the development of teletext services.

**3762** P M Lewis *Community Television and Cable in Britain* British Film Institute 1978. A study of five experimental cable systems in Britain in the 1970s.

*(iii) Radio*

**3763** S G Sturmy *The Economic Development of Radio* Duckworth 1958. A background history 1920–56.

**3764** D Parker *Radio: The Great Years* David and Charles 1977. A popular account of personalities and programmes from the 1920s to the 1970s.

**3765** Kate Whitehead *The Third Programme* Clarendon 1989. A history of the BBC arts channel 1957–70. It concentrates on the drama, poetry and fiction which the Third Programme stimulated and largely ignores its music, history and philosophy broadcasting.

**3766** F Kalkan 'The Development of Local Broadcasting in the United Kingdom' Keele MA Thesis 1973–4. A particular aspect of this is examined in Asa Briggs 'Local and Regional in Northern Sound Broadcasting' *Northern History* 10 1975 pp 165–87. This is an account of BBC radio broadcasting from the relay station at Leeds/Bradford from 1924 to the start of local BBC radio in 1967. M Baron *Independent Radio: The Story of Independent Radio in the UK* Dalton 1975 is largely concerned with the development of independent local radio after 1973 but it also covers pirate radio and stations such as Radio Luxembourg. Developments since 1973 are also surveyed in David Manasian 'Local Radio's Bigger Boom' *Management Today* Sept 1979 pp 82–9. A study of one the stations established after 1973, Manchester Piccadilly, is P Radcliffe *The Piccadilly Story: Profile of a Radio Station* Blond and Briggs 1979.

**3767** Paul Harris *Broadcasting from the High Seas: The History of Offshore Radio in Europe 1958–1976* Paul Harris 1977. A revised and updated edition of a study of pirate radio first published in 1968. It provides an excellent survey of the pirate radios, but is of less value on the changes in broadcasting policy, leading to the establishment of Radio 1, the growth of legal commercial stations and a general relaxation of former restrictions, which they helped to encourage. These aspects are dealt with more fully in John Hind and Stephen Moser *Rebel Radio: The Full Story of British Pirate Radio* Pluto 1985. J Venmore-Rowland *Radio Caroline: The Story of the First British Off-Shore Radio Station* Landmark Press 1967 is in part an account of the most famous of the pirate stations and in part an examination of the case for and against pirate radio. On Caroline see also Bob Noakes *Last of the Pirates: A Saga of Life on Board Radio Caroline* Paul Harris 1984. Peter Alex *Who's Who in Pop Radio* New English Library 1966 is a well illustrated collection of brief biographies of pirate radio disc jockeys, many of whom remained prominent for a considerable time afterwards.

**3768** J Clarricoats *World at their Fingertips: The Story of Amateur Radio in the United Kingdom and a History of the Radio Society of Great Britain* Radio Society of Great Britain 1967.

### (iv) External Broadcasting

**3769** Gerald Mansell *Let Truth be Told: 50 Years of BBC External Broadcasting* Weidenfeld and Nicolson 1982. A history of the BBC external broadcasts 1932–82 by the then recently retired director of external broadcasting. See also Andrew Walker *Voice from the World: 50 Years of Broadcasting to the World 1932–1982* BBC External Services 1982. J Beresford Clark 'The BBC's External Services' *International Affairs* 35 1959 pp 170–80 provides the reflections of the then director of external broadcasting on its history, functions, constitutional position and organization. Another examination of the role of the external broadcasting services and their relationship to foreign policy and relations with foreign countries by the current director is John Tusa 'Between Academe and Foreign Policy: The Work of the BBC External Services' *LSE Quarterly* 2 1988 pp 287–303.

**3770** *The European Service of the BBC: Two Decades of Broadcasting to Europe 1938–1959* BBC 1959. A short account.

**3771** Maurice Latey *Broadcasting to the USSR and East Europe* BBC 1964. A short lecture by the Head of the BBC East European Service, as is *Through the Iron Curtain: The BBC and the Cold War on the Air* BBC 1952. For a more recent study see Peter Frankel 'The BBC External Services: Broadcasting to the USSR and Eastern Europe' in K R M Short (ed) *Western Broadcasting over the Iron Curtain* Croom Helm 1986 pp 139–57.

### (v) Biographies

**3772** Eamonn Andrews *This is My Life* Macdonald 1963. His autobiography. In it he comments on once being snubbed by Lord Reith because he represented, 'much of what was frivolous and worthless, by his great standards, on television and radio'. See also Gus Smith *Eamonn Andrews: His Life* W H Allen 1988 and Tom Brennand *Eamonn Andrews* Weidenfeld and Nicolson 1989.

**3773** Michael Aspel *Polly Wants a Zebra* Weidenfeld and Nicolson 1974. The autobiography of the disc jockey and television presenter.

**3774** Thomas Barman *Diplomatic Correspondent* Hamilton 1968. The well regarded and informative memoirs of a BBC foreign correspondent.

**3775** Michael Barrett *Michael Barrett* Wolfe 1973. Autobiography of a television journalist.

**3776** G C Beadle *Television: A Critical Review* Allen and Unwin 1963. An autobiographical account of the growth of BBC television. Beadle joined the BBC in 1923 and retired as director of television broadcasting in 1961.

**3777** Reginald Bosanquet *Lets Get Through Wednesday: My Twenty Five Years with ITN* Michael Joseph 1980. The autobiography of an ITN newscaster.

**3778** Thelma Cazalet-Keir, a director of the BBC from 1956, see [5603].

**3779** Charles Curran *A Seamless Robe: Broadcasting Philosophy and Practice* Collins 1979. A semi-autobiographical analysis of the BBC by the Corporation's then recently retired Director-General.

**3780** Sir Robin Day *Grand Inquisitor: Memoirs* Weidenfeld and Nicolson 1989. The autobiography of the most famous of post-war political interviewers and political broadcasters. His *Day by Day: A Dose of My Own Hemlock* Kimber 1975 is a set of semi-autobiographical views on political reporting on ITV and BBC. See also his earlier *Television: A Personal Report* Hutchinson 1961.

**3781** Jack De Manio *Life Begins Too Early: A Sort of Autobiography* Hutchinson 1970. The autobiography of a BBC broadcasting personality.

**3782** Jonathan Dimbleby *Richard Dimbleby: A Biography* Hodder and Stoughton 1975. A filial tribute to a celebrated broadcaster. See also L Miall (ed) *Richard Dimbleby, Broadcaster, by his Colleagues* BBC 1966.

**3783** Robert Dougall *In and Out of the Box* Collins Harvill 1973. The autobiography of a celebrated newscaster.

**3784** Donald Edwards *The Two Worlds of Donald Edwards* Hutchinson 1970. Edwards was a former editor of the BBC news and current affairs before becoming managing director of ITN.

**3785** Willi Frischauer *David Frost* Michael Joseph 1972. A biography of the television presenter and interviewer.

**3786** Sandy Gall *Don't Worry About the Money Now* Hamilton 1983. After a period working for Reuters Gall became a television presenter and newscaster.

**3787** Val Gielgud *Years in a Mirror* The Bodley Head 1964. A memoir of 35 years at the BBC by the former head of BBC drama.

**3788** Sir Hugh Greene *The Third Floor Front: A View of Broadcasting in the Sixties* The Bodley Head 1969. Mixed reminiscences (in the form of a collection of lectures, speeches and broadcasts) of his time as the BBC's Director-General 1960–69. It also includes reflections on some of the controversial developments at the BBC during his time there and on the role of the BBC in the advent of the permissive society of the 1960s. See also Michael Tracey *A Variety of Lives: A Biography of Sir Hugh Greene* The Bodley Head 1983.

**3789** F Grisewood *My Story of the BBC* Odhams 1959. An autobiographical account of the BBC by a prominent member of its staff.

**3790** Harman Grisewood *One Thing at a Time: An Autobiography* Hutchinson 1968. Grisewood was the assistant to the BBC's Director-General 1955–64.

**3791** R Storey *Gilbert Harding, by his Private Secretary* Barrie and Rockliff 1961. Reminiscences of an important broadcasting personality of the early post-war years who died in 1960. Gilbert Charles Harding *Along My Line* Putnam 1953 is an autobiography and his *Master of None* Putnam 1958 is a volume of reminiscences. See also Wallace Reyburn *Gilbert Harding: A Candid Portrayal* Angus and Robertson 1978.

**3792** R Heppenstall *Portrait of the Artist as a Professional Man* Owen 1969. The autobiography of a former BBC features producer.

**3793** Charles Hill *Behind the Screen: The Broadcasting Memoirs of Lord Hill of Luton* Sidgwick and Jackson 1974. Memoirs of his time as successively chairman of the Independent Television Authority and the BBC in the 1960s and early 1970s. For his memories of his broadcasting experiences and his role in broadcasting policy as Postmaster-General 1955–7 see [824].

**3794** Sir Brian Horrocks *A Full Life* revised ed, Cooper 1974. The autobiography of a noted television pundit. See also Philip Warner *Horrocks: The General Who Led From the Front* Hamilton 1984.

**3795** Jeremy Isaacs *Storm Over 4* Weidenfeld and Nicolson 1989. The story of his years as the founding chief executive of Channel 4.

**3796** David Jacobs *Jacob's Ladder* Peter Davies 1963. Autobiography of a broadcaster and disc jockey.

**3797** Ludovic Kennedy *On My Way to The Club* Collins 1989. The autobiography of a leading political journalist.

**3798** For Sir Robert Lusty, a former Vice-Chairman of the BBC, see [3872].

**3799** Ian McDougall *Foreign Correspondent* Muller 1980. Memoirs of a celebrated BBC foreign correspondent.

**3800** Alisdair Milne *'DG': The Memoirs of a Broadcaster* Hodder and Stoughton 1988. These memoirs of a former BBC Director General (1982–87) are rather disappointing in that they reveal little of the Corporation's difficulties with the government in the 1980s or of the manner of his dismissal.

**3801** Leslie Mitchell *Leslie Mitchell Reporting . . .* Hutchinson 1981. The autobiography of a political commentator and interviewer who had previously worked on newsreel. He had a much less aggressive style of interviewing than the new generation of political interviewers introduced by ITN in the 1950s and typified by Robin Day and was Sir Anthony Eden's favourite interviewer. This memoir is therefore also useful for his reminiscences of his political friends.

**3802** Jimmy Savile *As It Happens: Jimmy Savile OBE: His Autobiography* Barrie and Jenkins 1974. The autobiography of the disc jockey and indefatigable worker for a whole range of charities. He helped to popularize Rock'n'Roll as a disc jockey with Radio Luxembourg in the 1950s and 1960s. See also his *Love Is An Uphill Struggle* Coronet 1976.

**3803** Mary D Stocks *Ernest Simon of Manchester* Manchester University Press 1963. A Liberal MP in the inter-war years Simon was most important in the post-war period as Chairman of the BBC Board of Governors 1947–52.

**3804** Howard Thomas *With An Independent Air: Encounters During a Lifetime of Broadcasting* Weidenfeld and Nicolson 1977. A very informative autobiography. Thomas was the producer in chief for the newsreel company Pathé 1944–55 and after that moved to a career in independent television.

**3805** For Lord Thomson of Fleet see [3709].

**3806** Ian Trethowan *Split Screen* Hamilton 1984. Trethowan's career in broadcasting culminated in his period as Director-General of the BBC 1977–82.

**3807** Alan Whicker *Within Whicker's World* Elm Tree Books 1982. The autobiography of a television presenter.

**3808** Terry Wogan *Wogan on Wogan* Penguin 1987. Reminiscences by the radio and television personality and presenter. See also Gus Smith *Wogan* W H Allen 1987.

**3809** Robert Wood *A World in Your Ear: The Broadcasting of an Era 1923–64* Macmillan 1979. The semi-autobiographical account of the development of broadcasting by the man who was responsible for the technical arrangements behind many of the outside broadcasts of this period.

**3810** Jimmy Young *Jimmy Young* Michael Joseph 1982. The autobiography of the radio broadcaster.

## (c) Newsreel

It was not until the 1950s that television began to compete seriously with the newsreel companies as a source of news and information and the last newsreel company did not disappear until the 1970s. The Universities Film and Video Council have produced two very useful works which both analysis the value of newsreel as a historical source and provide a bibliography on newsreel and the newsreel companies. These can be found in the literature on Pictures, Photographs, Film, Video and Sound Archives in the section on General Historical Sources [161–72].

**3811** Philip Norman 'The Newsreel Boys' *Sunday Times Magazine* 10/1/1971 pp 8–15. An affectionate and well illustrated look at the work of the cameramen, news editors and commentators on the newsreel crews.

**3812** J C Hulbert 'The British Cinema Newsreels' Treatment of the British Military 1948–1960' Keele MA Thesis 1978.

**3813** Peter Hopkinson *Split Focus: An Involvement in Two Decades* Hart-Davis 1969. Memoirs of a career in newsreels. Ronnie Noble *Shoot First! Assignments of a Newsreel Cameraman* Harrap 1955 is an anecdotal autobiography of his assignments and of the competition between the newsreel companies. Another autobiography by a newsreel cameraman is Paul Wyand *Useless If Delayed* Harrap 1959. For Howard Thomas' career in newsreels see [3804].

## (d) Video

The recent growth of the video industry has yet to be analysed in any detail. This is despite its phenomenal growth, large number of retail outlets and the considerable concern about its impact in the 1980s.

**3814** *Ten Years of Video* Video Trade Weekly 1989. This charts the phenomenal development of the industry in the 1980s and its legal history. It contains full statistics.

**3815** Martin Barker (ed) *The Video Nasties: Freedom and Censorship in the Media* Pluto 1984. The only substantive piece of work on the video industry analyses the background to the concern in the mid-1980s about the number of distasteful videos on the market and the changes in the law then proposed to deal with them. The legislative reaction to concern about the video industry is examined in David Marsh, Peter Gowin and Melvyn Read 'Private Members Bills and Moral Panic: The Case of the Video Recordings Bill (1984)' *Parliamentary Affairs* 39 1986 pp 179–96.

## (e) Publishing

### (i) General

**3816** Marjorie Deane 'United Kingdom Publishing Statistics' *Journal of the Royal Statistical Society* Series A 114 1951 pp 468–89. A guide to sources.

**3817** Peter J Curwen *The UK Publishing Industry* Pergamon 1981. A survey of the state of the industry. See also Michael Lane and Jeremy Booth *Books and Publishers: Commerce Against Culture in Postwar Britain* Lexington Books, Lexington, Massachusetts 1980. On the development of the smaller publishers and presses in the post-war period see also B E Bellamy *Private Presses and Publishing in England Since 1945* Clive Bingley 1980.

**3818** P Thomas 'Micropublishing in Britain Today' *British Book News* 36 1976 pp 629–36. A survey of changing production techniques and the growth of microform publishing.

**3819** George Greenfield *Scribblers For Bread: Aspects of the English Novel Since 1945* Hodder and Stoughton 1989. This is a good study of literary publishing in the post-war years and the influences changing the market. J A Sutherland *Fiction and the Fiction Industry* Athlone Press 1978 surveys the literary agencies, publishers and public lending systems that link the writers with their public.

3820   J A Snider 'A Study of Art Book Publishing in Great Britain, with Special Reference to Development After 1945' Wales MLib Thesis 1983.

3821   Ian Norrie *Sixty Precarious Years: A Short History of the National Book League 1925–1985* National Book League 1985.

3822   For the history of Allen and Unwin see [3877].

3823   Leslie Gardiner *Bartholomew: 150 Years* Bartholomew 1976. A celebration of the cartographic publishers.

3824   Arthur L P Norrington *Blackwells 1879–1979: The History of a Family Firm* Blackwell 1983. A history of the academic publishing firm.

3825   J W Lambert and Michael Ratcliffe *The Bodley Head 1887–1987* The Bodley Head 1988. An excellent account of the history of this publishing firm. It also looks at the publishing work of Allen Lane and his launch of Penguin, the paperback publishers.

3826   H Kay Jones *Butterworths: History of a Publishing House* Butterworths 1980. A history of the firm that specializes in legal publishing, 1818–1978.

3827   M H Black *Cambridge University Press 1584–1984* Cambridge University Press 1984. This general history is good on the post-war history of the press and its crises in the 1960s and 1970s.

3828   Michael S Howard *Jonathan Cape, Publisher* Penguin 1977. This traces the history of the publishing firm from its foundation in 1921 to 1971.

3829   Simon Nowell-Smith *The House of Cassell 1848–1958* Cassell 1958.

3830   Carlene Mair *The Chappell Story 1811–1961* Chappell 1961. This history of the music publishers has virtually no material on the post-war years.

3831   Oliver Warner *Chatto and Windus: A Brief Account of the Firm's Origins, History and Development* Chatto and Windus 1973. A history of the publishing house.

3832   H Simon *Song and Words: A History of the Curwen Press* Allen and Unwin 1973.

3833   *Good Books Come From Devon: The David and Charles Twenty-First Birthday Book* David and Charles 1981.

3834   *The Bell House Book: Celebrating Sixty Years of a Literary Agency 1919–1979* Hodder and Stoughton 1979. A history of the literary agency, John Farquharson Ltd.

3835   Timothy d'Arch Smith *R A Caton and the Fortune Press: A Memoir and a Hand-List* Bartram Rota 1983. A memoir of the press of the eccentric specialist publisher.

3836   Sheila Hodges *Gollancz: The Story of a Publishing House 1928–1978* Gollancz 1978. A good history of a publishing house with important Left-Wing political traditions.

3837   Dorothy A Harrop *A History of the Gregynog Press* Private Libraries Association 1980. An artistic small press that largely expired with the Second World War the Gregynog Press was revived as an imprint by the University of Wales in the early 1970s.

3838   *Partners in Progress: Some Recollections of the Past Quarter Century at 182 High Holborn* privately printed 1962. A history and reminiscences of Harraps 1937–62.

3839   Jeff Clew *Haynes Publishing: The First 25 Years* Haynes 1985. A history of the specialist publisher.

3840   Alan Hill *In Pursuit of Publishing* Murray 1988. A memoir of the development of Heinemann Educational publishing in Britain and the Commonwealth.

3841   Hugh Barty-King *HMSO: The Story of the First 200 Years 1786–1986* HMSO 1986. The history of Her Majesty's Stationery Office, the government publishing service.

3842   John Attenborough *A Living Memory: Hodder and Stoughton Publishers 1868–1975* Hodder and Stoughton 1975.

3843   *Footprints on the Sands of Time 1863–1963: The Story of the House of Livingstone, Medical, Scientific, Nursing and Dental Publishers* Livingstone 1963.

3844   Asa Briggs (ed) *Essays in the History of Publishing in Celebration of the 250th Anniversary of the House of Longman 1724–1974* Longman 1974. Several of the essays in this collection are of use for the post-war historian and cover, for instance, such changes as the development of the paperback market.

3845   Anthony Rudolf *From Poetry to Politics: The Menard Press 1969–1984* Menard Press 1984. This traces the move of this small press into the publication of anti-nuclear tracts.

3846   Simon Nowell-Smith (ed) *Letters to Macmillan* Macmillan 1967. This is not a history of the publishing firm but is more of a scrapbook drawn from the firm's correspondence files.

**3847** Maureen Duffy *A Thousand Capricious Chances: A History of the Methuen List 1889–1989* Methuen 1989. A good history of the publishing house and its authors.

**3848** John Dreyfus, Davis McKitterick and Simon Rendell *A History of the Nonesuch Press* Nonesuch Press 1981. This was established by Francis Meynell in 1923 and later incorporated into The Bodley Head.

**3849** Nicholas Barker *The Oxford University Press and the Spread of Learning 1478–1978: An Illustrated History* Clarendon 1978.

**3850** *Penguin's Progress 1935–60: Published on the Occasion of the Silver Jubilee of Penguin Books* Penguin 1960. A collection of short commemorative articles on the imprint which, by the introduction of paperbacks, revolutionized publishing.

**3851** George M Thomson Martin *Secker and Warburg: The First Fifty Years: A Memoir* Secker and Warburg 1986. A short memoir of the publishing house.

**3852** William H Brock and A Jack Meadows *The Lamp of Learning: Taylor and Francis and the Development of Science Publishing* Taylor and Francis 1984.

**3853** Trevor Craker *Opening Accounts and Closing Memories: Thirty Years with Thames and Hudson* Thames and Hudson 1985.

**3854** Edward Liveing *Adventure in Publishing: The House of Ward Lock 1854–1954* Ward Lock 1954.

**3855** Arthur King and A F Stuart *The House of Warne: One Hundred Years of Publishing* Warne 1965.

*(ii) Biographies*

**3856** Ralph Arnold *Orange Street and Brickhole Lane* Hart-Davis 1963. This autobiography gives an insight into the work of this medium sized publishing firm in the early post-war years.

**3857** Diana Athill *Instead Of A Letter* Deutsch 1976. Autobiographical reflections on the foundation of the publishing firm of André Deutsch in 1951 and its subsequent development. Athill is Deutsch's partner.

**3858** Deryck Abel *Ernest Benn: Counsel for Liberty* Benn 1960. A biography of the Right-Wing publisher and author.

**3859** *The Letters of John Calman 1951–1980* Murray 1986. Calman was a publisher, journalist and man of letters.

**3860** Brooke Crutchley *To Be A Printer* The Bodley Head 1980. Crutchley worked at Cambridge University Press 1946–74.

**3861** Lovat Dickson *The House of Words* 2v, Macmillan 1963. Reminiscences of his career with Macmillan and Jonathan Cape.

**3862** Edward England *An Unfading Vision: The Adventure of Books* Hodder and Stoughton 1982. Personal reflections on religious publishing with Hodder and Stoughton.

**3863** Sir Norman Flower *Just As It Happened* Cassell 1954. In his publishing career Flower rose to be Chairman of Cassell.

**3864** Ruth Dudley Edwards *Victor Gollancz: A Biography* Gollancz 1987. A candid and sympathetic biography of the Left- Wing publisher and pamphleteer. Among his post-war crusades were calls for the alleviation of suffering in occupied Germany, Arab relief in Palestine (neither of which made him popular with his fellow Jews) and the abolition of capital punishment. See also Victor Gollancz *My Dear Timothy: An Autobiographical Letter to his Grandson* Gollancz 1952 and *More For Timothy: Being the Second Instalment of an Autobiographical Letter to his Grandson* Gollancz 1953.

**3865** Mark Goulden *Mark My Words! The Memoirs of a Journalist/Publisher* W H Allen 1978. His days as a journalist were largely before the Second World War. The climax of his career in publishing was his period as Chairman of W H Allen.

**3866** *Jamie: An 80th Birthday Tribute From His Friends* privately printed 1980. A tribute volume to the publisher Hamish Hamilton.

**3867** Rupert Hart-Davis *The Arms of Time: A Memoir* Hamilton 1979. Hart-Davis was a Director of the synonymous publishing firm 1946–68. His memoirs are also of interest because of his many literary contacts.

**3868** David Higham *Literary Gent* Cape 1978. The autobiography of a literary agent which is also useful on the many authors with whom he was acquainted.

**3869** Alan Hill *In Pursuit of Publishing* Murray 1988. An autobiography by a leading figure at the firm of William Heinemann.

**3870** Richard Joseph *Michael Joseph: Master of Words* Ashford 1986. Michael Joseph was the Chairman and Managing Director of the publishing firm that bears his name.

**3871**  Jack E Morpurgo *Allen Lane: King Penguin* Hutchinson 1979. Allen Lane was the founder of Penguin Books. William E Williams *Allen Lane: A Personal Portrait* The Bodley Head 1973 is a much less substantial account.

**3872**  Sir Robert Lusty *Bound to Be Read* Cape 1975. Lusty was with Michael Joseph 1935–56 and with Hutchinson, where he rose to be Managing Director, 1956–73.

**3873**  For Robert Maxwell, the owner of Pergamon Press, see [3684].

**3874**  Sir Francis Meynell *My Lives* The Bodley Head 1971. Meynell was a book designer, publisher and poet. He founded the Pelican and later the Nonesuch Press, which was later amalgamated with The Bodley Head.

**3875**  S C Roberts *Adventures With Authors* Cambridge University Press 1966. Reminiscences of a career at Cambridge University Press.

**3876**  Roy Stokes *Michael Sadleir 1888–1957* Scarecrow Press 1980. Sadleir was an important figure in the publishing firm of Constable.

**3877**  Sir Stanley Unwin *The Truth About a Publisher: An Autobiographical Record* Macmillan 1960. Sir Stanley in this autobiography also traces the publishing firms that became Allen and Unwin from 1848–1955. Philip Unwin *The Publishing Unwins* Heinemann 1978 traces the history of the family and their publishing firm down to the death of Sir Stanley in 1968. It includes some autobiographical references. David Unwin *Fifty Years With Father: A Relationship* Allen and Unwin 1982 is a biography of Sir Stanley Unwin.

**3878**  Frederic John Warburg *All Authors Are Equal: The Publishing Life of Frederic Warburg 1936–1971* Hutchinson 1971. The autobiography of Frederic Warburg, who was the joint founder of Secker and Warburg in 1936. See also the earlier autobiography *An Occupation for Gentlemen* Hutchinson 1959.

**3879**  Leonard Woolf *The Journey Not The Arrival Matters: An Autobiography of the Years 1939 to 1969* Hogarth Press 1969. Woolf continued to be active on the Hogarth Press in these years. However, this final volume of his autobiography concentrates on the final years of the life of Virginia Woolf before her suicide in 1941 and conveys little of his work in publishing, his editorships of the *Political Quarterly* and the *New Statesman* or his activities on behalf of the Labour Party. Of rather more

value is Duncan Wilson *Leonard Woolf: A Political Biography* Hogarth Press 1978.

### (iii) Printing and Bookbinding

**3880**  Michael Twyman *Printing 1770–1970: An Illustrated History of its Development and Uses in England* Eyre and Spottiswoode 1970.

**3881**  John Lewis *The Twentieth Century Book: Design and Illustration* Studio 1967. This is partly a history and partly an anthology on the typefaces, illustration, layout, binding and dust jackets of twentieth century books. See also Roy Harley Lewis *Fine Bookbinding in the Twentieth Century* David and Charles 1984.

**3882**  James Moran *'Fit to be Styled a Typographer': A History of the Society of Typographic Designers 1928–1978* Westerham Press 1978. A short commemorative history. The Society was originally called the British Typographers Guild.

**3883**  Ellic Howe *The British Federation of Master Printers 1900–50* the Federation 1950.

**3884**  James Moran *The Double Crown Club: A History of Fifty Years* Westerham Press 1974. A commemorative illustrated history of the the dining club of typographers whose members included all the leading figures in this profession.

**3885**  James Moran *Clays of Bungay* Richard Clay 1978. A history of the printing firm.

**3886**  Robert Leach *Let The Ink Flow: The History of the First Fifty Years of Fishburn Ink* Fishburn Printing Ink Co Ltd 1980. A history of a manufacturer of printing materials.

**3887**  Philip Unwin *The Printing Unwins: A Short History of Unwin Brothers, the Gresham Press 1826–1976* Allen and Unwin 1976. A history of the printing firm.

**3888**  James Moran *Stanley Morison: His Typographic Achievement* Lund Humphries 1971. A study particularly of Morison's contribution to typography, design and printing. On Morison see also [3688].

### (f) Comics

**3889**  Denis Gifford *The British Comic Catalogue 1874–1974* Mansell 1975. A comprehensive and informative reference guide.

**3890** *Penny Dreadfuls and Comics: English Periodicals for Children from Victorian Times to the Present Day* Victoria and Albert Museum 1983. An informative and well illustrated exhibition catalogue.

**3891** Frederick Alderson *The Comic Postcard in English Life* David and Charles 1970. A social history of the English comic postcard.

## (g) The Record Industry

Some of the literature in the section on Popular Music is also of relevance.

**3892** Peter Gammond and Raymond Horricks (eds) *The Music Goes Round and Round: A Cool Look at the Record Industry* Quartet 1980. A well illustrated collection of essays looking at the work of the producers, engineers, executives and promoters in the record industry. It includes an outline of the industry's history and transcripts of interviews with some of those who work in it. Michael Wale *Voxpop: Profiles of the Pop Process* Harrap 1972 looks at the roles in the popular music industry of the managers, the record company executives, the producers, the promoters, the session musicians and the stars. Martin Plummer *The Rock Factory* Proteus 1982 is a survey of the contemporary music business. See also Simon Frith 'The Making of the British Record Industry 1920–1964' in James Curran, Anthony Smith and Pauline Wingate (eds) *Impacts and Influences: Essays on Media Power in the Twentieth Century* Methuen 1987 pp 278–90.

**3893** R Miller *The Incredible Music Machine* Quartet 1982. A history of EMI, the record industry to electrical goods group. Brian Southall *Abbey Road: The Story of the World's Most Famous Recording Studio* Stephens 1982 is a detailed history of the EMI studio by the company's press officer. It is well illustrated and useful for tracing the development of recording techniques. On EMI see also [3498].

**3894** Bert Muirhead *Stiff: The Story of a Record Label 1976–1982* Blandford 1983. The history of the punk rock record label.

**3895** Mick Brown *Richard Branson: The Inside Story* Michael Joseph 1988. A biography of the pop entrepreneur and owner of the Virgin company. Branson's interests now include records, retailing, publishing and air transport.

**3896** John Culshaw *Putting the Record Straight* Secker and Warburg 1981. The autobiography of a recording manager and the musical director of Decca Records. It is useful both for his reflections on the record industry and on his relations with great conductors and performers.

**3897** George Martin with Jeremy Hornsby *All You Need is Ears* Macmillan 1979. An autobiographical account of the development of record production during the thirty years of Martin's career. Martin was most famous for his work in recording and producing the Beatles.

## (h) Postal Services

**3898** Jean Farrugia *A Guide to Post Office Archives* Post Office Archives 1986. A good annotated guide. Unfortunately little on the post-war era is yet available.

**3899** Martin J Daunton *The Post Office Since 1840* Athlone Press 1985. A well illustrated history. Unfortunately it only has a epilogue on the post-war period. See also Nancy Martin *The Post Office: From Carrier Pigeon to Confravision* Dent 1969.

**3900** Michael Corby *The Postal Business 1969–79: A Study in Public Sector Management* Kogan Page 1979. This reviews the performance of the postal side of the Post Office in the first decade since it became a public corporation rather than a department of state. An authoritative and balanced account which criticizes the effect of continued government intervention.

**3901** *Report of the Post Office Review Committee* Cmnd 6850, *Parliamentary Papers* 1976–77. The report of the committee chaired by C F Carter. It suggested that the Post Office should be split into its functions of posts and telecommunications (subsequently implemented) and that there should be a reappraisal of management and pricing. On the difficulties of the Post Office in the 1970s see R J S Baker 'The Postal Service: A Problem of Identity' *Political Quarterly* 47 1976 pp 59–70.

## (i) Telecommunications

**3902** Douglas Pitt *The Telecommunications Function in the British Post Office: A Case Study of Bureaucratic Adaptation* Saxon House 1980. A political analysis of the telecommunications part of the Post Office from 1878 ending with the establishment of the Post Office Corporation in 1969. The telecommunications function was later separated from the Post Office as British Telecom. *Britain's Public Telephones: A Social History* British Telecom 1984 is a more conventional history of the development of Britain's telephone network and its social impact.

**3903** Nicholas Garnham 'Telecommunications Policy in the United Kingdom' *Media, Culture and Society* 7 1985 pp 7–30. A useful survey of contemporary policy.

**3904** Karin Newman *The Selling of British Telecom* Holt, Rinehart and Winston 1986. In 1984 the state-owned British Telecom was privatized. This is an analysis of the policy and the process of sale during the first major privatization of the Thatcher government. See also Jeremy Moon and P Smart 'The Privatisation of British Telecom: A Case Study of the Extended Process of Legislation' *European Journal of Political Research* 14 1986 pp 339–55. Francis Hawkings 'Selling British Telecom' *Policy Studies* 7 1987 pp 1–20 focuses on the criticism that the share price fixed by the government was too low, thus enabling massive profit-taking by speculators at the government's expense, but it also covers the logistics of the operation.

**3905** Hugh Barty-King *Girdle Round the World: The Story of Cable and Wireless and its Predecessors to Mark the Group's Jubilee 1929–1979* Heinemann 1979. The Dominions had expressed the view at a 1944 Commonwealth conference that a public utility company in Britain should be set up in Britain to co-ordinate imperial cable and wireless services. Cable and Wireless, which had been set up in 1929, was accordingly nationalized in 1946 and remained in the public sector until privatized by the Thatcher government.

**3906** Peter Young *Power of Speech: A History of Standard Telephones and Cables 1883–1983* Allen and Unwin 1983. Now known as STC.

(j) Advertising

**3907** Sally King *The Economist Pocket Guide to Advertising* Blackwell 1989. A well illustrated dictionary.

**3908** Terry R Nevett *Advertising in Britain: A History* Heinemann 1982. A general historical survey which is much more useful for the nineteenth than the twentieth century. The growth, increasing professionalism and impact of the advertising industry is analysed in Douglas C West 'The Growth and Development of the Advertising Industry Within the United Kingdom 1920–1970' Leeds PhD Thesis 1985. See also *75 Years of Advertising* Society of British Advertisers 1975.

**3909** John Pearson and Graham Turner *The Persuasion Industry* Eyre and Spottiswoode 1965. An analysis of the advertising and public relations industries. It consists mostly of case studies. The section on the public relations industry contains some useful reflections on public relations for the Conservative and Labour parties and other efforts in political public relations. Jeremy Tunstall *The Advertising Men in London Advertising Agencies* Chapman and Hall 1964 is another collection of case studies of advertising, market research, public relations for political parties and other clients and of the industry in general. Denis Thomas *The Visible Persuaders* Hutchinson 1967 is a defence of the advertising industry.

**3910** Ralph Harris and Arthur Seldon *Advertising in Britain* Hutchinson 1962. A booklet on the objectives and results of advertising in Britain based on seventy case studies.

**3911** D S Dunbar *Almost Gentleman: The Growth and Development of the Advertising Agent 1875–1975* privately printed 1976. The histories of several organizations involved in the sales promotion industry, and especially that of the British Sales Promotion Association, which was established in 1933, are traced in Faith Legh 'Half a Century of Professional Bodies in Sales Promotion' *Journal of Advertising History* 9 1986 pp 27–40.

**3912** Brian Henry *British Television Advertising: The First Thirty Years* Century Benham 1986. See also J Gable *The Tuppenny Punch and Judy Show: 25 Years of TV Commercials* Michael Joseph 1980. This surveys the history of television advertising, charts the history of some outstanding campaigns and reflects on how society is reflected in and affected by television advertising. Walter Taplin *The Origins of Television Advertising in the United Kingdom* Pitman 1961 is a short account of its early years.

**3913** Allan Halstead *F H Brown 40 Years: Advertising Special* privately printed 1969. A history of the advertising firm of F H Brown Ltd.

**3914** G H Saxon Mills *There is a Tide* Heinemann 1954. A study of the career in advertising of Sir William Crawford, of his firm and of the history of British advertising since 1914.

**3915** Stanley Piggott *OBM: A Celebration: One Hundred and Twenty Five Years in Advertising* Ogilvy, Benson and Mather 1975. A history of the firm.

**3916** Ivan Fallon *The Brothers: The Rise and Rise of Saatchi and Saatchi* Century Hutchinson 1988. A study of the advertising agency set up by the Saatchi brothers in the 1960s, briefly the largest advertising agency in the world, and a biography of its creators. It also considers their work for the Conservative Party and their impact on the world of advertising. See also Philip Klieman *The Saatchi and Saatchi Story* Weidenfeld and Nicolson 1987.

**3917** Douglas C West 'From T-Square to T-Plan: The London Office of the J Walter Thompson Advertising Agency 1919–70' *Business History* 29 1987 pp 199–217. A history of the London operations of this American agency.

**3918** David Mackenzie Ogilvy *Blood, Brains and Beer* Hamilton 1978. The autobiography of the Chairman of Ogilvy, Benson and Mather. See also his earlier *Confessions of An Advertising Man* Hutchinson 1964.

**3919** *A History of Bovril Advertising Compiled by Peter Hadley* Bovril Ltd 1970. On the history of the advertising of other products see *The First 25 Years: History as Mirrored in the Advertising of Shell-Mex and BP Ltd 1932–1957* Shell-Mex/BP 1957 and B Sibley *The History of Guinness Advertising* Guinness Books 1985.

**3920** Brian Ash *Tiger in Your Tank* Cassell 1969 is an anatomy of the celebrated use of the symbol of the tiger in the advertising campaigns of the Esso petrol company.

## (10) Food and Drink Industries

### (a) Food and Non-Alcoholic Beverages

**3921** R W D Mackintosh *Frozen Foods: The Growth of an Industry* Refrigeration Press 1962. A history of the development of frozen food technology, industry and retailing in Britain.

**3922** W J Reader *Birds Eye: The Early Years* Birds Eye 1963. A history of the food company.

**3923** J B Bibby and C L Bibby *A Miller's Tale: A History of J Bibby and Sons Ltd, Liverpool* J Bibby and Sons 1978.

**3924** Godfrey Harrison *Borthwick's: A Century in the Meat Trade 1863–1963* Borthwick 1963. A history of Thomas Borthwick and Sons Ltd.

**3925** David Wainwright *Brooke Bond: A Hundred Years* Newman Neame 1970. The history of the company's stock cube, Oxo, launched in 1905, is traced in Penny Vinchezi *Taking Stock* Collins 1985.

**3926** *Industrial Challenge: The Experience of Cadburys of Bournville in the Post-War Years* Pitman 1964. A study of the Birmingham-based chocolate manufacturers.

**3927** Wynford Vaughan-Thomas *Dalgety: The Romance of a Business* Melland 1984. A history of the international food business.

**3928** Patrick Beaver *Yes! We Have Some: The Story of Fyffes* Publications for Companies 1976. The history of the food importers.

**3929** T A B Corley *Quaker Enterprise in Biscuits: Huntley and Palmers of Reading 1822–1972* Hutchinson 1972.

**3930** Hugh Barty-King *Food For Man And Beast: The Story of the London Corn Trade Association, the London Cattle Food Trade Association and the Grain and Feed Trade Association, 1878–1978* Hutchinson Benham 1978. A short history.

**3931** Louise Wright *The Road from Aston Cross: An Industrial History 1875–1975* HP-Smedley Foods 1975. A short history of the company.

**3932** P Chalmin *Tate and Lyle: Sugar Giant* Harvard Academic 1987. An analysis of one of the largest food companies in the world. In the post-war period it withdrew from sugar production in the face of nationalizations in the developing world and became a multi-national sugar refiner, though ironically it was later invited back to manage the nationalized sugar industries of Jamaica and Trinidad. See also his 'The Strategy of a Multinational in the World Sugar Economy: The Case of Tate and Lyle 1870–1980' in Alice Teichova, Maurice Lévy and Helga Nussbaum (eds) *Multinational Enterprises in Historical Perspective* Cambridge University Press 1986 pp 103–15. Another history of the company is J A C Hugill *Sugar And All That: A History of Tate and Lyle* Gentry Books 1978.

**3933** James S Adams *A Fell Fine Baker: The Story of United Biscuits* Hutchinson Benham 1974.

**3934** Phillip Knightley *The Vestey Affair* Macdonald 1981. A study of the Vestey family and their wealth, which is especially derived from food-processing, meat and agriculture.

**3935** Gervas Huxley *Both Hands: An Autobiography* Chatto and Windus 1970. This autobiography is useful to the post-war historian for its reflections on the tea trade, which was important in the post-war period for the sterling balances as an earner of dollars, on the Colonial Office, and on the creation of the National Parks.

**3936** Harold Vincent Mackintosh *By Faith and Works: The Autobiography of the Rt Hon the First Viscount Mackintosh DL LLD* Hutchinson 1966. This autobiography of the chocolate manufacturer is also useful on his work for the Methodist Church.

## (b) Alcoholic Beverages

The drink industry has traditionally been one of the most heavily regulated. It is also an industry which has considerable social impact. It is the general literature, the literature on the industry per se (the brewing and distilling firms), and on the public houses, that appears below. So does material relating to the licensing law, though the material on the law on drink-driving has instead been included in the section on the law [2544]. That which is concerned with patterns of consumption, with temperance or with drunkenness can be found in the section on Lifestyles [6026–33].

**3937**  E J Higgs 'Research into the History of Alcohol Use and Control in England and Wales: The Available Sources in the Public Record Office' *British Journal of Addiction* 79 1984 pp 41–7.

**3938**  *Liquor Licensing Statistics for England and Wales* HMSO 1970–. Annual statistics.

**3939**  David M Fahey 'Drink and Temperance in the United Kingdom: Works Appearing 1940–1980' *Alcohol and Temperance History Group Newsletter* 3 1981.

**3940**  Gwylmor Prys Williams and George Thompson Brake *Drink in Great Britain 1900–1979* Edsall 1980. A worthy successor to George Bailey Wilson *Alcohol and the Nation* Nicholson and Watson 1940. The standard history of the development of the drink trade, of liquor licensing and of changes in the patterns of drunkenness in the twentieth century, amply supported by statistics.

**3941**  *Report of the Departmental Committee on Liquor Licensing* Cmnd 5154, *Parliamentary Papers* xiv 1972–73. This committee, chaired by Lord Erroll of Hale, recommended that on-licences should be allowed to open from 10 am to midnight and that off-licences' hours should be extended to 8.30 am to midnight, that the age limit should be reduced to seventeen, and that sixteen year olds should be allowed some drinks in restaurants. It was not implemented but the 1988 Licensing Act marked a move towards its recommendations. Rob Baggott 'Licensing Law Reform and the Return of the Drink Question' *Parliamentary Affairs* 40 1987 pp 501–16 surveys the development of licensing law since 1945. The tendency in these years has been towards liberalization, and after the Licensing (England and Wales) Act 1961, which allowed supermarkets to sell drink, the number of off-licences doubled in the next twenty years. At the same time concern about alcohol abuse was growing leading to measures such as the Sporting Events (Alcohol Control) Act 1985. This inconsistency, particularly under the Thatcher government, between general liberalization and a tightening of regulation in certain circumstances is also considered in the context both of post-war history and of the various pressure groups attempting to influence licensing policy in Baggott's 'Alcohol, Politics and Social Policy' *Journal of Social Policy* 15 1986 pp 467–88.

**3942**  K H Hawkins and C L Pass *The Brewing Industry: A Study in Industrial Organisation and Public Policy* Heinemann 1979. A political analysis of the brewing industry from the nineteenth century to the 1970s and of its current organization. Also of use is John Mark 'Changing in the Brewing Industry in the Twentieth Century' in Derek S Oddy and Derek J Miller (eds) *Diet and Health in Modern Britain* Croom Helm 1985 pp 81–101. An earlier study is John Vaisey *The Brewing Industry 1886–1951: An Economic Study* Pitman 1960. Technical change and investment in technical change in the post-war industry is examined in K A Marsden 'Technical Change in the British Malting Industry' Salford PhD Thesis 1985. See also H D Watts 'Market Areas and Spatial Rationalisation: The British Brewing Industry After 1945' *Tijdschrift voor Economische en Social Geographie* 68 1977 pp 224–40. Also of interest is the history of the first fifty years of the Allied Brewery Traders Association, 'The ABTA Golden Jubilee' *Brewers Guardian* 86 1957 pp 61–70.

**3943**  K H Hawkins *A History of Bass Charrington* Oxford University Press 1978. A history of Britain's largest brewer. For other histories of breweries see J Norman Slater *A Brewer's Tale: The Story of Greenall Whitley and Co Ltd Through Two Centuries* Greenall Whitley 1980, R G Wilson *Greene King: A Business and a Family History* The Bodley Head 1983, John Falcon Brown *Guinness and Hops* Arthur Guinness 1980, George Benson *Kemberley Ale: The Story of Hardys and Hensons: Kimberley 1932–1982* Melland 1982, Henry Hurford Janes *Albion Brewery 1808–1958: The Story of Mann, Crossman and Paulin Ltd* Harley Publishing 1959 and Terry R Gourvish *Beers from English Barley: A History of Steward and Patteson 1793–1963* Centre of East Anglian Studies, University of East Anglia 1987. This last firm was taken over by Watneys in 1963. On Watneys see Henry Hurford Janes *The Red Barrel: A History of Watney Mann* Murray 1963. See also *Trumans: The Brewers 1666–1966* Newman Neame 1966. W J Reader *Grand Metropolitan: A History 1962–1987* Oxford University Press 1988 is a history of the brewing to hotelier leisure industry group.

**3943A**  Sir Sydney Oswald Nevile *Seventy Rolling Years* Faber 1958. Nevile was a director of Whitbread 1919–68, active in the Brewers' Society and other brweing organizations and on the management of the State Management Districts 1921–55.

**3944**  James Saunders *Nightmare: The Ernest Saunders Story* Hutchinson 1989. A filial defence of his father's business career, which culminated in his chairmanship at Guinness and the controversial takeover of Distillers.

**3945** Asa Briggs *Wine for Sale: Victoria Wine and the Liquor Trade 1860–1984* Batsford 1985. A history of the chain of off-licences.

**3945A** George Bruce *A Wine Day's Work: The London House of Deinhard 1835-1985* Deinhard 1985. A history of a family-owned vintners.

**3946** L W Hagan and M J Waterson *The Relationship Between Alcohol Advertising and Consumption: A Preliminary Study* 1980. A study over the previous twenty years to see if advertising has influenced the growth of consumption over the period. It concludes that it has not because it is brand-related and only affects the brand shares of the market. On alcohol advertising see also H S Goodwin *Ten Years of Advertising Alcohol: A Study of Expenditure and Trends in the Sales Promotion of Alcoholic Drinks* Christian Economic and Social Research Foundation 1969. Consumption is examined in Tony McGuinness 'An Econometric Analysis of the Total Demand for Alcoholic Beverages in the UK 1956–75' *Journal of Industrial Economics* 29 1980 pp 85–109.

**3947** *The Good Beer Guide* CAMRA 1974–. An informative annual guide published by the Campaign for Real Ale. It is most useful for tracing the effect of the Campaign and changes in the beer industry in recent years. Richard Boston *Beer and Skittles* Collins 1976 is partly a history of CAMRA and partly an examination of the contemporary public house both as a purveyor of drinks and as a social institution. Also on the public house as a social institution see M A Smith '"Protestant" Asceticism and Working Class Conviviality: A Sociological Study of the Public House, with Special Reference to the Post-War Period' London PhD Thesis 1981. The most thorough examination of the public house in the post-war period is Gwylmor Prys Williams and George Thompson Brake *The English Public House in Transition* Edsall 1982. See also Christopher Hutt *The Death of the English Pub* Hutchinson 1973. Michael Jackson *The English Pub* Collins 1976 is a well-illustrated guide to the beers, pub arts and entertainments and activities. A general history of the public house which includes some useful information on sales and drinks in the post-war era is H A Monckton *A History of the English Public House* The Bodley Head 1969.

**3948** L P Wilkinson *Bulmers of Hereford: A Century of Cider-Making* David and Charles 1987. A history of the company.

(c) Tobacco

**3949** Peter Taylor *Smoke Ring: The Politics of Tobacco* The Bodley Head 1984. This is a good journalistic examination of the power and worldwide activities of British and American tobacco multinationals. It also traces the growth of the campaign against smoking. Another study of the British and American tobacco giants is M Corina *Trust in Tobacco: The Anglo-American Struggle for Power* Michael Joseph 1975.

**3950** G T Popham 'Government and Smoking: Policy Making and Pressure Groups' *Policy and Politics* 9 1981 pp 331–43. On government policy on smoking 1974–79 see Mike Daube 'The Politics of Smoking: The Labour Record' *Community Medicine* 1 1979 pp 306–14.

**3951** P H Mack *The Golden Weed: A History of Tobacco and of the House of Andrew Chambers 1865–1965* Newman Neame 1965. Other relevant company histories are W T Davies *Fifty Years of Progress: An Account of the African Organisation of the Imperial Tobacco Company 1907–57* Imperial Tobacco 1958 and B W E Alford *W D and H O Wills and the Development of the UK Tobacco Industry 1786–1965* Methuen 1973.

**3952** Mary Dunhill *Our Family Business* The Bodley Head 1979. An autobiography in which she reflects on the history of Dunhill International, the tobacco and luxury goods firm founded by her father, in which she worked for most of her life.

### (11) Other Industries

(a) Furniture and Furnishings

**3953** J L Oliver *The Development and Structure of the Furniture Industry* Pergamon 1966.

**3954** *Working Party Report on the Furniture Trade* HMSO 1946. This reports the state of the industry at the end of the war and under post-war austerity.

**3955** Jack Pritchard *View From a Long Chair* Routledge and Kegan Paul 1984. Memoirs of the Furniture Design Council and the furniture industry.

**3956** Nigel Whiteley '"Semi-Works of Art": Consumerism, Youth Culture and Chair Design in the 1960s' *Furniture History* 23 1987 pp 108–26. A study of the effects of the growth of consumerism on design in the 1960s from the advent of Terence Conran's Habitat shops to Peter Murdoch's paper chair.

**3957** Pat Kirkham, Rodney Mace and Julia Porter *Furnishing the World: The East London Furniture Trade 1830–1980* Journeyman 1987. The industry in this area has been in decline in the post-war period. This is a history of the making of the furniture and its distribution and marketing, making some use of oral history. It has a useful bibliography.

**3958** Sutherland Lyall *Hille: 75 Years of British Furniture* Elron Press 1981. An exhibition catalogue and history of the furniture company which began as a manufacturer of reproduction furniture and became a leader in the field of modern furniture after 1945.

**3959** E Myer *Myer's First Century 1876–1976: The Story of Myer's Comfortable Beds* the Company 1976.

**3960** Barbara Tilson 'Stones of Banbury (1870–1978): A Casualty of the Recession' *Furniture History* 23 1987 pp 98–107. A good history up to the demise of the company in the 1970s.

(b) Overseas Traders

**3961** Stephanie Jones *Two Centuries of Overseas Trading: The Origins and Growth of the Inchcape Group* Macmillan 1986. Whilst useful on the confusing amalgamation of the companies operating in the Inchcape Group in 1958 this history is generally thin on analysis and she does not, as she declares that she is going to, examine the vital but neglected topic of the marketing of British goods abroad. The history is also a little weak on the company's difficulties in recent years.

**3962** Suzanne Cronjé, Margaret Ling and Gillian Cronjé *Lonrho: Portrait of a Multinational* Julian Friedmann 1976. A study of the very diverse, high profile multinational trader. Richard Hall *My Life With Tiny: A Biography of Tiny Rowland* Faber 1983 is a study of the company's leading figure.

**3963** H E W Braund *Calling to Mind: Being some Account of the First Hundred Years (1870 to 1970) of Steel Brothers and Company Limited* Pergamon 1975. The history of an international trading and holding company.

(c) Paper and Related Industries

**3964** A H Shorter *Paper Making in the British Isles: An Historical and Geographical Survey* David and Charles 1971. This includes some information on the post-war development of the industry. See also S N Morris 'The United Kingdom Paper Trade: A Case Study of Business Behaviour in the Short Period 1948–1954' Cambridge PhD Thesis 1957–8.

**3965** W J Reader *Bowater: A History* Cambridge University Press 1981.

(d) Other

**3966** C H Ward-Jackson *The 'Cellophane' Story: Origins of a British Industrial Group* British Cellophane Ltd 1977.

**3967** Debbie Moore *When a Woman Means Business* Michael Joseph 1989. The autobiography of the model who founded the Pineapple Dance Studios in 1982.

**3968** R J Hercock and G S Jones *Silver by the Ton: A History of Ilford Limited 1879–1979* McGraw-Hill 1979. A good history of the film-making and processing firm, which also analyses aspects of the firm such as technical development, industrial relations or marketing.

**3969** R A Church *Kenricks in Hardware: A Family Business 1791–1966* David and Charles 1969. The history of a foundry and domestic hardware firm. It has quite a lot of material on the post-war period.

**3970** M J G Cattermole and A F Wolfe *Horace Darwin's Shop: A History of the Cambridge Scientific Instruments Company 1878 to 1968* Adam Hilger 1987. A study of the appliance of experimental science. A history of this company of instrument makers with case studies of the development of particular of its products.

**3971** Patrick Beaver *The Match Makers* Melland 1985. A history of Bryant and May, the manufacturers of matches and household goods. See also Walter Lucas *Making Matches 1861–1961* Newman Neame 1961.

**3972** C S Dingley *The Story of BIP 1894–1962* British Industrial Plastics 1963.

**3973** James McMillan *The Dunlop Story* Weidenfeld and Nicolson 1989. A centenary history of the company which produced the first pneumatic rubber tyre. On aspects of the rubber industry see also D Todd 'The Development of the Synthetic Rubber Industry and its Competitive Position with Respect to Natural Rubber' Manchester MA (Econ) Thesis 1964–5.

**3974** J Whitaker *The Best: A History of H H Martyn and Co: Carvers in Wood, Stone and Marble* privately printed 1985. An extensive company history.

**3975** Edward Bryan Latham *History of the Timber Trade Federation of the United Kingdom: The First 70*

*Years* Benn 1965. The history of a firm which grows, processes and markets timber is examined in Patrick Beaver *The Alsford Tradition: A Century of Quality Timber 1882–1982* Melland 1982. Augustus Muir *Anderson's of Islington: The History of C F Anderson and Son Ltd 1863–1963* Newman Neame 1963 is a history of a firm of timber merchants.

**3976**  P Trench *Model Cars and Road Vehicles* Pelham 1983. A history of British die-cast manufacturers of model toy cars from the 1930s to the 1980s.

**3977**  John Gray 'Growing a New Industry' *Design* 85 1956 pp 13–9. A survey of the British watch industry since 1945.

## D. ENERGY

### (1) General

**3978**  *Digest of United Kingdom Energy Statistics* HMSO 1972–. An essential annual collection of statistics. The Department of Energy also publishes the monthly *Energy Trends*.

**3979**  John Fernie *A Geography of Energy in the United Kingdom* Longman 1980. A review of the changing geography of the energy industry since 1945 and the environmental and ecological problems of the future.

**3980**  Lynn F Pearson *The Organisation of the Energy Industry* Macmillan 1981. A comprehensive guide. It is very detailed on the structure of the industry but less so on the policy making. It is also very useful on the organization of the Department of Energy.

**3981**  G L Reid, Kevin Allen and D J Harris *The Nationalised Fuel Industries* Heinemann 1973. A historical treatment in turn of the coal, gas and electricity industries. See also William G Shepperd *Economic Performance Under Public Ownership: British Fuel and Power* Yale University Press, New Haven, Connecticut 1965. On the role of the coal industry in fuel policy see also E S Simpson *Coal and the Power Industries in Postwar Britain* Longmans 1966.

**3982**  Alex J Robertson *The Bleak Midwinter: Britain and the Fuel Crisis of 1947* Manchester University Press 1987. A good study of the fuel crisis that hit in 1947 in the midst of the worst winter on record. He argues that this crisis, and the Attlee government's failure to avert it, was a major turning point in the life of the post-war Labour government, undermining economic recovery and government morale and demonstrating the hollowness of the claim for the efficiency of economic planning. This is thus also a major contribution to the historiography of the Attlee government. The crisis led to the decisions to develop nuclear power and to shift away from a dependence on coal and make increasing use of oil.

**3983**  *Domestic Fuel Policy* Cmnd 6762, *Parliamentary Papers* xii 1945–46. The report of the Fuel and Power Advisory Council chaired by Sir Ernest Simon set up to consider and advise on the use of fuels and the provision of heat in domestic circumstances, and especially on their efficient use and the prevention of pollution. It recommended smokeless solid fuel and minimum standards for heating appliances and stressed the corresponding importance of the development of central heating.

**3984**  *Report of the Committee on National Policy for the Use of Fuel and Power Resources* Cmnd 8647, *Parliamentary Papers* xii 1951–52. The report of the committee, chaired by Viscount Ridley, which called for more efficient use of energy resources in the light of the fuel crisis of 1947.

**3985**  S Mandel 'An Analysis of the Patterns of Energy in the United Kingdom and Scotland During the Period 1955–1974' Stirling PhD Thesis 1977.

**3986**  D Pearce *United Kingdom Energy Policy: An Historical Overview 1945–1982* University of Aberdeen 1982. See also J N Solomos 'The Political Economy of Energy Policy in Britain: A Study in the Form and Functions of State Intervention 1960–1978' Sussex MPhil Thesis 1980.

**3987**  *Fuel Policy* Cmnd 3438, *Parliamentary Papers* xxxix 1967–68. A White Paper issued in the light of the discovery of North Sea gas. The development of fuel policy in the wake of this White Paper is traced in Michael V Posner *Fuel Policy: A Study in Applied Economics* Macmillan 1973.

**3988**  Peter James *The Politics of Energy Technology: Britain's Energy Policy 1973–86* Macmillan 1986. A study of the development of energy policy since the energy crisis caused by the the dramatic rise in oil prices in 1973.

### (2) Coal

Items dealing with the coal industry in Scotland or Wales can be found under their respective national headings. Some items with relevance to the history of the coal industry can also be found in the section on mining and quarrying. The literature on the history of industrial relations in the industry and of its unions should also be consulted.

**3989** *National Coal Board Report and Accounts* National Coal Board 1946–. Until 1972/73 this annual report was published by HMSO as a *House of Commons Paper*. Since then it has been published by the National Coal Board, now known as British Coal. See also the annual *National Coal Board Statistical Tables*.

**3990** John Benson, Robert G Neville and Charles H Thompson *Bibliography of the British Coal Industry: Secondary Literature, Parliamentary and Departmental Papers, Mineral Maps and Plans and a Guide to Sources* Oxford University Press 1981. A comprehensive bibliography with some annotations.

**3991** A R Griffin *The British Coalmining Industry – Retrospect and Prospect* Macmillan 1977. A reasonably comprehensive and concise general history which is rather focused on developments in the East Midlands. Michael P Jackson *The Price of Coal* Croom Helm 1974 is a history of the industry in the twentieth century, especially in the context of its market position, the selling price of coal and poor returns.

**3992** William Ashworth *The History of the British Coal Industry Vol 5: 1946–1982* Clarendon 1986. An official history covering the period from the nationalization of the industry to the resignations of Derek Ezra as Chairman of the NCB and Joe Gormley as President of the National Union of Mineworkers. A detailed and comprehensive account. The history of the industry since nationalization is also examined in G Manners *Coal in Britain* Allen and Unwin 1981, Israel Berkovitch *Coal on the Switchback: The Coal Industry Since Nationalisation* Allen and Unwin 1977 and Joel Krieger *Undermining Capitalism: State Ownership and the Dialectic of Control in the British Coal Industry* Princeton University Press, Princeton, New Jersey 1983. On the contraction of the industry over the post-war period see A Stander 'The Role of Political, Economic and Technological Factors in the Contraction of the British Coal Industry' Manchester MSc Thesis 1973–4. On NCB policy see E F Schumacher 'Some Aspects of Coal Board Policy 1947–1967' *Economic Studies* 4 1969 pp 3–29.

**3993** Barry Supple *The History of the British Coal Industry Vol 4: 1913–1946: The Political Economy of Decline* Clarendon 1987. An excellent contribution to the official history which provides an essential backdrop to the nationalization of the industry. It concentrates on the evolution of public policy and the economic performance and structure of the industry, providing a classic study of the inability and unwillingness of the industry under private ownership to adapt to technical and economic change and of the resulting social consequences.

Another good history of the years leading up to nationalization is Maurice W Kirby *The British Coalmining Industry 1870–1946: A Political and Economic History* Macmillan 1977. The background to nationalization is also traced, rather more from the coalowners point of view, in W A Lee *Thirty Years in Coal 1917–1947: A Review of the Coalmining Industry Under Private Enterprise* Mining Association of Great Britain 1954.

**3994** G E Graham 'The Organisational Structure of the National Coal Board' London PhD Thesis 1962–3.

**3995** D M Kelly and D J Forsyth (eds) *Studies in the British Coal Industry* Pergamon 1969. This includes useful essays on the post-war contraction of the industry and its mechanization. The massive capital investment in the industry after nationalization transformed the previously slow rate of technological development, as S C A Walker 'Development of Mining Electrical Technology, with Special Reference to the South Midlands Area' Nottingham PhD Thesis 1986 reveals. On technological change in Yorkshire see R Hepworth *et al* 'The Effects of Technological Change in the Yorkshire Coalfield 1960–1965' *Economic Studies* 4 1969 pp 221–37.

**3996** N C Brewer 'Some Aspects of the British Coking Industry in the Twentieth Century, with Emphasis on Plants in Yorkshire and Derbyshire' Loughborough PhD Thesis 1981.

**3997** Sir Guy Nott-Bower and R H Walkerdine (eds) *National Coal Board: The First Ten Years: A Review of the First Decade of the Nationalised Coal Mining Industry in Great Britain* Colliery Guardian 1956. The first decade of nationalization is also surveyed in G E Baldwin *Beyond Nationalisation – Problems of the Coal Industry* Harvard University Press, Cambridge Massachusetts 1955 and W Haynes *Nationalisation in Practice: The British Coal Industry* Bailey Brothers 1953. See also A Young, H A Longdon and B L Metcalf 'Post-War Developments in the Coal Mining Industry' *Proceedings of the Institute of Civil Engineers* 6 1957 pp 662–708 and T M Thomas 'Recent Trends and Developments in the British Coal Mining Industry' *Economic Geography* 34 1958 pp 19–41. On the organization of the industry during the first years of nationalization see D W Kelly 'The Study of the Administration of the Coal Industry in Great Britain Since 1946 with Special Reference to the Problem of Decentralisation' Wales MA Thesis 1952–3.

**3998** C M Knight 'A Geographical Analysis of the Effects Upon Selected Communities of Closure and Reorganisation of Collieries in the Northern Coalfield Since 1957' Newcastle MLitt Thesis 1968–9.

**3999** Alfred Robens *Ten Years Stint* Cassell 1972. A memoir of his period as Chairman of the NCB 1961–71.

4000   Jim Bullock *Them and Us* Souvenir Press 1972. The autobiography of a Yorkshire miner who became the National President of the Association of Colliery Management 1956–69.

4001   M A Walker 'The Coal Miner this Century: Social and Economic Relationships in the Light of the Changing Labour Process' Keele MA Thesis 1981. See also C E Jencks 'Social Status of Coal Miners in Britain Since Nationalisation' *American Journal of Economics and Sociology* 26 1967 pp 301–12, L J Hardy 'Absenteeism and Attendance in the British Coal-Mining Industry: An Examination of Post-War Trends' *British Journal of Industrial Relations* 6 1968 pp 27–50 and R E Goffee 'Kent Miners: Stability and Change in Work and Community 1927–1976' Kent PhD Thesis 1979.

4002   A Moyes 'Post-War Changes in Coalmining in the West Midlands' *Geography* 59 1974 pp 111–20.

4003   A R Griffin *The Nottinghamshire Coalfield 1881–1981: A Century of Progress* Moorland Publications 1981. A good general history. R J Weller *The Dukeries Transformed: The Social and Political Development of a Twentieth Century Coalfield* Clarendon 1983 is a study, rich in its use of oral sources, of the history of this Nottinghamshire coalfield up to the middle of the century, an area of relatively large, well organized, paternalistic colliery companies.

4004   D-M O'Donnell 'The Anticipated Impact of Modern Colliery Development on Agriculture : The Case of the Selby Coalfield, North Yorkshire' Hull MPhil Thesis 1982. The steep rise in oil prices in 1973–4 stimulated interest in the development of the large Selby coalfield. This study concentrates on the public inquiries and agricultural opposition in this rich farming area.

## (3) Oil and Gas Extraction

Some literature on North Sea oil which particularly applies to Scotland can also be found in the section on energy in Scotland.

4005   *United Kingdom Offshore Oil and Gas Yearbook* Telford 1982. A guide to offshore operations.

4006   *Offshore Abstracts* Offshore Information Literature 1974–. A bimonthly guide to recent literature on offshore gas and oil extraction.

4007   Elaine M Dunphy *Oil: A Bibliography* Aberdeen and North of Scotland Library and Information Co-operative Services 1977. A detailed guide to the literature which is excellent on the material on North Sea oil. For the literature published since this bibliography appeared *Information Offshore* HMSO 1979–, the Department of Energy Library's occasional select bibliography, should be consulted. Richard Ardern (comp) *Offshore Oil and Gas: A Guide to Sources of Information* Capital Planning Information 1978 is a well organized and indexed guide to sources of information and their publications. See also Ian Maclean *North Sea Oil Information Sources: A Source Guide Bibliography and Media Data Summary* Kogan Page 1975 and A J Macauley (comp) *North Sea Oil: A Select List: Periodical and Newspaper Articles* Edinburgh College of Commerce 1974.

4008   Roy Hayman *The Institute of Fuel: The First Fifty Years* Institute of Fuel 1977. A history of the professional body which oversees the education of fuel scientists and engineers and promotes the professional interests of fuel technologists.

4009   Danny Hann *Government and North Sea Oil* Macmillan 1986. An examination of British oil policy since 1964. A fascinating study of all aspects of policy over this period and of the background of a constantly changing tax regime. M A Scoones 'The Development of the UK National Regime for Oil and Gas 1934–1981' Open University MPhil Thesis 1985 is largely concerned with government involvement in the development of the North Sea oil and gas fields since the 1960s. Also on government policy see Donald Cameron Watt 'Britain and North Sea Oil: Policies Past and Present' *Political Quarterly* 47 1976 pp 377–97 and J C Woodliffe 'State Participation in the Development of United Kingdom Offshore Petroleum Resources' *Public Law* 1977 pp 249–71. On the conflict of interest between the government and the oil companies over the development of these resources in the 1970s see Peter R Odell and Kenneth E Rosing *Optimal Development of the North Sea's Oil Fields: A Study in Divergent Government and Company Interests and Their Reconciliation* Kogan Page 1976.

4010   Bryan Cooper and T F Gaskell *The Adventure of North Sea Oil* Heinemann 1976. A survey of the problems involved in exploration and production. The exploration for oil and gas in the North Sea is discussed in Clive Callow *Power from the Sea: The Search for North Sea Oil and Gas* Gollancz 1973. See also John Fernie 'The Development of North Sea Oil and Gas Resources' *Scottish Geographical Magazine* 93 1977 pp 21–31. Institute of Petroleum *A Guide to North Sea Oil and Gas Technology* Heyden 1978 collects nineteen papers on the exploration, production, transport and storage of North Sea oil and gas and on oil and gas resources on the mainland. A similarly comprehensive discussion British oil resources, their extraction and transportation, with good diagrams and detailed statistics, is M Lovegrove *Our Island's Oil* Witherby 1975.

**4011** Keith Chapman *North Sea Oil and Gas: A Geographical Perspective* David and Charles 1976. This study is particularly strong on the political aspects of the distribution of the licences for offshore drilling and the development cost/revenue equation, the discoveries of deposits in 1964–74 and its on-shore impact.

**4012** Adrian Hamilton *North Sea Impact: Off-Shore and the British Economy* International Institute for Economic Research 1978. A history of the exploration for North Sea oil and a study of its initial impact on the British economy. See also D I Mackay and G A Mackay *The Political Economy of North Sea Oil* Robertson 1975. This focuses particularly on its effect on the Scottish economy.

**4013** Mervyn Jones *The Oil Rush* Quartet 1976. A well illustrated guide to the people and places of the oil boom of the 1970s.

**4014** Chris Rowland and Danny Hann *The Economics of North Sea Oil Taxation* Macmillan 1987. A critique of tax policy which they see as having been both inconsistent and a brake on investment. Alexander G Kemp *Taxation and the Profitability of North Sea Oil* Fraser of Allander Institute, Glasgow 1976 is a critical analysis of the 1975 Oil Taxation Act.

**4015** Robert Matro *et al The Market for North Sea Crude Oil* Oxford University Press 1986.

**4016** Michael Jenkin *British Industry and the North Sea: State Intervention in a Developing Industrial Sector* Macmillan 1981. The initial intervention by the government was prompted by the failure of British industries to respond to the challenge. This is an excellent study of the development of the government's policy to try and encourage a greater British role in the supply of the offshore oil industry as moderated through the Offshore Supplies Office.

**4017** Luke Johnson *Shell Expro: A History* Weidenfeld and Nicolson 1989. A history of the company's 25 years of exploration in the North Sea.

### (4) The Oil Industry

**4018** *Institute of Petroleum Abstracts* Institute of Petroleum, London 1969–. The principal bibliographical source for the industry.

**4019** *UK Petroleum Industry Statistics* Institute of Petroleum, London 1970–2. Statistics on consumption and refinery production.

**4020** George Sell (ed) *The Post-War Expansion of the UK Petroleum Industry* Institute of Petroleum, London 1954. The proceedings of a conference.

**4021** *Our Industry Petroleum: A Handbook Dealing with the Organisation and Functions of an Integrated International Oil Company, with Particular Reference to the British Petroleum Company Ltd* 5th ed, British Petroleum 1977. A very informative guide to the worldwide activities of the company. It was previously published as *Our Industry*. The only existing general history of BP is Henry Hayhurst *Adventure in Oil: The Story of British Petroleum* Sidgwick and Jackson 1959. A more detailed history is in preparation but nothing as yet has been published on the post-war period. The company's operations in the Middle East and its attempts to diversify away from the area in the wake of the 1951–3 Anglo-Iranian dispute and Suez are examined in J R L Andersen *East of Suez: A Study of Britain's Greatest Trading Enterprise* Hodder and Stoughton 1969. The gradual shift of the company towards refining in Europe rather than near to the point of source is analysed in Mari E W Williams 'Choices in Oil Refining: The Case of BP 1900–1960' *Business History* 26 1984 pp 307–28.

**4022** *History of Burmah Oil* Burmah 1972. A more detailed company history is in preparation.

**4023** E G D Liveing *Pioneers of Petrol: A Centenary History of Carless, Capel and Leonard 1859–1959* Witherby 1959.

**4024** W H Mitchell and L A Sawyer *Sailing Ship to Supertanker: The Hundred Year Story of British Esso and Its Ships* Terence Dalton 1988. A well illustrated account which also looks at the development of the distribution system in Britain.

**4025** Paul Atterbury and Julia Mackenzie *A Golden Adventure: The First 50 Years of Ultramar* Hurtwood Press 1985. This company was founded in 1935 to develop the Venezuela oilfields and is now a worldwide integrated oil and gas company. A well illustrated history.

**4026** Anthony N Stranges 'From Birmingham to Billington: High Pressure Coal Hydrogenisation in Great Britain' *Technology and Culture* 26 1985 pp 726–57. A history of the manufacture of synthetic oil in Britain. This was successfully manufactured in the inter-war years but, unable to compete with the price of Middle Eastern oil, the plant closed down in 1958.

## (5) The Gas Industry

**4027** *Gas Council Annual Report and Accounts* HMSO 1948/50–1972/73. The Gas Council was established in May 1949 under the terms of the 1948 Gas Act and had responsibility for the area gas councils. Its reports were published as House of Commons Papers until 1972/73. Since then the reports have been published by the British Gas Corporation as *British Gas Corporation Annual Report and Accounts*.

**4028** *Gas Directory and Who's Who* Benn 1898–. This annual directory gives information on the gas industry, including a biographical guide, statistics and material on the organization of British Gas.

**4029** Trevor I Williams *A History of the British Gas Industry* Oxford University Press 1981. A general history. The technical and administrative development of the gas industry is surveyed in Malcolm W H Peebles 'The United Kingdom' in his *Evolution of the Gas Industry* Macmillan 1980 pp 21–49. *The Development of the British Gas Industry* British Gas Corporation 1983 is a general chronology.

**4030** Malcolm Falkus *Always Under Pressure: A History of North Thames Gas Since 1949* Macmillan 1988. A study of its history from nationalization to privatization in 1986. This is the first substantial history of the gas industry or of any of the gas boards in the post-war years.

**4031** Sir Kenneth Hutchison *High Speed Gas: An Autobiography* Duckworth 1987. A good memoir of the transformation of the gas industry in the post-war period by someone who rose to be deputy chairman of the Gas Council before his retirement in 1966. It is especially useful on research and development.

## (6) Atomic Energy

**4032** L J Anthony *Sources of Information on Atomic Energy* Pergamon 1966. A useful bibliographical guide.

**4033** *United Kingdom Atomic Energy Authority Annual Report* HMSO 1955–.

**4034** *The Development of Atomic Energy 1939–1984: Chronology of Events* 2nd ed, United Kingdom Atomic Energy Authority 1984. An illustrated chronology which also lists important appointments and maps all the nuclear power stations in Britain.

**4035** Tony Hall *Nuclear Politics: The History of Nuclear Power in Britain* Penguin 1986. A detailed critical account. Another critical study is W Patterson *Going*

*Critical: An Unofficial History of British Nuclear Power* Paladin 1985. Dave Elliott *et al The Politics of Nuclear Power* Pluto 1978 is a collection of essays critically assessing aspects of the development of the atomic energy industry. Roger Williams *The Nuclear Power Decisions: British Policies 1953–1978* Croom Helm 1980 is useful on policy making and especially on the growing public concern about the safety of the industry leading to public challenges to Whitehall's monopoly on decision making and an increasing recourse to public inquiries. Also on the nature of policy making see G Donn 'The Rationales for Nuclear Power and Their Importance in Nuclear Power Decision Making 1956–1981' Strathclyde PhD Thesis 1984. Another study which includes case studies of the development of the independent fuel cycle industry, the 1977–8 Windscale inquiry and the joint European Torus is A Massey 'An Analysis of the Influence of Professional Experts as a Factor in Shaping Britain's Nuclear Energy Policy' London PhD Thesis 1986. All of the published works listed above are written from a standpoint more or less hostile to nuclear power. A more balanced account which includes a useful chronology is John Walker 'The Road to Sizewell: The Origins of the UK Nuclear Power Programme' *Contemporary Record* 1/3 1987 pp 44–50. On the origins of nuclear power in Britain see [2220].

**4036** Rowland Francis Peacock *Nuclear Power: Its Development in the United Kingdom* Institute of Nuclear Engineers 1977. A technological rather than a political account of the atomic energy industry.

**4037** Stephen Fothergill and Gordon MacKerron *The Economics of Nuclear Power* Macmillan 1988. An examination of the economics of nuclear power in Britain in historical context. See also Peter Lloyd Jones *The Economics of Nuclear Power Programmes in the United Kingdom* Macmillan 1984.

**4038** C E S Franks 'Parliament and Atomic Energy' Oxford DPhil Thesis 1974.

**4039** E J S Clarke 'Harwell and its Impact on the Oxford Region' in Trevor Rowley (ed) *The Oxford Region* Oxford Department of External Studies 1980 pp 185–201. A survey of the history of the research station since it was established in 1946, of its importance in attracting other research work to the region, and of the sociology of its employees. See also R Spence 'Twenty One Years at Harwell' *Nature* 214 1967 pp 343–4 and 436–8.

**4040** Rolt Hammond *British Nuclear Power Stations* Macdonald 1961.

**4041** D W Pearce, Lynne Edwards and Geoff Beuret *Decision Making for Energy Futures: A Case Study of the Windscale Inquiry* Macmillan 1979. A study of the

Windscale public inquiry set up in 1977 to investigate the proposal to build a thermal oxide reprocessing plant at Windscale. A good account of the mechanics of the nuclear power decision-making process is Brian Wynne *Rationality and Ritual: The Windscale Inquiry and Nuclear Decisions in Britain* British Society for the History of Science 1982. This is an examination of the Windscale public inquiry into the 1977 application by British Nuclear Fuels to build a thermal oxide reprocessing plant on the site. The report by Roger Jocelyn Parker *The Windscale Inquiry* 3v, HMSO 1978, concluded that that construction of the plant should go ahead.

**4042** Timothy O'Riordan, Ray Kemp and Michael Purdue *Sizewell B: An Anatomy of the Inquiry* Macmillan 1988. The Sizewell B inquiry, chaired by Sir Frank Layfield, was set up in January 1983. Four years later it reported in *Sizewell B Public Inquiry: Report on Applications by the Central Electricity Generating Board for Consent for the Construction of a Pressurized Water Reactor and a Direction that Planning Permission be Deemed Granted for that Development* 8v, HMSO 1987 that 'consent and deemed planning permission' for a pressurized water reactor, the first of its kind in Britain, should be given. This study is a good analysis of the public inquiry process which traces in detail the Sizewell B inquiry. It does however concentrate rather overmuch on the inquiry itself at the expense of the context of the development of nuclear power in Britain.

**4043** James Cutler and Rob Edwards *Britain's Nuclear Nightmare* Sphere 1988. This criticizes the Black Report [5522] which failed to find evidence of a link between nuclear power and cancer levels in the vicinity and impugns the safety levels at Sellafield in the light of incidents such as the 1957 Windscale fire. See also S M MacGill *The Politics of Anxiety: Sellafield's Cancer-Link Controversy* Pion 1987.

### (7) Electricity

**4044** Central Electricity Authority *Report and Statement of Accounts* HMSO 1947/49–1957. This was established as the British Electricity Authority in 1948 with responsibility for the area electricity boards. Under the 1957 Electricity Act it was superseded by the Central Electricity Generating Board and the Electricity Council in charge respectively of the supply and distribution of electricity. The *Central Electricity Generating Board Annual Report and Accounts 1958/59–* were published by HMSO as a House of Commons Paper until 1972/73. Since then they have been published by the Board. The Central Electricity Generating Board also publish an annual *Statistical Year Book.* The same publishing history has been followed by the annual reports of the Electricity Council and the area boards.

**4045** *Electricity Supply in Great Britain: A Chronology from the Beginnings of the Industry* 4th ed, Electricity Council 1987. A chronology up to the 1980s.

**4046** M Ince *Energy Policy: Britain's Electricity Industry* Junction Books 1982. A critical examination of the current structure and policy of the industry.

**4047** Leslie Hannah *Engineers, Managers and Politicians: The First Fifteen Years of Nationalised Electricity Supply in Britain* Macmillan 1982. A highly regarded study. This carries on from his *Electricity Before Nationalisation: A Study of the Development of the Electricity Supply Industry in Britain to 1948* Macmillan 1979. Christopher, Lord Hinton of Bankside *Heavy Current Electricity in the United Kingdom: History and Development* Pergamon 1979 traces the development of electricity supply up to nationalization and critically analyses Britain's poor performance and technological backwardness in this field. On a particular aspect of the development of the industry during the early years of nationalization see R W Bates 'The Determinants of Investment in the Nationalised Electricity Supply Industry in Great Britain, with Special Reference to the Period 1948–1960' Sheffield PhD Thesis 1964–5.

**4048** J L Ferns 'Electricity Supply and Industrial Archaeology' *Industrial Archaeology Review* 17 1982 pp 10–8. A study focusing on technical developments in the industry 1881–1982.

**4049** Walter Citrine *Two Careers* Hutchinson 1967. This, the second volume of his autobiography, covers his career from 1939. He remained General Secretary of the TUC until 1946. However this volume is most useful to the post-war historian for his service in the electricity industry as Chairman of the Central Electricity Authority 1947–57.

**4050** H R Burroughes 'Political and Administrative Problems of Development Planning: The Case of the CEGB and the Supergrid' *Public Administration* 49 1974 pp 131–48. A study of policy development.

**4051** J Carlton and D Heald 'Restructuring the Electricity Supply Industry' *Public Administration Bulletin* 29 1979 pp 43–60. A study of attempts to reorganize the industry in the 1970s.

**4052** Sidney Robinson *Seeboard: The First Twenty-Five Years* South-Western Electricity Board 1974. A short history, as is Stanley F Steward *Twenty-Five Years of South-Western Electricity: A Short History of a State Industry* South-Western Electricity Board 1973. On electricity supply in the South East see B Gordon *One Hundred Years of Electricity 1881–1981* South Eastern Electricity Board 1981. Another area board history is *A Record of Ten Years Progress 1948–1958* North-Western Electricity Board 1963. See also William Edward Eyles *Electricity in Bath 1890–1974* Bath City Council/South West Electricity Board 1974.

**4053** D G Tucker 'Refuse Destructors and Their Use for Generating Electricity: A Century of Development' *Industrial Archaeology Review* 2 1977–8 pp 5–27.

## E. FINANCE AND RELATED SERVICES

### (1) General

**4054** Derrick G Hanson *Dictionary of Banking and Finance* Pitman 1985. A comprehensive reference guide.

**4055** *The City Directory* Woodhead-Faulkner 1976/77–. An irregularly published comprehensive guide to the City of London. This includes essays surveying the institutions and professional bodies of the City and recent developments in the UK financial markets.

**4056** Stan Mason *The McGraw-Hill Handbook of British Finance and Trade* McGraw-Hill 1983. A detailed guide whose scope is wider than its title suggests. It provides useful information on recent developments.

**4057** Gerry M Smith *The Financial Activities of the City of London: A Select Bibliography* Business School Press 1976. A short, unannotated bibliography.

**4058** William Manning Dacey *The British Banking Mechanism* 5th ed Hutchinson 1964. A survey of the working of the banking and financial system since 1931. To some extent it is also a critique of monetary policy since the war. Jack Revell *The British Financial System* Macmillan 1973 is a useful in-depth analysis. David Kent Sheppard *The Growth and Role of UK Financial Institutions 1880–1962* Methuen 1971 is a rather technical reference book full of useful statistical tables.

**4059** Frank Welsh *Uneasy City: An Insider's View of the City of London* Weidenfeld and Nicolson 1986. A good discursive survey of the City, and particularly of the important issues of the 1980s. Each type of financial institution is examined in turn. William M Clarke *Inside the City: A Guide to London as a Financial Centre* 2nd ed, Allen and Unwin 1983 is highly regarded guide to the City and the innovations which have enabled it to remain the largest financial centre in the world. The conclusion surveys the prospects for the City maintaining its world lead. See also his earlier study of the place of the City in global financial markets, *The City in the World Economy* revised ed, Penguin 1967. Another use-

ful guide, with plenty of historical details, to the various financial activities carried out in the City is Hamish McRae and Frances Cairncross *Capital City: London as a Financial Centre* 3rd ed, Methuen 1984. See also Philip Coggan *The Money Machine: How the City Works* Penguin 1986. H Carter and I Partington *Applied Economics in Banking and Finance* 3rd ed, Oxford University Press 1984 is a textbook guide.

**4060** Charles Goodhart, David Currie and David Llewellyn (eds) *The Operation and Regulation of Financial Markets* Macmillan 1987. A collection of essays on such subjects as UK banking supervision and the 1984 Johnson Mathey Affair, structural changes in the British capital markets, monetary growth in Britain and France 1970–84 or the variability in some major UK assets markets since the mid 1960s. The importance of the City is examined in 'London as an International Financial Centre' *Bank of England Quarterly Bulletin* 29 1989 pp 516–30.

**4061** Jerry Coakley and Lawrence Harris *The City of Capital* Blackwell 1983. A critical study of the power and lack of accountability of the City. An earlier critical study both of these aspects and its perceived close links with the Conservative Party and apparent ignorance of and indifference to the needs of the rest of the economy is Richard Spiegelberg *The City: Power Without Responsibility* Blond and Briggs 1973.

**4062** Michael Moran 'Finance Capital and Pressure Group Politics in Britain' *British Journal of Political Science* 11 1981 pp 381–404. A study of the City as a pressure group.

**4063** Rowan Bosworth-Davies *Too Good to be True: How to Survive the Casino Economy* The Bodley Head 1987. A study of fraud and corrupt practices in the City. Financial scandals in the banks, Lloyds and stock exchange in the 1980s are examined in Michael Clarke *Regulating the City: Competition, Scandal and Reform* Open University Press 1986.

**4064** Bernard Taylor and Guy de Moubray (eds) *Strategic Planning for Financial Institutions* The Bodley Head 1974. This is useful for an assessment of the City in the 1970s. See also Christopher Johnson *Anatomy of UK Finance 1970–75* 2nd ed, Longman 1977.

**4065** Maximilian Hall *The City Revolution: Causes and Consequences* Macmillan 1987. A study of the pressure for reform from the 1970s. This was intensified by the abolition of exchange controls in 1979. This study culminates with an assessment of the City in the wake of the Big Bang of 27th October 1986. The changing attitude to the regulation of the financial markets over the same period is analysed in his *Financial Deregula-*

*tion: A Comparative Study of Australia and the United Kingdom* Macmillan 1987.

**4066**  *Committee to Review the Functioning of Financial Institutions Interim Report: Financing of Small Firms* Cmnd 7503, *Parliamentary Papers* 1978–79. A study of the role of financial institutions and their value to the economy, especially in the provision of funds for trade and industry. This committee, chaired by Sir Harold Wilson, recommended the encouragement of investment in small firms. Its final *Report and Appendices* Cmnd 7937, *Parliamentary Papers* 1979–80 traces in great detail the historical development of the various sectors of the British financial system, especially since the late 1950s. See also A D Bain 'The Wilson Report Three Years On' *Three Banks Review* 138 1983 pp 3–19.

**4067**  John Plender and Paul Wallace *The Square Mile: A Guide to the New City of London* Century 1985. A detailed study of the restructuring of the ownership and regulation of City institutions 1983–5.

**4068**  L C B Gower *Review of Investor Protection Part I: Report* Cmnd 9125, *Parliamentary Papers* 1983–84. A report which forms part of the background to the 1986 Financial Services Act and the end of the City's self-regulation. Regulation of the City since 1945 is surveyed in the context of the 1986 Act and the paradoxical growth of regulation of the City under the most free market government since the war in Michael Moran 'Thatcherism and Financial Regulation' *Political Quarterly* 59 1988 pp 20–7.

**4069**  Margaret Reid *All-Change in the City: The Revolution in Britain's Financial Sector* Macmillan 1988. A scrutiny of the reshaping of the City in the 1980s, particularly in the wake of the Big Bang in 1986. Separate chapters deal with changes in each financial sector. Changes in the City in the 1980s are also surveyed in her *Anatomy of the City* Macmillan 1988. Anthony Hilton *City Within a State: A Portrait of Britain's Financial World* I B Tauris 1987 is a critical analysis of trends in the City in the 1980s, especially since the Big Bang. It studies developments up to the Guinness scandal that broke in 1987. Events in the City from the Big Bang of October 1986 to the Great Crash of the following October are traced in Charles Jennings *The Confidence Trick: The City's Progress from Big Bang to Great Crash* Hamilton 1988. This concentrates on the Stock Exchange and is useful for its pithy reflections on both that institution and on Lloyds.

**4070**  P Unwin *The Stationer's Company 1918–1977: A Livery Company in the Modern World* Benn 1978. A history of one of the traditional livery companies of the City.

**4071**  Geoffrey Wansell *Tycoon: The Life of Sir James Goldsmith* Grafton 1986. A biography of the financier.

## (2) The Exchanges and Money Markets

### (a) The Stock Exchange and Money Markets

**4072**  *The Stock Exchange Official Handbook* Skinner 1934–80 (Macmillan 1981–). An annual guide.

**4073**  A G Ellinger *et al The Post-War History of the Stock Market 1945–72* Investment Research 1973. See also Edward Victor Morgan and William Arthur Thomas *Stock Exchange: Its History and Functions* Elek 1970. Also of use is A J Merrett and Allen Sykes 'Return on Equities: Fixed Interest Securities 1919–66' in R J Lister (ed) *Studies in Optimal Financing* Macmillan 1973 pp 28–38.

**4074**  A J Merrett and Allen Sykes 'Return of Equities and Fixed Interest Securities 1919–1966' *District Bank Review* 158 1966 pp 29–44.

**4075**  Malcolm Craig *The Sterling Money Markets* Gower 1976. A comprehensive guide.

**4076**  Jean-Claude Chouraqui *Le Marché Monétaire de Londres Depuis 1960* Presses Universitaires de France, Paris 1969. On the money markets in the 1960s see also E R Shaw 'The London Money Markets 1959–1971' Liverpool MA Thesis 1971–2 and G D A Wills 'A Study of the Equity Market, Risks and Returns, with Special Emphasis on the Period 1960–69' Birmingham MCom Thesis 1971–2. An earlier study is Norman MacRae *The London Capital Market* 2nd ed, Staples Press 1957.

**4077**  W R White 'The Authorities and the United Kingdom Gilt-Edged Market 1952–1966' Manchester PhD Thesis 1968–9. A study of the regulation and operation of the market in government stocks.

**4078**  Ian Kerr *A History of the Eurobond Market: The First 21 Years* Euromoney 1984. The development of the Eurobond market in the 1960s was of major importance in the revival of the City as a major financial centre. The first Eurobond was issued by S G Warburg in 1963. A Dequae Report on the Eurodollar Market Council of Europe 1971 is a report on the early development of the market. The background to the development of the Eurobond market is examined in Paul Einzig *The Euro-Dollar System* Macmillan 1964.

**4079**  A B Curry 'A Study of the Liverpool New Issue Market 1953–65' Liverpool MA Thesis 1970–1.

**4080**  J Moyle *The Pattern of Ordinary Share Owner-ship 1957–70* Cambridge University Press 1971.

**4081**  W J Reader *A House in the City: A Study of the City and of the Stock Exchange Based on the Records of Foster and Braithwaite 1825–1975* Batsford 1979. The last chapter examines the firm's post-war history up to 1971.

(b) Other

**4082**  Graham Lloyd Rees *Britain's Commodity Markets* Elek 1976.

**4083**  Hugh Barty-King *The Baltic Exchange: The History of a Unique Market* Hutchinson 1977.

**4084**  J R T Gibson-Harvie *The London Metal Exchange: A Commodity Market* Woodhead-Faulkner 1983. See also The Economist Intelligence Unit *The London Metal Exchange* London Metal Exchange 1958. G P Harrison *VYB: A Century of Metal Broking 1859–1959* Vivian, Younger and Bond 1959 is a history of the metal broking firm of Vivian, Younger and Bond.

### (3) Investment and Unit Trusts

**4085**  K J Lyall 'Investment Trust Companies 1971–1980' Edinburgh PhD Thesis 1983.

**4086**  W Hood 'Portfolio Selection Under Uncertainty – A Study of British Unit Trusts' Oxford BLitt Thesis 1972.

**4087**  Adrienne Gleeson *People and Their Money: 50 Years of Private Investment* M&G Group 1981. A history of M&G Group, the unit trust group.

### (4) Banking

**4088**  L S Pressnell and John Orbell *A Guide to the Historical Records of British Banking* Gower 1985. A guide to archives listed by company. This builds on *Survey of the Records of British Banking* 3v, Royal Commission on Historical Manuscripts 1980.

**4089**  *The Bankers' Almanac and Yearbook* Skinner 1844–. The standard international reference book and directory.

**4090**  Michael Collins *Money and Banking in the UK: A History* Croom Helm 1988. A history from 1826 of UK banking and the impact of monetary policy. Part III covers 1939–86. Banking since 1945, and especially in

the context of the response of British banks to an increasingly interdependent financial world and the invasion of foreign banks into London, is examined in detail in Derek F Channon *British Banking Strategy and the International Challenge* Macmillan 1977. See also Anthony Sampson *The Money Lenders* Hodder and Stoughton 1981.

**4091**  Edward P M Gardener *UK Banking Supervision: Evolution, Practice and Issues* Allen and Unwin 1986. The 1973–5 secondary banking crisis proved a watershed in the supervision of the British banking sector, leading as it did to the replacement of the traditional Bank of England supervision with closer regulation and intervention.

**4092**  D Rowan 'Banking and Credit Under the Labour Government 1945–49' *Journal of Politics* 12 1950 pp 290–322.

**4093**  John Grady and Martin Weale *British Banking 1960–85* Macmillan 1986. A study of change from the first impact of the secondary banks that grew up in the 1960s and of the increasing internationalization of the London banking world. It contains a mass of statistical data and benefited from an unrestricted access to deposits up to the secondary banking crisis of 1973–5.

**4094**  J E Wadsworth (ed) *The Banks and the Monetary System in the UK 1959–1971* Methuen 1972. A useful collection of essays. Robin Pringle *A Guide to Banking in Britain* Knight 1973 provides an analysis of the contemporary situation and an assessment of developments in the 1960s and 1970s.

**4095**  Michael Moran *The Politics of Banking: The Strange Case of Competition and Credit Control* 2nd ed, Macmillan 1986. A case study of the transformation of banking in the 1970s. It includes an epilogue on the 1984 Johnson Mathey Affair. The removal of the gentleman's agreements and the introduction of more competitive regulations in 1971 are also examined in D R Dobbs 'Changes in Asset and Liability Management in Banking in the United Kingdom Since 1971' Wales MSc Thesis 1986, particularly in the context of the consequent increased importance of good asset and liability management.

**4096**  W Mullineux *UK Banking After Deregulation* Croom Helm 1987. An examination of the situation after the deregulation of the 1980s. The effects of deregulation are also examined in Tim Clarke and William Vincent *Banking Under Pressure – Breaking the Chains* Butterworths 1989.

**4097**  Sidney Pollard 'The Nationalisation of the Banks: The Chequered History of a Socialist Proposal' in David E Martin and David Rubenstein (eds) *Ideology* *and the Labour Movement: Essays Presented to John Saville* Croom Helm 1979 pp 167–90. An analysis of the history of this proposal up to the 1970s.

**4098** J Reeder 'The History and Development of Corporate Loan Financing, with Special Reference to the Law Relating to the Floating Charge' Birmingham PhD Thesis 1976–7.

**4099** Edwin Green *Debtors to Their Profession: A History of the Institute of Bankers 1879–1979* Institute of Bankers 1979. A good history of the professional body.

**4100** J A Sargent 'Pressure Group Development in the EC: The Role of the British Bankers' Association' *Journal of Common Market Studies* 20 1982 pp 269–85.

**4101** Edward Nevin and E W Davis *The London Clearing Banks* Elek 1970. A dated study but still of considerable value on the development of the clearing banks in the post-war period. On particular aspects of the clearing banks' experience in this period see also N Perra 'The Sensitivity of the London Clearing Banks Profits to Changes in Bank Rate 1951–1970' *Applied Economics* 12 1980 pp 11–18, A Saunders 'The Regulation and the Behaviour of the London Clearing Banks 1965–1977' London PhD Thesis 1982, and W N Thompson 'Portfolio Behaviour of the London Clearing Banks 1953–1969' Southampton PhD Thesis 1980.

**4102** John Matatko and David Stafford *Key Developments in Personal Finance* Blackwell 1985. This charts the growth and change in the personal finance industry since 1960. It looks both at the development of new financial products but also the entry of new competitors to the market, such as the building societies or the National Girobank. D G Hanson *Service Banking: The Arrival of the All-Purpose Bank* 2nd ed, Institute of Bankers 1982 is an important study concentrating on the developments in retail banking over the previous twenty-five years, which also discusses such diverse innovations as corporate trusteeships and business advisory services. It also includes a useful chronology. Developments in retail banking and the movement into this sector by the building societies and, to some extent, the insurance companies, are analysed in Margaret Rothwell and Paul Jowett *Rivalry in Retail Financial Services* Macmillan 1988. See also J B Howcroft and J Lavis *Retail Banking: The New Revolution in Structure and Strategy* Blackwell 1986. Patrick Kirkman *Electronic Funds Transfer Systems: The Revolution in Cashless Banking and Payment Methods* Blackwell 1987 is an interesting account of the rise of cash dispensers, home and office banking, electronic payment systems and other innovations ushered in by new technology in recent years.

**4103** Philip Geddes *Inside the Bank of England* TV South 1987. A study, derived from a television series, on the Bank of England over the last twenty years up to the time of the Big Bang. Stephen Fay *Portrait of an Old Lady: Turmoil at the Bank of England* Viking 1987 concentrates more on the decline of the Bank's supervisory role in his analysis of the Governorships of Gordon Richardson (1973–83) and Robin Leigh-Pemberton (1983–). See also V H Hewitt and J M Keyworth *As Good as Gold: 300 Years of British Bank Note Design* British Museum Publications 1987.

**4104** G A Fletcher *The Discount Houses in London: Principles, Operations and Change* Macmillan 1976. A general history of the discount houses and their role in monetary policy which concentrates on the period 1951–70 and the changing situation in the 1970s after the reforms in monetary controls introduced in 1971. Richard S Sayers *Gilletts in the London Money Market 1867–1967* Clarendon 1968 is a history of the London discount house of Gilletts Brothers.

**4105** Jack Revell *Changes in British Banking: The Growth of a Secondary Banking System* Hill Samuel 1968. The first authoritative account of the growth of secondary and 'fringe' banking services. Their growth up to and including the 1973–5 secondary banking crisis is analysed in J W Grady 'The Growth of the British Non-Clearing Banks 1960–1975' Cambridge PhD Thesis 1982. Their role in the instalment credit industry in relation to the clearing banks and to monetary policy is examined in D B Jones 'An Investigation into the Instalment Credit Industry in the United Kingdom, 1st January 1960 to 31st December 1975, with Particular Reference to the Effects of Monetary Policy and Official Control on the Structure and Behaviour of Finance Houses' Brunel MPhil Thesis 1981.

**4106** Margaret Reid *The Secondary Banking Crisis 1973–75: Its Causes and Course* Macmillan 1982. An analysis of this major crisis and the 'lifeboat plan' that was required to rectify the situation. See also M C Williams 'Social Organisation and Moral Order in the Financial System, with Special Reference to the Banking Crisis of 1973–5' Oxford MPhil Thesis 1981. On the scandal that engulfed the Crown Agents at the time see Christopher Hood 'The Crown Agents Affair' *Public Administration* 56 1978 pp 297–304.

**4107** Richard Anthony Johns *Tax Havens and Offshore Finance: A Study of Transnational Economic Development* Pinter 1983. This incorporates a case study of offshore financial centres in the Channel Islands and the Isle of Man since the 1950s. Charles Raw, Godfrey Hodgson and Bruce Page *Do You Sincerely Want to be Rich? Bernard Cornfield and IOS: An International Swindle* Deutsch 1971 is an account of a notorious offshore banking scandal.

**4108** Tony Lorenz *Venture Capital Today: A Guide to the Venture Capital Market in the United Kingdom* Woodhead-Faulkner 1985. A useful and informative analysis of the development of venture capital operations in Britain. Developments since 3i was established by the Bank of England and the clearing banks in 1945 and particularly, under government encouragement, since the establishment of the Unlisted Securities Market in 1980, are traced in Rodney Clark 'Venture Capital in the United Kingdom' in his *Venture Capital in Britain, America and Japan* St Martins Press, New York 1987 pp 65–97.

**4109** T J Watsham 'The Role of Banks in the Provision of External Finance to Developing Countries, with Particular Reference to UK Banks Between 1970–1980' London PhD Thesis 1984.

**4110** Geoffrey Jones 'British Overseas Banks in the Middle East 1920–70: A Study in Multinational Middle Age' in Alice Teichova, Maurice Levy-Leboyer and Helga Nussbaum (eds) *Multinational Enterprise in Historical Perspective* Cambridge University Press 1986 pp 218–31. In the post-war period these banks gradually weakened, partly because of the decline of sterling, partly because of the increasing presence of American and British and European domestic banks and the development of indigenous banks, and partly because they were too small to any longer fulfil the needs of the market.

**4111** Geoffrey Jones 'Lombard Street on the Riviera: The British Clearing Banks and Europe 1900–1960' *Business History* 24 1982 pp 186–210. An analysis of the general lack of success attendant on the efforts of some independent British banks to establish a presence in Europe.

**4112** Andrew Lamb 'International Banking in London 1975–85' *Bank of England Quarterly Bulletin* 26 1986 pp 367–78. This concentrates on the growing importance in London of Japanese banks. It includes useful statistical tables. On American banks in Britain see I I Thomas 'The Expansion of American Banks from London to the Regions: A Study in Regional Financial Infiltration' Wales PhD Thesis 1976.

**4113** A W Tuke and R J H Gillman *Barclays Bank 1926–1969: Some Recollections* Barclays Bank 1972. The history of the overseas branch of the bank is told in Sir Julian Crossley and John Blandford *The DCO Story: A History of Banking in Many Countries* Barclays Bank International Ltd 1975. This traces the clearing and international banking history of the firm formed by the merger of the Dominion, Colonial and Overseas in 1925 until the change of name to Barclays International in 1971.

**4114** Augustus Muir *Blythe, Greene, Jourdain and Company 1810–1960* Newman Neame 1961. A short history of the merchant bankers.

**4115** Geoffrey Jones *Banking and Oil: The History of the British Bank of the Middle East* Vol 2 Cambridge University Press 1987. Originally known as the Imperial Bank of Persia it changed its name in 1952. This valuable study of a bank that often acted as an instrument of British policy in the area charts its decline from the 1930s to its merger with the Hongkong Bank in 1960.

**4115A** Laurie Dennett *The Charterhouse Group 1925–1979* Gentry Books 1979.

**4116** Bo Bramsen and Kathleen Wain *The Hambros 1779–1979* Michael Joseph 1979.

**4117** J R Winton *Lloyd's Bank 1918–69* Oxford University Press 1982. A history of the major clearing bank.

**4118** Edwin Green *The Making of a Modern Banking Group: A History of the Midland Bank Since 1900* St George's Press 1979. The gradual decline of Midland from being the largest to the fourth largest of the British banks is charted in A R Holman and Edwin Green *Midland: 150 Years of Banking Business* Batsford 1986. This is an excellent business history. It does not however really answer whether poor management has been the bank's problem and, for various reasons, does not cover the disastrous Croker purchase in the USA.

**4119** Kathleen Burk *Morgan Grenfell 1838–1988: The Biography of a Merchant Bank* Oxford University Press 1989. Whereas a number of histories of banks only have epilogues on the more recent period this excellent official history, written with full access to the bank's records, goes right up to the events of the 1980s. The 1980s are covered, though without the same benefit of official access to the bank's records, in Dominic Hobson *The Pride of Lucifer* Hamilton 1989. This is an account of the bank's expansion in the deregulated climate of the 1980s and the hard times that followed the Guinness scandal that broke in December 1986.

**4120** G W Tyson *100 Years of Banking in Asia and Africa 1863–1963* National and Grindlay's Bank 1963.

**4121** Glyn Davies *National Giro: Modern Money Transfer* Allen and Unwin 1973. A history of the development of the idea up to the establishment of the National Girobank in 1968.

**4122** Richard Reed *National Westminster Bank: A Short History* National Westminster Bank 1983.

**4123** Derek Wilson *Rothschild: A Story of Wealth and Power* Deutsch 1988. A history of the family of merchant bankers and the institutions they founded.

**4124** Richard Roberts *A History of Schroders* Macmillan 1988. A history of one of the largest and most prestigious of London merchant bankers since 1818, much of which deals with the post-war period.

**4125** Charles Raw *Slater Walker: An Investigation of a Financial Phenomenon* Deutsch 1977. Slater Walker were one of the fringe banking phenomenons of the 1960s and 1970s. See also Jim Slater *Return To Go: My Autobiography* Weidenfeld and Nicolson 1977. For Peter Walker see [867].

**4126** J A Henry and H A Siepmann (eds) *The First Hundred Years of the Standard Bank* Standard Bank 1963. This is updated by *Standard Chartered Bank Ltd: A Story Brought Up to Date* Standard Chartered Bank 1983. Standard Chartered was formed from the merger of the Chartered Bank of India, Australia and China with the Standard Bank. Compton Mackenzie *Realms of Silver: One Hundred Years of Banking in the East* Routledge and Kegan Paul 1954 is a history of the Chartered Bank. Richard Fry *Bankers in West Africa: The Story of the Bank of British West Africa Limited* Hutchinson Benham 1976 is a good history of this bank until its merger with the Standard Bank in 1965.

**4127** I C Ross 'Trustees Savings Banks: Historical Development, Current Structure and International Perspective' Heriot-Watt MSc Thesis 1980.

**4128** *The Way It Was: An Oral History of Twenty Years of Finance* Institutional Investor 1987. A collection of interviews with leading figures in the international financial world. The only British figures featured are David Scholey of S G Warburg and Denis Healey, Chancellor of the Exchequer 1974–9.

**4129** John Kinross *Fifty Years in the City: Financing Small Business* Murray 1982. The autobiography of a investment banker.

**4130** Jacques Attali *A Man of Influence: Sir Siegmund Warburg 1902–82* Weidenfeld and Nicolson 1986. A good biography of an important merchant banker.

### (5) Insurance

**4131** H A L Cockerell and Edwin Green *The British Insurance Business 1547–1970* Heinemann Education 1976. An introductory guide to the historical records of British insurance companies.

**4132** *Insurance Business: Annual Report* HMSO 1975–. A short report on the state of the industry and government activities under the 1974 Insurance Companies Act. Since then it has been published as *Insurance Annual Report*.

**4133** R T D Wilmot (ed) *Who's Who in Insurance* Graham and Trotman 1975. A biographical guide to some 3,000 top executives.

**4134** *The Insurance Index* Insurance Index Ltd 1980–. This monthly index claims to be the comprehensive reference system for all the latest developments, news comments and statistics relating to the insurance industry. It contains briefly annotated entries under some forty subjects derived from the press and periodicals.

**4135** *Insurance Reading List: A Selection of Useful Books and Periodicals on Insurance and Related Subjects* 6th ed, Chartered Insurance Institute Library 1984. A useful select, semi-annotated list.

**4136** G Clayton *British Insurance* Elek 1971. A full account of the development of the insurance industry since 1945.

**4137** Julian Tapp 'Regulation of the UK Insurance Industry' in Jörg Finsinger and Mark V Pauly (eds) *The Economics of Insurance Regulation: A Cross-National Study* Macmillan 1986 pp 27–61. The British market, one of the most competitive in the world, is also one of the most unregulated in the world.

**4138** D J Wilson *100 Years of the Association of Average Adjusters 1869–1969* Association of Average Adjusters 1969. On other professional associations see C Hewer *A Problem Shared: A History of the Institute of London Underwriters 1884–1984* Witherby 1984, H A L Cockerell *60 Years of the Chartered Insurance Institute 1897–1957* Chartered Insurance Institute 1957 and W L Catchpole and E Elverston *BIA Fifty 1917–1967: Fifty Years of the British Insurance Association* PH Press 1967.

**4139** Peter J Franklin and Caroline Woodhead *The UK Life Assurance Industry: A Study in Applied Economics* Croom Helm 1980. An introductory textbook. See also John Johnston and G W Murphy *The Growth of Life Insurance in the United Kingdom Since 1880* Manchester Statistical Society 1957.

**4140** James Colin Dodds *The Investment Behaviour of British Life Insurance Companies* Croom Helm 1979. A critical analysis of investment policy 1962–76. See also W Harrigan 'Investment Policy of British Life Offices Since 1929' Wales MA Thesis 1955–6. There are detailed statistics, graphs and historical information on the administration of pension fund investment by life insurance companies in 'Life Assurance Company and Private Pension Fund Investment 1962–84' *Bank of England Quarterly Bulletin* 26 1986 pp 546–57. See also K Richards and D Colenutt 'Concentration in the UK Ordinary Life Assurance Market' *Journal of Industrial Economics* 24 1975 pp 147–60.

**4141**   E F Cato Carter *The Real Business: A Narrative of the Vital Role Developed by Loss Adjusters* Robins Davies and Little 1972. A study of the development of loss adjustment through the history of the firm of Robins Davies and Little 1872–1972.

**4142**   Anthony Brown *Hazard Unlimited: The Story of Lloyd's of London* 2nd ed, Peter Davies 1978. A thematic history. It is quite informative on its post-war history. The administration of Lloyd's is featured strongly. Godfrey Hodgson *Lloyd's of London: A Reputation at Risk* Allen Lane 1984 concentrates on the changes and the scandals of 1970s and 1980s. See also H A L Cockerell *Lloyd's of London: A Portrait* Woodhead-Faulkner 1984, Raymond Flower and Michael Wynn Jones *Lloyd's of London: An Illustrated History* 3rd ed, Lloyd's of London Press 1987 and F Martin *The History of Lloyds Marine Insurance in Great Britain* Lloyds 1976.

**4143**   Edward Liveing *A Century of Insurance: The Commercial Union Group of Insurance Companies 1861–1961* Witherby 1961.

**4144**   Ronald George Garnett *A Century of Co-operative Insurance: The Co-operative Insurance Society 1867–1967: A Business History* Allen and Unwin 1968. A useful account of an important company.

**4145**   David Tregoning and Hugh Cockerell *Friends for Life: Friends Provident Life Office 1832–1982* Melland 1982.

**4146**   George Bruce *Poland's at Lloyds* Melland 1979. A history of the firm of John Poland and Co.

**4147**   Stanley D Chapman 'Hogg Robinson: The Rise of a Lloyd's Broker' in Oliver M Westall (ed) *The Historian and the Business of Insurance* Manchester University Press 1984 pp 173–89. This traces the lineage of one of the top of Lloyd's brokers to the present day and especially through the mergers and growth since 1945.

**4148**   E V Francis *London and Lancashire History: The History of the London and Lancashire Insurance Company Limited* London and Lancashire Insurance 1962.

**4149**   C R McDonald *Covering Seventy-Five Years: The Continuing Story of Municipal Mutual Insurance Ltd 1903–1978* Municipal Mutual Insurance 1978.

**4150**   Barry Supple *The Royal Exchange Assurance: A History of British Insurance 1720–1970* Cambridge University Press 1970. A major history of an important insurance company.

**4151**   W Gore Allen *We The Undersigned: A History of the Royal London Insurance Society Limited and its Times 1861–1961* Newman Neame 1961. Apart from some reflections of the effect of the social welfare provisions of the Attlee government on the insurance companies this has little material on the post-war period.

**4152**   B Watson *A Unique Society: A History of the Salvation Army Assurance Society Ltd* Salvationist Publishing 1968.

## (6) Accountancy

**4153**   R H Parker *British Accountants: A Biographical Sourcebook* Arno Press 1980.

**4154**   J Kitchen *Accounting: A Century of Development* University of Hull 1978. A history of the development of the profession and changes in accounting. There are a number of histories of professional accountants' bodies. Leon Hopkins *The Hundredth Year* Macdonald and Evans 1980 is a centenary history of the Institute of Chartered Accountants in England and Wales. See also Sir Harold Howitt *et al The History of the Institute of Chartered Accountants in England and Wales 1880–1965 and of its Founder Accountancy Bodies 1870–80: The Growth of a Profession and its Influence on Legislation and Public Affairs* Heinemann 1965. For histories of other professional bodies see William Ashworth *Fifty Years: The Story of the Association of Certified and Corporate Accountants 1904–1954* the Association 1954 and Alexander Adnett Garrett *History of the Society of Incorporated Accountants 1885–1957* Oxford University Press 1961.

**4155**   R Winsbury *Thomson McLintock and Co – The First Hundred Years 1877–1977* Seeley Service 1977. A useful business history. Another business history is Edgar Jones *Accountancy and the British Economy 1840–1980: The Evolution of Ernst and Whinney* Batsford 1981. For a biography of Sir Ellis Hunter of the accountancy firm of Dorman Long see [3345].

**4155A**   A B Richards *Touche Ross and Co 1899–1981: The Origins and Growth of the United Kingdom Firm* Touche Ross 1981.

**4156**   Sir Kenneth Cork *Cork on Cork: Sir Kenneth Cork Takes Stock* Macmillan 1988. Cork was a senior partner in Cork, Gully, the insolvency specialists, from 1946 to 1983. As such he was often involved with government industrial policy. In 1978–9 he was Lord Mayor of London. He also reflects on his post-retirement work in the patronage of the arts.

**4157** Michael Gillard *In the Name of Charity: The Rossminster Affair* Chatto and Windus 1987. A study of Roy Tucker and Ronald Plummer, two accountants who in the 1970s became famous through their adeptness at finding loopholes in the tax system for their clients. This journalistic investigation also gives a history of tax avoidance from 1960–85.

### (7) Pawnbroking

**4158** Kenneth Hudson *Pawnbroking: An Aspect of British Social History* The Bodley Head 1982. The final chapter deals with the decline of pawnbroking since 1945.

## F. COMMERCE

### (1) Domestic Commerce

#### (a) General

**4159** *Distributive Trades Survey* Confederation of British Industry 1983–. A monthly and quarterly guide and survey of trends and business confidence.

**4160** National Economic Development Office *Distributive Trade Statistics: A Guide to Official Sources* HMSO 1970. This is marred by imprecise citation of titles and incomplete information on access to these.

**4161** N A H Stacey and A Wilson *The Changing Pattern of Distribution* Pergamon 1965. The standard study of post-war retailing and distribution. T S Ward *The Distribution of Consumer Goods: Structure and Performance* Cambridge University Press 1973 is an analysis of labour productivity in retailing and changes in the distribution of consumer goods since the 1950s. It contains useful statistical information.

**4162** P Simmons 'Evidence on the Impact of Consumer Demand in the UK 1955–1968' *Review of Economic Studies* 1980 pp 893– 906.

#### (b) Prices

See also the category on Consumer Society in the section on Lifestyle [5770–8] for material on the cost of living and consumer spending.

**4163** *Retail Prices Indices 1914–1986* HMSO 1987. Most of the statistics in here are in fact 1956–86 and there are none before 1947. The coverage, reflecting the increasing sophistication of its compilers, grows more detailed and complex after 1974. See also *A Short Guide to the Retail Price Index* HMSO 1987, which gives details of the history, methods of compiling and calculation of the index. The Retail Price Index appears monthly in *Employment Gazette* (formerly *Ministry of Labour Gazette*).

**4164** C R Ross 'Price Stability in the United Kingdom' *Bulletin of the Oxford University Institute of Statistics* 20 1958 pp 265–84. A survey since 1945.

#### (c) Marketing and Market Research

**4165** Max K Adler *Marketing and Market Research* Crosby Lockwood 1967. A good analysis of the growth of market research. It also reflects on the effect of market research on products and packaging and on marketing and market research overseas. See also Max K Adler (ed) *Leading Cases in Market Research* Business Books 1971. This includes a number of case histories of marketing exercises, of women's attitudes to marketing and of the impact of shopping centres.

**4166** T A B Corley 'Consumer Marketing in Britain 1914–60' *Business History* 29 1987 pp 65–83. A good study of the place of marketing in company strategy and of the failings of British marketing. Further research on this subject, and of the relationship between poor marketing and industrial decline, is much needed.

#### (d) Retailing

**4167** *Stores, Shops, Supermarkets* Newman Books 1939–. An annual comprehensive directory of the retail trade. Also valuable for understanding retailing and patterns of consumption are the periodicals *Retail Business* 1958– and *Market Intelligence* 1972–.

**4168** *Retail Planning Methods: Bibliography* Unit for Retail Planning Information Ltd 1980. The same firm also published *Managed Shopping Centres: Bibliography and Research* in 1979. See also Ross L Davies and David J Bennison *British Town Centre Shopping Schemes: A Statistical Digest* Unit for Retail Planning Information Ltd 1979.

**4169** Grenville Havenhand *Nation of Shopkeepers* Eyre and Spottiswoode 1970. A general survey of the retail trade based on extensive interviews with people involved at all levels of the trade. Separate chapters cover the various aspects of the retail trade. On the major changes that have taken place in the retail trade in the latter part of the post-war period see *British Shopping Developments 1965–1982* Hillier, Parker, May and Rowden 1983. A study of the changing environment of retailing is C Guy *Retail Location and Retail Planning in Britain* Gower 1980.

**4170** James B Jeffreys *Retail Trading in Britain 1850–1950: A Study of Trends in Retailing with Special Reference to the Development of Co-operative, Multiple Shop and Departmental Store Methods of Trading* Cambridge University Press 1954. An excellent study which remains of great value. It provides a good statement of the state of the retail trade in 1950 and is well illustrated and supported by informative statistical tables.

**4171** Sidney Pollard and J D Hughes 'Costs in Retail Distribution in Great Britain 1950–7' *Oxford Economic Papers* n.s. 13 1961 pp 166–83.

**4172** P Shepherd and D Thorpe *Urban Redevelopment and Changes in Retail Structure 1961–1971* Manchester Business School 1977. A detailed examination of the impact of population change and housing clearance on changes in the number of shops. The response of retailers to similar developments in the 1970s is analysed in R Davies *Urban Change in Britain and the Retail Response* Oxford Institute of Retail Management 1987. The growth of large multiples, the steady rise in average store size, the development of new forms of retailing and the widespread adoption of new techniques, such as self-service, in the 1970s, are examined in J A N Bamfield 'Changing Face of British Retailing' *National Westminster Bank Quarterly Review* May 1980 pp 33–45.

**4173** Paul Regan 'The 1986 Shops Bill' *Parliamentary Affairs* 41 1988 pp 218–35. A study of the factors that led to government to try to amend the Sunday trading laws and the reasons for the defeat of the Bill.

**4174** Ross L Davies and Jonathan Reynolds *The Development of Teleshopping and Teleservices* Longman 1983. This charts the growing possibilities of home shopping.

**4175** Wyn Grant and David Marsh 'The Representation of Retail Interests in Britain' *Political Studies* 22 1974 pp 168–77. A study of retailers as a pressure group.

**4176** P A Raveh 'Managerial Behaviour in Retailing' London Business School PhD Thesis 1977.

**4177** D J Bennison and R L Davies *The Impact of Town Centre Shopping Schemes in Britain: Their Impact on Traditional Retail Environments* Pergamon 1980. A study of the development of self-contained shopping

centres, the planning philosophy behind them, the regional varieties in their growth, their impact on existing retailers and their economic, social and environmental effect. It includes a detailed case study of the Eldon Square development in Newcastle. On Eldon Square see also R G Chapman *et al* 'Eldon Square: Concept and Reality: The Genesis of a Shopping Centre' *Retail and Distribution Management* 5/1 1977 pp 46–50. Eldon Square and other developments in the North East are also discussed in R L Davies 'Shopping Centre Development in Newcastle upon Tyne and Tyne and Wear Metropolitan County' in John A Dawson and J Dennis Lord (eds) *Shopping Centre Development: Policies and Prospects* Croom Helm 1985 pp 161–84. Russell Schiller 'Land Use Controls in UK Shopping Centres' in the same volume pp 40–56 is an excellent survey of the post-war development and planning of these centres. One of the most successful of these is the one opened at Brent Cross in 1976. Its impact is assessed in P Downey *The Impact of Brent Cross* Reviews and Studies Series 2, Greater London Council 1980. This should be examined with his earlier research, *Brent Cross Shopping Centre Impact Study: Preliminary Analysis of Shop Vacancies and Changes in NW London 1971–1976* Greater London Council 1977 and with A J Bruce and H R Mann *The Brent Cross Shopping Centre Impact Study: The Results of the First Diary Study of Housing Shopping Trips* Greater London Council 1977.

**4178** David A Kirby 'The Decline and Fall of the Smaller Retail Outlet: A Geographical Study' *Retail and Distribution Management* 2 1974 pp 14–8. A study of the declining numbers of shops, which are being replaced by large multiple chains in larger units. The largest contraction is in the co-operative movement. On the problems of small shops see also R K Berry 'Small Unit Retailing in Urban Britain – A Review of Present Trends and the Policies Affecting the Small Shop' Wales MA Thesis 1977. John A Dawson and David A Kirby *Small Scale Retailing in the UK* Saxon House 1979 is based on detailed studies of small shops in Derby, Port Talbot and Exeter. It argues that increased operation costs and the increased overload of VAT are the major problems for small retailers.

**4179** N Mackeith *The History and Conservation of Shopping Arcades* Mansell 1986. A history from the eighteenth century onwards. The material on the modern period is largely concerned with efforts to conserve historic arcades.

**4180** J Henneberry 'The Evolution of the Retail Warehouse and its Impact on Other Retail Outlets' *Property Management* 5 1987 pp 254–61. A study of their emergence in the late 1960s and subsequent growth.

**4181** K Hudson *Behind the High Street* The Bodley Head 1982. A study of changes in urban shopping areas in the twentieth century, with particular reference to Bath. Changes in the Nottingham area are analysed in P T Whysall 'The Changing Pattern of Retail Structure in Greater Nottingham 1912–1971' Nottingham PhD Thesis 1974–6. C J Thomas 'The Growth and Functioning of an Unplanned Retail Park: The Swansea Enterprise Zone' *Regional Studies* 21 1987 pp 297–300 examines the decanting of retailers out from the city centre.

**4182** G I Jackson 'British Retailers' Expansion into Europe' Manchester PhD Thesis 1976.

**4183** D G Harris 'The Effects of Microelectronics in Supermarkets' Brunel PhD Thesis 1985. A study over the last fifty years of the technological changes in the groceries trade.

**4184** L Sparks *The Impact of the Recession on Retail Unemployment* Department of Business Studies, University of Stirling 1984. A paper on the changing composition of the retail workforce since 1960 and the effects of the recession of the early 1980s and structural changes in the industry on the workforce.

**4185** Robin Myers *The British Book Trade: A Bibliographical Guide* Deutsch 1973. For other bibliographies which contain material on the bookselling trade see [6652]. On that specialized form of bookselling, the book club, see Michael Byrne *The History and Contemporary Significance of Book Clubs* Birmingham Polytechnic 1978. Graham Watson *Book Society* Deutsch 1980 is an autobiography by someone in this line of trade. The restrictions on the number of Left-Wing journals carried by major newsagents and booksellers such as W H Smith are criticized in Liz Cooper, Charles Landry and Dave Berry *The Other Secret Service: Press Distribution and Press Censorship* Minority Press Group/Campaign for Press Freedom 1980. It should be noted that in the course of the 1980s W H Smith have begun to carry rather more Left-Wing titles than was at one time the case. On the Net Book Agreement see [3116].

**4186** M A Ali 'An Analysis of Demand for Motor-Cars in the United Kingdom in the Post-War Period' Leeds MA Thesis 1964–5.

**4187** Tom Salter *Carnaby Street* Margaret and Jack Hobbs 1970. An account of the fashionable centre of the swinging London of the 1960s. See also Ken and Kate Baynes 'Behind the Scene (Carnaby Street)' *Design* 212 1966 pp 18–29.

**4188** M Trewby 'Expresso Madness' *Design* 419 1983 pp 42–9. A study of the increasing popularity of expresso and filter coffee and of coffee bars in the 1950s.

**4189** J C Beasley 'A Study of Corporate Objectives for the Retailing of Menswear in the United Kingdom Since 1970' Leeds MPhil Thesis 1985. A detailed study of the major retailers and their response to the shift towards demand for more casual wear.

**4190** J F Lowe 'Competition in the UK Retail Petrol Market 1960–1973' *Journal of Industrial Economics* 24 1976 pp 203–20. See also E Tzanetis 'The Demand for Petrol in the United Kingdom 1955–1973: An Empirical Investigation' Surrey PhD Thesis 1977–8.

**4191** Peter Mathias *Retailing Revolution: A History of Multiple Retailing in the Food Trade Based upon the Allied Suppliers Group of Companies* Longmans 1967. A history of a supermarket chain.

**4192** D W Peel *A Garden in the Sky: The Story of Barker's of Kensington 1870–1957* W H Allen 1960. A history of the department stores Barkers, Pontings and Derry and Toms.

**4193** Rowan Benthall *My Store of Memories* W H Allen 1974. Memoirs of Benthall's department store, of which he was managing director and chairman.

**4194** B Hulanicki *From A to Biba* Hutchinson 1983. Biba was a celebrated and innovatory department store in the 1960s.

**4195** Bryan Little *David Jones 1862–1962: A Hundred Years of Wholesale Grocery* Newman Neame 1962. A short history.

**4196** Maurice Corina *From Silks and Oak Counters: Debenhams 1778–1978* Hutchinson Benham 1978. A history of the department stores group.

**4197** Bryan Stanford Morgan *Express Journey 1864–1964: A Centenary History of the Express Dairy Company Ltd* Newman Neame 1964. A history of the milk delivery and dairy firm.

**4198** *Great Universal Stores: 25 Years of Progress 1932–1957* Great Universal Stores 1957. A short history of the mail order company.

**4199** Barty Phillips *Conran and the Habitat Story* Weidenfeld and Nicolson 1984. This charts the progress of Sir Terence Conran from designer through the establishment of the Habitat chain of stores retailing innovative designs in furniture and furnishings. He went on to build the Storehouse group which also includes stores with similar products, such as Heals, as well chains such as Mothercare or British Home Stores. For the history of Heals see Susanna Gooden *At the Sign of the Four Poster: A History of Heals* Heals 1984. Jennifer Hawkins Opie 'Geoffrey Dunn and Dunns of Bromley: Selling Good Design – A Lifetime Commitment' *Journal of the Decorative Arts Society: 1850 to the Present* 10 1986 pp 34–9 is a profile of the previous owner of Heals, who acquired it as an addition to his chain of designer furniture and furnishings stores in 1963. Dunns folded in the recession of the 1970s and 1980s.

**4200** Tim Dale *Harrods: The Store and the Legend* Pan 1981. A history of the Knightsbridge department store. On the management of Harrods under the House of Fraser regime of Sir Hugh Fraser see George Pottinger *The Winning Counter: Hugh Fraser and Harrods* Hutchinson 1971. The history of House of Fraser is told in Michael Moss and Alison Turton *A Legend of Retailing: House of Fraser* Weidenfeld and Nicolson 1989.

**4201** Asa Briggs *Friends of the People: The Centenary History of Lewis's* Batsford 1956. A history of the department store group.

**4202** *John Speden Lewis 1885–1963* John Lewis Partnership 1985. A biography of a figure who was important in the development of the co-operative polity of the John Lewis Partnership.

**4203** Alison Adburgham *Libertys: A Biography of a Shop* Allen and Unwin 1975. A centenary history of the London department store that specializes in fabrics. See also M Coleman 'Liberty's Lives!' *Crafts* 1975 pp 34–41.

**4204** Goronwy Rees *St Michael: A History of Marks and Spencer* Weidenfeld and Nicolson 1969. The most thorough history of the company. Asa Briggs *Marks and Spencer 1884–1984* Octopus Books 1984 is a much shorter centenary history. K K Tse *Marks and Spencer: Anatomy of Britain's Most Efficiently Managed Company* Pergamon 1985 is a good appraisal of the successful management of Marks and Spencer by a Hong Kong management analyst. He points to the company as a model for British industry. It has certainly been used as a model for the Civil Service, as he points out. He devotes considerable space to the import of Marks and Spencer techniques into the Civil Service under the guise of the Rayner reviews initiated by Sir Derek Rayner, the company's joint managing director, during his period of part-time secondment to Whitehall in 1979–84. In addition there are a number of memoirs which cast light on the history of Marks and Spencer. The most important of these is that of Israel Sieff, Lord Sieff *Memoirs of Israel Sieff* Weidenfeld and Nicolson 1970, who was a leading member of the company from 1926 until his death in 1972. Also of great value is that of his successor, Marcus Sieff *Don't Ask The Price: The Memoirs of the President of Marks and Spencer* Weidenfeld and Nicolson 1987. Flora Solomon and Barnet Litvinoff *Baku to Baker Street: Memoirs of Flora Solomon* Collins 1984

is the memoir of an important Marks and Spencer employee.

**4205** Leslie Gardiner *The Making of John Menzies* John Menzies 1983. Centenary history of the newsagents and booksellers.

**4206** George Davis *What Next* Century Hutchinson 1989. The autobiography of the man who transformed the Next (formerly Hepworths) fashion retailing empire in the 1980s.

**4207** James Boswell (ed) *JS 100: The Story of Sainsburys* J Sainsbury 1969. A short centenary history of the supermarket chain.

**4208** R G Honeycombe *Selfridges Seventy-Five Years: The Story of the Store 1909–1984* Park Lane Press 1984. A history of the London department store.

**4209** Charles Wilson *First With The News: The History of W H Smith 1792–1972* Cape 1985. A history of the booksellers and newsagents. The final section covers the period from 1949, when Smiths became a public company, to 1972.

**4210** Maurice Corina *Pile It High, Sell it Cheap: The Authorised Biography of Sir John Cohen* Weidenfeld and Nicolson 1971. The biography of the founder of the Tesco chain of supermarkets.

(e) Rationing

**4211** Alida Harvie *The Rationed Years* Regency 1982. Rationing is a seriously under investigated topic. This, the only substantial work to concentrate on the subject, looks at rationing and its impact 1939–53. The nutritional effects of rationing are examined in Dorothy F Hollingsworth 'Rationing and Economic Constraints on Food Consumption Since the Second World War' in Derek S Oddy and Derek J Miller (eds) *Diet and Health in Modern Britain* Croom Helm 1985 pp 255–73.

(f) Hire Purchase and Consumer Credit

**4212** *Consumer Credit: Report of the Committee* Cmnd 4596, *Parliamentary Papers* ix 1970–71. This committee, chaired by Lord Crowther, reviewed the historical background and the licensing and regulation of consumer credit.

**4213** N Runcie 'A Study of Hire Purchase in the United Kingdom and Three Dominions, Australia, Canada and New Zealand, Since 1945' London PhD Thesis 1959–60. See also J K Ghandhi 'Hire Purchase in the

United Kingdom 1948–57' Cambridge PhD Thesis 1960–1.

**4214** Janet Ford *The Indebted Society: Credits and Default in the 1980s* Routledge 1988. An overview of consumer credit and personal indebtedness in the 1980s. It includes a discussion of borrowers' experiences and their management of debt.

### (g) Consumer Protection

**4215** *Consumer Protection: Interim Report of the Committee* Cmnd 1011, *Parliamentary Papers* xii 1959–60, *Final Report* Cmnd 1781, *Parliamentary Papers* xii 1961–62. This detailed report of the committee chaired by J T Molony covers standards and labelling, marks, seals, testing, civil redress and advertising and sales practice. On the history of consumer protection policy the only substantial study is W D B Roberts 'The Formation of Consumer Protection Policy in Britain 1943–1973' Kent PhD Thesis 1975–6.

### (h) The Co-operative Movement

**4216** *Report of the Annual Co-operative Congress* Co-operative Union 1869–. Information on the various co-operative societies in the British Isles is contained in the annual *The Co-operative Directory* Co-operative Union 1887–. This largely concentrates on the traditional co-operative movement of distributive and retail societies. In recent years however it has given increasing space to the new productive and special co-operatives which have grown up, particularly since the 1970s. For more material on these see [4611–3]. The annual *Co-operative Statistics* Co- operative Union 1946, 1949–, should also be consulted.

**4217** Beatrice Potter *The Co-operative Movement in Great Britain* Gower 1987. A useful general study. An earlier study by the then Secretary of the Co-operative Party (which is affiliated to the Labour Party) is Jack Bailey *The British Co-operative Movement* Hutchinson's University Library 1955. A general history of the movement is Arnold Bonner *British Co-operation: The History, Principles and Organisation of the British Co-operative Movement* 2nd ed, Co-operative Union 1970. See also Desmond Flanagan *1869–1969: A Centenary Story of the Co-operative Union of Great Britain and Ireland* Co-operative Union 1969.

**4218** G N Ostergaard and A H Halsey *Power in Co-operatives: A Study of the Internal Politics of British Retail Societies* Blackwell 1965. This political analysis of the retail societies has plenty of information on their gradual decline in the first twenty years of the post-war

period. Their failings are assessed in the context of the national organization and the London Co-operative Society in S R Lawrence 'A Critique of the Post-War Consumers' Co- operative Movement' Wales MSc (Econ) Thesis 1981.

**4219** Sir W Richardson *The CWS in War and Peace 1938–76: The Co-operative Wholesale Society in the Second World War and Post-War Years* Co-operative Wholesale Society 1977.

**4220** J Gaffin and D Thomas *Caring and Sharing: The Centenary History of the Co-operative Women's Guild* Co- operative Union 1983. Once an important part of working class life the Guild has suffered decline since 1939. The social and philanthropic side of the movement which it represents has been overshadowed by the need in the post-war period for efficient management in order to survive. The creation of the Welfare State also left it without a clear role.

**4221** J A N Bamfield 'The Revival of the Co-ops' *Retail Distribution Management* 6/2 1978 pp 18–23 and 6/3 1978 pp 14–18. This examines the problems of the co-operative movement and argues that the retail societies had experienced something of a revival in the 1960s and 1970s. If so, it proved short term because within five years S Eliot 'The Crisis in the Co-operative Movement' *Retail Distribution Management* 11/4 1983 pp 8–14 was again pointing to decline stemming from organizational fragmentation and out of date retailing methods. Greater London Council Economic Policy Group *The Co-op: Can It Still Care?* Greater London Council 1984 is a short paper charting the decline of co-operative societies in London, attempts to halt the decline and options for GLC assistance.

**4222** John B Smethurst (comp) *A Bibliography of Co-operative Societies' Histories* Co-operative Union n.d. (1970?). A good list of local society histories and other such material. Some of the works listed here are substantial pieces which are of considerable value for the post-war historian.

### (2) Overseas Trade

### (a) General

**4223** *Overseas Trade Statistics of the UK* 5v, HMSO 1848–. This is issued monthly and annually. It was formerly known as *Overseas Trade Accounts of the United Kingdom* and before that *Annual Statement of the Overseas Trade of the United Kingdom*. An annual survey published over the years under various titles. The first part of this summarizes exports and imports. The second analyses imports by commodity and country of origin. The third does the same for exports by commodity and country of destination. The fourth provides figures of imports and exports by trading partner. Finally the fifth examines trade at British ports.

**4224** Joan Mitchell 'The UK Balance of Payments 1946–55' *Bulletin of Oxford University Institute of Statistics* 20 1958 pp 29–53. A review of trends and of the impact of the Korean War.

**4225** D Connell *The UK's Performance in Export Markets: Some Evidence from International Trade* National Economic Development Office 1979. The poor performance of manufacturing exports under the Thatcher government, during which time Britain became a net importer of manufactured goods for the first time since the Industrial Revolution, is assessed in M Landesmann and A Snell 'The Consequences of Mrs Thatcher for UK Manufacturing Exports' *Economic Journal* 99 1989 pp 1–27. M Panic and T Seward 'The Problems of UK Exports' *Bulletin of Oxford University Institute of Statistics* 28 1966 pp 19–32 is an earlier reflection on Britain's poor export performance.

**4226** Leonard Rayner 'British Foreign Trade and the Imperial Hangover' *Round Table* 300 1986 pp 354–61. A critique of the detrimental effects on British trade of the dominance of its financial sector, the poor performance of the Foreign and Commonwealth Office as an agency for securing trade and the unmerited complacency of British companies about the security of Commonwealth markets which does not seem to have been lost even after the markets were.

**4227** Ann D Morgan *British Imports of Consumer Goods: A Study of Import Penetration* Cambridge University Press 1985. Notwithstanding that she has decided not to include either food or motor vehicles in her considerations this is a useful, if short, study. A more general study of British imports in the post-war period is T S Barker 'The Major Determinants of Britain's Visible Imports 1949–1966' Cambridge PhD Thesis 1972–3. Imports in the period 1899–1959 are discussed in G F Ray 'British Imports of Manufactured Goods' *National Institute Economic Review* 8 1960 pp 12–29. See also C Kevork 'The United Kingdom's Demand for Imports 1946–1957: A Discussion of Attempts to Measure Elasticities of Selected Commodities' London PhD Thesis 1959–60.

**4228** *Britain's Invisible Earnings: The Report of the Committee on Invisible Exports* HMSO 1967. A report into the performance of a major export earner chaired by William M Clarke. Nicholas Sowels *Britain's Invisible Earnings* Gower 1989 is a thorough survey. Britain's sources of invisible earnings are not only the financial services of the City of London, but educational services,

transport, management consultancy, accounting, legal services and entertainment copyrights and franchises. All of these are examined in David Liston and Nigel Reeves *The Invisible Economy: A Profile of Britain's Invisible Exports* Pitman 1988, a study of the history and performance of Britain's invisible earnings sector and the challenges it faces.

### (b) Effects of Government Policy and Devaluation

**4229** M F W Hemming, C M Miles and G F Ray 'A Statistical Summary of the Extent of Import Controls in the United Kingdom Since the War' *Review of Economic Studies* 26 1959 pp 75–109.

**4230** J A P Treasure 'Reducing Export Risks: A Study of Certain Aspects of the Post-War Export Drive 1945–1952' Cambridge PhD Thesis 1955–6.

**4231** M June Flanders 'The Effects of Devaluation on Exports: A Case Study, United Kingdom 1949–1954' *Bulletin of the Oxford University Institute of Economics and Statistics* 25 1963 pp 165–98. A study of the effects of the 1949 devaluation.

**4232** D S Higham 'The Effects of Exchange Rate Changes on the UK Balance of Payments, with Special Reference to the Devaluation of 1967' Oxford DPhil Thesis 1982. In 1967 the sterling/dollar parity was dropped from $2.80 to the pound to $2.40 to the pound. This thesis disputes the traditional view that this had only a small impact on visible trade. He argues it reduced the volume of imports and had made a difference to the balance of trade of about £1,000m by 1970. The effect of the 1967 devaluation is also analysed in Jocelyn Horne 'The Effect of Devaluation on the Balance Payments and the Labour Market: United Kingdom 1967' *Economica* 46 1979 pp 11–25.

### (c) Balance of Payments

**4233** Central Statistical Office *United Kingdom Balance of Payments* HMSO 1946/47–. An annual statistical guide, commonly known as the Pink Book.

**4234** A P Thirlwall *Balance of Payments Theory and the UK Experience* 3rd ed, Macmillan 1982. A lucid textbook and survey of the literature. It focuses on import penetration and the non-price factors in the UK performance. On the problems of the balance of payments in the post-war period see W G P Lynch 'The Balance of Payments Crises of the United Kingdom 1945–1965, with Special Reference to the Sterling Area' Strathclyde PhD Thesis 1969–70 and A S Papageorghiou 'The Post-War Balance of Payments Problem of the United Kingdom: A Consideration of Certain Structural Exogenous and Institutional Factors' Edinburgh PhD Thesis 1956–7.

**4235**  O Nankivell 'The Recovery of the United Kingdom Balance of Payments 1951–54' Manchester MA (Econ) Thesis 1963–4.

**4236**  K Richards 'The United Kingdom Balance of Payments 1958–65' Wales MA (Econ) Thesis 1969–70.

(d) EFTA and other Free Trade Agreements

**4237**  Frederick Victor Meyer *The Seven: A Provisional Appraisal of the European Free Trade Association* Barrie and Rockliff 1960. EFTA was a free trade association (from which agricultural products were specifically excluded) of Britain, Norway, Sweden, Denmark, Portugal, Austria and Switzerland which was formally established in January 1960. The negotiations which led to its establishment are discussed in Miriam Camps *The Free Trade Area Negotiations* Political and Economic Planning 1959 and G St John Barclay 'Negotiation Under Threats: The Diplomacy of the Free Trade Area Discussions 1956–58' *Australian Outlook* 20 1966 pp 278–95.

**4238**  G St John Barclay 'Background to EFTA: An Episode in Anglo-Scandinavian Relations' *Australian Journal of Politics and History* 11 1965 pp 185–97. See also T C Archer 'The Politics of the United Kingdom-Scandinavian Relationship Within the Context of the European Free Trade Association' Aberdeen PhD Thesis 1974–6.

**4239**  C Truninger 'Swiss Relations with the United Kingdom in the Formation and Development of EFTA Until 1967' Aberdeen PhD Thesis 1976.

**4240**  Dermot McAleese and John Martin *Irish Manufactured Imports from the UK in the Sixties: The Effects of AIFTA* Economic and Social Research Institute, Dublin 1973. A study of the Anglo-Irish Free Trade Area set up in 1965.

(e) Trade with the Commonwealth

**4241**  John Southgate *The Commonwealth Sugar Agreement 1951–1974* C Czarnikow 1985. This agreement signed in 1951 guaranteed a market for Commonwealth sugar producers and assured the UK and some other Commonwealth members of a sugar supply. It was replaced by the Lomé Convention in 1975.

**4242**  I R Thomas 'Anglo-Canadian Trade 1946–1960' Exeter MA Thesis 1961–2.

**4243**  R G Bingham 'The Performance of United Kingdom Export of Manufactures in the Australian Market 1960–1966' Kent MA Thesis 1979.

**4244**  D J Morgan 'Imperial Preference in the West Indies in the British Caribbean 1929–55: A Quantitative Analysis' *Economic Journal* 72 1962 pp 104–33.

(f) Trade with Western Europe

**4245**  Frederick Victor Meyer *United Kingdom Trade with Europe* Bowes and Bowes 1957. See also R W R Price 'The Competitive Position of the United Kingdom vis-à-vis the Countries of the European Economic Communities Evidenced by Changes in the Flow of Trade in Manufactured Goods Since 1952' Manchester PhD Thesis 1970–1 and R T Maddock 'Movements for Freer Trade in Western Europe Since the War, with Special Reference to the Effect of the Creation of the European Economic Community and European Free Trade Area on British Trade in Western Europe' Wales MA Thesis 1962–3. On the consequences of the British entry into the European Community on manufacturing trade see N H Ezz Moustafa 'Performance of British Manufacturing Industries in the EEC Market 1973–75' Bath PhD Thesis 1978.

**4246**  E H Lindsay 'Trade Between Northern Ireland and the Republic of Ireland 1950–1974' Queens MSc (Econ) Thesis 1978.

**4247**  Brinley Thomas 'The Changing Pattern of Anglo-Danish Trade 1913–1963' in Birgit Nuchel Thomsen and Brinley Thomas *Anglo-Danish Trade 1661–1963* University Press of Aarhus, Aarhus 1966 pp 337–423.

(g) Trade with other Areas

**4248**  D S Swamy 'Demand for British Exports in the United States During the Post-War Period' Leeds MA Thesis 1963–4.

**4249**  A Y A Mohammed 'The Suez Canal and the Trends of British Trade to and from the Middle and the Far East During the Period 1854–1966' St Andrews PhD Thesis 1967–8.

**4250**  Malcolm R Hill 'Soviet and East European Company Activity in the United Kingdom and Ireland' in Geoffrey Hamilton (ed) *Red Multinationals or Red Herrings? The Activities of Enterprises from the Socialist*

*Countries in the West* Pinter 1986 pp 17–87. A survey of these companies, most of which are concerned with developing trade and were established in the 1960s and 1970s when trade was growing rapidly. It includes some case studies.

**4251** M I Lipman *Memoirs of a Socialist Businessman* Lipman Trust 1982. As a commercial traveller in Eastern Europe after 1945 Lipman helped to establish British trade links in this area.

## G. TRANSPORT

It should be noted that a vast amount of material, largely in the form of short specialist books for enthusiasts, is published by publishers such as Ian Allan, on all aspects of transport history. Ian Allan also publish magazines such as *Railway World* or *Buses*, which contain a certain amount of information of interest. I have however only included a limited amount of this type of material, focusing on the titles more likely to be of interest to the academic historian and the general reader, rather than the enthusiast.

### (1) General

**4252** Denys Lawrence Munby *Inland Transport Statistics, Great Britain 1920–1970 Vol I: Railways, Road Passenger Transport, London's Transport* Clarendon 1978. A major work of painstaking scholarship. Unfortunately Munby's death prevented any further volumes. This volume indeed had to be completed after Munby's death by A H Watson.

**4253** *Transport Statistics, Great Britain* HMSO 1974–. An annual comprehensive collection of statistics.

**4254** *Journal of Transport History* 1953–. This regularly carries a large bibliography of recently published relevant material. The Chartered Institute of Transport Library regularly issues typescript bibliographies on various aspects of transport.

**4255** Derek H Aldcroft *British Transport Since 1914: An Economic History* David and Charles 1974. A good analysis of most aspects of developments in transportation in the twentieth century. It does however fail to give due weight to some developments of great importance, such as the rise of the motorway network. Also of use is his 'A New Chapter in Transport History: The Twentieth Century Revolution' *Journal of Transport History* n.s. 3 1975–76 pp 217–39, not least on the social and environmental changes that have been wrought. Enid Wistrich *The Politics of Transport* Longman 1983 is a good and comprehensive analysis of transport since

1945. It is particularly strong on transport policy. Transport policy is also assessed in K M Gwilliam *Transport and Public Policy* Allen and Unwin 1964.

**4256** Derek H Aldcroft *Studies in British Transport History 1870–1970* David and Charles 1974. Three of these essays deal with the post-war period. These examine the delay in moving to diesel and electrification on the railways, the changing pattern of demand for passenger transport, and the 1970 Rochdale inquiry into the shipping industry.

**4257** A W J Thomson and L C Hunter *The Nationalised Transport Industries* Heinemann 1973. Studies of the state of the nationalized rail, coach and air transport industries.

**4258** D Maltby and H P White *Transport in the United Kingdom* Macmillan 1982. A useful textbook.

**4259** D N M Starkie 'Transportation Planning and Public Policy' *Progress in Planning* 1 1973 pp 315–89. A study of transport planning in the 1960s and 1970s.

**4260** Michael R Bonavia *The Nationalisation of British Transport: The Early Years of the British Transport Commission 1948–53* Macmillan 1987. The 1947 Transport Act attempted to create an integrated inland transport monopoly. It initially included in its ambit rail, docks, road haulage, canals and waterways and London transport. This is a good study of its early years up until the 1953 Transport Act which denationalized road haulage. For contemporary assessments of the creation of the Transport Commission see B R Williams 'Transport Act 1947: Some Benefits and Dangers' *Journal of the Institute of Transport* 24 1951 pp 153–8 and B R Williams 'Nationalisation and After' *Journal of the Institute of Transport* 25 1952 pp 13–19. It remained in being for another ten years, being broken up after the 1962 Transport Act. For its reports and accounts see British Transport Commission *Annual Report and Accounts* HMSO 1948–62. See also D R Steel 'The British Transport Commission 1948–1962: A Study in the Managerial Autonomy of a Public Corporation' Oxford DPhil Thesis 1974–6. Some of its functions passed to the Transport Holding Company for which see its *Annual Report and Acounts* HMSO 1963–9.

**4261** J J Richardson 'The Formation of Transport Policy in Britain 1950–1956' Manchester PhD Thesis 1970–1.

**4262** Norman Lee 'Current Transport Policy in Britain' *District Bank Review* 160 1966 pp 20–40. A study of transport policy in the 1960s.

**4263** Mayer Hillman 'An Evaluation of Transport Policy in the 1970s' *Political Studies* 3 1982 pp 71–87. See also K J Button 'Transport Policy in the United Kingdom 1968–1974' *Three Banks Review* 103 1974 pp 26–48.

**4264** Anthony Harrison and John Gretton (eds) *Transport UK 1987: An Economic, Social and Policy Audit* Policy Journals 1987. Essays on developments of the 1980s such as deregulation, community transport, road safety policy, and changes in the nature of air, rail and bus services.

**4265** George Charlesworth *A History of the Transport and Road Research Laboratory* Avebury 1987. A good semi-official history emphasizing the laboratory's growing role in policy making.

**4266** J Sleeman 'The Rise and Decline of Municipal Transport' *Scottish Journal of Political Economy* 9 1962 pp 46–64. The effect of the new rate support structure for municipal transport after the 1974 Local Government Act is examined in P J Mackie 'The New Grants System for Local Transport – The First Five Years' *Public Administration* 58 1980 pp 187–206.

**4267** J M A Smith 'The Impact of the Motor Car on Public Transport' *Journal of the Institute of Transport* 29 1961 pp 41–8. An analysis of the detrimental effect of the spread of car ownership.

**4268** Peter J Mackie 'The New Grant System for Local Transport – The First Five Years' *Public Administration* 58 1980 pp 187–206. This argues that the rationalization of the central government grant for local transport services into a block grant has been an improvement on the old system.

**4269** P R White 'Travelcard Tickets in Urban Public Transport' *Journal of Transport Economics and Policy* 15 1981 pp 17–34. A survey of the rise of travelcards giving public transport passengers access to the whole urban public transport network in cities such as London, Edinburgh, Manchester and the West Midlands.

**4270** Peter J Mackie, David Simon and Anthony E Whiteing *The British Transport Industry and the European Community: A Study of Regulation and Modal Split in the Long Distance and International Freight Market* Gower 1987. A good analysis of road and rail freight traffic both before and after Britain's entry to Europe in the context of the effect of that entry.

**4271** Michael F Collins and Timothy M Pharoah *Transport Organisation in a Great City: The Case of London* Allen and Unwin 1974. A study of the development of transport in London since the mid-nineteenth century it is of great value for the post-war period and includes a number of case studies. It focuses particularly on transport policy in London since the 1960s. Policy in the same period, especially in the context of relations between planners and pressure groups, is also analysed in P Filian 'Transport Policies in London 1965–1980: A Study of Political Conflict and Social Injustice' Kent PhD Thesis 1983. The history of the various means of crossing the Thames, down to the construction of the Dartford tunnel, is traced in J Pudney *Crossing London's River: The Bridges, Ferries and Tunnels Crossing the Thames Tideway in London* Dent 1976. On the history of London Transport see Theodore Cardwell Barker and Michael Robbins *A History of London Transport: Passenger Travel and the Development of the Metropolis Vol 2: The Twentieth Century to 1970* 2nd ed, Allen and Unwin 1976. The history of London Transport is also examined in two illustrated histories; Oliver Green and John Reed *The London Transport Golden Jubilee Book 1933–1983* Daily Telegraph 1983 and Oliver Green *The London Underground: An Illustrated History* Ian Allan 1987.

**4272** Ian Black, Richard Gillie, Richard Henderson and Terry Thomas *Advanced Urban Transport* Saxon House 1975. A study of urban transportation systems and policy between the 1950s and the 1970s, especially in the context of case studies of Coventry.

**4273** J A Grant 'An Analysis of Urban Transportation Planning and Policy Making in Three County Boroughs 1947–1974' Reading PhD Thesis 1974–6.

**4274** John M Bailey 'The Evolution of Transport Policy in Oxford' in Trevor Rowley (ed) *The Oxford Region* Oxford University Department for External Studies 1980 pp 97–124. A study of planning since the 1940s. Oxford was particularly active in trying schemes of traffic restraint and was responsible for the innovative 'Park and Ride' scheme which was widely admired in the 1970s.

**4275** D Scrafton 'An Analysis of Public Passenger Transport Services in West Yorkshire 1896–1963' London PhD Thesis 1967–8.

**4276** D F Glenn *Roads, Rail and Ferries of the Solent Area 1919–1969* Ian Allan 1980.

**4277** D Fletcher 'Metro' *Local Government Policy Making* 8 1982 pp 127–34. A study of the development of the Tyne and Wear Metro as an integrated urban transport system.

## (2) Roads

**4278** *Roads in England and Wales: Report by the Minister of Transport* HMSO 1956/57–1964/65. A fascinating and detailed annual Command Paper with lots of illustrations. It was preceded by Ministry of Transport and Civil Aviation *Road Fund: Report on the Administration of the Road Fund* HMSO 1920/21–1955/56. Since the creation of the Welsh Office separate reports have been issued for England and Wales.

**4279** *Basic Road Statistics* British Road Federation 1938–. An annual statistical guide.

**4280** Road Research Laboratory *Road Abstracts* HMSO 1934–. A monthly collection of some 150 abstracts.

**4281** J Dunnett 'The Relationship Between Central and Local Government in Planning and Execution of Road Schemes' *Public Administration* 40 1962 pp 253–65.

**4282** W Rees Jeffreys *The Kings Highway: An Historical and Autobiographical Record of the Developments of the Past Sixty Years* Batchworth Press 1949. A survey from the 1890s which ends with an account of the creation of the British Transport Commission.

**4283** David Starkie *The Motorway Age: Road Traffic Policies in Post-War Britain* Pergamon 1982. The first motorway was built at the end of the 1950s. This study examines the increasing importance of motorways and roads in post-war transport policy. A major influence on roads policy is studied in William Plowden *The Motor Car and Politics 1896–1970* The Bodley Head 1971. This is a good study of the impact of the motor car on road planning and the role of motorists' pressure groups in road policy making. The history of the largest of these is examined in Hugh Barty-King *The AA: A History of the First 75 Years of the Automobile Association 1905–1980* Automobile Association 1980. The social, environmental and economic impact of the car, and especially its impact on towns and town traffic, is well assessed by one of the most important urban planners of the post-war years in Colin Buchanan *Mixed Blessing: The Motor in Britain* Leonard Hill 1958.

**4284** J G Taylor 'Post-War Trends in Road-Planning and Construction' *Journal of the Institute of Transport* 25 1954 pp 400–5.

**4285** *Traffic in Towns: A Study of the Long Term Problems of Traffic in Urban Areas: Report of the Working Group* HMSO 1963. An influential report by a committee chaired by Colin Buchanan. Its major contributions were in broadening the concept of urban traffic problems to include environmental effects and in drawing attention to the limited capacity to absorb traffic. It involved a number of case studies. Buchanan, in his reassessment, '"Traffic in Towns": An Assessment After Twenty Years' *Built Environment* 9 1983 pp 93–8 concludes that they basically got it right. Mayer Hillman 'The Wrong Turning: Twenty Years on from Buchanan'

*Built Environment* 9 1983 pp 104–12 is a much more critical assessment. See also Colin Buchanan *Traffic in Towns* Penguin 1964.

**4286** R J Nicholson and N Topham 'Urban Road Provision in England and Wales 1962–8' *Policy and Politics* 4 1975 pp 3–30.

**4287** Stephen Plowden *Towns Against Traffic* Deutsch 1972. A study of public resistance to urban road schemes in the 1960s, with particular reference to developments in Oxford and London.

**4288** George Charlesworth *A History of British Motorways* Telford 1984. A useful history. *20 Years of British Motorways: Proceedings of the Conference held in London 27–28 February 1980* Institute of Civil Engineers 1980 is a symposium on the role of motorways in roads policy, standards and design, construction and maintenance, usage and operation and their social and economic effects.

**4289** John Tyme *Motorways Versus Democracy* Macmillan 1978. This is largely a chronicle of the motorway construction inquiries in which this inveterate opponent of motorways has participated. He sees them as a device of technocrats acting under pressure from the powerful road lobby and in the process obliterating communities. This covers inquiries on a whole range of motorways and major roads. Public opposition and pressure group activity in various motorway schemes is analysed in Ian D Twinn *Public Involvement or Public Protest: A Case Study of the M3 at Winchester 1971–1974* Department of Town Planning, Polytechnic of the South Bank 1978, Roy Gregory 'The Minister's Line: Or the M4 comes to Berkshire' *Public Administration* 45 1967 pp 113–20, 269–86 and C J Ham 'Protest Group Politics: The Case of the A2 Group' Kent MPhil Thesis 1977.

**4290** Colin Buchanan *London Road Plans 1900–1970* Research Report 11, GLC Research and Intelligence Unit 1970. A study of road planning in the capital up to the proposal for a motorway box around London, put forward in *Greater London Development Plan* GLC 1969. The history and politics of plans for urban motorways in London, culminating in this proposal, is critically reviewed in Simon Jenkins 'The Politics of London Motorways' *Political Quarterly* 44 1973 pp 257–70. See also Peter Hall 'London's Motorways' in his *Great Planning Disasters* Weidenfeld and Nicolson 1980 pp 56–86. The history of the rise and fall of the 1969 motorway plan is traced in Douglas A Hart *Strategic Planning in London: The Rise and Fall of the Primary Road Network* Pergamon 1976.

**4291** W B Bell *M63: Motorway Through a Town* Old Vicarage Publications 1983. An illustrated account of the construction of the M63 urban motorway.

**4292**  R Baker and C Fraser (eds) *The M25 – Planning and Development Implications: A Bibliography* Faculty of the Built Environment, Polytechnic of the South Bank 1984. A short bibliography of reports, newspaper and periodical articles published between 1978 and 1984. The planning and design of the M25 are discussed in D I Evans *et al* 'M25 London Orbital Motorway' *Highway Transportation* 33 1986 pp 6–27.

**4293**  E J Cleary and R E Thomas *The Economic Consequences of the Severn Bridge and Associated Motorways* Bath University Press 1973. A study of the impact of this direct link between South Wales and the West Country. On the construction of the Humber bridge, the longest suspension bridge in the world, see K Brown 'The Humber Story' *Construction News Magazine* 1981 pp 18–24.

**4294**  M Hawkins *Devon Roads* Devon Books 1989. A history of roads in the county since Roman times.

**4295**  H McLintock 'Planning for the Cycling Revival' *Town Planning Review* 53 1982 pp 383–402. A study of the growing trend towards cycle tracks and the use of cycle lanes in road planning.

### (3) Road Transport

#### (a) General

**4296**  A Lane *Austerity Motoring 1939–1950* Shire Publications 1987. A short well illustrated account of motoring during the years of petrol rationing.

**4297**  P P Scott and P A Willis *Road Casualties in Great Britain During the First Year with Seat-Belt Legislation* Research Report 9, Transport and Road Research Laboratory 1985. This finds a clear reduction in casualty figures since the introduction of compulsory wearing of seat-belts in front seats in January 1983.

#### (b) Buses and Coaches

**4298**  John Hibbs 'A History of the Motor Bus Industry: A Bibliographical Survey' *Journal of Transport History* 2nd series 2 1973–4 pp 41–55.

**4299**  *National Bus Company Annual Report and Accounts* HMSO 1969–1971/72. In these years the annual report of this state-owned bus and coach company was published as a House of Commons Paper. Since then it has been published by the company itself. For earlier reports see those of the Transport Holding Company (which also included road haulage) 1963–69, and before that those of the British Transport Commission 1948–62 [4260].

**4300**  John Hibbs *The Bus and Coach Industry: Its Economics and Organisation* Dent 1975. The best general survey of the industry. Stephen Glaister and Corinne Mulley *Public Control of the British Bus Industry* Gower 1983 is a study of the licensing and regulation of the industry from before the 1930 Road Traffic Act to the 1980 Transport Act. It includes case studies on licensing and legal oversight. London, which has a different licensing system, is however excluded from the study. Regulation from 1930 to the deregulation of 1985 is examined in K J Button 'Developments in the Regulation of the United Kingdom Bus Industry' *Transport Journal* 25 1986 pp 43–59.

**4301**  Neil J Douglas *A Welfare Assessment of Transport Deregulation: The Case of the Express Coach Market Since 1980* Gower 1987. The 1980 Transport Act deregulated coach services, ended institutionalized monopolies and ushered in unfettered competition for long-haul passengers between coaches and rail. Douglas argues that this has led to significant reductions in fares and improvements in service quality, a view with which R P Kilvington and A K Cross *Deregulation of Express Coach Services in Britain* Gower 1986, largely concur. See also E H Davies 'Express Coaching Since 1980: Liberalisation In Practice' *Fiscal Studies* 5 1984 pp 76–86.

**4302**  Ian Savage *The Deregulation of Bus Services* Gower 1985. An examination of the deregulation of 1984.

**4303**  Ken Fuller *Radical Aristocrats: London Busworkers from the 1880s to the 1980s* Lawrence and Wishart 1985. A good history from a committed Left-Wing perspective.

**4304**  David Kaye *Buses and Trolleybuses Since 1945* Blandford Press 1968. A comprehensive enthusiast's guide to the vehicles. A similar, if smaller and less comprehensive guide is B H Vanderveen *Buses and Coaches from 1940* Warne 1974. See also Gavin Booth *The British Motor Bus: An Illustrated History* Ian Allan 1977, Doug Jack *The Leyland Bus* Transport Publishing 1977, S Morris 'The Ups and Downs of the British Double Decker' *Modern Transportation* 10 1980 pp 57–64 and E L Cornwell and John Parke *British Buses in the Forties* Ian Allan 1977. On the trolleybus, which gradually disappeared in this period, see Nicholas Owen *History of the British Trolleybus* David and Charles 1974.

**4305**  P Kelly *Liverpool's Buses* Transport Publishing 1986. This also discusses the long dominance of trams in Liverpool's public transport network. It was only in the post-war period that the decision to phase out trams was made. The last tram ran in 1957. This history then traces the city's bus services up until their merger into the Merseyside Passenger Transport Executive in 1969.

**4306** C R Warn 'The Development of Motor Bus Services in Northumberland 1904–1975' Newcastle MA Thesis 1977. The development of these services peaked in 1949–56. By 1968 public support was necessary to maintain the network.

**4307** Eric Watts *Fares Please: The History of Passenger Transport in Portsmouth* Milestone 1987. A history 1840–1986.

**4308** M E Beesley and J Politi 'A Study of the Profits of Bus Companies 1960–1966' *Economica* 36 1969 pp 151–71.

**4309** R J C Crawley, D R MacGregor and F D Simpson *The Years Between 1909 and 1969 Vol 2: The Eastern National Story from 1930* Oxford Publishing 1984. A well illustrated and very informative history of Eastern Counties bus services with substantial appendices. The jubilee of London's Green Line buses was marked by two histories: A W McCall *Green Line: The History of London's Country Bus Services* New Cavendish Books 1980 and K Warren *Fifty Years of the Green Line* Ian Allan 1980. Another company history is P Gray, M Keeley and J Scale *Midland Red: A History of the Company and its Vehicles from 1940 to 1970* Transport Publishing Company 1979. R C Anderson and I Frankis *History of Royal Blue Express Services* David and Charles 1970 is a good history of a large motor coach network. Other company histories are Nigel Watson *'United': A Short History of United Automobile Services Ltd 1912–87* privately printed 1987 and R M Warwick *An Illustrated History of United Counties Omnibus Limited* privately printed 1981.

(c) Trams

**4310** R J Buckley *History of Tramways* David and Charles 1975. A general history. In the post-war period trams have been phased out everywhere except Blackpool.

(d) Taxis

**4311** G N Georgano *A History of the London Taxicab* David and Charles 1972. A useful history of the design of the cabs and the regulation of the industry up to the time of the Maxwell Stamp Report, *London Taxicab Trade: Report of the Interdepartmental Committee* Cmnd 4483, *Parliamentary Papers* li 1970–71, chaired by A Maxwell Stamp.

(e) Road Haulage

**4312** Michael Seth-Smith *The Long Haul: A Social History of the British Commercial Vehicle Industry* Hutchinson 1975. A history of the road haulage industry.

**4313** M A Cundill and B A Shane *Trends in Road Goods Transport 1962–77* Research Report 72, Transport and Road Research Laboratory 1980. This discusses matters such as vehicle stock, registration, goods movement, the length of haul and the operating costs.

**4314** Sir Arthur Armitage *Report of the Inquiry into Lorries, People and the Environment, December 1980* HMSO 1980. This recommended certain environmental ameliorations but did not reject the introduction of higher weight limits on lorries. The policy of allowing heavier lorries on the roads up to the time of the Armitage Report is analysed in John Wardroper *Juggernaut* Temple Smith 1981. This also features a bibliography.

**4315** E Schenker 'Nationalisation and Denationalisation of Motor Carriers in Great Britain' *Local Economics* 1963 pp 219–30. Road haulage was nationalized as part of the Transport Commission in 1947. It was denationalized in 1953. On the 1953 deregulation see J J Richardson 'The Administration of Denationalisation: The Case of Road Haulage' *Public Administration* 49 1971 pp 385–402.

**4316** B T Bayliss *The Road Haulage Industry Since 1968* HMSO 1973. A study of the industry since the creation of the National Freight Corporation.

**4317** Peter G Hollowell *The Lorry Driver* Routledge and Kegan Paul 1968. A sociological study.

**4318** *National Freight Corporation Annual Report and Accounts* HMSO 1969–71. In these years the report was published as a House of Commons Paper. Thereafter it has been published by the company. For previous reports see those of the Transport Holding Company 1963–9, and before that, the British Transport Commission 1948–62 [4260]. On the selling off of the National Freight Corporation to its managers and employees in 1981 see Sandy McLachlan *The National Freight Buy-Out* Macmillan 1983.

**4319** T C Barker *The Transport Contractors of Rye: John Jempson and Son: A Chapter in the History of Road Haulage* Athlone Press 1982. A short business history. Another business history is William Joseph Reader *Hard Roads and Highways: SPD Limited 1918–1968: A Study* *in Distribution* Batsford 1969. Gerald L Turnbull *Traffic and Transport: An Economic History of Pickfords* Allen and Unwin 1979 is a history of the removal firm.

## (4) Air Transport

**4320** *British Airways Annual Report and Accounts* British Airways 1972/73–. British Airways was created by the merger of the state-owned BOAC and BEA. For the reports of these companies see British European Airways Corporation *Annual Report and Accounts* HMSO 1946/47–1971/72 and British Overseas Airways Corporation *Annual Report and Accounts* HMSO 1946/47–1971/72. See also British South American Airways Corporation *Annual Report and Statement of Accounts* HMSO 1946/47–1948/49. This corporation, nationalized, as was BEA, under the 1946 Civil Aviation Act, was merged with BOAC in 1949.

**4321** *British Airports Authority Annual Report and Accounts* HMSO 1965/67–1971/72. This was published as a House of Commons Paper in these years. Since 1971/72 it has been published by the Authority itself.

**4322** *Civil Aviation Authority Annual Report and Accounts* Civil Aviation Authority 1972–. The Civil Aviation Authority also annually publishes *UK Airlines and UK Airports*.

**4323** John Stroud *Annals of British and Commonwealth Air Transport 1919–1960* Putnam 1962.

**4324** Kenneth Munson *Pictorial History of BOAC and Imperial Airways* Ian Allan 1970. See also the short history *Highways of the Air: The Development of British Civil Aviation Through Imperial Airways and BOAC* BOAC 1964. Imperial Airways was the inter-war precursor of BOAC, which was formed, under state ownership, in 1940. For the development of BEA see Gary May *The Challenge of BEA: The Story of a Great Airline's First 25 Years* Wolfe 1971. On the nationalizations of 1940 and 1946 see J W S Brancker 'The Effect of Nationalisation on Air Transport' *Journal of the Institute of Transport* 23 1949 pp 108–12.

**4325** Günter Endres *British Airways* Ian Allan 1988. A short enthusiast's history. The preparation for privatization over the period 1979–86 is analysed in Duncan Campbell-Smith *The British Airways Story: Struggles for Take-Off* Coronet 1986. The successful reorganization and return to profitability in these years is studied in Alison Corke *British Airways: The Path to Profitability* Pinter 1986.

**4326** Sir Basil Smallpeice *Of Comets and Queens* Airlife 1981. An autobiography which usefully reflects on his work at BOAC and the Cunard shipping line in the 1950s and 1960s.

**4327** R H McIntosh with Jeffery Spry-Leverton *All-Weather Mac* Macdonald 1963. This autobiography includes a little information on his post-war career with British United Airways.

**4327A** R E G Davies *Rebels and Reformers of the Airways* Airlife 1987 pp 205–80. This section of this most useful book features studies of British entrepreneurs who set up independent airlines, including Edmund Fresson and Eric L Gandar Dower, who developed air transport in the Highlands and Islands, Sir Freddie Laker and Sir Adam Thomson of British Caledonian.

**4328** A C Morton Jones *British Independent Airlines Since 1945* 4v, LAAS International 1976. A general guide to a large range of companies. See also B K Humphreys 'The Economics and Development of the British Independent Airlines Since 1945' Leeds PhD Thesis 1973–4. Humphreys has also published two articles on this subject; on 'Nationalisation and the Independent Airlines in the United Kingdom 1945–1951' *Journal of Transport History* n.s. 3 1975–76 pp 265–81 and 'Trooping and the Development of the British Independent Airlines' *Journal of Transport History* n.s. 5 1978 pp 46–59. This latter reflects on the great part work for the military played in the development of the independents 1950–70, until chartered holiday flights began to be important in the 1960s. The history of a major charter airline for holidaymakers is told in Geoffrey Cuthbert *Flying to the Sun: Quarter Century of Britannia Airways, Europe's Leading Leisure Airline* Hodder and Stoughton 1987.

**4328A** B G Cramp *British Midland Airways* Airline Publications 1979. A history.

**4329** Christopher Monckton and Ivan Fallon *The Laker Story* Christiansen 1982. A short account of the failed airline run by Sir Freddie Laker and the events that led to its demise. See also Howard Banks *The Rise and Fall of Freddie Laker* Faber 1982 and Barry Ritchie *Fly Me, I'm Freddie* Weidenfeld and Nicolson 1980.

**4330** Christopher Brewin 'British Plans for International Operating Agencies for Civil Aviation 1941–45' *International History Review* 4 1982 pp 91–110. Despite these plans the regulatory framework which was eventually adopted was that which the Americans favoured. On the British regulatory body, the Civil Aviation Authority, see G R Baldwin 'A British Independent Regulatory Agency: The Civil Aviation Authority, its Evolution and Operation' Edinburgh PhD Thesis 1977.

**4331** R B Connolly 'A Study of the Development of Airports in the UK in Relation to Their Social, Political and Economic Environment' Bath MSc Thesis 1971–2. Ron Blake 'The Siting of British Airfields Since 1909' London PhD Thesis 1989 examines in great detail locational policy behind the siting of civil and military airfields since the beginnings of organized aviation in Britain.

**4332** P M Butler *An Illustrated History of Liverpool Airport* Merseyside Aviation Society 1983. The history of the most important English airport outside London is examined in R A Scholefield and M D McDonald *First and Foremost: 50 Years of Manchester's Civic Airports* Manchester International Airport Authority 1978 and K P Brookes 'Development of Manchester Airport 1919–64' Manchester MA (Econ) Thesis 1964–5.

**4333** J E Kitchen 'The Expansion of Luton Airport: The Involvement of Organisations in a Public Policy-Making Process, with Special Reference to the Role of Regional Planning Agencies' Glasgow PhD Thesis 1972–3.

**4334** Peter W Brooks 'A Short History of London's Airports' *Journal of Transport History* 3 1957–58 pp 23–30. This includes brief details on each site used.

**4335** *Commission on the Third London Airport: Report* HMSO 1971. The extensive deliberations of this Commission, chaired by Mr Justice Roskill, ended with the recommendation that a third airport should be constructed at Cublington in Berkshire. The *Papers and Proceedings* of this Commission were published by HMSO 1969–71, the final volume of which is a guide to the documentation. Airport planning policy in London since 1920, with particular reference to the debate over a third airport, is examined in David McKie *A Sadly Mismanaged Affair: A Political History of the Third London Airport* Croom Helm 1973. This debate is also critically assessed in Peter Hall 'London's Third Airport' in his *Great Planning Disasters* Weidenfeld and Nicolson 1980 pp 15–55. The resistance to the Cublington site suggested by the Roskill Commission is examined in David Perman *Cublington: A Blueprint for Resistance* The Bodley Head 1973. The policy making behind the alternative of Maplin Sands is critically assessed Peter Bromhead *The Great White Elephant of Maplin Sands: The Neglect of Comprehensive Transport Planning in Government Decision Making* Elek 1973. Neither the Cublington nor the Maplin options have been pursued. There has however been some development of facilities at Stansted. Of some use is the 200 item unannotated *Stansted and Maplin Airports – Bibliography* Department of the Environment/Department of Transport Library 1981.

## (5) Railways

**4336** George Ottley *Railway History: A Guide to Sixty-One Collections in Libraries and Archives in Great Britain* Library Association 1973. An annotated and informative guide.

**4337** Michael Freeman and Derek H Aldcroft *The Atlas of British Railway History* Croom Helm 1985. A very useful popular history. Well illustrated sections describe the nationalization of British Railways, the Beeching cuts, the competition from road and air transport and the growth of railway preservation societies among other aspects of post-war railway history.

**4338** Clifford J Wignall *Complete British Railways Map and Gazetteer from 1830–1981* Oxford Publishing 1983. This maps extant and closed lines. The use of red and green in these maps is rather unfortunate and makes this book virtually useless as far as colour blind people are concerned. A bibliography of the extensive literature on closed lines and stations (too long to list here) would also have been helpful. The nearest there is to this is C R Clinker *Register of Closed Passenger Stations and Goods Depots in England, Scotland and Wales 1830–1977* 3rd ed, Avon Anglia Publications 1979.

**4339** *British Railways Board Annual Report and Accounts* HMSO 1963–71. In these years the report appeared as a House of Commons Paper. It has since been published by the Board itself. Before 1963 British Rail was part of the Transport Commission (see [4260]).

**4340** George Ottley (comp) *A Bibliography of British Railway History* 2nd ed, HMSO 1983. A semi-annotated, classified, well-indexed and massive bibliography. E T Bryant *Railways: A Reader's Guide* Clive Bingley 1968 is an international bibliography with a bias towards British material. It covers publications 1945–67 with lively annotations. *Railways: A Basic List of Publications and Sources* Department of the Environment/British Railways Board Library 1972 is a short guide to bibliographies, abstracts and sources.

**4341** T R Gourvish *British Railways 1948–73: A Business History* Cambridge University Press 1986. A good and thorough official history. See also M R Bonavia 'The Organisation of British Railways 1948–1964' London PhD Thesis 1967–8. As a nationalized service it might have been expected that the management of British Rail would be torn by the tension between its social role and commercial goals. I Lapsley 'The Influence of Financial Measures in United Kingdom Railway Policy' *Journal of Public Policy* 3 1983 pp 285–300, in a study of the period 1948–83, however argues that financial considerations took precedence under both Conservative and Labour governments.

**4342** John Glover *BR Diary 1958–1967* Ian Allan 1987. See also his *BR Diary 1968–1985* Ian Allan 1985. Both are well illustrated enthusiast's histories stronger on technical details and the development of design than on the history of British Rail.

**4343** Derek H Aldcroft *British Railways in Transition: The Economic Problems of Britain's Railways Since 1914* Macmillan 1968. A good survey of the economic and financial problems of the industry. It has little on the staff or the industrial relations problems of the industry. Harold Pollins *Britain's Railways: An Industrial History* David and Charles 1971 does cover industrial relations reasonably well in this study of the industry from the early nineteenth century to 1970. It is not however good on the role and nature of government policy since 1919. See also Frank Fernyhough *History of Railways in Britain* Osprey 1975. Geoffrey Freeman Allen and Patrick Whitehouse (eds) *The Illustrated History of British Railways* Barker 1985 is a coffee table history.

**4344** *Bulletin of the Oxford University Institute of Statistics* 24 1962 pp 1–184. A whole issue devoted to railway economics, mainly in Britain.

**4345** C H Ellis *British Railway History: An Outline from the Accession of William IV to the Nationalisation of the Railways Vol 2: 1877 1947* Allen and Unwin 1959. A popular and well illustrated history.

**4346** J Williamson *Railways Today* 2nd ed, Oxford University Press 1951. On the situation in the 1950s see also J St John *Britain's Railways Today* Naldrett Press 1954 and A J Pearson 'Developments and Prospects in British Transport with Special Reference to Railways' *Journal of the Institute of Transport* 25 1953 pp 118–26.

**4347** N Lee 'Factors Responsible for the Financial Results of British Railways 1948–1958' London PhD Thesis 1962–3.

**4348** British Railways Board *The Reshaping of British Railways* HMSO 1963. The famous report by Sir John Beeching which led to considerable closures of lines and an attempt to concentrate activities on a profitable core. The closures that ensued are examined in R J Brent 'The Minister of Transport's Social Welfare Functions: A Study of the Closure Factors Behind Railway Closure Decisions 1963–1970' Manchester PhD Thesis 1975.

**4349** Richard Pryke and John Dodgson *The Rail Problem* Robertson 1975. A critique of policy since the 1968 Transport Act. Policy in this period is also analysed in John Harris and Glyn Williams *Corporate Management and Financial Planning: The British Rail Experience* Elek/Granada 1980.

**4350** Philip S Bagwell *End of the Line? The Fate of British Railways Under Thatcher* Verso 1985. A critique of the impact of the Thatcher government's transport policy on the railways. The broad outline of his indictment of Conservative hostility remains valid. The decision that the Channel Tunnel should provide a rail rather than a road link, against the Prime Minister's wishes, has however necessitated a more positive attitude in the last few years.

**4351** *Committee on the Review of Railway Finances Report* 2v, HMSO 1983. A rather negative view of the future of the railways, chaired by Sir David Serpell.

**4352** Kevin P Jones *Steam Locomotive Development: An Analytical Guide to the Literature on British Steam Locomotive Development 1923–1962* Library Association 1969. The phasing out of steam after the 1955 modernization plan is analysed in Oswald Stevens Nock *The Last Years of British Railways Steam: Reflections Ten Years After* David and Charles 1978. Steam was gradually replaced by diesel and the last regular steam service disappeared in 1968. Nock also reflects on the extent steam has continued to be used since then. See also Tom Heavyside *Steam Renaissance: The Rise and Decline of Steam Locomotives in Britain* David and Charles 1984. Oswald Stevens Nock *The British Steam Locomotive Vol 2: 1925–1965* Ian Allan 1966, F C Poultney *British Express Locomotive Development 1896–1948* Allen and Unwin 1952, P Ransome-Wallis *The Last Steam Locomotives of British Railways* Ian Allan 1974, Brian Reed *150 Years of British Steam Locomotives* David and Charles 1975 and E D Brutton *British Steam 1948–1955* Ian Allan 1977 deal more with the engines themselves.

**4353** J A B Hamilton *Trains to Nowhere: British Steam Train Accidents 1906–1960* Allen and Unwin 1981.

**4354** Roger Ford and Brian Perren *HSTs at Work* Ian Allan 1988. An enthusiast's account of the high speed train which has helped to improve long-distance travel in the 1970s and 1980s.

**4355** Edgar J Larkin and John G Larkin *The Railway Workshops of Britain 1823–1986* Macmillan 1988. A comprehensive and well illustrated history.

**4356** Oswald Stevens Nock *British Railway Signalling: A Survey of Fifty Years Progress* Allen and Unwin 1969.

**4357** R J Essery, D P Rowland and W D Steel *British Goods Wagons from 1887 to the Present Day* David and Charles 1970.

**4358** Michael Hervis, Roger Ford and Brian Perren *InterCity: 21 Years of Progress* Ian Allan 1987. The development of the InterCity network.

**4359** R S Joby *The Railwaymen* David and Charles 1984. A social history of the life and work of railwaymen over the past 150 years drawing on reminiscences and interviews. Another useful social history is Frank McKenna *The Railway Workers 1840–1970* Faber 1980. Richard Davey *My Life on the Footplate* Peco Publications 1974 is the autobiography of an engine driver. Other memoirs are Len Bedale *Station Master: My Lifetime's Railway Service in Yorkshire* Turntable Publications 1976 and *No Steam Without Fire: Memories of Life on the Footplate at Wolverhampton, Kidderminster and Newton Abbot* Uralia Press 1979.

**4360** Sir John Elliot *On and Off the Rails* Allen and Unwin 1982. An autobiography which covers his varied business career. It however concentrates on his period with British Rail, culminating with his time on the British rail executive up to 1953.

**4361** Gerald Fiennes *I Tried to Run a Railway* Ian Allan 1967. The autobiography of a British Rail manager.

**4362** For Sir Richard Marsh see [738].

**4363** Sir Peter Parker *For Starters: The Business of Life* Cape 1989. Parker was Chairman of British Rail 1976–83.

**4364** Adrian Vaughan *Signalman's Morning* Murray 1981. This is continued by *Signalman's Twilight* 1983 and *Signalman's Nightmare* 1987, the last volume of which carries these fascinating and detailed memoirs up to 1975.

**4365** David St John Thomas and Patrick Whitehouse *The Great Days of the Country Railway* David and Charles 1986. This does not contain much on the post-war period but what it does is informative. For instance, it shows the social and economic importance of many of the branch lines lopped off in the Beeching cuts.

**4366** David St John Thomas and C R Clinker (eds) *A Regional History of the Railways of Great Britain* David and Charles 1960–. Volumes published so far are David St John Thomas *The West Country* 6th ed, 1988, H P White *Southern England* 3rd ed, 1981, H P White *Greater London* 2nd ed, 1971, K Hoole *North-East England* 4th ed, 1973, D J Gordon *Eastern Counties* 1968, J Thomas *Scotland: The Lowland and the Borders* 1972, R Christiansen *The West Midlands* 1973, D A W Joy *South and West Yorkshire* 1975, R Leleux *The East Midlands* 1976, G O Holt *The North West* 1978, P E Baughan *North and Mid Wales* 1980, D S Barrie *South Wales* 1980 and R Christiansen *Thames and Severn* 1981.

**4367** Donald J Ross *New Street Remembered: The Story of Birmingham's New Street Railway Station 1854–1967* Barbryn 1984.

**4368** Patrick Whitehouse and David St John Thomas (eds) *The Great Western Railway: 150 Glorious Years* David and Charles 1984. See also Oswald Stevens Nock *The Great Western Railway in the 20th Century* Ian Allan 1964.

**4369** J R L Currie *The Northern Counties Railway Vol II: Heyday and Decline 1903–72* David and Charles 1974.

**4370** K Hoole 'Railway Electrification on Tyneside 1902–67' *Transport History* 2 1969 pp 258–83.

**4371** C R Clinker (comp) *London and North-Western Railway: A Chronology of Opening and Closing Dates of Lines and Stations Including Joint Worked and Associated Undertakings 1900–60* David and Charles 1961.

**4372** C F Klapper *London's Lost Railways* Routledge and Kegan Paul 1976. A study of the decline of the overland railway system in the twentieth century. On London's suburban trains see George Thomas Moody *Southern Electric: The History of the World's Largest Suburban Electrified System* 3rd ed, Ian Allan 1960.

**4373** Henry Frederick Howson *London's Underground* Ian Allan 1988. An enthusiast's account. See also A A Jackson and D F Croome *Rails Through the Clay: A History of London's Tube Railways* Allen and Unwin 1962, John Robert Day *The Story of London's Underground* London Transport 1974 and Hugh Douglas *The Underground Story* Hale 1963. For other relevant material see [4271].

## (6) Shipping

**4374** P Mathias and A W H Pearsall (eds) *Shipping: A Survey of Historical Records* David and Charles 1971. Brief histories and statements of the present activities of the shipping companies are followed by details of their records. The second half of the book is a guide to archives and record office material.

**4375** D S Buchanan *Merchant Shipping: A Guide to Government Publications* HMSO 1975. An unannotated list of Acts, statutory instruments, reports and Command Papers relating to shipping.

4376   J Calvert and J McConville *The Shipping Indus-try: Statistical Sources* Sir John Cass Faculty of Transport, City of London Polytechnic 1983. A classified guide to world statistical sources. The authors take a broad interpretation of their brief and provide useful annotations.

4377   *British Shipping Review* General Council of British Shipping 1978–. An annual statistical guide.

4378   George Blake *Lloyds' Register of Shipping 1760–1960* Lloyds 1960. This specialist publication is the primary source on shipping and shipping insurance.

4379   *Committee of Inquiry into Shipping: Report* Cmnd 4337, *Parliamentary Papers* xxvii 1969–70. A review of the shipping industry's history and contemporary situation chaired by Viscount Rochdale. A detailed analysis.

4380   *Decline in the UK Registered Merchant Fleet* HC Paper 94, *Parliamentary Papers* 1986–87. A useful study of this trend by a committee chaired by Gordon A T Bagier.

4381   L H Powell *The Shipping Federation: A History of the First 60 Years 1890–1950* Shipping Federation 1950.

4382   C R V Gibbs *British Passenger Liners of the Five Oceans. A Record of the British Passenger Lines and Their Liners from 1838 to the Present Day* Putnam 1963. The decline of the passenger liner with the growth of air is charted in William Henry Miller *British Ocean Liners: A Twilight Era 1960–85* Stephens 1985. See also his *Transatlantic Liners 1945–1980* David and Charles 1981 and his *Famous Ocean Liners: The Story of Passenger Shipping from the Turn of the Century to the Present Day* Stephens 1987.

4383   Tony Lane *Grey Dawn Breaking: British Merchant Seafarers in the Late Twentieth Century* Manchester University Press 1986. A good oral history of a disappearing industry. On merchant navy officers, of which he was one, see also his 'Neither Officers nor Gentlemen' *History Workshop* 19 1985 pp 128–43.

4384   William Webb *Coastguard! An Official History of HM Coastguard* HMSO 1976. This short account also describes the contemporary situation. The main responsibilities of the coastguards are search and rescue, prevention of pollution and meteorology. See also Bernard Scarlett *Shipminder: The Story of HM Coastguard* Pelham 1971 and Nancy Martin *Search and Rescue: The Story of the Coastguard Service* David and Charles 1974.

4385   Oliver Warner *The Life-Boat Service: A History of the Royal National Life-Boat Institution 1824–1974* Cassell 1974. Other histories are Cyril Jolly *SOS: The Story of the Life-Boat* Service 2nd ed, Cassell 1974 and A D Farr *Let Not the Deep: The Story of the Royal National Lifeboat Institution* Impulse Books 1973. Local histories include Robert Malster *Saved From The Sea: The Story of Life-Saving Services off the East Anglian Coast* Dalton 1974 and Grahame Farr *Wreck and Rescue on the Dorset Coast: The Story of the Dorset Lifeboats* Bradford Barton 1971. Henry Parry *Wreck and Rescue on the Coast of Wales* 2v, Bradford Barton 1969–73 is a station by station collection of histories.

4386   Tony Parker *Lighthouse* Hutchinson 1975. An anecdotal sociological study of the life of the lighthouse keeper.

4387   A H Booth *A Liverpool Merchant House: Being the History of Alfred Booth and Company 1863–1958* Allen and Unwin 1959.

4388   D E Keir *The Bowring Story* The Bodley Head 1962. A history of C T Bowring.

4389   F E Hyde *Cunard and the North Atlantic 1840–1973: A History of Shipping and Financial Management* Macmillan 1975. A general history of the passenger line which was taken over by Trafalgar House in 1971. On the post-war years see W H Mitchell *The Cunard Line: A Post-War History (1945–1974)* Marinart Ltd 1975. There are some reflections on Cunard in the post-war years in [4326].

4390   P N Davies *The Trade Makers: Elder Dempster in West Africa 1852–1972* Allen and Unwin 1973.

4391   S Sedgwick and R F Sprake *London and Overseas Freighters Limited 1949–1977: A Short History* World Ship Society 1977.

4392   R Finch *A Cross in the Topsail: An Account of the Shipping Interests of R&W Paul Ltd, Ispwich* Boydell Press 1979.

4393   David Howarth *The Story of P and O: The Peninsular and Orient Steamship Navigation Company* Weidenfeld and Nicolson 1986. A history celebrating 150 years of the company. See also *Neil McCart 20th Century Passenger Ships of the P and O* Stephens 1985.

4394   For Trafalgar House see [3533].

4395   A Long and R Long *A Shipping Venture: Turnbull Scott and Company 1872–1972* Allen and Unwin 1973.

**4396** P N Davies *Henry Tyrer: A Liverpool Shipping Agent and his Enterprise 1879–1979* Croom Helm 1979. A history of Henry Tyrer and Co Ltd.

## (7) Docks

**4397** *Statistical Abstract of the UK Ports Industry* British Ports Association 1982–. Published quarterly and annually.

**4398** *British Transport Docks Board Annual Report and Accounts* 1963–81. This was initially published as a House of Commons Paper and latterly by the Board itself. The Board was established as a result of the break-up of the Transport Commission under the 1962 Transport Act.

**4399** J Bird *The Major Seaports of the United Kingdom* Hutchinson 1963. An analysis by region of their physical setting, history, dock system, markets and industries.

**4400** R E Takel *Industrial Port Development: With Case Studies from South Wales and Elsewhere* Scientechnica 1974. This is a comparative account focusing on the revolution in port operations since the Second World War in Britain. It is also useful on the accompanying infrastructure.

**4401** *Committee of Inquiry into Certain Matters Concerning the Port Transport Industry: First Report* Cmnd 2523, *Parliamentary Papers* xxi 1964–65, *Final Report* Cmnd 2734, *Parliamentary Papers* xxi 1964–65. This report, by the committee chaired by Lord Devlin, led to the curtailment of the large numbers of firms competing for dockside labour, the end of restrictive practices and the simplification of the wages system. Its consequences are examined in Michael Mellish *The Docks After Devlin* Heinemann 1972 and B Nicholson 'The First Year of Devlin: A Review of the Docks' *Trade Union Register* 1969 pp 211–22.

**4402** G K Wilson 'Planning: Lessons from the Ports' *Public Administration* 61 1983 pp 266–81. This is mainly an analysis of the failure of the National Ports Council between its establishment in 1964 and its demise in 1982, to produce a national ports plan. It also reflects on technical and economic changes and the political pressures on the ports industry.

**4403** K Y Chu 'The Growth and Decline of Major British Seaports: An Analysis of Foreign Non-Fuel Cargo Traffic 1965–1974' London PhD Thesis 1978.

**4404** L S Greeves *London Docks 1800–1980: A Civil Engineering History* Telford 1980. This is useful on post-war reconstruction, the modernization of cargo handling, the development of Tilbury and the redevelopment of docklands in the 1970s. On the Port of London Authority see *Liquid History: To Commemorate Fifty Years of the Port of London Authority 1909–59* privately printed 1960. The social and geographical impact of changes in the docks are reviewed in D J Connolly 'Social Repercussions of New Cargo Handling Methods in the Port of London' *International Labour Review* 105 1972 pp 543–68.

**4405** D Hilling 'The Restructuring of the Severn Estuary Ports' in B S Hoyle and D Hilling (eds) *Seaport Systems and Spatial Change: Technology, Industry and Development Strategies* Wiley 1984 pp 257–76. The post-war decline of colonial and transatlantic trade hit these ports and they were on the wrong side of the country to be helped by the growth of trade with the continent. This is useful on the attempts to cope with these problems. One effort was the 1966 Portbury dock proposal. The decision by the Ministry of Transport to reject this is reviewed in M L Senior 'The British Ministry of Transport's Study of the Portbury Dock Proposal 1966: A Reappraisal of the Spatial Analysis' *Environment and Planning C: Government and Policy* 1 1985 pp 85–105.

**4406** Hugh Conway-Jones *Gloucester Docks: An Illustrated History* Alan Sutton/Gloucester County Library 1984.

**4407** S Mountfield *Western Gateway – A History of the Mersey Docks and Harbour Board* Liverpool University Press 1965.

**4408** R B Oram *The Dockers' Tragedy* Hutchinson 1970. A sympathetic portrayal of the London docker. This has a few references to mechanization and containerization after the Second World War. Stephen Hill *The Dockers: Class and Tradition in London* Heinemann 1976 is a sociological study of limited value. A useful autobiography is Joe Bloomberg *Looking Back: A Docker's Life* Stepney Books 1979.

**4409** *The Dock Worker* University of Liverpool Press 1955. A study of Manchester dockers since 1945.

## (8) Inland Waterways

**4410** L A Edwards (comp) *Inland Waterways of Great Britain and Ireland* Imray, Lawrie, Noria and Wilson 1972. This provides systematic imformation on some 180 canals and rivers.

**4411** H Salter (ed) *The Broads Book* Link House Publications 1973–. An annual publication, as is his *The*

*Canals Book* Link House Publications 1976–. Both of these are essentially guides for holidaymakers to these waterway systems.

**4412** *British Waterways Board Annual Report and Accounts* 1963–. This was published as a House of Commons Paper in these years. It has since been published by the Board itself. The Board was created by the break-up of the Transport Commission under the 1962 Transport Act.

**4413** Charles Hadfield *British Canals: An Illustrated History* 7th ed, David and Charles 1984. The last chapter of this general history covers the post-war period, ending with the current revival of traffic on the waterways. Hadfield also wrote a survey of the contemporary situation of the waterways in the 1950s, *Introducing Canals: A Guide to British Waterways Today* Benn 1955, which remains of some value. The post-war history of the canals is examined in M W Baldwin 'The Post-1948 Development of and Prospects for, Inland Waterway Transport in Britain' London PhD Thesis 1978.

**4414** J J Richardson and Richard Kimber 'The British Waterways Board: A Neglected Asset' *Public Administration* 52 1974 pp 303–18.

**4415** Roger W Squires *Canals Revisited: The Story of the Waterways Restoration Movement* Moonraker Press 1979. A history of the Inland Waterways Association and the canal restoration movement of the post-war period with a good bibliography. This effort by small groups of enthusiasts and the development of cruise hire on the canals since the 1950s are two of the most important developments in the post-war history of the inland waterways. Squires has also written the complementary *The New Navvies: A History of the Modern Waterways Restoration Movement* Phillimore 1973. This looks at the restoration programme region by region. It also has a section on the related boat hire industry. There is a chronology and list of canal societies in this well illustrated history. It is updated in his 'Waterway Restoration: Public Money, Private Muscle' in Mark Baldwin and Anthony Burton (eds) *Canals: A New Look: Studies in Honour of Charles Hadfield* Phillimore 1984 pp 110–29. Robert Aickman *The River Runs Uphill: A Story of Success and Failure* J M Pearson 1986 is an account of the establishment of the Inland Waterways Association, in which he was closely involved, up to the Market Harborough festival of 1950. On canal conservation see Peter White 'What is Conservation?' in the same volume pp 93–109. See also P J G Ransom *Waterways Restored* Faber 1974.

**4416** Kenneth R Clew *The Exeter Canal* Phillimore 1984. A history up to the present day. See also his *The Kennet and Avon Canal* 2nd ed, David and Charles 1973.

**4417** D A Fernie *The Manchester Ship Canal and the Rise of the Port of Manchester 1894–1975* Manchester University Press 1980. In 1947–8 Manchester was the third port in the realm. The shift in economic power to the South East, enhanced by entry into Europe, led to the decline of the port. Adapting to the rise of road transport the company that administers the canal went into road haulage in the 1970s. On the canal see also David Owen *The Manchester Ship Canal* Manchester University Press 1983.

### (9) Channel Tunnel

**4418** G A Davies *The Channel Tunnel* Cardig Liason Centre, Coventry 1973. A short classified bibliography which covers newspaper articles as well as more usual material. Another bibliography is Anthony G Brown *Channel Tunnel Bibliography* Channel Tunnel Association 1969.

**4419** Michael Robert Bonavia *The Channel Tunnel Story* David and Charles 1987. A good general history up to the current attempt to create a tunnel linking Britain to France. There are eight essays appraising the history of the various schemes that have been attempted in B Jones (ed) *The Channel Tunnel and Beyond* Horwood 1987. Earlier histories of the various schemes are Peter Haining *Eurotunnel: An Illustrated History of the Channel Tunnel Scheme* New English Library 1972 and Deryck Abel *Channel Underground* Pall Mall Press 1961. On the current project see Nicholas Henderson *Channels and Tunnels: Reflections on Britain and Abroad* Weidenfeld and Nicolson 1987. This disparate collection of reflections includes a frank account of the 1984–5 background to the Anglo-French negotiations and of how his Channel Tunnel Group won the contract. He also shows how the scheme gained initial impetus from Mrs Thatcher's enthusiasm for a road tunnel, why the engineers rejected this in favour of a rail tunnel and why, for reasons of prestige, it was by then too late for Mrs Thatcher to back out.

### H. TOURISM AND THE LEISURE INDUSTRY

Leisure has more generally been dealt with by the social rather than the economic historian. Much material on trends in leisure and tourism therefore appears in the relevant part of the social history section, as well as below.

## (1) General

**4420** Countryside Recreation Research Advisory Group *Trends in Tourism and Recreation 1968–78* Countryside Commission 1980. A statistical survey.

**4421** K Bradbury *Leisure, Recreation and Tourism: Sources of Information* Aslib 1973.

**4422** J Christopher Holloway *The Business of Tourism* Macdonald and Evans 1983. A comprehensive textbook survey of the tourist industry, concentrating on the post-war period. A J Burkhart and S Medlik *Tourism: Past, Present and Future* 2nd ed, Heinemann 1981 is a very informative survey of the contemporary state of the industry with considerable detail on its historical background. It contains a number of useful statistical tables and appendices and a chronology. Earlier surveys are Economist Intelligence Unit *The British Travel Industry – A Survey* Association of British Travel Agents 1968 and L J Lickorish and A G Kershaw *The Travel Trade* Practical Press 1958.

**4423** Brian Asher *The Impact of Domestic Tourism* University of Wales Press 1973. A study of the local social and economic impact of the tourist industry.

**4424** C Cooper 'The Changing Administration of Tourism in Britain' *Area* 19 1987 pp 249–53. A study of changes in government policy and developments in the industry since 1979. Trends in employment in the industry in the 1980s are surveyed in D Parsons 'Tuning into Trends: Tourism and Related Leisure Jobs' *Employment Gazette* 95 1987 pp 337–45.

**4425** Derek Taylor and David Bush *The Golden Age of British Hotels* Northwood 1974. A history of the hotel business 1837–1974. Another general illustrated history is Derek Taylor *Fortune, Fame and Folly: British Hotels and Catering from 1878–1978* IPC Business Press 1977. In recent years business custom and conferences have become an increasingly important element in this business, as indicated in G D Credland 'Changes in the British Market for UK Hotel Accommodation 1960–1980' London MPhil Thesis 1981.

**4426** S F Witt 'The Demand for Foreign Holidays' Bradford PhD Thesis 1977.

**4427** Ronald Hamilton *Now I Remember: A Holiday History of Britain* 2nd ed, Chatto and Windus 1983. A social history.

**4428** James Walvin *Beside the Seaside: A Social History of the Popular Seaside Holiday* Allen Lane 1978. A useful study which goes up to the 1970s. M J Pickup 'Development of the English Seaside Resort' Edinburgh MPhil Thesis 1979 concentrates on the problems of post-war decline when faced with competition from package holidays to the continent. See also Felicity Stafford and Nigel Yates *The Later Kentish Seaside (1840–1974)* Sutton 1985, J A Barrett 'The Seaside Resort Towns of England and Wales' London PhD Thesis 1968 and B J H Brown 'Survey of the Development of Leisure Industries of the Bristol Region, with Special Reference to the History of Seaside Resorts' Bath PhD Thesis 1971–2.

**4429** S H Adamson *Seaside Piers* Batford 1977. An illustrated survey from the nineteenth century onwards which examines their impact on leisure and urban history.

**4430** Chloe Stallibrass 'Seaside Resorts and Holiday Accommodation Industry: A Case Study of Scarborough' *Progress in Planning* 13 1980 pp 103–74.

**4431** John K Walton *The Blackpool Landlady: A Social History* Manchester University Press 1978. A social study of tourism in England's most popular seaside resort up to the 1970s.

**4432** C Ward *Goodnight Campers! The History of the British Holiday Camp* Mansell 1986. A social history. See also Jill Drower *Good Clean Fun: The Story of Britain's First Holiday Camp* Arcadia Books 1983. On the most famous of holiday camp companies see Rex North *The Butlin Story* Jarrolds 1962. Sir William H E C Butlin and Peter Dacre *The Billy Butlin Story: 'A Showman to the End'* Robson 1982 is an autobiography of the company's founder.

**4433** Mike Stabler and Brian Goodall 'Timeshare: A New Dimension in Tourism' *Built Environment* 15 1989 pp 101–24. An account of the development of the timeshare market in the 1980s.

**4434** J R Lidster *Yorkshire Coast Lines: A Historical Record of Railway Tourism on the Yorkshire Coast* Hendon Publishing 1983. A short account of outings and railway tours to the Yorkshire coast from the county's industrial heartland from the 1840s to the 1960s.

**4435** Edmond Swinglehurst *Cook's Tours: The Story of Popular Travel* Blandford 1982. A history of the original tour operator.

**4436** Roy Gregory 'Court Line, Mr Benn and the Ombudsman' *Parliamentary Affairs* 30 1976–77 pp 269–92. An account of the government handling of the 1974 collapse of what was then Britain's largest tour operator, Court Line.

**4437** Hugh Montgomery-Massingberd and D Watkin *The London Ritz: A Social and Architectural History*

Aurum Press 1981. A history of the leading London hotel 1906–80. Another history of a great London hotel is Stanley Jackson *The Savoy: The Romance of a Great Hotel* Muller 1964.

**4438** Lord Forte *Forte: The Autobiography of Charles Forte* Sidgwick and Jackson 1986. The autobiography of the founder of the restaurant and hotel group Trust House Forte.

**4439** Egon Ronay *The Unforgettable Dishes of My Life* Gollancz 1989. A memoir of his life in the food industry by Ronay, who has been publishing restaurant and hotel guides since 1957.

**4440** C A Miller 'The Organisation and Development of Student Travel in the United Kingdom Since 1970' Strathclyde MSc Thesis 1979.

**4441** Edward Francis Williams *Journey into Adventure: The Story of the Worker's Travel Association* Odhams 1960. A history from its establishment in 1921.

**4442** Howard Bass *Glorious Wembley: The Official History of Britain's Foremost Entertainment Centre* Guiness Superlatives 1982.

## I. AGRICULTURE, FORESTRY AND FISHERIES

### (1) Agriculture

**4443** *Guide to the Institute of Agricultural History and Museum of English Rural Life* University of Reading 1982. An annotated guide to the museum, library and archives, oral history material and other resources which are held at this centre which specializes in rural life, agricultural bodies and agricultural trade unionism.

**4444** Central Statistical Office *Agricultural and Food Statistics: A Guide to Sources* HMSO 1974. A short guide.

**4445** *Agricultural Statistics, United Kingdom* HMSO 1867–. An annual statistical survey. *A Century of Agricultural Statistics: Great Britain 1866–1966* HMSO 1968 describes various statistical series. It also contains some maps. Alison Burrell, Berkeley Hill and John Medland *Statistical Handbook of UK Agriculture* Macmillan 1985 has statistical tables which run from c1960 (and in some cases 1950) to c1984. It provides plenty of supporting text and a good short bibliography.

**4446** J M Stratten and Jack Houghton Brown *Agricultural Records AD 220 to 1977* 2nd ed, John Baker 1978.

This attempts to relate the prevailing weather to the seasonal yield. They argue that the weather has made little difference to the yield since 1947. This survey is conducted year by year. The information on the weather and yield for the twentieth century is particularly detailed. There are appendices showing patterns of rainfall and prices.

**4447** *Agricultural Land Commission Report* HMSO 1948–63. This was established in 1947 under the 1947 Agriculture Act to manage and farm land vested with the Ministry of Agriculture. It was dissolved in 1963 and its powers passed to the Ministry of Agriculture, Fisheries and Food.

**4448** J T Coppock *An Agricultural Atlas of England and Wales* Faber 1976.

**4449** G P Lilley *Information Sources in Agriculture and Food Sciences* Butterworths 1981. An informative guide and bibliography.

**4450** *Agricultural History Review* 1953–. This has annual lists of books, articles and pamphlets on agricultural history.

**4451** B A Holderness *British Agriculture Since 1945* Manchester University Press 1984. A short but illuminating account with a good bibliography. Another good account of changes in agriculture since 1945 and their impact on the countryside is Quentin Seddon *The Quiet Revolution: Farming and the Countryside in the 21st Century* BBC 1989. David Grigg *English Agriculture: An Historical Perspective* Blackwell 1989 examines the origins, causes and consequences of the major revolution in agriculture since the 1930s and 1940s and puts this in the context of the history of agriculture over the past 300 years. V H Beynon *Agriculture and Economics* University of Exeter 1979 is a short paper on the period 1920–77.

**4452** Peter Self and Herbert J Storing *The State and the Farmer* Allen and Unwin 1962. An analysis of agricultural policies and politics 1945–61. This is particularly in the context of the state guidance of agriculture in this period and the response of the National Farmers' Union. Agriculture during this period is also examined in G Hallett 'Aspects of Post-War British Agricultural Policy' Wales PhD Thesis 1962–3 and F C H Pooley 'Some Economic Aspects of British Agriculture Since 1946' Exeter MA Thesis 1960–1.

**4453** J Ashton and S J Rogers (eds) *Economic Change and Agriculture* Oliver and Boyd 1967. A collection of essays on such subjects as the role of agriculture in the economy, agricultural productivity, consumption and marketing, the pressure on the land, forestry, research and education or the attitudes of the National Farmers'

Union. Subjects such as land, finance and farming technology are covered in Angela Edwards and Alan Rogers (eds) *Agricultural Resources: An Introduction to the Farming Industry of the United Kingdom* Faber 1974. Another useful introductory textbook is Frank H Garner *Modern British Farming Systems: An Introduction* Elek 1972.

**4454** Brian Davey, T E Josling and Alister McFarquhar (eds) *Agriculture and the State: British Policy in a World Context* Macmillan 1976. This examines British agriculture in the context of world trade and the impact upon it of the EC's Common Agricultural Policy.

**4455** Richard Body *Agriculture: The Triumph and the Shame* Temple Smith 1982. A critique of the economic and environmental effects of the subsidizing of British agriculture since 1945 by a farmer and Conservative MP. See also Richard W Howarth *Farming for Farmers? A Critique of Agricultural Support Policy* Institute of Economic Affairs 1985.

**4456** John Weller *Modern Agriculture and Rural Planning* Architectural Press 1968. A study of post-war agriculture from a novel perspective, that of the planner. About half the book is therefore about the growth of developmental pressures on the land and the problems of planning in rural areas. It also analyses in some detail changes in the nature and organization of farming. It is a useful history with informative appendices.

**4457** E F Nash *Agricultural Policy in Britain* University of Wales Press 1965. A selection of papers on the policy and the policy environment. See also R C Hine and A M Houston *Government and Structural Change in Agriculture* Department of Agriculture, University of Nottingham 1973. On the historical development of policy see J H Kirk *The Development of Agriculture in Germany and the UK Vol 2: UK Agricultural Policy 1870–1970* Centre for European Agricultural Studies, Wye College, University of London 1979 and A V Vickery 'An Historical Review of the Development of British Agricultural Policies and Programmes Since 1900' Oxford BLitt Thesis 1958–9. Another comparative study, which concentrates on developments in the USA, is Graham K Wilson *Special Interests and Policymaking: Agricultural Policies and Politics in Britain and the United States of America 1956–70* Wiley 1977. The pursuit of efficiency and the harm to the countryside that has tended to result since the 1947 Agriculture Act is examined in John K Bowers 'British Agricultural Policy Since the Second World War' *Agricultural History Review* 33 1985 pp 66–76. That the industry has also been considerably successful since the 1947 Act is remarked in Raymond J G Wells 'British Agriculture – A Rare Success Story' *Round Table* 289 1984 pp 86–92. See also M E Tracy 'Fifty Years of

Agricultural Policy' *Journal of Agricultural Economics* 27 1976 pp 331–49.

**4458** Edith H Whetham and C A Royce *A Record of Agricultural Policy 1947–1952* School of Agriculture, University of Cambridge 1952. This was followed by similar short studies of agricultural policy *1952–1954, 1954–1956, 1956–1958* and *1958–1960.*

**4459** G K Wilson 'The Politics of Subsidising Agriculture in Britain and the USA 1957–70' Oxford DPhil Thesis 1974–6.

**4460** Edith H Whatham *British Farming 1939–49* Nelson 1953. This was a period of considerable change in agriculture, not least because of wartime controls. There are a number of useful reflections on farming in this period by a former adviser to the Ministry of Agriculture in Anthony Hurd *A Farmer in Whitehall: Britain's Farming Revolution 1939–1950 and Future Prospects* Country Life 1951. The state of agriculture at the end of the war is examined in Viscount Astor and B Seebohm Rowntree *Mixed Farming and Muddled Thinking* Macdonald 1946. They comment, 'We are now at the beginning of a second agricultural revolution which is inaugurating a new farming system based upon the specialised and mechanised production of milk, eggs, vegetables and fruit.' Jonathan Brown *Agriculture in England 1870–1947* Manchester University Press 1987 examines agriculture up to the 1947 Agriculture Act. Finally, there are useful reflections on changes in agriculture up to the 1940s in James Keith *Fifty Years of Farming* Faber 1954. This is a semi-autobiographical account by a very successful farmer.

**4461** K E Hunt and K R Clarke *The State of British Agriculture* Agricultural and Economic Research Institute, University of Oxford 1966. The contemporary state of agriculture.

**4462** Ministry of Agriculture, Fisheries and Food *The Changing Structure of Agriculture 1968–1975* HMSO 1977.

**4463** A E Buckwell, D R Harvey, K J Thomson and K A Parton *The Costs of the Common Agricultural Policy* Croom Helm 1982. On another aspect of the impact of Britain's entry into the European Community on British agriculture see W Grant 'The Politics of the Green Pound 1974–1979' *Journal of Common Market Studies* 19 1981 pp 313–29.

**4464** Ian Niall *To Speed the Plough: Mechanisation comes to the Farm* Heinemann 1977. See also J Ashton and R F Lord (eds) *Research, Education and Extension in Agriculture* Oliver and Boyd 1969 and W Harwood Long 'The Development of Mechanisation in English Farming' *Agricultural History Review* 11 1963 pp 15–

26. The relationship between output prices and technological change is examined in D P Godden 'Technological Change and Demand for Output at the Farm Level in United Kingdom Agriculture 1950–80' London PhD Thesis 1986. This finds that technological change is positively influenced by output price.

4465   Malcolm Sargent *Agricultural Co-operation* Gower 1982. On one aspect of agricultural co-operation see G A Bridger 'The Development of the Joint Use of Farm Machinery Since 1939 with Special Reference to England and Wales' Manchester MA Thesis 1956–7.

4466   G Darley *The National Trust Book of the Farm* National Trust/Weidenfeld and Nicolson 1981. A study of the evolution of farm buildings in England and Wales from mediaeval times to the present day. This is largely conducted by a region to region study.

4467   L Easterbrook *et al* 'Fifty Fighting Years: History of the National Farmers' Union' *British Farmer* 10 1958 pp 6–18. See also George Allen 'The National Farmers' Union as a Pressure Group' *Contemporary Review* 195 1959 pp 257–68 and 321–34 and P L H Walters 'Farming Politics in Cheshire: A Study of the Cheshire County Branch of the National Farmers' Union' Manchester PhD Thesis 1969–70.

4468   M Hiles *The Young Farmers' Club Movement* National Federation of Young Farmers' Clubs 1956. A short history of this organization since its foundation in 1921. It is not so much of a pressure group as the National Farmers' Union and is more concerned with agricultural education and mutual support.

4469   M C Ryan 'A Pressure Group Prepares for Europe: The Country Landowners Association 1961/72' *Parliamentary Affairs* 26 1973 pp 307–17. A study of their responses to the prospects of entry to the EC and the impact of the Common Agricultural Policy.

4470   P J Giddings *Marketing Boards and Ministers; A Study of Agricultural Marketing Boards as Political and Administrative Instruments* Saxon House 1974. The only authoritative account. On the activities of the individual boards see below.

4471   Sir E J Russell *A History of Agricultural Science in Great Britain 1620–1954* Allen and Unwin 1966. A useful general survey. Russell was Director of Rothhamsted Experimental Station for more than thirty years. On the work of other agricultural research stations see Henry Cecil Pawson *Cockle Park Farm: An Account of the Work of the Cockle Park Experimental Station from 1896 to 1956* Oxford University Press 1960 and Sir J Hutchinson and A C Owers *Change and Innovation in Norfolk Farming: Seventy Years in Experiment and Advice at the Norfolk Agricultural Station, Michaelmas 1908 to Michaelmas 1978* Packard Publishing 1980.

4472   *The Changing Structure of the Agricultural Labour Force in England and Wales: An Analysis of Statistical Information for the Years 1945–1965* Ministry of Agriculture, Fisheries and Food 1967. The changing structure of the agricultural labour force is also examined in G J Tyler 'Factors Affecting the Size of the Labour Force and the Level of Earnings in UK Agriculture 1948–1965' *Oxford Agrarian Studies* 1 1972 pp 143–60 and J D Hughes 'A Note on the Decline in Numbers of Farmworkers in Great Britain' *Farm Economist* 8 1957 pp 34–9. On farmworkers themselves see A K Giles and W J G Cowie *The Farm Worker: His Training, Pay and Status* Bradley 1964. Howard Newby *The Deferential Worker: A Study of Farm Workers in East Anglia* Allen Lane 1977 is an influential sociological study of farm workers, their conditions, their trade unions and activities from 1850–1976.

4473   C J Lines 'The Development and Location of the Specialist Agricultural Engineering Industry, with Special Reference to East Anglia' London MSc (Econ) Thesis 1960–1. The illustrated history of a specialist agricultural engineering firm is well presented in Theo Sherwen *The Bomford Story: A Century of Service to Agriculture* Bomford and Evershed Ltd 1978.

4474   G E Jones 'Factors Affecting the Adoption of New Farm Practices, with Particular Reference to Central Wales and the East Midlands of England' Oxford BLitt Thesis 1960–1. Also on farming in the East Midlands see R Bennett Jones *The Pattern of Farming in the East Midlands* School of Agriculture, University of Nottingham 1954.

4475   Vance Hall *A History of the Yorkshire Agricultural Society 1837–1987* Batsford 1987. Also on farming in Yorkshire see G I Ramsdale 'Twenty-Five Years of Agricultural Change in the East Riding 1931–1956' Hull MA Thesis 1956–7.

4476   Henry Cecil Pawson *A Survey of the Agriculture of Northumberland* Royal Agricultural Society of England 1961. A survey of developments in the county in the twentieth century.

4477   J V Beckett *Laxton: England's Last Open Field System* Blackwell 1989. A study of the last unenclosed village in England (in Nottinghamshire) and how and why it has survived up to the present.

4478   A M Blair 'Spatial Effects of Urban Influences on Agriculture in Essex 1960–1977' London PhD Thesis 1978. A study of the pressure of urban spread on agricultural land to the North East of London.

4479   S Wilson 'Farms in the City' *Architects Journal* 12 1978 pp 63–5. A study of the development of urban farms in the 1970s.

4480   J J Richardson, A G Jordan and R H Kimber 'Lobbying, Administrative Reform and Policy Styles: The Case of Land Drainage' *Political Studies* 25 1978 pp 47–64.

4481   P Clarke 'The Land Settlement Association 1934–1948: The Evolution of a Social Experiment' London PhD Thesis 1985. The Land Settlement Association established full-time agricultural smallholdings and tried to create co-operative colonies of these smallholdings. On the development of smallholdings see also B A Wood 'The Development of the Nottinghamshire County Council Smallholdings Estate 1907–1980' *East Midland Geographer* 8 1982 pp 25–35.

4482   *Report of the Technical Committee to Enquire into the Welfare of Animals Kept Under Intensive Livestock Husbandry Systems* Cmnd 2836, *Parliamentary Papers* iv 1965–66. This committee was set up under F W R Brambell because of public indignation at intensive factory farming. It stressed the need for better education and training, a state veterinary scheme and a farm animal welfare standing advisory committee.

4483   R J Colley 'Inter-Relationships of Price and Production for Major Livestock Products of the United Kingdom 1955 to 1963 with Special Reference to State Policies' Aberdeen PhD Thesis 1965–6.

4484   Robert William Bell *The History of the Jersey Cattle Society of the United Kingdom 1878–1978* Jersey Cattle Society 1979.

4485   R L White and H D Watts 'The Spatial Evolution of an Industry: The Example of Broiler Production' *Transactions of the Institute of British Geographers* n.s. 2 1977 pp 175–91. A study of the production of broiler chickens in the East Midlands.

4486   Stanley Baker *Milk to Market: Forty Years of Milk Marketing* Heinemann 1973. A history of the Milk Marketing Board. On the economics of milk production see Phyllis Manning *A History of the National Investigation into the Economics of Milk Production 1934–51* Agricultural Economics Research Institute, University of Oxford 1960 and R C Simpkin 'A Study of the Effects of Statutory Regulations on Selling Prices and Distributive Margins for Milk in England and Wales 1933–1961' London PhD Thesis 1961–2. See also A S Foot 'Changes in Milk Production 1930–70' *Royal Agricultural Society Journal* 131 1970 pp 30–42. The influence of the National Farmers' Union on policy towards dairy produce during the first 75 years of their existence, 1908–83, is examined in S J Lawrence 'The Role of the National Farmers' Union of England and Wales vis-à-vis British Dairy Policy' Hull MPhil Thesis 1983.

4487   *Export of Animals for Slaughter: Report of the Committee* Cmnd 5566, *Parliamentary Papers* iii 1974. This committee, chaired by Lord O'Brien did not recommend the abolition of this trade but did suggest various improvements. Government policy on the British slaughter industry is examined in M Haines 'A Study of British Government Policy in the Livestock Slaughter Industry and its Impact on the Financial Viability of the Public Sector of the Industry Today' Wales PhD Thesis 1978. See also R H Tuckwell 'The United Kingdom Meat Market 1920–59' Cambridge MSc Thesis 1963–4.

4488   A M Walker 'The Marketing of British Wool' Leeds PhD Thesis 1984. British sheep are now largely reared for meat rather than wool. Walker sees this as being in part the result of the failure of the British Wool Marketing Board. This was established in 1950. It compares unfavourably with organizations in Australia and New Zealand and is here indicted for sticking to traditional methods of classing and marketing and for not developing schemes to improve textile standards and the value of the British clip.

4489   Gerald Egerer 'The Political Economy of British Wheat 1920–60' *Agricultural History* 40 1966 pp 295–310. See also his 'Protection and Imperial Preference in Britain: The Case of Wheat 1925–60' *Canadian Journal of Economic and Political Science* 31 1965 pp 382–9.

4490   J E Wrathall 'The Oilseed Rape Revolution in England and Wales' *Geography* 63 1978 pp 42–5. An account of the spreading cultivation of oilseed rape.

## (2) Horticulture

4491   Harold R Fletcher *The Story of the Royal Horticultural Society 1804–1968* Oxford University Press 1969. An authoritative, well illustrated study.

## (3) Forestry

4492   *Annual Report of the Forestry Commission* HMSO 1944/45–.

4493   N D G James *A History of English Forestry* Blackwell 1981. See also his *A Forestry Centenary: The History of the Royal Forestry Society of England, Wales and Northern Ireland* Blackwell 1982.

4494   George Ryle *Forest Service: The First Forty Five Years of the Forestry Commission of Great Britain* Augustus M Kelley, New York 1969. A good history of the Forestry Commission and its work which includes informative appendices.

**4495** C Watkins 'Woodlands in Nottinghamshire Since 1945: A Study of Changing Distribution, Type and Use' Nottingham PhD Thesis 1983.

**4496** B J Rendle *Fifty Years of Timber Research: A Short History of the Forest Products Research Laboratory, Princes Richborough* HMSO 1976.

### (4) Fisheries

**4497** *Sea Fisheries: Statistical Tables* HMSO 1948–. An annual statistical guide.

**4498** Godfrey Michael Graham *The Fish Gate* revised ed, Faber 1949. A study of the UK fishing industry. See also Godfrey Michael Graham (ed) *Sea Fisheries: Their Investigation in the United Kingdom* Arnold 1956.

**4499** T D Kennea 'Changes of the Sea Fishing Industry of Southern England Since the Second World War' London PhD Thesis 1968–9.

**4500** S Vickers 'The Transformation of British Fisheries Policy 1967–83' Warwick PhD Thesis 1986. A study of Britain's gradual shift from a support for freedom of shipping to the idea of 200 mile fishing limits. An important factor in this process was Britain's entry into the European Community. Another was the Cod War with Iceland. Iceland's extension of her territorial waters from three to, eventually, 200 miles from 1958 onwards was eventually recognized by Britain in 1976. On this dispute see H Jonsson *Friends in Conflict: The Anglo-Icelandic Cod War and the Law of the Sea* Christopher Hurst 1982 and Leslie S Green 'The Territorial Sea and the Anglo-Icelandic Dispute' *Journal of Public Law* 9 1960 pp 53–72.

**4501** Maritime Museum for East Anglia, Museum Parade, Great Yarmouth, Norfolk. This museum has an oral archive on the life and work of East Anglian fishermen. Oral history work has also produced P Frank 'Women's Work in the Yorkshire Inshore Fishing Industry' *Oral History* 4 1976 pp 57–72. Jeremy Tunstall *The Fishermen* MacGibbon and Kee 1962 is a sociological study of deep-sea fishermen.

**4502** R A Taylor *The Economics of White Fish Distribution in Great Britain* Duckworth 1960. A useful study.

## J. LABOUR

### (1) General

**4503** *Employment Gazette* HMSO 1971–. The principal source for labour statistics and trends. It was originally published as *Board of Trade Labour Gazette* 1893–1917, becoming *Labour Gazette* 1917–22, *Ministry of Labour Gazette* 1922–68 and *Employment and Productivity Gazette* 1968–70.

**4504** *British Labour Statistics – Historical Abstract 1886–1968* HMSO 1971. The statistical series contained in this volume were updated in *British Labour Year Book* HMSO 1969–76. This latter was discontinued with the 1976 edition (published in 1979).

**4505** Kenneth Walsh, Ann Izatt and Richard Pearson *The UK Labour Market: The IMS Guide to Information* Kogan Page 1980. A comprehensive guide to useful sources of information. It also features a directory of labour market organizations.

**4506** *British Journal of Industrial Relations*. In 1982–4 this carried a large and detailed annual bibliography.

**4507** R Wragg and J Robertson *Post-War Trends in Employment, Productivity, Output, Labour Costs and Prices by Industry in the United Kingdom* Department of Employment Research Paper 3, HMSO 1977.

**4508** Guy Routh *Occupation and Pay in Great Britain 1906–79* 2nd ed, Macmillan 1980. A study of changes in occupational structure and pay with useful statistical tables. See also Martyn Andrews and Stephen Nickell *Unions, Real Wages and Employment in Britain 1951–79* Centre for Labour Economics Discussion Paper 152, London School of Economics, University of London 1983.

**4509** A F Young *Social Services in British Industry* Routledge and Kegan Paul 1968. A useful study of the development and contemporary state of industrial training, the employment service, health and safety legislation, wages councils, employment protection and redundancy provisions and provision for the employment of the disabled.

**4510** Margaret Stewart *Britain and the ILO: The Story of Fifty Years* HMSO 1969. A history of relations between the British government and the International Labour Office which was set up after the First World War.

**4511** Keith Mason *Front Seat: A Summing Up of 22 Years Reporting on Industry* privately printed 1981. A memoir of his years as an industrial journalist 1955–77.

It includes good reflections on most of the major developments of this period.

**4512** Arthur Primrose Young *Across The Years: The Living Testament of an Engineer with a Mission* Knight 1971. Young was most important in the post-war period in the development of bodies such as the British Works Management Association and the Industrial Welfare Society and for his contribution to industrial relations.

## (2) Labour Law

**4513** R Blanpain *International Encyclopaedia for Labour Law and Industrial Relations* Kluwer 1986. A looseleaf encyclopaedia helpfully arranged by country. The section on the United Kingdom is quite substantial and informative and the entries invariably have a historical dimension. Another looseleaf encyclopaedia is B A Hepple and P O'Higgins *Encyclopaedia of Labour Relations Law* Sweet and Maxwell 1972–. This is now published in three volumes with six supplements per year. A similar and equally valuable reference work is *Harvey on Industrial Relations and Employment Law* Butterworths 1972–.

**4514** B A Hepple, J M Neeson and Paul O'Higgins *A Bibliography of British and Irish Labour Law* Mansell 1975. An extensive classified bibliography. The same authors (with Paula Stirling) produced the supplementary *Labour Law in Great Britain and Ireland to 1978* Sweet and Maxwell 1981.

**4515** *Industrial Law Journal* 1974–. This annually carries a bibliography of periodical literature on employment and labour law.

**4516** T Smith and Sir J C Wood *Industrial Law* 2nd ed, Butterworths 1983. An excellent textbook. See also Roger William Rideout *Rideout's Principles of Labour Law* 4th ed, 1983 and B A Hepple and S Fredman *Labour Law and Industrial Relations in Great Britain* Kluwer 1986. K W Wedderburn *The Worker and the Law* 2nd ed, Penguin 1971 has a useful bibliography.

**4517** Roy Lewis 'The Historical Development of Labour Law' *British Journal of Industrial Relations* 14 1976 pp 1–17.

**4518** Charles Drake *The Trade Union Acts* Sweet and Maxwell 1985. A textbook analysis which goes up to the 1984 legislation. See also Charles Drake and Brian Bercusson *The Employment Acts 1974–80* Sweet and Maxwell 1981. This provides the texts of these acts with a helpful commentary and cross-references to case law. The Conservative Employment Acts of 1980 and 1982

are analysed in David Newell *The New Employment Law Legislation* Kogan Page 1983.

**4519** R Kidner *Trade Union Law* 2nd ed, Stevens 1983. An excellent textbook. A good earlier textbook is C Grunfeld *Modern Trade Union Law* Sweet and Maxwell 1966.

## (3) Industrial Relations

### (a) General

**4520** Arthur Marsh *Concise Encyclopaedia of Industrial Relations* 2nd ed, Gower 1979. An informative reference work. The 3,000 entries in this encyclopaedia are mainly concerned with British and Irish industrial relations.

**4521** J T Ward and W Hamish Fraser (eds) *Workers and Employers: Documents on Trade Unions and Industrial Relations in Britain Since the Early Nineteenth Century* Macmillan 1980. A collection of primary sources on all aspects of trade unionism and industrial relations down to 1974.

**4522** *Industrial Relations Law Reports* Eclipse Productions 1972–. A monthly report of cases with indexes.

**4523** *British Journal of Industrial Relations* 1963–. Each quarterly issue features a chronicle of industrial relations in Britain, which is indexed annually.

**4524** William Pidduck (ed) *Conflict and Consensus in British Industrial Relations 1916–1948* Harvester 1985. A microfilm collection with a printed listing and guide.

**4525** George Sayers Bain and Gillian B Woolven *A Bibliography of British Industrial Relations* Cambridge University Press 1979. A very comprehensive, classified, though unannotated bibliography. It is updated by George Sayers Bain and J D Bennett *A Bibliography of British Industrial Relations 1971–1979* Cambridge University Press 1985, covering material published 1971–79. An earlier and shorter bibliography is A W Gottschalk and T G Whittingham *British Industrial Relations: An Annotated Bibliography* Department of Adult Education, University of Nottingham 1969. George Sayers Bain and Gillian B Woolven 'The Literature of Labour Economics and Industrial Relations: A Guide to its Sources' *Industrial Relations Journal* 1/1 1970 pp 30–42 is a guide to bibliographical material appearing in the various specialist journals.

**4526** Arthur Marsh *Employee Relations Bibliography and Abstracts* Oxford Employee Relations Bibliography and Abstracts 1985–. This supplies abstracts of excellent quality in two supplements per year. The material concentrates on the period since 1960.

**4527** Jack Jones and Max Morris *A–Z of Trade Unionism and Industrial Relations* Heinemann 1982.

**4528** Hugh Armstrong Clegg *The Changing System of Industrial Relations in Great Britain* 4th ed, Blackwell 1979. The standard work. Alan Fox *History and Heritage: The Social Origins of the British Industrial Relations System* Allen and Unwin 1985 is a good historical account of industrial relations in Britain since 1914. He also surveys management attitudes since 1945 in his 'British Management and Industrial Relations: The Social Origins of a System' in M J Earl (ed) *Perspectives on Management: A Mulitdisciplinary Analysis* Oxford University Press 1983 pp 6–39. The changing nature of industrial relations in the twentieth century is also examined in E H Phelps-Brown *The Growth of British Industrial Relations* Macmillan 1965. E G A Armstrong *Industrial Relations: An Introduction* Harrap 1969 is an introductory textbook.

**4529** Colin Crouch *The Politics of Industrial Relations* Manchester University Press 1979. A good study of developments since 1945. See also Kevin Hawkins *British Industrial Relations 1945–75* Barrie and Jenkins 1976.

**4530** David Coates *The Crisis of Labour: Industrial Relations and the State in Contemporary Britain* Philip Allan 1989. A survey of the interplay of industrial relations and politics since 1951. It also attempts to examine the difficulties encountered by the whole labour movement in this period.

**4531** Richard Clutterbuck *Industrial Conflict and Democracy: The Last Chance* Macmillan 1984. A rather doom-laden look at industrial relations and their impact on the economy in recent years. It consists mostly of brief chapters, many of which are case studies of industrial strife in particular industries or of the impact of Japanese management techniques on British industrial relations.

**4532** Kevin Hawkins 'The Decline of Voluntarism' *Industrial Relations Journal* 2 1971 pp 24–41. This argues that increased government intervention is more the symptom than the cause of the decline of voluntarism in industrial relations.

**4533** Gustav Schmidt (ed) *Industrial Relations and Industrial Democracy in Great Britain* Studienverlag Dr N Brockmeyer, Bochum 1984. This has some useful essays, notably on the lack of trade union interest in worker control on the nationalized industries and on industrial relations under the Attlee government.

**4534** N H Cuthbert and Kevin Hawkins *Company Industrial Relations Policies: The Management of Industrial Relations in the 1970s* Longman 1973. A rare look at industrial relations from the point of view of company strategy. There is quite a lot of useful historical detail in the various essays in this collection.

**4535** Eric Batstone *The Reform of Workplace Industrial Relations: Theory, Myth and Evidence* 2nd ed, Clarendon 1988. This charts changes in workplace industrial relations and attempts at reform from the 1960s onwards.

**4536** W W Daniel and Neil Millward *Workplace Industrial Relations in Britain* Heinemann Education 1983. The results of the first Workplace Industrial Relations Survey conducted 1975–80. One of its most interesting findings was the growth of joint consultation committees. The second survey was published as Neil Millward and Mark Stevens *British Workplace Industrial Relations 1980–1984* Gower 1986. This survey is commented on Neil Millward and Mark Stevens (eds) 'Symposium: British Workplace Industrial Relations 1980–1984' *British Journal of Industrial Relations* 25 1987 pp 275–94. The relationship between technical change and workplace industrial relations is analysed using data from the second British Workplace Industrial Relations Survey in W W Daniel *Workplace Industrial Relations and Technical Change* Pinter 1987. An earlier survey of workplace industrial relations is M G Wilder and S R Parker 'Changes in Workplace Industrial Relations 1966–72' *British Journal of Industrial Relations* 13 1975 pp 14–22. W E J McCarthy and S R Parker *Workplace Industrial Relations: A Social Survey* HMSO 1968 was a survey conducted for the Donovan Royal Commission [4553].

**4537** Edward Benson *The Law of Industrial Relations* Macmillan 1987. A good legal textbook. See also J G Riddal *The Law of Industrial Relations* Butterworths 1981.

**4538** Derek Sawbridge, David Bright and Robin Smith 'Industrial Relations in the North East England' *Employee Relations* 6/4 1984 pp 1–34.

**4539** H S Kirkcaldy 'Industrial Relations in Great Britain: A Survey of Post-War Developments' *International Labour Review* 68 1953 pp 468–92. See also Arnold A Rogow 'Labor Relations Under the British Labor Government' *American Journal of Economics and Sociology* 14 1955 pp 357–76.

**4540** A J Allen *Management and Men: A Study in Industrial Relations* Hallam Press 1967. An analysis of industrial relations in the 1960s largely based on interviews. It is written particularly from a personnel management perspective.

**4541** George Sayers Bain (ed) *Industrial Relations in Britain* Blackwell 1983. An authoritative collection of essays on developments in industrial relations in Britain between the Donovan Royal Commission of 1968 and 1980. See also E Owen Smith 'United Kingdom' in E Owen Smith (ed) *Trade Unions in the Developed Economies* Croom Helm 1981 pp 123–54.

**4542** Kevin Hawkins *Case Studies in Industrial Relations* Kogan Page 1982. Textbook analyses of developments in the 1970s. William A Brown (ed) *The Changing Contours of British Industrial Relations: A Survey of Manufacturing Industry* Blackwell 1981 mainly deals with developments of the late 1970s.

**4543** Gerald A Dorfman *British Trade Unionism Against the Trades Union Congress* Macmillan 1983. The Social Contract formula for incomes policy in the 1970s put the TUC at the centre of the pay bargaining process. The TUC however did not have the ability to hold its constituent unions in line, as the 'Winter of Discontent' was to show. Robert Taylor *et al* 'Symposium: The Winter of Discontent' *Contemporary Record* 1/3 1987 pp 34–43 is a witness seminar on the industrial unrest of 1978–79 which helped to undermine the Callaghan government. See also William Rodgers 'Government Under Stress: Britain's Winter of Discontent 1979' *Political Quarterly* 55 1984 pp 171–9.

**4544** Michael Fogarty and Douglas Brook *Trade Unions and British Industrial Development* 2nd ed, Policy Studies Institute 1989. A review of developments in British industrial relations since 1979. Richard Hyman *The Political Economy of Industrial Relations: Theory and Practice in a Cold Climate* Macmillan 1989 is a Marxist analysis concentrating on the problems for the trade unions in the 1980s. The changes in the law which have helped to create these problems for the unions are examined in P Fosh and C Littler *Industrial Relations and the Law in the 1980s* Gower 1985. The unions have also faced problems because of industrial decline. There are a number of case studies of the industrial politics of industrial decline in the Thatcher years in Hugh Levie, Denis Gregory and Nick Lorentzen *Fighting Closures: De-Industrialisation and the Trade Unions 1979–1983* Spokesman 1984. One of the consequences has been the introduction of no strike agreements in the 1980s. This trend is analysed in Philip Bassett *Strike Free: New Industrial Relations in Britain* Macmillan 1986. Tim Claydon 'Union Derecognition in Britain in the 1980s' *British Journal of Industrial Relations* 27 1989 pp 214–224 draws on case studies of withdrawal of recognition for trade unions in various firms in the 1980s.

**4545** Noel Hibbert 'Historical Changes in the Conservative Party's Industrial Relations Philosophy' *Employee Relations* 7/3 1985 pp 9–14.

**4546** Peter J Buckley and Peter Enderwick *The Industrial Relations of Foreign Owned Firms Based in Britain* Macmillan 1984. A short study. See also John Gennard and M D Steuer 'The Industrial Relations of Foreign Owned Subsidiaries in the United Kingdom' *British Journal of Industrial Relations* 9 1971 pp 143–59.

**4547** John Child 'Quaker Employers and Industrial Relations' *Sociological Review* n.s. 13 1964 pp 293–315. Quaker employers and the Society of Friends in general have made considerable efforts in the twentieth century to analyse and improve industrial relations and to establish good working conditions and some form of worker consultation.

(b) Government Policy

(i) General

**4548** Eric Wigham *Strikes and the Government 1893–1981* 2nd ed, Macmillan 1982. A good history which particularly considers the role of governments in mediating in industrial disputes since the establishment of the Labour Department of the Board of Trade in 1893.

**4549** Gerald A Dorfman *Wage Politics in Britain 1945–1967: Government Versus the TUC* Knight 1974. In the 1960s particularly governments began to grapple with the need to secure agreement with the trade unions on industrial relations, productivity and restraint of wage claims. Dorfman's analysis of how governments dealt with these problems is continued in his *Government Versus Trade Unions in British Politics Since 1968* Macmillan 1979. Government handling of industrial relations is also analysed in D F Macdonald *The State and Trade Unions* 2nd ed, Macmillan 1976 and V L Allen *Trade Unions and the Government* Longmans 1960.

**4550** Colin Crouch *Class Conflict and the Industrial Relations Crisis: Compromise and Corporatism in the Policies of the British State* Heinemann Educational 1977. This traces incomes policy and government attempts to reform industrial relations since the creation of the Council for Prices, Productivity and Incomes in 1957. It includes a good bibliography.

**4551** R V Sires 'The Repeal of the Trade Disputes and Trade Union Act of 1927' *Industrial and Labour Relations Review* 6 1953 pp 227–38. One of the first acts of the Attlee government was to repeal this piece of legislation, thus lifting its restrictions on the political levy and on the unions' right to picket or take sympathetic action.

**4552** Denis Barnes and Eileen Reid *Government and Trade Unions: The British Experience 1964–79* Heinemann 1980. An analysis of attempts to improve industrial relations and enforce wage restraint since the early 1960s. It concentrates on the period 1964–74. See also J F B Goodman 'Great Britain: Towards the Social Contract' in S Barkin (ed) *Worker Militancy and its Consequences 1965–75* Robertson/Praeger 1976 pp 39–81 and D Strinati 'The Political Organisation of Capital, the State and Industrial Relations Policy in Britain 1960–1975' London PhD Thesis 1982.

**4553** *Royal Commission on Trade Unions and Employers' Associations* Cmnd 3623, *Parliamentary Papers* xxxii 1967–68. A Royal Commission which generated a considerable amount of research and evidence. It was set up under Lord Donovan to make recommendations to improve industrial relations. Its deliberations are analysed in J D Derbyshire 'The Royal Commission on Trade Unions and Employers' Associations 1965–1968: An Analysis of a Royal Commission as an Instrument for Public Policy Making' London PhD Thesis 1976. George H Doughty 'The Donovan Report: A Sugar Coated Pill with a Bitter Centre' *Trade Union Register* 1969 pp 41–52 is a critique from the trade unions' point of view. For another commentary see R F Banks 'The Reform of British Industrial Relations: The Donovan Report and the Labour Government's Policy Proposals' *Relations Industrielle* 24 1969 pp 333–82. This also examines the subsequent White Paper.

**4554** Eric Batstone *Working Order* Blackwell 1984. An important study of attempts to reform British industrial relations since the Donovan Commission. It is weakest on management behaviour since 1980.

**4555** Barbara Castle *In Place of Strife: A Policy for Industrial Relations* Cmnd 3888, *Parliamentary Papers* liii 1968–69. The White Paper which followed the Donovan Report and which went beyond it in certain important respects, not least in suggesting penal sanctions against unofficial strikes. The struggle in the Wilson government over the Donovan Report and the White Paper and the reactions of the trade unions to this policy is analysed in Peter Jenkins *The Battle of Downing Street* Knight 1970. This detailed account remains highly regarded.

**4556** Michael Moran *The Politics of Industrial Relations: The Origins, Life and Death of the 1971 Industrial Relations Act* Macmillan 1977. After the failure of the Wilson government to deal with the damage being done to the economy by strikes the Heath government attempted to tackle the same problem with this piece of legislation which made collective bargaining enforceable at law and established a National Industrial Relations Court to enforce it. This is a good account of the origins of the Act, the opposition it generated from the trade unions, and its eventual repeal when Labour returned to power in 1974. The objectives and failings of the Act are also analysed in B Weekes, M Mellish, L Dickens and J Lloyd *Industrial Relations and the Limits of the Law: The Industrial Effects of the Industrial Relations Act 1971* Blackwell 1975. C G Heath *A Guide to the Industrial Relations Act* Sweet and Maxwell 1971 is a good contemporary commentary on the Act. Other useful contemporary commentaries are Alan Campbell *The Industrial Relations Act* Longman 1971 and Cyril Crabtree *The Industrial Relations Act* Knight 1971. A W J Thompson and Stephen R Engleman *The Industrial Relations Act: A Review and Analysis* Robertson 1975 is an attempt to assess the Act's impact in the light of its repeal. Other reflections on the Act are B James and R Clifton 'Labour Relations in the Firm: The Impact of the Industrial Relations Act' *Industrial Relations Journal* 5 1974 pp 11–25, Sir Otto Kahn-Freund 'The Industrial Relations Act 1971: Some Retrospective Reflections' *Industrial Law Journal* 3 1974 pp 186–200, A Campbell 'The Industrial Relations Act 1971: Reflections of a Practitioner' *Cambrian Law Review* 5 1974 pp 1–11 and J E King 'Penal Clauses in Labour Relations Legislation: The Case of the British Industrial Relations Act 1971–74' *Journal of Industrial Relations* 18 1976 pp 142–55. See also A R Benstead 'The Industrial Relations Act 1971, a Traditionalist Alternative to Donovan: An Analysis of the Acceptibility of the Major Provisions of the Industrial Relations Act to Trades Unionists and Management in the Engineering Industry of the West Midlands' Keele LLM Thesis 1978. J Lervez 'Syndicalisme et Politique: Les Syndicats Britanniques face au Gouvernment Conservateur 1970–1974' *Revue Française de Science Politique* 25 1975 pp 919–45 provides an overview of Heath's industrial relations policy and the confrontation between his government and the trade unions as does N A Smith 'Government Versus Trade Unions in Britain' *Political Quarterly* 46 1975 pp 293–303. The operation of the National Industrial Relations Court that the Act introduced is reviewed in D H Hills 'National Industrial Relations Court in 1972 – A Personal History' *British Journal of Industrial Relations* 11 1973 pp 259–85.

**4557** B Perrins *Labour Relations Law* Butterworths 1975. An analysis of the state of the law after the repeal of the 1971 Industrial Relations Act which includes text and commentary on the 1974 Trade Union and Labour Relations Act.

**4558** Peter Hain *Political Strikes: The State and Trade Unionism in Britain* Viking 1986. An analysis of conflicts between governments and trade unions in the 1970s and 1980s. A similarly critical analysis is Jim Arnison *The Shrewsbury Three* Lawrence and Wishart 1974. He alleges that the charges against these building workers, of conspiracy and affray on the picket lines, were politically motivated. For the conflict between government and trade unions during the 'Winter of Discontent' see [4543].

**4559** *Advisory, Conciliation and Arbitration Service Annual Report* ACAS 1975–. ACAS was established in 1974 to mediate in industrial disputes. Its record is examined in Ramsumair Singh 'Mediation and Industrial Disputes in Britain' *Industrial Relations Journal* 17 1986 pp 24–31. See also George Tyrell 'The Politics of a Hived-Off Board: The Advisory, Conciliation and Arbitration Service' *Public Administration* 58 1980 pp 225–34 and H Concannon 'The Growth of Arbitration Work on ACAS' *Industrial Relations Journal* 9 1978 pp 12–18.

**4560** John MacInnes *Thatcherism at Work: Industrial Relations and Economic Change* Open University Press 1987. A critical assessment of industrial relations policy and its impact under the Thatcher government. See also F I Magee *The Thatcher Government and the Unions 1979–83* Longman Resources Unit 1983 and S McBride 'Mrs Thatcher and the Post-War Consensus: The Case of Trade Union Policy' *Parliamentary Affairs* 39 1986 pp 330–40.

*(ii) Control of Industrial Disputes*

**4561** R Geary *Policing Industrial Disputes 1893 to 1985* Cambridge University Press 1985. A good analysis of the state's handling of industrial disputes up to and including the miner's strike of 1984–5. Geary has also commented on the increased violence in industrial confrontation in the 1980s, with police training now emphasizing riot control rather than public order training, in his 'The Return to Battle: Contemporary Industrial Confrontation' *Police Journal* 58 1985 pp 100–10. The contrast between declining violence in the policing of industrial disputes in the early part of the century with the resurgence of violent confrontations since 1970 is also examined in Robert Reiner 'Policing Strikes: An Historical U Turn' *Policing* 1 1985 pp 138–48. The government's handling of and contingency planning for and during industrial disputes is also well analysed in Keith Jeffery and Peter Hennessy *States of Emergency: British Governments and Strike-Breaking Since 1919* Routledge and Kegan Paul 1983. This contingency planning is also commented on in Peter Hennessy 'Whitehall Contingency Planning for Industrial Disputes' in Peter J Rowe and Christopher J Whelan (eds) *Military Intervention in Democratic Societies* Croom Helm 1985 pp 94–109. See also G S Morris 'A Study of the Protection of Public and Essential Services in Labour Disputes 1920–1976' Cambridge PhD Thesis 1978.

**4562** Geoff Ellen 'Labour and Strikebreaking 1945–51' *International Socialism* 24 1984 pp 45–73. A critical

analysis of the Attlee government's handling of the unofficial strikes of the time.

*(iii) Employment Protection and Redundancy Law*

**4563** S D Anderson *Law of Unfair Dismissal* 2nd ed, Butterworths 1985. A good legal textbook. The law of unfair dismissal is now a major part of labour law.

**4564** C Brown *Redundancy Law and Practice* Butterworths 1983. A good legal textbook which has useful coverage on cases of redundancy and business streamlining necessitated by the recession of the early 1980s.

**4565** Linda Dickens *et al Dismissal – A Study of Unfair Dismissal and the Industrial Tribunal System* Blackwell 1985. In 1971 statutory protection against unfair dismissal was introduced. This examines its origins, nature and effectiveness. Another study is Michael J Goodman *Industrial Tribunals Procedure* 2nd ed, Oyez 1979. K Williams 'Unfair Dismissal: Myths and Statistics' *Industrial Law Journal* 12 1983 pp 157–65 examines the record 1972–81.

(c) Personnel Management

**4566** M M Niven *Personnel Management 1913–63: The Growth of Personnel Management and the Development of the Institute* Institute of Personnel Management 1967. A history of the Institute of Personnel Management and of the growth of personnel management in industry. The Institute also periodically issues bibliographies on recent developments in personnel management.

**4567** Keith Sisson (ed) *Personnel Management in Britain* Blackwell 1989. A collection of essays on all major aspects of personnel management.

**4568** Peter Anthony and Anne Crichton *Industrial Relations and the Personnel Specialists* Batsford 1969. This has some useful reflections on the growth of personnel management and its role in British industrial relations.

**4569** T G P Rogers 'Recent Advances in Personnel Management' *Political Quarterly* 27 1956 pp 260–9. See also Anne Crichton 'The IPM in 1950 and 1960' *Personnel Management* 43 1961 pp 253–70.

**4570** Lesley Mackay and Derek Torrington *The Changing Nature of Personnel Management* Institute of Personnel Management 1986. An examination of personnel management in the 1970s and 1980s.

**4571** T M Higham 'Thirty Years of Psychology in an Industrial Firm' *Occupational Pyschology* 29 1955 pp 232–9. A study at Rowntrees.

**(d) Wages and Conditions Bargaining**

*(i) General*

**4572** E H Phelps-Brown 'New Wine in Old Bottles: Reflections on the Changed Working of Collective Bargaining in Great Britain' *British Journal of Industrial Relations* 11 1973 pp 329–37.

**4573** M Reiss 'Compulsory Arbitration as a Method of Settling Industrial Disputes, with Special Reference to British Experience Since 1940' Oxford BLitt Thesis 1963–4.

**4574** I Sharp *Industrial Conciliation and Arbitration in Great Britain* Allen and Unwin 1950.

**4575** B M Swift 'The Duration of Wage Negotiations 1950–1958' *Royal Statistical Society Journal* series A, 126 1963 pp 300–14.

**4576** B C Roberts and Sheila Rothwell 'Recent Trends in Collective Bargaining in the United Kingdom' *International Labour Review* 106 1972 pp 543–72. This assesses the trends towards plant and company bargaining, unofficial action and public sector militancy since 1945.

**4577** William Brown *The Structure and Processes of Pay Determination in the Private Sector 1979–86* Confederation of British Industry 1988.

*(ii) Productivity Bargaining*

**4578** L C Hunter 'Productivity Agreements' *Scottish Journal of Political Economy* 11 1964 pp 260–86. A review of the Fawley productivity agreements of the 1950s.

**4579** Ray Collins 'Trends in Productivity Bargaining' *Trade Union Register* 1970 pp 86–108.

**4580** David Metcalf 'Water Notes Dry Up: The Impact of the Donovan Reform Proposals and Thatcherism at Work on Labour Productivity in British Manufacturing Industry' *British Journal of Industrial Relations* 27 1989 pp 1–32. A comparison of two government efforts to improve productivity in British industry.

**4581** J Kelly 'Productivity Bargaining in the British Steel Industry 1964–74' Warwick PhD Thesis 1980.

**4582** A Ferner 'Political Constraints and Management Strategies: The Case of Working Practices in British Rail' *British Journal of Industrial Relations* 23 1985 pp 47–70. A detailed case study of the productivity initiatives introduced under political pressure by British Rail in 1979, and of their consequences.

**4583** P D Periton 'The Significance of Productivity Deals for Lower Paid Workers, with Special Reference to Local Authority Manual Workers 1966–71' Oxford BLitt Thesis 1973–4.

*(iii) Comparability Bargaining*

**4584** J F B Goodman and G M Thomson 'Cost of Living Indexation Agreements in Post-War British Collective Bargaining' *British Journal of Industrial Relations* 11 1973 pp 181–210. See also his 'Cost of Living Indexation Agreements in Wage Bargaining with Special Reference to Great Britain Since 1945' Manchester MA (Econ) Thesis 1972–3. Although comparability has been an important factor both in prices and incomes policy and in many important post-war disputes, and not least during the disputes of the early 1970s, there has been little research done in this field. Comparability in bargaining in British Rail in the 1960s has however been analysed in C D Jones 'The Uses of Coparability in Salary Bargaining: The Evidence from British Railways 1960–1968' *Bulletin of Economic Research* 24 1972 pp 98–110.

**(e) The Closed Shop**

**4585** W E J McCarthy *The Closed Shop in Britain* Blackwell 1964. Still the standard work on the subject. On the early post- war period see also J T McKelvey 'The "Closed Shop" Controversy in Postwar Britain' *Industrial and Labor Relations Review* 7 1954 pp 550–74. The closed shop since the 1960s is examined in Stephen Dunn and John Gennard *The Closed Shop in British Industry* Macmillan 1984. They argue that the closed shop had little impact on industrial relations in this period despite the fears of its detrimental effects which were expressed at the time. Developments since the 1960s are also examined in W W Daniel 'Changes in the Closed Shop in Britain' *Policy Studies* 4 1983 pp 58–71. There are reflections on the closed shop in the National Health Service and more generally in S R Harrison 'The Closed Shop and the National Health Service' Warwick MPhil Thesis 1983.

## (f) Shop Stewards and Shop Stewards Movements

**4586** Eric Batstone, Ian Boraston and Stephen Frankel *Shop Stewards in Action: The Organisation of Workplace Conflict and Accommodation* Blackwell 1984. A useful sociological study of an understudied group. W E J McCarthy *The Role of Shop Stewards in Industrial Action* HMSO 1966 was a research paper for the Donovan Royal Commission.

**4587** Edmund and Ruth Frow *Engineering Struggles: Episodes in the Story of the Shop Stewards Movement* Working Class Movement Library 1982. There are a number of studies of the shop stewards movement during and after the First World War. This very informative compilation of episodes covers 1914 to the 1960s.

**4588** R T Buchanan 'The Shop Steward Movement 1935–1947' *Scottish Labour History Society Journal* 12 1978 pp 34–55.

**4589** Jonathan Zeitlin 'The Emergence of Shop Steward Organisation and Job Control in the British Car Industry: A Review Essay' *History Workshop* 10 1980 pp 119–37. This is responded to in D Lyddon 'Workplace Organisation in the British Car Industry' *History Workshop* 15 1983 pp 131–40.

## (g) Strikes

Accounts of individual strikes and disputes can be found in the material on industrial relations in particular industries.

**4590** James E Cronin *Industrial Conflict in Modern Britain* Croom Helm 1979. An innovative and persuasive attempt to create a theory to explain the various strike waves that have hit Britain since the 1880s. Another attempt to examine strike patterns is C J Baldry 'A Sociological Examination of the Causes of British Inter-Industrial Strike Patterns 1950–1969' Durham PhD Thesis 1977.

**4591** H A Turner *Is Britain Really Strike-Prone? A Review of the Incidence, Character and Costs of Industrial Conflict* Cambridge University Press 1969. In the face of the contemporary concern about the damaging effects of industrial disputes Turner asserts that it is not strikes which are the problem so much as resistance to change and low productivity. It has also of course been shown that when statistics are compared Britain is not noticeably more strike-prone than her competitors (see for instance E H Phelps-Brown 'What is the British Predicament?' *Three Banks Review* 116 1977 pp 3–29). It should be noted however that the work-to-rule, the go-slow and the overtime ban are also much used parts

of the British trade unions armoury. These, which contributed significantly to the sense of industrial chaos that pervades the news media of the late 1960s and early 1970s, are however not also reflected in the statistics. They have been largely overlooked in the literature on industrial disputes.

**4592** J W Durcan, W E J McCarthy and G P Redman *Strikes in Post-War Britain: A Study of Stoppages of Work due to Industrial Disputes 1948–1973* Allen and Unwin 1983. A descriptive account based on Department of Employment records.

**4593** R A Leeson (comp) *Strike: A Live History 1887–1971* Allen and Unwin 1973. The last two chapters cover the post-war years up to the Postmen's Strike of 1971. It largely consists of pieces written by the principal actors in the various disputes. The contributors are not just trade union leaders but shop stewards and other officials.

**4594** E W Evans and S W Creigh (eds) *Industrial Conflict in Britain* Cass 1977. A selection of previously published articles on post-war disputes.

**4595** J E T Eldridge *Industrial Disputes: Essays in the Sociology of Industrial Relations* Routledge and Kegan Paul 1968. A collection of essays on unofficial strikes, and disputes in the shipbuilding, engineering and steel industries. It includes a useful bibliography.

**4596** P Galambos and E W Evans 'Work Stoppages in the United Kingdom 1951–64: A Quantitative Study' *Bulletin of Oxford University Institute of Economics and Statistics* 28 1966 pp 33–62. This is continued by their 'Work Stoppages in the United Kingdom 1965–70: A Quantitative Survey' *Bulletin of Economic Research* 25 1973 pp 22–42. Strikes in the period 1960–79 and the impact of the ensuing recession on strike activity are analysed in Paul Edwards 'Britain's Changing Strike Problem' *Industrial Relations Journal* 13 1982 pp 5–20.

**4597** John Gennard *Financing Strikers* Macmillan 1977. A useful analysis of the history and practice of strike pay. It concentrates more on the experience of the strikers than on how trade unions finance strikes. It ends with a discussion of the debate over what should be done about the state subsidy to strikers (in the form of welfare) in the 1970s. Also on this debate see J W Durcan and W E J McCarthy 'The State Subsidy Theory of Strikes: An Examination of Statistical Data for the Period 1956–70' *British Journal of Industrial Relations* 12 1974 pp 26–47 and L C Hunter 'The State Subsidy Theory of Strikes – A Reconsideration' *British Journal of Industrial Relations* 12 1974 pp 438–44.

**4598** W E J McCarthy 'The Reasons Given for Striking: An Analysis of Official Statistics 1945–1957' *Bulletin of Oxford University Institute of Economics and*

*Statistics* 21 1959 pp 17–29. See also M P Jackson 'A Critical Assessment of the Ministry of Labour's Method of Analysing the Cause of Stoppages – With Special Reference to Major Stoppages in the Port, Transport and Coal Mining Industries Between 1963 and 1966 (Inclusive)' Hull MA Thesis 1971–2.

**4599** K G Knight 'Strikes and Wage Inflation in British Manufacturing Industry 1950–1968' *Bulletin of Oxford University Institute of Economics and Statistics* 34 1972 pp 281–94.

**4600** K G J C Knowles *Strikes – A Study in Industrial Conflict: With Special Reference to British Experience Between 1911 and 1947* Blackwell 1952.

**4601** Michael Silver 'Recent British Strike Trends: A Factual Analysis' *British Journal of Industrial Relations* 11 1973 pp 66–104. Statistical tables and analysis of trends since 1959. See also J F B Goodman 'Strikes in the United Kingdom: Recent Statistics and Trends' *International Labour Review* 45 1967 pp 465–81 and R Bean and D A Peel 'A Quantitative Analysis of Wage Strikes in Four UK Industries 1962–1970' *Journal of Economic Studies* 1 1974 pp 88–97.

**4602** C T B Smith *et al Strikes in Britain: A Recent Study of Industrial Stoppages in the United Kingdom* Manpower Papers 15, Department of Employment 1978.

**4603** Stephen Evans 'The Use of Injunctions in Industrial Disputes' *British Journal of Industrial Relations* 23 1985 pp 133–7. An analysis of the growing use of injunctions in industrial disputes in the 1980s. This is updated by his 'The Use of Injunctions in Industrial Disputes May 1984–April 1987' *British Journal of Industrial Relations* 25 1987 pp 419–35.

## (h) Industrial Democracy

### (i) Work-ins and Sit-ins

**4604** Ken Coates *Work-ins, Sit-ins and Industrial Democracy: The Implications of Factory Occupations in Great Britain in the Early Seventies* Spokeman 1981. An analysis of the wave of factory occupations of the early 1970s. The reasons for this are analysed in A J Mills 'Workers' Occupations 1971–1975: A Socio-Historical Analysis of the Development and Spread of Sit-ins, Work-ins and Workers' Co-operatives in Britain' Durham PhD Thesis 1982. There is a mass of material on the most famous of these, the Upper Clyde Shipbuilders work-in. For this material see [8214, 8224].

**4605** A G Tuckman 'Industrial Action and Hegemony: Workplace Occupation in Britain 1971 to 1981' Hull PhD Thesis 1985. A study which includes a number of case studies.

### (ii) Worker Participation and Worker Directors

**4606** Campbell Balfour (ed) *Participation in Industry* Croom Helm 1973. Essays on workers' co-operatives, worker participation in management in various industries, worker directors in British Steel and other such themes. J Y Tabb and A Goldfarb *Workers' Participation in Management – Expectations and Experience* Pergamon 1970 is a useful analysis. M D Gold 'Industrial Democracy, Incorporation and Control: Britain 1945–1980' Edinburgh PhD Thesis 1983 provides a general, if rather jargon-ridden analysis of developments and attitudes towards industrial democracy since the Second World War. See also W Stanley 'Workers' Control in Twentieth Century Britain: A Critical Review' Manchester MSc Thesis 1979. On trade union attitudes to worker participation in the post-war period see J Eaton and A Fletcher 'Workers' Participation in Management: A Survey of Post-War Organised Opinion' *Political Quarterly* 47 1976 pp 82–92.

**4607** J R Street 'The Origins and Development of Trade Union Attitudes to Worker Involvement in the Management and Control of British Industry, Especially Nationalised Industry 1930–1951' Oxford DPhil Thesis 1981. An attempt to explain why the trade unions did not attempt to secure workers' control in the nationalized industries. He argues that they wanted industrial participation but not workers' control.

**4608** John Elliott *Conflict or Co-operation? The Growth of Industrial Democracy* Kogan Page 1978. A good study of developments, mostly in the period 1968–78, between the Donovan and Bullock Reports. On worker participation in this period see also P L Davies 'Employee Representation on Company Boards and Participation in Corporate Planning' *Modern Law Review* 38 1975 pp 254–73.

**4609** *Report of the Committee on Industrial Democracy* Cmnd 6707, *Parliamentary Papers* xvi 1976–77. This committee, chaired by Lord Bullock, recommended increased worker participation and worker directors in industry. It is commented on in W B Creighton 'The Bullock Report: Coming of the Age of Democracy' *British Journal of Law and Society* 4 1977 pp 1–17 and Roy Lewis and Jon Clark 'The Bullock Report' *Modern Law Review* 40 1977 pp 323–38.

**4610**  Peter Brennen *et al The Worker Directors* Hutchinson 1976. A study of worker directors in British Steel.

### (iii) Workers' Co-operatives

The studies of particular co-operatives can be found in the literature on the industries to which they belonged. For instance the material on the Meriden co-operative can be found in [3444] or the material on the *Scottish Daily News* in [8213].

**4611**  Catherine Luyster (ed) *The New Co-operatives: A Directory and Resource Guide* 3rd ed, Blackrose Press 1984. The foreword of this directory outlines the development of these co- operatives, which was particularly encouraged in the 1970s by measures such as the Industrial Common Ownership Act 1976 and by the efforts, supported by the Labour government and Labour local authorities, of the Industrial Common Ownership Movement. It also comments on the nature of these co-operatives before details of co-operative enterprises region by region. It includes details on the traditional co-operative movement and other sponsoring bodies and also a useful bibliography.

**4612**  Ken Coates *The New Workers' Co-operatives* Spokesman 1976. A survey of the rise of workers' co-operatives in the early 1970s. See also P Chaplin and R Cowe *A Survey of Contemporary British Worker Co-operatives* Working Paper 36, Manchester Business School 1977.

**4613**  Chris Cornforth 'The Role of Local Co-operative Development Agencies in Promoting Workers' Co-operatives' in Terry Faulkner, Graham Beaver, John Lewis and Allan Gibb (eds) *Readings in Small Business* Gower 1986 p 328–67. In the wake of the 1976 Industrial Common Ownership Act local independent Co-operative Development Agencies began to appear. This is a survey of these and their activity and that of the National Co-operative Development Agency set up in 1978.

### (i) Industrial Relations in the Public Sector

### (i) Civil Service

**4614**  Henry Parris *Staff Relations in the Civil Service: Fifty Years of Whitleyism* Allen and Unwin 1973. See also J D Thomas *Staff Relations in the Civil Service: Fifty Years of Whitleyism in the Inland Revenue 1920–1970* Inland Revenue 1970, Sir William Armstrong 'Whitleyism in the Civil Service' *Whitley Bulletin* 49

1969 pp 136–9 and 151–5, T R Jones 'The War Years and After' *Whitley Bulletin* 49 1969 pp 100–6.

**4615**  I J Beardwell 'The Impact of Trade Union Structure on Collective Bargaining in the British Civil Service' London PhD Thesis 1984. A detailed analysis of developments and conflicts between the Priestley Royal Commission of 1956 and the Megaw Committee of 1982.

**4616**  S J Frankel 'Arbitration in the British Civil Service' *Public Administration* 38 1960 pp 197–211.

**4617**  Sir William Armstrong *Personnel Management in the Civil Service* Civil Service Department 1971. A collection of lectures.

**4618**  Michael P Kelly *White Collar Proletariat: The Industrial Behaviour of British Civil Servants* Routledge and Kegan Paul 1980. An inadequate and heavily theoretical investigation into increasing militancy in the Civil Service since 1945.

**4619**  Gavin Drewry 'The GCHQ Case – A Failure of Government Communications' *Parliamentary Affairs* 38 1985 pp 371–86. An analysis of the Thatcher government's decision in 1984 to ban trade unions at the signals intelligence establishment GCHQ.

### (ii) Nationalized Industries in General

**4620**  J D M Bell 'The Development of Industrial Relations in Nationalised Industries in Post-War Britain' *British Journal of Industrial Relations* 13 1975 pp 1–13. See also G D H Cole 'Labour and Staff Problems Under Nationalisation' *Political Quarterly* 21 1950 pp 160–70. A F Sturmthal 'Nationalisation and Workers' Control in Britain and France' *Journal of Political Economy* 61 1953 pp 43–79 is a comparative study of the evolution of policy and the degree of worker participation in management.

### (iii) Coal

**4621**  Roy Church, Quintin Outram and David N Smith 'Essay in Historiography: Towards a History of British Miners' Militancy' *Bulletin of the Society for the Study of Labour History* 54 1989 pp 21–36.

**4622**  Brian J McCormick *Industrial Relations in the Coal Industry* Macmillan 1979. A historical treatment of developments in the post-war period. See also C E Jencks 'British Coal: Labor Relations Since Nationalisation' *Industrial Relations* 6 1966 pp 95–110, Frederic Meyers 'Nationalisation, Union Structure and Wages

Policy in the British Coalmining Industry' *Southern Economic Journal* 24 1958 pp 421–33, L J Handy 'Wage Policy in the Coal Mining Industry Since Nationalisation: A Case Study of National Wage Bargaining' Cambridge PhD Thesis 1978. The initial effect of nationalization on industrial relations in the industry is assessed in S K Saxena *Nationalisation and Conflict: Example of British Coal Mining* Nijhoff, Den Haag 1955. Industrial conflict in the industry, after being relatively rare for much of the post-war period, has become much more common since the early 1970s. Joel Krieger *Undermining Capitalism: State Ownership and the Dialectic of Control in the British Coal Industry* Princeton University Press 1984 offers useful perspectives on the causes and nature of these conflicts. Trends in industrial conflict in the industry are reviewed in Lisa M Lynch 'Strike Frequency in British Coal Mining 1950–74' *British Journal of Industrial Relations* 16 1978 pp 95–98. See also I Rutledge 'Changes in the Mode of Production and the Growth of "Mass Militancy" in the British Mining Industry 1954–1974' *Science and Society* 41 1977 pp 410–29.

**4623** Brian J McCormick 'Strikes in the Yorkshire Coalfield 1947–1963' *Economic Studies* 4 1969 pp 171–97.

**4624** C Slaughter 'The Strike of the Yorkshire Mineworkers in May 1955' *Sociological Review* 6 1958 pp 241–59.

**4625** Malcolm Pitt *The World on Our Backs: The Kent Miners and the 1972 Miners' Strike* Lawrence and Wishart 1979. See also David Winchester 'The British Coal Mine Strike of 1972' *Monthly Labour Review* 95/10 1972 pp 30–6. Nothing as yet has been written specifically on the 1974 dispute which was instrumental in bringing down the Heath government.

**4626** Martin Adeney and John Lloyd *The Miners' Strike 1984–5: Loss Without Limit* Routledge and Kegan Paul 1986. Probably the best general account of the strike. Other more instant accounts are Geoffrey Goodman *The Miners' Strike* Pluto 1985 and Sunday Times Insight Team *Strike* Coronet 1985. The only material on the strike which does not appear below is that which deals with the handling of the dispute in the media. For this see [3557].

**4627** Hywel Francis and Gareth Rees (eds) *Class, Community and the Miners: The British Coalfields and the 1984–85 Strike* Lawrence and Wishart 1988. These collected essays dissect the strike in every coalfield, its strengths and weaknesses, its local peculiarities and its aftermath, particularly in the context of the split between the National Union of Mineworkers and the Union of Democratic Miners (the breakaway Nottinghamshire union). Every aspect of the strike is explored from a sympathetic point of view. A similarly sympathetic collection of essays on the strike is Huw Beynon (ed) *Digging Deeper: Issues in the Miners' Strike* Verso 1985. Phil Scraton and P Thomas (eds) 'The State v the People: Lessons from the Coal Dispute' *Journal of Law and Society* 12 1985 pp 251–403 is a collection of papers which reflect, in a hostile fashion, on a number of aspects of the handling of the dispute by the authorities. One of the papers is also concerned with the role of folk memories of previous disputes in the coalfields during the strike of 1984–5.

**4628** Ian Macgregor with Rodney Tyler *The Enemies Within: The Story of the Miners' Strike 1984–5* Collins 1986. A useful account of the strike from the management point of view by the then Chairman of the National Coal Board. It is also useful on the politics and the government handling of the dispute. In this context [867] should also be consulted. See also John Saville 'An Open Conspiracy – Conservative Politics and the Miners' Strike 1984–85' *Socialist Register* 1985–86 pp 295–329. A particular aspect of government policy is critically examined in L Sutcliffe and B Hill *Let Them Eat Coal: The Political Use of Social Security during the Miners' Strike* Canary 1985.

**4629** Roy Ottey *The Strike* Sidgwick and Jackson 1985. The inside account of the strike by the former Secretary of the Power Group of the NUM (up to July 1984). It is very critical of Arthur Scargill's leadership of the union into and during the dispute.

**4630** David Cooper and Trevor Hooper (eds) *Debating Coal Closures: Economic Calculations in the Coal Dispute 1984–85* Cambridge University Press 1988. An important set of analyses on the economic background to the dispute.

**4631** Raphael Samuel, Barbara Bloomfield and Guy Boanas (eds) *The Enemy Within: Pit Villages and the Miners' Strike of 1984–5* Routledge and Kegan Paul 1986. A study which focuses on the ordinary people caught up in the dispute and not their leaders. It largely consists of interviews, diaries and letters reflecting on the strike. Since it covers to the end of 1985 it also covers the aftermath of the strike in the coalfields.

**4632** Vicky Seddon (ed) *The Cutting Edge: Women and the Pit Strike* Lawrence and Wishart 1987. A good analysis of women's response to and support for the 1984–5 strike, both inside and outside the coalfields. It is also strong on personal reminiscences, as is Chrys Salt and Jim Layzell (eds) *Here We Go: Women's Memories of the Miners' Strike* London Political Committee, Co-operative Retail Services Ltd 1985. See also Jean Stead *Never the Same Again: Women and the Miners' Strike* Women's Press 1987.

**4633** Jonathan Winterton and Ruth Winterton *Coal, Crisis and Conflict: The 1984–85 Miners' Strike in Yorkshire* Manchester University Press 1989. An authoritative study of the origins, development and ultimate defeat of the strike in the area in which it began drawing on access to NUM records and extensive interviewing. It also features a valuable bibliography. There are a number of other studies of the strike in particular communities and localities, such as Roger Seifert and John Seifert *Struggle Without End: The 1984–85 Miners' Strike in North Staffordshire* Penrhos 1987. Peter Gibbon and David Steyne (eds) *Thurcroft: A Village and the Miners' Strike: An Oral History* Spokesman 1986 is an oral history of the strike in a South Yorkshire village. Tony Parker *Red Hill: A Mining Community* Heinemann 1986 is an oral history of the strike in a pit village in the North East. The names of the village and its inhabitants have been changed. Unlike most of the oral histories of the strike it does not just concentrate on the miners and their families but also contains interviews with local NCB officials and policemen. See also Huw Beynon 'The Miners' Strike in Easington' *New Left Review* 148 1984 pp 104–15.

**4633A** B Jackson and T Wardle *The Battle for Orgreave* Canary 1986. A committed account of the picketing of the Orgreave coking works during the 1984–5 strike.

**4634** Eric Jones, Margaret Jones and John King 'It's our Fight too: Solidarity and Support in Lancaster During the Miners' Strike of 1984–85' *North West Labour History* 11 1985 pp 71–83.

**4635** Bob Fine and Robert Millar (eds) *Policing the Miners' Strike* Lawrence and Wishart 1985. A collection of essays critically examining various aspects of the policing of the dispute. These essays were presented as evidence to a National Council for Civil Liberties inquiry into the police conduct during the strike. The policing of the strike is also critically examined in Jim Coulter, Susan Miller and Martin Walker *A State of Siege: Politics and Policing of the Coalfields Miners' Strike 1984* Canary 1984. The issues raised by the policing of the dispute are examined in Sarah McCabe *et al The Police, Public Order and Civil Liberties: Legacies of the Miners' Strike* Routledge 1988. See also S Spencer *Police Authorities During the Miners' Strike* Cobden Trust 1985, a short paper on their activities during the dispute. P A J Waddington *The Effect of Manpower Depletion during the NUM Strike 1984–85* Police Foundation 1985 examines the effects of the policing of the strike on police manpower levels, arrests, crime rates and officer stress.

**4636** *Policing the Coal Dispute in South Yorkshire* South Yorkshire Police 1985. This collects the official report of the Chief Constable of South Yorkshire Police, the report of the inquiry into police policy during the strike by the special sub-committee of the South Yorkshire Police Committee and the police reply. Another local study of the policing of the strike is T Leonard 'Policing the Miners in Derbyshire' *Policing* 1 1985 pp 96–101.

**4637** Ray Richardson and Stephen Wood 'Productivity Change in the Coal Industry and the New Industrial Relations' *British Journal of Industrial Relations* 27 1989 pp 33–56. An attempt to explain productivity improvement in the coal industry after the 1984–85 strike.

*(iv) Other Nationalized Industries*

**4638** R D V Roberts and H Sallis 'Joint Consultation in the Electricity Supply Industry 1949–1959' *Public Administration* 37 1959 pp 115–33. Industrial relations in the industry.

**4639** P J White 'Gasworkers' Strike 1972–3: An Analysis of Causes' *Industrial Relations Journal* 5 1974 pp 27–37.

**4640** Hugh Armstrong Clegg *Labour Relations in London Transport* Blackwell 1950.

**4641** Eric Batstone, Anthony Ferner and Michael Terry *Consent and Efficiency: Labour Relations and Management Strategy in the State Enterprise* Blackwell 1984. A study of industrial relations in the Post Office 1960–80. See also Anthony Ferner and Michael Terry *'The Crunch had to Come': A Case Study of Changing Industrial Relations in the Post Office* Warwick Papers in Industrial Relations 1, University of Warwick 1985.

**4642** Charles Macleod *All Change: Railway Industrial Relations in the Sixties* Gower 1970. A survey of developments since the Guillebaud committee of inquiry into railway pay in 1958–60 established comparability which then became an increasingly important facet of incomes policy.

**4643** Eric Taylor *The Better Temper: The History of the Midland Iron and Steel Wages Board 1876–1976* Iron and Steel Trades Confederation 1976. A history of the oldest conciliation board in the industry. It concentrates on the period before the First World War.

**4644** Charles Doherty *Steel and Steelworkers: The Sons of Vulcan* Heinemann Education 1983. An account of the three month long strike in 1980. See also Jean Hartley, John Kelly and Nigel Nicholson *Steel Strike* Batsford 1983 and Loraine Downing *A Consideration of the 1980 Strike Within the British Steel Corporation with*

*Particular Regard to the Government's Role* Sheffield City Polytechnic 1981.

### (v) The National Health Service

**4645** Stuart J Dimmock 'Incomes Policy and Health Services in the United Kingdom' in Amarjit Singh Sethi and Stuart J Dimmock (eds) *Industrial Relations and Health Services* Croom Helm 1982 pp 325–41. An account of incomes policy in the NHS since it was established in 1948. The same volume also contains M Carpenter 'The Labour Movement in the National Health Service (NHS) UK' pp 74–90 and S D Anderson, J H Angel and R Meilly 'Legislations Governing Industrial Relations in the National Health Service UK' pp 139–67. Other general analyses of industrial relations in the NHS are Maurice H W Cuming *Personnel Management in the National Health Service* Heinemann 1978, H A Clegg and T E Chester *Wage Policy and the Health Service* Blackwell 1957 and S B Herd *Industrial Relations in the National Health Service* Health Service Management Unit, Department of Social Administration, University of Manchester 1980.

**4646** Theodore R Marmor and David Thomas 'Doctors, Politics and Pay Disputes: "Pressure Group Politics" Revisited' *British Journal of Political Science* 2 1972 pp 421–42.

**4647** R V R Felgate 'The Emergence of Militancy in the Nursing Profession 1960–1972' Surrey PhD Thesis 1977–8. See also M J Carpenter 'The Development of Trade Union Activity Among Nurses in Britain 1910–76' Warwick PhD Thesis 1985.

**4648** Susan Treloar 'The Junior Hospital Doctors' Pay Dispute 1975–1976: An Analysis of Events, Issues and Conflicts' *Journal of Social Policy* 10 1981 pp 1–30.

**4649** M McDonough 'The 1982 NHS Pay Dispute: National and Local' Hull MSc Thesis 1983.

**4650** Jonathan Neale *Memoirs of a Picket: Working for the NHS* Pluto 1983. Memoirs of a NUPE shop steward in the NHS which includes reflections on the 1982 dispute.

### (vi) Other

**4651** A Fowler *Personnel Management in Local Government* Institute of Personnel Management 1975.

**4652** Martin Laffin *Managing Under Pressure: Industrial Relations in Local Government* Macmillan 1988. A study of industrial relations in the straitened financial circumstances of local government in the 1980s, illustrated by case studies. Militancy amongst council staff in the 1970s is examined in a particular context in P C Joyce 'Shop Steward Militancy: A Case Study in a London Borough During the 1970s' London PhD Thesis 1983. The conciliation machinery in local government is assessed in L Kramer 'Reflections on Whitleyism in English Local Government' *Public Administration* 37 1958 pp 47–69.

**4653** R J Thornton 'Teacher Unionism and Collective Bargaining in England and Wales' *Industrial and Labour Relations Review* 35 1982 pp 177–91.

**4654** Vincent Burke *Teachers in Turmoil* Penguin 1971. An outline of the growing militancy in the teaching profession leading to the 1970 strike. The strike is examined in T Griffiths *The Teachers' Strike (1969–70)* National Union of Teachers 1970 and in Peter Price 'The Teacher's Strike' *Trade Union Register* 1970 pp 173–7.

### (j) Industrial Relations in the Private Sector

### (i) The Motor Industry

**4655** David Marsden, Timothy Morris, Paul Willman and Stephen Wood *The Car Industry: Labour Relations and Industrial Adjustment* Tavistock 1985. Another general analysis is H A Turner, G Clack and G Roberts *Labour Relations in the Motor Industry* Allen and Unwin 1967. See also John Bescoby and H A Turner 'An Analysis of Post-War Labour Disputes in the British Car Manufacturing Firms' *Manchester School of Economic and Social Studies* 29 1961 pp 133–60 and D G Rhys 'Employment, Efficiency and Labour Relations in the British Motor Industry' *Industrial Relations Journal* 5 1974 pp 4–26.

**4656** Henry Friedman and Sander Meredeen *The Dynamics of Industrial Conflict: Lessons From Fords* Croom Helm 1980. An analysis of the 1968 strike by Ford sewing machinists which is also quite useful on industrial relations at Ford in general. This dispute was a benchmark strike which led to the Equal Pay Act 1970 and thence to the Sex Discrimination and Employment Protection Acts of 1975.

**4657** Freddy Silberman 'The 1969 Ford Strike' *Trade Union Register* 1970 pp 222–31.

**4658** John Mathews *Ford Strike: The Workers' Story* Panther 1971. A study of the 1970–1 dispute in the context of a critical history of labour relations at Ford based on interviews with union officials and workers.

**4659** Alan Thornett *From Militancy to Marxism: A Personal and Political Account of Organising Car Workers* Left View Books 1987. Thornett began work at Cowley in 1959 and was a militant shop steward there from 1963 until he was sacked during Sir Michael Edwardes' stewardship of British Leyland. This autobiography traces militancy at the factory 1959–74. Industrial relations at British Leyland from the 1975 Ryder Report, and especially during the Edwardes period, are traced in Paul Willman 'Labour Relations Strategy at BL Cars' in Steven Tolliday and Jonathan Zeitlin (eds) *The Automobile Industry and its Workers Between Fordism and Flexibility* Polity 1986 pp 305–27.

## (ii) Docks

**4660** David F Wilson *Dockers: The Impact of Industrial Change* Fontana 1972. An analysis of post-war developments and particularly those of the 1960s, when casual labour was at last abolished and the container revolution began to affect the docks. Another useful history, concentrating on the post-war period, is Michael P Jackson *Labour Relations on the Docks* Saxon House 1973.

**4661** Gordon Phillips and Noel Whiteside *Casual Labour: The Unemployment Question in the Port Transport Industry 1880–1970* Clarendon 1985. The central focus of this study is the gradual eradication of casual labour in the docks. Developments 1940–70 are dealt with only in an epilogue.

**4662** *Review of the British Dock Strikes 1949* Cmnd 7851, *Parliamentary Papers* xxix 1948–49. A survey of the course and cost of the strikes, with some documentation. Kenneth Knowles 'The Post-War Dock Strikes' *Political Quarterly* 22 1951 pp 266–89 is a good survey of these unofficial disputes, with some statistics. See also Peter Weiler 'British Labour and the Cold War: The London Dock Strike of 1949' in James E Cross and Jonathan Schneer (eds) *Social Conflict and the Political Order in Modern Britain* Croom Helm 1982 pp 146–78.

**4663** Fred Lindop 'Unofficial Militancy in the Royal Group of Docks 1945–67' *Oral History* 11 1983 pp 21–33.

## (iii) Engineering

**4664** A I Marsh *et al Workplace Industrial Relations in Engineering* Engineering Employers' Federation 1971. See also A I Marsh *Industrial Relations in Engineering* Pergamon 1965.

**4665** M Derber 'Adjustment Problems of a Long-Established Industrial Relations System: An Appraisal of British Engineering 1954–1961' *Quarterly Review of Economics and Business* 3 1963 pp 37–48.

**4666** Paul Edwards and Hugh Scullion 'The Local Organisation of a National Dispute: The British 1979 Engineering Strike' *Industrial Relations Journal* 13 1982 pp 57–63.

**4667** Huw Beynon and Hilary Wainwright *The Workers' Report on Vickers* Pluto 1979. A shop stewards' combine committee report on work, wages, rationalization and rank and file organization in a British multinational. It surveys developments since 1945 and especially since 1970. It is particularly useful on the shop stewards themselves.

**4668** Jim Arnison *The Million Pound Strike* Lawrence and Wishart 1970. An account of a strike for equal pay for women at the Roberts-Arundel works in Stockport in 1967–8 which led to the closure of the company. Arnison reflects both on the course and the policing of the dispute.

**4669** Colin Love *Conflicts Over Closure: The Lawrence Scott Affair* Avebury 1988. The account of the year-long resistance by the employees to the employer's determination to close a Manchester engineering works in 1981–2.

## (iv) Grunwick

**4670** Jack Dromey and Graham Taylor *Grunwick: The Workers' Story* Lawrence and Wishart 1978. An inside history of the 1976–8 industrial action at the North London film-processing plant. They are critical of the lack of trade union assistance hitherto to the unorganized, mainly Asian women involved in the dispute. Joe Rogaly *Grunwick* Penguin 1977 is good on the various issues raised by the dispute. It includes a chronology and the report of the Scarman Court of Inquiry and the Grunwick reply in its appendices. The course of the strike is examined in the context of trade union attitudes and their pre-existing record on organizing coloured workers in Annie Phizacklea and Robert Miles 'The Strike at Grunwick' *New Community* 6 1978 pp 268–78.

**4671** George Ward *Fort Grunwick* Temple Smith 1977. A view of the strike and the issues raised by the managing director of Grunwick. It is also useful on the strike-breaking tactics adopted.

## (v) Media and Printing

**4672**   Keith Sisson *Industrial Relations in Fleet Street* Blackwell 1975. An excellent account. See also P Hartman 'Industrial Relations in the News Media' *Industrial Relations* 6 1976 pp 107–24. The impact of new technology on industrial relations in Fleet Street in the 1970s and 1980s is surveyed in Roderick Martin *New Technology and Industrial Relations in Fleet Street* Clarendon 1981 and John Gennard and S Dunn 'The Impact of New Technology on the Structure and Organisation of Craft Unions in the Printing Industry' *British Journal of Industrial Relations* 21 1983 pp 17–37.

**4673**   H C Strick 'British Newspaper Journalism 1900–1956: A Study in Industrial Relations' London PhD Thesis 1956–7.

**4674**   Eric Jacobs *Stop Press: The Inside Story of The Times Dispute* Deutsch 1980. An account of the eleven month lock-out by the management of Times newspapers 1978–9.

**4675**   M Dickinson *To Break a Union: The Messenger, the State and the NGA* Manchester Free Press 1984. An account of the dispute between Eddie Shah of the *Stockport Messenger* and the National Graphical Association.

**4676**   John Child *Industrial Relations in the British Printing Industry: The Quest for Security* Allen and Unwin 1967. The last chapter of this history covers the post-war years. See also John Gennard 'Major Post-War Disputes in the Printing Industry' Manchester MA (Econ) Thesis 1967–8.

## (vi) Shipbuilding

**4677**   James McGoldrick 'Industrial Relations and the Division of Labour in the Shipbuilding Industry Since the War' *British Journal of Industrial Relations* 21 1983 pp 197–220.

**4678**   G C Cameron 'Post-War Strikes in the North-East Shipbuilding and Ship-Repairing Industry 1946–1961' *British Journal of Industrial Relations* 2 1964 pp 1–22.

**4679**   P A Oakley 'Demarcation and Amalgamation: A Study of Union Antagonism Between the Shipwrights and Boilermakers in the Cammel Laird Shipyard, Birkenhead 1953–64' Manchester MA (Econ) Thesis 1967–8.

## (vii) Other

**4680**   Timothy Morris *Innovations in Banking: Business Strategies and Employee Relations* Croom Helm 1986. A study of industrial relations in banking.

**4681**   David P Waddington *Trouble Brewing: A Social Psychological Analysis of the Ansells Brewery Dispute* Avebury 1987. A study of the 1981 strike at the brewery. It was the largest ever dispute in an industry with a tradition of good industrial relations.

**4682**   C Gill, R Morris and J Eaton *Industrial Relations in the Chemicals Industry* Saxon House 1978.

**4683**   T B Austrin 'Industrial Relations in the Construction Industry: Some Sociological Considerations on Wage Contracts and Trade Unionism (1914–1973)' Bristol PhD Thesis 1978.

**4684**   Michael Chanon *Labour Power in the British Film Industry* British Film Institute 1976.

**4685**   N A Godman 'Historical and Contemporary Issues in the Catching Sector of the British Fishing Industry' Heriot-Watt PhD Thesis 1982. A historical examination of industrial relations in the fishing industry during its post-war decline.

**4686**   Eric Armstrong 'The Conciliatory Negotiation of Change: A Case Study of the Norwich Footwear Arbitration Board 1909–80' *Industrial Relations Journal* 13 1982 pp 43–56.

**4687**   Tony Lane and K Roberts *Strike at Pilkingtons* Fontana 1971. Another account of this strike is Norman McCord 'St Helens 1970' in his *Strikes* Blackwell 1980 pp 105–15.

**4688**   J G Capey 'The Pottery Labour Force with Special Reference to the Effects of the Industrial Relations Act 1971' Keele MSc Thesis 1977.

**4689**   J McConville 'Industrial relations in the UK Shipping Industry Since the Second World War' Warwick PhD Thesis 1982. G Foulser *Seamen's Voice* Macgibbon and Kee 1961 concentrates particularly on the seamen's strike of 1960. On this see also J M Doxey 'The Seamen's Strike of 1960' Manchester MA (Econ) Thesis 1962–3.

## (4) Trade Unions

Much material of interest can also be found in the sections on the Labour party and on various aspects of economic policy, especially industrial and incomes policy. The literature listed in the section on industrial relations should obviously also be consulted.

## (a) General

**4690** Arthur Marsh and Victoria Ryan *Historical Directory of Trade Unions* 3v, Gower 1980–87. An exhaustive guide. Volume one covers white collar unions, including defunct unions. These are listed alphabetically. A historical sketch and information on sources and publications is provided for each. The second volume lists unions in engineering, shipbuilding and minor metal trades, coal mining, iron and steel, agriculture, fishing and chemicals. The third volume covers unions in building and construction, transport, woodworkers, leatherworkers and tobacco-workers. Arthur Marsh *Trade Union Handbook* 3rd ed, Gower 1984 is a guide and directory to the structure, membership, policy and personnel of British trade unions. It also contains a bibliography of official union histories. A similar directory is Jack Eaton and Colin Gill *The Trade Union Directory: A Guide to all TUC Unions* 2nd ed, Pluto 1983.

**4691** N Robertson and K I Sams *British Trade Unionism: Select Documents* 2v, Blackwell 1972. These documents concentrate on the period 1914–69, with an appendix covering 1970. Another collection of documents is John Dennis Hughes and Harold Pollins (eds) *Trade Unions in Great Britain* David and Charles 1974.

**4692** *Trade Union Register* Merlin 1969–. An annual register of events and developments.

**4693** Ruth Frow, Edmund Frow and Michael Katanka *The History of British Trade Unions: A Select Bibliography* Historical Association 1969.

**4694** Henry Pelling *A History of British Trade Unionism* 4th ed, Macmillan 1987. The standard general history, which takes the story up to the 1980s. Eric L Wigham *Trade Unions* 2nd ed, Oxford University Press 1969 is a useful, thematically arranged history. See also Allen Hutt *British Trade Unionism: A Short History* 6th ed (with a concluding chapter by John Gollan), Lawrence and Wishart 1975.

**4695** Mark Stephens *Roots of Power: 150 Years of British Trade Unions: A Personal View* SPA Books 1986. An idiosyncratic view of trade union history. The second half of the book deals in detail with developments since the Donovan Report.

**4696** Ben Pimlott and Chris Cook (ed) *Trade Unions in British Politics* Longman 1982. A good collection of papers. It includes six essays on the trade unions since

1945 on subjects such as their relations with CND, or with the media.

**4697** Michael Jackson *Trade Unions* 2nd ed, 1989. A general textbook. See also Ken Coates and Tony Topham *Trade Unions in Britain* Spokesman 1980.

**4698** V L Allen *Militant Trade Unionism* Merlin 1966. An examination of militancy in the unions since 1947.

**4699** Brian Burkitt and David Bowers 'The Degree of Unionisation 1948–1968' *Bulletin of Economic Research* 26 1974 pp 79–100. This is responded to in K Mayhew 'The Degree of Unionisation 1948–1968' *Bulletin of Economic Research* 29 1977 pp 51–6. See also Brian Burkitt and David Bowers 'The Determination of the Rate of Unionisation in the United Kingdom 1924–1966' *Applied Economics* 10 1978 pp 161–72 and Robert J Price and George Sayer Bain 'Union Growth Revisited: 1948–1974 in Perspective' *British Journal of Industrial Relations* 14 1976 pp 339–55.

**4700** George Douglas Howard Cole *British Trade Unionism Today: A Survey with the Collaboration of Trade Union Leaders and Other Experts* Methuen 1945. Opinions on the contemporary state of trade unionism.

**4701** R Undy, V Ellis, W E J McCarthy and A M Halmos *Changes in Trade Unions: The Development of UK Unions Since the 1960s* Hutchinson 1981. The tactics used by the unions to influence public policy and their role in the state since 1960 is studied in Timothy C May *Trade Unions and Pressure Group Politics* Saxon House 1975. Another account of the trade unions since the 1960s is P B Beaumont *The Decline of Trade Union Organisation* Croom Helm 1986.

**4702** George Sayer Bain and Robert J Price *Union Growth and Employment Trends in the United Kingdom 1964–1970* Industrial Relations Research Unit, University of Warwick 1972. See also J D Hughes 'British Trade Unionism in the Sixties' *Socialist Register* 1966 pp 86–113.

**4703** Robert Taylor *The Fifth Estate: Britain's Unions in the Modern World* 2nd ed, Pan 1980. An invaluable and excellent account of the unions in the 1970s. It includes a good bibliography. Innis MacBeath *Votes, Virtues and Vices: Trade Union Power* Associated Business Press 1979 gives a survey of the unions and their leaders in the 1970s. On the unions in the 1970s see also Stephen Milligan *The New Barons* Temple Smith 1976. This is perhaps a little oversimplified but very readable. Its title derives from the view of union power that prevailed in the 1970s. The trade union response to the economic difficulties of the 1970s is examined in Adam Sharples 'Alternative Economic Strategies: Labour

Movement Responses to the Crisis' *Socialist Economic Review* 1 1981 pp 71–91.

**4704** William Brierley (ed) *Trade Unions and the Economic Crisis of the 1980s* Gower 1987. A collection of essays. The effect of the legislation of the Thatcher government on the unions is analysed in David Marsh and Jeff King *The Trade Unions Under Thatcher* Essex Papers in Politics and Government 27, Department of Government, University of Essex 1985.

**4705** Derek Fatchell *Trade Unions and Politics in the 1980s: The 1984 Trade Union Act and Political Funds* Croom Helm 1987. The 1984 Act required trade unions affiliated to the Labour party to ballot their membership on the retention of the political levy. This, and the successful campaign to retain the levy, is analysed here. The ballots are reviewed in John W Leopold 'Trade Union Political Funds: A Retrospective Analysis' *Industrial Relations Journal* 17 1986 pp 287–303 and David Grant 'Mrs Thatcher's Own Goal: Unions and the Political Funds Ballots' *Parliamentary Affairs* 40 1987 pp 57–73.

**4706** Martin S Estey 'Trends in Concentration of Union Membership 1897–1962' *Quarterly Journal of Economics* 80 1966 pp 343–60.

**4707** Rosemary Hutt 'Trade Unions as Friendly Societies 1912–1952' *Yorkshire Bulletin of Economic and Social Research* 7 1955 pp 69–87. See also Arthur I Marsh and Peter Cope 'The Anatomy of Trade Union Benefits in the 1960s' *Industrial Relations Journal* 1/1 1970 pp 4–18.

**4708** John Hemingway *Conflict and Democracy: Studies in Trade Union Government* Clarendon 1978. This focuses on government and administration in the Seamen's Union, the NUR and USDAW. There are a number of case studies, including studies of other bodies. Earlier studies of trade union government and administration are B C Roberts *Trade Union Government and Administration in Great Britain* Bell 1957 and V L Allen *Power in Trade Unions* Longmans 1954.

**4709** Hugh Armstrong Clegg, A J Killick and Rex Adams *Trade Union Officers: A Study of Full Time Officers, Branch Secretaries and Shop Stewards in British Trade Unions* Blackwell 1961. A useful sociological study.

**4710** Shirley W Lerner *Breakaway Unions and the Small Trade Union* Allen and Unwin 1961. This includes both a series of case studies of breakaway unions, notably of the Chemical Workers Union, and an examination of the disadvantages suffered by small unions under the TUC's Bridlington Agreement governing inter-union disputes.

**4711** David F Selvin 'Communications in Trade Unions: A Study of Union Journals' *British Journal of Industrial Relations* 1 1963 pp 73–93.

**4712** E N Farthing 'British Trade Unions and European Integration: The Development of Attitudes 1945–1982' Warwick MA Thesis 1984. The response of the unions to Britain's entry into Europe is analysed in P Teague 'Labour and Europe: The Response of British Trade Unions to Membership of the European Communities' London PhD Thesis 1984. The trade union reaction to the initial attempt to join Europe is discussed in R Colin Beever 'Trade Unions and the Common Market' *Planning* 28 1962 pp 73–109. R Colin Beever 'Trade Union Re-Thinking' *Journal of Common Market Studies* 2 1963 pp 140–54 traces trade union thought on European integration 1956–62 using TUC records.

**4713** John Gennard *Multinational Corporations and British Labour: A Review of Attitudes and Responses* British-North American Committee 1972. A study of the attitude of British trade unions towards multinationals, and especially American multinationals.

**(h) The Trades Union Congress**

**4714** *Trade Union Congress: General Council Minutes 1921–* Harvester 1975–. A microfiche publication. It is chronologically arranged and unindexed.

**4715** John Lovell and B C Roberts *A Short History of the TUC* Macmillan 1968. A centenary history. See also Lionel Birch (ed) *The History of the TUC 1868–1968: A Pictorial Survey of a Social Revolution: Illustrated with Contemporary Prints, Documents and Photographs* TUC 1968 and V L Allen 'The Centenary of the British Trades Union Congress 1868–1968' *Socialist Register* 1968 pp 231–52.

**4716** Ross M Martin *TUC: The Growth of a Pressure Group 1868–1976* Clarendon 1980. The narrow focus on the TUC's role as a pressure group in this work obscures its place in British politics. Also on the TUC as a pressure group see S E Finer 'The Political Power of Organised Labour' *Government and Opposition* 8 1973 pp 391–406.

**4717** Shirley W Lerner 'The TUC Jurisdictional Dispute Settlement 1924–1957' *Manchester School of Economics and Social Studies* 26 1958 pp 222–40. A study of the TUC mechanism for the settlement of inter-union disputes.

**4718** Stephen Bornstein and Peter Gourevitch 'Unions in a Declining Economy: The Case of the British TUC' in Peter Gourevitch *et al Unions and Economic Crisis:*

*Britain, West Germany and Sweden* Allen and Unwin 1984 pp 13–88. This focuses on the TUC 1974–9.

**4719** D I Davies 'The Politics of the TUC's Colonial Policy' *Political Quarterly* 35 1964 pp 23–34.

### (c) General Federation of Trade Unions

**4720** Alice Prochaska *History of the General Federation of Trade Unions 1889–1980* Allen and Unwin 1982. This is basically a strike insurance fund. Marginalized by the 1981 reform of the TUC it nevertheless remains a servicing agency for the smaller unions. See also Arthur Marsh and M Speirs 'The General Federation of Trade Unions 1945–1970' *Industrial Relations Journal* 2/3 1971 pp 22–34.

### (d) Trade Councils

**4721** Alan Clinton 'The History of Trades Councils' *Bulletin of the Society for the Study of Labour History* 29 1974 pp 37–50. A bibliographical essay which analyses the archive holdings and histories of trades councils in alphabetical order. Local trades council histories which are of some use for the post-war period are John Corbett *The Birmingham Trades Council 1866–1966* Lawrence and Wishart 1966, Andy Durr (ed) *A History of Brighton Trades Council and Labour Movement 1890–1970* Brighton Trades Council 1974, Malcolm Wallace *Nothing To Lose, A World to Win: History of Chelmsford and District Trades Council* the author 1979, Barry Burke *Rebels With A Cause: The History of Hackney Trades Council 1900–1975* Hackney Trades Council/Hackney Workers Education Association 1975, Edmund and Ruth Frow *A History of the Manchester and Salford Trades Council* E J Marten 1976, Dave Russell *Southwark Trades Council 1903–78* Southwark Trades Council 1978 and Angela Tuckett *Up With All That's Down! A History of Swindon Trades Council 1891–1971* Quill Press 1971.

### (e) Women in the Trade Union Movement

**4722** Sarah Boston *Women Workers and the Trade Unions* 2nd ed, Lawrence and Wishart 1987. A history of women workers and their struggle to organize and to be recognized by employers and male trade unionists from the early nineteenth century to 1986. Other useful histories are Sheila Lewenhak *Women and Trade Unions: An Outline History of Women in the British Trade Union Movement* Benn 1977 and Norbert C Solden *Women in British Trade Unions 1874–1976* Gill and Macmillan, Dublin 1978. See also Barbara Drake *Women in Trade Unions* Virago 1984 and Ruth Elliott

'How far have we come? Women's Organisation in the Unions in the United Kingdom' *Feminist Review* 16 1984 pp 64–73.

### (f) White Collar Unionism

**4723** George Sayer Bain and Harold Pollins 'The History of White Collar Unions and Industrial Relations: A Bibliography' *Bulletin of the Society for the Study of Labour History* 11 1965 pp 20–64. A historiographical guide to the literature.

**4724** George Sayer Bain *The Growth of White Collar Unionism* Clarendon 1970. The standard history. See also his *Trade Union Growth and Recognition with Special Reference to White Collar Unions in Private Industry* 1967. The 1970s were marked by increasing militancy amongst white collar unions, which is reflected in Clive Jenkins and Barrie Sherman *White Collar Unionism: The Rebellious Salariat* Routledge and Kegan Paul 1979, a short and detailed history. Also of use on such developments is Richard Hyman and Robert Price (eds) *The New Working Class? White Collar Workers and their Organisation: A Reader* Macmillan 1983. Other general accounts of white collar unionism in Britain are R Lumley *White Collar Unionism in Britain* Methuen 1973 and Jean Bocock 'The Politics of White Collar Unionisation' *Political Quarterly* 44 1973 pp 294–303. Guy Routh 'United Kingdom' in Adolf Sturmthal (ed) *White Collar Trade Unions: Contemporary Developments in Industrialised Societies* University of Illinois Press, Champaign, Illinois 1966 pp 165–204 is a useful survey which largely pre-dates the rise of white collar militancy.

**4725** B C Roberts *et al Reluctant Militants: A Study of Industrial Technicians* Heinemann 1972. A study of technicians, draughtsmen and other technical unions and their attitudes to industrial relations.

**4726** R Roslender 'Trade Unionism among Scientific Workers in Great Britain 1960–1975' Leeds PhD Thesis 1983. This covers the growth of trade unionism among scientists, engineers and technologists.

**4727** V L Allen and Sheila Williams 'The Growth of Trade Unionism in Banking' *Manchester School of Economic and Social Studies* 28 1960 pp 299–381. The story is traced further in J C Heritage 'The Growth of Trade Unionism in the London Clearing Banks 1960–1970: A Sociological Interpretation' Leeds PhD Thesis 1978. The banks have tended to try and resist unionization amongst their workers. Both they and the building societies have instead provided staff associations. On these see Olive Robinson 'Representation of the White Collar Worker: The Bank Staff Associations in Britain'

*British Journal of Industrial Relations* 7 1969 pp 19–41 and A I R Swabe and Patricia Price 'Building a Permanent Association? The Development of Staff Associations in the Building Societies' *British Journal of Industrial Relations* 22 1984 pp 195–204. In the case of the building societies most of these had only developed in the 1970s.

**4728** Paul Joyce, Paul Corrigan and Mike Hayes *Striking Out: Social Work and Trade Unionism 1970–1985* Macmillan 1988. The first account of the development of trade unionism amongst social workers and its impact on the existing trade unions. It is seen in the context of the explosion of white collar unionism in the 1960s and 1970s and of the growth of the Left in local government.

**4729** K L Jones 'The Growth and Development of White Collar Trade Unionism in the British Steel Industry' London PhD Thesis 1977.

**4730** Peter Seglow *Trade Unionism in Television: A Case Study in the Development of White Collar Militancy* Saxon House 1978. An examination of the traditions of the main BBC and ITV unions and the differing attitudes to industrial relations that result.

(g) Unionism in Particular Industries

**4731** B A Hepple and P O'Higgins *Public Employee Trade Unionism in the United Kingdom* Institute of Labor and Industrial Relations, Detroit, Michigan 1971. This is especially good on the approach of these unions to collective bargaining.

**4732** H A Turner *Trade Union Growth, Structure and Policy: A Comparative Study of the Cotton Unions* Allen and Unwin 1962. A thematic history of the unions in the cotton industry up to the 1950s.

**4733** R D Coates *Teachers Unions and Interest Group Politics: A Study of the Behaviour of Organised Teachers in England and Wales* Cambridge University Press 1972. A useful study of unionism in the teaching profession.

(h) Individual Trade Unions

**4734** M W Nuttal 'The Development of White Collar Trade Unionism in the UK Since 1945, with Particular Reference to the Growth and Character of the North-East Area of the CAWU (now APEX)' Leeds PhD Thesis 1979.

**4735** Jim Sweeney *A History of Trade Unionism in the North Staffordshire Textile Industry Part 2: The Amal-gamated Society of Textile Workers and Kindred Trades 1919–71* Department of Adult Education, University of Keele 1971.

**4736** Larry James *Power in a Trade Union: The Role of the District Committee in the AUEW* Cambridge University Press 1984. There is no general account of the post-war history of the engineering workers' union. This is a somewhat theoretical analysis of the Manchester district of the union. It is useful for the structure of the union, but does not always show a good grasp of history. Edmund and Ruth Frow and Ernie Roberts *Democracy in the Engineering Union* Institute for Workers Control 1982 is a polemic against what they see as the erosion of democracy in the union in recent years. On democracy in the union see also Roger Undy 'The Electoral Influence of the Opposition Party in the AUEW Engineering Section 1960–75' *British Journal of Industrial Relations* 17 1979 pp 19–33. I Bernstein 'The Interpretation of International Affairs by British Trade Union Leaders: A Case Study of the Amalgamated Engineering Union 1945–1951' Edinburgh PhD Thesis 1981 looks at the role of the Cold War in winning the union's support for the Attlee government's economic policies, and not least its imposition of pay restraint.

**4737** H J Fryth and Henry Collins *The Foundry Workers: A Trade Union History* Amalgamated Union of Foundry Workers 1959. An official history 1809–1959. It is quite informative on the post-war period.

**4738** Colin Gill, R S Morris and Jack Eaton 'APST: The Rise of a Professional Union' *Industrial Relations Journal* 8 1977 pp 50–61. A history of the Association of Professional Scientists and Technologists.

**4739** Angela Tuckett *The Blacksmiths' History: What Smithy Workers Gave Trade Unionism* Lawrence and Wishart 1974. A history of the Association of Blacksmiths' Forge and Smithy Workers up to their merger with the Boilermakers in 1961.

**4740** James E Mortimer *A History of the Association of Engineering and Shipbuilding Draughtsmen* the Association 1960. A good institutional history of this union, established in 1913.

**4741** Nonita Glendey and Mary Price *Reluctant Revolutionaries: A Century of Headmistresses 1874–1974* Pitman 1974. A history of the Association of Headmistresses.

**4742** Sandra Turner *Social Class Status and Teacher Trade Unionism: The Case of Public Sector Further and Higher Education* Croom Helm 1988. An analysis of the Association of Polytechnic Teachers and the Association of Teachers in Technical Institutes. A good analysis of the history and difficulties of the latter body, particularly in the context of the circumstances that led to it becoming the first academic union to affiliate to the TUC in 1967 is Ronald E Kowalski 'Professional Association or Teachers' Trade Union: The ATTI and the Question of TUC Affiliation' *Albion* 11 1979 pp 259–73.

**4743** Archie Kleingartner and Evelyn Hunt *Academic Unionism in British Universities* Institute of Industrial Relations, University of California, Los Angeles, California 1986. A study of the Association of University Teachers.

**4744** Malcolm Speirs *One Hundred Years of a Small Trade Union: A History of the Card Setting Machine Tenters' Society* the Society 1972.

**4745** Eric Wigham *From Humble Petition to Militant Action: A History of the Civil and Public Services Association 1903–1978* Civil and Public Services Association 1980. A union covering the lower ranks of the Civil Service which is constantly losing its best members by promotion. It has been increasingly militant since the 1960s.

**4746** Bernard Newman *Yours for Action* Civil Service Clerical Association 1953. A history of its first fifty years.

**4747** Kathleen L Edwards *The Story of the Civil Service Union* Allen and Unwin 1975. A short history from 1917 onwards.

**4748** F Hughes *By Hand and Brain: The Story of the Clerical and Administrative Workers' Union* Lawrence and Wishart 1953.

**4749** Mick Carpenter *Working for Health: The History of COHSE* Lawrence and Wishart 1988. A good history of the Confederation of Health Service Employees since its amalgamation in 1946.

**4750** John Lloyd *Light and Liberty: One Hundred Years of the EETPU* Weidenfeld and Nicolson 1989. A good union history. An earlier history is *The Story of the ETU: The Official History of the Electrical Trades Union* ETU 1953. See also R Bean 'Militancy, Policy Formation and Membership Opposition in the Electrical Trades Union 1945–1961' *Political Quarterly* 36 1965 pp 181–90.

**4751** Joseph McLeod *The Actors Right to Act* Lawrence and Wishart 1981. A history of the actors' union, Equity.

**4752** F H Radford *'Fetch the Engine': The Official History of the Fire Brigade Union* the Union 1951.

**4753** James E Mortimer and Valerie A Ellis *A Professional Union: The Evolution of the Institution of Professional Civil Servants* Allen and Unwin 1980. The official history of the first sixty years of union representation of 100,000 civil servants in the professional and specialist grades. In recent years its history has been marked by affiliation to the TUC, increasing militancy and the struggle to achieve parity of pay with their generalist colleagues. See also Edward Hewlett 'The Institution' *State Service* 43 1963 pp 40–5 and 56–7.

**4754** Sir Arthur Pugh *Men of Steel by One of Them: A Chronicle of Eighty-Eight Years of Trade Unionism in the British Iron and Steel Industry* Iron and Steel Trades Confederation 1951. A semi-autobiographical account by the former union leader.

**4755** Andrew Bullen *The Lancashire Weavers' Union: A Commemorative History* Amalgamated Textile Workers' Union 1984.

**4756** *Progress Report 1909–59: The First Fifty Years in the History of the London County Council Staff Association* the Association 1959.

**4757** National Association of Colliery Overmen, Deputies and Shotfirers *Midland Area 1908–1962: A Short History* J R Rudd 1962.

**4758** Alec Spoor *White Collar Union: Sixty Years of NALGO* Heinemann 1967. A massive history of the National Association of Local Government Officers up until its affiliation to the TUC in 1965. The story is continued by George Newman *Path to Maturity: NALGO 1965–1980* Co-operative Press 1982. For a contemporary comment on its TUC affiliation see D Volker 'NALGO's Affiliation to the TUC' *British Journal of Industrial Relations* 4 1966 pp 59–76. See also T C Barton *A History of the Manchester Municipal Officers Guild (Branch of NALGO) 1906–1956* the Guild 1956.

**4759** John Robert Newman *The NAOP Heritage: A Short Historical Review of the Growth and Development of the National Association of Operative Plasterers 1860–1960* the Association 1960.

**4760** B Morton *Action 1919–1969* National Association of Schoolmasters 1969. A history of the union. See also G Latta 'The NAS: A Historical Analysis' Warwick MA Thesis 1969. For other material of relevance see [4733].

**4761** James Moran *NATSOPA Seventy-Five Years: The National Society of Operative Printers and Assistants 1889–1964* Heinemann 1964.

**4762** Renée Danziger *Political Powerlessness: Agricultural Workers in Post-War England* Manchester University Press 1988. This is not a history of the agricultural workers' union. The only such history to venture into the post-war period is F D Mills 'The National Union of Agricultural Workers' Reading PhD Thesis 1964–5. What Danziger's book does provide is an analysis of the poor industrial bargaining position of the agricultural workers in the post-war period and the failure of the union to improve this position.

**4763** Alan Fox *A History of the National Union of Boot and Shoe Operatives 1874–1957* Blackwell 1958.

**4764** Hew Reid *The Furniture Makers: A History of Trade Unionism in the Furniture Trade 1865–1972* Malthouse Press 1986. An institutional history of the National Union of Furniture Trades Operatives and its predecessors.

**4765** Hugh Armstrong Clegg *General Union in a Changing Society: A Short History of the National Union of General and Municipal Workers 1889–1964* Blackwell 1984. An attractive short history of the transformation of this general union from a fiery organization to an efficient bureaucracy.

**4766** Richard Gurnham *A History of the Trade Union Movement in the Hosiery and Knitwear Industry 1776–1976: The History of the National Union of Hosiery and Knitwear Workers, its Evolution and Predecessors* the Union 1976.

**4767** Clement J Bundock *The National Union of Journalists: A Jubilee History 1907–1957* Oxford University Press 1957. See also Harry Christian 'The Development of Trade Unionism and Professionalism among British Journalists: A Sociological Enquiry' London PhD Thesis 1984.

**4768** Robert G Neville and John Benson 'Labour in the Coalfields' *Bulletin of the Society for the Study of Labour History* 31 1975 pp 45–59. A bibliographical essay on labour and union history in the coalfields. There is no general history of the National Union of Mineworkers in the post-war period. Robin Page Arnot's history of miners' unionism did not get beyond the volume which covers the period up to the nationalization of the industry, *The Miners: One Union, One Industry: A History of the National Union of Mineworkers 1939–46* Allen and Unwin 1979. On the early history of the NUM, which was created from the old Miners' Federation of Great Britain in 1945, see also George B Baldwin 'Structural Reform in the British Miners' Union' *Quarterly Journal of Economics* 67 1953 pp 576–97. Reasons for the revival of militancy in the union in the 1970s are explored in I Rutledge 'Changes in the Mode of Production and the Growth of Mass Militancy in the British Mining

Industry 1954–74' *Science and Society* 41 1977/78 pp 410–29. Analysing the industrial unrest of the 1970s up to the the strikes against pit closures in 1981 V L Allen *The Militancy of British Miners* Moor Press 1981 seeks to explain it in the context of the demoralization of the 1960s in the face of a massive contraction of the industry. This is however a somewhat careless book which should be handled with care. One facet of this increased militancy was the rise of the Left in the union after the strikes of 1972 and 1974. Their subsequent advance is analysed in Adrian Campbell and Malcolm Warner 'Changes in the Balance of Power in the British Mineworkers' Union: An Analysis of National Top-Office Elections 1974–84' *British Journal of Industrial Relations* 23 1985 pp 1–24. Another general study of the union is M J Ball 'The Miners and Politics: A Sociological Case Study' Hull MA Thesis 1976. In addition there are a number of studies of unionism in particular coalfields. Andrew Taylor *The Politics of the Yorkshire Miners* Croom Helm 1984 traces the internal politics of the Yorkshire NUM from 1945 to the triumph of the Left after 1972. W R Garside *The Durham Miners 1919–1960* Allen and Unwin 1971 is a good study of the union in a declining coalfield. So is Raymond Challinor *The Lancashire and Cheshire Miners* Graham 1972. David Howell *The Politics of the NUM: A Lancashire View* Manchester University Press 1989 is a study of the NUM in the North West region during and after the 1984–5 strike. A R Griffin *The Nottinghamshire Coalfield 1881–1981: A Century of Progress* Moorland Publishing 1981 is a pictorial centenary history of the Nottinghamshire miners. James Eccles Williams *The Derbyshire Miners: A Study in Industrial and Social History* Allen and Unwin 1962 has no more than an epilogue on the post-war period. This can however be supplemented by Cliff Williams *The Derbyshire Miners 1880–1980: A Pictorial History* Derbyshire NUM 1980.

**4769** Clement J Bundock *The Story of the National Union of Printing, Bookbinding and Paper Workers* Oxford University Press 1959. This is of limited value for the post-war years.

**4770** R Fryer, A Fairclough and T Manson *Organisation and Change in NUPE* National Union of Public Employees 1974.

**4770A** Philip S Bagwell *The Railwaymen: The History of the National Union of Railwaymen* Allen and Unwin 1963. A very highly regarded official union history. It covers from 1830 to the Beeching Report. Its high quality is maintained in his *The Railwaymen Volume 2: The Beeching Era and After: The History of the National Union of Railwaymen* Allen and Unwin 1982. See also A E Grigg *In Railway Service: The History of the Bletchley Branch of the National Union of Railwaymen* the Branch 1972.

**4771** Ted Brake *Men of Good Character* Lawrence and Wishart 1985. A profusely illustrated official history of the National Union of Sheet Metal Workers, Coppersmiths, Heating and Domestic Engineers.

**4772** Margaret Stewart and Leslie Hunter *The Needle is Threaded: The History of an Industry* Heinemann 1964. A history of the National Union of Tailors and Garment Workers.

**4773** W Roy *The Teachers' Union* Schoolmaster Press 1968. An account of the National Union of Teachers. See also Ken Jones 'The National Union of Teachers (England and Wales)' in Martin Lewin (ed) *The Politics of Teacher Unionism: International Perspectives* Croom Helm 1985 pp 279–301. Roger V Seifert 'Some Aspects of Factional Opposition: Rank and File and the National Union of Teachers 1967–1982' *British Journal of Industrial Relations* 22 1984 pp 372–90 is a study of Rank and File Teachers, a Trotskyite faction within the union. See also [4733].

**4774** J O French *Plumbers in Unity: History of the Plumbing Trades Union 1865–1965* the Union 1965. See also [4750].

**4775** Frank Bealey *The Post Office Engineering Union: The History of the Post Office Engineers 1870–1970* Bachman and Turner 1976. See also J Golding *75 Years: A Short History of the Post Office Engineering Union* the Union 1962.

**4776** Frank Burchill and Richard Ross *A History of the Potters, Ceramic and Allied Trades' Union* the Union 1977. A useful analysis of the union from the early nineteenth century to the 1970s.

**4777** P A Walley 'A Storm from Liverpool: British Seaman and their Union 1920–1970' Liverpool PhD Thesis 1985. This traces the history of the union and the decline of consensual industrial relations which paralleled the decline of the industry.

**4778** David Dougan *The Shipwrights: The History of the Shipconstructors and Shipwrights Association 1882–1963* Graham 1975.

**4779** Greg Bamber *Militant Managers? Managerial Unionism and Industrial Relations* Gower 1986. A study of the origins and growth of the Steel Industrial Management Association from 1949 onwards. It includes a chronology and a useful bibliography.

**4780** Chris Smith *Technical Workers: Class, Labour and Trade Unionism* Macmillan 1987. An analysis of trade unionism amongst technical workers based on research at a British Aerospace factory in Bristol. It incorporates a post-war history of TASS and a bibliography.

**4781** Joseph Goldstein *The Government of British Trade Unions* Allen and Unwin 1952. A study of the Transport and General Workers' Union exaggerating the power of small minorities within it. On the TGWU see also Roger Undy 'The Devolution of Bargaining Levels and Responsibilities in the Transport and General Workers' Union 1965–1975' *Industrial Relations Journal* 9 1978 pp 44–56. See also [4303].

**4782** Leslie W Wood *A Union to Build: The Story of UCATT* Lawrence and Wishart 1979. The history of the construction workers' union. W S Hilton *Foes to Tyranny: A History of the Amalgamated Union of Building Trade Workers* the Union 1963 is a history of one of its predecessor organizations.

**4783** Alan Clinton *Post Office Workers: A Trade Union and Social History* Allen and Unwin 1984. A history from the 1840s. See also Michael Moran *The Union of Post Office Workers: A Study in Political Sociology* Macmillan 1974.

**4784** Sir William Richardson *A Union of Many Trades: The History of USDAW* Union of Shop, Distribution and Allied Workers 1979. USDAW was formed by the merger of two unions in 1946. This useful history traces its story up to the 1970s.

**4785** Linda Dickens 'UKAPE: A Study of a Professional Union' *Industrial Relations Journal* 3/3 1972 pp 2–16. A study of the United Kingdom Association of Professional Engineers, founded in 1969.

**4786** Harry Hignett *The History of the United Kingdom Pilots Association* the Association 1984.

(i) Memoirs and Biographies

**4787** Olga Cannon and J R L Anderson *The Road From Wigan Pier: A Biography of Les Cannon* Gollancz 1973. Cannon was General Secretary of the Electrical, Electronic, Telecommunications and Plumbing Union and began the fight against Communist influence in the union.

**4788** Frank Chapple *Sparks Fly* Michael Joseph 1984. The autobiography of Cannon's successor as leader of the Electrical, Electronic, Telecommunication and Plumbing Union 1966–84. This is largely concerned with the continuing fight against the Communists.

**4789** Geoffrey Goodman *The Awkward Warrior: Frank Cousins: His Life and Times* Spokesman 1984. A good biography of the General Secretary of the TGWU 1956–69. Cousins also served as Minister of Technology 1964–66. See also 'Frank Cousins "Face to Face": Interview with John Freeman on BBC Television' *The Listener* 66 1961 pp 637–41.

**4790** Jack Dash *Good Morning Brothers!* Lawrence and Wishart 1969. The autobiography of the leader of the London dockers in the 1967 strike. Dash was an official in the TGWU and a life-long member of the Communist Party.

**4791** V L Allen *Trade Union Leadership: Based on a Study of Arthur Deakin* Longmans 1957. This is not a biography of Arthur Deakin but a study of the power and influence of trade union leaders in the context of a study of the leader of the most powerful union, the TGWU. An informative study.

**4792** Eric Silver *Victor Feather TUC* Gollancz 1973. Feather was Assistant General Secretary of the TUC 1960–9, and General Secretary 1969–73.

**4793** Joe Gormley *Battered Cherub* Hamilton 1982. The autobiography of the President of the NUM 1971–82.

**4794** Sir Ronald Gould *Chalk up the Memory* George Philip Alexander 1976. An autobiography. Gould was the General Secretary of the National Union of Teachers 1947–70.

**4795** William W Craik *Sydney Hill and the National Union of Public Employees* Allen and Unwin 1968. A biographical study of Hill, who was General Secretary of NUPE 1962–8.

**4796** Arthur Horner *Incorrigible Rebel* Lawrence and Wishart 1960. Horner was General Secretary of the NUM 1946–59.

**4797** Jack Jones *Union Man: The Autobiography of Jack Jones* Collins 1986. A good autobiography by the leader of the TGWU 1969–78 during the difficult corporatist years of the 1970s.

**4798** J F Clarke 'An Interview with Sir William Lawther' *Bulletin of the Society for the Study of Labour History* 19 1969 pp 14–21. This concentrates on Lawther's inter-war career. Lawther was the first post-war President of the NUM. See also Robin Smith 'Sir William Lawther 1889–1976: Obituary Article' *North East Group for the Study of Labour History Bulletin* 10 1976 pp 27–33.

**4799** Peggy Kahn 'Tommy Mullany' *Bulletin of the Society for the Study of Labour History* 44 1982 pp 49–58. An interview with a member of the executive of

the Yorkshire NUM. It is supported with good notes and biographical sketches.

**4800** Will Paynter *My Generation* Allen and Unwin 1972. The autobiography of the General Secretary of the NUM 1959–68. Hywel Francis 'Tribute to Will Paynter (1903–1984)' *Llafur* 4/2 1985 pp 4–9 is an obituary tribute both to his work for the NUM and the Communist Party.

**4801** For Wesley Perrins see [751].

**4802** William W Craik *Bryn Roberts and the National Union of Public Employees* Allen and Unwin 1955. A biography of the General Secretary of NUPE 1935–62.

**4803** 'The Role of Militancy: Interview with Hugh Scanlon' *New Left Review* 46 1967 pp 3–15. As President of the Amalgamated Union of Engineering Workers 1968–78 Scanlon was subsequently one of the most powerful union leaders at the height of union power.

**4804** Michael Crick *Scargill and the Miners* Penguin 1985. A well regarded biographical study of Arthur Scargill, the militant President of the NUM since 1981, and of the rise of the Left in the union. Scargill played a leading role in the mining disputes of 1972 and 1974, on which he comments in his 'The New Unionism' *New Left Review* 92 1975 pp 3–33.

**4805** Bill Sirs *Hard Labour* Sidgwick and Jackson 1985. Memoirs of the leader of the Iron and Steel Trades Confederation 1975–85.

**4806** Sidney Weighell *On the Rails* Orbis 1983. Weighell was General Secretary of the National Union of Railwaymen 1975–83. See also his *A Hundred Years of Railway: Three Generations of a Railway Family* Robson 1984.

### (5) Professional Associations

Other relevant material can be found in the sections on accountancy and insurance.

**4807** Kenneth Prandy *Professional Employees: A Study of Scientists and Engineers* Faber 1965. A sociological study of professional associations and trade unions and their members. See also Roy Lewis and Angus Maude *Professional People* Phoenix House 1952.

**4808** Robert Trow-Smith *Power on the Land: A Centenary History of the Agricultural Engineers Association 1875–1975* Agripress Publicity Ltd 1975.

**4809** Association of Consulting Engineers *Fifty Years 1913–63* Newman Neame 1963.

**4810** *The Chartered Institute of Secretaries 1891–1951: A Review of Sixty Years* Chartered Institute of Secretaries 1951.

**4811** Graham D Clifford (ed) *A 20th Century Professional Institution: The Story of the Brit IRE* Council of the British Institute of Radio Engineers 1960. A history from its establishment in 1925.

**4812** Rowland Caplan 'A Short History of the Institute of Engineering Inspection' *Quality Engineer* 33 1969 pp 5–20.

**4813** E S Cox 'The History of the Institute of Locomotive Engineers: The Ten Years to the Golden Jubilee' *Institute of Locomotive Engineers Journal* 50 1960/61 pp 682–6.

**4814** B C Curling *History of the Institute of Marine Engineers* Institute of Marine Engineers 1961.

**4815** J Garth Watson *The Civils: The Story of the Institution of Civil Engineers* Telford 1988. A good institutional history.

**4816** William Joseph Reader *A History of the Institution of Electrical Engineers* Peregrinus 1987. An excellent history.

**4817** W T G Braunholtz *The Institution of Gas Engineers: The First Hundred Years 1863–1963* Institution of Gas Engineers 1963.

**4818** L T C Rolt *The Mechanicals: Progress of a Profession* Heinemann 1967. A history of the Institution of Mechanical Engineers.

**4819** K C Barnaby *The Institution of Naval Architects 1860–1960* Allen and Unwin 1960.

**4820** O S Nock *Fifty Years of Railway Signalling* Ian Allan 1962. A history of the Institution of Railway Signal Engineers.

**4821** J F Clarke *A Century of Service to Engineering and Shipbuilding* North East Coast Institution of Engineers and Shipbuilders 1985.

### (6) Pay and Hours

**4822** *Time Rates of Wages and Hours of Work* HMSO 1946–. A through collection of data on the previous year's agreements. It is updated monthly by *Changes in Rates of Wages and Hours of Work*.

**4823** R F Elliott and H C Shelton 'A Wage Settlement Index for the United Kingdom 1950–1975' *Bulletin of Oxford University Institute of Economics and Statistics* 40 1978 pp 303–19. See also Ely Devons, J R Crossley and W F Maunder 'Wage Rate Indexes by Industry 1948–1965' *Economica* n.s. 35 1968 pp 392–423.

**4824** Roger Tarling and Frank Wilkinson 'Changes in the Inter-Industry Structure of Earnings in the Post-War Period' *Cambridge Journal of Economics* 6 1982 pp 231–48. See also David Newlands and Andrew Tylecote *The Causes of Changes in Relative Earnings among UK Industries 1959–1975* Department of Political Economy, University of Aberdeen 1981, P Haddy and R E Currell 'British Inter-Industrial Earnings Differentials 1924–55' *Economic Journal* 68 1958 pp 104–11 and J C Shapiro 'Inter-Industry Wage Determination: The Post-War United Kingdom Experience' London PhD Thesis 1965–6.

**4825** R Penn 'The Course of Wage Differentials Between Skilled and Non-Skilled Manual Workers in Britain Between 1856 and 1964' *British Journal of Industrial Relations* 21 1983 pp 69–90.

**4826** A J H Dean 'Earnings in the Public and Private Sectors 1950–1975' *National Institute Economic Review* 74 1975 pp 60–70. A comparison of pay relativities.

**4827** R J Apps 'Wage Inflation and Labour Market Behaviour in the UK 1950–1975' Manchester PhD Thesis 1982. A study of the factors causing wage inflation. Over the post-war period views on the determinants have shifted from emphasizing demand/supply factors (as identified in the Phillips curve [2948]) to stressing the real income aspirations of unions and workers. The unions' role is examined in Brian Burkitt and David Bowers 'Wage Inflation and Union Power in the United Kingdom 1949–1967' *Applied Economics* 8 1976 pp 289–300 and A G Hines 'Trade Unions and Wage Inflation in the United Kingdom 1893–1961' *Review of Economic Studies* 31 1964 pp 221–52. Unemployment as a factor is examined in R L Thomas and P J M Stoney 'Unemployment Dispersion as a Determinant of Wage Inflation in the UK 1925–1966' *Manchester School of Economic and Social Studies* 39 1971 pp 83–116. See also L A Dicks-Mireaux and J C R Dow 'The Determinants of Wage Inflation: United Kingdom 1946–1956' *Royal Statistical Society Journal* series A, 122 1959 pp 145–84.

**4828** P B Beaumont 'Experience under the Fair Wages Resolution of 1946' *Industrial Relations Journal* 8 1977 pp 34–42.

**4829** F J Bayliss *British Wages Councils* Blackwell 1962. A history and study of the contemporary situation. These councils, each covering a particular industry, were for the protection of the low paid. See also Christine Craig, Jill Rubery, Roger Tarling and Frank Wilkinson *Abolition and After: The Cutlery Wages Council* HMSO 1980. The same authors have produced *Abolition and After: The Jute Wages Council* HMSO 1980 and *Abolition and After: The Paper Box Wages Council* HMSO 1980.

**4830** Colin Duncan *Low Pay: Its Causes and the Post-War Trade Union Response* Wiley 1981. This seeks to provide a detailed study of low pay, its causes and relationship to the level of poverty, and of the trade union response since 1945. The role of incomes policy is also examined.

**4831** John L Fullick 'The Growth of Top Salaries in the Post-War Period' *Industrial Relations Journal* 8 1977 pp 4–13.

**4832** David Marden 'Youth Pay Compared with France and FR Germany Since 1966' *British Journal of Industrial Relations* 23 1985 pp 399–414.

**4833** E H Phelps Brown and Margaret H Browne 'Earnings in Industries of the United Kingdom 1948–1959' *Economic Journal* 72 1962 pp 517–49. See also K G J C Knowles and E M F Thorne 'Wage Rounds 1948–1959' *Bulletin of Oxford University Institute of Economics and Statistics* 23 1961 pp 1–26 and R K Wilkinson 'Differences in Earnings and Changes in the Distribution of Manpower in the UK 1948–1957' *Yorkshire Bulletin of Economic and Social Research* 14 1962 pp 46–57.

**4834** Leslie Godfrey and Jim Taylor 'Earnings Changes in the United Kingdom 1954–1970: Excess Labour Supply, Exported Inflation and Union Influence' *Bulletin of Oxford University Institute of Economics and Statistics* 35 1973 pp 197–216. On earnings in the 1960s see P E Hart 'The Dynamics of Earnings 1963–1973' *Economic Journal* 86 1976 pp 551–65 and George Zis 'The 1969–70 Wage Explosion in the United Kingdom' *National Westminster Bank Quarterly Review* Feb 1978 pp 55–64.

**4835** Trevor Noble 'Inflation and Earning Relativities in Britain After 1970' *British Journal of Sociology* 36 1985 pp 238–58. Relativities and inflation were key issues in the 1970s.

**4836** A Bowey *et al Effects of Incentive Payments Systems: United Kingdom 1977–80* Department of Employment Research Paper 36, HMSO 1982.

**4837** R F Elliott and J L Fullick *Pay in the Public Sector* Macmillan 1981. A study focusing on the period 1951–75. This does not supersede Hilda R Kahn *Salaries in the Public Services in England and Wales* Allen and Unwin 1962. This is an exhaustive, sector-by-sector study.

**4838** P J Lund *et al Wages and Employment in Agriculture: England and Wales 1960–80* Ministry of Agriculture, Fisheries and Food 1983. The low pay and status of agricultural workers is examined in S Winyard *Cold Comfort Farm: A Study of Farmworkers and Low Pay* Low Pay Unit 1982. See also E Mejer *Agricultural Labour in England and Wales Part 2: Farm Workers' Earnings 1917–51* School of Agriculture, University of Nottingham 1951.

**4839** R A Hart and D I Mackay 'Engineering Earnings in Britain 1914–1968' *Journal of the Royal Statistics Society* series A, 138 1975 pp 32–50.

**4840** Alan A Carruth and Andrew J Oswald 'Miners' Wages in Post-War Britain: An Application of a Model of Trade Union Behaviour' *Economic Journal* 95 1985 pp 1003–21. See also K J W Alexander 'Wages in Coalmining Since Nationalisation' *Oxford Economic Papers* n.s. 8 1956 pp 164–80 and M Barratt Brown 'Determinants of the Structure and Levels of Wages in the Coal Mining Industry Since 1956' *Bulletin of Oxford University Institute of Economics and Statistics* 29 1967 pp 139–70.

### (7) Working Conditions

**4841** *Health and Safety Statistics* HMSO 1977–. An annual statistical guide on accidents at work.

**4842** Grenville Janner *Janner's Compendium of Health and Safety Law* 3rd ed, Business Books 1982. A comprehensive guide to the law on health and safety at work. *Encyclopaedia of Factories, Shops and Offices: Law and Practice* Sweet and Maxwell 1962– (which has been entitled *The Encyclopaedia of Health and Safety at Work: Law and Practice* since 1978) is a looseleaf guide with updated inserts. Possibly the most useful textbook on the subject, from the historian's point of view, is C D Drake and F B Wright *Law of Health and Safety at Work: The New Approaches* Sweet and Maxwell 1983. This includes statistics on prosecutions and pays attention to famous accidents.

**4843** *Her Majesty's Inspectors of Factories 1833–1983: Essays to Commemorate 150 Years of Health and Safety Inspection* HMSO 1983. This includes quite a lot on aspects of work in recent years, including case studies.

**4844** P W J Bartrip *Workman's Compensation in Twentieth Century Britain: Law, History and Social Policy* Gower 1987.

**4845** 'The Development of Factory Safety Legislation' *British Journal of Industrial Safety* 6 1963 pp 27–33.

**4846** D J Turner-Samuels 'Industrial Injuries Acts 1946–1948' *Industrial Law Journal* 6 1952 pp 266–78.

**4847** *Health, Wealth and Safety in Non-Industrial Employment: Hours of Employment of Juveniles: Report of the Committee of Inquiry* Cmnd 7664, *Parliamentary Papers* xv 1948–49. The report of the committee chaired by Sir Ernest Gowers.

**4848** *Safety and Health at Work: Report of the Committee 1970–72* Cmnd 5034, *Parliamentary Papers* xii 1971–72. This report, by the committee chaired by Lord Robens, led to the 1974 Health and Safety at Work Act and the establishment of the Health and Safety at Work Executive. Union attitudes to safety at work before and after the 1974 Act are discussed in P B Beaumont *Safety at Work and the Unions* Croom Helm 1983.

**4849** *Industrial Health Services: Report of the Committee of Enquiry* Cmnd 8170, *Parliamentary Papers* xv 1950–51. The report of the committee chaired by Edgar T Dale. The history of industrial health services up to the Dale Committee is traced in Irene H Charley *The Birth of Industrial Nursing: Its History and Development in Great Britain* Baillière Tindall and Cox 1954.

## (8) Unemployment

**4850** J Micklewright *A Selective Bibliography of Recent Research on Unemployment in Britain* Unemployment Project Working Note 7, Department of Health and Social Security 1981.

**4851** Brian Showler and Adrian Sinfield (ed) *The Workless State: Studies in Unemployment* Robertson 1981. A collection of essays on unemployment and policies to deal with it since 1945, concentrating particularly on the 1970s. Unemployment since the war and the factors that have created it are analysed in Martyn Andrews and Stephen Nickell *Unemployment in the United Kingdom Since the War* Centre for Labour Economics Discussion Paper 102, London School of Economics, University of London 1982. See also A S Fowkes 'Structural Unemployment and Employers' Labour Requirements in Great Britain 1952/1971' Leeds PhD Thesis 1978, P N Junankar 'Econometric Analysis of Unemployment in Great Britain 1952–1975' *Oxford Economic Papers* 33 1981 pp 387–400 and John Salt 'Post-War

Unemployment in Britain: Some Basic Considerations' *Transactions of the Institute of British Geographers* 46 1969 pp 93–104.

**4852** B Crick (ed) *Unemployment* Methuen 1981. A collection of essays reprinted from the *Political Quarterly* on unemployment policy, the impact of unemployment, youth unemployment and regional patterns of unemployment.

**4853** W R Garside *The Measurement of Unemployment: Methods and Sources in Great Britain 1850–1979* Blackwell 1980. A good discussion of the nature and sources of unemployment statistics. The measurement of unemployment is also examined in G D N Worswick (ed) *The Concept and Measurement of Involuntary Unemployment* Allen and Unwin 1976, P A Hildreth 'The Measurement of British Unemployment: A Study of the Theory and Empirical Evidence Relating to the Recent Criticism of the Official Unemployment Statistics' Wales MSc (Econ) Thesis 1977 and J K Bowers 'Unemployment Statistics 1966–1970: A Note' *British Journal of Industrial Relations* 9 1973 pp 286–96. Nothing substantial has, as yet, been written on the changes in the measurement of unemployment introduced under the Thatcher government.

**4854** T F Cripps and Roger Tarling 'An Analysis of the Duration of Male Unemployment in Great Britain 1932–1973' *Economic Journal* 84 1974 pp 289–316.

**4855** J L Baxter 'Long-Term Unemployment in Great Britain 1953–1971' *Bulletin of Oxford University Institute of Economics and Statistics* 34 1972 pp 329–44.

**4856** Graham Smith, Linda S Keates, Andrew Rix and Pauline Beresford *Youth Unemployment and Special Measures: An Annotated Bibliography (Revised and Updated January 1983)* Manpower Services Commission 1983. An informative bibliography covering writings on the subject since the 1940s. Peter E Hart *Youth Unemployment in Great Britain* Cambridge University Press 1988 is a history of youth unemployment and youth unemployment policy since the 1930s. T L Rees and P Atkinson (eds) *Youth Unemployment and State Intervention* Routledge and Kegan Paul 1982 is a collection of essays on youth unemployment and related issues such as education, the response of the unions and the development of special training programmes. On youth unemployment in the 1970s see J Payne and C Payne 'Youth Unemployment 1974–81: The Changing Importance of Age and Qualifications' *Quarterly Journal of Social Affairs* 1 1985 pp 177–92.

**4857** I F McMaster 'The Industrial and Regional Adjustment of Wages and Employment, UK 1961–1982' London PhD Thesis 1985. In this thesis McMaster argues that the market acts very slowly to remove inter-regional variations in unemployment and that active intervention is required for the purpose. The regional pattern of unemployment is also examined in Frank P R Brechling 'Trends and Cycles in British Regional Unemployment' *Oxford Economic Papers* n.s. 19 1967 pp 59–74, C P Harris and A P Thirlwall 'Inter- Regional Variations in Cyclical Sensitivity to Unemployment in the UK 1949–1964' *Bulletin of Oxford University Institute of Economics and Statistics* 31 1968 pp 55–66 and J Taylor 'A Regional Analysis of Hidden Unemployment in Great Britain 1951–1966' *Applied Economics* 3 1971 pp 291–303. The contrast between areas of recession and high unemployment and those of relative prosperity was already being drawn in F W Paish 'The Two Britains' *The Banker* 114 1964 pp 88–98, on regional differences in unemployment. On these regional variations see also Keith Cowley and David Metcalf 'Wage- Unemployment Relationships: A Regional Analysis for the UK 1960–1965' *Bulletin of Oxford University Institute of Economics and Statistics* 29 1967 pp 31–9 and A R Townsend 'Recession and the Regions in Great Britain 1976–1980: Analyses of Redundancy Data' *Environment and Planning A* 14 1982 pp 1389–1404. This latter focuses particularly on Wales, the West Midlands and the North West.

**4858** C Jenkins and B Sherman *The Collapse of Work* Eyre and Methuen 1979. A study of the impact of new technology and automation on the growth in unemployment. The impact of new technology on the labour market and the responses in terms of the growth of work-sharing and re-training is also examined in D A Bell *Unemployment in the Age of Drastic Change: The Future with Robots* Abacus Press 1984.

**4859** Penny Farmer (ed) *The Social and Economic Impact of Unemployment 1979–1985: A Select Bibliography* Technicals Communications 1985. A classified guide to the material covering the social and psychological impact of this period of high unemployment. Another short bibliography is Lesley Grayson (ed) *Unemployment and Health: A Review of the Literature 1979–1986* Technical Communications 1986. The impact on family life and health is studied in L Fagin and M Little *The Forsaken Families: The Effects of Unemployment on Contemporary British Life* Penguin 1984. See also D Marsden *Workless: Some Unemployed Men and Their Families* 2nd ed, Croom Helm 1981, which is based on detailed interviews with unemployed men and their families. L Burghes and R Lister (eds) *Unemployment: Who Pays the Price* Child Poverty Action Group 1981 is a collection of essays on the extent and the distribution of unemployment, its social effects, its causes, the government reaction and the government's attitudes to benefit claimants.

**4860** D Gujarati 'The Behaviour of Unemployment and Unfilled Vacancies: Great Britain 1958–1971' *Economic Journal* 82 1972 pp 195–204. There is a reply to this by J Taylor 'The Behaviour of Unemployment and Unfilled Vacancies: Great Britain 1958–1971: An Alternative View' *Economic Journal* 82 1972 pp 1352–65. The question is also addressed in R A Bewley 'The Dynamic Behaviour of Unemployment and Unfilled Vacancies in Great Britain 1958–1971' *Applied Economics* 11 1979 pp 303–8. See also Alan Evans 'Notes on the Changing Relationship Between Registered Unemployment and Notified Vacancies 1961–1966 and 1966–1971' *Economica* 44 1977 pp 179–96.

**4861** Nicholas Bosanquet and Guy Standing 'Government and Unemployment 1966–1970: A Study of Policy and Evidence' *British Journal of Industrial Relations* 10 1972 pp 180–92.

**4862** Frank Field (ed) *The Conscript Army: A Study of Britain's Unemployed* Routledge and Kegan Paul 1977. An analysis of unemployment in the 1970s. The measurement of unemployment is criticized and the government response to unemployment assessed. There is a case study of unemployment in Liverpool. A survey of unemployment in the 1970s, well stocked with statistics, is W W Daniel *A National Survey of the Unemployed* Political and Economic Planning 1974. The reasons for the increase in unemployment in the 1970s are analysed in David Metcalf 'Unemployment: History, Incidence and Prospects' *Policy and Politics* 8 1980 pp 21–37. The geography of job losses in the recession of the late 1970s is assessed in A R Townsend 'Geographical Perspectives on Major Job Losses in the UK 1977–80' *Area* 13 1984 pp 31–8. The government response to unemployment since 1970 is examined in Jeremy Moon 'The Responses of British Governments to Unemployment' in Jeremy J Richardson and Roger Henning (eds) *Unemployment: Policy Responses of Western Democracies* Sage 1984 pp 15–39. On government policy see also D A Lovett 'Unemployment and Public Policy in Britain 1970–1976' London MPhil Thesis 1978. Lovett has also assessed the role of the class structure, the labour market and government policy in the unemployment of the 1970s in his *Unemployment and Class Conflict in Britain During the 1970s Town Planning* Discussion Paper 35, University College, London 1980. The unemployment of the 1970s is compared with that of the 1930s in Keith Middlemas 'Unemployment: The Past and Future of a Political Problem' *Political Quarterly* 51 1980 pp 464–80 and P D Travers 'The Experience of Unemployment in the 1930s and the 1970s' Oxford MPhil Thesis 1981.

**4863** Sheila Allen, Alan Watson, Kate Purcell and Stephen Wood (eds) *The Experience of Unemployment* Macmillan 1986. A collection of essays on the effect of unemployment, the interpretation of unemployment in the media, female unemployment, youth and Asian youth unemployment, rural unemployment and re-training in the 1980s. Alan Gordon *The Crisis of Unemployment* Christopher Helm 1988 is a textbook on unemployment in the 1980s. The determinants and geography of the job losses of the recession of the late 1970s and early 1980s are analysed in Doreen Massey and Richard Meegan *The Anatomy of Job Loss: The How, Why and Where of Employment Decline* Methuen 1982. This includes a number of case studies. The impact of this recession is examined in R Taylor *Workers and the New Depression* Macmillan 1982. The range of measures adopted by the Thatcher government to try and reduce unemployment and their massaging of the unemployment statistics is assessed in Jeremy J Richardson and Jeremy Moon 'The Politics of Unemployment in Britain' *Political Quarterly* 55 1984 pp 29–37. The various job creation schemes of the Thatcher government are also assessed in Jeremy Moon 'Policy Change in Direct Government Responses to United Kingdom Unemployment' *Journal of Public Policy* 3 1983 pp 301–30. On the public response and public assistance to the unemployed see A A McArthur 'Public Responses to the Growth of Unemployment in the United Kingdom, with Particular Reference to Action at the Local Scale' Glasgow PhD Thesis 1984.

**4864** A Barker, P Lewis and M McCann 'Trade Unions and the Organisation of the Unemployed' *British Journal of Industrial Relations* 22 1984 pp 391–404. A study of the trade union response to the mass unemployment of the 1980s.

**4865** Jeremy Moon and Jeremy J Richardson 'The Unemployment Industry' *Policy and Politics* 12 1984 pp 391–411. A study of the emergence of business, trade union, voluntary and research groups connected with the unemployment issue and their role in influencing and implementing government policy.

**4866** Jeremy Seabrook *Unemployment* Quartet 1982. A humane portrait of the mass unemployment of the early 1980s largely told in their own words by his interviewees. His images of people's experiences were largely drawn from interviewing in Birmingham, Sunderland and Bolton.

**4867** M J Hill, R M Harrison, A V Sargeant and V Talbot *Men Out Of Work: A Study of Unemployment in Three English Towns* Cambridge University Press 1973. A sociological study of unemployment in the early 1970s in Hammersmith, Coventry and Newcastle-upon-Tyne.

**4868** Roy Gregory 'The Local Government Response to Unemployment in the UK' in Jeremy J Richardson and Roger Henning (eds) *Unemployment: Policy Responses of Western Democracies* Sage 1984 pp 40–56. This is largely a case study of Hounslow.

**4869** Brian Showler 'An Analysis of the Characteristics of Adult Unemployment in the Sub-Region of Humberside Since 1951' Hull MSc Thesis 1968–9.

**4870** J J Oakeshott *Unemployment in London* Greater London Council 1975. Statistics and a report on the differences between unemployment in London and the rest of the South East in 1971–4.

**4871** John Salt 'A Consideration of some Post-War Unemployment Problems in the Merseyside and Manchester Conurbations' Liverpool PhD Thesis 1966–7. Unemployment and its consequences on Merseyside is also discussed in F F Ridley 'View from a Disaster Area: Unemployed Youth in Merseyside' *Political Quarterly* 52 1981 pp 16–27.

**4872** M Jones *Life on the Dole* David-Poynter 1972. A case study of unemployment in Merthyr Tydfil.

**4873** Ben Pimlott 'Unemployment and the Unemployed in North East England' *Political Quarterly* 56 1985 pp 346–60.

## (9) Training

The education system has always figured strongly in training policy. For material on education and training the literature in the section on Education should also be consulted, particularly that dealing with Technical Education.

**4874** *The Industrial Training Yearbook* Kogan Page 1967/68–1972. Continued as *Personnel and Training Management Yearbook and Directory* Kogan Page 1973–. A directory which includes chapters on current personnel and training issues.

**4875** B O Pettman *The Industrial Training Act and the Work of the Industrial Training Boards: A Selective and Annotated Bibliography* Institute of Scientific Business 1978. A bibliography that focuses on the arguments leading to the 1964 Industrial Training Act and its consequences. It also covers training legislation since 1935. Short historical notes and informative appendices are provided.

**4876** John Sheldrake and Sarah Vickerstaff *The History of Industrial Training in Britain* Avebury 1987. See also E A Taylor 'A Critical Examination of the Post-War Education Problems Within Industry' Leicester PhD Thesis 1960–1 and A J Redpath 'Corporatism and Planning: The Evolution of British Industrial Training Policy' London MPhil Thesis 1982. R Entwistle 'Industrial Training Policy: A Study of Influences on Government Intervention 1958–62' Manchester MA (Econ) Thesis

1964 studies government intervention 1914–62 particularly in the context of the changes in attitudes taking place in 1958–62. The progress of the Industrial Training Service set up in this period is reviewed in P Meade 'Industrial Training Twenty Years On' *Personnel Management* 12 1980 pp 32–6.

**4877** S J Prais *et al Productivity, Education and Training: Britain and Other Countries* National Institute of Economic and Social Research 1989. This collects research on Britain's comparatively poor record on training and its macroeconomic effects.

**4877A** J Lang *City and Guilds of London Institute Centenary 1878–1978: An Historical Commentary* City and Guilds Institute 1978. A history of the training validating body.

**4878** E Donnelly 'Tomorrow's Industrial Training Officer – The Challenge of Change' *Journal of European Industrial Training* 39 1985 pp 1–36. This examines the role of the training officer before the 1964 Industrial Training Act, the effects of the Act, and the areas of concern in the 1980s.

**4879** *Central Training Council: Report to the Minister* HMSO 1965. The Council was set up under the 1964 Industrial Training Act. This report was periodically followed by others, generally at two year intervals, until the Council was superseded.

**4880** G T Page *The Industrial Training Act and After* Deutsch 1967. A useful assessment of the 1964 Act. *Industrial Training Since the 1964 Industrial Training Act: Report of a Conference of Trade Union Members of Industrial Training Boards* Trade Union Congress 1969 is a discussion of the establishment, composition and financial operation of the boards, the objectives and achievements of the Act and the Central Training Council and its objectives. The impact of the Act in a particular industry is assessed in Keith Hartley and Peter Mancini 'The Industrial Training Act and the Hotel and Catering Industry: A Case Study' *Industrial Relations Journal* 4/2 1973 pp 37–44. On the Act itself see P J C Perry 'The Industrial Training Act 1964: Its Origins, Purposes, Provisions and Effects' London PhD Thesis 1976 and J Haigh 'The State Provision of Education and Training: The Industrial Training Act 1964 and the Concept of Apprenticeship' London MA Thesis 1970–1. On the impact of the Act in particular areas of training or in the different regions of the country see W J Giles 'A Critical Assessment of the Initial Impact of the Industrial Training Act 1964 on Selected Industrial Training Schemes' Nottingham MA Thesis 1968–9, W T Hamilton 'Innovation and Change in Further Education: The Influence of the 1964 Industrial Training Act' Loughborough MSc Thesis 1977, R Winders 'The Industrial Training Act 1964: Sunderland a Sample Study'

Durham MEd Thesis 1969–70 and B O Pettman 'The Industrial Training Act 1964: A Review of Progress and Discussion of Several Sub-Optimal Results, with Particular Reference to Small Engineering Firms in the London Area' City PhD Thesis 1970–1.

**4881** *Manpower Services Commission: Annual Report* Manpower Services Commission 1974–. The growth and evolution of the MSC is traced in David J Howells 'Manpower Services Commission: The First Five Years' *Public Administration* 58 1980 pp 305–32. See also R Grover *et al Work and the Community: A Report on the Manpower Services Commission's Programmes for the Unemployed* Bedford Square Press 1980, T Keller 'The Manpower Services Commission: Ideology, Policy and Politics Concerning Unemployment 1979–84' Essex PhD Thesis 1987 and Mo Kah Kui 'Manpower Services Commission and the Voluntary Sector: An Appraisal of the Relationship Founded on Special Employment Measures (1976–1982)' London MPhil Thesis 1984.

**4882** A Oliver 'Skill Shortages' *Economic Trends* 323 1980 pp 102–9. An analysis of skill shortages in the period of growing unemployment in the 1970s. The poor results of training initiatives in response to this problem are examined in Gordon and Michael Stephens *The British Malaise: Industrial Performance Education and Training in Britain Today* Falmer 1982.

**4883** Pat Ainsley *From School to YTS: Education and Training in England and Wales 1944–1987* Open University Press 1987. Training initiatives for youth are also examined in the essays in T L Rees and P Atkinson (eds) *Youth Unemployment and State Intervention* Routledge and Kegan Paul 1983. Dan Finn *Training Without Jobs: From Raising the School Leaving Age to the Youth Training Scheme* Macmillan 1987 also provides an overview of developments since the raising of the school leaving age under the 1944 Education Act but concentrates on developments in the 1980s.

**4884** Kenneth Roberts *From School to Work: A Study of the Youth Employment Service* David and Charles 1971. A study of its origins and development since 1909. It includes a bibliography. Another history of the service and study of its work is H Higenbotham *The Youth Employment Service* Methuen 1957. See also Robert James 'The Youth Employment Service' *Industrial Law Review* 8 1953 pp 52–61 and G Cook 'Development and Administrative Control of the Youth Employment Service Since 1939' Manchester MA (Econ) Thesis 1964–5. The report on its work, *Report on the Work of the Youth Employment Service* National Youth Employment Council, was published triennially after 1950.

**4885** D M Silberston *Youth in a Technical Age* Parrish 1959. A history and study of the purpose and content of day release schemes. The Post Office scheme is taken as a case study.

**4886** *The Careers Service 1974–1979* Department of Employment 1979. An outline of the organization of the careers service and its work in schools and colleges.

**4887** R Fiddy (ed) *In Place of Work: Policy and Provision for the Young Unemployed* Falmer 1983. A critical assessment of the Youth Opportunities Programme. D S Edwards 'The History and Politics of the Youth Opportunities Programme 1978–1983' London PhD Thesis 1985 analyses of the programme's history. There is a case study of its operation in Portsmouth. The establishment of the successor Youth Training Scheme is also examined. A short criticism of the programme from the point of view of one of the sponsors of one of its schemes is *A Critique of the Youth Opportunities Programme* Camden Council of Social Service 1980.

**4888** P N Junankar (ed) *From School to Unemployment? The Labour Market for Young People* Macmillan 1988. This includes essays touching on the Youth Training Scheme. The chances of ethnic minorities on the scheme are assessed in M Cross and D Smith (eds) *Black Youth Futures: Ethnic Minorities and the YTS* National Youth Bureau 1987.

**4889** Kenneth Lysons *A Passport to Employment: A History of the London Chamber of Commerce and Industry Education Scheme 1887–1987* Pitman 1988.

**4890** P W Musgrove 'The Growth in Demand for Training in the Iron and Steel Industry 1945–1964' *Vocational Aspects of Secondary and Further Education* 18 1966 pp 10–16.

**4891** R M Lindley 'Demand for Apprentice Recruits by the Engineering Industry 1951–1971' *Scottish Journal of Political Economy* 22 1975 pp 1–29.

**4892** J Haines 'In-Service Training for Community Work in the United Kingdom: A Review of Recent Experience' *Community Development Journal* 15 1980 pp 41–52. A review of the previous ten years.

**4893** Department of Employment and Productivity *Ryhope: A Pit Closes, A Study in Redeployment* HMSO 1970. An in-depth study of the consequences of the closure of a coal mine and the re-training of its workers.

## (10) The Labour Force

### (a) General

**4894** Guy Routh *Occupations of the People of Great Britain 1801–1981* Macmillan 1987. The statistics are drawn from censuses. Chapters examine employment changes over time. Another useful statistical guide is Clive Howard Lee *British Regional Employment Statistics 1841–1971* Cambridge University Press 1979.

**4895** *Ministry of Labour Gazette* HMSO 1893–1968. This subsequently became *Employment and Productivity Gazette* 1968–70, *Department of Employment Gazette* 1971–79 and *Employment Gazette* 1979–. It is the main statistical source and also includes articles and tables of the retail price index.

**4896** *Labour Force Survey* HMSO 1973–. This contains detailed employment statistics from the Department of Employment and the European Community.

**4897** N K Buxton, D I Mackay and C L Wood *British Employment Statistics: A Guide to Sources and Methods* Blackwell 1977. Much more than a guide to the sources from the nineteenth century to the 1970s. It provides a critical analysis of the methods of collecting and dealing with the statistics. In the process it provides a historical analysis of some of the post-war statistical series. Also on employment statistics see K Allen and D Yuill *The Accuracy of Pre-1971 Employment Data* Discussion Papers in Economics 12, University in Glasgow 1975.

**4898** R C O Matthews 'Why has Britain had Full Employment Since the War?' *Economic Journal* 78 1968 pp 555–69. A seminal paper which argued that the full employment that Britain enjoyed in the first two decades after the war was the result not of Keynesian deficit finance but of high levels of private investment and the long boom in world trade.

**4899** J C R Dow and L A Dicks-Mireaux 'The Excess Demand for Labour: A Study of Conditions in Great Britain 1946–1956' *International Labour Review* 77 1958 pp 147–59. See also L C Hunter 'Cyclical Variations in the Labour Supply: British Experience 1951–1960' *Oxford Economic Papers* 15 1963 pp 140–53.

**4900** Geoff Briscoe and D A Peel 'The Specification of the Short-Run Employment Function: The Demand for Labour in the UK Manufacturing Sector 1955–1972' *Bulletin of the Oxford University Institute of Economic Statistics* 37 1975 pp 115–42.

**4901** M Frost and M Spence 'The Changing Structure and Distribution of the British Workforce' *Progress in*

*Planning* 21 1984 pp 69–146. A study of changes in the structure of employment 1971–7.

**4902** R Layard and S Nickell *The Performance of the British Labour Market* Centre for Labour Economics, London School of Economics, University of London 1986. An analysis of changes in the 1980s, not least the surge in productivity. Geographical aspects of the labour market in the 1980s are examined in A R Townsend 'The Location of Employment Growth after 1978: The Suprising Significance of Dispersed Centres' *Environment and Planning A* 18 1986 pp 529–45.

**4903** Brian Showler *Public Employment Service* Longman 1976. A survey of the functions and role of the national employment service. It reviews employment policy trends since 1945, concentrating on the developments of the 1970s, and also covers such themes as employment service provision for special groups, training and re-training. Also on the employment service see C B Efstratoglou 'An Appraisal of the Employment Service Policy in Great Britain 1909–1978: The Case of the ESA – Job Centres' York MPhil Thesis 1979.

**4904** Derek H Aldcroft *Full Employment: The Elusive Goal* Harvester 1984. An analysis of employment policies. The failings of selective employment policies are traced in Geoffrey Shepherd 'United Kingdom: A Resistance to Change' in François Duchêne and Geoffrey Shepherd (eds) *Managing Industrial Change in Western Europe* Pinter 1987 pp 145–77.

**4905** Jim Tomlinson *Employment Policy: The Crucial Years 1939–55* Clarendon 1987. An important book which undermines the myth that post-war employment policy was founded upon Keynesianism. See also C Farrar 'The Manpower Policy of the British Government 1945–1950' London PhD Thesis 1951–2.

**4906** *The Economic Consequences of Full Employment* Cmnd 9725, *Parliamentary Papers* xxxvi 1955–56. The government White Paper which for the first time questioned the priority of full employment over price stability. It ushered in the period of stop-go economic policies.

**4907** *Employment: The Challenge to the Nation* Cmnd 9474, *Parliamentary Papers* 1984–85. Statement of policy by the Thatcher government.

**4908** David Lockwood *The Black Coated Worker: A Study in Class Consciousness* 2nd ed, Clarendon 1989. This second edition of a seminal work first published in 1958 adds a postscript on the changes over thirty years and a critical appraisal of the theory of white collar proletarianization. An example of this theory is Rosemary Crompton and Gareth Jones *White-Collar Proletariat: Deskilling and Gender in Clerical Work* Macmillan 1984. This focuses on recent changes and the growth of female labour in office work. On white collar workers see also R F Elliott 'The Growth of White Collar Employment in Great Britain 1951–1971' *British Journal of Industrial Relations* 15 1977 pp 30–44 and P Galambos 'On the Growth of the Employment of Non-Manual Workers in the British Manufacturing Industries 1948–1962' *Bulletin of Oxford University Institute of Economic Statistics* 26 1964 pp 369–87. Spatial changes in office work in London and the drift of office work away from London over the period 1966–81 are examined in I Longhurst *Office Workers in London* Statistical Series 55, London Research Centre 1986.

**4909** R M Price 'The Growth of Scientific Institutions and Employment of Natural Science Graduates in Britain 1900–1960' London MSc (Econ) Thesis 1974–6.

**4910** L Morton *Part Time Predicament: The Rise of Part-Time Employment in Britain* West Midlands Low Pay Unit 1987. A study of the rise of part-time work which has occurred particularly amongst women, focusing on the West Midlands area. The geographical aspects of what is discribed as 'one of the most radical changes in employment structure this century' are examined in A R Townsend 'Spatial Aspects of the Growth of Part-Time Employment in Britain' *Regional Studies* 20 1986 pp 313–30. See also J Wallace 'An Examination of the Influence of Labour Demand on the Growth of Part-Time Employment in Great Britain 1951–1984' Bath PhD Thesis 1985 and C J Chesterman 'Women in Part-Time Employment: An Investigation of the Growth of Part-Time Employment in Britain Since World War II with Particular Reference to Patterns of Employment in Coventry' Warwick MA Thesis 1978.

**4911** J D Alden and S K Sahey 'A Regional Analysis of Double Job-Holding in the UK 1969–1975' *Regional Studies* 14 1980 pp 367–79. A study of the impact of this phenomenon on income levels, unemployment and industry.

**4912** Richard Perry *United Kingdom Public Employment: Patterns of Change 1951–1978* Centre for the Study of Public Policy 62, University of Strathclyde 1980. See also his *The Territorial Dimension in United Kingdom Public Employment* Centre for the Study of Public Policy 65, University of Strathclyde 1980. Moses Abramovitz and Vera F Eliasberg *The Growth of Public Employment in Great Britain* Oxford University Press 1957 examines the growth of public employment from 1890–1950. The government's efforts to be a model employer are critically examined in P B Beaumont *Government as Employer – Setting an Example?* Royal Institute of Public Administration 1981.

**4913** S Fothergill, M Kitson and S Monk *Unequal Growth: Urban and Regional Employment Change in* the UK Heinemann 1982. See also P Tyler *The Growth of Male and Female Manufacturing Employment across the Regions of the UK 1952–76* Department of Land Economy Discussion Paper 6, University of Cambridge 1982 and F Brechling 'Trends and Cycles in British Regional Employment' *Oxford Economic Papers* 19 1967 pp 1–21.

**4914** J Hodgson 'Changes in the Structure of Employment in the Northern Region of England 1921–71' Newcastle MA Thesis 1975.

**4915** J J Flagg 'Spatial Change in Manufacturing Employment in Greater Leicester 1947–1970' *East Midlands Geographer* 5 1973 pp 400–15.

**4916** D P W Knight, A Tsapatsaris and J Jaroszak *The Structure of Employment in Greater London 1961–80* Research Memorandum 501, GLC 1977.

**4917** A Moyes 'Employment Change in the North Staffordshire Conurbation 1951–1966' *North Staffordshire Journal of Field Studies* 12 1972 pp 83–100.

**4918** D Jeffrey and J C Adams 'Spatial-Sectoral Patterns of Employment Growth in Yorkshire and Humberside 1963–1975: A Time-Series Factor Analytic Approach' *Regional Studies* 14 1980 pp 441–53.

## (b) Labour Mobility

**4919** R D Sleeper 'Inter-Industry Labour Mobility in Britain Since 1959' Oxford DPhil Thesis 1972–3. See also P W T Moreton 'Labour Turnover and its Relationship to Levels of Employment and Unemployment in some Sectors of British Manufacturing Industry Since 1948' Hull PhD Thesis 1970–1 and R M Lindley 'Inter-Industry Mobility of Male Employees in Britain 1959–1968' *Journal of the Royal Statistical Society* series A 139 1976 pp 56–79.

**4920** Stephen Fothergill and Graham Gudgin 'Regional Employment Change: A Sub-Regional Explanation' *Progress in Planning* 12 1979 pp 155–219.

**4921** G Thomas *The Mobility of Labour in Great Britain 1945–1949* HMSO 1952. An analysis of the patterns and characteristics of labour mobility compared with trends in industry and the labour market. This is continued by Amelia I Harris and Rosemary Clausen *Labour Mobility in Great Britain 1953–63* HMSO 1967, which also includes data on the reasons given for moving.

**4922** M Waugh 'The Changing Distribution of Professional and Managerial Staff in England and Wales Between 1961 and 1966' *Regional Studies* 3 1969 pp 157–69.

**4923** John Salt and Robin Flowerdew 'Labour Migration from London' *London Journal* 6 1980 pp 36–50. See also Robert Dennis 'The Decline of Manufacturing Employment in Greater London 1966–1974' *Urban Studies* 15 1978 pp 63–73. Employment mobility within London and its impact on the housing market is assessed in D Palmer and D Gleave 'Employment, Housing and Mobility in London' *London Journal* 7 1981 pp 177–93.

**4924** D L Saunders *Employment Mobility and the North West: 1945–1966 and 1966–1970* Merseyside Structure Plan Team 1973.

## (c) Women

**4925** *Bibliography on Women Workers 1861–1965* International Labour Office 1970. This contains a large number of references for Great Britain, including a number of relevant ILO reports. Thus, although now dated, it remains useful.

**4926** G Joseph *Women at Work: The British Experience* Philip Allan 1983. An examination of trends in female participation in the labour market in the twentieth century. See also Heather Joshi, Richard Layard and Susan Owen *Female Labour Supply in Post-War Britain: A Cohort Approach* Centre for Labour Economics, London School of Economics, University of London 1981, V Hammond 'Working Women Abroad – Great Britain' *Equal Opportunities International* 5 1986 pp 8–16, K Galen and P Marks 'Twentieth Century Trends in the Work of Women in England and Wales' *Journal of the Royal Statistical Society* series A 1937 1974 pp 60–74 and E James 'Women at Work in Twentieth Century Britain: The Changing Structure of Female Employment' *Manchester School of Economic and Social Studies* 30 1962 pp 283–300.

**4927** J C Lewis 'Regional Development in Post-War Britain: The Role of Women in the Labour Market' London PhD Thesis 1984. A study of the growth of women's work in the North East, particularly of routine and low paid jobs in labour intensive and declining industries.

**4928** *Royal Commission on Equal Pay 1944–1946: Report* Cmnd 6937, *Parliamentary Papers* xi 1945–46. A wide ranging examination of the socio-economic consequences of adopting equal pay for men and women chaired by Sir Cyril Asquith.

**4929** William Crofts 'The Attlee Government's Pursuit of Women' *History Today* 36 1986 pp 29–35. A study of the efforts of the Attlee government to persuade women to rejoin the workforce.

**4930** Allen M Potter 'The Equal Pay Campaign Committee' *Political Studies* 1957 pp 49–64. A study of the efforts of women to secure equal pay culminating in the granting of equal pay for equal work in the public services in 1955. See also Paolo Roberti 'Did the UK trend towards equality really come to an end in 1957?' *International Journal of Social Economics* 2 1975 pp 52–9.

**4931** Audrey Hunt (ed) *Women and Paid Work: Issues of Equality* Macmillan 1988. A set of essays examining various issues in the question of women's equality at work over the period 1965–81. See also Brian Chaplin and Peter Stone 'Sexual Discrimination in the Labour Market' *British Journal of Industrial Relations* 12 1974 pp 371–402. The effect of and the developments in the wake of the equal pay legislation of the late 1960s are studied in A Zabalza and Z Tzannotos *Women and Equal Pay: The Effects of Legislation on Female Employment and Wages in Britain* Cambridge University Press 1985. They argue that this legislation has been successful in considerably eroding the gap between men and women's pay. On the campaigns for equality see also Elizabeth Meehan *Women's Rights at Work: Campaigns and Policy in Britain and the United States* Macmillan 1984. The 1972 Act is seen as largely symbolic in L J Henderson 'The Impact of the Equal Employment Opportunity Act of 1972 on Unemployment Opportunities for Women and Minorities in Municipal Government' *Policy Studies Journal* 7 1978 pp 234–43. Progress up to the Sex Discrimination Act 1975 is traced in J Hebden 'Men's and Women's Pay in Britain 1968–1975' *Industrial Relations Journal* 9 1978 pp 56–70. The consequences of this legislation are assessed in C L Gough 'Pay Parity and Policy: An Appraisal of Past and Present Sex Discrimination Legislation in Britain and its Consequences for Women Workers' Wales MSc (Econ) Thesis 1979.

**4932** *Equal Opportunities Commission Annual Report* HMSO 1976–. The annual report of the commission set up as a watchdog in the Sex Discrimination Act 1975. The effectiveness of both this and the Commission for Racial Equality set up as a watchdog on discrimination against ethnic minorities, particularly in the workplace, is assessed in G Appleby and E Ellis 'Formal Investigations: The Commission for Racial Equality and the Equal Opportunities Commission as Law Enforcement Agencies' *Public Law* 1984 pp 236–76.

**4933** W B Creighton *Working Women and the Law* Mansell 1979. A study of the development of the law relating to the employment of women. David Pannick *Sex Discrimination Law* Clarendon 1985 is an assessment of the state of the law ten years after the Sex Discrimination Act. B A Hepple *Equal Pay and the Industrial Tribunals* Sweet and Maxwell 1984 and M Rubenstein *Equal Pay for Work of Equal Value* Macmillan 1984 are good surveys of the workings of the law.

**4934** Harriet Bradley *Men's Work, Women's Work: A History of the Sex-Typing of Jobs in Britain* Polity 1989. A set of sociological case studies of gender-based jobs.

**4935** Gregory Anderson (ed) *The White Blouse Revolution* Manchester University Press 1989. Studies of the feminization of office work.

**4936** Shelley Pennington and Belinda Westover *A Hidden Workforce: Women Homeworkers in Britain 1850–1985* Macmillan 1988. A study of the types and geographical locations of homeworkers, attempts to improve their lot and the prospects for the future. The final chapter covers 1945–85.

**4937** Michael P Fogarty, Isobel Allen and Patricia Walters *Women in Top Jobs 1968–1979* Heinemann Education 1981. A study of the extent to which women have succeeded in penetrating the upper professional echelons of the labour force and of the effects on their domestic life. An earlier study is Michael P Fogarty (ed) *Women in Top Jobs: Four Studies in Achievement* Allen and Unwin 1971. See also Constance E Arreger (ed) *Graduate Women at Work* Oriel Press 1966.

(d) The Disabled

**4938** S Simpson *Employment for Handicapped People* Reedbooks Ltd/Disabled Living Foundation n.d.? 1982. A short bibliography.

**4939** M Riviere 'Rehabilitation of the Disabled – with Special Reference to the Administration of the Disabled Persons (Employment) Act 1944' Oxford DPhil Thesis 1954–5. See also N Phillips 'The Disabled Persons (Employment) Act 1944: A Study of its Administration with Special Reference to the North West Region of the Ministry of Labour and National Service' Manchester MA (Econ) Thesis 1954–5.

**4940** J L Edwards 'Remploy: An Experiment in Sheltered Employment for the Severely Disabled in Great Britain' *International Labour Review* 77 1958 pp 147–59. See also W L Buxton 'Industrial Rehabilitation Units: A British Experiment' *International Labour Review* 67 pp 1953 pp 535–48.

**4941** R Hertzog 'The Provision of Day Training Centres for the Severely Subnormal in the North West 1959–64' Manchester MEd Thesis 1966–7.

# 8 ENVIRONMENTAL HISTORY

## A. THE PHYSICAL ENVIRONMENT

### (1) General

**4942** Stanley P Johnson *The Politics of Environment: The British Experience* Stacey 1973. An analysis of the evolution of the legislation and political machinery for handling environmental issues. It includes a section on the work of the Department of the Environment. Tony Aldous *Battle for the Environment* Fontana 1972 assesses the then new Department and some of the contentious environmental issues that emerged in the late 1960s. Malcolm Slesser *The Politics of Environment* Allen and Unwin 1972 focuses on the evils of large-scale industrialization, especially in Scotland.

**4943** J Cripps *The Countryside Commission: Government Agency or Pressure Group?* Town Planning Discussion Paper 31, Bartlett School of Architecture and Planning, University College, London 1979. The Countryside Commission replaced the National Parks Commission in the late 1960s. The author of this assessment of it and its activities was its chairman for eight years.

**4944** Michael Allaby *The Eco-Activists: Youth Fights for a Human Environment* Knight 1971. Semi-autobiographical account of some of the environmental battles of the late 1960s.

**4945** Jonathon Porritt and David Winner *The Coming of the Greens* Fontana 1988. An account of the rise of Green issues in the 1980s.

**4946** Andrew Blowers 'Transition or Transformation? Environmental Policy under Thatcher' *Public Administration* 65 1987 pp 277–95. A critical appraisal.

### (2) Rural Conservation

**4947** John Sheil *Nature in Trust: The History of Nature Conservation in Britain* Blackie 1976. A full history. See also Sir Laurence Dudley Stamp *Nature Conservation in Britain: With a list of Conservation Areas in England, Wales and Scotland* Collins 1970.

**4948** D Lowenthal and M Binney (eds) *Our Past Before Us: Why do We Save It?* Temple Smith 1981. An analysis and justification of conservation efforts in both urban and rural contexts.

**4949** John Sheil *Pesticides and Nature Conservation: The British Experience 1950–1975* Oxford University Press 1985. See also B F Gillespie 'British Control of Pesticide Technology, with Reference to the Occupational, Environmental and Consumer Hazards Associated with the use of Aldrin and Dieldrin' Manchester PhD Thesis 1977.

**4950** John Sheil 'Grassland Management and the Early Development of British Ecology' *British Journal of the History of Science* 19 1986 pp 283–99.

**4951** Marion Shoard *The Theft of the Countryside* Temple Smith 1980. A polemic against the threat posed to the preservation of the countryside by intensive farming methods. She tells the story of the struggle of conservationists against threats such as these in her *This Land is Ours: The Struggle for Britain's Countryside* Paladin 1987. See also P Lowe *et al Countryside Conflicts: The Politics of Farming, Forestry and Conservation* Gower 1986. The impact of changes in farming and of growing recreational use upon the countryside since 1945 are examined Victor Bonham Carter *The Survival of the English Countryside* Hodder and Stoughton 1971.

**4952** I D Brotherton 'Party Political Approaches to Rural Conservation in Britain' *Environment and Planning* A 18 1986 pp 151–60. This brings out the differences between the Conservatives and Labour in rural conservation. See also the reply by A Flynn and P Lowe 'The Problems of Analysing Party Politics: Labour and Conservative Approaches to Rural Conservation' *Environment and Planning* A 19 1987 pp 409–14 which also brings ideological differences and the importance of environmental pressure groups.

**4953** Geoffrey Berry and Geoffrey Beard *The Lake District: A Century of Conservation* Bartholomew 1980. A well illustrated history of the defence of the Lake District from tourists and new roads.

**4954** Peter Scott *The Eye of the Wind* revised ed, Hodder and Stoughton 1977. The autobiography of the naturalist and conservationist. *Sir Peter Scott at 80: A Retrospective* Sutton 1989 is a posthumously published collection of tributes. See also George Edward Baker *Peter Scott* Cassell 1964.

**4955** E Barton Worthington *The Ecological Century: A Personal Appraisal* Clarendon 1983. A memoir by the leading naturalist and conservationist.

### (3) Climate

Some of the material in the section on Agriculture should also be consulted.

**4956** T J Chandler and S Gregory *The Climate of the British Isles* Longman 1976. A detailed analysis with useful statistics. It also includes a good bibliography. See also H H Lamb *The English Climate* 2nd ed, English Universities Press 1964 and H H Lamb 'Britain's Changing Climate' *Geographical Journal* 130 1967 pp 445–68.

**4957** Gordon Manley *Climate and the British Scene* Collins 1952. Some of his views on the influence of climate on man seem somewhat dubious. Much of the book is also historical rather than contemporary. Nevertheless this well illustrated book contains much useful information.

**4958** *British Rainfall* HMSO 1862–. Annual statistics.

**4959** T J Chandler *The Climate of London* Hutchinson 1965. See also W A L Marshall *A Century of London Weather* HMSO 1952.

**4960** Bob Ogley *In the Wake of the Hurricane* Froglets Publications 1988. Pictures and text show the damage done in Southern England and the Channel Islands by the great storm of October 1987.

### (4) Water

**4961** *Water Statistics* Institute of Municipal Treasurers and Accountants 1964–. An annual publication. Since 1973 the Institute has been the Chartered Institute of Public Finance and Accountancy.

**4962** E B Funnell and R D Hey (eds) *The Management of Water Resources in England and Wales* Saxon House 1974. A series of analyses at the time of the reorganization of the water authorities under the 1973 Water Act. A comprehensive examination of the industry is D J Parker and E C Penning-Rowsell *Water Planning in Britain* Allen and Unwin 1980. See also C Kirby *Water in Britain* Penguin 1979. On the pre-1973 organization of the water industry see K Smith *Water in Britain* Macmillan 1972.

**4963** A G Jordan, J J Richardson and R H Kimber 'The Origins of the Water Act of 1973' *Public Administration* 55 1977 pp 317–34. The ensuing reorganization of water management into ten water authorities in England and Wales is examined in D A Okun *The Regionalisation of Water Management* Applied Science Publishers 1977. A good study of the organization and responsibilities of these authorities is Elizabeth Porter *Water Management in England and Wales* Cambridge University Press 1978.

**4964** K Hawkins *Environment and Enforcement: Regulation and the Social Definition of Pollution* Oxford University Press 1984. Based on two years observation of staff in two regional water authorities. It examines the part played by the criminal law in protecting the purity of the water supply.

**4965** D C Renshaw *et al* 'Some Recent European Legislation in Water Pollution Control and Implications for the United Kingdom' *Water Pollution Control* 79 1979 pp 178–223. An assessment of EC directives on water control and quality.

**4966** Jack Brand 'The Politics of Fluoridisation: A Community Conflict' *Political Studies* 19 1971 pp 430–9. On the campaign to fluoridize the water supply see also A G Walt 'Policy-Making in Britain: A Comparative Study of Fluoridisation and Family Planning 1960–1974' London PhD Thesis 1976 and A P Brier 'The Decision Process in Local Government: A Case Study of Fluoridisation in Hull' *Public Adminstration* 48 1970 pp 153–68.

**4967** J C Doornkamp, K J Gregory and A S Burn *Atlas of Drought in Britain 1975–1976* Institute of British Geographers 1980. It is argued in C D Andrews *We didn't wait for the rain* Water Council 1976 that the ability of the water authorities to control regional water resources meant that fewer restrictions on supply during the drought of 1976 had to be imposed than would otherwise have been the case.

**4968** Terry Marsh *The 1984 Drought* Institute of Hydrology, Wallingford 1985. 1984, a hot summer like that of 1976, also led to water shortages.

**4969** *London's Water Supply 1903–53: A Review of the Work of the Metropolitan Water Board* Staples 1953. See also A K Mukhopadhyay 'The Politics of London Water Supply' London PhD Thesis 1972–73. Mukhopadhyay has also published 'The Politics of London Water' *London Journal* 1 1975 pp 207–25.

**4970** S J Dolbey 'The Politics of Manchester's Water Supply 1961– 1967' Manchester PhD Thesis 1968–69.

**4971** David L Rydz 'The Formation of the Great Ouse Water Authority' *Public Administration* 49 1971 pp 163–84, 245–68. A case study.

### (5) Floods and Flood Prevention

**4972** M D Newson *Flooding and the Flood Hazard in the United Kingdom* Oxford University Press 1975.

**4973** Dudley Barker *The Official Story of the Great Floods of 1947 and Their Sequel* Board of Agriculture 1948.

**4974** D Summers *The East Coast Floods* David and Charles 1978. A study of the major flooding of 1953. Hilda E P Grieve *The Great Tide: The Story of the 1953 Flood Disaster in Essex* Essex County Council 1959 is an illustrated account of the floods and the damage they caused. Also on the storm floods of 1953 see J A Steers 'The East Coast Floods January 31 to February 1 1953' *Geographical Journal* 119 1953 pp 280–95, J R Rossiter 'The North Sea Storm Surge of 31 January and 1 February 1953' *Philosophical Transactions of the Royal Society, London* series A 246 1954 pp 371–99 and A Robinson 'The Sea Floods around the Thames Estuary' *Geography* 38 1953 pp 170–6.

**4975** Stuart Gilbert and Ray Horner *The Thames Barrier* Telford 1984. The disastrous floods of 1953 led to the decision to build the Thames Barrier to protect the capital from the threat of flooding. The twenty years of debate and ten years of construction are traced in this useful history. Both of the authors were heavily involved in the project throughout its history. The successful completion of the barrier was celebrated with a special issue of *Construction News* 18/11/1982.

**4976** J A Steers *et al* 'The Storm Surge of 11 January 1978 on the East Coast of England' *Geographical Journal* 145 1979 pp 195–205.

### (6) Pollution

**4977** C M Lambert (ed) *Environmental Pollution: Sources of Information on Environmental Pollution in* the UK Department of the Environment/Department of Transport Library 1983. This lists and details sources of information. Kay Henderson (ed) *Pollution: Sources of Information* Library Association 1972 is a valuable and well-produced sourcebook.

**4978** G D Cuzner *Pollution: A Select Bibliography* Manchester Public Libraries 1972. A useful record of the literature published 1950–71 covering all aspects of pollution. In addition the Department of the Environment Library periodically publishes bibliographies on air, environmental, marine and coastal pollution.

**4979** *Digest of Environmental Pollution Statistics* HMSO 1978–. This subsequently became the Digest of Environmental Pollution and Water Statistics and is now known as Digest of Environmental Protection and Water Statistics.

**4980** J Bugler *Polluting Britain* Penguin 1972. This includes a number of detailed case studies.

**4981** G Richardson *Policing Pollution: A Study of Regulation and Enforcement* Clarendon 1982. See also A Walker *Law of Industrial Pollution Control* George Godwin 1979.

**4982** *Royal Commission on Environmental Pollution: 1st Report* Cmnd 4585, *Parliamentary Papers* xvi 1970– 71 (Chairman Sir Eric Ashby). The Royal Commission has existed as a standing body since 1970, periodically publishing reports. *2nd Report: Three Issues in Industrial Pollution* Cmnd 4894 xii 1971–72 (Sir Eric Ashby), *3rd Report: Pollution in Some British Estuaries and Coastal Waters* 5054 xii 1971–72 (Sir Eric Ashby), Elizabeth Porter *Pollution in Four Industrial Estuaries: Studies in Relations to Changes in Pollution and Industrial Development (Tees, Mersey, Humber and Clyde Estuaries)* HMSO 1973, *4th Report: Pollution Control: Progress and Problems* 5780 ix 1974–75 (Sir Brian Flowers), *Report 5: Air Pollution Control: An Integrated Approach* 6371 xii 1975–76 (Sir Brian Flowers), *Report 6: Nuclear Power and the Environment* 6618 xii 1975– 76 (Sir Brian Flowers), *Report 7: Agriculture and Pollution* 7644 1979–80 (Sir Hans Kornberg), *Report 8: Oil Pollution of the Sea* 8358 1980–81 (Sir Hans Kornberg), *Report 9: Lead in the Environment* 8852 1982–83 (T R E Southwood), *10th Report: Tackling Pollution – Experience and Prospects* 9149 1983–84 (Sir Richard Southwood), *11th Report: Managing Waste: The Duty of Care* 9675 1985–86 (Sir Richard Southwood) and *12th Report: Best Practicable Environmental Option* 310 1987–88 (Sir Jack Lewis).

**4983** *National Smoke Abatement Society Annual Report* National Smoke Abatement Society 1930–50. This continued as *National Smoke Abatement Society Year Book* 1951–56 and as *Clean Air Year Book* 1957–.

**4984** Eric Ashby and Mary Anderson *The Politics of Clean Air* Clarendon 1981. A history of air pollution and attempts to control it. A good analysis of air pollution legislation from the appointment of the Beaver Committee in 1952 is Howard A Scarrow 'The Impact of British Domestic Air Pollution Legislation' *British Journal of Political Science* 2 1972 pp 261–82. This argues that the Clean Air Act of 1956 has had minimal effect. Andris Auliciems and Ian Burton 'Trends in Smoke Concentration Before and After the Clean Air Act of 1956' *Atmospheric Environment* 7 1973 pp 1063–70 agrees with this and points, in a study of the county of Kent, to resistance to the use of smokeless fuel as a factor.

**4985** *Ministry of Health Mortality and Morbidity during the London Fog of December 1952* HMSO 1954. An official analysis of the great smog of 5–8 December 1952. See also E T Wilkins 'Air Pollution Aspects of the London Fog of December 1952' *Quarterly Journal of the Royal Meteorological Society* 80 1954 pp 267–78.

**4986** *Committee on Air Pollution: Interim Report* Cmnd 9011, *Parliamentary Papers* viii 1953–54. The Report was Cmnd 9322, *Parliamentary Papers* viii 1953–54. The report of the committee chaired by Sir Hugh Beaver which led to the 1956 Clean Air Act. On the Act see J B Sanderson 'The National Smoke Abatement Society and Clean Air Act 1956' Manchester MA (Econ) Thesis 1959–60. Sanderson published an article of the same title in *Political Studies* 9 1962 pp 236–53.

**4987** R Garner and R Gow *Clean Air – Law and Practice* 4th ed Shaw 1976. A legal textbook.

**4988** P Brimblecombe *The Big Smoke: A History of Air Pollution in London Since Mediaeval Times* Methuen 1987. This traces the development of control of air pollution in the capital. M J R Schwar and D J Bell *Thirty Years on: A Review of Air Pollution in London* GLC 1983 reviews progress since the great smog and summarizes the present quality of the air.

**4989** *Twenty Years Review of Air Pollution Control in the Area of the Council* Manchester Area Council for Clean Air and Noise Control 1976. A review of improvements in Manchester since 1956. The success in smoke control leading to increasing visibility in Manchester is demonstrated in C M Wood 'Visibility and Sunshine in Greater Manchester' *Clean Air* 3 1973 pp 15–24.

**4990** Geoffrey Wall 'Public Response to Air Pollution in South Yorkshire, England' *Environment and Behavior* 5 1973 pp 219–48. This study found that fear of losing concessionary coal (in an area where many were miners) meant there was little enthusiasm for smokeless fuel.

**4990A** G O Allen 'Sixteen Years: A Saga of Smoke Control' *Clean Air* 3 1973 pp 12–15. An analysis of progress since 1956 in Scunthorpe.

**4991** Andrew Blowers *Something in the Air: Corporate Power and the Environment* Harper and Row 1984. An insider account of the struggle between environmentalists and the London Brick Company 1978–83 over industrial emissions. This includes a large theoretical section and a detailed account of the takeover of this Bedfordshire company by Hanson Trust.

**4992** Basil A Alexander *Acid Rain and the Environment: Sources of Information* British Library Science Reference and Information Services 1985. A bibliography, guide to the library's holdings, list of databases and source guide to interested organizations. See also the short, select bibliography *Acid Rain* Department of Energy Library 1984.

**4993** *UK Review Group on Acid Rain Acid Deposits in the United Kingdom* Warren Spring Laboratory 1983. A report on acid rain deposits 1978–80. It includes a useful bibliography.

**4994** Des Wilson *The Lead Scandal: The Fight to Save Children from Damage by Lead in Petrol* Heinemann 1983. A campaigning book by the leader of the Campaign for Lead Free Air.

**4995** Alan Irwin and Kenneth Lucas 'The Control of Chemical Carcinogens in Britain' *Policy and Politics* 11 1983 pp 439–60.

**4996** J M Ferguson 'Managing Clinical Waste' *Wastes Management* 77 1987 pp 144–55. This examines the management of clinical waste, the growing concern in the 1980s about its disposal in the London area and attempts to develop a policy on the issue.

**4997** John H Bates *United Kingdom Marine Pollution Law* Lloyds of London Press 1985. A comprehensive guide. It includes tables of statutes, cases and other relevant legislation and a useful bibliography.

**4998** D S Moulder and A Varley (comp) *A Bibliography on Marine and Estuarine Oil Pollution* Marine Biological Association of the UK 1971.

**4999** *The Torrey Canyon: Report of the Committee of Scientists on the Scientific and Technological Aspects of the Torrey Canyon Disaster* HMSO 1968. A report chaired by Sir Solly Zuckerman on the disaster that befell the oil tanker the *Torrey Canyon*. See also the instant histories, Richard Petrow *The Black Tide: In the Wake of the Torrey Canyon* Hodder and Stoughton 1968 and Crispin Gill, Frank Booker and Tony Soper *The Wreck of the Torrey Canyon* David and Charles 1967.

**5000** J Doxat *The Living Thames: The Restoration of a Great River* Hutchinson Benham 1977. An account of the attempts to clean up the river in the post-war years. The considerable success in cleaning up the Thames estuary and re-introducing fish into its waters is celebrated in A C Wheeler *The Tidal Thames: The History of the River and its Fishes* Routledge and Kegan Paul 1979.

**5001** C Penn *Noise Control* Shaw 1980. A practical work based on his own experience in environmental health work.

**5002** C M Wood *et al The Geography of Pollution: A Study of Greater Manchester* Manchester University Press 1974.

## (7) Environmental Groups

**5003** Philippa Bassett (comp) *Lists of Historical Records of Environmental Organisations* Centre for Urban and Regional Studies, University of Birmingham/Institute of Agricultural History, University of Reading 1980. This comprises details on the history and the historical records of a large array of environmental organizations.

**5004** Michael J C Barber *Directory for the Environmental Organisations in Britain and Ireland 1986–7* Routledge and Kegan Paul 1986. The second edition of a directory first published in 1984. It contains information on the aims, activities, status, publications and who to contact in a large and diverse range of bodies. It also contains a bibliography.

**5005** Philip Lowe and Jane Goyder *Environmental Groups in Politics* Allen and Unwin 1983. The fullest survey of environmental pressure groups. The nature and history of each group is examined. There is a useful bibliography.

**5006** R H Kimber and J J Richardson (eds) *Campaigning for the Environment* Routledge and Kegan Paul 1974. A study of the campaigning groups concerned with the protection of the environment. See also S K Brookes and J J Richardson 'The Environmental Lobby in Britain' *Parliamentary Affairs* 28 1975 pp 312–28 and S K Brookes, A G Jordan, R H Kimber and J J Richardson 'The Growth of the Environment as a Political Issue in Britain' *British Journal of Political Science* 6 1976 pp 245–55.

**5007** Philip Lowe 'Amenity and Equity: A Review of Local Enviromental Pressure Groups in Britain' *Environment and Planning* A 9 1977 pp 35–58. An analysis of the campaigning activities and the effects of a disparate range of local environmental pressure groups such as civic preservation societies, residents and tenants associations or community action groups.

**5008** G Griesbach 'Some Aspects of Environmentalism – The Case of Nuclear Power Development in Britain' London MPhil Thesis 1976. A study of environmental groups protesting about nuclear power.

**5009** Michael Brown and John May *The Greenpeace Story* Dorling Kindersley 1989. A history of the leading campaigning environmental pressure group.

**5010** John Gaze *Figures in a Landscape: A History of the National Trust* Barrie and Jenkins 1989. An institutional history of the body founded in 1895 to preserve landscapes and buildings for the nation. See also Robin Fedden *The National Trust: Past and Present* Cape 1974. James Lees-Milne *Prophesying Peace* Chatto and Windus 1977 is the autobiography of an author who served on the staff of the National Trust 1936–66, during 1951–66 as adviser on historical buildings.

## (8) Animal Welfare

**5011** Richard North *The Animals Report* Penguin 1983. A journalistic investigation into the use and abuse of animals in the 1970s and 1980s.

**5012** J E Hampson 'Animal Experimentation 1876–1976: Historical and Contemporary Perspectives' Leicester PhD Thesis 1978. A history and contemporary analysis of government policy on the use of animals in experiments and of the pressure group activities of anti-vivisectionists.

**5013** 'The Economics of Domestic Pets' *Planning* 23 1957 pp 198–211. An audit of the British fondness for pets, their numbers, costs, social aspects and the protection of pets.

**5014** *Report of the Committee on Cruelty to Wild Animals* Cmnd 8266, *Parliamentary Papers* viii 1950–51. An inquiry into cruelty, including blood sports, chaired by John Scott Henderson. It did not suggest the abolition of blood sports but wanted to mitigate the cruelty involved. The fullest analysis of the arguments for and against hunting, the pressure groups who oppose it and the attempts to legislate against it is Richard Thomas *The Politics of Hunting* Gower 1983. This analysis is continues in his 'Hunting as a Political Issue' *Parliamentary Affairs* 39 1986 pp 19–30. See also Vera Sheppard *My Head Against the Wall: A Decade in the Fight Against Blood Sports* Moonraker Press 1979.

**5015** Anthony Brown *Who Cares for Animals* Heinemann 1974. A history of the first 150 years of the Royal Society for the Prevention of Cruelty to Animals. An earlier history is A W Moss *Valiant Crusade: The History of the RSPCA* Cassell 1961.

**5016** Richard Fitter and Peter Scott *The Penitent Butchers: The Fauna Preservation Society 1903–1978* Fauna Preservation Society 1978. A short history.

**5017** Iain Patterson *The British Veterinary Profession 1791–1948* W H Allen 1984.

**5018** G Cottisloe *The Story of the Battersea Dogs' Home* David and Charles 1979. The history of the Metropolitan Police's dogs' home.

### (9) National Parks

**5019** Ann and Malcolm MacEwen *Greenprints for the Countryside: The Story of Britain's National Parks* Allen and Unwin 1987. A critical history of the post-war creation of the National Parks and subsequent policy towards them.

**5020** M Bell (ed) *Britain's National Parks* David and Charles 1975. A guide. There are interesting comments on the parks and the situation in which they were created and why in Harold M Abrahams (ed) *Britain's National Parks* Country Life 1959 and Roger Bush *The National Parks of England and Wales: Together with Areas of Outstanding Natural Beauty and Long-Distance Footpaths and Bridleways* Dent 1973.

**5021** John Sheil 'The Concept of National Parks in Great Britain 1900–1950' *Transactions of the Institute of British Geographers* 66 1975 pp 41–56.

**5022** John Dower *National Parks in England and Wales: Report* Cmnd 6628, *Parliamentary Papers* v 1944–45. A report commissioned in wartime by the Ministry of Town and Country Planning on the problems of establishing National Parks. This was followed by *Report of the National Parks Committee (England and Wales)* Cmnd 7121, *Parliamentary Papers* xiii 1946–47. However, most of the recommendations of this committee, chaired by Sir Arthur Hobhouse, were not in fact incorporated into the ensuing legislation.

**5023** Gordon E Cherry *Environmental Planning 1939–1969 Volume II: National Parks and Recreation in the Countryside* HMSO 1975. Part of the official peacetime history series on environmental planning. This examines the origins and implementation of the national parks programme and other aspects of countryside planning in the 1940s.

**5024** P W Richwood 'The National Land Fund 1946–80: The Failure of a Policy Initiative' *Leisure Studies* 6 1987 pp 15–23. This was set up to develop the national parks and access to the countryside. It was supposed to accept land and property in lieu of estate duty. Its failure down to its closure in 1980 is traced in this article.

**5025** *National Park Policies Review Committee Report* HMSO 1974. The report by the committee chaired by Lord Sandford. This recommended that National Park authorities be given more power and resources but had few concrete results.

**5026** Ann and Malcolm McEwen *National Parks: Conservation or Cosmetics* Allen and Unwin 1982. A critical appraisal focusing particularly on what are seen as inadequate planning controls in the national parks.

**5027** Crispin Gill *The First Ten Years: An Account of the Work of Dartmoor National Park 1951–1961* Devon County Council 1965. On the Lake District see [4953].

## B. THE HUMAN ENVIRONMENT

### (1) Town and Country Planning

#### (a) Reference Works

**5028** Brenda White *The Literature and Study of Urban and Regional Planning* Routledge and Kegan Paul 1974. A splendid work of reference covering sources of information on planning, the history and modern development of planning and major planning actions. It also contains a wealth of bibliographical material. In addition there are 262 annotated entries in J Barrich *Town and Country Planning: Sources of Information* Department of the Environment/Department of Transport Library 1979.

**5029** Bernard Taylor and Heinz Redwood (eds) *British Planning Databook* Pergamon 1983. Data and statistics on planning 1960–80.

**5030** *Directory of Official Architecture and Planning* Longman 1956–. Annual. Not just a directory, it also summarizes the development of planning policy each year.

**5031** Anthony Sutcliffe *The History of Urban and Regional Planning: An Annotated Bibliography* Mansell 1981. An international bibliography but with a strong British section. *Land Use Planning and the Social Sciences: A Selected Bibliography, Literature on Town and Country Planning and Related Social Sciences in Great*

*Britain 1930–1963* Centre for Urban Studies 1964 is an unannotated guide to the literature published between those dates. There was also a supplement covering 1964–70. In addition the typescript bibliographies on various subjects which the Royal Town Planning Institute Library has periodically issued since 1972 are well worth consulting.

**5032** S Job *The New Development Plan System: An Annotated Bibliography* Centre for Environmental Studies 1980. This new system was introduced by the Town and Country Planning Act 1968 and the complementary Act for Scotland in 1969. The material in this bibliography was published 1965–79.

**5033** *Major Planning Enquiries: Bibliography* Department of the Environment/Department of Transport Library 1981. A short select bibliography on planning appeals and inquiries.

**5034** *Sage Urban Studies Abstracts* Sage 1973–. An international abstracting service. It nevertheless contains a good range of abstracts of reports, books and articles on British planning issues. *Planning and Transport Abstracts* GLC 1969–86 is a monthly collection of about 100 abstracts.

**5035** PLANEX. The database of the Planning Exchange, Glasgow. This has been covering material on planning, local government finance and administration, housing, environment, economic planning and local economic development. See also the weekly *Information Bulletin* and the monthly *Planning Information Digest*.

(b) General

**5036** J B Goddard and A G Champion (eds) *The Urban and Regional Transformation of Britain* Methuen 1983. A good study of the post-war changes to the human and planned environment since the war. Peter Hall *et al The Containment of Urban England* 2v, Allen and Unwin 1973 is an ambitious and detailed study of these changes. Volume I is a study of urban growth and planning procedures to contain this since 1945. Volume II examines the planning system. See also David Donnison and P Soto *The Good City: A Study of Urban Development and Policy in Britain* Heinemann 1980.

**5037** Lionel Esher *A Broken Wave: The Rebuilding of Britain 1940–1980* Allen Lane 1981. An excellent inside history by Lord Esher. He focuses on the peculiar challenges presented by London, Newcastle, Sheffield, Liverpool and Milton Keynes. It supplies a well illustrated guide to the history of post-war planning from the high hopes and idealism of 1940s to the distaste with which the post-war planners' work is now generally

viewed. Francis Gladstone *The Politics of Planning* Temple Smith 1976 is a critical account of recent urban planning policy. It concentrates on Sheffield, Middlesborough, South Hampshire and Liverpool. Post-war planning is also critically assessed in Alison Ravetz *The Government of Space: Town Planning in Modern Society* Faber 1986, which places contemporary planning issues in historical context. B Raggett 'Post-War Urban Renewal: Past and Present Partnership Schemes' *Built Environment* 12 1986 pp 189–97 discusses partnerships between local authorities and landlords and developers in urban redevelopment since the 1950s.

**5038** John Barry Cullingworth *Town and Country Planning in Britain* 10th ed, Unwin Hyman 1988. The standard textbook on the development of planning. Gordon E Cherry *The Politics of Town Planning* Longman 1982 traces the development of the town planning from its origins as a movement into a function of government and examines the nature of contemporary town planning. Peter Hall *Urban and Regional Planning* Penguin 1980 is a survey of developments in planning from the 1940 Barlow Report [5043] onwards. Lincoln Allison *Environmental Planning: A Political and Philosophical Analysis* Allen and Unwin 1975 examines the relationship between planning and political theory. He notes the increasing stress on conservationism from the late 1960s. John Ratcliffe *An Introduction to Town and Country Planning* Hutchinson 1974 is a good textbook. See also M J Hebbert 'The Evaluation of British Town and Country Planning' Reading PhD Thesis 1977, P M Dawson 'The Development of the British State after World War Two: The Case of Town Planning' London MPhil Thesis 1979 and I Haywood 'The Changing Concept of the Urban Planning Operation in Great Britain Since 1947' Edinburgh MSc Thesis 1969–70.

**5039** Jeremy Alden and Robert Morgan *Regional Planning: A Comprehensive View* Leonard Hill 1974. An analysis that focuses on the impact of regional planning. It is perhaps more theoretical than historical.

**5040** G R R Hart *et al Development Control – Thirty Years On* Sweet and Maxwell 1979.

**5041** Sir Patrick Abercrombie *Town and Country Planning* 3rd ed, Oxford University Press 1959. A classic work by one of the greatest British planners. It includes an annex reviewing the history of planning, particularly 1940–59.

**5042** William Ashworth *The Genesis of Modern British Town Planning* Routledge and Kegan Paul 1954. The first history of town and country planning. It remains useful as a reflection of the views and aspirations of the immediate post-war period. The final chapter covers 1909–47. Focusing more particularly on the planning of the immediate post-war period is James W R Adams *Modern Town and Country Planning* Churchill 1952.

**5043** *Royal Commission on the Distribution of the Industrial Population* Cmnd 6153, *Parliamentary Papers* iv 1939–40. The Royal Commission chaired by Montague Barlow which was the fundamental starting point for post-war planning.

**5044** H Myles Wright 'The First Ten Years: Post-War Planning and Development in England' *Town Planning Review* 26 1955 pp 73–91. A progress report on the impact of post-1945 legislation. The legislation which laid the foundations of post-war planning is discussed in Frank Schaffer 'The Town and Country Planning Act 1947' *The Planner* 60 1974 pp 690–5 and in H S Kilner 'The Contribution of Labour Party Policy to the 1947 Town and Country Planning Act' London MPhil Thesis 1982. On the 1952 Act see P Tsitas 'The Consequences of the Town Planning Act 1952' London MA Thesis 1965–66.

**5045** D T Cross and M R Bristow (eds) *English Structure Planning: A Commentary on the Procedure and Practice in the Seventies* Methuen 1982. See also D G Hayman 'English Planning and Environmental Law and Administration: The 1970s' *American Planning Association Journal* 46 1980 pp 162–71. M J Bruton 'Local Plans, Local Planning and Development Plan Schemes in England 1974–1982' *Town Planning Review* 54 1983 pp 4–23 examines and reviews (except in Greater London) the development plan schemes that were required as a consequence of the 1974 local government reorganization.

**5046** Tim Brindley, Yvonne Rydin and Gerry Stoker *Remaking Planning: The Politics of Urban Change in the Thatcher Years* Unwin Hyman 1988. They agree that planning has been under a cloud during the Thatcher years, but do not go as far as critics like A Thornley *Thatcherism and Town Planning* School of Environment, Central London Polytechnic 1981 who argues that the Thatcher government was dismantling planning controls for the sake of market forces.

**5047** Desmond Heap (ed) *Encyclopaedia of the Law of Town and Country Planning* Sweet and Maxwell 1959–. A looseleaf compilation which is regularly updated. His *An Outline of Planning Law* 6th ed, Sweet and Maxwell 1973 is more digestible and deals with England and Wales only. A E Telling and R M C Duxbury *Planning Law and Procedure* 7th ed, Butterworths 1986 is a useful legal textbook. See also M Grant *Urban Planning Law* Sweet and Maxwell 1982. A somewhat outdated, but nevertheless still useful study of the development of British planning law by an American jurist is Beverley J Pooley *The Evolution of British Planning Legislation*

University of Michigan Law School, Ann Arbor, Michigan 1960.

**5048** John Punter 'A History of Aesthetic Control Part 1: 1909–1953' *Town Planning Review* 57 1986 pp 351–81. A well illustrated history of aesthetic controls on planning and architecture. The second part, covering the years 1953–85 appeared in *Town Planning Review* 58 1987 pp 29–62.

**5049** Andrew Blowers *The Limits of Power: The Politics of Local Planning Policy* Pergamon 1981. A study of the relationship between planners and politicians, incorporating a number of case studies. See also John Gyford *Town Planning and the Practise of Politics* Bartlett School of Architecture and Planning, University College, London 1978.

**5050** Gladys Keable *Tomorrow Slowly Comes: A Brief Account of Sixty Years of Work for Better Towns in an Unspoilt Countryside* Town and Country Planning Association 1963. A personal account of the development of the Garden Cities Association and the Garden Cities and of the Town and Country Planning Association 1899–1959. Colin Ward 'Say it again, Ben! An Evocation of the First Seventy-Five Years of the Town and Country Planning Association' *Bulletin of Environmental Education* 43 1974 pp 5–19 is a somewhat polemical account of the Association's development. On the Town and Country Planning Association see also Donald L Foley 'Idea and Influence: The Town and Country Planning Association' *Journal of the American Institute of Planners* 28 1962 pp 10–17. On other planning associations see Gordon E Cherry *The Evolution of British Town Planning: A History of Town Planning in the United Kingdom during the 20th Century and of the Royal Town Planning Institute 1914–74* Leonard Hill 1974 and, on the Glasgow-based Planning Exchange, a non-profit company established by central and local government to provide planning information, J B Cullingworth *The Planning Exchange: A Personal Account of its Establishment and Early Experience* Centre for Environmental Studies 1977.

**5051** D E C Eversley and Mary Moody *The Growth of Planning Research Since 1961* Social Science Research Council 1976.

**5052** H W E Davies and H W F Davies *British Planning Practice and Planning Education in the 1970s and 1980s* Department of Town Planning, Oxford Polytechnic 1983. On planning education see also A H Thomas 'An Analysis of Changes in Planning Education 1965–1975' London MPhil Thesis 1979.

**5053** D E C Eversley *The Planner in Society: The Changing Role of a Profession* Faber 1973. On the changing nature of the profession since 1947 see P

Healey 'The Professionalisation of Planning in Britain: Its Form and Consequences' *Town Planning Review* 56 1984 pp 492–506.

**5054**   Gordon E Cherry (ed) *Pioneers in British Planning* Architectural Press 1981. Post-war figures in this volume of detailed biographical studies include George Pepler, Sir Patrick Abercrombie, Thomas Sharpe, Colin Buchanan and Francis Osborn.

**5055**   A Barker and M Couper 'The Art of Quasi-Judicial Administration: The Planning Appeal and Inquiry System in England' *Urban Law and Policy* 6 1984 pp 363–476. An analysis of the workings of the planning appeal and inquiry system.

**5056**   *People and Planning: Report of the Committee on Public Participation in Planning* HMSO 1969. This report of the committee chaired by Arthur M Skeffington made important recommendations about increasing public participation and consultation in the planning process. The impact of public participation is examined in A R Long 'Participation and the Community' *Progress in Planning* 5 1975 pp 61–134 and Noel Boaden, Michael Goldsmith, William Hampton and Peter Stringer 'Planning and Participation in Practice: A Study of Public Participation in Structure Planning' *Progress in Planning* 13 1980 pp 1–102. On public participation in Newham, Islington, Westminster and Richmond see Prue Chamberlayne 'The Politics of Participation: An Enquiry into Four London Boroughs' *London Journal* 4 1978 pp 49–68.

**5057**   Norman Dennis *Public Participation and Planners' Blight* Faber 1972. A detailed study of radical proposals to redevelop an old residential area of Sunderland and of the efforts of local residents to influence them.

**5058**   R Alterman, D Harris and M Hill 'The Impact of Public Participation on Planning: The Case of the Derbyshire Structure Plan' *Town Planning Review* 55 1984 pp 177–96. Under the 1971 Town and Country Planning Act adequate public participation is required before structure plans can be approved. In the light of this study these provisions seem to have had little effect.

**5059**   M F Tanner 'The Problems of Planned "Town Expansion" in South Eastern England 1952–61' London MSc Thesis 1962–3.

**5060**   John Holliday (ed) *City Centre Redevelopment: A Study of British City Centre Planning and Case Studies of Five English City Centres* Knight 1973. The case studies are in Birmingham, Coventry, Leicester, Liverpool and Newcastle-upon-Tyne. There is a good introduction on the recent history of central area renewal.

**5061**   A Jones *For the Record – Bedford 1945–74: Land Use and Financial Planning* Roberts Publishing 1981.

**5062**   James L Macmorran *Municipal Public Works and Planning in Birmingham: A Record of the Administration and Achievements of the Public Works Committee and Department of the Borough and City of Birmingham 1852–1972* City of Birmingham Public Works Committee 1973. An official account by a former senior officer. Roger Smith 'Post-War Birmingham: Planning and Development' *Town Planning Review* 45 1974 pp 189–206 is a succinct and account of planning in the city since 1945. See also M B Stedman and P A Wood 'Urban Renewal in Birmingham: An Interim Report' *Geography* 50 1965 pp 1–17, M J Ryan 'Comprehensive Redevelopment in Birmingham: The Work of the Corporation with Special Reference to the Town and Country Planning Act 1944' Birmingham MSocSci Thesis 1976–7 and J M H Parke 'The Post-War Redevelopment of the Central Area of Birmingham' Birmingham MA Thesis 1974–5.

**5063**   Hilda Jennings *Societies in the Making: A Study of Development and Redevelopment within a County Borough* Routledge and Kegan Paul 1962. A study of the redevelopment of the slum area of Barton Hill in East Bristol and the sociological impact of the redevelopment.

**5064**   M Long 'The Post-War Planning Office: Coventry's Department of Architecture and Planning 1957–66' Liverpool PhD Thesis 1986. This concentrates on the planning methods used rather than, as is more common, the built environments that were created.

**5065**   J Brierley 'Exeter 1939–1974: The Reconstruction of a City' Manchester MA Thesis 1980.

**5066**   James W R Adams *Report of the Work of the Planning Department from 1948–1959 with some Reference to Earlier Town and Country Planning Activities in Kent* Kent County Council 1959. An offical study by the county's Chief Planning Officer.

**5067**   Donald L Foley *Controlling London's Growth: Planning the Great Wen 1940–1960* University of California Press, Berkeley, California 1963. A detailed study of the preparation and application of the Greater London Plan 1944, concentrating on the problems raised by the strategy of containing the outward spread of the capital. See also P L Garside 'Town Planning in London 1930–1961: A Study of Pressures, Interests and Influences Affecting the Formation of Policy' London PhD Thesis 1980.

**5068**   Peter Self *Metropolitan Planning: The Planning System of Greater London* Weidenfeld and Nicolson

1971. An account of the planning system of London in the 1960s in the light of the local government reorganization that took place. Another study of the effects of the 1965 reorganization of local government is I W Currie 'Local Authority Planning Administration in London before and after 1965' London MPhil Thesis 1970–1. John M Hall 'A Mighty Maze! But not without a Plan' *London Journal* 2 1976 pp 117–26 is an account of the history of the modified Greater London Development Plan of 1965. D A Hart 'A Policy Biography of the Greater London Council: Planning and Transport' *Built Environment* 10 1984 pp 100–12 is a digest of the strategic planning in London 1957–83.

**5069**   Peter Hall *London 2001* Unwin Hyman 1988. This follows on from his visionary *London 2000* 2nd ed, Faber 1969. It is an analysis of the planning problems and needs of London in the 1980s and of what went wrong with the planning dreams of the 1960s.

**5070**   T Christensen *Neighbourhood Survival: The Struggle for Covent Garden's Future* Prism 1979. A history of the largely successful struggle waged by the Covent Garden Community Association against GLC planners in the 1960s and 1970s. The confrontation between planners and the local residents in Notting Hill in 1966–74 is told in J O'Malley *The Politics of Community Action: A Decade of Struggle in Notting Hill* Bertrand Russell Peace Foundation, Nottingham 1977. Another story of successful struggle between tenants and, on this occasion, property developers focuses on the battle since 1957 over the redevelopment of an area of Camden. This is told in N Wates *The Battle for Tolmer Square* Routledge and Kegan Paul 1976.

**5071**   J G Davies *The Evangelistic Bureaucrat: A Study of Planning Exercise in Newcastle upon Tyne* Tavistock 1974. A celebrated and influential study. A sustained critical polemic against the planners.

**5072**   Steve Hopkins *Planning in Oxford – An Historical Survey and Bibliography* Department of Town Planning Working Paper 21, Oxford Polytechnic 1978. Part I is a historical survey 1923–77. The second part is an annotated bibliography on planning in Oxford.

## (2) Land Use

**5073**   *Land Use Planning and the Social Sciences: A Selected Bibliography* Centre for Urban Studies 1964. An extensive bibliography. A number of supplements have since appeared.

**5074**   D R Denham *et al Bibliography of Rural Land Economy and Land Ownership 1900–1957: A Full List of Works Relating to the British Isles and Selected Works from the United States and Western Europe* Cambridge University Press 1958. A bibliography of some 6,500 titles.

**5075**   Robin H Best *Land Use and Living Space* Methuen 1981. The best general survey of land use in Britain. Robin H Best and J T Coppock *The Changing Use of Land in Britain* Faber 1962 and Laurence Dudley Stamp *The Land of Britain: Its Use and Misuse* 3rd ed, Longmans 1962 are also worth consulting.

**5076**   N Lichfield and H Davis-Drabkin *Land Policy in Planning* Allen and Unwin 1980. A critical history of land use policy up to the mid-1970s and a review of possibilities beyond the Community Land Scheme. See also L J Sharpe 'Innovation and Change in British Land Use Planning' in J E S Hayward and Michael Watson (eds) *Planning, Politics and Public Policy* Cambridge University Press 1975 pp 316–57 and John H Westergaard 'Land Use Planning Since 1951: The Legislative and Administrative Framework' *Town Planning Review* 35 1964 pp 219–37.

**5077**   J B Cullingworth *Environmental Planning 1939–69 Volume 4: Land Values, Compensation and Betterment* HMSO 1981. The final volume of the official peacetime history of post-war environmental planning. See also John Ratcliffe *Land Policy: An Exploration of the Nature of Land in Society, the Problem of Community Created Land Values and the Twin Processes of Planning and Development* Hutchinson 1976. The various attempts to redistribute land values from the Town and Country Planning Act 1947 to the Community Land Tax Act 1976 are surveyed in H L Leung 'Towards a New Methodolgy of Public Policy Evaluation: A Re-Examination of British Policies Since 1945 for Redistributing Land Values' Cambridge MSc Thesis 1982. See also A G C Williams 'A Consideration of the Post-War Legislation with Respect to Town and Country Planning, Including those Enactments Relating to Land Values and the Assessment of Compensation' Sheffield LLM Thesis 1958–9.

**5078**   Andrew Cox *Adversary Politics and Land: The Conflict over Land and Property Policy in Post-War Britain* Cambridge University Press 1984. This focuses on the different attitudes in the political parties and argues that the alternation between the policy initiatives of governments of either party have in turn hindered urban development or generated property speculation. The politics of the land question, and not least the question of the taxing of land values, is discussed in Roy Douglas *Land, People and Politics: A History of the Land Question in the UK 1878–1952* Allison and Busby 1976. On the Labour Party's attitude to land use policy see S F Morser 'The Labour Party and Land 1947–1970' London MPhil Thesis 1981.

**5079** P Healey *Local Plans in British Land Use Planning* Pergamon 1983. An analysis of the nature, purpose and operation of development plans, focusing especially on local plans, and their effect on land development and land use over the post-war period.

**5080** J B Cullingworth *Environmental Planning 1939–1969 Volume 1: Reconstruction and Land Use Planning 1939–1947* HMSO 1975. A blow by blow account of government thinking on land use policy and planning during and immediately after the war.

**5081** Christopher J Duerksen 'England's Community Land Act: A Yankee's View' *Urban Law Annual* 12 1976 pp 49–76. This traces the background to and assesses the 1975 Community Land Act which provided for the eventual control by local authorities of all land available for development. The historical context, passage and application of the Act is also examined in C A Johnston 'The Genesis and Initial Implementation of the Community Land Act 1975: A Legislative Case History' Warwick LLM Thesis 1977.

**5082** Robin H Best and A G Champion *Regional Conversions of Agricultural Land to Urban Use in England and Wales 1945–1967* Centre for Environmental Studies 1970. See also A G Champion 'A Comparative Analysis of Evolving Land Use Patterns on the Urban Fringe of Selected Large Towns in England and Wales, with Particular Reference to the Relationship between Urban Expansion and Population Changes Since 1945' Oxford DPhil Thesis 1972–3 and G S Swinnerton 'An Analysis of the Quality of Agricultural Land being Converted to Urban Use in England and Wales, with Special Reference to the Period Since 1950' London PhD Thesis 1974.

**5083** Institute of Terrestrial Ecology, Natural Environment Research Council *Upland Land Use in England and Wales* Countryside Commission 1978. An analysis covering the period 1951–71. It includes a case study of Cumbria.

**5084** *Royal Commission on Common Land 1955–1958: Report* Cmnd 462, *Parliamentary Papers* x 1957–58. This was set up under the chairmanship of Sir Ivor Jennings to investigate the laws relating to common land and the changes that are desirable to promote their better use and enjoyment. It recommended registration, management and improvements and led to the 1965 Commons Registration Act. W G Hoskins and Laurence Dudley Stamp *The Common Lands of England and Wales* Collins 1963 is a useful study which includes in its appendices the first county by county list of known commons, village greens, common gravel pits and fuel allotments.

**5085** Robin H Best and A W Rogers *The Urban Countryside: The Land Use Structure of Small Towns*

*and Villages in England and Wales* Faber 1973. See also R C Fordham 'Urban Land Use Change in the United Kingdom during the Second Half of the 20th Century' *Urban Studies* 12 1975 pp 71–84.

**5086** J Barr *Derelict Britain* Penguin 1969. This and K Wallwork *Derelict Land* David and Charles 1974 are the best examinations of the nature, origins and distribution of derelict land in Britain. G C Dickinson and M G Shaw 'Land Use in Leeds 1957–1976: Two Decades of Change in a British Society' *Environment and Planning A* 14 1982 pp 343–58 shows how urban land use change in Britain is largely the result of the reuse of derelict land.

### (3) Urban History

**5087** *Urban History Yearbook 1974–*. This annually publishes an international current bibliography of urban history.

**5088** Gareth Rees and John Lambert *Cities in Crisis: The Political Economy of Urban Development in Post-War Britain* Arnold 1985. A socialist analysis and critique of post-war urban policy. Another good study of urban policy in the post-war years is David H McKay and Andrew W Cox *The Politics of Urban Change* Croom Helm 1979.

**5089** Phil Cooke (ed) *Localities: The Changing Face of Urban Britain* Unwin Hyman 1989. A study of the urban and regional system in Britain.

**5090** Nigel Spence *et al British Cities: An Analysis of Urban Change* Pergamon 1982. A descriptive snapshot of social and employment changes in Britain's cities since the 1950s. See also *British Cities: Urban Population and Employment Trends 1951–71* Research Report 10, Department of the Environment 1976 and Claus Adolf Moser and Wolf Scott *British Towns: A Statistical Study of their Social and Economic Differences* Oliver and Boyd 1961.

**5091** Paul Lawless and Frank Brown *Urban Growth and Change in Britain: An Introduction* Harper and Row 1986. A well regarded textbook.

**5092** Thomas Walter Freeman *The Conurbations of Great Britain* 3rd ed, Manchester University Press 1966. See also Roy Drewett, John Goddard and Nigel Spence 'Urban Britain, Regional Containment' in Brian J L Berry (ed) *Urbanization and Counterurbanization* Vol XI Sage 1976 pp 43–79. This is a study of the decline of the conurbations in the 1960s and the concentration of population growth in smaller satellites and in medium-sized free-standing units, especially in the Home Counties.

**5093** George Gordon (ed) *Regional Cities in the UK 1890–1980* Harper and Row 1986. An analysis of planning and urban ranking. Birmingham, Manchester, Liverpool and Merseyside, Glasgow and Clydeside, Leeds, Edinburgh, Cardiff, Belfast and London are all well analysed.

**5094** Chris Hamnett 'The Post-War Restructuring of the British Housing and Labour Markets' *Environment and Planning* A 16 1984 pp 147–61. An analysis of the growing divide between the suburbs and the inner city in the post-war years. This polarization between the outer and inner city, despite the gentrification of parts of inner London, is also examined in his 'The Changing Socioeconomic Structure of London and the South East 1961–1981' *Regional Studies* 20 1986 pp 391–406. See also Chris Hamnett and Peter Williams 'Social Change in London: A Study of Gentrification' *London Journal* 6 1980 pp 51–66.

**5095** P T Kivell 'Postwar Urban Residential Growth in North Staffordshire' in A D M Phillips and B J Turton (eds) *Environment, Man and Economic Change: Essays Presented to S H Beaver* Longman 1975 pp 441–58.

**5096** J N Tern 'Urban Regeneration: The Conservation Dimension' *Town Planning Review* 56 1985 pp 245–68. An analysis of the evolution since the late nineteenth century of thinking on urban conservation as reflected in legislation. This period has seen a gradual shift in emphasis from individual buildings to whole environments. It has also seen increasing public awareness of the issue. The article ends with a review of the contemporary situation. The activities of the Civic Trust in the field of urban conservation since its foundation in 1957 are examined in K A Oliver 'Places, Conservation and the Care of Streets in England 1957–1980' London PhD Thesis 1983. *Bath: A Study in Conservation* HMSO 1968, *Chester: A Study in Conservation* HMSO 1968, *Chichester: A Study in Conservation* HMSO 1968, and *York: A Study in Conservation* HMSO 1968 are studies of urban conservation in particular cities commissioned by the Ministry of Housing and Local Government.

**5097** A J Youngson *Urban Development and the Royal Fine Art Commissions* Edinburgh University Press 1989. A study of the role of the Commissions in urban conservation over the past sixty years.

**5098** *Houses of Outstanding Historical or Architectural Interest: Report* of the Committee HMSO 1950. This report by the committee chaired by Sir Ernest Gowers led to the establishment of the various Historic Buildings Councils of England, Wales and Scotland. Many fine houses have nevertheless been demolished over the post-war years. Roy Strong *et al The Destruction of the Country House 1875–1975* Thames and Hudson 1974 is a well illustrated study of and lament for the decline of the country house and an examination of the chances and problems of preserving the surviving houses and their gardens.

## (4) New Towns

The term 'New Town' is generally held to apply to the government designated new towns to which population was decanted from old established cities in the 1940s and the 1960s. There were 28 such towns established before increasing concern about the social and economic health of the inner cities led to a switch of emphasis. From the late 1960s the focus was increasingly on revitalizing the inner cities rather than decanting population from them. The shift of emphasis is also apparent in the literature on the new towns programme. The triumphalism of the early literature has been replaced by works which have questioned whether the new towns programme has in fact contributed to the modern problems of the inner city.

The towns established by the government's new towns programme are not however the only ones covered in the section below. New towns are here interpreted to include the garden cities and major developments such as the GLC's Thamesmead estate in South London.

The new towns programme had implications for housing policy in London and other affected cities. The material in the section on housing should therefore also be consulted for the literature on some of the consequences of the programme.

**5099** *New Town Development Corporations Annual Reports 1948/49–*. Until 1972/73 these various reports were published as House of Commons Papers and bound with the Parliamentary Papers. See also *Commission of New Towns Annual Report and Accounts* HMSO 1962/63–1985, which was also published as a House of Commons Paper.

**5100** A G Champion, K Clegg and R L Davies Facts about the *New Towns: A Socio-Economic Digest* Academic 1983. Details on each new town with diagrams and statistics.

**5101** *New Towns – Bibliography* 65 Department of the Environment Headquarters Library 1976. A 2,635 reference international bibliography. A J Veal *New Communities in the UK: A Classified Bibliography* Centre for Urban and Regional Studies, University of Birmingham 1973 is an unannotated bibliography covering the new towns, the expanded towns and major post-war housing estates. A supplement was published in 1975. Jean Viet *New Towns: A Selected Annotated Bibliography* UNESCO 1960 is both international and somewhat outdated.

**5102** J B Cullingworth *Environmental Planning 1939–1969* Volume 3: New Towns Policy HMSO 1980. The official peacetime history of the new towns programme. Frederic J Osborn and Arnold Whittick *New Towns: Their Origins, Achievements and Progress* Leonard Hill 1977 is a well illustrated if rather unanalytical guide to the development of each new town. Meryl Aldridge *The British New Towns: A Programme without a Policy* Routledge and Kegan Paul 1979 is in contrast a critical appraisal of the new towns programme, not least in the context of its effect on regional growth and inner city decline. David Thompson 'Britain: The New Towns Revisited' in Mahlon Apgar IV (ed) *New Perspectives on Community Development* McGraw-Hill 1976 pp 23–37 surveys the new towns and criticizes them for a different reason, for what he sees as their inadequate social infrastructure. Frank Schaffer *The New Town Story* Paladin 1972 instead presents the new towns as one of the great achievements of the post-war welfare state from the point of view of a civil servant who was closely involved in the development of policy from the late 1940s. Hazel Meyrick Evans (ed) *New Towns: The British Experience* Knight 1972 contains a number of interesting perspectives, including an essay by Dame Evelyn Sharp, the former Permanent Secretary at the Ministry of Housing and Local Government. British new towns are contrasted with those in America in Carol Corden *Planned Cities: New Towns in Britain and America* Sage, Beverley Hills 1977. M Haggerty *The New Towns* New Towns Association 1981 is a brief history of the new towns programme. See also Frederick J Osborn and Arnold Whittick *The New Towns* 2nd ed, Leonard Hill 1973, *New Towns: The British Experience* Knight 1973, E P Hopkins 'The Contribution of the New Towns Idea, Especially to Urban Dispersal, in Britain' Edinburgh MSc Thesis 1970–1 and H Rosing 'A Study between Philosophy and Development of Selected British New Towns' Edinburgh MSc Thesis 1970–1.

**5103** Lloyd Rodwin *The British New Towns Policy* Harvard University Press, Cambridge, Massachusetts 1956. A penetrating analysis of the early development of the programme. Another early analysis is A C Duff *New Towns: An Experiment in Living* Pall Mall Press 1961. Duff was the General Manager of the Stevenage Development Corporation 1947–57, though he has not made much use of that experience in this account.

**5104** *New Towns Committee: Interim Report* Cmnd 6759, *Second Interim Report* Cmnd 6794, and *Final Report* Cmnd 6876, *Parliamentary Papers* xiv 1945–46. The report by Lord Reith which led to the New Towns Act of 1946 and the designation of the first batch of new towns. The New Towns Act is assessed in J Wood 'The History, Purpose and Application of the New Towns Act 1946' Liverpool MA Thesis 1952–3.

**5105** P H Levin *Government and the Planning Process: An Analysis and Appraisal of Government Decision-Making Processes with Special Reference to the Launching of the New Towns and Town Development Schemes* Allen and Unwin 1976. Two case studies of the process of designating town expansion areas under the Town Development Act 1957 and the New Towns Act 1965.

**5106** Ray Thomas *London's New Towns: A Study of Self- Contained and Balanced Communities* Political and Economic Planning 1969. A critical and evaluative study as is his *Aycliffe to Cumbernauld: A Study of Seven New Towns in their Regions* Political and Economic Planning 1969.

**5107** A G Champion 'The Changing Land Requirements of Planned Urban Development, with Particular Reference to the Land Use Structure and Land Provisions Adopted by British New Towns Since 1960' London MPhil Thesis 1969–70.

**5108** S Potter 'The Alternative New Towns' *Town and Country Planning* 53 1984 pp 306–12. A review of the 'expanded towns' designated under the 1952 Town Development Act.

**5109** B J Heraud 'Social Class and the New Towns' *Urban Studies* 5 1968 pp 33–58. A study of the social mix in the new towns focusing on Crawley. See also L Bokvell *et al* 'Social Class in a New Town: A Comment' *Urban Studies* 6 1969 pp 93–6.

**5110** A M Fields and C Crofts *Some Aspects of Planned Migration to New and Expanding Towns* GLC 1977. A rather inconclusive analysis of population and industrial migration to new towns of the South East and the effects this has had upon London. See also R G Walker 'Population and Employment Growth in the London and Glasgow New Towns 1951–64' Birmingham PhD Thesis 1968–9. S Fothergill *et al* 'The Impact of the New and Expanded Town Programme on Industrial Location in Britain 1960–1978' *Regional Studies* 17 1983 pp 251–60 finds that the new towns had considerable effect on industrial location in the 1960s but that this was small in the 1970s.

**5111** Henry Dupree *Urban Transportation: The New Town Solution* Gower 1987. A good well illustrated analysis. It is mostly concerned with the road network but also deals with pedestrian areas and rail services in each of the new towns.

**5112** Peter Lucas *A Reporter's Look at the Development of one of Britain's Biggest New Towns* privately printed 1985. Basildon was one of the first wave of new towns to be designated after the war.

**5113** Robert Steel *Basingstoke Town Development: A Review of the First Six Years* Basingstoke Development Group 1967.

**5114** Philip A Henslowe *Ninety Years On: An Account of the Bourneville Village Trust* Bourneville Village Trust 1984. A brief account up to the 1980s Although now rather outdated *The Bourneville Village Trust 1900–1955* Bourneville Village Trust 1956 is in many ways more informative.

**5115** H and J Parris *Bracknell: The Making of Our New Town* Bracknell Development Corporation 1981. A history of the planning and development of Bracknell since 1949. See also Audrey Ogilvy *Bracknell and its Migrants: Twenty-One Years of New Town Growth* HMSO 1975.

**5116** Geoffrey L Woodcock *Planning, Politics and Communications: A Study of the Central Lancashire New Town* Gower 1986. The Central Lancashire new town was the last to be designated, in 1970. This is an examination of its development, especially in the context of public consultation and participation in the planning process.

**5117** B G Clarke 'Decision Making and the Land Development Process: A Study in Politics and Land Development, with Special Reference to Crawley New Town' Sussex DPhil Thesis 1971–2.

**5118** Kathleen M Slack *Henrietta's Dream: A Chronicle of the Hampstead Garden Suburb 1905–1982* the author 1982.

**5119** Frederick Gibberd, Ben Hyde Harvey, Len White *et al Harlow: Story of a New Town* Publications for Companies 1980. An official account of the development of the town from its designation in 1947 until the dissolution of the development corporation in 1980. A well illustrated account which draws on the reminiscences of the authors and contains numerous useful appendices. See also W Eric Adams *The Development of the New Town of Harlow* Harlow Development Corporation 1963.

**5120** C B Purdom *The Letchworth Achievement* Dent 1963. A history of the first garden city 1903–62. It is particularly useful on the crisis that hit the company that developed the town in 1956–62, in which Purdom was personally involved. See also M Miller 'Letchworth Garden City Eighty Years On' *Built Environment* 9 1983 pp 167–84.

**5121** Derek Walker *The Architecture and Planning of Milton Keynes* Architectural Press 1982. Milton Keynes was designated in 1967. It was planned as a city of up to 250,000 inhabitants, much larger than most of the new

towns. Walker, its Chief Architect and Planner 1970–76, describes its planning and development. The background to the development of Milton Keynes is examined in detail in P L Mortimer 'Urban Development in North Buckinghamshire 1930–1970' Open University MPhil Thesis 1984. Progress at Milton Keynes is reviewed in W Bor 'Milton Keynes New City – Ten Years On' *Ekistics* 46 1979 243–52 and R Thomas 'Milton Keynes – City of the Future?' *Built Environment* 9 1983 pp 245–54. The landscaping of the new city is discussed in N Higson 'Milton Keynes: City of Trees' *Landscape Design* 168 1987 pp 24–9.

**5122** Hugh Barty-King *Expanding Northampton* Secker and Warburg 1985. A well illustrated official history covering the period between Northampton's designation for expansion in 1968 and the replacement of the development corporation by the Commission for the New Towns in 1985.

**5123** Gordon Anstis *Redditch: Success in the Heart of England: The History of Redditch New Town 1964–85* Publications for Companies 1985. A well illustrated official history tracing the history of the new town up to the dissolution of the development corporation in 1985. Walter Stranz *Overspill, Anticipation and Reality: A Case Study of Redditch* Centre for Urban and Regional Studies Occasional Paper 23, University of Birmingham 1972 examines the failure to expand the town under the Town Development Act 1952 and its growth as a new town in the 1960s.

**5124** Jack Balchin *First New Town: An Autobiography of the Stevenage Development Corporation 1946–1980* Stevenage Development Corporation 1980. An anecdotal and allusive official account of the development of the new town up to the winding up of the development corporation in 1980 using official records and oral testimony. The politics of the planning of Stevenage are examined in Bob Mullan *Stevenage Ltd: Aspects of the Planning and Politics of Stevenage New Town 1945–78* Routledge and Kegan Paul 1980. See also Harold Orlans *Stevenage: A Sociological Study of a New Town* Routledge and Kegan Paul 1952.

**5125** Michael Harloe *Swindon: A Town in Transition: A Study in Urban Development and Overspill Policy* Heinemann 1975. A detailed analysis of the expansion of the town 1953–66.

**5126** I Skinner *Thamesmead* GLC 1976. A 104 reference bibliography on the new GLC estate in South London.

**5127** Stephen Holley *Washington: Quicker by Quango: The History of Washington New Town 1964–1983* Publications for Companies 1983. A good account of the successes and failures of the development of the new town and a defence of the record of the development corporation. The special problems of development in an area of economic decline are examined in W V Hole, I M Adderson and M T Pountney *Washington New Town: The Early Years* HMSO 1979. See also J D Peart 'The Aims and Objectives of New Towns: An Investigation into the Attainment of Selected Planning Objectives at Washington New Town' Newcastle Polytechnic MPhil Thesis 1980.

**5128** R Filler *A History of Welwyn Garden City* Phillimore 1986. A general history of the garden city.

**5129** D Deakin (ed) *Wythenshawe: The Story of a Garden City Volume 2: 1926 to 1984* Northenden Civic Society 1984.

## (5) Inner Cities

Other sections, most notably that on housing should also be consulted. The celebrated Church of England report, *Faith in the City*, can be found in the section on the Churches and Social Problems [2646, 8062].

**5130** Nigel J Thrift and Martin Clarke *British Inner Cities: A Research Bibliography* School of Geography, University of Leeds n.d. (1979?). A quite well organized, unannotated bibliography.

**5131** Paul Lawless *Britain's Inner Cities – Problems and Policies* Harper and Row 1981. A good analysis of the causes of the decay of the inner cities and the various programmes and initiatives put forward since the 1960s to try and tackle it. Another useful analysis of the problems of the inner city and the policies put forward to solve them is M S Gibson and M J Longstaff *An Introduction to Urban Renewal* Hutchinson 1982. This includes case studies of Birmingham and Leeds. *The Costs of Industrial Change* Community Development Project 1981 examines the impact of inner area economic decline in the context of studies of Benwell (in Newcastle), North Shields, Batley, Saltley (in Birmingham) and Lavington. Colin Jones (ed) *Urban Deprivation and the Inner City* Croom Helm 1979 considers aspects of the inner city problem such as population decline, unemployment, housing, the planning of renewal and the historical growth of the problem through a series of case studies. See also J S Forman and P P A Gripaios 'Inner City Problems and Inner City Policies' *Regional Studies* 11 1977 pp 401–12. Alison Ravetz 'Changing Attitudes – The Idea of Value in the Inner City' *Built Environment* 4 1978 pp 177–82 concentrates on the problem posed by under-investment in the inner city.

**5132** Peter Hall (ed) *The Inner City in Context: The Final Report of the Social Science Research Council*

*Inner Cities Working Party* Heinemann 1981. An impressive series of studies of the problems and the roots of the problems of the inner cities. Alan Evans and D E C Eversley (eds) *The Inner City: Employment and Industry* Heinemann 1980 is a collection of papers on the decline of manufacturing industry, the effects of regional policy, changes in the urban labour market, housing, small firms, manpower and planning in the inner city. It includes case studies. See also Kenneth J Button 'Employment and Industrial Decline in the Inner Areas of British Cities: The Experience of 1962–1977' *Journal of Industrial Affairs* 6 1978 pp 1–6, P Elias and G Keogh *Industrial Decline and Unemployment in the Inner City Areas of Britain: A Review of the Evidence* Manpower Research Group Discussion Paper 12, University of Warwick 1980 and M W Danson, W F Lever and J F Malcolm 'The Inner City Employment Problem in Great Britain 1952–1976: A Shift-Share Approach' *Urban Studies* 17 1980 pp 193–210. The implications for the cities of their declining population, partly as a result of the new towns programme, are examined in P A Stone 'The Implications for the Conurbations of Population Changes (with Particular Reference to London)' *Regional Studies* 12 1978 pp 95–123.

**5133** Crispin Cross *Ethnic Minorities in the Inner City: The Ethnic Dimension in Urban Deprivation in England* Commission for Racial Equality 1978. A special report.

**5134** Joan Higgins, Nicholas Deakin, John Edwards and Malcolm Wicks *Government and Urban Poverty: Inside the Policy Making Process* Blackwell 1983. A history of inner city policy since 1967 and especially of the policy making process. A dismal story of enthusiastic projects foundering through bureaucratic inertia, lack of funds and an overly narrow focus and an examination of why the policies have not had more success. It includes a chronology. Urban policy is also critically assessed in Paul Lawless *Urban Deprivation and Government Initiative* Faber 1979. Brian Robson *Those Inner Cities: Reconciling the Social and Economic Arms of Urban Policy* Clarendon 1988 is a useful overview of inner city policy. See also John Edwards and Richard Batley *The Politics of Positive Discrimination: An Evaluation of the Urban Programme 1967–77* Tavistock 1978 and Martin Loney and Mark Allen (ed) *The Crisis of the Inner City* Macmillan 1979. Paul Lawless *The Evolution of Spatial Policy: A Case Study of Inner City Policy in the United Kingdom 1968–1981* Pion 1986 is more theoretical than empirical. Lee Bridges 'The Ministry of Internal Security: British Urban Social Policy 1968–74' *Race and Class* 16 1975 pp 375–86 and 'Keeping the Lid On: British Urban Social Policy 1974–1981' *Race and Class* 23 1981–82 pp 171–85 sees inner city policy largely in terms of social control.

**5135** D McKay and A Cox 'Confusion and Reality in Public Policy: The Case of the British Urban Programme' *Political Studies* 26 1978 pp 491–506. This rejects the conventional explanation that urban policy developed as Labour's response to Enoch Powell's 'Rivers of Blood' speech of 1968 and instead argues that amorphous academic ideas and bureaucratic pressure are the best explanations.

**5136** John Edwards and Richard Batley *The Politics of Positive Discrimination: An Evaluation of the Urban Programme 1967–1977* Tavistock 1978. A study of the development and implementation of the Home Office's policy. See also Nicholas Deakin 'Fits and Snarks: The Search for a Solution for Inner City Deprivation' *Local Government Policy Making* 8 1981 pp 81–94.

**5137** *Policy for the Inner Cities* Cmnd 6845, *Parliamentary Papers* xliv 1976–77. The outcome of a major policy review announced by Callaghan in September 1976 this White Paper sets out his government's view of the inner city problem and its policies to combat it. On inner city policy since the White Paper see M Stewart 'Ten Years of Urban Policy: A Review' *Local Link* 10 1987 pp 6–11 and R Hambleton 'Implementing Inner City Policy: Reflections from Experience' *Policy and Politics* 9 1981 pp 51–7.

**5138** T R Hornby 'Urban Renewal: The Financial Institutions and Whitehall' *Management in Government* 4 1982 pp 206–18. A case study of the co-operation in urban regeneration between private industry and the government through the Department of the Environment Financial Institutions Group set up in 1981.

**5139** *Gilding the Ghetto: The State and the Poverty Experiments* Community Development Project 1977. A short report on the Community Developments Projects. The first part runs down all the projects set up. The second part looks at the roots of inner city decline and the rise of government concern since the 1960s. The final part is an assessment of the projects. This is updated by *Community Development – Towards a National Perspective of the Work of the Community Development Projects Foundation 1978–1982* Community Development Projects Foundation 1982. The Community Development Project was launched in July 1969. On its development see also Ray Lees and G Smith (eds) *Action Research in Community Development: Papers Relating to the Home Office's Community Development Project* Routledge and Kegan Paul 1975 and 'The British National Community Development Project 1969–74' *Community Development Journal* 9 1974 pp 162–86. Martin Loney *Community against Government: The British Community Development Project 1968–78 – A Study of Government Incompetence* Heinemann Educational 1983 is a critical assessment of the implementation of this policy. He also brings out the way in which local

Community Development Projects were radicalized by activists. Harry Specht *The Community Development Project* Paper 2, National Institute for Social Work 1976 is a critique of the strategy of the action team directors and the failings of the policy 1969–74.

**5140** S Spooner *The Politics of Partnership* Planning Studies 6, School of Environment Planning, Polytechnic of Central London 1980. An analysis of the Inner City Partnership programme. This involved central and local government in schemes such as the provision of small industrial units. The various initiatives of the programme and its inadequacies are assessed in P A Richardson 'Government Policy for the Inner Cities: A Case Study of Small Premises Provision in the Partnership Areas' Reading PhD Thesis 1985. The failure to integrate and involve the local population is one of the principal charges laid against them by Michael Parkinson and S R M Wilks 'Managing Urban Decline: The Case of the Inner City Partnerships' *Local Government Studies* 9 1983 pp 23–39, a case study of these partnerships in Manchester/Salford and Liverpool.

**5141** J Hall *et al* 'The Redevelopment of Britain's Urban Docklands' *Town and Country Planning* 51 1982 pp 19–131. Five linked articles on redevelopment in docklands.

**5142** Nigel Moor and Paul Waddington *From Rags to Ruins: Batley, Woollen Textiles and Industrial Change* Community Development Project 1980. A study of urban decline in Batley focusing on the years 1966–75.

**5143** Chris Paris and Bob Blackaby *Not Much Improvement: Urban Renewal Policy in Birmingham* Heinemann 1979. A study which focuses on slum clearance and housing policy. The establishment, aims, organization and effectiveness of the city's Inner City Partnership in the period 1979–84 is assessed in Public Sector Management Research Unit, University of Aston *Five Year Review of the Birmingham Inner City Partnership* Department of the Environment 1985. *Unequal City: Final Report of the Birmingham Inner Area Study* HMSO 1977 is a very informative and in-depth study of the nature of inner city problems in Birmingham, concentrating on Small Heath.

**5144** C Vereker and J B Mays *Urban Redevelopment and Social Change: A Study of Social Conditions in Central Liverpool 1955–6* Liverpool University Press 1961. The urban renewal programme in Liverpool in the 1960s is analysed in David M Muchnick *Urban Renewal in Liverpool* Bell 1970. See also P J Moran 'Local Authority Involvement in Community Development: Liverpool 1965–1970 – A Case Study' Liverpool MA Thesis 1971–2. A vast amount of information and statistics on inner city problems in Liverpool is contained in *Change and Decay: Final Report of the Liverpool Inner*

*Area Study* HMSO 1977. The work of the Community Development Project in Liverpool is assessed in P Toppin and G Smith *Government against Poverty? Liverpool Community Development Project 1970–1975* Social Evaluation Unit, University of Oxford 1977. On other efforts to regenerate Liverpool; the Merseyside Docklands Development Corporation, set up in 1981, is assessed in B Adcock 'Regenerating Merseyside Docklands: The Merseyside Development Corporation 1981–1984' *Town Planning Review* 55 1984 pp 265–89. The Task Force set up by Michael Heseltine in the wake of the 1981 Toxteth riots is assessed in Michael Parkinson and James Duffy 'Government's Response to Inner City Riots: The Minister for Merseyside and the Task Force' *Parliamentary Affairs* 37 1984 pp 76–96.

**5145** R Nabarro and D Richards *Wasteland: A Thames Television Report* Associated Book Publishers 1980. A study of derelict land in inner London, and especially Tower Hamlets, and the reasons and history behind the poor use of land. Industrial decline in inner London is examined in P Damesick 'The Inner City Economy in Industrial and Post-Industrial London' *London Journal* 6 1980 pp 23–35. Population change in inner London is surveyed in Nicholas Deakin and Clare Ungerson *Leaving London: Planned Mobility and the Inner City* Heinemann 1977. Focusing on moves to the new towns from Islington in 1966–71 they conclude that whoever gained from the new towns programme it was not the deprived households left behind in the inner city. The decanting of population increased rather than decreased the problems of the inner areas. So did the social segregation that resulted from the gentrification of certain areas, as Chris Hamnett 'Social Change and Social Segregation in Inner London 1961–1971' *Urban Studies* 13 1976 pp 261–72 argues.

**5146** P A Roberts 'The Quality of the Residential Environment in the Inner City: A Case Study of Battersea 1961 to 1981' Reading PhD Thesis 1983.

**5147** J Anderson *London Docklands: A Bibliography on Social Change and Public Policy* Open University Press 1980. A short bibliography. J M Hall 'East London's Future: Visions Past and Present' *East London Papers* 14 1972 pp 5–24 is a history of attempts to plan and redevelop the East End culminating with the 1971 London Docklands Study. The next innovation was the creation, by the local authorities, of the Docklands Joint Committee. Its history, and that of the Docklands Land Board, is reviewed in *London Docklands: Past, Present and Future* Docklands Joint Committee 1980. On schemes to redevelop docklands in the 1970s see also N P Falk 'The Planning and Development of London's Docklands (1970–75)' London PhD Thesis 1984. The failings of the schemes of these years are also discussed in Falk's article, 'London's Docklands: A Tale of Two Cities' *London Journal* 7 1981 pp 65–80. Grant Ledger-

wood *Urban Innovation: The Transformation of London's Docklands 1968–84* Gower 1985 is an examination of the development and effect of urban policy in the London docklands up to the creation of the London Docklands Development Corporation. The plan of 1978 is evaluated in M Mayo, I Newman and N Sharman 'Rebuilding London's Docklands: The Strategic Plan – Two Years On' *Community Development Journal* 15 1980 pp 60–8. The creation of the latest innovation in docklands redevelopment planning in 1981 is described in D Billingham *The Creation of the London Docklands Development Corporation* Planning Studies 13, Polytechnic of Central London 1981. Its policies and activities are outlined by its chairman in N Broacken 'The Regeneration of London's Docklands' *Journal of the Royal Society of Arts* 132 1984 pp 105–17. See also W J Tuckley 'Politics and Planning in Docklands: The Case of the London Docklands Development Corporation' London MPhil Thesis 1984. The attempt to encourage tourism in Docklands is discussed in Stephen Page and M Thea Sinclair 'Tourism and Accommodation in London: Alternative Policies and the Docklands Experience' *Built Environment* 15 1989 pp 125–37.

**5148** A McEwan 'The Lansbury Story' *East London Papers* 3 1960 pp 67–86. A history of the scheme for planning the Lansbury estate in Poplar commencing with its designation as a Comprehensive Development Area in the 1950s.

**5149** Stephen Hatch, Enid Fox and Charles Lagg *Research and Reform: The Case of Southwark 1969–72* Urban Deprivation Unit, Home Office 1977. A blow-by-blow account of the activities of the Community Development Project in Southwark and of some of its research findings.

**5150** *Final Report of the Lambeth Inner Area Study* HMSO 1977 An in-depth study of the inner city problems of this south London borough.

**5151** P N Balchin *Housing Improvement and Social Inequality: Case Study of an Inner City* Saxon House 1979. A study of policy on improvements to the housing and social environment of West London since 1969.

**5152** P E Lloyd and C M Mason 'Manufacturing Industry in the Inner City: A Case Study of Greater Manchester' *Transactions of the Institute of British Geographers* n.s. 3 1978 pp 66–90. Industrial decline in Manchester was mainly the result of the closure of small firms. On another aspect of inner city problems and policies in Manchester see G T Stoker 'The Politics of Urban Renewal in Withington Village, Manchester 1962–1983' Manchester PhD Thesis 1985.

**5153** W Hamilton and I Walkland *Byker Community Development Project 1974–1978* Council for Voluntary

Service, Newcastle-upon-Tyne 1980. See also *West Newcastle in Growth and Decline: A Picture History* Benwell Community Development Project, Newcastle-upon-Tyne 1981.

## (6) Suburbia

**5154**  Arthur M Edwards *The Design of Suburbia: A Critical Study in Environmental History* Pembridge Press 1981. A good illustrated history of the planning and design of suburbs since the eighteenth century and the economic and social factors affecting their development.

**5155**  F M L Thompson (ed) *The Rise of Suburbia* Leicester University Press 1982. Studies of suburban development in Ealing, Acton, Bromley, Bexley and Headingley in the nineteenth and twentieth centuries. On suburban development in areas such as Bromley and Bexley see also M Waugh 'Suburban Growth in North-West Kent 1861–1961' London PhD Thesis 1967–8 and M C Carr 'The Growth and Characteristics of a Metropolitan Suburb – Bexley Borough, North-West Kent 1880–1963' London PhD Thesis 1970–1.

**5156**  Guy R Williams *London in the Country: The Growth of Suburbia* Hamilton 1975.

## (7) Green Belts

**5157**  David Thomas *London's Green Belt* Faber 1970. A good history. Richard Munton *London's Green Belt: Containment in Practice* Allen and Unwin 1983 examines the pressures on the green belt in the 1980s, as a result of the construction of the M25 motorway and changes in land use. It also contains a useful bibliography. The pattern of acquisition of the green belt and its significance to land use planning over the period 1920–80 is examined in detail for the first time in E G Sharp 'The Acquisition of the London Green Belt Estates: A Study of Inter-Authority Relations' London PhD Thesis 1986.

**5158**  D I Scargill 'Conservation and the Oxford Green Belt' in Trevor Rowley (ed) *The Oxford Region* Department for External Studies, University of Oxford 1980 pp 125–38. Informally established in the 1950s it was approved in 1975.

**5159**  Gerald Haythornthwaite *The Sheffield Green Belt* Sheffield and Peak District Branch, Council for the Protection of Rural England 1984. Though first approved in 1938 its existence did not prevent overspill building in Sheffield in the 1950s. Only in 1983 was a green belt with a degree of legal protection established.

## (8) Rural Planning

**5160**  *Countryside Planning Yearbook* Geo Books 1980–. An annual guide.

**5161**  Andrew W Gilg *Countryside Planning: The First Three Decades 1945–76* Methuen 1979. The standard account. M Blacksell and Andrew W Gilg *The Countryside: Planning and Change* Allen and Unwin 1981 assesses the impact of planning proliferation over the same period and criticizes a perceived lack of planning coordination. See also Gordon Clark *Housing and Planning in the Countryside* Research Studies Press 1982 and J M Reid 'Planning and the Rural Landscape: The Origin and Development of Post-War Policy' Birmingham PhD Thesis 1982–3.

**5162**  Martin Voorhees Associates *Review of Rural Settlement Policies 1945–1980* Department of the Environment 1981. A critical examination of post-war development plans. It is particularly critical of the key settlements idea. Though recognizing that it has sometimes been useful it argues that there is no universally applicable solution to the problems of planning in rural areas.

**5163**  D J Parsons 'A Geographical Examination of the Twentieth Century Theory and Practice of Selected Village Development in England' Nottingham PhD Thesis 1979. A study of the post-war practice of categorizing villages according to their function in rural planning, making use of case studies in South Nottinghamshire and North Norfolk. A particular example of this is the planned development of Ivybridge in the 1960s and 1970s described in Anne Glyn-Jones *Village into Town: A Study of Transition in South Devon* Devon County Council/University of Exeter 1977. At the opposite end of the categories were 'D' villages. The designation of and effect of such designation on these villages is sympathetically analysed in D B Walsh '"D" Village Policy in Durham County 1951–79: A Study in the Co-ordination of Physical Planning and Employment Generation' Strathclyde MSc Thesis 1979. The effects, not least the social effects, of this policy in Durham are examined and condemned in R Snowden '"Condemned to Die . . .": Housing Action and Social Justice in South West Durham 1949–1979' Durham MA Thesis 1979.

**5164**  Anne Glyn-Jones *Rural Recovery: Has it begun? A study of a Parish in North-West Devon 1964–1978* Devon County Council/University of Exeter 1979. Designated a key settlement Hatherleigh had at last turned round and begun to increase its population, employment and services by the end of the 1970s.

**5165** D L W Sherry 'Socio-Economic Changes in some Dorset Villages 1871–1974 with Reference to Rural Planning' Manchester PhD Thesis 1974–6.

**5166** M C Dunn 'Patterns of Population Change and Movement in Herefordshire 1951–1971 and their Implications for Rural Planning' Birmingham PhD Thesis 1978–9.

**5167** Y Oyama 'Post-War Rural Settlement Policy in Britain, with Special Reference to Hertfordshire' Birmingham PhD Thesis 1979–80.

### (9) Rural Life

In addition to the literature listed below there are a considerable number of historical and sociological studies of rural areas which are to be found in the section on Local History.

**5168** Simon Neate *Rural Deprivation: An Annotated Bibliography of Economic and Social Problems in Rural Britain* Geo Abstracts 1981. A well organized bibliography with informative annotations. It focuses on issues such as planning or the disappearance of amenities.

**5169** David Phillips and Allan Williams *Rural Britain: A Social Geography* Blackwell 1984. A good textbook with a good bibliography.

**5170** Howard Newby *Green and Pleasant Land? Social Change in Rural England* Hutchinson 1979. A study of the transformation of the landscape in the agricultural revolution since the war and the ensuing social changes, which have seen villages transformed from working communities into commuter dormitories, and the resulting problems of conservation. Changes in rural life are also examined in Gwyn Evans Jones *Rural Life: Problems and Processes* Longman 1973.

**5171** H E Bracey *English Rural Life* Routledge and Kegan Paul 1959. A comprehensive survey of all aspects of rural life. See also W P Baker *The English Village* Oxford University Press 1953.

**5172** David Phillips and Allan Williams *Rural Britain: A Social Geography* Blackwell 1984. A very useful study of the state of and processes of change in the countryside, the rural economy, rural planning, rural society and amenities. It includes a good bibliography.

**5173** J Ashton and W H Lang (eds) *The Remoter Areas of Britain* Oliver and Boyd 1972. A collection of papers on farming, tourism, the disappearance of amenities and other economic and social changes in these areas.

**5174** John Saville *Rural Depopulation in England and Wales 1851–1951* Routledge and Kegan Paul 1957. This includes a considerable amount of material on contemporary problems stemming from this flight to the towns. See also H E Bracey 'Some Aspects of Rural Depopulation in the United Kingdom' *Rural Sociology* 23 1958 pp 385–91 and T P Jones 'Rural Depopulation in an Area of South Devon Since 1945' London MA Thesis 1967–8. The reversal of depopulation trends in some rural areas as a result of influxes of commuters or retired people in the 1970s is examined in Paul Cloke 'Counterurbanisation: A Rural Perspective' *Geography* 70 1985 pp 113–22.

**5175** J Martin Shaw (ed) *Rural Deprivation and Planning* Geo Books 1979. A good collection of essays on local politics and rural deprivation in services and amenities. The role of planning in the disappearance of these services is also brought out. Perhaps the most influential publication on this process is Standing Conference of Rural Community Councils *The Decline of Rural Services* National Council of Social Service 1978. It focuses on villages in the South West. It found that the smaller the village the faster its services disappeared. The less mobile inhabitants became increasingly deprived. The report concluded by making a number of important recommendations for the prevention and alleviation of this decline in services. One of these services is examined in detail in David St John Thomas *The Rural Transport Problem* Routledge and Kegan Paul 1963.

**5176** Alan Walker (ed) *Rural Poverty: Property Deprivation and Planning in Rural Areas* Child Poverty Action Group 1978. A collection of papers on the effects of landownership, pay, housing, social services, health provision, transport, education, access to recreation facilities and welfare rights on the quality of life in rural areas. See also Sue Cooper *Rural Poverty in the United Kingdom* Policy Studies Institute 1981.

**5177** Malcolm J Moseley *Social Issues in Rural Norfolk* Centre of East Anglian Studies, University of East Anglia 1978. A survey of an area of population decline in the period 1951–71. It examines social change and the declining quality of services and amenities. See also John Packman and M H C Terry *Services in Rural Norfolk 1950–1980: A Survey of the Changing Patterns of Service in Rural Norfolk over the Last Thirty Years* Norfolk County Council 1981. These same problems and planning failures in the period 1975–81 are analysed in Reg Harman 'Rural Services: Change in North-East Norfolk' *Policy and Politics* 10 1982 pp 477–94.

**5178** D M Bell 'The Social Effects of the Closure of Village Schools in Northumberland' Durham MA (Ed) Thesis 1985. This argues that the evidence to support the view that the closure of village schools leads to the death of villages is minimal. Amenities and rural life in Northumberland are examined more generally, despite its title, in Heather H Aitken *Northumberland Village Halls* Northumberland Rural Community Council 1959.

# 9 SOCIAL HISTORY

## A. GENERAL

In addition to the works listed below there are a number of local sociological studies which have been published. These can be found in the section on local histories.

**5179** David Rhind *A Census User's Handbook* Methuen 1983. An indispensable guide to the nature and use of the data produced as a result of the censuses which are taken every ten years (though there was an attempt to increase the frequency to once every five years in the 1960s). See also the *Guide to Census Reports, Great Britain 1801–1966* HMSO 1977. The material derived from the censuses of the 1961 and 1966 is used to good effect to show demographic and domestic trends in *People in Britain: A Census Atlas* HMSO 1971. A successor volume using material from the 1971 census appeared as *People in Britain: A Census Atlas* HMSO 1980. On changes to the census and its increasing quality see I Mills 'Developments in Census Taking Since 1841' *Population Trends* 48 1987 pp 37–44.

**5180** Alan F Sillitoe *Britain in Figures: A Handbook of Social Statistics* 2nd ed, Penguin 1973.

**5181** *Social Trends* HMSO 1970–. An annual audit of social change in Britain. *General Household Survey* HMSO 1970– is an annual survey of private households, focusing on education, health, housing and employment. It includes special surveys in some years.

**5182** Victor F Gilbert (comp) *Labour and Social History Theses: American, British and Irish University Theses and Dissertations in the Field of British and Irish Labour History Presented between 1900 and 1978* Mansell 1982. A classified unannotated bibliography.

**5183** Arthur Marwick *British Society Since 1945* 2nd ed Penguin 1990. An excellent short history with a good bibliography. His *Britain In Our Century: Images and Controversies* Thames and Hudson 1984 is a well illustrated social history. His *The Explosion of British Society 1914–1970* Macmillan 1971 also remains useful. T Noble *Modern Britain: Structure and Change* Batsford 1975 is an excellent general work on social change in the

post-war period. Guy Arnold *Britain Since 1945* Blandford 1989 is a useful social history of the post-war period. See also John Colville *The New Elizabethans 1952–77* Collins 1977.

**5184** A H Halsey *Change in British Society* 3rd ed, Oxford University Press 1986. The standard social history of Britain in the twentieth century. The same broad range of fields is covered in A H Halsey (ed) *British Social Trends Since 1900: A Guide to the Changing Social Structure of Britain* Macmillan 1988.

**5185** Francois Bedarida *A Social History of England 1851–1975* Methuen 1979. A well regarded French perspective on modern British social history. Theo Barker and Michael Drake (eds) *Population and Society in Britain 1850–1980* Batford 1982 is a good collection of essays on unemployment, children, domestic life, mortality, health, women and families and immigration. David C Marsh *The Changing Social Structure of England and Wales 1871–1961* 3rd ed, Routledge and Kegan Paul 1978 is a useful, if rather dry account. See also Judith Ryder and Harold Silver *Modern British Society: History and Structure 1850–1970* 2nd ed, Methuen 1977, Peter Maugher and Leslie Smith *The British People 1902–1968* Heinemann Educational 1972, John Salt and B J Elliott *British Society 1870–1970* Hulton 1975 and Charles Furth *Life Since 1900* Allen and Unwin 1956.

**5186** Philip Abrams and Richard Brown (eds) *UK Society: Work, Urbanism and Inequality* 2nd ed, Weidenfeld and Nicolson 1984. Useful historical perspectives on contemporary social problems such as urban change, sex discrimination, privilege, crime, poverty and one-parent families. See also Roy Bailey and Jock Young (eds) *Contemporary Social Problems in Britain* Saxon House 1973. E A John *The Social Structure of Modern Britain* 3rd ed, Pergamon 1979 is a rather anodyne textbook guide to contemporary British society. Another textbook is Nicholas Abercrombie *et al Contemporary British Society: An Introduction to Sociology* Polity 1988. Changes in culture, occupation and class structure, women's impact on the labour market, the effects of privatization and the widening of the north-south divide in the 1980s are among the issues addressed in Chris Hamnett, Linda McDowell and Philip Sarre (eds) *Restructuring Britain: The Changing Social Structure* Sage 1989.

**5187**   E Ellis Cashmore *United Kingdom Class, Race and Gender Since the War* Unwin Hyman 1989. A good analysis of changes in these aspects of British society.

**5188**   Richard Dennis and H Clout *A Social Geography of England and Wales* Pergamon 1980. A well regarded geography textbook.

**5189**   Martin Joseph *Sociology For Everyone* Polity 1989. A good textbook.

**5190**   Daniel Snowman *Kissing Cousins: Britain and America: An Interpretation of their Cultures 1945–1975* Temple Smith 1977. An examination of Britain's postwar interaction with its most important cultural partner.

**5191**   Harry Hopkins *The New Look: A Social History of the Forties and Fifties in Britain* Secker and Warburg 1963. A good piece of contemporary history which evocatively describes the trends and events of the period under review. See also Roland Marx *La Vie Quotidienne Angleterre en Temps de l'expérience Socialiste (1945–1951)* Hachette, Paris 1983.

**5192**   Benjamin Seebohm Rowntree and George R Lavers *English Life and Leisure* Longmans 1951. A detailed, if somewhat impressionistic study of social life, attitudes and leisure drawing on case studies of High Wycombe and York. Geoffrey Gorer *Exploring English Character* Cresset Press 1955 concentrates on attitudes towards subjects such as housing, friendship, love, marriage, law and order and religion. Like Rowntree and Lavers this study is based on questionnaires. Social changes and attitudes over the twentieth century, especially in the areas of sexual morality, women's lives, violence and mental illness are assessed in G M Carstairs *This Island Now* Hogarth Press 1963. Other similar studies of this period are Theodore Cauter and J S Downham *The Communication of Ideas: A Study of Contemporary Influences on Urban Life* Chatto and Windus 1954 and Ferdynand Zweig *Labour, Life and Poverty* Gollancz 1948.

**5193**   Michael Dunlop Young *The Rise of the Meritocracy 1870–2033* Thames and Hudson 1958. An examination of general social trends which is partly historical and partly prophetic.

**5194**   Raymond Williams *The Long Revolution* Chatto and Windus 1961. A cultural and social history which includes a useful final section on British society in the 1960s.

**5195**   Jeremy Seabrook *What Went Wrong? Working People and the Ideals of the Labour Movement* Gollancz 1978. A rather sad exploration of the erosion of values and the loss of a sense of identity and community in the face of the rise of the consumer society. It is basically an oral account, or a set of oral testimonies as Seabrook lets his respondents speak in their own bleak and alienated language in interviews held, mostly informally, in Rhondda, Wigan, Coventry, Blackburn, Milton Keynes, Northampton, Hackney, Bradford and Nottingham. It is also useful on attitudes to race, the family and the inner city. Beryl Bainbridge *Forever England: North and South* BBC 1987 is a similar journalistic exploration of Britain in the 1980s. The towns focused on are Liverpool, Hastings, Barnsley, Bentley, and Birmingham.

**5196**   Eric Jacobs and Robert Worcester *Britain under the MORIScope* Weidenfeld and Nicolson 1989. A comprehensive study of attitudes, values and sentiments using the opinion polls compiled by MORI as a database.

**5197**   Paul Barker (ed) *The Other Britain: A New Society Compilation* Routledge and Kegan Paul 1982. A collection of essays on aspects of modern British society from skinheads to vegetarians, from Welsh chapels to soccer hooligans.

**5198**   Peter Trudgill (ed) *Language in the British Isles* Cambridge University Press 1984. See also Peter Trudgill and Arthur Hughes *English Accents and Dialects: An Introduction to Social and Regional Varieties of British English* Arnold 1979. Changes in accents and the increasing prevalence of received pronunciation are assessed in John Honey *Does Accent Matter: The Pygmalion Factor* Faber 1989.

**5199**   Jeremy Tunstall *Old and Alone: A Sociological Study of Old People* Routledge and Kegan Paul 1966. A thorough investigation of the life and experience of the elderly.

**5200**   Geoffrey Gorer *Death, Grief and Mourning in Contemporary Britain* Cresset Press 1965. A survey of attitudes towards and the observance of mourning.

**5201**   Ronald Frankenburg *Communities in Britain: Social Life in Town and Country* Penguin 1966. A social and anthropological study of communities in Gosforth, Glossop, Banbury, Bethnal Green and assorted urban housing estates.

**5202**   Anne Grimshaw *The Horse: A Bibliography of British Books 1851–1976: With a Narrative Commentary on the Role of the Horse in British Social History, as Revealed by the Contemporary Literature* Library Association 1982. The works in this bibliography on the horse in the post-war period particularly relate to the horse in sport.

## B. POPULATION

### (1) General

**5203** *Population Trends* HMSO 1975–. This supersedes *Registrar-General's Quarterly Return for England and Wales* HMSO 1950–74. A quarterly compendium of social statistics and short articles on demographic trends.

**5204** *Population and Health Statistics in England and Wales* Office of Population, Censuses and Surveys 1980. A guide to sources and the methods whereby the statistics are compiled. It includes some bibliographical material and some information on the history and pre-history of the Office of Population, Censuses and Surveys, which was created out of the merger of the General Register Office and the Government Social Survey. See also the companion volume *Vital Registration and Marriage in England and Wales* Office of Population, Censuses and Surveys 1980.

**5205** Rosalind Mitchison *British Population Change Since 1860* Macmillan 1977. A brief presentation of the key population trends up to the 1960s. It includes useful bibliographical material. See also John Craig 'Changes in the Population Composition of England and Wales Since 1841' *Population Trends* 48 1987 pp 27–36. Michael Anderson 'The Emergence of the Modern Life Cycle in Britain' *Social History* 10 1986 pp 69–87 examines the emergence of the life cycle of the 1960s and 1970s over the previous centuries.

**5206** Heather Joshi (ed) *The Changing Population of Britain* Blackwell 1989. An important series of essays surveying recent demographic and social trends and some of the social policy problems that these present.

**5207** John Ermisch *The Political Economy of Demographic Change: Causes and Implications of Population Trends in Great Britain* Heinemann 1983. A study of the role and problems of population policy in the twentieth century. Population policy, particularly in the context of immigration control, is examined in John Simons 'The Development of Population Policy in Britain' *International Journal of Health Services* 3 1973 pp 855–62.

**5208** Roger Keith Kelsall *Population* 2nd ed, Longman 1972. A short textbook.

**5209** *Royal Commission on Population: Report* Cmnd 7695, *Parliamentary Papers* xix 1948–49. Chaired by Sir Hubert Henderson this report surveys contemporary population trends and considers what measures should be taken to influence future trends.

**5210** A E Holmans 'Current Population Trends in Britain' *Scottish Journal of Political Economy* 11 1964 pp 31–56. A study of population trends in the post-war period. There is more consideration of regional patterns and population density in R Lawton 'Recent Trends in Population and Housing in England and Wales' *Sociological Review* 11 1963 pp 303–21. See also Ian Bowen 'A Note on Urbanization and Population Growth in England and Wales Since 1931' *Yorkshire Bulletin of Economic and Social Research* 10 1958 pp 63–94. R H Osborne 'Population Changes in England and Wales 1951–1961' *East Midland Geographer* 2 1961 pp 41–50. The stability in population trends in the 1970s and 1980s is discussed in R I Armitage 'English Regional Fertility and Mortality Patterns 1975–1985' *Population Trends* 47 1987 pp 16–23.

**5211** A G Champion 'Evolving Patterns of Population Distribution in England and Wales 1951–1971' *Transactions of the Institute of British Geographers* n.s. 1 1976 pp 401–20. The reasons for the population decentralization into non-metropolitan areas in the 1970s is examined in Chris Hamnett and W Randolph 'The Changing Population Distribution of England and Wales 1961–1981: Clean Break or Consistent Progression?' *Built Environment* 8 1983 pp 272–80. This population shift is also examined in M Brittan 'Recent Population Changes in Perspective' *Population Trends* 44 1986 pp 33–41. See also S Robert and W Randolph 'Beyond Decentralisation: The Evolution of Population Distribution in England and Wales 1961–1981' *Geoforum* 14 1983 pp 75–102.

**5212** John Craig *Population Density and Concentration in Great Britain 1931, 1951 and 1961* HMSO 1975. A study using census data. See also his *Population Density and Concentration in Great Britain 1951, 1961 and 1971* HMSO 1980.

**5213** *Births Statistics* HMSO 1974–. Annual. Before 1974 the statistics appeared in *Registrar-General's Statistical Review of England and Wales* and in the *Annual Report of the Registrar-General for Scotland* and the *Annual Report of the Registrar-General for Northern Ireland*.

**5214** Alison Macfarlane *Birth Counts: Statistics of Pregnancy and Childbirth* HMSO 1984. Statistics covering the period from the introduction of state registration in 1836 up to 1983. Most of the essays in D F Roberts and R Chester (eds) *Changing Patterns of Conception and Fertility* Academic Press 1981 deal with aspects of fertility trends in Britain, covering such subjects as artificial insemination by donor, teenage pregnancy, in vitro fertilization and contraception.

**5215** Jean Thompson and Malcolm Brittan 'Some Socio-Economic Differentials in Fertility in England

and Wales' in R W Hiorns (ed) *Demographic Patterns in Developed Societies* Taylor and Francis 1980 pp 1–10. See also B Werner 'Fertility Trends in Different Social Classes 1970 to 1983' *Population Trends* 41 1985 pp 5–13.

**5216** Lynn Iliffe 'Estimated Fertility Rates of Asian and West Indian Immigrant Women in Britain 1969–74' *Journal of Biosocial Science* 10 1978 pp 189–97. Racists have often focused on what they see as the relatively high birth rates of ethnic minorities as a cause for concern. This article shows that although birth rates amongst these communities remains closer to that of the country of origin it is declining towards that of the host population.

**5217** Kirsty Stevens with Emma Dolly *Surrogate Mother: One Woman's Story* Century 1985. Pseudonymous autobiography of a woman who agreed to bear a child for an infertile couple in the early 1980s. The question of surrogate motherhood became an important issue in the field of medical ethics in the 1980s.

**5218** *Mortality Statistics* HMSO 1974–. Annual. The previous sources for these statistics are the same as those mentioned in [5213].

**5219** Office of Population, Censuses and Surveys *Trends in Mortality 1951 1975* HMSO 1978. Trends in mortality are also discussed in T McKeown, R G Record and R D Turner 'An Interpretation of the Decline of Mortality in England and Wales 1951–1971' *Population Studies* 29 1975 pp 391–422. See also A M Adelstein and J S A Ashley 'Recent Trends in Mortality and Morbidity in England and Wales' in R W Hiorns (ed) *Demographic Patterns in Developed Societies* Taylor and Francis 1980 pp 143–70.

**5220** W R Ackroyd and J P Keveny 'Mortality in Infancy and Early Childhood in Ireland, Scotland, England and Wales 1871–1970' *Ecology of Food and Nutrition* 2 1973 pp 11–19. On the effects on poverty and unemployment on infant mortality rates see Jay Winter 'Unemployment, Nutrition and Infant Mortality in Britain 1920–50' in Jay Winter (ed) *The Working Class in Modern British History: Essays in Honour of Henry Pelling* Cambridge University Press 1983 pp 232–56.

**5221** M G Marmot, A M Adelstein and I Bulusu *Immigrant Mortality in England and Wales 1970–78* HMSO 1984. A very detailed and useful study.

**5222** I Bulusu and M Alderson 'Suicides 1950–1982' *Population Trends* 35 1984 pp 11–17. Trends and statistics. See also R Farmer, T Preston and S O'Brien 'Suicide Mortality in Greater London: Changes during the Past 25 Years' *British Journal of Preventive Social Medicine* 31 1977 pp 171–7. G M G McClure 'Recent

Changes in Suicide among Adolescents in England and Wales' *Journal of Adolescence* 9 1986 pp 135–43 traces trends in suicide since 1950 and the changes in the preferred means of death.

**5223** K J M Smith 'Assisting in Suicide – The Attorney-General and the Voluntary Euthanasia Society' *Criminal Law Review* 1983 pp 579–86. Suicide ceased to be an offence under the 1961 Suicide Act. However the law on those assisting suicides remains unclear, as the case in 1983 over the booklet produced by the Voluntary Euthanasia Society recommending various ways of suicide made apparent. This article traces the development and current state of the law.

**5224** C M Law and A M Warnes 'The Changing Geography of the Elderly in England and Wales' *Transactions of the Institute of British Geographers* n.s. 1 1976 pp 453–71. This comments on the concentrations of retired people developing in particular areas, especially on the South Coast. See also their 'The Movement of Retired People to Seaside Resorts' *Town Planning Review* 4 1973 pp 373–90. Valerie A Karn *Retiring to the Seaside* Routledge and Kegan Paul 1977 is a sociological study of this trend towards retirement by the seaside, based on research and extensive interviewing at Clacton and Bexhill, mainly conducted in 1968. Importantly she examines not only the social reasons for this migration to the seaside but also the implications for local social services and the problems that they have had in adapting.

**5225** Sarah Harper 'The Impact of the Retirement Debate on Post-War Retirement Trends' in Tony Gorst, Lewis Johnman and W Scott Lucas (eds) *Postwar Britain 1945–64: Themes and Perspectives* Pinter 1989 pp 95–108. An examination of the growth of retirement in the period 1945–64 despite labour shortages and government efforts to retain workers in the labour market. A contemporary study of the post-war retirement debate is *Retirement: A Study of Current Attitudes and Practices* Acton Society Trust 1960.

## (2) Migration

### (a) Internal Migration

**5226** D Friedlander and R J Roshier 'A Study of Internal Migration in England and Wales Part 1: Geographical Patterns of Internal Migration 1851–1951' *Population Studies* 19 1965–66 pp 239–80. This was followed by their 'A Study of Internal Migration in England and Wales Part 2: Recent Internal Migrants: Their Movements and Characteristics' *Population Studies* 20 1967 pp 45–59. The effects of regional development and new towns policy on internal migration are assessed in D E C Eversley 'Population Changes and Regional Policies Since the War' *Regional Studies* 5 1971 pp 211–28. Despite the efforts of regional policy population has tended to gravitate towards the South of England, as R H Osborne 'The Drift South Continues' *Tidjschrift voor Economische en Sociale Geografie* 51 1960 pp 286–89 comments in his examination of net regional migration patterns 1931–58. The attraction of the South lay in its relative economic success.

**5227** A A Ogilvy 'Migration – The Influence of Economic Change' *Futures* 1979 pp 383–94. This points out that in the economic recession of the 1970s internal migration was much reduced.

## (b) Emigration

### (i) General

**5228** Norman Henry Carter and James R Jeffrey *External Migration: A Study of the Available Statistics 1815–1950* HMSO 1953.

**5229** Julius Isaac *British Post-War Migration* Cambridge University Press 1954. This reflects the continuing interest in encouraging emigration to the Commonwealth that persisted until the 1950s. Emigration since the Second World War of war brides to America or more generally to the Commonwealth is examined in the text and in detailed appendices. At the same time there is, with hindsight, a remarkable lack of concern about immigration. Isaac even suggests that if emigration became excessive a positive immigration policy could be implemented to mitigate the resulting demographic and economic effects.

**5230** Gillian Wagner *Children of the Empire* Weidenfeld and Nicolson 1982. A history of emigration to the Commonwealth up to 1952. This history is also surveyed in G F McCleary *Peopling the British Commonwealth* Faber 1954. McCleary is also interesting in that he reflects various attitudes of the 1950s, such as the concern that Britain was on the verge of over-population and needed to encourage emigration, the belief in the Britishness of the white Commonwealth with which this study largely deals, and the Malthusian need to keep the birth rate up in the empire as a whole. Another history of emigration to the Commonwealth is G F Plant *Overseas Settlement: Migration from the United Kingdom to the Dominions* Oxford University Press 1951. This however contains very little material on the post-war period.

**5231** Una Monk *New Horizons: A Hundred Years of Women's Migration* HMSO 1963. A history of the Women's Migration and Overseas Appointments Society and its predecessor organizations. It contains little information on the post-war years.

**5232** R T Appleyard *British Emigration to Australia* Weidenfeld and Nicolson 1964. Australia was the most popular destination for British emigrants in the early post-war era. This study surveys emigration to Australia 1945–58, the demographic and economic background to this, the migration policies of both Britain and Australia which encouraged this, and the social and economic aspirations of a sample of migrants in 1959. On the development of Australia's post-war immigration policy see W D Borrie *Immigration: Australia's Problems and Prospects* Australian Institute of International Affairs/Institute of Pacific Relations 1949. This short account traces the development of policy from the establishment of an Australian Department of Immigration in July 1945 to June 1948. On Australian policy in this period see also L F Fitzhardinge 'Immigration Policy – A Survey' *Australian Quarterly* 21 1949 pp 7–19. The assisted passage scheme of the late 1940s and early 1950s whereby emigrants to Australia could obtain their passage for just £10 is examined in Betka Zamowska *The Ten Pound Fare: Experiences of British People who Emigrated to Australia in the 1950s* Viking 1988. She also looks at the aspirations of the emigrants and their experiences and reflections on the policy of assisted migration after their arrival in Australia. Richard Bosworth 'Australia and Assisted Immigration from Britain 1945–1954' *Australian Journal of Politics and History* 34 1988 pp 187–200 also reflects upon this scheme. His emphasis however is principally on the running down of the scheme and the ending of the 'white Australia' policy. As W D Borrie '"British" Immigration to Australia' in A F Madden and W H Morris-Jones (eds) *Australia and Britain: Studies in a Changing Relationship* Cass 1980 pp 109–16 points out Britain (and the Commonwealth) nevertheless remained a major source of immigrants into Australia.

### (ii) Brain Drain

**5233** *Committee on Manpower Resources for Science and Technology: The Brain Drain: Report of the Working Group on Migration* Cmnd 3417, *Parliamentary Papers* xxxix 1966–67. This committee, under the chairmanship of Dr F E Jones was appointed in the face of growing concern at the emigration of skilled personnel from Britain. It calculated that the number of engineering and technology graduates going abroad for a year or more had increased from 24 per cent in 1961 to 42 per cent in 1966, with nearly half of these going to North America. Another report is *Emigration of Scientists from the United Kingdom: Report of a Committee Appointed by the Council of the Royal Society* The Royal Society

1963. On the brain drain to North America see James A Wilson 'The Depletion of National Resources of Human Talent in the United Kingdom: A Special Aspect of Migration to North America 1952–64' Queens PhD Thesis 1964–5. Wilson has also published 'The Emigration of British Scientists' *Minerva* 5 1966 pp 20–9. Another reflection on the emigration of skilled manpower in the 1950s and 1960s and the governmental response is Sir Gordon Sutherland 'The Brain Drain' *Political Quarterly* 38 1967 pp 51–61.

5234   Science and Engineering Policy Studies Unit *The Migration of Scientists and Engineers to and from the UK* The Royal Society/The Fellowship of Engineering 1987. After the 1960s concern about the brain drain temporarily subsided, though, as this report makes clear, the problem continued. In the 1980s this report and David Parsons and Richard Pearson *The Bio-Technology Brain Drain: A Report Prepared for the Bio-Technology Directorate of the Science and Engineering Research Council by the Institute of Manpower Studies* The Directorate 1983 have tried to draw attention once again to this problem.

5235   J R Searle 'Medical Emigration from Britain 1930–1961' *British Medical Journal* 17/3/1962 pp 782–6. This is updated by O Gish 'British Doctor Migration 1962–67' *British Journal of Medical Education* 4 1970 pp 279–88.

## (c) Immigration

The literature which is mentioned below deals particularly with the process of immigration and the growth of immigration controls since 1962. Other material dealing with immigrants is dealt with in the section on Race Relations, which should certainly be consulted.

### (i) General

5236   James Walvin *Passage to Britain* Penguin 1984. A history of immigration to Britain focusing on the period during and immediately after the Second World War. It also deals with the related issues of immigration control, the rise of race relations as a political issue, the range of communities that have become established in Britain and the reactions of the host community. The large scale immigration in waves of first Irish, then Jewish (from Eastern Europe) and finally New Commonwealth settlers since the late nineteenth century and their impact on Britain is examined in Colin Holmes *John Bull's Island: Immigration and British Society 1871–1971* Macmillan 1988. The final chapter deals with New Commonwealth immigration since 1945.

5237   Zig Layton-Henry 'Immigration into Britain: The New Commonwealth Migrants 1945–1962' *History Today* 35 1985 pp 27–32.

5238   Ceri Peach 'British Unemployment Cycles and West Indian Immigration 1955–1974' *New Community* 7 1979 pp 40–4. An examination of the correlation between the two. V Robinson 'Correlates of Asian Immigration 1959–1974' *New Community* 8 1980 pp 115–22 found that a similar correlation also exists in the case of Asian immigration, albeit not so strongly.

5239   K Jones and A D Smith *The Economic Impact of Commonwealth Immigration* Cambridge University Press 1970. This argues, using data drawn from the 1961 and 1966 censuses, that immigration has had a generally beneficial effect. Immigrants, it is contended, have made low demands on the social services whilst helping to improve living standards and to stock the labour force. See also Oscar Gish 'Color and Skill: British Immigration 1955–1968' *International Migration Review* 3 1968 pp 19–35, 'Britain and Commonwealth Migration' *Planning* 23 1957 pp 198–211 and [5321].

5240   Hugh Tinker *The Banyan Tree: Overseas Emigration from India, Pakistan and Bangladesh* Oxford University Press 1977. A survey of migration from the sub-continent, largely but not entirely to Britain, by a distinguished Commonwealth historian.

5241   Ceri Peach *West Indian Migration to Britain: A Social Geography* Oxford University Press 1968. An examination of where immigrants have come from in the Caribbean and their distribution in Britain once they have settled. It is argued that the principal determination of their distribution in Britain was the distribution of employment opportunities, which were largely concentrated in the main conurbations. Joyce Eggington *They Seek a Living* Hutchinson 1957 examines the West Indian migration to Britain from the viewpoint of the settlers. See also John Figueroa 'British West Indian Immigration to Great Britain' *Caribbean Quarterly* 5 1958 pp 116–20, Gene Tildrick 'Some Aspects of Jamaican Emigration to the United Kingdom 1953–1962' *Social and Economic Studies* 15 1966 pp 22–9 and George E Cumper 'Working Class Emigration from Barbados to the United Kingdom 1955' *Social and Economic Studies* 6 1957 pp 76–83.

5242   Geoffrey, Lord Elton *The Unarmed Invasion: A Study of Afro-Asian Immigration* Geoffrey Bles 1965. A brief description of the growth of immigration and a call for restrictions. It usefully illustrates the state of the debate about immigration in the mid-1960s.

5243   Tom Stacey *Immigration and Enoch Powell* Tom Stacey 1970. An analysis of the effect Powell had, in the wake of his 'Rivers of Blood' speech in 1968, on attitudes to immigration. The full text of this speech is reproduced in *Race* 10 1968 pp 94–103, together with the responses of Edward Heath, Quentin Hogg (Lord Hailsham) and Roy Jenkins. See also A Fox 'Attitudes to Immigration: A Comparison of Data from the 1970 and 1974 general election surveys' *New Community* 4 1975 pp 167–78.

**5244**  Nicholas Deakin 'The Immigration Issue in British Politics (1948–1964) with Special Reference to Three Selected Areas' Sussex DPhil Thesis 1972–3. Political attitudes are also examined in N C Duncan 'British Party Attitudes to Immigration and Race, with Particular Reference to Special Areas 1955–1971' Manchester PhD Thesis 1977. See also Stephen Deakin 'Immigration Control: The Liberal Party and the West Midlands Liberals 1950–1970' *Immigrants and Minorities* 3 1984 pp 297–311. In contrast to the libertarian attitude of the national party the West Midlands Liberals favoured stricter immigration controls than those put forward by either the Labour or Conservative parties.

**5245**  Elizabeth Skedulis 'The Resettlement of Displaced Persons in the United Kingdom' *Population Studies* 5 1952 pp 207–37. A survey of the principles behind and the results of the schemes launched by the government in 1946 onwards to attract refugees to Britain.

**5246**  F X Kirwin and A G Nairn 'Migrant Employment and the Recession – The Case of the Irish in Britain' *International Migration Review* 17 1983–84 pp 672–81. An examination of migration flows 1971–77.

*(ii) Immigration Control*

**5247**  *Control of Immigration Statistics, United Kingdom* HMSO 1980–. Annual.

**5248**  Vaughan Bevan *The Development of British Immigration Law* Croom Helm 1986. A valuable examination of the developments of immigration law since the Norman Conquest and of its current practice. The development of nationality law and its implications, especially for would-be Commonwealth immigrants, is traced in Anthony Lester *Citizens Without Status* Runnymede Trust 1972. The development of immigration and nationality law is also surveyed in W H Liu 'The Evolution of Commonwealth Citizenship and UK Statutory Control over Commonwealth Immigration' *New Community* 5 1977 pp 426–47.

**5249**  Iain Macdonald *Immigration Law and Practice in the United Kingdom* Butterworths 1983. A good legal textbook.

**5250**  J Rayner 'Immigration Control: Policy and Practice 1945–1981' Oxford MLitt Thesis 1982. Less of a history of immigration controls and more of a diatribe against their contemporary operation and nature is Robert Moore and Tina Wallace *Slamming the Door: The Administration of Immigration Control* Robertson 1975. An early account is 'British Immigration Policy' *Planning* 14 1947 pp 17–36.

**5251**  *Immigration Appeals: Report of the Committee* Cmnd 3387, *Parliamentary Papers* xxxvi 1966–67. The recommendations of this committee chaired by Sir Roy Wilson led to the Immigration Appeals Act 1969 which set up the Immigration Appeals Tribunal to hear appeals against decisions taken in the administration of the Commonwealth Immigrants and Aliens Acts. The work of the tribunal is reported in *Immigration Appeal Reports* HMSO 1972–. The development and state of the legal definition of the illegal immigrant is examined in Kristin Couper and Ulysses Santamaria 'An Elusive Concept: The Changing Definition of the Illegal Immigrant in the Practice of Immigration Control in the United Kingdom' *International Migration Review* 18 1984 pp 437–52. On the handling of illegal immigrants see P Gordon *Policing Immigration: Britain's Internal Controls* Pluto 1985. This is a history of the development of internal controls on immigrants since the 1914 Status of Aliens Act. It draws attention to the increasing intertwining of the immigration and welfare systems from the 1970s onwards, with welfare officers being obliged to enforce immigration controls and deal with illegal immigration. This development is also examined in H Storey 'United Kingdom Immigration Controls and the Welfare State' *Journal of Social Welfare Law* 1984 pp 14–28. On another aspect of internal controls see his *Passport Raids and Checks: Britain's Internal Immigration Controls* Runnymede Trust 1981. See also S d'Orey *Immigration Prisoners: A Forgotten Minority* Runnymede Trust 1984. This is a history of the detention of immigrants in Britain since 1905, a review of the contemporary situation and a set of recommendations for change.

**5252**  D W Dean 'Coping with Coloured Immigration: The Cold War and Colonial Policy, the Labour Government and Black Communities in Great Britain 1945–51' *Immigrants and Minorities* 6 1987 pp 305–34. A detailed analysis of the Attlee government's attitude to New Commonwealth (at that time essentially West Indian) immigration. On the 1948 British Nationality Act see [3548].

**5253**  Bob Carter, Clive Harris and Shirley Joshi 'The 1951–55 Conservative Government and the Racialisation of Black Immigration' *Immigrants and Minorities* 6 1987 pp 335–47. A study of the attitude of Churchill's peacetime administration.

**5254**  Nicholas Deakin 'Harold Macmillan and the Control of Commonwealth Immigration' *New Community* 4 1975 pp 191–4. An examination of the Macmillan government's attitudes to immigration, which increased greatly during their term of office, and their grounds for introducing and passing the 1962 Commonwealth Immigration Act.

**5255**  David Steel *No Entry: The Background and Implications of the Commonwealth Immigrants Act 1968* Christopher Hurst 1969. A commentary on the Act by one of the Liberal MPs who opposed it in parliament.

**5256**  Hannan Rose 'The Immigration Act 1971: A Case Study in the Work of Parliament' *Parliamentary Affairs* 26 1972–73 pp 69–91. An examination of the process of passing the Bill, from the drafting of the legislation and the role of pressure groups in the framing of its terms, concentrating on its treatment in the Commons at the committee stage and in the Lords. On parliamentary attitudes to the Immigration Rules that were subsequently introduced see Philip Norton 'Intra-Party Dissent in the House of Commons: A Case Study: The Immigration Rules 1972' *Parliamentary Affairs* 29 1976 pp 404–20. On the rules themselves see Richard Plender 'The New Immigration Rules' *New Community* 2 1973 pp 168–76. On the consequences of the Act see also Hannan Rose 'The Politics of Migration after the 1971 Act' *Political Quarterly* 44 1973 pp 183–96.

**5257**  Laurie Fransman *British Nationality Law and 1981 Act* Fourmat Publishing 1982. An examination of the British Nationality Act 1981 in the context of the development of nationality law since 1948. David Dixon 'Thatcher's People: The British Nationality Act 1981' *Journal of Law and Society* 10 1983 pp 161–80 is a critical assessment of the Act.

**5258**  Jacqueline Bhabha, Francesca Klug and Sue Shutter (eds) *Worlds Apart: Women under Immigration and Nationality Law* Pluto 1985.

**5259**  *2nd Report from the Home Affairs Committee: Immigration from the Indian Sub-Continent* 2v, HC Paper 67, *Parliamentary Papers* 1985–86. The report and evidence of the committee chaired by Sir Edward Gardner.

**5260**  Ranjit Sondhi *Divided Families: British Immigration Control in the Indian Sub-Continent* Runnymede Trust 1987. An examination of the delaying tactics of the entry clearance system and of the effect of British immigration controls on families.

### (3) Marriage and the Family

**5261**  *Marriage and Divorce Statistics* HMSO 1974–. An annual collection of statistics. For previous years consult the annual reports of the Registrar-Generals of, respectively, England and Wales, Scotland and Northern Ireland.

**5262**  K D Sell and B H Sell (eds) *Divorce in the United States, Canada and Great Britain: A Guide to Information Sources* Gale 1978. A well organized reference guide and bibliography.

**5263**  R N Rapoport, M P Fogarty and R Rapoport (eds) *Families in Britain* Routledge and Kegan Paul 1982. More of a sociological than a historical text. It also suffers from a rather poor quality of print. It nevertheless encompasses studies of most aspects of change affecting the family and of the policy issues arising. It also includes a good bibliography.

**5264**  *Royal Commission on Marriage and Divorce 1951–1955* Cmnd 9678, *Parliamentary Papers* xxiii 1955–56. This Royal Commission, chaired by Lord Morton of Henryton, recommended the introduction of new grounds for divorce and other changes in the marriage law.

**5265**  *Report of the Committee on the Age of Majority* Cmnd 3342, *Parliamentary Papers* xxi 1966–67. An inquiry into the law relating to marriage contracts and wards of court. It recommended tidying up the pre-existing law so that 18 became the general age of majority. Although they did not consider the political consequences of this recommendation it did lead to the lowering of the age at which people gained the vote to 18 in 1969.

**5266**  Archbishop's Commission on the Christian Doctrine of Marriage *Marriage, Divorce and the Church: The Report of a Commission Appointed by the Archbishop of Canterbury to Prepare a Statement on the Christian Doctrine of Marriage* SPCK 1971. The report of the Commission chaired by Professor H Root. See also *Marriage and the Church's Task: Report by the General Synod Marriage Commission* CIO Publishing 1978, which was chaired by Rt Rev K Skelton, Bishop of Lichfield.

**5267**  Ronald Fletcher *The Shaking of the Foundations* Routledge 1988. A review of trends in divorce and the resulting instability of the institutions of marriage and the family. His companion volume, *The Abolitionists: Family and Marriage Under Attack* Routledge 1988, is a defence of both institutions in difficult times. One of the principal factors placing strain upon the stability of the family has been the growing importance of women within the workforce. L Rimmer and J Popay *Employ-*

*ment Trends and the Family Study* Commission on the Family 1982 analyses the effects of trends in employment and the labour market on the family over the last fifty years and the reciprocal effects of trends in family structures and functions on the nature of the labour supply. This interaction between changes in the labour market and employment and changes in the family is also examined in R Rapoport and M Sierakowski *Recent Social Trends in Family and Work in Britain* Institute of Family and Environmental Research/Policy Studies Institute 1982.

**5268** D A Coleman 'Recent Trends in Marriage and Divorce in Britain and Europe' in R W Hiorns (ed) *Demographic Patterns in Developed Societies* Taylor and Francis 1980 pp 83–124. See also R Schoen and J Baj 'Twentieth Century Cohort Marriage and Divorce in England and Wales' *Population Studies* 38 1984 pp 439–50 and Robert Chester 'Contemporary Trends in the Stability of English Marriage' *Journal of Biosocial Science* 3 1971 pp 69–91.

**5269** Richard Leete *Changing Patterns of Family Formation and Dissolution in England and Wales 1964–76* Office of Population, Censuses and Surveys Studies in Medical and Population Subjects 39, HMSO 1979. On trends affecting the family in the 1960s see also Ronald Fletcher *The Family and Marriage in Britain* 3rd ed, Penguin 1973.

**5270** Geoffrey Gorer *Sex and Marriage in England Today: A Study of the Views and Experience of the Under-45s* Nelson 1971. A splendid impressionistic survey of attitudes based on extensive interviewing.

**5271** Kathleen E Kiernan and Sandra M Eldridge 'Age at Marriage: Inter- and Intra-Cohort Variations' *British Journal of Sociology* 38 1987 pp 44–65. A study of variations in marriage patterns 1921–81. See also Kathleen Kiernan *A Demographic Analysis of First Marriages in England and Wales 1950–1980* Centre for Population Studies, London School of Hygiene and Tropical Medicine 1985 and John Ermisch 'Economic Opportunities, Marriage Squeezes and the Propensity to Marry: An Economic Analysis of Period Marriage Rates in England and Wales' *Population Studies* 35 1981 pp 347–56.

**5272** Rachel M Pierce 'Marriage in the "Fifties"' *Sociological Review* n.s. 2 1963 pp 315–40.

**5273** Kathleen E Kiernan and Sandra M Eldridge *A Demographic Analysis of First Marriages in England and Wales 1950–1980* Centre for Population Studies, London School of Hygiene and Tropical Medicine, University of London.

**5274** John Haskey 'Trends in Marriage: Church, Chapel and Civil Ceremonies' *Population Trends* 22 1980 pp 19–24. This draws attention to the rapid decline in the proportion of religious wedding ceremonies. What is not clear is the extent to which this is a function of the increasing proportion of marriages which are between divorced people, the large majority of which do not take place in a religious setting.

**5275** Avril Lansdell *Wedding Fashions 1860–1980* Shire Publications 1983. A well illustrated pamphlet which serves as a historical guide to the ceremonies of all different churches and creeds.

**5276** P R Jones 'Ethnic Intermarriage in Britain' *Ethnic and Racial Studies* 5 1982 pp 223–8.

**5277** Oliver Ross McGregor *Divorce in England: A Centenary Study* Heinemann 1957. A history of trends and developments in the law of divorce since the 1857 Divorce Act. It includes statistics and a critique of the Morton Commission [5264].

**5278** John Haskey 'Social and Socio-Economic Differentials in Divorce in England' *Population Studies* 38 1984 pp 419–38. A study of class specific differences in divorce rates.

**5279** B H Lee 'The Divorce Reform Act 1969: Its Background and Passage' Oxford DPhil Thesis 1971–2.

**5280** John Haskey 'Recent Trends in Divorce in England and Wales: The Effects of Legislative Changes' *Population Trends* 44 1986 pp 9–16. An interim study of the effect of the change in the law of divorce introduced in 1984 (allowing couples to petition for divorce after only one year of marriage instead of the three years which had hitherto been obligatory) and the resultant surge in marriage breakdowns.

**5281** Barry Kosmin *Divorce in Anglo-Jewry 1970–1980: An Investigation* West-Central Community Development Centre 1982.

**5281A** *Report from the Select Committee in Marriage* House of Commons Paper 553, *Parliamentary Papers* xxxv 1974–75. The evidence and report of a select committee investigation into violence towards wives. A subsequent report, also encompassing evidence and detailed statistics, on violence in the family towards children is *First report from the Select Committee on Violence in the Family: Violence to Children* 3v, House of Commons Paper 329, *Parliamentary Papers 1976–77*.

**5282** *Report of the Committee on One-Parent Families* Cmnd 5629, *Parliamentary Papers* xvi 1974. This committee was set up under the chairmanship of Sir Morris Finer to inquire into the implications for social policy, not least in the fields of housing, social security and unemployment, of the growth of one- parent families. The report includes a considerable amount of historical research into the nature and growth of one-parent families. See also J Haskey 'One-Parent Families in Great Britain' *Population Trends* 45 1986 pp 5–13.

**5283** B Werner 'Recent Trends in Illegitimate Births and Extra- Marital Conception' *Population Trends* 30 1982 pp 9–15. This draws attention to the rapidly rising number of pregnancies and births outside wedlock.

**5284** Tony Parker *In No Man's Land: Some Unmarried Mothers* Heinemann 1972. A journalistic study of their life, problems and attitudes.

**5285** Anthea Duquesin 'Who Doesn't Marry and Why?' *Oral History* 12 1984 pp 40–7. An investigation based on interviews.

## C. SOCIAL WELFARE

### (1) The Welfare State

#### (a) The State and Social Policy

**5286** *Guide to the Social Services* Family Welfare Association 1882–. An annual reference guide. This gives details, a directory and descriptive essays on the organization and administration of all types of social services, including health, legal, housing, social security, race relations, education and consumer services; both those provided by the state and those provided by voluntary bodies.

**5287** *Year Book of Social Policy in Britain* Routledge and Kegan Paul 1971–. Since 1987 this has been published by Longman and in 1989 it changed its name to *Social Policy Review*. It contains a number of essays on selected recent social policy developments and legislation. These are furnished with useful bibliographies.

**5288** *A Guide to Health and Social Service Statistics* Department of Health and Social Security 1974. A guide to the government's statistics and the methods whereby they are compiled.

**5289** *Health and Personal Social Services Statistics for England* HMSO 1969–. An annual statistical digest. See also the annual *Local Health Service Statistics* Institute of Municipal Treasurers and Accountants 1951–, now published as *Local Health and Social Service Statistics* by the Chartered Institute of Public Finance and Accountancy.

**5290** Rex Pope, Alan Pratt and Bernard Hoyle (eds) *Social Welfare in Britain 1885–1985* Croom Helm 1986. A collection of documents, speeches and commentaries designed for teaching purposes. James Roy Hay (ed) *The Development of the British Welfare State 1880–1975* Arnold 1978 and Brian Watkin (comp) *Documents on Health and Social Services 1834 to the Present Day* Methuen 1975 are earlier collections of documents.

**5291** Tessa Blackstone (ed) *Social Policy and Administration: A Bibliography* Pinter 1975. An extensive unannotated bibliography on contemporary social policy. See also G H Williams (comp) *Poverty and Policy in the United Kingdom: A Classified Bibliography* Policy Studies Institute 1980.

**5292** *DHSS-DATA*. The on-line database of the Department of Health/Department of Social Security library since 1983. Approximately 12,000 titles per year are added to this database each year covering social policy, the social services, social security and health service administration.

**5293** Nicholas Deakin *The Politics of Welfare* Methuen 1987. A general history of social policy and welfare from the Beveridge Report of 1942. A more interpretative study is William A Robson *Welfare State and Welfare Society: Illusion and Reality* Allen and Unwin 1976. This argues that there is a tension between the existence of the welfare state and the prevailing social attitudes and ends by asserting that 'to some extent the dissatisfaction which prevails in contemporary Britain may be due to the absence of a philosophy of the welfare state, or any coherent ethical doctrine to support it'. Richard Morris Titmuss *The Gift Relationship: From Human Blood to Social Policy* Allen and Unwin 1970 could be seen as an attempt by one of the leading influences on post-war social policy to express the philosophy that Robson feels is lacking. In stressing the social responsibilities of each for all expressed in the willingness to give blood, which serves as Titmuss' starting point and illustration of the gift relationship, he tries to develop a picture of the relationship between the welfare state and the society it serves. Other interpretative studies of the nature and development of the welfare state are David C Marsh *The Welfare State: Concept and Development* Longman 1980 and A K Sen *Collective Choice and Social Welfare* Oliver and Boyd 1970.

**5294** Richard Berthoud and Joan C Brown with Steven Cooper *Poverty and the Development of Anti-Poverty Policy in the United Kingdom* Heinemann 1981. An analysis of policies since 1945 designed to eliminate poverty and re-distribute income and welfare towards the poorer members of society.

**5295** Richard Morris Titmuss *Essays on 'The Welfare State'* Allen and Unwin 1958. A collection of lectures on social administration, the social division of welfare, pension systems and population change, war and social policy, the impact of industrialization on welfare and the creation of the National Health Service. Important comments on these issues by a leading figure in post-war British social policy thinking. Another collection of essays by an influential figure is Peter Townsend *Sociology and Social Policy* Penguin 1976. These appraise aspects of social policy since 1960.

**5296**  P Bean and S Macpherson (eds) *Approaches to Welfare* Routledge and Kegan Paul 1983. A collection of essays addressing a range of social policy issues covering the whole of the post- war period. These include not just studies of particular policies but also interpretative studies of the nature of the welfare state. S Bennett and C Fudge (eds) *Policy and Action: Essays on the Implementation of Public Policy* Methuen 1981 is a collection of essays on the implementation of social policy. David Donnison and Valerie Chapman (eds) *Social Policy and Administration: Studies in the Development of Social Services at the Local Level* Allen and Unwin 1965 is a collection of case studies on slum clearance, the National Assistance Board, the home help service, the Children's Department of the Home Office and secondary education in Croydon.

**5297**  Victor George and Paul Wilding *The Impact of Social Policy* Routledge and Kegan Paul 1984. A study of the effects and consequences of social policy since 1945. They argue that social services are conducive to economic growth and are the most important mechanism in enhancing social and economic well-being, though they are somewhat inefficient in reducing inequality.

**5298**  A M Rees *T H Marshall's Social Policy in the Twentieth Century* 5th ed, Hutchinson 1985. The standard textbook guide. Another similar work which has detailed in successive editions the state and administration of social policy is Muriel Brown *Introduction to Social Administration in Britain* 6th ed, Hutchinson 1986. Another interesting textbook is Phoebe Hall *et al Change, Choice and Conflict in Social Policy* Heinemann 1976. Gordon A Causer (ed) *Inside British Society: Continuity, Challenge and Change* Wheatsheaf 1987 is a collection of essays on the contemporary state of various areas of social policy as is David C Marsh (ed) *Introducing Social Policy* Routledge and Kegan Paul 1979. See also A J Culyer *The Political Economy of Social Policy* Robertson 1980, Alan Cawson *Social Policy and State Intervention in Britain* Heinemann Educational 1982, Thomas Wilson and Dorothy J Wilson *The Political Economy of the Welfare State* Allen and Unwin 1982, Alistair Young *The Politics of the Welfare State* Longman 1986 and David C Marsh *The Welfare State* Longman 1970.

**5299**  D Pollard *Social Welfare Law* Oyez Longman 1977–. A two volume looseleaf encyclopaedia which is updated bimonthly with annual supplements.

**5300**  P Alcock and P Harris *Welfare Law and Order* Macmillan 1982. A critical analysis which approaches welfare in the context of its role in social control.

**5301**  Paul Lawless and Colin Raban (eds) *The Contemporary British City* Harper and Row 1986. A collection of essays concentrating on welfare provision in urban areas.

**5302**  Maurice Bruce *The Coming of the Welfare State* Batsford 1961. The establishment of a welfare state in the immediate aftermath of the war is splendidly put in its historical context in Asa Briggs 'The Welfare State in Historical Perspective' *Archives Européenes de Sociologie* 2 1961 pp 221–58. It is examined in the context of social policy before and during the war in Bentley Brinkerhoff Gilbert 'British Social Policy and the Second World War' *Albion* 3 1971 pp 103–15. See also Ross Ganston *Legal Foundations of the Welfare State* Weidenfeld and Nicolson 1985. R A Pearson (ed) *The Guardian Book of the Welfare State* Wildwood House 1988 is a collection of excerpts from the *Manchester Guardian* (as it then was) from the period 1945–8 (with additional editorial comment). These are ordered in chronologically arranged sections on housing, education, health and welfare and social security. The Labour party's attitude to welfare up to the creation of the National Health Service in 1948 is examined in Arthur Marwick 'The Labour Party and the Welfare State in Britain 1900–1948' *American Historical Review* 73 1967 pp 380–403.

**5303**  J Dryzek and R E Goodin 'Risk-Sharing and Social Justice: The Motivational Foundations of the Post-War Welfare State' *British Journal of Political Science* 16 1986 pp 1–34. This argues that the shared risks of the wartime period led to a greater ability and willingness to share burdens, and that this explains the post-war enthusiasm for a welfare state.

**5304**  J S Morgan 'The Break-up of the Poor Law in Britain 1907–1947: An Historical Footnote' *Canadian Journal of Economics and Political Science* 14 1948 pp 209–19. The welfare programme of the Attlee government finally removed the last vestiges of the nineteenth century Poor Law. On the record of the Attlee government see Barbara Wootton 'Record of the Labour Government in the Social Services' *Political Quarterly* 20 1949 pp 101–12.

**5305**  Barbara Wootton 'Is There a Welfare State? A Review of Recent Social Change in Britain' *Political Science Quarterly* 78 1963 pp 179–97.

**5306** Rodney Lowe 'Resignation at the Treasury: The Social Services Committee and the Failure to Reform the Welfare State 1955–57' *Journal of Social Policy* 18 1989 pp 505–26. This article questions the orthodox view that there was a consensus over social policy in the 1950s, resurrecting as it does the battle over welfare expenditure in 1955–7 which culminated in the Treasury's defeat and the resignation of the Treasury ministers headed by Chancellor of the Exchequer Peter Thorneycroft early in 1958.

**5307** Keith Banting *Poverty, Politics and Policy: Britain in the 1960s* Macmillan 1979. A study of the social policy process and the factors shaping the policy. It draws attention to the lack of success, despite the policy initiatives of the 1960s, in changing poverty or income distribution. The disappointment of the high hopes of progress in just such fields is apparent in Peter Townsend and Nicholas Bosanquet (eds) *Labour and Inequality* Fabian Society 1972, a review of the social policy of the 1964–70 Labour government.

**5308** Rudolf Klein *et al Joint Approaches to Social Policy: Rationality and Practice* Cambridge University Press 1988. A description and analysis of attempts to co-ordinate social policy by the governments of the 1970s. Nick Bosanquet and Peter Townsend (eds) *Labour and Inequality: A Fabian Study of Labour in Power 1974–79* Heinemann 1980 is a critical and disappointed study of social policy under the second Wilson and the Callaghan government.

**5309** Philip Brown and Richard Sparks *Beyond Thatcherism: Social Policy, Politics and Society* Open University Press 1989. A critical study of social policy under the Thatcher government 1979–89. Geraint Perry (ed) 'Welfare State and Welfare Society' *Government and Opposition* 20 1985 is a whole issue devoted to a review of the development and prospects of the welfare state under Thatcher.

**5310** Alan Walker and Carol Walker (eds) *The Growing Divide: A Social Audit 1979–1987* Child Poverty Action Group 1987. A critical assessment of social policy under Thatcher and its effects. It also suggests an alternative strategy. The appendix contains a chronology of policies affecting the poor 1979–87. M Wicks *A Future For All: Do we need the Welfare State?* Penguin 1987 is an examination of Conservative social policy since 1979 in the context of the history of the welfare state and the arguments for and against it. It too is somewhat partisan in its criticism of the Thatcher government. Another critical study is Martin Loney *The Politics of Greed: The New Right and the Welfare State* Pluto 1986. This is a study of the hostility of the New Right to the welfare state, an analysis of the effect of New Right thinking on social policy since 1979 and an indictment of its effects.

**5311** Rudolf Klein (ed) *Social Policy and Public Expenditure* Centre for Studies in Social Policy 1974–76. Annual reviews of social spending budgets and expenditure on social policy.

**5312** G C Peden *British Economic and Social Policy: Lloyd George to Margaret Thatcher* Philip Allan 1988. An outline history of twentieth century social policy which places social policy in the context of economic and financial policy, both in terms of their effects on social policy and in terms of their effects on social expenditure. These relationships are also examined in Alan Walker (ed) *Public Expenditure and Social Policy: An Examination of Social Spending and Social Priorities* Heinemann 1982. Howard Glennerster *Social Service Budgets and Social Policy* Allen and Unwin 1975 and his subsequent *Paying for Welfare* Blackwell 1985 are textbook studies on the financing of welfare services.

**5313** Timothy A Booth (ed) *Planning for Welfare: Social Policy: The Expenditure Process* Blackwell/Robertson 1979. Essays on various aspects of social expenditure, including examinations of the determinants of expenditure and its planning and control, the financial relationship between central and local government in the financing of social services and a number of case studies of budgeting within the social services.

**5314** Frank Gould and Barbara Roweth 'Public Spending and Social Policy: The United Kingdom 1950–1977' *Journal of Social Policy* 9 1980 pp 337–57. A review of the growth of expenditure on social policy over this period. See also Edward J Mishon 'A Survey of Welfare Economics 1939–51' *Economic Journal* 70 1960 pp 197–265.

**5315** Victor George and Paul Wilding *Ideology and Social Welfare* Routledge and Kegan Paul 1976. An examination of the social theory and influence of four important groups of thinkers. These are grouped as anti-collectivists (Friedrich von Hayek, Milton Friedman and Enoch Powell), Keynesians (J M Keynes, William Beveridge and J K Galbraith), Fabians (R H Tawney, Richard Titmuss and Anthony Crosland) and Marxists (Harold Laski, John Strachey and Ralph Miliband). This study concentrates on the two middle groups which the authors clearly favour most. On the influence of social thinkers and social scientists on policy see also G C Fimister 'The Influence of Social Science on Government Policy (with Particular Reference to Britain)' Loughborough MSc Thesis 1972–3.

**5316** Paul Barker (ed) *Founders of the Welfare State* Heinemann 1984. This includes essays on Seebohm Rowntree, William Beveridge, R H Tawney, Eleanor Rathbone, Aneurin Bevan and Richard Titmuss and an overview by David Donnison.

**5317** José Harris *William Beveridge: A Biography* Oxford University Press 1977. A well regarded biography of the man whose report on social insurance in 1942 was to be one of the foundation documents for the post-war welfare state. Beveridge's own autobiography is *Power and Influence* Hodder and Stoughton 1953. See also P B Mair *Shared Enthusiasm: The Story of Lord and Lady Beveridge by their Son* Ascent 1982. A number of important pieces by Beveridge are collected in Karel Williams and John Williams (eds) *A Beveridge Reader* Unwin Hyman 1988.

**5318** Asa Briggs *Social Thought and Social Action: A study of the Work of Seebohm Rowntree* Longmans 1961. A good study of the work of the Quaker social reformer and pioneering social scientist.

**5319** D A Reisman *Richard Titmuss: Welfare and Society* Heinemann Educational 1977. A good assessment of Titmuss' work and attitudes towards social policy. Titmuss was Professor of Social Administration at the London School of Economics. Tributes to Titmuss are paid in Paul Wilding 'Richard Titmuss and Social Welfare' *Social and Economic Administration* 10 1976 pp 147–66, Margaret Gowing 'Richard Morris Titmuss (1907–1973)' *Proceedings of the British Academy* 61 1975 pp 401–28 and David Donnison 'Social Policy Since Titmuss' *Journal of Social Policy* 8 1979 pp 145–56. Some of Titmuss' principal work is collected in Brian Abel-Smith and Kay Titmuss with S M Miller (eds) *The Philosophy of Welfare: Selected Writings of Richard M Titmuss* Unwin Hyman 1987.

**5320** Paul F Whiteley and Stephen J Winyard *Pressure for the Poor: The Poverty Lobby and Policy Making* Methuen 1987. A study of pressure groups active in the field of social policy, concentrating on the Child Poverty Action Group. See also their 'The Poverty Lobby in British Politics' *Parliamentary Affairs* 41 1988 pp 195–208. The Child Poverty Action Group was founded in 1966. Its activities in the 1970s are reviewed in Frank Field *Poverty and Politics: The Inside Story of the Child Poverty Action Group's Campaigns in the 1970s* Heinemann Educational 1982. Field was its Director 1969–79. See also M A McCarthy *Campaigning for the Poor: CPAG and the Politics of Welfare* Croom Helm 1986 and Patrick Seyd 'The Child Poverty Action Group' *Political Quarterly* 47 1976 pp 189–202.

**5321** Catherine Jones *Immigration and Social Policy in England* Tavistock 1977. This details the social welfare problems presented by successive waves of immigrants since the mid-nineteenth century, and the response of social services. By far the greatest problems have been experienced by New Commonwealth immigrants since 1945. Jones supplies a detailed examination of the ad hoc responses of social policy makers and social services to their arrival. See also N Engin 'New Commonwealth Immigration and Welfare Effects on the United Kingdom Economy' Surrey PhD Thesis 1975–6.

**5322** Clare Ungerson (ed) *Women and Social Policy: A Reader* Macmillan 1985. Collected articles, speeches, reports and other documents on how women are affected by various areas of social policy.

## (b) Charities and Voluntary Welfare

**5323** *Charities Digest* Charity Organisation Society 1882–. An annual guide published by a body which is now known as the Family Welfare Association. Since there are now over 170,000 registered charities (and rising) not all of these can be listed in the digest, which therefore concentrates on national charities and those in the London area. It includes information on the law relating to charities and the Charity Commissioners. Another guide to voluntary organizations is *Voluntary Social Service: A Directory of National Organisations* National Council of Social Service 1928–. The National Council of Social Service has now become the National Council of Voluntary Organisations. Its directory is a useful reference guide revised annually.

**5324** *Annual Report of the Chief Registrar of Friendly Societies* 1894–1974. This is now known as the *Annual Report of the Certification Officer*.

**5325** Frank Prochaska *The Voluntary Impulse: Philanthropy in Modern Britain* Faber 1988. This concentrates on the nineteenth century but also goes up to the post-war period.

**5326** Madeleine Rooff *Voluntary Societies and Social Policy* Routledge and Kegan Paul 1957. A study of voluntary bodies in the fields of child welfare, mental health and the blind since 1945.

**5327** Maria Brenton *The Voluntary Sector in British Social Services* Longman 1985. The voluntary sector has become more important since 1979 because of the New Right emphasis on self-help, the demoralizing effects of state welfare and the potential of the voluntary sector. This study therefore concentrates on the changes in the voluntary sector since 1979. The appendices provide lists of relevant legislation since 1944 and relevant documents.

**5328** Stephen Hatch *Outside the State: Voluntary Organisations in Three English Towns* Croom Helm 1980. A study of voluntary organizations in the 1970s. The identities of the three towns are disguised by pseudonyms.

**5329** J Finch and D Groves *Labour of Love: Women, Work and Caring* Routledge and Kegan Paul 1983. An examination of the work of women as unpaid carers in the home of the handicapped and the elderly and their relationship with the social security system. It includes a useful bibliography.

**5330** C K Lysons 'Some Aspects of the Historical Development and Present Organisation of Voluntary Welfare Societies for Adult Deaf Persons in England 1840–1963' Liverpool MA Thesis 1964–5.

**5331** M Morris *Social Enterprise* National Council of Social Service 1962. A study of the activities of voluntary societies and voluntary workers in Halifax 1937–57.

**5332** Madeleine Rooff *A Hundred Years of Family Welfare: A Study of the Family Welfare Association (Formerly Charity Organisation Society) 1869–1969* Michael Joseph 1972.

**5333** Margaret Brasnett *Voluntary Social Action: A History of the National Council of Social Service 1919–69* National Council of Social Service 1969.

**5334** H R Poole *The Liverpool Council of Social Service 1909–59* Liverpool Council of Social Service 1960.

**5335** Asa Briggs and Anne Macartney *Toynbee Hall: The First Hundred Years* Routledge and Kegan Paul 1984. A centenary history of the original settlement which was established amongst the poor of the East End in 1884. J Rimmer *Troubles Shared: The Story of a Settlement 1899–1979* Phlogiston Publications 1980 is a history of the settlement in Birmingham.

**5336** Anke Weihs and Joan Talls (eds) *Camphill Villages* 2nd ed, Camphill Press 1988. A history of the charity which has run integrated community schools for children with special needs around the world since the first was established in Aberdeen in 1940.

**5337** William Robertson *Welfare in Trust: A History of the Carnegie United Kingdom Trust 1913–1963* Carnegie United Kingdom Trust 1964. A analysis of the work of the trust based on its annual reports.

**5338** June Rose *For the Sake of the Children: Inside Dr Barnardo's: 120 Years of Caring for Children* Hodder and Stoughton 1987. A history of the children's charity. An earlier history, published to mark the centenary, is Janet Hitchman *They Carried the Sword* Gollancz 1966.

**5339** Richard Gordon Carter *White Harnesses: The Story of Guide Dogs for the Blind* Sherratt 1961. On another charity for the blind see Mary G Thomas *The Royal National Institute for the Blind 1868–1956* Royal National Institute for the Blind 1957.

**5340** L E Waddicombe *Private Philosophy and Public Welfare: The Joseph Rowntree Memorial Trust 1954–1979* Allen and Unwin 1983. A history of the activities of the philanthropic trust.

**5341** P Leonard *Venture in Faith* Liverpool and District Family Service Unit 1963. The story of the work of this body and its work with problem families compiled from its records.

**5342** Sue Graham-Dixon *Never Darken My Door: Working for Single Parents and their Children 1918–1978* National Council for One-Parent Families 1978. A well illustrated history of this body.

**5343** V Shennan *Our Concern – The Story of the Royal Society 1946–1980* National Society for Mentally Handicapped Children 1981. The history of this society. It received a royal charter in 1981.

**5344** Anne Allen and Arthur Morton *This is Your Child: The Story of the National Society for the Prevention of Cruelty to Children* Routledge and Kegan Paul 1961. An official history. The adjustment to the increased role of the state in the protection of children in the twentieth century and the new roles the society found in the post-war years are the central themes of C A Sherrington 'The NSPCC in Transition 1884–1983: A Study of Organisational Survival' London PhD Thesis 1985.

**5345** R W Clark *A Biography of the Nuffield Foundation* Longman 1972. A history of the philanthropic organization.

**5346** R T Clarke *Personal Social Services Council 1973–1980: The Case History of an Advisory Non-Governmental Organisation* Personal Social Services Council 1981. A study of an advisory body working in the fields of child care, handicapped people, the elderly, health and community services.

**5347** Beryl Lucey *A Village Where the World is One: The Story of the Pestalozzi International Children's Village in England* Regency Press 1984.

**5348** Chad Varah (ed) *The Samaritans: Befriending the Suicidal* 2nd ed, Constable 1987. This is mainly a counsellor's book. It however includes a history by Varah, an Anglican priest who founded the Samaritans in the early 1950s.

**5349** Sue Ryder *Child of My Love: An Autobiography* Collins Harvill 1986. A large and revealing biography, much of which deals with her considerable involvement in charity work, not least with the charities founded by her and her husband Leonard Cheshire. On Leonard Cheshire see Russell Reading Braddon *Cheshire VC: A Story of War and Peace* Evans 1970 and Andrew Boyle *No Passing Glory: The Biography of Group Captain Cheshire* Collins 1959. On the Cheshire Homes they founded see Wilfrid Russell *New Lives for Old: The Story of the Cheshire Homes* Gollancz 1963.

**5350** P Russell 'Profile: The Voluntary Council for Handicapped Children' *Child Care Health Development* 5 1979 pp 359–66. A description of the council and its unique comprehensive advisory service.

## (2) Social Security

**5351** *Social Security Statistics* HMSO 1972–. An annual digest.

**5352** Peter Alcock *Poverty and State Support* Longman 1987. A history of post-war social security and benefit provision policy. See also Victor George *Social Security: Beveridge and After* Routledge and Kegan Paul 1968 and E M Burns 'Social Security in Britain: Twenty Years after Beveridge' *Industrial Relations* 2 1963 pp 15–32. A now rather outdated history is H E Raynes *Social Security in Britain: A History* 2nd ed, Pitman 1960. Victor George *Social Security and Society* Routledge and Kegan Paul 1973 looks at social security in the context of the levels of poverty, low pay, unemployment and old age. The impact of social security on poverty is examined in Wilfrid Beckerman and Stephen Clark *Poverty and Social Security in Britain Since 1961* Oxford University Press 1982.

**5353** T Lynes *Family Income Support Part 7: Maintaining the Value of Benefits* Policy Studies Institute 1985. A study of efforts to maintain the real value of social security payments.

**5354** J C Kincaid *Poverty and Equality in Britain: A Study of Social Security and Taxation* Penguin 1973. A somewhat partisan study of the development of social security in the context of low wages and taxes. It particularly concentrates on organizations like the Claimants' Union.

**5355** Paul O'Higgins and Martin Partington *Social Security Law in Britain and Ireland: A Bibliography* Mansell 1986. This is neither annotated nor particularly easy to use. The standard legal textbook is A Ogus and E Berendt *The Law of Social Security* 2nd ed, Butterworths 1982. See also Harry Greenall Calvert *Social Security Law* 2nd ed, Sweet and Maxwell 1978. The practice of social security law is scrutinized in Kathleen Bell *Tribunals in the Social Services* Routledge and

Kegan Paul 1969. The handling of the claims of the unemployed by tribunals and other forms of administrative justice is examined in Julian Fulbrook *Administrative Justice and the Unemployed* Mansell 1978.

**5356** Alan Deacon and Jonathan Bradshaw *Reserved for the Poor: The Means Test in British Social Policy* Blackwell/Robertson 1983. A history of the means test in the post-war period and a discussion of its objectives and the extent to which governments have succeeded in making (through the use of means testing) their social security more selective and targeted more clearly on the poor. It also reviews the problems associated with the use of means testing.

**5357** Sir William Beveridge *Social Insurance and Allied Services Report* Cmnd 6404 (Appendix G Cmnd 6405), *Parliamentary Papers* vi 1942–43. Few government reports can have made the immediate impact and sold as well as the Beveridge Report did. It proposed in trenchant language a comprehensive system of compulsory social insurance.

**5358** A B Atkinson *Poverty in Britain and the Reform of Social Security* Cambridge University Press 1969. The exposure of relative poverty in the late 1960s by Peter Townsend and others led to renewed concern about the extent to which social security was dealing with poverty. This book is really concerned with making recommendations on how the system should be changed but in the process is quite revealing on the social security system in the late 1960s.

**5359** David Donnison *The Politics of Poverty* Robertson 1982. In effect this is his memoirs of his work on the Supplementary Benefits Commission 1973–80, of which he was Chairman 1975–80. It includes case studies of social security and poverty and concludes with a lengthy examination of the Social Security Act 1980. The background to and nature of the 1980 Act is also examined in C Walter *Changing Social Policy: Case of the Supplementary Benefit Review* Bedford Square Press 1983.

**5360** A Weale *et al Lone Mothers, Paid Work and Social Security: A Study of the Tapered Earnings Disregard* Bedford Square Press 1984. Tapered Earnings Disregard, which was introduced in November 1980, was designed to relate earnings and benefit and to help people to begin earning whilst still on benefit. This examines the reasons for the development of this policy and its consequences.

**5361** Sir R Micklethwait *The National Insurance Commissioners* Stevens 1976. An account of their work by the then Senior Commissioner. On national insurance see Katherine Hood *Room at the Bottom: National Insurance in the Welfare State* Lawrence and Wishart 1960

and David Walker 'National Insurance Contributions 1946–1955' *Manchester School of Social and Economic Studies* 23 1955 pp 228–44. On the use of designated friendly societies in the provision of benefits until 1948 see Glyn Carpenter 'National Health Insurance 1911–1948: A Case Study in the use of Private Non-Profit Making Organisations in the Provision of Welfare Benefits' *Public Administration* 62 1984 pp 71–90.

5362   S Cooper *Family Income Support Part 5: The Health Benefits* Policy Studies Institute 1985. An account of the development of health benefits, the criteria for entitlement, their value as a form of income support, the levels of take-up and recent reforms.

5363   J Macnicol *The Movement for Family Allowances* Heinemann 1980. Family allowances were introduced in 1945 before the end of the war. Their history since then is also commented on. See also Eleanor F Rathbone *Family Allowances: A New Edition of 'The Disinherited Family' with an Epilogue by Lord Beveridge and a New Chapter on the Family Allowance Movement 1924–47 by Eva M Hubback* Allen and Unwin 1949. Rathbone was a leading campaigner for the introduction of family allowances.

5364   Joan C Brown and S Small *Family Income Support Part 9: Maternity Benefits* Policy Studies Institute 1985. A survey of their development in the twentieth century and of the contemporary situation.

5365   Frank Field *Family Income Support Part 6: What Price a Child? A Historic Review of the Relative Cost of Dependents* Policy Studies Institute 1985. An account of social security provision for dependents. On child benefits as well see M A McCarthy 'Trade Unions, the Family Lobby and the Callaghan Government: The Case of Child Benefits' *Policy and Politics* 11 1983 pp 461–86.

5366   J Creedy *State Pensions in Britain* Cambridge University Press 1982. A general account of their development since 1908. Bryan Ellis *Pensions in Britain 1955–75* HMSO 1989 is an examination of each pension scheme developed and in turn supplanted after the shortcomings of the Beveridge system of flat-rate contributions and pensions became clear in the mid 1950s as governments searched for a new bipartisan formula which eventually found again, temporarily, in the mid–1970s. Michael Pilch and Victor Wood *Pension Schemes: A Guide to Principles and Practice* Gower 1979 is a textbook with some historical details. The history of post-war pensions policy is traced in S K Kim 'A Study of the Development of Retirement Pensions Policy in the British Welfare State' Aberdeen PhD Thesis 1982. E J Shragge 'The Development of State Retirement Pensions in Britain 1940–1975' Kent PhD Thesis 1982 is a Marxist analysis of pensions policy in the post-war years.

5367   J Roebuck 'When does "Old Age" Begin? The Evolution of the English Definition' *Journal of Social Policy* 12 1979 pp 416–28.

5368   D M Groves 'Women and Occupational Pensions 1870–1983: An Exploratory Study' London PhD Thesis 1986. This seeks to account for the under-representation of women in employer pension schemes and to throw light on poverty amongst elderly women.

5369   Gerald Rhodes *Public Service Pensions* Allen and Unwin 1965. A massive, detailed study of pensions schemes in all sections of public employment. One of these schemes is examined in depth in Sir Douglas Logan *The Birth of a Pension Scheme: A History of the Universities Superannuation Scheme* Liverpool University Press 1985.

5370   Leslie Hannah *Inventing Retirement: The Development of Occupational Pensions in Britain* Cambridge University Press 1986. A good historical study of pension schemes set up by private sector firms for their employees.

5371   M Upton 'The Provision of Social Security Benefits to the Unemployed in the United Kingdom Since the Second World War' Leeds MPhil Thesis 1982. See also Sir F Tillyard *Unemployment Insurance in Great Britain 1911–1948* Thames Bank Publishing 1949 and P Fenn 'Sources of Disqualification for Unemployment Benefit 1960–1976' *British Journal of Industrial Relations* 18 1980 pp 240–53.

5372   Alan Deacon 'The Scrounging Controversy: Public Attitudes towards the Unemployed in Contemporary Britain' *Social and Economic Administration* 12 1978 pp 120–35. In the 1970s there was a widespread feeling that the unemployment benefit system was being abused, a feeling that largely disappeared with the mass unemployment of the 1980s. This controversy is an easily missed and yet important facet of the 1970s.

5373   Sally Coetzee *Flat Broke: How the Welfare State Collapsed in Birmingham* Pluto 1984. An account of the social security strike of 1982–3.

5374   R Franey *Poor Law: The Mass Arrest of Homeless Claimants in Oxford* Campaign for Single Homeless People and Others 1983. An investigation of the police operation against claimants suspected of fraud in September 1982.

## (3) Personal Social Services

### (a) General

**5375** *Social Services Yearbook* Longman 1983–. A guide to information on social services and advice centres. *Guide to the Social Services* Family Welfare Association 1913– is a detailed annual source of information on all aspects of the social services.

**5376** *Personal Social Services Statistics* Chartered Institute of Public Finance and Accountancy 1974–. An annual statistical digest.

**5377** Joan Clegg *Dictionary of Social Services Policy and Practice* 3rd ed, Bedford Square Press 1980. A not very detailed dictionary covering a limited range of subjects. It however has some uses as a reference work.

**5378** R W Stacey and Arthur T Collin (eds) *British Association of Social Workers: Catalogue and Guide to the Archives of Predecessor Organisations 1890–1970* British Association of Social Workers 1987. This is a guide to the papers of the various bodies of specialist social workers who came together to form the present association.

**5379** David Streatfield *Social Work: An Information Sourcebook* Capital Planning Information 1982. A useful work with an unconventional format. J Hurstwit and M Webley *Information in Social Welfare: A Survey of Resources* National Institute for Social Work 1977 is a guide to developments in information sources in the 1970s and a bibliography.

**5380** *Social Services Abstracts* Department of Health and Social Security Library 1977–. This is now published by HMSO. It provides monthly summaries of selected articles, reports, books and pamphlets. These cover the whole range of personal social services. The abstracts are classified and indexed with a cumulative index appearing annually. *Current Literature on Personal Social Services* Department of Health and Social Security Library 1974– gives short indications of the contents of selected articles, books and reports.

**5381** NATIONAL INSTITUTE FOR SOCIAL WORK INFORMATION SERVICE. A database specializing in the personal social services set up by the National Institute for Social Work in 1985.

**5382** Gill Stewart (comp) *Personal Social Services Bibliography* Department of Social Administration, University of Lancaster 1978. This has been updated by two supplements. It provides a classified guide to the literature on the personal social services in Britain with some annotations many of which however are far from illuminating. It covers a wide range of material. Unfortunately it is also very badly printed and contains an unacceptable number of typographical errors. *Bibliography of Social Work and Administration: A Classified List of Articles from Selected British Periodicals 1930–1952* Joint University Council for Social and Public Administration 1954 is a listing which has been updated by a number of supplements. See also *Some Books on the Social Services* National Council of Social Service 1969.

**5383** Eileen Younghusband *Social Work in Britain: 1950–1975* 2v, Allen and Unwin 1978. A comprehensive historical survey which examines the changing role of the voluntary and professional sectors and the changes in policy towards and the organization of the personal social services. See also her *The Newest Professions: A Short History of Social Work* Business Press 1981. The post-war expansion of social work is traced in P Seed *The Expansion of Social Work in Britain* Routledge and Kegan Paul 1973. For other general histories see K Woodroofe *From Charity to Social Work* Routledge and Kegan Paul 1962 and Robert Pinker 'Social Work and Social Policy in the Twentieth Century: Retrospect and Prospect' in Martin Bulmer, Jane Lewis and David Piachaud (eds) *The Goals of Social Policy* Unwin Hyman 1989 pp 84–107.

**5384** Michael H Cooper (ed) *Social Work: A Survey of Recent Developments* Blackwell 1973. Articles on recent change in social work in the fields of education, health, housing, social security, care for the elderly and children and probation work.

**5385** John Mays with Anthony Forder and Olive Keiden (eds) *Penelope Hall's Social Services of England and Wales* 10th ed, Routledge and Kegan Paul 1983. A very useful standard textbook. The essays it contains cover most aspects of the social services and each has a short historical introduction. Another textbook is Eric Sainsbury *The Personal Social Services* Pitman 1977.

**5386** Alan Walker (ed) *Community Care: The Family, the State and Social Policy* Blackwell/Robertson 1982. Studies of the growth and effectiveness of community care policies over the last thirty years, the assumptions of that policy. By means of case studies it assesses the effects of community care policies on the family and the state.

**5387** Ronald G Walton *Women in Social Work* Routledge and Kegan Paul 1975. A good history of women in the caring professions and voluntary social work 1860–1975. It looks at the development of theories as well as the practice of social work.

**5388** Ken Judge *Rationing Social Services: A Study of Resource Allocation and the Personal Social Services* Heinemann 1978.

**5389** C Hallett *The Personal Social Services in Local Government* Allen and Unwin 1982. Personal social services are here considered in the context of the political and administrative functions of local authorities. See also J E G Utting *Social Accounts of Local Authorities* Cambridge University Press 1953 and M Brown 'The Development of Local Authority Welfare Services from 1948–1965 under Part III of the National Assistance Act 1948: A Study of the Relationship between Legislative Intention and Administrative Activity with regard to the Formation of Policy" Manchester PhD Thesis 1972–3.

**5390** *Social Workers in the Local Authority Health and Welfare Services: Report of the Working Party* HMSO 1959. Chaired by Eileen Younghusband its recommendations led to the rapid growth of social work in the 1960s.

**5391** Eileen Younghusband (ed) *New Developments in Casework* Allen and Unwin 1966. A collection of studies of developments in social work techniques in the 1950s and 1960s.

**5392** Phoebe Hall *Reforming the Welfare* Heinemann 1976. An account of developments in the personal social services in the 1960s. The movement towards unified social service departments (social work departments in Scotland) in this period, particularly in the wake of the Seebohm Report, is traced in Joan D Cooper *The Creation of the British Personal Social Services 1962–1974* Heinemann Educational 1983.

**5393** *Report of the Committee on Local Authority and Allied Personal Social Services* Cmnd 3703, *Parliamentary Papers* xxxii 1967–68. This committee recommended the immediate unification of local authority social services, leading to major changes in the local government organization of these services and an increase in their relative importance. The report is reassessed by the committee's chairman, Frederic Seebohm, in the three papers collected in his *Seebohm: Twenty Years On* Policy Studies Institute 1989.

**5394** Adrian Webb and Gerald Wistow *Social Work, Social Care and Social Planning: The Personal Social Services Since Seebohm* Longman 1987. A study of contemporary issues and problems in the context of developments since the Seebohm Report. Unrest in the new social services departments created in the wake of that report is examined in B Glastonbury (ed) *Social Work in Conflict: The Practitioner and the Bureaucrat* Croom Helm 1980.

**5395** Richard Bryant 'Professionals in the Firing Line' *British Journal of Social Work* 3 1973 pp 161–74. A study of the impact of the 1972 miners' strike on the social services.

**5396** Adrian Webb and Gerald Wistow *Planning, Need and Scarcity: Essays on the Personal Social Services* Allen and Unwin 1986. An examination of change in the 1980s. See also their *Whither State Welfare: Policy and Implementation in the Personal Social Services 1979–80* Royal Institute of Public Administration 1982 which studies the initial progress of the Thatcher government towards achieving its avowed aims of reducing public expenditure and its minimalist vision of the social services.

**5397** Marilyn Taylor, Frances Presley and Gabriel Chanon *Community Work in the UK 1982–6* Library Association 1987. A well annotated bibliography. The lengthy introduction explores the growth of community work in the 1980s, and not least of voluntary community work.

**5398** R Hadley, P Dale and P Sills *Decentralising Social Services: A Model for Change* Bedford Square Press 1984. An analysis of the pioneering experiment in East Sussex in the 1980s where social services have been decentralized to locally based financially responsible teams.

**5399** A F Young *Social Service in British Industry* Routledge and Kegan Paul 1968. This is a largely contemporary study which is principally concerned with the social services concerned with the needs of workers in an industrial setting.

**5400** Dorothy Clarissa Keeling *The Crowded Stairs: Recollections of Social Work of Liverpool* National Council of Social Service 1961.

**5401** Kathleen Jones *Eileen Younghusband: A Biography* Bedford Square Press 1984. A useful biography of a figure who had a formative influence on the development of the personal social services in the post-war period.

**5402** A E Hartshorn *Milestone in Education for Social Work: The Carnegie Experiment 1954–1958* National Institute for Social Work 1982. A study of an important stage in the development of the training of social workers.

**5403** Barbara N Rodgers and Julia Dixon *Portrait of Social Work* Oxford University Press 1960. A record and discussion of the education and social services in a northern town in the late 1950s. Barbara N Rodgers and June Stevenson *A New Portrait of Social Work: A Study of the Social Service in a Northern Town from Young-*

*husband to Seebohm* Heinemann Educational 1973 is a sequel covering the period 1959–68.

**5404** *Welfare in London 1948–1954: An Account of the Work of the Welfare Department of the London County Council* London County Council 1955. See also S P Pinch 'The Geography of Local Authority Housing, Health and Welfare Resource Allocation in London 1965–73' London PhD Thesis 1976.

**5405** J Baker *The Neighbourhood Advice Centre: A Community Project in Camden* Routledge and Kegan Paul 1978. A study of the establishment of an advice centre in London and the reaction of the local community. *The FAC Book: A History of the Moss Side Family Advice Centre* Youth Development Centre 1981 is on an advice centre in Manchester.

**(b) The Disabled**

**5406** Sheila Dale *The Handicapped Persons in the Community: Using the Literature* Open University Press 1975. A useful annotated bibliography.

**5407** David Lane, Sheila Noble, Michael Tidball and Sam Twigg *The Quiet Revolution: The Planning, Development and Provision of Community Services for the Mentally Handicapped* Macmillan 1983. A useful case study drawing on case studies. See also J L Mansell "Residential Care and Mental Handicap: An Examination of the Debate with Particular Reference to the Years 1954–1977" Wales MSc (Econ) Thesis 1981. Edie Topliss *Provision for the Disabled* 2nd ed, Robertson/Blackwell 1979 is a general text on provision for the disabled in the social security and personal social services.

**5408** D Thomps *The Experience of Handicap* Methuen 1982. A review of autobiographical writings by handicapped people.

**5409** Edie Topliss and G Gould *A Charter for the Disabled: The Chronically Sick and Disabled Persons Act 1970* Blackwell 1981. A study of the background and passage of this piece of legislation. A Morris *No Feet To Drag* Sidgwick and Jackson 1972 also provides an account of events leading up to the passage of the act.

**(c) The Elderly**

**5410** C Godlove and A Mann 'Thirty Years of the Welfare State: Current Issues in British Social Policy for the Aged' *Aged Care and Services Review* 2 1980 pp 1–13. A review of the literature on and the issues in the field of welfare for the elderly.

**5411** Peter Townsend *The Last Refuge: A Survey of Residential Institutions and Homes for the Aged in England and Wales* Routledge and Kegan Paul 1964. A model of research which produces an excellent study of a rather grim subject. See also his *The Development of Home and Welfare Services for Old People 1946–1960* Association of Directors of Welfare Services 1961.

**5412** Idris Williams *The Care of the Elderly in the Community* Croom Helm 1979. From the 1960s onwards there was a shift in policy away from providing residential care and towards the provision of welfare in the home. This trend and its effects is also surveyed in A C Bebbington ' Changes in the Provision of Social Services to the Elderly in the Community over Fourteen Years' *Social Policy Administration* 13 1979 pp 111–23. This trend and the reports, like that of Townsend, which led to the drastic reduction of residential care for the elderly from the 1960s onwards, are criticized in J R Jack 'Last Chance for the Last Refuge' *Social Policy Administration* 21 1987 pp 147–56.

**5413** Hazel Qureshi and Alan Walker *The Caring Relationship: Elderly People and their Families* Macmillan Education 1983. A study of the care of the elderly by their relatives.

**(d) Child Care and Youth Work**

On the provision of day nurseries, playgroups and other child care facilities see the section on education [6455–8].

**5414** *Year Book of the Youth Service in England and Wales* Youth Service Information Centre, Leicester 1970–. An annual information digest.

**5415** *Youth Social Work* National Youth Bureau 1973–. A bimonthly collection of abstracts.

**5416** Maria Johnstone (comp) *A Bibliography of Youth Social Work including Intermediate Treatment* National Youth Bureau 1974. An unannotated listing which was largely superseded by [5997].

**5417** Jean Packman *The Child's Generation: Child Care Policy in Britain* 2nd ed, Blackwell/Robertson 1981. A historically structured textbook on developments in child care policy and services over the post-war period. Post-war developments are also traced in Jean S Heywood *Children in Care: The Development of the Service for the Deprived Child* 3rd ed, Routledge and Kegan Paul 1978. This includes useful chronologies and a good bibliography. A J Jeffs *Young People and the Youth Service* Routledge and Kegan Paul 1979 concentrates on the history, organization and deficiencies of the

Youth Service, drawing attention to its apparent rejuvenation after the Albemarle Report in 1960 [5420]. A J Jeffs and Mark Smith (eds) *Welfare and Youth Work Practice* Macmillan 1988 is a collection of studies of the impact of social, economic and political changes on youth work in the 1970s and 1980s.

**5418** Rick Rogers *Crowther to Warnock: How Fourteen Reports tried to Change Children's Lives* Heinemann Educational 1980. A guide to various important reports on the youth care services and education in the period 1959–78, their recommendations and implementation. The reports are; the Crowther Report 1959 on raising the school leaving age, the Platt Report 1959 on the welfare of children in hospitals, the Albemarle Report 1960 on the youth service, the Newsom Report 1963 on the schooling of less able children, the Plowden Report 1967 on primary schools, the Latey Report 1967 on the age of majority, the Halsey Report 1972 on educational priority areas, the Houghton Report 1972 on adoption, the Finer Report 1975 on one-parent families, the Bullock Report 1975 on the reading and use of English in schools, the Select Committee repors on violence in the family 1975 and 1977, the Court Report 1976 on child health services, the Taylor Report 1977 on the government of schools and the Warnock Report 1978 on special educational needs.

**5419** *Training in Child Care: Interim Report of the Child Care Committee* Cmnd 6760, *Care of Children Committee Report* Cmnd 6922, *Parliamentary Papers* x 1945–46. The recommendations of this committee, chaired by Dame Myra Curtis, led to the 1948 Children Act, which established a statutory duty of local authorities to provide orphanages and residential care and maintenance for children under 18. On the 1948 Act see L M Mitchell 'The Children Act 1948: Problems arising in the Operation of its Provisions' Aberdeen PhD Thesis 1959–60 and J Wareham 'The History of the Children Bill in a County Borough 1946–1948: A Case Study in Social Policy, Construed for the Social Work Administrator' Manchester MA (Econ) Thesis 1966–7.

**5420** *The Youth Service in England and Wales: Report of a Committee Appointed by the Minister of Education in November 1958* Cmnd 929, *Parliamentary Papers* xxi 1959–60. A report which led to the re-shaping of the Youth Service. It was chaired by the Countess of Albemarle.

**5421** B E Stimpson 'The Children and Young Persons Act 1969 – A Survey and Review' Leicester MA Thesis 1974.

**5422** P Vass 'Parental Rights and Child Care Legislation: The Children Act 1975 and its Historical Context' Exeter MA Thesis 1979. A study of history of attempts to protect children from parental abuse, concentrating particularly on the 1975 Act and its consequences. The case of Maria Colwell (who was returned to her natural mother by the social services and was subsequently battered to death), which had a major influence on the framing of the 1975 Act, is recounted and examined in John G Howells *Remember Maria* Butterworths 1974.

**5423** F Briggs 'The Development of Nursery Nursing and the Changing Role of the Nursery Nurse (1870–1975)' Sheffield MA Thesis 1978. Over this period their prestige has declined but their duties have increased enormously. This has presented problems for those who design the training courses. Nursery provision in the NHS is examined in T M Ryan *Day Nursery Provision under the Health Service: England and Wales 1948–1963* National Society of Children's Nurseries 1964.

**5424** M Harrison 'Home-Start: A Voluntary Home Visiting Scheme for Young Families' *Child Abuse and Neglect* 5 1981 pp 441–7. An account of a voluntary home-visiting scheme to families in difficulties which started in Leicester in the early 1970s. It succeeded in reducing the levels of abuse of children through intensive preparation and support.

**5425** R G Walton 'The Development of the Residential Care of Deprived Children Since 1900' Manchester MA (Econ) Thesis 1966–7. See also A Shearer *Handicapped Children in Residential Care: A Study of Policy Failure* Bedford Square Press 1980. This is a critical study of the development of policy on the residential care for handicapped children since 1945.

**5426** *Report of the Departmental Committee on the Adoption of Children* Cmnd 5107, *Parliamentary Papers* xxxviii 1971–72. This committee, chaired by F A Stockdale, recommended various changes in the law relating to adoption and custody in the light of social trends. On adoption see also G Roberts 'Social and Legal Policy in Child Adoption in England and Wales 1913–1958' Leicester PhD Thesis 1974.

**5427** S Bunt and R Gargrave *The Politics of Youth Clubs* National Youth Bureau 1982. A history of their development since the late nineteenth century. See also Frank Dawes *A Cry from the Streets: The Boys Club Movement in Britain from the 1850s to the Present Day* Wayland 1975.

**5428** C L Bibby *Shaftesbury Boys' Clubs* Shaftesbury Boys' Clubs 1974 is a history of these social clubs for working class lads from their establishment in 1886.

**5429** J Bradshaw *The Family Fund: An Initiative in Social Policy* Routledge and Kegan Paul 1980. This is an account of the fund set up in 1973 to ease the burden of families who had thalidomide children. It was unprecedented as it involved the distribution of public money by a private trust. This evaluation concludes that this arrangement was neither adequate nor equitable.

## (4) Health Services

### (a) General

The material below is largely concerned with the development of health policy and health services. The literature on medical developments and on the professional medical bodies as well as the biographies of doctors is all to be found elsewhere in the section on Medicine [6848–77], which is part of the section on Intellectual History.

**5430** *The Medical Directory* H K Lewis 1845–. An annual guide to the medical profession and to the health organizations and medical education establishments.

**5431** *The Hospitals and Health Services Year Book* Institute of Health Services Management 1889–. An annual directory of the various bodies concerned with the policy-making and administration of both the public and private health services. It also contains a digest of recent statutory instruments and government circulars, a summary of recent government reports and a select, books only, bibliography.

**5432** *Health Care UK* Policy Journals 1984–. An annual privately conducted audit of the welfare state, monitoring the state of health care.

**5433** *Digest of Health Statistics for England and Wales* HMSO 1969–.

**5434** K W Chaplin (ed) *Health Care in the United Kingdom – Its Organisation and Management* Kluwer Medical 1982. An extensive examination of the organization of the National Health Service and of private health care services. This dichotomy between the public and private health services and the struggle between governments and the medical profession over the making of health policy is analysed in Vincente Navarro *Class Struggle: The State and Medicine: An Historical and Contemporary Analysis of the Medical Sector in Great Britain* Robertson 1978. Good comparative studies of health policy are Daniel M Fox *Health Policies, Health Politics: The British and American Experience 1911–1965* Princeton University Press 1986 and J Roger Hollingsworth *A Political Economy of Medicine: Great Britain and the United States* John Hopkins Press, Baltimore 1986.

**5435** Sir Kenneth Stowe *On Caring for the National Health* Nuffield Provincial Hospitals Trust 1988. An overview of the problems and the costs involved in comparative context by a former permanent secretary of the Department of Health and Social Security.

**5436** Tom Jones and Malcolm Prowle *Health Service Finance: An Introduction* Certified Accountants Educational Trust 1984. A textbook study.

**5437** J Eyles and K J Woods *The Social Geography of Medicine and Health* Croom Helm 1983. An examination of the distribution of health care provision.

**5438** James Parkhouse *Medical Manpower in Britain* Churchill Livingstone 1979. A history of manpower planning since the Goodenough Report on medical schools in 1944. A detailed examination which includes a number of statistical tables.

**5439** *Medical Practitioners: Report of the Committee to Consider the Future Numbers of Medical Practitioners and the Appropriate Intake of Medical Students* HMSO 1957. The report of the committee chaired by Sir Henry Willink.

**5440** *Royal Commission on Medical Education 1965–68: Report* Cmnd 3569, *Parliamentary Papers* xxv 1967–68. This commission, chaired by Lord Todd, had a similar remit to that of the Willink committee. It however also considered the need to re-shape medical education in the light of changing technology and the possible future patterns of health care. It includes detailed analysis and appendices.

**5441** *Royal Commission on Doctors' and Dentists' Remuneration: Report* Cmnd 939, *Supplement to the Report: Further Statistical Appendix* Cmnd 1064, *Parliamentary Papers* xii 1959–60. This commission, chaired by Sir Harry Pilkington, surveyed the remuneration of the medical profession since the establishment of the National Health Service in 1948 and made various recommendations, not least for a standing review body.

**5442** R E O Williams *Microbiology for the Public Health: The Evolution of the Public Health Laboratory Services 1939–1980* Public Health Laboratory Services 1985.

**5442A** Reginald Pound *Harley Street* Michael Joseph 1967. A history of a street famous for its doctors in private practice, with some criticisms of what he perceives as its post-war decline.

### (b) The National Health Service

**5443** *On the State of the Public Health Annual Report of the Chief Medical Officer of the Ministry of Health*

HMSO 1920–. Since 1968 the Ministry of Health has been replaced by the Department of Health and Social Security. This is a very informative annual report.

**5444** *Health Service Abstracts* Department of Health and Social Security 1985–. A monthly collection of abstracts of recent literature. It was the result of the merger of three monthly abstracting and bibliographical services, *Hospital Abstracts* 1961–85, *Current Literature on the Health Services* 1974–85 and *Current Literature on General Medical Practice* 1974–85.

**5445** Nancy M Mathers (comp) *National Health Service: A Bibliography* Nuffield Centre for Health Service Studies, University of Leeds 1978. An unannotated and unindexed listing, mainly focusing on official and serial reports. K W Best *A Select Bibliography on the National Health Service* Department of Health and Social Security 1980 is a brief, unannotated guide to the literature.

**5446** Charles Webster *The Health Services Since the War Vol 1: Problems of Health Care: The National Health Service before 1957* HMSO 1988. The first volume of the official peacetime history. It examines the haphazard health services of Britain in the 1930s and the establishment of the National Health Service. The development of and attitudes towards this new body are traced up to the Guillebaud Report [5456] which concluded that notwithstanding the idealism which had led to the creation of the National Health Service a comprehensive health service was utopian and that the country could not afford it. Rudolf Klein *The Politics of the National Health Service* 2nd ed, Longman 1989 is a political analysis of the development of the NHS since 1948, contemporary policy issues and possible future developments. Another textbook analysis of the history of the NHS is Judith Allsop *Health Policy and the National Health Service* Longman 1984. This focuses on the distribution of the services, the funding and management of the NHS and the policy problems facing governments since the 1970s. It concludes with an examination of the 1982 reorganization which, it is argued, did little to provide a more equitable geographical distribution of health care. Another history which looks particularly at the organization of the NHS is Brian Watkin *The National Health Service: The First Phase 1948–74 and After* Allen and Unwin 1978. R G S Brown *The Changing National Health Service* 2nd ed, Routledge and Kegan Paul 1978 is a succinct study of its history up to the 1970s. Brian Abel-Smith *The National Health Service: The First Thirty Years* HMSO 1978 is even shorter. See also John E Pater *The Making of the National Health Service* Kings Fund Centre 1981 and F J Dougan 'The National Health Service in England and Wales' National University of Ireland PhD Thesis 1967–8. The initial history of the NHS is traced in Almont Lindsay *Socialized Medicine in England and Wales: The National Health Service 1948–61* Oxford University Press 1962.

This, like Harry Eckstein *The English Health Service: Its Origins, Structure and Achievement* Harvard University Press, Cambridge, Massachusetts 1958, presents an interesting American perspective on the creation and early years of the NHS. See also Paul F Gammill *Britain's Search for Health: The First Decade of the National Health Service* Pennsylvania University Press, Philadelphia, Pennsylvania 1960. Another early account is D McI Johnson *The British National Health Service* Johnson 1962. On the relations between the medical profession and the state in the creation and development of the NHS see G Forsyth *Doctors and the State: A Study of the British Health Service* Pitman Medical 1966. For other material of this kind see the section on the British Medical Association [5513–7].

**5447** Christopher Ham *Health Policy in Britain: The Organisation and Politics of the NHS* 2nd ed, Macmillan 1985. A well reviewed textbook on contemporary issues and policy problems in the NHS. See also John Vaizey *National Health* Robertson 1984.

**5448** Keith Barnard and Kenneth Lee (eds) *Conflicts in the National Health Service* Croom Helm 1977. A collection of essays on subjects such as the medical profession, the growth of militancy amongst ancillary workers, the inadequacy of planning or the growth of community medicine.

**5449** David Owen *Our NHS* Pan 1988. A tract in which the leader of the SDP examines the past, present and future of the NHS. See also his earlier *In Sickness and In Health: The Politics of Medicine* Quartet 1976, written when he was a junior minister at the Department of Health and Social Security. Steve Iliffe *The NHS: A Picture of Health?* Lawrence and Wishart 1983 is a political examination of the NHS from a rather different perspective.

**5450** J Finch *Health Services Law* Sweet and Maxwell 1981. A legal textbook.

**5451** Stuart C Heywood and A Alasziewski *Crisis in the Health Service: The Politics of Management* Croom Helm 1980. An examination of management and decision making in the NHS. One of the principal problems in this area is the large role the medical profession has in the management of health care. This is examined in the context of attempts to give high priority to community health care in the 1980s in Heywood's 'The Politics of Management in Health Care: A British Perspective' *Journal of Health Politics, Policy and Law* 8 1983 pp 424–43. See also Howard Elcock and Stuart C Heywood *The Buck Stops Where? Accountability and Control in the National Health Service* Institute for Health Studies, University of Hull 1980.

**5452** Stuart C Heywood *et al The Curate's Egg . . . Good in Parts: Senior Officers' Reflections on the NHS* Institute for Health Studies, University of Hull 1979. Reflections on health service management.

**5453** A F Long and G Mercer (eds) *Manpower Planning in the National Health Service* Gower 1981. An analysis of manpower planning and training and education planning. For examination of medical manpower planning in particular see [5438–40]. See also W J Neufeld 'Manpower Planning in the National Health Service' Brunel PhD Thesis 1980.

**5454** Sir James Stirling Ross *The National Health Service in Great Britain: An Historical and Descriptive Study* Oxford University Press 1952. A well regarded study of the origins, establishment and early contours of the NHS. It includes useful maps. A good reassessment of the foundation of the NHS and the struggle between the doctors and Bevan is Frank Honigsbaum *Health, Happiness and Security* Routledge 1989. John and Sylvia Jewkes *The Genesis of the British National Health Service* Blackwell 1961 is a short account. The creation of the NHS is viewed from the perspective of the British Medical Association which mounted such opposition to Bevan's plans in Charles Hill and C Woodcock *The National Health Service* Johnson 1949. Hill was the Secretary of the British Medical Association at the time. A French perspective on the creation of the NHS is provided in Yves Vincetot *La Service de Santé en Grande Bretagne* Armand Colin, Paris 1952. An insider's perspective on its creation is presented in Patrick Benner 'The Early Years of the National Health Service – An Insider's View' in Tony Gorst, Lewis Johnman and W Scott Lucas (eds) *Postwar Britain 1945–64: Themes and Perspectives* Pinter 1989 pp 43–52. The Labour Party's attitudes towards and role in the framing of the NHS is examined in Charles Webster 'Labour and the Origins of the National Health Service' in Nicholas A Rupke (ed) *Science, Politics and the Public Good* Macmillan 1988 pp 184–202 and R J Earwicker 'The Labour Movement and the Creation of the National Health Service 1906–1948' Birmingham PhD Thesis 1982–3.

**5455** James M Mackintosh *Trends of Opinion about the Public Health 1901–1951* Oxford University Press 1953. The final section deals with the debate over the cost of the service and the decision to introduce prescription charges in 1951.

**5456** *Report of the Committee of Inquiry into the Cost of the National Health Service* Cmnd 9663, *Parliamentary Papers* xx 1955–56. Although this report concluded that hopes of a publicly funded comprehensive health service were utopian it argued that there was no need for fundamental restructuring of the NHS and thus ended, for a time, the debate about the cost of the NHS. The committee that framed this report was chaired by C W Guillebaud. Brian Abel-Smith and Richard Morris Titmuss *The Cost of the National Health Service in England and Wales* Cambridge University Press 1956 was a detailed contribution to this debate over the cost of the service that the Guillebaud Report helped to end.

**5457** W A J Ferndale *Trends in the National Health Service* Pergamon 1964.

**5458** D E Allan 'The Development of the 1962 Hospital Plan: A Case Study in Decision Making' Manchester PhD Thesis 1976.

**5459** Stephen Ingle and Philip Tether *Parliament and Health Policy: The Role of MPs 1970–75* Gower 1981. A study of the parliamentary oversight of every aspect of health policy.

**5460** Ruth Levitt and Andrew Wall *The Reorganised National Health Service* 3rd ed, Croom Helm 1984. A detailed examination of the reorganizations of the administration, and not least its geography, of the NHS in 1974 and 1982. The 1974 reorganization was an attempt to streamline the administration. It is critically assessed in R G S Brown *Reorganising the National Health Service: A Case Study in Administrative Change* Blackwell/Robertson 1979. The background to the reorganization is assessed in R C Brewer 'The Reorganisation of the National Health Service 1965–74' Open University MPhil Thesis 1980. See also S Shivananda 'Health Service Reorganisation and the Public Interest: A Study of the Politics of Participation' Glasgow PhD Thesis 1978.

**5461** *Royal Commission on the National Health Service: Report* Cmnd 7615, *Parliamentary Papers* 1979–80. This commission, under Sir Alex Merrison, was set up in the light of concern at the effects of the 1974 reorganization. It led to a the further reorganization of 1982 which removed the area tier of administration, as well as a number of other developments in the administration and parliamentary oversight of the NHS and the introduction of the compulsory wearing of seat belts in the front seats of cars. See also C Farrell 'The Royal Commission on the National Health Service' *Policy and Politics* 8 1980 pp 189–202. N Chaplin *Getting It Right? The 1982 Reorganisation of the National Health Service* 2nd ed, Institute of Health Services Administrators 1982 provides a brief introduction and survey of the 1982 reorganization.

**5462** *Inequalities in Health: Report of a Research Working Group* Department of Health and Social Security 1980. This report by a group chaired by Sir Douglas Black concluded that there was a direct link between standards of living and working conditions and health and called for more preventive medicine and action to tackle problems like child poverty. The report was subsequently shelved by the Thatcher government. The Black Report is reassessed and the political decision to shelve it is commented on Peter Townsend and Nick Davidson (eds) *Inequality in Health: The Black Report* Penguin 1982.

**5463** Edwina Currie *Life Lines* Sidgwick and Jackson 1989. A semi-autobiographical account and assessment of health policy during her period as a junior minister at the Department of Health in 1986–8.

**5464** Nick Davidson *A Question of Care: The Changing Face of the National Health Service* Michael Joseph 1987. A discussion of the contemporary problems of the NHS. Neil Small *Politics and Planning in the NHS* Open University Press 1989 discusses the main issues in the debate over the NHS in the 1980s.

**5465** *Welfare of Children in Hospital: Report of the Committee of the Central Health Services Council* HMSO 1959. The report of the committee chaired by Sir Harry Platt. A subsequent report on the need to improve child health care services is that of the committee chaired by S D M Court, *Fit for the Future: Report of the Committee on Child Health Services* 2v, Cmnd 6684, *Parliamentary Papers* xi 1976–77.

**5466** Howard Elcock 'Regional Government in Action: The Members of Two Regional Health Authorities' *Public Administration* 56 1978 pp 379–97. An analysis of the personnel and attitudes to policies of the members of the Yorkshire and Northern regional health authorities which were set up in the 1974 reorganization.

**5467** Bradford Heritage Recording Unit, Industrial Museum, Moorside Road, Eccleshill, Bradford (tel: 0274 631756). One of this body's oral history projects was the recording of interviews with people involved in the administration of the local health services. These interviews are mostly available in transcript form.

**5468** Christopher Ham *Policy Making in the National Health Service: A Case Study of the Leeds Regional Hospital Board* Macmillan 1981. An analysis of the relative roles of doctors, administrators and the public in resource allocation and services.

**5469** Kevin J Woods 'The National Health Service in London: A Review of the Impact of NHS Policy Since 1976' *London Journal* 9 1983 pp 165–83.

**5470** B M Barrows *A County and Its Health: A History of the Development of the West Riding Health Services 1889–1974* Kirklees Area Health Authority 1974.

(c) Hospitals

Histories of individual hospitals are too numerous to list in this bibliography. The best sources for these histories are the bibliographies listed under [5477].

**5471** Brian Abel-Smith *The Hospitals 1800–1948: A Study in Social Administration in England and Wales* Heinemann 1964.

**5472** John Martin *Hospitals in Trouble* Robertson 1984. An inquiry into malpractices in hospital administration over the previous fifteen years.

**5473** Simon Domberger, Shirley Meadowcroft and David Thompson 'The Impact of Competitive Tendering on the Costs of Hospital Domestic Services' *Fiscal Studies* 8 1987 pp 39–54. A study of the effects of the contracting out of hospital domestic services in the 1980s.

**5474** 'The Institute of Hospital Administrators: The First Fifty Years 1902–1952' *Hospital* 48 1952 pp 285–321.

**5475** J F Moham 'State Policies and Public Facility Location: The Hospital Services of North East England 1948–1982' Durham PhD Thesis 1983. This concentrates on the implications for hospital location of changes in the local economy. See also his 'Planners, Politicians and the Development of the Hospital Services of Newcastle-upon-Tyne 1948–1969' *Environment and Planning C: Government and Policy* 2 1984 pp 471–84.

**5476** G Rivett *The Development of the London Hospital System 1823–1982* Kings Fund Centre 1982. See also Peter Cowan 'Some Observations Concerning the Increase of Hospital Provision in London between 1850 and 1960' *Medical History* 14 1970 pp 42–52. This points out that the main influence on provision is not legislation but long-term population changes.

(d) Nursing and the Other Caring Professions

**5477** Alice M C Thompson (ed) *A Bibliography of Nursing Literature 1859–1960* Library Association 1968. This covers much more than simply material on nursing published between these dates. It is also the best source of hospital histories. It is updated by Alice M C Thompson (ed) *A Bibliography of Nursing Literature 1961–1970* Library Association 1974 and Frances Walsh (ed) *A Bibliography of Nursing Literature 1971–1975* Library Association 1985.

**5478** Brian Abel-Smith *A History of the Nursing Profession* Heinemann 1960. See also Rosemary White

*Social Change and the Development of the Nursing Profession: A Study of the Poor Law Nursing Service 1848–1948* Henry Kimpton 1978.

**5479** *Committee on Nursing: Report* HMSO 1972. The report of the committee on the nursing profession chaired by Asa Briggs. See also J A Birch 'Anxiety in Nursing Education (with Particular Reference to the Report of the Committee on Nursing: Chairman Professor Asa Briggs HMSO 1972)' Newcastle PhD Thesis 1978.

**5480** Eve R D Bendall and Elizabeth Raybould *A History of the General Nursing Council for England and Wales 1919–1969* H K Lewis 1969. An institutional history of the governing body of the profession.

**5481** G Bowman *The Lamp and the Book: The Story of the Royal College of Nursing 1916–1966* Queen Anne Press 1967. A jubilee history of the main nurses' association and trade union.

**5482** B Colwell and D Wainwright *Behind the Blue Door: The History of the Royal College of Midwives 1881–1981* Ballière and Tindall 1981.

**5483** Monica E Baly *A History of the Queen's Nursing Institute: 100 Years 1887–1987* Croom Helm 1987. A short official history which provides a stimulating account of district nursing. See also Mary D Stocks *A Hundred Years of District Nursing* Allen and Unwin 1960.

**5484** Patricia Young 'A Short History of the Chartered Society of Physiotherapy' *Physiotherapy* 55 1969 pp 271–8. See also Sybil M Evans 'To Thy Heritage be True' *Physiotherapy* 41 1955 pp 302–7.

**5485** M F Weller 'Seventy Years On: Inaugural Lecture at the Annual Conference of the Health Visitors' Association, held in Folkestone in October 1966' *International Journal of Nursing Studies* 4 1967 pp 233–43. The problems of health visiting in the 1960s are discussed, using case studies of Leeds, in Joyce M Akester and Angus N MacPhail *Health Visiting in the Sixties* Macmillan 1963. J Clark *What Do Health Visitors Do? A Review of the Research 1960–1980* Royal College of Nursing 1981 is useful as a guide to the literature on the changing role of the health visitor. On their training see Elaine Wallace *A History of the Council of the Education and Training of Health Visitors: An Account of its Establishment and Field of Activities 1962–75* Allen and Unwin 1979.

(e) Community Health

**5486** Jane Lewis *What Price Community Medicine? The Philosophy, Practice and Politics of Public Health Since 1919* Wheatsheaf 1986. The nearest to a standard history, though better on the philosphy than the practice of community health. This is however a comparatively neglected field and much remains to be explored. One aspect of it is covered in Frank Honigsbaum *The Division in British Medicine: A History of the Separation of General Practice from Hospital Care 1911–1968* Kogan Page 1979.

**5487** John R Butler *Family Doctors and Public Policy: A Study of Manpower Distribution* Routledge and Kegan Paul 1973. A study of the spatial distribution of general practitioners conducted for the Department of Health and Social Security. It points to the scarcity of these doctors in certain areas. The work of general practitioners is examined, mainly in the contemporary context, in Jonathon Gathorne-Hardy *Doctors: The Lives and Work of GPs* Weidenfeld and Nicolson 1984.

**5488** M Ryan 'Health Centre Policy in England and Wales' *British Journal of Sociology* 19 1968 pp 34–46.

**5489** Rudolf Klein and Jane Lewis *The Politics of Consumer Representation: A Study of Community Health Councils* Centre for Studies in Social Policy 1976. These councils were created as an afterthought of the 1974 health service reorganization. This is a portrait of their membership and an analysis of their activities in their first year of existence. See also D R Phillips 'Establishing Community Health Councils: An Analysis of the Creation and Implementation of an Innovation in Social Policy' York MPhil Thesis 1978. Phillips has also published 'The Creation of Consultative Councils in the NHS' *Public Administration* 58 1980 pp 47–66. On the development of the Community Health Councils see Ruth Levitt *The People's Voice in the NHS: Community Health Councils after Five Years* Kings Fund Centre 1980.

(f) Mental Health

**5490** S S Segal *Mental Handicap: A Select Annotated Bibliography* National Foundation for Educational Research 1972.

**5491** Nigel Malin, David Race and Glenys Jones *Services for the Mentally Handicapped in Britain* Croom Helm 1980. A detailed assessment of the development of services and of contemporary problems.

**5492** Clive Unsworth *The Politics of Mental Health Legislation* Clarendon 1987. A study of changes in legislation and civil commitment procedures since the end of the nineteenth century, examining particularly the 1959 Mental Health Act. Kathleen Jones *A History of the Mental Health Services* Routledge and Kegan Paul 1972 is a history from the eighteenth century. It is however quite useful on post-war developments. The changes in the mental health services between the Mental Health Acts of 1959 and 1983 are charted in F M Martin *Between The Acts: Community Mental Health Services 1959–1983* Nuffield Provincial Hospitals Trust 1984.

**5493** H Freeman and J Farndale (eds) *Trends in Mental Health Services: A Symposium of Original and Reprinted Papers* Pergamon 1963. See also their subsequent collection of edited essays, *New Aspects of Mental Health Services* Pergamon 1967.

**5494** Noel Timms *Pyschiatric Social Work in Great Britain 1939–1962* Routledge and Kegan Paul 1964.

**5495** Tom Butler *Mental Health, Social Policy and the Law* Macmillan 1985. A well regarded legal examination.

**5496** *Royal Commission on the Law Relating to Mental Illness and Mental Deficiency 1954–1957* Cmnd 169, *Parliamentary Papers* xvi 1956–57. An in-depth analysis of the development and future needs of the mental health services chaired by Lord Percy of Newcastle. Its recommendations led to the 1959 Mental Health Act. Alysia Wingfield *The Inside of the Cup* Angus and Robertson 1958 is an account of her experiences in a mental hospital and a critique of the mental health system before the 1959 Act.

**5497** Alan Maynard and Rachel Tingle 'The Objectives and Performance of the Mental Health Services in England and Wales' *Journal of Social Policy* 4 1975 pp 151–68. A study in the failure of policy objectives set in the early 1960s.

**5498** G S Donges *Policymaking for the Mentally Handicapped* Gower 1982. One of the main facets of this study of contemporary policy-making is his enthusiasm for the trend in the 1980s towards caring for the mentally handicapped and the mentally ill in the community rather than in institutions. See also Nigel Malin (ed) *Reassessing Community Care (with Particular Reference to Provision for People with Mental Handicap and for People with Mental Illness)* Croom Helm 1987. The proposals of the 1980s are put in their historical context in P Noble 'Mental Health Services and Legislation – An Historical Review' *Medicine, Science and the Law* 21 1981 pp 16–24.

**5499** *Better Services for the Mentally Handicapped* Cmnd 4683, *Parliamentary Papers* xx 1970–71. An important White Paper. Subsequent progress is reviewed

by Peter Mittler in *Mental Handicap: Progress, Problems and Priorities: A Review of Mental Handicap Services in England Since the 1971 White Paper 'Better Services for the Mentally Handicapped'* HMSO 1987.

**5500** K A Stanton 'The Employment of Nurses in Public Mental Hospitals (England and Wales) 1909–1975' London PhD Thesis 1984.

**5501** Greta Jones *Social Hygiene in Twentieth Century Britain* Croom Helm 1986. A study of the concern about mental defectives that was a strong characteristic of the inter-war years and of the eugenics schemes that were mooted as solutions. Only one chapter deals with the post-war period when the experiments of the Nazis had given eugenics a bad name and the full employment of the early post-war years curbed fears about mental defectives, leading to the disappearance of interest in such matters.

**5502** Hugh Freeman 'Mental Health Services in an English County Borough before 1974' *Medical History* 28 1984 pp 111–28. A study of Salford. See also R Bhaduri 'A Study of Mental Health Social Services in Salford from 1950 to 1974' Manchester MA (Econ) Thesis 1976.

**5503** G Gaton *Let's Go . . . An Account of the BBC's Mental Handicap Project 1976–9* BBC 1980. A short evaluation by the producer of the series.

(g) Ambulance Services

**5504** *Ambulance Service Statistics* Institute of Municipal Treasurers and Accountants 1955–. In 1973 the Institute changed its name to the Chartered Institute of Public Finance and Accountancy.

**5505** Ronnie Cole-Mackintosh *A Century of Service to Mankind: A History of the St John Ambulance Brigade* Century Hutchinson 1986. A useful centenary history. J Clifford *A Good Uniform: The St John Story* Hale 1967 is not just a history of the ambulance brigade but also of the St John Ophthalmic Hospital.

(h) Private Health Care

**5506** *Directory of Independent Hospitals and Health Services* MMI 1980–84, since then Longman. An annual comprehensive reference guide to the burgeoning private health sector.

**5507** Joan Higgins *The Business of Medicine: Private Health Care in Britain* Macmillan 1988. This explores the history of private medicine since the foundation of the NHS. The growth of the private sector in the 1970s, especially with the advent of American-owned profit-orientated companies, is explained. So are the reasons for people choosing private health care. It concludes with a dispassionate assessment of the benefits and disadvantages of a dual health care system and a discussion of the morality of profit making in medicine. Another, more critical assessment of the growth of private medicine and of contracting out within the NHS is Ben Griffith, Steve Iliffe and Geof Rayner *Banking on Sickness: Commercial Medicine in Britain and the USA* Lawrence and Wishart 1987.

## (i) Dentists and Opticians

**5508**  *The Advance of the Dental Profession: A Centenary History 1880–1980* Southern Publishing 1979. A history of the Dental Association.

**5509**  G H Giles *The Ophthalmic Services Under the National Health Services Acts 1946–1952* Hammond Hammond 1953.

**5510**  Hugh Barty-King *Eyes Right: The Story of Dolland and Aitchison, 1750–1985* Quiller Press 1986. A company history.

## (j) Hospices

**5511**  Shirley du Boulay *Cecily Saunders: Founder of the Modern Hospice Movement* Hodder and Stoughton 1984. Saunders has been chairman of St Christopher's Hospice since 1985. She founded this, the first hospice to be established in the post-war period, in 1967. It has been an important example in the re-establishment of the principle of the provision of a caring environment for the terminally ill.

**5512**  A W M Ward 'The Impact of the Provision of a Terminal Care Nursing Home in Sheffield 1971–1972' Sheffield PhD Thesis 1975.

## (k) The British Medical Association and Other Medical Pressure Groups

**5513**  British Medical Association, BMA House, Tavistock Square, London WC1. The BMA has a small but significant collection of taped interviews and films, including material on the establishment of the National Health Service.

**5514**  Paul Vaughan *Doctors' Commons: A Short History of the British Medical Association* Heinemann 1959. A general history of the doctors' professional association up to 1956. Instead of adopting a chronological approach it reviews in turn the various activities of the association. E Grey-Turner and F M Sutherland *History of the British Medical Association Vol 2: 1932–81* British Medical Association 1982 is a short official history.

**5515**  Harry Eckstein *Pressure Group Politics: The Case of the British Medical Association* Allen and Unwin 1960. A celebrated study of the association as a pressure group. Philip R Jones *Doctors and the BMA: A Case Study of Collective Action* Gower 1981 is an organizational study of the association and an attempt to account for the high voluntary membership. Its role in the creation and development of the NHS is also examined.

**5516**  A J Willcocks *The Creation of the National Health Service: A Study of Pressure Groups and a Major Social Policy Decision* Routledge and Kegan Paul 1967. A still useful study of the pressure group activities of the British Medical Association and other organizations in the creation of the NHS. The role of one of these other organizations is examined in D S Murray *Why a National Health Service? The Part Played by the Socialist Medical Association* Pemberton 1972.

**5517**  Steve Watkins *Medicine and Labour: The Politics of a Profession* Lawrence and Wishart 1987. This reflects on the power of the British Medical Association from a Left-Wing point of view. He also considers discrimination against black and women doctors. The core of the book however is the activities of the TUC-affiliated Medical Practitioners' Union.

## (5) Diseases

**5518**  G M Howe *National Atlas of Disease Mortality in the United Kingdom* Nelson 1963. A pioneering work showing the spatial patterns of mortality. It includes a statistical appendix. See also M J Gardner, Paul D Winter and D J P Barker *Atlas of Mortality from Selected Diseases in England and Wales 1968–1978* Wiley 1984.

**5519**  W P D Logan and Eileen M Brooke *The Survey of Sickness 1943 to 1952* HMSO 1958.

**5520**  *British Empire Cancer Campaign Annual Report* 1924–74. Since 1974 this has been known as *Cancer Research Campaign Annual Report*. This report by the leading cancer research body contains useful information but few statistics.

**5521**  W P D Logan *Cancer Mortality by Occupation and Social Class 1851–1971* HMSO 1982. A statistical analysis of socioeconomic trends in cancer mortality in

England and Wales. See also Medical Research Council Environmental Epidemiology Unit/Office of Population, Censuses and Surveys *Trends in Cancer Mortality 1951–1980* HMSO 1983, Office of Population, Censuses and Surveys *Cancer Mortality 1911–1970* Studies in Medical and Population Subjects 29, HMSO 1977 and R A M Case 'Cohort Analysis of Cancer Mortality in England and Wales 1911–54 by Site and Sex' *British Journal of Preventative and Social Medicine* 10 1956 pp 172–99.

**5522** *Investigation of the Possible Increased Incidence of Cancer in West Cumbria: Report of the Independent Advisory Group* HMSO 1984. This group, chaired by Sir Douglas Black, was set up by the government in the wake of a Yorkshire television programme which drew attention to cancer levels in the vicinity of Sellafield (formerly Windscale). The Black Report was inconclusive and could detect no clear link. Neither could P J Cook-Mozaffari *et al Cancer Incidence in Mortality in the Vicinity of Nuclear Power Installations in England and Wales 1959–80* HMSO 1987. This is a detailed study which includes extensive statistical tables.

**5523** Jane R Toms (ed) *Trends in Cancer Survival in Great Britain: Cases Registered between 1960 and 1974* Cancer Research Campaign 1982. A detailed and informative study illustrating progress and increasing success in controlling certain types of cancer.

**5524** Lesley Doyd *et al Cancer in Britain: The Politics of Prevention* Pluto 1983. This is a detailed study of the private interests resisting regulation and control of carcinogens in the workplace, in goods and in the environment.

**5525** Linda Bryder *Below the Magic Mountain: A Social History of Tuberculosis in Twentieth Century Britain* Clarendon 1988. A study of the major campaign for the eradication of tuberculosis in the twentieth century. This looks not only at the medical administration of this campaign but also at the patients and at the social impact of tuberculosis. See also Office of Population, Censuses and Surveys *Trends in Respiratory Mortality 1951–1975* HMSO 1981 and W P D Logan and B Benjamin *Tuberculosis Statistics for England and Wales 1938 to 1955 – An Analysis of Trends and Geographical Distribution* HMSO 1957.

**5526** K P Bell and H Purcell 'Recent Trends in Coronary Mortality and their Implications for the UK: Are we Winning or Losing?' *Postgraduate Medical Journal* 60 1984 pp 1–46.

**5527** S C Rogers and J A C Weatherall *Anencephalus, Spina Bifida and Congenital Hydrocephalus: England and Wales 1964–1972* HMSO 1976. An examination of the statistics with a historical introduction which analyses the incidence of these diseases in the context of the environment and social class.

**5528** *3rd Report from the Social Services Committee Session 1986–87: Problems Associated with Aids* HC Paper 182, *Parliamentary Papers* 1986–87. The report and evidence of the committee chaired by Reneé Short.

## D. CLASS AND INEQUALITY

### (1) General

**5529** Ivar Reid *Social Class Differences in Britain: A Sourcebook* Open Books 1977.

**5530** Gordon Marshall, David Rose, Howard Newby and Carolyn Vogler *Social Class in Modern Britain* revised ed, Unwin Hyman 1989. A good textbook study. Another major study of class divisions and their changing nature is David Rose (ed) *Social Stratification and Economic Change* Unwin Hyman 1988.

**5531** Richard Mabey (ed) *Class: A Symposium* Anthony Blond 1967. A collection of essays on the nature of class, class attitudes and class distinctions in Britain. There are valuable observations on these subjects in George Douglas Howard Cole *Studies in Class Structure* Routledge and Kegan Paul 1956.

**5532** John Westergaard and Henrietta Riesler *Class in a Capitalist Society: Society in Contemporary Britain* Heinemann 1975. A general textbook.

**5533** John Scott *The Upper Classes: Property and Privilege in Britain* Macmillan 1982. A detailed historical analysis. Roy Perrott *The Aristocrats: A Portrait of Britain's Nobility and their Way of Life Today* Weidenfeld and Nicolson 1968 is more of a sociological study of contemporary aristocratic mores, society, wealth and politics. Hugh Montgomery-Massingberd *Great British Families* Debretts/Webb and Bower 1988 is a series of accounts of the fortunes of the aristocracy in the twentieth century focusing on their social habits, lifestyle, marriages and the media response to them. See also Andrew Gossip *A History of High Society from 1920 to 1970* Hamilton 1978.

**5534** Nancy Freeman Mitford (ed) *Noblesse Oblige: An Enquiry into the Identifiable Characteristics of the English Aristocracy* Hamilton 1956. A collection of essays on aristocratic mores and attitudes. It includes the essay which defined the idea of U and Non-U speech patterns and accents.

**5535** Philip Stanworth and Anthony Giddens (eds) *Elites and Power in British Society* Cambridge University Press 1974. Essays in elites in politics, industry, finance, property, the civil service, academia and the Church of England. W D Rubinstein 'Education and the Social Origins of British Elites' in his *Elites and the Wealthy in Modern British History: Essays in Social and Economic History* Harvester 1987 pp 172–221 is a study of the effect of education on elite recruitment. political elites see [292].

**5536** Roy Lewis and Angus Maude *The English Middle Class* Phoenix House 1949. An influential sociological study. Roger King and John Raynor *The Middle Class* 2nd ed, Longman 1981 draws attention to the increasingly heterogenous nature of the middle class as a result of changes in occupation structure. They argue that in consequence the middle class values enunciated by Mrs Thatcher are no longer widely held by the middle classes and point to the rise of environmental concerns and of a middle class left. Ian Bradley *The English Middle Classes are Alive and Kicking* Collins 1982 nevertheless argues that the Thatcher years have seen a resurgence of confidence amongst the middle classes. On the defensiveness of the middle class during the 1970s see [1081].

**5537** John Clarke, Charles Critcher and Richard Johnson (eds) *Working Class Culture: Studies in History and Theory* Hutchinson 1979. This includes essays on football, culture and leisure.

**5538** James E Cronin *Labour and Society in Britain 1918–1979* Batsford Academic 1984. A detailed examination of the working class in the twentieth century drawing on much under-utilized material. It is particularly good on voting patterns. If there is a weakness in this work it is in its description of the structural changes in the working class since the 1950s. These structural changes and the resulting changes in working class attitudes are also analysed in A Russell 'The Quest for Security: The Changing Working Conditions and Status of the British Working Class in the Twentieth Century' Lancaster PhD Thesis 1983. The impact of changing technology on these changes in structure and attitudes are examined in Roger Penn *Class, Power and Technology: Skilled Workers in Britain and America* Polity 1989.

**5539** Ferdynand Zweig *The British Worker* Penguin 1952. A social and psychological study of the working class and their activities, work and attitudes. Similar technques of sampling and interviewing with the workforce in selected factories are used in his *The Worker in an Affluent Society: Family Life and Industry* Heinemann 1961. This study focuses particularly on lifestyles, living standards and beliefs.

**5540** J H Goldthorpe, David Lockwood, Frank Bechofer and Jennifer Platt *The Affluent Worker* 3v, Cambridge University Press 1968–69. The research for this was conducted in Luton. Volume 1 covers political attitudes and behaviour, volume 2 the affluent worker in the class structure and volume 3 his industrial attitudes and behaviour.

**5541** Trevor Blackwell and Jeremy Seabrook *A World Still to Win: The Reconstruction of the Post-War Working Class* Faber 1985. An impressionistic account of working class culture and attitudes since the 1940s.

**5542** Richard Hoggart *The Uses of Literacy* 2nd ed, Penguin 1958. An influential and well regarded study of working class culture in the context of a literary analysis of popular publications of the previous thirty or forty years.

**5543** Ken Worpole *Bibliography of Working Class Autobiographies and Autobiographical Novels Published in Britain Since the 1930s* Language and History, Proceedings of History Workshop 14, 1980. A more detailed bibliography is John Burnett, David Vincent and David Mayall (eds) *The Autobiography of the Working Class: An Annotated Critical Bibliography Vol II 1900–1945* Harvester 1987. This does not cover works published in that period but works mainly concerned with that period, some of which are also useful for the post-war era. Succinct information is provided on the autobiographies of 1,113 people.

**5544** Centreprise Trust Ltd, 136 Kingsland High Street, London E8. This has an oral archive of interviews with local working class people. See also Ron Barnes *A Licence to Live: Scenes from a Post-War Working Life in Hackney* Centerprise 1974.

**5545** Arthur Marwick 'Images of the Working Class Since 1930' in Jay Winter (ed) *The Working Class in Modern British History: Essays in Honour of Henry Pelling* Cambridge University Press 1983 pp 215–31. A study of how the working class has been presented in literature and in the cinema. See also [7193, 7342 and 7394].

## (2) Social Mobility

**5546** A H Halsey, A F Heath and J M Ridge *Origins and Destinations: Family, Class and Education in Modern Britain* Clarendon 1980. A good series of discussions of the various factors which influence social class mobility. It is based on a sample of 10,000 males tracing the effect of their education from the 1930s to the 1960s. They conclude by arguing that the 1944 Education Act has failed to create a more meritocratic society. An important earlier study, based originally on research conducted in 1949, is D V Glass (ed) *Social Mobility in Britain* 2nd ed, Routledge and Kegan Paul 1963. See also Richard Breen and Christopher T Whelan 'Vertical Mobility and Class Inheritance in the British Isles' *British Journal of Sociology* 36 1985 pp 175–92.

**5547** R Miller *The New Classes* Longmans 1966. An analysis of the increasing social mobility and blurring of social classes as a result of changing lifestyles and the rise of consumer society and consumer credit.

**5548** J H Goldthorpe, C Llewellyn and C Payne *Social Mobility and Class Structure in Modern Britain* 2nd ed, Oxford University Press 1987. This concentrates on the extent and pattern of class mobility in recent decades and the consequences of mobility on social relations.

**5549** A F Heath *Social Mobility* Fontana 1981. An excellent textbook and succinct statement of the state of research on the subject.

**5550** A H Halsey 'The Relation betweem Education and Social Mobility, with Particular Reference to the Grammar School Since 1944' London PhD Thesis 1954–5.

### (3) Income Distribution and Inequality

**5551** William D Rubenstein *Wealth and Inequality in Britain* Faber 1986. A good history with comparisons with other countries. It concludes that there has been increasing inequality in the distribution of wealth in the 1980s. A B Atkinson and A J Harrison *Distribution of Personal Wealth in Britain* Cambridge University Press 1978 also traces the recent history of inequalities in wealth distribution. See also Atkinson's *Unequal Shares: Wealth in Britain* Penguin 1974. J C Kincaid *Poverty and Equality in Britain* 2nd ed, Pelican 1975 is a well regarded general text.

**5552** A B Atkinson (ed) *The Personal Distribution of Incomes* Allen and Unwin 1976. A good collection of papers on the distribution of wealth and income. A B Atkinson (ed) *The Economics of Inequality* 2nd ed, Clarendon 1983 includes essays examining the concept of inequality and its causes. The essays in Dorothy Wedderburn (ed) *Poverty, Inequality and Class Structure* Cambridge University Press 1974 examine the measurement of inequalities in income and wealth distribution and the effects on class consciousness. It includes a number of case studies. See also Richard Morris Titmuss *Income Distribution and Social Change: A Study in Criticism* Allen and Unwin 1962. See also H F Lydall and D G Tipping 'The Distribution of Personal Wealth in Britain' *Bulletin of Oxford University Institute*

*of Economic Statistics* 23 1961 pp 83–104 on the distribution of wealth in the 1950s.

**5553** Thomas Stark *The Distribution of Personal Income in the United Kingdom 1949–1963* Cambridge University Press 1972. This shows the persistence of great differences in income distribution and of poverty despite the rising affluence of the period. It thus presents a rather different picture from that which appears in Dudley Sears *The Levelling of Incomes Since 1938* 2nd ed, Blackwell 1957.

**5554** W G Runciman *Relative Deprivation and Social Justice: A Study of Attitudes to Social Inequality in Twentieth Century England* Routledge and Kegan Paul 1966. An important history of class and wealth distribution in the twentieth century in terms of his theory of relative deprivation. This is brought more up to date by W W Daniel *Survey on Inflation* Political and Economic Planning 1978.

**5555** *Royal Commission on the Distribution of Income and Wealth* Cmnd 6171, Cmnd 6172, *Parliamentary Papers* xxxii 1974–75, Cmnd 6383, *Parliamentary Papers* xli 1975–76, Cmnd 6626, *Parliamentary Papers* xlii 1975–76, Cmnd 6999, Cmnd 7175, *Parliamentary Papers* 1977–78, Cmnd 7595, Cmnd 7679, *Parliamentary Papers* 1979–80. This was established by the second Wilson government with the intention that it should be a standing Royal Commission. It was chaired through all these reports by Lord Diamond, and existed continuously during the Labour governments of 1974–79. It was however wound up by Mrs Thatcher when she came to power.

**5556** Stewart Lansley 'Changes in Inequality and Poverty in the UK 1971–1976' *Oxford Economic Papers* 32 1980 pp 134–50.

**5557** John Rentoul *The Rich Get Richer: The Growth of Inequality in Britain in the 1980s* Unwin Hyman 1987. A study of growing inequality in the distribution of wealth and the rise of the extremely rich under the Thatcher government. Government policies as factors in this process are critically assessed. The effects of changes in taxation and social security scales during the Thatcher years on the distribution of income are examined in *Taxation and Social Security 1979–1989* Institute for Fiscal Studies 1989. See also Paul Johnson and Graham Stark 'Ten Years of Mrs Thatcher: The Distributional Consequences' *Fiscal Studies* 10 1989 pp 29–37.

**5558** Elsie R Pamuk 'Social Class Inequality in Mortality from 1921 to 1972 in England and Wales' *Population Studies* 39 1985 pp 17–32. This traces increasing differences in the mortality rates between the classes over this period.

**5559** Frank Field *Inequality in Britain: Freedom, Welfare and the State* Fontana 1981. This looks particularly at attempts through welfare policy to re-distribute wealth. See also R A-H E El-Shiekh 'The Redistribution of Incomes through Public Finance in the United Kingdom 1948–1958' Leeds PhD Thesis 1961–2. Attempts to use health policy to promote greater equality are assessed and found wanting in A Maynard and A Ludbrook 'Inequality, the Health Service and Health Policy' *Journal of Public Policy* 2 1982 pp 97–116.

**5560** K E Bigsworth 'Public Sector Housing and the Distribution of Income: The Impact of Housing Policies on the Income Distribution of Public Sector Households in Great Britain 1952–1977' Cambridge PhD Thesis 1981. An assessment of the influence of housing policy on the distribution of income. This argues that the pattern of housing subsidies has been too indiscriminate and that, far from being targeted on those in greatest need, the most needy have, in some cases, received less subsidy than those with much greater resources.

**5561** C D Hanbury and D M W Hitchins *Inheritance and Wealth Inequality in Britain* Allen and Unwin 1979. Inheritance continues to be an important way of perpetuating wealth. This is first historical study of its role in wealth distribution.

**5562** William D Rubenstein *Men Of Property: The Very Wealthy in Britain Since the Industrial Revolution* Croom Helm 1981. A study of the very wealthy and changes in their composition since the early nineteenth century. Frank Field (ed) *The Wealth Report* 2v, Routledge and Kegan Paul 1979–83 is a conscious attempt to examine the wealthy and to shift the debate about poverty and income distribution onto new ground. Volume 2 analyses the findings of the Royal Commission on the Distribution of Income and Wealth and the effects on the rich of the coming to power of the Thatcher government. See also R J Lampman *The Share of Top Wealth Holders in National Wealth 1922–1956* National Bureau for Economic Research 1962 and R G D Allen 'Changes in the Distribution of Higher Incomes' *Economica* 24 1957 pp 138–53.

**5563** George Taylor and N Ayres *Born and Bred Unequal* Longman 1969. A study of the regional variations in income distribution and inequality. See also P J Devine 'Inter-Regional Variations in the Degree of Inequality of Income Distribution: The United Kingdom 1949–1965' *Manchester School of Social and Economic Studies* 37 1969 pp 141–59 and J A Schofield 'Distribution of Personal Incomes at the Regional Level: An Analysis for the Period 1965–66 to 1970–71' *Bulletin of Oxford University Institute of Economic Statistics* 37 1975 pp 1–11.

## (4) Poverty

**5564** P Ashley *The Money Problems of the Poor: A Literature Review* Heinemann 1983.

**5565** S Macgregor *The Politics of Poverty* Longman 1981. A good history of the poverty issue, levels of poverty, changing perceptions of poverty and the rise of pressure groups specifically concerned with it since 1945. See also G C Fieghen, P S Lansley and A D Smith *Poverty and Progress in Britain 1953–73: A Statistical Study of Low Income Households – Their Number, Types and Expenditure Patterns* Cambridge University Press 1977. This also draws attention to the problems of measuring poverty and to the changes to its extent over time.

**5566** Peter Townsend *Poverty in the United Kingdom* Allen Lane 1979. A massive and influential study which consciously sought to establish a successor to the pioneering work of Charles Booth and Seebohm Rowntree. It seeks to establish the nature and extent of poverty drawing on case studies. Muriel Brown and Nicola Madge *Despite the Welfare State* Heinemann Educational 1982 is a specially commissioned study of the persistence of poverty, its characteristics and causes based on research conducted in the 1970s.

**5567** Jeremy Seabrook *Landscapes of Poverty* Blackwell 1985. An impressionistic insight into poverty in Britain.

**5568** Peter Townsend *Poverty: Ten Years after Beveridge* Political and Economic Planning 1952. A study of progress towards the eradication of poverty in the wake of the 1942 Beveridge Report on Social Insurance.

**5569** Dorothy Wedderburn 'Poverty in Britain to-day: The Evidence' *Sociological Review* 10 1962 pp 257–82.

**5570** Frank Field *Poverty: The Facts* Child Poverty Action Group 1975. An examination of poverty and the poor and of regional patterns of poverty in the 1970s. See also P S Lansley 'Changes in Inequality and Poverty in the UK 1971–1976' *Oxford Economic Papers* n.s. 32 1980 pp 134–50.

**5571** J Mack and P S Lansley *Poor Britain* Allen and Unwin 1985. A good study of the contemporary extent of poverty and of attitudes towards the poor. Beatrix Campbell *Wigan Pier Revisited: Poverty and Politics in the 1980s* Virago 1984 is an impressionistic portrait of poverty and the poor in the 1980s drawing on visits paid to various parts of the country. *Ten Years On: The Poor Decade* Low Pay Unit 1989 is a report on poverty and low pay during the Thatcher years and the effects in these areas of government policies.

**5572** Caroline Glendinning and Jane Miller (eds) *Women and Poverty in Britain* Wheatsheaf 1987. Essays on women and poverty in the twentieth century, racism and women's poverty, low paid work, women as carers and women and welfare. These are most informative, especially for the most recent period. See also P J Sloane (ed) *Women and Low Pay* Macmillan 1980.

**5573** P Harrison *Inside The Inner City: Life under the Cutting Edge* Penguin 1983. An investigation into poverty and the life of the poor in Hackney, in inner London, in the 1980s.

**5574** Peter Townsend, Paul Corrigan and Ute Kowerzik *Poverty and Labour in London* Low Pay Unit 1987. A slim volume published to mark the centenary of Booth's massive work of social investigation. Examining poverty in London in the 1980s it draws attention to increasing disparities of incomes, deprivation, the cost of living and the feminization of poverty.

**5575** Ken Coates and Richard Silburn *Poverty: The Forgotten Englishmen* Penguin 1968. This is largely a case study of poverty in the slum (now cleared) of St Anne's in Nottingham.

**5576** Benjamin Seebohm Rowntree and George R Lavers *Poverty and the Welfare State: A Third Social Survey of York dealing only with Economic Questions* Longmans 1951. An attempt to throw light on to how far welfare has affected poverty by comparison with Rowntree's earlier surveys in 1901 and 1936. This includes an examination of malnutrition amongst the poor. Rowntree found a clear improvement in people's condition in 1951. This study is followed up by A B Atkinson, A K Maynard and C G Trinder *Parents and Children: Income in Two Generations* Heinemann 1983.

## E. STATUS OF WOMEN

### (1) General

**5577** Ruth Cowley *What About Women? Information Sources for Women's Studies* Fanfare Press 1986. A descriptive list of most women's organizations in Britain.

**5578** Anne Crawford *et al* (eds) *The Europa Biographical Dictionary of British Women* Europa Publications 1983. A collection of short biographies of notable women throughout British history, including some which are of use for the post-war period.

**5579** *Women's Studies Abstracts* Rush Publishing, Rush, New York 1972–. A quarterly abstracting service

which is classified and contains about 200 abstracts per issue. It has a distinct North American bias.

**5580** M Ritchie *Women's Studies: A Checklist of Bibliographies* Mansell 1980. This has 489 annotated entries.

**5581** *Bibliofem* Fawcett Library, City of London Polytechnic 1978–86. A bibliography of material on women based on the collections of the Fawcett Library and the Equal Opportunities Commission. It was issued as a microfiche at monthly intervals in classified form. *Women's Work and Women's Studies* Bernard College Women's Center, New York 1972– is an annual bibliography of books, articles, pamphlets and research papers about women and feminism.

**5582** Linda Frey, Marrsha Frey and Joanna Schneider (eds) *Women in Western European History: A Select, Chronological and Topical Bibliography: The Nineteenth and Twentieth Centuries* Greenwood 1984. A well organized but unannotated bibliography. It contains a fair amount of material on British women since 1945. The first supplement appeared in 1986. See also Victor F Gilbert and Darshan Singh Tatla *Women's Studies: A Bibliography of Dissertations 1870–1982* Blackwell 1985.

**5583** Diana Souhami *Woman's Place: The Changing Picture of Women in Britain* Penguin 1987. A history of women's changing life and role in society. Monica Charlot (ed) *Les Femmes dans la société Britannique* Armand Colin, Paris 1977 contains a collection of historical essays on women and society, and education, women's sexuality, work, the women's movement and women in politics, the churches or the cinema. See also E Whitelegg *et al The Changing Experience of Women* Robertson 1982. On women and politics 1850–1980 see Vicky Randell *Women and Politics* Macmillan 1982. Jane Lewis *Women in England 1870–1970: Sexual Divisions and Social Change* Wheatsheaf 1984 looks at family, motherhood and women's employment taking account of class-related differences. Mary Ingham *Now We Are Thirty* Eyre Methuen 1981 surveys women's social conditions 1907–80. The social, and particularly the living conditions, of working class women 1920–84 are discussed in Violet Cowley *Over My Shoulder* Stockwell 1985.

**5584** April Carter *The Politics of Women's Rights* Longman 1988. A history of women's changing position since 1945 which concentrates on the struggle to gain equal rights and the efforts of the feminist movement. A good study which includes a useful bibliography. Elizabeth Wilson *Only Halfway to Paradise: Women in Postwar Britain 1945–1968* Tavistock 1980 essays an explanation of the relative quietism of campaigners for women's rights within the broad history of women's changing conditions in the immediate aftermath of the war followed by the emergence of militant feminism in the 1960s. Those who have been active in the feminist movement, like Wilson, are perhaps inclined to give it a relatively large place in their account of the changes in the position of women in society in the post-war era. It has however been argued by E J Mishon 'Was the Women's Liberation Movement Really Necessary?' *Encounter* 64 1985 pp 7–20 that social and economic factors have been much more important in changing women's position in society.

**5585** K O'Donovan *Sexual Divisions in Law* Weidenfeld and Nicolson 1985. A study of the unequal legal status of men and women in the 1980s. I Reid and E Wormald (eds) *Sex Differences in Britain* Grant McIntyre 1982 examines inequality in treatment and opportunity between men and women in fields such as education, health, the labour market, social security, politics or crime.

**5586** Liz Heron (ed) *Truth, Dare or Promise: Girls Growing Up in the Fifties* Virago 1985. A collection of reminiscences by 12 women of their youth and growth towards feminism in the 1950s. Carol Dix *Say I'm Sorry to Mother: Growing up in the Sixties* Pan 1978 is the recollections of four girls of their teenage years in the 1960s and of the impact rock music, the Pill, abortions and feminism made upon them.

**5587** Georgina Ashworth and Lucy Bonnerjea (eds) *The Invisible Decade: UK Women and the UN Decade 1976–85* Gower 1985. An indictment of lack of progress towards greater equality for women during the UN decade of women. Veronica Beachey and Elizabeth Whitelegg (eds) *Women in Britain Today* 2nd ed, Open University Press 1986 examines the contemporary situation.

**5588** Germaine Greer *The Female Eunuch* MacGibbon and Kee 1970. An influential account of the situation of women and the way they are treated.

**5589** Ann Oakley *Housewife* Penguin 1976. A history of the development of the housewife's role and a summary of the contemporary situation. It includes four case histories. See also R Adam *A Woman's Place 1910–75* Chatto and Windus 1976. Suzanne Lowry *The Guilt Cage: Housewives and a Decade of Liberation* Elm Tree Books 1980 assesses the effects of the women's movement on the role of housewives.

**5590** Charmian Kenner *No Time for Women: Exploring Women's Health in the 1930s and Today* Pandora Press 1985. See also Elaine Showalter *The Female Malady: Women, Madness and English Culture 1830–1980* Pantheon, New York 1985. Attitudes and policy towards childbirth in the immediate aftermath of the Second

World War are explored in Denise Riley 'The Free Mothers: Pronatalism and Working Women in Industry at the End of the Last War in Britain' *History Workshop* 11 1981 pp 59–119.

**5591** J Pahl *A Refuge for Battered Women: A Study of the Role of a Women's Centre* HMSO 1978. A study of the establishment in the mid-1970s of the Canterbury Women's Centre, the women in it and their experiences which led them to seek refuge.

### (2) Women's Organizations

**5592** I Grant *National Council of Women of Great Britain: The First Sixty Years 1895–1955* National Council of Women of Great Britain 1955.

**5593** Dorothy V Hall *Making Things Happen: History of the National Federation of Business and Professional Women's Clubs of Great Britain and Northern Ireland* the Federation 1963.

**5594** Betty Jarman *The Lively-Minded Women: The First Twenty Years of the National Housewives Register* Heinemann 1981. This was set up to provide a forum and meeting place for women with young children, as a relief from the home. It is now known as the National Women's Register.

**5595** S Goodenough *Jam and Jerusalem: A History of the Women's Institute* Collins 1977. See also I Jenkins *The History of the Women's Institute Movement of England and Wales* National Federation of Women's Institutes 1953.

### (3) The Feminist Movement

**5596** Pat Darter *The Women's Movement* Library Association 1983. A short annotated bibliography and guide to the main periodicals.

**5597** Olive Banks *Faces Of Feminism: A Study of Feminism as a Social Movement* Martin Robinson 1981. A history of feminism in Britain and America since the early nineteenth century in relation to three intellectual traditions, the enlightenment, evangelicalism and socialism. Liz Heron *Changes of Heart: Reflections on Women's Independence* Pandora 1986 reflects on the impact of the feminist movement on women's lives through interviews and autobiographical fragments from a feminist perspective.

**5598** Anna Coote and Beatrix Campbell *Sweet Freedom* 2nd ed, Blackwell 1987. A history of the development of the women's movement since the late 1960s. It includes reflections on feminist involvement in the peace movement and the miners' strike of 1984–5 and on the black women's movement as well as on campaigns against sexual harassment or for equal pay. Angela Neustatter *Hyenas in Petticoats: A Look at Twenty Years of Feminism* Penguin 1989 concentrates more particularly on the feminist movement. Another history of the movement since the late 1960s is David Bourchier *The Feminist Challenge: The Movement for Women's Liberation in Britain and the USA* Macmillan 1983. Sheila Rowbotham *The Past Before Us: Feminism in Action Since the 1960s* Unwin Hyman 1989 selects a number of issues and cases and analyses them in depth. See also Jane Humphries 'The Emancipation of Women in the 1970s and 1980s: From the Latent to the Floating' *Capital and Class* 20 1983 pp 6–28.

**5599** Juliet Mitchell *Women's Estate* Penguin 1971. A study of the influences which led to the rise of the women's liberation movement in the late 1960s, which she sees as being principally transatlantic in flavour. It provides a good introduction on the state of the movement in the late 1960s. See also Sue O'Sullivan 'Passionate Beginnings: Ideological Politics 1969–72' *Feminist Review* 11 1982 pp 20–87.

**5600** Michelle Wandor (ed) *The Body Politic: Writings from the Women's Liberation Movement in Britain 1969–1972* Stage 1 1972. A collection of writings illustrating trends in thought and the prevailing ideas in this formative period of the movement.

**5601** Anna Paczuska *Sisters and Workers: Ten Years of the Struggle for Women's Liberation and Socialism* Women's Voice 1980. A study of the development of socialist feminism as is Angela Weir and Elizabeth Wilson 'The British Women's Movement' *New Left Review* 148 1984 pp 74–103.

**5602** Bridget Hutter and Gillian Williams (ed) *Controlling Women: The Normal and the Deviant* Croom Helm 1980. Essays on motherhood, prostitution, women and alcohol, abortion, old age and women in prison.

**5603** Thelma Cazalet-Keir *From The Wings* The Bodley Head 1967. Her autobiography. A Conservative MP between the wars she was very active in women's issues after the war. As Chairman of the Equal Pay Campaign Committee 1947–56 she helped to secure equal pay for equal work in the public services in 1955. She was also President of the Fawcett Society 1956–61. Her autobiography also throws light on the origins of the Arts Council, in which she was also active. She was also well connected in Bohemian London with figures like Augustus John.

**5604** Rosalind Messenger *The Doors of Opportunity: A Biography of Dame Caroline Haslett DBE, Companion IEE* Femina Books 1967. Haslett was important in pointing the way for women to become electrical engineers and pursue other professions. She was active in the British Federation of Business and Professional Women and also served on various government committees in the late 1940s.

**5605** Dora Russell *The Tamarisk Tree Vol 3: Challenge to the Cold War* Virago 1985. The autobiography of a feminist, important figure in the birth control movement, pacifist and socialist. This final part of her autobiography covers from 1945 until shortly before her death in 1986. See also Dale Spender (ed) *The Dora Russell Reader: 57 Years of Writing and Journalism 1925–1982* Routledge and Kegan Paul 1983.

**5606** Prunella Stack *Movement Is Life: The Autobiography of Prunella Stack* Collins and Harvill 1973. The autobiography of the leading light of the Women's League of Health and Beauty since she and her mother founded it in 1930.

**5607** Mary Stott *Forgetting's No Excuse: The Autobiography of Mary Stott, Journalist, Campaigner and Feminist* Faber 1973. Stott was the women's editor of *The Guardian* 1957–72, a founder of Women in Media and active in the women's movement. See also her further autobiography *Before I Go: Reflections on My Life and Times* Virago 1985.

**5608** Andro Linklater *An Unhusbanded Life* Hutchinson 1979. A feminist autobiography. For other biographies by feminist activists see Ann Oakley *Taking It Like A Woman* Cape 1983 and Elizabeth Wilson *Mirror Writing: An Autobiography* Virago 1982.

## F. RACE RELATIONS

Race relations has been one of the most emotive social issues of the post-war years. This has been partly because of the scale of immigration from the New Commonwealth, principally the West Indies and the Indian sub-continent, for much of the period. It has also been because immigrant settlement has tended to be concentrated in certain areas. Furthermore differences of culture and most obviously of colour were rather more glaring in this case than in previous and smaller immigration waves.

The importation of labour in view of the full employment prevailing in Britain, and the British Nationality Act of 1948, which extended British citizenship to the Commonwealth and colonies, were the two main catalysts of New Commonwealth immigration from the late 1940s onwards. In the 1950s this immigration caused increasing concern. Signs of growing racial tension, not least the 1958 race riots in Nottingham and Notting Hill, encouraged the development of policies designed to restrict both immigration and racial discrimination. Not all the material that is relevant to the study of this subject is to be found in the following pages. The literature on immigration and immigration control is to found in the appropriate section. So is the material on media reactions to racial issues. Studies on both the racist vote and the votes of ethnic minorities are to be found in the section on Electoral History. There is a considerable literature on the educational disadvantage that ethnic minority children, particularly those of West Indian background, have tended to suffer. This can be found in the section on Education [6424–30].

### (1) General

#### (a) Reference Works

**5609** Radical Statistics Race Group *Britain: Black Population* Heinemann Educational 1980. Statistics on the population and discussions of the problems with the statistics. Various aspects of the black experience are also reflected in statistical terms.

**5610** J Akinsanya and L Dada *A Bibliography of Race and Race Relations* New Dimension Publications 1984. This is the most recent general bibliography on the subject of race relations with over 4,500 titles listed on the situation in Britain. Raj Madan *Coloured Minorities in Britain: A Comprehensive Bibliography 1970–1977* Aldwych Press 1979 exhaustively covers works published in that period. This is the sequel to Ambalavaner Sivanandan *Coloured Minorities in Britain* 3rd ed, Institute of Race Relations 1969, which covers works published between 1950 and 1969. Both were compiled from the extensive holdings of the Institute of Race Relations and provide lists of relevant journals and concerned organizations. Madan's bibliography is much the larger, reflecting the growing literature on the subject. Unfortunately neither is annotated. A more select, and also unannotated, bibliography is Paul Gordon and Francesca Klug *Racism and Discrimination in Britain: A Select Bibliography 1970–83* Runnymede Trust 1984. This is the sequel to *Ethnic Minorities in Britain: A Select Bibliography* Runnymede Trust 1977. See also Zig Layton-Henry *Race and Politics in Britain: A Select Bibliography* Research Unit on Ethnic Relations 1979.

**5611** *Race Relations in Britain: A Select Bibliography* Community Relations Commission (now the Commission for Racial Equality) 1970–. An irregularly published serial bibliography which includes some annotations. Another serial bibliography is the Institute of Race Relations' biennial *Coloured Immigrants in Britain: A Select Bibliography*. Immigrants and Mi-

norities has annually published a short bibliography on race and labour in Britain since 1979.

**5612** Victor F Gilbert and Darshan Singh Tatla *Immigrants, Minorities and Race Relations: A Bibliography of Theses and Dissertations Presented at British and Irish Universities 1900–1981* Mansell 1984.

**5613** Sage *Race Relations Abstracts* 1975–. Although international in scope this tends to include abstracts of major works relating to British race relations. The distortingly partisan tone of some of the abstracts however reduces their value since they sometimes convey a totally misleading impression of the work under review. This publication also features useful bibliographical essays focusing on trends in the literature on various aspects of race relations. See also *Race Relations Abstracts* Institute of Race Relations 1968–.

**5614** Gideon Ben-Tovim and John Gabriel 'The Politics of Race in Britain 1962–1970: A Review of the Major Trends and of the Recent Literature' Sage *Race Relations Abstracts* 4/4 1979 pp 1–56. A good bibliographical essay covering the various trends in the literature in this period from a committed standpoint. J Bourne and Ambalavaner Sivanandan 'Cheer Leaders and Ombudsmen: The Sociology of Race Relations in Britain' *Race and Class* 21 1980 pp 331–51 is another bibliographical essay which reviews the literature on the sociology of race relations. The literature on the attitudes of ethnic minorities, and especially of West Indians and Asians, is reviewed in S Field *The Attitude of Ethnic Minorities* Study 80, Home Office Research Unit 1984.

#### (b) General Histories and Surveys

**5615** E J B Rose (ed) *Colour and Citizenship: A Report on British Race Relations* Oxford University Press 1969. A massive and comprehensive history of all aspects of race relations in the post-war period. Another useful history is Clifford S Hill *Immigration and Integration: A Study of the Settlement of Coloured Minorities in Britain* Pergamon 1970.

**5616** Brian D Jacobs *Racism In Britain* Christopher Helm 1988. A general textbook. It is good on immigration policy and less good on the employment of ethnic minorities. See also Chris Mullard *Black Britain* Allen and Unwin 1977. This latter includes reflections on developments at the Institute of Race Relations.

**5617** Paul Gilroy *There Ain't No Black in the Union Jack: The Cultural Politics of Race and Nation* Hutchinson 1989. A good analysis of the cultural aspects of race relations in Britain. Robert Miles and Annie Phizacklea *Labour and Racism* Routledge and Kegan Paul 1980 sets out to examine the postion of blacks in British political culture. There are lots of useful quotes amongst the extensive tables and examinations of racial attitudes both towards and among the black minorities. A useful comparative study is G P Freeman *Immigrant Labor and Racial Conflict in Industrial Societies: The French and British Experience 1945–1975* Princeton University Press 1979.

**5618** Robert Miles and Annie Phizacklea *White Man's Country: Racism in British Politics* Pluto 1984. A committed analysis of what they see as the institutionalization of racism in post-war Britain. Another work which focuses particularly on a theoretical debate about the nature of 'state racism' in Britain is John Solomos *The Politics of Racism: Theories and Practice in Contemporary Britain* Macmillan 1988. See also Ambalavaner Sivanandan *Race, Class and the State: The Black Experience in Britain* Institute of Race Relations 1976.

**5619** Robert Miles and Annie Phizacklea (eds) *Racism and Political Action in Britain* Routledge and Kegan Paul 1979. A collection of essays covering race relations issues from the early nineteenth century. These focus particularly on white racism. In the literature on this subject there is however little on white opposition to racism. Another collection of historical essays is Kenneth Lunn (ed) *Race and Labour in Twentieth Century Britain* Cass 1986. Unfortunately the relevant essays on immigrant labour in the 1940s and 1950s and on Indian foundry workers 1945–62 are not amongst the best in the volume and tend to reflect sociological hypotheses, not historical evidence.

**5620** Nathan Glazer and Ken Young (eds) *Ethnic Pluralism and Public Policy: Achieving Equality in the United States and Britain* Heinemann Educational 1983. In fact most of the essays relate to Britain. They include analyses of race relations policy in fields such as education, housing or policing. There is also an essay on the political representation of ethnic minorities. Simon Abbott (ed) *The Prevention of Racial Discrimination in Britain* Oxford University Press 1971 is a good collection of essays on the situation of New Commonwealth and recent developments in race relations legislation. Frank Field and Patricia Haskin (eds) *Black Britons* Oxford University Press 1971 is a book of readings and extracts of articles on various aspects of race relations. See also Ivor Crewe (ed) *British Political Sociology Yearbook Vol 2: The Politics of Race* Croom Helm 1975.

**5621** W W Daniel *Racial Discrimination in England* Penguin 1967. The first in a series of studies of reports by Political and Economic Planning and its successor organization, the Policy Studies Institute. It was followed by David J Smith *Racial Disadvantage in Britain* Penguin 1977 and Colin Brown, Elizabeth Worth and Eileen Reid *Black and White Britain: The Third PSI Survey* Heinemann 1984. These are all based on extensive interviewing to discover ordinary people's experience. They find that discrimination is not really decreasing.

**5622** John Haskey 'Families and Households of the Ethnic Minority and White Populations of Great Britain' *Population Trends* 57 1989 pp 8–19. A useful statistically based survey.

**5623** Andy Thomas 'Racial Discrimination and the Attlee Government' *New Community* 10 1982 pp 270–8. A survey of the reactions of this government to immigration and race relations problems 1945–51 in the light of recently released papers at the Public Record Office.

**5624** Sydney Collins *Coloured Minorities in Britain: Studies in British Race Relations based on African, West Indian and Asiatic Immigrants* Lutterworth 1957. A useful early study of race relations before either the riots of 1958 or the introduction of immigration controls. This includes case studies of negro, Muslim and Chinese communities. Contemporary studies of race relations and attitudes are Michael Banton *White and Coloured: The Behaviour of British People Towards Coloured Immigrants* Cape 1959 and James Wickenden *Colour in Britain* Oxford University Press 1958. The results of the 1951 attitude survey are used to show how the threat to jobs from the influx of coloured workers and the end of empire changed racial attitudes in the 1950s in Michael Banton 'The Influence of Colonial Status upon Black-White Relations in England 1948–58' *Sociology* 17 1983 pp 546–59.

**5625** Christopher Temple Husbands *'Race' in Britain: Continuity and Change* 2nd ed, Hutchinson Educational 1987. An eclectic and not very well arranged study of the main trends and developments in race relations 1962–79. See also the short paper, S Field *Ethnic Minorities in Britain: A Study of Trends in their Position Since 1961* HMSO 1981.

**5626** Nicholas Deakin (ed) *Colour, Citizenship and British Society* Panther 1970. A comprehensive report on the state of race relations after the legislation of the late 1960s based on the reports which produced [5615]. Another comprehensive study is Sheila Patterson *Immigration and Race Relations in Britain 1960–67* Oxford University Press 1969. Richard Hooper (ed) *Colour in Britain* BBC 1965 covers various aspects of race relations in the 1960s. It is based on a BBC radio series. Public opinion on race relations in the 1960s is assessed in Donley T Studlar 'British Public Opinion, Colour Issues and Enoch Powell: A Longitudinal Analysis' *British Journal of Political Science* 4 1974 pp 371–81. He argues that public opinion on the issue was fairly constant from 1960 onwards and was only slightly affected by events such as Powell's 'Rivers of Blood' speech in 1968. Indeed he claims that political decisions were far more affected by public opinion than vice versa.

**5627** Centre for Contemporary Cultural Studies *The Empire Strikes Back: Race and Racism in 70s Britain* Hutchinson 1982. This picks out issues such as race relations during a period of economic crisis, the efforts of the National Front or the stress on black criminality which was a feature of the decade. 'Immigration and Race Relations' *Political Social Economic Review* 14 1978 pp 1–31 is a survey of the effect on public opinion of Mrs Thatcher's speech about the fear of being swamped by immigrants in 1978. It argues that the speech had a considerable effect, which worked in favour of the Conservatives.

**5628** Michael Banton 'The Beginning and the End of the Racial Issue in British Politics' *Policy and Politics* 15 1987 pp 39–47. A study of race relations as a political issue. It argues that it has diminished in importance because of immigration controls and a measure of integration, but it remains a factor because of the association of this issue with poverty and inner city deprivation. Brian D Jacobs *Black Politics and Urban Crisis in Britain* Cambridge University Press 1986 looks particularly at the attitudes of the black community to race relations in the 1980s. He emphasizes that despite the riots of the 1980s the leadership of the community remains moderate, respectable and anxious to integrate. Whereas most books on race relations concentrate on the experience of New Commonwealth immigrants Philip Cohen and Harwant S Bains (eds) *Multi-Racist Britain* Macmillan Education 1988 also looks at groups such as the Jews and the Irish. This is a series of studies of issues in race relations in the 1980s based on interviews with people involved in education, youth policy or skinhead activities. It particularly looks at race relations as they affect the young.

**5629** Alfred Davey *Learning To Be Prejudiced: Growing up in Multi-Racial Britain* Arnold 1983. A study of socialization.

**5630** D A Coleman (ed) *Demography of Immigrants and Minority Groups in the UK* Academic Press 1982. Historical and geographical perspectives and statistics covering a good range of the ethnic minorities in Britain.

**5631** S M Poulter *English Law and Ethnic Minority Customs* Butterworths 1986. An analysis of the difficulties presented in the enforcement of the law by ethnic and religious differences.

**5632** Michael Stubbs (ed) *The Other Languages of England* Routledge and Kegan Paul 1985. A history and background of the various linguistic minorities. These are comprehensively covered. On a special scheme set up to teach English to ethnic minorities in North London

see R Grant and E Self (eds) *'Can You Speak English?' A History of Neighbourhood English Classes Based on the Recollected Experiences of some of its Members and Friends* Neighbourhood English Classes 1984.

**5633** Nancy Stepan *The Idea of Race in Science: Great Britain 1800–1960* Macmillan 1982. A study of racial theories.

**5634** Gideon Ben-Tovim, John Gabriel, Ian Law and Kathleen Shredder *The Local Politics of Race* Macmillan 1986. A study of the processes which create racial tensions and issues, drawing on case studies.

**5635** John Brown *The Unmelting Pot: An English Town and its Immigrants* Macmillan 1970. A study of race relations in Bedford, a town which has attracted a wide variety of ethnic groups.

**5636** John Lambert *Crime, Police and Race Relations: A Study in Birmingham* Oxford University Press 1970. The post-war history of race relations in the Handsworth area of Birmingham is studied in depth in John Rex and Sally Tomlinson *Colonial Migrants in a British City – A Class Analysis* Routledge and Kegan Paul 1979. Handsworth, where many immigrants settled, is also studied in Peter Ratcliffe *Racism and Reaction: A Profile of Handsworth* Routledge and Kegan Paul 1981. The black community in Handsworth is examined in detail in Augustine John *Race in the Inner City* Runnymede Trust 1972. All aspects of race relations in another area of Birmingham are examined in depth and historical detail, including a chronology, in John Rex and Robert Moore *Race, Community and Conflict: A Study of Sparkbrook* Oxford University Press 1967.

**5637** Bradford Heritage Recording Unit, Industrial Museum, Moorside Road, Eccleshill, Bradford (tel: 0274 631756). Bradford has been one of the main centres of immigrant settlement. During and immediately after the war many East European refugees arrived in the city. This was followed by a much larger wave of immigration from India and Pakistan, partly attracted by Bradford's textiles industries. Even before 1939 the city supported substantial immigrant, mainly Irish, communities. It is now one of the most racially mixed populations in Britain. This oral history project records the experience of all the various ethnic minorities in Bradford. The tapes are catalogued and in many cases transcripts are available.

**5638** A H Richmond *Immigration and Race Relations in an English City: A Study in Bristol* Oxford University Press 1973. A good study.

**5639** Simon Jenkins *Here To Live: A Study of Race Relations in an English Town* Runnymede Trust 1971.

A study focusing on the experiences of Sikhs in Leamington Spa.

**5640** Ian Law *A History of Race and Racism in Liverpool* Merseyside Community Relations Commission 1982. Liverpool has a long history of racial and sectarian conflict. Racial attitudes in the particular context of eugenics and concern about moral decline resulting from mixed marriages are examined in Paul B Rich 'Philanthropic Racism in Britain: The Liverpool University Settlement, the Anti-Slavery Society and the Issue of "Half-Caste" Children 1919–1951' *Immigrants and Minorities* 3 1984 pp 30–48.

**5641** Chaim Bermant *Point Of Arrival: A Study of London's East End* Eyre Methuen 1975. A study of this area as a racial melting pot in the nineteenth and twentieth centuries, up to the Brick Lane riot of 1970.

**5642** Tim Mason 'Residential Succession, Community Facilities and Urban Renewal in Cheetham Hill, Manchester' *New Community* 6 1977–78 pp 78–87. This area had an influx of Jews and East Europeans in the aftermath of the war. As these dispersed they were succeeded by Sikhs and Pakistanis. The influence of the housing market in these residential patterns is examined in detail.

**5643** Daniel Lawrence *Black Migrants and White Natives: A Study of Race Relations in Nottingham* Cambridge University Press 1974. After the 1958 race riot Nottingham gained a reputation for good race relations. Lawrence explores the extent to which this reputation was justified.

**5644** Campaign Against Racism and Fascism/Southall Rights *Southall: The Birth of a Black Community* Institute of Race Relations/Southall Rights 1981. A history of the black community in the Southall area of North London from the 1950s to the confrontation with the National Front on 23rd April 1979. It includes a chronology.

**5645** Edwin Eames and Howard Robboy 'Racism Ltd, British Ethnocentrism and the Punjabi Migrant' *International Journal of Contemporary Sociology* 18 1981 pp 77–101. A study of racism and the efforts to deal with it in Wolverhampton 1955–79.

**(c) The Institute of Race Relations and Similar Bodies**

**5646** Chris Mullard *Race, Power and Resistance* Routledge and Kegan Paul 1986. A history of the Institute from 1950. It focuses on ideological conflict within it and on the radical change in 1969–72 during which a white elite were replaced within the Institute by a black leadership. See also Ambalavaner Sivanandan *Race and Resistance: The IRR Story* Race Today 1974.

**5647** Benjamin W Heinemann Jr *The Politics of the Powerless: A Study of the Campaign Against Racial Discrimination* Oxford University Press 1972. A study of this mainly West Indian body which was established in 1964. Tensions between its various members and its objectives led to its demise in 1967.

**5648** Ambalavaner Sivanandan *A Different Hunger: Writings on Black Resistance* Pluto 1982. Writings from the 1940s to the 1980s collected and analysed.

**(2) Race Relations Policy**

**5649** Zig Layton-Henry *The Politics of Race in Britain* Allen and Unwin 1984. A succinct and thorough account of post-war developments in race relations and the management of the tensions attendant on mass immigration. See also Dipak Nandy *The Politics of Race Relations* Fontana 1980 and John Carson 'A Matter of Policy: The Lesson of Recent British Race Relations Legislation' *Albion* 8 1976 pp 154–77. The response to this mass immigration is analysed in a comparative context drawing on case studies in Ira Katznelson *Black Men, White Cities: Race, Politics and Immigration in the United States 1900–30 and Britain 1948–68* Oxford University Press 1973. A critical account of the handling of immigration and race relations and the reaction of the host community is Paul Foot *Immigration and Race in British Politics* Penguin 1965.

**5650** John Solomos *Black Youth, Racism and the State: The Politics of Ideology and Policy* Cambridge University Press 1983. A comprehensive and critical analysis of state policy towards young blacks in the post-war period and of the process whereby they came to be seen as a social problem.

**5651** B A Hepple *Race, Jobs and the Law* 2nd ed, Penguin 1970. An examination of the state of the law. The concepts, not least the concept of race, which were instrumental in framing the law are analysed in E J Fry 'Race, Discrimination and Law: An Analysis of Normative Arguments, with Reference to the Race Relations and Immigration Acts' Manchester PhD Thesis 1983.

**5652** Robert Miles 'The Riots of 1958: Notes on the Ideological Construction of "Race Relations" as a Political Issue in Britain' *Immigrants and Minorities* 3 1984 pp 252–75. An examination of the effects of the 1958 riots on the development of immigration control and race relations policy.

**5653** I Walker 'An Analysis of Questions in the House of Commons in the Field of Race Relations and Commonwealth Immigration 1959–1964' Bradford MSc Thesis 1973–4.

**5654** Michael Banton *Promoting Racial Harmony* Cambridge University Press 1985. An excellent account of policy on race relations since the 1960s focusing on the Community Relations Commission and committees set up in the 1960s and the Commission for Racial Equality which replaced them after the 1976 Race Relations Act. It provides a judicious analysis of the difficulties faced by these bodies, their efforts and their failings. On the committees established after the 1965 Race Relations Act see Michael J Hill and Ruth Issacharoff *Community Action and Race Relations: A Study of Community Relations Committees in Britain* Oxford University Press 1971. The 1965 Act, under Section 6, also prohibited utterances and publication and distribution of material of a racist nature. The background to Section 6, and its enforcement is examined in Richard P Longaker 'The Race Relations Act of 1965: An Evaluation of the Incitement Provision' *Race* 11 1969 pp 125–56. *Commission for Racial Equality Report* HMSO 1978– is the annual report of the body set up after the 1976 Act. On progress since the 1976 Act see also Ken Young and Naomi Connelly 'After The Act: Policy Review for Local Authorities under the Race Relations Act 1976' *Local Government Studies* 10 1984 pp 13–25.

**5655** Zig Layton-Henry and Paul B Rich *Race Government and Politics in Britain* Macmillan 1986. This focuses particularly on policy and the problems of handling race relations issues in areas such as policing or education by the Thatcher government. Policy in the area of employment is criticized in Richard Jenkins and John Solomos (eds) *Racism and Equal Opportunity Policies in the 1980s* Cambridge University Press 1987.

### (3) Spatial Patterns of Race

**5656** N Karnalijnslyper and R Ward *The Housing Position and Residential Distribution of Ethnic Minorities in Britain: A Bibliography* Social Science Research Unit on Ethnic Relations, University of Aston 1982.

**5657** J Henderson and Valerie A Karn *Race, Class and State Housing: Inequality and the Allocation of Public Housing in Britain* Gower 1987. An examination of the distribution of housing amongst social and racial groups. Susan J Smith *The Politics of 'Race' and Residence: Citizenship, Segregation and White Supremacy in Britain* Polity 1988 is a rather jargon-ridden look at patterns of racial distribution. See also P N Jones 'The Distribution and Diffusion of the Coloured Population in England and Wales 1961–71' *Transactions of the Institute of British Geographers* n.s. 3 1978 pp 515–32.

**5658** Hazel Flett 'The Practice of Racial Dispersal in Birmingham 1969–1975' *Journal of Social Policy* 8 1979 pp 289–309. This details the implementation and failure of Birmingham's attempt to use public sector housing to disperse immigrants throughout the city in the interests of racial integration.

**5659** Vaughan Robinson *The Segregation of Asians within a British City: Theory and Practice* School of Geography, University of Oxford 1979. An examination of the spatial structure of the Asian community in Blackburn.

**5660** M Dalton and J M Seaman 'The Distribution of New Commonwealth Immigrants in the Borough of Ealing 1961–6' *Transactions of the Institute of British Geographers* 58 1973 pp 21–40. This study of a London borough illustrates that as the numbers increase they are gathered in greater clusters, thus increasing their segregation from the host population.

**5661** Ian Law 'White Racism and Black Settlement in Liverpool: A Study of Local Inequalities and Policies, with Particular Reference to Council Housing' Liverpool PhD Thesis 1985. A historical account of the concentration, increased by local housing policy in the 1980s, of black people in the lowest quality housing stock. The racial implications of the Militant-controlled Liverpool City Council in the early 1980s, particularly in the field of public housing, are critically assessed in Liverpool Black Caucus *The Racial Politics of Militant in Liverpool* Merseyside Area Profile Group/Runnymede Trust 1986.

**5662** T R Lee *Race and Residence: The Concentration and Dispersal of Immigrants in London* Clarendon 1977. This concentrates on the experience of West Indians 1961–71. See also Ceri Peach and S Shah 'The Contribution of Council House Allocation to West Indian Desegregation in London 1961–1971' *Urban Studies* 17 1980 pp 333–41. John Parker and Keith Dugmore *Colour and the Allocation of GLC Housing: The Report of the GLC Lettings Survey 1974–5* GLC 1976 found that a disproportionate amount of the Greater London Council's oldest and most unpopular accommodation was allocated to coloured people, but explained that this was partly the result of the structure of the housing lists and partly because a high proportion of blacks made their first preference an inner London location.

**5663** A Simpson *Stacking the Decks: A Study of Race, Inequality and Council Housing in Nottingham* Nottingham Community Relations Council 1981. The result of a three year study which argues that the allocation and transfer system in public housing works against black people. See also Ira Katznelson 'The Politics of Racial Buffering in Nottingham 1954–1968' *Race* 11 1970 pp 431–46.

## (4) Race Relations in Industry

**5664**  Peter Braham, Ed Rhodes and Michael Pearn (eds) *Discrimination and Disadvantage in Employment: The Experience of Black Workers* Harper and Row 1981. A collection of essays of varying quality, including a number of case studies. The earnings disadvantage of minorities and their exploitation in low paid jobs is examined in K Mayhew and B Rosewell 'Immigrants and Occupational Crowding in Great Britain' *Bulletin of Oxford University Institute of Economic Statistics* 40 1978 pp 223–48. See also Frank Cousins 'Race Relations in Employment in the United Kingdom' *International Labour Review* 102 1970 pp 1–13.

**5665**  A H Richmond 'Relation between Skill and Adjustment of a Group of West Indian Negro Workers in England' *Occupational Psychology* 25 1957 pp 153–65. There is a need for more recent studies of the extent of success in adjusting to life and work in Britain of different types of immigrant workers.

**5666**  R Jain *Employment-Unemployment Amongst Black Youths: A Bibliography* Scope Publications 1978. A short listing. David Beetham *Immigrant School Leavers and the Youth Employment Service in Birmingham* Institute of Race Relations 1967 is a short study. The stereotyping and racial prejudice of employers in the operation of the Youth Training Scheme is examined in E de Sousa 'Racism in the YTS' *Critical Social Policy* 20 1987 pp 66–73.

**5667**  Malcolm Rimmer *Race and Industrial Conflict: A Study in a Group of Midlands Foundries* Heinemann Educational 1972. A brief study. See also Mark Duffield 'Rationalisation and the Politics of Segregation: Indian Workers in Britain's Foundry Industry 1945–62' *Immigrants and Minorities* 4 1985 pp 142–72.

**5668**  Dennis Brooks *Race and Labour in London Transport* Oxford University Press 1975. A good sociological study on race relations in a major employer of coloured labour. Importantly it reveals the inter-island rivalries of West Indians and the racial tensions between ethnic minorities as well as against them by the host population.

**5669**  Paul Gordon 'Guest Workers of the Sea: Racism in British Shipping' *Race and Class* 28 1986 pp 73–81. A study of a history of a discrimination in an industry which was excluded from the provisions of the 1968 and 1976 legislation. It is very critical of the role of the National Union of Seamen.

**5670**  John K Chadwick-Jones 'The Acceptance and Socialisation of Immigrant Workers in the Steel Industry' *Sociological Review* n.s. 12 1964 pp 169–83.

**5671**  B G Cohen and P J Jenner 'The Employment of Immigrants: A Case Study within the Wool Industry' *Race* 10 1968 pp 41–56.

**5672**  Peter L Wright *The Coloured Worker in British Industry with Special Reference to the Midlands and the North of England* Oxford University Press 1968. A major piece of work based on research conducted in 1961–4.

**5673**  Sheila Allen, Stuart Bentley and Joanna Bornet *Work, Race and Immigration* Bradford University Press 1977. 'A unique historical portrait of the employment structure and processes of a major industrial city and the part which coloured immigrant groups played in it' based on research carried out in Bradford in 1966–9.

**5674**  Sheila Patterson *Immigrants in Industry* Oxford University Press 1968. An analysis of the employment of various groups of immigrants, principally Irish, Poles and West Indians, in Croydon 1958–60.

## (5) Attitudes of Political Parties and Trade Unions

**5675**  Frank Reeves *British Racial Discourse: A Study of British Political Discourse about Race and Race Related Matters* Cambridge University Press 1983. An analysis of party attitudes to racial issues over the post-war period. Party attitudes and ethnic minority support for political parties are examined in Muhammad Anwar *Race and Politics: Ethnic Minorities and the British Political System* Tavistock 1986 and Marion Fitzgerald *Black People and Political Parties in Britain* Runnymede Trust 1987.

**5676**  Anthony M Messina 'Race and Party Competition in Britain: Policy Formation in the Post-Consensus Period' *Parliamentary Affairs* 38 1985 pp 423–36. A study of party attitudes in the 1970s and 1980s. On attempts to woo the black vote and party attitudes to the immigration issue in the 1970s see Zig Layton-Henry 'Race Electoral Strategy and the Major Parties' *Parliamentary Affairs* 31 1978 pp 268–81.

**5677**  Marion Fitzgerald *Political Parties and Black People: Participation, Representation and Exploitation* Runnymede Trust 1984. A study in London of the attitudes of the major parties to blacks as voters, activists and candidates and vice versa.

**5678** Shirley Joshi and Bob Larter 'The Role of Labour in the Creation of a Racist Britain' *Race and Class* 25 1984 pp 53–70. A critical assessment of Labour's record on race relations, focusing particularly on the Attlee government. The volte face from the Race Relations Act 1965 to the Commonwealth Immigration Act 1968 is examined in Robert Moore 'Labour and Colour 1965–1968' *Institute of Race Relations Newsletter* 1968 pp 383–90.

**5679** S Taylor 'The Liberal Party and Immigration Control: A Study in Political Deviants' *New Community* 8 1980 pp 107–14. A study of the attitude of the party since 1962 and why its opposition to immigration restrictions had not cost it seats. There was a contrast in the 1960s between the liberal attitudes of the national party on immigration and race relations and the demand for strict controls of the West Midlands Liberals. This is explored in Stephen Deakin 'Immigration Control: The Liberal Party and the West Midlands Liberals 1950–1970' *Immigrants and Minorities* 3 1984 pp 297–309.

**5680** Robert Miles *The TUC, Black Workers and New Commonwealth Immigration 1954–1973* Working Papers on Ethnic Relations 6, Research Unit on Ethnic Relations, Social Science Research Council 1977. A survey of the response of the union movement to the influx of coloured workers from the West Indies and the Indian sub-continent. This analysis is continued in Robert Miles and Annie Phizacklea 'The TUC and Black Workers 1974–76' *British Journal of Industrial Relations* 16 1978 pp 195–207. See also Beryl Radin 'Coloured Workers and British Trade Unions' *Race* 8 1966 pp 157–73. For further reflections on the response of the unions to coloured workers see [4670–1].

## (6) Racial Tension

For the riots of the 1980s see the section on Public Order [6218–29].

**5681** Tony Kushner and Kenneth Lunn (eds) *Traditions of Intolerance: Historical Perspectives on Fascism and Race Discourse in Britain* Manchester University Press 1989. This includes useful essays on the impact of imperial decline, racial vigilantism and political racism.

**5682** Colin Holmes 'Violence and Race Relations in Britain 1953–1968' *Phylon* 36 1975 pp 113–24. A general study of racial tension in this period. This peaked with the race riots in Nottingham and Notting Hill in 1958. Edward Pilkington *Beyond The Mother Country: West Indians and the Notting Hill Riots 1958* I B Tauris

1988 is a good narrative account of one of these episodes and the background and consequences of it.

**5683** Ken Leech *Brick Lane 1978: The Events and the Significance* All Faiths for One Race 1980. An account of the causes and the course of the racial violence against Bengalis in the East End in 1978.

**5684** A F Dickey 'Organised Racial Incitement and the Law in England 1945–1965' Kent PhD Thesis 1972–3. An examination of developments up to the 1965 Race Relations Act.

**5685** Gus John and Derek Humphrey *Because They're Black* Penguin 1971. A study of racial hatred. See also M H Lyon 'An Enquiry into the Origins of British Racism' Aberdeen PhD Thesis 1980. Zig Layton-Henry 'Racial Attacks in Britain' *Patterns of Prejudice* 16 1982 pp 3–13 traces the growth of racial violence since the 1960s. Racial attacks in the 1980s are examined in *3rd Report from the Home Affairs Committee: Racial Attacks and Harassment* House of Commons Paper 409, *Parliamentary Papers* 1985–86 (chaired by Sir Edward Gardner). Racial violence in the 1980s is also examined in Keith Thompson *Under Siege: Racial Violence in Britain Today* Penguin 1988.

**5686** *The Fight Against Racism: A Pictorial History of Asians and Afro-Caribbeans in Britain* Institute of Race Relations 1986. An exhibition catalogue which briefly outlines and illustrates organization and resistance to racism by immigrant communities since 1945.

**5687** *Racial Harassment in London: Report of a Panel of Inquiry set up by the Greater London Council Police Committee* GLC 1984. A study of the causes and nature of racial attacks and of attempts to deal with this problem. An earlier survey of colour prejudice in London is Clifford S Hill *How Colour Prejudiced is Britain?* Gollancz 1965. *Racialist Activity in Ealing 1979–81* Ealing Community Relations Council 1981 is a brief analysis of racialist activity in the London Borough of Ealing, a chronology of incidents and a collection of documents and cuttings relating to these. On racism in London's East End see Christopher Temple Husbands 'East End Racism 1900–1980' *London Journal* 8 1982 pp 3–26.

**5688** *Racial Harassment in Manchester and the Response of the Police 1980–1985* Manchester Council for Community Relations 1986.

**5689** *Silence Gives Consent: Racist Attacks in Redbridge: What Is To Be Done?* Redbridge Community Relations Council 1986. A study of racial harassment in the North London borough.

**5690** Mary Winters and J Hatch 'Colour Persecution on Tyneside: A Historical Note' *Race and Class* 24 1982

**5690** Mary Winters and J Hatch 'Colour Persecution on Tyneside: A Historical Note' *Race and Class* 24 1982 pp 134–8. An edited version of a piece written in 1947, showing harassment of blacks, discrimination in allocation of housing and other forms of abuse.

## (7) Policing

**5691** Paul Gordon 'Police and Black People in Britain: A Bibliographical Essay' *Sage Race Relations Abstracts* 10/2 1985 pp 3–33. A good bibliographical essay concentrating on works published between 1969–84. The quality and range of the literature is also well assessed in his 'Black People and the British Criminal Justice System: A Bibliographical Essay' *Sage Race Relations Abstracts* 11/2 1986 pp 3–17.

**5692** Paul Gordon *White Law: Racism in the Police, Courts and Prisons* Pluto 1983. A committed account of what he sees as institutionalized racism in the criminal justice system.

**5693** John Benyon *A Tale of Failure: Race and Policing* Centre for Research in Ethnic Relations, University of Warwick 1986. A study of the policing of black crime and of the handling of complaints about racism in the police force. It has a historical dimension but focuses on the 1980s. *Policing Against Black People: Evidence Compiled by the Institute of Race Relations* Institute of Race Relations 1987 reports over 200 cases of police harrassment of blacks 1979–87. These include the effects of over-policing, the concentration of special squads in black areas, failures of the police complaints procedures and the lack of response to racial violence.

**5694** D Bishton and B Homer (eds) *Talking Blues: The Black Community Speaks about its Relationship with the Police* All Faiths for One Race 1978. A short account based on oral testimonies of the frustration and sense of injustice amongst young blacks at police behaviour.

**5695** M Tuck and P Southgate *Ethnic Minorities, Crime and Policing: A Survey of the Experience of West Indians and Whites* HMSO 1982. A Home Office study of the Moss Side area of Manchester which shows considerable use of and satisfaction with the police amongst the West Indian population (similar to that amongst the white population in fact) in a high crime, inner city area.

**5696** *Police/Immigrant Relations in England and Wales* Cmnd 5438, *Parliamentary Papers* xxxi 1972–73. The government's reponse to the recommendations on policing in the *Select Committee on Race Relations and Immigration* 3v, HC Paper 405, *Parliamentary Papers* xxx and xxxi 1972–73.

**5697** David Wilson, Simon Holdaway and Christopher Spenser 'Black Police in the United Kingdom' *Policing* 1 1984 pp 20–30. A survey based on interviews of the attitudes of serving black officers to recruitment policies, their experiences of policing and their experience of racism in the police force.

## (8) Ethnic Minorities

### (a) General

In most cases the literature in this section in fact refers exclusively to the two main groups of New Commonwealth settlers, the West Indians and the Asians from the Indian sub-continent. A number of works are however more comprehensive and this will be noted where appropriate.

**5698** Dilip Hiro *Black British, White British* revised ed, Pelican 1973. A dispassionate and well regarded general history of the West Indian and Asian communities in Britain. Peter Fryer *Staying Power: The History of Black People in Britain* Pluto 1984 is a useful reminder of the long history of coloured communities in Britain. It is a detailed history from the sixteenth century. However, it has relatively little on the post-war period. Recent history gets rather more coverage in Edward Scobie *Black Britannia: A History of Blacks in Britain* Johnson Publishing, Chicago 1972. N File and C Power *Black Settlers in Britain 1555–1968* Heinemann Educational 1981 is only a short history.

**5699** Ron Ramdin *The Making of the Black Working Class in Britain* Gower 1987. A history up to 1986. It is not so much a narrative as a directory of facets of all facets of black life. It is useful on such aspects as black-led churches or the initial shabby treatment of blacks by trade unions.

**5700** James Lee Watson (ed) *Between Two Cultures: Migrants and Minorities in Britain* Blackwell 1977. A collection of essays on Sikhs, Pakistanis, Montserratians, Jamaicans, West Africans, Chinese, Poles, Italians and both Greek and Turkish Cypriots. Ernest Krausz *Ethnic Minorities in Britain* Macgibbon and Kee 1971 is a survey covering all the ethnic minorities in Britain.

**5701** Sheila Allen *New Minorities, Old Conflicts: Asian and West Indian Migrants in Britain* Random House, New York 1971. A general study.

**5702** *Colonial Students in Britain* Political and Economic Planning 1956. Both this and the follow up study, *New Commonwealth Students in Britain* Political and

Economic Planning 1965 refer particularly to students from East Africa and their experiences in Britain. Their experiences are told in their own words in Henri Taffel and John Dawson (eds) *Disappointed Guests: Essays by African, Asian and West Indian Students* Oxford University Press 1965. These accounts the ubiquitous nature of the racism they faced. See also A T Carey *Colonial Students: A Study of the Adaptation of Colonial Students in London* Secker and Warburg 1956.

**5703** J A G Griffith *et al Coloured Immigrants in Britain* Oxford University Press 1960. Essays on various aspects of their situation in the 1950s.

**5704** R B Davison *Black British: Immigrants to England* Oxford University Press 1966. A report on the New Commonwealth immigrants in the 1960s.

**5705** Valerie Amos 'Black Women in Britain: A Bibliographical Essay' *Sage Race Relations Abstracts* 7 1982 pp 1–11. A short survey of the literature.

**5706** Eric Butterworth *Immigrants in West Yorkshire: Social Conditions and the Lives of Pakistanis, Indians and West Indians* Institute of Race Relations 1967.

**5707** D A Vaughan *Negro Victory: The Life Story of Dr Harold Moody* Independent Press 1950. Moody was a West Indian who campaigned against what was then known as the colour bar in both Britain and the empire. He founded the League of Coloured Peoples in 1931. Its history is traced in Roderic J Macdonald 'Dr Harold Arundel Moody and the League of Coloured Peoples 1931–47: A Retrospective' *Race* 14 1973 pp 291–310.

## (b) West Indians

**5708** Donald Hines *Journey To An Illusion: The West Indian in Britain* Heinemann 1966. This is a good, even-handed account of how the myth of the mother country was shattered by the reality of prejudice in Britain. To a large extent it draws on oral testimony. This same tale of disillusionment and rejection is told in Trevor Carter *Shattering Illusions: West Indians in British Politics* Lawrence and Wishart 1986. This is a semi-autobiographical account by a West Indian who arrived in 1954. In addition there are a number of other oral testimonies of the West Indian experience in Britain. Thomas J Cottle *Black Testimony: The Voices of Britain's West Indians* Wildwood House 1978 reflects the experience of West Indians in London. *Forty Winters On: Memories of Britain's Post-War Caribbean Immigrants* South London Press 1988 is another collection of reminiscences. See also Elizabeth Thomas-Hope 'Hopes and Reality in the West Indian Migration to Britain' *Oral History* 8 1980 pp 35–42.

**5709** Colin Brock (ed) *The Caribbean in Europe: Aspects of the West Indian Experience in Britain, France and the Netherlands* Cass 1986. In fact most of these essays are concerned with Britain. They cover such subjects as labour, government response to their arrival, settlement patterns, education, music, literature, youth and sport.

**5710** Roy Kerridge *Real Wicked Guy: A View of Black Britain* Blackwell 1983. A racy and anecdotal portrait of blacks in Britain ranging from the 1950s to the present, principally in London and Birmingham. It is largely concerned with West Indians.

**5711** Winston James 'A Long Way from Home: On Black Identity in Britain' *Immigrants and Minorities* 5 1986 pp 258–84. A good examination of the creation of a West Indian self-identity as white hostility broke down inter-island and class barriers and the growing realization of the existence of a deprived white working class destroyed assumptions of white superiority. These problems are compounded for the second generation who do not even have the choice of comparison with the poverty of the Caribbean. This article is also useful in that it provides a rare look at the often hostile relations with the Asian community.

**5712** G Llewellyn Watson 'The Sociology of Black Nationalism: Identity, Protest and the Concept of "Black Power" among West Indian Immigrants to Britain' York DPhil Thesis 1972.

**5713** K L Little *Negroes in Britain: A Study of Racial Relations in English Society* Kegan Paul, Trench, Trubner and Co 1947. This predates the arrival of the SS *Empire Windrush* in 1948 and the beginning of mass immigration from the Caribbean. It looks at the history of negroes in Britain and their contemporary situation, making use of a case study of Cardiff.

**5714** S K Ruck (ed) *The West Indian comes to England* Routledge and Kegan Paul 1960. A collection of essays on the situation in the 1950s, mainly dealing with London. Settlement and problems in the 1950s are also reported in R B Davison *West Indian Migration to Britain 1955–56* Oxford University Press 1962 and C Senior and D Manley *West Indians in Britain* Tract 179, Fabian Colonial Bureau 1956. See also 'Post-War Migration of West Indians to Great Britain' *International Labour Review* 74 1956 pp 193–209.

**5715** D Sutcliffe *British Black English* Blackwell 1982. A history of West Indian dialects, focusing particularly on Jamaican creole. It includes a bibliography and glossary.

**5716** Beverley Bryan, Stella Dadzie and Suzanne Scafe *The Heart of the Race: Black Women's Lives in*

*Britain* Virago 1985. This documents the lives of West Indian women in Britain over the post-war years looking at their experiences in fields such as education, social life, welfare, housing or confrontation with racial prejudice.

**5717** Jeffrey P Green 'John Alcindor and James Jackson Brown – Afro-Caribbean Doctors in London 1899–1953' *Journal of Caribbean History* 20 1985–6 pp 49–77. Both of these doctors are shown as middle class and fairly well assimilated. Green argues that white attitudes in this period before mass immigration were based more on class than race.

**5718** Anthony H Richmond *Colour Prejudice in Britain: A Study of West Indian Workers in Liverpool 1941–51* Routledge and Kegan Paul 1954. A good study.

**5719** Ruth Glass and Harold Pollins *Newcomers: The West Indians in London* Allen and Unwin 1960. A study of events and attitudes in the late 1950s, both amongst the West Indians and amongst the racist opposition they faced. A more impressionistic set of observations on the West Indians in London in the 1950s is Clifford S Hill *Black and White in Harmony: The Drama of West Indians in the Big City from a London Minister's Notebook* Hodder and Stoughton 1958. Hill was a Congregational minister at the time. On West Indian settlers in London see also N Foner *Jamaica Farewell: Jamaican Migrants in London* Routledge and Kegan Paul 1979 and Sheila Patterson *Dark Strangers: A Sociological Study of the Absorption of a Recent West Indian Group in Brixton, South London* Tavistock 1963. A good study of West Indian and African sailors and settlers in Stepney, East London in 1940–50 is Michael Banton *The Coloured Quarter: Negro Immigrants in an English City* Cape 1951.

**5720** D G Pearson *Race, Class and Political Activism: A Study of West Indians in Britain* Gower 1980. A study of West Indian community organisations, families, religion and political activism in the West Midlands.

## (c) Indians, Pakistanis and Bangladeshis

For material which is specifically concerned with the Sikh community see the relevant category in the section on Religious History.

**5721** Amrit Wilson *Finding a Voice – Asian Women in Britain* Virago 1978. A study based on oral accounts, with the chapters focusing on different aspects of their lives, such as family, work, education and marriage.

**5722** K Vadyama *India in Britain: The Indian Contribution to the British Way of Life* Royce 1984. See also

R Desai *Indian Immigrants to Britain* Oxford University Press 1963.

**5723** G S Betts 'Working Class Asians in Britain: Economic, Social and Political Changes 1959–1979' London MPhil Thesis 1981. An analysis within a Marxist framework. See also G S Aurora 'Indian Workers in England: A Sociological and Historical Survey' London MSc (Econ) Thesis 1959–60.

**5724** John De Witt *Indian Workers' Associations in Britain* Oxford University Press 1969.

**5725** Muhammad Anwar *The Myth of Return: Pakistanis in Britain* Heinemann Educational 1979. A good study of adaptation. It includes extensive statistical information on the size and character of the Pakistani community. Badr Dahya 'Pakistanis in Britain: Transients or Settlers?' *Race* 14 1973 pp 241–78 is a sociological analysis of Pakistani communities in various parts of the Midlands and the North of England based on observations since 1956.

**5726** *1st Report from the Home Affairs Committee: Bangladeshis in Britain* 3v, HC Paper 96, *Parliamentary Papers* 1986–87. The report, evidence and appendices of the committee chaired by Sir Edward Gardner.

## (d) East African Asians

**5727** Vaughan Robinson *Transients, Settlers and Refugees: Asians in Britain* Clarendon 1986. This examines why these people arrived in such numbers in the late 1960s and early 1970s in the face of Africanization in Kenya and their expulsion from Idi Amin's Uganda, their culture and lifestyles, and their assimilation both into the host population and into the resident Asian population.

**5728** Derek Humphrey and Michael Ward *Passports and Politics* Penguin 1974. An investigation into the low budget relief operations set up to help and rehouse expelled Ugandan Asians to resettle in Britain. The government's response to the situation is also critically assessed in Mike Bristow 'Britain's Response to the Ugandan Asian Crisis: Government Myth versus Political and Resettlement Realities' *New Community* 5 1976 pp 302–10. E Nelson Swinerton, William G Knepper and G Lynne Lacky *Ugandan Asians in Great Britain: Forced Migration and Social Absorption* Croom Helm 1975 is kinder to the authorities but it does bring out the inadequacies of the Resettlement Board. A short analysis, it includes case studies of resettlement in Wandsworth and Slough.

**5729** Valerie Marett *Immigrants Settling in the City: Ugandan Asians in Leicester* Leicester University Press 1988. A study of the unwelcoming attitude of the city council, which went to the length of putting notices in the Ugandan press, which is contrasted with the positive efforts in resettlement made by the voluntary sector. It also examines the local Ugandan Asian community as it developed.

(e) Jews

**5730** *The Jewish Year Book* Jewish Chronicle Publications 1896–. A guide to all sorts of Jewish institutions and activities. It also features a biographical guide to Jewry and a necrology.

**5731** Ruth D Lehmann *Anglo-Jewish Bibliography 1937–1970* Jewish Historical Society of England 1973. A comprehensive, if unannotated, bibliography. Lloyd P Garner 'A Quarter Century of Anglo-Jewish Historiography' *Jewish Social Studies* 48 1986 pp 105–26 is a survey of recent books and articles on Anglo-Jewish history.

**5732** Stephen Brook *The Club: The Jews of Modern Britain* Constable 1989. A good, journalistic account of the 350,000 strong Jewish community (as defined by religion rather than by race). See also S L Lipman and V D Lipman (eds) *Jewish Life in Britain 1962–1977* K G Saur 1981 and I Bild *The Jews in Britain* Batsford 1984.

**5733** Geoffrey Alderman *The Jewish Community in British Politics* Oxford University Press 1983. A study of Jewish political attitudes, Jewish pressure groups and Jews in politics. The significant role of Jews in London politics is examined in detail in his impressive *London Jewry and London Politics 1889–1986* Routledge 1989. See also his 'Anglo-Jewry: The Politics of an Image' *Parliamentary Affairs* 37 1984 pp 160–82 which examines the high degree of success of this slowly shrinking minority.

**5734** Chaim Bermant *The Cousinhood: The Anglo-Jewish Gentry* Eyre and Spottiswoode 1971. A history of the gradual anglicization of the great Jewish families up to the present. It includes plenty of biographical information.

**5735** V D Lipman *Social History of the Jews in England 1850–1950* Watts and Co 1954. See also Norman Bentwich 'The Social Transformation of Anglo-Jewry 1883–1960' *Jewish Journal of Sociology* 2 1960 pp 16–24.

**5736** Julius Gould and Saul Esh (eds) *Jewish Life in Modern Britain* Routledge and Kegan Paul 1964. A collection of essays on aspects of the Anglo-Jewish community in the 1960s.

**5737** Stanley Waterman and Barry Kosmin *British Jewry in the Eighties: A Statistical and Geographical Study* Board of Deputies of British Jews 1986. A short analysis.

**5738** Barry Kosmin 'Localism and Pluralism in British Jewry 1900–1980' *Transactions of the Jewish Historical Society of England* 28 1981–82 pp 111–25. A study of gradual assimilation and the loss of a distinctive Jewish identity.

**5739** D Newman 'Integration and Ethnic Spatial Concentration: The Changing Distribution of the Anglo-Jewish Community' *Transactions of the Institute of British Geographers* n.s. 10 1985 pp 360–76. See also Barry Kosmin 'Jewish Circumcision and the Demography of British Jewry 1968–1982' *Jewish Journal of Sociology* 27 1985 pp 5–11, S J Prais 'Synagogue Statistics and the Jewish Population of Great Britain 1900–1970' *Jewish Journal of Sociology* 14 1972 pp 215–28 and S J Prais and Marlena Schmool 'The Size and Structure of the Anglo-Jewish Population 1960–1965' *Jewish Journal of Sociology* 10 1968 pp 5–34.

**5740** V D Lipman 'Trends in Anglo-Jewish Occupations' *Jewish Journal of Sociology* 2 1960 pp 202–18. A history up to the present day.

**5741** Sidney Saloman *Anti-Semitism and Fascism in Post-War Britain: The Work of the Jewish Defence Committee* Woburn Press 1950. This briefly surveys Anti-Semitism and the work of the Jewish Defence Committee to combat this in the immediate aftermath of the war.

**5742** L M Waldenberg 'The History of Anglo-Jewish Responses to Immigration and Racial Tension 1950–1970' Sheffield MA Thesis 1972–3.

**5743** V D Lipman *A Century of Social Service 1859–1959: The Jewish Board of Guardians* Routledge and Kegan Paul 1959. A history of a Jewish philanthropic body in London.

**5744** Ruth Sebag-Montifiore *A Family Patchwork: Five Generations of an Anglo-Jewish Family* Weidenfeld and Nicolson 1987. A study of the distinguished Montifiore family in the twentieth century.

## (f) Chinese

**5745** *2nd Report from the Home Affairs Committee: Chinese Community in Britain* 3v, HC Paper 102, *Parliamentary Papers* 1984–85. The report, proceedings and minutes of evidence of the committee chaired by Sir Edward Gardner. It examines the background of Chinese immigration, the size of the Chinese community and its social and linguistic problems. 'The Chinese Community in Britain' *Race and Immigration* 1985 pp 8–15 is a brief discription of its size, distribution and characteristics. See also Douglas Jones 'The Chinese in Britain' *New Community* 7 1979 pp 397–402 and M Broady 'The Chinese in Great Britain' in M H Fried (ed) *Colloquium on Overseas Chinese* Institute of Race Relations 1958.

**5746** Ng Kwee Choo *The Chinese in London* Oxford University Press 1968. A history of Chinese immigration and a survey of the economic and social activities of the Chinese in London.

**5747** Douglas Jones 'Chinese Schools in Britain: A Minority Response to its own Needs' *Trends in Education* 1980 pp 15–18. These have been established since 1928 to teach and preserve Chinese language and culture.

## (g) Irish

**5748** Maureen Hartigan, Mary J Hickman and Angela Lynch *The History of the Irish in Britain: A Bibliography* Irish in Britain History Centre, London 1986. A select, unannotated bibliography which includes some material on the post-war period.

**5749** Kevin O'Connor *The Irish in Britain* Sidgwick and Jackson 1972. A study of the Irish in contemporary Britain. A more historical study, which nevertheless contains much information on the Irish in post-war Britain, is J A Jackson *The Irish in Britain* Routledge and Kegan Paul 1963.

## (h) Gypsies

**5750** Don Kennington *Gypsies and Travelling People* 3rd ed, Capital Planning Information 1986. A well annotated and introduced booklet guide to documentary and organizational sources of information. It includes lists of relevant organizations.

**5751** Thomas Acton *Gypsy Politics and Social Change: The Development of Ethnic Ideology and Pressure Politics Among British Gypsies from Victorian Reformism to Romany Nationalism* Routledge and Kegan Paul 1974. A good history of the gypsies since 1800. On the post-war years it concentrates legal and economic changes and the establishment of pressure groups, notably the Gypsy Council which was established in 1966.

**5752** Denis Harvey *The Gypsies: Waggon-Time and After* Batsford 1979. A well illustrated and rather nostalgic evocation of the traditional gypsy waggons and the way of life that went with them which has now, as gypsies have become motorized, almost disappeared. Much of the book focuses on recent developments in the lifestyle of the gypsy. The greater part of Jeremy Sandford *Gypsies* Secker and Warburg 1973 is an account of this lifestyle and of gypsy customs based on oral testimonies. The main purpose of this book however is a plea for better treatment of gypsies in the wake of the 1968 Caravan Sites Act. G E C Webb *Gypsies: The Secret People* Herbert Jenkins 1960 is an impressionistic view of gypsy life. Gypsies and other travelling folk are also discussed in Norman N Dodds *Gypsies, Didecois and Other Travellers* Johnson Publications 1966, Jan Yoors *The Gypsies* Allen and Unwin 1967. The lifestyle of the gypsy is also evoked in Betsy Whyte *The Yellow on the Broom* Chambers 1979, the autobiography of a Scottish traveller. Another gypsy autobiography which is useful on gypsy customs is Manfri Frederick Wood *In the Life of a Romany Gypsy* Routledge and Kegan Paul 1973.

**5753** Thomas Acton (ed) *Current Changes Amongst British Gypsies and Their Place in International Patterns of Development* National Gypsy Educational Council 1971. Relevant essays in this collection examine linguistic change, gypsy education and gypsies and travellers relations with the settled population in Scotland.

**5754** John Cripps *Accommodation For Gypsies: A Report on the Working of the Caravan Sites Act 1968 Presented to the Secretary of State for the Environment, December 1976* HMSO 1977. This made various recommendations for speeding up the hitherto slow application of the Act. A short gypsy comment on the Act and on discrimination against and harassment of gypsies is *The Romany Guild Looks at the Caravan Sites Act Eight Years on – Who Cares* Romany Guild 1976.

**5755** Barbara Adams *et al Gypsies and Government Policy in England: A Study of the Travellers' Way of Life in Relation to Policies and Practices of Central and Local Government* Heinemann 1975. A major piece of research analysing how local authorities were coping with the duty to provide managed caravan sites under the 1968 Caravan Sites Act, how the gypsies were reacting and how those still on the road were faring.

**5756** D Sibley *Outsiders in Urban Societies* Blackwell 1981. A study of prejudice in planning and the designation of caravan sites drawing on case studies in Hull and Sheffield. The unwillingness of local politicians to provide sites in North Humberside is examined in Howard Elcock 'Politicians, Organisations and the Public – The Provision of Gypsy Sites' *Local Government Studies 5* 1979 pp 43–54. See also R K Home 'The Caravan Sites Act 1968: Progress and Problems with Designation' *Journal of Planning and Environment Law* 1984 pp 226–34, R K Connell 'Planning for Gypsies: Aspects of Current Policies and Practices' Leeds Polytechnic MSc Thesis 1976 and R P Dowdeswell 'Planning for Gypsies and Travellers' Oxford Polytechnic MSc Thesis 1977.

### (i) Displaced Europeans

**5757** Francesca M Wilson *They Came As Strangers: The Story of Refugees to Great Britain* Hamilton 1959. A general history of fugitives seeking refuge in Britain. The epilogue has some information on wartime refugees and their successor communities. See also Maud Bulbring 'Post-War Refugees in Great Britain' *Population Studies* 8 1954 pp 99–112.

**5758** Jerzy Zubrzycki *Polish Immigrants in Britain: A Study of Adjustment* Nijhoff, Den Haag 1956. A history and study of the contemporary situation of the Polish community. There were 250,000 Poles in exile in Britain when the Attlee government recognized the Communist government that had been installed by the Russians in Warsaw after the war. British policy on dealing with these Polish forces is examined in Keith R Sword ' "Their Prospects will not be Bright": British Responses to the Problem of the Polish "Recalcitrants" 1946–49' *Journal of Contemporary History* 21 1986 pp 367–90. The 'Recalcitrants' were Polish forces who refused to decide whether to be repatriated or to be resettled outside Poland.

**5759** Murdoch Rodgers 'Immigration into Britain: The Lithuanians' *History Today* 35 1985 pp 14–20. Many Lithuanians came to Britain as refugees during and after the war.

### (j) Other

**5760** R E Oakley 'Cypriot Migration and Settlement in Britain' Oxford DPhil Thesis 1971–2. See also V Nearchou 'The Cypriot Community in London' Nottingham MA Thesis 1959–60.

**5761** U Marin *Italiani in Gran Bretagna* Centro Studi Emigrazione, Roma 1975. The Italians form the largest group of white immigrants in Britain, over 100,000 strong. The mechanics of immigration from Italy, the regions of origin and the nature of the Italian community

is examined in R King 'Italian Migration to Great Britain' *Geography* 62 1977 pp 176–86. See also P Garigue and R W Firth 'Kinship and Organisation of Italians in London' in R W Firth (ed) *Two Studies of Kinship in London* Athlone Press 1956 pp 65–93.

**5762** Geoff Dench *Maltese in London: A Case Study in the Erosion of Ethnic Consciousness* Routledge and Kegan Paul 1975. A study of Maltese immigration and the Maltese community in the post-war period.

**5763** Atmaram R Mannick *Mauritians in London* Dodo Books 1987.

**5764** P R Jones *Vietnamese Refugees: A Study of their Reception and Resettlement in the United Kingdom* HMSO 1982. An examination of the socio-demographic characteristics of the Vietnamese refugees who have been allowed to settle in Britain since 1979, the problems faced and the agencies that have been set up to help their resettlement. Progress is reported in *Refugees and Asylum with Special Reference to the Vietnamese* HMSO 1985. See also P Edholm *et al Vietnamese Refugees in Britain* Commission for Racial Equality 1983 and Felicity Somerset 'Vietnamese Refugees in Britain: Resettlement Experiences' *New Community* 10 1983 pp 454–63.

## G. LIFESTYLE

### (1) Diet

**5765** James P Johnson *A Hundred Years Eating: Food, Drink and the Daily Diet in Britain Since the Late Nineteenth Century* Gill and Macmillan, Dublin 1977. See also John Burnett *Plenty and Want: A Social History of Diet in England from 1815 to the Present Day* 3rd ed, Scolar Press 1989.

**5766** Christopher Driver *The British At Table 1940–1980* Chatto and Windus 1983. A journalistic guide to changes in diet and the concern about the need to eat healthier foods. Recent dietary trends and changes in palate are also examined in L J Angel and G E Hurdle 'The Nation's Food – 40 Years of Change' *Economic Trends* 294 1978 pp 97–105. Changes in diet by class and household size are examined in J P Greaves and Dorothy F Hollingsworth 'Trends in Food Consumption in the United Kingdom' *World Review of Nutrition and Dietetics* 6 1966 pp 34–89. R C Garry (chair) 'Food Habits in Britain' *Proceedings of the Nutrition Society* 20 1961 pp 25–51 includes papers on changing food habits since the war, case studies and an analysis of the effect of recent legislation and advertising. On nutrition policy in the light of wartime and post-war rationing see

Dorothy F Hollingsworth 'Nutritional Policies in Great Britain 1939–46' *Journal of the American Dietetic Association* 23 1947 pp 96–100.

**5767** Royston Lambert *Nutrition in Britain 1950–1960: A Critical Discussion of the Standards and Findings of the National Food Survey* Occasional Papers in Social Administration 6, Codicote Press 1964. Increasing concern about malnutrition in large families was a major factor in dietary change in the 1950s.

**5768** *Food Quality and Safety: A Century of Progress* HMSO 1976. A symposium to mark the centenary of the Sale of Food and Drugs Act 1875.

**5769** Forrest Capie 'Consumer Preference: Meat in England and Wales' *Bulletin of Economic Research* 28 1976 pp 85–94.

### (2) Consumer Society

**5770** *Family Expenditure Survey* HMSO 1957–. This annual publication monitors the expenditure of private households and provides useful economic and social data on trends in consumer spending.

**5771** John Burnett *A History of the Cost of Living* Penguin 1969. The final section of this history of living costs and standards since the middle ages deals with the events of the period since the First World War. Peter Wilsher *The Pound in Your Pocket 1870–1970* Cassell 1970 looks at the causes and effects of a number of crises which have affected consumer spending. The relevant crises for the post-war period are in 1949, 1957, 1967 and 1970. See also J F Wright 'Real Wage Resistance: Eighty Years of the British Cost of Living' *Oxford Economic Papers* 36 1984 pp 152–67.

**5772** D Piachaud *Family Incomes Since the War* Study Commission on the Family 1982. Family expenditure is examined in T Schultz 'Income, Family Structure and Food Expenditure before and after the War' *Bulletin of Oxford University Institute of Economic Statistics* 24 1962 pp 447–68 and V Borooah and D R Sharpe 'Household Income, Consumption and Savings in the United Kingdom 1966–82' *Scottish Journal of Political Economy* 32 1985 pp 234–56.

**5773** D Elliston Allen *British Tastes: An Enquiry into the Likes and Dislikes of the Regional Consumer* Hutchinson 1968. A study of regional patterns in consumer taste based on a number of surveys conducted over the previous ten years. It provides a very interesting analysis of these regional differences.

**5774** Rodney Bennett-England *As Young As You Look: Male Grooming and Rejuvenation* Peter Owen 1970. Reflections on men's self images, male cosmetics, toiletries and male attempts to improve their bodies by everything from keep-fit to cosmetic surgery.

**5775** Mark Abrams *The Teenage Consumer* London Press Exchange 1959. A study of the post-war rise of the teenager as a conspicuous consumer and as a principal target of advertising and market research and of the trends which explain the rise of the teenage consumer. A similarly valuable (if much later) study of another important group of consumers is his *The Elderly Consumer* National Consumer Council 1982.

**5776** *Influence of Car Ownership on Shopping Habits* Kent County Council Planning Department 1964. Cars have increased mobility and led to the increasing use of larger shopping centres.

**5777** Andrew David Bain *The Growth of Television Ownership in the United Kingdom* Cambridge University Press 1964. A short paper.

**5778** R Wraith *The Consumer Cause* Royal Institute of Public Administration 1976. A study of consumer pressure groups. John Martin and George W Smith *The Consumer Interest* Pall Mall 1968 examines the economic and social changes leading to the development of consumer organizations. See also R J Kendle 'An Evaluation of Institutional Activity on Behalf of Consumers in the Last Decade' Manchester MA (Econ) Thesis 1968–9.

### (3) Leisure and Recreation

#### (a) General

**5779** Anthony J Veal *Recreation Planning in New Communities: A Review of British Experience* Memorandum 46, Centre for Urban and Regional Studies, University of Birmingham 1975. Not a comprehensive bibliography since it is largely concerned with recreation facilities in new towns and new housing estates. Nor is it annotated. It is however extensive and has a most informative introduction. S R Parker *Annotated Bibliography of Leisure* European Centre for Leisure and Recreation 1972 is a bibliography on leisure provision in Britain 1962–72.

**5780** Ian Appleton (ed) *Leisure Research and Policy* Scottish Academic Press 1974. A detailed history and study of the contemporary state of leisure policy and provision, largely by reference to Scotland. There are useful reflections on problems in recreational management and the accompanying social pressures, with particular reference to London and Torquay, in Fred P Bossalman *In the Wake of the Tourist: Managing Special Places in Eight Countries* Conservation Foundation, Washington DC 1978. See also J Allen Patmore *Land and Leisure in England and Wales* David and Charles 1970, J B Cullingworth 'Planning for Leisure' *Urban Studies* 1 1964 pp 1–26 and J G H Howells 'Recreational Planning in Cities, with Particular Reference to Plymouth 1943–1976' Manchester MEd Thesis 1978.

**5781** D Hanson 'The Development of Community Centres in County Durham 1919–1968' Newcastle MEd Thesis 1971–2. See also D Payne 'The Development of Community Centres, with Special Reference to Yorkshire' Manchester MEd Thesis 1967–8.

**5782** *United Kingdom Social Clubs* Data Research Group 1975–. An annual informative guide to over 6,000 clubs listed under their respective locations. See also *United Kingdom Workingmen's Clubs* Data Research Group 1977–. The history of the largest group of workingmen's clubs, the Club and Institute Union, which covers over 4,000 clubs, is told in George Tremlett *Clubmen: The History of the Working Men's Club and Institute Union* Secker and Warburg 1987. The history of a rather different sort of club is told in Anthony Lejeune and Malcolm Lewis *The Gentlemen's Clubs of London* Macdonald and Janes 1979. This contains well illustrated historical sketches of each of these clubs. It usefully brings out the decline in recent years of the various clubs which are attached to the political parties. It also provides some bibliographical information. For the histories of individual London clubs see also F R Cowell *The Athenaeum: Club and Social Life in London 1824–1974* Heinemann 1975 and P G Cambray *Club Days and Ways: The Story of the Constitutional Club* Constitutional Club 1963. On the Reform Club see George Woodbridge *The Reform Club 1836–1978: A History from the Club's Records* Reform Club 1978 and J M Crook *The Reform Club* Reform Club 1973. Barry Phelps *Power and the Party: A History of the Carlton Club 1832–1982* Macmillan 1983 is a history of the club closely associated with the Conservative Party which includes the text of the 1982 lecture by Harold Macmillan. See also Sir Charles Petrie *The Carlton Club* revised ed, White Lion Publishers 1972.

**5783** Stephen Knight *The Brotherhood: The Secret World of the Freemasons* Granada 1983. This analysis of the network of lodges, their activities and of their supposed influence is taken further by Martin Short *Inside The Brotherhood: Further Secrets of the Freemasons* Collins 1989. This is better than Knight on the social background of Freemasonry. However his case against the Freemasons, especially in the police and the law, remains largely circumstantial. In addition to these

there are a number of short commemorative histories of individual lodges, many of which are listed in [50].

**5784** S B Burrell 'The Leisure Pool' *Chartered Municipal Engineer* 7 1981 pp 176–84. This reviews the development of indoor sports centres over the previous twenty years and describes, in technical detail, the characteristics of leisure pools.

**5785** Joe Benjamin *In Search of Adventure* National Council of Social Service 1961. A survey of the development of adventure playgrounds since 1948. It details various projects and includes a bibliography.

**5786** A C J Reed 'A Geographical Investigation into the Provision of Coastal Moorings and Marinas in England and Wales and some of the Consequences of their Development' Southampton MPhil Thesis 1981. An examination of this aspect of the post-war leisure boom in the context of the lack of attendant planning. See also J D Godfrey 'An Approach to Interest Group Success: the Case of the Brighton Marina' Sussex MA Thesis 1968.

**5787** Frank Baron *The Town Moor Hoppings: Newcastle's Temperance Festival 1882–1982* Newbury Lovell Baines 1984. A history of the largest travelling fair in Europe.

**5788** E John *et al Masquerading: The Art of the Notting Hill Carnival* Arts Council 1986. Essays on the history and music of the Carnival and on its roots in West Indian culture. The Carnival was started in 1965. Its history is traced in Abner Cohen 'Drama and Politics in the Development of a London Carnival' in Ronald Frankenberg (ed) *Custom and Conflict in British Society* Manchester University Press 1982 pp 313–44.

**(b) Access to the Countryside and Outdoor Recreation**

An important aspect of access to the countryside policy was the setting up of the National Parks. The literature on these can be found in the section on the Environment [5019–27].

**5789** Tom Stephenson (edited by Ann Holt) *Forbidden Land* Manchester University Press 1989. This chronicles the campaign for access to the countryside, mountains and moorlands of Britain. Stephenson was a seasoned campaigner in this cause and was centrally involved in the 1949 Access to the Countryside Act. Another book by an activist tracing the development of the movement and of progess on the issue since the 1860s is Howard Hill *Freedom To Roam – The Struggle for Access to Britain's Moors and Mountains* Moorland

Publishing 1980. See also J P Rossiter 'An Analytical Study of the Public Use of Private Land for Outdoor Recreation in England 1949–1968' Cambridge PhD Thesis 1972.

**5790**   *Footpaths and Access to the Countryside: Report of the Special Committee (England and Wales)* Cmnd 7207, *Parliamentary Papers* x 1946–47. A survey of all rights of way under Sir Arthur Hobhouse. It took up the suggestion of the creation of new long-distance and coastal footpaths of the National Parks Commission and also recommended a Country Code of behaviour. The history of calls for such footpaths and of their development since the Access to the Countryside Act 1949 is traced in R S Henshaw 'The Development and Impact of Formal Long-Distance Footpaths in Great Britain' Edinburgh PhD Thesis 1984.

**5791**   O Coburn *The Youth Hostel Story* National Council of Social Service 1950. A history of the first twenty years of the movement. This is updated by *A Short History of the YHA* Youth Hostels Association 1966.

**5792**   D James (ed) *Outward Bound* Routledge and Kegan Paul 1957. An account of the work and aims of the outward bound movement. James Martin Hogan *Impelled into Experiences – The Story of the Outward Bound Schools* Educational Productions Ltd 1968 is a personal account by the founder of the first school of this type. He also looks at the influence of the movement on formal education. John Ridgeway *Flood Tide* Hodder and Stoughton 1988 is the second part of the autobiography of the adventurer and transatlantic oarsman. It concentrates on the development of the Ardmore School of Adventure he established in 1969 in Sutherland, Scotland. The first part of his autobiography, *Journey to Ardmore* Hodder and Stoughton 1971, traces his life in the army and susequent adventures up to the establishment of Ardmore.

**5793**   D Wainwright *Youth in Action: Duke of Edinburgh's Award Scheme 1956–1966* Hutchinson 1966. A detailed study of the aims and success of the award.

(c) Parks and Gardens

There is also a certain amount of literature on the related topic of landscape gardening and architecture which has been included in the section on architecture.

**5794**   Edward S Hyams *The English Garden* Abrams, New York 1966. This includes a chapter on contemporary English gardens. Miles Hadfield *A History of British Gardening* Murray 1979 only has an appendix on the post-war years.

**5795**   A Crowe *The Parks and Woodlands of London* Fourth Estate 1987. A detailed history and guide of each of over 100 of London's open spaces. The evolution, character and management of the Royal Parks of London is described in H Thurston *Royal Parks for the People: London's Ten* David and Charles 1974.

**5796**   W Addison *Portrait of Epping Forest* Hale 1977. A history of its preservation and management, concentrating on the period since the 1878 Act which passed control to the Corporation of London.

**5797**   Joyce Bellamy 'Burgess Park: The History of a New Metropolitan Park' *Greater London Intelligence Quarterly* 34 1976 pp 5–16. A history of the development of this South London park from old bomb sites and displacements of population since 1945.

(d) Sport

Sport has generated a tremendous amount of memorabilia and quasi-historical material. Much of this is of ephemeral or of extremely specialized interest. One facet of this is the large number of sports biographies and autobiographies, often of limited value. The literature listed below is therefore necessarily a selection.

Biographies and autobiographies of sports journalists appear elsewhere with those of other journalists.

*(i) General*

**5798**   Richard W Cox *Sport – A Guide to Historical Sources in the UK* Sports Council 1983. An informative guide to archives and repositories.

**5799**   B S Duffield *et al A Digest of Sports Statistics* Sports Council 1983. A compendium of figures on participation in organized and casual sport in the 1970s. It also provides information on facilities, equipment, sports bodies and their spending and sports magazines.

**5800**   Richard W Cox 'A Survey of Literature on the History of Sport in Britain' *British Journal of Sport History* 1 1984 pp 41–59.

**5801**   *British Journal of Sports History* 1984–6. This journal, which has now changed its name to *The International Journal of the History of Sport* 1987–, carries an annual bibliography of material on the history of sport.

**5802**   Richard W Cox *Theses and Dissertations on the History of Sport, Physical Education and Recreation Accepted for Higher Degrees and Advanced Diplomas* *in British Universities 1900–1981* Bibliographical Centre for the History of Sport, Liverpool 1982. See also his *American Theses on the History of British Sport and Physical Education* Bibliographical Centre for the History of Sport, Liverpool 1982.

**5803** S Mangia *Artificial Sports and Playing Surfaces: A Select Bibliography* Research Documents Guide 14, GLC 1981. An annotated bibliography.

**5804** Tony Mason (ed) *Sport in Britain: A Social History* Cambridge University Press 1989. The various chapters of this book analyse the historical development of various major sports. John Hargreaves *Sport, Power and Culture: A Social and Historical Analysis of Popular Sports in Britain* Polity 1986 is a general historical analysis. See also his 'The State and Sport: Programmed and Non-Programmed Intervention in Britain' in Lincoln Allison (ed) *The Politics of Sport* Manchester University Press 1986 pp 242–61. D L Willey *Sport, Commerce and the State* Centre for Leisure Studies, University of Salford 1981 surveys the changing attitudes towards the finance of sport over the previous hundred years.

**5805** H Justin Evans *Service To Sport: The Story of the CCPR 1935–1972* Sports Council 1974. A history of the Central Council of Physical Recreation, its effect on the concept and provision of education, its organization and its eventual absorption into the Sports Council.

**5806** Peter McIntosh and Valerie Charlton *The Impact of Sport For All Policy 1966–1984 and A Way Forward* Sports Council 1985. An evaluation of the development of policy, organizational innovation, such as the foundation of the Sports Council in 1964, funding and the extent to which the sport for all policy has been successful.

**5807** John Bale *Sport And Place: A Geography of Sport in England, Scotland and Wales* Christopher Hurst 1982. A good historical survey. See also his 'Sport and National Identity: A Geographical View' *British Journal of Sport History* 3 1986 pp 18–41.

**5808** P Stefanuti 'Safety at Sports Grounds' *Building Control* 22 1987 pp 69–75. A study of the development of legislation since the Wheatley Report [5809].

**5809** *Report of the Inquiry into Crowd Safety at Sports Grounds* Cmnd 4952, *Parliamentary Papers* ix 1971–72. The report of the committee set up under Lord Wheatley after the 1971 Ibrox disaster when many people were killed when barriers collapsed at Glasgow Rangers ground. Its recommendations led to the 1975 Safety of Sports Grounds Act.

**5810** *Committee of Inquiry into Crowd Safety and Control at Sports Grounds: Interim Report* Cmnd 9585,

*Parliamentary Papers* 1984–85 and *Final Report* Cmnd 9710, *Parliamentary Papers* 1985–86. The interim report of this inquiry set up under Oliver Popplewell covers the Bradford City fire in May 1985 and the serious crowd disorder of the same day at Birmingham City. The final report looks at the extent of hooliganism and its causes, the history of such inquiries and of the Safety of Sports Ground Act 1975 and at the crowd disorders, in which 38 were killed, in the Heysel disaster in May 1985. Its recommendations touched on the availability of alcohol, the idea of club membership cards and the responsibilities of clubs.

**5811** R W Palmer 'The Development of Student Sports Bodies in Britain Since 1919' Leicester MEd Thesis 1974.

**5812** T Mannington 'A Socio-Historical Study of the Development and Present Popularity and Viability of Industrial Sports Clubs with Particular Reference to the Birmingham Area' Birmingham MA Thesis 1972–3.

**5813** Ernest Cashmore *Black Sportsmen* Routledge and Kegan Paul 1983. An examination of why so many West Indians are so active and successful in sport. He suggests that it is as a result of setbacks in education and integration which means that sport offers a better chance of achievement to West Indians than many other pursuits. It includes a useful bibliography.

## (ii) Cricket

It should be noted that there are vast numbers of cricketing biographies and autobiographies. The ones listed below are a select list of the works on the more eminent of post-war cricketers. It should be noted that most of these, particularly in the case of autobiographies, were written before the end of their subjects' careers. It should also be noted that, in addition to the histories listed below, all the county cricket clubs publish annual year books.

**5814** *Wisden's Cricketers' Almanack* Wisden 1864–. An annual, exhaustive guide to the previous season's play with commentaries, statistical records and articles, often of a historical nature. It also contains a certain amount of bibliographical information. Another useful year book is *Cricket Year Book* Pelham 1979–, now published as *Benson and Hedges Cricket Year*.

**5815** Fred Trueman and Don Mosey *Cricket Statistics Year by Year 1946–1987* Stanley Paul 1988.

**5816** E W Padwick (comp) *A Bibliography of Cricket* 2nd ed, Library Association 1984. A bibliography of over 8,000 entries containing material published up to 1979.

**5817** Philip Bailey *Who's Who of Cricketers* Newnes/Association of Cricket Statisticians 1984. A guide to first class cricketers.

**5818** Michael Down *Is It Cricket? Power, Money and Politics Since 1945* Queen Anne Press 1985. An account of the intrusion of money and politics into the international game since the war. A more traditional, if elite, history of the international game is E W Swanton *A History of Cricket* vol 2, Allen and Unwin 1962. This includes a useful bibliography. The best general social history of the game up to the 1977 Packer Affair is Christopher Brookes *English Cricket: The Game and its Players Through the Ages* Weidenfeld and Nicolson 1978. See also John Arlott *Rothman's Jubilee History of Cricket 1890–1965* Barker 1965.

**5819** Keith A P Sandiford 'The Professionalization of Modern Cricket' *British Journal of Sport History* 2 1985 pp 270–89. A good study of the dramatic decline of the amateur in the post-war game and of the major changes that have taken place in the finances of cricket. The contemporary financial problems and opportunities of cricket in the 1950s, including that of the leagues as well as the first class game, is analysed in 'The Cricket Industry' *Planning* 22 1956 pp 158–71.

**5820** Tony Lewis *Double Century: The Story of MCC and Cricket* Hodder and Stoughton 1987. An illustrated history of the club and its ground, Lord's. It includes some reflections on the declining influence of the MCC in national and international cricket in recent years. On the MCC and its ground see also Diana Rait Kerr and Ian Peebles *Lords 1945–1970* Harrap 1971. Another useful history is Geoffrey Moorhouse *Lords* Hodder and Stoughton 1983.

**5821** Gordon Ross *The Testing Years: The Story of England's Rise to the Top in Post-War Cricket* Stanley Paul 1958. A journalistic account of international success in early post-war cricket.

**5822** David Frith (ed) *England v. Australia: Test Match Records 1877–1984* 5th ed, Willow 1984. The history of the Ashes encounters between these two countries is told in Ray Illingworth and Kenneth Gregory *The Ashes: A Centenary History* Collins 1982. See also Ralph Hammond Barker and Irving Rosenwater *England v Australia: A Compendium of Test Matches between the Countries 1877–1968* Batsford 1969, Edward Dexter (ed) *Rothmans Book of Test Matches: England Versus Australia 1946–1963* Barker 1964 and James Maurice Kilburn *Cricket Decade: England v Australia 1946 to 1956* Heinemann 1959. On test match records against other countries see S C Caple *The Springboks at Cricket: England versus South Africa 1888–1960* Littlebury 1960, S C Caple *England Versus India 1886–1959* Littlebury 1959 and S C Caple *England Versus the West Indies 1895–1957* Littlebury 1957.

**5823** Basil D'Oliveira *The D'Oliveira Affair* Collins 1969. An account of the cancellation of the 1968–9 tour to South Africa because of the inclusion of D'Oliveira, a Cape coloured, in the England side.

**5824** Derek Humphrey *The Cricket Conspiracy* National Council for Civil Liberties 1975. A study of the successful 1969–70 campaign against sporting links with South Africa which was particularly directed against proposed cricket and rugby union tours by the South Africans. It largely deals with the ensuing trial of Peter Hain, who was one the principal organizers behind the campaign. Peter Hain has also written on the campaign in his *Don't Play With Apartheid: The Background to the Stop the Seventy Tour Campaign* Allen and Unwin 1971.

**5825** Henry Blofeld *The Packer Affair* Collins 1978. An account of the episode in the 1970s when the Australian entrepreneur Kerry Packer set up his own international cricket organization in Australia (involving English players) in defiance of the international cricket authorities.

**5826** Roy Webber *The County Cricket Championship: A History of the Competition from 1873 to the Present Day* Phoenix Sports Books 1957. A history of the main domestic cricket competition. See also Trevor Bailey *Championship Cricket: A Review of County Cricket Since 1945* Muller 1961.

**5827** Christopher Martin-Jenkins *Twenty Years On* Collins 1984. A history of limited overs cricket. On the history of the original one-day limited overs competition see Gordon Ross *The Gillette Cup 1963 to 1980* Queen Anne Press 1981.

**5828** John Shawcroft *A History of Derbyshire County Cricket Club 1870–1970* Ripley 1972.

**5829** Grahame Parker *Gloucester Road* Pelham 1983. A history of Gloucestershire County Cricket Club.

**5830** Peter Wynne-Thomas *The History of Hampshire County Cricket Club* Christopher Helm 1988. A good county history.

**5831** Robert Arrowsmith *Kent* Barker 1971. A history of Kent County Cricket Club.

**5832** Vernon Addison and Brian Bearshaw *Lancashire Cricket at the Top* Stanley Paul 1971. A study of Lancashire county cricket, concentrating particularly on the post-war years. The best general history of the county cricket club is John Kay *Lancashire* Barker 1972. See also A W Ledbrooke *The Official History of the Lancashire County and Manchester Cricket Club 1864–1953* Phoenix House 1954. Another history is Rex Pogson *Lancashire County Cricket* Convoy Publications 1952.

**5833**   Edward Eric Snow *Leicestershire Cricket 1949–1977* Stanley Paul 1977. A history of Leicestershire county cricket.

**5834**   David Lemmon *The Official History of Middlesex County Cricket Club* Christopher Helm 1988. A good county history. Other histories are Anton Rippon *The Story of Middlesex County Cricket Club* Moorland 1982, Evelyn Wellings *Middlesex* Barker 1972 and Terence Prittie *Middlesex County Cricket Club* Convoy Publications 1952. Material on Middlesex can also be found in [5820].

**5835**   James Desmond Coldham *Northamptonshire Cricket: A History* Heinemann 1959. A history of Northamptonshire County Cricket Club.

**5836**   Ron Roberts *Sixty Years of Somerset Cricket* Westaway 1952. A history of Somerset County Cricket Club.

**5837**   Gordon Ross *Surrey* Barker 1971. A history of Surrey county cricket. See also Louis Palgrave *The Story of the Oval and the History of Surrey Cricket 1902 to 1948* Cornish Brothers 1949.

**5838**   John Norman Marshall *Sussex Cricket: A History* Heinemann 1959. Another history is Sir Home Seton Charles Montagu Gordon *Sussex County Cricket* Convoy Publications 1950.

**5839**   Leslie Duckworth *The Story of Warwickshire Cricket: A History of Warwickshire County Cricket Club and Ground 1882–1972* Stanley Paul 1974.

**5840**   David Lemmon *The Official History of Worcestershire County Cricket Club* Christopher Helm 1989. See also Wilfred Rowland Chignell *A History of the Worcester County Cricket Club 1844–1950* Littlebury 1951 and Roy Genders *Worcestershire County Cricket* Convoy Publications 1952.

**5841**   Don Mosey *We Don't Play It For Fun* Methuen 1988. A passionate history of Yorkshire cricket, and particularly of the disputes that have wracked the county side during its long fallow period since it last won the county championship in 1968. See also John Callaghan *Yorkshire's Pride: 150 Years of County Cricket* Pelham 1984, Mike Stevenson *Yorkshire* Barker 1972, James Kilburn *A History of Yorkshire Cricket* Stanley Paul 1970 and J M Kilburn *et al History of Yorkshire County*

*Cricket 1924–1949* Yorkshire County Cricket Club 1950.

**5842**   Alan Gibson *The Cricket Captains of England: A Survey* Cassell 1979.

**5843**   Bill Frindall *England Test Cricketers: The Complete Record from 1877* Willow 1989. A comprehensive, well illustrated alphabetically arranged biographical guide which includes masses of statistical information. Peter Walker *Cricket Conversations* Pelham 1978. This includes interviews with Ray Illingworth, Tom Cartwright, Alan Knott, Basil D'Oliveira and Brian Close.

**5844**   Dennis Amiss with Michael Carey *In Search of Runs: An Autobiography* Reader's Union 1977. A short autobiography by the England opening batsman. Ken Barrington *Playing It Straight* Stanley Paul 1968 is the autobiography of the great batsman. See also his *Running Into Hundreds* Stanley Paul 1963. Barrington's career and contribution to the game is also assessed in Brian Scovell *Ken Barrington: A Tribute* Harrap 1982. Alec and Eric Bedser *Our Cricket Story* Evans 1950 is a memoir which was followed by their subsequent *Following On* Evans 1954. Don Mosey *Botham* 2nd ed, Sphere 1987 is the best biography of the England all-rounder Ian Botham. See also Patrick Murphy *Botham: A Biography* Dent 1988. William Eric Bowes *Express Deliveries* Stanley Paul 1949 is the autobiography of the fast bowler. Don Mosey *Boycott* Methuen 1985 is a study of the Yorkshire batsman. It is rather more interesting than Geoffrey Boycott's own, rather pedestrian efforts, *Boycott: The Autobiography* Macmillan 1987. It should be borne in mind however that it is also somewhat hostile towards Boycott. On Boycott see also John Callaghan *Boycott* Pelham 1982. A leading player of the immediate post-war period recalls his career in F R Brown *Cricket Musketeer* Nicholas Kaye 1954. Brian Close with Don Mosey *I Don't Bruise Easily* Macdonald and Janes 1978 is the autobiography of a former England captain. Denis Compton *End Of An Innings* Oldbourne 1958 is the autobiography of the greatest batsman of the early post-war years. Another great batsman and former England captain remembers his career in Colin Cowdrey *MCC: The Autobiography of a Cricketer* Hodder and Stoughton 1976. Mike Denness *I Declare* Barker 1977 is the autobiography of a former England captain, as is Edward Dexter *Ted Dexter Declares* Stanley Paul 1966. On Dexter see also Derek Lodge *The Test Match Career of Ted Dexter* Nutshell 1989. Basil D'Oliveira *Time to Declare* Dent 1980 is the autobiography of a leading England player of the 1960s. See also his *D'Oliveira: An Autobiography* Collins 1968 and [5823]. William John Edrich *Round The Wicket* Muller 1959 is the autobiography of a leading batsman. His brother, who was also a fine batsman, remembers his career in John Edrich *Runs In The Family* Stanley Paul 1969. Thomas Godfrey Evans *Behind The Stumps* Hodder and Stoughton 1951 is the reminiscences of his career by the England wicketkeeper. Keith Fletcher *Captain's Innings* Stanley Paul 1983 is the autobiography of a former England captain. Mike Gatting *Leading From The Front: The Autobiography of Mike Gatting* Macdonald 1988 is a pugnacious autobiography which got him into trouble with the game's authorities and helped to lose him the England captaincy. Graham Gooch with Alan Lee *Out of the Wilderness* revised ed, Grafton 1986 is the autobiography by a leading batsman and England captain of the 1980s who suffered a ban from international cricket after leading a rebel tour of South Africa in the early part of the decade. David Gower with Alan Lee *With Time To Spare* Ward Lock 1980 is an autobiography of a batsman early in his career. Tom Graveney *The Heart of Cricket* Barker 1983 is the autobiography of a leading batsman, and subsequently cricket commentator. A former England captain recalls his career in Tony Greig *My Story* Stanley Paul 1980. Gerald Howat *Walter Hammond* Allen and Unwin 1984 is a biography of the great batsman and the first England captain of the post-war era. See also Ronald Mason *Walter Hammond: A Biography* Hollis and Carter 1962. John Hampshire *Family Argument* Allen and Unwin 1983 is the autobiography of the Yorkshire and England batsman. A great spin bowler recalls his career in Eric Hollies *I'll Spin You A Tale* Museum Press 1955. Sir Leonard Hutton with Alex Bannister *Fifty Years in Cricket* Stanley Paul 1984 is the autobiography of a great batsman and former England captain. Ray Illingworth with Don Mosey *Yorkshire and Back* Queen Anne Press 1980 is the autobiography of the spin bowler and former England captain. Alan Knott *Stumper's View* Stanley Paul 1972 is the autobiography of the England wicketkeeper. Jim Laker *Over To Me* Muller 1960 is the reminiscences of a great spin bowler, as is Graeme Anthony Richard Lock *For Surrey and England* Hodder and Stoughton 1957. Peter May with Michael Melford *A Game Enjoyed: An Autobiography* Stanley Paul 1985 remembers a career as a leading batsman in the 1950s. He also served as England captain and, for most of the 1980s, as chairman of the England selectors. See also Robert Rodrigo *Peter May* Phoenix House 1960. Jim Parks published two volumes of reminiscences, *Time To Hit Out* Stanley Paul 1967 and *Runs in the Sun* Stanley Paul 1961. Ian Peebles *Spinner's Yarn* Collins 1977 is the autobiography of the spin bowler. Derek Randall *The Sun Has Got His Hat On* Willow 1984 is a memoir by the batsman. The England captain (and future Bishop of Woolwich and Liverpool) David Sheppard writes of his cricket career in *Parson's Pitch* Hodder and Stoughton 1964. Another distinguished career is recalled in E J Smith *'Tiger' Smith of Warwickshire and England* Lutterworth 1981. John Snow *Cricket Rebel: An Autobiography* Hamlyn 1976 and John Brian Statham *Flying Bails* Stanley Paul 1961 are both autobiographies of fast bowlers. David Steele *Come In Number 3* Pelham 1977 is the autobiography of the number three batsman. An England wicketkeeper remembers his career in Bob Taylor *Standing Up, Standing Back* Collins 1985. Fred Trueman *Ball Of Fire: An Autobiography* Willow 1984 is the memoirs of the celebrated fast bowler. See also John Arlott *Fred: Portrait of a Fast Bowler* Methuen 1983. Another great fast bowler recalls his career in Frank Tyson *A Typhoon Called Tyson* Heinemann 1961. Derek Underwood *Beating The Bat* Stanley Paul 1975 is the autobiography of the spin bowler. Other autobiographies of leading cricketers include Bob Woolmer *Pirate and Rebel: An Autobiography* Barker 1984, Robert Wyatt *Three Straight Sticks* Stanley Paul 1951 and Norman Yardley *Cricket Campaigns* Stanley Paul 1950.

**5845** Rachel Heyhoe-Flint and N Rheinberg *Fair Play: The Story of Women's Cricket* Angus and Robertson 1976. A general history. Rachel Heyhoe-Flint *Heyhoe!* Pelham 1978 is the autobiography of the most celebrated female cricketer of the post-war era.

*(iii) Association Football*

The biographies, autobiographies and club histories listed below are a select list. This is because so much of the material of this kind is of strictly limited value. Furthermore most football autobiographies, as with sports autobiographies in general, are written well before the end of the career of their subjects.

Material on football hooligans can be found in the section on public order [6231–2].

**5846** *Rothmans Football Yearbook* Queen Anne Press 1970–. A directory, overview of the past season and collection of statistical records.

**5847** Phil Soar (ed) *Encyclopedia of British Football* 3rd ed, Willow 1983. A useful reference guide.

**5848** George W Keeton *The Football Revolution: A Study of the Changing Pattern of Association Football* David and Charles 1972. This is a good guide to all aspects of the modern game. On the organization, administration and finance of the game see also Peter Douglas *The Football Industry* Howard House 1974. A similar guide to the players, managers, press and fans is Arthur Hopcraft *The Football Men: People and Passions in Soccer* Penguin 1968. Desmond Morris *The Soccer Tribe* Cape 1985 supplies some useful sociological insights supported by excellent colour photography.

**5849** Stephen Wagg *The Football World: A Contemporary Social History* Harvester 1984. A social history of the game and its supporters, particularly since 1918, examining the changing nature of the game and themes such as the fight against the maximum wage or the impact of television. Another useful social history is Charles Critcher 'Football Since the War' in John Clarke, Charles Critcher and Richard Johnson (eds) *Working Class Culture* Hutchinson 1979 pp 161–84. A more general history of the game since pre-industrial times is James Walvin *The People's Game: A Social History of Football* Allen Lane 1975. The last two chapters deal with developments since 1939. There is also some social history in Percy Marshall Young *A History of British Football* Arrow 1973. For other general histories see also Dennis Signy *A Pictorial History of Soccer* 2nd revised ed, Hamlyn 1970 and Morris Marples *A History of Football* Secker and Warburg 1954.

**5850** Nicholas Fishwick *English Football and Society 1910–1950* Manchester University Press 1989. A major monograph on football at the time of its peak popularity, and on its place in the social life particularly of the working classes.

**5851** Geoffrey Green *Soccer In The Fifties* Ian Allan 1974. Not a social history but an account of the features of the professional game in the 1950s.

**5852** Simon Inglis *Soccer In The Dock: A History of British Football Scandals 1900 to 1965* Willow 1985. A good study of bribery, the fight for an end to the maximum wage, Sunday football, ownership scandals and match-rigging.

**5853** B Walker 'The Demand for Professional League Football and the Success of Football League Teams: Some City Size Effects' *Urban Studies* 23 1986 pp 209–19. This argues that success can be ranked with city size. This however has not always been the case.

**5854** Simon Inglis *League Football and the Men Who Made It: The Official Centenary History of the Football League 1888–1988* Willow 1988. See also Bryan Butler *The Football League 1888–1988: The Official Illustrated History* Macdonald 1987, Reginald Charles Churchill *Sixty Seasons of League Football* 2nd ed, Nicholas Kaye 1961 and Maurice Golesworthy *We Are The Champions: A History of the Football League Champions 1888–1972* Pelham 1972.

**5855** Tony Pawson *100 Years of the FA Cup: The Official Centenary History* Heinemann 1972. A history of the competition. See also Geoffrey Green *The Official History of the FA Cup* Naldrett Press 1949. On the Football Association see Geoffrey Green *History of the Football Association* 2nd ed, Heinemann 1960.

**5856** Bob Barton *Servowarm History of the FA Amateur Cup* Barton 1984. A history of the competition.

**5857** Lionel Francis *Seventy-Five Years of Southern League Football* Pelham 1969.

**5858** J R Bale 'Changing Regional Origins of an Occupation: The Case of Professional Footballers in 1950 and 1980' *Geography* 68 1983 pp 140–8. The strength of the Professional Footballers' Association, particularly since changes to the retain and transfer system in 1978, is examined in Braham Dabscheck 'Beating the Off-Side Trap: The Case of the Professional Footballers' Association' *Industrial Relations Journal* 17 1986 pp 350–61.

**5859** Brian Woolnough *Black Magic: The Rise of the Black Footballer* Pelham 1983. A useful study.

**5860** Morley Farror and Douglas Lamming *A Century of English International Football 1872–1972* Hale 1972. See also Anton Rippon *England: The Story of the National Soccer Team* Moorland Publishing 1981. The record in the oldest international fixture in the world is recorded in Brian James *England v Scotland* Pelham 1969. The story of the finest hour of English football, the 1966 World Cup which England both hosted and won, is told in David Miller *England's Last Glory: The Boys of '66* Pavilion 1986.

**5861** Stephen Kelly *You'll Never Walk Alone: The Official Illustrated History of Liverpool FC* Queen Anne Press 1987. A rather superficial history of the most successful club of the post-war years, and especially of the 1970s and 1980s. See also Derek Hodgson *The Liverpool Story* revised ed, Mayflower 1979, Matthew Graham *Liverpool* Hamlyn 1984 and David Prole *Come On The Reds: The Story of Liverpool FC* Hale 1967. The history of its Merseyside rival receives similar treatment in his *Forever Everton: The Official Illustrated History of Everton FC* Queen Anne Press 1987. On Everton see also Derek Hodgson *The Everton Story* Barker 1979 and John Roberts *Everton* Mayflower 1978. The history of these two clubs calls out for more scholarly study, putting their history in the social and economic context of Liverpool. This is not just because of the peculiar intensity of football support in the city but because there seems to be a need for an explanation of the success of the two clubs, particularly Liverpool, in recent years, despite the economic decline of their native city. This is not achieved in Percy Marshall Young *Football on Merseyside* Stanley Paul 1965. The history of another notably successful club is told in Phil Soar and Martin Tyler *Arsenal: The Official History* 2nd ed, Hamlyn 1989. See also Ralph Leslie Finn *Arsenal: Chapman to Mee* Hale 1969 and Bernard Joy *Forward Arsenal: A History of the Arsenal Football Club* Phoenix House 1952. The history of another distinguished North London club, Tottenham Hotspur, is traced in Phil Soar *And The Spurs Go Marching In* 2nd ed, Hamlyn 1985 and Ralph Leslie Finn *enham Hotspur FC: The Official History* Hale 1972. The club's history between 1958–74 is also examined in Bill Nicholson *Glory Glory* Macmillan 1984. Chelsea's history is examined in John Moynihan *The Chelsea Story* Barker 1982, Ralph Leslie Finn *A History of Chelsea Football Club* Pelham 1969 and Albert Sewell *Chelsea Champions! The History of the 1954–55 Football League Champions from 1905 to the Jubilee Year* Phoenix Sports Books 1955. The social and economic context of football is fully brought out in Charles Korr *West Ham United: The Making of a Football Club* University of Illinois Press, Champaign, Illinois 1986 (on West Ham see also John Moynihan *The West Ham Story* Barker 1984). This traces the history of this East London club from its foundation in 1895 to 1968. There are however no comparable scholarly club histories. Oxford United is analysed in Vic Couling *Anatomy of a Football Club* New Horizon 1983. Geoffrey Green *There's Only One United: The Official Centenary History of Manchester United 1878–1978* Hodder and Stoughton 1978 is a massive account of the history of a great club. A further official history is Tom Tyrell *Manchester United* Hamlyn 1988. The Munich air disaster that killed several of the team in 1958 and its impact is examined in Frank Taylor *The Day A Team Died* Souvenir Press 1983 and John Roberts *The Team That Wouldn't Die* Mayflower 1979. The internal politics and difficulties of Manchester United since it last won the league championship in 1967 are examined in Michael Crick *Manchester United: The Magic and the Money* Pelham 1988. See also Derek Hodgson *The Manchester United Story* Barker 1977, Eric Thornton *Manchester United: Barson to Busby* Hale 1971 and Percy Marshall Young *Manchester United* Heinemann 1960. The history of the other Manchester club is told in Andrew Ward *Manchester City Story* Breedon 1984. On another distinguished club see Ian Johnson *The Aston Villa Story* Barker 1981 and Peter Morris *Aston Villa: The History of a Great Football Club 1874–1960* Naldrett Press 1960. Dave Smith and Paul Taylor *Of Fossils and Foxes* Polar Publishing 1989 is an official history of Leicester City. Michael Lidbury *Wimbledon Centenary* Wimbledon FC 1989 and Denis Clareborough *The First 100 Years* Sheffield United FC 1989 are other useful official histories. On football in Sheffield see also Percy Marshall Young *Football in Sheffield* Stanley Paul 1962. Other club histories are Robin Daniels *Blackpool Football: The Official Club History* Hale 1972, Percy Marshall Young *Bolton Wanderers* Stanley Paul 1961, David Wiseman *Up The Clarets: The Story of Burnley Football Club* Hale 1973, Roy Peskett *The Crystal Palace Story* the author 1969, Dennis Turner *A History of Fulham Football Club 1879–1979* Fulham FC 1979, Charles Ekberg *The Mariners* Sporting and Leisure 1983 (a history of Grimsby Town FC), John Gibson *The Newcastle United FC Story* Pelham 1969, Keith Warsop *The Magpies* Sporting and Leisure 1984 (Nottingham County), John Lawson *Forest 1865–1978* Mayflower 1979 (Nottingham Forest), Mike Neasom, Mick Cooper and Doug Robinson *Pompey: The History of Portsmouth*

*Football Club* Milestone 1984, Dennis Signy *A History of Queen's Park Rangers Football Club* Pelham 1969, John Staff *The History of Scunthorpe United Football Club* John Staff Enterprises 1980, Keith Farnsworth *Wednesday! The History of Sheffield's Oldest Professional Football Club* Sheffield City Libraries 1982 (Sheffield Wednesday), G A Willmore *West Bromwich Albion* Hale 1979 and Percy Marshall Young *Centenary Wolves* Wolverhampton Wanderers 1976.

**5862** Brian Pead *Liverpool: A Complete Record 1892–1986* Breedon 1986. Each title in this series contains detailed club statistics, a chronology and reports season by season. Other titles include Gerald Mortimer *et al Derby County* 1984, Ian Ross and Gordon Smailes *Everton* 1985, Leo Triggs *Grimsby Town* 1989, Ed Law *Hartlepool United* 1989, Tony Matthews *Birmingham City 1875–1989* 1989, Simon Marland *Bolton Wanderers 1877–1989* 1989, Mike Purkiss and Nigel Sands *Crystal Palace 1905–1989* 1989, Chris Elton *Hull City 1904–1989* 1989, Martin Jarred and Malcolm Macdonald *Leeds United 1919–1989* 2nd ed, 1989, Harry Glasper *Middlesborough 1876–1989* 1989, Paul Joannou *Newcastle United 1882–1986* 1986, Andy and Roger Howland *Oxford United 1893–1989* 1989 and Brian Knight *Plymouth Argyle 1903–1989* 1989.

**5863** Ted Croker *The First Voice You Will Hear Is* Willow 1986. The reminiscences of a football bureaucrat who was General Secretary of the Football Association 1977–89.

**5864** Alan Hardaker *Hardaker of the League* Pelham 1977. The memoirs of a former Secretary of the Football League

**5865** Stanley Rous *Football Worlds: A Lifetime in Sport* Faber 1978. Rous, a universally well regarded football administrator, was Secretary of the Football Association 1934–61 and President of FIFA 1961–74.

**5866** Ron Atkinson with Joe Melling *United To Win: An Autobiography of Ron Atkinson* Sidgwick and Jackson 1984. An autobiography of a distinguished footballer and manager. Alan Ball *It's All About A Ball* W H Allen 1978 is an autobiography covering a distinguished England career. Gordon Banks *Banks of England* Futura 1981. The autobiography of the England goalkeeper. There are also biographies and autobiographies of a number of other leading players, including the England striker Trevor Brooking *Trevor Brooking* Pelham 1981. Sir Matt Busby *Soccer At The Top: My Life in Football* Weidenfeld and Nicolson 1973 is the autobiography of the great Manchester United manager. See also Matt Busby *My Story, as Told to David R Jack* Souvenir Press 1957. David Miller *Father of Football: The Story of Sir Matt Busby* Stanley Paul 1970 is a good biography. Ron Burgess *Football – My Life* Souvenir Press 1952, Bobby

Charlton *Forward With England* Stanley Paul 1967 and Jackie Charlton *For Leeds And England* Stanley Paul 1967 are all autobiographies by distinguished players. Tony Francis *Clough* Stanley Paul 1987 is a biography of the celebrated manager, Brian Clough. Clough's longtime collaborator writes of him in Peter Taylor *With Clough* revised ed, New English Library 1981. George Eastham *Determined To Win* Stanley Paul 1964 reflects both on his career with England and Arsenal and his fight for the reform of players' pay and of the administration of the league. Tom Finney *Football Round the World* Museum Press 1953, Ron Flowers *For Wolves and England* Stanley Paul 1962 and Trevor Francis *The World To Play For* Sidgwick and Jackson 1982 are all memoirs of distinguished England careers. Ron Greenwood *Yours Sincerely* Willow 1984 is the autobiography of the West Ham and England manager. Jimmy Greaves and Reg Gutteridge *Let's Be Honest* Pelham 1972 is the reminiscences of a celebrated striker. See also Jimmy Greaves *This One's On Me* Barker 1979. The autobiography of another leading England striker is Roger Hunt *Hunt For Goals* Pelham 1969. Emlyn Hughes *Crazy Horse* Barker 1980 is the autobiography of the Liverpool player capped over 50 times by England. Kevin Keegan *Kevin Keegan* Barker 1978 looks at the career of the Liverpol and England player. Tommy Lawton *When the Cheering Stopped: The Rise the Fall Golden Eagle* 1973 is an autobiography by a former England captain. See also his *My Twenty Years of Soccer* Heirloom Library 1955. Nat Lofthouse *Goals Galore* Stanley Paul 1954 is the autobiography of the great striker. Stanley and Mila Matthews *Back in Touch* Barker 1981 is the reminiscences of the great winger. See also Stanley Matthews *The Stanley Matthews Story* Oldborne 1960 and Stanley Matthews *Feet First* Ewen and Dale 1948. Joe Mercer *The Great Ones* Oldborne 1964 is a memoir of a distinguished career. Phil Neal *Life at the Kop* Queen Anne Press 1986 recalls a career with Liverpool and England. Jeff Powell *Bobby Moore: The Authorised Biography* Everest 1976 is a biography of the man who captained England to their World Cup triumph in 1966. See also Bobby Moore *England! England!* Stanley Paul 1970 and *My Soccer Story* Stanley Paul 1966. Another celebrated footballer recalls his career in Stanley Mortensen *Football Is My Game* Sampson, Low, Marston and Co 1949. Martin Peters *Goals from Nowhere* Stanley Paul 1969 is the autobiography of an England player. Alfred Ramsey *Talking Football* Stanley Paul 1952 is the nearest to an autobiography of the man who later as England manager guided them to the World Cup triumph of 1966. Another autobiographical piece by a player who was later to manage first Leeds then England is Don Revie *Soccer's Happy Wanderer* Museum Press 1955. Another autobiography written before its subject became England manager is Bobby Robson *Time On The Grass* Barker 1982. Bryan Robson *United I Stand* is the autobiography of the Manchester United and England midfielder. A distinguished England captain reflects on his career in William

Wright *Captain of England* Stanley Paul 1950 and *The World's My Football Pitch* Stanley Paul 1953.

### (iv) Rugby Football

**5867**   *Rothmans' Rugby Yearbook* Queen Anne Press 1972–.

**5868**   Eric Dunning and Kenneth Stead *Barbarians, Gentlemen and Players: A Sociological Study of the Development of Rugby Football* Robertson 1979. A general social history of the game.

**5869**   Val Addison Titley and Allan Ross MacWhirter *Centenary History of the Rugby Football Union* Rugby Football Union 1970. An official history.

**5870**   Terry Godwin *The International Championship 1883–1983* Collins 1984. A history of the Home Championship between the four home rugby unions and that of France. There are also a number of studies of individual series against South Africa, New Zealand or Australia. These can best be traced using [7].

**5871**   Wallace Macdonald Reyburn *The Lions* Stanley Paul 1967. A general history of the British Lions (the team selected from the best of the four home unions) since 1888.

**5872**   Reg Sweet *Pride of the Lions* Bailey Brothers and Swinfen 1962. A history of contests between the British Lions and the South African Springboks since 1891.

**5873**   Nigel Starmer-Smith *The Barbarians: The Official History of the Barbarians Football Club* Macdonald and Janes 1977.

**5874**   Wallace Macdonald Reyburn *The Men In White: The Story of English Rugby* Pelham 1975. See also John Griffiths *The Book of English International Rugby 1971–1982* Willow 1982 and B M Bowker *England Rugby: A History of the National Side 1871–1976* Cassell 1976.

**5875**   Tom Salmon *The First Hundred Years* Cornwall Rugby Football Union 1983. The history of another county union is traced in John Reed (ed) *Surrey Rugby: 100 Years* Regency Press 1978.

**5876**   Bill Beaumont *Thanks To Rugby* Stanley Paul 1982. The autobiography of a former England rugby union captain. See also Sean Pryor *Billy Beaumont* Star 1983. The amateur code has tended to militate against the writing of autobiography by rugby union players. However there is Mike Burton *Never Stay Down* Queen Anne Press 1982, Fran Cotton *Fran* Queen Anne Press

1981, David Duckham *Dai For England* Pelham 1980, Dusty Hare *Dusty* Queen Anne Press 1985, Gus Risman *Rugby Renegade* Stanley Paul 1958, Robert Scott *The Bob Scott Story* Herbert Jenkins 1956, Steve Smith with Geoff Green *The Scrum Half of My Life: An Autobiography* Stanley Paul 1984, Roger Uttley *Pride In England* Stanley Paul 1981 and Peter Wheeler *Rugby From The Front* Stanley Paul 1983.

5877  J V Smith *'Good Morning President': Rugby from the Top* Allen and Unwin 1985. The autobiography of a rugby administrator.

5878  *Playfair Rugby League Annual* Queen Anne Press 1984–. This annual guide to the sport later became the Rothmans Annual.

5879  Robert Gate *Rugby League: An Illustrated History* Barker 1989. An official history of the game and the league. See also Keith Macklin *The Story of Rugby League* Stanley Paul 1984.

5880  Robert Gate *The Struggle for the Ashes* privately printed 1985. A history of rugby league test matches between Great Britain and Australia.

## (v) *Tennis*

5881  Max Robertson *Wimbledon* 2nd ed, BBC Books 1981. The fullest history of the lawn tennis championships. See also James Medlycott *100 Years of the Wimbledon Tennis Championships* Hamlyn 1977 and Lance Tingay *100 Years of Wimbledon* Guinness Superlatives 1977.

5882  Ted Tinling *Tinling: Sixty Years in Tennis* Sidgwick and Jackson 1983. The autobiography of the celebrated tennis couturier. See also the earlier Ted Tinling with Robert Oxby *White Ladies* Stanley Paul 1963. The more prosaic sportswear designer and inter-war tennis champion, Fred Perry, recalls his career in *Fred Perry* Hutchinson 1984.

5883  Angela Mortimer *My Waiting Game* Muller 1962. The autobiography of the 1961 Wimbledon ladies champion. Other tennis autobiographies are Christine Truman *Tennis Today* Barker 1961, Virginia Wade *Courting Triumph* Hodder and Stoughton 1978 and Bobby Wilson with John Cottrell *My Side of the Net* Stanley Paul 1964.

## (vi) *Golf*

5884  Joseph S F Murdoch (comp) *The Library of Golf 1743–1966: A Bibliography of Golf Books* Gale, Detroit, Michigan 1968. An annotated bibliography.

5885  Geoffrey Cousins *Golf In Britain: A Social History from the Beginnings to the Present Day* Routledge and Kegan Paul 1975. A useful general history. Bernard Darwin *et al A History of Golf in Britain* Cassell 1952 contains essays on the development of the game, its rules, implements and courses and on women's golf.

5886  K Wadd 'The Development of Golf in England: An Essay in the Sociology of Leisure' Leeds MA Thesis 1964–5. A study of golf as a mass social activity.

5887  Rosalynde Cossey *Golfing Ladies: Five Centuries of Golf in Britain and Ireland* Orbis 1984. A history of women's golf.

5888  Peter Alliss *The Open: The British Open Golf Championship Since the War* Collins 1984. A well written history. See also Charles Gordon Mortimer and Fred Pignon *The Story of the Open Golf Championship 1860–1950* Jarrolds 1952.

5889  Nick Faldo *The Rough with the Smooth* Stanley Paul 1980. In common with many sporting autobiographies this appeared early in its subject's career and its value is accordingly limited. Tony Jacklin *The First Forty Years* Macdonald 1985 is an autobiography by one of the most successful British golfers of the post-war years. See also his *Jacklin: The Champion's Own Story* Barker 1970 and Liz Kahn *Tony Jacklin* Hamlyn 1979. Another golfing autobiography is James Sheridan *Sheridan of Sunningdale: My Fifty-Six Years as Caddy-Master* Country Life 1967.

## (vii) *Horse Racing*

5890  Eileen P Loder *Bibliography of the History and Organisation of Horse Racing and Thoroughbred Breeding in Great Britain and Ireland: Books Published in Great Britain and Ireland 1565–1973* J A Allen 1978. A classified bibliography consisting of 1,817 briefly annotated entries.

5891  Tony Morris and John Randall *Horse-Racing: Records, Facts and Champions* 2nd ed, Guinness 1988.

5892  Christopher R Hill *Horse Power: The Politics of the Turf* Manchester University Press 1987. An excellent study of the state of the horse racing industry in all its aspects from the breeding to the betting and of all the changes that have affected it during the post-war years.

Another social study of those involved in horse racing is Jocelyn De Mowbray *Horse-Racing and Racing Society: Who Belongs and How It Works* Sidgwick and Jackson 1985. The best general history of horse-racing is Dennis Craig *Horse Racing: The Breeding of Thoroughbreds and a Short History of the English Turf* J A Allen 1982. See also Barry Campbell *Horse Racing in Britain* Michael Joseph 1977.

**5893** Roger Mortimer *The Jockey Club* Cassell 1958. A history of the leading authority in the sport.

**5894** Michael Ayres and Gary Newton *Over The Sticks* David and Charles 1971. A history of National Hunt racing.

**5895** Michael Williams *The Continuing Story of Point to Point Racing* Pelham 1970.

**5896** Ernest A Bland (ed) *Flat-Racing Since 1900* Dakers 1950.

**5897** Richard Onslow *Headquarters: A History of Newmarket and its Racing* Great Ouse Press 1983. A history of the flat- racing racecourse and of the surrounding breeding and training industry.

**5898** Roger Mortimer *The History of the Derby Stakes* 3rd ed, Michael Joseph 1984. A history of the classic flat race. See also Vincent Robert Orchard *The Derby Stakes: A Complete History from 1900 to 1953* Hutchinson 1954 and George Melton *The Derby 1919–1947* Knapp, Drewett and Sons 1947.

**5899** Michael Seth-Smith, Peter Willett, Roger Mortimer and John Lawrence *The History of Steeplechasing* Michael Joseph 1966. See also Germaine Eliot *Portrait of a Sport: A History of Steeplechasing* Longmans 1958.

**5900** Reg Green *A Race Apart: The History of the Grand National* Hodder and Stoughton 1988. A lavishly illustrated book which is in some senses more a chronology than a history. See also Peter King *The Grand National* Quartet 1983, Clive Graham and Bill Curling *The Grand National: An Illustrated History of the Greatest Steeplechase in the World* Barrie and Jenkins 1972 and Vian Crocker Smith *The Grand National: A History of the World's Greatest Steeplechase* Stanley Paul 1969.

**5901** John Welcome *The Cheltenham Gold Cup: The Story of a Great Steeplechase* 3rd ed, Pelham 1984.

**5902** Tim Fitzgeorge-Parker *Jockeys of the Seventies* Pelham 1980.

**5903** Terry Biddlecombe *Winner's Disclosures: An Autobiography* Stanley Paul 1982. The life of a leading trainer is told in Bill Curling *The Captain: A Biography of Captain Sir Cecil Boyd-Rochfort, Royal Trainer* Barrie and Jenkins 1970. There are a number of autobiographies and biographies of leading jockeys, for instance Harry Carr *Queen's Jockey* Stanley Paul 1966. Claude Duval *Willie Carson: A Biography* Stanley Paul 1980 is a biography of the leading flat season jockey. Bob Champion *Bob Champion's Story: A Great Human Triumph* Fontana 1982 and Joe Childs *My Racing Reminiscences* Hutchinson 1952 are jockey's autobiographies. Tim Fitzgeorge-Parker *Ever Loyal: The Biography of Neville Cramp* Stanley Paul 1987 is a biography of a famous national hunt trainer. The career of another trainer is recorded in Alan R Bennett *Horsewoman: The Extraordinary Mrs D: A Biography of Louie Dingwall, Racehorse Trainer* Dorset Publishing 1979. A jockey remembers his career in Dick Francis *The Sport of Queens: The Autobiography of Dick Francis* 2nd ed, Michael Joseph 1982. John Francombe *Born Lucky* Pelham 1985 is the autobiography of the leading national hunt jockey. Quentin Gilbey *Fun Was My Living* Hutchinson 1970 is another jockey's autobiography, as are Jack Jarvis *They're Off: An Autobiography* Michael Joseph 1969 and Jack Leach *Sods I Have Cut On The Turf* Gollancz 1961. Marcus Marsh *Racing With The Gods* Pelham 1968 is a trainer's autobiography. The life of the leading flat season jockey, Lester Piggott, is told in Dick Francis *Lester: The Official Biography* Charnwood 1987. See also Claude Duval *Lester: A Biography* Stanley Paul 1972. The life of another great jockey is examined in Michael Seth-Smith *Knight of the Turf: The Life and Times of Sir Gordon Richards* Hodder and Stoughton 1980. Richards rode more winners than any other British jockey. See also Sir Gordon Richards *My Story* Hodder and Stoughton 1955. Charles James William Smirke *Finishing Post* Oldborne 1960 is another autobiography by a jockey, as is Douglas Smith with Peter Willett *Five Times Champion: The Autobiography of Doug Smith* Pelham 1963 Eph Smith *Riding To Win* Stanley Paul 1968 and Tommy Weston *My Racing Life* Hutchinson 1952. The career of a leading jockey and trainer is traced in David Hedges *Mr Grand National: The Story of Fred Winter, Jockey and Trainer* Pelham 1969.

*(viii) Motorsport*

**5904** Maurice Hamilton *The British Grand Prix* Crowood Press 1989. A history of the race. See also Richard Alexander Hough *British Grand Prix: A History* Hutchinson 1958.

**5905** Louis Klemantaski and Michael Frostick *British Racing Green 1946–1956* The Bodley Head 1957. A well-illustrated account of British motor car racing after the war.

**5906** G S Davison *Racing Through the Century: Memoirs of Fifty Years of Motor Cycle Sport* TT Special 1951. A history of British motor cycle racing.

**5907** Bob Holliday *Racing Round The Island* David and Charles 1976. A history of the Isle of Man Tourist Trophy motor cycle races. See also Peter Arnold (ed) *TT Races: Diamond Jubilee 1907–1967* BP Retail Division 1967 and Richard Alexander Hough *Tourist Trophy: The History of Britain's Greatest Motor Race* Hutchinson 1957.

**5908** Maurice Hamilton *RAC Rally 1932–1986* Partridge Press 1987. A good account of the history of the race.

**5909** Marcus Chambers *Seven Year Twitch* Foulis 1962. An account of British rallying and especially of the BMC team 1955–61.

**5910** Martin Rogers *An Illustrated History of Speedway* Studio Publications 1978. A speedway autobiography is Johnie Hoskins *Speedway Walkabout* Studio Publications 1977.

**5911** S C H Davis *Great British Drivers* Hamilton 1957. This includes pieces on John Cobb, Reginald Parnell and Stirling Moss.

**5912** Gina Campbell with Michael Meech *Bluebirds: The Story of the Campbell Dynasty* Sidgwick and Jackson 1988. The story of three generations of a speed racing family, from Sir Malcolm who held world speed records on land and water in the 1930s, through Donald, who gained world speed records on land and water until his death on Coniston Water in 1966 to Donald's daughter, Gina, who has also set world speed records on water. See also Philip Drackett *Like Father Like Son: The Story of Malcolm and Donald Campbell* Clifton Books 1969, Douglas James *Donald Campbell: An Informal Biography* Neville Spearman 1968 and Arthur Knowles and Dorothy Campbell *Donald Campbell CBE* Allen and Unwin 1969.

**5913** Derek Bell and Alan Harry *Derek Bell: My Racing Life* Stephens 1988. An autobiography of a motor racing driver. Another motor racing autobiography is John Bolster *Motoring Is My Business* Autosport 1958. Cliff Brown *George Brown: Sprint Superstar* Haynes 1981 is a biography of a motorcycle racer. Jim Clark, the great Formula 1 world champion, recalls his career in his *Jim Clark At The Wheel: The World Motor Racing Champion's Own Story* Barker 1964. Biographies and tributes that appeared after Clark's death in 1966 include Graham Gould *Jim Clark Remembered* 2nd ed, Stephens 1984 and Bill Gavin *The Jim Clark Story* Frewin 1967. John Cooper with John Bentley *John Cooper – Grand Prix Carpetbagger* Haynes 1977 is his reminiscences of the Cooper motor racing firm, their grand prix team and other racing successes and the development of the mini coopers. Patrick MacNaughton *Piers Courage 27 May 1942–21 June 1970* privately printed 1972 is a biography, including tributes, of the Formula 1 racing driver. Peter Lewis *Alf Francis: Racing Mechanic* Foulis 1957 is a memoir based on interviews with its subject. Ted Macauley *Mike: The Life and Times of Mike Hailwood* Buchan and Enright 1984 is the biography a former motorcycling world champion. See also Mike Hailwood *Hailwood* Transport Bookman Publications 1978. Mike Hawthorn *Challenge Me The Race* Kimber 1958 is the autobiography of a motor racing driver. Graham Hill with Neil Ewart *Graham* Hutchinson 1976 is a posthumously published autobiography of the Formula 1 racing driver. An earlier autobiography is his *Life At The Limit* Kimber 1969. See also the memoir by his wife, Bette Hill *The Other Side of the Hill* Stanley Paul 1978 and the tribute biography Tony Rudlin *Mr Monaco: Graham Hill Remembered* Stephens 1983. James Hunt *James Hunt Against All Odds* Hamlyn 1978 is the autobiography of the Formula 1 world champion of 1976. Innes Ireland *All Arms and Elbows* Pelham 1967 is the autobiography of a motor racing driver. Nigel Mansell and Derick Allsop *Driven To Win: An Autobiography* Stanley Paul 1988 is an autobiography of the motor racing driver. On Mansell see also Christopher Hilton *Nigel Mansell: The Making of a Champion* 2nd ed, Corgi 1988. David McDonald *Fifty Years with the Speed Kings* Stanley Paul 1961 are the memoirs of a support mechanic and the drivers and cars he knew. It is also a record of the involvement of the tyre-making firm of Dunlop in motor racing. Jeremy Walton *Only Here For The Beer: Gerry Marshall* Haynes 1978 is a biography of a saloon car racing driver. Derek Minter *Racing All My Life* Barker 1965 is a memoir of a motorcycle racing career. Pat Moss *The Story So Far* Kimber 1967 is the autobiography of a rally driver. Stirling Moss with Doug Nye *Stirling Moss: My Cars and My Career* Stephens 1987 is a rather shallow autobiography of the great motor racing driver. Earlier memoirs of his (and British) successes of the 1950s are *A Turn At The Wheel* Kimber 1961 and *In the Track of Speed* Muller 1953. Probably the best memoir however, despite its title, is Stirling Moss and Lawrence Pomeroy *Design and Behaviour of the Racing Car* Kimber 1963. Ken W Purdy *All But My Life* Kimber 1963 is based on interviews with Moss. On Moss see also Edmund Holley Burke *Stirling Moss* Ario Publications 1962. The career of a former motorcycling world champion is told in Phil Read *Phil Read: The Real Story* Macdonald and Janes 1977. An earlier autobiography is his *Prince of Speed* Barker 1970. John Redman *Wheels of Fortune* Stanley Paul 1966 contains motorcycle racing reminiscences. A motorcycling world champion recalls his career in Barry Sheene *Leader of the Pack* Queen Anne Press 1983. See also Michael Scott *Barry Sheene* W H Allen 1984. Jackie Stewart and Eric Dymock *World Champion* Pelham 1970 is an account of Stewart's Formula 1 championship winning year in 1969 with his career before 1969 briefly sketched in. Jackie Stewart and Peter Manso *Faster!* Kimber 1971 is a diary of the 1970 championship. John Surtees *Speed: John Surtees' Own Story* Barker 1963 is an account of Surtees' career as a motorcycle champion and racing car driver. Sheila Van Damm *No Excuses* Putnam 1957 is a rally driving memoir. She also comments on the celebrated Windmill Theatre, a London theatre famous for its saucy revues, of which her father was manager.

### (ix) Athletics

**5914**   Peter Lovesey and T McNab *The Guide to British Track and Field Literature 1275–1968* Athletics Arena 1969. A bibliography of material published in Britain.

**5915**   Peter Lovesey *The Official Centenary History of the Amateur Athletic Association* Guinness Superlatives 1979. The history of the sport's governing body.

**5916**   D A Young 'The History of the English Schools' Athletics Association 1925–1980' Manchester MEd Thesis 1981.

**5917**   L N Richardson *The History of the International Cross-Country Union 1903 to 1953: Jubilee Souvenir* Richardson 1954.

**5918**   Bill Smith *Stud Marks on the Summits: A History of Amateur Fell Racing 1861–1983* SKG Publications 1985. An informative history.

**5919**   *The Official Report* Organising Committee for the XIV Olympiad 1948. The report on the 1948 London Olympic Games.

**5920**   Roger Bannister *First Four Minutes* Putnam 1955. The autobiography of the first man to run a mile in less than four minutes, in 1954. James Coote *The Dave Bedford Story* Penta Publications 1971 is a short life of the long distance record-breaker. David Emery *Lillian* Coronet 1972 is a biography of the sprinter Lillian Board. Brian Vine *Zola: The Official Biography* Stanley Paul 1984 is a populist biography of the controversial runner from South Africa, Zola Budd. Linford Christie with Tony Ward *An Autobiography* Stanley Paul 1985 is the autobiography of the sprinter. Sebastian Coe with David Miller *Running Free* Sidgwick and Jackson 1981 is an autobiography of the very successful middle distance runner. See also David Miller *Seb Coe – Coming Back* Sidgwick and Jackson 1984. Jack Crump *Running Round the World* Hale 1965 is the autobiography of an athletics coach who was British team manager 1937–57. Brendan Foster *Brendan Foster* Heinemann 1978 is the autobiography of a long distance runner. Brian Hewson

with Peter Bird *Flying Feet* Stanley Paul 1962 is the reminiscences of a middle distance runner. Dorothy Hyman *Sprint to Fame* Stanley Paul 1964 is the autobiography of a sprinter. The career of a middle distance runner is recorded in Terry O'Connor *Four Minute Smiler: The Derek Ibbotson Story* Stanley Paul 1960. David Hemery *Another Hurdle* Heinemann 1976 is the autobiography of a former Olympic 400 metre hurdles champion. David Moorcroft *Running Commentary* Stanley Paul 1984 is the autobiography of the long-distance runner. Bill Nankeville *The Miracle of the Mile* Stanley Paul 1956 reminiscences over his middle distance running career. Simon Turnbull *Steve Ovett: Portrait of an Athlete* W H Allen 1983 is a biography of a record-breaking middle distance runner. See also the biography by Ovett's coach, Harry Wilson *Steve Ovett* Stanley Paul 1982 and the recollections of the athlete himself in Steve Ovett with John Rodda *Ovett: A Biography* Willow 1984. The autobiography of another middle distance runner is Gordon Pirie *Running Wild* W H Allen 1961. Mary Rand *Mary Mary (An Autobiography)* Hodder and Stoughton 1969 is an account of her career as pentathlete and sprinter. Arthur Rowe *Champion in Revolt* Stanley Paul 1963 is the autobiography of a shot putter (and rugby league player) in which he critically reflects on the administration of athletics in Britain. Tessa Sanderson with Leon Hickman *My Life in Athletics* Willow 1986 recalls the career of the javelin throwing Olympic champion. Skip Rozin *Daley Thompson: The Subject is Winning* Arrow 1984 is a biography of the double Olympic and World decathalon champion. Fatima Whitbread and Andrianna Blue *Fatima: The Autobiography of Fatima Whitbread* Pelham 1988 traces her life up to her triumph in the javelin at the 1988 Olympics. Harry Wilson *Running Dialogue: A Coach's Story* Stanley Paul 1982 recalls a coaching career during which his charges included Steve Ovett.

### (x) Mountaineering

**5921**   Jill Neate *Mountaineering Literature: A Bibliography of Material Published in English* revised ed, Cicerone 1986. An alphabetically arranged guide to journals, biographies, club records and accounts of expeditions. There is some annotation.

**5922**   Ronald William Clark and Edward Charles Pyatt *Mountaineering in Britain: A History from the Earliest Times to the Present Day* Phoenix House 1957. A far from profound general history is Robert Lock Graham Irving *A History of British Mountaineering* Batsford 1955.

**5923**   Michael Banks *Commando Climber* Dent 1955. Mountaineering memoirs. Christian Bonington *I Chose to Climb* Gollancz 1966 is the first part of the distinguished climber's autobiography. This is continued by his *The Next Horizon: Autobiography* Gollancz 1973. His *The Everest Years: A Climber's Life* Viking 1986 is a memoir of expeditions to Mount Everest in which he participated. Joe Brown *The Hard Years: An Autobiography* Gollancz 1967 recalls the career of a major post-war mountaineer. Leo Dickinson *Filming the Impossible* Cape 1982 is the autobiography of a mountaineering cameraman. Dennis Gray *Rope Boy* Gollancz 1970 is another memoir. D Hastan *In High Places* Cassell 1972 is the autobiography of a leading Scottish climber. Edmund Hillary and Peter Hillary *Ascent: Two Lives Explored: The Autobiographies of Sir Edmund and Peter Hillary* Doubleday 1986. The New Zealander Sir Edmund Hillary was part of the 1953 British mountaineering expedition which finally conquered Everest and was one of the two men who were the first to stand on its summit. The leader of that expedition recalls it in Henry John Cecil Hunt *The Ascent of Everest* Hodder and Stoughton 1953. See also Hunt's autobiography *Life is Meeting* Hodder and Stoughton 1978. Hamish MacInnes *Beyond the Ranges* Gollancz 1984 recalls his mountaineering experiences. Gwen Moffat *Space Below my Feet* Hodder and Stoughton 1961 is an autobiography by a professional mountain guide, continued in her *On my Home Ground* Hodder and Stoughton 1968 and *Survival Count: A Personal Journey Towards Conservation* Gollancz 1972. Another mountaineering autobiography is Nea F Morin *A Woman's Reach* Eyre and Spottiswoode 1968. Other memoirs are Eric Shipton *That Untravelled World: An Autobiography* 2nd ed, Hodder and Stoughton 1969, Showell Styles *Blue Remembered Hills* Faber 1965, Joe Tasker *Savage Arena* Methuen 1982, Michael Phelps Ward *In This Short Span: A Mountaineering Memoir* Gollancz 1972 and Donald Whillans and Alick Ormerod *Don Whillans: Portrait of a Mountaineer* Penguin 1976.

### (xi) Sailing

**5924**  Bob Fisher *The Admiral's Cup* Pelham 1985. A history of the triennial international sailing competition held off Cowes.

**5925**  Cecil Mead *The History of the Royal Cornwall Yacht Club 1871–1949* Underhill 1951. This includes a survey of contemporary sailing in Cornwall. Other club histories are Sir Gerald Duke *The History of the Royal Engineers Yacht Club* Tulett 1982 and Frank Hussey *The Royal Harwich: A Short History of the RHYC* Boydell Press 1972.

**5926**  Anita Walker *Francis Chichester: A Biography* Walker, New York 1975. A biography of the round the world yachtsman. See also John Rowland *Lone Adventurer: The Story of Sir Francis Chichester* Lutterworth

1968. Augustine Courtauld *Man the Ropes* Hodder and Stoughton 1957 is a yachting autobiography. June Dixon *Uffa Fox: A Personal Biography* Angus and Robertson 1978 is a life of a yachtsman. Edward Heath *Sailing: A Course of my Life* Sidgwick and Jackson 1975 is a memoir by the former Prime Minister of an ocean racing career which included captaining Britain to victory in the Admiral's Cup in 1971. Robin Knox-Johnston *A World of my own* Grafton 1969 is the autobiography of the round the world yachtsman. Other autobiographies are Owen Parker *Tack Now, Skipper* Adlard Coles 1979 and A C Sandison *To Sea in Carpet Slippers: The Autobiography of an Ocean Racing Cook* Adlard Coles 1966.

### (xii) Boxing

**5927**  Frank Butler *A History of Boxing in Britain: A Survey of the Noble Art from its Origins to the Present Day* Barker 1972.

**5928**  Leslie Bell *Inside the Fight Game* Rockliff 1952. A study of the sport, its administration, the business aspects and the conduct of the sport.

**5929**  Harry Mullin *Heroes and Hard Men* Stanley Paul 1989. A celebration of British boxing heroes. Freddie Mills *Battling for a Title* Stanley Paul 1954 is a memoir of fighters he knew and a collection of reflections on the sport. There are also a number of boxing autobiographies such as Edward Broadribb *Fighting is my Life* Muller 1951, the memoir of a boxing manager and trainer. John Conteh *I Conteh: An Autobiography* Harrap 1982 is the autobiography of a former light-heavyweight world champion. Henry Cooper *An Autobiography* Coronet 1974, supplemented by his *H for 'Enry: More than just an Autobiography* Willow 1984 is by the former heavyweight boxer. A boxing referee recalls his career in Moss Deyong *Everybody Boo . . .* Stanley Paul 1951. Terry Downes *My Bleeding Business* Stanley Paul 1964 is the autobiography of the former world middleweight champion in which he reflects usefully on the administration of the sport. A heavyweight tells his story in Chris Finnegan *Finnegan* Macdonald and Jane's 1976. Eugene Henderson *Boxing On* Stanley Paul 1957 is a memoir of a boxing referee. Jack Birtley *Freddie Mills* New English Library 1977 is a biography of the former world light-heavyweight champion. Mills' own autobiography is *Twenty Years* Nicholson and Watson 1950. Another former champion recalls his career in Alan Minter with Claude Duval *Minter: An Autobiography* Queen Anne Press 1980. Jack Solomons *Jack Solomons Tells All* Rich and Cowan 1951 is the autobiography of a boxing promoter. Jack Birtley *The Tragedy of Randolph Turpin* New English Library 1975 is a good biography of the former world middleweight champion. Bruce Woodcock *Two Fists and a Fortune* Hutchinson 1951 is a memoir of a boxing career.

### (xiii) Equestrian Sports

**5930**  Dorian Williams *Horse of the Year: The Story of a Unique Horseshow* David and Charles 1976. A history of the show-jumping event. Michael Clayton and Dick Tracey *Hickstead: The First Twelve Years* Pelham 1972 is a history of another major show-jumping event.

**5931**  Sir Mike Ansell *Soldier On: An Autobiography* Peter Davies 1973. The post-war section of this autobiography is largely concerned with show-jumping and equestrian sport. Ansell was the manager of the gold medal winning show-jumping team in the 1952 Olympics. David Barker with Kenneth Ligertwood *One Thing and Another: An Autobiography* Pelham 1964 is the autobiography of a show-jumper. John Board *From Point to Point* Christopher Johnson 1953 is the autobiography of an equestrian journalist. Malcolm Severs *Caroline Bradley: A Tribute* Harrap 1983 is a biography of a three-day eventer. Another three-day eventer recalls her career in Jane Bullen and Genevieve Murphy *The Galloping Nurse: The Story of Jane Bullen* Stanley Paul 1970. One of Britain's most successful show-jumpers recalls his career with David Broome with Brian Giles *Twenty Five Years in Show Jumping* Stanley Paul 1981. The careers and successes of a husband and wife team of show-jumpers are recorded in Ann Martin *The Edgars for Ever* Pelham 1984. Jack Hance *Riding Master* Hale 1960 is another show-jumping autobiography. Jane Vere Nicoll *Take Off! The Story of International Show Jumper Johnny Kidd* Pelham 1972 is a biography of the show-jumper and polo player. Ann Moore with Ann Martin *Clear to Win* Stanley Paul 1973 is another show-jumper's autobiography. Angela Rippon *Mark Phillips: The Man and his Horses* David and Charles 1982 is a biography of the three-day eventer (and husband of Princess Anne). Elwyn Hartley-Edwards *Lucinda Prior-Palmer* Hamilton 1982 is a short profile of the three-day eventer. Harvey Smith *Harvey* Arrow 1976 is the autobiography of a show-jumper. Anneli Drummond-Hay *Anatomy of a Show-Jumper* Barker 1970 is a biography of Patricia Smythe. Dorian Williams, the show-jumper and commentator has published two autobiographies, *Master of One: An Autobiography* Dent 1978 and *Between the Lines: Further Reminiscences* Methuen 1984.

### (xiv) Cycling

**5932**  George a'Green *This Great Club of ours: The Story of the CTC* Cyclists' Touring Club 1953. A history of the club's first 75 years.

**5933**  Chas Messenger *Where There's a Wheel* Pelham 1972. An account of the League of Racing Cyclists and the Tours of Britain he organized for them 1958–64.

**5934**  Reg Harris *Two Wheels to the Top* W H Allen 1976. The autobiography of a leading cyclist. See also George Pearson *Reg Harris: An Authoritative Biography* Temple Press 1950. For other autobiographies see Barry Hoban *Watching the Wheels go Round* Stanley Paul 1981, Hugh Porter *Champion on Two Wheels* Hale 1975, Eileen Sheridan *Wonder Wheels: The Autobiography of Eileen Sheridan* Nicholas Kaye 1956 and Tommy Simpson *Cycling Is My Life* Stanley Paul 1966.

### (xv) Other

**5935**  Godfrey R Bolsover *Who's Who and Encyclopaedia of Bowls* Rowland Publishers 1959. A massive reference guide.

**5936**  D M C Pritchard *The History of Croquet* Cassell 1981.

**5937**  *Modern British Fencing: A History of the Amateur Fencing Association 1964–81* Amateur Fencing Assocation 1984.

**5938**  Marjorie Pollard (ed) *Hilda M Light: Her Life and Times* All England Women's Hockey Association 1972. A biography of a hockey administrator. Ian Taylor *Behind the Mask* Queen Anne Press 1989 is the autobiography of the England men's hockey goalkeeper in the 1988 Olympics gold medal winning team.

**5939**  Jayne Torvill *Torvill and Dean* David and Charles 1984. An account of the very successful ice-skating career of the ice-dance partners Jayne Torvill and Christopher Dean. On John Curry, another Briton to win Olympic gold, see Keith Money *John Curry* Michael Joseph 1978. His successor, who also took the men's Olympic gold, has recalled his career in Robin Cousins *Skating For Gold* Sphere 1981.

**5940**  B C Goodger 'The Development of Judo in Britain: A Sociological Study' London PhD Thesis 1981. A study of its development over the past sixty years and the changes in the process both in terms of the people who have pursued it and the gradual replacement of its moral and philosophical attributes with simple treatment as a sport.

**5941**  *Henley Royal Regatta 1939–1962* The Stewards of Henley Royal Regatta 1969. Mainly a collection of results from this premier event in the world of rowing. The history of the other major annual event in the British rowing calendar is told in Christopher Dodd *The Oxford* *and Cambridge Boat Race* Stanley Paul 1983. This account is poorest in its treatment of the most modern period.

**5942** Rex Bellamy *The Story of Squash* Cassell 1978. A general international history of the sport with some appendices on past champions. Ross Reyburn *Jonah* Dent 1983 is a biography of Jonah Barrington, one of the most successful squash players of the post-war era. See also Jonah Barrington with Clive Everton *The Book of Jonah* Stanley Paul 1972.

**5943** *Benson and Hedges Snooker Yearbook* Pelham 1984–. An annual guide to the sport and its events. Steve Davis with Brian Redford *Frame and Fortune* Barker 1982, Fred Davis *Talking Snooker* 2nd ed, Black 1983, Terry Griffiths *Griff: The Autobiography of Terry Griffiths* Pelham 1989 and Ray Reardon and Peter Buxton *Ray Reardon* David and Charles 1982 are all autobiographies or reminiscences by world snooker champions.

**5944** Sam Rockett *It's Cold in the Channel* Hutchinson 1956. A history of attempts to swim the English Channel. Sharron Davies *Against The Tide* Willow 1984 is a swimming autobiography.

**5945** Marion Connock *The Precious Mackenzie Story* Pelham 1975. A biography of the weightlifter.

**5946** Joe Cornelius *Thumbs Up* W H Allen 1984. The autobiography of a wrestler. Sir Atholl Oakeley *Blue Blood on the Mat: The All-In Wrestling Story* Stanley Paul 1971 is the autobiography of a wrestler and wrestling promoter.

### (e) Gambling

**5947** *Gambling Statistics: Great Britain 1968–78* Cmnd 7897, *Parliamentary Papers* 1979–80.

**5948** D B Cornish *Gambling: A Review of the Literature* HMSO 1978. This examines the economic and social significance of the major forms of commercial gambling and seeks to establish whether or not it is harmful.

**5949** *Royal Commission on Betting, Lotteries and Gaming: 1949–1951 Report* Cmnd 8190, *Parliamentary Papers* viii 1950–51. This Commission under Sir Henry Willink reviewed developments since the 1928 and 1934 Acts.

**5950** *Lotteries: Report of the Interdepartmental Working Party* Cmnd 5506, *Parliamentary Papers* iii 1973–74. The report of the working group chaired by K P Witney.

**5951** *Royal Commission on Gambling* Cmnd 7200, *Parliamentary Papers* 1977–78. The report of the Commission chaired by Lord Rothschild which was generally in favour of greater latitude towards the gambling industry.

**5952** R Dixey 'It's a Great Feeling When You Win: Women and Bingo' *Leisure Studies* 6 1987 pp 199–214. An analysis of the attraction of bingo for working class women using national data and a Leeds case study.

**5953** N Kent-Lemon 'Significant Influences on the United Kingdom Casino Industry Since 1960' *The Annals* 474 1984 pp 72–9. A study of the growth of casinos in Britain since the 1960s.

### (4) The Permissive Society

### (a) General

**5954** Susan Lipshitz *Sexual Politics in Britain: A Bibliographical Guide with Historical Notes* Harvester 1977. A guide to the publications of various feminist, gay and similar organizations. It also provides historical notes on these organizations. It has since been updated on an annual basis.

**5955** W H G Armytage (ed) *Changing Patterns of Sexual Behaviour* Academic Press 1980. A collection of essays on changing attitudes to sex, sexual mores and morality. Changes in these fields since 1900 are examined in C H Whiteley and W W Whiteley *The Permissive Morality* Methuen 1964 in the context of changes in family life and public morality. Growing permissiveness in the 1950s and 1960s, not just in terms of sexual attitudes but also in drugs culture and reforms in the penal system, is reflected on in Frank Pakenham, Lord Longford 'The Permissive Society' in Norman Autton (ed) *Christianity and Change* SPCK 1971 pp 15–27.

**5956** Wayland Young *Eros Denied* 2nd ed, Weidenfeld and Nicolson 1967. A detailed analysis of obscenity, pornography and sex through the ages. There is useful section on contemporary prostitution in London on pp 121–43.

**5957** *Report of the Committee on Homosexual Offences and Prostitution* Cmnd 247, *Parliamentary Papers* xiv 1956–57. This committee, chaired by Sir John Wolfenden, recommended the decriminalizing of male homosexual acts between consenting adults in private. It suggested the extension of the laws governing prostitution to male prostitutes and a clarification of these laws, leading to the 1959 Street Offences Act.

**5958** Christie Davies *Permissive Britain: Social Change in the Sixties and Seventies* Pitman 1975. A well regarded study of the transformation of attitudes in this period. The development of issues of conscience such as capital punishment, homosexuality, abortion, censorship, divorce and the Sabbath and parliament's handling of these issues in the 1960s is examined in Peter Godfrey Richards *Parliament and Conscience* Allen and Unwin 1970. See also National Deviancy Conference (ed) *Permissiveness and Control: The Fate of the Sixties Legislation* Macmillan 1980 and O R McGregor 'Equality, Sexual Values and Permissive Legislation: The English Experience' *Journal of Social Policy* 1 1972 pp 44–59. John Selwyn Gummer *The Permissive Society* Cassell 1971 is a critique by a Conservative MP and Anglo-Catholic churchman of the assumptions and values of the youth culture of the late 1960s.

**5959** Steve Humphries *A Secret World of Sex: Forbidden Fruit: The British Experience 1900–1950* Sidgwick and Jackson 1988. A good oral history.

**5960** Michael Schofield *The Sexual Behaviour of Young People* Longmans 1965. This argues, on the basis of random sampling techniques, that the received picture of increasing promiscuity was still far from the truth.

**5961** Bridget A Pym *Pressure Groups and the Permissive Society* David and Charles 1974. A study of the various groups campaigning both for permissive legislation and of those seeking restrictions on pornography or abortion.

(b) Family Planning

**5962** Audrey Leathard *The Fight For Family Planning: The Development of Family Planning Services in Britain 1921–74* Macmillan 1980. A history from the establishment of the first clinics by Marie Stopes in the 1920s to the acceptance of responsibility by the government in 1974. It is both a story of the changing nature and provision of family planning and of the changing attitudes towards it. See also Robert E Dowse and John Peel 'The Politics of Birth Control' *Political Studies* 13 1965 pp 179–97.

**5963** Jean Aitken-Swan *Fertility Control and the Medical Profession* Croom Helm 1977. A study of the changes in the attitudes of the medical profession towards birth control and abortion since the 1967 Abortion Act.

**5964** Constance Rover *Love, Morals and the Feminists* Routledge and Kegan Paul 1970. The most useful part of this book is the examination in the epilogue of the

response to the condemnation of birth control delivered in the 1968 Papal encyclical *Humanae Vitae*.

**5965** Jane Lewis with Fenella Connell 'The Politics of Motherhood in the 1980s: Warnock, Gillick and Feminists' *Journal of Law and Society* 13 1986 pp 321–43. A feminist view of the 1984 Warnock Report on artificially aided reproduction and the Gillick case on provision of the pill to the under sixteens.

**5966** Barbara Evans *Freedom To Choose: The Life and Work of Dr Helena Wright, Pioneer of Contraception* The Bodley Head 1984. Wright was the only doctor among those who founded the Family Planning Association in the 1930s and long remained a leading figure in this body.

(c) Abortion

**5967** *Abortion Statistics* HMSO 1974–. An annual guide to the statistics on legal abortions.

**5968** Barbara Brookes *Abortion in Britain 1900–1967* Croom Helm 1988. A history up to the legalization of abortion in the 1967 Abortion Act, which concentrates particularly on the inter-war years and the background to the formation of the Abortion Law Reform Association in the 1930s. See also L J F Smith 'The Abortion Controversy 1936–77: A Case Study in the "Emergence of Law"' Edinburgh PhD Thesis 1980. The history of the attitudes of the medical profession towards abortion and their reactions to and influence on the form of the 1967 Act is examined in I J Keown 'Some Aspects of the Legal Regulation of Abortion in England from 1803 to 1982, with Particular Reference to the Influence of the Medical Profession on the Development of the Law and of the Law on the Practice of Abortion by the Medical Profession' Oxford DPhil Thesis 1985.

**5969** Keith Hindell and Madeleine Simms *Abortion Law Reformed* Peter Owen 1971. A history of the struggle for reform of the abortion law and the framing and passage of the 1967 Act. It benefited from free access to the files of the Abortion Law Reform Association and private papers of campaigners.

**5970** *Abortion Act: Committee on the Working of the Act: Report* Cmnd 5579, *Parliamentary Papers* vi 1974–75. The report of the committee chaired by E K Lane. Experience under the Act is also reviewed in Anthony Horden *Legal Abortion: The English Experience* Pergamon 1971, Richard Leete 'Some Comments on the Demographic and Social Effects of the 1967 Abortion Act' *Journal of Biosocial Science* 8 1976 pp 229–51, Madeleine Simms 'Abortion Act after three years' *Political Quarterly* 42 1971 pp 269–86 and F Munoz-Perez

'Douze ans d'avortement légal en Angleterre-Gallas' *Population* 36 1981 pp 1105–38. Paul Cavadiso 'Illegal Abortions and the Abortion Act 1967' *British Journal of Criminology* 16 1976 pp 63–7 argues that it failed to stop illegal abortions.

**5971** David Marsh and Joanna Chambers *Abortion Politics* Junction Books 1981. A study of parliamentary votes and scrutiny and pressure group activity on an issue that has been far from settled by the 1967 Act. It looks in particular detail at the debates over John Carrie's Abortion (Amendment) Bill in 1979–80. Pro- and anti-abortion pressure groups are examined in detail in A H Clarke 'The Abortion Campaign: A Study of Moral Reform and Status Protest' Nottingham PhD Thesis 1984.

(d) Homosexuality

**5972** V L Bullough *et al An Annotated Bibliography of Homosexuality* Garland 1976. Most of the references in this volume are to American works.

**5973** Harford Montgomery Hyde *The Other Love: An Historical and Contemporary Survey of Homosexuality in Britain* Heinemann 1970. The standard history of homosexuality in Britain up to the aftermath of the Wolfenden Report [5957]. See also Jeffrey Weeks *Coming Out: Homosexual Politics in Britain from the Nineteenth Century to the Present* Quartet 1977.

**5974** Bob Cant and Susan Hemmings (eds) *Radical Records: Thirty Years of Lesbian and Gay History 1957–1987* Routledge 1988. A series of recollections reflecting on key events, trends, pressure groups and characteristics of gay life since the Wolfenden Report [5957]. It focuses particularly on links between the gay movement and radical politics, though it notes that in the 1980s the male homosexual scene has been increasingly depoliticized and commercialized.

**5975** Kenneth Plummer (ed) *The Making of the Modern Homosexual* Hutchinson 1981. This is a useful collection of articles on homosexuals, lesbians, transvestites and transsexuals. It features a very useful bibliography. Another collection of articles is Aubrey Walter (ed) *Come Together – The Years of Gay Liberation 1970–73* Gay Men's Press 1980. This tells of the early years of the Gay Liberation Front in Britain in the introduction and through people's stories of their homosexuality from edited extracts from the GLF's newspaper, *Come Together*.

**5976** Michael Schofield *A Minority: A Report on the Life of the Male Homosexual in Great Britain* Longmans 1960. A survey conducted at a time when male homo-

sexual acts were still illegal. It includes a good bibliography. J Tudor Rees and Harley V Osill (eds) *They Stand Apart: A Critical Survey of the Problem of Homosexuality* Heinemann 1955 is useful on attitudes, especially in the establishment, before the Wolfenden Report. See also G Westwood *Society and the Homosexual* Gollancz 1952.

**5977** Simon Shepherd and Mick Wallis *Coming On Strong: Gay Politics and Culture* Unwin Hyman 1989. Perspectives on gay politics and culture in the 1980s. Jamie Gough and Mike McNair *Gay Liberation in the Eighties* Pluto 1985 is a guide to and statement for radical gay politics.

**5978** *Building the London Gay Community* London Gay Workshops Collective 1982.

**5979** Charlotte Wolff *Love Between Women* Duckworth 1971. A sociological study.

**5980** Roberta Cowell *Roberta Cowell's Story* Heinemann 1954. The autobiography of Britain's first transsexual. Another transsexual autobiography is Jan Morris *Conundrum* Faber 1974. Tula (whose real name is Caroline Cossey) *I Am A Woman* Sphere 1982 is the autobiography of a transsexual which includes reflections on transsexuality and on the gay scene in the 1960s and 1970s and on her career as a fashion model.

**5981** Quentin Crisp *The Naked Civil Servant* Cape 1968. A good autobiography which had additional impact when it was used as the basis for a television drama-documentary. His *How To Become A Virgin* Duckworth 1981 is a further volume of autobiography. Other useful autobiographies are Michael Davidson *Some Boys* Bruce 1970 and Robert Hutton *Of Those Alone* Sidgwick and Jackson 1958.

**5982** Jim Harris *Menlove: The Life of John Menlove Edwards* Gollancz 1985. A biography of a leading campaigner for toleration of homosexuality. See also Geoffrey Sutton and Wilfrid Noyce (eds) *Samson: The Life and Writings of Menlove Edwards* Cloister Press 1961.

**5983** Peter Wildeblood *Against The Law* Weidenfeld and Nicolson 1956. The first-hand account by a journalist of his arrest, trial and imprisonment for involvement in the 1954 Lord Montagu case. It is also useful as a prison memoir.

(e) Pornography and Prostitution

**5984** Geoffrey Robertson *Obscenity: An Account of Censorship Laws and their Enforcement in England and Wales* Weidenfeld and Nicolson 1979. A study of the state and operation of the law since the Obscene Publications Act 1959 and of developments in pornographic media since then. John Sutherland *Offensive Literature: Censorship in Britain 1960–1982* Junction Books 1982 is largely a series of case histories of books and publications which have been faced with prosecution for pornography in this period, including D H Lawrence's *Lady Chatterley's Lover*, the *Oz* trial and the blasphemy prosecution of *Gay News* in 1977. See also M Yaffé 'The Law Relating to Pornography: A Pschological Overview' *Medicine, Science and the Law* 20 1980 pp 20–7 and Roy Brown 'Literature and the Permissive Society' *Library World* 72 1971 pp 257–62. On the Lady Chatterley case see C H Rolph *The Trial of Lady Chatterley* Penguin 1961. The history of legislation against pornography and the difficulties of defining the offence are discussed in I Donaldson 'Is Obscenity Obsolescent?' *Police Journal* 60 1987 pp 112–7. In the 1970s there was considerable concern about the use of children in pornography. M A McCarthy and R A Moodie 'Parliament and Pornography: The 1978 Child Protection Act' *Parliamentary Affairs* 34 1981 pp 47–62 is a case study of the parliamentary passage of the measure to ban this.

**5985** Philip Purser and Jenny Wilkes *The One and Only Phyllis Dixey* Futura 1978. A biography of the prominent strip show artiste of the 1940s and 1950s.

**5986** R L Archdale *Prostitution And Persecution: Some Comments on the Street Offences Act 1959* Pall Mall Press 1960. Comments on the Act passed in the wake of the Wolfenden Report [5957].

**5987** Frank Pakenham, Lord Longford *Pornography: The Longford Report* Coronet 1972. This private report by a leading Labour and Catholic peer recommended changes in the obscenity laws in the light of changing social morality.

**5988** *Report of the Committee on Obscenity and Film Censorship* Cmnd 7772, *Parliamentary Papers* 1979–80. This committee under Bernard Williams largely dealt with film censorship and made recommendations on the consolidation of the law. It made no mention of videos which became increasingly popular over the next decade.

**5989** M Tomlinson *The Pornbrokers: The Rise of the Soho Sex Barons* Virgin Books 1982. A survey of the rise of London's sex barons since the 1960s and their activities in the fields of pornography and gambling.

**5990** Jeremy Sandford *Prostitutes* revised ed, Abacus 1977. An account of his observations of prostitutes' pressure groups 1975–7. It incorporates interviews with various types of prostitutes (including male), reflections on pimps and on the law as it relates to prostitution. Another study of this type is Iain Scarlet *The Profession-*

*als: Prostitutes and their Clients* Sidgwick and Jackson 1972. Judith Priceman *Research Into Prostitution* Josephine Butler Educational Trust 1973 is a good pamphlet. A useful earlier study is Rosalind Wilkinson *Women of the Streets* Secker and Warburg 1955.

**5991** Paul Bailey *An English Madam: The Life and Work of Cynthia Payne* Cape 1982.

**5992** Gloria Lovett and Pam Cockerill *A Nice Girl Like Me* Columbus 1988. The autobiography of a prostitute. It highlights the sex abuse she suffered when in care and the high proportion of prostitutes who have been in institutional care as children, the attitudes of the police towards prostitutes and the exploitation of the girls by clients and pimps. Norma Levy *I, Norma Levy* Blond and Briggs 1973 is the autobiography of a high class prostitute whose clients included Lord Lambton (the ensuing scandal led to his resignation from the Heath government).

### (f) Campaigners Against the Permissive Society

**5993** E J Bristow *Vice and Vigilance: Purity Movements in Britain Since 1700* Gill and Macmillan, Dublin 1977. A useful overview.

**5994** D Morrison and M Tracey *Opposition To The Age: A Study of NVALA* Social Science Research Council 1978. A report on the National Viewers' and Listeners' Association. This campaigns particularly against sex and violence on the mass media. Mary Whitehouse *Cleaning Up: From Protest to Participation* Blandford Press 1967 describes the growth of the clean up TV movement (of which she was a co-founder), which developed into the NVALA.

**5995** Mary Whitehouse *Who Does She Think She Is?* New English Library 1971. An account of her campaigns against sex and violence on the mass media. It also reflects on other movements with which she was involved such as the Festival of Light. A further autobiography is her *A Most Dangerous Woman?* Lion Publishing 1982. M Caulfield *Mary Whitehouse* Mowbrays 1975 is a sympathetic biography. M Tracey and D Morrison *Whitehouse* Macmillan 1979 is a biography which overstates its case.

### (5) Youth, Youth Organizations and Youth Cultures

There is also a considerable amount of useful information on youth cultures in the literature in the section on Rock Music and, to some extent, in the section on Student Politics.

**5996** Eleanor Grey *Children In The UK: Signposts to Statistics* National Children's Bureau 1982. A guide to the statistics, their sources and the organizations that produce them.

**5997** Deborah Derrick (comp) *Selected and Annotated Bibliography of Youth, Youth Work and Provision for Youth* National Youth Bureau 1976. A bibliography on youth, adolescence and the youth services. It features books only. See also *The History of Childhood and Youth: A Guide to the Literature* Department of Humanities, Oxford Polytechnic 1982.

**5998** Kenneth Roberts *Youth and Leisure* Allen and Unwin 1983. A general history since 1945. The social history and impact on patterns of consumption of the teenager, a product particularly of growing affluence since the Second World War, is traced in Peter Everett *You'll Never Be 16 Again: An Illustrated History of the British Teenager* BBC 1986.

**5999** Steve Humphries, Joanna Mack and Robert Perks *A Century of Childhood* Sidgwick and Jackson 1988. A well illustrated study of the changing nature of and attitudes towards childhood during the twentieth century by a group of researchers involved in the Oral History Society. Aspects of childhood are also examined in Ken Fogelman (ed) *Growing Up In Great Britain: Collected Papers from the National Child Development Study* Macmillan 1983. John Springhall *Coming of Age: Adolescence in Britain 1860–1960* Gill and Macmillan, Dublin 1986 has little on the post-war period beyond some comments on the Teddy Boys of the 1950s.

**6000** John and Elizabeth Newson *The Extent of Physical Punishment in the UK* Approach 1989. A detailed study on physical punishment of children (usually by mothers) based on research into the histories of 700 Nottingham families since the 1950s. They found that attitudes in the home to physical punishment had scarcely changed in the period despite great changes in attitude in the media and in schools, and that the smacking or beating of children remained widespread. Their conclusions argue that such children are more likely to be troublesome adolescents or to have a criminal record by the time they are twenty.

**6001** John Springhall, Brian Fraser and Michael Hoare *Sure And Steadfast: A History of the Boys' Brigade 1883 to 1983* Collins 1983. A very good centenary history. The history of the other celebrated uniformed organization for boys is told in Henry Collis, R Hazelwood and F Huril *BP's Scouts: An Official History* Collins 1961. See also P B Nevill *Scouting In London 1908–1965* Trustees of London Scout Council 1966. On the girls' equivalent see R Kerr and Alix Liddell *Story of the Girl Guides* 2v, Girl Guides Association 1976. The history of another uniformed organization for girls is briefly told in E M Want *The Ray's Outsprung – Story of the Girls' Life Brigade* 2v, Girls' Life Brigade 1952–62.

**6002** D Prynn 'The Woodcraft Folk and the Labour Movement 1925–1970' *Journal of Contemporary History* 18 1983 pp 79–95. This youth organization was founded in 1925 as an antithesis to what was seen as the militaristic tone of the scouts.

**6003** Elizabeth Nelson *The Roots, Rise and Fall of the British Counter-Culture* Macmillan 1988. A good general study of youth cultures and their music and other attributes. Dick Hebdige *Subculture: The Meaning of Style* Methuen 1979 is a perceptive analysis of the rise and fall of successive youth cultures in the post-war period as is Paul E Willis *Profane Culture* Routledge and Kegan Paul 1978. Mike Brake *The Sociology of Youth Culture and Youth Subcultures: Sex and Drugs and Rock'n'Roll?* Routledge and Kegan Paul 1980 is a sociological analysis which is marred by its jargon-ridden style and its banal conclusions. The empirical material it contains, including research on the development of youth culture amongst the immigrant communities, is however most interesting. It also has a good bibliography. On youth cultures see also Stuart Hall and Tony Jefferson (eds) *Resistance Through Rituals: Youth Cultures in Postwar Britain* Hutchinson 1976, Iain Chambers *Urban Rhythms and Popular Culture* Macmillan 1985, Kenneth Leech *Youthquake: The Growth of a Counter-Culture Through Two Decades* Sheldon Press 1973, Paul Corrigan and Simon Frith 'The Politics of Youth Culture' *Working Papers in Cultural Studies* 7 1975 pp 231–9 and T M Beveridge 'Post-War Youth Sub-Cultures: Class, Sex and the Search for Space' Dundee MEd Thesis 1979.

**6004** Colin MacInnes *English, Half English* Macgibbon and Kee 1961. A critical examination of the development of youth culture in the 1950s, particularly in the context of two of its most important attributes, teenage consumption and pop music. See also Timothy Raison (ed) *Youth in New Society* Hart-Davis 1966.

**6005** Peter York *Style Ware* Sidgwick and Jackson 1980. A study of youth cultures 1960–80.

**6006** Frank Musgrove *Youth and the Social Order* Routledge and Kegan Paul 1964. A sociological examination of youth cultures in the early 1960s. This was followed by his *Ecstacy and Holiness: Counter Culture and the Open Society* Methuen 1974, researched in 1971–3.

**6007** Geoff Mungham and Geoff Pearson (eds) *Working Class Youth Culture* Routledge and Kegan Paul 1976. The essays in this volume cover such subjects as mods, glamrock, education, racial attitudes and sex.

**6008** Stanley Cohen *Folk Devils and Moral Panics: The Creation of the Mods and Rockers* Macgibbon and Kee 1972. A detailed study. It is better on the Rockers than the Mods. On the Mods see J Mays *The Young Pretenders* Michael Joseph 1965. Richard Barnes (comp) *Mods* Eel Pie Publishing 1979 is an essay on Mod culture supplemented by an excellent collection of photographs, press cuttings and adverts which reflect the Mods lifestyle and music.

**6009** Simon Jones *Black Culture, White Youth: The Reggae Tradition from JA to UK* Macmillan 1988. A study of the impact of Jamaican reggae culture on young white people in contemporary Britain (focusing on Birmingham). The culture of reggae, rude boys and skinheads is examined in Dick Hebdige 'Reggae, Rastas and Rudies' in James Curran, Michael Gurevitch and Janet Woollacott (eds) *Mass Communication and Society* Arnold 1977 pp 427–39.

**6010** Jim Haynes *Thanks For Coming: An Autobiography* Faber 1984. An autobiography by an American who was heavily involved in the alternative scene in Britain in the 1960s. He founded the Traverse Theatre in Edinburgh, was active on the *International Times*, ran a pioneering pornographic magazine and mixed with the rock stars of the period. This book is as much an anthology of material as a structured autobiography.

### (6) Drugs and Alcohol Abuse

### (a) Drugs

**6011** J Zacune and C Hensman *Drugs, Alcohol and Tobacco in Britain* Heinemann 1971. A concise, clear and unbiased presentation of the statistics on patterns of use.

**6012** Philip Bean *The Social Control of Drugs* Robertson 1974. The first part of this work examines the growth of the drugs control system since the 1920 Dangerous Drugs Act. The second part examines the changing social composition of the drug takers. It includes useful appendices and a chronology.

**6013** M M Glatt *et al The Drug Scene in Great Britain* Arnold 1987. A study of drugtakers and their lifestyles. Jock Young *The Drugtakers* Paladin 1971 is a sociological study. See also Sean O'Callaghan *Drug Addiction in Britain* Hale 1970 and T H Bewley 'Drug Abuse in the United Kingdom' *Addictive Diseases* 3 1977 pp 27–32.

**6014** Maurice Partridge 'Drug Addiction – A Brief Review' *International Journal of the Addictions* 2 1967 pp 207–20. An analysis of addiction 1836–1960. Since 1960 the problem has grown dramatically as the type of addict and the principal drug has changed (to heroin). The growth of addiction in the 1960s through the use of drugs, especially heroin, for non-therapeutic purposes, is examined in detail in D M Hepworth 'Addiction in Britain: Patterns of Narcotic Abuse in the Mid-Sixties' London PhD Thesis 1982. See also Philip Bean 'Drug Abuse in England and Wales Since 1900' London MSc Thesis 1970–1.

**6015** Griffith Edwards and Carol Busch (eds) *Drug Problems in Britain: A Review Of Ten Years* Academic Press 1981. A review of the problems as revealed in research 1966–76.

**6016** Richard Law *Controlled Drugs: Law and Practice* Butterworths 1984. A historical examination of the development of the legislation and the administration controlling drugs in the context of the changing patterns of drug abuse. Charles G Jeffery 'Drug Control in the United Kingdom' in Richard V Phillipson (ed) *Modern Trends in Drug Dependence and Alcoholism* Butterworths 1970 pp 60–74 is an interesting article on this subject. See also Virginia Berridge 'Drugs and Social Policy: The Establishment of Drug Control in Britain 1900–1980' *British Journal of Addiction* 79 1984 pp 17–29.

**6017** *Drug Addiction: Report of the Interdepartmental Committee* HMSO 1961. The report of the committee chaired by Sir Russell Brain. A second report, also chaired by (by then) Lord Brain, was published in 1965. The implementation of this second report is examined in Richard V Phillipson 'The Implementation of the Second Report of the Interdepartmental Committee on Drug Addiction' in Richard V Phillipson (ed) *Modern Trends in Drug Dependence and Alcoholism* Butterworths 1970 pp 75–98. The shifts in policy after the second Brain Report are assessed in Carol Smart 'Social Policy in Drug Addiction: A Critical Study of Policy Development' *British Journal of Addiction* 79 1984 pp 31–39. Developments in the late 1960s are examined in Griffith Edwards 'British Policies on Opiate Addiction: Ten Years Working of the Revised Response and Option for the Future' *British Journal of Psychiatry* 134 1979 pp 1–13.

**6018** *Advisory Council on the Misuse of Drugs: Treatment and Rehabilitation* HMSO 1982. See also *Advisory Council on the Misuse of Drugs: Prevention* HMSO 1984. Developments in British drugs policy in the 1980s are analysed in G V Stimson 'British Drug Policies in the 1980s: A Preliminary Analysis and Suggestions for Research' *British Journal of Addiction* 82 1987 pp 477–88.

**6019** W J Lanouette 'Legislative Control of Cannabis: A Comparison of the Use of Information about Cannabis by Members of the House of Commons and the US House of Representatives in the Course of Legislating for Drug Control 1969–1971' London PhD Thesis 1972–3.

**6020** *Directory of Organisations Concerned with Drug Misuse* Charities Aid Foundation 1981–. An annual directory which gives details on each organization working with drug addicts, its type of work, geographical area and foundation date. The large number of foundations, together with the foundation of the directory in the 1980s, illustrate the recent growth of the problem. The growth of drugs clinics for treating addicts is examined in the context of drugs control policy in P H Connell 'The British Experience' in P H Connell (ed) *Addicts and Drug Users: Current Approaches to the Problem* Twayne, Boston, Massachusetts 1971 pp 145–64. In addition there are a number of accounts of particular projects working with addicts. Anne Jamieson, Alan Glanz and Suzanne MacGregor *Dealing With Drug Abuse: Crisis Intervention in the City* Tavistock 1984 is a history of City Roads, a crisis intervention centre for drug takers in London set up in 1978. The story of another such project, based in a Baptist church, is told in E Blakeborough *No Quick Fix: A Church's Mission to the London Drugs Scene* Marshall Pickering 1984. There are reflections on the experience in this work of a religious community in Surrey in Sister Mildred Rebecca 'Nine Decades of Experience In the Treatment of Alcoholism and Drug Dependence' in Richard V Phillipson (ed) *Modern Trends in Drug Dependence and Alcoholism* Butterworths 1970 pp 206–22. R Yates *Out From The Shadows: Lifeline Project Tenth Anniversary Report* National Association for the Care and Resettlement of Offenders 1981 is an account of a day centre for drug addicts in Manchester. See also [2813].

**6021** J Picardie and D Wade *Heroin: Chasing the Dragon* Penguin 1985. An investigation into the rising tide of addiction to heroin since the 1960s. This includes an attempt to examine how the drug is distributed and why it is so cheap and widely available. Attempts to control the ensuing problem are analysed in G V Stimson and E Oppenheimer *Heroin Addiction: Treatment and Control in Britain* Tavistock 1982.

**6022** H B Spear 'The Growth of Heroin Addiction in the United Kingdom' *British Journal of Addiction* 64 1969 pp 245–55. An examination of the growth of heroin addiction in the 1960s.

**6023** Nicholas Dorn and Nigel South (eds) *A Land Fit for Heroin? Drug Policies, Prevention and Practice in Britain in the 1980s* Macmillan 1987. A clear account of the effects and incidence of heroin abuse, the development of policy to deal with the growing problem and the pattern of distribution of the drug. It includes a useful bibliography. There are also a number of studies of

heroin abuse in particular areas in the 1980s. Geoffrey Pearson, Mark Gibson and Shirley McIver *Young People and Heroin: An Examination of Heroin Use in the North of England* Gower 1987 is a short study. Heroin abuse in the North West and its social consequences are examined in H Parker and R Newcombe 'Heroin Use and Acquisitive Crime in an English Community' *British Journal of Sociology* 38 1987 pp 331–50. The relationship between heroin abuse and crime is also discussed in the context of the housing estates of North Southwark in A Burr 'Chasing the Dragon: Heroin Misuse, Delinquency and Crime in the Context of South London Culture' *British Journal of Criminology* 27 1984 pp 333–57. The growth of addiction on Merseyside in the 1980s is examined in H Parker, R Newcombe and K Bakx 'The New Heroin Users: Prevalence and Characteristics in Wirral, Merseyside' *British Journal of Addiction* 82 1987 pp 147–57.

**6024** Joyce M Watson *Solvent Abuse: The Adolescent Epidemic?* Croom Helm 1986. Solvent abuse emerged as a problem, especially in the inner cities, in the 1970s. This examination of solvent abuse and attempts to control is based on a study of Strathclyde.

**6025** Charles Webster 'Tobacco Smoking Addiction: A Challenge to the National Health Service' *British Journal of Addiction* 79 1984 pp 7–16. An account of policy towards smoking and the rise of the anti-tobacco lobby in the post-war years.

(b) Alcohol

Much material of value on this subject appears in the section on alcoholic beverages in the section on Industry.

**6026** *Offences of Drunkenness, England and Wales* HMSO 1950–. An annual guide to statistics of convictions for drunkenness.

**6027** Nicholas Dorn *Alcohol, Youth and the State: Drinking Practice Controls and Health Education* Croom Helm 1983. An examination of policies and practice. Health education on the consequences of alcohol is also examined in a historical context in Celia A Hudson and David J Jeremy *A Survey of Alcohol Education in the United Kingdom* Christian Economic and Social Research Foundation 1985.

**6028** R E Kendell 'The Beneficial Consequences of the United Kingdom's Declining Per Capita Consumption of Alcohol in 1979–82' *Alcohol and Alcoholism* 19 1984 pp 271–6. Consumption rose steadily in the 1970s but fell by 11 per cent during the 1979–82 recession, resulting in a fall in mortality, drink-driving and other drink related problems. An earlier study of consumption is Tony McGuinness 'An Econometric Analysis of Total Demand for Alcoholic Beverages in the UK 1956–75' *Journal of Industrial Economics* 29 1980 pp 85–109.

**6029**  Gwylmor Prys Williams *Supermarket Off-Licences and the Growth of Drunkenness Among Young Women and Young Persons Since 1966* Alliance News 1975. A short report on the development of supermarket outlets which has had a major effect on consumption patterns.

**6030**  A Hawker *Adolescents And Alcohol: Report of an Enquiry into Adolescent Drinking Patterns Carried Out From October 1975 to June 1976* Edsall 1978. A survey which helped to alert concern to a growing problem. It examines patterns of drinking and influences upon them.

**6031**  T Cook *Vagrant Alcoholics* Routledge and Kegan Paul 1975. A report on the work of the Alcoholics Recovery Project, based in South London, in 1966–74. It includes a useful bibliography.

**6031A**  Mark H C Hayler *The Vision of a Century: The United Kingdom Alliance in Historical Perspective* UK Alliance 1953. Reflections on the history of a major temperance organization. The history of another temperance organization is told in *A Century of Service 1976–1976* National British Women's Total Abstinence Union n.d. (1977?).

**6032**  Wilfred Winterton *Breath-Taking History* UK Alliance 1968. An account of the campaign to introduce the breath test as a deterrent to drunken drivers which was crowned with success in the 1967 Road Safety Act. Winterton however perhaps exaggerates his own role in the campaign. There are also reflections on this campaign and on the temperance movement (as well on banking trade unionism) in his autobiography, *Harvest Of The Years* Templar Press 1969.

**6033**  Gwylmor Prys Williams and George Thompson *Brake Drink: Ups and Downs of Methodist Attitudes to Temperance* Oliphants 1974. A critical appraisal published in the year that the Methodist conference decided to make temperance a matter of individual conscience for its church members. The main development in Methodist witness on temperance witness since then is the report *Through A Glass Darkly* Division of Social Responsibility, Methodist Church 1987.

## (7) Communes

**6034**  Andrew Digby *Alternative Realities: A Study of Communes and their Members* Routledge and Kegan Paul 1974. A study of a whole variety of communes,

from the political to the religious, and of their history and salient characteristics. See also his *Communes in Britain* Routledge and Kegan Paul 1974.

## H. HOUSING

### (1) General

**6035**  *British Housing and Planning Yearbook* National Housing and Town Planning Council 1950–. An annual directory and guide. *Housing Year Book* Longman 1983– is a directory of organizations involved in housing and other interested bodies. Another annual directory is *Institute of Housing Yearbook* Institute of Housing 1953–61.

**6036**  Mary Smith *Guide To Housing* 2nd ed, Housing Centre Trust 1977. An informative guide to all aspects of contemporary British housing. It includes a useful bibliography. T Newson and P Potter *Housing Policy In Britain: An Information Sourcebook* Mansell 1984 is a good guide to the sources of housing information and their issuing bodies. See also Department of the Environment/Department of Transport *Library Sources of Information on Housing* HMSO 1979. Michael Norton *Housing* Wildwood House 1981 is a guide to alternative, non-governmental, sources of information.

**6037**  W V Hole and M T Poutney *Trends in Population, Housing and Occupancy Rates 1861–1971* HMSO 1971. A statistical examination of the long-term trends in housing tenure. See also Alan S Murie *Housing Tenure in Britain: A Review of Survey Evidence 1958–71* Centre for Urban and Regional Studies Research Memorandum 30, University of Birmingham 1974.

**6038**  *Housing and Construction Statistics* HMSO 1972–. This replaced *Housing Statistics and Monthly Bulletin of Construction Statistics*. It is a quarterly and annual statistical guide to housing policy, finance and construction. See also *Housing Statistics* Institute of Municipal Treasurers and Accountants 1951–.

**6039**  Pat Ellender *Housing in Britain* Department of the Environment/Department of Transport Library 1975. An extensive and well annotated and classified bibliography covering all aspects of British housing. There was a supplement published in 1979 covering material published 1975–8. Tony Newson *Housing Policy: An International Bibliography* Mansell 1986 is a classified bibliography whose ambit is much wider than its title would suggest. It is annotated to some extent. John M Stewart *et al A Housing Bibliography* Centre for Urban and Regional Studies, University of Birmingham 1980 covers work published up to 1980. Though unannotated it does point out which periodicals carry literature on housing and housing policy. It is updated by T Newson *A Housing Bibliography* Centre for Urban and Regional Studies, University of Birmingham 1982. Department of the Environment/Department of Transport *Library Housing Publications 1971–1981* HMSO 1983 is a listing of the publications in this period of the government departments responsible for housing and housing policy in England and Wales.

**6040** AREA INFORMATION SERVICES 1983–. A database on local authority and Housing Corporation housing programmes in England run by the Faculty of Construction, Liverpool Polytechnic.

**6041** John Short *Housing In Britain: The Post-War Experience* Methuen 1982. A concise and clear history. Martin J Daunton *A Property-Owning Democracy? Housing In Britain* Faber 1987 is an excellent overview placing the policy problems and objectives of the 1980s in a long historical context. The inadequacies of British housing provision and policy since 1919 are critically assessed in Fred Berry *Housing: The Great British Failure* Knight 1974. The private rented, public and owner-occupied sectors of the housing market in the period 1945–72 are examined in Roger H Duclaud-Williams *The Politics of Housing in Britain and France* Heinemann 1978. John Burnett *A Social History of Housing 1815–1985* 2nd ed, David and Charles 1986 examines the social history of the development of mass housing for the middle and working classes. The final part deals with the period since 1918. The social dimension of housing is also examined in the essays in M Edwards, F Gray, S Merrett and J Swann (eds) *Housing and Class in Britain* Political Economy of Housing Workshop, London 1975, which look at subjects such as high rise housing or inner area gentrification.

**6042** Herbert Ashworth *Housing In Great Britain* Skinner 1957. A good survey of housing developments, supply and demand in the 1950s. The appendix provides a guide to post-war legislation.

**6043** Frank Allaun *No Place Like Home: Britain's Housing Tragedy (from the Victims' View) and How to Overcome It* Deutsch 1972. A critical assessment of recent housing policy and commentary on poor quality housing, often in the words of those who dwell in such accommodation with a series of recommendations.

**6044** Peter Malpass (ed) *The Housing Crisis* Croom Helm 1986. This identifies a growing housing crisis and shortage in the 1970s and 1980s as a result of declining public expenditure and the deterioration of housing stock. It critically reviews government policy, not least the privatization programme and the encouragement of owner-occupation, which have been pursued whilst at the margins of the housing market the young and the elderly have faced difficulties in entering the market and there has been a considerable increase in homelessness. The growing inbalance between supply and demand for housing in the 1970s is traced in M Fleming and J Nellis 'A New Housing Crisis?' *Lloyds Bank Review* 144 1982 pp 38–53.

**6045** E Corrales Roa 'Housing Policy and the Building Industry in Postwar Britain' Edinburgh MPhil Thesis 1981. A study of the relation between the construction industry and housing starts, local authority housing provision and the cost of private sector housing.

**6046** A Arden and M Partington *Housing Law* Sweet and Maxwell 1983 (with periodic updating supplements since). A compendious account of the state of the law.

**6047** Alan Murie *Housing Inequality and Deprivation* Heinemann Educational 1983. A study of over-crowding and poor quality housing.

**6048** *Local Housing Statistics* HMSO 1967–. A quarterly guide to house-building in England and Wales. It replaced *Housing Returns for England and Wales*.

**6049** Valerie A Karn *Aycliffe Housing Survey: A Study of Housing in a New Town* Centre for Urban and Regional Studies 9, University of Birmingham 1970. She has also conducted surveys of housing in *Stevenage Housing Survey: A Study of Housing in a New Town* Centre for Urban and Regional Studies 10, University of Birmingham 1970, and *Crawley Housing Survey: A Study of Housing in a New Town* Centre for Urban and Regional Studies 11, University of Birmingham 1970.

**6050** A G S Fidler 'Post-War Housing in Birmingham' *Town Planning Review* 25 1955 pp 25–47.

**6051** P J Shoebridge 'The Nature and Location of Post-War Housing Development in the Coalfield Area of County Durham' Durham PhD Thesis 1969–70.

**6052** M M Griffiths 'The Housing of Ipswich 1840–1973' Essex PhD Thesis 1985. An account of the development and implementation of housing policy in the borough.

**6053** R Bradbury 'Post-War Housing in Liverpool' *Town Planning Review* 27 1957 pp 145–63.

**6054** J Barelli *et al London Housing Statistics* London Research Centre Housing and Surveys Group 1987. A detailed guide to sources of information and their issuing bodies.

**6055** *Housing in Greater London: Report of the Committee* Cmnd 2605, *Parliamentary Papers* xvii 1964–65. The report of the committee set up under Sir Milner

Holland in the wake of the scandal over the private rented properties of Perec Rachman in 1963. It argued that the private rented sector needed to be encouraged but that the law on landlords needed to be tightened. It also found that the post-war decanting of population to the new towns had failed to solve London's housing problems. The relationship between the new town programme and housing in London is examined in B J Heraud 'The New Towns and London's Housing Problem' *Urban Studies* 3 1966 pp 8–21. One of the consequences was inner area population decline as examined in J M Dobson 'population Decline and Housing Policy in Central London, with Special Reference to Holborn 1945–1975' London PhD Thesis 1982. Developments in the wake of the Milner Holland Report, especially in terms of the policies of the Greater London Council, are charted in G H Taylor *A Review of Housing in London 1966–1976* GLC 1978. It also looks at changes in housing standards and stock. Changes in housing tenure in London are examined in Chris Hamnett and Bill Randolph 'The Changing Structure of the Greater London Housing Market 1961–1981' *London Journal* 9 1983 pp 153–64.

**6056** *North Shields: Working Class Politics and Housing 1900–1977* North Tyneside Community Development Project 1978. A short study.

### (2) Design

**6057** E R Scoffham *The Shape of British Housing* George Godwin 1984. A study of domestic architecture since 1945 in terms of its planning and its social impact rather than from an architectural or aesthetic point of view. Designs between 1952–77 are critically assessed in S Pepper 'The People's House' *Architectural Review* 96 1977 pp 269–73.

**6058** A Powers and C Aslet *The National Trust Book of the English House* Viking 1985. A well illustrated guide to domestic architecture since the middle ages.

**6059** S Martin Gaskell *Model Housing From the Great Exhibition to the Festival of Britain* Mansell 1987. A good study.

**6060** Alice Coleman *Utopia On Trial: Vision and Reality in Planned Housing* Hilary Shipman 1985. A critical examination of post-war planning. It argues that leaving the design and planning to bureaucrats and architects without consultation with the occupants themselves has led to the inhuman, decaying estates of the 1950s and 1960s, rife with social problems and crime. C Ward 'Community architecture: What a time it took for the penny to drop' *Built Environment* 13 1987 pp 7–14 is a condemnation of the post-war experiments in social engineering of the architects and planners of housing and

welcomes the return towards human scale domestic architecture in the 1980s. E R Scoffham 'Xenophobic Housing' *International Journal of Housing Science* 9 1985 pp 15–28 emphasizes the alien nature of much post-war housing design and calls for a return to the enduringly popular vernacular architecture.

**6061** Department of the Environment Housing Development Directorate *An Investigation of Difficult to Let Housing* 3v, HMSO 1980–81. An inquiry into the defects that make particular council estates difficult to let. Volume 1 covers general findings. Volume 2 is a collection of case studies of seven post-war estates. Defects identified include poor design, high density, poor sound insulation, anonymous public spaces, drab presentation and inhuman scale and poor maintenance. Volume 3 examines the defects of five selected pre-war estates. Another useful survey is *Defects In Housing* 3v, Association of Metropolitan Authorities 1983–85. The first examines the defects of non-traditional dwellings of the 1940s and 1950s. The second deals with industrial and system built dwellings of the 1960s and 1970s and the third with repair and modernization of traditional built buildings.

**6062** A E Power 'The Development of Unpopular Council Housing Estates and Attempted Remedies 1895–1984' London PhD Thesis 1985. The first part of this thesis examines the history of the unpopular estates, both in terms of their design and of the lettings policy adopted by the councils. The second part discusses the realization of the problem in the 1970s whilst the third assesses attempts since then to improve unpopular estates. F E A Down 'The Clearance of Purpose Built Local Authority Estates in Britain' London MPhil Thesis 1983 is an investigation of the defects of unpopular estates based on fourteen case studies. P J Taylor *'Difficult to Let'*, *'Difficult to Live in'* and sometimes *'Difficult to get out of': An Essay on Provision of Council Housing with Special Reference to Killingworth* Centre for Urban and Regional Studies Discussion Papers 16, University of Newcastle 1978 is a study of an estate on Tyneside.

**6063** R S Haynes 'Design and Image in English Urban Housing 1945–1957' London MPhil Thesis 1976.

**6064** D Crawford *A Decade of British Houses 1963–1973* Architectural Press 1975. A study of design and provision in this period.

**6065** *Homes for Today and Tomorrow: Report of a Sub-Committee of the Central Housing Advisory Committee* HMSO 1961. This report, by the committee chaired by Sir Parker Morris, led to the establishment of new housing standards. Subsequent developments, not least the relaxation of standards in the 1980s, are reviewed in B Goodchild and R Furbey 'Standards in Housing Design: A Review of the Main Changes Since the Parker Morris Report (1961)' *Land Development Studies* 3 1986 pp 79–99.

**6066** B D Finnimore 'The Industrialisation of Building: Building Systems and Social Housing in Welfare Britain 1942–1975' London PhD Thesis 1986. A study of the politics, design and construction of mass produced, system built housing of the post-war period. See also R C Mullick 'Techniques of Mass Production used in Local Authority Housing in England 1946–56' Liverpool MArch Thesis 1963–4.

**6067** Oonagh Gay 'Prefabs: A Study in Policy Making' *Public Administration* 65 1987 pp 407–22. A critical study of the planning and administration of the programme of construction of prefabricated houses to replace bomb-damaged ones in 1946–8.

**6068** Brian Finnimore 'The AIROH House: Industrial Diversification and State Building Policy' *Construction History* 1 1985 pp 60–71. The Aircraft Industries Research Organisation for Housing was established during the Second World War and during the period of great scarcity after the war its aluminium housing was used until priorities changed and the government withdrew its subsidies.

**6069** C Bacon *The Rise and Fall of Deck Access Housing* Department of Town and Regional Planning, University of Sheffield 1986. A history of the development of such estates, the theories which led to their popularity with architects and the reasons for their increasing decline and demolition.

**6070** J Lever *Home Sweet Home: Housing Designed by the London County Council and Greater London Architects 1888–1975* Academy Editions 1976. A study of municipal domestic architecture in the London area.

### (3) Housing Policy

### (a) Central Government Policy

**6071** A E Holmans *Housing Policy in Britain: A History* Croom Helm 1987. A history of twentieth century housing policy emphasizing its economic and financial aspects. Policy since 1918 is assessed in Alan Murie, Pat Niner and Christopher Walton *Housing Policy and the Housing System* Allen and Unwin 1976. Peter Malpass and Alan Murie *Housing Policy and Practice* 2nd ed, Macmillan 1987 is a good textbook examining post-war housing policy. P N Balchin *Housing Policy and Housing Needs* Macmillan 1981 is a useful overview of all aspects of housing policy. Another good recent textbook is David V Donnison and Clare Ungerson *Housing Policy* Penguin 1982. This is a total rewrite of David V Donnison *The Government of Housing* Penguin 1967, necessitated by the transformation of the policy formation environment and the disappearance of the post-war consensus in the intervening period. See also David V Donnison *Housing Policy Since the War* Codicote Press 1960.

**6072** John Barry Cullingworth *Essays On Housing Policy: The British Scene* Allen and Unwin 1979. A series of case studies.

**6073** John Barry Cullingworth *Housing and Local Government in England and Wales* Allen and Unwin 1966. A detailed historical study and analysis of the contemporary role of local government in housing policy.

**6074** Lawrence R Murphy 'Rebuilding Britain: The Government's Role in Housing and Town Planning 1945–1957' *The Historian* 32 1970 pp 410–27. A rather shallow analysis. The policy of the 1945–51 Attlee government is examined in detail in J A Chenier 'The Development and Implementation of Post-War Housing Policy under the Labour Government' Oxford DPhil Thesis 1984.

**6075** *Housing Corporation Annual Report and Accounts* HMSO 1964–72. In this period this report was published as a House of Commons Paper. Since 1972/73 it has been published by the Housing Corporation.

**6076** R Thomas 'The 1972 Housing Finance Act and the Demise of the New Town and Local Authority Housing Programmes' *Urban Law and Policy* 5 1982 pp 107–26. The abolition of subsidies for council housing under this Act provoked fierce resentment which is examined in L Sklair 'The Struggle against the Housing Finance Act' *Socialist Register* 1975 pp 250–92. The most celebrated of these struggles, involving the councillors of Clay Cross in Derbyshire, is described in Dennis Skinner and Julia Langdon *The Story of Clay Cross* Spokesman 1974. See also Austin Mitchell 'Clay Cross' *Political Quarterly* 1974. Richard Minns 'The Significance of Clay Cross: Another Look at District Audit' *Policy and Politics* 2 1973–74 pp 303–29 looks at the role of the district auditor and the process of surcharging in the context of the surcharging of the Clay Cross councillors in 1973 for not implementing the 1972 Housing Finance Act.

**6077** Stephanie Cooper *Public Housing and Private Property* 1970–1984 Gower 1985. An examination of the changing philosophy and provisions of the 1972, 1975 and 1980 Housing Acts and an exploration of the state's role in housing provision in relation to theories of property.

**6078** A Kirby 'The Housing Corporation 1974–1979: An Example of State Housing Policy in Britain' *Environment and Planning A* 13 1981 pp 1295–1303. A study of the Corporation's activities with particular reference to regional shortfalls in local government housing provision. The Housing Corporation's policy in the 1970s is also examined, particularly with respect to its responsibilities in the field of improvement policy, in D J Noble 'Imperfect Administration: A Study of the Implementation of the 1974 Housing Act by the Housing Corporation' Birmingham MSocSci Thesis 1979–80.

**6079** R Prentice 'The Governance of British Public-Housing Investment in the Late 1970s: Central Encouragement of Comparative Local Diversity' *Environment and Planning C: Government and Policy* 2 1984 pp 325–41. This argues that this happened particularly in Wales.

**6080** P Hall 'Housing, Planning, Land and Local Finance: The British Experience' *Urban Law and Policy* 6 1983 pp 75–83. An examination of the policy changes under the Thatcher government and particularly of the provisions of the 1980 Housing Act. Another general examination of housing policy under Thatcher is C Whitehead 'Housing under the Conservatives: A Policy Assessment' *Public Money* 3 1983 pp 15–21.

**6081** Ray Forrest and Alan Murie *Selling the Welfare State: The Privatisation of Council Housing* Routledge and Kegan Paul 1987. A study of the policy of council house sales which has been one of the most important facets of housing policy under Thatcher, the ensuing social and economic effects and the geography and variety of local approaches to the sales. The evolution and implementation of this policy is evaluated in the context of post-war council housing policy in B Barker 'The Sale of Council Houses: A Housing Policy and Political Issue' Oxford Polytechnic MSc Thesis 1980. Its impact of the policy is assessed in A D H Crook 'Privatisation of Housing and the Impact of the Conservative Government's Initiatives on Low-Cost Homeownership and Private Renting Between 1979 and 1984 in England and Wales: The Privatisation Policies' *Environment and Planning A* 18 1986 pp 639–59, 827–36. The introduction of this policy and the philosophy behind it is critically assessed in Michael Harloe and Chris Paris 'The Decollection of Consumption: Housing and Local Government Finance in England and Wales 1979–1981' in Ivan Szelenyi (ed) *Cities in Recession: Critical Responses to the Urban Policies of the New Right* Sage 1984 pp 70–98. The variations in policy on council house sales depending on the political control of the local authority, with many local Labour councils initially resisting outright the right to buy enshrined in the 1980 Housing Act, are examined in K Hoggart 'Political Party Control and the Sale of Local Authority Dwellings 1974–1983' *Environment and Planning C:*

*Government and Policy* 3 1985 pp 463–74. The resulting pattern of sales was rather uneven. Richard Dunn, Ray Forrest and Alan Murie 'The Geography of Council House Sales in England 1979–1985' *Urban Studies* 24 1987, pp 47–59 suggests that sales were highest in areas which already had high levels of owner-occupation. See also K Bassett 'The Sale of Council Houses as a Political Issue' *Policy and Politics* 8 1980 pp 290–307.

**6082** J McHugh 'The Labour Party and the Politics of Housing 1918–1963' Salford MSc Thesis 1975.

**6083** B Stafford and J Doling *Rent Control and Rent Regulation in England and Wales 1915–80* Centre for Urban and Regional Studies Occasional Papers 2, University of Birmingham 1981. An overview of policy. P Beirre *Fair Rent and Legal Fiction: Housing Rent Legislation in a Capitalist Society* Macmillan 1977 is a Marxist critique of the state regulation of rents up to the 1972 Housing Finance Act.

**6084** M J Barnett *The Politics of Legislation: The Rent Act 1957* Weidenfeld and Nicolson 1969. A good study of the framing and passage of a controversial piece of legislation which removed some rent controls and allowed rent increases in the hope of encouraging private landlords to repair properties and put more houses on the private rented market. The effects of the Act are examined in the context of the expectations at the the time of its passage in David V Donnison, Claud Cockburn and T Corlett *Housing Since the Rent Act* Occasional Papers on Social Administration 3, University of London 1961.

**6085** L Reynolds *Some Effects of the 1974 Rent Act in London* Middlesex Polytechnic 1977. An assessment of the impact of the Act, which was designed to give security of tenure to tenants of private rented furnished accommodation.

**6086** D A Kirby *Slum Housing and Residential Renewal: The Case in Urban Britain* Longman 1979. A study of the achievements of British governments in the field of slum clearance since 1918. John English, Ruth Madigan and Peter Norman *Slum Clearance: The Social and Administrative Context in England and Wales* Croom Helm 1976 is a collection of case studies and studies of the attitudes of residents. Slum clearance in Sunderland 1930–70 is examined in Norman Dennis *People and Planning: The Sociology of Housing in Sunderland* Faber 1970. Aspects of slum clearance in Leeds are discussed in R Wilkinson 'A Statistical Analysis of Attitudes to Moving' *Urban Studies* 2 1965 pp 1–14.

**6087** E F Derrick *House and Area Improvement in Britain: Bibliography and Abstracts* Centre for Urban and Regional Studies, University of Birmingham 1976. Housing improvement policy, particularly since the 1960s, is examined in K Cook 'Housing Improvement

Policy in Britain 1949–1979' *International Journal for Housing Science* 7 1983 pp 65–83. A local study of the implementation of housing improvement policy is C H Balch 'The Development of Housing Improvement Policies in England and Wales, with Special Reference to Newcastle-upon-Tyne' Edinburgh MPhil Thesis 1976. The main pieces of post-war legislation affecting improvement policy are the 1969 and 1974 Housing Acts. On the 1969 Act see D W Smith 'The Housing Act 1969: Local House Improvement Policies and Practice' Birmingham PhD Thesis 1979–80. T L C Duncan *Housing Improvement Policies in England and Wales* Centre for Urban and Regional Studies 28, University of Birmingham 1973 is a commentary on the effects of the 1969 Act and the subsequent establishment of General Improvement Areas, drawing on detailed case studies of Coventry, Plymouth and Winchester. On the implementation of the 1974 Act by the Housing Corporation see [6078]. The 1974 Act also set up Housing Action Areas. These are assessed in Elizabeth Mary Monck *Housing Action Areas: Success and Failure* Centre for Environment Studies, London 1980, A Kirby *Housing Action Areas in Great Britain 1975–1977* Department of Geography Paper 60, University of Reading 1977, Chris Paris 'Housing Action Areas' *Roof* 2 1977 pp 9–14 and E C Higgins 'Improvement Policy and Access to Housing: A Study of the Part played by Housing Action Areas' East Anglia PhD Thesis 1984. The latter includes a case study of the Housing Action Area set up in Islington. The impact of the Housing Action Area in inner Bristol is assessed in J R Short and K A Bassett 'Housing Improvement in the Inner City: A Case Study of Changes Before and After the 1974 Housing Act' *Urban Studies* 15 1978 pp 333–42 and also in their 'Housing Policy and the Inner City in the 1970s' *Transactions of the Institute of British Geographers* n.s. 6 1981 pp 293–312. A D Thomas *Area Based Renewal: Three Years in the Life of a Housing Action Area* Centre for Urban and Regional Studies, University of Birmingham 1979 is a lengthy report on the Beeches Road Housing Action Area in Sandwell. See also G Lomas Clough *Street Housing Action Area, Burnley, Lancashire: A Case Study* Centre for Environmental Studies, London 1978 and N F Rowe 'Housing and Environmental Improvements in the Inner City: A Case Study of a Housing Action Area in Birmingham, Little Green, Small Heath' Edinburgh MPhil Thesis 1979.

**6088**   A A Nevitt *Housing Taxation and Subsidies: A Study of Housing in the United Kingdom* Nelson 1966. An historical examination of these financial provisions and the policy that guides them.

**(b) Local Government Policy**

**6089**   Pat Niner *Local Authority Housing Policy and Practice – A Case Study Approach* Centre for Urban and Regional Studies 31, University of Birmingham 1975. Detailed analyses of policy in West Bromwich, Warley, Wolverhampton, Halesowen, Stafford and Ludlow.

**6090**   S P Morgan 'Local Housing and Planning Policies: A Study of the South Coast of England 1961–1971' London PhD Thesis 1977.

**6091**   Owen A Hartley 'Housing Policy in Four Lincolnshire Towns 1919–59' Oxford DPhil Thesis 1969–70.

**6092**   P A T Goodwin 'Housing Needs and Planning Policy in Greater London 1945–1971' Edinburgh MSc Thesis 1970–1. Ken Young and J Kramer *Strategy and Conflict in Metropolitan Housing: Suburbia versus the Greater London Council 1964–75* Heinemann 1978 evaluates the GLC strategy of opening out suburbia to the inner urban poor and its eventual failure as a result of opposition from the suburban local authorities.

## (4) Housing Pressure Groups

**6093**   M Brynin 'Young Homeless: Pressure Groups, Politics and the Press' *Youth Policy* 20 1987 pp 24–34. In 1986 the Board and Lodging Information Programme was set up as part of a response to a rapid growth in the numbers of young homeless people and changes in the benefit system. This article focuses upon this new body and its work.

**6094**   *Ten Years of Campaigning for Single Homeless People* Campaign for the Homeless and Rootless 1982. A short review of the work of the Campaign.

**6095**   J Morton *A Decade of Housing Aid: SHAC 1970/1980* Shelter Housing Aid Centre 1980. An account of the development and work of the housing aid and advice centre run by Shelter in London. Patrick Seyd 'Shelter: The National Campaign for the Homeless' *Political Quarterly* 46 1975 pp 418–31 is a study of Shelter as a pressure group.

## (5) Homelessness

**6096**   Lionel Rose *'Rogues and Vagabonds': Vagrant Underworld in Britain 1815–1985* Routledge 1988. An investigation of government and social attitudes to vagrants. It does not sufficiently examine the causes of vagrancy. Jeremy Sandford *Down and Out in Britain* Peter Owen 1971 is a report on the conditions of the homeless. It does reflect on some of the causes of homelessness and on how they are treated by the social services. He researched for it, in part, by living among homeless people. Another examination of the experience of homelessness is Alan S Murie and Syd Jeffers (eds) *Living in Bed and Breakfast: The Experience of Homelessness in London* School for Advanced Urban Studies 71, University of Bristol 1987. T Wilkinson *Down and Out* Quartet 1981 is an account of a month spent living as a tramp in London. See also [2734].

**6097**  Jeremy Sandford *Cathy Come Home* Pan 1967. This is based on his influential television play of the same name on the plight of homeless young people. The play was first broadcast in 1966.

**6098**  Ron Bailey and Joan Ruddock *The Grief Report* Denny Brothers 1972. A report on temporary accommodation provision and those who use it for the housing pressure group Shelter.

**6099**  M Martin 'A Study of the Relationship between Homelessness and Housing Policy at both National and Local Levels in England and Wales Since 1948' Manchester MA (Econ) Thesis 1968–9.

**6100**  Patricia J Woodward and Elizabeth M Davidge 'Homelessness Four Years on' *Journal of Planning and Environment Law* 1982 pp 158–67. A study of how the good intentions of the 1977 Housing (Homeless Persons) Act were being lost in the interpretations being placed upon it in the courts and the resulting effect on provisions for homeless people. See also P F Smith 'The Housing (Homeless Persons) Act 1977 – Four Years On' *Journal of Planning and Environment Law* 1982 pp 143–57.

**6101**  Valerie A Karn *No Place That's Home: A Report on Accommodation for Homeless Young People in Birmingham* Centre for Urban and Regional Studies 32, University of Birmingham 1974.

**6102**  John M Stewart *Of No Fixed Abode: Vagrancy and the Welfare State* Manchester University Press 1975. An examination of policy on and administrative provision for homeless people in the North West of England since 1948.

**6103**  A M Dale 'Homeless Families in a London Borough: A Case Study of Policy and Practice from 1965–1972' London MPhil Thesis 1977.

### (6) Squatting

**6104**  Chris Paris and Gerry Popplestone *Squatting: A Bibliography* Centre for Environmental Studies, London

1978. A short list of material, including newspaper articles, to have appeared on the issue in the 1970s.

**6105**  Ron Bailey *The Squatters* Penguin 1973.

**6106**  James Hinton 'Self-Help and Socialism: The Squatters Movement of 1946' *History Workshop* 25 1988 pp 100–26. After the war there was a great shortage of housing. This looks at the organized squatting in disused army camps and empty housing that resulted, the role of the Communist Party in this and the Attlee government's reaction to it.

**6107**  A Franklin *Squatting in England 1969–79: A Case Study of Social Conflict in Advanced Industrial Capitalism* School for Advanced Urban Studies, University of Bristol 1984. There was a substantial growth in squatting in the 1970s, especially in London. This process and the attempt, in the 1977 Criminal Law Act, to deal with the problem is examined in Chris Paris and Gerry Popplestone 'Squatting and the Criminal Law Act: Problem or Solution' *Centre for Environmental Studies Review* 2 1977 pp 38–45.

### (7) Types of Housing

#### (a) High-Rise

**6108**  Anthony Sutcliffe (ed) *Multi-Storey Living: The British Working Class Experience* Croom Helm 1974. A collection of essays on the sociology of high-rise housing since the middle of the eighteenth century.

**6109**  Patrick Dunleavy *The Politics of Mass-Housing in Britain 1945–1975: A Study of Corporate Power and Professional Influence in the Welfare State* Oxford University Press 1981. A study of the interests influencing the development of post-war high-rise building in this period. It includes case studies of the influence of planners on policy in Newham, Birmingham and Bristol. The reasons for the vogue in high-rise developments and for its eventual rejection are analysed in Joan Ash 'The Rise and Fall of High-Rise Housing in England' in Clare Ungerson and Valerie Karn (eds) *The Consumer Experience of Housing* Gower 1980 pp 93–123. See also W V Hole 'The Origin and Development of High Density Housing Policies in the UK 1945–1970' *Planning History Bulletin* 3 1981 pp 2–6 and R McCutcheon 'High Flats in Britain 1945 to 1971: Factors Affecting their use by Local Authorities and some of the Implications' Sussex MSc Thesis 1972.

**6110**  E Gittus *Flats, Families and the Under Fives* Routledge and Kegan Paul 1976. A study of the problems of bringing up young children in high-rise local authority housing in Tyneside in the 1960s.

## (b) Public-Rented Housing

Literature on policy developments affecting public sector housing, and not least the privatization programme under the Conservatives in the 1980s, can also be found above in the section on Housing Policy.

**6111** Stephen Merrett *State Housing in Britain* Routledge and Kegan Paul 1979. A review of policy and the development of council estates since the First World War. David Whitham 'The First Sixty Years of Council Housing' in John English (ed) *The Future of Council Housing* Croom Helm 1982 pp 9–33 briefly surveys the development of policy and legislation over the same period. See also J A Dales 'Public Housing, England and Wales 1919–1969' London PhD Thesis 1977. Policy since 1945 is examined in Peter Malpass 'The Development of Public Housing Policy in Britain: A Study of Continuity and Change in the Modernisation of Housing Tenure' Bristol PhD Thesis 1986. This argues, in contrast with those who feel that the privatization programme of the 1980s marks a clear break with earlier post-war policy, that there has been considerable continuity in government attitudes since the 1950s.

**6112** Anne Power *Property Before People: The Management of Twentieth Century Council Housing* Unwin Hyman 1987. A detailed study which argues that councils concentrated on management of property and not on responding to people's needs.

**6113** Alan S Murie and Ray Forrest *Monitoring the Right to Buy 1972–1982* School for Advanced Urban Studies 40, University of Bristol 1984. A study of the sale of council houses to their tenants, greatly encouraged by the policy of the Thatcher government in the 1980s.

**6114** Patricia L Garside 'Intergovernmental Relations and Housing Policy in London 1919–1970 with Special Reference to the Density and Location of Council Housing' *London Journal* 9 1983 pp 39–57. The history of council housing in different parts of London is told in *East End Housing: A Review of the LCC's Post-War Housing Achievements in Bethnal Green, Poplar and Stepney* London County Council 1963 and Neil McIntosh *Housing for the Poor? Council Housing in Southwark 1925–1975* Southwark Community Development Project 1975.

**6115** *History of the Growth and Location of the Corporation Housing Schemes* Sheffield City Council 1959.

**6116** C L Andrews *Tenants and Town Hall* Department of the Environment 1979. A detailed study of relations between the tenants' group and the local housing department on an inner London estate. A Power *Holloway Tenant Co-operative Five Years On* Holloway Tenant Co-operative 1977 is an account of the history and current activities of this London tenants' body. Tenants' organizations in Sheffield are examined in P A Baldock 'Tenants' Voice: A Study of Council Tenants' Organisations, with Particular Reference to those in the City of Sheffield 1961–71' Sheffield PhD Thesis 1971.

## (c) Private Rented Housing

The literature on developments in rent control and regulation designed to affect the private rented sector is in the section on Housing Policy.

**6117** M Davies *Public Control of Private Rented Housing* Gower 1984. An examination of the gradual decline of this type of housing since 1945 and of the legislation and regulations that govern it. It includes a detailed investigation of the implementation of fair rents legislation. The decline of this sector in the face of policies designed to encourage wider home ownership is also examined in John Short 'Decline of the British Landlord' *Geographical Magazine* 53 1981 pp 787–92.

**6118** S Cooper *Public Housing and Private Property 1970–1984* Gower 1985. An evaluation of attempts to revive the private rented sector during this period.

**6119** J Greve *Private Landlords in England* Bell 1965. A sociological study of landlords and their reasons for acquiring property for rent. S Green *Rachman* Michael Joseph 1971 is a biography of Perec Rachman, who became so notorious for his exploitation of his slum property tenants that a new word, Rachmanism, was coined to describe this.

**6120** L M Clements 'The "Demise" of Tied Cottages – Rent (Agriculture) Act 1976' *The Conveyancer and Property Lawyer* 42 1978 pp 259–76. Tied cottages are rented out to the tenant so long as he employed by the farmer. This is an account of an attempt to end this practice.

**6121** Chris Hamnett and Bill Randolph *Cities, Housing and Profits: Flat Break-up and the Decline of Private Renting* Hutchinson 1988. A study of an aspect of the decline of the private rented sector in London. It was more profitable to sell off flats than to rent them. The decline of the private rented sector and its consequences are also analysed in Malcolm S Allen 'A Future in Private Renting' *Built Environment* 2 1976 pp 298–304.

**6122** D Burn *Rent Strike St Pancras 1960* Pluto 1972. A detailed account. See also David Mathieson *The St Pancras Rent Strike 1960: A Study in Consensus Politics* Labour Heritage 1977.


### (d) Owner-Occupied Housing


**6123** *Homes, People, Prices and Places* Abbey National Building Society 1978–. A quarterly guide to price movements in each region, changes in the availability of property and the structure of demand. It includes commentaries on trends in the housing market.


**6124** Stephen Merrett and F Gray *Owner-Occupation in Britain* Routledge and Kegan Paul 1982. A description of the changing housing market and profile of owner-occupiers since 1918 and of the principal influences upon them, notably government policy and the actions of the building societies. On the post-war housing market see A J Cornford 'The Market for Owned Houses in England and Wales Since 1945' Oxford DPhil Thesis 1976 and G Hadjimatheou *Housing and Mortgage Markets: The UK Experience* Saxon House 1976.


**6125** Colin Jones 'The Demand for Home Ownership' in John English (ed) *The Future of Council Housing* Croom Helm 1982 pp 115–31. An examination of the demand for ownership amongst former council tenants at the height of the Thatcher government's privatization programme.


**6126** P B Fairest *Mortgages* 2nd ed, Sweet and Maxwell 1980. A good legal textbook. An earlier textbook which remains of use to historians is C H M W Waldock *The Law of Mortgages* 2nd ed, Stevens/Sweet and Maxwell 1950.


**6127** K A Bassett and J R Short 'Patterns of Building Society and Local Authority Mortgage Lending in the 1970s' *Environment and Planning A* 12 1980 pp 279–300.


**6128** John Doling, Janet Ford and Bruce Stafford (eds) *The Property-Owning Democracy* Avebury 1988. An examination of the nature and causes of the growing mortgage arrears in the 1980s.


**6129** M C Fleming and J G Nellis *House Price Statistics for the United Kingdom: A Survey and Critical Review of Recent Developments* Department of Economics, University of Loughborough 1984. A study of the surge in house prices in the 1970s and 1980s. The influence of the building societies on this process is examined in D G Mayes *The Property Boom: The Effects of Building Society Behaviour on House Prices* Robertson 1979. Regional variations in the house price rise are analysed in Chris Hamnett 'Regional Variations in House Prices and House Price Inflation 1969–1981' *Area* 15 1983 pp 97–109 and I D McAvinchey and D Maclennan 'A Regional Comparison of House Price Inflation Rates in Britain 1967–76' *Urban Studies* 19 1982 pp 43–57. The role of housing quality in price movements 1900–70 is assessed with respect to Doncaster and Halifax in R K Williamson 'The Quality of Housing and the Measurement of Long-Term Changes in Prices' *Urban Studies* 13 1976 pp 273–84.


**6130** M J Vipond 'Fluctuations in Private Housebuilding in Great Britain 1950–1966' *Scottish Journal of Political Economy* 16 1969 pp 196–211.


**6131** D Jachnick *House Prices in the GLC Area 1939–1971* Department of Geography, University of Reading 1978. A commentary which contrasts prices in greater London in 1939 with those of 1967–71.


**6132** Edward Craven 'Private Residential Expansion in Kent 1956–64: A Study of Patterns and Process in Urban Growth' *Urban Studies* 6 1969 pp 1–16. This concentrates on the strategy of the developers who were building these residential developments.


### (e) Second Homes


**6133** C L Bielckus, A W Rogers and G P Wibberley *Second Homes in England and Wales: A Study of the Distribution and Use of Rural Properties Taken Over as Second Residences* Studies in Rural Land Use 11, Wye College, University of London 1972. A major study commissioned by the Countryside Commission in 1968 analysing the implications of the growing trend towards rural second homes. The implications are also examined in J T Coppock (ed) *Second Homes: Curse or Blessing?* Pergamon 1977. See also C L Bielckus 'A Study of the Development of Second Homes, with Particular Reference to the Countryside and Coast of England and Wales' London MPhil Thesis 1972–3.


### (f) Rural Housing


**6134** M Dunn *et al Rural Housing: Competition and Choice* Allen and Unwin 1981. A detailed study of the history and contemporary state of rural housing including case studies.


### (g) Housing for the Elderly


**6135** C M Lambert *Housing for the Elderly: A Select List of Material in the DoE/DTp Library* Department of the Environment/Department of Transport Library

1983. Another unannotated listing is Richard Thomas *Sheltered Housing and the Elderly: A Selected Classified Bibliography* National Building Agency 1976.

**6136** L F Heumann 'Sheltered Housing for the Elderly: The Role of the British Warden' *The Gerontologist* 20 1980 pp 318–30. A study of the development of the role of the wardens who oversee sheltered housing.

**6137** Cyril James Davey *Home From Home: The Story of the Methodist Homes for the Aged* Epworth 1976. His subsequent *Home For Good: The Methodist Homes for the Aged 1943–1983* Methodist Homes for the Aged 1983 is much less substantial but does to some extent update the larger work.

### (8) Building Societies

**6138** *Building Societies Year Book* Building Societies Association 1927–. A review of the societies' activities and statistics. See also *Building Societies Fact-Book* Building Society Association 1984–. The Association also periodically publishes *A Compendium of Building Society Statistics 1964–* (formerly Building Society Statistics). This both presents the statistics and discusses the history of these and the methods whereby they are compiled.

**6139** Herbert Ashworth *The Building Society Story* Franey 1980. A history of the societies since the eighteenth century as is E J Cleary *The Building Society Movement* Elek 1965.

**6140** Martin Boddy *The Building Societies* Macmillan 1980. A study of their historical growth and their financial and organizational structure and activities. See also M Pawley *Home Ownership* Architectural Press 1978.

**6141** Mark Boleat *The Building Society Industry* 2nd ed, Allen and Unwin 1986. A excellent textbook review of the state of the industry in the post-war period and the issues it faced in the 1980s.

**6142** E C L Butler *The Building Societies Institute 1934–1978* CBSI Ltd 1979. A history of the body that oversees the profession.

**6143** Mark Boleat 'United Kingdom' in his *National Housing Finance Systems: A Comparative Survey* Croom Helm 1985 pp 40–59. This looks at all aspects of the housing finance system, including the role of banks and local authorities. The changing activities involved in this sector are discussed in 'The Housing Finance Market: Recent Growth in Perspective' *Bank of England Quarterly Bulletin* 25 1985 pp 80–91.

**6144** Paul Barnes *Building Societies: The Myth of Mutuality* Pluto 1984. An analysis of recent frauds and scandals and a call for more regulation and accountability.

**6145** Debrapriya Ghosh *The Economics of Building Societies* Saxon House 1974. A study of building society activities 1959–73. See also C St J O'Herlihy and J E Spencer 'Building Societies' Behaviour 1955–70' *National Institute Economic Review* 61 1972 pp 40–52.

**6146** *Studies in Building Society Activity 1974–79* Building Societies Association 1980. This includes articles on their operations and on the state of the housing and savings markets.

**6147** J Foster 'The Redistributive Effect of Inflation on Building Society Shares and Deposits 1961–1974' *Bulletin of Economic Research* 28 1976 pp 67–76.

**6148** P Williams 'Building Societies and the Inner City' *Transactions of the Institute of British Geographers* 3 1978 pp 23–34. A commentary on the reluctance of societies to lend in the inner city and its effects.

**6149** Martin Davis *Every Man His Own Landlord: A History of Coventry Building Society* Coventry Building Society 1985.

**6150** Sir O R Hobson *A Hundred Years of the Halifax: The History of the Halifax Building Society 1853–1953* Batsford 1953. A history of the largest building society.

**6151** Michael Cassell *Inside Nationwide: One Hundred Years of Co-operation* Lund Humphries 1982. A good institutional history up to the financial innovations of the 1970s and 1980s and the move towards banking facilities such as current accounts.

**6152** S J Price *From Queen to Queen: The Centenary Story of the Temperance Permanent Building Society 1854–1954* Franey 1954.

**6153** Charles Harvey 'Old Traditions, New Departures: The Later History of the Bristol and West Building Society' in Charles E Harvey and Jon Press (eds) *Studies in the Business History of Bristol* Bristol Academic Press 1988 pp 239–72. A history from the 1930s to the 1980s.

### (9) Housing Associations and Co-operatives

**6154** *Housing Association Yearbook* National Federation of Housing Associations 1981–.

**6155** P Jones *The Jubilee Album: A Celebration of the Housing Association Movement 1935–1985* Liverpool

Housing Trust 1985. A history of voluntary housing and housing associations in Britain and of their influence on policy and legislation.

**6156** Ian S Emsley *The Development of Housing Associations: With Special Reference to London including a Case Study of the London Borough of Hammersmith* Garland 1986. A history since 1840. The housing associations had only a minor role until the 1974 Housing Act established them as a major arm of policy. This study includes a case history of the work of the Notting Hill Housing Trust.

**6157** *50 Years: The Story of a Housing Association from 1928 to 1978* Merseyside Improved Houses 1979.

**6158** *25 Years of Housing 1935–1960* North Eastern Housing Association Ltd 1960. A commemorative history of a Newcastle-upon-Tyne housing association.

**6159** J Gowing *For Ever Building: A Short History of the St Pancras Housing Society 1925–54* St Pancras Housing Society 1955. A history of a London housing association.

**6160** A McDonald *The Waller Way: The Story of the Waller Streets Housing Co-operative* Faber 1986. An account of a house building co-operative set up by a group of Liverpudlians and the nature of its operations.

## I. CRIME AND POLICING

### (1) Reference Works

**6161** *Criminal Statistics, England and Wales* HMSO 1950–. This very useful annual statistical collection was published as *Judicial Statistics* HMSO 1856–1949. A guide to criminal and prosecution statistics and their sources is provided in Nigel Walker *Crimes, Courts and Figures: An Introduction to Criminal Statistics* Penguin 1971.

**6162** A Harrison and J Gretton (eds) *Crime UK 1986: An Economic, Social and Policy Audit* Policy Journals 1986–. An annual analysis of crime and of policy to deal with it and with its victims.

**6163** Martin Wright (ed) *Use of Criminology Literature* Butterworths 1974. A good collection of bibliographical essays. It is international in scope but covers Britain more than adequately. The sections on the police and the prison service are particularly good. The article on official publications is also useful, not least because of its lists of relevant government inquiries.

**6164** *Abstracts on Criminology and Penology* Kluwer 1961–. In 1980 the Criminologica Foundation retitled this *Criminology and Penology Abstracts* and Kugler became the publishers. It is a well indexed collection of abstracts which are international in flavour, with American and British journals being the main ones abstracted.

### (2) Crime

**6165** Terence Morris *Crime and Criminal Justice Since 1945* Blackwell 1989. An excellent overview of crime and the changing attitudes towards it and handling of it by the criminal justice system. It includes a chronology and useful bibliographical information. There are good, historically flavoured reflections on crime, delinquency and drugs and on the responses of the criminal justice system in David James George Hennessy, Lord Windlesham *Responses to Crime* Clarendon 1987. Another analysis by an influential and respected figure is Frank Pakenham, Lord Longford *Causes of Crime* Weidenfeld and Nicolson 1958. F H McClintock and N Howard Avison *Crime in England and Wales* Heinemann 1968 surveys trends in crime, detection, convictions, recidivism and crime prevention since 1900. See also K I Wolpin 'An Economic Analysis of Crime and Punishment in England and Wales 1894–1967' *Journal of Political Economy* 86 1978 pp 815–40.

**6166** Philip Norton (ed) *Law and Order and British Politics* Gower 1984. A collection of essays surveying the handling of the problem of crime and the political attitudes towards crime. I R Taylor 'Social Democracy and the Crime Question in Britain 1945 to 1980' Sheffield PhD Thesis 1982 examines political attitudes to the rising crime rate of the post-war years.

**6167** Clive Borrell and Brian Cashinella *Crime in Britain Today* Routledge and Kegan Paul 1975. A survey of trends in crime 1960–74.

**6168** Richard Kinsey, John Leo and Jock Young *Losing the Fight Against Crime* Blackwell 1986. Despite the increases in police manpower in the 1980s the crime rate has, as this analysis points out, continued to increase. It especially discusses crime on Merseyside. The relationship between crime and the high unemployment of the 1980s best discussed in Steven Box *Recession, Crime and Punishment* Macmillan 1987.

**6169** Nigel Walker *Crime and Insanity in England* 2v, Edinburgh University Press 1968. A comprehensive analysis of how the law on the mentally disordered and the crimes committed by the mentally disordered has developed since Saxon times. Volume 1 presents historical perspectives on this issue. Volume 2 surveys the contemporary use of hospital orders since the 1959 Mental Health Act.

**6170** M G Maxwell *Fear of Crime in England and Wales* Home Office Research Unit Report 78, HMSO 1984. This is based on the first British Crime Survey conducted in 1982 (*The British Crime Survey* Home Office Research Unit Report 76, HMSO 1983). It is an impressionistic reflection of people's perceptions of the dangers and risks of crime. This fear of crime has led to initiatives such as Neighbourhood Watch, victim support schemes or renewal of council housing estates.

**6171** F H McClintock *Crimes of Violence* Macmillan 1963. An inquiry into crimes of violence against the person in London. It provides a detailed assessment of trends in reporting of these crimes, the detection rates, the convictions, the nature of the criminals and their punishment.

**6172** Geoffrey Pearson *Hooligan: A History of Respectable Fears* Macmillan 1983. A good history which seeks to show by reference to the nineteenth century that the modern moral panic about violent crime and hooliganism is not new. It finishes by examining the concern about hooliganism and moral degeneracy in the face of the behaviour of the mods and rockers in the 1950s and 1960s.

**6173** J H H Gaute and R Odell *The Murderers' Who's Who* Methuen 1979. A collection of biographical sketches of 360 murderers, mostly British. It suffers from a poor arrangement and a faulty subject index.

**6174** Douglas Wynn *Settings for Slaughter: Thirteen Macabre Murders* Hale 1988. A collection of case histories 1912–69. Alan Sewart *Murder in Lancashire* Hale 1988 is a collection of fourteen case histories spanning the period 1830–1984. Another similar collection is Peter N Walker *Murders and Mysteries from the North York Moors* Hale 1988. This culminates with an account of the manhunt for the Yorkshire Ripper (Peter Sutcliffe) in 1982. Conrad Phillips *Murderer's Moon* Barker 1956 includes studies of Neville Heath, John George Haigh and John Christie.

**6175** Peter Beveridge *Inside the CID* Evans 1957. This reveals little of the CID. It is mostly a series of case studies of murders and other metropolitan crimes with which he had to deal.

**6176** Allen Andrews *Intensive Inquiries: Seven Chief Constables Open CID Files on Their Most Remarkable Murder Investigations* Harrap 1973. Detailed case studies of a number of post-war murders.

**6177** Patrick Wilson *Murderess: A Study of the Women Executed in Britain Since 1823* Michael Joseph 1971. See also Renee Huggett and Paul Berry *Daughters of Cain: The Story of Eight Women Executed Since Edith Thompson in 1923* Chivers 1985.

**6178** Evelyn Gibson and Sidney Klein *Murder 1957 to 1968: A Home Office Statistical Division Report on Murder in England and Wales* HMSO 1969. A short report assessing the consequences of the Homicide Act 1957 on murder rates. It includes an annexe on murder in Scotland. Terence Morris and Louis Blom-Cooper *A Calendar of Murder: Criminal Homicide in England Since 1957* Michael Joseph 1964 is an analysis of every case of murder indicted in England and Wales between the 1957 Act and the end of 1962.

**6179** Elwyn Jones *The Last Two To Hang* Pan 1964. An account of the cases and execution of Peter Allen and Gwyn Evans in 1964.

**6180** David A Yallop *To Encourage the Others* W H Allen 1974. On the case of Derek Bentley and Christopher Craig. Bentley was hanged after his accomplice, who was too young to suffer the same fate, murdered a policeman. The latest of the numerous studies of the legal and social implications of this case, and one which offers some new evidence on aspects of it, is Christopher Berry-Dee and Robin Odell *Dad, Help Me Please* W H Allen 1989. See also Francis Selwyn *Gangland: The Case of Bentley and Craig* Routledge 1988 and David A Yallop *To Encourage the Others* W H Allen 1971. William George Bentley *My Son's Execution* W H Allen 1957 is an account of Derek Bentley's life, trial and death. H Montgomery Hyde (ed) *Trial of Christopher Craig and Derek William Bentley* Hodge 1954 is an edited version of the trial from the notable British trials series.

**6181** Emlyn Williams *Beyond Belief: A Chronicle of Murder and its Detection* Hamilton 1967. A study of the moors murders of Ian Brady and Myra Hindley in the 1960s. Jonathan Goodman (ed) *The Trial of Ian Brady and Myra Hindley: The Moors Case* 2nd ed, David and Charles 1986 is an edited version of the case from the celebrated trials series. On the moors murders see also David Marchbanks *The Moors Murders* Frewin 1966 and Robert Wilson *Devil's Disciples* Javelin 1986. The murderers themselves are examined in Fred Harrison *Bradley and Hindley: Genesis of the Moors Murders* Ashgrove 1989. Hindley's personality is explored in Jean Ritchie *Myra Hindley: Inside the Mind of a Murderess* Angus and Robertson 1988.

**6182** Rupert Furneaux *The Two Stranglers of Rillington Place* Panther 1961. On the case of John Reginald Halliday Christie and Timothy John Evans. F Tennyson Jesse (ed) *Trials of Timothy John Evans and John Reginald Halliday Christie* William Hodge 1957 is an edited version of the trials from the notable British trials series.

On Christie see also Molly Lefebvre *Murder With A Difference: Studies of Haigh and Christie* Heinemann 1958. Doubts, which have since been vindicted, are cast on the guilt of Evans, in Ludovic Kennedy *Ten Rillington Place* Gollancz 1961. The verdict of the trial was supported by *Report of an Inquiry into Certain Matters Arising Out of the Deaths of Mrs Beryl Evans and of Geraldine Evans* and out of the *Conviction of Timothy John Evans of the Murder of Geraldine Evans: Report by Mr J Scott Henderson QC* Cmnd 8896 *Parliamentary Papers* ix 1952–53 but was discredited by *The Case of Timothy John Evans: Report of an Inquiry by The Hon Mr Justice Brabin* Cmnd 3101 *Parliamentary Papers* xxvi 1966–67.

**6183** Tony Parker *The Plough Boy* Hutchinson 1965. On the crimes and trial of Michael J Davies.

**6184** Jonathan Goodman and Patrick Pringle (eds) *The Trial of Ruth Ellis* David and Charles 1974. On the case of Ruth Ellis, the last British woman to be executed for murder, from the notable British trials series. See also Robert Hancock *Ruth Ellis: The Last Woman to be Hanged* Barker 1963.

**6185** Arthur Joseph La Bern *Haigh: The Mind of a Murderer* W H Allen 1973. On Haigh's life and crimes see also Stanley Jackson *John George Haigh* Odhams 1953 and Gerald Byrne *John George Haigh: Acid Bath Killer* Headliner Publications 1950. Patrick Theobald Tower Butler, Lord Dunboyne (ed) *The Trial of John George Haigh – The Acid Bath Murder* Hodge 1953 is a transcript of the trial from the notable British trials series. See also [6182].

**6186** Louis Blom-Cooper *The A6 Murder: Regina v. James Hanratty: The Semblance of Truth* Penguin 1963. A critical examination of the handling of the case by the criminal justice system, raising doubts about the guilt of Hanratty, who was executed for this murder.

**6187** Francis Selwyn *Rotten to the Core: The Life and Death of Neville Heath* Routledge 1988. The most valuable of the studies of the brutal murderer of two young women in 1946. See also Paull Hill *Portrait of a Sadist* Neville Spearman 1960 and Gerald Byrne *Borstal Boy: The Uncensored Story of Neville Heath* John Hill Publications 1954. MacDonald Critchley (ed) *The Trial of Neville George Clevely Heath* Hodge 1951 is an edited version of Heath's trial, from the notable British trials series.

**6188** Tom Tullett *Portrait of a Bad Man* Evans 1956. A biography of John Donald Merrett, a murderer and smuggler, who committed suicide in 1954.

**6189** Gordon Burn *Somebody's Husband, Somebody's Son: The Story of the Yorkshire Ripper* Viking 1985. An account of the murders of and manhunt for the Yorkshire Ripper, Peter Sutcliffe, in the early 1980s. See also Baron Boulos *The Yorkshire Ripper: A Case Study of the Sutcliffe Papers* Department of Sociology, Manchester University 1983.

**6190** Michael Pratt *Mugging as a Social Problem* Routledge and Kegan Paul 1980. A view of the contemporary problem of mugging from the point of view of the Metropolitan Police. The moral panic about mugging and the rise in violent crime in the 1970s is examined in a sociological context in Stuart Hall *et al Policing the Crisis: Mugging, the State and Law and Order* Macmillan 1978. This also looks at the growing civil disorder of the 1970s and the policing problems arising.

**6191** R Harding 'Firearms Use in Crime' *Criminal Law Review* 1979 pp 765–74. An examination in the context of the 1973 Green Paper on the control of firearms. It looks at the changing use of firearms and concludes that this is not excessive or alarming.

**6192** John George Pearson *The Profession of Violence: The Rise and Fall of the Kray Twins* 3rd ed, Granada 1984. A study of the criminal careers of the notorious Kray twins, London gangland bosses and murderers. See also Brian MacConnell *The Evil Firm: The Rise and Fall of the Brothers Kray from an Investigation by a 'Daily Mirror' Team* Mayflower 1969. Reg and Ron Kray with Fred Dineage *Our Story* Sidgwick and Jackson 1988 is a candid autobiography charting their criminal careers, trial and imprisonment. Another biography is Charles Kray with Robin McGibbon *Me and My Brothers* Grafton 1988. John Dickson *Murder Without Conviction: Inside the World of the Krays* Sidgwick and Jackson 1986 is a memoir by a former member of the Kray gang which paints a vivid picture of the brutal world they moved in.

**6193** Tony Parker *The Courage of His Convictions* Heinemann 1962. A good biography of Robert Allerton, a professional thief. Tony Parker *A Man of Good Abilities* Hutchinson 1967 is a portrait of a petty but persistent criminal. Another study of a recidivist is his *The Unknown Citizen* Hutchinson 1963. His *Five Women* Arrow 1965 is a series of studies of female criminals.

**6194** Peta Fordham *The Robbers' Tale* Hodder and Stoughton 1965. An account of the great train robbery of August 1963.

**6195** Karl Klockars *The Professional Fence* Tavistock 1975. A sociological study of professional receivers of stolen goods.

**6196** J Munice *The Trouble With Kids Today: Youth and Crime in Post-War Britain* Hutchinson 1984. A history of juvenile crime and delinquency. John Pitts *The*

*Politics of Juvenile Crime* Sage 1988 concentrates more on contemporary developments and the shift back towards retributive justice in the 1980s. See also T R Fyvel *The Insecure Offender: Rebellious Youth in the Welfare State* Chatto and Windus 1961. The problem of delinquency is linked to marriage break-up in Claud Mullins *Marriage Failures and the Children* Epworth 1954.

**6197** *Committee on Children and Young Persons: Report* Cmnd 1191, *Parliamentary Papers* ix 1959–60. The report of this inquiry into juvenile delinquency chaired by Lord Ingleby led to the Children and Young Persons Act 1963 which raised the age of criminal responsibility from eight to ten.

**6198** D P Farrington 'La déjudiciarisation des mineurs en Angleterre' *Déviance Société* 4 1980 pp 257–77. A study of the consequences of the 1969 Children and Young Persons Act which greatly altered the work of the juvenile courts and enormously enhanced the role of social workers in the treatment of juvenile offenders.

**6199** Jean Davies and Nancy Goodman *Girl Offenders Aged 17–20 Years* HMSO 1972. A statistical survey on juvenile female offenders, recidivism and after-care in the 1960s. K Sullivan *Girls Who Go Wrong* Gollancz 1956 is an impressionist study of female juvenile delinquents.

**6200** A E Bottoms 'Delinquency amongst Immigrants' *Race* 8 1967 pp 352–83. A statistical survey.

**6201** David Downes *The Delinquent Solution* Routledge and Kegan Paul 1966. A study of juvenile crime and delinquency in London's East End. Terence Morris *The Criminal Area* Routledge and Kegan Paul 1958 is a similar study of Croydon, and John Barron Mays *Growing Up in the City* Liverpool University Press 1958 of Liverpool. Policing responses to the problem are explored in Paul Lerman 'Policing Juveniles in London: Shifts in Guiding Discretion 1893–1968' *British Journal of Criminology* 24 1984 pp 168–84. W J P Sprott, Pearl Jephcott and M P Carter *The Social Background of Delinquency* University of Nottingham 1954 examines delinquency in the Nottinghamshire mining village of Hucknall. For another local study see E H Hulland 'The Changing Attitudes towards the Problems of Juvenile Deliquency in this Country in the Twentieth Century with Special Reference to the Developments in the West Riding of Yorkshire' Leeds MEd Thesis 1956–7.

**6202** P Farmer *Vandalism: A State of the Art Review and Guide to Sources of Information* Capital Planning Information 1983.

**6203** Tony Parker *The Twisting Lane: Some Sex Offenders* Hutchinson 1969. A portrayal of the characteristics of some sex offenders, their problems and the reasons for their crimes.

**6204** Nigel Parton *The Politics of Child Abuse* Macmillan 1985. A comprehensive account of the nature and growing awareness of child abuse as a major social problem.

**6205** Mike Hepworth 'The Criminalization of Blackmail' in Hermanus Bianchi, Mario Simond and Mike Hepworth (eds) *Deviance and Control in Europe* John Wiley 1975 pp 189–206.

**6206** Mihir Bose and Cathy Gunn *Fraud: The Growth Industry of the Eighties* Unwin Hyman 1989. A study of all aspects, including computer crime, of the growth of fraud in the City in the 1980s.

**6207** Charles Black and Michael Horsnell *Counterfeiter: The Story of a British Master-Forger* New English Library 1989. Black's autobiography.

**6208** Dermot Walsh *Shoplifting: Controlling a Major Crime* Macmillan 1978. An excellent account of shop theft and researches into it. Shoplifting increased considerably with changing retail methods and patterns of consumption in the 1960s. An early analysis is T C N Gibbens and J Prince *Shoplifting* Institute for the Study and Treatment of Delinquency, London 1962.

**6209** James Vasey *In the Net* Stockwell 1983. A study of salmon poaching in the 1940s.

**6210** David Peirce, Peter N Grabosky and Ted Robert Gurr 'London, The Politics of Crime and Conflict 1800 to the 1970s' in Ted Robert Gurr, Peter N Grobosky and Richard C Huta (eds) *The Politics of Crime and Conflict: A Comparative History of Four Cities* Sage 1977 pp 33–214. A study of trends in crime in the capital and of the administrative response. L Taylor *In The Underworld* Blackwell 1984 reveals London's criminal underworld through interviews with various types of criminal. Gilbert Kelland *Crime in London: From Post-War Soho to Present Day Supergrasses* The Bodley Head 1986 presents an eyewitness account of London's underworld from the viewpoint of a leading figure in the Metropolitan Police, and of some the leading London crimes of the previous years.

### (3) Public Order

The literature in this section examines riots, public disturbances, football hooliganism and the making of policy and policing designed to maintain public order. It does not include literature on public disturbances during industrial disputes, which can be found in the section on the Control of Industrial Disputes. Nor does it include the literature on the Race Riots of 1958 in Notting Hill and Nottingham, which is instead to be found in the section on Discrimination and Racial Tension in the Race Relations category.

**6211** E Edwards, R Golland and S Leach *Urban Riots and Public Order: A Select Bibliography 1975–1985* Technical Communications 1986. This is based on material collected on the Greater London Council's databases. It covers works published in this period. It particularly concentrates on the riots of 1981 and 1985 but also reflects on the policing of race relations and industrial disputes, the media response to riots and on football hooliganism. It covers not only books and reports but also articles, including articles in the press. Furthermore it is very well annotated.

**6212** George Gaskell and Robert Benewich (eds) *The Crowd in Contemporary Britain* Sage 1987. This examines why public order should have become a problem since the 1970s in contrast to the rest of post-war history. It concentrates on the nature of public order problems in the 1980s.

**6213** Garry Northam *Shooting in the Dark: Riot Police in Britain* Faber 1988. A study of the developments in riot control by the police since such problems began to be of increasing importance since the 1960s.

**6214** Mary Grigg *The Challenor Case* Penguin 1965. An account of the framing of a demonstrator against the Queen of Greece in London in 1963 by a policeman who turned out to be mentally ill.

**6215** James D Halloran, Philip Elliott and Graham Murdock *Demonstrations and Communications: A Case Study* Penguin 1970. The definitive study of the Grosvenor Square demonstration in 1968 outside the American embassy in protest at American policy in Vietnam.

**6216** Sir Leslie Scarman *The Red Lion Square Disorders of 15 June 1974: Report of Inquiry* Cmnd 5919, *Parliamentary Papers* xxx 1974–75. The Scarman inquiry into this demonstration against the National Front is critically assessed in Tony Gilbert *Only One died: An Account of the Scarman Inquiry into the Events of 15th June 1974 in Red Lion Square Where Kevin Gately Died Opposing Racism and Fascism* Beauchamp 1975.

**6217** Tony Ward *Death and Disorder: Three Case Studies of Public Order and Policing* Inquest 1986. A pamphlet which examines the deaths at the demonstrations at Red Lion Square in 1974, Southall in 1979 and of Cynthia Jarrett in 1985 (an incident which helped to provoke the Broadwater Farm riot) and the policing on each occasion.

**6218** A T H Smith 'Public Order Law 1974–1983: Developments and Proposals' *Criminal Law Review* 1984 pp 643–51. A survey of developments in the law. One aspect of this, the 1982 Police and Criminal Evidence Bill introduced in the light of the growing public disorder problems for the police since the 1972 miners' strike, is examined in Lee Bridges and Tony Bunyan 'Britain's New Urban Policing Strategy: The Police and Criminal Evidence Bill in Context' *Journal of Law and Society* 10 1983 pp 85–107.

**6219** John Benyon and John Solomos 'The Simmering Cities: Urban Unrest during the Thatcher Years' *Parliamentary Affairs* 41 1988 pp 402–22. An assessment of the riots and the extent to which their causes have been dealt with.

**6220** *Southall 23rd April 1979: The Report of the Unofficial Committee of Inquiry* National Council for Civil Liberties 1980. An inquiry into the causes, policing and reporting and the events in Southall, North London just before the 1979 general election where a demonstration against a National Front march developed into a riot during which Blair Peach was killed, apparently by a police truncheon. David Ransom *The Blair Peach Case: Licence to Kill* Friends of Blair Peach Committee 1980 is an inquest into Peach's death.

**6221** H Joshua, T Wallace and H Booth *To Ride the Storm: The 1980 Bristol 'Riot' and the State* Heinemann 1983. A study of the disturbances in the St Pauls district of Bristol and its consequences. The causes of the disturbances are briefly examined in *Slumbering Volcano? Report of an Inquiry into the Origins of the Eruption in St Pauls, Bristol on 2nd April 1980* Bristol Trades Council 1981.

**6222** Martin Kettle and L Hodges *Uprising: The Police, the People and the Riots in Britain's Cities* Pan 1982. An instant history of the riots that took place in the summer of 1981 in Brixton, Southall, Toxteth and Mosside, their historical and social context, the responses to the rioting and the implications for policing in the inner city. *Race and Riots '81* New Society 1982 is a collection of essays on a whole range of aspects of the 1981 urban riots and the issues arising. So is P J Waller *et al* '1981 in Retrospect: Urban Riots, Scarman, Police Reactions' *New Community* 9 1982 pp 344–80. The geography of these riots is examined in Ceri Peach 'A Geographical Perspective on the 1981 Urban Riots in England' *Ethnic and Racial Studies* 9 1986 pp 396–411. They are placed in the context of the increased fear of crime and mugging, and in consequence of heavier policing, in the 1970s, in D Garland 'The Civil Disorders in English Cities: Their Political Context and Significance' *Panopticon* 6 1985 pp 7–20. J P Bowrey 'The 1981 Urban Riots in England' London M.Phil Thesis 1984 sees the riots as the product of alienated inner city youth responding to racism, unemployment, heavy policing and powerlessness. In the process he compares and contrasts the 1981 riots with those which were so common in the eighteenth century. The causes of the riots are interpreted in similar terms in C Unsworth 'The Riots of 1981: Popular Violence and the Politics of Law and Order' *Journal of Law and Society* 9 1982 pp 63–85 and John Rex 'The 1981 Urban Riots in Britain' *International Journal of Urban and Regional Research* 6 1982 pp 100–13. M Brake 'Under Heavy Manners: A Consideration of Racism, Black Youth Culture and Crime in Britain' *Crime and Social Justice* 20 1983 pp 1–15 places more emphasis on racial discrimination as a catalyst. It is the political, cultural and economic marginalization of the West Indian community that is seen as crucial in J Lea and J Young 'Urban Violence and Political Marginalisation: The Riots in Britain Summer 1981' *Critical Social Policy* 1 1982 pp 56–69. The role of Left-Wing revolutionaries in these events and particularly their activities in Brixton before and after 1981 (with brief references to Toxteth and Southall) is considered in Peter Shipley 'The Riots and the Far Left' *New Community* 9 1981 pp 194–8.

**6223** D Cowell, T Jones and J Young (eds) *Policing the Riots* Junction Books 1982. This presents the perspectives of policemen, politicians and academics on the causes of and problems of policing the 1981 riots and of the issues in policing which they raised. Policing methods are indicted as one of the causes of the riots. This volume includes a chronology on the events of 1981. The techniques of policing and developments in riot control are examined through interviews with senior officers in D W Jackson '"Public Police Thyselves": Deadly Force and Public Disorder, Two Crises in British Community Policing' *Police Studies* 8 1985 pp 132–48. The various responses to the riots and the implications for policing are discussed in C F J Vick 'Ideological Responses to the Riots' *Police Journal* 55 1982 pp 262–77.

**6224** John Solomos *Riots, Urban Protest and Social Protest: The Interplay of Reform and Social Control* Centre for Research in Ethnic Relations, University of Warwick 1986. A short analysis of the official response to the riots of 1980–1 which he compares with the response to those of 1985. In both cases he argues the reform that followed was limited, contradictory and symbolic.

**6225** *The Brixton Disorders 10–12 April 1981: Report of an Inquiry by the Rt Hon The Lord Scarman OBE* Cmnd 8427 *Parliamentary Papers* 1981–82. The most important of the official responses to the 1981 riots. It examines the social context of the riots, criticized a number of aspects of police tactics and made recommendations that led to the growing emphasis on community policing in the rest of the 1980s. The Scarman Report is assessed in John Benyon (ed) *Scarman and After: Re-*

*flecting on Lord Scarman's Report, the Riots and Their Aftermath* Pergamon 1984 by a symposium of community leaders, policemen, journalists, politicians, pressure group leaders and academics. It is critically examined in Martin Baker and Anne Baezer 'The Language of Racism – An Examination of Lord Scarman's Report on the Brixton Riots' *International Socialism* 2 1983 pp 108–25, which argues that the report is itself riddled with racist language and assumptions. A particular aspect of the causes of the Brixton riots is scrutinized in Louis Blom-Cooper and Richard Drabble 'Police Perceptions of Crime: Brixton and the Operational Response' *British Journal of Criminology* 22 1982 pp 184–7. This argues that the police reaction to their view that Brixton was a uniquely criminal area by saturation policing was effectively a self-fulfilling prophecy.

**6226** Paul Cooper 'Competing Explanations of the Merseyside Riots of 1981' *British Journal of Criminology* 25 1985 pp 60–9. This argues that coercive policing of marginalized communities was the main cause of the riots in Toxteth in July 1981. See also P J Waller 'The Riots in Toxteth, Liverpool: A Survey' *New Community* 9 1982 pp 344–53.

**6227** Paul Gordon 'Inquiring into the "Riots": A Review of Reports on the 1985 Urban Disorders' *Sage Race Relations Abstracts* 12 1987 pp 3–22. A critical assessment of the police and local authority reports into the riots of 1985.

**6228** *The Broadwater Farm Inquiry: Report of the Independent Inquiry into the Disturbances of October 1985 at Broadwater Farm Estate, Tottenham* Broadwater Farm Inquiry 1986. The report of an independent inquiry set up by Haringey Council under Lord Gifford into the riot on this North London housing estate which led to the death of a policeman. It examines the social and economic context and the policing of the estate. Martin Loney 'Imagery and Reality in the Broadwater Farm Riot' *Critical Social Policy* 17 1986 pp 81–6 is a short commentary on the background, press coverage and aftermath of the riot in the context of the police dissatisfaction at the way in which it was handled. It concludes that crime clear-up rates would be more likely to improve through better community relations than through the deployment of more officers, the tactic that had helped to provoke the riot. This police dissatisfaction is articulated in T Judge 'The Battle of Broadwater Farm' *Police* 18 1985 pp 10–5.

**6229** Geoffrey Dear *Report of the Chief Constable of West Midlands, Handsworth/Lozells* West Midlands Police 1985. The police report on the 1985 Handsworth riots. This alleges that the riots were orchestrated by local drug dealers hoping to protect their trade in the face of a clampdown by the police. This view is challenged in the report commissioned by Birmingham City Council, Julius Silverman *The Handsworth-Lozells Riots: Report of an Inquiry by Mr Julius Silverman* Birmingham City Council 1986. He argues that the principal causes were unemployment, racial discrimination and racist policing.

**6230** F E C Gregory 'The Concept of "Police Primary" and its Application in the Policing of the Protests against Cruise Missiles in Great Britain' *Police Studies* 9 1986 pp 59–67. An examination of the policing of protesters at cruise missiles bases since 1981.

**6231** Eric Dunning, Patrick Murphy and John Williams *The Roots of Football Hooliganism: A Historical and Sociological Survey* Routledge and Kegan Paul 1988. A good examination of the recent history and the contemporary problem of football hooliganism and of the policies adopted to try and contain the problem. James Walvin *Football and the Decline of Britain* Macmillan 1986 adopts an even broader approach to the problem, seeing it in the context of social malaise. Another useful study is P Marsh *et al The Rules Disorder* Routledge and Kegan Paul 1978. The problem of soccer hooliganism in the 1950s and 1960s is studied in Ian Taylor 'Football Mad: A Speculative Sociology of Football Hooliganism' in Eric Dunning (ed) *Sport: Readings from a Sociological Perspective* Cass 1971 pp 352–77. The attitudes of football hooligans are examined in David Robins *We Hate Humans* Penguin 1984. J A Maguire 'The "Limits of Decent Partisanship": A Sociogenetic Investigation of the Emergence of Football Spectating as a Social Problem' Leicester PhD Thesis 1985 surveys the history of football violence since the 1880s which he sees in the context of class/cultural conflict. The history of football hooliganism is also examined in P Mackay 'The Fall and Rise of Football Hooliganism' *Police Journal* 49 1986 pp 198–207. R Ingham, S Hall *et al Football Hooliganism: The Wider Context* Inter-Action Imprint 1978 is a more sociological study of the nature of football fans and their attitudes to the game and self-images and of their treatment by the press.

**6232** *Football Spectator Violence: Report of an Official Working Group* HMSO 1984. The report commissioned from the group chaired by D V Teasdale after violence at England football matches in Luxembourg and France in late 1983 and early 1984. It outlines the problems, the steps already taken and makes further recommendations. The problem of the behaviour of English fans abroad is also examined, on the basis of three studies of their behaviour and methods of control conducted in 1982, in John Williams, Eric Dunning and Patrick Murphy *Hooligans Abroad: The Behaviour and Control of England Fans in Continental Europe* Routledge and Kegan Paul 1984.

## (4) The Police

The literature on the policing of race relations appears in the section on Race Relations [5691–7] and also to some extent in the section above on public order. The material on the policing of industrial relations can be found in the sections on Control of Industrial Disputes and on disputes in the coal industry.

**6233** *Police and Constabulary Almanac* R Hazell 1861–. A directory to police forces and the criminal justice and civil defence system. It is mainly useful for tracing office holders.

**6234** *Report of Her Majesty's Chief Inspector of Constabulary* HMSO 1934–. A short annual report on the police in England and Wales outside the Metropolitan area.

**6235** J R Thackrah 'Police Archives in Britain' *Police Studies* 5/3 1982 pp 58–61. An introductory survey.

**6236** Dennis T Brett (comp) *The Police of England and Wales: A Bibliography 1829–1979* 3rd ed, Police Staff College 1979. A comprehensive if poorly arranged and only semi-annotated bibliography. It can be updated by the monthly *Additions to the Library* Police College Library, Bramshill. One of bibliography's strengths is that it lists lots of histories of local police forces. Consequently the histories of local forces listed below are only either those which are more substantial or those which have appeared since Brett's bibliography was published.

**6237** International Police Association *International Bibliography of Selected Police Literature* M and W Publications 1968. This bibliography has quite a large section on Britain.

**6238** *Police Science Abstracts* Kugler 1980–. This was formerly Abstracts on Police Science Kluwer 1973–. International in scope the main journals abstracted are American and British.

**6239** T A Critchley *A History of Police in England and Wales* 2nd ed, Constable 1978. The last three chapters of this standard history deal with the post-war period. See also G P Davies 'The Police Service of England and Wales between 1918 and 1964, with Particular Reference to Problems of Personnel, Recruitment and Command' London PhD Thesis 1972–3.

**6240** Simon Holdaway *Inside the British Police* Blackwell 1983. An in-depth sociological study of the British police force, its attitudes, structures and characteristics. Simon Holdaway (ed) *The British Police* Arnold 1979 surveys various issues such as the growth of police unionism, the police's public image, and the contemporary nature of police work. Another useful collection of essays on a range of police issues is J C Alderson and P J Stead (eds) *The Police We Deserve* Wolfe 1973.

**6241** Robert Reiner *The Politics of the Police* Wheatsheaf 1985. A good study of the reasons why the police and policing have become controversial political issues since the 1970s and of the events which have helped to raise these controversies. Phil Scraton *The Politics of the Police* Pluto 1985 has a wider historical scope. However the second part of the book concentrates on the issues in policing, particularly with respect to the policing of the inner city and of industrial disputes, in the 1980s. It includes a case study on the policing of Merseyside in the 1980s. See also 'Great Britain' in John D Brewer *et al The Police, Public Order and the State* Macmillan 1988 pp 6–46. The police's role in society is also examined in Maureen Cain *Society and the Policeman's Role* Routledge and Kegan Paul 1973.

**6242** W Hewitt *British Police Administration* C C Thomas 1965. This describes the adminstrative structure of British police forces.

**6243** J P Martin and Gail Wilson *The Police: A Study in Manpower: The Evolution of the Service in England and Wales 1829–1966* Heinemann Educational 1969. A history with a particular emphasis on personnel and finance.

**6244** *Royal Commission on the Police: Interim Report* Cmnd 1222 *Parliamentary Papers* xx 1960–61 and *Final Report* Cmnd 1728 *Parliamentary Papers* xx 1961–62. This Commission under Sir Henry Willink was appointed in the light of concern about some disciplinary incidents in the 1950s. The interim report led to substantial police pay increases. The final report led to the Police Act 1964, which made some changes in the organization and administration of the police and some developments in the handling of complaints against the police. The effects of the changes in organization brought about by the 1964 Act are assessed in J H B Nicholson 'The Effects of Police Force Amalgamations, Resulting from the 1964 Police Act' London MSc Thesis 1974–5. Developments in the wake of the Act are examined in A F Wilcox 'Police 1964–1973' *Criminal Law Review* 1974 pp 144–57.

**6245** Michael Banton *The Policeman in the Community* Tavistock 1964. A study of contemporary policing in the 1960s. See also Ben Whitaker *The Police* Eyre and Spottiswoode 1964. Stuart Bowes *The Police and Civil Liberties* Lawrence and Wishart 1966 examines cases of the police exceeding their powers in the 1960s.

**6246** M Weatheritt *Innovations in Policing* Croom Helm 1986. A synopsis of recent developments in policing technique and equipment in the face of changing pressures and circumstances and the demands of central government. P K Manning 'British Policing: Continuities and Change' *Howard Journal of Criminal Justice* 25 1986 pp 261–78 looks at changes of the 1970s and 1980s focusing on changes in management, public image and crime control.

**6247** Ben Whitaker *The Police in Society* Eyre Methuen 1979. A sympathetic study of the problems of contemporary policing introduced by Lord Scarman. J R Thackrah (ed) *Contemporary Policing: An Examination of Society in the 1980s* Sphere Reference 1985 is a collection of essays by members of the staff at the Police Staff College, Bramshill on the current state of policing and police management. A more critical collection of perspectives on contemporary policing issues is Phil Scraton (ed) *Law, Order and Authoritarian State: Readings in Critical Criminology* Oxford University Press 1987. Another collection of essays is David Pope and Norman Weiner (eds) *Modern Policing* Croom Helm 1981. Roger Graef *Talking Blues* Collins Harvill 1989 is a study of police attitudes nationwide to a whole range of contemporary issues in policing based on extensive interviewing.

**6248** L H Leigh *Police Powers in England and Wales* 2nd ed, Butterworths 1983. A statement of the state of the law on police powers. The development of the discretionary powers of the police since before the 1964 Police Act is examined in L Lustgarten *The Governance of Police* Sweet and Maxwell 1986. See also S H Bailey and D J Birch 'Recent Developments in the Law of Police Powers' *Criminal Law Review* 1982 pp 475–84 and 547–57.

**6249** J D Christian 'A Planning, Programming, Budgeting System in the Police Service in England and Wales between 1969 and 1974' Manchester MA (Econ) Thesis 1982. This is an evaluation of the establishment of this system by a Home Office concerned about rising police expenditure, and of its subsequent abandonment.

**6250** D E Williams 'Provisional Police Training in Britain: Continuity and Reform 1947–1985' Oxford DPhil Thesis 1985. The first detailed examination of police training in the post-war period.

**6251** Stuart Morris 'British Chief Constables: The Americanization of a Role?' *Political Studies* pp 352–64. A study of the growing public role and importance of chief constables.

**6252** Anthony Judge *The First Fifty Years: The Story of the Police Federation* Police Federation 1968. An institutional history of the body which represents the bulk of the rank and file members of the force. Robert Reiner *The Blue-Coated Worker: A Sociological Study of Police Unionism* Cambridge University Press 1978 is a good study of police attitudes to unionism incorporating reflections on the history and structure of the Police Federation.

**6253** Joan Lock *The British Policewoman: Her Story* Hale 1979. A history of the role of women in the police force.

**6254** Barry Cox, John Shirley and Martin Short *The Fall of Scotland Yard* Penguin 1977. A journalistic account of corruption in the Metropolitan Police in the 1960s and 1970s, with particular chapters focusing on graft in the drug squad, the CID and the obscene publications squad. It also evaluates the success of Sir Robert Mark's drive against corruption in the Metropolitan Police in the 1970s. Corruption in this period is also examined in Maurice Punch *Conduct Unbecoming* Tavistock 1985. Richard Hobbs *Doing the Business: Entrepreneurship, the Working Class and Detectives in the East End of London* Clarendon 1988 is a study of corruption in the police in the East End in the nineteenth and twentieth centuries.

**6255** Ian Oliver *Police, Government and Accountability* Macmillan 1987. This provides a detailed study of the debate over the constitutional position of the police and their accountability since before the 1962 Willink Report, concentrating on the debate over accountability in the 1980s. It includes a useful bibliography. Questions of police accountability are also considered in detail in Peter Hain (ed) *Policing the Police* 2v, John Calder 1979–80. The first of these volumes *The Complaints System, Police Powers and Terrorism Legislation* examines the development of the complaints system and the problems in controlling police activities posed by the prevention of terrorism legislation. The second volume, *The Politics of Policing and the Policing of Politics, Society under Surveillance, the Special Patrol Group* looks at the lack of democratic accountability, the growth of surveillance technology and at the concern over the activities of the Special Patrol Group. The concerns about police accountability which led to the establishment of the Willink Royal Commission are examined in Geoffrey Marshall 'Police Accountability Revisited' in David Butler and A H Halsey (eds) *Policy and Politics: Essays in Honour of Norman Chester* Macmillan 1978 pp 51–65. Two case studies of police accountability, in the aftermath of the disturbances in Southall in 1979 and Brixton in 1981, are considered in the context of the history of police accountability in T Jefferson and R Grimshaw *Controlling The Constable: Police Accountability in England and Wales* Muller/Cobden Trust 1984.

**6256** B Loveday 'Police Complaints Procedure: An Overview' *Social Policy and Administration* 19 1985 pp 134–44. This review the development of the complaints procedure since the 1964 Police Act. See also P E G De La Rue 'Origin and Operation of the Procedure for Dealing with Complaints against the Police: A Review (England and Wales)' *Bramshill Journal* 1/3 1981–82 pp 5–12.

**6257** *The Handling of Complaints Against the Police: Report of the Working Group for England and Wales* Cmnd 5582, *Parliamentary Papers* xiv 1974. This report by the group chaired by A D Gordon-Brown considered the history of complaints procedure and made the recommendations which led to the 1976 Police Act and the setting up of the Police Complaints Board. The work of this body is reviewed in C Philips *et al Police Complaints Board: Final Review Report 1977–1985* HMSO 1985. There had been criticisms of it which led to the establishment of the working party under Lord Plowden. The report produced by the Plowden working party, *Establishment of an Independent Element in the Investigation of Complaints Against the Police: Report of a Working Party* Cmnd 8193, *Parliamentary Papers* 1980–81, led to the provisions in the 1984 Police and Criminal Evidence Act which replaced the Police Complaints Board with a Police Complaints Authority with an independent element. This process, and the differences between the two complaints authorities, are described in J Bell 'PACE and Complaints against the Police' *Policing* 2 1986 pp 283–93.

**6258** H R M Johnson 'Deaths in Police Custody in England and Wales' *Forensic Science International* 19 1982 pp 231–6. A study of the causes of deaths in police custody 1970–79 and of the ensuing inquest verdicts. The deaths of some 300 people in police custody in London are investigated in Melissa Benn and Ken Worpole *Death in the City: An Examination of Police Related Deaths in London* Canary Press 1986.

**6259** Ann Brogden '"Sus" is dead: But what about "Sas"?' *New Community* 9 1981 pp 44–58. The use of arrests on suspicion under the 1824 Vagrancy Act was one of the most controversial issues in policing in the late 1970s. It was repealed in the 1981 Criminal Law Amendment Act but was already being replaced by the use of stop and search powers the operation of which in Liverpool is the subject of this article.

**6260** Lee Bridges 'The British Left and Law and Order' *Sage Race Relations Abstracts* 8/1 1982. This is a bibliographical essay on the Left's growing criticism in the 1970s of the police and of policing methods. The reasons for this criticism and the impact of perceptions of the 1981 and 1981 urban riots on the Left's critique of the police are examined in Martin Kettle 'The Left and the Police' *Policing* 1 1985 pp 165–73.

**6261** Paul Lerman 'Policing Juveniles in London: Shifts in Guiding Discretion 1893–1968' *British Journal of Criminology* 24 1984 pp 168–84.

**6262** R Morgan and C Maggs *Following Scarman? A Survey of Formal Police/Community Consultation Arrangements in Provincial Police Authorities in England and Wales* Centre for the Analysis of Social Policy, University of Bath 1984. One of the key aspects of the Scarman Report on the 1981 Brixton riots [6225] was its emphasis on the need for better relations between the police and the local community. Formal consultation arrangements within which to discuss ways to improve community policing began to appear in 1982. This is an interim report on the development and operation of these committees, which was required under the 1984 Police and Criminal Evidence Act. The intentions and effects of this Act are analysed in R Morgan and C Maggs *Setting the PACE: Police Community Consultation Arrangements in England and Wales* Centre for the Analysis of Social Policy, University of Bath 1985. The report assessing the resulting developments in community policing, D Brown and S Iless *Community Constables: A Study of a Policing Initiative* Research and Planning Unit 30, Home Office 1985, nevertheless found that officers were insufficiently trained for the public relations skills required in community policing.

**6263** John Baldwin 'The Police and Tape Recorders' *Criminal Law Review* 1985 pp 695–704. A history of the debate over the use of tape recorders in police interrogation which attempts to account for the dramatic shift in their favour in the 1980s. The first trials with tape recorders are assessed in C Willis *The Tape Recording of Police Interviews with Suspects: An Interim Report* HMSO 1984. Case studies of interrogation practice before the introduction of tape recording are provided in P Softley *et al Police Interrogation: An Observational Study in Four Police Stations* HMSO 1980 and B Irving *Police Interrogation: A Case Study of Current Practice* HMSO 1980.

**6264** S Mainwaring-White *The Policing Revolution: Police Technology, Democracy and Liberty in Britain* Harvester 1983. A study of the increasing sophistication of police technology and use of computers in the 1970s and 1980s. The growing use of computers and of sophisticated riot control and other technology and the effects on policing methods are also examined in T Cornford *et al Technocop: New Police Technologies* Free Association Books 1985. The developing use of computers in the 1970s is described in B Luetchford and M A J Godley 'Police and Computer Technology – UK Police Force Computers – Ten Years of Development' *Police Research Bulletin* 38 1982 pp 4–15. M Hough 'Managing with less Technology: The Impact of Information Technology on Police Management' *British Journal of Criminology* 20 1980 pp 344–57 argues that the police initially made poor use of information technology. The development of a particular information technology, the Home Office Large Major Enquiry System, is discussed in R C Barrington and D M S Pearce 'HOLMES: The Development of a Computerised Major Crime Investigation System' *Police Journal* 58 1985 pp 207–33. The development of the Police National Computer which was established in 1970 is charted in G W A Duguid 'The Police National Computer' *Police Research Bulletin* 34 1980 pp 4–12.

**6265** Roger Tarling and J Burrows 'The Investigation of Crime in England and Wales' *British Journal of Criminology* 27 1987 pp 229–51. This reviews the changing nature of criminal investigation over the last twenty years in the face of growing crime and declining clear-up rates.

**6266** R W Gould and M J Waldren *London's Armed Police 1829 to the Present* Arms and Armour Press 1986. A history of the use of firearms by London officers and not least in recent cases such as the sieges in Balcombe Street and at the Iranian Embassy. George Brock *Six Days at the Iranian Embassy* Macmillan 1980 is an instant history of the 1980 siege.

**6267** Ronald Seth *The Specials: The Story of the Special Constabulary in England, Wales and Scotland* Gollancz 1961. A comprehensive history of this body which reinforces the regular police force and survey of its contemporary state.

**6268** Tom Bowden 'Men in the Middle: The UK Police' *Conflict Studies* 68 1976 pp 1–20. A study of the effects of terrorism on the role and methods of the police. See also K Bryett 'The Effects of Political Terrorism on the Police in Great Britain and Northern Ireland Since 1969' Aberdeen PhD Thesis 1987.

**6269** *Report of the Commissioner of Police of the Metropolis* HMSO 1869–. An extensive annual report which usefully details recent policing problems and developments in police policy in London. The history of London's police is told in David Ascoli *The Queen's Peace: The Origins and Development of the Metropolitan Police 1829–1979* Hamilton 1979. See also Alastair Clark and Nigel Hinton (eds) *Scotland Yard: A 150 Year History* Hamlyn 1979. The operations of the Special Branch and its responsibilities in the field of internal security are assessed in Rupert Allason *The Branch: A History of the Metropolitan Police Special Branch 1883–1983* Secker and Warburg 1983. This however has little material on the post-war period. David J Smith *Police and People in London* 4v, Policy Studies Institute 1983 is a critical study of contemporary policing methods. So is *Policing London: Collected Reports of the GLC Police Committee* Greater London Council 1986. The articles in this collection are taken from the twice monthly journal *Policing London* 1982–, which acts as a critical watchdog on the Metropolitan Police.

**6270** W Indge Short *History of the Berkshire Constabulary 1856–1956* Berkshire Constabulary 1956. There are many histories of local police forces, most of which are listed in [6236]. Other reasonably substantial local histories of this kind include S P Thompson *Maintaining The Queen's Peace: A Short History of the Birkenhead Borough Police* Birkenhead Constabulary 1958, R J Goslin *Duty Bound: A History of the Bolton Borough Police Force 1839–1969* Bolton Borough Council 1970, Gordon H Smith *Bradford's Police* Bradford Constabulary 1974, *Review of the Years 1946–1965* Devonshire Constabulary 1966, R V Kyrke *History of the East Sussex Police 1840–1967* Sussex Police Authority 1970, J Woodgate *The Essex Police* Terence Dalton 1985, Ian A Watt *A History of the Hampshire and Isle of Wight Constabulary 1839–1966* Hampshire and Isle of Wight Constabulary 1967, Neil Osborn *The Story of the Hertfordshire Police* Hertfordshire Constabulary 1969, Ewart W Clay (ed) *Leeds Police 1836–1974* West Yorkshire Police 1975, Denis Taylor *999 And All That* Oldham Corporation 1968 (a history of Oldham police 1849–1968), Douglas J Elliott *Policing Shropshire 1836–1967* Brewin 1985, Charles A Darwin *Southport County Borough Police 1870–1969* Southport Constabulary 1969, J D Wheeler *History of the West Suffolk Constabularies* West Suffolk Constabulary 1967 and Colin Glover *A History of the Worcester City Police 1833–1967* Worcester Constabulary 1967.

**6271** J McClure *Spike Island: Portrait of a Police Division* Macmillan 1980. An extensive and well regarded study of life as a police officer with A division of the Merseyside police working in inner city Liverpool in the late 1970s.

**6272** G Hardwicke *Keepers of the Door: The History of the Port of London Authority Police* Peel Press 1979. The history of a special police force.

**6273** John Alderson and B Franklin 'The Youth and Policy Interview' *Youth and Policy* 11 1984–85 pp 6–11. An interview with Alderson, the former Chief Constable of Devon and Cornwall in which he discusses many contemporary policing issues.

**6274** Dave Brady *Yankee One and George* Police Review 1985. Personal recollections of the Metropolitan Police 1955–83.

**6275** Frank Bunn *No Silver Spoon* the author 1970. The autobiography of a policeman who served in provincial forces around the country.

**6276** Frank Cater and Tom Tullett *Sharp End: The Fight against Organised Crime* The Bodley Head 1988.

Memoirs of a leading Metropolitan Police officer. His last post was as commander of the flying squad investigating the Brinks Mat gold bullion robbery of 1984.

**6277** Macdonald Hastings *The Other Mr Churchill: A Lifetime of Shooting and Murder* Harrap 1963. A biography of Robert Churchill, the forensic science expert.

**6278** Harry Cole *Policeman's Progress* Firecrest 1985. Memoirs of his service in the Metropolitan Police 1952–79.

**6279** Gilbert Kelland *Crime in London* The Bodley Head 1986. A memoir of police work in London in the post-war years.

**6280** Sir David McNee *McNee's Law* Collins 1983. The autobiography of the Commissioner of the Metropolitan Police 1977–82, reflecting on many of the policing problems and key issues of the day. McNee was previously Chief Constable of Glasgow 1971–5 and of Strathclyde 1975–7.

**6281** Sir Robert Mark *In the Office of Constable* Collins 1978. A good autobiography by the Commissioner of the Metropolitan Police 1972–7 who was charged with dealing with many of the controversial issues of the 1970s, all of which are discussed in this work. Mark was previously Deputy Commissioner 1968–72 and Chief Constable of Leicester 1957–67.

**6282** Harold Scott *Scotland Yard* Deutsch 1954. Scott was the Metropolitan Police's first post-war commissioner.

**6283** Jack Slipper *Slipper of the Yard* Sidgwick and Jackson 1981. A memoir of the flying squad.

**6284** For John Stalker see [8546].

**6285** Henry James Walls *Expert Witness: My Thirty Years in Forensic Science* Lang 1972. Memoirs of a leading forensic scientist.

### (5) Private Security

**6286** Thomas Clayton *The Protectors: The Inside Story of Britain's Private Security Forces* Oldbourne 1967. The growth of private security firms in the post-war period has gone largely unrecorded and unanalysed. This journalistic study concentrates on Securicor and Factoryguards, the two largest firms.

## (6) Capital Punishment

**6287** *Report of the Royal Commission on Capital Punishment* Cmnd 8932, *Parliamentary Papers* vii 1952–53. This Commission under Sir Ernest Gowers was not asked to review whether or not capital punishment should be retained and accordingly did not threaten the status quo. However Sir Ernest Gowers later published *A Life for a Life? The Problem of Capital Punishment* Chatto and Windus 1956 in which he explained the reasons for his subsequent conversion to the abolitionist cause.

**6288** James B Christoph *Capital Punishment and British Politics: The British Movement to Abolish the Death Penalty 1945–1957* Allen and Unwin 1962. A useful study of the debate over capital punishment up to the 1957 Homicide Act which modified but did not abolish capital punishment. See also Elizabeth Tuttle *The Crusade Against Capital Punishment in Britain* Stevens 1961. The history of the debate is taken up to the 1965 Murder Act, which abolished capital punishment for murder for a trial period (confirmed by parliament in 1969) in Frank Dawtry 'The Abolition of the Death Penalty in Britain' *British Journal of Criminology* 6 1966 pp 183–92. That capital punishment nevertheless remained a controversial issue (it has indeed remained the subject of frequent parliamentary votes ever since) is confirmed in Gavin Drewry 'Parliament and Hanging: Further Episodes in an Undying Saga' *Parliamentary Affairs* 27 1973–4 pp 251–61.

**6289** Louis Blom-Cooper (ed) *The Hanging Question: Essays on the Death Penalty* Duckworth 1969. Examinations of the hanging debate from different, including historical, perspectives.

**6290** Arthur Koestler and C H Rolph *Hanged by the Neck: An Exposure of Capital Punishment in England* Penguin 1961. An abolitionist polemic which includes brief descriptions of the fate of every murderer executed between 1949 and 1960.

**6291** Maurice Christopher Hollis *The Homicide Act* Gollancz 1964. A study of the 1957 Homicide Act which includes its full text.

## (7) The Penal System

### (a) General

**6292** *Report of the Commissioners of Prisons* HMSO 1878–1964. An annual report on the state of the prison service and on current developments. This became *Report on the Work of the Prison Department* HMSO 1965–. See also *Report of HM Chief Inspector of Prisons* HMSO 1982–.

**6293** Mick Ryan *The Politics of Penal Reform* Longman 1983. A good history of the changing nature of penal policy in the post-war period, and the various problems it has encountered such as prison overcrowding or, partly as a result of this, prison riots. Another useful treatment is J E Hall Williams *The English Penal System in Transition* Butterworths 1970. Mike Fitzgerald and J Sim *British Prisons* 2nd ed, Blackwell 1982 is more a study of the contemporary state of the penal system. Also more sociological than historical in its treatment is the earlier but comprehensive and well organized study, Nigel Walker *Crime and Punishment in Britain: An Analysis of the Penal System in Theory, Law and Practice* 2nd ed, Edinburgh University Press 1968. See also Hugh Klare *People in Prison* Pitman 1973. Earlier examinations of the development and contemporary state of the penal system are D L Howard *The English Prisons* Methuen 1960, Sewell Stokes *Come To Prison: A Tour Through British Prisons Today (A Personal Report)* Longmans 1957 and Winifred A Elkin *The English Penal System* Penguin 1957. Lionel W Fox *The English Prison and Borstal Systems* Routledge and Kegan Paul 1952 was for many years the standard description of the penal system.

**6294** David Downes *Contrasts In Tolerance: Post-War Penal Policies in the Netherlands and England and Wales* Oxford University Press 1988. This contrasts British penal policy with the liberal policies pursued in the Netherlands.

**6295** Barbara Wootton *Crime and Penal Policy* Allen and Unwin 1978. Wootton was an important influence on social policy in post-war Britain. In this volume she reflects in an erudite fashion on fifty years of sentencing policy, the work of the Advisory Council on the Penal System and other bodies with which she was involved and the changing contours of the penal system.

**6296** Louis Blom-Cooper (ed) *Progress in Penal Reform* Clarendon 1974. A useful collection of essays on aspects of penal history, penal policy, the prison service, the experience of prisoners and the development of non-custodial sentencing through devices such as the community service order. Another wide ranging and useful collection of essays is Paul Halmos (ed) *Sociological Studies in the English Prison Service* University of Keele 1965. Nigel Walker (ed) *Penal Policy-Making in England* Institute of Criminology, University of Cambridge 1977 presents a number of different perspectives and examinations of different problems in policy-making. Rupert Cross *Punishment, Prison and the Public* Stevens 1971 is a collection on penal policy in the twentieth century. It however concentrates on the pre-1939 era.

**6297** L J Fox 'English Prisons Since the War' *Annals of the American Academy of Political Science* 293 1954 pp 118–29.

**6298** *Prisons, Borstal Institutions, Approved Schools and Remand Homes: Report of a Committee to Review Punishments Part 1 and 2: Prisons and Borstal Institutions* Cmnd 8256, and *Part 3 and 4: Approved Schools and Remand Homes* Cmnd 8429, *Parliamentary Papers* xviii 1950–51. The report of the committee chaired by H W F Franklin.

**6299** *Advisory Council on the Treatment of Offenders Imprisonment: Alternatives to Short Terms of Imprisonment* HMSO 1957. The report of a committee chaired by the Earl of Drogheda which led to the introduction of the non-custodial community service orders.

**6300** *Penal Practice in a Changing Society: Aspects of Future Developments (England and Wales)* Cmnd 645, *Parliamentary Papers* xxv 1958–59. The 1959 White Paper which marked the first major shift in penal policy since the liberalizing 1948 Criminal Justice Act. It called for a major rebuilding programme and the replacement of antiquated prisons. The further policy review and statement *The War Against Crime in England and Wales 1959–1964* Cmnd 2296, *Parliamentary Papers* xxv 1963–64 led to the establishment of a Royal Commission on the Penal System. This was however disbanded without having ever produced a report in 1966. The only result of this Commission, which was chaired by Viscount Amory, was the five volumes of evidence published by HMSO in 1967.

**6301** *Crime: A Challenge To Us All* Labour Party 1964. The report of a Labour Party Study Group on Crime and the Penal System chaired by Lord Longford. It effectively set the agenda for the incoming Labour government, recommending important changes in the penal system and in sentencing, in the treatment of young offenders and in the law of murder.

**6302** *Prison Escapes and Security: Report of the Inquiry* Cmnd 3175, *Parliamentary Papers* xlvii 1956–57. The report of the inquiry set up under Earl Mountbatten of Burma in the wake of the escape of the spy George Blake from Wormwood Scrubs in 1966. It made major recommendations affecting the security classification of prisoners, the security of prisons and the nature of prison administration.

**6303** Michael Wolff *Prison* Eyre and Spottiswoode 1967. A good survey of the state of the penal system in the late 1960s.

**6304** *People in Prison (England and Wales)* Cmnd 4214, *Parliamentary Papers* xvii 1969–70. A White Paper reviewing the work of the prison service in the post-war period and laying out plans for a building and modernization programme.

**6305** S Grant 'The European Convention on Human Rights and Issues in English Penal Practice Since 1966' Institute of Criminology, University of Cambridge Dip Thesis 1977.

**6306** Joy Mott *Adult Prisons and Prisoners in England and Wales 1970–1982: A Review of the Findings of Social Research* HMSO 1985. A study of the problems and aims of policy in the 1970s. It concludes that policy mistakenly concentrated upon the character of the inmates and failed to concentrate on the main obstacle to the provision of a better prison regime, which was overcrowded prisons and overstretched staff.

**6307** J E Hall Williams *Changing Prisons* Peter Owen 1975. A good study of the problems in the prison regime in the light of the prison overcrowding and disturbances and prisoner protest groups which emerged in the late 1960s and early 1970s. The reasons for the increase in the prison population and its changing composition are explored in J C Baldock 'Why the Prison Population has grown Larger and Younger?' *Howard Journal of Penology and Crime Prevention* 19 1980 pp 142–56. The pressures on the penal system are also considered in P Evans *Prison Crisis* Allen and Unwin 1980 and Roy D King and Kathleen McDermott 'British Prisons 1970–1987: The Ever-Deepening Crisis' *British Journal of Criminology* 29 1989 pp 107–28. Richard Sparks *Local Prisons: The Crises in the English Penal System* Heinemann 1971 is a prescient statement on the growing crisis.

**6308** Vivien Stern *Bricks of Shame: Britain's Prisons* Penguin 1987. A critical examination of the contemporary state of the penal system and of changes in sentencing policy and the resulting changes in the prison population.

**6309** *The United Kingdom Prison Services: Report of the Committee of Inquiry* Cmnd 7673, *Parliamentary Papers* 1979–80. A response to the problem of increasing overcrowding of often antiquated prison accommodation, this committee under J D May was also charged to look at the management of work in prisons. It suggested that sentencing policy should be re-examined with a view to reducing the prison population, Dartmoor should be closed and Peterhead substantially redeveloped and that managerial practice and industrial relations in prison work should be improved.

**6310** *Peter J Prior Report of the Committee on the Prison Disciplinary System* Cmnd 9641, *Parliamentary Papers* 1984–85. A response to the growing problem of prison riots and prisoner violence. This committee under Peter J Prior suggested a Prison Disciplinary Tribunal, a new criminal offence of prison mutiny and other new offences to deal with the problem of hostage taking, violence and barricading. The riots which led to the setting up of this committee, and particularly the one at Hull, are examined in J E Thomas and R Pooley *Exploding Prisons: Prison Riots and the Case of Hull* Junction Books 1980. A further series of riots and demonstrations are investigated in *Report of an Inquiry by Her Majesty's Inspectorate of Prisons for England and Wales into the Disturbances in Prison Service Establishments between 29 April–2 May 1986* HC Paper 42, *Parliamentary Papers* 1987–88.

**6311** A Rutherford 'Deeper into the Quagmire: Observations on the Latest Prison Building Programme' *Howard Journal of Criminal Justice* 23 1984 pp 129–37. Critical observations on the building programme of the Thatcher years, designed to greatly increase the amount of prison accommodation, in the context of the other two building programmes since 1959. On the programme launched in 1959 see N Johnston 'Recent Trends in Correctional Architecture' *British Journal of Criminology* 1 1961 pp 317–38.

**6312** E Stockdale 'A Short History of Prison Inspection in England' *British Journal of Criminology* 23 1983 pp 209–28. A history of prison inspection 1773–1982.

**6313** Gordon Rose *The Struggle for Penal Reform: The Howard League and Its Predecessors* Stevens 1961. A good history of the oldest of the pressure groups trying to influence penal policy. It includes a good bibliography. Enid Huws Jones *Margery Fry: The Essential Amateur* Oxford University Press 1966 is a biography of a Quaker who was an activist in the cause of the Howard League for Penal Reform and the crusade for the abolition of capital punishment. The Howard League is compared with the much more recent and more radical pressure group, Radical Alternatives to Prison, in Mick Ryan *The Acceptable Pressure Group – Inequality in the Penal Lobby: A Case Study of the Howard League and RAP* Saxon House 1978. The growth of organized pressure group tactics amongst prisoners themselves in the early 1970s and the protests and demonstration which led to the creation of Preservation of Rights of Prisoners are discussed in Mike Fitzgerald *Prisoners of Revolt* Penguin 1977. See also his 'The British Prisoners' Movement: Aims and Methods' in H Bianchi, M Simondi and I Taylor (eds) *Deviance and Control in Europe* Wiley 1985 pp 97–108.

**6314** *Corporal Punishment: Report of the Advisory Council on the Treatment of Offenders* Cmnd 1213, *Parliamentary Papers* xiii 1960–61. Corporal punishment had been formally abolished in 1948. This committee under Sir P K Barry was set up to consider whether it should be reintroduced in cases of violent crime or sexual offences. Its report includes some reflections on the experience of corporal punishment in the Isle of Man.

It was decided that corporal punishment should not be reintroduced in Britain.

**6315** S Dell 'The Detention of Diminished Responsibility Homicide Offenders' *British Journal of Criminology* 23 1983 pp 50–60. A study of the patterns of use and character of hospital orders used in the case of men convicted of manslaughter on the grounds of diminished responsibility 1966–77.

**6316** P Birkinshaw 'The Control Unit Regime: Law and Order in Prison' *Howard Journal of Penology and Crime Prevention* 20 1981 pp 69–80. A examination of the reasons for the 1974 establishment and the operation of the Control Unit at Wakefield prison.

**6317** N Morgan 'The Shaping of Parole in England and Wales' *Criminal Law Review* 1983 pp 137–51. An overview of the development and implementation of parole. Since 1967 parole has increasingly been used as a method for reducing the prison population and expenditure.

**6318** A E Bottoms 'The Suspended Sentence in England 1967–1978' *British Journal of Criminology* 21 1981 pp 1–26. This reviews the use of the suspended sentence, re-assesses its place in the penal system and casts doubt upon its value.

**6319** K Pease and W McWilliams (eds) *Community Service by Order* Scottish Academic Press 1980. A study of British experience with this alternative to custodial sentences. Pilot schemes were started in 1973. By the late 1970s their use was widespread. The relationship of community service orders to the rest of British penal policy is highlighted. This examination can be updated by K Pease 'Community Service Orders' in M Tonry and N Morris (eds) *Crimes and Justice: An Annual Review of Research* vol 6, University of Chicago Press 1985 pp 51–94. This account is partly based on his *Community Service Orders* Howard League 1982. See also P Ralphs 'Community Service: A Going Concern, But Where To?' *International Journal of Offender Therapy and Comparative Criminology* 24 1980 pp 234–40 and W A Young 'Community Service Orders: The Development of a New Penal Measure' Cambridge PhD Thesis 1978.

**6320** S Jones 'Deferment of Sentence: An Appraisal Ten Years On' *British Journal of Criminology* 23 1983 pp 381–93. A general assessment of the impact of deferred sentences which were introduced in 1972. They have proved less popular than probation, suspended sentences or community service orders and their use has been most common in magistrates courts.

**6321** Norval Morris *The Habitual Criminal* London University Press 1951. In 1908 a special sentence of preventive detention for persistent offenders was introduced. It was little used and succeeded only in incarcerating petty but persistent offenders for very long periods. This was amended in 1948 and abolished in 1967, when it was replaced by a little used opportunity of recourse to extended sentences. The history of habitual offender legislation in England and Wales is traced in 'Incapacitating the Habitual Criminal: The English Experience' *Michigan Law Review* 78 1980 pp 1307–89.

**6322**   J E Thomas 'From Caprice to Anarchy: The Role of the English Prison Governor' *International Journal of Offender Therapy and Comparative Criminology* 25 1981 pp 222–31. An examination of the changing role of the prison governor and the effect on his role by the development of the prison system and the unionization of prison officers. John Vidler *If Freedom Fails* Macmillan 1964 is the memoirs of a prison governor who spent an innovatory ten years at Maidstone. Another set of memoirs by a former prison governor is B P H Bell *Prison was my Parish* Heinemann 1956. Mary Size *Prisons I Have Known* Allen and Unwin 1957 is an autobiographical account of her career in the women's prison service.

**6323**   J E Thomas *The English Prison Officer Since 1850* Routledge and Kegan Paul 1972. A well regarded account. Harley Cronin *The Screw Turns* Lang 1967 is an autobiography by a former General Secretary of the Prison Officers' Association. Another prison officer's autobiography is L Merrow-Smith *Prison Screw* Jenkins 1962.

**6324**   Peter Baker *Time Out of Life* Heinemann 1961. A good memoir by a former prisoner. Another celebrated prison memoir is John McVicar *McVicar by Himself* revised ed, Arrow 1979. Don Thomson *Victims and Victors: The Life of a Wilful Survivor* Pluto 1985 reflects on prison life 1939–55. Trevor Hercules *Labelled a Black Villain* Fourth Estate 1989 is an account of his seven years in gaol for armed robbery. In the process it casts useful light on the experiences of West Indians in prison. Rod Caird *A Good and Useful Life: Imprisonment in Britain Today* Hart-Davis, MacGibbon 1974 is an account of a year spent in prison.

**6325**   Ken Smith *Inside Time* Harrap 1989. An account of the time he spent 1985–87 as writer in residence at Wormwood Scrubs and his reflections upon the prison.

**6326**   Ann D Smith *Women In Prisons: A Study in Penal Methods* Stevens 1962. A history of women's prisons in Britain. The final part covers the years 1921–61. It includes a good bibliography. See also Xenia Field *Under Lock and Key: A Study of Women in Prison* Max Parrish 1963. Joan Henry *Who Lie in Gaol* Gollancz 1952 is reminiscences of life in Holloway and Askham Grange prisons. Dorothy Crisp *A Light in the Night* Holborn Publishing Co 1960 is the autobiography of a

woman imprisoned for bankruptcy in 1958. It has some useful reflections on her experiences in prison and also on her role as chairman of the National Housewives League set up to criticize shortages during the Attlee government. Rosie Johnston *Inside Out* Michael Joseph 1989 is a sympathetic and thought-provoking account of six months spent in women's prisons in 1987.

**6327**   G Coggan and M Walker *Frightened For My Life: An Account of Deaths in British Prisons* Fontana 1982. This looks at an issue which became of considerable political importance in the 1980s.

**6328**   D L Howard (ed) *The Education of Offenders* Institute of Criminology, University of Cambridge 1971. An annotated and select bibliography. Frances Bank *Teach Them to Live: A Study of Education in English Prisons* Max Parrish 1958 examines the post-war development and contemporary state of prison education services.

**6329**   W J Gray 'The English Prison Medical Service: Its Historical Background and More Recent Developments' in *Medical Care of Prisoners and Detainees* Associated Book Publishers 1973 pp 129–42.

**6330**   J M Wells 'Group Counselling in Prisons and Borstals in England and Wales 1958–1967' Southampton MPhil Thesis 1968–9.

**6331**   Terence Morris and Pauline Morris *Pentonville: A Sociological Study of an English Prison* Routledge and Kegan Paul 1963. A good study of the London prison. Tom Tullett *Inside Dartmoor* Muller 1966 is a journalistic history of another prison. Tony Parker *The Frying Pan: A Prison and its Prisoners* Basic Books, New York 1970 is a unique portrayal of the inmates of the psychiatric prison at Grendon.

### (b) Youth Custody

**6332**   Keith Hawkins *Select Bibliography on Deprivation of Liberty as a Means of Treating Juvenile Delinquency in Great Britain 1940–1965* Institute of Criminology, University of Cambridge 1966. This listing can be updated by A Skinner *A Bibliography of Intermediate Treatment 1968–1984* National Youth Bureau 1985.

**6333**   Simon Stevenson 'Some Social and Political Tides affecting the Development of Juvenile Justice 1938–64' in Tony Gorst, Lewis Johnman and W Scott Lucas (eds) *Postwar Britain 1945–64: Themes and Perspectives* Pinter 1989 pp 68–94. A good examination of the development of the handling of juvenile offenders by the criminal justice and the penal system. The initial development of policy up to the Criminal Justice Act 1948 is traced in V Bailey *Delinquency and Citizenship: Reclaiming the Young Offender 1914–1948* Clarendon 1987. On the treatment of these offenders see R F Sparks and Roger Hood (eds) *The Residential Treatment of Disturbed and Deliquent Boys* Institute of Criminology, University of Cambridge 1968.

**6334** *Treatment of Young Offenders: Report of the Advisory Council on the Treatment of Offenders* HMSO 1959. The report of the group chaired by Sir P R Barry. *Report of the Committee on Children and Young Persons* Cmnd 1191, *Parliamentary Papers* ix 1959–60 is the result of the inquiry chaired by Viscount Ingleby into the juvenile criminal justice system and the treatment of young offenders.

**6335** N Tutt 'A Decade of Policy' *British Journal of Criminology* 21 1981 pp 246–56. An analysis of the shifts in policy on the treatment of young offenders in the 1970s in the context of the 1980 White Paper *Young Offenders* HMSO 1980 which led to the setting up of a more retributive system of treatment. He argues that this reflected ideological concern in the light of the rediscovery of the juvenile deliquent and the mugger in the 1970s rather than empirical research. The result of this was the replacement of borstals with a new youth custody regime under the 1982 Criminal Justice Act. The final years of borstals and the transition to this new system is assessed in D A Godfrey 'The Development and Effectiveness of Borstal Training 1965–1977 and the Introduction of Youth Custody' Leeds MPhil Thesis 1986. The initial impact of the new regime is evaluated in David Thornton *Tougher Regimes in Detention Centres: Report of an Evaluation* HMSO 1984.

**6336** Roger Hood *Borstal Re-Assessed* Heinemann 1965. A history and critical assessment of borstals reflecting contemporary concern about them. It contains a useful chronology.

**6337** Julius Carlebach *Caring for Children in Trouble* Routledge and Kegan Paul 1970. A history of approved schools. Gordon Rose *Schools for Young Offenders* Tavistock 1967 outlines their history and examines the situation in the 1960s. It includes a good bibliography. See also R J Clough 'The History of Reformatory and Approved Schools 1850–1967' London MPhil (Econ) Thesis 1971.

**6338** W D Wills *Spare the Child: The Story of an Experimental Approved School* Penguin 1971. An account of the Cotswold Community School, detailing the successful experiment in changing a hierarchical and authoritarian system into a caring community.

**6339** W D Wills *A Place Like Home* Allen and Unwin 1970. An account of Reynolds House, Bromley, Kent, a

pioneer hostel for boys who have left schools for the maladjusted with nowhere else to go.

**6340** B Dunlop *Junior Attendance Centres* HMSO 1980. A Home Office study of how these Saturday attendance centres were operating in 1976. As an alternative to custody it was felt that, although there were problems with absenteeism, the fact that 60 per cent of boys did not reoffend during their order period meant that they were reasonably successful.

**6341** Caroline Brown *Lost Girls* Gollancz 1955. An account of her experiences as a teacher at a remand home for girls.

(c) Probation

**6342** Dorothy Bochel *Probation and After Care* Scottish Academic Press 1976. A full length administrative history of the development of the probation service in England and Wales. See also D Haxby *Probation: A Changing Service* Constable 1978, F V Jarvis *Advise, Assist and Befriend: A History of the Probation and After-Care Service* National Association of Probation Officers 1972 and A W Hunt 'Developments in the use of Probation: A Critical Examination of Principles, Practices and Trends in the Probation Service' Nottingham MA Thesis 1968–9.

**6343** Joan King *The Probation and After Care Service* 2nd ed, Butterworths 1970. This is a good description of the contemporary situation. The first edition was published in 1958. Subsequent developments in the probation service are discussed in Joan King (ed) *Pressures and Changes in the Probation Service* Institute of Criminology, University of Cambridge 1979. The development of the service since it was made statutory under the provisions of the 1948 Criminal Justice Act and its contemporary state are discussed in C G Cartledge 'United Kingdom' in C G Cartledge, P J P Tak and M Tomi-Malic (eds) *Probation in Europe* European Assembly for Probation and After-Care 1981 pp 453–508.

**6344** *Report of the Departmental Committee on the Probation Service* Cmnd 1650, *Parliamentary Papers* xxiii 1961–62. An inquiry under R P Morison into the service and the approved probation hostel system. It argued that there was a need for improved training facilities as the rapid expansion of the service in the post-war period had not kept pace with the increasing amount of work.

**6345** *Work and Pay of Probation Officers and Social Workers: Report of the Butterworth Inquiry* Cmnd 5076, *Parliamentary Papers* xxxiv 1971–72. A report chaired by J B Butterworth.

**6346** Dorothy Bochel 'A Brief History of NAPO' *Probation* 10 1962 pp 33–6 and 53–5. A history of the National Association of Probation Officers.

**6347** J B Coker and J P Martin *Licensed To Live* Blackwell 1985. The abolition of capital punishment in 1965 has led to an increase in probation work with former lifers. This is an analysis of how the probation service has risen to the challenge. It concludes that there is no evidence that probation prevents recidivism and casts doubt on the efficacy of supervision in preventing offences.

**6348** R G Green 'Probation and the Black Offender' Aston PhD Thesis 1986. This argues that black people are disadvantaged by the 'colour-blind' approach of the probation service which focuses on explaining crime with reference to pathology and not to social structures and discrimination. This problem is analysed particularly in the context of the probation service's response to the urban riots of 1981 and 1985.

**6349** *The Police and Children* 2nd ed, Liverpool Constabulary 1962. A description of the juvenile liaison scheme by its pioneers. See also Marilyn Taylor *Study of the Juvenile Liason Scheme in West Ham 1961 to 1965* HMSO 1971.

**6350** *Discharged Prisoners' Aid Societies: Report of a Committee* Cmnd 8879, *Parliamentary Papers* ix 1952–53. The report of the committee chaired by Sir Alexander Maxwell. It surveyed the history of after care for prisoners up to 1950 and recommended that prison welfare officers should assist with care and that the grants to aid societies should be simplified.

**6351** *Advisory Council on the Treatment of Offenders The Organisation of After-Care* HMSO 1963. A report chaired by B J Hartwell. This report foreshadowed a great increase in after-care provision for adult prisoners and the assumption by the probation (henceforth the probation and after-care service) service of all after-care functions.

**6352** J P Martin 'After-Care in Transition' in Tadeusz Grygier, Howard Jones and John C Spencer (eds) *Criminology in Transition: Essays in Honour of Hermann Mannheim* Tavistock 1965 pp 88–108. A survey of the development and of recent changes in the field of after-care. One aspect of the changes was experimentation with schemes such as that which is examined in K L Soothill 'The APEX Project: An Evaluation of an Experimental Employment Agency for Ex-Prisoners' London PhD Thesis 1978.

## J. FIRE SERVICES

**6353** *Report of HM Chief Inspector of Fire Services* HMSO 1949–. This appears annually as a Command Paper.

**6354** *Report of the Departmental Committee on the Fire Services* Cmnd 4371, *Parliamentary Papers* xiii 1969–70. Developments in the fire services are one the most neglected aspects of post-war British history. This report by the committee chaired by Sir Ronald Holroyd is the nearest there is to a history of the fire services in this period. Reviewing developments it then points to the need for larger units and areas in view of the impending change in local government in the wake of the 1969 Redcliffe-Maud Report.

**6355** *Report of the Cunningham Inquiry into the Work of the Fire Service* Cmnd 4807, *Parliamentary Papers* xiii 1971–72. The report by Sir Charles Cunningham which evaluated the fireman's job and made proposals about his pay and conditions.

**6356** Frank Eyre and E C R Hadfield *The Fire Service Today* 2nd ed, Oxford University Press 1953. A contemporary study. B G Thomas *Fire Fighting in Maidstone* Phillimore 1976 is a useful local history containing plentiful material on developments since 1945. For other local histories see Jack Farmer *Epping Town Fire Brigade: A History* Epping Forest District Museum 1986, B S Veriod *A History of the Norwich City Fire Brigade* the author 1986 and D J Osbourne *A History of the Borough of Thetford Fire Brigade* the author 1988.

# 10 EDUCATION

There is also material on educational disadvantage among coloured immigrants in the section on Race Relations [5691–7]. Some of the material in the section on the Health Services is also of use for those interested in medical education and policy affecting it.

## A. GENERAL

### (1) Reference Works

**6357** *Department of Education and Science Report* HMSO 1965–. The annual report of the responsible government department, which has appeared under different titles as a Command Paper since 1928.

**6358** *Education Statistics for the United Kingdom* HMSO 1967–. Now known as *Statistics for Education*. This comes in six volumes, dealing with schools, school leavers, school examinations, further education, teachers, finance and awards and universities.

**6359** J Stuart Maclure (ed) *Educational Documents: England and Wales: 1816 to the Present Day* 4th ed, Methuen 1979. A useful collection of documents which includes quite a lot of material from the post-war period.

**6360** *British Education Index* Library Association 1954–1969. A quarterly publication. Since 1970 this has been published by the British Library Bibliographical Services Division. It references over 200 English language journals, the majority of which are British publications.

**6361** *Sociology of Education Abstracts* Carfax Publishing 1965–. This contains about 600 detailed abstracts per year. See also *Education Abstracts* UNESCO, Paris 1949–.

**6362** EMIE 1981–. The education management information exchange database produced by the National Foundation for Educational Research on educational policy and provision. It is also the source of *Education Management Abstracts*.

**6363** George Baron *A Bibliographical Guide to the English Educational System* 3rd ed, Athlone Press 1965. A good, well annotated and classified bibliography. D A Howell *A Bibliography of Educational Administration in the United Kingdom* National Foundation for Educational Research 1978 is to some extent an update, but it is unannotated. See also S Kimmerance *A Guide to the Literature of Education* Institute of Education, University of London 1961.

**6364** Peter Cunningham *Local History of Education in England and Wales: A Bibliography* Leeds Museum of the History of Education 1971. This provides some 3,000 largely unannotated entries arranged by county and town. It also covers the Isle of Man and the Channel Islands.

**6365** *Educational Developments at Home and Abroad: A Select List of Recent Additions to the Library* Department of Education and Science Library 1972–. A monthly list of some 100 titles.

**6366** Victor F Gilbert and Colin Holmes *Theses and Dissertations on the History of Education Presented at British and Irish Universities between 1900 and 1976* History of Education Society 1979. A listing.

**6367** J E Vaughan and Michael Argyles *British Government Publications Concerning Education: An Introductory Guide* 4th ed, School of Education, University of Liverpool 1982. A good descriptive guide.

**6368** Harold Silver 'Education and the Labour Movement' *History of Education* 2 1973 pp 173–202. A bibliographical essay which covers all aspects of the relationship between the Labour Movement and education, from the education policies of the Labour Party to the trade unions involvement in adult education.

**6369** *School, University and College Registers and Histories in the Library of the Society of Genealogists* Society of Genealogists 1988. There are a large number of these which are conveniently listed in this catalogue.

**6370**  Richard Aldrich and Peter Gordon *Dictionary of British Educationalists* Woburn 1989. An excellent alphabetically arranged guide to prominent figures in the field of education in the nineteenth and twentieth centuries.

**6371**  Peter Gordon and Denis Lawton *A Guide to English Educational Terms* Batsford 1984. A useful historical and contemporary guide.

## (2) General

**6372**  Peter Gordon *Education Since the Second World War* Robertson 1983. A useful study of post-war developments. See also Roy Lowe *Education in the Post-War Years: A Social History* Croom Helm 1988. Peter Gosden *The Education System Since 1944* Robertson 1983 concentrates rather more on the development of policy. Janet Finch *Education as Social Policy* Longman 1984 puts this in the context of the broader development of social policy. W Kenneth Richmond *Education in Britain Since 1944: A Personal Retrospect* Methuen 1978 is an impressionistic account which focuses somewhat critically on post-war educational ideas, theories and objectives.

**6373**  Harold Collett Dent *1870–1970: A Century of Growth in English Education* Longman 1970. A history since the important 1870 Education Act. The history of education over this period is also examined in Bernard Lawrence *The Administration of Education in Great Britain* Batsford 1972 and A D C Peterson *100 Years of Education* 3rd ed, Duckworth 1971. G A N Lowndes *The Silent Social Revolution: An Account of the Expansion of Public Education in England and Wales 1895–1965* 2nd ed, Oxford University Press 1969 surveys developments since education was made a compulsory requirement. An earlier study of education in the twentieth century is S J Curtis *Education in Britain Since 1900* Dakers 1952. W H G Armytage *Four Hundred Years of English Education* Cambridge University Press 1970, despite its broad historical sweep, has quite good coverage on the post-war era.

**6374**  Michael Sanderson *Educational Opportunity and Social Change in England* Faber 1987. A study of changing access to education in the twentieth century and the failings of skills training.

**6375**  Peter Gosden *The Development of Educational Administration in England and Wales* Blackwell 1966. An administrative history. Robert Peers *Fact and Possibility in English Education* Routledge and Kegan Paul 1963 is a general survey of selected issues in policy and administration in education since the 1902 Education Act. Willem van der Eyken *Adventures in Education* Penguin 1975 looks at innovations in education 1914–61.

**6376**  Stewart Ranson and John Tomlinson (eds) *The Changing Government of Education* Allen and Unwin 1986. A study of the contemporary adminstration of the education system and of the organization and adminstration of its various constituent elements in the context of developments since 1944. A more historical study is Nigel Middleton and Sophie Weitzman *A Place For Everyone: A History of State Education from the End of the 18th Century to the 1970s* Gollancz 1976. Keith Fenwick and Peter McBride *The Government of Education in Britain* Robertson 1981 is a useful textbook which contains many historical details. The various advisory bodies which influence policy making are examined in Maurice Kogan and Tim Packwood *Advisory Councils and Committees in Education* Routledge and Kegan Paul 1974. See also G Fowler, V Morris and G Ozja (eds) *Decision Making in British Education* Heinemann 1974.

**6377**  Peter Gordon (ed) *The Study of Education: A Collection of Inaugural Lectures* 3v, Woburn 1980–8. An introduced and edited collection of inaugural lectures by professors of education and heads of major educational establishments on the idea, philosophy and practice of education and the place of education in society. The volumes are useful as a source and demonstrate the changing nature of education. The first volume covers lectures to 1965, the second lectures 1965–78 and the third lectures 1977–84.

**6378**  Peter Gordon and John White *Philosophers and Educational Reformers: The Influence of Idealism on British Educational Thought and Practice* Routledge and Kegan Paul 1979. An excellent study of the history of British educational philosophy and its moral objectives. See also R F Dearden 'Philosophy of Education 1952–1982' *British Journal of Educational Studies* 30 1982 pp 57–71. An important aspect of educational philosophy and policy is examined in H-C Kang 'Educational Policy and the Concept of Equality of Opportunity in England 1900–1970' Oxford DPhil Thesis 1982.

**6379**  J Lello *The Official Position on Education* Pergamon 1964. This is a classified summary of the major reports affecting legislation over the period 1944–64. Sir William Alexander and F Barraclough *Education Acts Amended* Councils and Education Press 1969 lists all the various amendments to the 1944 Education Act down to 1969.

**6380**  John Vaizey *The Economics of Education* Macmillan 1973. See also John Vaizey and John Sheehan *Resources for Education: An Economic Study of Education in the United Kingdom 1920–1965* Allen and Unwin 1968. The changing finance of education is analysed in the context of the relative roles of local and central government in D Williams 'Education and Finance: A Local Government Perception: A Study of the Finance of Education Since 1945, with Regard to the Role of the Local Education Authority' Leeds MEd Thesis 1985. This is studied in the immediate post-war period in W E D Stephens 'A Critical Examination of Developments in the Adminstrative and Financial Relationship between the Ministry of Education and Local Education Authorities in the Period 1944–1954' London PhD Thesis 1955–6.

**6381** Harold Collett Dent *Education in England and Wales* 2nd ed, Hodder and Stoughton 1982. The standard textbook picture of the contemporary state of education. It supersedes his earlier series of contemporary impressions of the educational system which culminated with his *The Education System in England and Wales* 5th ed, Athlone Press 1971. See also N D C Grant and R E Bell *Patterns of Education in the British Isles* Allen and Unwin 1977.

**6382** A H Halsey, Jean Floud and C Arnold Anderson (eds) *Education, Economy and Society: A Reader in the Sociology of Education* Collier Macmillan 1985. This is mostly concerned with the USA. It however includes essays on subjects such as the growth of universities in Britain, the social profile of Oxbridge or teacher recruitment.

**6383** K Jeffreys 'R A Butler, the Board of Education and the 1944 Education Act' *History* 69 1984 pp 415–31. The 1944 Education Act, for which Butler was the Minister responsible, was of crucial importance in establishing the main contours of the post-war education system and also led to the raising of the school leaving age to 15 in 1947. Its principal author looks back on it in R A Butler *The Education Act and After* Longmans 1965. Other perspectives on the Act are Brian Simon 'The 1944 Education Act: A Conservative Measure?' *History of Education* 15 1986 pp 31–43, Nigel Middleton 'Lord Butler and the Education Act of 1944' *British Journal of Education Studies* 20 1972 pp 178–91 and Stuart Maclure 'Forty Years On' *British Journal of Education Studies* 33 1985 pp 117–34.

**6384** Harold Collett Dent *Growth in English Education 1946–52* Routledge and Kegan Paul 1954. A survey of post- war developments. See also P Wann 'The Collapse of Parliamentary Bipartisanship in education 1945–1952' *Journal of Educational Administration and History* 3 1971 pp 24–34. The work of the Labour Ministers of Education of this period is examined in D W Dean 'Planning for a Post-War Generation: Ellen Wilkinson and George Tomlinson at the Ministry of Education 1945–51' *History of Education* 15 1986 pp 95–117.

**6385** D J O'Keefe 'Some Aspects of Raising the School Leaving Age in England and Wales in 1947' *Economic History Review* 2nd series 28 1975 pp 500–16. The background debate to the raising of the school leaving age which eventually culminated in this implementation of the 1944 legislation is examined in C Barber 'The Raising of the School Leaving Age 1870–1947' Manchester PhD Thesis 1976.

**6386** Brian Simon 'The Tory Government and Education 1951–60: Background to Breakout' *History of Education* 14 1985 pp 283–98. A seminal study of why the Conservative view that only a limited number of people were sufficiently gifted to benefit from higher education was gradually abandoned in the 1950s.

**6387** Maurice Kogan *The Politics of Education: Edward Boyle and Anthony Crosland in Conversation with Maurice Kogan* Penguin 1971. Conversations with two of the most important policy-makers of the 1960s. Boyle was Minister of Education 1962–4 and Crosland was Secretary of State at the new Department of Education and Science 1965–7. Sir William Alexander *Education in England* 2nd ed, Newnes 1964 is a well regarded survey of the educational system in the 1960s.

**6388** Maurice Kogan *The Politics of Educational Change* Fontana 1978. This contends that education was a central and controversial issue in the 1970s. It examines many of the particular issues and events as well as the conflicts over curricula and standards and the increasing militancy of teachers in the context of the place of the 1970s in the history of post-war educational developments. The failure to make much progress despite attempts to launch a national debate on education by Prime Minister James Callaghan is assessed in the essays on educational change in the 1970s and 1980s in Max Morris and Clive Griggs (eds) *Education: The Wasted Years? 1973–1986* Falmer 1988. Policy in the 1960s and 1980s is examined in Edgar Litt and Michael Parkinson *US and UK Educational Policy: A Decade of Reform* Praeger 1979. The debate over education in the 1960s and 1970s between progressives and the supporters of the Black Papers [6395] is examined in the essays in Gerald Bernbaum (ed) *Schooling in Decline* Macmillan 1979.

**6389** L M Crosby 'The Raising of the School Leaving Age from 15 to 16 in 1972: A Case Study in Educational Policy-Making' Exeter MA Thesis 1977. This focuses on thinking on the issue of raising the leaving age since the 1944 Education Act. A local aspect of the implementation of the raising of the school leaving age in the early 1970s is analysed in R Burgess 'The Implementation of the Raising of the School Leaving Age in Devon 1973–74' Bath MEd Thesis 1974–5.

**6390** J Ahier and M Flude (eds) *Contemporary Education Policy* Croom Helm 1983. This reflects the situation in the 1980s. Ken Jones *Right Turn: The Conservative Revolution in Education* Hutchinson Radius 1989 is a useful assessment of the educational policies of the Thatcher government.

**6391** Rodney Barker *Education and Politics 1900–1951: A Study of the Labour Party* Oxford University Press 1972. A good study. For the later development of Labour policy, particularly towards comprehensives, see A Brooke 'The Labour Party's Educational Policy and the Sociology of Education' CNAA MPhil Thesis 1982.

**6392** S Shaw 'Political Ideas, Values and Ideology: A Study of Conservative Party Views on Education 1944–1966' Nottingham PhD Thesis 1979–80.

**6393** Maurice Kogan *Educational Policy-Making: A Study of Interest Groups and Parliament* Allen and Unwin 1975. A study of policy change and the influence on policy of various pressure groups, such as the teachers' unions, the press, parliament, parents or the Roman Catholic church, between 1960 and the fall of the Heath government in 1974. It includes a number of case studies. Probably the most imporant pressure groups are the teachers' unions. Their influence on policy is analysed in Ronald A Manser *Teachers and Politics: The Role of the National Union of Teachers in the Making of National Educational Policy in England and Wales Since 1944* Manchester University Press 1970 and in R D Coates *Teachers' Unions and Interest Group Politics* Cambridge University Press 1972. The history of a much older pressure group up to its disbandment in 1959 (when its functions, which by then were largely to represent Nonconformist interests, were taken over by the Free Church Federal Council) is examined in Arnold P Derrington 'The National Education Association of Great Britain 1889–1959' Manchester MEd Thesis 1970–1 and also in his 'The National Education Association of Great Britain 1889–1959: A Short Account and Bibliography' *History of Education Society Bulletin* 11 1973 pp 18–33. Another body is studied in J R Brooks 'The Council for Educational Advance during the Chairmanship of R H Tawney 1942–9' *Journal of Educational Administration and History* 9 1977 pp 42–8 and J R Brooks 'R H Tawney and the Politics of Educational Reform 1903–1953' *Durham and Newcastle Research Review* 9 1982 pp 322–34.

**6394** Institute of Christian Education *Institute of Christian Education at Home and Overseas 1935–56* Religious Education Press 1956. A short anniversary history of the work of the Institute.

**6395** C B Cox and A E Dyson (ed) *Fight for Education* Critical Quarterly Society 1969. The first of the celebrated black papers which critically assessed the current state of education and many of the contemporary fashions in educational theory and called for a return to traditional educational values. This and the subsequent black papers; C B Cox and A E Dyson (eds) *Black Paper Two: The Crisis in Education* Critical Quarterly Society 1969, C B Cox and A E Dyson (eds) *Black Papers on Education* Davis Poynter 1971, C B Cox and Rhodes Boyson (eds) *Black Paper 1975: The Fight for Education* Dent 1975 and C B Cox and Rhodes Boyson *Black Paper 1977* Temple Smith 1977, set out much of the educational agenda of the New Right which has since been pursued by the Thatcher government.

**6396** K A Williams 'Educational Maintenance Allowances: The Evolution of a Public Policy' Birmingham MEd Thesis 1981. A history of policy on these grants.

**6397** G Sutherland *Ability, Merit and Measurement: Mental Testing and English Education 1880–1950* Oxford University Press 1984. A rather critical look at the origins of the selective system based on the Eleven Plus introduced by the 1944 Education Act over a long historical perspective.

**6398** D E Regan *Local Government and Education* Allen and Unwin 1977. A survey of the education system since 1944 from the point of view of the local education authorities in all its various aspects. Robert E Jennings *Education and Politics: Policy Making in Local Education Authorities* Batsford 1977 is a well documented study of the extent to which the local administration of education has been politicized drawing on studies of three outer London boroughs and three English counties conducted in 1973–4. Jack Brand 'Ministry Control and Local Autonomy in Education' *Political Quarterly* 36 1965 pp 154–63 argues that there is diminishing local autonomy in the local education service.

**6399** *The First Fifty Years* Association of Education Committees 1953. This traces local government administration of local education since control passed to local councils under the 1902 Education Act.

**6400** Maurice Kogan and Willem van der Eyken *County Hall: The Role of the Chief Education Officer* Penguin 1973. This set of transcripts of interviews with the Chief Education Officers of Devon, Hillingdon and Leeds illustrates the problems of management, of partisan attitudes to education and the finance of education. So does the subsequent volume, Tony Bush and Maurice Kogan *Directors of Education* Allen and Unwin 1982. This examines changes in the role of these officers, not least their change of title, in the decade since the first book, drawing on interviews with the Directors of Education in South Glamorgan, Coventry, the Inner London Education Authority and Avon. See also H Booth 'The Chief Officer in English Education 1870–1968' Manchester MEd Thesis 1970–1.

**6401** Michael J Apter *The New Technology of Education* Macmillan 1968. A textbook on the growing use of broadcasting, computers and other innovations in education. On broadcasting for schools see K V Bailey *The Listening Schools: Educational Broadcasting by Sound and Television* BBC 1957. This is a brief but comprehensive account which includes a good short bibliography. See also the brief survey *Broadcasts and Teacher Education: The Contribution of BBC Education Broadcasting from 1970 to 1980* BBC 1981. The use of broadcasting in education since 1939 is surveyed in Helen Coppen (ed) 'Symposium on Mass Media in the United Kingdom' *Year Book of Education* 1960 pp 294–312.

**6402** Rosemary Deem *Women and Schooling* Routledge and Kegan Paul 1978. A historical survey of women's education. See also her 'State Policy and Ideology in the Education of Women 1944–80' *British Journal of Sociology of Education* 2 1981 pp 131–43, which relates changes in policy on women's education to changing economic and social circumstances. She has also edited *Schooling for Women's Work* Routledge and Kegan Paul 1980, which is a collection of essays reflecting on girls' education c1912–1979.

**6403** Peter Chisholm McIntosh *Physical Education in England Since 1800* revised ed, Bell 1968. A useful general history. See also Sheila Fletcher *Women First: The Female Tradition in English Physical Education 1880–1980* Athlone Press 1984.

**6404** Frank Field (ed) *Education and the Urban Crisis* Routledge and Kegan Paul 1977. A study of the educational element in the inner city crisis of the 1970s, the state of inner city schools and the response of the policy-makers through devices such as the Educational Priority Areas.

**6405** C A Wood 'Educational Policy in Bristol' Bristol MSc Thesis 1973. This is useful not least for secondary school reorganization in the 1960s.

**6406** A G Geen 'Educational Policy-Making in Cardiff 1944–1970' *Public Administration* 59 1981 pp 85–104. A study of the handling of issues, not least comprehensive education.

**6407** K H Wood-Allum 'A Review of the Education Service in the Borough of Chesterfield 1944–1967' Durham MEd Thesis 1969–70.

**6408** B Rigby 'The Planning and Provision of Education in the Foundation and Development of a Post-War New Town: Crawley, Sussex 1947–66' Southampton PhD Thesis 1974–5. A case study.

**6409** Mildred M Cullen *Education in Darlington 1900–74* Local History Publications 5, Darlington Public Library 1974. A short survey up to the local government reorganization of 1974.

**6410** C Asher 'An Analysis of the Work of an Exempted District: Educational Provision in the Borough of Keighley 1944–1974' Leeds PhD Thesis 1985. Excepted districts were an administrative compromise set up under the 1944 Education Act which were abolished under the 1972 Local Government Act.

**6411** John Fox *Education in Gillingham 1893–1974* Gillingham Public Libraries 1974.

**6412** J Stuart Maclure *One Hundred Years of London Education 1870–1970* Allen Lane 1970. A useful history. An official report on progress in the first post-war decade is *Education in London 1945–54: A Report by the Education Officer* London County Council 1955. D A Howell and Roger Brown *Educational Policy Making: An Analysis* Heinemann Educational 1983 provides case studies of the introduction of the Bachelor of Education degree in London in 1963–70 and of the Inner London Education Authority's review of vocational higher education in 1970–73.

**6413** Donald Jones *Stewart Mason: The Art of Education* Lawrence and Wishart 1988. A biography of the innovatory Director of Education who was largely responsible for the progressive education for which Leicestershire became famous in the post-war period.

**6414** F F Ridley *Education Policy-Making in Four Merseyside County Boroughs* Social Science Research Council 1974. See also J C Humphrey 'The Reorganisation of Education in the County Borough of Wallasey 1961–1968' Durham MEd Thesis 1969–70.

**6415** Peter Gosden and P R Sharp *The Development of an Educational Service: The West Riding 1889–1974* Robertson 1978. A good history of the educational service in the West Riding of Yorkshire until it was swept away in the local government reorganization of 1974. Keith Fenwick (ed) *Yorkshire Studies in Education 1983* School of Education, University of Leeds 1983 collects post-graduate essays on subjects like the reorganization of middle schools in Bradford in the 1960s, the effect of falling school roles or management of education in Yorkshire.

**(3) Technical Education in Schools, Further and Higher Education**

**6416** J Heywood *Bibliography of British Technological Education and Training* Hutchinson 1971. A useful guide to the literature.

**6417** Michael Argyles *South Kensington to Robbins: An Account of English Technical and Scientific Education Since 1851* Longman 1964. A useful general account concentrating on technical education down to the 1963 Robbins Report on higher education. The changing philosophy of technical education since the nineteenth century is examined in A J Peters 'The Changing Idea of Technical Education' *British Journal of Educational Studies* 11 1963 pp 142–66.

**6418** Stephen F Cotgrove *Technical Education and Social Change* Allen and Unwin 1958. The opening statement: 'The present shortage of trained scientific manpower in England is without precedent. Moreover, in spite of post-war increases in the output from the universities and technical colleges, the numbers of trained technologists and technicians in England compare very unfavourably with those in other advanced countries', remains depressingly familiar. This is a detailed enquiry into the failings of the education system in this area. It includes a good bibliography.

**6419** R C Mudie 'Education and Industry: A Study of Developments in the Relationship between Education and Industry Since 1960' Dundee MEd Thesis 1982. By the 1970s there was increasing concern that the progressive education of the 1960s had failed to produce trained and skilled personnel. This thesis examines this, the 'great debate on education' initiated by the government and the subsequent growth in emphasis on vocationalism and training in the context of education's role as a provider of personnel for industry.

**6420** Peter William Musgrave 'Constant Factors in the Demand for Technical Education 1860–1960' *British Journal of Educational Studies* 14 1965–6 pp 173–87.

**6421** Jeremy Moon and J J Richardson 'Policy-Making with a Difference? The Technical and Vocational Education Alternative' *Public Administration* 62 1984 pp 23–33. A study of the background to the launch of TVEI by the Thatcher government in the early 1980s as a device to try and improve vocational training in schools. The policy is critically assessed in the context of New Right thinking in Daniel Wincott *Interpreting the Technical and Vocational Education Initiative: A Critical Study of 'Conservative Neo-Liberalism'* Manchester Papers in Politics 5, Department of Government, Victoria University of Manchester 1989. E A Fennell 'The Technical and Vocational Education Initiative: What's it all about' *Newscheck* 2 1984 pp 3–8 is a detailed analysis of the scheme to stimulate training for 14–18 year olds across the ability range which was in 1984 still being tested in fourteen localities.

**6422** R Dandy 'Factors and Institutions which have affected the Teaching of Handicrafts in the Twentieth Century, with Particular Reference to the Institute of Craft Education' Sheffield MA Thesis 1977.

**6423** R P Gaskell 'Trends in Technical Education in the West Midlands 1938–1964' Birmingham MA Thesis 1964.

### (4) Multi-Racial Education

**6424** Sally Tomlinson 'Race and Education in Britain 1960–1977: An Overview of the Literature' *Sage Race Relations Abstracts* 2/3 1976 pp 3–33. A useful bibliographical essay. A further essay reviewing the research on the subject is her 'The Educational Performance of Ethnic Minority Children' *New Community* 8 1980 pp 213–38. See also M Purushothaman *The Education of Children of Caribbean Origin: Select Research Bibliography* Centre for Information and Advice on Educational Disadvantage 1978. The West Indian creole language has often been associated with the low educational attainments of West Indian children in Britain. The works on this subject are reviewed in Viv Edwards 'Black British English: A Bibliographical Essay on the Language of Children of West Indian Origin' *Sage Race Relations Abstracts* 5 1980 pp 1–25.

**6425** David L Kirp *Doing Good by Doing Little: Race and Schooling in Britain* University of California Press 1979. A critical appraisal.

**6426** M Stone *The Education of the Black Child in Britain* Fontana 1981. See also R Giles *The West Indian Experience in British Schools* Heinemann 1977. The response of local education authorities is examined in H E R Townsend *Immigrant Pupils in England: The LEA Response* National Foundation for Educational Research 1971.

**6427** G K Verma *et al Ethnicity and Educational Achievement in British Schools* Macmillan 1986. A report on the influence of cultural variables on educational achievement.

**6428** *West Indian Children in our Schools: Interim Report of the Committee of Inquiry into the Education of Children from Ethnic Minority Groups* Cmnd 8273, *Parliamentary Papers* 1980–81. The report of the committee chaired by Anthony Rampton.

**6429** *Education For All: The Report of the Committee of Inquiry into the Education of Children from Ethnic Minority Groups* Cmnd 9453, *Parliamentary Papers* 1984–85. This report by the committee chaired by Lord Swann contains much important research into the contemporary state of the education and the educational achievements of ethnic minority children. It draws attention to under-achievement amongst West Indians and Bangladeshis. Fifteen years of research into the education of West Indian children is critically reviewed in Monica J Taylor *Caught Between: A Review of Research into the Education of Pupils of West Indian Origin* National Foundation for Educational Research/Nelson 1981.

**6430** Bernard Coard *How the West Indian Child is made Educationally Sub-Normal in the British School System* New Beacon 1971. A disproportionate number of West Indians were being placed in schools for the educationally sub-normal. This work examines this tendency and the nature and function of these schools. The history of the debate over the over-representation of West Indians in these schools from the first complaints in 1965 is traced in Sally Tomlinson 'West Indian Children and ESN Schooling' *New Community* 4 1978 pp 235–42.

## B. SCHOOLS

### (1) General

**6431** Alan Arthur Coulson *School Administration and Management: A Selected Annotated Bibliography* Flag Publications 1975. A short bibliography.

**6432** Michael Hyndman *Schools and Schooling in England and Wales: A Documentary History* Harper and Row 1978. A collection of edited documents.

**6433** Keith Evans *The Development and Structure of the English School System* Hodder and Stoughton 1985. A useful history and survey. Another survey is George Baron *Society, Schools and Progress in England* Pergamon 1965.

**6434** G S Osborne *Scottish and English Schools: A Comparative Study of the Past Fifty Years* Longmans 1966. A good comparative study, focusing particularly on state schools.

**6434A** *Half Our Future: Report of the Central Advisory Council for Education (England)* HMSO 1963. A report into the education of less able children chaired by Sir John Newsom.

**6435** George Baron and D A Howell *The Government and Management of Schools* Athlone Press 1974. This study begins with two excellent chapters on the history of the government of schools and then provides a good survey of the contemporary nature of the way in which central and local government run the schools system.

**6436** *New Partnership for our Schools: Report of the Committee of Inquiry* HMSO 1977. This report of the committee chaired by Tom Taylor looked to an increased role for parents and teachers in school government and thus pointed towards the Education Reform Act of 1988. The government of schools since 1944, especially in the context of parental pressure groups and the Taylor Report, is examined in George Baron 'Political Parties and School Government in England and Wales' in George Baron (ed) *The Politics of School Government* Pergamon 1981 pp 81–104.

**6437** T R P Brighouse 'Britain's Schools: End of Term Report' *Political Quarterly* 58 1987 pp 263–75. A critical assessment of initiatives in the field of schools policy in the 1980s such as Technical and Vocational Educational Initiative or the national curriculum.

**6438** Margaret B Sutherland 'Whatever Happened about Coeducation?' *British Journal of Education Studies* 33 1985 pp 155–63. Coeducational schooling became the norm after 1944 as an unplanned consequence of the 1944 Education Act. In the 1980s however there has been growing demands for single sex schooling from Muslims. The persistence of single sex schooling is analysed in A Weinberg 'Analysis of the Persistance of the Single Sex School in the English Education System' Sussex DPhil Thesis 1979.

**6439** J Stuart Maclure *Educational Development and School Building: Aspects of Public Policy 1945–73* Longman 1984. This looks at the success of the school building programme developed in Hertfordshire and subsequently adopted nationally. An architectural history focusing on the design of schools as a representation of educational and social policy and theory in the post-war period is Andrew Saint *Towards a Social Architecture: The Role of School-Building in Post-War England* Yale University Press 1987. Malcolm Seaborne and Roy Lowe *The English School: Its Architecture and Organisation: Vol 2 1870–1970* Routledge and Kegan Paul 1971 is a history of the design and building of schools. The building programme necessitated by the raising of the school leaving age and the commitment to secondary schooling for all in the 1944 Education Act is examined in terms of the respective roles of central and local government in the programme and the competing claims on public money in the period made by govenment housing and health programmes in J R Dunford 'A Study of the Influence of the Association of Education Committees on School Building Policy in England and Wales 1944–1964' Leeds PhD Thesis 1984. See also Ministry of Education *The Story of Post-War School Building* Pamphlet 33, HMSO 1957. Local school building and buildings are examined in Ron Ringshall, Margaret Miles and Frank Kelsall *The Urban School: Buildings for Education in London 1870–1980* Architectural Press 1983 and P E Edwards 'Post-War School-Building with

Special Reference to the Problems faced by the Hampshire Local Education Authority' Durham MEd Thesis 1962–3.

**6440** P W Musgrave 'Morality and the Medical Department 1907–1974' *British Journal of Education Studies* 25 1977 pp 136–54. This is largely concerned with the attempts, largely inspired by Sir George Newman, the inter-war Chief Medical Officer, to influence certain aspects of national morality through the school system and the school curriculum. Another body with a similar interest is examined in G W Whitmarsh 'Society and the School Curriculum: The Association for Education in Citizenship 1934–1957' Birmingham MEd Thesis 1972–3. Another aspect of curriculum control is discussed in Peter Fisher 'Curriculum Control in England and Wales: The Birth of the Schools Council 1964' *Journal of Educational Administration and History* 16 1984 pp 35–44.

**6441** Denis Lawton and Peter Gordon *HMI* Routledge and Kegan Paul 1987. An excellent history of Her Majesty's Inspectors of Schools. Another historical study is E L Edmonds *The School Inspector* Routledge and Kegan Paul 1962. John Blackie *Inspecting the Inspectorate* Routledge and Kegan Paul 1970 is short and rather sketchy. See also Leonard Clark *The Inspector Remembers: Diary of one of Her Majesty's Inspectors of Schools 1936–70* Dobson 1976.

**6442** David Garner 'Education and the Welfare State: The School Meals and Milk Service 1944–80' *Journal of Education Administration and History* 17 1985 pp 63–8. The history of another schools service, the health service, is traced up to its transfer to the National Health Service in 1973 in P Henderson *The School Health Service 1908–1974: Report of the Chief Medical Officer of the DES and Presenting an Historical Review by Dr Peter Henderson, Principal Medical Officer of the DES* HMSO 1975. Another service's history is examined in J F Fulton 'Factors Influencing the Growth and Pattern of the Child Guidance Services and School Psychological Services in Britain from 1900 to the Present Time' Queen's, Belfast MA Thesis 1963–4.

**6443** N P Hampton 'A Study of the Raising of the School Leaving Age, with Special Reference to its Implications in Cheshire Since 1947' Keele MA Thesis 1979. A study of the effects on schools and school building in Cheshire.

**6444** E Webster 'Halifax Schools 1870–1970' *Transactions of the Halifax Antiquarian Society* 1975 pp 1–50.

**6445** D C S Child-Thomas 'The Development of Community Schools in Hampshire' Reading MPhil Thesis 1982. A study of the development, use and constitution of community schools in Hampshire since 1944.

**6446** J A H Mander 'Freedom and Constraint in a Local Education Authority: A Case Study of Some Historical, Logistic and Socio- Economic Aspects of the Establishment of Primary and Secondary Schools in the City of Leicester between 1944 and 1974' Leicester PhD Thesis 1975. See also J A Brand 'The Implementation of the 1944 Education Act in Leicester: A Case Study in Administrative Relationships' London PhD Thesis 1962–3.

**6447** Stewart C Mason *In Our Experience: The Changing Schools of Leicestershire* Longman 1970. An assessment by the innovatory director of education in Leicestershire.

## (2) Teachers

The material on teachers' trade unions is in the section on Trade Unions. On the influence of teachers on policy making see [6393].

**6448** J D Turner and J Rushton (eds) *The Teacher in a Changing Society* Manchester University Press 1974. A study of the changing relative position of teachers both in terms of their pay and their position in society and the resulting increase in teacher militancy. The history of the profession since 1850 is told through the the the records of the National Union of Teachers in Asher Tropp *The School Teachers* Heinemann 1957.

**6449** G M Mungham 'A Critical Review of Welfare Professions: A Case Study of Changes in the Professional Careers, Attitudes and Behaviour of Secondary School Teachers during the Post-War Period of Educational Reorganisation' Oxford BLitt Thesis 1972–3. See also Asher Tropp 'The Changing Status of the Teacher in England and Wales' *Year Book of Education* 1953 pp 143–70.

**6450** P H J H Gosden *The Evolution of a Profession: A Study of the Contribution of Teachers' Association to the Development of School Teaching as a Professional Occupation* Blackwell 1972. A good history of the role of teachers in the development of teaching since 1850.

**6451** E J Brent 'The Training, Recruitment and Conditions of Service of the London Senior (Elementary) Secondary Modern School Teacher 1939–1961' London PhD Thesis 1964.

**6452** Vivienne C Greenhalgh 'The Movement of Teachers' Salaries 1920–1968' *Journal of Educational Administration and History* 1 1968 pp 22–36. The system influencing teachers' pay and promotion is assessed in W F Dennison 'Points, Unit-Totals, Age-Weightings and Promoted Posts – Their Effects on the Development of the English Schooling System' *British Journal of Education Studies* 28 1980 pp 325–39. The history of the workings of the committees in which salary and other negotiations took place is traced in R J Garner 'A Study of the Work of the Standing Joint and Burnham Committees 1919–71' Leicester MEd Thesis 1976.

**6453** I G Booth 'The Movement for a Teachers' Council 1949–70 with Special Reference to the Work of the Main Committee for the Proposed Teachers' General Council: An Administrative and Political Study' Durham MEd Thesis 1971–2.

**6454** Geoffrey Partington *Women Teachers in the Twentieth Century in England and Wales* National Foundation for Educational Research 1976.

### (3) Nurseries and Play Groups

**6455** Tessa Blackstone *A Fair Start: The Provision of Pre-School Education* Allan Lane 1971. A lucid account of the development of nursery education 1900–65 which includes case studies and an analysis of why the growth of nursery provision was so slow in many areas. Another short study of the growth of the nursery school is N Whitbread *The Evolution of the Nursery Infant School: A History of Infant and Nursery Education in Britain 1800–1970* Routledge and Kegan Paul 1972.

**6456** *Education: A Framework for Expansion* Cmnd 5174, *Parliamentary Papers* vii 1972–73. The White Paper which announced the launching of a new policy to encourage the education of the under fives. However, progress since then has still been slow.

**6457** Brenda Crowe *The Playgroup Movement* Allen and Unwin 1973. An authorized study and history of the movement founded in 1962 to provide a safe and creative environment for pre-school children and support for their mothers.

**6458** Marjorie Allen and Mary Nicholson *Memoirs of an Uneducated Lady* Thames and Hudson 1975. The autobiography of Lady Allen of Hurtwood. The widow of the inter-war Labour politician Clifford Allen, she was a leading figure in the Nursery Schools Association and in the movement to improve playground facilities and preschool education.

### (4) Denominational Schools

**6459** Marjorie Cruikshank *Church and State in English Education 1870 to the Present Day* Macmillan 1963. A study of the role of the churches in debates on education, the changing situation of church schools and the wrangles over the funding of these, both between the churches and the state and between the various churches. See also James Murphy *Church, State and Schools in Britain 1800–1970* Routledge and Kegan Paul 1971.

**6460** P Price 'The History of the Voluntary Schools Since the 1944 Education Act: Development within an Egalitarian Structure' Leeds PhD Thesis 1986. The 1944 Education Act finally settled the wrangle between the churches which had helped to stymie attempts to raise the school leaving age in the inter-war years and which had been rumbling on since 1902. It involved a 50 per cent direct grant which was raised to 75 per cent in 1959 and even further in subsequent instalments. This thesis traces this process and considers the place of the voluntary-aided school in the education system. The conflict over denominational schools up until the 1959 legislation is examined in D Huot 'Denominational Schools as a Political Problem in England and Wales 1940–1959' Oxford DPhil Thesis 1961–2.

**6461** S E Kelly 'The Schools of the Established Church of England: A Study of Diocesan Involvement Since 1944' Keele PhD Thesis 1978. The activities in a particular diocese are scrutinized in Lois M R Louden 'The Managers of Blackburn Diocese and the Implementation of the 1944 Education Act in Lancashire' *Journal of Educational Administration and History* 15 1983 pp 27–34 and K Halliwell 'Church of England Schools in the Diocese of Manchester and the Education Acts 1936 and 1944–1953' Manchester MEd Thesis 1957–8. On Anglican education see also R Clark 'A Critical Survey of the Church's Involvement in Church and State Schools 1870–1970 with Special Reference to the Church of England' London MPhil Thesis 1977, A Pomfret 'The Reaction of the Established Church to Educational Legislation 1918–1959' London MA Thesis 1969 and M E Boddington 'The Part played by Anglican Women's Religious Communities in the Education of Children in England' Hull MEd Thesis 1975.

**6462** F R Phillips 'An Investigation into the Development of Catholic Educational Policy in England and Wales from 1944 to 1949' London MA Thesis 1964–5. He has also produced the sequel, 'The Consolidation of Catholic Educational Policy in England and Wales 1950–1959' London PhD Thesis 1979. Policy in a particular diocese is examined in J-A Upton 'Non-Elementary and Secondary Education in the Roman Catholic Diocese of Nottingham 1870 to 1970' Hull MEd Thesis 1976. See also C A Middleton 'The Contribution of the Salenian Order to the Development of Catholic Education in North West England' Liverpool MEd Thesis 1977.

**6463** S E Kelly 'The Voluntary Schools in Four Lancashire County Boroughs 1903–1963: A Study of Policies and Provision' Keele MA Thesis 1968–9. Kelly has also published an article of the same title in the *Journal of Educational Administration and History* 3 1971 pp 42–52. Local voluntary school provision in Liverpool with its large Catholic population is examined in Kelly's 'Voluntary School Provision in Liverpool 1936–1961' Manchester MEd Thesis 1963–4.

**6464** M B Steinberg 'Provisions for Jewish Schooling in Great Britain 1939–1960' London MA Thesis 1962–3.

**6465** Nazar Mustafa 'Muslim Education in the United Kingdom' *Islamic Quarterly* 29 1985 pp 108–17. A study of the growing demand for and provision of Muslim schools.

## (5) Primary Schools

**6466** Roy Lowe (ed) *The Changing Primary School* Falmer 1987. A collection of essays reviewing the architecture, policy towards, training of teachers for, and curriculum of primary schools in the post-war period. It also reflects on the effects of multicultural education, changing attitudes to gender, the Black Papers and progressivism on the primary school. See also D N Hubbard 'English Primary Education 1930–1980: The Structure, Process and Change of its Teachers' Roles' Sheffield PhD Thesis 1982. See also M M P Beeson 'Infant School Methods from 1870–1970' Liverpool MEd Thesis 1972–3.

**6467** *Children and Their Primary Schools: A Report of the Central Advisory Council for Education (England)* 2v, HMSO 1967. Volume 1 is the report and volume 2 the research and surveys. This was an influential report on educational deprivation by the committee chaired by Lady Plowden. It is scrutinized in R Peters (ed) *Perspectives on Plowden* Routledge and Kegan Paul 1968. The plan to set up educational priority areas however fell down on inter-departmental wrangling.

**6468** Adrian Bell and Alan Sigsworth *The Small Rural Primary School: A Matter of Quality* Falmer 1987. A good assessment of the process of closures and amalgamations in recent years and of the future of small rural schools.

**6469** A D Lee 'An Analysis of Middle School Policy in Crawley New Town 1967–1983' Sussex MPhil Thesis 1984. The development of middle schools, which cater for children from nine to twelve, is traced here by someone who was closely involved in the development of the middle school policy in Crawley.

**6470** P F J Vallom 'The Reform of Primary Mathematics during the Post-War Years: A Study of Teacher Reaction' Southampton MPhil Thesis 1976.

**6471** R Eaton 'The Development of Music in the English Primary School 1960–1980: A Synoptic Study' Sheffield MA Thesis 1982.

**6472** B R Steven 'A Study of the Factors Governing the Development of Science Teaching in Junior Schools 1945–1965' Sheffield MSc Thesis 1969–70.

**6473** J T Calvert 'The Primary School Network in North Yorkshire: Policy and Practice at Local Authority Level 1944–1980' Manchester MEd Thesis 1983.

**6474** John Gretton and Mark Jackson *William Tyndale: Collapse of a School – Or a System?* Allen and Unwin 1976. A journalist's study of the troubles that engulfed a North London primary school in the early 1970s, winning nationwide attention. See also T Ellis *et al William Tyndale: The Teachers' Story* Writers and Readers Publishing Cooperative 1976.

## (6) Secondary Schools

There are far too many histories of individual schools for inclusion below. Many of the works of this type can however be found listed in [6369].

### (a) General

**6475** Harry Judge *A Generation of Schooling: English Secondary Schools Since 1944* Oxford University Press 1984. A useful general history. Roy Lowe (ed) *The Changing Secondary School* Falmer 1989 reviews various aspects of developments since 1945. See also John Gray, Andrew F McPherson and David J Raffe *Reconstructions of Secondary Education: Theory, Myth and Practice Since the War* Routledge and Kegan Paul 1983.

**6476** Harold Collett Dent *Secondary Education For All: Origins and Development in England* Routledge and Kegan Paul 1949. A study of the 1944 Education Act and its implementation.

**6477** R Woods 'Margaret Thatcher and Secondary Reorganisation' *Journal of Educational Administration and History* 13 1981 pp 33–42. On changes introduced whilst Mrs Thatcher was Secretary of State for Education in 1970–4.

**6478** Michael Parkinson *The Labour Party and the Organisation of Secondary Education 1918–65* Routledge and Kegan Paul 1970. A study of the movement towards a commitment to comprehensive education.

**6479** Peter Gordon *Selection for Secondary Education* Woburn 1980. A good history of schools selection and of selective education in Britain. See also B A Fisher 'The Development of Bilateral Secondary Education in England Since 1940' Sheffield PhD Thesis 1965–6.

**6480** Denis Lawton *The Politics of the School Curriculum* Routledge and Kegan Paul 1980. This examines attitudes to the curriculum and curriculum control since 1944 and the influence of the Schools Council and examinations on the curriculum. A more general history concentrating on the nineteenth century is Peter Gordon and Denis Lawton *Curriculum Change in the Nineteenth and Twentieth Centuries* Hodder and Stoughton 1978. Peter Gordon (ed) *The Study of the Curriculum* Batsford 1981 is a textbook collection of studies of values in the curriculum, the history of the curriculum, its role in policy and the nature of curriculum planning.

**6481** P Fisher 'The Influence of the Association of Education Committees upon the Development of Secondary School Examinations in England 1943–1964' Leeds PhD Thesis 1980. The history of the Certificate of Secondary Education, the less academic of the two tier system of examinations that subsequently developed, is traced in Hugo Radice 'A Short History of the CSE' *Capital and Class* 10 1980 pp 43–9. J A Petch *Fifty Years of Examining: The Joint Matriculation Board 1903–1953* Harrap 1953 is the history of the northern universities examining board. Another aspect of the history of school examinations in the post war period is covered in P Fisher *External Examinations in Secondary Schools in England and Wales 1944–64* Museum of the History of Education, University of Leeds 1982.

**6482** R J Brown and P M Ribbins 'Policy Making in English Local Government: The Case of Secondary School Reorganisation' *Public Administration* 57 1979 pp 182–202. A general survey, and guide to the existing literature. Most literature on this subject deals with the shift of policy in particular localities in the direction of comprehensive schooling. Comparative studies of policy in a number of areas are E M Byrne 'Demand and the Allocation of Resources in Secondary Education (1945–1965) in the Cities of Lincoln and Nottingham and the County of Northumberland' London Ph.D Thesis 1972–3, David Peschek and Jack Brand *Policies and Politics in Secondary Education: Case Studies in West Ham and Reading* London School of Economics, University of London 1966 and P T White 'The Reorganization of Secondary Education in Bath and Southampton' Southampton MPhil Thesis 1975.

**6483** I G Keith Fenwick The *Comprehensive School 1944–1970: The Politics of Secondary Reorganisation*

Methuen 1976. A good account of the political and educational pressure to move away from the selective system set up by the 1944 Education Act and the resulting development and spread of comprehensive education. It examines policy making particularly in Coventry, Croydon, Leicestershire, Liverpool, Manchester and the West Riding of Yorkshire.

**6484** M H Parkinson *Politics of Urban Education* University of Liverpool 1973. A study of secondary school reorganization in the Merseyside local authorities of Birkenhead, Bootle, Wallasey and Liverpool.

**6485** Richard Batley, Oswald O'Brien and Henry Parris *Going Comprehensive: Educational Policy-Making in Two County Boroughs* Routledge and Kegan Paul 1972. A useful short study. It contrasts the easy triumph of comprehensive education in Labour-dominated Gateshead with the slower progress made in marginal Darlington where a thorough-going comprehensive education system was only set up by 1970.

**6486** E Keane 'Reorganisation of Secondary School Education in Bath 1963–8' Bristol MEd Thesis 1968.

**6487** J Hurst 'Developments in Secondary Education 1944–65, Exemplified in the County of Berkshire' Reading MPhil Thesis 1985.

**6488** Kester Isaac-Henry 'The Politics of Comprehensive Education in Birmingham 1957–67' Birmingham MSocSci Thesis 1969–70.

**6489** J K Cowgill 'Problems of Secondary School Organisation in Bolton Since 1947' Manchester MEd Thesis 1973–4.

**6490** B Bishop 'Secondary Education in Bournemouth from 1902–1965 with Special Reference to the Provision made by the Local Education Authority' Southampton MA Thesis 1965–6.

**6491** A Dark 'A Historical Study of Secondary Reorganisation in England and Wales up to 1965 with Special Reference to Bradford' Durham MEd Thesis 1967–8.

**6492** S G Whitehead 'Secondary Education in Cheshire 1944–68: A Study of Policy Formation' Manchester MEd Thesis 1971–2.

**6493** Geoffrey C Firth *Comprehensive Schools in Coventry and Elsewhere* City of Coventry Education Committee 1963. A survey of the implementation of the City Council's plans for comprehensive education with some comparisons.

**6494** Gerald T Rimmington *The Comprehensive School Issue in Leicester 1945–1974 and other essays*

Iota 1984. A study of policy making in a progressive local authority.

6495  R E Smith 'The Development of Secondary Education in Liverpool 1947–68' Liverpool MEd Thesis 1969–70.

6496  Margaret E Bryant *The London Experience of Secondary Education* Athlone Press 1986. A general study. On the movement towards comprehensive schooling in London see *London Comprehensive Schools: A Survey of Sixteen Schools* London County Council 1961. This is a survey of the implementation of policy since the Council's 1947 plan. The development of policy on secondary school reorganization is assessed in Richard Bourne 'Going Comprehensive in Greater London' *London Journal* 2 1976 pp 85–96. See also R Cole 'A Study in the Origins and Development of Comprehensive Schools in the London Area up to 1961' Sheffield MA Thesis 1961–2. The process of going comprehensive in a particular London borough is assessed in R R Lewis 'Secondary School Reorganization in the Outer London Boroughs with Special Reference to the London Borough of Merton' London MA Thesis 1968.

6497  Rene Saran *Policy Making in Secondary Education: A Case Study* Clarendon 1973. A study based on his thesis on secondary policy in Middlesex 1944–64. In the published version, because of his confidential access, he has felt obliged to give fictitious names to many of the places and characters.

6498  M A Stern 'Policy Formation in the Reorganization of Secondary Schools in Manchester along Comprehensive Lines 1953–1967' *Diploma in Public Administration,* London School of Economics, University of London 1971.

6499  S John Eggleston 'Going Comprehensive' *New Society* 8 22/12/1966 pp 944–6. A study of secondary school reorganization in Northamptonshire.

6500  J N Hewitson *The Grammar School Tradition in a Comprehensive World* Routledge and Kegan Paul 1969. A study of the process of going comprehensive in Norwich and its effects.

6501  A M Spencer 'The Local Implementation of National Secondary Education Policy 1965–1978' Manchester PhD Thesis 1982. A study of the interaction between local and national policy and the lack of consensus between the two examined in the context of Stockport.

6502  W Ellis 'The Development of Secondary Education in Sunderland 1945–70' Newcastle MEd Thesis 1973–4.

6503  P R Eccles 'Secondary Reorganisation in Tynemouth 1962–69' *Journal of Educational Administration and History* 6 1974 pp 35–44. A study of the process of going comprehensive in a county borough.

6504  R Jones 'A Study of Secondary Education as it has Developed in the Borough of Widnes, as seen against the National Background and with Particular Reference to the Period 1941–1967' Liverpool MEd Thesis 1967–8.

6505  E A Elton *Secondary Education in the East Riding of Yorkshire 1944–74* Museum of the History of Education, University of Leeds 1974.

(b) Selective Schools

There is a dearth of material which specifically focuses on secondary modern, technical or grammar schools.

6506  William Taylor *The Secondary Modern School* Faber 1963. A study of the secondary modern schools introduced under the tripartite system brought in by the 1944 Education Act. See also Harold Loukes *Secondary Modern* Harrap 1956. The development of these schools is traced and the arguments for and against them are rehearsed in 'Secondary Modern Schools' *Planning* 22 1956 pp 70–83.

6507  E P T Duggan 'Extended Courses, External Examinations and Vocational Influences in Secondary Modern Schools 1955–1964' London PhD Thesis 1968–9.

6508  G F Taylor 'Developments in Secondary Technical Education 1944–1960' Sheffield MA Thesis 1965–6. For other material of interest see the section on Technical Education.

6509  A D Edwards 'The Grammar School Sixth Form 1917–65: A Study of Administrative and Social Factors Influencing its Development' London MPhil Thesis 1966–7.

(c) Comprehensive Schools

There are a large number of case studies of secondary reorganization which examine the gradual shift of local authority policy in the direction of comprehensive schools. Because this literature is tangential to the decline of the tripartite system as well as the rise of comprehensive schools it has been included in the general section above [6482–6505].

**6510**  W J Bunton *Comprehensive Education: A Select Annotated Bibliography* National Foundation for Educational Research 1971. A short bibliography.

**6511**  Caroline Benn and Brian Simon *Half Way There: Report on the British Comprehensive School Reform* 2nd ed, Penguin 1972. A committed account of the shift towards comprehensive schooling. This gives a detailed survey of the debate 1944–70 and then adopts a thematic approach looking at the various schemes pursued and the debates over appropriate subjects, organization and examinations. It contains a wealth of information about the growth of the comprehensive school in Britain. See also David Rubinstein and Brian Simon *The Evolution of the Comprehensive School 1926–1972* 2nd ed, Routledge and Kegan Paul 1973. Case studies of the transformation of schools and educational districts to the comprehensive system are provided in E Halsall (ed) *Becoming Comprehensive: Case Histories* Pergamon 1970. See also Robin Pedley *The Comprehensive School* 3rd ed, Penguin 1979.

**6512**  Billy Hughes and David Rubenstein 'Labour Governments and Comprehensive Schooling 1945–51' *History Workshop* 7 1979 pp 156–69. Ellen Wilkinson's reluctance to depart from the provisions of the 1944 Act as she sought, as Minister of Education 1945–7, to implement the raising of the school leaving age, in order to promote comprehensive (or as it was then known, multilateral) education, has meant that she has suffered considerable posthumous vilification from the Left. This presents a debate in which Hughes defends her from such charges. Caroline Benn 'Comprehensive School Reform and the 1945 Labour Government' *History Workshop* 10 1980 pp 197–204 is a rejoinder.

**6513**  M L Mackenzie 'The Road to the Circulars – A Study of the Evolution of Labour Party Policy with Regard to the Comprehensive School' *Scottish Education Studies* 1 1967 pp 25–33. A historical survey of the background to the policy which encouraged the rapid spread of comprehensive schools from the 1960s.

**6514**  R Richmond 'The Conservative Party's National Policy on Comprehensive Education 1944–1971' Durham MEd Thesis 1975. See also M Pattison 'Resistance or Reform? The Politics of Comprehensive Education 1965–1980, with Special Reference to Conservative Controlled Local Education Authorities' Open University PhD Thesis 1983.

**6515**  C G Hall 'The Social and Educational Significance of External Examinations in the Non-Selective Schools in England and Wales between 1945 to 1965' Sheffield MA Thesis 1970–1. A study up to the introduction of the Certificate of Secondary Education in 1965.

**6516**  L Berg *Rising Hill – Death of a Comprehensive School* Penguin 1968. An account of the controversial coeducational comprehensive in Islington which was closed down in 1965.

(d) Public Schools

**6517**  *The Public and Preparatory Schools Year Book: The Official Book of Reference for the Headmasters' Conference and of the Incorporated Association of Preparatory Schools* Black 1891–. This is now titled *Independent Schools Year Book* and is published in two volumes covering girls' and boys' schools.

**6518**  Geoffrey Walford (ed) *British Public Schools: Policy and Practice* Falmer 1984. A sociological study. It includes essays on the demand for places at these schools, the teachers, ex- public schoolboys' dominant role in public life, the assisted places scheme introduced to replace the direct grant in the 1980s and the perceptions of the schools by parents and politicians. Geoffrey Walford *Life in Public Schools* Methuen 1986 is another sociological study which reflects, amongst other things, on the introduction of girls at sixth form level in boys' public schools and on the ex-public school presence in the civil service. For an earlier study see John Wakeford *The Cloistered Elite: A Sociological Analysis of the English Public Boarding School* Macmillan 1969.

**6519**  John Rae *The Public School Revolution: Britain's Independent Schools 1964–1979* Faber 1981. A study of changes in the public schools and changes in policy towards them. The attitudes of the Labour Party are examined in J M Collins 'The Labour Party and the Public Schools: A Conflict of Principles' *British Journal of Education Studies* 17 1969 pp 301–11.

**6520**  R Lambert *et al The Hothouse Society* Weidenfeld and Nicolson 1968. A celebrated sociological investigation of public schools at a time when they were being savaged by films like *If.*

**6521**  Graham Kalton *The Public Schools: A Factual Survey of Headmasters' Conference Schools in England and Wales* Longmans 1966. A survey of contemporary conditions. James McConnell *English Public Schools* W W Norton 1985 is a pictorial guide to 25 of the greatest public schools. See also Michael L Landon 'The Position of the "Public Schools" in Post-War Britain' *Social Studies* 1967.

**6522**  T W Bamford *The Rise of the Public Schools: A Study of Boys' Public Boarding Schools in England and Wales from 1837 to the Present Day* Nelson 1967.

**6523** Mallory Wober *English Girls' Boarding Schools* Allen Lane 1971. A sociological study. Arthur Marshall *Giggling in the Shrubbery: The Splendours and Miseries of Girls' Boarding Schools as Recalled by Former Pupils* Collins 1985 is a wittily compiled and presented anecdotal social history of girls' public schools.

**6524** Donald Leinster-Mackay *The Rise of the English Prep School* Falmer 1984. A social history of independent preparatory schools. It is good on the problems of adjusting to the post-war situation and the amalgamations, closures and changes in funding that have resulted.

### (e) Experimental Schools

**6525** Maurice Punch *Progressive Retreat: A Sociological Study of Dartington Hall School 1926–57 and some of its Former Pupils* Cambridge University Press 1977. The heyday of experimental schools, of which Dartington Hall was arguably the most celebrated, was the inter-war years. This is a stimulating, if flawed, sociological study of the school in its days of greatest influence. See also Victor Bonham-Carter *Dartington Hall: The History of an Experiment* Phoenix House 1958. Maurice Ash *et al Who Are The Progressives Now?* Routledge and Kegan Paul 1969 is a useful source on the confrontation between progressives of modernist and classical persuasions at Dartington Hall in 1965.

**6526** G W Phillips *Smile, Bow and Pass On: A Biography of an Avant-Garde Headmistress, Miss Iris M Brooks MA (Cantab) Malvern Girls' College (1928–54)* St Michael's Abbey Press 1980.

### (f) Special Schools

**6527** W A Axford *Handicapped Children in Britain: Their Problems and Education* Library Association 1959. A guide to books and articles on the subject published between 1944–58.

**6528** *Special Education Abstracts* Association for Special Education 1967–. Abstracts of books and articles, mostly drawn from British journals.

**6529** J S Hurt *Outside The Mainstream: A History of Special Education* Batsford 1988. See also Stephen Jackson *Special Education in England and Wales* 2nd ed, Oxford University Press 1969.

**6530** L Barton and S Tomlinson *Special Education: Policy, Practices and Social Issues* Harper and Row 1982. An examination of policy and its implementation. See also W K Brennan *Changing Special Education* Open University Press 1982.

**6531** *Special Educational Needs: Report of the Committee of Inquiry into the Education of Handicapped Children and Young People* Cmnd 7212, *Parliamentary Papers* x 1977–78. The report of the committee chaired by Baroness Warnock. Some of the effects of the Warnock Report are examined in detail in A Brownhill 'Children with Special Educational Needs in the Normal Classroom: An Examination of the Effects of the Warnock Report and the 1981 Education Act upon Local Authority Policy and Attitudes in some Derby Schools' Nottingham MPhil Thesis 1983.

**6532** R Gallop 'The Development of Special Education within the Administrative County of Worcestershire up to 1970' Wales MEd Thesis 1973–4.

**6533** Richard C Fletcher *The College on the Ridge* the author 1984. A history of Worcester College for the Blind 1959–80. Another school history is provided in K G Fothergill 'The Development of a School for Visually-Handicapped Children in the Light of Educational Thought and Practice, with Special Reference to the Period 1944–74' Liverpool MEd Thesis 1977.

**6534** A W G Ewing 'The Education for the Deaf: History of the Department of Education of the Deaf, University of Manchester 1919–1955' *British Journal of Education Studies* 4 1956 pp 103–28. A detailed study of a technique of teaching the deaf up to its gradual rejection in the 1960s is provided in M G McLoughlin 'A Study of the Ascendance of Oralism in the History of the Education of the Deaf 1880–1960' Liverpool MPhil Thesis 1986.

**6535** Ministry of Education *Education of the Handicapped Pupil 1945–55* HMSO 1956. See also D G Pritchard *Education and the Handicapped 1760–1960* Routledge and Kegan Paul 1963.

**6536** Robert A Laslett *Changing Perceptions of Maladjusted Children 1945–1981* Association of Workers with Maladjusted Children 1984. A study of changing perceptions and changes in the legal definition of maladjusted children and their effects on policy on the education of psychologically or emotionally disturbed children.

### (g) Development of Particular Subjects

**6537** G Sutton *Artisan or Artist? A History of the Teaching of Arts and Crafts in English Schools* Pergamon 1967. Another history is G D Gilbride 'Art in the Curriculum: An Historical and Comparative Study 1835–1982' Hull MPhil Thesis 1985. About half of this thesis deals with art in secondary education in the post-war period. Mike Steveni 'Dick Field (1912–1986): A

Personal Appreciation' *Journal of Art and Design Education* 6 1987 pp 131–7 is a tribute to a teacher who made an important contribution to the development of art education in schools from the 1950s. See also D Hanson 'The Development of a Professional Association of Art Teachers' *Studies in Design Education* 3 1971 pp 30–40.

**6538** Paul Brazier *Art History in Education: An Annotated Bibliography and History* Heinemann Education 1985. A short bibliography on art history education in Britain and America since 1800.

**6539** P R Youakim 'A Critical Survey of the Teaching of Biology in English Grammar Schools Since 1945' Sheffield MSc Thesis 1965–6. See also G W Tracey 'The Place and the Role of the Biological Sciences in English School Curricula 1902–1956' Sheffield MSc Thesis 1960–1.

**6540** A G Geen 'The Teaching of Classics in England and Wales in the Twentieth Century' Wales MEd Thesis 1973–4. R W Prescott 'The Changing Role of Classics in English Secondary Education from 1860 to the Present Day' Bristol MEd Thesis 1970–1.

**6541** H N Bryant 'Drama in Education: Its Development in Bristol between 1944 and 1970' Bristol MLitt Thesis 1973–4.

**6542** *A Language for Life* HMSO 1975. A report into the reading and use of English in schools in the light of concern about declining standards generated by the Black Papers and chaired by Sir Alan Bullock. The best general history is A P R Howard *A History of English Language Teaching* Oxford University Press 1984. David Allen *English Teaching Since 1965: How Much Growth?* Heinemann Educational 1980 is an unsatisfactory study of recent developments. See also W R Mullins 'A Study of Significant Changes in the Theory of the Teaching of English to Older Pupils in Elementary and Secondary Modern Schools 1860–1960' Leicester MEd Thesis 1967–8. Another aspect of the teaching of English is covered in W Simister 'Broadcasting to Secondary Schools Relating to the Teaching of English from 1955' Manchester MEd Thesis 1977. An aspect of the ideological construction of English courses is examined in Eleanor M Wright 'The Representation of Women and Girls in Post- War Secondary School English Course Books' *History of Education Society Bulletin* 31 1983 pp 25–33 and 32 1983 pp 32–42.

**6543** L E Cottrell 'A Study of the French Course-Book and its Relation to Teaching Methods in England 1900–1958' Liverpool MA Thesis 1958–9. See also E Forbes 'A Study of French Readers for the Age Group 12–14 in English Schools during the period 1902–1960' Liverpool MEd Thesis 1967–8.

**6544** G E Gilchrist 'Curriculum Developments in Geography 1945–70' Liverpool MEd Thesis 1981.

**6545** G Blackford *A History of Handicraft Teaching* Christophers 1961. See also [6537].

**6546** Incorporated Association of Assistant Masters in Secondary Schools *The Teaching of History in Secondary Schools* 3rd ed, Cambridge University Press 1965. A guide rather than a history of the teaching of the subject. The history of the teaching of the subject in the twentieth century is traced in T D Cook 'Changing Attitudes to the Teaching of History in Schools 1900–1970' Lancaster MLitt Thesis 1970–1. An aspect of the ideological construction of history teaching is examined in F J Glendinning 'Attitudes to Colonialism and Race in British and French History Textbooks' *History of Education* 3 1974 pp 57–72.

**6547** D A Taylor 'Trends and Factors in the Teaching of School Music in Britain, with Particular Reference to the 1965–1975 Decade' Sheffield MA Thesis 1977. A report on a period of expansion.

**6548** A C Woodward 'The Development of Physical Education in Schools in England and Wales' Manchester MEd Thesis 1968.

**6549** J J Woodin 'A Critical Evaluation of Politics Teaching in British Secondary Schools 1935 to 1980' Nottingham MPhil Thesis 1980.

**6550** Colin Alves *Religion and the Secondary School* SCM Press 1968. A detailed survey conducted on behalf of the British Council of Churches. It draws attention to the weaknesses of religious education in schools, the common failure of schools to comply with either the spirit or the letter of the 1944 Education Act's provision covering religious assemblies and the too often inadequate quality of the teachers and the teaching of religious studies. Growing concern at the state and nature of religious education, the provisions for which had been, at the time, seen as one of the major achievements of the 1944 Act, is one of the key themes of W N Todd 'Church and State in Religious Education 1944–1984' Durham MEd Thesis 1985. At the same time religious education has, since the 1960s, become more multi-faith in its approach and the specifically Christian character of religious education before then has been condemned as an attempt to indoctrinate. This view is reassessed and dismissed by C E Mitchell 'Christian Education and the Christian Nation: A Study of the Role Envisaged for Religious Education in the British State Schools c1920–65' Cambridge MLitt Thesis 1985, who argues that the object of Christian education was transformed, enlightened and morally responsible schools and individuals rather than the gaining of church members. Religious education in this period is also examined in N Chetwood

'Religious Teaching in Grammar Schools, with Special Reference to the period after 1944' Nottingham MEd Thesis 1958–9.

**6551** J F Kerr 'Some Sources for the History of the Teaching of Science in England' *British Journal of Educational Studies* 7 1958–59 pp 149–60. The standard history of science teaching is Gary McCulloch, Edgar Jenkins and David Layton *Technological Revolution? The Politics of School Science and Technology in England and Wales Since 1945* Falmer 1985. This is a good study of curriculum development in a subject in which there has been considerably political interest in view of the national need for scientifically trained personnel. It also includes a good bibliography. This concern about the need for scientifically trained personnel also led to the introduction of the Nuffield science teaching project in 1962, the background to which is examined in Mary Waring 'Background to Nuffield Science' *History of Education* 8 1979 pp 223–37. The development of the curriculum up to the introduction of the Nuffield project is assessed in E W Jenkins *From Armstrong to Nuffield: Studies in Twentieth Century Science Education in England and Wales* Murray 1979. See also R H Millar 'Curriculum and Control: The Rhetoric of School Science Curriculum Innovation 1960–1980' Edinburgh MPhil Thesis 1981 and E W Jenkins 'The Practice and Rationale of School Science Education in England and Wales 1900–1962 with Particular Reference to Grammar Schools' Leeds MEd Thesis 1978. On science teaching to girls see E W Jenkins 'The Scientific Education of Girls Since 1902' *Durham Research Review* 7 1973–74 pp 873–86. The teaching of the history of science and its considerable growth since 1945 is examined in W J M Sherratt 'History of Science in Education: An Investigation into the Role and Use of Historical Ideas and Material in Education, with Particular Reference to Science Education in the English Secondary School Since the Nineteenth Century' Leicester PhD Thesis 1980.

## C. HIGHER AND FURTHER EDUCATION

### (1) Higher Education: General

**6552** *Research into Higher Education Abstracts* Society for Research into Higher Education, University of Surrey 1967–. Initially quarterly this now appears three times a year. It provides classified abstracts drawn from about 200 journals. There are about 200 abstracts per issue.

**6553** W A C Stewart *Higher Education in Postwar Britain* Macmillan 1988. A good general history which examines developments in their economic, social, cultural and political contexts.

**6554** *Report of the Committee Appointed by the Prime Minister under the Chairmanship of Lord Robbins 1961–1963* Cmnd 2154, *Parliamentary Papers* xi–xiv 1962–63. This report into higher education had enormous immediate impact and was formally accepted in a White Paper within 24 hours of its publication. It recommended a massive expansion in the student population (particularly in science and technology), important institutional changes, not least the creation of the Council for National Academic Awards, the broadening of university degrees, various amendments in the fields of finance, teacher training, postgraduate studies, staffing and adult education, the creation of two business schools and much else besides. The 178 recommendations left virtually no aspect of higher education untouched. The evidence to the committee was published separately by HMSO in six volumes. John Carswell *Government and the Universities in Britain: Programme and Performance 1960–1980* Cambridge University Press 1985 is an excellent analysis of the Robbins Report and of subsequent developments. It finds that not all of Robbins goals were achieved and that the financial strains in the expansion programme led governments to redefine their relations with the University Grants Committe and the financially dependent higher education sector in the 1970s and 1980s. The consequent growth of central control of the universities is analysed in J M Fraser 'The Decline of Autonomy of British Universities in the Robbins Era 1963–1983' Stirling MEd Thesis 1983. The Robbins Report and its initial impact is also examined in R Layard *et al The Impact of Robbins* Penguin 1969, Sir Charles Morris *et al* 'Second Thoughts on Robbins' *Universities Quarterly* 18 1963–64 pp 119–68, Sir Charles Morris 'The Robbins Report' *British Journal of Educational Studies* 13 1964 pp 5–15 and V C-C Chen 'The Robbins Report on Higher Education' Oxford BLitt Thesis 1969–70. The implementation of the Robbins Report is reconsidered in the context of the financial problems of higher education in the 1980s in Noel Annan 'The Reform of Higher Education in 1986' *History of Education* 16 1987 pp 217–26.

**6555** H J Butcher and Ernest Rudd (eds) *Contemporary Problems in Higher Education* McGraw-Hill 1972. This includes useful comments on contemporary problems such as academic performance, student unrest and change in teaching methods and organization.

**6556** Maurice Kogan with David Kogan *The Attack on Higher Education* Kogan Page 1983. A critical study of the cuts in higher education and increases in fees for overseas students under the Thatcher government and an examination of the reaction of the universities. See also K T Smith 'A Critical Review of the Higher Education Policies of the Conservative Governments Since 1979'

Hull MEd Thesis 1985 and J M Ashworth 'Reshaping Higher Education in Britain' *Journal of the Royal Society of Arts* 130 1982 pp 713–29. The hardest hit have been the arts and social science faculties which have, as Sara Delamont and Martin Head *The Effects of the Cuts '80–'86 on Arts and Social Science Faculties* Social Research Unit, University of Wales, Cardiff 1989 points out, suffered a cut in staff of 10 per cent whilst student numbers have increased by 10 per cent over the same period.

**6557** R H Vipond 'A Study of Government Policy-Making in Higher Technological Education 1944–68' Leeds PhD Thesis 1982. Far- reaching reforms were suggested in this area but, beyond the creation of the polytechnics little more than incremental progress was made. A related aspect of technological education policy is considered in G L Price 'Origins of Government Policy for Higher Education in Science and Technology 1939–1964: Determination of the Social and Academic Status of Technological Education' Manchester MSc Thesis 1974–6. See also P W Taylor 'The Development of Higher Technological Education in Britain 1945–1951' *Journal of Educational Administration and History* 8 1975 pp 20–30 and J Heywood 'An Evaluation of Certain Post-War Developments in Higher Technological Education' Lancaster MLitt Thesis 1968–9.

**6558** Gareth Williams, Tessa Blackstone and David Metcalf *The Academic Labour Market: Economic and Social Aspects of a Profession* Elsevier Scientific Publishing 1974. A sociological study, with copious statistics, of the academic profession as it expanded with the expansion of the universities in the 1960s. A H Halsey and M A Trow *The British Academics* Faber 1971 is a more rounded and historical study.

**6559** F D Klingender 'Changing Patterns of Student Recruitment in England' *Universities Quarterly* 9 1954–55 pp 168–76. The history and organization of post-graduate education is submitted to thorough investigation in Ernest Rudd with Renate Simpson *The Highest Education: A Study of Graduate Education* Routledge and Kegan Paul 1975. Peter Williams *The Overseas Student Question: Studies for a Policy* Heinemann 1981 examines the development and current state of policy on overseas students, the costs and benefits of overseas students and the commercial and foreign policy implications of encouraging overseas students. British policy and its outcome is in the process contrasted with that of other developed countries. For other material on overseas students see [5702].

**6560** J Makkison 'The Development of Higher and Further Education in Sunderland Since 1908' Durham MEd Thesis 1969–70.

## (2) The Universities

**6561** Harold Silver and S John Teague (comp) *The History of British Universities 1800–1969, excluding Oxford and Cambridge: A Bibliography* Society for Research into Higher Education, London 1970. A useful guide to the literature. J P Powell (comp) *Universities and University Education: A Select Bibliography* 2v, National Foundation for Educational Research 1966 is a classified bibliography which has a certain amount of material on British universities.

**6562** Sir Eric Ashby *Adapting Universities to a Technological Society* Jossey Bass Publishers, San Francisco 1974. A collection of essays which reflect on the idea of a university, investment in higher education, the role of students in university government, academics, the social responsibilities of science and technology and the implications of mass education for higher education. Another survey by a university administrator of their finances, contemporary state and relations with government is Sir Sydney Caine *British Universities: Purpose and Prospects* The Bodley Head 1969. The alterations in the concept of the nature and purpose of a university through successive waves of expansion up to the 1960s are examined in Thomas William Heyck 'The Idea of a University in Britain 1870–1970' *History of European Ideas* 8 1987 pp 205–19.

**6563** Graeme C Moodie and Rowland Eustace *Power and Authority in British Universities* Allen and Unwin 1974. A useful analysis of the administration of the universities (excepting the administration and maintenance of the buildings themselves) including some case work and a valuable bibliography. Darman Christopherson *The University at Work* SCM Press 1973 provides a personal statement on university administration by the then Vice-Chancellor of Durham (and previously Chairman of the Vice-Chancellor's Committee in 1967–70).

**6564** Graeme C Moodie 'Buffer, Coupling and Broker: Reflections on 60 Years of the UGC' *Higher Education* 12 1983 pp 331–47. Further reflections on the role of the University Grants Committee as a clearing house in relations between the universities and the government, especially in financial matters, are provided in M Shattock and Robert O Berdahl 'The British University Grants Committee 1919–83: Changing Relationships with Government and the Universities' *Higher Education* 13 1984 pp 471–500. The development of the UGC from the background to its creation in 1919 to the changes of 1946 which turned it into a sort of planning commission for the universities is traced in Christine Helen Shinn *Paying The Piper: The Development of the UGC 1910–1946* Falmer 1986. On the early history of the UGC see also Margery Fry 'The University Grants

Committee: An Experiment in Administration' *Universities Quarterly* 2 1947–48 pp 221–30.

**6565** W H G Armytage 'The Civic Universities and Social Re- Adjustment 1944–1954' *Universities Review* 26 1954 pp 52–7. The greatest problem in this period was the adjustment to the return to peacetime conditions. See also Sir Hector Hetherington 'The British University System 1914–54' *Aberdeen University Review* 36 1955 pp 1–13.

**6566** Robert O Berdahl *British Universities and the State* Cambridge University Press 1959. A good study of the funding and administration of the universities in the 1950s.

**6567** R M Mawditt 'Universities in Great Britain: A Study of Comparative Costs to 1975' Bath MSc Thesis 1983. In the 1960s there was a rapid expansion of higher education with all party support in the light of the commitment to allow all the opportunity to benefit from a university education that was enshrined in the Robbins Report. The student unrest with which the decade closed and increasing economic difficulties however led to growing concern about cost. This is a detailed examination of funding patterns in this important period.

**6568** *Review of the University Grants Committee* Cmnd 81, *Parliamentary Papers* 1986–87. The report produced by Lord Croham which critically reviewed the financial efficiency and flexibility of the universities. It led to the White Paper, *Higher Education: Meeting the Challenge* Cmnd 114, *Parliamentary Papers* 1986–87, which pointed to the replacement of the UGC with the University Funding Council which was established in 1989.

**6569** Sir P Venables *Higher Education Developments: The Technological Universities 1956–1976* Faber 1978. A study of the growth of the new technological universities designed to produce a scientifically trained graduate population in the post-war years.

**6570** Tony Birks *Building the New Universities* David and Charles 1972. A well illustrated guide to the expansion of the universities in the 1960s. It concentrates on the design and building of Sussex, York, East Anglia, Kent, Essex, Warwick and Lancaster. On the establishment of this same group of universities see Michael Beloff *The Plateglass Universities* Secker and Warburg 1968.

**6571** Maureen Woodhall and Mark Blaug 'Productivity Trends in British University Education 1938–62' *Minerva* 3 1964–65 pp 483–98. A study of efficiency in the throughput of students.

## (3) Individual Universities

**6572** Geoffrey Walford *Restructuring Universities: Politics and Power in the Management of Change* Croom Helm 1987. This uses Aston, a university which was particularly hard hit, as a case study in the restructuring of the universities in the 1980s. It demonstrates the relative success of the university in coping with rapid changes enforced by government budgetary decisions which led to a cut in the student body by a third and in the academic body of a half and the closure of half the university's departments. At the same time the university pursued major innovations such as a science park and campus redevelopment. This useful study of these developments is marred by a poor typeface and a overly theoretical approach.

**6573** Sir Robert Stephenson *Administration of a University: An Account of the Management of Academic Affairs in the University of Birmingham* University of London Press 1966.

**6574** J Topping *The Beginnings of Brunel University: From Technical College to University* Oxford University Press 1981.

**6575** Eric Homberger, William Janeway and Simon Schama *The Cambridge Mind: Ninety Years of the Cambridge Review 1879–1969* Cape 1970. A history of the university review. The experience of women at Cambridge and their gradual acceptance is analysed in Rita McWilliam-Tullberg *Women at Cambridge* Gollancz 1975. The history of the first women's (now co- educational) college at Cambridge is told in M C Bradbrook *'That Infidel Place': A Short History of Girton College 1869–1969 with an essay on the Collegiate University in the Modern World* Chatto and Windus 1969 and Barbara Megson and Jean Lindsay *Girton College 1869–1959: An Informal History* Heffer 1961. Sir Harry Godwin *Cambridge and Clare* Cambridge University Press 1985 is a history of Clare College since 1919. The background to the establishment of the much younger Churchill College in 1961, especially the fear of a technological gap opening up between her competitors and Britain, is examined in Peter Carpenter 'Churchill and his "Technological" College' *Journal of Educational Administration and History* 17 1985 pp 69–75. On Homerton College see [6617]. Another college history is L P Wilkinson *A Century of King's 1873–1972* King's College, Cambridge 1980. R Murray *New Hall 1954–1972: The Making of a College* New Hall, Cambridge 1980 is a brief history of a women's college. Richard Deacon *The Cambridge Apostles: A History of Cambridge University's Elite Intellectual Secret Society* Robert Royce 1985 is a history tracing the Apostles from their origins in the early nineteenth century to its more eminent recent members such as the spies Burgess and Maclean, or Peter Shore and Jonathan Miller.

**6576** S J Teague *The City University: A History* City University 1980.

**6577** T A Whitworth *Yellow Sandstone and Mellow Brick: An Account of Hatfield College, Durham 1846–1971* Hatfield College, University of Durham 1971.

**6578** T W Bamford *The University of Hull: The First Fifty Years* Oxford University Press 1978. A good history, half of which deals with developments since the Robbins Report. John Heyward 'Responses to Contraction: The University of Hull 1979–1984' *Minerva* 24 1986 pp 74–97 is a study of the ways in which Hull has sought to combat the financial stringency in the 1980s.

**6579** Sir James Mountford *Keele: A Historical Critique* Routledge and Kegan Paul 1972. A study of the development of the prototype new university established in 1949. W B Gallie *A New University: A D Lindsay and the Keele Experiment* Chatto and Windus 1960 is a study of the early years of the university in praise of A D Lindsay, the university's first Vice-Chancellor and former Master of Balliol College, Oxford. On Lindsay see also Drusilla Scott *A D Lindsay* Blackwell 1971.

**6580** Peter Gosden and A J Taylor (eds) *Studies in the History of a University 1874–1974: To Commemorate the Centenary of the University of Leeds* Arnold 1975. See also S T Anning *A History of the Leeds School of Medicine: One and a Half Centuries 1831–1981* Leeds University Press 1982.

**6581** Jack Simmons *New University* Leicester University Press 1958. This traces the development of the University of Leicester from its origins.

**6582** Thomas Kelly *For Advancement of Learning: The University of Liverpool 1881–1981* Liverpool University Press 1981. The history of the School of Tropical Medicine 1899–1971 is traced in B G Macgraith 'History of the Liverpool School of Tropical Medicine' *Medical History* 16 1972 pp 59–86.

**6583** Negley Harte *The University of London 1836–1986* Athlone Press 1986. An official, well illustrated history. Percy Dunsheath and Margaret Miller *Convocation in the University of London: The First Hundred Years* Athlone Press 1958 is a history of the university's graduate body. There are also a number of histories of some of the colleges, institutes and medical schools that make up the university. These include D Dymond (ed) *The Forge: The History of Goldsmith's College* 1905–55 Methuen 1955, A Rupert Hall *Science for Industry: A Short History of the Imperial College of Science and Technology and its Antecedents* Imperial College,

University of London 1982, C W Dixon *The Institute: A Personal Account of the History of the University of London Institute of Education 1932–1972* Institute of Education, University of London 1986 (which supersedes *Studies and Impressions 1902–1952* Institute of Education 1952), G Huelin *King's College, London 1828–1978* King's College, London 1978, G P Moss and M V Saville *From Palace to College: An Illustrated Account of Queen Mary College (University of London)* Queen Mary College, University of London 1985, Caroline Bingham *The History of Royal Holloway College 1886–1986* Constable 1987 (see also Moreton Moore (ed) *Royal Holloway and Bedford New College: Centenary Lectures 1886–1986* Royal Holloway and Bedford New College, University of London 1988), C H Philips *The School of Oriental and African Studies, University of London 1917–67: An Introduction* School of Oriental and African Studies, University of London 1967 and Janet Sondheimer *Castle Adamant in Hampstead: A History of Westfield College 1882–1982* Westfield College, University of London 1983. The history of individual medical schools and medicine related institutions is told in J Calnon *The Hammersmith 1935–1985: The First 50 Years of the Royal Postgraduate Medical School at Hammersmith Hospital* MTP 1985, Catherine M Clark and James M Mackintosh *The School and the Site: A Historical Memoir* H K Lewis 1954 (a history of the London School of Hygiene and Tropical Medicine), D Ranger *The Middlesex Hospital Medical School: Centenary to Sesquintenary 1935–1985* Hutchinson Benham 1985, T E Wallis *History of the School of Pharmacy, University of London* Pharmaceutical Press 1964 and W R Merrington *University College Hospital and Its Medical School: A History* Heinemann 1976.

**6584** Leonard M Cantor and Geoffrey F Matthews *Loughborough: From College to University: A History of Higher Education at Loughborough 1909–1966* Loughborough University of Technology 1977. This includes an epilogue on events 1966–76.

**6585** E M Bettenson *The University of Newcastle-upon-Tyne: A Historical Introduction 1834–1971* University of Newcastle-upon-Tyne 1971.

**6586** *A University of the Air* Cmnd 2922, *Parliamentary Papers* xiii 1965–66. The White Paper that led to the foundation of the Open University which used the resources of radio and television to give large numbers of people the opportunity of a university education. It thus represented a new departure in the field of adult education. D G Hewbridge *The Open University: A Select Bibliography* 2nd ed, Open University Press 1975 is a listing of books and articles on Open University. This was first conceived by Harold Wilson in 1963 and opened to its first students in 1971. Its origins, students, courses and use of the media are examined in Jeremy Tunstall *The Open University Opens* Routledge and

Kegan Paul 1974. Its origins are also examined in D A Hoult 'The Open University: Its Origins and Establishment (September 1963 to June 1969)' Hull MEd Thesis 1975. Walter Perry *Open University: A Personal Account by the First Vice-Chancellor* Open University Press 1976 is an account of the establishment of the Open University, its finance and administration, its students and its future. John Ferguson *The Open University From Within* University of London Press 1978 is a highly personal account of the University by its Dean and the Director of Arts. The growth of the University is also examined in H and S Cowper 'The Open University: Ten Years Old' *Scottish Journal of Adult Education* 4 1979 pp 19–23, which assesses its advantages and disadvantages. The development of the University's Institute of Educational Technology is analysed in P Northcott 'Institute of Educational Technology, The Open University: Structure and Operations 1969–1975' *Programmed Learning* 13 1976 pp 11–24.

**6587** F H Lawson *The Oxford Law School 1850–1965* Clarendon 1968. There is no general history of Oxford University in the post-war period. David Walter *The Oxford Union: Playground of Power* Macdonald 1985 is a history of the University's debating society. This continues to be an important nursery of a large number of leading politicians of all parties. This useful work examines its history up to 1984. See also Maurice Christopher Hollis *The Oxford Union* Evans 1965. Vivian Green *The Commonwealth of Lincoln College 1427–1977* Oxford University Press 1979 is a useful college history. Nuffield College was founded during the inter-war years. The stewardship of Norman Chester during his period as Warden of this College 1954–78 is examined in A H Halsey 'Norman Chester and Nuffield College' in David Butler and A H Halsey (eds) *Policy and Politics: Essays in Honour of Norman Chester* Macmillan 1978 pp 1–12. The history of the University's oldest ladies' colleges is told in Penny Griffin (ed) *St Hugh's: One Hundred Years of Women's Education in Oxford* Macmillan 1986. David Footman *Antonin Besse of Aden: The Founder of St Antony's College, Oxford* Macmillan 1986 is a biography of the French businessman who founded St Antony's after the Second World War. The history of the benefaction set up by Cecil Rhodes to enable promising scholars from the USA and the Commonwealth to study in Oxford is told in Godfrey, Lord Elton *The First Fifty Years of the Rhodes Trust and the Rhodes Scholarships 1903–1953* Blackwell 1955.

**6588** Martin Harris 'The University of Salford: Integration and Innovation' *Manchester Memoirs* 1 1980–81 pp 100–12. A study of the development of the organization of and curriculum at Salford, which originated as the Royal Technical Institute in 1896 and became a university in 1967. See also M C Gordon 'The Foundation of the University of Salford' Salford MSc Thesis 1967–8.

**6589** A W Chapman *The Story of a Modern University: A History of the University of Sheffield* Oxford University Press 1955.

**6590** Alfred Temple Patterson *The University of Southampton: A Centenary History of the Evolution and Development of the University of Southampton 1862–1962* University of Southampton Press 1962.

**6591** Roger Blin-Stoyle and Geoff Ivey (eds) *The Sussex Opportunity: A New University and the Future* Harvester 1986. A history of Sussex University since its establishment in 1961 and a study of the perceptions of its students and the courses it offers. The origins and foundation of the University are examined in David Daiches (ed) *The Idea of a New University: An Experiment in Sussex* Deutsch 1964. See also G Lockward 'An Analysis of the Planning Process in 1968–73 in the Context of the History of the University of Sussex and of the Management of Universities' Sussex DPhil Thesis 1981.

**6592** Lord James of Rusholme 'The Start of a New University' *Transactions of the Manchester Statistical Society* 1965–66 pp 1–26. On the foundation of York University in the 1960s.

### (4) Further Education

**6593** J Skelding 'Developments in Further Education 1944–1982' Bath PhD Thesis 1983. A study of developments since the idea of county colleges was put forward in the 1944 McNair Report. The expansion of the training college network, the development of day release and training courses and the extent to which the ideals of 1944 have been realized are all analysed. It includes a case study of Basingstoke. The development of policy is also traced in J R Lukas 'The Formation of Government Policy over Further Education 1939–65' Oxford DPhil Thesis 1974–6. See also J B Soden 'A Study of the Development of Further Education 1956–1972' Edinburgh MEd Thesis 1986.

**6594** M C Davis 'The Council for National Academic Awards 1964–74: A Study of a Validating Agency' Loughborough PhD Thesis 1979. The CNAA oversees awards from colleges of further education and polytechnics. This thesis examines its policies, organization and decision making and those of its predecessor organization, the National Council for Technical Awards 1955–64.

**6595** G Harrison 'Further Education Policy in England and Wales Since 1944, with Particular Reference to Manchester' Salford MSc Thesis 1969–70.

**6596** H V Wyatt 'Cats and Robbins' *Universities Quarterly* 19 1964–5 pp 23–32. An examination of the proposals in the Robbins Report concerning colleges of advanced technology. The development of such colleges since 1944 is analysed in P F R Venables 'The Emergence of Colleges of Advanced Technology in Britain' *Year Book of Education* 1959 pp 224–36.

**6597** E Twigg 'Trends in Teacher Training and Staff Development in Technical Colleges and Colleges of Further Education in the Yorkshire and Humberside Council for Further Education Region 1945/75' Leeds MEd Thesis 1975–6.

**6598** H Arrowsmith *Pioneering in Education for the Technologies: The Story of Battersea College of Technology* University of Surrey 1966.

**6599** David Warren Piper (ed) *Readings in Art and Design Education* 2v, Davis Poynter 1973. Examinations of developments, the second volume of which concentrates on the period since the 1960 Coldstream Report. D M Sellers 'Post-War English Art Education' Sheffield MA Thesis 1982 is a general history. On design education see John Eggleston *Developments in Design Education* Open Books 1976.

**6600** Dick Field *Change in Art Education* Routledge and Kegan Paul 1970. An examination of the great changes wrought in the field of art education by the 1960 report of the National Advisory Council on Art Education chaired by Sir William Coldstream.

**6601** Sir William M Coldstream *National Advisory Council on Art Education: First Report* HMSO 1960. An influential report. This was followed by his further reports, *Vocational Courses in Colleges and Schools of Art: Second Report of the National Advisory Council on Art Education* HMSO 1962, *Post-Diploma Studies in Art and Design: Third Report of the National Advisory Council on Art Education* HMSO 1964 and *Structure of Art and Design Education in the Further Education Sector: Report of a Joint Committee of the National Advisory Council on Art and Education and the National Council for Diplomas in Art and Design* HMSO 1970.

**6602** Christopher Frayling *The Royal College of Art: One Hundred and Fifty Years of Art and Design* Barrie and Jenkins 1987. A useful analysis, although it is not a systematic history. See also *Graphics RCA: 15 Years*

*Work of the School of Graphic Design* Royal College of Art 1963.

**6603** C Ashwin *A Century of Art Education 1882–1982* Middlesex Polytechnic 1982. A history of the arts faculty at the polytechnic.

**6604** M Allthorpe-Gayton and J Stevens *A Happy Age: A School of Art in Norwich 1845–1982* Jarrold 1982.

**6605** Hugh Barty-King *Guildhall School of Music and Drama: A Hundred Years' Performance* Staines and Bell 1980. Other music college histories are H C Colles and John Cruft *The Royal College of Music: A Centenary Record 1883–1983* Prince Consort Foundation 1982 (which supersedes G Warrack *Royal College of Music: The First Eighty-Five Years 1883–1968* and Beyond Royal College of Music n.d. (1979?) and Michael Kennedy *The History of the Royal Manchester College of Music 1893–1971* Manchester University Press 1971.

## (5) Art and Music Education

## (6) Teacher Training

**6606** Michael Barry *Teacher Training Institutions in England and Wales: A Bibliographical Guide to their History* Society for Research into Higher Education, University of Surrey 1973. A useful, semi-annotated bibliography.

**6607** Harold Collett Dent *The Training of Teachers in England and Wales 1800–1975* Hodder and Stoughton 1977. The last part of this short history usefully examines the post-war period. See also M G Bruce 'Teacher Education Since 1944: Providing the Teachers and Controlling the Providers' *British Journal of Education Studies* 33 1985 pp 164–72.

**6608** P M Gardner 'Poor Relations: A Study of the Curriculum of Teacher Education, with Particular Reference to Four Colleges in the Cambridge Institute of Education 1944–1984' London MPhil Thesis 1986. A good study in a local context of the factors affecting teacher education, the reorganization of the 1960s involving the introduction of degree courses and other attempts to shake off the unacademic image of teacher education and the development of the curriculum.

**6609** M A B Jones 'The Emergency Training Scheme for Teachers: An Adventure in Administration' *Public Administration* 26 1948 pp 92–9. An account of the emergency scheme set up to train sufficient teachers in the aftermath of the Second World War to enable the government to implement the raising of the school leaving age in 1947.

**6610** E M Thompson 'National Policy in Relation to the Training and Supply of Teachers in England and Wales 1960–1970' Hull MEd Thesis 1976. A decade which saw attempts to end the notional inferiority of teacher education. The introduction of the academic qualification, the Bachelor of Education degree, as part of this is examined in D A Howell 'The Introduction of the Bachelor of Education Degree: A Case Study in British University Decision Making 1963–1970' London PhD Thesis 1976.

**6611** *Teacher Education and Training: Report by a Committee of Enquiry* HMSO 1972. The report of the committee chaired by Lord James of Rusholme. The state of teacher training at the time the committee was established is critically reviewed in T Burgess (ed) *Dear Lord James: A Critique of Teacher Education* Penguin 1971. J P Parry *The Lord James Tricycle* Allen and Unwin 1972 is a hostile response to the report.

**6612** Joan D Brown *Teachers of Teachers: A History of the Association of Teachers' Colleges and Departments of Education* Hodder and Stoughton 1979. The ATCDE was founded in 1943 to discuss matters relating to the education of teachers and to safeguard the interests of those engaged in this activity. The role of this body as a pressure group helping to shape the administration of teacher training is examined in I G Booth 'The Control and Administration of Training Colleges from the McNair Report 1944 to the Education (No 2) Act with Special Reference to the Policies of the ATCDE' Durham PhD Thesis 1981.

**6613** P S Gedge 'The Church of England Colleges of Education Since 1944' *Journal of Educational Administration and History* 13 1981 pp 33–42. See also R N Powell 'Tradition and Change in Church of England Teacher Training Colleges 1944–1974' Manchester MEd Thesis 1978.

**6614** D Corrigan *The Catholic Teachers' Colleges in the United Kingdom 1850–1960* Catholic University of America Press, Washington DC 1961. See also M Turketine 'Some Aspects of Social Change in Catholic Colleges of Education in the Twentieth Century' Leicester MEd Thesis 1968 and M M Cullen 'The Growth of Roman Catholic Training Colleges for Women during the Nineteenth and Twentieth Centuries' Durham MEd Thesis 1964.

**6615** A Mary Shaw *When Were You There: Reflections on Edgehill College 1884–1984* the author 1984. Reminiscences and history.

**6616** Francesca Mary Wilson *Rebel Daughter of a Country House: The Life of Eglantine Jebb* Allen and Unwin 1967. A biography of the influential educationa-list who was the Principal of the Froebel Educational Institute, Roehampton 1932–55.

**6617** T H Simms *Homerton College 1695–1978: From Dissenting Academy to Approved Society in the University of Cambridge* Trustees of Homerton College 1979. A history of the teacher training college in Cambridge.

**6618** I M Webb 'The History of Chelsea College of Physical Education with Special Reference to Curriculum Development 1898–1973' Leicester PhD Thesis 1977. Chelsea College of Physical Education trains women PE teachers. See also I M Webb 'Women's Physical Education in Great Britain 1800–1966, with Special Reference to Teacher Training' Leicester MEd Thesis 1967.

**6619** E J M Smith 'Art Teacher Training in Britain (1852–1985) with Special Reference to Leeds' *Journal of Art and Design Education* 4 1985 pp 103–46. A good survey up to the problems with cutbacks in government funding in the 1980s.

## (7) Student Politics

**6620** Eric Ashby and Mary Anderson *The Rise of the Student Estate in Britain* Macmillan 1970. A history from 1815 culminating in the statement the Committee of Vice-Chancellors and Principals issued in 1968 on the part that students should play in the management of universities, thereby rightly drawing attention to the the importance of this issue in the student unrest of the late 1960s. This is particularly emphasized in Anthony Arblaster *Academic Freedom* Penguin 1974. This is not a history but a survey of the grievances of the students in the 1960s, not least against undemocratic academic structures, and of the activities of the Council for Academic Freedom and Democracy, of which he was a leading member. See also A B Denis 'The Changing Role of Students in Relation to the Government of British Universities 1935–1968: A Sociological Analysis' London PhD Thesis 1968–9.

**6621** F A Rhodes 'The National Union of Students 1922–67' Manchester MEd Thesis 1968–9. The NUS in the period 1968–78 is examined in R J Holden 'Democracy in British Student Politics: The National Union of Students' Exeter PhD Thesis 1980.

**6622** Arthur Marwick 'Youth in Britain 1920–1960: Detachment and Commitment' *Journal of Contemporary History* 5 1970 pp 37–51. A study of student politics and attitudes. It largely concentrates on the period before 1945.

**6623** Bryan Wilson *The Youth Culture and the Universities* Fabian Society 1970. A collection of essays on student attitudes and protest, hippies and youth culture and the social context of the student problem in the 1960s.

**6624** *Select Committee on Education and Science: Student Relations* HC Paper 449, *Parliamentary Papers* vii–x 1968–69. This report examines the historical background to the international wave of student unrest in 1968. It urged various schemes of university reorganization, the introduction of careers advice, greater student participation, and a reconsideration of courses.

**6625** Stanley Rothman and S Robert Lichter *Roots of Radicalism: Jews, Christians and the New Left* Oxford University Press 1983. An examination of radical student movements spawned by the New Left in the 1960s.

**6626** David Adelstein (ed) *Teach Yourself Student Power* Radical Student Alliance 1968. A radical critique of the organization of higher education since the nineteenth century. Particular essays focus on what was seen as the cultural schism in the binary system of universities and polytechnics set up by Crosland in 1965, the origins of the Radical Student Alliance, and the sit-ins in London in 1967 and 1968.

**6627** M A Rooke *Anarchy and Apathy: Student Unrest 1968–70* Hamilton 1971. A useful general account of the student unrest of the late 1960s. See also J R Searle *The Campus War* Penguin 1972, David Martin *Anarchy and Culture: The Problem of the Contemporary University* Routledge and Kegan Paul 1969, C Crouch *The Student Revolt* The Bodley Head 1970 and A H Halsey and S Marks 'British Student Politics' *Daedalus* 97 1968 pp 116–36. The role of the Far Left in the students' movement of this period is examined in A Z Ehrlich 'The Leninist Organisation in Britain and the Student Movement 1966–1972' London PhD Thesis 1981. Student links with the trade union movement and perceptions of the students from within the union movement are discussed in Ken Tarbuck 'Students and Trade Unions' *Trade Union Register* 1969 pp 101–5. Joan Abbott *Student Life in a Class Society* Pergamon 1971 is a sociological work which has some reflections on the student unrest of the 1960s.

**6628** Tessa Blackstone, K Gales, Roger Hadley and W Lewis *Students in Conflict: LSE in 1967* Weidenfeld and Nicolson 1970. An account of the sit-in at the London School of Economics in 1967. See also P Hoch and V Schoenbach *LSE: The Natives are Restless* Sheed and Ward 1969, H Kidd *The Troubles at LSE* Oxford University Press 1969 and Ben Brewster and Alexander Cockburn 'Revolt at the LSE' *New Left Review* 43 1967 pp 11–26.

**6629** Hornsey College of Art *The Hornsey Affair* Penguin 1969. An account of the six week takeover of the college in May 1968 by students and some of the staff. It was written by those involved by this experiment in communal education.

**6630** Keith Jacka, Caroline Cox and John Marks *Rape of Reason: The Corruption of the Polytechnic of North London* Churchill 1975. A critical account of the intolerant activities of far left students and the corrupting of academic standards.

**6631** E P Thompson (ed) *Warwick University Ltd* Penguin 1970. A sympathetic account of the seizure of the university registry by the students in February 1970 and its consequences. It features some of the documents captured. In part both the students action and the book is an attack on links between business and universities. It pleas that universities should be 'centres of free discussion and action, tolerating and even encouraging "subversive thought and activity" – rather than simply providing "pre-packed intellectual commodities which meet the demands of management"'.

## D. ADULT EDUCATION

The material on the Open University [6586], in many ways the greatest and most significant innovation in the field of adult education in the post-war period, can be found in the section on Individual Universities [6586].

**6632** *Adult Education in 1961* – National Institution of Adult Education 1961–. A year book, and reference guide which includes an annual bibliography.

**6633** J E Thomas and J H Davies (eds) *A Select Bibliography of Adult Continuing Education in Great Britain* National Institute of Adult Education 1984. A useful annotated bibliography of works published up to the end of 1981. It builds on but does not entirely supersede Thomas Kelly *A Select Bibliography of Adult Education in Great Britain* 3rd ed, National Institute of Adult Education 1974. W E Styler *A Bibliographical Guide to Adult Education in Rural Areas 1918–1978* Department of Adult Education, University of Hull 1973 is a comprehensive guide to the literature.

**6634** David Ben Rees *Preparation for Crisis: Adult Education 1945–80* Hesketh 1982. A critical assessment of adult education provision in the post-war years. See also S G Raybould (ed) *Trends in British Adult Education* Heinemann 1959.

**6635** Roger Fieldhouse *Adult Education and the Cold War: Liberal Values under Siege 1946–51* Leeds Studies in Adult and Continuing Education, Department of Adult Education, University of Leeds 1985. This includes some reflections on adult education in the forces but is largely concerned with the idea of state influence on adult education and emphasis on containing Marxist subversions, drawing attention to the witchhunting of Communists in university extra-mural departments and also amongst those involved in adult education in the colonial empire.

**6636**  *Organisation and Finance of Adult Education in England and Wales: The Report of the Committee* HMSO 1954. This report of the committee chaired by Eric Ashby also contains useful reflections on the purpose of adult education.

**6637**  F J Brown and D C Galleymore 'Adult Education and Local Government Reorganisation: The Effects of Change in Three Local Education Authorities 1973–5' *Studies in Adult Education* 8 1976 pp 29–42. A study of local education authorities in the North East of England in the light of the changes brought in by the 1972 Local Government Act.

**6638**  Stuart Marriott *Extramural Empires: Service and Self- Interest in English University Adult Education 1873–1983* Department of Adult Education, University of Nottingham 1984. See also John A Blyth *English University Adult Education 1908–1958: The Unique Tradition* Manchester University Press 1983 and H V Wiseman 'University Extension Work Since 1945' *Adult Education* 24 1957 pp 180–92.

**6639**  Roger Fieldhouse 'The Ideology of English Responsible Body Adult Education 1925–1950' Leeds PhD Thesis 1984. The responsible bodies referred to are the universities, the National Council of Labour Colleges and the Workers' Education Association. This thesis examines the political aspects of their adult education work, especially affinities with the Labour Movement, and other conflicts, not least the constraints imposed on adult education in the forces by the military authorities in 1939–50. J P M Millar *The Labour College Movement* NCLC Publishing 1979 is a history of the Left-Wing National Council of Labour Colleges set up in the 1920s by one of its prominent members. On the WEA see Mary D Stocks *The Workers' Education Association: The First Fifty Years* Allen and Unwin 1953 and Cecil Alexander Scrimgeour *Fifty Years A-Growing: A History of the North Staffordshire District, the Workers Educational Association 1921–1971* North Staffordshire District, Workers Educational Association 1974.

**6640**  John Allaway *The Education Centres Movement 1909–77* National Institution of Adult Education n.d 1977–8?.

**6641**  H J Edwards *The Evening Institute: Its Place in the Education System of England and Wales* National Institution of Adult Education 1961. A history up to 1961 and a survey of the contemporary situation. It lists legislation affecting evening institutes.

**6642**  W Arnold Hall *The Adult School Movement in the Twentieth Century* Department of Adult Education, University of Nottingham 1985. A good history of the oldest of adult education bodies tracing its development in the twentieth century and its declining links with the Society of Friends. Another good study is John Fletcher Clews Harrison *Learning and Living 1790–1960: A Study of the English Adult School Movement* Routledge and Kegan Paul 1961. On the most famous of the Quaker adult education colleges which have developed in the twentieth century see R Davis (ed) *Woodbrooke College 1903–53: A Brief History of a Quaker Experiment in Religious Education* Bannisdale Press 1953. The history of this Quaker adult education college in Birmingham is continued in F Ralph Barlow *Woodbrooke 1953–1978: A Documentary Account of Woodbrooke's Third 25 Years* William Sessions.

**6643**  'Trade Union Education in the United Kingdom' *Labor Studies Journal* 4/3 1980. A special issue devoted to the subject. This series of essays looks at subjects such as the establishment of the Northern College in the 1970s, or the post-war shift from liberal to vocational courses. See also J Atkins 'The TUC and Trade Union Education 1909–1964' *WEA Trade Union and Industrial Studies Newsletter* 3 1979 pp 1–21. The links of the NUM to the adult education movement are explored in the short research paper, Graham Mee *Miners, Adult Education and Community Service 1920–1984* Nottingham Working Papers in the Education of Adults, Department of Adult Education, University of Nottingham 1984, which however fails to examine the role of adult education in forming union consciousness.

**6644**  Harold Pollins *The History of Ruskin College Occasional Publications* 3, Ruskin College Library 1984. A short history of this trade union college at Oxford which concentrates on the period 1909–39. Al Nash *Ruskin College: A Challenge to Adult and Labor Education* New York State School of Industrial and Labor Relations, Cornell University 1981 is a rather bland study which contains some factual errors. See also J G Blumler 'The Effects of Long-Term Residential Adult Education in Post-War Britain with Particular Reference to Ruskin College, Oxford' Oxford DPhil Thesis 1961–2.

**6645**  J Robinson *Learning Over The Air: 60 Years of Partnership in Adult Learning* BBC 1982. A study of the efforts of the BBC and the IBA to help adult education through the provision of general interest and adult education programmes and of the responses of the adult education agencies.

**6646** Wendy Hay (comp) *Adult Literacy in Britain: An Annotated Bibliography* Library Association 1978. A useful guide. D Hargreaves *On The Move: The BBC's Contribution to the Adult Literacy Campaign in the United Kingdom between 1972 and 1976* BBC 1977 is a short account by the project leader on the exercise.

**6647** William A Devereux *Adult Education in Inner London 1870–1980* Shepheard and Walwyn 1982. Adult education provision in recent years in this area by the Inner London Education Authority is examined in M Newman *The Poor Cousin* Allen and Unwin 1979.

**6648** M L Shaw 'Local Authority Provision of Post-Compulsory Educaiton in Nelson and Colne, Lancashire Since 1955' Manchester MEd Thesis 1978.

## E. LIBRARIES AND MUSEUMS

### (1) Libraries

**6649** *The Libraries, Museums and Art Galleries Year Book* James Clarke and Co 1897–. A somewhat irregular publication.

**6650** *The Year's Work in Librarianship* Library Association 1928–50. An irregular state of the art survey of developments in the Association's various branches in all aspects of library work. This detailed work was carried on by P H Sewell *Five Years Work in Librarianship* 3v, 1958–68. Volume 1 covers 1951–55, volume 2 covers 1956–60 and volume 3 1961–65. This work was continued by H A Whatley (ed) *British Librarianship and Information Science* 2v, Library Association 1972–77. The first of these volumes covers 1966–70 and the second 1971–75.

**6651** Denis F Keeling (ed) *British Library History Bibliography 1962–8* Library Association 1972. The first of a series of annotated historical bibliographies. The subsequent volumes have tended to cover three rather than six years at a time.

**6652** *Bibliography in Britain* Oxford Bibliographical Society 1962–67. An annual guide to works on the history of the printed word, with sections covering such subjects as libraries, typography, bookbinding, publishing, newspapers and so on. A similar, successor publication is the *Annual Bibliography of the History of the Printed Book and Libraries* Nijhoff, Den Haag 1973–. This series covers works published since 1970 on a similar range of subjects. It is however international in scope, though it offers good coverage on works relating to Britain. For major works it also tends to list the references for all the important reviews.

**6653** Peter J Taylor (ed) *Library and Information Studies in the United Kingdom and Ireland 1850–1974: An Index to Theses* Aslib 1976. This is unannotated but has a good index. It can be supplemented by Laurence John Taylor *FLA Theses: Abstracts of all Theses Accepted for the Fellowship of the Library Association from 1964* British Library/Library Association Library 1979.

**6654** Margaret Mann *Archival Problems of Audiovisual Materials: A Select, Annotated Bibliography* Department of Information Science, University of Sheffield 1982. This briefly reviews the main literature on the problems of audiovisual archives since 1970.

**6655** *Library Science Abstracts* Library Association 1950–68. Since 1968 its title has been *Library and Information Science Abstracts*. It appears bi-monthly and is international in scope. Since 1969 the information which appears in the abstracts has also been available on the Library Association's database, LISA. Contact the Library Association, 7 Ridgmount Street, Store Street, London WC1E 7AE, for further details.

**6656** T Landau (ed) *Who's Who in Librarianship and Information Science* 2nd ed, Abelard-Schuman 1972. A collection of alphabetically arranged potted biographies.

**6657** Thomas A Kelly *A History of Public Libraries in Great Britain 1845–1975* 2nd ed, Library Association 1977. The standard work on the subject which includes a good bibliography. The final section covers 1939–75. J E Pemberton *Politics and Public Libraries in England and Wales 1850–1970* Library Association 1977 is an analysis of the political forces affecting public library policy and legislation, concentrating on the twentieth century. See also R J B Morris *Parliament and the Public Libraries: A Survey of Legislative Activity Promoting the Municipal Library Service in England and Wales 1850–1976* Mansell 1977. This chronologically examines the legislation affecting libraries as it went through parliament and tabulates the progress of all the 66 Bills of this period. It also deals with parliamentary questions in a similarly exhaustive fashion. William Arthur Munford 'Our Recent Past: A Review Article' *Journal of Librarianship* 15 1983 pp 216–24 reviews British librarianship 1928–80. See also P Sykes 'Attitudes and Use: A Critical Study of Factors Influencing the Establishment, Development and Relevance of British Public Libraries 1850–1977' Sheffield MA Thesis 1977.

**6658** Keith Barr and Maurice Line (eds) *Essays on Information and Libraries: Festschrift for Ronald Urquhart* Clive Bingley 1975. A collection of essays on subjects such as special libraries, the national lending library, the British Library or Urquhart himself.

**6659** *The Structure of the Public Lending Service in England and Wales: Report of the Committee Appointed by the Minister of Education in September 1957* Cmnd 660 *Parliamentary Papers* xvi 1958–59. This report by the committee chaired by Sir Sydney Roberts led to the setting up of advisory bodies for England and Wales and required the county councils to submit schemes for the administration of libraries, leading to changes in the county service.

**6660** N A Webber 'Public Libraries in Britain' *Contemporary Review* 226/1309 pp 1975 pp 91–6. An outline history of developments in the 1960s.

**6661** W L Saunders (ed) *British Librarianship Today* Library Association 1976. A useful broad survey of the contemporary state of librarianship published for the centenary of the Library Association. It also traces the evolution of the Association.

**6662** William Arthur Munford (ed) *Annals of the Library Association 1877–1977* Library Association 1977. The standard account. The role of the Library Association as a political pressure group is reviewed in J E Pemberton 'A Century of Library Politics' *Library Association Record* 79 1977 pp 181, 184–5. He argues that it became more effective in pressing for better libraries from 1959 onwards. The background to this is analysed in D D Haslam 'The Fighting Fifties: An Informal Review of the Association's Activities during 1950–59' *Library Association Record* 62 1960 pp 2–10. See also the short branch history, Christopher W J Harris *Fifty Years of Progress: The London and Home Counties Branch of the Library Association 1923–1973* London and Home Counties Branch, Library Association 1973.

**6663** Peter J Taylor (ed) *Essays on Aslib* Aslib 1978. Essays examining various aspects of the history of the Association of Special Libraries and Information Bureaux. There is also a useful bibliography.

**6664** William Arthur Munford *Who Was who in British Librarianship 1800–1985: A Dictionary of Dates with Notes* Library Association 1987. A reference guide. On women librarians and their struggle for equal treatment in a profession in which women have traditionally been a high proportion of the workforce see K Weibel *et al* (eds) *The Role of Women in Librarianship 1876–1976: The Entry, Advancement and Struggle for Equalisation in one Profession* Mansell 1979.

**6665** Ronald J Edwards *In-Service Training in British Libraries: Its Development and Present Practice* Library Association 1977. The history of librarian training is also told in Gerald Bramley *Apprentice to Graduate: A History of Library Education in the UK* Clive Bingley 1981. See also Alec Ellis *Librarianship on the Mersey: An Account of the School of Librarianship and Informa-* *tion Studies, Liverpool Polytechnic 1962–1987* Liverpool Polytechnic Press 1987.

**6666** Ronald Staveley 'From Lancashire to University College: Raymond Urwin and Professional Librarianship' *Library Review* 34 1985 pp 153–9. Urwin championed rural libraries and was important in post-war planning by the Library Association.

**6667** Norman Roberts 'Ten Years of Library Journals 1969–1979' *Journal of Librarianship* 11 1979 pp 163–82. An account not least of the development of the journal in which it was published.

**6668** Graham Jones (ed) *'This Emphatically British Library': The First Ten Years of the British Library* McDougall 1983. A study of the establishment, development and various services of the British Library. F Dolores Donnelly 'The British Library: Phenomenon of the Seventies or Prototype of National Library Planning' *Library History* 16 1981 pp 380–93 is an examination of the background to the establishment of the British Library as a national library from what used to be the British Museum Library. The background to the establishment of the British Library and its subsequent development is traced in D J Urquhart 'Some Thoughts on the British Library' *Journal of Documentation* 37 1981 pp 125–33. A more critical assessment of the establishment of the British Library and the planning for the new building at St Pancras in London is Peter Hall 'Two New Disasters: California's New Campuses and Britain's National Library' in his *Great Planning Disasters* Weidenfeld and Nicolson 1980 pp 152–84. The history of the catalogue of the British Library and its predecessor is told in A H Chaplin *150 Years of the General Catalogue of the British Museum* Scolar 1987. The history of the Newspaper Library section at Colindale in North London, which was established in 1932, is told in *Newspaper Library Newsletter* Aug 1982, the whole issue of which is devoted to the subject.

**6669** M L Ward *Readers and Library Users: A Study of Reading Habits and Library Use* Library Association 1977. A useful survey of reading habits and public library use 1900–76. B Luckham 'Decline and Fall: Social Regression in Public Library Service' *Information and Library Manager* 1 1981 pp 74–80 uses statistical tables to chart declining readership over the period 1850–1970s.

**6670** Victor Bonham-Carter *The Fight for Public Lending Rights 1951–1979* Exmoor Press 1988. The ninth Bill of the post-war period seeking to give authors of popular books at public lending libraries some financial reward was finally passed in 1979.

**6671** Anthony H Thompson *Censorship in Public Libraries in the United Kingdom during the Twentieth Century* Bowker 1975. A good and interesting study.

**6672** Kenneth Alan Stockham (ed) *British County Libraries 1919–69* Deutsch 1969. A short history interspersed with biographical sketches. It includes a good bibliography. See also L V Paulin 'County Libraries: Half a Century's Achievement' *Library Association Record* 71 1969 pp 347–52.

**6673** G I J Orton *An Illustrated History of Mobile Library Services in the United Kingdom: With Notes on Travelling Libraries and Early Public Transport* Mobile Libraries Group of the Library Association 1980. The history and contemporary operations of this type of library is examined in C R Eastwood *Mobile Libraries and other Public Library Transport* Association of Assistant Librarians 1967. See also P M Long 'The Commercial Circulating Library in the 1970s' *Library History* 6 1981 pp 185–93.

**6674** Thomas A Kelly 'Public Libraries in Adult Education' *Journal of Librarianship* 2 1970 pp 145–59. Libraries had a large role in adult education in the nineteenth century but financial constraints in the twentieth century has meant that they have concentrated on book provision.

**6675** Alec Ellis *Library Services for Young People in England and Wales 1830–1970* Pergamon 1971. This is partly added to and updated by his 'Public Library Services for Children in England and Wales 1943–1959' *Journal of Librarianship* 4 1972 pp 14–31 and 'Public Library Services for Children in England and Wales 1960–1974' *Journal of Librarianship* 6 1974 pp 10–27.

**6676** W Hay *Library Services for the Handicapped People: An Annotated Bibliography of British Material*

*1970–1981* Library Association 1982. A classified guide to 132 items. A list of interested organizations is provided in the brief introduction.

**6677** Charles Parish *The History of the Literary and Philosophical Society of Newcastle upon Tyne 1896–1989* the Society 1989. A history of the society and its well regarded library in its second century.

## (2) Museums and Galleries

**6678** Stuart Davies *By the Gains of Industry: Birmingham Museum and Art Galleries 1885–1985* Birmingham Museums and Art Galleries 1985.

**6679** Malcolm Rogers *Museums and Galleries of London* Benn 1983. A guide. There are histories of several of the national museums and galleries in London. These include Edward Miller *That Noble Cabinet: A History of the British Museum* Deutsch 1975, F Sheppard 'The Museum of London' *London Journal* 3 1977 pp 212–20 (a brief description of the new Museum of London which opened in December 1976), William T Stearn *The Natural History Museum at South Kensington: A History of the British Museum (Natural History) 1753–1980* Heinemann 1981 (and also the illustrated history, Peter Whitehead *The British Museum (Natural History)* Wilson 1981), *The Science Museum: The First Hundred Years* HMSO 1957, S Fox-Pitt 'The Tate Gallery Archive of Twentieth Century British Art, Its Formation and Development' *Archives* 74 1985 pp 94–106 and J Physick *The Victoria and Albert Museum: The History of the Building* Phaidon/Christie's 1982.

**6680** R G L Rivis *The Gunnersbury Park Museum 1927–55* privately printed 1960.

# 11 INTELLECTUAL AND CULTURAL HISTORY

## A. GENERAL

**6681** Roland Turner (ed) *Thinkers of the Twentieth Century* St James Press 1987. A collection of biographies of major intellectual figures in twentieth century world history, each of which is complemented by a useful bibliography. It includes a good range of British philosophers, historians, theologians and scientists. A similar work is Alan Bullock and Oliver Stallybrass (eds) *The Fontana Dictionary of Modern Thought* revised ed, Fontana 1988.

**6682** C B Cox and A E Dyson (eds) *The Twentieth Century Mind: History, Ideas and Literature in Britain Vol 3: 1945–1965* Oxford University Press 1973. An all embracing study of thought, science, culture and the arts in post-war Britain, though it is less successful in its treatment of the arts and music than of academic thought and literature.

**6683** L H C Tippett 'Annals of the Royal Statistical Society 1934–71' *Journal of the Royal Statistical Society* 135 1972 pp 545–68. A history of the society.

## B. HUMANITIES

### (1) Philosophy

**6684** Geoffrey J Warnock *English Philosophy Since 1900* 2nd ed, Oxford University Press 1969. A short selective guide.

**6685** C A Mace (ed) *British Philosophy in Mid-Century: A Cambridge Symposium* 2nd ed, Allen and Unwin 1966. A collection of essays by eminent philosophers, reflecting on recent trends in the various branches of philosophy.

**6686** S G Shanker (ed) *Philosophy in Britain Today* Croom Helm 1986. Reflections on contemporary issues in philosophy. It also includes an autobiographical passage by Anthony Flew.

**6687** Bryan Magee *Modern British Philosophy* Oxford University Press 1986. A collection of interviews with important philosophers about current concerns in British philosophy. It includes biographical information. Bryan Magee (ed) *Modern British Philosophy* Secker and Warburg 1971 is a similar earlier volume. J H Muirhead and H D Lewin (eds) *Contemporary British Philosophy: Personal Statements* 4v, Allen and Unwin 1976 collects brief accounts of the life and work of eminent philosophers. It includes a bibliography.

**6688** Alan P F Sell *The Philosophy of Religion 1875–1980* Croom Helm 1988. A study of the relations between Western, largely British, philosophy and religion and theology since the nineteenth century. He argues that there has been a more pluralistic philosophical climate less inimical to religion since 1945.

**6689** Alfred J Ayer *Part of My Life* Collins 1977. An autobiography up to the late 1940s. See also his *More of My Life* Collins 1984 which goes up to 1963.

**6690** Neil MacCormick *H L A Hart* Arnold 1981. A study of the life and thought of the distinguished Oxford legal philosopher.

**6691** Nancy Cunard *GM: Memories of George Moore* Hart-Davies 1956. A personal memoir of the great ethical philosopher. His work is assessed in Alice Ambrose and Morris Lazerowitz (eds) *G E Moore: Essays in Retrospect* Allen and Unwin 1970.

**6692** Karl Popper *Unended Quest: An Intellectual Autobiography* revised ed, Fontana 1976. An autobiography by one of the dominant figures in post-war British philosophy. See also Bryan Magee *Popper* Fontana 1973. There is also considerable material on Popper's *The Open Society* and on his political philosophy in the section on Political Thought.

**6693** Werner Martin *Bertrand Russell: A Bibliography of his Writings 1895–1976* Linnet, Hampden, Connecticut 1981. The best biography of the Cambridge philosopher is Ronald W Clark *The Life of Bertrand Russell* Cape/Weidenfeld and Nicolson 1975. Russell's own autobiography, *The Autobiography of Bertrand Russell Vol 3: 1944–1967* Allen and Unwin 1969, conceals as much as it reveals. Its deficiencies and message is assessed in Robert H Bell 'Confession and Concealment in the Autobiography of Bertrand Russell' *Biography* 8 1985 pp 318–35. Another biographical study is H Gottschalk *Bertrand Russell: A Life* Baker 1965. Katherine Tait *My Father, Bertrand Russell* Gollancz 1976 is an interesting assessment of Russell's life and attitudes. Tributes are paid to the great philosopher in George W Roberts (eds) *Bertrand Russell: Memorial Volume* Allen and Unwin 1979. Alfred J Ayer *Russell* Woburn Press 1974 is a study of Russell's life and work by another distinguished British philosopher. It includes a useful bibliography. Ralph Schoeman (ed) *Bertrand Russell: Philosopher of the Century* Little Brown, Boston, Massachusetts 1967 is a collection of essays on the man and the philosopher. Russell's philosophy and writings are also assessed in Paul Grimley Kuntz *Bertrand Russell* Twayne, Boston, Massachusetts 1986. Alan Ryan *Bertrand Russell: A Political Life* Allen Lane 1988 is a political biography which largely concentrates on the earlier part of his career and examines Russell's links with the Labour Party, his work for pacifist causes and for CND and his role in the creation of a more permissive society.

**6694** Francois H Lapointe *Ludwig Wittgenstein: A Comprehensive Bibliography* Greenwood 1980. The life of Wittgenstein is explored in Norman Malcolm *Ludwig Wittgenstein: A Memoir* Oxford University Press 1958. On Wittgenstein, an Austrian who became a naturalized British citizen in the late 1930s, and on his philosophy of logic see also *Ludwig Wittgenstein: Personal Recollections* Blackwell 1981, David Francis Pears *Ludwig Wittgenstein* Penguin 1977 and Kuang Tih Fann (ed) *Ludwig Wittgenstein: The Man and His Philosophy* Dell Publishing, New York 1967.

## (2) Psychology

**6695** Grogorio Kohon (ed) *The British School of Psychoanalysis: The Independent Tradition* Yale University Press 1986. An analysis of the distinctiveness of the British school of thought.

**6696** Hannah Steinberg (ed) *The British Psychological Society 1901–61* British Psychological Society 1961. A short history.

**6697** Anita M Menden and Harold J Fine 'A Short History of the British School of Object Relations and Ego Psychology' *Bulletin of the Menninger Clinic* 40 1976 pp 357–82.

**6698** L S Hearnshaw *Cyril Burt: Psychologist* Hodder and Stoughton 1979. A good biography (including a bibliography of Burt's work) of the distinguished psychologist whose reputation has become tainted since his death in 1971 by denigration of his academic integrity, an accusation that is borne out here.

**6699** H B Gibson *Hans Eysenck: The Man and His Work* Owen 1981. A biography of a leading psychologist. Eysenck achieved notoriety in the 1970s because of some controversial comments about genetic conditioning. It is such aspects of psychology that are briefly examined in M Billig *Psychology, Racism and Fascism* Searchlight 1977.

## (3) Economics

Much useful material can also be found in the section on General Economic Policy. This section also includes the biographical material on a number of leading economists, notably John Maynard Keynes and James Meade, who also served as economic advisers to the government.

**6700** R P Sturges *Economists' Papers 1750–1950: A Guide to Archives and Other Manuscript Sources for the History of British and Irish Economic Thought* Macmillan 1975. A finding list. It includes material on post-war figures such as Keynes or the economic historian R H Tawney.

**6701** A E Booth and A W Coats 'The Market for Economists in Britain 1944–1975' *Economic Journal* 88 1978 pp 436–54.

**6702** A W Coats and S E Coats 'The Changing Social Composition of the Royal Economic Society 1890–1960 and the Professionalisation of British Economics' *British Journal of Sociology* 24 1973 pp 165–87. A study of the changing nature of the economic profession.

**6703** Christopher L Gilbert *The Development of British Econometrics 1945–85* Institute of Economics and Statistics, University of Oxford 1986. A short analysis.

**6704** M Bleaney *The Rise and Fall of Keynesian Economics* Macmillan 1985. A study of the economic orthodoxy that dominated most of the post-war period.

**6705** Robert Locke 'Educational Traditions and the Development of Business Studies after 1945 (An Anglo-

French-German Comparison)' in R P T Davenport-Hines and Geoffrey Jones (eds) *The End of Insularity: Essays in Comparative Business History* Cass 1988 pp 84–103. A comparative study of the development of economic studies, business history and courses for the Master of Business Administration qualification.

**6706** J R Gould 'Opportunity Lost: The London Tradition' in Harold Edey and B S Yamey (eds) *Debts, Credits, Finance and Profits* Sweet and Maxwell 1974 pp 91–107. A study of George Thirlby and the economists at the London School of Economics between the 1930s and 1950s.

**6707** Brian Pollitt and Bruce McFarlane (eds) *Selected Papers of Maurice Dobb* 2v, Lawrence and Wishart 1986. Dobb was a leading Marxist economist and a socialist theoretician of international stature. This collection of his papers attempts to present a rounded portrait of his work. See also [6718].

**6708** Lionel Charles Robbins *Autobiography of an Economist* Macmillan 1971. Robbins was Professor of Economics at the London School of Economics 1929–61, the chairman of the 1961–3 committee on higher education and the first Chancellor of Stirling University 1968–78. His life and work is assessed in detail in the well regarded biography, Dennis Patrick O'Brien *Lionel Robbins* Macmillan 1988. There is also the collection of his speeches in the House of Lords, Lionel Charles Robbins *Against Inflation: Speeches in the Second Chamber 1965–1977* Macmillan 1979.

**6709** Harvey Gram and Vivian Walsh 'Joan Robinson's Economics in Retrospect' *Journal of Economic Literature* 21 1983 pp 518–50. An assessment of a controversial economist and her work.

### (4) History

**6710** Charles A Watson *The Writing of History in Britain: A Bibliography of Writings about British Historians and Biographers* Garland 1982. A detailed bibliography of writings about historians.

**6711** Gertrude Himmelfarb *The New History and the Old: Critical Essays and Reappraisals* Harvard University Press 1987. This includes some reflections on British historiographical trends. Geoffrey Elton *Modern Historians on British History 1485–1945: A Critical Bibliography 1945–1969* Methuen 1970 is a well regarded study of British historiographical trends. Richard Schlatter (ed) *Recent Views on British History: Essays on Historical Writing Since 1966* Rutgers University Press, New Brunswick, New Jersey 1986 is a collection of essays by North American scholars reviewing the

most significant trends and developments in writings on British history in recent years.

**6712** *The Historical Association 1906–1956* Historical Association 1957.

**6713** M D Knowles 'Academic History' *History* 47 1962 pp 222–32. A view of the teaching of history at the universities. See also George Kitson Clark 'A Hundred Years of the Teaching of History at Cambridge 1873–1973' *Historical Journal* 16 1973 pp 535–53 and A J Taylor 'History at Leeds 1877–1974: The Evolution of a Discipline' *Northern History* 10 1975 pp 141–64.

**6714** D C Coleman *History and the Economic Past: An Account of the Rise and Decline of Economic History in Britain* Clarendon 1987. A study of the writing and changing nature of economic history covering the period from the Scottish enlightenment to the present. The rise of business history as a discipline and the work of the Business Archives Council is examined in Peter Mathias 'The First Half Century: Business History, Business Archives and the BAC' *Business Archives* n.s. 5 1984 pp 1–16.

**6715** Harold Perkin 'Social History in Britain' *Journal of Social History* 10 1976 pp 129–43. A study of the development and contemporary state of the discipline as it emerged from the shadow of economic history to equal status by one of its principal exponents. Intellectual trends and fashions in areas of interest are examined in Negley B Harte 'Trends in Publications on the Economic and Social History of Great Britain and Ireland 1925–74' *Economic History Review* 2nd series, 30 1977 pp 20–41.

**6716** Peter Gordon and Richard Szreter *History of Education: The Making of a Discipline* Woburn 1989. A history of the study of education and educational philosophy. Brian Simon 'The History of Education in the 1980s' *British Journal of Educational Studies* 30 1982 pp 85–96 is a study of the contemporary state of the discipline and a review of its development.

**6717** John Terraine 'Twenty-Five Years of Military History 1945–1970' *Journal of the Royal United Services Institute for Defence Studies* 116 1971 pp 13–23. A historiographical review.

**6718** Harvey J Kaye *The British Marxist Historians: An Introductory Analysis* Polity 1984. A historigraphical analysis of the work and interpretations of Maurice Dobb (on whom see also [6707]), Rodney Hilton, Christopher Hill, Eric Hobsbawm and E P Thompson. See also Raphael Samuel 'British Marxist Historians 1880–1980' *New Left Review* 120 1980 pp 21–96. Marxist historians are also examined in Eric Hobsbawm 'The Historians' Group of the Communist Party' in Maurice Cornforth (ed) *Rebels and their Causes: Essays in Honour of A L*

*Morton* Lawrence and Wishart 1978 pp 21–48. The work and methods of History Workshop, a journal of and for socialist and feminist historians, is examined in David Selbourne 'On the Methods of History Workshop' *History Workshop* 9 1980 pp 150–61 and Raphael Samuel 'On the Methods of History Workshop: A Reply' *History Workshop* 9 1980 pp 162–76.

**6719**  S William Halperin (ed) *Some 20th Century Historians: Essays on Eminent Europeans* University of Chicago Press, Chicago, Illinois 1961. This includes essays on G M Trevelyan, Herbert Butterfield, Sir Charles Webster and G P Gooch.

**6720**  Institute of Historical Research, Senate House, Malet Street, London WC1E 7HU. The Institute has produced a number of videotapes of distinguished historians in interview talking about their work. These include Moses Finley, Christopher Hill, Lawrence Stone, Eric Hobsbawm, Henry Pelling, Margaret Gowing, Joseph Needham (on whom see also [6790]), Rodney Hilton, Geoffrey Dickens, Geoffrey Elton, Joan Thirsk, Peter Laslett and Hugh Clegg.

**6721**  P Street *Arthur Bryant: Portrait of a Historian* Collins 1979. A biography and study of the work of the historian and successful popularizer of the discipline.

**6722**  Sir Denis Brogan 'Sir Herbert Butterfield as a Historian: An Appreciation' in J H Elliott and H G Koenigsberger (eds) *The Diversity of History: Essays In Honour of Sir Herbert Butterfield* Routledge and Kegan Paul 1970 pp 1–16. See also John Derry 'Herbert Butterfield' in John Cannon (ed) *The Historian at Work* Allen and Unwin 1980 pp 171–87. Butterfield and his work are also considered in Geoffrey Elton 'Herbert Butterfield and the Study of History' *Historical Journal* 27 1984 pp 329–43. His philosophy of international relations is fully explored in A R Coll *The Wisdom of Statecraft: Sir Herbert Butterfield and the Philosophy of International Politics* Duke University Press, Durham, North Carolina 1986. Butterfield is contrasted with the late nineteenth century historian, Lord Acton, in Owen Chadwick 'Acton and Butterfield' *Journal of Ecclesiastical History* 38 1987 pp 386–405. Butterfield's work, particularly on the philosophy of history, and his attempts to analyse history within a Christian framework are analysed in J Munsey Turner 'The Christian and the Study of History: Sir Herbert Butterfield (1900–79)' *Proceedings of the Wesley Historical Society* 46 1987 pp 1–12.

**6723**  Tamara Deutscher 'E H Carr: A Personal Memoir' *New Left Review* 137 1983 pp 78–86. A tribute to the historian of the Soviet Union.

**6724**  Maurice Ashley *Churchill as Historian* Secker and Warburg 1968. A good study of Churchill's strengths and failings as a historian.

**6725**  Richard Cobb *Something To Hold Onto: Autobiographical Sketches* Murray 1988. The autobiography of the specialist on revolutionary France who was Professor of Modern History at Oxford 1973–84.

**6726**  Christina Scott *A Historian and His World: A Life of Christopher Dawson 1889–1970* Sheed 1984. A useful life of the Catholic church and social historian which includes a good bibliography.

**6727**  J E King and O M Westall (eds) *Innovation and Labour during British Industrialisation: A Celebration of the Life and Work of Henry Dutton 1947–1984* Huntingdon Publications 1985. A memorial tribute to an economic historian.

**6728**  David Cannadine 'Urban History in the United Kingdom: The "Dyos Phenomenon" and After' in David Cannadine and David Reader (eds) *Exploring the Urban Past: Essays in Urban History by H J Dyos* Cambridge University Press 1982 pp 203–21. This traces the growth of the discipline of urban history through the life and work of its leading exponent, H J Dyos, the first Professor of Urban History to be appointed in Britain. Dyos discusses his life and work in B M Stave 'A Conversation with H J Dyos: Urban History in Great Britain' *Journal of Urban History* 5 1979 pp 469–500. See also Seymour J Mandelbaum 'H J Dyos and British Urban History' *Economic History Journal* 38 1985 pp 437–47.

**6729**  George Ewart Evans *The Strength of the Hills: An Autobiography* Faber 1983. The autobiography of the pioneering oral historian.

**6730**  Frank Eyck *G P Gooch* Macmillan 1982. Gooch was an eminent historian and the editor of the *Contemporary Review* 1911–60. G P Gooch *Under Six Reigns* Longmans 1958 is a rather unsatisfactory autobiography.

**6731**  Adrian Morey *David Knowles: A Memoir* Darton, Longman and Todd 1979. A biography of the first Benedictine monk to become Regius Professor of Modern History (1954–63) at Cambridge. It includes a bibliography of Knowles' writings on church history. See also C N L Brooke *David Knowles* Oxford University Press 1975.

**6732**  Maurice Cornforth 'A L Morton: Portrait of a Marxist Historian' in Maurice Cornforth (ed) *Rebels and Their Causes: Essays in Honour of A L Morton* Lawrence and Wishart 1978 pp 7–20.

**6733** Julia Namier *Lewis Namier: A Biography* Oxford University Press 1971. A useful biography of the historian of the eighteenth century by Namier's second wife. Namier's work is appreciated in John Cannon 'Lewis Bernstein Namier' in John Cannon (ed) *The Historian at Work* Allen and Unwin pp 136–53. For Namier's links with the Zionist movement see [1454].

**6734** Sir Charles Petrie *A Historian Looks at the World* Sidgwick and Jackson 1972. Autobiographical reminiscences of an eminent historian.

**6735** Irene Roth *Cecil Roth: Historian Without Tears* Sepher-Hennon 1983. A biography of an Anglo-Jewish historian.

**6736** For R H Tawney see [771 and 932].

**6737** Chris Wrigley *A J P Taylor: A Complete Annotated Bibliography and Guide to his Historical and other Writings* Harvester 1980. A comprehensive guide which even includes references to his broadcasts and his letters to newspapers. There is some autobiographical material in A J P Taylor *An Old Man's Diary* Hamilton 1984. See also Eva Haraszti *Taylor A Life with Alan: The Diary of A J P Taylor's Wife Eva from 1978 to 1985* Hamilton 1987. There is a mixture of autobiographical material and assessments of Taylor's work as a historian in A J P Taylor *et al Journal of Modern History* 49 1977 pp 1–72. Michael Foot 'Alan Taylor' in Chris Wrigley (ed) *Warfare, Diplomacy and Politics: Essays in Honour of A J P Taylor* Hamilton 1986 pp 189–209 is an appreciation of his work and politics.

**6738** Bryan D Palmer *The Making of E P Thompson* New Hogtown Press, Toronto 1981. A study of the life and work of the Marxist historian and CND activist.

**6739** S Fiona Morton *A Bibliography of Arnold J Toynbee* Oxford University Press 1980. A comprehensive bibliography arranged by year of publication. It also lists the reviews of his work. The only substantial biography is William H McNeill *Arnold J Toynbee: A Life* Oxford University Press 1989. This is a scholarly if uninspiring life which nevertheless goes some way to reassessing Toynbee's reputation. Christian B Peper *An Historian's Conscience* Oxford University Press 1987 collects the correspondence between Toynbee and Columba Cary-Eleves, a monk of Ampleforth.

**6740** Mary Moorman *George Macaulay Trevelyan: A Memoir* Hamilton 1980. See also George Macaulay Trevelyan *An Autobiography and other Essays* Longmans 1949. Trevelyan's work and reputation is assessed in Joseph M Hernon Jr 'The Last Whig Historian and Consensus History: George Macaulay Trevelyan 1876–1962' *American Historical Review* 81 1976 pp 66–97.

**6741** Sir John Wheeler-Bennett *Friends, Enemies and Sovereigns* Macmillan 1976. The third volume of memoirs by the historian covering the period 1945–72, commenting in particular on his work as editor-in-chief of the captured German archives, on the Nuremberg trials and as official biographer of George VI.

### (5) Archaeology and Palaeontology

**6742** Kenneth A Hudson *A Social History of Archaeology: The British Experience* Macmillan 1981. A general history.

**6743** Ronald Miller *The Piltdown Man* Gollancz 1972. A popular history of one of the greatest of all scientific hoaxes, the 'discovery' of Piltdown man in 1912 and its exposure as a hoax in 1953.

**6744** Sally Green *Prehistorian: A Biography of V Gordon Childe* Moonraker 1981. See also Bruce G Trigger *Gordon Childe: Revolutions in Archaeology* Columbia University Press, New York 1980.

**6745** Osbert Guy Stanhope Crawford *Said and Done: The Autobiography of an Archaeologist* Weidenfeld and Nicolson 1955.

**6746** Glyn Daniel *Some Small Harvest* Thames and Hudson 1986. The autobiography of a Cambridge archaeologist.

**6747** Sonia Cole *Leakey's Luck: The Life of Louis Seymour Bazett Leakey 1903–1972* Collins 1975. A biography of the palaeontologist who spent most of his life working in the Rift Valley of East Africa. Another biography is Mulvey Mina White *Digging Up Adam: The Story of L S B Leakey* McKay, New York 1965. See also his autobiography, Louis S B Leakey *By the Evidence: Memoirs 1932–1951* Harcourt, Brace, Jovanovitch, New York 1974. Mary D Leakey *Disclosing the Past* Doubleday 1984 is the autobiography of his wife. The autobiography of his son, who has carried on his work, is told in Richard Leakey *One Life: An Autobiography* Michael Joseph 1978.

**6748** Jacquetta Hawkes *Adventurer in Archaeology: The Biography of Sir Mortimer Wheeler* Weidenfeld and Nicolson 1982. A life of an important archaeologist and a great and successful popularizer of his subject. See also Norman McCord 'Mortimer Wheeler' in John Cannon (ed) *The Historian at Work* Allen and Unwin 1980 pp 154–70.

## (6) Sociology

**6749** Martin Bulmer (ed) *Essays on the History of British Sociological Research* Cambridge University Press 1985. A good collection of essays considering the development of the subject and its uses as well as particular aspects such as the government social surveys, studies of poverty, methodology or the work of Mass Observation. See also his 'Theory and Method in Recent British Sociology: Whither the Empirical Impulse?' *British Journal of Sociology* 40 1989 pp 393–417. Raymond A Kent *A History of British Empirical Sociology* Gower 1981 usefully traces changing fashions in empirical research over the period since the 1830s. Recent trends in empirical and theoretical sociology are examined in J Eldridge *Recent British Sociology* Macmillan 1981. In the 1970s social science came under increasing criticism. Patricia Thomas *The Aims and Outcomes of Social Policy* Croom Helm 1985 is an investigation into its nature which attempts to justify sociological research with reference to work carried out between the 1960s and 1980s. The post-war development of the sociological profession is examined in A H Halsey 'Provincials and Professionals: The British Post-War Sociologists' *LSE Quarterly* 1 1987 pp 43–74. On the nature and methodology of British social research see Colin Ball and S Encck (eds) *Inside the Whale: Ten Personal Accounts of Social Research* Pergamon 1978.

**6750** Ramesh Mishra 'The Academic Tradition in Social Policy: The Titmuss Years' in Martin Bulmer, Jane Lewis and David Piachaud (eds) *The Goals of Social Policy* Unwin Hyman 1989 pp 64–83. A study of the growth of social administration as an academic discipline in the post-war years. The Social Administration department at the London School of Economics, of which Richard Titmuss was at one time professor, is examined in David Donnison 'Taking Decisions in a University' in David Donnison and Valerie Chapman (eds) *Social Policy and Administration Revisited* Allen and Unwin 1975 pp 253–85.

**6751** Penny Summerfield 'Mass Observation: Social Research on Social Movement' *Journal of Contemporary History* 20 1985 pp 439–52. Mass Observation was a unique organization which sought to use anthropological techniques to study British social life and conditions. Its work covered the period 1937–48. Much of its material remains underused in the archive at Sussex University.

**6752** Paul Rock (ed) *A History of British Criminology* Clarendon 1988. A history and study of the contemporary state of criminology, from the British Journal of Criminology 28 1988. It includes extensive bibliographies.

**6753** Lord Butler 'The Foundation of the Institute of Criminology in Cambridge' in Roger Hood (ed) *Crime, Criminology and Public Policy: Essays in Honour of Sir Leon Radzinowicz* Heinemann 1974 pp 1–10. The institute was established in 1959.

**6754** H Parker and H Giller 'More or less the same: British Delinquency Research Since the Sixties' *British Journal of Criminology* 21 1981 pp 230–45. A study of changing perspectives, not least because of the growing impact of New Right thinking and the fragmented response to it.

**6755** Robert Bocock 'British Sociologists and Freud: A Sociological Analysis of the Absence of a Relationship' *British Journal of Sociology* 32 1981 pp 346–61. A sociological study of absence of Freudian analysis in British sociology.

**6756** Sandra Acker 'No Woman's Land: British Sociology of Education 1960–1979' *Sociological Review* 29 1981 pp 77–104. A consideration of the development of the sociology of education from a feminist perspective.

**6757** A H Halsey 'T H Marshall: Past and Present 1893–1981: President of the British Sociological Association 1964–1969' *Sociology* 18 1984 pp 1–18. A biographical tribute.

**6758** For Richard Morris Titmuss see [5295, 5315–6, 5319].

**6759** J P Ward *Raymond Williams* University of Wales Press 1981. A short study of Williams' life and thought. Raymond Williams *Politics and Letters: Interviews with New Left Review* New Left Books 1979 includes a chronology of Williams' life and work and interviews about his life, work and views on culture and politics. E P Thompson *et al* 'Remembering Raymond Williams' *Cambridge Review* 109 1988 pp 51–61 is a collection of tributes to the sociologist and cultural historian who was a major intellectual figure on the Left until his death in 1988. His work is assessed in Alan O'Connor *Raymond Williams: Writing, Culture, Politics* Blackwell 1989. See also K Davey 'The Development of the Work of Raymond Williams 1939–1961' Kent MA Thesis 1985.

**6760** Barbara Wootton *In a World I Never Made: Autobiographical Reflections* Allen and Unwin 1967. Useful memoirs by a socialist intellectual particularly concerned with social policy. Terence Morris 'In Memoriam: Barbara Wootton 1897–1988' *British Journal of Sociology* 40 1989 pp 310–8 is a tribute to the influential sociologist and criminologist.

## (7) Anthropology

**6761** Adam Kuper *Anthropology and Anthropologists: The Modern British School* 2nd ed, Routledge and Kegan Paul 1983. A critical history of British social anthropology in the twentieth century.

**6762** E E Evans-Pritchard *A Bibliography of the Writings of E E Evans-Pritchard* Tavistock 1974. Evans-Pritchard was the Professor of Social Anthropology at Oxford 1946–70. Mary Douglas *Edward Evans-Pritchard* Fontana 1980 is a useful biography.

## (8) Human Geography

**6763** Ronald John Johnston *Geography and Geographers: Anglo-American Human Geography Since 1945* 3rd ed, Arnold 1987. See also T W Freeman *A History of Modern British Geography* Longman 1980, which is a history since the 1880s. It includes biographical sketches of the eminent geographers of the period. See also G R Crone 'British Geography in the Twentieth Century' *Geography Journal* 130 1964 pp 197–220.

**6764** Robert W Steel *The Institute of British Geographers: The First Fifty Years* Institute of British Geographers 1984.

**6765** *The First Ten Years 1966 to 1976: Including the Annual Report 1975–1976* Centre for Urban and Regional Studies, University of Birmingham 1977. This reviews the history of the centre and its research. It also gives a full list of the centre's publications.

**6766** A D M Phillips and B J Turton 'S H Beaver: An Introduction', followed by an appreciation by M J Wise in A D M Phillips and B J Turton (eds) *Environment, Man and Economic Change: Essays Presented to S H Beaver* Longman 1975 pp 1–28. A tribute to the distinguished human geographer.

## (9) Political Studies

**6767** Leonard Tivey *Interpretations of British Politics: The Image and the System* Harvester 1988. A textbook discussing the range of interpretations of the British political system since 1945.

**6768** Joni Lovenduski *The Profession of Political Science in Britain* Centre for the Study of Public Policy 84, University of Strathclyde 1981. A study of the growth of the political science profession in the post-war years. The growth of political science is also examined in D Norman Chester 'Political Studies in Britain: Recollections and Comments' *Political Studies* 23 1975 pp

29–42 and W A Robson 'The Study of Public Administration Then and Now' *Political Studies* 23 1975 pp 61–70. See also W Harrison 'The Early Years of Political Studies' *Political Studies* 23 1975 pp 43–60. On the development of political science at Oxford see D Norman Chester *Economics, Politics and Social Studies at Oxford 1900–85* Macmillan 1986. This detailed account particularly looks at the growth of the Faculty of Social Studies, which was founded in 1903 and is now the largest in the university, and at the development of Nuffield College.

**6769** Austin Ranney 'Review Article: Thirty Years of Psephology' *British Journal of Political Science* 6 1976 pp 217–30. A review of the work of the Nuffield series of general election studies and of the development of the discipline of psephology.

**6770** John Pinder (ed) *Fifty Years of Political and Economic Planning (PEP): Looking Forward 1931–1981* Gower 1981. PEP was born in the wave of enthusiasm for planning as a way of avoiding the economic and social affects of the Slump which engulfed the country in the early 1930s. In 1978 it merged with the Centre for Studies in Social Policy and became the Policy Studies Institute. See also 'PEP 1931–56' *Planning* 22 1956 pp 142–55.

**6771** Raymond Nottage and Freida Stack 'The Royal Institute of Public Administration 1922–72' *Public Administration* 50 1972 pp 281–302, 419–46.

**6772** For Harold Laski and John Pitcairn Mackintosh see [729, 735].

## (10) Classics

**6773** Hugh Lloyd-Jones (ed) *Maurice Bowra: A Celebration* Duckworth 1974. Bowra was a classicist, an Oxford Professor of Poetry and an acclaimed university administrator as Warden of Wadham College 1938–70 and Vice-Chancellor of Oxford University 1951–4. This is a collection of tributes.

**6774** Duncan Wilson *Gilbert Murray OM 1855–1957* Clarendon 1987. A biography of the Oxford classicist with important connections with the Liberal Party. See also Francis West *Gilbert Murray: A Life* Croom Helm 1984 and Jean Smith and Arnold J Toynbee (eds) *Gilbert Murray: An Unfinished Autobiography* Allen and Unwin 1960.

## (11) Linguistic, Oriental and African Studies

**6775** R E F Smith *A Novelty: Russian at Birmingham University 1917–67* University of Birmingham 1987. It was not until the 1960s that Russian began to be a generally more popular subject.

**6776** *Oriental Studies in Britain* Central Office of Information 1975. A study of the development of oriental studies as an academic discipline and of its contemporary state. The resources, societies, libraries and publications involved in this field are also detailed.

**6777** *The Royal Asiatic Society: Its History and Treasures* Brill 1979.

**6778** Peter Carey *Maritime Southeast Asian Studies in the United Kingsdom: A Survey of their Post-War Development and Current Resources* JASO 1986. A study of an important field of research. It is also an important subject given the large numbers of overseas students in Britain who come from that part of the world. It has however suffered from declining funding in the 1980s. See also David K Bassett 'Southeast Asian Studies in the United Kingdom' in Tunku Shamsul Bahrin, Chandran Jeshurun and A Terry Rambo (eds) *A Colloquium on Southeast Asian Studies* Institute of Southeast Asian Studies, Singapore 1981 pp 58–71.

**6779** Mona Macmillan *Champion of Africa: The Second Phase of the Work of W H Macmillan (1934–1974)* the author 1985. Macmillan was an influential writer on African affairs and the Director of Colonial Studies at St Andrews University.

### C. SCIENCE

Material of relevance to this section can also be found in the section on Science Policy (under Economic History).

### (1) General

**6780** *Scientific and Learned Societies of Great Britain: A Handbook Compiled from Official Sources* 5th ed, Allen and Unwin 1964. A classified arrangement with brief details on the various societies listed.

**6781** *History of Science: An Annual Review of Literature, Research and Teaching* Cambridge University Press 1962–. The subtitle of this annual review was changed slightly in 1973.

**6782** *Year Book of the Royal Society of London* Royal Society of London 1897–. The annual publication of the premier scientific society. *Notes and Records of the Royal Society of London* 1938– regularly carries a bibliography on the history of the Society and on the lives and work of its fellows.

**6783** Margaret Gowing 'The Contemporary Scientific Archives Centre' *Notes and Records of the Royal Society of London* 34 1979 pp 123–31. A guide to the setting up of the centre in Oxford in 1973 and to its holdings. See also L R Day 'Resources for the History of Science in the Science Museum Library' *British Journal of the History of Science* 18 1985 pp 71–6, a guide to resources in the Science Museum in London.

**6784** Magda Whitrow (ed) *ISIS Cumulative Bibliography 1913–1965* 5v, Mansell 1971–82. An unannotated bibliography of the history of science. It is well indexed and classified and is continued by John Neu (ed) *ISIS Cumulative Bibliography 1966–1975* 2v, Mansell 1980–85. These are based on the works listed in the annual publication which has appeared since 1913. This is international in scope but contains much material on modern British science and is easy to use.

**6785** Roy M MacLeod and James R Friday (eds) *Archives of British Men of Science* Mansell 1972. A microfilm guide to the papers of British scientists who flourished between 1800 and 1950, including a few who were active after the latter date.

**6786** *Biographical Memoirs of Fellows of the Royal Society* the Royal Society of London 1955–. An annual publication which provides full biographies of important scientists who have recently died. There is also a fulsome bibliography for each subject. More biographical material is provided in *Who's Who of British Scientists* 3rd ed, Simon Books 1980. An earlier biographical guide is J G Crowther *British Scientists of the 20th Century* Routledge 1952.

**6787** Greta Jones *Science, Politics and the Cold War* Routledge 1988. A study of the role of science in social and defence policy and in politics since the 1930s. It concentrates on British politics and scientists and on the extent to which scientists seem to offer solutions to contemporary problems. The key themes pursued are eugenics, technology policy and nuclear weapons. Dissatisfaction with and declining public confidence in the Mephistophelian scientist is examined in D W Ashcroft 'A Study of the Contemporary "Anti-Science" Movement: Reality of Illusion?' Manchester MEd Thesis 1974–6.

**6788** Roy MacLeod and Peter Collins (eds) *The Parliament of Science: The British Association for the Advancement of Science 1831–1981* Science Reviews 1981. The last chapter covers the Association since 1945.

**6789** Gwendy Caroe *The Royal Institution: An Informal History* Murray 1985. The Royal Institution was established in 1799 as a scientific institute with a particular emphasis on education. This history is quite useful on its post-war history.

**6790** P Gary Werskey *The Visible College* Allen Lane 1978. A collective biography of five Left-Wing scientists, J D Bernal, J B S Haldane, Lancelot Hogben, Hyman Levy and Joseph Needham (on whom see also [6720]). It concentrates on Bernal and on the influence of this group on science and technology policy and on the 1964–70 Labour government. Martin Green 'The Visible College in British Science' *American Scholar* 47 1977 pp 105–77 discusses C P Snow, J B S Haldane, J D Bernal and P M S Blackett.

**6791** Tom Bower *The Paperclip Conspiracy: The Hunt for the Nazi Scientists* Little, Brown, Boston, Massachusetts 1987. A study of Allied efforts to acquire German scientists after 1945. See also Clarence Lasby *Project Paperclip* Athenaeum 1971.

## (2) Physics

**6792** Jerry Gaston *Originality and Competition in Science: A Study of the British High Energy Community* Chicago University Press 1973. A study of the contemporary work and organization of high energy physics research in Britain.

**6793** Rudolph E Peierls 'Britain in the Atomic Age' *Bulletin of the Atomic Scientists* 26 1970 pp 40–6. Peierls had been the head of the British mission to Los Alamos in Nevada where the first atomic weapons were tested. This is a general review of developments in British atomic physics since.

**6794** James G Crowther *The Cavendish Laboratory 1874–1974* Macmillan 1974. A history of the celebrated laboratories at Cambridge University.

**6795** Henry Lipson 'The Last Fifty Years of Physics at Manchester' *Manchester Memoirs* 1 1980–81 pp 87–99. This looks especially at physics at Manchester University in 1927–53 under W L Bragg and P M S Blackett.

**6796** S T Keith and Paul K Hoch 'Formation of a Research School: Theoretical Solid State Physics at Bristol 1930–1954' *British Journal of the History of Science* 19 1986 pp 19–44.

**6797** Eric Edward Smith *Radiation Science at the National Physical Laboratory 1912–1955* National Physical Laboratory 1975.

**6798** John Hendry 'The Scientific Origins of Controlled Fusion Technology' *Annals of Science* 44 1987 pp 143–68. An examination of the emergence of the appreciation of fusion as an energy source since the 1930s, with the first detailed proposals being put forward by G P Thomson and P C Thonemann working in Britain in the late 1940s.

**6799** Ronald Clark *Sir Edward Appleton* Pergamon 1971. Appleton was the Secretary of the Department of Scientific and Industrial Research 1939–49. In 1947 he won the Nobel Prize for Physics.

**6800** Maurice Goldsmith *Sage: A Life of J D Bernal* Hutchinson 1980. A biography of an important scientist who, through his links with the Labour Party, had considerable influence on the science policy of the 1964–70 Labour government. He was Professor of Physics 1937–63 and Professor of Crystallography 1963–68 at Birkbeck College, London.

**6801** Sir Bernard Lovell *P M S Blackett: A Biographical Memoir* The Royal Society of London 1976. A memoir of the Left-Wing atomic physicist who was a life peer and the President of the Royal Society in the late 1960s.

**6802** Max Born *My Life: Recollections of a Nobel Laureate* Scribner, New York 1978. The autobiography of a leading physicist who won the Nobel Prize in 1954.

**6803** Sir Lawrence Bragg 'Reminiscences of Fifty Years Research' *Proceedings of the Royal Institution of Great Britain* 41 1966 pp 92–100. Reminiscences of his work in the field of crystallography.

**6804** For Lord Cherwell, physicist, astrophysicist and chemist, see [802].

**6805** For Sir John Cockcroft see [2227].

**6806** Behram N Kursunoghu and Eugene P Wigner (eds) *Reminiscences about a Great Physicist: Paul Adrien Maurice Dirac* Cambridge University Press 1987. A collection of tributes and scientific papers.

**6807** Otto R Frisch *What Little I Remember* Cambridge University Press 1979. The autobiography of a Cambridge nuclear physicist.

**6808** John Boslough *Stephen Hawking's Universe* Morrow 1984. A study of the life and thought of the Cambridge mathematician and astrophysicist.

**6809** Leonard S Kenworthy 'Kathleen Lonsdale: Eminent Scientist and Concerned Quaker' in Leonard S Kenworthy (ed) *Living in the Light: Some Quaker Pioneers of the Twentieth Century Vol 2: In the Wider World*

Friends General Conference and Quaker Publications, Kennett Square, Pennsylvania 1985 pp 129–44. Lonsdale was an x-ray crystallographer.

**6810** Sir Nevill Mott *A Life in Science* Taylor and Francis 1986. The autobiography of a Cambridge physicist. Mott was Cavendish Professor of Physics at the University 1954–71. He was awarded a Nobel Prize in 1977.

**6811** Sir Rudolph Peierls *Bird of Passage: Recollections of a Physicist* Princeton University Press, Princeton, New Jersey 1985. Peierls was a leading nuclear physicist who led the British mission to Los Alamos during the Second World War.

**6812** Nancy Arms *A Prophet in Two Countries* Pergamon 1966. A life of Sir Francis Simon who was an important figure in the Oxford scientific community and a leading figure in the fields of low temperature physics and atomic energy.

### (3) Engineering

**6813** *Who's Who of British Engineers* 5th ed, Simon Books 1980. A biographical guide

**6814** Henry George Taylor *An Experiment in Co-operative Research: An Account of the First Fifty Years of the Electrical Research Association* Hutchinson 1970.

**6815** T J N Hilken *Engineering at Cambridge University 1783–1965* Cambridge University Press 1967.

**6816** E R Laithwaite *A History of Linear Electric Motors* Macmillan 1987. This traces developments since the late nineteenth century, giving due weight to his own work in this field. Through international comparisons he shows how Britain has in this field failed to reap rewards for conducting the initial research. There is an extensive bibliography.

### (4) Astronomy

**6817** Peter Haining *Eyewitness to the Galaxy: Britain's Contribution to Research in Space* W H Allen 1985. A general account.

**6818** R J Tayler (ed) *History of the Royal Astronomical Society Vol 2: 1920–1980* Blackwell Scientific 1987. The history of the Royal Observatory 1836–1975 is covered in A J Meadows *The Royal Observatory at Greenwich and Herstmonceux 1675–1975 Vol 2: Recent History* Taylor and Francis 1975.

**6819** Bernard Lovell 'The Early History of the Anglo-Australian 150 Inch Telescope (AAT)' *Quarterly Journal of the Royal Astronomical Society* 26 1985 pp 393–455.

**6820** R E Jennings 'History of British Infrared Astronomy Since the Second World War' *Quarterly Journal of the Royal Astronomical Society* 27 1986 pp 454–61.

**6821** David Owen Edge and Michael J Mulkay *Astronomy Transformed: The Emergence of Radio Astronomy in Britain* Wiley 1976. A good account. Radio astronomy was established after the Second World War by Bernard Lovell, who reflects on this initial period in his 'The Emergence of Radio Astronomy in the UK after World War II' *Quarterly Journal of the Royal Astronomical Society* 28 1987 pp 1–9. On the radio telescopes Lovell went on to establish at Jodrell Bank see Bernard Lovell *The Story of Jodrell Bank* Oxford University Press 1968 and Bernard Lovell *The Jodrell Bank Telescopes* Oxford University Press 1985.

**6822** Fred Hoyle *The Small World of Fred Hoyle: An Autobiography* Michael Joseph 1986. Hoyle was Professor of Astronomy and Experimental Philosophy at Cambridge 1958–72.

**6823** Zdenek Korpal *Of Stars and Men* Adam Hilger 1986. The autobiography of an astronomer at Manchester University.

**6824** Dudley Saward *Bernard Lovell: A Biography* Hale 1984. The authorized biography of the father of British radio astronomy. In part it is also a criticism of the failure of successive post-war governments to fully support Lovell or to capitalize on the technological lead in the field that he gave. Bernard Lovell *Out of the Zenith* Harper and Row 1973 contains some autobiographical reminiscences.

### (5) Earth Sciences

**6825** G S Sweeting (ed) *The Geologists' Association 1858–1958* Benham 1958.

**6826** Harold E Wilson *Down To Earth: One Hundred and Fifty Years of the British Geological Survey* Scottish Academic Press 1985. An illustrated history with a bibliography.

**6827** Henry Frankel 'Arthur Holmes and Continental Drift' *British Journal of the History of Science* 11 1978 pp 130–50. An examination of Holmes' work on continental drift and the movement of tectonic plates.

## (6) Exploration

**6828** P G Mott *Wings Over Ice: An Account of the Falklands Islands and Dependencies Aerial Survey Expedition 1955–57* the author 1986.

**6829** Ingrid Cranfield *The Challengers: British and Commonwealth Adventure Since 1945* Weidenfeld and Nicolson 1976. This gives accounts of scientific expeditions, exploration of polar regions and of mountaineering and sailing feats of the post-war period.

**6830** Ranulph Fiennes *Living Dangerously: An Autobiography* Macmillan 1987. An autobiography which covers both his military career and his later career as an explorer of the arctic regions.

## (7) Botany

**6831** David Ellaston Allen *The Botanists: A History of the Botanical Society of the British Isles through a Hundred and Fifty Years* St Pauls Bibliographies 1986.

**6832** A T Gage and W T Stearn *A Bicentenary History of the Linnean Society of London* Academic Press 1988. An institutional history of this distinguished botanical society. It is an update of Gage's history published in 1938 with additional chapters.

**6833** Phillada Ballard *An Oasis of Delight: The History of Birmingham Botanical Gardens* Duckworth 1983.

**6834** S M Walters *The Shaping of Cambridge Botany: A Short History of Whole-Plant Botany in Cambridge from the Time of Ray to the Present Century: Published on the Occasion of the Sesquincentenary of Henslow's New Botanic Gardens 1831–1981* Cambridge University Press 1981.

**6835** Ronald King *Royal Kew* Constable 1985. A history of the Royal Botanical Gardens at Kew, South London. The history of the Commonwealth Mycotological Institute at Kew is told in Geoffrey C Ainsworth 'CMI 1920–1980' *Review of Plant Pathology* 59 1980 pp 249–55. F Nigel Hepper (ed) *Plant Hunting for Kew* HMSO 1989 is a collection of accounts of twenty recent expeditions.

## (8) Biology

**6836** G Vevers *London's Zoo: An Anthology to Celebrate 150 Years of the Zoological Society of London with its Zoos at Regents Park and Whipsnade in Bed-*

*fordshire* The Bodley Head 1976. More a history of the zoos than of zoology.

**6837** Greta Jones 'British Scientists, Lysenko and the Cold War' *Economy and Society* 8 1979 pp 26–58. A study of the response of British scientists to the heterodox and ultimately discredited biological theories of the Soviet scientist Lysenko within the contemporary political context. See also Diane B Paul 'A War on Two Fronts: J B S Haldane and the Response to Lysenkoism in Britain' *Journal of the History of Biology* 16 1986 pp 1–37.

**6838** A J Southward and E K Roberts 'The Marine Biological Association 1884–1984: One Hundred Years of Marine Research' *Report and Transactions: Devonshire Association for the Advancement of Science, Literature and Art* 116 1984 pp 155–99.

**6839** Ronald Clark *JBS: The Life and Work of J B S Haldane* Hodder and Stoughton 1968. A study of the Marxist geneticist. Haldane's work is also assessed in Krishna R Dronamraju (ed) *Haldane and Modern Biology* Johns Hopkins University Press, Baltimore, Maryland 1968. More political aspects of Haldane's life and work are also assessed in Krishna R Dronamraju *Haldane: The Life and Work of J B S Haldane with Special Reference to India* Aberdeen University Press 1985. See also the memoir by Haldane's sister, Naomi Mitchison 'The Haldanes: Personal Notes and Historical Lessons' *Proceedings of the Royal Institution of Great Britain* 47 1974 pp 1–21.

**6840** J R Baker *Julian Huxley: Scientist and World Citizen: A Biographical Memoir* UNESCO, Paris 1978. This examines not only Huxley's scientific work but also his political thinking and work. It includes a bibliography of Huxley's writings. See also Huxley's autobiography, *Memories* 2v Allen and Unwin 1970–72.

**6841** Peter Medawar *Memoir of a Thinking Radish: An Autobiography* Oxford University Press 1986. Medawar is a zoologist and immunologist.

## (9) Chemistry

**6842** R C Chirnside and J H Hamence *The Practising Chemists: A History of the Society for Analytical Chemistry 1874–1974* Society for Analytical Chemistry 1974.

**6843** Maurice Stacey and David J Manners 'Edmund Langley Hirst 1890–1975' *Advances in Carbohydrate Chemistry* 35 1978 pp 1–29. An obituary notice.

**6844** G B Kaufmann (ed) *Frederick Soddy (1877–1956): Early Pioneer in Radio Chemistry* Reidal 1986.

Soddy was an important figure in radio- and electro-chemistry.

## (10) Biochemistry

**6845** Trevor W Goodwin (ed) *British Biochemistry Past and Present* Academic Press 1970. Goodwin has also written the *History of the Biochemistry Society 1911–1986* Biochemical Society 1987. See also R A Morton 'Biochemistry at Liverpool 1902–1971' *Medical History* 16 1972 pp 321–53.

**6846** James D Watson *The Double Helix: A Personal Account of the Discovery of the Structure of DNA: A New Critical Edition including text, commentary, reviews, original papers (edited by Gunther S Stent)* Weidenfeld and Nicolson 1981. Watson was the American who, together with the British scientists Francis Crick and Maurice Wilkins did the work on unravelling the secret of DNA, the results of which were announced in a short article in *Nature* in 1953. See also Mahlon Hoagland *Discovery: The Search for DNA's Secrets* Houghton Mifflin, Boston, Massachusetts 1981, Robert Olby *The Path to the Double Helix* Macmillan 1974 and James D Watson and John Tooze *The DNA Story: A Documentary History of Gene Cloning* Freeman, San Francisco 1981.

**6847** Joseph D Robinson 'Appreciating Key Experiments' *British Journal of the History of Science* 19 1986 pp 51–6. A history of Peter Mitchell's chemiosmotic theory of bioenergetics (which drastically revised understanding of how cells produce and store energy) which was confirmed in 1966.

## D. MEDICINE

Material on the medical profession can also be found in the section on the Health Services. There is some literature on medical education in the section on Universities under the Education History section.

## (1) General

**6848** *Bibliography of the History of Medicine* US Department of Health, Education and Welfare, Bethesda, Maryland 1940–. An annual publication with regular cumulations. It supplies massive, if unannotated, coverage of the current literature. It is also easier to use, in some ways, than the similarly international serial bibliography, *Current Work in the History of Medicine* Wellcome Institute for the History of Medicine 1954– (quarterly), not least because it is divided into national sections.

**6849** David Armstrong *Political Anatomy of the Body: Medical Knowledge in Britain in the Twentieth Century* Cambridge University Press 1983.

## (2) The Royal Colleges

**6850** John Fry, Lord Hunt of Fawley and R J F H Pinsent (eds) *A History of the Royal College of General Practitioners: The First 25 Years* MTP Press 1983. A good series of essays on the establishment in 1952, organization and activities of the College.

**6851** Royal College of Physicians, 11 St Andrews Place, London NW1. The College holds a small but significant collection of tapes and films. This includes material on leading physicians and on such matters as the conquest of tuberculosis. The official history of the College unfortunately does not really cover the post-war period. Alexander M Cooke *A History of the Royal College of Physicians of London: Vol 3* Clarendon 1972 covers from the 1858 Medical Act to the setting up of the National Health Service in 1948 and has yet to be updated.

**6852** Sir William F Shaw *Twenty-Five Years: The Story of the Royal College of Obstetricians and Gynaecologists 1929–54* Churchill 1954.

**6853** M Davidson *The Royal Society of Medicine: The Realization of an Ideal (1805–1955)* Royal Society of Medicine 1955. A story of its origins and development, especially since the various amalgamations of 1905.

**6854** Enid Hutchinson *A History of the British Dietetic Association* Newman Books 1961.

## (3) Biography

**6855** William Munk *Lives of the Fellows of the Royal College of Physicians of London Vol 5: Continued to 1965* Royal College of Physicians 1968. A good collection of full biographies of members deceased before 1965. There is a similar series of biographies of members of the Royal College of Surgeons. The relevant volumes are Sir D'arcy Power and W R Le Fanu *The Lives of the Fellows of the Royal Collge of Surgeons of England Vol 3: 1930–51* Royal College of Surgeons 1953, R H O B Robinson and W R Le Fanu *Vol 4: 1952–64* Livingstone 1970 and Sir James Paterson Ross and W R Le Fanu *Vol 5: 1965–1973* Pitman Medical 1981. Biographies of the members of the Royal College of Obstetricians and Gynaeocologists since its establishment in 1929 can be found in Sir John Peel (ed) *The Lives of the Fellows of the Royal College of Obstetricians and Gynaeocologists 1929–1969* Heinemann Medical 1976.

**6856** Willis J Elwood and A Fèlicitè Tuxford (eds) *Some Manchester Doctors: A Biographical Collection to Mark the 150th Anniversary of the Manchester Medical Society* Manchester University Press 1984. An account of the history of the society with biographies of selected Manchester doctors up to the 1980s.

**6857** Hugh McLeave *A Time to Heal: The Life of Ian Aird, the Surgeon* Heinemann 1964. Aird was the Professor of Surgery at the Postgraduate Medical School at Hammersmith Hospital, London.

**6858** S V Humphries *The Life of Hamilton Bailey: Surgeon, Author and Teacher of Surgery* Ravenswood 1973.

**6859** Geoffrey Howard Bourne *We Met at Bart's: The Autobiography of a Physician* Muller 1963. Bourne was a dietician and physician.

**6860** Ronald Clark *The Life of Ernst Chain: Penicillin and Beyond* Weidenfeld and Nicolson 1985. Chain was one of the team that worked on the development of penicillin before the war. He was awarded the Nobel Prize in 1945 for this work. In 1961–73 he was Professor of Biochemistry at Imperial College, London.

**6861** W C Noble *Coli – Great Healer of Men: The Biography of Dr Leonard Colebrook* Heinemann Medical 1974. Colebrook was the director of the Burns Investigation Unit at Birmingham 1944–8 and a member of the scientific staff of the Medical Research Council until 1948.

**6862** Alfred Noyes Thomas *Doctor Courageous: The Story of Dr Grantley Dick-Read* Heinemann 1957. Dick-Read was an obstetrician and an advocate of natural childbirth.

**6863** For Herbert Ellis's autobiography, which includes reflections on the development of aviation medicine see [2282].

**6864** Gwyn Macfarlane *Howard Florey: The Making of a Great Scientist* Oxford University Press 1979. Florey also played an important part in the discovery of penicillin. He was Professor of Pathology at Oxford 1935–62. See also Trevor I Williams *Howard Florey: Penicillin and After* Oxford University Press 1984 and Lennard Bickel *Rise up to Life: A Biography of Howard Walter Florey who gave Penicillin to the World* Angus and Robertson 1972.

**6865** Reginald Pound *Gillies: Surgeon Extraordinary: A Biography* Michael Joseph 1964. A life of Sir Harold Delf Gillies, the New Zealand born pioneer of plastic surgery in Britain.

**6866** T M Horder *The Little Genius: A Memoir of the First Lord Horder* Duckworth 1966. Horder was a famous physician who died in 1955. This is a memoir by his successor.

**6867** William Sargant *The Unquiet Mind: The Autobiography of a Physician in Psychological Medicine* Heinemann 1967. This reflects on progress since the 1930s in medical and surgical treatments of mental illness.

**6868** W Melville Capper and Douglas Johnson (eds) *The Faith of a Surgeon: Belief and Experience in the Life of Arthur Rendle Short* Paternoster 1976. A biography of the surgeon and leading member of the Plymouth Brethren.

## (4) Medical Research

**6869** J Jaramillo-Arango *The British Contribution to Medicine* Livingstone 1953. This concentrates on recent developments. It contains detailed studies of work on typhoid and paratyphoid fevers, infection and the development of penicillin, anti-biotics, malaria, vitamins and the conquest of nutritional diseases and research on cancer.

**6870** *Medical Research Council Annual Report* HMSO 1920–. An annual report of research in progress which has appeared as a Command Paper since 1926. See also A Landsborough Thomson *Half a Century of Medical Research* 2v, HMSO 1973–75. Volume one looks at the origins, development and policy of the Medical Research Council. Volume two examines its activities and programme.

**6871** A R Hall and B A Bambridge *Physic and Philanthropy: A History of the Wellcome Trust 1936–1986* Cambridge University Press 1986. An account of its origins, evolution and work and an appraisal of its impact on medical science in Britain.

**6872** *Report of the Committee of Inquiry into Human Fertilization and Embryology* Cmnd 9314, *Parliamentary Papers* 1983–84. An examination of ways of regulating embryo research and the fertility services in the light of the development of in vitro fertilization which was chaired by Dame Mary Warnock. It also touched on artificial insemination by donor and recommended that surrogate motherhood be outlawed. Henry Leese *Human Reproduction and IVF* Macmillan 1988 is a textbook history of in vitro fertilization and the debate over medical ethics aroused by embryo research, giving due weight to the conclusions of the Warnock committee. The regulation of genetic research in the light of the Warnock Report is analysed in David Bennett, Peter Glasner and

David Travis *The Politics of Uncertainty: Regulating Recombinant DNA Research in Britain* Routledge and Kegan Paul 1986. The development of in vitro fertilization, embryo transfer and artificial insemination by donor is also discussed in Josephine Barnes 'Artificial Motherhood' *Contemporary Review* 249 1986 pp 297–301.

### (5) Particular Branches of Medicine

**6873** Jennifer Beinart *A History of the Nuffield Department of Anaesthetics, Oxford 1937–1987* Oxford University Press 1987.

**6874** Eric G Forbes 'The Professionalisation of Dentistry: The United Kingdom' *Medical History* 29 1985 pp 169–81. A history from the 1840s to the 1983 Dentists Act.

**6875** J Purdon Martin 'British Neurology in the last 50 years: Some Personal Experiences' *Proceedings of the Royal Society of Medicine* 64 1971 pp 1055–9.

**6876** Hans S Baer 'The Drive for Professionalisation in British Osteopathy' *Social Science and Medicine* 19 1984 pp 717–25. Osteopathy was introduced to Britain at the turn of the century from America. This examines the search for recognition for a calling distrusted by the medical profession, in the course of the twentieth century.

**6877** Shulamit Ramon *Psychiatry in Britain: Meaning and Policy* Croom Helm 1985. A study of developments since the 1920s. See also D H Clark 'Administrative Psychiatry 1942–1962' *British Journal of Psychiatry* 109 1963 pp 178–201.

### E. THE ARTS

### (1) General

**6878** *Art Bibliographies* Modern Clio 1972–. This appears twice a year. It is international in scope and unannotated. The classification and indexing system however makes it easy to use and it contains much material of interest. It was preceded by *LOMA: Literature on Modern Art 1969–71*.

**6879** *Arts Council of Great Britain: Annual Report and Accounts* Arts Council of Great Britain 1946–. The Arts Council grew out of CEMA which was set up to entertain civilians during the Second World War. In addition to this annual guide to its activities all the regional arts associations publish annual reports.

**6880** *Facts About The Arts* Policy Studies Institute 1983 and 1986. A selection of statistics and analyses of the arts, museums and galleries, the performing and visual arts, crafts, literature, film and broadcasting over recent years. In 1989 it was replaced by the new quarterly *Cultural Trends*.

**6881** Boris Ford (ed) *The Cambridge Guide to the Arts in Britain Vol 9: Since the Second World War* Cambridge University Press 1988. An excellent survey with essays examining the cultural and social context as well as the developments in the various fields such as music, the visual and performing arts, architecture, industrial design, film and broadcasting. Another of its many virtues is the extensive and semi-annotated bibliography it contains. Alan Sinfield *Literature, Politics and Culture in Postwar Britain* Blackwell 1989 is a general cultural history of the period from a Marxist perspective.

**6882** J Minchan *The Nationalisation of Culture: The Development of State Subsidies to the Arts in Great Britain* Hamilton 1977. A study of the state's role in subsidizing the arts from the early nineteenth century and of the development of the Arts Council in the postwar years. H Baldray *The Case for the Arts* Secker and Warburg 1981 traces the origins of the arts funding system and the development of all its aspects. These include not only the Arts Council but also the funding provided by the regional arts associations, local government and by business. It also looks at the role of the arts in education.

**6883** Eric Walter White *The Arts Council in Great Britain* Davis-Poynter 1975. After tracing the pre-history of the Arts Council in the wartime CEMA organization to the establishment of the Arts Council in 1946 this traces its history, administration and finance and the history of its policy in fields such as drama, opera, ballet, music, visual arts and literature. It also includes personal reflections on its history and informative appendices. Robert Hutchinson *The Politics of the Arts Council* Sinclair Browne 1982 is a critical look at the history of the Arts Council and its policies, activities and relations with central government by a former employee. It argues that the secrecy and centralization of the Arts Council has been detrimental. Roy Shaw *The Arts and the People* Cape 1987 is an impassioned critique of recent government attitudes to the funding of the arts by the Secretary General of the Arts Council 1975–83. It especially examines arts policy and attitudes to arts funding under Thatcher. See also [723].

**6884** D Mitchell 'Art Patronage by the London County Council (LCC) 1948–1965' *Leonardo* 10 1977 pp 207–12. A detailed picture of the LCC patronage programme and a critical of the (then) more parsimonious provision of its successor, the Greater London Council.

**6885** Ivor Brown *The Way of My World* Collins 1954. A view of the theatre. It is however most useful for the light it casts on the origins of the Arts Council. See also [5603].

**6886** N Pearson *The State and the Visual Arts* Open University Press 1982. An examination of patterns in the relationship 1760–1980, scrutinizing the funding bodies, the providers of the visual arts and the influence of politics on visual arts policy.

**6887** D J Dougan 'Public Subsidy for the Arts in the Northern Region: the Development of a Structure for Subsidising the Arts in the Northern Region of England 1945–1975' City PhD Thesis 1982.

**6888** John Myerscough *The Economic Importance of the Arts in Britain* Policy Studies Institute 1988. The first real assessment of the economic significance of the arts. It also examines funding. This study is complemented by John Myerscough *The Economic Importance of the Arts in Merseyside* 1988, John Myerscough *The Economic Importance of the Arts in Ipswich* 1988 and John Myerscough *The Economic Importance of the Arts in Glasgow* 1988.

**6889** Robert Hewison *The Heritage Industry: Britain in a Climate of Decline* Methuen 1989. A cultural history of attitudes to the national heritage since the foundation of the National Trust. It especially concentrates on attacking the ahistorical excesses of the heritage industry which burgeoned in the 1980s.

**6890** Robert Hutchinson and Susan Forrester *Arts Centres in the UK* Policy Studies Institute 1987. A survey of forty years of local arts centres, their aims and the range of activities undertaken.

**6891** Hugh David *The Fitzrovians: A Portrait of Bohemian London 1900–1955* Michael Allen 1988. A good depiction of the era and of the brilliant artists who moved in these licentious coteries. A timely reassessment of a group who have been in the shadow of the Bloomsbury Group for too long.

**6892** Robert Hewison *In Anger: Culture in the Cold War 1945–60* Weidenfeld and Nicolson 1981. An excellent general cultural history of the period set in its political and social context. This is followed by his equally valuable *Too Much: Art and Society in the Sixties 1960–75* Methuen 1986. This series of studies begins with his *Under Siege: Literary Life in London 1939–45* revised ed, Methuen 1988.

**6893** Bryan Appleyard *The Pleasures of Peace: Art and Imagination in Post-War Britain* Faber 1989. A useful general cultural history.

**6894** L Johnson *The Cultural Critics from Matthew Arnold to Raymond Williams* Routledge and Kegan Paul 1979. Assessments of the development of cultural criticism and cultural history since the nineteenth century.

**6895** Martin Green *Children of the Sun: A Narrative of 'Decadence' in England after 1918* Constable 1977. A description of the imaginative life of English culture 1918–58, particularly in the context of Harold Acton and Brian Howard and their friends. He argues that they presented a new view of England, but that older themes reasserted themselves after 1958.

**6896** Geoffrey Grigson *Recollections: Mainly of Artists and Writers* Chatto and Windus/Hogarth 1984. His reminiscences of friends and acquaintances such as W H Auden, Louis MacNeice, Stephen Spender, Dylan Thomas, Henry Moore and John Piper.

**6897** Meryle Secrest *Kenneth Clark: A Biography* Weidenfeld and Nicolson 1984. A good biography, though one which perhaps concentrates overmuch on Clark's emotional life. Clark was a professor of the history of art, the chairman of the Arts Council 1953–60 and a notable television presenter and popularizer. Kenneth Clark *The Other Half: A Self-Portrait* Hamilton 1977 is the second volume of his autobiography, covering the period from the Second World War onwards. It includes useful biographical sketches of a number of other important figures in the art world.

**6898** Margaret Gardiner *A Scatter of Memories* Free Association Books 1989. Gardiner was an intimate of figures such as Barbara Hepworth, W H Auden and Louis MacNeice, the founder of an art gallery on Orkney and an art collector.

**6899** Charles Osborne *Giving It Away: The Memoirs of an Uncivil Servant* Secker and Warburg 1986. The autobiography of the Australian-born Arts Council administrator.

**6900** C F James *The Story of the Performing Rights Society* Performing Rights Society 1951. A history of an organization which works to protect intellectual copyright.

**6901** K Owusu *The Struggle for Black Arts in Britain: What Can We Consider Better Than Freedom* Comedia 1986. A history of black arts in Britain. It looks at the role of the Arts Council and other bodies, notably the Greater London Council, in providing funding and at the importance of the Notting Hill Carnival as a catalyst.

## (2) The Fine Arts

Material on design is to be found under the appropriate heading in the section on Business History. Material on art education can be found under the appropriate headings in the sections on Education.

### (a) General

**6902** Charlotte Parry-Cooke (ed) *Contemporary British Artists* Bergstrom and Boyle 1979. A who's who of contemporary artists. Wendy Beckett *Contemporary Women Artists* Phaidon 1987 is a well regarded study.

**6903** Tate Gallery Archive, Millbank, London SW1. This includes the largest oral archive on cultural subjects in Britain. It includes audio-visual material, taped interviews, BBC transcripts and offcuts of films.

**6904** Frances Spalding *British Art Since 1900* Thames and Hudson 1986. A well illustrated history which examines trends in art within their social, political and economic context. Sir John Rothenstein *British Art Since 1900: An Anthology* Phaidon 1962 is a pictorial survey of paintings and sculpture 1900–55 with a brief introductory essay.

**6905** S C Hutchinson *The History of the Royal Academy 1768–1968* Chapman and Hall 1968. See also [6914].

**6906** Herbert Read *Contemporary British Art* Penguin 1957. A short survey of painting and sculpture in the 1940s and 1950s. Bevis Hillier *Austerity Binge: The Decorative Arts of the Forties and Fifties* Studio Vista 1975 is a general introduction to the art of that period.

**6907** Susan Compton (ed) *British Art in the Twentieth Century: The Modern Movement* Royal Academy 1987. A well illustrated exhibition catalogue.

**6908** Mario Amaya *Pop in Art: A Survey of the New Sugar Realism* Studio Vista 1965. An instant history of the Pop Art movement on both sides of the Atlantic. It examines its roots, defining characteristics and main exponents. The role of the Independent Group in the origins of the movement is re-examined and challenged in K A Massey 'The Independent Group: Towards a Redefinition' Newcastle Polytechnic PhD Thesis 1985.

**6909** Dennis Farr 'Eighty Years On: The Achievements of the National Art-Collections Fund in a Changing World' *Apollo* Jan 1983 pp 14–20. A history of the fund established to secure the British arts heritage.

**6910** William Bywater *Clive Bell's Eye* Wayne State University Press, Detroit, Michigan 1975. A biographical study of the art critic and member of the Bloomsbury set. It includes a useful bibliography.

### (b) Painting, Prints and Etchings

**6911** *Who's Who in Art* 23rd ed, Art Trade Press 1988. A biennial alphabetical arrangment of potted biographies.

**6912** Edward Lucie-Smith, Carolyn Cohen and Judith Higgins *The New British Painting* Phaidon 1988. A good study of twentieth century British art. Richard Shone (comp) *The Century of Change: British Painting Since 1900* Phaidon 1977 consists largely of illustrations. Art history since the sixteenth century is traced in Simon Wilson *British Art from Holbein to the Present Day* Tate Gallery/The Bodley Head 1979.

**6913** F Constantine and J Spalding *British Painting 1900–1960* Mappin Art Gallery, Sheffield 1975 is an exhibition catalogue covering most of the major themes and movements of the period.

**6914** Paul Huxley (ed) *Exhibition Road: Painters at the Royal Academy of Art* Phaidon/Christies 1988. A well illustrated catalogue with historical essays, mainly looking at the relationship between painters and the Royal Academy in recent years.

**6915** Adrian Vincent *100 Years of Traditional English Painting* David and Charles 1989. A well illustrated account. The decline of traditionalist painting and of the Royal Academy's influence, with the simultaneous rise of modernism, which reached its apogee in the late and early 1970s, is traced in A Brighton 'Where are the Boys of the Old Brigade? The Post-War Decline of the British Traditionalist Painting' *Oxford Art Journal* 4 1981 pp 35–43.

**6916** A K Mabbutt 'Aspects of Modern Developments of the British Landscape Painting Tradition' MLitt Thesis 1983. This argues that this tradition retains vitality despite the rise of modern and abstract movements.

**6917** Edward Lucie-Smith 'The Way We Were' *Art and Artists* 12 1977 pp 14–7. A study of trends in painting in the 1960s in relation to the buying policy of the Tate Gallery.

**6918** Andrew Crozier and David Mellor (eds) *A Paradise Lost: The Neo-Romantic Imagination in Britain 1935–1955* Lund Humphries 1987. A catalogue to a major exhibition reassessing neo-romantic art.

6919 A Lewis 'British Avant-Garde Painting 1945–1956 Part 1' *Artscribe* Mar 1982 pp 17–33. A study of trends.

6920 T Cross *Painting the Warmth of the Sun: St Ives Artists 1939–1975* Lutterworth 1984. The St Ives group were originally abstract artists. They later became very avant-garde and ceased to be a very coherent school after about 1960. D Lewis, D Brown and O Watson *St Ives 1939–1964: Twenty-Five Years of Painting* Tate Gallery 1985 is an exhibition catalogue which includes reminiscences about the group.

6921 J Lemon and M Lemon *A World of Their Own: Twentieth Century British* Naïve Painters Pelham 1985. A chronologically arranged survey of 44 artists.

6922 Nina Maria Corazzo 'Post-War British Painting: The Kitchen Sink School' Indiana PhD Thesis 1981. A study of a group of painters who achieved notoriety through their 'kitchen sink' subjects.

6923 John Rothenstein *Modern English Painters* 3v, Macdonald 1984. A collection of studies of the life and work of most of the major twentieth century figures.

6924 Gabriel White *Edward Ardizonne: Artist and Illustrator* The Bodley Head 1979.

6925 Dawn Ades *Francis Bacon* Thames and Hudson 1985. A study of Bacon's life and work. See also John Russell *Francis Bacon* Thames and Hudson 1979. David Sylvester *Brutality of Fact: Interviews with Francis Bacon* 3rd ed, Thames and Hudson 1987 consists of edited transcripts of interviews with Bacon conducted since 1962.

6926 *Peter Blake* Tate Gallery 1983. An exhibition catalogue of the work of the pop artist. It includes a bibliography.

6927 Richard Cork *David Bomberg* Yale University Press 1987. A well-illustrated biography of the artist. See also his exhibition catalogue *David Bomberg* Tate Gallery 1988. William Lipke *David Bomberg: A Critical Study of his Life and Work* Adams and Mackay 1967.

6928 *Edward Burra: A Painter Remembered by his Friends* Deutsch 1982. A tribute volume. John Rothenstein *Edward Burra* Tate Gallery 1973, Andrew Causey *Burra: The Complete Catalogue* Phaidon 1985 and *Edward Burra* Arts Council of Great Britain 1985 are all catalogues of Burra's work. See also William Chappell (ed) *Well Dearie: The Letters of Edward Burra* Fraser 1985.

6929 William Anderson *Cecil Collins: The Quest for the Great Happiness* Barrie and Jenkins 1988. A biography and study of Collins' art and beliefs.

6930 Lawrence Gowing *Lucien Freud* Thames and Hudson 1982. A good biography.

6931 *Gilbert and George: The Complete Pictures 1971–1985* Thames and Hudson 1986. This is the nearest to a biographical study of Gilbert and George and their work.

6932 Grey Gowrie *Derek Hill: An Appreciation* Quartet 1987. A study of a portrait and landscape painter.

6933 Marco Livingstone *David Hockney* revised ed, Thames and Hudson 1987. A good study of his life and work. See also Peter Webb *Portrait of David Hockney* Chatto and Windus 1988. David Hockney *David Hockney* Thames and Hudson 1977 is a useful, well-illustrated autobiography. *David Hockney: A Retrospective* Thames and Hudson 1988 is an exhibition catalogue.

6934 Michael Spender 'Ken Howard ARA' *Old Water-Colour Society's Club Annual* 60 1985 pp 70–85. Howard is a watercolourist and was the Imperial War Museum's official artist in Northern Ireland 1973–80.

6935 Michael Holroyd *Augustus John: A Biography* 2v, Weidenfeld and Nicolson 1973–74.

6936 Marco Livingstone *R B Kitaj* Phaidon 1985. A biography of the artist. Kitaj's work is studied in John Ashbery, Joe Shannon, Jane Livingstone and Timothy Hyman *Kitaj: Paintings, Drawings, Pastels* Thames and Hudson 1983.

6937 Frank Whitford *Oskar Kokoschka: A Life* Weidenfeld and Nicolson 1986. A biography of the Austrian born artist who was a leading figure in the modern movement. See also Oskar Kokoschka *My Life* Thames and Hudson 1974.

6938 Shelley Rohde *Private View of L S Lowry* revised ed, Methuen 1987. An attempt to explore Lowry's enigmatic character. Tilly Marshall *Life With Lowry* Hutchinson 1981 is a memoir of the artist. Allen Andrews *The Life of L S Lowry 1887–1976* Jupiter Books 1977 is a short biography.

6939 Richard Morphet *Cedric Morris* Tate Gallery 1984. An exhibition catalogue.

6940 Jean Goodman *What a Go! The Life of Alfred Munnings* Collins 1988. A warts-and-all biography of the great figurative painter and his lifelong campaign against the modern movement. The final speech of his term as President of the Royal Academy 1944–9, a notorious attack on modern art, and his attempts to persecute Stanley Spencer after his reinstatement by the Royal Academy in 1950, are covered in full. Reginald Pound *The Englishman: A Biography of Sir Alfred Munnings* Heinemann 1962 is also a useful biography which fully covers Munnings' controversial role in post-war art politics. There are also three volumes of autobiography, *An Artist's Life* Museum Press 1950, *The Second Burst* Museum Press 1951 and *The Finish* Museum Press 1952. These however reveal more of the period than the man.

**6941**  Anthony West *John Piper* Secker and Warburg 1979. A study of the artist and his life.

**6942**  Jean Goodman *Edward Seago: The Other Side of the Canvas* Collins 1978. A biography of the landscape painter.

**6943**  David Shepherd *The Man Who Loves Giants: An Artist among Elephants and Engines* Coronet 1977. The autobiography of the wildlife painter is continued in *The Man Who Loves Giants: The Continuing Story of an Artist* David and Charles 1989.

**6944**  Mervyn Levy *Ruskin Spear* Weidenfeld and Nicolson 1985. A short study of Spear's life and work.

**6945**  John Rothenstein *Stanley Spencer The Man: Correspondence and Reminiscences* Elek 1979. A memoir of the artist.

**6946**  Roger Berthoud *Graham Sutherland: A Biography* Faber 1982. A well regarded study.

**6947**  Robin Tanner *Double Harness* Impact Books 1988. The autobiography of an eminent etcher, especially of rural scenes.

**6948**  Keith Vaughan *Journals 1939–1977* Murray 1989. The illuminating journals and diaries of the artist.

**6949**  Barbara Wadsworth *Edward Wadsworth: A Painter's Life* Michael Russell 1989. A biography of her father, the vorticist painter who died in 1948.

**6950**  Josephine Walpole *Vernon Ward: Child of the Edwardian Era* Antique Collectors Club 1988. A biography of a figurative painter in an age that preferred modern art.

**6951**  Frank Wootton *The Landscape Paintings of Frank Wootton* David and Charles 1989. A semi-autobiographical guide to his art and techniques.

**6952**  Josephine Walpole *Anna: A Memorial Tribute to Anna Zinkeisen* Royle Publications 1978. A biography and tribute to the portrait painter, artist and designer.

## (c) Sculpture

**6953**  Michel Seuphor *The Sculpture of this Century: Dictionary of Modern Sculpture* Zwemmer 1960. An illustrated international reference guide including pieces on sculpture in twentieth century Britain, Henry Moore and Barbara Hepworth and alphabetically arranged short biographies.

**6954**  Sandy Nairne and Nicholas Serota (eds) *British Sculpture in the Twentieth Century* Whitechapel Art Gallery 1981. This illustrated exhibition catalogue examines developments and trends in sculpture, the media used and the nature of patronage. A Gouk 'Too much too soon' *Artscribe* Feb 1982 pp 22–33 attempts to revise the view of post-war sculpture presented in Nairne and Serota. Perspectives on post-war sculpture are presented in Terry Ann Neff (ed) *A Quiet Revolution: British Sculpture Since 1945* Thames and Hudson 1987.

**6955**  H M B Gresty 'Sculpture in Britain in the Early '70s' London MPhil Thesis 1984. See also B Jones 'A New Wave in Sculpture: A Survey of Recent Work by Ten Younger Sculptors' *Artscribe* Sept 1977 pp 14–9.

**6956**  R C Rossi 'Sculpture in Great Britain 1960–66: The Saint Martin's Group' New York PhD Thesis 1978. A history and critical study of an influential group of British sculptors.

**6957**  Penelope Curtis (ed) *Patronage and Practice: Sculpture on Merseyside* Tate Gallery 1989. An exhibition catalogue.

**6958**  Alan Bowness *Lynn Chadwick* Methuen 1962. A short illustrated biography of the sculptor with a listing of her exhibitions and a select bibliography.

**6959**  *Tony Cragg* Arts Council of Great Britain 1987. An exhibition catalogue.

**6960**  Jacob Epstein *Let There Be Sculpture: Epstein: An Autobiography* 2nd ed, Vista 1963. This second edition was issued with a new introduction after the death of the controversial sculptor in 1963.

**6961**  Elizabeth Frink *Sculpture: Catalogue Raisonné* Harpvale 1984. A guide to her work.

**6962**  Barbara Hepworth *A Pictorial Autobiography* Adams and Dart 1970. The life and work of the sculptor is also examined in Abraham Hammacher *Barbara Hepworth* revised ed, Thames and Hudson 1981.

**6963**  Edward H Teague *Henry Moore: Bibliography and Reproduction Index* Bailey and Swinfen 1981. This includes a potted biography. The best biography is Roger

Berthoud *The Life of Henry Moore* Faber 1987. See also David Finn *Henry Moore* Thames and Hudson 1977. Susan Compton with Richard Cork and Peter Fuller *Henry Moore* Weidenfeld and Nicolson 1988 is an exhibition catalogue.

## (d) Photography

**6964** W Messer 'The British Obsession: About To Pay Off?' *British Journal of Photography* 124 1977 pp 1042–7, 1065–8, 1072–3, 1078–81, 1086–7, 1094–7, 125 1978 pp 16–9, 26–9, 43. A study of the development of creative photography in Britain since 1939.

**6965** A Ellis 'Playback: British Photography 1955–1965' *British Journal of Photography* 130 1983 pp 420–5.

**6966** Val Williams *Women Photographers: The Other Observers 1900 to the Present Day* Virago 1986. A photographic and cultural history. The relevant chapters are those on women and *Picture Post*, portraiture in the studio 1900–55 and feminist photography 1979–86.

**6967** Hugo Vickers *Cecil Beaton: The Authorised Biography* Hodder and Stoughton 1985. A useful biography of the royal and society photographer. *Cecil Beaton* Barbican Art Gallery 1986 is an exhibition catalogue. Cecil Beaton *Photobiography* Odhams 1951 is an illustrated autobiography. Two volumes of diaries on the post-war period have been published. These are Cecil Beaton *The Restless Years: Diaries 1955–63* Weidenfeld and Nicolson 1976 and *The Parting Years: Diaries 1963–74* Weidenfeld and Nicolson 1978. There is also Richard Buckle (ed) *Self-Portrait With Friends: The Selected Diaries of Cecil Beaton 1926–74* Weidenfeld and Nicolson 1979.

**6968** Frances Spalding *Vanessa Bell* Weidenfeld and Nicolson 1983. A biography of the photographer and member of the Bloomsbury group.

**6969** For Bert Hardy see [3662].

**6970** Patrick Lichfield *Not The Whole Truth: An Autobiography* Constable 1986.

**6971** Norman Parkinson *Lifework* Weidenfeld and Nicolson 1983. A photographic autobiography.

**6972** David Sinclair *Snowden: A Man Of Our Times* Proteus 1982. An illustrated biography of the photographer and erstwhile husband of Princess Margaret.

**6973** Jo Spence *Putting Myself in the Picture: A Political, Personal and Photographic Autobiography* Camden Press 1986. The autobiography of a feminist photographer.

## (e) Architecture

Material of relevance can also be found in the sections on Town and Country Planning, New Towns, Inner Cities, Schools and Housing.

**6974** *Architects' Yearbook* Elek 1945–74. An irregular series of 14 volumes, each of which had a different theme. They contained essays, plans and information.

**6975** A Mace and R Thorne *The Royal Institute of British Architects: A Guide to its Archives and History* Mansell 1986. A guide to the archives of the Institute since its establishment in 1834 which includes a short history of the Institute.

**6976** G M Waters *Dictionary of British Architects Working 1900–1950* 2v, Eastbourne Fine Art 1975–76. Volume 1 supplies brief biographical data on 5,500 architects working in the period. The second volume contains supplementary information.

**6977** Ann Lee Morgan and Colin Naylor (eds) *Contemporary Architects* 2nd ed, St James Press 1987. A collection of biographies which is international in scope. It includes a number of British architects, supplying full biographies, criticism of their work and a list of their buildings and projects.

**6978** L Wodehouse (ed) *British Architects 1840–1975: A Guide to Information Sources* Gale, Detroit, Michigan 1978. This has about 2,000 annotated entries. The first part is a classified bibliography of books and articles on architecture and the second is a biobibliography of 288 architects. See also Howard M Colvin *English Architectural History: A Guide to Sources* Pinhorns 1976.

**6979** Ruth H Kamen *British and Irish Architectural History: A Bibliography and Guide to Sources of Information* Architectural Press 1981. A good bibliography. It is well annotated and contains a select guide to sources. The one drawback is that it only lists published books and does not include articles. Valerie J Bradfield (ed) *Information Sources in Architecture* Butterworths 1983 is a collection of bibliographical essays which, whilst international in scope are biased towards British sources. These supply detailed information on all sorts of information sources.

**6980** *Architecture Journal* 1894– includes a useful annual bibliography.

**6981** *Architectural Periodicals Index* Royal Institute of British Architects 1972–. A quarterly classified index to articles appearing in journals taken in the Institute's library. This replaces the *RIBA Library Bulletin*, which in turn replaced the 'RIBA Annual Review of Periodical Articles' which appeared in the *RIBA Journal*.

**6982** Hugh Casson 'Twenty Five Years of Architectural Development' *Contemporary Review* 231 1977 pp 302–7. A survey of developments during the reign of Elizabeth II. Peter Murray and Stephen Trombley (eds) *Modern British Architecture Since 1945* Muller 1984 is a catalogue, by regions, of the major buildings of the period.

**6983** Anthony Jackson *The Politics of Architecture: A History of Modern Architecture in Britain* Architectural Press 1970. An account of the work of the modern movement in architecture since the 1920s concentrating on the period either side of the Second World War.

**6984** Bruce Allsopp *Towards a Humane Architecture* Muller 1974. A *cri de coeur* against many of the features of modern architecture, such as the high-rise block of flats and the design of buildings which are insensitive to their surroundings. The most celebrated of critics of modern architecture in Britain is the Prince of Wales. His *A Vision of Britain* Doubleday 1989 encapsulates his critique of modern architecture and his enthusiasm for classical architecture and sets forth the principles which he feels should govern good design. See also the critical response to the Prince's views of the then President of the Royal Institute of British Architects, Maxwell Hutchinson *The Prince of Wales: Right and Wrong* Faber 1989. Though this later work takes issue with the way in which the Prince has intervened in the debate about post-war architecture and with some of his views it is significantly not a defence of many of the buildings or styles that have been condemned.

**6985** S Harvey and S Rettig (eds) *Fifty Years of Landscape Design 1934–1984* Landscape Press 1985. A collection of essays examining all aspects of the recent history of landscape architecture. See also Jane Brown (ed) *The Art and Architecture of English Gardens: Designs for the Garden from the Collection of the Royal Institute of British Architects, 1609 to the Present Day* Weidenfeld and Nicolson 1989. The history of the Institute of Landscape Architects is told in L J Fricker 'Forty Years A-Growing' *Journal of the Institute of Landscape Architects* 86 1969 pp 8–15.

**6986** Trevor Dannatt *Modern Architecture in Britain: Selected Examples of Recent Buildings* Batsford 1959. A survey of work conducted in 1945–58. See also J Summerson (ed) *Ten Years of British Architecture 1945–55* Arts Council 1956. There are studies of fifteen examples of various important buildings of different types of this period in Edward D Mills *The New Architecture in Britain 1945–53* Standard Catalogue 1953.

**6987** Rayner Banham *The New Brutalism: Ethic or Aesthetic?* Architectural Press 1966. A study of the development in the 1950s of the movement primarily associated with Alison and Peter Smithson.

**6988** Michael Webb *Architecture in Britain Today* Country Life 1969. A pictorial survey of architecture in Britain 1958–68 by building type.

**6989** Sutherland Lyall *The State of British Architecture* Architectural Press 1980. A critical review of architecture in the 1970s. *British Architecture* Architectural Design 1982 surveys the range of styles in contemporary architecture and the development of student work.

**6990** Sutherland Lyall *Dream Cottages: From Cottage Ornée to Stockbroker Tudor: Two Hundred Years of the Cult of the Vernacular* Hale 1988. A history of cottage vernacular architecture, including a little on the post-war neo-vernacular revival.

**6991** Bruce Allsopp (ed) *Modern Architecture of Northern England* Oriel Press 1969. A pictorial representation of the range of developments in the North in the 1960s.

**6992** Charles McKean *Architectural Guide to Cambridge and East Anglia Since 1920* Royal Institute of British Architects 1982. A good guide.

**6993** C Stansfield-Smith 'Developments in Social Architecture in Hampshire' *Transactions of the Royal Institute of British Architects* 3 1984 pp 38–47. An illustrated appraisal of the work of the local authority's architects over the previous ten years.

**6994** L Lloyd Smith and R J B Keene *1872–1972: The First Hundred Years of the Leicestershire and Rutland Society of Architects* the Society 1972.

**6995** Charles McKean and Tom Jenkins (eds) *Modern Buildings in London: A Guide* Warehouse 1976. An illustrated glossary of new buildings constructed between 1965 and 1975. S Cantacuzino 'The Barbican Development, City of London' *Architectural Review* 9 1973 pp 66–90 is a critical review of the history and design of this central development. M Spring 'The Natwest Tower' *Building* 23/1/1981 pp 38–51 is a review of the design and construction of the tallest office block in Britain. D Hutchinson and S Williams 'South Bank Saga' *Architectural Review* 160 1976 pp 156–62 reviews the controversy which has raged over the merits of the South Bank arts complex ever since it was constructed for the 1951 Festival of Britain.

**6996** Deyan Sudjic *Norman Foster, Richard Rogers, James Stirling: New Directions in British Architecture* Thames and Hudson 1986. An exhibition catalogue on the work of three of the most distinguished of post-war British architects.

**6997** Lionel Brett *Our Selves Unknown: An Autobiography* Gollancz 1985. Brett was president of the Royal Institute of British Architects and active in the Royal College of Art. However, this autobiography is not very informative and is best on the architecture of the 1960s.

**6998** Gordon E Cherry and Leith Penny *Holford: A Study in Architecture, Planning and Civic Design* Mansell 1986. A biography of Lord Holford, who had a multifarious role in post-war planning even if he was an indifferent architect. This is a reassessment of the work of a man who was once held in much higher regard than he or his work is now.

**6999** K Wharton *Adventure in Architecture: A Profile of the Owen Luder Partnership* Lund Humphries 1977. A history from its foundation in 1958.

**7000** S Houfe *Sir Albert Richardson: The Professor* White Crescent Press 1980. Richardson was Professor of Architecture at London University 1919–46.

**7001** Raglan Squire *Portrait of an Architect* Colin Smythe 1984. A good, well-illustrated autobiography by an internationally successful architect.

## (f) Other

**7002** Paul Ride and Christopher Gowing *British Studio Ceramics in the 20th Century* Barrie and Jenkins 1989. A good history tracing developments from the factory productions of the turn of the century to the extraordinary variety of studio work in the 1980s. The work of the leading artists is examined in depth in terms of its interest and influence. The book is well illustrated with examples of this work. Studio ceramics of the 1980s are discussed in Michael Casson 'British Ceramics Today' *Ceramics Monthly* 30 1982 pp 54–60.

**7003** Elizabeth Cameron and Philippa Lewis *Potters on Pottery* Evans Brothers 1976. Studio pottery has had growing commercial viability in the post-war period. This is a well-illustrated guide to the views of various contemporary British ceramic artists on their craft with potted biographies. Those covered include Alan and Ruth Barrett-Danes, Svend Bayer, Alan Caiger-Smith, Michael Cardew, Michael Casson, Elizabeth Fritsch, Ian Godfrey, Mo Jupp, David Leach, Denka Napiorkowska and Roger Mitchell, Bryan Newman, Siddig A El'Ni-

goumi, Mary Rogers, Peter Starkey, Geoffrey Swindell and Yeap Poh Chap.

**7004** Garth Clark *Michael Cardew: A Portrait* Faber 1978. A biography of the ceramic artist.

**7005** Carol Hogben (ed) *The Art of Bernard Leach* Faber 1978. Studies of the work of the ceramic artist.

**7006** John Webber and Henry Hammond 'William Staite Murray' *Crafts* 14 1975 pp 25–34. A memoir of the potter.

**7007** *Katherine Pleydell-Bouverie: A Potter's Life 1895–1985* Crafts Council 1986. A short biography.

**7008** Marigold Coleman 'Charles Vyse' *Crafts* 12 1975 pp 18–24. A review of the potter's work.

**7009** A Waugh *300 Years of British Glass: 1675–1975* Wolverhampton Art Galleries and Museums 1975. An exhibition catalogue.

**7010** M Timmers *The Way We Live Now: Designs for Interiors 1950 to the Present Day* Victoria and Albert Museum 1979. An exhibition catalogue. Mary Gilliatt *English Style in Interior Decoration* The Bodley Head 1967 examines trends in style since the 1951 Festival of Britain. Elizabeth Dickson *Colefax and Fowler: The Best in English Interior Design* Barrie and Jenkins 1989 is a history of the firm of interior designers.

**7011** Peter Hinks *Twentieth Century British Jewellery 1900–1980* Faber 1983. An illustrated study. A more international study of post-war trends is Peter Dormer and Ralph Turner *The New Jewelry: Trends and Traditions* Thames and Hudson 1985.

## (2) Music

### (a) Classical

#### (i) General

**7012** Stanley Sadie (ed) *The New Grove Dictionary of Music and Musicians* 20v, Macmillan 1981. The standard reference work. Each entry contains bibliographical references.

**7013** *British Music Year Book* Classical Music 1972–. An annual mine of information. It includes a directory, obituaries, details of record releases and a survey of events.

**7014** *The Music Index* Information Services, Detroit, Michigan 1949–. The key source on current periodical literature on music. Another serial bibliography is *British Catalogue of Music* Council of the British National Bibliography 1951–.

**7015** Cyril Ehrlich *The Music Profession Since the Eighteenth Century* Clarendon 1985. A history of musicians which contains some information on the post-war period.

**7016** Peter J Pirie *The English Musical Renaissance* Gollancz 1979. A history from Elgar and Delius in the 1890s to Maxwell Davies and Harrison Birtwhistle in the 1970s. It is a chronological account setting the music in its social and political context. Another good account, which includes a useful bibliography, is Michael J Trend *The Music Makers: Heirs and Rebels of the English Musical Renaissance: Edward Elgar to Benjamin Britten* Weidenfeld and Nicolson 1985. This however has rather less coverage on the post-war period. See also Frank Stewart Howes *The English Musical Renaissance* Secker and Warburg 1966 and H Wood 'English Contemporary Music' in Howard Hertog (ed) *European Music in the Twentieth Century* Pelican 1961 pp 145–70. Percy Marshall Young *A History of British Music* Benn 1967 has a useful final chapter.

**7017** Frank Stewart Howes *Music 1945–1950* Longmans 1951. A short survey for the British Council.

**7018** Barrie Hall *The Proms and the Man Who Made Them* Allen and Unwin 1981. A well illustrated history of the Proms since Henry Wood inaugurated the greatest music festival in Europe, which is held annually in London, in 1895. It is especially useful on the organization and management of the promenade concerts. In analysing this he was able to draw on the files of the BBC, who have organized the event since 1927. Hall also supplies the first account of the 1980 musicians' dispute which disrupted the Proms that year. Useful earlier histories are David Cox *The Henry Wood Proms* BBC 1980 and Ates Orga *The Proms* David and Charles 1974. Leslie Ayre *The Proms* Frewin 1968 is a short, anecdotal history.

**7019** Thomas Russell *Philharmonic Project* Hutchinson 1952. An examination of the problems of symphony orchestras in Britain at the time and a plea for better help and funding.

**7020** Nicholas Kenyon *The BBC Symphony Orchestra: The First Fifty Years 1930–1980* BBC 1980. An official and yet sometimes critical review of the formation and achievements of the orchestra.

**7021** Michael Kennedy *The Hallé 1858–1983: A History of the Orchestra* Manchester University Press 1882.

A good history of the famous Manchester-based orchestra. See also the centenary histories Michael Kennedy *The Hallé Tradition: A Century of Music* Manchester University Press 1960 and C B Rees *One Hundred Years of the Hallé* MacGibbon and Kee 1957.

**7022** Maurice Pearton *The LSO at 70: A History of the Orchestra* Gollancz 1974. A history not only of the London Symphony Orchestra as an institution but also a social history of changing tastes amongst concert-goers, how the orchestra has responded, and the changing nature of the orchestra. Alan Smyth (ed) *The London Symphony Orchestra: To Speak For Ourselves* Kimber 1970 is a collection of interviews with the then current players.

**7023** Stephen J Pettitt *Philharmonia Orchestra: A Record of Achievement 1945–1985* Hale 1985. A good history of the orchestra's foundation, development and surmounting of its financial difficulties in the 1960s.

**7024** R A Edwards *And The Glory: The Huddersfield Choral Society 1836–1986* W S Maney 1986. A history of a distinguished choral society which continues to commission choral works and influence composers.

**7025** Kenneth Thompson *A Dictionary of Twentieth Century Composers 1911–1971* Faber 1973. A useful reference work, which includes entries on all the more distinguished of twentieth century British composers.

**7026** Diane McIveagh *et al Twentieth Century English Masters: Elgar, Delius, Vaughan Williams, Holst, Walton, Tippett* Macmillan 1984. A collection of studies of the most significant British composers of the twentieth century, of whom Vaughan Williams, Walton, Tippett and Britten were still working in the post-war period.

**7027** Alan Frank *Modern British Composers* Dennis Dobson 1953. This collection of biographies of contemporary composers features Ralph Vaughan Williams, John Ireland, Arnold Bax, Arthur Bliss, Arthur Benjamin, E J Moeran, Gordon Jacob, Edmund Rubbra, William Walton, Lennox Berkeley, Michael Tippett, Alan Rawsthorne, Constant Lambert, Herbert Murrill and Benjamin Britten.

**7028** Murray Schafer *British Composers in Interview* Faber 1961. A collection of interviews with John Ireland, Egon Willesz, Arthur Benjamin, Alan Bush, Edmund Rubbra, William Walton, Lennox Berkeley, Michael Tippett, Elizabeth Lutyens, Benjamin Britten, Humphrey Searle, Peter Racim Fricken, Malcolm Arnold, Iain Hamilton, Alexander Goehr and Peter Maxwell Davies.

**7029** Francis Routh *Contemporary British Music* Macdonald 1972. This includes studies of Peter Maxwell Davies, Iain Hamilton, Nicholas Maw, Anthony Milner and Thea Musgrave. It also includes a large bibliography.

**7030** Lewis Foreman (ed) *British Music Now: A Guide to the Work of Younger Composers* Elek 1975. A collection of studies of the contemporary composers Thea Musgrave and Gordon Grosse, Ronald Stevenson, Alexander Goehr, Hugh Wood, Harrison Birtwhistle, Peter Maxwell Davies, Alun Hoddicott and William Mathias, Nicholas Maw, Richard Rodney Bennett, David Blake, David Bedford, Kenneth Leighton and John McCabe, John Tavener, Justin Connolly, Jonathan Harvey, Roger Smalley, Anthony Payne, Tristam Cary, Anthony Milner, Christopher Headington, Robin Holloway, David Ellis and Christopher Shaw. There is also a selection of potted biographies on other composers and a bibliography and discography on composers featured.

**7031** Paul Griffiths *New Sounds: New Personalities: British Composers of the 1980s* Faber 1985. A collection of short interviews with Alexander Goehr, George Benjamin, Peter Maxwell Davies, Simon Bainbridge, Jonathan Harvey, Oliver Knussen, Brian Ferneyhough, John Casten, David Matthews, Colin Matthews, John Tavener, Robin Holloway, Nigel Osborne, Tim Souster, Stephen Oliver, Gavin Bryars, Dominic Muldowney, Nicholas Maw, Robert Sexton and Harrison Birtwhistle.

**7032** Michael Kennedy *Barbirolli: Conductor Laureate: The Authorised Biography* MacGibbon and Kee 1971. A biography of the great conductor, most famous for his long association with and revival of the fortunes of the Hallé orchestra 1943–70. See also Charles Reid *John Barbirolli* Hamilton 1971 and Charles Rigby *John Barbirolli* John Sherratt 1948.

**7033** Lewis Foreman 'Bibliography of Writings on Arnold Bax' *Current Musicology* 10 1970 pp 124–40. This consists of 210 items listed alphabetically. Foreman has since written a biography of this Master of the King's Musick who died in 1953, Lewis Foreman *Bax: A Composer and His Times* Scolar Press, Berkeley, California 1983. See also Colin Scott-Sutherland *Arnold Bax* Dent 1973.

**7034** Alan Jefferson *Sir Thomas Beecham: A Centenary Tribute* Macdonald and Jane's 1979. A biography of celebrated conductor. See also Charles Reid *Thomas Beecham: An Independent Biography* Gollancz 1971. Neville Cardus *Sir Thomas Beecham: A Memoir* Collins 1961 is a tribute volume. Humphrey Proctor-Gregg *Beecham Remembered* Duckworth 1976 is a short biography followed by a collection of appreciations.

**7035** Michael Hall *Harrison Birtwhistle* Robson 1984. A study of Birtwhistle's life and music.

**7036** James Blades *Drum Roll: A Professional Adventure from the Circus to the Concert Hall* Faber 1977. An entertaining autobiography by a leading percussionist.

**7037** S R Craggs 'The Life and Music of Sir Arthur Bliss: A Catalogue and Commentary' Strathclyde PhD Thesis 1982. A four volume work. The first examines his life and music. The rest is an annotated catalogue to his work. Arthur Bliss *As I Remember* Faber 1970 is a collection of reminiscences and letters by the composer. See also Christopher Palmer *Bliss* Novello 1976.

**7038** Michael Kennedy *Adrian Boult* Hamilton 1987. A biography of the famous conductor drawing on unrestricted access to Boult's papers. See also Sir Adrian Boult's autobiography, *My Own Trumpet* Hamilton 1973.

**7039** Arnold Whitall *The Music of Britten and Tippett: Studies in Themes and Techniques* Cambridge University Press 1982. A chronological study of the development of the music of these two great composers. The best biography of Benjamin Britten is Michael Kennedy *Britten* Dent 1981. See also Imogen Holst *Britten* 3rd ed, Faber 1980 and Ronald Duncan *Working With Britten: A Personal Memoir* Rebel Press 1981. Alan Blyth (ed) *Remembering Britten* Hutchinson 1981 is a volume of tributes and reminiscences. Christopher Palmer (ed) *The Britten Companion* Faber 1984 supplies a useful reference guide to Britten's life and music. Britten's operatic work is particularly examined in Eric Walter White *Benjamin Britten: His Life and Operas* 2nd ed, Faber 1983.

**7040** Michael Hurd *Immortal Hour: The Life and Period of Rutland Broughton* Routledge and Kegan Paul 1962. The biography of a communist composer.

**7041** B B Daubrey 'Benjamin Burrows 1891–1966: The Life and Music of the Leicester Composer' Leicester MPhil Thesis 1979.

**7042** Alan Bush *In My Eighth Decade and Other Essays* Kahn and Averill 1980. A collection of autobiographical reminiscences. He feels that his communist views handicapped acceptance of his music in Britain. He was however popular behind the Iron Curtain.

**7042A** Harriet Cohen *A Bundle of Time: The Memoirs of Harriet Cohen* Faber 1969. The autobiography of the concert pianist who died in 1967.

**7043** Paul Griffiths *Peter Maxwell Davies* 2nd ed, Robson 1982. A study of the composer's life and music drawing on interviews with its subject.

**7044** Carol Easton *Jacqueline du Pré: A Biography* Hodder and Stoughton 1989. A biography of the distinguished cellist.

**7045** Maurice Leonard *Kathleen: The Life of Kathleen Ferrier 1912–1953* Century Hutchinson 1988. A biography of the celebrated contralto. See also the biography by her sister, Winifred Ferrier *The Life of Kathleen Ferrier* Hamilton 1955, Charles Rigby *Kathleen Ferrier: A Biography* Hale 1955 and Peter Lethbridge *Kathleen Ferrier* Cassell 1959. Neville Cardus (ed) *Kathleen Ferrier: A Memoir* Hamilton 1954 is a collection of tributes.

**7046** Charles Rigby (ed) *Philip Godlee by his Friends* Dolphin Press 1954. A tribute memoir of the chairman of the committee governing the Hallé orchestra.

**7047** Christopher Palmer *Herbert Howells: A Study* Novello 1978. A study of the life and work of this composer best known for his choral compositions.

**7048** John Langmire *John Ireland: Portrait of a Friend* John Baker 1969. A portrayal of the composer. Muriel V Searle *John Ireland: The Man and His Music* Midas Books 1979 is an anecdotal biography. See also Colin Scott-Sutherland *John Ireland* Triad Press 1980.

**7049** Richard Stead *Constant Lambert* Simon Publications 1973. This study of the English composer who died in 1951 shortly after his last work, the ballet 'Teiresias', was declared a critical flop, incorporates a memoir by Anthony Powell. A more biographical study is Andrew Motion 'Constant' in his *The Lamberts: George, Constant and Kit* Chatto and Windus 1986 pp 119–259.

**7050** Meirion and Susie Harries *A Pilgrim Soul* Michael Joseph 1989. A good biography of Elizabeth Lutyens. The memoirs of Lutyens are told in her *A Goldfish Bowl* Cassell 1972.

**7051** Sir Robert Mayer *My First Hundred Years* Van Duren 1979. An autobiography on the occasion of the celebrated conductor's hundredth birthday.

**7052** Yehudi Menuhin *Unfinished Journey* Macdonald and Jane's 1977. His autobiography. See also Robin Daniels *Conversations with Menuhin* Macdonald and Janes 1979 is an excellent collection of interviews. Robert Magidoff and Henry Rayner *Yehudi Menuhin: The Story of the Man and the Musician* 2nd ed, Hale 1973 is a useful biography.

**7053** Geoffrey Self *The Music of E J Moeran* Toccato Press 1986. This is the first full length study of Moeran and his music. See also Stephen Wild *E J Moeran* Triad Press 1973. Lionel Hill *Lonely Waters: The Diary of a Friendship with E J Moeran* Thames Publishing 1985 is also of use.

**7054** Gerald Moore *Am I Too Loud? Memoirs of an Accompanist* Penguin 1979. The anecdotal memoirs of an accompanist and raconteur. Further volumes of memoirs *Farewell Recital: Further Memoirs* Hamilton 1978 and *The Unashamed Accompanist* revised ed, McRae 1984.

**7055** Steve Race *Musician at Large* Eyre Methuen 1979. The autobiography of a music broadcaster. It includes well considered reflections on the performers and trends in classical music and also, to a lesser extent, in popular music.

**7056** Nicholas Kenyon *Simon Rattle* Faber 1987. A biography of an important conductor of the post-war generation.

**7057** Hugh Ottaway *Edmund Rubbra: An Appreciation* Alfred Lengnick 1981. A study of the composer. See also Lewis Foreman (ed) *Edmund Rubbra* Triad Press 1977. Frederic Vanson 'Edmund Rubbra at Seventy-Five' *Contemporary Review* 230 1977 pp 318–22 is an interview with the composer.

**7058** Charles Reid *Malcolm Sargent: A Biography* Hamilton 1968. A biography of the great conductor. See also Phyllis Matthewman *Sir Malcolm Sargent* Cassell 1959.

**7059** Cyril Scott *Bone Of Contention: Life Story and Confessions* Aquarian Press 1969. The autobiography of the composer.

**7060** Paul Robinson *Solti* Macdonald and Jane's 1979. A biography of the great composer Sir Georg Solti.

**7061** Lionel Tertis *My Viola And I: A Complete Autobiography* Elek 1974. The autobiography of a great musician.

**7062** Garry O'Connor *The Pursuit of Perfection: A Life of Maggie Teyte* Gollancz 1979. The last performances of Teyte, one of the greatest English singers of the twentieth century, were in the 1950s.

**7063** Paul D Andrews 'Sir Michael Tippett – A Bibliography' *Brio* 15 1978 pp 33–46. This lists 171 items about Tippett alphabetically. The best study of the composer and his work is Ian Kemp *Tippett: The Composer and his Music* Eulenberg Books 1984. Tippett's operatic work is examined in Eric Walter White *Tippett and his Operas* Barrie and Jenkins 1979. See also Meirion Bowen *Michael Tippett* Robson 1982, Michael Hurd *Tippett* Novello 1978 and David Matthews *Michael Tippett: An Introductory Study* Faber 1980. On the chronological development of Tippett's music see also [7039].

**7064** Ursula Vaughan Williams *RVW: A Biography of Ralph Vaughan Williams* Oxford University Press 1964. The best biography of the composer. See also Roy Douglas *Working With RVW* Oxford University Press 1972 and Percy Marshall Young *Vaughan Williams* Dennis Dobson 1953 and Hubert Foss Ralph *Vaughan Williams: A Study* Harrap 1952. Wilfrid Mellors *Vaughan Williams and the Vision of Albion* Barrie and Jenkins 1989 attempts to set Vaughan Williams' music in context.

**7065** Michael Kennedy *Portrait of Walton* Oxford University Press 1989. A candid biography of the composer William Walton and an assessment of his music drawing on his correspondence. Susana Walton *William Walton: Behind the Facade* Oxford University Press 1988 is a memoir by his wife. Neil Tierney *William Walton: His Life and Music* Hale 1984 is a good study of Walton's life and music. It includes a useful bibliography.

*(ii) Opera*

**7066** Cameron Northouse *Twentieth Century Opera in England and the United States* Prior 1976. The history of opera from the sixteenth to twentieth centuries is examined in Eric Walter White *A History of English Opera* Faber 1983. The final chapter examines twentieth century works, productions and companies.

**7067** Frances Donaldson *The Royal Opera House in the Twentieth Century* Weidenfeld and Nicolson 1982. A short general musical and architectural history is Andrew Saint *A History of the Royal Opera House: Covent Garden 1732–1982* Royal Opera House 1982.

**7068** John Higgins (ed) *Glyndebourne: A Celebration* Cape 1984. A collection of essays on various aspects of the development of the annual opera festival held at Glyndebourne. See also Spike Hughes *Glyndebourne: A History of the Festival Opera* Methuen 1985. Wilfrid Jasper Walter Blunt *John Christie of Glyndebourne* Geoffrey Bles 1968 is a biography of one of the leading organizers of the festival opera.

*(iii) Ballet*

**7069** Joan W White (ed) *Twentieth Century Dance in Britain: A History of Major Dance Companies in Britain* Dance 1985. A history of ballet and contemporary dance companies, with articles on Ballet Rambert, the Royal Ballet and Sadler's Wells Royal Ballet, the London

Festival Ballet, the London Contemporary Dance Ballet and Scottish Ballet.

**7070** Clive Barnes *Ballet in Britain Since the War* Thrift Books 1953. A summary of ballet in London since 1945.

**7071** Alexander Bland *Observer of the Dance 1958– 1982: In Memory* Dance Books 1985. A collection of his dance journalism and a commentary on the development of ballet from his pieces for *The Observer* as dance critic 1955–82.

**7072** Alexander Bland *The Royal Ballet: The First Fifty Years* Threshold/Sotheby Parke Bernet 1981. A very thorough history which includes a useful chronology. The development of the company is traced by one who was closely involved in Ninette de Valois *Step by Step: The Formation of an Establishment* W H Allen 1977. An earlier history of this company is Mary Clarke *The Sadler's Wells Ballet: A History and an Appreciation* Black 1955.

**7073** Clement Crisp, Anya Sainsbury and Peter Williams (eds) *Ballet Rambert: 50 Years and On* revised ed, Ballet Rambert 1981. An earlier history of the company founded in 1926 is Mary Clarke *Dancers of Mercury: The Story of Ballet Rambert* Black 1962.

**7074** Zöe Dominic and John Selwyn Gilbert *Frederick Ashton: A Choreographer and his Ballets* Harrap 1971. A life and study of the work of Sir Frederick Ashton.

**7075** Ninette de Valois *Come Dance With Me: A Memoir 1898–1956* Hamilton 1957. The memoirs of a major ballet teacher who played an important role in the development of many of the leading dancers of post-war ballet.

**7076** Sir Anton Dolin *Last Words: A Final Autobiography (edited by Kay Hunter)* Century 1985. Dolin became the first great British male ballet star during the inter-war period. See also the two memorial tributes, Andrew Wheatcroft (comp) *Dolin: Friends and Memories* Routledge and Kegan Paul 1982 and *A Pictorial Tribute to Sir Anton Dolin: The First British Ballet Star 1904–1983* Gala Committee 1984.

**7077** Margot Fonteyn *Autobiography* W H Allen 1975. The autobiography of a great British ballerina. See also Keith Money *The Art of Margot Fonteyn* Dance Books 1975, Keith Money *Fonteyn: The Making of a Legend* Collins 1973, Elizabeth Frank *Margot Fonteyn* Chatto and Windus 1958, James Monahan *Fonteyn: A Study of the Ballerina in her Setting* Black 1957 and Gordon Anthony *Margot Fonteyn* Phoenix House 1950.

**7078** David Gillard *Beryl Grey: A Biography* W H Allen 1977. The first major study of the great ballerina and Festival Ballet administrator. See also Gordon Anthony *Beryl Grey* Phoenix House 1952.

**7079** Arnold Haskell *Balletomane at Large: An Autobiography* Heinemann 1972. Haskell was a teacher at the Royal Ballet School established after the Second World War and a leading ballet critic.

**7080** Elizabeth Salter *Helpmann: The Authorised Biography of Sir Robert Helpmann CBE* Angus and Robertson 1978. A biography of the Australian who as dancer, teacher and administrator made a massive contribution to post-war British ballet.

**7081** Edward Thorpe *Kenneth Macmillan: The Man and his Ballets* Hamilton 1985. A biography of the great post-war choreographer whose first major production was for the Royal Ballet in 1965.

**7082** Alicia Markova *Giselle and I* Barrie and Rockliff 1960. The title of this autobiography refers to the most famous role of the great ballerina. See also Anton Dolin *Markova: Her Life and Art* W H Allen 1953 and Gordon Anthony *Alicia Markova* Phoenix House 1951.

**7083** Margaret Morris *My Life in Movement* Owen 1969. An autobiography by the founder of the Margaret Morris School of Dancing.

**7084** Marie Rambert *Quicksilver: The Autobiography of Marie Rambert* Macmillan 1972. The autobiography of the founder of Ballet Rambert.

**7085** Lynn Seymour with Paul Gardner *Lynn: The Autobiography of Lynn Seymour* Granada 1984. The autobiography of the famous ballerina. See also Richard Austin *Lynn Seymour: An Authorised Biography* Angus and Robertson 1980.

**7086** Barbara Newman *Antoinette Sibley: Reflections of a Ballerina* Hutchinson 1986. A biography.

**7087** Christopher Sexton *Peggy Van Praagh: A Life of Dance* Macmillan 1985. Van Praagh was important in the development of post-war ballet first as a dancer and then as a teacher, and had a leading role in the development of the Sadler's Wells, now Royal, Ballet.

(b) Popular Music

*(i) General*

**7088** Leslie Drow *Directory of Popular Music 1900–1965* Peterson 1975. A massive and reliable source of information. It supplies chronological lists of songs published since 1900 and of musicals for stage and screen.

**7089** Paul Gambaccini, Tim Rice and Jo Rice *British Hit Singles* 7th ed, Guinness Books 1989. An illustrated guide to hit singles since 1952 arranged alphabetically according to the name of the recording artist or group. It is well organized and indexed. A different approach to the same subject is taken in the unindexed compilation of record charts, Tony Jasper *British Record Charts 1955–1982* 4th ed, Blandford Press 1982.

**7090** Tim Rice *et al The Guinness Hit Albums* 2nd ed, Guinness Superlatives 1986. An illustrated guide to hit albums since 1958 arranged alphabetically according to the name of the recording artist or group.

**7091** Sheila Tracy *Who's Who in Popular Music: The British Music Scene* World's Work 1984.

**7092** Paul Taylor *Popular Music Since 1955: A Critical Guide to the Literature* Mansell 1985. An excellent bibliography, which perhaps concentrates particularly on rock music. It is both well indexed and well and extensively annotated. The classification system is helpful as are the biographical notes.

**7093** Bert Muirhead (comp) *The Record Producers File: A Directory of Rock Album Producers 1962–1984* Blandford 1984.

**7094** Edward Lee *Music of the People: A Study of Popular Music in Great Britain* Barrie and Jenkins 1970. The second half of this general history is on the development of popular music in the twentieth century, the extent of American influence on this music and on the establishment reactions to it. Iain Chambers *Urban Rhythms: Pop Music and Popular Culture* Macmillan 1985 is a chronologically arranged cultural history of popular, and particularly of rock music, in the post-war period which attempts to place it in its social and political context. The development of popular music in the post-war period in Britain and the effects of stardom are examined with case studies and statistics in the useful survey, Michael Cable *The Pop Music Inside Out* W H Allen 1977.

**7095** Charlie Gillett *The Sound of the City: The Rise of Rock and Roll* revised ed, Souvenir Press 1983. This is a classic history of rock up to 1971. Only the last part deals with British bands.

**7096** Peter Gammond *A Guide to Popular Music* Phoenix 1960. A survey of the popular music scene in the 1950s by an insider. The emphasis is on dance bands and musicals rather than on the still novel rock music which arrived in the course of the decade from America.

**7097** George Melly *Revolt Into Style: The Pop Arts in Britain* Allen Lane 1970. A perceptive analysis of the evolution of a popular culture associated with popular music styles in the 1950s and 1960s by a leading jazz performer and critic. It remains an essential work, as is Richard Middleton *Pop Music and the Blues: A Study of the Relationship and its Significance* Gollancz 1972 on the importance of the influence of the blues on rock in the 1960s.

**7098** Derek Jewell *The Popular Voice: A Musical Record of the 60s and 70s* Sphere 1980. A collection of pieces from two decades as a jazz and popular music critic which provides a good outline of trends in the period, albeit with a bias towards jazz music.

**7099** Tony Jasper *The 70s: A Book of Records* Macdonald Futura 1980. A reference guide to the popular music scene in the 1970s. It includes essays on developments in the 1970s, a chronology, bibliography, filmography and discography and a good survey of the music press. John van der Kinte *Roxeventies: Popular Music in Britain 1970–79* Kawabata Press 1982 is a short but illuminating essay on trends in the 1970s.

## (ii) Rock

There are a number of studies of particular groups and artists listed below. In addition there are numerous pieces of fan- orientated material which, whilst providing some sort of insight into the sociology of the rock scene, are of strictly limited value to the historian. These have therefore been excluded. See also the sections on the record industry and on youth culture.

**7100** Nick Logan and Bob Woffinden (eds) *The Illustrated Encyclopedia of Rock* 3rd ed, Salamander 1982. A disappointing update of the standard reference work, particularly for the British rock scene. It is alphabetically arranged by artist and musical form. Each entry supplies well written notes and discographies.

**7101** William York *Who's Who in Rock Music* Barker 1982. The most complete biographical reference guide, even if it has something of an American bias as well as various omissions.

**7102** Charlie Gillett (ed) *Rockfile* Pictorial Presentations 1972. This also appeared, published by Panther, in 1974–8. It included useful historical and sociological essays surveying the recording business and various trends in the music and youth culture. It also supplied useful statistics. The *Rock Yearbook* 1981– Virgin Books 1980– has since become the standard annual reference work. It is well illustrated and includes a chronology of the previous year, a review of the current situation and trends in most areas of the music, as well as statistics and reviews of relevant books, films and albums.

**7103** John Tobler and Peter Frame *25 Years of Rock* Hamlyn 1980. An outline history 1955–80 of the impact of rock on the popular music scene. Each chapter covers a different year.

**7104** Simon Frith *Sound Effects: Youth, Leisure and the Politics of Rock* Constable 1983. A well regarded study focusing on rock, the record industry and youth culture in contemporary Britain. It is both a detailed analysis of the music industry in all its aspects from the musicians to the disc jockeys and music press and an in-depth examination of the impact of the music on cultural attitudes. Malcolm Doney *Summer in the City: Rock Music and Way of Life* Lion 1978 is a short survey of the growth of rock music and its influence on youth culture. It provides an interesting analysis of this from a far from intrusive Christian standpoint.

**7105** Peter Leslie *FAB: The Anatomy of a Phenomenon* MacGibbon and Kee 1965. An early attempt to seriously examine the relationship between the music, fashion and teenage culture. It still offers useful insights into the scene in the early 1960s and provides good information about the rock industry and the youth subcultures at this time. It includes case studies on Lonnie Donegan, Tommy Steele, Adam Faith, Cliff Richard and the Beatles.

**7106** Richard Mabey *The Pop Process* Hutchinson Education 1969. A sociology of the fashion, music, style, audience, industry, and music press of the rock world in the late 1960s, mostly in Britain. It also looks at the subcultures associated with it such as the Hippies, the Mods and the Teddy Boys.

**7107** Jeremy Sandford and Ron Reid *Tomorrow's People* Jerome Publishing 1974. A brief outline of the history of pop festivals, which started in Britain in the 1950s is here followed by a detailed analysis of the festivals held 1967–73. It is well illustrated sociological analysis.

**7108** Nicholas Schaffner *British Invasion: From the First Wave to the New Wave* McGraw-Hill 1982. An excellent account of the impact of British rock music in

America since the arrival of the Beatles in the 1960s. It is in fact best on the initial impact in the 1960s.

**7109** Dave Rodgers *Rock'n'Roll* Routledge and Kegan Paul 1982. A history of rock'n'roll music in Britain, its initial impact in the 1950s, the Teddy Boys and the revival of rock'n'roll in the 1970s.

**7110** Bob Groom *The Blues Revival* Studio Vista 1971. This traces the growth of the blues in Britain and especially of the blues revival of the 1950s and 1960s which had so much influence on the rock scene of the 1960s.

**7111** Chris May and Tim Phillips *British Beat* Socion Books 1974. An account of the development of the beat scene from its origins on Merseyside in the period 1962–7 organized by geographical areas.

**7112** Simon Frith and Howard Horne *Art into Pop* Methuen 1987. This study starts from the observation that a large number of British rock musicians since the 1960s have started off in art school and examines the cross-fertilization between art and rock over the ensuing period. It argues that the success of British rock is partly because of this art-conscious input of style and image. It goes on to examine the influence of this not just on the music and its packaging but on rock culture in general.

**7113** Julie Burchill and Tony Parsons *The Boy Looked At Johnny: The Obituary of Rock and Roll* Pluto 1978. A short and cynical study of the punk rock of the mid–1970s.

**7114** Dave Hill *Designer Boys and Material Girls: Manufacturing the '80s Pop Dream* Blandford Press 1986. Studies of the music, videos, packaging and theatrical style of groups of the early 1980s, including the Police, Wham!, Eurythmics, Madness, Spandau Ballet, Duran Duran, Paul Weller, Howard Jones, the Thompson Twins, Elvis Costello, the Human League, Frankie Goes To Hollywood and Culture Club. It includes discographies.

**7115** David Widgery *Beating Time: Riot'n'Race'n'Rock'n'Roll* Chatto and Windus 1986. An illustrated account of the Rock Against Racism movement which rose out of the Anti-Nazi League's confrontations with the National Front in the 1970s.

**7116** Gary Johnson *The Story of Oi: A View from the Dead-End of the Street* Babylon Books 1981. A rather short and superficial account of Oi!; skinhead music which is characterised by aggressive, nihilistic and often overtly racism vocals and a toneless wall of sound.

**7117** Allen J Weiner (ed) *The Beatles: A Recording History* McFarland 1986. The Beatles have inspired a plethora of reference books and material, of which this discography is one of the most useful. Carol D Terry *Here, There and Everywhere: The First International Beatles Bibliography 1962–1982* Pierion, Ann Arbor, Michigan 1985 is both useful for tracing the extensive literature on the group and for assessing their global impact. Mark Lewisohn *The Beatles: 25 Years in the Life* Sidgwick and Jackson 1987 is a chronology of the Beatles and of the activities of its former members since the group split up in 1970. Philip Norman *Shout! The True Story of the Beatles* Corgi 1982 is the best study of the group, although there are some minor inaccuracies. Geoffrey Stokes *The Beatles* W H Allen 1988 is a useful account which reassesses some of the myths about the group. See also Howard A DeWitt *The Beatles: Untold Tales* Horizon, Fremont, California 1985. Hunter Davies *The Beatles: The Authorised Biography* revised ed, Mayflower 1978 is an inadequate revision of the useful study which he originally published with Heinemann in 1968 when the Beatles were at the height of their fame. Elizabeth Thomson and David Gutman (eds) *The Lennon Companion: Twenty-Five Years of Comment* Macmillan 1987 is a collection of new articles and of reprints of important critical essays on the Beatles' music from the 1960s and 1970s. It also supplies a comprehensive bibliography and discography on the Beatles and their subsequent careers. Geoffrey Guiliano *The Beatles: A Celebration* Sidgwick and Jackson 1986 is a coffee table book on the group. Peter Brown *The Love You Make: An Inside Story of the Beatles* Macmillan 1983 is a candid, not to mention explicit, inside story of the group by the former manager of their business affairs which gets behind the wholesome image they tended to project, particularly in the early years. The tangled story of the Apple Corporation that the Beatles set up is told in-depth in the insider account by Richard DiLello *The Longest Cocktail Party* Charisma Books 1973. On Apple see also Peter McCabe and Robert D Schonfield *Apple to the Core: The Unmaking of the Beatles* Martin Brian and O'Keefe 1977. The failure of Apple is also covered in detail in John Blake *All You Needed Was Love: The Beatles after the Beatles* Hamlyn 1981. This dates the beginning of the end from the death of Brian Epstein in 1967 and examines in-depth both the break-up of the group and the lives of each one of them since. It is a good study. Ray Coleman *Brian Epstein: The Man Who Made the Beatles* Viking 1989 is an excellent biography of the man who managed the Beatles through their early successes. There are a number of biographies of John Lennon, the Beatle who was murdered in 1980. The most recent is the acclaimed study by Albert Goodman, *The Lives of John Lennon* Bantam Press 1988. Another well regarded biography is Ray Coleman *John Winston Lennon* 2v, Sidgwick and Jackson 1984. The first volume covers his life 1940–66 and the second 1967–80. Another biography is Jan Weiner *Come Together: John Lennon in his Time* Faber 1985. Cynthia Lennon *A Twist of Lennon* Star 1978 is a useful memoir of her life as

Lennon's first wife. Another memoir is Julia Baird with Geoffrey Guiliano *John Lennon: My Brother* Grafton 1988. On the other leading songwriter in the Beatles, Paul McCartney, see Chet Flippo *McCartney: The Biography* Sidgwick and Jackson 1988 and Chris Salewicz *McCartney: The Definitive Biography* St Martins, New York 1986. George Harrison *I, Me, Mine* Genesis Publications 1980 is the autobiography of another member of the band.

7118   Peter and Leni Gillman *Alias David Bowie* Hodder and Stoughton 1986. A well regarded biography. See also Jerry Hopkins *Bowie* Macmillan 1985, Henry Edwards and Tony Zametta *Stardust: The David Bowie Story* McGraw-Hill 1986 and Kerry Juby *David Bowie* Midas Books 1982. Dave Thompson *David Bowie: Moonage Daydream* Plexus 1987 is a well illustrated coffee table book.

7119   Kerry Juby *Kate Bush – The Whole Story* Sidgwick and Jackson 1988. A good biography and assessment of her music.

7120   Ray Coleman *Survivor: The Authorised Biography of Eric Clapton* Sidgwick and Jackson 1985. A study of the celebrated blues guitarist. See also John Pidgeon *Eric Clapton: A Biography* Panther 1976.

7121   Dave Rimmer *Like Punk Never Happened: Culture Club and the New Pop* Faber 1985. An account of the rise of Culture Club and new romantic music in the early 1980s.

7122   Barbarian, Steve Sutherland and Robert Smith *The Cure: Ten Imaginary Years* Zomba Books 1988. An illustrated account of the group.

7123   Mike Oldfield *Dire Straits* Sidgwick and Jackson 1983. A good study.

7124   Spencer Bright *Peter Gabriel: An Authorised Biography* Sidgwick and Jackson 1988. An in-depth biography of the former lead singer with Genesis who has pursued a successful solo career since 1975.

7125   Bob Geldof *Is That It?* Sidgwick and Jackson 1986. The acclaimed autobiography of the Irish singer and leader of the Irish band the Boomtown Rats. It deals both with the rock world and with his efforts to raise money for famine victims in Ethiopia in the 1980s.

7126   Armonado Gallo *Genesis: Evolution of a Rockband* Sidgwick and Jackson 1978. An illustrated study.

7127   Barry Toberman *Elton John: A Biography* Weidenfeld and Nicolson 1988.

7128   Johney Rogers *The Kinks: The Sound and the Fury* Elm Tree 1984. The first substantial study of an underrated band who pioneered heavy rock and concept albums in the 1960s.

7129   Howard Mylett *Led Zeppelin* 3rd ed, Panther 1981. See also Stephen Davis *Hammer of the Gods: The Led Zeppelin Saga* Morrow, New York 1985.

7130   Lulu *Lulu: Her Autobiography* Granada 1985. The autobiography of the Scottish singer.

7131   Ray Coleman *Gary Numan: The Authorized Biography* Sidgwick and Jackson 1982. A biography of one of the prime exponents of the synthesizer in the late 1970s and early 1980s.

7132   Cliff Richard *Which One's Cliff? The Autobiography* Coronet 1981. A useful autobiography of a figure who has been consistently successful since the 1950s which also covers his film and television career. Biographies include John Tobler *25 Years of Cliff* Optimum 1983, Patrick Doncaster and Tony Jasper *Cliff* Sidgwick and Jackson 1981, Tony Jasper *Survivor: A Tribute to Cliff* Marshall Pickering 1989 and George Tremlett *The Cliff Richard Story* Futura 1975. See also [7136].

7133   Mary Laverne Dimmick *The Rolling Stones: An Annotated Bibliography* revised ed, University of Pittsburgh Press, Pittsburgh 1979. This annotates 455 items, mostly articles, written 1962–77. It also provides some scholarly essays on the group's history and a chronology. Philip Norman *The Stones* Elm Tree 1984 is a useful study of the group, though not up to the standard of the one he wrote on the Beatles. He has also written *The Life and Good Times of the Rolling Stones* Century 1989. Another major study of the group is Stanley Booth *The True Adventures of the Rolling Stones* Heinemann 1985. For other studies of the group see Tim Dowley *The Rolling Stones* Midas 1983, Dezo Hoffman *The Rolling Stones* Vermilion 1984, Robert Palmer *The Rolling Stones* Sphere 1984, George Tremlett *The Rolling Stones Story* White Lion Publishers 1976 and Philippe Bas Rabérin *Les Rolling Stones* Albin Michel, Paris 1972. An early view of the group is *Our Own Story by the Rolling Stones as we told it to Pete Goodman* Transworld Publishers 1964. Carey Schofield *Jagger* Methuen 1983 is a good biography of the Rolling Stones' lead singer. It is particularly useful in that it sets the group in the context of the blues revival in the 1950s and 1960s and of social trends and of the reaction of the establishment to the Rolling Stones in the 1960s. The life and death of group member, Brian Jones, is examined in Mandy Aftel *Death of a Rolling Stone: The Brian Jones Story* Sidgwick and Jackson 1982.

7134   Johney Rogan *Roxy Music: Style with Substance: Roxy's First Ten Years* Star Books 1982. A superior study of Roxy Music, one of the principal products of the glam rock of the early 1970s.

**7135** Fred and Judy Vermorel (ed) *The Sex Pistols: The Inside Story* Star Books 1978. This assembles plenty of material on the notorious punk band of the mid–1970s and on the hype, posturing and attitudes surrounding the punk phenomenon. Paul Taylor *Impresario: Malcolm MacLaren and the British New Wave* MIT Press, Cambridge, Massachusetts 1988 is the study of the man who, as their manager, was widely credited with masterminding their rise to infamy. He has since pursued an eclectic career within the music business.

**7136** Mike Read (ed) *The Story of the Shadows: An Autobiography* Elm Tree 1983. Transcripts of interviews with the most successful British band of the early 1960s, often in association with Cliff Richard (see [7132]). They split up and reformed, very successfully, in 1975. Bruce Welch *Rock'n'Roll: I Gave You the Best Years of My Life: A Life in the Shadows* Viking 1989 is the autobiography of a member of the group.

**7137** Lucy O'Brien *Dusty* Sidgwick and Jackson 1989. A biography of 1960s singing star Dusty Springfield.

**7138** John Shearlaw *Status Quo: The Authorised Biography* 2nd ed, Sidgwick and Jackson 1986. A bland biography of the unsophisticated band formed in 1962.

**7139** John Kennedy *Tommy Steele* Souvenir Press 1958. A biography published to capitalise on Steele's relative success in the 1950s at a time when he was being promoted as a British alternative to American rock imports.

**7140** Luke Crampton *Wham! The Official* Biography Virgin 1986. A glossy account of the successes of the pop group of the early 1980s. See also Johny Rogan *Wham! Confidential: The Death of a Supergroup* Omnibus 1987 and Darlene Fredericks *Wham!* Ballantine, New York 1985.

**7141** George Tremlett *The Who* Futura 1975. A short popular biography of a band whose importance in the development of British rock music does not seem to have won it much attention. See also Andrew Motion 'Kit' in his *The Lamberts: George, Constant and Kit* Chatto and Windus 1986 pp 261–76. Kit Lambert was the manager and producer of the Who.

**7142** Alan Clayson *Back in the High Life: A Biography of Steve Winwood* Sidgwick and Jackson 1988. Since working with the Spencer Davis Group, Traffic and the first supergroup, Blind Faith, in the 1960s Winwood has pursued a solo career.

**7143** Dan Hedges *Yes: The Authorised Biography* Sidgwick and Jackson 1981. A study of the group.

*(iii) Jazz and Jazz-Related Music*

**7144** D Kennington and D L Read *The Literature of Jazz* 2nd ed, Library Association 1980. An international bibliography with some annotation. It essentially only covers books on the subject. Bernhard Hefele *Jazz Bibliography* K G Saur 1981 is an international bibliography on jazz, blues, spiritual and ragtime music. It is poorly organized and unannotated.

**7145** David Boulton *Jazz in Britain* W H Allen 1958. A history. See also Jim Godbolt *A History of Jazz in Britain 1919–50* Quartet 1985.

**7146** Ian Carr *Music Outside: Contemporary Jazz in Britain* Latimer New Dimensions 1973. This well written study is based on lengthy interviews with the leading contemporary British musicians and composers. It includes a good bibliography.

**7147** Ivan Berg and Ian Yeomans *Trad: An Illustrated A to Z Who's Who of the British Traditional Jazz Scene* Foulsham 1962. A guide produced at the height of the popularity of the trad scene.

**7148** Leo Walker and Brian Rust *British Dance Bands* Storyville 1973. A study of the great dance bands which were at the height of their popularity in the 1940s. Ted Heath *Listen To My Music: An Autobiography* Muller 1957 is the autobiography of the leader of one of the best loved bands of the 1940s and 1950s.

**7149** Brian Bird *Skiffle: The Story of a Folk-Song with a Jazz-Beat* Hale 1958. The foreword to this study published at the height of the skiffle boom of the late 1950s is by its prime exponent, Lonnie Donegan. The book provides a concise history of jazz and its growth in Britain. It sees skiffle as emerging from jazz and as very much a British phenomenon. The style and nature of skiffle is defined. This is followed by potted biographies of the leading skiffle groups.

**7150** Graham Collier *Cleo and John: A Biography of the Dankworths* Quartet 1976. A good biography of the British jazz performer and his versatile wife.

**7151** Jim Godbolt *All This and 10%* Hale 1976. The autobiography of an important manager, especially in the jazz world. It includes useful reflections on the growth and impact of modern popular music in Britain.

**7152** Humphrey Lyttleton *I Play As I Please: The Memoirs of an Old Etonian Trumpeter* MacGibbon and

Kee 1954. A collection of amusing and interesting comments on the British jazz scene 1945–54. His *Second Chorus* MacGibbon 1958 takes the story up to 1958. See also his *Take It From The Top: An Autobiographical Scrapbook* Robson 1975.

**7153** George Melly *Owning Up* Weidenfeld and Nicolson 1965. The thoughtful reminiscences of the jazz singer and critic of the jazz scene in the 1950s. His *Rum, Bum and Concertina* Weidenfeld and Nicolson 1977 is a further volume of reminiscences.

**7154** Ronnie Scott *Some of My Best Friends are Blues* W H Allen 1979. Scott is one of the leading figures in the British jazz scene and the proprietor of the famous club in London in London which bears his name. On the club see also Benny Green *Jazz Decade: Ten Years at Ronnie Scott's* Kings Road Publishing 1969.

*(iv) Folk*

**7155** Douglas Neil Kennedy *English Folk Dancing Today and Yesterday* Bell 1964.

**7156** J R A MacKenzie 'Contemporary English Folk Music: The Social Context of Stylistic Change' Keele MA Thesis 1977. This examines the social and economic context of the revival of folk music since the 1950s.

**7157** Dave Laing *et al The Electric Muse: The Story of Folk into Rock* Eyre Methuen 1975. This concentrates on folk-rock in the US but the final quarter of the book looks at folk-rock in Britain from the revival of traditional folk music in the 1950s to the experimentation of Fairport Convention and Steeleye Span.

**7158** David Phillips *Jimmy Shand* D Winter and Sons 1976. A biography of the popular Scottish folk music artiste.

*(v) Other*

**7159** Cilla Black *Step Inside* Dent 1985. The autobiography of the singer.

**7160** Max Bygraves *After Thoughts* W H Allen 1988. The second volume of autobiography from the singer who started his successful career in the music halls in the early post-war years.

**7161** Andrea Kon *This Is My Song: Biography of Petula Clark* Comet 1984. A biography of the singer.

**7162** Tony Bernard Smith *Farewell Mr Blackpool: A Souvenir Tribute to Reginald Dixon* Cinema Organ Society 1985. A brief tribute to the cinema organist.

**7163** Val Doonican *The Special Years: An Autobiography* Elm Tree 1980. The autobiography of the Irish singer and television presenter.

**7164** Colin Macfarlane *Tom Jones: The Boy From Nowhere* W H Allen 1988. A biography of the Welsh-born singer.

**7165** Vera Lynn *Vocal Refrain: An Autobiography* W H Allen 1975. The singer's autobiography of her life in show business up to her television work in the 1970s.

## (4) Literature

(a) General

**7166** T H Howard-Hill *Bibliography of British Literary Bibliographies* 2nd ed, Clarendon 1987. An annotated, classified guide. David Daiches *Introduction to English Literature Vol 5: The Present Age from 1920* Cresset Press 1958 is a survey guide to the trends in the literature of the period which includes an extensive bibliography.

**7167** *Annual Bibliography of English Language and Literature* Modern Humanities Research Association 1962–. Before 1962 this was published by Cambridge University Press. A well organized guide to critical, historical, biographical and general writings on English language and literature. It covers English literature in the Commonwealth, Ireland and America as well as in Britain.

**7168** Stanley J Kunitz and Howard Haycraft (eds) *Twentieth Century Authors: A Biographical Dictionary of Modern Literature* H W Wilson, New York 1942. A good collection of full biographies (with appended bibliographies) of eminent contemporary authors. It concentrates on British and American writers. It is supplemented by Stanley J Kunitz with Vineta Colby (eds) *Twentieth Century Authors: First Supplement* H W Wilson, New York 1955. A further supplement covering those writers who came to prominence in the period mentioned in the title is John Wakeman (ed) *World Authors 1950–1970: A Companion Volume to Twentieth Century Authors* H W Wilson, New York 1975, as are the successor volumes, John Wakeman (ed) *World Authors 1970–1975* H W Wilson, New York 1980 and Vineta Colby (ed) *World Authors 1975–1980* H W Wilson, New York 1985.

**7169** *Contemporary Authors: A Bio-Bibliographical Guide to Current Authors and Their Work* 4v, Gale, Detroit, Michigan 1962–63. This bibliographical guide to critical and other writings on contemporary authors has subsequently been updated on a semi-annual basis.

**7170** Peter Scott, Bert Moore-Gilbert and Simon Edwards *Studies in a Fragmentary Culture: British Writing Since 1930* Macmillan 1987. A good study of trends in literature and the way in which literature has handled and reflected contemporary themes such as the end of empire or the break up of family life. A similar approach is taken in Hugh Kenner *A Sinking Island: The Modern British Writers* Barrie and Jenkins 1988, a powerful study of British literature since 1895 which sees national decline as having been paralleled by a loss of literary vision. Alan Sinfield (ed) *Society and Literature 1945–1970* Methuen 1983 presents essays on the reflection of social, religious and sexual themes in the various branches of literature in the post-war years. Harry Blamires *Twentieth Century English Literature* 2nd ed, Macmillan 1986 is a textbook history up to the 1980s which also tries to put the literature in its social and political context. It also features chronological tables. See also Alfred Charles Ward *Twentieth Century English Literature 1901–1960* Methuen 1964. The short section on post-war British literature in Walter Allen *Tradition and Dream: A Critical Survey of British and American Fiction From the 1920s to the Present Day* Penguin 1965 provides a good general account. There are some useful essays on themes such as the novel, poetry, drama, popular fiction and literary criticism, generally only covering the period 1900–60, in Bernard Bergonzi (ed) *History of Literature in the English Language Vol 7: The Twentieth Century* Barrie and Jenkins 1970. This includes a useful chronology. Another useful collection of essays is Boris Ford (ed) *A Guide to English Literature Vol 7: The Modern Age* Cassell 1964.

**7171** Richard Findlater *Author! Author! A Selection from The Author, the Journal of the Society of Authors Since 1890* Faber 1984. See also the history of the Society of Authors, Victor Bonham Carter *Authors by Profession* The Bodley Head 1984. Another literary organization is analysed in R A Wilford 'The PEN Club 1930–1950' *Journal of Contemporary History* 14 1979 pp 99–116. This examines this international association of left-leaning writers and intellectuals from an anglocentric perspective.

**7172** Andrew Sinclair *War Like a Wasp* Hamilton 1989. A study of literature in the 1940s. Andrew Sinclair (ed) *The War Decade* Hamilton 1989 is an accompanying anthology of the literature of what he feels has been an undeservedly neglected decade.

**7173** Harry Ritchie *Success Stories: Literature and the Media in England 1950–9* Faber 1988. The first attempt to reassess some of the myths about the literature of the 1950s. It argues that the Angry Young Men phenomenon to which commentators at the time pointed was to some extent a hype and demonstrates that the working class credentials of many of them were certainly suspect. A good contemporary assessment of the literature of the 1950s, and particularly of the attitudes of the Angry Young Men, is Kenneth Allsop *The Angry Decade: A Survey of the Cultural Revolt of the Nineteen-Fifties* Peter Owen 1958.

**7174** Ronald Hayman *The Novel Today 1967–1975* Longman 1976. A short study for the British Council.

**7175** J Morey '"The Movement": A Critical and Historical Study, with Particular Reference to Kingsley Amis, Donald Davie, Philip Larkin and John Wain' Birmingham M Litt Thesis 1979–80. The Movement was the general title given to a group of novelists and poets who emerged in the post-war period, though it was somewhat misleading, since there was little cohesion and no programme binding the group that was so described.

**7176** Efraim Sicher *Beyond Marginality: Anglo-Jewish Literature after the Holocaust* State University of New York Press, Albany, New York 1985. A study of post-war Anglo-Jewish literature. Authors covered include many of the most important figures in British literature of the period, such as Wolf Mankowitz, Arnold Wesker, Harold Pinter, Peter Shaffer, Frederick Raphael and Dannie Abse. It includes a useful bibliography.

**7177** D L Kirkpatrick (ed) *Contemporary Novelists* 4th ed, St James Press 1986. A collection of critical biographies of contemporary novelists, mainly British and American, with appended bibliographies. B Oldsey (ed) *British Novelists 1930–1959* 2v, Gale, Detroit, Michigan 1983 is a collection of full critical biographies of 59 writers with bibliographies and useful appendices.

**7178** Randall Stevenson *The British Novel Since the Thirties: An Introduction* Batsford 1986. A critical history. See also Harvey Curtis Webster *After The Trauma: Representative British Novelists Since 1920* University of Kentucky Press, Lexington, Kentucky 1970.

**7179** Neil McEwan *The Survival of the Novel: British Fiction in the Later Twentieth Century* Macmillan 1981. A vigorous and sympathetic argument for the main strengths of comtemporary British fiction. Rubin Rabinovitz *The Reaction Against Experimentation in the English Novel 1950–1960* Columbia University Press 1967 is a study mainly with reference to Kingsley Amis, Angus Wilson and C P Snow.

**7180** Margaret Crosland *Beyond The Lighthouse: English Women Novelists in the Twentieth Century* Constable 1987. A good study. The title refers to the story by Virginia Woolf. See also Elaine Showalter *A Literature of Their Own: British Women Novelists from Brönte to Lessing* Princeton University Press, Princeton, New Jersey 1977 and H Roberts 'Women and Fiction: A Sociological Study of British Fiction by and for Women Since the Turn of the Century' Sussex DPhil Thesis 1976.

**7181** Patrick Swinden *The English Novel of History and Society 1940–1980* Macmillan 1984. This incorporates studies of the work of Richard Hughes, Henry Green, Anthony Powell, Angus Wilson, Kingsley Amis and V S Naipaul.

**7182** J N McEwan 'Perspective in Historical Fiction by British Writers 1953–1983' Stirling PhD Thesis 1984. This concentrates on the historical novels of Mary Renault, John Fowles and William Golding.

**7183** David Rubin *After The Raj: British Novels of India Since 1947* University Press of New England, Hanover, New Hampshire 1986. A critical appraisal of British fictional portrayals of British India and adjustment to Indian independence, especially concentrating on *The Raj Quartet* of Paul Scott. Fictional accounts of imperial withdrawal elsewhere are examined in S A Arab 'The Novel as Chronicle of Decolonisation in Africa' Sussex DPhil Thesis 1979. Post-war writings about empire, in the context of the work of the popular novelist, Nevil Shute, are analysed in Donald Lammers 'Nevil Shute and the Decline of the "Imperial Idea" in Literature' *Journal of British Studies* 16 1977 pp 121–42. This is an excellent analysis of the impossibility of writing about empire, in the post-war period, in the way John Buchan had done, and of the varying reactions, as portrayed in their novels, to imperial retreat of novelists as varied as Alec Waugh, John Masters, Nicholas Montserrat, Anthony Burgess, Ian Fleming and Nevil Shute.

**7184** M A Marshment 'Ideology and Fictional Form: A Study of the treatment of the Ideology of Racism in Contemporary British Popular Fiction' Birmingham PhD Thesis 1976–7.

**7185** Kingsley Amis *The James Bond Dossier* Cape 1965. A study of the genre of the spy thriller. The career of Ian Fleming's creation of James Bond as a popular hero from the 1950s to the 1980s is comprehensively analysed in Tony Bennett and Janet Woollacott *Bond and Beyond: The Political Career of a Popular Hero* Macmillan 1987. This examines not only the Fleming novels and the films which they have given rise to but also the representation of Bond in the press, fanzines and soft pornography.

**7186** John M Reilly (ed) *Twentieth Century Crime and Mystery Writers* 2nd ed, St James Press 1985. A collec-

tion of short critical biographies with appended bibliographies.

**7187** David R Mesher 'Science and Technology in Modern British Fiction: The Two Cultures' *Essays in Arts and Sciences* 13 1984 pp 73–82. A study of attitudes towards science and technology.

**7188** Curtis C Smith (ed) *Twentieth Century Science Fiction Writers* 2nd ed, St James Press 1986. A collection of short critical biographies with appended bibliographies. It includes a short section on what it terms fantasy writers, including figures such as Tolkien. See also D J Berry 'The Science Fiction Novel 1930–1970: An Analysis of some Major Themes' Birmingham MA Thesis 1973–4 and Brian Stapleford *Scientific Romance in Britain 1890–1950* Fourth Estate 1985.

**7189** J S Ryan 'Modern English Myth-Makers: An Examination of the Imaginative Writings of Charles Williams, C S Lewis and J R R Tolkien' Cambridge PhD Thesis 1967–8. A study of the writings of this Oxford circle. Williams died in 1945 but the other continued to flourish in the post-war period. See also A Swinfen 'The Sub-Creative Art: An Examination of some Aspects of Fantasy, Principally in English Children's Literature 1945–1975' Dundee PhD Thesis 1979.

**7190** James Vinson (ed) *Twentieth Century Western Writers* Macmillan 1982. A collection of short critical biographies of authors (including British authors) of wild west stories with appended bibliographies.

**7191** James Vinson (ed) *Twentieth Century Romance and Gothic Writers* Macmillan 1982. A collection of short critical biographies of authors of romantic stories and historical romances with appended bibliographies.

**7192** D L Kirkpatrick (ed) *Twentieth Century Children's Writers* 2nd ed, Macmillan 1983. A collection of biographies examining the life and work of children's writers with full accompanying bibliographies. See also Frank Eyre *British Children's Books in the Twentieth Century* revised ed, Longmans 1971. Mary Cadogan and Patricia Craig *You're a Brick Angela: A New Look at Girl's Fiction 1839–1975* Gollancz 1976 is a history of schoolgirls' popular fiction and its portrayal of adolescent feelings and fantasies.

**7193** Stuart Laing *Representations of Working Class Life 1957–1964* Macmillan 1986. John Lehmann in the 1950s proclaimed the death of working class literature just before its remarkable flowering in the late 1950s. This study of the gritty social realism of the period also looks at the films and television representations of working class life of the period. See also D Craig 'The British Working Class Novel Today' *Zeitschrift fur Anglistik* *und Amerikanistik* 11 1963 pp 29–41. See also [5545, 7342 and 7394].

**7194** David Smith *Socialist Propaganda in the Twentieth Century British Novel* Macmillan 1978. A useful history and criticism of an interesting strain in the twentieth century British novel. Unfortunately it does not venture far beyond Doris Lessing's *Retreat to Innocence* published in 1956, and while good on the political context is not quite as good on the literary context. On socialist writers see also R A Wilford 'The Political Involvement and Ideological Alignments of Left-Wing Literary Intellectuals in Britain 1930–1950' Wales PhD Thesis 1974–6.

**7195** Dennis Vannatta (ed) *The English Short Story 1945–1980: A Critical History* Twayne, Boston, Massachusetts 1985.

**7196** M E Gingerich *Contemporary Poetry in America and England 1950–1975: A Guide to Information Sources* Gale, Detroit, Michigan 1983. This useful bibliography has an American bias.

**7197** James Vinson and D L Kirkpatrick (eds) *Contemporary Poets* 4th ed, St James Press 1985. A collection of short critical biographies with full bibliographies. V B Sherry Jr (ed) *Poets of Great Britain and Ireland 1945–1960* Gale, Detroit, Michigan 1984. This features critical biographical studies with appended bibliographies. The previous volume, D E Stansford (ed) *British Poets 1914–1945* Gale, Detroit, Michigan 1983 also includes many figures who remained active into the post-war period. Anthony Thwaite *Twentieth Century English Poetry* Heinemann Education 1978 is a short account, mainly through the medium of short critical biographies of most of the major poets of the century. Michael Schmidt *A Reader's Guide to Fifty Modern English Poets* Barnes and Noble 1979 is a collection of critical biographies, including studies of many lesser known poets. Each entry includes a full bibliography.

**7198** Donald Davie *Under Briggflatts* Carcanet 1989. A history of British poetry since 1960 which provides a mordant and compelling account of the social climate to which the poems were a response and a call for more attention to modern poetry and to neglected poets. Martin Booth *British Poetry 1964 to 1984: Driving Through The Barricades* Routledge and Kegan Paul 1985 is partly a history and partly a work of literary criticism. Anthony Thwaite *Poetry Today – A Critical Guide to British Poetry 1960–84* Longman 1985 is a British Council guide. Peter Jones and Michael Schmidt (eds) *British Poetry Since 1970: A Critical Survey* Carcanet 1980 is partly an anthology and partly a critical survey of developments and the new poets who emerged during the decade. It regards the 1970s as a decade of low achieve-

ment. Alan Robinson *Instabilities in Contemporary British Poetry* Macmillan 1988 is a study of poetry in the 1970s and 1980s in the context of literary theory, social conditions, the growth of feminism and other cultural influences. An earlier short study is Derek Stanford *Movements in English Poetry 1900–1958* Centaur Press 1959.

**7199** Eric Walter White (ed) *Poetry Book Society: The First Twenty Five Years* Poetry Book Society 1979. This society was set up to advise on Arts Council poetry policy. The book largely consists of a selection of contributions to the society's publications.

**7200** Brian Finney *The Inner I: British Literary Autobiography in the Twentieth Century* Oxford University Press 1985. A literary study.

**7201** Humphrey Carpenter *The Brideshead Generation: Evelyn Waugh and his Friends* Weidenfeld and Nicolson 1989. An excellent piece of literary and social history. Figures examined in this study, in addition to Waugh, include Harold Acton, John Betjeman, Cyril Connolly, Maurice Bowra, Graham Greene, Lord Berners, Nancy Mitford, Anthony Powell, Diana Cooper and Randolph Churchill.

**7202** Peter Parker *Ackerley: A Life of J R Ackerley* Constable 1989. J R Ackerley was an unprolific writer and friend of E M Forster who died in 1967. Francis King (ed) *My Sister and Myself: The Diaries of J R Ackerley* Hutchinson 1982 is a selection from Ackerley's diaries 1948–57.

**7203** Harold Acton *Memories of an Aesthete* Methuen 1948 and *More Memoirs of an Aesthete* Methuen 1970. The memoirs of a man of letters and friend of many leading writers and artists.

**7204** Richard Eugene Smith *Richard Aldington* Twayne, Boston, Massachusetts 1977. A short study of the author's life and work, which includes a brief chronology. See also Norman Gates *A Checklist of the Letters of Richard Aldington* Feffer and Simons 1977 and *Richard Aldington: Literary Lifelines: The Richard Aldington-Lawrence Durrell Correspondence* Faber 1981.

**7205** Walter Allen *As I Walked Down New Grub Street: Memories of a Writing Life* Heinemann 1981. The memoirs of an author, man of letters and critic.

**7206** Dale Salwak *Kingsley Amis: A Reference Guide* G K Hall 1978. A listing of nearly 1,800 items about Amis. Paul Gardner *Kingsley Amis* Twayne, Boston, Massachusetts 1981 is a critical biography which includes a brief chronology of the author's life and work and a bibliography.

**7207** B C Bloomfield and Edward Mandelson *W H Auden: A Bibliography 1924–1969* 2nd ed, University Press of Virginia, Charlottesville, Virginia 1972. Humphrey Carpenter *W H Auden: A Biography* Allen and Unwin 1981 is a study of the poet. Charles Osborne *W H Auden: The Life of a Poet* Eyre Methuen 1980 is a good chronologically organized biography. A L Rowse *The Poet Auden: A Personal Memoir* Methuen 1987 is a memoir which particularly focuses on Auden's period as Professor of Poetry at Oxford.

**7208** Martha Fodasti *George Barker* Twayne, Boston, Massachusetts 1969. A short critical biography of the poet which includes a chronology and bibliography.

**7209** Herbert Ernest Bates *An Autobiography* 3v, Michael Joseph 1967–72. The autobiography of the novelist.

**7210** David Cecil *Max: A Biography* Constable 1964. The official biography of Max Beerbohm. Rupert Hart-Davis (ed) *Letters of Max Beerbohm 1892–1956* Murray 1988 is a useful selection.

**7211** Patrick Taylor-Martin *John Betjeman: His Life and Work* Allen Lane 1983. A sympathetic study and biography of the poet laureate 1969–84. See also Derek Stanford *John Betjeman: A Study* Neville Spearman 1961.

**7212** B J Kirkpatrick *A Bibliography of Edmund Blunden with a Personal Introduction by Rupert Hart-Davis* Clarendon 1979. A massive bibliography of the writings by and about the poet and his work. Thomas Mallon *Edmund Blunden* Twayne, Boston, Massachusetts 1983 is a short critical biography which includes a chronology and bibliography.

**7213** Barbara Storey *Enid Blyton: A Biography* Hodder and Stoughton 1974. A study of Blyton's life and her children's stories. Blyton's work has been loved by children and reviled by adults the world over. Blyton and the strong reactions aroused, which even included attempts to exclude her books from public libraries, are examined in Sheila G Ray *The Blyton Phenomenon: The Controversy Surrounding the World's Most Successful Children's Writer* Deutsch 1982.

**7214** J'nan M Sellery *Elizabeth Bowen: A Descriptive Bibliography* Texas University Press 1977. An annotated guide to critical examinations of her novels. Victoria Glendinning *Elizabeth Bowen: Portrait of a Writer* Weidenfeld and Nicolson 1977 is a good biography.

**7215** Dale Salwak *John Braine and John Wain: A Reference Guide* G K Hall 1980. A bibliography of writings on the two novelists' work. James W Lee *John Braine* Twayne, Boston, Massachusetts 1968 is a short critical biography which includes a chronology of his life and work.

**7216** Agatha Bailey *Vera Brittain* Penguin 1987. A biography of the writer who died in 1970. Vera Brittain *Testament of Experience: An Autographical Story of the Years 1925–1950* Macmillan 1957 is a good autobiography.

**7217** Carroll F Terrell (ed) *Basil Bunting: Man and Poet* National Poetry Foundation, Orone, Maine 1981. A short biography, critical essays and a bibliography are collected in this volume.

**7218** Anthony Burgess *Little Wilson and Big God* Heinemann 1987. The first part of the novelist's autobiography. A A De Vitis *Anthony Burgess* Twayne, Boston, Massachusetts 1972 and Samuel Coale *Anthony Burgess* Ungar, New York 1981 are short critical biographies which include useful chronologies. They also provide intelligent insights into the influence of Burgess's experiences in colonial outposts 1943–60 on his subsequent writings.

**7219** Peter Alexander *Roy Campbell: A Critical Biography* Oxford University Press 1982. A good study of the life and work of the poet which corrects many of the distortions in Campbell's last autobiographical work published just five years before his death, *Light On a Dark Horse* Hollis and Carter 1951.

**7220** Alan Bishop *Gentleman Rider: A Biography of Joyce Cary* Michael Joseph 1989. A biography of the novelist who is especially noted for his novels on British power and decolonization in Africa. Malcolm Foster *Joyce Cary: A Biography* Michael Joseph 1968 is another good biography. Dennis Hall *Joyce Cary: A Reappraisal* Macmillan 1983 is a re-examination of Cary's work which attempts to get past the novelist's self-explanations. R W Noble *Joyce Cary* Oliver and Boyd 1973 is a chronological study of Cary's novels and the development of his narrative skills which seeks to summarize his achievement and his place in twentieth century British literature. Another critical work is Barbara Fisher *Joyce Cary: The Writer and His Theme* Smythe 1980.

**7221** Harry Chambers (ed) *Causley at 70* Peterloo Poets 1987. An appreciation of and tribute to the poet Charles Causley.

**7222** Agatha Christie *An Autobiography* Collins 1977. A life of the crime and mystery writer. The fullest biography is Janet Morgan *Agatha Christie: A Biography* Collins 1984. See also Charles Osborne *The Life and Crimes of Agatha Christie* Collins 1982. Mary S Wagoner *Agatha Christie* Twayne, Boston, Massachusetts 1986 is a short critical biography which includes a bibliography and a chronology.

7223 Arthur C Clarke *Astounding Days: A Science Fictional Autobiography* Gollancz 1989. The autobiography of the doyen of science fiction writers who was also the first, in 1945, to demonstrate the possibility of geostationary satellites. There are also some semi-autobiographical passages in Clarke's *The View from Serendip* Gollancz 1978.

7224 Hilary Spurning *Secrets of a Woman's Heart: The Later Life of Ivy Compton-Burnett 1920–1969* Hodder and Stoughton 1984. A good biography of the novelist. See also Elizabeth Sprigge *The Life of Ivy Compton-Burnett* Gollancz 1973. Cecily Craig *Ivy Compton-Burnett: A Memoir* Garnstone Press 1972 is a memoir by Compton-Burnett's typist 1945–69. Kay Dick *Ivy and Stevie: Ivy Compton-Burnett and Stevie Smith: Conversations and Reflections* Duckworth 1971 is a collection of interviews held with the novelist and the poet in the 1960s.

7225 Michael Shelden *Friends of Promise: Cyril Connolly and the World of Horizon* Hamilton 1989. A critical study of the novelist's work. Stephen Spender *Cyril Connolly: A Memoir* Tagara Press 1978 is a brief tribute. Cyril Connolly *Enemies of Promise* Deutsch 1973 is an autobiography which was originally published in 1948. Some of Connolly's correspondence is collected in Noel Blakiston (ed) *A Romantic Friendship: The Letters of Cyril Connolly to Noel Blakiston* Constable 1975.

7226 Mary Cadogan *Richmal Crompton: The Woman Behind William* Allen and Unwin 1986. A serious, well-written biography of the author of the popular William books for children.

7227 Anne Chisholm *Nancy Cunard* Sidgwick and Jackson 1979. A biography of the radical poet and author. See also Hugh Ford (ed) *Nancy Cunard: Brave Poet, Indomitable Rebel* Chilton Book Company, Radnor, Pennsylvania 1968.

7228 Roald Dahl *Boy: Tales of Childhood* Cape 1984. An autobiographical account of the writer's youth up to the start of his first job.

7229 Donald Davie *Trying to Explain* Carcanet 1980. A collection of essays which includes some autobiographical material. The life and work of the poet is also commented on in the collection of critical essays, George Dekker (ed) *Donald Davie and the Responsibilities of Literature* Carcanet 1983.

7230 Joseph N Riddell *C Day Lewis* Twayne, Boston, Massachusetts 1971. A short critical biography including a chronology and bibliography. Day Lewis's is a difficult career to assess. A radical poet in the 1930s, in association with Auden and Spender, in the post-war period his reputation declined and so did his Left-Wing commitment. In 1968 he became poet laureate. C Day Lewis *The Buried Day* Chatto and Windus 1960 is an autobiography.

7231 Doris Ross *Walter de la Mare* Twayne, Boston, Massachusetts 1966. A short critical biography of the poet with a chronology and bibliography.

7232 Patric Dickinson *The Good Minute: An Autobiographical Study* Gollancz 1965. The autobiography of the poet.

7233 Cecil Woolf *A Bibliography of Norman Douglas* Hart-Davies 1954. The best biography is Mark Holloway *Norman Douglas: A Biography* Secker and Warburg 1976. Nancy Cunard *Grand Man: Memories of Norman Douglas* Secker and Warburg 1954 is a personal memoir of the writer and man of letters who died in 1952. For other studies of Douglas see Ralph Donald Lindeman *Norman Douglas* Twayne, New York 1965 and Ian Greenlees *Norman Douglas* Longmans 1957.

7234 Lynn Veach Sadler *Margaret Drabble* Twayne, Boston, Massachusetts 1986. A short critical biography of the novelist with a chronology and bibliography. A similar, balanced study of her life and of her work and critical acclaim is Joanne Creighton *Margaret Drabble* Methuen 1985.

7235 Richard Kelly *Daphne du Maurier* Twayne, Boston, Massachusetts 1987. A short critical biography of the novelist with a chronology and bibliography.

7236 Ronald Frederick Henry Duncan *All Men Are Islands: An Autobiography* Hart-Davis 1964. The subsequent volumes of autobiography by this writer, poet and dramatist are *How To Make Enemies* Hart-Davis 1968 and *Obsessed: A Third Volume of Autobiography* Michael Joseph 1977.

7237 John A Weigel *Lawrence Durrell* Twayne, Boston, Massachusetts 1964. A short critical biography of the novelist with a chronology and bibliography. George Wickes (ed) *Lawrence Durrell, Henry Miller: A Private Correspondence* Faber 1965 is a selection of the letters which passed between Durrell and the American playwright up to 1959. Further relevant correspondence is collected in [7204].

7238 Beatrice Ricks (comp) *T S Eliot: A Bibliography of Secondary Works* Scarecrow 1980. A good, classified bibliography of over 4,000 entries covering all aspects of Eliot's work. See also Ronald Gallup *T S Eliot: A Bibliography* revised ed, Faber 1952. There is also a comprehensive bibliography of Eliot's works in Caroline Behr *T S Eliot: A Chronology of his Life and Works* Macmillan 1983. Eliot, though most remembered as a poet, was also a dramatist and publisher (in the firm of Faber and Faber). Lyndall Gordon *Eliot's New Life* Oxford University Press 1988 is a masterly biography of Eliot's mature years. Peter Ackroyd *T S Eliot* Hamilton 1984 is another good biography. Allen Tate (ed) *T S Eliot: The Man and his Work* Chatto and Windus 1967 is a collection of memorial essays in which friends and colleagues reflect upon his life and work. See also F B Pinion *A T S Eliot Companion: Life and Works* Macmillan 1985.

**7239** Roma Gill (ed) *William Empson: The Man and His Work* Routledge and Kegan Paul 1974. A collection of tributes and reflections on his life and work by friends and acquaintances.

**7240** John George Pearson *The Life of Ian Fleming* Cape 1966. A biography of the creator of James Bond.

**7241** Sanford Sternlicht *C S Forester* Twayne, Boston, Massachusetts 1981. A biography and study of the work of the popular historical novelist which includes a chronology and bibliography.

**7242** B J Kirkpatrick *A Bibliography of E M Forster* 2nd ed, Clarendon 1985. A guide to writings by and about the novelist and his work. Francis King *E M Forster* Thames and Hudson 1978 is a useful biography. See also John Colmer *E M Forster: The Personal Voice* Routledge and Kegan Paul 1975 and P N Furbank *E M Forster Vol 2: Polycrates' Ring (1914–1970)* Secker and Warburg 1978. Also of use is Mary Iago and P N Furbank (eds) *Selected Letters of E M Forster Vol 2: 1921–1970* Harvard University Press 1985.

**7243** Robert Huffaker *John Fowles* Twayne, Boston, Massachusetts 1980. A short critical biography of the novelist with a chronology and bibliography.

**7244** Allan E Austin *Roy Fuller* Twayne, Boston, Massachusetts 1979. A short critical biography of the poet seen as the father-figure of the Movement which includes a chronology and bibliography.

**7245** Bernard F Dick *William Golding* revised ed, Twayne, Boston, Massachusetts 1987. A short critical biography, novel by novel, including a chronology and bibliography, of the Nobel Laureate of 1985. John Carey (ed) *William Golding: The Man and His Books: A Tribute on his 75th Birthday* Faber 1986 is a collection of tribute essays examining his work which includes some biographical material. It also includes a rare interview conducted in 1985. Jack I Bilen *Talk: Conversations with William Golding* Harcourt, Brace, Jovanovitch, New York 1970 is a collection of interviews. See also [7307].

**7246** Hallman Bell Bryant *Robert Graves: An Annotated Bibliography* Garland 1986. The life and work of the poet, critic and historical novelist is throughly analysed in Martin Seymour-Smith *Robert Graves: His Life and Work* Hutchinson 1982. Paul O'Prey (ed) *In Broken Images: Selected Letters of Robert Graves 1914–1946* Hutchinson 1982 is a selection with a commentary and notes. This is continued in Paul O'Prey (ed) *Between Moon and Moon: Selected Letters of Robert Graves 1946–1972* Hutchinson 1984.

**7247** Keith C Odom *Henry Green* Twayne, Boston, Massachusetts 1978. A short critical biography of the work of the novelist and industrialist which includes a chronology and bibliography.

**7248** R A Wobbe *Graham Greene: A Bibliography and Guide to Research* Garland 1979. A useful guide to the writings about Greene. A A De Vitis *Graham Greene* revised ed, Twayne 1986 is a short critical biography of the novelist with a chronology and bibliography. Graham Greene *A Sort of Life: An Autobiography* The Bodley Head 1971 is a volume of memoirs which is continued by *Ways Of Escape* The Bodley Head 1980. Marie-François Allain *The Other Man: Conversations with Graham Greene* The Bodley Head 1983 is a useful and illuminating series of interviews.

**7249** Jack W C Haystrom and George Bixby *Thom Gunn: A Bibliography 1940–1978* Bettam Rota 1979. A full descriptive bibliography of the poet's works.

**7250** Edward Trostler Jones *L P Hartley* Twayne, Boston, Massachusetts 1978. A short critical biography of the novelist with a chronology and bibliography.

**7251** Keith Sagar and Stephen Tabor *Ted Hughes: A Bibliography 1946–1980* Mansell 1983. A guide to writings on the work of the man who became poet laureate in 1984. Thomas West *Ted Hughes* Methuen 1985 is a short critical biography. Keith Sagar *The Achievement of Ted Hughes* Manchester University Press 1983 is a useful critical study.

**7252** Robert Green *R C Hutchinson: The Man and His Books* Scarecrow 1985. A study of the life and work of the novelist, with a useful bibliography. See also Ray Coryton *Hutchinson: Two Men of Letters: Correspondence between R C Hutchinson, Novelist, and Martyn Skinner, Poet, 1957–1974* Michael Joseph 1979.

**7253** Elven E Bass *Aldous Huxley: An Annotated Bibliography of Criticism* Garland 1981. A guide to literary criticism of the novelist's work. Sybille Bedford *Aldous Huxley: A Biography Vol 2: 1939–1963* Chatto and Windus/Collins 1974 is the standard study of Huxley's life and work. See also Keith M May *Aldous Huxley* Elek 1972. Julian Huxley (ed) *Aldous Huxley 1894–1963: A*

*Memorial Volume* Chatto and Windus 1965 is a collection of tributes and memoirs of the novelist. See also Grover Smith (ed) *Letters of Aldous Huxley* Chatto and Windus 1969.

**7254** Robert W Funk *Christopher Isherwood: A Reference Guide* Prior 1979. An earlier guide to writings by and about Isherwood is Selmer Westby and Clayton M Brown *Christopher Isherwood: A Bibliography 1923–1967* California State College at Los Angeles Foundation, Los Angeles, California 1968. The best biography of Isherwood is Brian Finney *Christopher Isherwood: A Critical Biography* Faber 1979, though as Finney points out the task is complicated by the extent to which all of Isherwood's works are semi-autobiographical. See also Jonathan Fryer *Isherwood: A Biography of Christopher Isherwood* New English Library 1977. John Lehmann *Christopher Isherwood: A Personal Memoir* Weidenfeld and Nicolson 1987 is largely based on the correspondence between the two and is not really biography. Claude J Summers *Christopher Isherwood* Ungar 1980 is a short critical biography. Christopher Isherwood *My Guru and Other Disciples* Eyre Methuen 1980 is a spiritual rather than a literary autobiography explaining his conversion to Vendanta Hinduism.

**7255** Storm Jameson *Journey From the North* 2v, Virago 1984. A reissue of the autobiographical account by the novelist first published in 1969.

**7256** Joanna Colenbrander *A Portrait of Fryn: A Biography of F Tennyson Jesse* Deutsch 1984. A biography of the novelist.

**7257** James Kirkup *I Of All People: An Autobiography of Youth* Weidenfeld and Nicolson 1988. A frank autobiography by the poet. It however does not really touch on the most notorious incident in Kirkup's career, when a poem he had published in *Gay News* was successfully prosecuted for blasphemy in 1977.

**7258** *Arthur Koestler: An International Bibliography* Ardis 1979. The most substantial study of Koestler's life and work is Iain Hamilton *Koestler: A Biography* Secker and Warburg 1982.

**7259** Barry Cambray Bloomfield *Philip Larkin: A Bibliography 1933–1976* Faber 1979. A guide to the works by and about the poet. George Hartley (ed) *Philip Larkin 1922–1985: A Tribute* Marvell 1988, Dale Salwak (ed) *Philip Larkin: The Man and his Work* Macmillan 1988, Harry Chambers (ed) *An Enormous Yes: In Memoriam: Philip Larkin 1922–1985* Peterloo Poets 1986 and *Larkin at Sixty* Faber 1982 are all tribute volumes containing personal memoirs of the poet and assessments of his work. Selem Kadhem Hassan *Philip Larkin and his Contemporaries: An Air of Authenticity* Macmillan 1988 is a useful critical study. Andrew Motion *Philip Larkin*

Methuen 1982 and David Timms *Philip Larkin* Oliver and Boyd 1973 are short critical biographies.

**7260** John Lehmann *The Ample Proposition: Autobiography III* Eyre and Spottiswoode 1966. An autobiography covering the period since 1945 during which the poet, literati, critic and broadcaster built and lost a publishing firm and literary magazines and continued to move in the bohemian circles on which he reflects here.

**7261** D Seligman *Doris Lessing: An Annotated Bibliography of Criticism* Greenwood 1981. A guide with 1,045 entries. Mona Knapp *Doris Lessing* Ungar 1984 is a short critical biography concentrating on the work of the radical, Rhodesian-born novelist. See also Michael Thorpe *Doris Lessing* Longman 1973.

**7262** Joe R Christopher and Joan K Ostlin *C S Lewis: An Annotated Checklist of Writings about him and his Works* Kent State University Press, Kent, Ohio 1975. A tutor at Oxford 1925–54 Lewis became Professor of Mediaeval and Renaissance Literature at Cambridge from 1954 until his death in 1963. He left behind a wide range of work in literary criticism, imaginative novels, writings for children and Christian apologetics. The authorized biography is Roger Lancelyn Green and Walter Hooper *C S Lewis: A Biography* Collins 1974. Joe R Christopher *C S Lewis* Twayne, Boston, Massachusetts 1987 is a short critical study of Lewis's life and work which includes a chronology and an up to date bibliography of writings by and about Lewis and his work. George Sayer *Jack: C S Lewis and his Times* Macmillan 1988 is an affectionate biography. Douglas Gresham *Lenten Lands* Collins 1989 is a memoir by Lewis's stepson. Lewis's letters are edited and introduced with a memoir by his brother in W H Lewis (ed) *Letters of C S Lewis* Geoffrey Bles 1966. There are also family reflections on the writer contained in Clyde S Kilby and Majorie Lamp Mead (eds) *Brothers and Friends: The Diaries of Major Warren Hamilton Lewis* Harper and Row 1982. Warren Lewis was C S Lewis's brother with whom he lived for many years. James T Como (ed) *C S Lewis at the Breakfast Table and Other Reminiscences* Collins 1980 is a collection of reminiscences and tributes by friends and acquaintances. Carolyn Keefe (ed) *C S Lewis: Speaker and Teacher* Zondervan 1971 includes a number of insights into aspects of Lewis's life. On Lewis and his marriage to Joy Davidman see Brian Sibley *Shadowlands: The True Story of C S Lewis and Joy Davidman* Hodder and Stoughton 1985.

**7263** Jeffrey Meyers *The Enemy: A Biography of Wyndham Lewis* Routledge and Kegan Paul 1980. A good biography of the novelist and artist. Although his political novels of the period 1939–50 showed a shift in his political attitudes and some of his best work appeared in the 1950s before his death in 1957 his reputation remained under a cloud because of his open sympathy for fascism for most of the inter-war period.

**7264** William H New *Malcolm Lowry: A Reference Guide* G K Hall, Boston, Massachusetts 1978. A guide to writings by and about Lowry. Douglas Day *Malcolm Lowry: A Biography* Oxford University Press 1974 is useful biography of the under-rated novelist. See also Tony Bareham *Malcolm Lowry* Macmillan 1989 and Ronald Binns *Malcolm Lowry* Macmillan 1984. Gordon Bowker *Malcolm Lowry Remembered* Ariel 1985 is a tribute volume. Tony Kilgannin *Lowry* Press Porcepic, Erin, Ontario 1973 is a study which examines particularly the mystical side to Lowry's novels. For his correspondence see Harvey Breit and Margerie Bonner Lowry (eds) *Malcolm Lowry: Selected Letters* Penguin 1967.

**7265** Tony Gould *Insider Outsider: The Life and Times of Colin MacInnes* Chatto and Windus 1983. A useful study of the novelist and critic who was a dominant figure in bohemian London in the 1950s and 1960s.

**7266** Elton Edward Smith *Louis MacNeice* Twayne, Boston, Massachusetts 1970. A short critical biography of the Anglo-Irish poet including a chronology and bibliography. A more detailed study of his life and work is Adolphe Heberer *Louis MacNeice 1907–1963: L'homme et la poésie* 2v, Atelier Nationale de Reproduction des Thèses, Lille 1986. Barbara Coulton *Louis MacNeice in the BBC* Faber 1980 is a study of the poet's life and work as a writer-producer in the BBC's radio features department 1941–63 which casts light on the impact of broadcasting on literary endeavour.

**7267** Ethel Mannin *Brief Voices* Hutchinson 1959. The third volume of the novelist's autobiography and the only one to touch upon the post-war period.

**7268** Constance Babington Smith *John Masefield: A Life* Oxford University Press 1978. A life of the poet laureate 1930–67.

**7269** C Saunders (comp) *W Somerset Maugham: An Annotated Bibliography of Writings about Him* Northern Illinois University Press, DeKalb, Illinois 1970. A useful guide to 2,355 items about the writer. Robert Calder *Willie: The Life of W Somerset Maugham* Heinemann 1989 is a well reviewed biographical reassessment making use of what material Maugham, who did not want a biography, did not destroy. Another good biography is Ted Morgan *Somerset Maugham* Cape 1980. Robin Maugham *Conversations With Willie: Recollections of W Somerset Maugham* W H Allen 1978 is a useful memoir by his novelist nephew. Frederic Raphael *W Somerset Maugham and his World* Thames and Hudson 1976 is an illustrated biography. Richard Albert Cordell *Somerset Maugham: A Writer for all Seasons: A Bio-*

*graphical and Critical Study* 2nd ed, Indiana University Press 1969 is not terribly deep as criticism but remains of some use as biography.

**7270** Selina Hastings *Nancy Mitford: A Biography* Hamilton 1985. An anecdotal biography of the novelist. See also Harold Acton *Nancy Mitford: A Memoir* Hamilton 1975.

**7271** John Mortimer *Clinging To The Wreckage: A Part of Life* Weidenfeld and Nicolson 1982. Autobiographical reminiscences by the novelist, screenwriter and playwright.

**7272** T T Tominaga and W Schneidermeyer *Iris Murdoch and Muriel Spark: A Bibliography* Scarecrow 1976. A comprehensive guide to the literature by and about these two novelists complete with chronologies. Richard Todd *Iris Murdoch* Methuen 1984 is a biography and a critical appraisal of her various novels. It includes a good bibliography.

**7273** Katherine Middleton Murry *Beloved Quixote: The Unknown John Middleton Murry* Souvenir Press 1989. A useful reassessment of the life of her father, the author, Christian pacifist and idealist. See also F A Lea *The Life of John Middleton Murry* Methuen 1959.

**7274** E C Bufkin *P H Newby* Twayne, Boston, Massachusetts 1975. A short critical biography with a chronology and bibliography. Newby is best known for his trilogy of novels on Egyptian-British relations published 1955–9.

**7275** Jeffrey and Valerie Meyers *Orwell: An Annotated Bibliography of Criticism* Garland 1977. A useful reference guide to writings on the work of George Orwell (real name Eric Blair), the novelist, essayist, journalist and critic. The best biography, and the first based on full access to his papers, is Bernard Crick *George Orwell: A Life* Secker and Warburg 1980. See also T R Fyvel *George Orwell: A Personal Memoir* Weidenfeld and Nicolson 1982. Peter Lewis *George Orwell: The Road to 1984* Heinemann Quixote 1981 is a short illustrated biography. Peter Stansky and William Abrahams *The Unknown Orwell* Constable 1972 and L Brander *George Orwell* Longmans 1954 are early and now outdated studies. Stephen Wadhams (ed) *Remembering Orwell* Penguin 1984 is a collection of interviews with contemporaries and friends as is Audrey Coppard and Bernard Crick (ed) *Orwell Remembered* BBC 1984. In addition there are four volumes of collected journalism and letters, the post-war period being covered in Sonia Orwell and Ian Angus (eds) *The Collected Essays, Journalism and Letters of George Orwell Vol 4: In Front of Your Nose 1945–1950* Secker and Warburg 1968. Orwell's journalism for the Labour Party's Left-Wing journal *Tribune* is examined in Paul O'Flinn 'Orwell and

*Tribune' Literature and History* 6 1980 pp 201–18. The roots and nature of Orwell's radical politics and vision are explored in Gordon B Beadle 'George Orwell and the Victorian Radical Tradition' *Albion* 7 1975 pp 287–99. The development and nature of these political attitudes and the rather different tone that came into his wartime and post-war writings as he came to stress the need to restore the traditional values that had been undermined by the hedonistic individualism he execrated is examined in Gregory Claeys 'Industrialism and Hedonism in Orwell's Literary and Political Development' *Albion* 18 1986 pp 219–45. Orwell remains the most widely read and influential British political writer of the twentieth century. His work, particularly the novel *Nineteen Eighty-Four*, is reassessed by political scientists and philosophers, literary critics and social historians in the useful collection of essays, Peter Buitenhuis and Ira Bruce Nadel (eds) *George Orwell: A Reassessment* Hamilton 1988. *1984* and other post-war work such as *Animal Farm* have often led to Orwell being seen as a prophetic opponent of the Left and yet he always described himself as a socialist. This tension in his relationship with the Left is analysed in detail in the highly acclaimed set of essays collected in Christopher Norris (ed) *Inside the Myth: Orwell: Views from the Left* Lawrence and Wishart 1984 in which Orwell's views on such subjects as the state, the Spanish Civil War and women are interpreted. Another examination of Orwell as a political writer which is now quite dated is David L Kubal *Outside The Whale: George Orwell's Art and Politics* University of Notre Dame Press, Notre Dame, Indiana 1972.

**7276** John Watney *Mervyn Peake* Michael Joseph 1976. A good biography of the novelist and illustrator. See also the moving memoir by Peake's widow, Maeve Gilmore *A World Away: A Memoir of Mervyn Peake* Gollancz 1970.

**7277** Peter Alexander *William Plomer: A Biography* Oxford University Press 1989. A good biography of the South African born writer.

**7277A** Paul Potts *Dante Called you Beatrice* Eyre and Spottiswoode 1960. The autobiography of the poet and author.

**7278** Anthony Powell *To Keep the Ball Rolling* 4v, Heinemann 1976–82. These autobiographical volumes reflect the novelist's interests and personality but not in a very succinct fashion. Nor are they arranged chronologically. Neil Brennan *Anthony Powell* Twayne, Boston, Massachusetts 1974 is a short critical biography with a chronology and bibliography.

**7279** Alan E Day *J B Priestley: An Annotated Bibliography* Ian Hodgkins 1980. The best biography of Priestley is Vincent Brome *J B Priestley* Hamilton 1988. As he points out, Priestley was a great wartime broadcaster and political writer whose 1957 article in *New Statesman* helped to spark off CND, but who was never accepted as a great as opposed to a popular novelist. The post-war period is covered in Priestley's own autobiography, *Instead of the Trees: A Final Chapter of Autobiography* Heinemann 1977. See also Susan Cooper *J B Priestley: Portrait of An Author* Heinemann 1970, which is an informal study of Priestley's life, work and politics written with the assistance of its subject.

**7280** Dean R Baldwin *V S Pritchett* Twayne, Boston, Massachusetts 1987. The only critical biography, as yet of the Left-Wing writer, especially of short stories. It includes a chronology and bibliography. See also V S Pritchett's successive volumes of autobiography, *A Cab At The Door* Chatto and Windus 1968, *Midnight Oil* Chatto and Windus 1971 and *The Turn of the Years* Michael Russell 1981.

**7281** Janice Rossen *The World of Barbara Pym* Macmillan 1987. This study assesses her significance within the development of the modern British novel and traces the maturation of her work and the cultural themes within it. Dale Salwak (ed) *The Life and Work of Barbara Pym* Macmillan 1987 is a collection of essays on her life and work. Hazel Holt and Hilary Pym (eds) *A Very Private Eye: The Diaries, Letters and Notebooks of Barbara Pym* Macmillan 1984 is a selection covers the novelist's life from her time at Oxford in the 1930s to her death in 1980.

**7282** Hugh Brogan *The Life of Arthur Ransome* Cape 1984. A scholarly account of the life of the journalist and children's writer.

**7283** Francis Berry *Herbert Read* revised ed, Longman 1981. A study of the poet and art critic. See also Robin Skelton (ed) *Herbert Read: A Memorial* Symposium Methuen 1971.

**7284** Peter Wolfe *Mary Renault* Twayne, Boston, Massachusetts 1969. A short critical biography of the historical novelist which includes a chronology and bibliography.

**7285** Victoria Glendinning *Vita: The Life of Vita Sackville-West* Weidenfeld and Nicolson 1983. A good biography of the novelist. Michael Stevens *V Sackville West: A Critical Biography* Michael Joseph 1973 is a study of her life and writings. It includes a chronology and bibliography. Nigel Nicolson *Portrait of a Marriage* Weidenfeld and Nicolson 1973 is an account by her son of her marriage to the politician and political diarist Harold Nicolson, for other material on whom see [674]. It casts light upon their lives and particularly upon their sexual inclinations and attitudes.

**7286** D Felicitas Corrigan *Siegfried Sassoon: Poet's Pilgrimage* Gollancz 1973. A useful and touching book. The introduction surveys the poet's life which is then illustrated by a selection of poems, diaries and letters.

**7287** James Brabazon *Dorothy L Sayers: The Life of a Courageous Woman* Gollancz 1981. The official biography of the mystery writer and playwright. Nancy M Tuschler *Dorothy L Sayers: A Pilgrim Soul* John Knox Press 1980 is particularly strong on the influence of Christianity on her life and work. Janet Hitchman *Such A Strange Lady: An Introduction to Dorothy L Sayers 1893–1957* New English Library 1975 is an informal and rather inadequate biography.

**7288** David E Gerard *Alan Sillitoe: A Bibliography* Mansell 1988. A guide to writings by and about the author. Stanley S Atherton *Alan Sillitoe: A Critical Assessment* W H Allen 1979 is a critical study of the novelist and short story writer who was one of the leading exponents of the northern social realism working class novel to emerge in the 1950s. Allan Richard Penner *Alan Sillitoe* Twayne, Boston, Massachusetts 1972 is a short study of his life and work, incorporating a chronology.

**7289** C H Sisson *On The Look Out* Carcanet 1989. The memoirs of the poet, novelist and former Whitehall mandarin. He takes as his starting point 1964 and works backwards from there.

**7290** For Martyn Skinner see [7252].

**7291** John Pearson *Facades: Edith, Osbert and Sacheverell Sitwell* Fontana 1980. A study of the three Sitwell poets. Of the three siblings Edith has received the most critical acclaim as well as the most attention from biographers. Victoria Glendinning *Edith Sitwell: A Unicorn Among Lions* Oxford University Press 1983 is a good biography. Geoffrey Elborn *Edith Sitwell: A Biography* Sheldon Press 1981 is also useful. Edith Sitwell *Taken Care Of: An Autobiography* Hutchinson 1965 is a posthumously published and not very revealing autobiography. On Edith see also John Lehmann and Derek Parker (eds) *Edith Sitwell: Selected Letters* Macmillan 1970, a collection which includes letters written up to her death in 1964. On Sacheverell see also Neil Ritchie *Sacheverell Sitwell: An Annotated and Descriptive Bibliography 1916–1986* Giardo Press, Florence 1989.

**7292** Frances Spalding *Stevie Smith: A Critical Biography* Faber 1988. Another good biography of the female poet who died in 1971 is Jack Barbara and William McBrian *Stevie: A Biography of Stevie Smith* Heinemann 1985. See also [7224].

**7293** John Halperin *C P Snow: An Oral Biography: Together with a Conversation with Lady Snow (Pamela Hansford Johnson)* Harvester 1983. Snow was best known for his novels. In addition he was a Cambridge physicist, a Civil Service Commissioner 1945–60 and a junior minister at the Ministry of Technology in 1964–6. These various careers are reflected on in the interviews which make up this book, which were conducted in 1979–80 shortly before Snow's death.

**7294** H B Kulkarni *Stephen Spender: Works and Criticism: An Annotated Bibliography* Garland 1976. Spender rose to prominence as a political poet in the 1930s. Stephen Spender *The Thirties and After: Poetry, Politics and People (1933–75)* Macmillan 1978 is a volume of memoirs drawing on extracts from his journals and other material. It is however rather thin after the 1940s. John Goldsmith (ed) *Stephen Spender Journals 1939–1983* Faber 1985 is a massive if discontinuous series of extracts from the Spender journals which is much fuller on the post-war period and is most detailed on the 1970s. It is complemented by an accompanying commentary.

**7295** Derek Stanford *Inside The Forties: Literary Memories 1937–1957* Sidgwick and Jackson 1977. The autobiography of a man of letters. In the process he attempts to present the story of the neo-romantic movement amongst the writers of his generation.

**7296** Angela Bull *Noel Streatfeild* Collins 1984. A biography of the writer of children's books.

**7297** D M Thomas *Memories and Hallucinations* Gollancz 1988. The salacious autobiography of the novelist and poet.

**7298** Humphrey Carpenter *J R R Tolkien: A Biography* Allen and Unwin 1977. A good literary biography of the philologist, author and Oxford Professor of ancient literature. Humphrey Carpenter with Christopher Tolkien (eds) *Letters of J R R Tolkien* Allen and Unwin 1981 is a selection which reflect on Tolkien and his friendships with contemporaries like C S Lewis and Charles Williams, his Catholicism, his writings and his work as a Oxford don.

**7299** Jessica Mitford *Faces of Philip: A Memoir of Philip Toynbee* Heinemann 1984. A biography of the novelist and journalist who died in 1981.

**7300** Denis Judd *Alison Uttley: The Life of a Country Child (1884–1976): The Authorised Biography* Michael Joseph 1986. A biography of the writer of rural belle-lettres and children's books.

**7301** Frederic I Carpenter *Laurens van der Post* Twayne, Boston, Massachusetts 1969. A short study of the life and work of the South African born writer.

**7302** John Wain *Sprightly Running: Part of an Autobiography* Macmillan 1962. Autobiographical material by one of the leading exponents of the northern social realism working class novel to emerge in the 1950s. Dale Salwak *John Wain* Twayne, Boston, Massachusetts 1981 is a short critical biography with a chronology and bibliography. See also [7215].

**7303** Claire Harman *Sylvia Townsend Warner* Chatto and Windus 1989. A biographical study. William Maxwell (ed) *The Letters of Sylvia Townsend Warner* Chatto and Windus 1982 is a selection of the letters of the novelist and poet up to her death in 1978. Another collection of letters is Wendy Mulford (ed) *This Narrow Place: Sylvia Townsend Warner and Valentine Ackland: Life, Letters and Politics 1930–1951* Pandora 1988. This includes a prologue and epilogue. Both these and the letters reflect on the Left-Wing politics and poetry of the two women. On their lives together and love see Valentine Ackland *For Sylvia: An Honest Account* Methuen 1985. This autobiography of her youth, written in the 1940s, appears with a useful introduction by Bea Howe.

**7304** Robert Murray Davis *et al Bibliography of Evelyn Waugh* Whitston, Troy, New York 1986. A guide to works by and about the novelist. Christopher Sykes *Evelyn Waugh: A Biography* Collins 1975 is a good biography. Another biography covering from 1948 until his death in 1966 is Frances Donaldson *Evelyn Waugh: Portrait of a Country Neighbour* Weidenfeld and Nicolson 1967. Michael Davie (ed) *The Diaries of Evelyn Waugh* Weidenfeld and Nicolson 1976 extract selections from Waugh's diaries 1911–65 with chronological tables. See also Mark Amory (ed) *The Letters of Evelyn Waugh* Weidenfeld and Nicolson 1980.

**7305** Victoria Glendinning *Rebecca West: A Life* Weidenfeld and Nicolson 1987. A good official biography of the novelist who died in 1983.

**7306** François Gallix *T H White: An Annotated Bibliography* Garland 1986. A guide to writings by and about White. Sylvia Townsend Warner *T H White: A Biography* Cape/Chatto and Windus 1967 is a rather dull biography by a fellow novelist. Also of use is François Gallix (ed) *Letters to a Friend: The Correspondence between T H White and L J Potts* Putnam 1982.

**7307** John Henry Stape *Angus Wilson: A Bibliography 1947–1987* Mansell 1988. A guide to writings by and about the novelist. Wilson's life and work is examined in Peter Faulkner *Angus Wilson: Mimic and Moralist* Secker and Warburg 1980. See also Danielle Escudié *Deux Aspects de l'aliénation dans le roman anglais contemporain 1945–1965: Angus Wilson et William Golding* Didier, Paris 1975.

**7308** David A Jasen *A Bibliography and Reader's Guide to the First Editions of P G Wodehouse* Barrie and Jenkins 1971. Frances Donaldson *P G Wodehouse: A Biography* Weidenfeld and Nicolson 1982 is the best biography of the writer of whimsical and comic novels. Benny Green *P G Wodehouse: A Literary Biography* Pavilion 1981 is also useful but is rather thin on the post-war period, as is David A Jasen *P G Wodehouse: A Portrait of a Master* Mason and Lipscomb 1974. Wodehouse's three autobiographical works, *Bring on the Girls* (with Hugh Jenkins), *Performing Fleas* (letters) and *Over Seventy* (reflections), which were first published in 1953–7, were reprinted as *Wodehouse on Wodehouse* Hutchinson 1980. Joseph Connolly *P G Wodehouse: An Illustrated Biography* Orbis 1979 is an amusing biography which has a complete bibliography.

## (b) Literary Criticism

**7309** Elmer Borklund (ed) *Contemporary Literary Critics* 2nd ed, Gale, Detroit, Michigan 1982. A collection of studies of various leading critics, especially American and British, with full bibliographies.

**7310** Frederick Brittain *Its A Don's Life* Heinemann 1972. The autobiography of a Cambridge tutor in English literature.

**7311** *The Leavises: Recollections and Impressions* Cambridge University Press 1984. Tributes to and memoirs of F R Leavis and his wife Q D Leavis, both of whom were literary critics of international standing. See also P J M Robertson *The Leavises on Fiction: An Historic Partnership* Macmillan 1981. The fullest study of F R Leavis' work is R P Billan *The Literary Criticism of F R Leavis* Cambridge University Press 1979. Other assessments of his life and work are Michael Bell *F R Leavis* Routledge and Kegan Paul 1976, William Walsh *F R Leavis* Chatto and Windus 1980 and Ronald Hayman *Leavis* Heinemann 1976.

**7312** John Dover Wilson *Milestones on the Dover Road* Faber 1969. The autobiography of a Shakespearian scholar.

## (5) The Dramatic Arts

### (a) The Theatre

**7313** D Howard (comp) *Directory of Theatre Research and Information Sources in the UK* Arts Council 1980. A survey of the relevant societies and associations and a directory and finding list of the various research resources and collections.

**7314** *British Theatre Directory* J Offord Publications 1972–. This annual publication supersedes *Stage Yearbook* 1948–69. It is a guide to the theatre, ballet and opera, alternative theatre, drama awards and other aspects and events of the world of the stage. It also lists most important productions each year.

**7315** Theatre Museum, Covent Garden, 1e Tavistock Street, London WC2. This has a collection of recorded interviews with leading figures in the fields of the theatre and ballet.

**7316** Ian Herbert with Christine Baxter and Robert E Finley (eds) *Who's Who in the Theatre: A Biographical Record of the Contemporary Stage* 2v, 17th ed, Gale, Detroit, Michigan 1981. The first volume is a collection of biographies of leading figures of the theatre in Britain and America. The second is an update on all the major productions and statistics of the London and New York stage. It has since been continued by *Contemporary Theatre, Film and Television* Gale, Detroit, Michigan 1984–. This is an expansion, annually updated, which is designed to include a wider range of individuals. However, the biographies seem less satisfactory and it no longer lists productions.

**7317** E K Mikhail *Contemporary British Drama 1950–1976: An Annotated Critical Bibliography* Macmillan 1976. A useful bibliography, though one which could be better organized.

**7318** John Courtenay Trewin *Drama in Britain 1945–1950* Longmans 1951. A short British Council survey. It was continued by his *Drama in Britain 1951–1964* Longmans 1965 and by Jack Walter Lambert *Drama in Britain 1964–1973* Longman 1974. After that the series was discontinued.

**7319** Richard F Dietrich *British Drama 1890 to 1950: A Critical History* G K Hall 1989. This is continued by Susan Rusinko *British Drama 1950 to the Present: A Critical History* G K Hall 1989. These cover all aspects of trends in the modern British theatre. H Hunt *et al The Revels History of Drama in English Vol 7: 1880 to the Present Day* Methuen 1978 is an examination of the modern theatre in all English- speaking countries.

**7320** John Elsom *Post-War British Theatre* 2nd ed, Routledge and Kegan Paul 1979. A compendious history tracing changes in style, acting, administration and finance, and the rise of repertory and fringe theatres. See also Peter Davison *Contemporary Drama: The Popular Dramatic Tradition in England* Macmillan 1982. Major trends and turning points in modern drama, such as the appearance of the kitchen sink dramas of the 1950s in the wake of John Osborne's *Look Back in Anger* are examined in Katherine Joyce Worth *Revolutions in Modern British Drama* Bell 1973. Colin Chambers and

Mike Prior *Playwright's Progress: Patterns of Post-War British Drama* Amber Lane Press 1988 concentrates particularly on aspects such as the presentation of the working class, or of women, or of political theatre. It has its unsatisfactory side, relying overmuch on unsubstantiated statements. It is nevertheless quite useful.

**7321** Harold Hobson *Theatre in Britain: A Personal View* Phaidon 1984. A critic's view of theatrical trends and productions 1920–82. Another critic's view is presented in Ronald Hayman *The Set-Up: An Anatomy of English Theatre Today* Eyre Methuen 1973. John Elsom (comp) *Post-War British Theatre Criticism* Routledge and Kegan Paul 1980 is a collection of critical perspectives.

**7322** Kathleen Tynan *The Life of Kenneth Tynan* Weidenfeld and Nicolson 1988. A good biography of the famous critic, essayist and leading figure of the permissive culture that emerged in the 1960s. Tynan's theatrical criticism is collected in his *A View of the English Stage 1944–65* Methuen 1984.

**7323** Charles Marowitz and Simon Trumler (eds) *Theatre at Work: Playwrights and Productions in the Modern British Theatre* Methuen 1967. A collection of interviews with leading playwrights, directors, actors and others involved in the world of the theatre.

**7324** John Russell Taylor *Anger and After: A Guide to the New British Drama* 2nd ed, Eyre Methuen 1977. A good study of the theatre of the 1950s and of the major changes that took place in that decade. Arnold P Hinchcliffe *British Theatre 1950–70* Blackwell 1974 particularly concentrates on 1956, the year of *Look Back in Anger*, and the European influence of Samuel Beckett and Bertolt Brecht. Trends in the theatre, the quality of writing and the avant-garde and alternative productions since the developments of the mid–1950s are critically assessed in Ronald Hayman *The British Theatre Since 1955: A Reassessment* Oxford University Press 1979. This includes a useful chronology. The impact of the new developments of the mid–1950s are also examined in F M G Le Blond '"Watch It Come Down": The Vision of Social Failure in Post-War British Drama 1956–1976' Birmingham PhD Thesis 1981–2. See also J S R Goodlad 'An Analysis of the Social Content of Popular Drama 1955–1965' London PhD Thesis 1969–70.

**7325** John Russell Taylor *The Second Wave: British Drama in the Sixties* 2nd ed, Eyre Methuen 1978. A good study of trends in the theatre in the 1960s.

**7326** Douglas Colby *As The Curtain Rises: On Contemporary British Drama 1966–1976* Associated Universities Presses 1978.

7327 Vera Gottlieb 'Thatcher's Theatre – After *Equus*' *New Theatre Quarterly* 4 1988 pp 99–104. A critique of what she sees as despair in the theatre and the resulting inadequacy of the social commentary of its productions, which she dates from Peter Shaffer's *Equus* in 1973.

7328 Richard Findlater *Banned! A Review of Theatrical Censorship in Britain* MacGibbon and Kee 1967. This reviews and expresses the increasing frustration being felt in a theatre which was changing in the wake of the new themes being explored in the 1950s and 1960s, with the continuing effect of theatrical censorship, a censorship which was removed in 1968. See also J A Florence 'Theatrical Censorship in Britain 1901–1968' Wales PhD Thesis 1980.

7329 John Courtenay Trewin *Shakespeare on the English Stage 1900–1964: A Survey of Productions* Barrie and Rockliff 1964. A useful survey. Laurence Olivier's productions and portrayals of Shakespeare's plays on stage and screen are assessed in P C Mason 'Olivier's Shakespeare' Birmingham PhD Thesis 1978–9.

7330 R J Ingram 'The Attempted Popularisation of Verse Drama in England 1945–1956' London MPhil Thesis 1967–8. An examination of the attempts of Christopher Fry, T S Eliot and others to revive the verse drama.

7331 S A Strehl 'The Absurd and its Experiments on the English Stage in the 1950s' Nottingham MPhil Thesis 1974–6. A study of the writing of theatre of the absurd by such dramatists as N F Simpson and of productions of theatre of the absurd in the decade when it was at its height.

7332 Leslie Smith *Modern British Farce: A Selective Study from Pinero to the Present Day* Macmillan 1988. A historical survey of a popular but under-studied genre.

7333 Niloufer Harben *Twentieth Century English History Plays: From Shaw to Bond* Macmillan 1987. A study of the handling of historical themes by playwrights such as George Bernard Shaw, T S Eliot, Robert Bolt, Peter Shaffer, John Osborne and Edward Bond.

7334 John Goodwin (ed) *British Theatre Design* Weidenfeld and Nicolson 1989. An illustrated celebration of British success in this field, including many essays on the subject by leading designers.

7335 Charles Wintour *Celebration: Twenty Five Years of British Theatre* W H Allen 1981. A survey of the West End theatre in London in the light of the *Evening Standard* drama awards 1955–80. On London's theatre in this period see also Warren L Chernaik 'Art and Politics: London Theatre Since the Fifties' *London Journal* 8 1982 pp 208–12.

7336 John Goodwin (ed) *Peter Hall's Diaries: The Story of a Dramatic Battle* Hamilton 1983. These diaries cover the period 1972–80 during which Hall was embroiled in setting up the National Theatre. They also include some reflections on Hall's previous work in setting up Britain's other national theatre company, the Royal Shakespeare Company and on early productions at the National Theatre. On the setting up of the National Theatre from the origins of the idea see John Elsom and Nicholas Tomalin *History of the National Theatre* Cape 1978. Tim Goodwin *Britain's National Theatre: The First 25 Years* National Theatre 1987 is a catalogue guide to productions.

7337 S Bearman *The Royal Shakespeare Company: A History of Three Decades* Oxford University Press 1982. See also D A Addenbrooke 'The Structure, Development and Production Work of the Royal Shakespeare Theatre Company over the Years 1960 to 1968' Warwick PhD Thesis 1971–2.

7338 G Rowell and A Jackson *The Repertory Movement: A History of Regional Theatre in Britain* Cambridge University Press 1984. A study particularly in the boom in regional theatre and in creativity in the regions since the 1950s. This is despite the detrimental effects of television which are blamed for the many closures in Yorkshire in D S Pinkney 'The Professional Repertory Theatre in Yorkshire 1945–1955' Leeds PhD Thesis 1986. On the provincial theatre see also John Elsom *Theatre Outside London* Macmillan 1971.

7339 Terry Browne *Playwright's Theatre: The English Stage Company at the Royal Court* Pitman 1975. The history of the innovatory company's organization, foundation and development since 1955. It covers the first production and impact of *Look Back in Anger* and the battles over the plays of Edward Bond with the Lord Chancellor which led to the end of theatre censorship in Britain. In the process the theatre attracted and nourished many of the most talented dramatists, directors, designers and actors of the 1950s and 1960s. Their reminiscences of the Royal Court's heyday are collected in Richard Findlater (ed) *At The Royal Court: 25 Years of the English Stage Company* Amber Lane 1981. Irving Wardle *The Theatre of George Devine* Cape 1978 is a masterly biography of the Royal Court's first artistic director. Philip Roberts *The Royal Court Theatre 1965–1972* Routledge and Kegan Paul 1986 surveys the key years under Devine's successor William Gaskill and Gaskill's battles over censorship with the Lord Chancellor's Department.

7340 *British Alternative Theatre Directory* J Offord Publications 1979–. A detailed annual guide to alternative and fringe theatre activities, finance, venues and productions. Andrew Davies *Other Theatres: The Development of Alternative and Experimental Theatre in Britain* Macmillan 1987 is the first history of their development since the nineteenth century. It however suffers from significant omissions, such as the Scottish and Welsh (not least Welsh language) new theatres and over abundant errors. It does however include coverage of experimental drama on radio and television. Clive Barker *British Alternative Theatre* Macmillan 1985 is a critical overview of developments during the boom in alternative theatre since the 1970s, examining its growth and variety, embracing everything from community theatre to cabaret, mime and dance, within the social and theatrical context. This period of growth is analysed by insider, committed essays on various aspects of alternative and political theatre in Sandy Craig (ed) *Dreams and Reconstructions: Alternative Theatre in Britain* Amber Lane 1980. See also Peter Ansporge *Disrupting The Spectacle: Five Years of Experimental and Fringe Theatre in Britain* Pitman 1975. The history of the most famous showcase for fringe theatre productions, the fringe at the annual Edinburgh festival, is examined in Alastair Moffat *The Edinburgh Fringe* Johnston and Bacon 1978.

**7341** David Ian Rabey *British and Irish Political Drama in the Twentieth Century: Implicating the Audience* Macmillan 1986. A study, especially in the context of mainstream rather than alternative theatre. It covers wide range of dramatists. Howard Goorney and Ewan MacColl (eds) *A git-Prop to Theatre Workshop: Political Playscripts 1930–50* Manchester University Press 1986 is a survey and collection. The development of socialist theatre and its revival in the 1970s is traced in D Watson 'British Socialist Theatre 1930–1979: Class Politics and Dramatic Form' Hull PhD Thesis 1985. The history of a Communist theatre is told in Colin Chambers *A History of Unity Theatre* Lawrence and Wishart 1986. This was established and at its height during the Popular Front period of the 1930s. It had difficulties in the Cold War era and was destroyed by fire in the 1970s.

**7342** A Storey 'Representations of Class in Modern British Drama' Nottingham PhD Thesis 1985. An examination of the treatment of class-related themes in the British theatre. It argues that by the 1980s only alternative theatres dependent on small subsidies were addressing such themes.

**7343** Michelene Wandor *Carry On Understudies: Theatre and Sexual Politics* 2nd ed, Routledge and Kegan Paul 1986. A study of feminist theatre and of female playwrights since 1969.

**7344** Kitty Black *Upper Circle: A Theatrical Chronicle* Methuen 1984. A study of the world and work of H M Tennant, the theatrical impressario, since the 1930s, especially during the war years and immediately afterwards. It includes a chronology 1936–73. Richard Huggett *Binkie Beaumont: Eminence Grise of the West End Theatre 1933–1973* Hodder and Stoughton 1989 is a biography of the co-founder and managing director of H M Tennant.

**7345** Caryl Brahms and Ned Sherrin *Too Dirty For The Windmill: A Memoir of Caryl Brahms* Constable 1986. The edited memoirs and interviews with Brahms are here collected by Sherrin. They cover her many theatrical interests and her occasional brushes with the law over productions.

**7346** Peter Brook *The Shifting Point: Forty Years of Theatrical Exploration 1946–1987* Methuen 1988. The memoirs of the most consistently innovatory director in London's West End. See also John Courtenay Trewin *Peter Brook: A Biography* Macdonald 1971. Brook's work is examined in Edward Throstle *Following Directions: A Study of Peter Brook* Lang, New York 1985. David Williams (comp) *Peter Brook: A Theatrical Casebook* Methuen 1988 reconstructs through eyewitness accounts many of Brook's most innovative productions and contains a complete chronology of his productions.

**7347** Gil Rowbottom 'Over 80 Years of Cinemas and Theatres in Coventry' *Coventry Local History* 3 1984 pp 11–27.

(b) Dramatists

**7348** S Weintraub (ed) *British Dramatists Since World War II* 2v, Gale, Detroit, Michigan 1982. A dictionary of literary biography which also includes Irish playwrights. Each entry also has an appended bibliography. The companion volume, S Weintraub (ed) *Modern British Dramatists 1900–1945* 2v, Gale, Detroit, Michigan 1982 is also useful since it includes biographical studies of a number of dramatists who remained active after 1945. D L Kirkpatrick (ed) *Contemporary Dramatists* 4th ed, St James Press 1988 is a collection of critical biographies of dramatists writing in English with attached bibliographies of their work and critical assessments of it. It has supplements on writers for the screen, radio and television, musical librettists and theatre groups.

**7349** Kimball King *Twenty Modern British Playwrights: A Bibliography 1956 to 1976* Garland 1977. An annotated bibliography with brief biographical details.

**7350** John Bull *New British Political Dramatists: Howard Brenton, David Hare, Trevor Griffiths and David*

*Edgar* Macmillan 1984. A well regarded examination of the work of various modern playwrights.

**7351** Emil Roy *British Drama Since Shaw* Feffer and Simons 1972. This includes studies of T S Eliot, Christopher Fry, John Osborne, John Arden, Harold Pinter, Arnold Wesker and John Whiting.

**7352** John Russell Brown *Theatre Language* Allen Lane 1972. A study of the drama of John Arden, John Osborne, Harold Pinter and Arnold Wesker.

**7353** Frances Gray *John Arden* Macmillan 1982. A critical biographical study of his work which includes a select bibliography. See also Ronald Hayman *Arden* Heinemann 1968 and Albert Hunt *Arden: A Study of his Plays* Eyre Methuen 1974.

**7354** Ian Watson *Conversations With Ayckbourn* Macdonald 1981. A well illustrated collection of interviews in which the playwright Alan Ayckbourn discusses his life and work. It includes a chronology.

**7355** Anna Sebba *Enid Bagnold: The Authorized Biography* Weidenfeld and Nicolson 1986. A good life of the playwright.

**7356** David L Hirst *Edward Bond* Macmillan 1985. A critical biographical study of the work of one of the leading political playwrights of the period. It includes a select bibliography.

**7357** Ronald Hayman *Robert Bolt* Heinemann Educational 1969. A short biography and study of his works.

**7358** Caryl Churchill 'The Common Imagination and the Individual Voice' *New Theatre Quarterly* 4 1988 pp 3–16. An interview with the political playwright on her work.

**7359** Sheridan Morley *A Talent To Amuse: A Biography of Nöel Coward* Pavilion 1969. A good biography published before Coward's death. Cole Lesley *The Life of Nöel Coward* Cape 1976 is a large, very informative but less dispassionate and rather more anecdotal biography. Another useful biography is Charles Castle *Nöel* W H Allen 1972. Frances Gray *Nöel Coward* Macmillan 1987 is a critical examination of his life and work concluding with an overview of the current state of critical opinion on his *oeuvre* and on his influence on the writers of the 1950s and 1960s. Another critical biography is Robert F Kiernan *Nöel Coward* Ungar, New York 1986. This includes a chronology and bibliography. See also C Lesley, G Payn and Sheridan Morley *Nöel Coward and His Friends* Weidenfeld and Nicolson 1979. Graham Payn and Sheridan Morley (eds) *The Nöel Coward Diaries* Weidenfeld and Nicolson

1982 edits Coward's diaries for 1941–69 covering both his life in the theatre and in high society.

**7360** J K Rook 'The Impact of T S Eliot on the English Drama of his Time: A Study of the Years 1919–1955' London MA Thesis 1955–6. See also [7238].

**7361** Derek Standford *Christopher Fry: An Appreciation* Peter Nevill 1951. A tribute to the work of the playwright who, with Eliot, tried to revive verse drama in the mid-century. Emil Roy *Christopher Fry* Feffer and Simons 1968 is a critical appraisal of Fry's work and account of his life.

**7362** Maurice Charney *Joe Orton* Macmillan 1984. A biographical study of his life and work which includes a select bibliography. John Lahr (ed) *Joe Orton's Diaries* Methuen 1986 covers in diary entries and letters the last 18 months of Orton's life before his murder in 1967 during which he at last became a successful playwright. They include useful reflections on the process of putting on a production in the late 1960s during the last years of theatrical censorship.

**7363** Cameron Northouse and Thomas P Walsh *John Osborne: A Reference Guide* G K Hall, Boston, Massachusetts 1974. The first section of this is a bibliographical catalogue of Osborne's works. The second gives a chronologically arranged list of literary criticisms of his work. John Osborne *A Better Class of Person: An Autobiography 1929–1956* Faber 1981 traces Osborne's life up to the eve of *Look Back in Anger*. Ronald Hayman *John Osborne* 2nd ed, Heinemann 1970 is a study of Osborne's life and work. Alan Carter *John Osborne* 2nd ed, Oliver and Boyd 1973 is both biography and literary criticism. Arnold P Hinchliffe *John Osborne* Twayne, Boston, Massachusetts 1984 is a short study with a bibliography and chronology.

**7364** Steven H Gale *Harold Pinter: An Annotated Bibliography* Prior 1987. A guide to the writings by and about the dramatist and his work. Bernard Frank Dukore *Harold Pinter* Macmillan 1982 is a biographical study of his life and work which includes a select bibliography. Other short studies are Guido Almansi *Harold Pinter* Methuen 1983, Ronald Hayman *Harold Pinter* 4th ed, Heinemann 1980, William Baker and Stephen Ely Tabachnick *Harold Pinter* Oliver and Boyd 1973 and Arnold P Hinchliffe *Harold Pinter* Macmillan 1976.

**7365** Michael Darlow and Gillian Hodson *Terence Rattigan: The Man and His Work* Quartet 1979. A good biography with the help of its subject. His popularity declined after the 1950s and he turned to scriptwriting for much of his remaining years.

**7366** C J Gianakaris *Peter Shaffer* Macmillan 1987. This traces Shaffer's career and assesses his work. It includes a select bibliography.

**7367** Dan H Lawrence *Bernard Shaw: A Bibliography* 2v, Clarendon 1984. A guide to the writings by and about the Anglo- Irish playwright and his work. See also J P Wearing *G B Shaw: An Annotated Bibliography of Writings About Him* Northern Illinois University Press, De-Kalb, Illinois 1987. Shaw's life and work is critically assessed in John O'Donovan *Bernard Shaw* Gill and Macmillan, Dublin 1983. Other biographies are Hesketh Pearson *Bernard Shaw: A Biography* Macdonald and Jane's 1975, Margery Morgan *Bernard Shaw Vol 2: 1907–1950* Profile 1982, Alfred Charles Ward *Bernard Shaw* Longmans 1951 and Margaret Shenfield *Bernard Shaw: A Pictorial Biography* Thames and Hudson 1962. Saint John G Ervine *Bernard Shaw: His Life, Work and Friends* Constable 1956 and Stephen Winsten *Jesting Apostles: The Life of Bernard Shaw* Hutchinson 1956 are biographical memoirs of the playwright. Colin Wilson *Bernard Shaw: A Reassessment* Macmillan 1981, Stanley Weintraub *The Unexpected Shaw: Biographical Approaches to George Bernard Shaw and His Work* Ungar, New York 1982, Arthur Ganz *George Bernard Shaw* Macmillan 1983, Eric Bentley *Bernard Shaw* 2nd ed, Methuen 1967 and Eldon C Hill *George Bernard Shaw* Twayne, Boston, Massachusetts 1978 are short studies of Shaw's life and work. Dan H Laurence and James Rambeau (eds) *Agitations: Letters to the Press 1875–1950* Ungar, New York 1985 is a collection of Shaw's letters.

**7368** R C Sherriff *No Leading Lady: An Autobiography* Gollancz 1968. The autobiography of the playwright.

**7369** Susan Rushinko *Tom Stoppard* Twayne, Boston, Massachusetts 1986. A short critical biography which includes a chronology and bibliography. His life and work is also assessed in Thomas R Whitaker *Tom Stoppard* Macmillan 1985, Michael Billington *Stoppard the Playwright* Methuen 1986 and Ronald Hayman *Tom Stoppard* 3rd ed, Heinemann Educational 1979. The development of Stoppard's art is examined in T J Brassell 'Tom Stoppard: An Assessment' Wales MA Thesis 1980.

**7370** Glenda Leeming *Arnold Wesker* Methuen 1983. A short critical biography. See also Ronald Hayman *Arnold Wesker* 3rd ed, Heinemann Educational 1979.

**7371** Ronald Hayman *John Whiting* Heinemann Educational 1969. A play by play analysis of Whiting's life and work.

**(c) Musicals**

**7372** Kurt Günzl *British Musical Theatre Vol 2: 1945–1984* Macmillan 1986. An acclaimed history from the continuing American influence of the 1940s, through the successes of Nöel Coward and Ivor Novello to the rock operas of the 1970s and the international success of Andrew Lloyd Webber in the 1980s. It critically analyses the lyrics and the music. It is also an excellent reference work, giving full details of all the British musicals to have appeared in London's West End in the post-war period. Another useful guide is Derek and Julia Parker *The Story and the Song: A Survey of English Musical Plays 1916–78* Elm Tree Books 1979.

**7373** Ronald Frederick Delderfield *Bird's Eye View: An Autobiography* Constable 1954. The reminiscences of a writer of musical comedy, continued by his *Overture for Beginners* Hodder and Stoughton 1970.

**7374** Michael Walsh *Andrew Lloyd Webber: His life and Works* Viking 1989. A study of the popular composer of musicals and other pieces. See also Gerald McKnight *Andrew Lloyd Webber* Granada 1984 and Christopher Headington *The Performing World of the Musician: With a Profile of Andrew Lloyd Webber* Hamilton 1981.

**7375** Sandy Wilson *Ivor* Michael Joseph 1975. A biography of Ivor Novello, the composer of musicals who died in 1951.

**(d) Television and Radio**

**7376** G W Brandt (ed) *British Television Drama* Cambridge University Press 1981. A good survey of television drama since the 1930s. It includes studies of the television work of various of the most important of modern dramatists. Productions, problems of censorship and the nature of the medium are examined in S Sutton *The Largest Theatre in the World: Thirty Years of Television Drama* BBC 1982. Drama on television in the various forms it takes is critically assessed in T C Worsley *Television: The Ephemeral Art* Alan Ross 1970.

**7377** S Sutton *The Largest Theatre in the World: The Fleming Memorial Theatre* BBC 1981. The then head of BBC television drama traces the development of television drama.

**7378** C F King 'The Influence of Documentary Methods upon BBC Television Drama, with Particular Reference to the Years 1946– 1962' Hull PhD Thesis 1975. See also A J Goodwin 'British Television Drama-Documentary 1946–80' Birmingham MA Thesis 1981– 2.

**7379** R Dyer *et al Coronation Street* British Film Institute 1982. A scholarly appraisal of the plots, characters and concern for realism in Granada Television's long-running soap opera. H V Kershaw *The Street Where I Live* Granada 1981 is a personal history of Coronation Street by a writer and producer who has worked on the programme from the beginning.

**7380** J Drakakis (ed) *British Radio Drama* Cambridge University Press 1981. A critical introduction to the development of radio drama since the 1920s which includes appraisals of many of the leading writers to have worked in the medium. See also P F Lewis (ed) *Radio Drama* Longman 1981. Developments from the 1920s to the 1960s are examined, especially in the context of technical advances affecting the style and presentation of plays, in I Rodger *Radio Drama* Macmillan 1982. An earlier historical survey by one closely involved is Val Gielgud *British Radio Drama 1922–1956* Harrap 1957.

**7381** G Baseley *'The Archers': A Slice of My Life* Sidgwick and Jackson 1971. The inside history of the first 21 years of the long-running radio soap opera.

(e) Cinema

**7382** Denis Gifford *The British Film Catalogue 1895–1985: A Reference Guide* 2nd ed, David and Charles 1986. A catalogue of all the British films made in this period arranged in chronological order, providing brief details on each. See also his *British Animated Films 1895–1985: A Filmography* McFarland 1986.

**7383** Leslie Halliwell *Halliwell's Film Guide* 6th ed, Grafton Books 1987. An indispensable reference guide, as is his *Halliwell's Filmgoer's and Video Viewers' Companion* Granada 1984.

**7384** Denis Gifford *The Illustrated Who's Who of British Films* Batsford 1978. This has about 1,000 entries on British actors and directors providing brief biographical and career information. See also David Thomson *A Biographical Dictionary of the Cinema* Secker and Warburg 1980, which is international in scope.

**7385** *Monthly Film Bulletin* British Film Institute 1934–. A quarterly which reviews every feature length film released in Britain plus a good selection of the more significant shorts. There are full details in the annual cumulative index.

**7386** John C Garlach and Lena Garlach *The Critical Index: A Bibliography of Articles on Film in English 1946–1973 Arranged by Name and Topics* Columbia University Teachers College, New York 1974. A classified catalogue to some 5,000 items drawn from American, Canadian and British film and general periodicals.

**7387** *International Index to Film Periodicals* International Federation of Film Archives 1972–. An annual annotated guide to articles appearing in nearly 100 of the world's leading film magazines. *Film Literature Index* State University of New York, New York 1973– is a quarterly with annual cumulations which is similar but less usefully organized.

**7388** George Perry *The Great British Picture Show* 2nd ed, Pavilion 1985. A good history of the British film industry. Charles Barr (ed) *All Our Yesterdays: 90 Years of British Cinema* British Film Institute 1986 is a a good collection of essays on the same subject. For general histories of the British cinema see also Gilbert Adair and Nick Roddick *A Night at the Pictures: Ten Decades of British Film* Columbus 1985, Ernest Betts *The Film Business: A History of British Cinema 1896–1972* Allen and Unwin 1973, Charles Oakley *Where We Came in: Seventy Years of the British Film Industry* Allen and Unwin 1964, Ivan Butler *Cinema in Britain* Tantivy Press 1973 and Patricia Warren *The British Film Collection 1896–1984: A History of the British Cinema in Pictures* Elm Tree Books 1984. Roy Armes *A Critical History of British Cinema* Secker and Warburg 1978 is a well-illustrated study of the cinema not as an industry but as an art-form in the context of the financial and international influences on the film-makers and the work of the individual directors.

**7389** Raymond Durgnat *A Mirror For England: British Movies from Austerity to Affluence* Faber 1970. A study of changing artistic trends in the British cinema. See also Raymond Lefevrè and Roland Lacourbe *Trente Ans de Cinema Brittanique* Editions 76 1976. The making and style of British films is examined in D Quinlan *British Sound Films: The Studio Years 1928–1959* Batsford 1984.

**7390** Leslie Halliwell *Seats In All Parts: Half a Lifetime at the Cinema* Granada 1985. A leading critic's memoirs and view of film and British cinemas 1930–80. Another useful autobiographical view from the stalls is [725]. These are also useful as evidence of the social impact of the cinema.

**7391** Jeffrey Richards and Anthony Aldgate *Best of British: Cinema and Society 1930–70* Blackwell 1983. A good analysis of ten selected important British films, though more investigation of the social impact of the films selected would have been useful.

**7392** James Curran and Vincent Porter (eds) *British Cinema History* Weidenfeld and Nicolson 1983. A disparate collection of essays on subjects such as the audience, state policy, Rank's attempts to break into the US market in 1944–9 or the Carry On films.

**7393**  Robert Murphy *Realism and Tinsel: Cinema and Society in Britain 1939–1948* Routledge 1989. A study of artistic trends in the cinema during and after the war and the representation of society in the cinema and its impact upon it.

**7394**  John Hill *Sex, Class and Realism: British Cinema 1956–1963* British Film Institute 1986. A good study of the new social realism of the cinema in a very creative period in which class, industrial and sexual issues were all addressed. The social realist cinema of this period is also reviewed in the context particularly of two films made in the period of contemporary working class novels by John Wain and Alan Sillitoe respectively in Arthur Marwick 'Room at the Top, Saturday Night, Sunday Morning and the "Cultural Revolution"' *Journal of Contemporary History* 19 1984 pp 127–52. See also [5545, 7193 and 7342].

**7395**  Peter John Graham *The Abortive Renaissance: Why Are Good British Films So Bad?* Axle Publications 1963. A critical assessment of the contemporary British cinema.

**7396**  Alexander Walker *Hollywood England: The British Film Industry in the Sixties* Michael Joseph 1974. A good study of the industry and trends in film-making in the 1960s. Ernest Betts *Inside Pictures: With Some Reflections from the Outside* Cresset Press 1960 is a useful contemporary guide to the organization and finance of the British and American film industries and the perennial problems of the former. See also Roger Manvell *New Cinema in Britain* Studio Vista 1969.

**7397**  Linda Wood (ed) *British Films 1971–1981* British Film Institute 1983. A catalogue of films for cinema and television made wholly or partly by British companies in the 1970s. The introduction traces the significant changes of the decade. Alexander Walker *National Heroes: British Cinema in the Seventies and Eighties* Harrap 1985 is a good survey of both the financial difficulties of the industry in this period and its artistic successes.

**7398**  Martyn Auty and Nick Roddick (eds) *British Cinema Now* British Film Institute 1985. An indispensable series of essays on the state of British film-making in the 1980s and the issues facing the industry.

**7399**  Margaret Dickinson and Sarah Street *Cinema and the State: The Film Industry and the Government 1927–84* British Film Institute 1985. A study of British government attempts to protect and nurture the domestic film industry in the face of the overwhelming dominance of Hollywood. The financial weakness of the British industry is examined in *The British Film Industry: A Report on its History and Present Organisation with Special Reference to the Economic Problems of British Feature Film Production* Political and Economic Planning 1952. British film policy is compared and contrasted with that of the French in D M Dickinson 'Government and the Film Industry: Britain and France 1945–1975' Edinburgh MPhil Thesis 1979. On the British Film Fund Agency set up under the 1957 Cinematographic Films Act to help channel funds into the industry see its *Annual Report and Statement of Accounts* HMSO 1957/58–.

**7400**  Paul Swann *The Hollywood Feature Film in Postwar Britain* Croom Helm 1987. This is an examination of the impact of American films on British society and culture, especially during the austerity years 1945–55. Though good on their appeal and on British government attempts to stem the tide he overstates the weakness of the British industry. One episode in the government's attempts to protect the domestic film industry in this period has been analysed in detail in Ian Jarvie 'British Trade Policy Versus Hollywood 1947–48: "Food before Flicks?"' *Historical Journal of Film, Radio and Television* 6 1986 pp 19–41. This is a study of the 75 per cent ad valorem duty slapped on American films in August 1947 to stop the dollar outflow.

**7401**  Ivan Butler *'To Encourage the Art of the Film'*: *The Story of the British Film Institute* Hale 1971. A history of the Institute which was established to encourage the British cinema and the preservation and study of film art in 1933.

**7402**  James C Robertson *The Hidden Cinema: British Film Censorship in Action 1913–1972* Routledge 1989. The law on film censorship and its historical development is examined in Neville March Hunnings *Film Censors and the Law* Allen and Unwin 1967. See also James C Robertson *The British Board of Film Censors: Film Censorship in Britain 1896–1950* Croom Helm 1985.

**7403**  J P Mayer *British Cinemas and their Audiences* Dobson 1948. A survey of audiences and their tastes. After the early 1950s audiences dropped under the impact of television. The factors involved in the economics and statistics of decline and the implications for cinema chains and film-makers were already being assessed in gloomy terms in John Spraos *The Decline of the Cinema: An Economist's Report* Allen and Unwin 1962. Other contemporary reports on the state of the industry are *The British Film Industry* Political and Economic Planning 1952 and *The British Film Industry* Political and Economic Planning 1958. See also John Watson 'The Changing Economics of the Cinema' *Three Banks Review* 102 1974 pp 35–54.

**7404** David Atwell *Cathedrals of the Movies: A History of British Cinemas and their Audiences* Architectural Press 1980. A good architectural history of the British picture palace placed in the context of the social importance of the cinema. See also Dennis Sharp *The Picture Palace and Other Buildings for the Movies* Hugh Evelyn 1969.

**7405** Charles Barr *Ealing Studios* Cameron and Tayleur 1977. A history of the studios where the celebrated Ealing comedies were made. On the Ealing comedies see J C P Ellis 'The Ealing Comedies 1947–57: Their Production and Use' Birmingham MA Thesis 1974–5. George Perry *George Perry Presents Forever Ealing: A Celebration of the Great British Film Studio* Pavilion 1985 is a tribute to the film-makers who worked at Ealing and the films they produced.

**7406** Patricia Warren *Elstree: The British Hollywood* Elm Tree Books 1983. A history of the complexes of studios at Elstree from their heyday to the 1980s when most of the surviving capacity is used as studios by the BBC.

**7407** George Perry *Movies from the Mansion: A History of Pinewood Studios* Elm Tree Books 1986. A history of the main complex of studios in post-war Britain.

**7408** Nicholas Pronay 'The British Post-Bellum Cinema: A Survey of the Films Relating to World War Two made in Britain between 1945 and 1960' *Historical Journal of Film, Radio and Television* 8 1988 pp 39–54.

**7409** Elizabeth Sussex *The Rise and Fall of British Documentary: The Story of the Film Movement founded by John Grierson* University of California Press 1975. An oral history and survey of the documentary film movement, in which the documentary was treated as art, up to its post-war decline.

**7410** P de K Dusinberre 'English Avant-Garde Cinema 1966–1974' London MPhil Thesis 1977.

**7411** *The House of Hammer: The Complete Story of Hammer Films* 2nd ed, Lorrimer 1981. A history of the British horror film company of the post-war period.

**7412** Jim Pines 'Blacks on Film – The British Angle' *Multiracial Education* 9 1981 pp 3–15. An analysis of the changing presentation of blacks on British film and television.

**7413** R J Minney *Puffin Asquith: A Biography* Frewin 1973. A biography of the film director son of the Liberal Prime Minister.

**7414** Sir Michael Balcon *Michael Balcon Presents – A Lifetime of Films* Hutchinson 1969. An autobiography. Balcon was involved as a film producer in many of the important films of the post-war years and was a director of many film companies.

**7415** Muriel Box *Odd Woman Out* Frewin 1974. The autobiography of a scriptwriter.

**7416** Adrian Brunel *Nice Work: The Story of Thirty Years in British Film Production* Forbes Robertson 1949. The memoirs of a film producer and scriptwriter.

**7417** T E B Clarke *This Is Where I Came In* Michael Joseph 1974. Memoirs of the scriptwriter of Ealing comedies such as *Passport to Pimlico*, *The Titfield Thunderbolt* and *The Lavender Hill Mob* (for which he won an Oscar).

**7418** Basil Dean *Mind's Eye: An Autobiography* Hutchinson 1973. The autobiography of the stage and film director and producer.

**7419** Roberto Vaccino *Blake Edwards* Le Nuova Italia, Firenze 1979. The only study of the film maker and his innovative work.

**7420** Bryan Forbes *Notes for a Life* Collins 1974. An autobiography by the film director.

**7421** Donald Spoto *The Life of Alfred Hitchcock: The Dark Side of Genius* Collins 1983. A warts and all biography of the director. John Russell Taylor *Hitch: The Life and Work of Alfred Hitchcock* Faber 1978 is less of an investigation into previously unexplored aspects of Hitchcock's character and more a critical assessment of his films and his approach to film-making. See also T Ryall 'Alfred Hitchcock and the British Cinema' CNAA MPhil Thesis 1979.

**7422** Derek Jarman *The Last of England* Constable 1987. An account of the film which includes an autobiographical fragment by the stage designer and film-maker.

**7423** Karol Kulik *Alexander Korda: The Man Who Could Work Miracles* W H Allen 1975. An excellent biography of the Hungarian-born director and producer. Korda was a key figure in the British film industry and its survival either side of the Second World War. It is also a useful general study of the film industry in these years. The appendices includes a filmography. See also P Tabori *Alexander Korda* Oldbourne 1959.

**7424** Alain Silver and James Ursini *David Lean and His Films* Frewin 1974. A study of the life and work of the film director. Michael A Anderegg *David Lean* Twayne, Boston, Massachusetts 1984 is a short assessment of the his life and work which includes a chronology, filmography and bibliography.

**7425** Michael Powell *A Life in Movies: An Autobiography* Heinemann 1986. Powell, in association with Emeric Pressberger, was one of the most important and influential film-makers of the early post-war period. This autobiography traces his career up to 1948. Kevin Gough-Yates (comp) *Michael Powell in Collaboration with Emeric Pressberger* British Film Institute 1971 is a celebration of the work of Powell and Pressberger, as is his *Michael Powell* Royal Film Archive of Belgium, Brussels 1973.

**7426** Andrew Yule *Enigma: David Putnam: The Story So Far* Mainstream 1988. A biography of the film producer who was one of the key figures behind the artistic, if not financial, revival of the British cinema in the early 1980s.

**7427** Alan Wood *Mr Rank: A Study of J Arthur Rank and British Films* Hodder and Stoughton 1952. Rank was a wealthy Methodist flour miller who saw films as a means of promoting Christian values and therefore built up a dominant position in the British film industry in the 1930s. His role in and influence on the industry is examined.

**7428** Robert F Moss *The Films of Carol Reed* Macmillan 1987. A study of the life and work of the film director.

**7429** Diane Rosenfeldt *Ken Russell: A Guide to References and Resources* Prior 1978. A guide to material on the life and work of the flamboyant film director. Ken Russell *A British Picture: An Autobiography* Heinemann 1989 is a chronicle of Russell's life and achievements, a tribute to Britain and the British cinema and a polemic on what they both should be. See also the authorised biography, John Baxter *An Appalling Talent: Ken Russell* Michael Joseph 1973.

**7430** Nancy J Brooker *John Schlesinger: A Guide to References and Resources* Prior 1978. A guide to material on the life and work of the film director.

**7431** Herbert Wilcox *Twenty-Five Thousand Sunsets* The Bodley Head 1967. The autobiography of the producer and director of films and husband of Anna Neagle.

**7432** Bill Harding *The Films of Michael Winner* Muller 1978. A guide to the work of the film director.

(f) Actors

**7433** S Palmer *A Who's Who of British Film Actors* Scarecrow 1981. A collection of potted biographies of about 1,400 actors and actresses including some Commonwealth actors and some British born actors who made their names and careers entirely outside the UK.

**7434** Michael Sanderson *From Irving to Olivier: A Social History of the Acting Profession in England 1880–1983* Athlone Press 1984.

**7435** Sandra L Richards *The Rise of the English Actress* Macmillan 1988. A social history of the rise of the actress over the centuries to the current status and respectability she now enjoys. The section on the twentieth century focuses on Dames Sybil Thorndike, Edith Evans and Peggy Ashcroft.

**7436** Hal Burton (ed) *Great Acting* BBC Books 1967. A collection of edited interviews with Laurence Olivier, Sybil Thorndike, Ralph Richardson, Peggy Ashcroft, Michael Redgrave, Edith Evans, John Gielgud and Noël Coward. The appendix supplies a chronological guide to their acting careers.

**7437** Richard Findlater *These Our Actors: A Celebration of the Theatre Acting of Peggy Ashcroft, John Gielgud, Laurence Olivier and Ralph Richardson* Elm Tree Books 1983.

**7438** Joss Ackland *I Must Be In There Somewhere* Hodder and Stoughton 1989. The autobiography of the actor.

**7439** For Betty Astell see [7509].

**7440** Michael Billington *Peggy Ashcroft* Murray 1988. The authorized biography of Dame Peggy Ashcroft. See also Robert Tonitch *Ashcroft* Hutchinson 1987.

**7441** Dirk Bogarde *A Postillion Struck by Lightning* Chatto and Windus 1977. The first of a series of autobiographies by the film actor which is continued by his *Snakes and Ladders* Chatto and Windus 1978, *An Orderly Man* Chatto and Windus 1983 and *Backcloth* Viking 1986. These are collected in Dirk Bogarde *Dirk Bogarde: The Complete Autobiography* Methuen 1988.

**7442** Tony Booth *Stroll On: An Autobiography* Sidgwick and Jackson 1989. The autobiography of an actor who has worked particularly in television.

**7443** Kenneth Branagh *Beginnings* Chatto and Windus 1989. The autobiography of one of the leading actors of the 1980s.

**7444** Peter Bull *Bull's Eye* Robin Clark 1985. The actor's memoirs selected and edited by Sheridan Morley. The appendix lists the details of Bull's career.

**7445**  Simon Callow *Being An Actor* Methuen 1984. This is partly an autobiography and partly a collection of acute observations on the profession.

**7446**  Timothy J Lyons *Charlie Chaplin: A Guide to References and Resources* Prior 1979. Chaplin had an enormous worldwide impact as the major comedy star of the first great form of mass entertainment in the Hollywood of the silent era. As such he is the subject of a massive literature. The most substantial biography is David Robinson *Chaplin: His Life and Art* Collins 1985. Other useful biographies are Maurice Bessy *Charlie Chaplin* Thames and Hudson 1985 and Denis Gifford *Chaplin* Macmillan 1974. Chaplin's own autobiography, *My Autobiography* The Bodley Head 1964 is a useful and in places moving work. See also Charles Spencer Chaplin *My Father, Charlie Chaplin* Longmans 1960. The second half of Chaplin's career, including his post-war film work, his troubles in America with McCartheyism during the Cold War and his eventual retirement, is traced in Jerry Epstein *Remembering Chaplin* Bloomsbury 1988.

**7447**  Michael Feeney Callan *Julie Christie* W H Allen 1984. A biography of the actress.

**7448**  John Courtenay Trewin *Alec Clunes* Rockliff 1958. A biography of the actor.

**7448A**  Joan Collins *Past Imperfect: An Autobiography* revised ed, Coronet 1985. See also Robert Levine *Joan Collins: Superstar: A Biography* 2nd ed, Chivers 1986 and Jill Rovin *Joan Collins: The Unauthorized Biography* 2nd ed, Bantam 1985.

**7449**  Sheridan Morley *Gladys Cooper: A Biography* Heinemann 1979. A biography of his actress grandmother. See also Sewell Stokes *Without Veils: The Intimate Biography of Gladys Cooper* Peter Davies 1953.

**7450**  Peter Cushing *Past Forgetting: Memoirs of the Hammer Years* Weidenfeld and Nicolson 1988. The autobiography of an actor particularly renowned for his work in Hammer's horror films.

**7451**  Gerald Jacobs *A Great Deal of Laughter: Judi Dench: An Authorised Biography* Weidenfeld and Nicolson 1985.

**7452**  John Courtenay Trewin *Robert Donat: A Biography* Heinemann 1968. A biography of the celebrated film actor of the inter-war and early post-war period.

**7453**  Diana Dors *Behind Closed Dors* W H Allen 1979. Other autobiographies by the actress are *Dors by Diana* Macdonald Futura 1981 and *For Adults Only* W H Allen 1978. See also Joan Florey *Diana Dors: Only A Whisper Away* Lennard 1987.

**7454**  Bryan Forbes *Ned's Girl: The Authorised Biography of Dame Edith Evans* Elm Tree Books 1977. See also Jean Battersby *Edith Evans: A Personal Memoir* Hart-Davis MacGibbon 1977. John Courtenay Trewin *Edith Evans* Rockliff 1954 is a well illustrated but rather early biography written when her career was still at its height.

**7455**  Trader Faulkner *Peter Finch: A Biography* Angus and Robertson 1979. A good biography of the distinguished Australian-born classical and film actor.

**7456**  Sir John Gielgud *An Actor and His Time* Sidgwick and Jackson 1979. A memoir. Gielgud became a leading figure in the acting profession in the inter-war years. The best biography is Ronald Hayman *John Gielgud* Heinemann 1971. Robert Tonitch *Gielgud* Harrap 1988 is an illustrated guide to his career. See also Gyles Brandreth *John Gielgud* Pavilion 1984.

**7457**  Hermione Gingold *How To Grow Old Disgracefully: An Autobiography* Gollancz 1988. A posthumously published autobiography by the actress and revue artiste.

**7458**  Stewart Granger *Sparks Fly Upward* Granada 1981. The autobiography of the film actor up to his divorce from Jean Simmons in 1960. It includes a filmography.

**7459**  Alec Guinness *Blessings in Disguise* Hamilton 1985. Autobiographical reminiscences of Sir Alec Guinness covering his long and distinguished career. John Russell Taylor *Alec Guinness: A Celebration* Pavilion 1984 is a well illustrated guide to his career.

**7460**  Sheila Hancock *Ramblings of an Actress* Arrow 1989.

**7461**  For Richard Harris see [7462].

**7462**  Rex Harrison *Rex: An Autobiography* Macmillan 1974. See also Roy Moseley, Philip Masheter and Martin Masheter *Rex Harrison: The First Biography* New English Library 1987. Elizabeth Harrison *Love, Honour and Dismay* Weidenfeld and Nicolson 1976 is the autobiography of the daughter of Lord Ogmore, a minister in the Attlee government, who was successively wife to Richard Harris and Rex Harrison.

**7463**  Paulene Stone *One Tear Is Enough: A Biography of Laurence Harvey* Michael Joseph 1975.

**7464**  Jack Hawkins *Anything for a Quiet Life* Elm Tree Books 1973. The autobiography of the celebrated screen actor.

**7465** Karen Moline *Bob Hoskins: An Unlikely Hero* Sidgwick and Jackson 1988. A biography of the actor.

**7466** Vivienne Howard *Trevor Howard: A Gentleman and a Player* Muller, Blond and White 1986. An anecdotal biography of the actor. Michael Munn *Trevor Howard: The Man and His Films* Robson 1989 is useful on his film career.

**7467** Ian Woodward *Glenda Jackson: A Study in Fire and Ice* Coronet 1986. The fullest biography of the Oscar-winning actress. See also David Nathan *Glenda Jackson* Spellmount 1984.

**7468** Peter Underwood *Horror Man: The Life of Boris Karloff With An Appendix Of The Films In Which He Appeared* Frewin 1972. Karloff (real name William Henry Pratt) was particularly known for his career in horror films.

**7469** Simon Callow *Charles Laughton: A Difficult Actor* Methuen 1987. An excellent biography of a great actor. See also Kurt D Singer *The Charles Laughton Story* Hale 1954.

**7470** Christopher Lee *Tall, Dark and Gruesome: An Autobiography* W H Allen 1977. The autobiography of the actor who made his name acting in Hammer Horror films. See also Robert W Pohle *The Films of Christopher Lee* Scarecrow 1983.

**7471** Alexander Walker *Vivien: The Life of Vivien Leigh* Methuen 1988. A good biography of the actress who rose to international stardom as Scarlett O'Hara in *Gone With The Wind* in 1939, tracing her career, her marriage to Laurence Olivier and her decline and death. See also John Russell Taylor *Vivien Leigh* Elm Tree Books 1984, Hugo Vickers *Vivien Leigh* Hamilton 1988, Anne Edwards *Vivien Leigh – A Biography* W H Allen 1977, Alan Dent *Vivien Leigh: A Bouquet* Hamilton 1969 and Gwen Robyns *Light of a Star* Frewin 1968. On her marriage to Olivier see [7483].

**7472** Joanna Lumley *Stand Back and Smile* Viking 1989. The autobiography of the actress.

**7473** Maurice Zolotow *Stagestruck – Alfred Lunt and Lynn Fontanne* Heinemann 1965. A biography of the husband and wife acting team.

**7474** Diana de Rosso *James Mason* Lennard Publishing 1989. The best biography of the distinguished screen actor. Sheridan Morley *James Mason: Odd Man Out* Weidenfeld and Nicolson 1989 is a good warts and all biography which elucidates many aspects of Mason's character which remain unrevealed in Mason's own autobiography, *Before I Forget* Hamilton 1981.

**7475** Sir John Mills *Up In The Clouds, Gentlemen Please* Weidenfeld and Nicolson 1980. The autobiography of the distinguished actor, including a list of his acting credits.

**7476** Paul Donovan *Dudley* W H Allen 1988. A biography of Dudley Moore from his role in satirical comedy in the 1960s, particularly in association with Peter Cook, to the Hollywood career he established in the 1980s.

**7477** Roy Moseley with Philip and Martin Masheter *Roger Moore: The First Biography* New English Library 1985. A biography of the film actor, most famous for his portrayal of James Bond.

**7478** Kenneth More *Happy Go Lucky: My Life* Hale 1959. The autobiography of the screen actor.

**7479** Robert Morley with Sewell Stokes *Robert Morley: 'Respectable Gentleman'* Heinemann 1966. A biographical study of Robert Morley drawn from his conversations with Sewell Stokes.

**7480** Anna Neagle *There's Always Tomorrow: An Autobiography* W H Allen 1974. The autobiography of Dame Anna Neagle.

**7481** John Courtenay Trewin *John Neville* Barrie and Rockliff 1961.

**7482** Sheridan Morley *The Other Side of the Moon: The Life of David Niven* Weidenfeld and Nicolson 1985. A good biography of the film actor. It critically assesses Niven's life and career. Niven's own autobiography, *The Moon's A Balloon* Hamilton 1971, whilst being very amusing and informative about Hollywood 1935–60 (the period covered in the book), reveals little of Niven himself. Niven's other autobiographical work, *Bring on the Empty Horses* Hamilton 1975 is more a memoir of Hollywood life, pictures and personalities in its heyday between 1930–60 than an account of his own career. On Niven see also Charles Francisco *David Niven: Endearing Rascal* W H Allen 1987.

**7483** Laurence Olivier *Confessions of an Actor* Weidenfeld and Nicolson 1982. The autobiography of Lord Olivier, held in high esteem as one of the finest, not to mention most versatile, actors to tread the boards in the twentieth century. Unfortunately it is rather elliptical and unrevealing. There are also autobiographical reflections on his career and profession in Olivier's *On Acting* Weidenfeld and Nicolson 1976. The latest biography, Anthony Holder *Olivier* Weidenfeld and Nicolson 1988, is a spirited but flawed attempt to fill the gaps left by Olivier's self-portrait and flesh out the man. Olivier has attracted numerous biographers and his recent death will no doubt encourage more. Amongst the most useful is

John Cottrell *Laurence Olivier* Weidenfeld and Nicolson 1975. For other biographies see Melvyn Bragg *Laurence Olivier* Hutchinson 1984, Thomas Kiernan *Olivier: The Life of Laurence Olivier* Sidgwick and Jackson 1981, Virginia Fairweather *Cry God for Larry: An Intimate Memoir of Sir Laurence Olivier* Calder and Boyers 1969, Raymond Lefèvre *Sir Laurence Olivier* Editions PAC, Paris 1980, Foster Hirsch *Laurence Olivier* Twayne, Boston, Massachusetts 1979 and Robert Tanitch *Olivier: The Complete Career* Thames and Hudson 1985. Garry O'Connor (ed) *Olivier: In Celebration* Hodder and Stoughton 1987 is a collection of tributes and memoirs by fellow actors, playwrights and directors. It includes a chronology of his career. A similar volume is Logan Gourlay (ed) *Olivier* Weidenfeld and Nicolson 1973. On Olivier's marriage to Vivien Leigh see Jesse Lasky *Love Scene: The Story of Laurence Olivier and Vivien Leigh* Sphere 1980 and Richard Felix Raine Barker *The Oliviers: A Biography* Hamilton 1953.

**7484** Nicholas Wapshott *Peter O'Toole: A Biography* New English Library 1983. The best biography. Michael Freedland *Peter O'Toole* St Martins, New York 1982 is a rather poor if colourful and anecdotal biography of the actor.

**7485** Sir Michael Redgrave *In My Mind's Eye: An Autobiography* Weidenfeld and Nicolson 1983. The autobiography of the distinguished actor.

**7486** Oliver Reed *Reed All About Me: The Autobiography of Oliver Reed* W H Allen 1979. An anecdotal autobiography by the film actor.

**7487** Garry O'Connor *Ralph Richardson: An Actor's Life* 2nd ed, Hodder and Stoughton 1986. A well regarded biography of Sir Ralph Richardson.

**7488** Brian Rix *Farce About Face* Hodder and Stoughton 1989. Rix made his name starring in the celebrated farces at the Whitehall Theatre in London in the 1950s and 1960s. This autobiography traces both his acting career and his later career as Secretary-General of Mencap, the charity for the mentally handicapped.

**7489** Alexander Walker *No Bells on Sunday: The Journals of Rachel Roberts* Sphere 1985. A biography and edited selection from the journals of the actress who committed suicide in 1982.

**7490** Kenneth Barrow *Flora: An Appreciation of the Life and Work of Dame Flora Robson* Heinemann 1981. A good, well illustrated biography. See also Janet Dunbar *Flora Robson* Harrap 1960.

**7491** Robert Tanitch *Leonard Rossiter* Robert Royce 1985. A biography.

**7492** Dame Margaret Rutherford *An Autobiography* W H Allen 1972. The life and career of the distinguished actress is also examined by her adopted daughter in Dawn Langley Simmons *Margaret Rutherford: A Blithe Spirit* Sphere 1985.

**7493** John Courtenay Trewin *Paul Scofield* Rockliff 1956. An early, and still the only, biographical study of the distinguished actor.

**7494** Alexander Walker *Peter Sellers: The Authorised Biography* Weidenfeld and Nicolson 1981. The life and career of the comic actor and former member of the Goons is also examined in Peter Evans *Peter Sellers: The Mask Behind the Mask* Saxon House 1981.

**7495** Donald Sinden *A Touch of the Memoirs* Hodder and Stoughton 1982. An anecdotal autobiography, continued in his *Laughter in the Second Act* Hodder and Stoughton 1985.

**7496** Terence Stamp *Stamp Album* Bloomsbury 1987. An autobiographical treatment of the early part of his life and career, continued by his *Coming Attraction* Bloomsbury 1988.

**7497** Elizabeth Taylor *Elizabeth Takes Off: An Autobiography* Macmillan 1988. On the much married film star see also Sheridan Morley *Elizabeth Taylor: A Celebration* Pavilion 1988 and Kitty Kelley *Elizabeth Taylor: The Last Star* Michael Joseph 1981.

**7498** Sheridan Morley *Sybil Thorndike: A Life in the Theatre* Weidenfeld and Nicolson 1977. A biography of the distinguished actress. See also Elizabeth Sprigge *Sybil Thorndike* Casson Gollancz 1971 and John Courtenay Trewin *Sybil Thorndike* Rockliff 1955.

**7499** Peter Ustinov *Dear Me* Heinemann 1977. The autobiography of the actor, author and playwright.

**7500** Jack Warner *Jack of All Trades: An Autobiography* W H Allen 1975. An autobiography of the actor most celebrated for his creation of the role of Dixon of Dock Green on film and television.

**7501** Ronald Hayman *Sir Donald Wolfit CBE* Secker and Warburg 1971. A good biographical study of one of the last of the great actor-managers.

## (g) Music Hall, Variety and Circuses

**7502** Roy Busby (ed) *British Music Hall: An Illustrated Who's Who from 1880 to the Present Day* Elek 1976. A well illustrated collection of biographical sketches.

**7503** R Mander and J Michenson *British Music Hall* Gentry Books 1974. A history up to the post-war period of decline and change. It includes useful appendices. See also John M Garrett *Sixty Years of British Music Hall* Chappell/Deutsch 1977. G J Mellor *The Northern Music Hall: A Century of Popular Entertainment* Frank Graham 1970 has a little on the decline of the music hall after 1945.

**7504** R Wilmut *Kindly Leave The Stage: The Story of Variety 1919–1960* Methuen 1986. During this period variety increasingly came to be dominated by and subordinate to broadcasting and the music halls, palaises and hippodromes gradually disappeared.

**7505** Denis Gifford *The Golden Age of Radio* Batsford 1985. A directory of light entertainment programmes and events from the 1930s to the 1950s (with some coverage of the 1920s and 1960s) after which television replaced radio as the main form of mass entertainment. This is a very useful reference guide to a form of entertainment in which most of the leading variety stars of this period served.

**7506** Maureen Owen *The Crazy Gang: A Personal Reminiscence* Weidenfeld and Nicolson 1986. A memoir of the music hall star comedians who were at the height of their powers from the 1930s to the late 1950s. Bud Flanagan *My Crazy Life* Muller 1961 is the autobiography of one of their leading members.

**7507** Arthur Askey *Before Your Very Eyes* Woburn 1975. The autobiography of the entertainer.

**7508** Jimmy Chipperfield *My Wild Life* Macmillan 1975. An autobiography of his life spent running circuses, zoos and safari parks.

**7509** Cyril Fletcher *Nice One Cyril: Being the Odd Odessey and Anecdotage of a Comedian* Barrie and Jenkins 1978. The memoirs of a comedian covering the music hall, pantomime, television work and his marriage to the actress Betty Astell.

**7510** Gracie Fields *Sing As We Go: The Autobiography of Gracie Fields* Muller 1960. The autobiography of the film and singing star who died in 1979. The best biography is Joan Moules *Our Gracie: The Life of Dame Gracie Fields* Hale 1983. This includes a filmography and discography. See also Muriel Burgess *Gracie Fields* W H Allen 1980.

**7511** Alan Randall and Ray Seaton *George Formby: A Biography* W H Allen 1974. The Lancashire comic made his last film in 1946 after which he concentrated on his music hall career. See also John Fisher *George Formby* Woburn 1975.

**7512** Peter Underwood *Life's a Drag: Danny La Rue and the Drag Scene* Frewin 1974. This is essentially a biography of Danny La Rue, who had a tremendously successful drag act in the 1960s and early 1970s.

**7513** Fred Lawrence Guiles *Stan* Michael Joseph 1980. A biography of Stan Laurel. Laurel and Hardy were among the leading Hollywood movie comedy acts of the inter-war years. After 1945 they were much less active, though they did tour the British music halls in the 1950s. See also John McCabe *The Comedy World of Stan Laurel* Robson 1975. Randy Skretvedt *Laurel and Hardy: The Magic Behind the Movies* Apollo 1987 is a massive study of their lives and comic genius.

**7514** John M East *Max Miller: The Cheeky Chappie* W H Allen 1977. A biography of the celebrated stand-up comedian who died in 1963. It includes tributes from contemporaries and a discography.

**7515** Albert Edward Wilson *Prime Minister of Mirth: The Biography of Sir George Robey CBE* Odhams 1956. A biography of one of the most celebrated figures in the music hall since before the First World War. See also Peter Cotes *George Robey: The Darling of the Halls* Cassell 1972.

**7516** Max Wall *The Fool on the Hill* Quartet 1979. The memoirs of one of the most notable music hall artistes and comedians of the post-war period.

(h) Comedy

**7517** D Nathan *The Laughtermakers: A Quest for Comedy* Peter Owen 1971. A history of the development and trends in British comedy in the post-war period, including comedy on television and radio.

**7518** Barry Took *Laughter in the Air: An Informal History of British Radio Comedy* 2nd ed, Robson/BBC 1981. Took himself is a notable writer and performer of radio comedy. This is an inside history of the development of BBC radio comedy since 1922.

**7519** Robert Hewison *Footlights: A Hundred Years of Cambridge Comedy* Methuen 1983. A good history. It provides a well illustrated guide to the development and productions of the Cambridge revue troupe.

**7520** R Wilmut *From Fringe to Flying Circus: Celebrating a Unique Generation of Comedy 1960–1980* Eyre Methuen 1980. A study of the importance of the Oxbridge influence on British comedy in this period.

**7521** Francis Worsley *'ITMA' 1939–1948* Vox Mundi Books 1948. The reminiscences of the producer of the popular radio comedy show. Bill Grundy *That Man: A Memory of Tommy Handley* Elm Tree Books 1976 is a biography of the star of the show.

**7522** R Wilmut and J Grafton *The Goon Show Companion: A History and Goonography* Robson 1976. A history and reference guide to the cult radio show of the 1950s. See also A Draper *et al The Story of the Goons* Everest 1976. Sir Harry Secombe *Arias and Raspberries* Robson 1989 is an autobiography covering his career from wartime army concert parties, through a spell at the Windmill Theatre in London after the war up to the beginning of the Goons. See also his earlier autobiographical reminiscences, *Goon Abroad* Robson 1982. The writer of the show, Spike Milligan has written six volumes of autobiography covering his war service and his immediate post-war experiences in an army concert party in Italy, culminating in his *Goodbye Soldier* Michael Joseph 1986. Milligan's post-war career as Goon, comedian and comic poet is traced in Pauline Scudamore *Spike Milligan: A Biography* Granada 1985 and Dominic Behan *Milligan: The Life and Times of Spike Milligan* Methuen 1988. For another member of the Goons, Peter Sellers, see [7494]. There are also some useful comments on the early history of the show in [7525].

**7523** George Perry *Life of Python* 2nd ed, Pavilion 1986. A history of Monty Python, the generic title of the group of Oxbridge graduates who made the cult BBC television show 1969–74 and of their subsequent films and television work. Their anarchic approach transformed television comedy. Robert Hewison *Monty Python: The Case Against* Eyre Methuen 1981 examines how they coped with censorship and the increasing unease of the BBC management with the series and the similar problems they have encountered since, not least over their controversial (and in some eyes, blasphemous) film, *Life of Brian*.

**7524** Ronnie Barker *Its Hello From Him* New English Library 1988. A good show business memoir.

**7525** Michael Bentine *The Long Banana Skin* Wolfe 1975. An autobiography covering his long career in variety and radio and television comedy, including his involvement in the early history of the Goons.

**7526** Joyce Grenfell *In Pleasant Places* Macmillan 1979. The autobiography of the comedienne. It includes reflections on her membership of the 1960 Pilkington committee on broadcasting. See also her *Requests the Pleasure* Macmillan 1976.

**7527** F Hancock and D Nathan *Hancock* Kimber 1969. A biography of Tony Hancock, the popular radio and television comedian of the 1950s and early 1960s. See also P Oakes *Tony Hancock* Woburn 1975 and R Wilmut *Tony Hancock: 'Artiste'* Eyre Methuen 1978.

**7528** John Smith *The Benny Hill Story* W H Allen 1988. A biography of the comedian.

**7529** N Hackforth *Solo for Horne: The Biography of Kenneth Horne* Angus and Robertson 1976. Kenneth Horne combined a successful career in industry with starring roles in a succession of popular wartime and post-war radio comedies culminating in the cult show of the 1960s, *Round the Horne*, which ended after his death in 1969.

**7530** Frankie Howerd *On The Way I Lost It: An Autobiography* W H Allen 1976. The autobiography of the comedian.

**7531** Joan Le Mesurier *Lady Don't Fall Backwards: A Memoir* Sidgwick and Jackson 1988. The memoirs of the wife of comic actor John Le Mesurier and the mistress of Tony Hancock.

**7532** Eric Morecambe and Ernie Wise *There's No Answer To That: An Autobiography With Help from Michael Freedland* Barker 1981. This covers their entire career from their music hall beginnings but concentrates on the 1970s when they had their own, extremely popular, show on television. Gary Morecambe *Funny Man: Eric Morecambe* Methuen 1982 is a memoir by his son and Joan Morecambe *Morecambe and Wife* Pelham 1985 a memoir by his wife.

**7533** Ned Sherrin *A Small Thing – Like an Earthquake – Memoirs* Weidenfeld and Nicolson 1983. A good memoir by a well connected and influential figure in the field of comedy, drama and entertainment. It also casts valuable light upon the inner workings of the BBC.

**7534** Michael Freedland *Kenneth Williams: A Biography* Weidenfeld and Nicolson 1989. A perceptive biography of the comedian. See also Kenneth Williams *Just Williams: An Autobiography* Fontana 1985.

**7535** Mike Yarwood *Impressions of My Life* Fontana 1986. The autobiography of an impressionist who enjoyed much popularity and success in the 1970s.

# 12 LOCAL HISTORY

## A. GENERAL

It should be noted that works which are in a sense local histories also appear elsewhere in the bibliography. Thus, for instance, the material on the various New Towns appears in the section on the development of New Town policy. Studies of race relations, industry, regional policy and so on in particular areas are covered in the relevant sections. Since much material of value is therefore scattered elsewhere throughout the bibliography the local historian is advised to consult the index for additional reading material on the history of his area of interest.

**7536**  W B Stephens *Sources for English Local History* Cambridge University Press 1981. This contains some useful guidance on the nature and availability of resources. Though most useful for historians of earlier periods it is still of some use to the post-war historian. See also Philip Riden *Local History: A Practical Handbook for Beginners* Batsford 1983.

**7537**  *Local Historian* 1952–. A quarterly journal. It contains informative articles on developments in local history, regular bibliographies and other useful information.

**7538**  *British Humanities Index: Regional Lists* Library Association 1954–68. An annual publication. The lists provide indexes of periodical articles covering each of the English counties.

**7539**  *County Magazine Index: An Index to Magazines Covering the Rural and Country Life of the Counties of England* Clover Publications 1979–. A quarterly index to about 27 magazines. It indexes about 3,500 articles per year, including some on Wales.

**7540**  Geoffrey Howard Martin and Sylvia McIntyre *A Bibliography of British and Irish Municipal History* Leicester University Press 1972. An annotated and classified bibliography of works published on municipal history between 1897 and 1967.

## B. LOCAL GOVERNMENT AND POLITICS

### (1) Reference Works

**7541**  Frederick A Youngs *Guide to the Local Administration Units of England Vol 1: Southern England* 2nd ed, Royal Historical Society 1981. A historical guide to the succession of local administrative units. *Godwin's Concise Guide to Local Authorities in England and Wales* George Godwin 1974 is a easy reference guide to the new local authorities set up in 1974 and the units they replaced. It is well furnished with maps.

**7542**  Lewis Golding *Dictionary of Local Government in England and Wales* English University Press 1962.

**7543**  Martin Minogue (ed) *Documents on Contemporary British Government Vol 2: Local Government in Britain* Cambridge University Press 1977. A collection of documents, maps and statistical tables, essentially covering the years since 1956.

**7544**  *Municipal Year Book and Public Services Directory* Municipal Journal 1898–. An annual directory, now published in two volumes. The first volume is a guide to relevant organizations. The second volume is a guide to local authority areas and the topography of their areas and to central government bodies.

**7545**  *Local Government Trends* Chartered Institute of Public Finance and Accountancy 1973–83, 1987. This appeared annually until 1983. It contains a mixture of statistical information and surveys of developments in various areas of the local government services.

**7546**  Mary Robinson (comp) *Local Authority Information Sources: A Guide to Publications, Databases and Services* Library Association 1986. A guide to current information sources and their publishers.

**7547**  D Halasz *Metropolis* Nijhoff, Den Haag 1967 pp 95–129. This is a select bibliography on administration in metropolitan areas around the world. It has a large section on Britain. The material is arranged chronologically without annotation. It concludes with a useful list of sources of information and material.

**7548** *Local Government Annotations Service* Central Library, Romford 1965–. This service publishes some 2,800 abstracts per annum on local government and related issues such as education, architecture, planning, transport, social work and environmental health.

**7549** W Barker *Local Government Statistics: A Guide to Statistics on Local Government Finance and Services in the United Kingdom at August 1964* Institute of Municipal Treasurers and Accountants 1965. This guide is now rather out date. However despite the fact that many of the titles referred to have since changed it remains useful. It is well annotated and refers to reports and other sources as well as serial publications.

**7550** *Local Government Financial Statistics* HMSO 1953–. An annual series. The best general statistical series on local government is now *Local Government Comparative Statistics* Chartered Institute of Public Finance and Accountancy 1981–.

**7551** *Who's Who in Local Government 1984/5* Carrick 1984. A guide to British local government officers.

**7552** Charles Cross and Stephen Bailey *Cross on Local Government Law* 7th ed, Sweet and Maxwell 1986. The latest edition of a legal textbook first issued in 1959. Each statement of the law affecting local government provides useful updates on the changes that occurred since the previous edition was published. Another good legal textbook is Keith Davies *Local Government Law* Butterworths 1983.

**7553** A J Little (ed) *Schofield's Local Government Elections* 8th ed, Shaw and Sons 1979. This reproduces and describes the relevant laws and statutory instruments in force.

### (2) General Works

**7554** Bryan Keith-Lucas and Peter Godfrey Richards *A History of Local Government in the Twentieth Century* Allen and Unwin 1978. The standard history of local government up to the reorganization carried out in 1974. Bryan Keith-Lucas *English Local Government in the Nineteenth and Twentieth Centuries* Historical Association 1977 is a useful short primer, though rather limited on the post-war period. I H Seeley *Local Government Explained* Macmillan 1978 is a useful study exploring the history of local government up until the 1974 reorganization.

**7555** Alan Alexander *The Politics of Local Government in the United Kingdom* Longman 1982. A good textbook tracing the major themes in the post-war history of local government. Alexander also provides an overview of the history of local government since 1945 in Alan Alexander and Chris Wrigley 'Symposium: Local Government' *Contemporary Record* 2/6 1989 pp 2–8 (Wrigley's piece is a case study of hung administration in Leicestershire County Council in the 1980s).

**7556** Martin Loughlin, M David Gelfand and Ken Young (eds) *Half a Century of Municipal Decline 1935–1985* Allen and Unwin 1985. This traces the weakening of the local government system and of local government power over this period, examining political, financial, economic and legal changes affecting local government.

**7557** Jack Brand *Local Government Reform in England 1888–1974* Croom Helm 1974. This examines the process of administrative change in local government from the setting up of the county councils to the reorganization of 1974. Administrative change over this period, especially in the context of the growing impact of central government on the organization and duties of local government, is also examined in Clifford Pearce *The Machinery of Change in Local Government 1888–1974: A Study of Central Involvement* Allen and Unwin 1980. T W Freeman *Geography and Regional Administration: England and Wales 1830–1968* Hutchinson 1968 is an analysis of local government reform from a spatial rather than an administrative point of view. See also W Thornhill (ed) *The Growth and Reform of English Local Government* Weidenfeld and Nicolson 1971 and B J Earley 'Local Government Reform in British Politics 1888–1958' Liverpool MA Thesis 1978.

**7558** Brian W Hogwood and Michael Keating (eds) *Regional Government in England* Clarendon 1982. A useful and detailed collection of essays and case studies. These cover regional government in its widest sense since they also embrace the regional organization of central government offices such as the Department of the Environment, regional policy and regional planning and regional water and health authorities. Howard Elcock *Local Government: Politicians, Professionals and the Public in Local Authorities* 2nd ed, Methuen 1986 is a textbook on regional government and its organization and aims which is even more comprehensive in its approach. See also H V Wiseman 'Regional Government in the United Kingdom' *Parliamentary Affairs* 19 1965–66 pp 56–82.

**7559** William A Robson *Local Government in Crisis* 2nd ed, Allen and Unwin 1968. A study of the loss of functions and utilities and the resulting changing relationship with central government. This superseded his earlier *The Development of Local Government* 2nd ed, Allen and Unwin 1954.

**7560** Tony Bryne *Local Government in Britain: Everyone's Guide to How It All Works* 5th ed, Penguin 1987. The most highly regarded study of the politics and organization of contemporary local government. It provides a good overview of trends in and affecting local government, as well as useful statistical and other appendices and a considerable bibliography. Another informative textbook which is particularly useful on developments in the 1980s is Gerry Stoker *The Politics of Local Government* Macmillan 1988. William Hampton *Local Government and Urban Politics* Longman 1987 is a study of the difficulties of local government in the 1970s and 1980s, concentrating on central/local relations. John Gyford, Steve Leach and Chris Game *The Changing Politics of Local Government* Unwin Hyman 1989 is another useful study, based on a research conducted for the Widdicombe Report [7573]. For studies interpreting the issues of the 1970s and 1980s see also C Cross and D Mallen *Local Government and Politics* 3rd ed, Longman 1987, Peter Godfrey Richards *The Local Government System* Allen and Unwin 1983 and John Gyford *Local Politics in Britain* Croom Helm 1984. The situation in the 1960s is explored in Richard Meredith Jackson *The Machinery of Local Government* 2nd ed, Macmillan 1965, W E Jackson *The Structure of Local Government in England and Wales* Longmans 1965 F W G Benemy *Whitehall – Town Hall* 6th ed, Harrap 1967. Another study which offers, in its succeeding editions, a picture of the changing nature of local government is J J Clarke *The Local Government of the United Kingdom* 20th ed, Pitman 1969. This series began before the Second World War. However its post-war editions were increasingly criticized. Another series of this kind which began before the Second World War was John Maud and Herman Finer *Local Government in England and Wales* 2nd ed, Oxford University Press 1953. This superseded Finer's *English Local Government* 3rd ed, Methuen 1950.

**7561** R A W Rhodes 'The Lost World of British Local Politics' *Local Government Studies* 1 1975 pp 39–59. A look back to the local government system of before the 1974 reorganization. It includes a good bibliography.

**7562** W W Crouch 'Local Government under the British Labour Government' *Journal of Politics* 12 1950 pp 232–59. See also J M Hawksworth 'Some Developments in Local Government 1944–1948' *Public Administration* 29 1948 pp 262–8.

**7563** H V Wiseman (ed) *Local Government in England 1958–69* Routledge and Kegan Paul 1970. This informative study covers a decade of considerable change in local government from the setting up of the English and Welsh boundary commissions to the report of the Redcliffe-Maud Royal Commission on Local Government [7565]. It also surveys events 1945–58.

**7564** Royston Greenwood, M A Lomer, C R Hinvigs and Stuart Ranson *The Organisation of Local Authorities in England and Wales 1967–75* Institute of Local Government Studies, University of Birmingham 1975.

**7565** *Royal Commission on Local Government in England 1966–1969* Cmnd 4040, *Parliamentary Papers* xxxviii 1968–69. This Royal Commission, chaired by Lord Redcliffe- Maud, produced three voluminous reports. It set the scene for the reorganization of local government, alongst lines rather different from those envisaged in the Commission's recommendations, enacted in the 1972 Local Government Act. The background to the decision to appoint the Commission is discussed in George W Jones 'Mr Crossman and the Reform of Local Government' *Parliamentary Affairs* 20 1966 pp 77–89. The background to, terms of reference, course and outcome of the Commission are all remembered in the Institute of Contemporary British History witness seminar of people closely involved in the event published as 'Symposium: Recliffe-Maud Royal Commission: Twenty Years On' *Contemporary Record* 2/6 1989 pp 30–5 and 3/1 1989 pp 36–8. Also of value for recapitulating the history of the Commission is L Welsh (ed) *Royal Commission on Local Government: Evidence in Brief: Summaries of Evidence to the Commission and of Other Material on the Subject Published in the Local Government Chronicle* Knight 1967. B Rose *England Looks to Maud* Justice of the Peace 1970 is an anthology of comments on the Commission and on the subsequent White Paper. The Commission is critically assessed in Roger W Benjamin 'Local Government in Post-Industrial Britain: Studies of the Royal Commission on Local Government' in Vincent Ostrom and Francis Bish (eds) *Comparing Urban Delivery Systems: Structure and Performance* Sage 1977 pp 149–72.

**7566** Bruce Wood *The Process of Local Government Reform 1966–74* Allen and Unwin 1976. An account of the whole process from the setting up of the Royal Commission. It has a foreword by Lord Redcliffe-Maud. The reformers are criticized as having concentrated more on function than democratic quality in L J Sharpe 'The Failure of Local Government Modernisation in Britain: A Critique of Functionalism' *Canadian Public Administration* 24 1981 pp 92–115. The importance of one of the major influences calling for reform is assessed in L P Barnhouse 'The Impact of Local Authority Associations on Local Government Reorganisation in England 1966–71' University of West Virginia PhD Thesis 1972.

**7567** Peter Godfrey Richards *The Local Government Act 1972: Problems of Implementation* Allen and Unwin 1975. A study of the 1972 Act reorganizing local government on lines significantly different from those recommended by the Royal Commission and of its subsequent implementation.

**7568** Department of the Environment *The New Local Authorities: Management and Structure: Report of a Study Group on Local Authority Management Structure* HMSO 1972. A report by a group chaired by M A Bains into one aspect of the implementation of the 1972 Act. Another aspect of the 1972 Act, the provisions which enabled non-elected persons to participate in the local government process through co-option on sub-committees with delegated powers, is examined in historical context in Ann Richardson 'Decision-Making by Non-Elected Members: An Analysis of New Provisions in the 1972 Local Government Act' *Journal of Social Policy* 6 1977 pp 171–84.

**7569** Department of the Environment/Welsh Office *Local Government in England and Wales: A Guide to the New System* HMSO 1974. An outline and a description of the new functions and electoral arrangements of the new authorities with maps. The reorganization affected not only local government but also local water, police and health authorities all of which are also covered in this guide.

**7570** *Conduct in Local Government: Prime Minister's Committee on Local Government Rules of Conduct* Cmnd 5636, *Parliamentary Papers* viii 1974. The report and recommendations of the committee chaired by Lord Redcliffe-Maud in the light of the Poulson scandal (see [289]). It investigated the Poulson Affair and its lessons and drew up a national code of conduct which was promulgated in October 1975.

**7571** Alan Alexander *Local Government Since Re-Organisation* Allen and Unwin 1982. This examines the situation and argues that the reformed system was based upon flawed legislation. Peter Godfrey Richards *The Reformed Local Government System* 4th ed, Allen and Unwin 1980 is a textbook which describes the background to the changes and the new institutions and framework that they created. John Dearlove *The Reorganisation of British Local Government: Old Orthodoxies and Political Perspectives* Cambridge University Press 1979 is a political science analysis of the changes in local government boundaries, administration, duties and finance after 1972. It has a good bibliography.

**7572** *Streamlining The Cities: Government Proposals for Re- Organising Local Government in Greater London and the Metropolitan Counties* Cmnd 9063, *Parliamentary Papers* 1983–84. The White Paper which outlined proposals, implemented in 1986, to abolish the metropolitan counties. All of these, with the exception of the Greater London Council, which had been established in 1965, had only been in existence since 1974.

**7573** Department of the Environment/Scottish Office *Local Authority Publicity: Interim Report of the Committee of Inquiry into the Conduct of Local Authority Business* HMSO 1985. This committee under David Widdicombe was set up in the light of renewed concern about the conduct of local authority business. Its final report, in five volumes, was *The Conduct of Local Authority Business: Report of the Committee of Inquiry into the Conduct of Local Authority Business* Cmnd 9797–9801, *Parliamentary Papers* 1985–86. It looks particularly at the rights and responsibilities of councillors and officers, the limits and conditions of discretionary spending and at ways of strengthening local democracy.

**7574** Bryan Keith-Lucas *The English Local Government Franchise* Blackwell 1952.

**7575** R E Jennings 'The Changing Representational Role of the Local Councillor in England' *Local Government Studies* 8 1985 pp 67–86. A study of changes since 1974 in the role and duties of the local councillor. It identifies an increasing centralization of power because of corporate planning, management schemes and the growth of formal party groupings.

**7576** S E Bristow 'Women Councillors: An Explanation of the Under-Representation of Women in Local Government' *Local Government Studies* 6 1980 pp 73–90. See also J Hills 'Women Local Councillors: A Reply to Bristow' *Local Government Studies* 8 1982 pp 61–71.

### (3) Types of Local Government

**7577** Kester Isaac-Henry 'The Association of Municipal Corporations and the County Councils Association: A Study of Influences and Pressures on the Reorganisation of Local Government 1945–1972' London PhD Thesis 1981. His article 'The English Local Authority Associations' *Public Administration Bulletin* 33 1980 pp 21–41 is based on material in this unpublished thesis. The record of the local authority associations since 1974 and their weakness vis-à-vis central government is critically assessed in his 'Taking Stock of the Local Authority Associations' *Public Administration* 62 1984 pp 129–46. The growth of party politics in the associations over this period is examined in John Gyford and Mari James 'The Development of Party Politics in the Local Authority Associations' *Local Government Studies* 8 1982 pp 23–46. The role and success of the associations as a conduit of local government pressure on central government in the period after reorganization is assessed in B J A Binder 'Relations between Central and Local Government Since 1975: Are the Associations Failing?' *Local Government Studies* 8 1982 pp 35–44.

**7578** P Bongers 'The British Sections of IULA and CEM' *Local Government Studies* 6 1980 pp 7–79. A study of the aims and work of the International Union of Local Authorities and of the Council of European Municipalities with especial emphasis on the British sections.

**7579** P Bassett *A List of the Historical Records of the County Councils Association (now the Association of County Councils)* Social Science Research Council 1980.

**7580** Ken Young (ed) *New Directions for County Government* Association of County Councils 1989. A volume of essays to mark the centenary of the foundation of the first county councils. The first part of the book examines their original objectives and their historical development. In the second part leading county chief officers appraise contemporary dilemmas and challenges. The final part is a political analysis of the nature of county government. It includes an excellent bibliographical review of the literature on county councils. The centenary was also marked by a special edition of the *Association of County Councils Gazette* 82/1 April 1989.

**7581** Jeffery Stanyer *County Government in England and Wales* Routledge and Kegan Paul 1967. A political science analysis and textbook. Bryan Keith-Lucas 'The Government of the County in England' *Western Political Quarterly* 9 1956 pp 44–55 is a political and historical analysis.

**7582** David Clark *Battle for the Counties: A Guide to the County Council Elections* Redrose 1977. A useful guide to the issues and the electoral system. It also covers the 1973 elections in detail. Another election guide is C Rallings and M Thrasher *The 1985 County Council Election Results in England* 2v, Plymouth Polytechnic 1986.

**7583** Keith Hoggart 'Explaining Policy Outputs: English County Boroughs 1949–74' *Local Government Studies* 9 1983 pp 57–68. A study of the county boroughs up to the reorganization of 1974. The impact of political control on local social policy is investigated in his 'Political Control and Urban Redistributive Policies: An Investigation of Social Well-Being Variation in 57 English Cities 1949–1974' London PhD Thesis 1984.

**7584** L J Sharpe (ed) *Voting in Cities: The 1964 Borough Elections* Macmillan 1967. A useful guide. Unfortunately publications such as this have not become regular features.

**7585** Charles Arnold-Baker *Parish Administration: Being a Treatise on the Administration of Rural Parishes by Parish Councils, Parish Meetings and Other Parish Authorities* Methuen 1958. The first half of this book provides detailed coverage on the history, organization, elections and duties of parish organizations. The second half of the book provides excerpts from relevant legislation. This was updated by his *The New Law and Practice of Parish Administration: Being a Treatise on the Civil Administration of Parishes in Rural Districts* Longcross Press 1966. See also J M Beck 'Parish Councils and their Representative Associations 1894–1970' Kent PhD Thesis 1971–2.

## (4) Parties in Local Politics

**7586** John Gyford and Mari Wilson *National Parties and Local Politics* Allen and Unwin 1983. A study of the relations between local and national parties, including a number of case studies. It is based on extensive interviews. Jim Bulpitt *Party Politics in English Local Government* Longmans 1967 remains a useful study, though politics has continued to grow in importance in local government since it was published. For an earlier perspective see J H Warren 'The Party System in Local Government' *Parliamentary Affairs* 5 1951–52 pp 179–94.

**7587** L J Sharpe and K Newton *Does Politics Matter? The Determinants of Public Policy* Clarendon 1984. A study which sets out to demonstrate that party politics are much more important than is generally thought in determining the level and priorities of local services using data from 1957–73. The party system in local government in the period after reorganization is analysed in S L Bristow 'Political Change and Party Systems in English and Welsh Local Government 1973–1979' Salford PhD Thesis 1985.

**7588** Steve Leach and Chris Game *Cooperation and Conflict: Politics in the Hung Counties* Common Voice 1989. A study of minority control and three party politics in the hung county councils of the 1980s. See also S Leach and J D Stewart 'The Politics and Management of Hung Authorities' *Public Administration* 66 1988 pp 35–55.

**7589** George W Jones and Alan Norton (eds) *Political Leadership in Local Authorities* Institute of Local Government Studies, University of Birmingham 1979.

**7590** D J Wilson and Michael Pinto-Duschinsky 'Conservative City Machines: The End of an Era' *British Journal of Political Science* 6 1976 pp 239–44. A requiem to the vanished autonomy of the provincial Tory city machine, its decline reflecting falling membership and diminishing success. It is particularly useful on Birmingham, Liverpool, Bradford and Manchester.

**7591** Howard Elcock 'Traditions and Change in Labour Party Politics: The Decline and Fall of the City Boss' *Political Studies* 39 1981 pp 439–47. A study of the decline of party machines.

**7592**  Stewart Lansley and Christian Wolmar *Councils in Conflict: The Rise and Fall of the Municipal Left* Macmillan 1988. A study of the power of the Labour Left in the town halls in the late 1970s and 1980s and its conflict with Westminster. It examines the ideological battle, the Left's record in power and its attempts to extend the activities of local government and the Thatcher government's attempts to contain the local Left. The local Left and its impact both on central government and on local government officers is also examined in John Gyford *The Politics of Local Socialism* Allen and Unwin 1985. See also M Boddy and C Fudge *Local Socialism?* Macmillan 1984. A Right-Wing analysis of the origins of the local Left and critique of its policies is offered in David Regan *The Local Left and Its National Pretensions* Centre for Policy Studies 1987.

**7593**  R Pinkney 'An Alternative Political Strategy? Liberals in Power in English Local Government' *Local Government Studies* 10 1984 pp 69–84. This seeks to demonstrate that the Liberals in the 1980s adopted a significantly different approach to common local government problems and to issues such as open government from their Conservative and Labour opponents. On the Liberals in local government in the 1970s and 1980s see also his 'Nationalising Local Politics and Localising a National Party: The Liberal Party in Local Government' *Government and Opposition* 18 1983 pp 347–58.

**7594**  Wyn Grant *Independent Local Politics in England and Wales* Saxon House 1978. A short analysis of the continuation of independent politics in local government and of independent movements such as ratepayers' associations. It draws on a number of case studies.

**7595**  Roger King and Neill Nugent 'Ratepapers' Associations in Newcastle and Wakefield' in John Garrard *et al* (ed) *The Middle Class in Politics* Saxon House 1978 pp 229–61. A couple of in-depth case studies. The Ratepayers' Association was set up in Newcastle in the 1960s. The one in Wakefield was set up as a result of a rates revolt after the 1974 reorganization.

### (5) Local Administration

**7596**  K P Poole *The Local Government Service in England and Wales* Allen and Unwin 1978. A survey of its contemporary organization with historical reflections, useful appendices and a good bibliography. This supersedes J H Warren *The Local Government Service* Allen and Unwin 1952.

**7597**  N Wilson 'The Local Government Service Since the War' *Public Administration* 30 1952 pp 131–8.

**7598**  Noel Boaden 'Innovation and Change in English Local Government' *Political Studies* 29 1971 pp 416–29. A study of contemporary developments.

**7599**  Royston Greenwood *et al Patterns of Management in Local Government* Robertson 1981. A study of all aspects of managerial developments since the 1974 reorganization. See also Royston Greenwood *et al In Pursuit of Corporate Rationality: Organisational Developments in the Post-Reorganisation Period* Institute of Local Government Studies, University of Birmingham 1977. The development of corporate planning in local government is analysed in R A W Rhodes and Arthur F Midwinter *Corporate Management: The New Conventional Wisdom in British Local Government* Centre for the Study of Public Policy 59, University of Strathclyde 1980. Royston Greenwood and J D Stewart *Corporate Planning in English Local Government: An Analysis with Readings 1967–72* Knight 1974 is a collection of documents drawn from various sources. On the development of corporate planning see also J D Stewart 'Developments in Corporate Planning in British Local Government: The Bains Report and Corporate Planning' *Local Government Studies* 5 1973 pp 13–30.

**7600**  Sir John Boynton *Job At The Top: The Role of the Chief Executive in Local Government* Longman 1986. A concise and informative study of each of the many areas of the main job in English local government, illustrated where necessary by Boynton's experience as chief executive of Cheshire County Council until 1979. The chief executive largely plays the role of the pre-reorganization town clerk. The work of the town clerk is discussed in T E Headrick *The Town Clerk in English Local Government* Allen and Unwin 1962. See also Sir C Barratt 'The Town Clerk in British Local Government' *Public Administration* 41 1963 pp 157–71.

**7601**  M Laffin and Ken Young 'The Changing Role and Responsibilities of Local Authority Chief Officers' *Public Administration* 63 1985 pp 41–59. This argues that there is an end of political consensus and increasing political impact on local government officers in the 1970s and 1980s.

**7602**  Thomas Llewellyn Poynton *et al The Institute of Municipal Treasurers and Accountants: A Short History 1885–1960* The Institute 1960. This has since become the Chartered Institute of Public Finance and Accountancy.

**7603**  R V Davies (ed) *Watchdog's Tales: The District Audit Service: The First 138 Years* HMSO 1986. A collection of essays and memoirs by former members of the District Audit Service (which was created in 1846 as an independent watchdog on the use of public funds by local government. The computerization of the service, the scandals and frauds it uncovered and its growing responsibilities up until its replacement in 1982 by the Audit Commission are also chronicled. Leonard Mervyn Helmore *The District Auditor* Macdonald and Evans 1961 is a valuable comprehensive account of the growth, functions and responsibilities of the service. See also A Wilson 'The District Audit Service' *Public Administration* 28 1950 pp 189–98. See also [6076].

7604   V Moore and H Sales *The Local Ombudsman: A Review of the First Five Years* JUSTICE 1980. A critical assessment of the Commission for Local Administration set up as a watchdog on local government under the Local Government Act 1974. Another useful study is Norman Lewis and Bernard Gateshill *The Commission for Local Administration: A Preliminary Appraisal* Royal Institute of Public Administration 1978. See also the review by a practising ombudsman, D C M Yardley 'Local Ombudsmen in England: Recent Trends and Developments' *Public Law* 1983 pp 522–31 and C M Chinkin and R J Bailey 'The Local Ombudsman' *Public Administration* 54 1976 pp 267–82.

7605   P Cook *Ombudsman: An Autobiography* BKT Publications 1981. This concentrates on his work as a local government ombudsman.

7606   Nicholas Deakin 'Research and the Policy-Making Process in Local Government' *Policy and Politics* 10 1982 pp 303–16. A study of the growth in the 1970s of policy research in local government.

## (6) Local Government Finance

7607   Tony Travers *The Politics of Local Government Finance* Allen and Unwin 1986. A clear and comprehensive statement outlining the major developments since the 1957 White Paper. It also makes clear the fiscal problems that have beset local government in the 1970s and 1980s. So does another useful textbook, K Newton and T J Karran *The Politics of Local Expenditure* Macmillan 1985. For another general statement on local government finance see N P Hepworth *The Finance of Local Government* 7th ed, Allen and Unwin 1984. An earlier study is Joseph Margach Drummond (revised by W A C Kitching) *The Finance of Local Government: England and Wales* 2nd ed, Allen and Unwin 1962.

7608   C D Foster, R A Jackson and M Perlman *Local Government in a Unitary State* Allen and Unwin 1980. A good study of contemporary developments in local government finance in the light of the vital importance of central government as a major source of revenue.

7609   P Pattinson 'Local Government Finance 1945–1955' Sheffield MA Thesis 1955–6.

7610   C Crawford and V Moore *The Free Two Pence: Section 137 of Local Government Act 1972 and Section 83 of the Local Government (Scotland) Act 1973* Chartered Institute of Public Finance and Accountancy 1983. A study of the constitutional significance and use of these sections which empowered local authorities to spend money above the expenditure on services for which local authorities have statutory responsibilities.

7611   *Local Government Finance: Report of the Committee of Inquiry* Cmnd 6453, *Parliamentary Papers* xxi 1975–76. This committee, chaired by Frank Layfield, was set up because of increasing concern about the growth of local government expenditure. The committee saw a need to apply greater responsibility and control over local government expenditure. It therefore drew attention to what it saw as the lack of accountability and fairness in the existing rating system and suggested a local income tax should replace it. The extent to which a new discipline was imposed in the wake of the report is assessed in Ian Ward and Peter Williams 'The Government and Local Accountability Since Layfield' *Local Government Studies* 18 1986 pp 21–32.

7612   P Birdseye and T Webb 'Why the Rate Burden is a Cause for Concern' *National Westminster Bank Quarterly Review* Feb 1984 pp 2–15. This analyses the rates burden and its effect on businesses as well as criticizing the rates system as unpredictable, likely to offer a poor return on services and unrelated to ability to pay.

7613   Tyrell Burgess and Tony Travers *Ten Billion Pounds: Whitehall's Takeover of the Town Halls* Grant McIntyre 1980. The Thatcher government's first response to the problem of growing local expenditure was the new block grant system of funding announced in 1980. This book is a critical study of this move and the background to it since the Layfield Report, which is seen as having been largely ignored.

7614   S Bailey and J Meadows 'High Spending Cities: An Historical Perspective' *Public Money* 4 1984 pp 21–6. This looks at spending over the previous thirty years in Manchester, Newcastle, Liverpool, Bristol, Birmingham and Leeds. It argues that there is supporting evidence for the government thesis of over-spending local authorities. T J Karran 'County Politics and Council Politics: Some Social and Political Determinants of County Council Expenditure 1950–71' Manchester PhD Thesis 1980 argues that party control does not seem to have had much impact on the amount of expenditure in county councils and points out that party politics was still not very strong on the councils before 1974. Another perspective on this question, looking at the fiscal problems of Labour-controlled authorities in the 1970s and 1980s, is Keith Hoggart 'Property Tax Resources and

Political Party Control in England 1974–1984' *Urban Studies* 23 1986 pp 33–46.

**7615** Richard Rose and Edward Page (eds) *Fiscal Stress in Cities* Cambridge University Press 1983. A collection of essays assessing the causes and consequences of the fiscal stress of local government in the 1970s and 1980s, caught between falling local revenues and governments anxious to keep down the grants to local authorities. P M Jackson, J Meadows and A B Taylor 'Urban Fiscal Decay in UK Cities' *Local Government Studies* 8 1985 pp 23–43 points to the problem of deteriorating infrastructures which both reduce the revenue and increase the costs of local government. This has been exacerbated by the desire of central government since the IMF crisis of 1976 to restrain its expenditure and not least its support for local government. The consequences of this for local government are examined in Keith Hoggart 'Responses to Local Fiscal Stress: Local Government Expenditures in England 1976–85' *Progress in Planning* 27 1987 pp 137–220.

**7616** Douglas E Ashford 'The Effects of Central Finance on the British Local Government System' *British Journal of Political Science* 6 1976 pp 305–22. An analysis of the years 1949–67. It argues that the heavy dependence on grants from central government in that period did not result in limited policy choices for local authorities. On central government funding see also A Crispin 'Local Government Finance: Assessing the Central Government's Contribution' *Public Administration* 54 1976 pp 45–61. The development of the Rate Support Grant, especially since 1974, is examined in R Atkinson *The Development of the Rate Support Grant (RSG) System* Department of Social Studies, Portsmouth Polytechnic 1984.

**7617** I D Ball 'Local Authority Capital Expenditure in the United Kingdom 1950–1973' Birmingham PhD Thesis 1976–7.

**7618** F R Oliver and Jeffery Stanyer 'Some Aspects of the Financial Behaviour of County Boroughs' *Public Administration* 47 1969 pp 169–84.

**7619** Royston Greenwood 'Changing Patterns of Budgeting in English Local Government' *Public Administration* 61 1983 pp 149–68. The growth of programme budgeting and corporate planning is examined in M M Bait-El-Mal 'An Investigation of Recent Developments in Government Budgeting with Particular Reference to British Local Government' Aston PhD Thesis 1978.

## (7) Relations with Central Government

**7620** R A W Rhodes *The National World of Local Government* Allen and Unwin 1986. This is especially useful on central/local relations and the role in this of the local authority associations. The nature of central/local relations are also explored in Rhodes' *Control and Power in Central-Local Relations* Gower 1981. The growth in conflict in central/local relations in the 1970s, particularly over local expenditure, is put the context of general government expenditure policy in his 'Continuity and Change in British Central-Local Relations: The "Conservative Threat"' *British Journal of Political Science* 14 1984 pp 261–83. His 'Intergovernmental Relations in the Post-War Period' *Local Government Studies* 8 1985 pp 35–56 summarizes developments in central/local relations in 1945–79 and seeks to explain why Conservative policy since then has highlighted the central/local conflict. The impact of the New Right on this conflict is examined with a case study approach to Lothian in Brian Elliott and David McCrone 'Austerity and the Politics of Resistance' in Ivan Szelenyi (ed) *Cities in Recession: Critical Responses to the Urban Policies of the New Right* Sage 1984 pp 192–216. For other recent studies of central/local relations drawing attention to this growing conflict see George W Jones *Central-Local Relations in Britain* Saxon House 1980 and Barrie Houlihan *The Politics of Local Government: Central-Local Relations* Longman 1986. This growing conflict is examined particularly in the context of the abolition of the metropolitan counties in 1986 in M Loughlin *Local Government in the Modern State* Sweet and Maxwell 1986.

**7621** Stewart Ranson, George W Jones and Kieron Walsh (eds) *Between Centre and Locality: The Politics of Public Policy* Allen and Unwin 1985. A good and extensive set of essays on central/local relations. They focus particularly on the growing crisis since the mid-1970s and the various attempts by central government to reduce the growth of expenditure of local government. There are also case studies of central/local relations in policy-making areas such as urban policy, transport, health or policing. See also M Goldsmith (ed) *New Research in Central-Local Relations* Gower 1986, Ken Young (ed) *National Interests and Local Government* Heinemann Educational 1983 and George W Jones (ed) *New Approaches to the Study of Central-Local Government Relations* Social Science Research Council/Gower 1980. An earlier study is Daniel Norman Chester *Central and Local Government: Financial and Administrative Relations* Macmillan 1951.

**7622** Central Policy Review Staff *Relations Between Central Government and Local Authorities* HMSO 1977. A review of the situation subsequent to the Layfield Report [7611].

**7623** Michael J Elliott *The Role of Law in Central-Local Relations* Social Science Research Council 1981. A study of the law governing central/local relations.

**7624** M Laffin *Professionalism and Policy: The Role of the Professions in the Central/Local Relationship* Gower 1986. This focuses more on relationships at the officer level rather than political and financial conflict. So, in exhaustive detail, does J A G Griffith *Central Departments and Local Authorities* Allen and Unwin 1966. Case studies of central/local relations in particular services over the previous thirty years are offered in Gerald Rhodes (ed) *Central-Local Relations: The Experience of the Environmental Health and Trading Services* Royal Institute of Public Administration 1986. Another case study of central/local relations is R J Newman 'The Relationship between Central and Local Government: A Case Study of the Oxford Inner Relief Road Controversy 1923–1974' Oxford DPhil Thesis 1976.

**7625** Brian Jacobs 'Labour Against the Centre: The Clay Cross Syndrome' *Local Government Studies* 10 1984 pp 75–87. A study of the willingness of Labour-controlled authorities, such as Clay Cross in the early 1970s over housing issues to challenge government policy or pursue their own policy in defiance of central government. On Clay Cross see also [6076].

**7626** Peter Godfrey Richards *Delegation in Local Government: County to District Councils* Allen and Unwin 1956. A study of the nature, legal and historical context and practice of such delegation. The only general study of county/district relations to appear since is S N Leach 'County/District Relationships in Shire and Metropolitan Counties' Birmingham MSocSci Thesis 1977. See also S N Leach and N Mogre 'County/District Relations in Shire and Metropolitan Counties in the Field of Town and Country Planning: A Comparison' *Policy and Politics* 7 1979 pp 165–79.

## (8) Local Government in Particular Areas

### (a) London

### (i) The London County Council and the Greater London Council

For a study of the role of Jews in London politics see [5733].

**7627** Sydney K Ruck and Gerald Rhodes *The Government of Greater London* Allen and Unwin 1970. An account of the working of the new system introduced in 1965 against its historical background.

**7628** Andrew Saint (ed) *Politics and the People of London: The London County Council 1889–1965* Hambledon Press 1989. Studies of the LCC from its origins. The best general history. William Eric Jackson *Achievement: A Short History of the London County Council* Longmans 1965 is an authoritative, if uncritical, official history concentrating on the period 1939–64. In the following year the LCC was replaced by the Greater London Council, an authority which covered a much wider area.

**7629** Herbert Morrison *How London is Governed* People's University Press 1949. A guide by the Labour leader of the pre- war London County Council.

**7630** *Royal Commission on Local Government in Greater London 1957–1960* Cmnd 1164, *Parliamentary Papers* xviii 1959–60. This report by the committee chaired by Sir Edwin Herbert advocated the restructuring of the government of London. Subsequently the existing boroughs were replaced by larger units and new London boroughs were created from existing district councils which came within the ambit of the newly created Greater London Council. The process of reform is examined in Gerald Rhodes *The Government of London: The Struggle for Reform* Weidenfeld and Nicolson 1970. See also F Smallwood *Greater London: The Politics of Metropolitan Reform* Bobbs-Merrill, Indianapolis, Indiana 1965 and Donald L Foley *Governing the London Region: Reorganisation and Planning in the Sixties* University of California Press, Berkeley, California 1972.

**7631** Gerald Rhodes (ed) *The New Government of London: The First Five Years* Weidenfeld and Nicolson 1972. This evaluates the new government system in London. It looks at the government of the new boroughs as well as of the Greater London Council.

**7632** Horace Cutler *The Cutler Files* Weidenfeld and Nicolson 1981. Cutler was the Conservative leader of the GLC in the 1970s. This is a critical reflection on London government rather than an autobiography.

**7633** Wally Seacombe 'Sheila Rowbotham on Labour and the Greater London Council' *Canadian Dimension* 21 1987 pp 32–7. An interview covering Labour policy on the Greater London Council in 1981–5. The policies of the Labour Left leading the authority in this period are critically assessed in a collection of articles on Livingstone's GLC in Anne Sofer *The London Left Takeover* privately printed 1987. Sofer left the Labour group on the council in 1981 and joined the SDP. The organization, direction and implementation of intervention, especially economic intervention, by the GLC under Livingstone is assessed in Maureen Mackintosh and Hilary Wainwright *A Taste of Power: The Politics of Local Economics* Verso 1987.

**7634** Brendan O'Leary 'Why Was The GLC Abolished?' *International Journal of Urban and Regional Research* 11 1987 pp 193–217. A critical appraisal of the decision and decision-making process which led to the abolition of the Greater London Council in April 1986. A Forrester, S Lansley and R Pauley *Beyond Our Ken: A Guide to the Battle for London* Fourth Estate 1985 is an account of the struggle against the Thatcher government's determination to abolish the GLC led by Ken Livingstone, then the authority's Labour leader.

**7635** *General Election of County Councillors* London County Council 1919–61. A guide published after each triennial election. On elections to the Greater London Council see F W S Craig *Greater London Votes 1: The Greater London Council 1964–1970* Political Reference Publications 1971. Thereafter the GLC published volumes on each GLC and London boroughs election. See also Gwyn Rowley 'The Greater London Council Elections of 1964 and 1967: A Study in Electoral Geography' *Transactions of the Institute of British Geographers* 53 1971 pp 117–32, Paul Cousins 'The GLC Election 1981' *London Journal* 8 1982 pp 39–62 and Jeff Bartley and Ian Gordon 'London at the Polls: A Review of the 1981 GLC Election and Analysis' *London Journal* 8 1982 pp 39–62.

**7636** Ken Young *Local Politics and the Rise of Party: The London Municipal Society and the Conservative Intervention in Local Elections 1894–1963* Leicester University Press 1975. The Municipal Society was the label under which the Conservatives contested seats on the London County Council. See also his 'The Conservative Strategy for London 1855–1975' *London Journal* 1 1975 pp 56–81.

**7637** H W Fulton 'The GLC's Parliamentary Business' *Greater London Intelligence Journal* 42 1979 pp 18–23. This describes the GLC's promotion of private bills either for its own purposes or on behalf of London boroughs. It also examines the GLC response to legislation affecting London.

**7638** R Mace (ed) *Taking Stock: A Documentary History of the Greater London Council Supplies Department Celebrating Seventy Five Years of Working for London* GLC 1984.

*(ii) London Boroughs*

**7639** Andrew D Glassberg *Representation and the Urban Community* Macmillan 1981. A study of Tower Hamlets, Bromley and Islington councils.

**7640** Christopher Temple Husbands 'The London Borough Council Elections of 6 May 1982: Results and Analysis' *London Journal* 8 1982 pp 177–90. The issues in the 1982 elections are analysed in P F Cousins '1982: The Battle for the Boroughs' *London Review of Public Administration* 15 1983 pp 12–24.

**7641** Christopher Temple Husbands 'The London Borough Council Elections of 8 May 1986: Results and Analysis' *London Journal* 12 1986 pp 146–66. This includes an appendix (pp 167–71) on by-elections 1982–6.

**7642** A M Rees and T A Smith *Town Councillors: A Study of Barking* Acton Society Trust 1964.

**7643** Enid Wistrich *Local Government Reorganisation: The First Years of Camden* London Borough of Camden 1972. A study of the process of local government reorganization in London as it affected the borough of Camden which was created as a result of the 1965 reorganization.

**7644** A M Messina 'Ethnic Minority Representation and Party Compensation in Britain: The Case of Ealing Borough' *Political Studies* 35 1987 pp 224–38. This argues that ethnic issues are avoided by both the Labour and Conservative parties in Ealing for fear of alienating white voters in marginal wards.

**7645** R Butterworth 'Islington Borough Council: Some Characteristics of Single-Party Rule' *Politics* 1 1966 pp 21–31. An analysis of Labour dominance of Islington politics.

**7646** John Dearlove *The Politics of Policy in Local Government: The Making and Maintenance of Public Policy in the Royal Borough of Kensington and Chelsea* Cambridge University Press 1973. A good account. It however has little on the minority Labour group on the council.

**7647** J Rodrigues 'Ted Knight Interviewed' *Marxism Today* 25 1981 pp 11–6. An interview with the then Left-Wing Labour leader of Lambeth council on the role of the local Labour parties, local government finance and confrontations with the Thatcher government.

**7648** Sue Goss *Local Labour and Local Government: A Study of Interests, Politics and Policy in Southwark 1919 to 1982* Edinburgh University Press 1989. A good well-reviewed history of Southwark local government since Labour first captured the council in 1919.

**7649** Janice Morphet 'Local Authority Decentralisation – Tower Hamlets goes all the way' *Policy and Politics* 15 1987 pp 119–26. This traces experiments in local government decentralization since 1980, and particularly the most thoroughgoing experiment carried out under Labour and Liberal administrations in Tower

Hamlets. P Hughes 'Decentralisation in Tower Hamlets' *Local Government Policy Making* 14 1987 pp 29–36 is an insider study of the development of the scheme.

**7650** Paul Beresford *Good Council Guide: Wandsworth 1978–1987* Policy Study 84, Centre for Policy Studies 1987. An account of policy and administration under the Conservative administration since 1978. Beresford has been leader of the council since 1983. A more critical appraisal of the Conservatives' policies is offered in 'Struggles in the Welfare State: Wandsworth – The Cuts and the Fightback' *Critical Social Policy* 1 1981 pp 67–94.

## (b) Other Cities and Boroughs

**7651** J G Bulpitt 'The Nature and Effect of Party Political Local Government with Special Reference to some North-Western Authorities' Manchester MA (Econ) Thesis 1961–2.

**7652** H J Black *History of the Corporation of Birmingham Vol 6: 1936–50* Birmingham City Council 1957. The social composition of the councillors is assessed D S Morris and Kenneth Newton 'The Social Composition of a City Council: Birmingham 1925–1966' *Social and Economic Administration* Jan 1971 pp 29–33 and D S Morris and Kenneth Newton *Profile of a Local Political Elite: Businessmen on Birmingham Council 1920–1966* Discussion Paper F6, Faculty of Commerce and Social Science, University of Birmingham 1969.

**7653** M J Le Lohé 'A Study of Local Elections in Bradford County Borough 1937–1967' Leeds PhD Thesis 1971–2.

**7654** Roger Victor Clements *Local Notables and the City Council* Macmillan 1969. A study of Bristol.

**7655** Denis Stuart *County Borough: The History of Burton upon Trent 1901–74: Part 2: 1914–74* Charter Trustees of Burton on Trent 1977.

**7656** B R Bentley 'Conventions in Local Government: A Study of Party System in Coventry' Birmingham MCom Thesis 1959–60.

**7657** E Shuttleworth 'Policy Making: Darlington Town Council 1962–1965' Durham MA Thesis 1968–9.

**7658** J C Aspden *A Municipal History of Eastbourne 1938–1974* Eastbourne Borough Council 1979.

**7659** L Corina 'The Working of Halifax County Borough Council Since 1945' Leeds PhD Thesis 1972–3.

**7660** H Victor Wiseman *Local Government at Work: A Case Study of a County Borough* Routledge and Kegan Paul 1967. This is a mixture of a case study of the operation of Leeds council in the post-war period and a memoir of his time as councillor (and eventually deputy leader) in the 1950s. On Leeds see also B M Powell 'A Study of the Change in Social Origins, Political Affiliations and Length of Service of Members of the Leeds City Council 1888–1953' Leeds MA Thesis 1957–8.

**7661** Michael Parkinson *Liverpool on the Brink: One City's Struggle Against Government Cuts* Policy Journals 1985. The best and fullest, albeit somewhat partisan, study of Liverpool's budget crisis and the confrontation between the Militant-led council and the Thatcher government (which ended in a victory for the government and the de-barring and financial penalization of the councillors in 1986). It is particularly useful on the background to the crisis since the 1970s. Arthur F Midwinter 'Setting the Rate: Liverpool Style' *Local Government Studies* 11 1985 pp 25–33 looks particularly at the crisis over the council's refusal to set a rate in 1985. The Militant view of the crisis is presented in Peter Taaffe and Tony Mulhearn *Liverpool: A City that Dared to Fight* Fortress Books 1988.

**7662** H H Heclo 'The Recruitment of Manchester City Councillors 1954–65' Manchester MA (Econ) Thesis 1966–7. Manchester's experiments in decentralization in the 1980s are discussed in A Seex 'Manchester's Approach to Decentralisation' *Local Government Policy Making* 14 1987 pp 21–7.

**7663** D G Green *Power and Party in an English City: An Account of Single-Party Rule* Allen and Unwin 1981. An account of policy-making in the ruling Labour group in Newcastle-upon-Tyne. It analyses party discipline, the relations with the party outside the council, the power of the committee chairman, the role of local patronage and the nature of the policy-making process.

**7664** S E Peacock *Borough Government in Portsmouth 1835–1974* Portsmouth City Council 1975. A short official history.

**7665** *Forty Years of Labour Rule in Sheffield* Sheffield Trades and Labour Council 1967. An account of Labour rule in the city since the party first captured the council in 1926.

**7666** George W Jones *Borough Politics: A Study of the Wolverhampton Town Council 1888–1964* Macmillan 1969. A well regarded study.

### (c) County Councils

**7667** *Bedfordshire County Council: A Hundred Years at your Service 1889–1989* Bedfordshire County Council 1988. The county councils were set up in 1889. This is one of several guides surveying the first hundred years work of the various authorities established then.

**7668** E R Davies *A History of the First Berkshire County Council* Berkshire County Council 1981. A substantial history of the council from its establishment in 1889 until the reorganization of 1974.

**7669** John Michael Lee *Social Leaders and Public Persons: A Study of County Government in Cheshire Since 1888* Clarendon 1963. A highly regarded study. The story of Cheshire County Council was taken up to reorganization in John Michael Lee and Bruce Wood *The Scope of Local Initiative: A Study of Cheshire County Council 1961–1974* Robertson 1974. T J Harrington 'Explaining Local Authority Policy-Making: Class Pressures, Professional Interests and Systems in Two County Councils' Kent PhD Thesis 1984 is a study of policy-making in Cheshire and in Clywd.

**7670** A L Davies (ed) *Cornwall County Council 1889–1989: A History of 100 Years of County Government* Cornwall County Council 1989.

**7671** *A Century of Service 1889–1989* Cumbria County Council 1989. A pamphlet on county government in Cumbria. Cumbria County Council was created in 1974, replacing Cumberland, Westmorland and a portion of Lancashire.

**7672** J Stanyer *A History of Devon County Council 1889–1989* Devon Books 1989.

**7673** C R V Bell *A History of East Sussex County Council 1889–1974* Phillimore 1975.

**7674** *100 Not Out: A Centenary of Service: Essex County Council 1889–1989* Essex County Council 1989.

**7675** G A Rushton *100 Years of Progress: Hampshire County Council 1889–1989* Hampshire County Council 1989.

**7676** G Sheldrick *The Hart Reguardant: Hertfordshire County Council 1889–1989* Hertfordshire Publications 1989.

**7677** Howard Elcock 'English Local Government Reformed: The Politics of Humberside' *Public Administration* 53 1975 pp 159–66. Humberside was one of the new counties created by reorganization in 1974.

**7678** P A Moylan *The Form and Reform of County Government: Kent 1889–1974* Leicester University Press 1978. A good account of the history of Kent County Council. Elizabeth Melling *History of the Kent County Council 1889–1974* Kent County Council 1975 is much less analytical but very informative.

**7679** John D Marshall and M E McClintock (eds) *The History of Lancashire County Council 1889–1974* Robertson 1977. A good collections of essays on the development of county government in Lancashire and on aspects of the county council's activities such as policy-making, planning or transport.

**7680** A Wickstead *Lincolnshire, Lindsey: The Story of the County Council 1889–1974* Lincolnshire and Humberside Arts 1978. A history of county government in Lindsey.

**7681** N J Frangopulo *Tradition in Action: The Historical Evolution of the Greater Manchester County* EP Publishing 1977. Greater Manchester was one of the new metropolitan counties created in 1974. It was abolished in 1986.

**7682** C Wilkins-Jones (ed) *Centenary: A Hundred Years of County Government in Norfolk 1889–1989* Norfolk County Council Library and Information Service 1989. A useful collection of essays on the development of county government. *Norfolk County Council 1889–1974* Norfolk County Council n.d (1974?) also remains worth consulting.

**7683** M Y Ashcroft (ed) *A History of the North Riding of Yorkshire County Council 1889–1974* North Riding of Yorkshire County Council 1974. A conventional study of an authority which disappeared in the reorganization of 1974.

**7684** G C Baugh *Shropshire and its Rulers: A Thousand Years* Shropshire Libraries 1979. The final section looks at the history of the county council.

**7685** D Fowkes *et al 100 Not Out: A Look Back at 100 Years of Staffordshire County Council* Staffordshire County Council 1989. A short account.

**7686** D J Mitchell *A History of Warwickshire County Council 1889–1989* Warwickshire County Council 1988.

**7687** J Godfrey *et al West Sussex County Council: The First Hundred Years* West Sussex County Council 1988.

**7688** B J Barber and M W Beresford *The West Riding County Council 1889–1974: Historical Studies* West Yorkshire Metropolitan County Council 1979. A good collection of essays on all aspects of the history of the

West Riding County Council. The West Riding was replaced by the metropolitan county of West Yorkshire in 1974. The background to the creation of the metropolitan county, the problems this process involved and its inherent weaknesses are assessed in D A Keighley 'The Metropolitan County Council with Special Reference to the Experience in West Yorkshire 1972–82' Leeds PhD Thesis 1984. See also E S Dixon 'Management in Local Government in West Yorkshire April 1974–March 1977' Bradford MSc Thesis 1978.

**7689** K Rogers *Wiltshire County Council: The First Hundred Years 1889–1989* Wiltshire County Council 1989. A short account.

### (9) Studies of Local Politics

**7690** William L Miller *Irrelevant Elections? The Quality of Local Democracy in Britain* Clarendon 1988. A detailed survey of public attitudes to local democracy and the reasons for and the implications of the generally low and declining turnout at local elections. Paul E Peterson and Paul Kantor 'Political Parties and Citizen Participation in English City Politics' *Comparative Politics* 9 1977 pp 197–217 attribute low participation in local politics to the lack of media attention and the lack of institutional opportunities for groups and organizations to discuss and criticize local policy. For an earlier study of participation and turnout in local democracy see 'Local Elections – How Many Vote?' *Planning* 15 1948 pp 163–78. A more general survey of local elections is 'Voting for Local Councils' *Planning* 21 1955 pp 49–64.

**7691** William G Andrews 'Social Change and Electoral Politics in Britain: A Case Study of Basingstoke 1964 and 1974' *Political Studies* 22 1974 pp 324–36.

**7692** Nigel Todd 'Labour Women: A Study of Women in the Bexley Branch of the British Labour Party (1945–1950)' *Journal of Contemporary History* 8 1973 pp 159–73. A case study of the role of women in the labour movement.

**7693** Kenneth Newton *Second City Politics: Democratic Processes and Decision Making in Birmingham* Oxford University Press 1976. A well-regarded political analysis of local government and electoral politics in Birmingham. For labour politics in Birmingham see Marion Large 'Sources of Labour History: Primary Material in the Social Sciences Department of Birmingham Reference Library' in A Wright and R Shackleton (eds) *Worlds of Labour: Essays in Birmingham Labour History* Department of Extra-Mural Studies, University of Birmingham 1983 pp 156–66, which is a guide to local Labour Party, trade union and labour activists archives.

**7694** Michael J Le Lohé 'The Effect of the Presence of Immigrants upon the Local Political System in Bradford 1945–77' in Robert Miles and Annie Phizacklea (eds) *Racism and Political Action* Routledge and Kegan Paul 1979 pp 184–203.

**7695** Dorothy Howell-Thomas *Socialism in West Sussex: A History of the Chichester Constituency Labour Party* Chichester Constituency Labour Party 1983.

**7696** Peter Hayden 'Culture, Creed and Conflict: Methodism and Politics in Cornwall c1832–1979' Liverpool PhD Thesis 1982. A study of the local political influence of the dominant church in Cornwall and its relationship with the relative strength of Cornish Liberalism.

**7697** C J James *MP for Dewsbury: One Hundred Years of Parliamentary Representation* the author 1970.

**7698** J R Robbins 'Electoral Politics in Doncaster 1945–1968' Leeds MPhil Thesis 1969–70.

**7699** A H Birch *Small Town Politics: A Study of Political Life in Glossop* Oxford University Press 1959. An excellent study of local political life and electoral politics since the early nineteenth century.

**7700** P R G Hornsby 'Party Politics and Local Government in Hampshire' Southampton MSc (Econ) Thesis 1957.

**7701** *Ince and Westhoughton Constituencies and Parts of Wigan Souvenir Booklet 1906–1956* Ince, Westhoughton and Wigan Constituency Labour Parties 1956. A celebration of fifty years of Labour representation of these constituencies in parliament.

**7702** *Ipswich Constituency Labour Party Jubilee Year Book 1923–83* Ipswich Constituency Labour Party 1983.

**7703** Philip Tether *Kingston Upon Hull Conservative Party: A Case Study of an Urban Tory Party in Decline* Hull Papers in Politics 19, Politics Department, University of Hull 1980.

**7704** David Berry *The Sociology of Grass Roots Politics: A Study of Party Membership* Macmillan 1970. A good study of party membership and adherence and political attitudes in Liverpool. The influence of the sectarian divide between Protestant and Catholic on Liverpool politics is examined in David A Roberts 'Religion and Politics in Liverpool Since 1900' London MSc Thesis 1965. R J Baxter 'The Liverpool Labour Party 1918–63' Oxford DPhil Thesis 1969 is a good study of the rise of the Labour Party in the city up to the death of John Braddock and the decline of its dependence on the Catholic vote.

**7705** John E Turner *Labour's Doorstep Politics in London* Macmillan 1978. A study of the local aspects of Labour Party electoral campaigning in the capital, especially in South Kensington, Bermondsey and Fulham.

**7706** Frank Bealey, Jean Blondel and W P McCann *Constituency Politics: A Study of Newcastle under Lyme* Faber 1965. An excellent study of local political life and electoral politics.

**7707** R W Johnson 'The Nationalisation of English Rural Politics: Norfolk South-West 1945–1970' *Parliamentary Affairs* 26 1972 pp 8–55. An excellent study of the growth of party politics and the declining electoral influence of religion (particularly Methodism) and agricultural trade unionism in both local and parliamentary politics in this constituency.

**7708** Alan Alexander *Borough Government and Politics: Reading 1835–1985* Allen and Unwin 1985. A good study focusing on local government. The local parties are usefully analysed in Jean Blondel 'The Conservative Association and the Labour Party in Reading' *Political Studies* 6 1958 pp 101–19. See also S C Coombs 'The Conservative Party in Reading 1945–1970' Reading MPhil Thesis 1969–70.

**7708A** Michael J Le Lohé and A R Goldman 'Race in Local Politics: The Rochdale Central Ward Election of 1968' *Race* 10 1969 pp 435–47. A study of the impact of a Pakistani Liberal candidate.

**7709** William Hampton *Democracy and Community: A Study of Politics in Sheffield* Oxford University Press 1970. A good study of the local political system, local parties and local electoral politics in this Labour-dominated city.

**7710** M T McVicar 'A Case Study of the Local Political System in the County Borough of Southend-on-Sea 1945 to 1972' Exeter MA Thesis 1976.

**7711** D Brown 'The Labour Movement in Wigan 1874–1967' Liverpool MA Thesis 1968–9. A study not only of the local Labour Party organization but also of the local trade unions and trades council and the relationship of these with the political party.

## C. LONDON

### (1) General

**7712** Alan Weinreb and Christopher Hibbert (eds) *The London Encyclopaedia* Macmillan 1986. A comprehensive reference guide to London, its history, government, commerce and life. See also Russell Ash (comp) *The Londoner's Almanac* Century 1985, Hunter Davies (ed) *The New London Spy* Anthony Blond 1966 and Robert Allen and Quentin Guirdham (eds) *The London Spy* Anthony Blond 1972.

**7713** *Greater London Local History Directory and Bibliography* Peter Marcan Publications 1988. A list of local history collections, museums, local societies and study groups and relevant publications 1983–87. It is a sequel to *London's Local History* Peter Marcan Publications 1983.

**7714** Philippa Dolphin, Eric Grant and Edward Lewis *The London Region: An Annotated Geographical Bibliography* Mansell 1981. An excellent, well annotated guide to the literature on the physical environment, historical growth, economy, transport, social patterns, planning and environmental problems of the capital.

**7715** Emrys Jones and D J Sinclair *Atlas of London and the London Region* 2 portfolios, Pergamon 1968–9. Seventy sheets comprising 240 distributive and thematic maps of London and South-East England with explanatory comments.

**7716** *Annual Abstract of Greater London Statistics* Greater London Council 1966–86. A useful statistical series which succeeded *London County Council Statistical Abstract* London County Council 1897–.

**7717** Ken Young and Patricia Garside *Metropolitan London: Politics and Urban Change 1837–1981* Arnold 1982. The standard history of the development of modern London. Social and economic developments of the post-war period are explored in Steve Humphries and John Taylor *The Making of Modern London 1945–1985* Sidgwick and Jackson 1986. This is a well illustrated and most enjoyable book.

**7718** J Shepherd *et al A Social Atlas of London* Clarendon 1974. An atlas of the social structure of the capital based on the 1971 census returns. Some of the maps are of rather poor quality. London's social structure is also explained and mapped in Christine Cooper *The Changing Social Structure of Greater London* Greater London Council 1982 and *A Social Review of Greater London* Greater London Council 1980. M J Mogridge *The Exploding City* Transport Studies Group 1979 is an exposition of the structure of London and the problems created by its rapid expansion in the twentieth century. See also M Ash *A Guide to the Structure of London* Adams and Dart 1972.

**7719** David V Donnison and D E C Eversley (eds) *London: Urban Patterns: Problems and Policies* Heinemann 1973. A collection of essays reflecting developments in the urban system in London in the 1960s.

**7720** Nicholas Shakespeare *Londoners* Sidgwick and Jackson 1986. A portrait of life and work of people of the city through individual accounts. Other impressionistic accounts of the metropolis are Michael Elliott *Heartbeat London: The Anatomy of a Supercity* Firethorn Press 1986, Richard Bourne *Londoners* Dent 1981 and Robert Clayton *Portrait of London* Hale 1980.

### (2) Parts of London

**7721** Sandra Wallman *et al Living in South London: Perspectives on Battersea 1871–1981* Gower 1982. Perspectives on the local social life and structure and local politics within the context of a study of life in the inner city.

**7722** Michael Young and Peter Willmott *Family and Kinship in East London* University of Liverpool Press 1954. A good sociological study of Bethnal Green in London's East End. Jocelyn Cornwell *Hard Earned Lives: Accounts of Health and Illness in East London* Tavistock 1984 is a useful follow-up study.

**7723** *Dockland: An Illustrated Historical Survey of Life and Work in East London* North East London Polytechnic/Greater London Council 1986. A study of economic decline, social change and developments in the built environment in the East End since the nineteenth century.

**7724** John A Richardson *A History of Erith Part 4: 1894–1965* Bexley Libraries 1979. A pamphlet on the history of this industrial waterfront area until the demise of the Erith Urban District Council and its incorporation into the London Borough of Bexley and the Greater London Council in the reorganization of 1965.

**7725** People's Autobiography of Hackney *The Island: The Life and Death of an East London Community 1870–1970* Centreprise 1979. An account of the Isle of Dogs derived from oral testimony. On Hackney see the extended annual local council report, *The London Borough of Hackney 1978–1982* London Borough of Hackney 1982.

**7726** Colin J Gray (comp) *Harrow Votes: Parliamentary and County Council Election Results 1945–1979: Middlesex County Council Election Results 1937–1961 and Greater London Council Election Results 1964–1981* the author 1983. See also his *Harrow Votes: Harrow Urban Council 1934–1954: A Handbook of Election Results* the author 1984.

**7727** D L Munby *Industry and Planning in Stepney* Oxford University Press 1951. An excellent in-depth study of the area.

**7728** Daniel Farson *Soho in the Fifties* Michael Joseph 1987. A brilliant photographic essay garnished by reminiscences of this quarter of the West End in the 1950s.

**7729** Peter Willmott and Michael Young *Family and Class in a London Suburb* Routledge and Kegan Paul 1960. A sequel to their study of Bethnal Green [7722]. A sociological study of Woodford.

**7730** Edward Francis Ernest Jefferson *The Woolwich Story 1895–1965* Woolwich and District Antiquarian Society 1970. An extensive history up to the point where the urban district council of this waterfront industrial area in South London became, as a result of local government reorganization, part of the London Borough of Greenwich and the Greater London Council.

## D. COUNTY AND LOCAL HISTORIES

**7731** Ronald Blythe *Akenfield: Portrait of an English Village* Allen Lane 1969. A celebrated study of a village in East Suffolk. It examines the social, political and demographic character of the village, drawing on oral testimony and provides a thorough picture of village life in the 1960s. The names of the village and the villagers have been changed.

**7732** Norman Dennis, Fernando Henriques and Clifford Slaughter *Coal Is Our Life: An Analysis of a Yorkshire Mining Community* 2nd ed, Tavistock 1969. A study of working class mining culture and community in Ashton. An important landmark study.

**7733** William Morgan Williams *A West Country Village – Ashworthy: Family, Kinship and Land* Routledge and Kegan Paul 1963. A useful sociological study.

**7734** Margaret Stacey *Tradition and Change: A Study of Banbury* Oxford University Press 1960. An influential sociological study in the context of Banbury's change from being a Home Counties market town after the introduction of industry in the 1930s. Margaret Stacey, Eric Batstone, Colin Bell, and Anne Murcott *Power, Persistence and Change: A Second Study of Banbury* Routledge and Kegan Paul 1975 is a follow-up study charting change since 1960 and looking at much the same themes. It is not as empirical or as satisfactory as the earlier work.

**7735** M H Haigh *The History of Batley 1800–1974* Haigh 1985. A history of the Yorkshire woollen town until the local government reorganization of 1974.

**7736** L R Conisbee *A Bedfordshire Bibliography with some Comments and Biographical Notes* Bedfordshire Historical Record Society 1962. This lists about 6,000 items with their locations. It was supplemented in 1967 and 1971.

**7737** *The Birmingham Post Year Book and Who's Who* Birmingham Post and Mail Ltd 1949–. A annual directory of local government, law, trades and professions, religion, charity, education, health and sports in Birmingham. Anthony Sutcliffe and Roger Smith *Birmingham 1939–1970* Oxford University Press 1974 is the third volume of the definitive official history of the city. *Birmingham and its Regional Setting: A Scientific Survey* Local Executive Committee for the British Association for the Advancement of Science 1950 is a guide produced for the meeting of the association in Birmingham that year. It contains a few useful essays on the local economy.

**7738** Jeremy Seabrook *City Close-Up* Allen Lane 1971. A study based on oral testimonies from Blackburn, reflecting the impact of immigration and social change, and changing working class and religious attitudes.

**7739** Gordon Readyhough *Bolton Town Centre: A Modern History* Richardson 1982. A history of the Lancashire cotton town. Bolton Oral History Project, which is held in the reference section of Bolton Central Library, contains a large number of catalogued interviews reflecting on aspects of local history. Many of these are transcribed, though the quality of typing is unfortunately not high.

**7740** Clement Richardson *A Geography of Bradford* University of Bradford 1976. A work of historical geography. The last four chapters are on the recent past and contemporary developments, particularly changes in the built environment and in the industrial and ethnic geography of the city.

**7741** C M MacInnes and W F Whittard (eds) *Bristol and its Adjoining Counties* Bristol Local Committee of the British Association for the Advancement of Science 1955. A collection of essays on the local climate, agriculture and education. It however does not contain much of value on the post-war period.

**7742** C Rippon *Buckinghamshire: A Bibliography* Library Association 1972. Over 5,000 entries arranged alphabetically by subject. It excludes periodical articles but is fully indexed.

**7743** J A Steers (ed) *The Cambridge Region 1965* Cambridge Local Executive Committee for the British Association for the Advancement of Science 1965. A guide to the physical, economic and social character of the Cambridge region produced for the meeting of the British Association for the Advancement of Science held in Cambridge that year.

**7744** G Birtill *The War and After* Guardian Press 1976. A history of Chorley since 1939 by a local journalist.

**7745** Minnie C Horton *The Story of Cleveland* Cleveland County Libraries 1979. This contains some material on the post- war period.

**7746** Kenneth Richardson *Twentieth Century Coventry* Macmillan 1972. An official history. It is useful on the rebuilding of the city after the devastation of 1940. It is however more a survey of institutions and personalities than a history, and is poor on subjects such as housing, education or poverty. These are covered much more fully in Bill Lancaster and Tony Mason (eds) *Life and Labour in a Twentieth Century City: The Experience of Coventry* Cryfield Press 1985. Essays in this volume examine the economy, industry, welfare, society and politics of Coventry.

**7747** H W Hodgson (comp) *A Bibliography of the History and Topography of Cumberland and Westmorland* Joint Archives Committee for Cumberland, Westmorland and Carlisle Record Office 1968. An annotated bibliographical guide to the literature. There is an oral archive covering all aspects of Lake District life and culture since the late nineteenth century held at Ambleside Library, Keswick Road, Ambleside, Cumbria, LA22 0BZ.

**7748** P Willmott *The Evolution of a Community: A Study of Dagenham after Forty Years* Routledge and Kegan Paul 1963. A good sociological study of the development of the community under the influence of the major Ford car plant situated there.

**7749** A Brockett (ed) *The Devon Union List: A Collection of Written Material Relating to the County of Devon* Exeter University Library 1977. Over 8,000 entries arranged alphabetically by author with a subject index.

**7750** *Doncaster: An Area Study* HMSO 1969. An economic survey conducted for the Department of Economic Affairs.

**7751** Martin Bulmer (ed) *Mining and Social Change: Durham County in the Twentieth Century* Croom Helm 1988. Sociological studies and personal documents. It is most valuable on planning and on the changing nature of work as the coal industry has declined. It is also useful on Labour Party dominance in the county. John C Dewdney (ed) *Durham County and City with Teeside* Durham Local Executive Committee of the British Association for the Advancement of Science 1970 is a collection of essays on the physical, economic and social character of the region. G H J Daysh, J S Symonds *et al West Durham: A Study of a Problem Area in North Eastern England* Blackwell 1953 is a useful analysis of the economic prospects, operation of regional policy and social character of an area hit by the declining coalfield.

**7752** *East Anglia Bibliography: A Check List of Publications in the British National Bibliography* Library Association Eastern Branch 1960–. A quarterly guide to recent literature on Cambridgeshire, Isle of Ely, Huntingdonshire, Norfolk and Suffolk. There is an oral archive of rural life in East Anglia held in the Museum of East Anglian Life, Abbot's Hall, Crowe Street, Stowmarket, Suffolk. Malcolm J Moseley (ed) *Power, Planning and People in Rural East Anglia* Centre of East Anglian Studies, University of East Anglia 1982 concentrates on planning issues in the region, but also covers subjects such as housing and services. This is a successor to Malcolm J Moseley (ed) *Social Issues in Rural Norfolk* Centre of East Anglian Studies, University of East Anglia 1978. The economic character of the region is examined in *East Anglia: A Study: A First Report by the East Anglia Planning Council* HMSO 1968. On the economic character of the region see also T Eastwood *Industry in the County Towns of Norfolk and Suffolk* Oxford University Press 1951.

**7753** *The East Midlands Bibliography* East Midlands Branch, Library Association 1970–. An annual guide to the literature which replaced *North Midlands Bibliography 1963–69*. It covers Derbyshire, Nottinghamshire, Lincolnshire, Leicestershire, Rutland, Northamptonshire, and the Soke of Peterborough. It includes articles and theses and has a five year cumulative index. The economic character of the region is assessed in East Midlands Economic Planning Council *The East Midlands Study* HMSO 1966.

**7754** Peter J Aspinall and Daphne M Hudson *Ellesmere Port: The Making of an Industrial Borough* Ellesmere Port Borough Council 1982. A history of the Cheshire port on the Manchester Ship Canal.

**7755** Jean Robin *Elmdon: Continuity and Change in a North-West Essex Village 1861–1964* Cambridge University Press 1980. An excellent study of rural social change.

**7756** Harvey Benham *Two Cheers for the Town Hall* Hutchinson 1964. This contains much material of relevance on recent Essex political and social history. It provides an impression of post-war Essex local government, society and religious life.

**7757** Frank Barlow (ed) *Exeter and its Region* University of Exeter 1969. A collection of essays on subjects such as the climate, economy, services and culture of Devon, and on the growth of and university of Exeter.

**7758** C N Riches 'The Development of Felixstowe 1870–1970' East Anglia PhD Thesis 1977. A study of the growth of the East coast port.

**7759** William Morgan Williams *The Sociology of a Village: Gosforth* Routledge and Kegan Paul 1956. A useful sociological study of village life.

**7760** Yorkshire and Humberside Economic Planning Council and Board *Halifax and Calder Valley: An Area Study* HMSO 1968. An economic survey of the town and region for the Department of Economic Affairs.

**7761** *Huddersfield and Colne Valley: An Area Study* HMSO 1969. An economic survey.

**7762** Edward Gillett *A History of Hull* Oxford University Press 1980. A history of the Humberside port. See also Hugh Calvert *A History of Kingston upon Hull* Phillimore 1978 and Kay Pearson *Life in Hull From Then Till Now* Bradley 1979.

**7763** David Symes (ed) *Humberside in the Eighties: A Spatial View of the Economy* Department of Geography, University of Hull 1987. A good collection of essays on the local economy with supporting statistics. See also J Craig *et al* 'Humberside: Employment, Unemployment and Migration – The Evolution of Industrial Structure 1951–1966' *Yorkshire Bulletin of Economic and Social Research* 22 1970 pp 123–42.

**7764** George Bennett (comp) *The Kent Bibliography: A Finding List of Kent Material in the Public Libraries of the County and of the Adjoining London Boroughs* Library Association, London and Home Counties Branch 1977. This has been updated by Wyn Burgess (comp) *Supplement to the Kent Bibliography* Library Association, London and Home Counties Branch, Kent sub-Branch 1981. S G McRae and C P Burnham (eds) *BA – 73: The Rural Landscape of Kent* Wye College, University of London 1973 is a collection of essays on the environment, agriculture and character of rural Kent produced for the 1973 meeting of the British Association for the Advancement of Science.

**7765** Derek Fraser (ed) *A History of Modern Leeds* Manchester University Press 1980. The last essay in this volume traces the city's history from 1945 to the local government reorganization of 1974. There are essays on the local climate, agriculture, urban environment, transport, economy and education system in M W Beresford and G R J Jones (eds) *Leeds and Its Region* Arnold 1967.

**7766** N Pye (ed) *Leicester and its Region* Leicester University Press 1972. A collection of essays on the climate, economy, society and culture of the region.

**7767** Dennis R Mills (ed) *Twentieth Century Lincoln-shire* History of Lincolnshire Committee 1989. A well-produced book, with essays on life and work, agriculture, industry, transport, the impact of the RAF, the coastline, planning, politics, education, religion and culture, supported by illustrations and statistics.

**7768** Madeleine Kerr *The People of Ship Street* Rout-ledge and Kegan Paul 1958. A good sociological study of life in a deprived part of Liverpool. Life and work in the deprived area of Toxteth in 1965–80 is examined in John Cornelius *Liverpool 8* Murray 1982.

**7769** G H Thomas *The Minutes Tell The Story: Lymm 1895–1974* Lymm and District History Society 1981. A short history up to local government reorganization.

**7770** H P White (ed) *The Continuing Conurbation: Change and Development in Greater Manchester* Gower 1980. A collection of essays recording and inter-preting change over the eighteen years since the British Association for the Advancement of Science, for whose annual meeting this volume was compiled, last met in Manchester. It concentrates on the urban environment and economy. The book prepared for the previous meet-ing of the British Association for the Advancement of Science in Manchester is Charles F Carter (ed) *Manches-ter and its Region: A Survey Prepared for the Meeting held in Manchester August 29 to 7 September 1962* Manchester University Press 1962. It examines the local climate, agriculture, industry, society and education. There is an extensive oral archive, which is unfortunately no longer being added to, held at the Manchester Studies Unit, Manchester Polytechnic, Hilton House, Hilton Street, Manchester M1 2FE. This is particularly strong on Manchester Jews, the cotton industry, political life and immigration. G Wilkinson (ed) *Lifetimes* Manches-ter Studies Group, Manchester Polytechnic 1976 is derived from this collection. C Makepeace *Manchester As It Was 6: War and its Aftermath* Hendon Publishing 1977 is a photographic record of Manchester 1939–52.

**7771** J R G Jennings 'Mansfield: The Evolution of an Urban Landscape 1863–1963' Nottingham PhD Thesis 1966–7.

**7772** Gladys A Swindells *A History of Marple* Marple Antiquarian Society 1974. Post-war developments are covered to some extent in this useful study of what is now a Cheshire suburb of Manchester.

**7773** William T S Gould and Alan G Hodgkiss (eds) *The Resources of Merseyside* Liverpool University Press 1982. A collection of essays which includes studies of the growth of the conurbation, the local economy, so-ciety and education and attempts to revive inner city Liverpool. An earlier compilation of essays for a meet-ing of the British Association for the Advancement of Science in Liverpool is Wilfrid Smith (ed) *A Scientific Study of Merseyside* University Press of Liverpool 1953. This features essays on the climate, population, social, economic and urban structure of the region and on Liverpool University. Also useful is R Lawton and C M Cunningham (eds) *Merseyside: Social and Economic Studies* Longman 1970. This examines subjects such as development policies or unemployment. Economic change and decline on Merseyside is also analysed in B L Anderson and P J M Stoney (eds) *Commerce, Industry and Transport: Studies in Economic Change on Mersey-side* Liverpool University Press 1983. The economic decline, which has been accompanied by a steady decline in the population and in the urban environment on Mer-seyside, and particularly in Liverpool itself, is assessed in L Cousins *et al Merseyside in Crisis* Merseyside Socialist Research Group 1982. The region's economy in the 1960s is surveyed in R Lawton (ed) *Merseyside in the Sixties* Longman 1969. *Problems of Merseyside* HMSO 1965 is a contemporary survey of the economic structure of the region and the prospects for development conducted for the then recently created Department of Economic Affairs. See also [7768].

**7774** E Darrock and B Taylor *A Bibliography of Nor-folk History* Centre of East Anglian Studies, University of East Anglia 1975. Over 7,000 unannotated but classi-fied entries.

**7775** *Northern History* 1966–. This quarterly journal carries an annual review of periodical literature and occasional publications on aspects of the history of the Northern counties of England. It includes material pub-lished by local history and antiquarian societies.

**7776** *Northern Bibliography* Northern Regional Li-brary System, Central Library, Newcastle-upon-Tyne 1979–. A quarterly listing of recent literature concerning the North East counties of Northumberland, Durham, Tyne and Wear and Cleveland. It is classified with an annual index. Norman McCord *North East England: An Economic and Social History* Batsford 1979 is the stand-ard history of the region. However only the final section deals with the post-war period. Richard A Chapman (ed) *Public Policy Studies: The North East of England* Edin-burgh University Press 1985 examines economic policy, planning, education and health policy in the region. There are essays on the region's climate, settlement pattern and economy in Peter C G Isaac and Ruth E A Allan (ed) *Scientific Survey of North-Eastern England* Newcastle Local Executive Committee of the British Association for the Advancement of Science 1949.

**7777** *North West Regional Atlas* Department of the Environment North West Regional Office 1976. Thirty-six looseleaf planning maps showing population, indus-trial and employment distribution in the region. Population trends, the economy, transport, and the built environment in the region are surveyed in Department of Economic Affairs *The North West: A Regional Survey* HMSO 1965.

**7778** Frank Briers (ed) *Norwich and its Region* Norwich Local Executive Committee of the British Association for the Advancement of Science 1961. A collection of essays on the local environment, economy, society and culture.

**7779** K C Edwards (ed) *Nottingham and Its Region* Nottingham Local Executive Committee of the British Association for the Advancement of Science 1966. A collection of essays on the local environment, economy, society and culture.

**7780** E W Martin *The Shearers and The Shorn: A Study of Life in a Devon Community* Routledge and Kegan Paul 1965. A good sociological study of life, politics and religion in Okehampton.

**7781** Trevor Rowley (ed) *The Oxford Region* Department of External Studies, Oxford University 1980. An excellent set of essays on subjects such as local transport, planning, politics, the development of the Harwell research laboratories or the recent history of the university. Essays on local society, transport and planning are the main features of C G Smith and D I Scargill (eds) *Oxford and Its Region* Oxford University Press 1975. There is little of value in A F Martin and R W Steel (eds) *The Oxford Region: A Scientific and Historical Survey* Oxford University Press 1954. On Oxford see also Jessie Parfit *The Health Of A City: Oxford 1770–1974* Amate Press 1987.

**7782** Peter Ambrose *The Quiet Revolution: Social Change in a Sussex Village 1871–1971* Chatto and Windus 1974. An excellent sociological case study of changing village life in Ringmer. It examines local society and politics as the village, from 1960 onwards, increasingly became dominated by commuters. It also assesses the impact of planning and changing service provision and is particularly critical of the declining ability of local people to afford housing which is instead being bought up by commuters.

**7783** Crispin Gill *The Isles of Scilly* David and Charles 1975. Something of a travelogue which reflects to some extent on recent developments.

**7784** David L Linton (ed) *Sheffield and Its Region: A Scientific and Historical Survey* Local Executive Committee of the British Association for the Advancement of Science 1956. Essays on the climate and the water supply, the urban structure and the economy of the region. Geoffrey Beattie *Survivors of Steel City: A Portrait of Sheffield* Chatto and Windus 1986 is an impressionistic study of Sheffield in the aftermath of the recession of the early 1980s. Edward Bramley *A Record of the Burgary of Sheffield, Commonly Called the Town Trust, from 1894 to 1955* J W Northend 1957 is the annals of the town charity, the main interest of which was improvements to Sheffield.

**7785** C M Mason and M E Witherick (eds) *Dimensions of Change in a Growth Area: Southampton Since 1960* Gower 1981. A collection of essays assessing urban and economic growth in industry, the port and in local on-shore oil wells such as Wytch Farm. There are essays on the local climate, land use and conservation, economy, built environment, culture and press in F J Monkhouse *A Survey of Southampton and its Region* Southampton University Press 1964. This also includes an essay on the Ordnance Survey, which is based in Southampton.

**7786** A V Steward (comp) *A Suffolk Bibliography* Suffolk Records Society 1979. Over 8,000 well indexed, classified entries on all aspects of Suffolk life and history. See also A O D Claxton *The Suffolk Dialect of the Twentieth Century* Brydell and Brewer 1968.

**7787** L C Silverthorne (ed) *A Current Bibliography of Surrey* Surrey County Library, Guildford 1977–. An annual mimeographed bibliography with alphabetically arranged classifications. John E Salmon (ed) *The Surrey Countryside: The Interplay of Land and People* University of Surrey 1975 is a collection of essays examining land use, planning, population and economic activity in the county.

**7788** *Sussex Bibliography* East Sussex County Library 1970–. An annual listing. Geography Editorial Committee (ed) *Sussex: Environment, Landscape and Society* Sutton 1983 is a collection of essays on the climate and environment, coastal protection, land use, conservation, transport, agriculture, society and employment in the county.

**7789** U Rayska and A Carr *Telford Past and Present* Shropshire Libraries 1978. A photographic history of the town with a short text.

**7790** Bill Williamson *Class, Culture and Community: A Biographical Study of Social Change in Mining* Routledge and Kegan Paul 1982. A study of social change in the declining mining community of Throckley, Northumberland observed through the life of the author's family.

**7791** D C Johnson 'Industry and Employment in Warrington 1890–1982' Manchester MA Thesis 1983.

**7792** Barbara Mary Dimond Smith and M MacDonald *A Bibliographic Profile of the West Midlands County in the 1970s* Memorandum 61, Centre for Urban and Regional Studies, University of Birmingham 1979. The

West Midlands county was created in the local government reorganization of 1974. Frank Joyce (ed) *Metropolitan Development and Change: The West Midlands: A Policy Review* Saxon House 1977 is a collection of essays assessing planning, economic, social and demographic change, transport and the built environment in the conurbation. The economic structure and prospects of the region are also assessed in Department of Economic Affairs *The West Midlands: A Regional Study* HMSO 1965.

7793   J Littlejohn *Westrigg: The Sociology of a Cheviot Parish* Routledge and Kegan Paul 1963. A sociological study of a rural community.

7794   Melvyn Bragg *Speak For England: An Oral History of England 1900–1975: Based on Interviews with Inhabitants of Wigton, Cumberland* Secker and Warburg 1976. A well regarded social history and observation of changing social and political attitudes in a rural community.

7795   *Wiltshire Records 1947–1987* Wiltshire County Record Office 1987. An account of the development of the record office with a guide to main records held.

7796   Sir Charles Ponsonby *Wootton: The Anatomy of an Oxfordshire Village 1945–1968* privately printed 1968. A short study.

7797   C H Feinstein (ed) *York 1831–1981: 150 Years of Scientific Endeavour and Social Change* Ebor Press 1981. An excellent collection of essays on local culture, religion, politics and society in York. See also *York Memories at Home: Personal Accounts of Domestic Life in York 1900–1960* York Castle Museum/York Oral History Project 1987.

7798   *Census Atlas of Yorkshire* Department of Geography, Sheffield University 1974. An atlas of the demography and social and economic structure of the county based upon the 1971 census returns. Yorkshire's economy and its economic prospects are examined in Yorkshire and Humberside Economic Planning Council *A Review of Yorkshire and Humberside* HMSO 1966, a study for the Department of Economic Affairs.

## E. ISLE OF MAN AND THE CHANNEL ISLANDS

The Isle of Man and the Channel Islands are possessions of the English crown but are not part of the United Kingdom, or of the European Community. The United Kingdom is responsible for their defence and foreign relations. The Isle of Man and the Bailiwicks of Jersey and Guernsey however have separate legislatures and constitutional arrangements. In the post-war period all have become increasingly important as offshore banking centres and have experienced considerable population growth.

### (1) Isle of Man

7799   *Journal of the Manx Museum* 1924–. This regularly produces bibliographical guides to the literature on the Isle of Man.

7800   *Isle of Man Digest of Economic and Social Statistics* Isle of Man Government 1975–. An annual guide to key economic, social and demographic trends. Demographic information also appears in the annual *Chief Registrar's Annual Report and Statistical Review* Isle of Man Government 1951–.

7801   *Subject Guide to the Acts of Tynwald* Isle of Man Government 1988. This lists the Acts of the Isle of Man parliament in chronological and alphabetical order revised to 1st February 1988. See also *Statutes of the Isle of Man* 1824–. This guide to legislation of the recent session has been published annually by Island Development Company since 1883. It includes details of UK Acts applying in the Isle of Man and Orders in Council extending UK Acts to the Isle of Man. It is supplemented by the annual Acts of Tynwald.

7802   *The Times Reports of Debates in the Manx Legislature* Island Development Company 1887–. Reports of the debates in the Tynwald.

7803   E H Stenning *Portrait of the Isle of Man* Hale 1958. A survey and impression of the character of the island. The economic character of the island is examined in Jack William Birch *The Isle of Man: A Study in Economic Geography* Cambridge University Press 1964.

7804   R H Kinvig *The Isle of Man: A Social, Cultural and Political History* Liverpool University Press 1975. The last chapter of this general history surveys twentieth century administrative, economic and social change.

7805   D G Kermode *Devolution At Work: A Case Study of the Isle of Man* Saxon House 1979. This is the nearest there is to a political history of the Isle of Man. It usefully examines the administration of the island in the context of its relations with the United Kingdom. On this relationship see also [273]. On the administrative history of the island see also J M Templeton 'Public Administration in the Isle of Man' CNAA MPhil Thesis 1982.

7806   T Sherratt *Isle of Man Parliamentary Election Results 1919–1979* the author 1979. A compilation of statistics.

7807 Jeff Richards 'Electoral Change in a Small Community: The Isle of Man Revisited' *Parliamentary Affairs* 40 1987 pp 388–408. This examines electoral change and nationalism in the context of the constitutional changes of the 1980s. The most important of these was the introduction of the single transferable vote for the 1986 elections (discussed in Richards 'The Single Transferable Vote in the Isle of Man' *Parliamentary Affairs* 41 1988 pp 423–7) which contributed to the creation of the office of Chief Minister in the island government. The impact of the economic background of the development of offshore banking and flag of convenience shipping on electoral and constitutional developments is also examined. An earlier study of electoral politics in the Isle of Man is Jacqueline Templeton and Jeff Richards 'Elections in a Small Community: The Case of the Isle of Man' *Parliamentary Affairs* 36 1981 pp 322–34.

7808 P H Craine 'Population and Taxation in the Isle of Man 1960–80' Liverpool MPhil Thesis 1982. A study of how Tynwald used the devolution of powers from the UK parliament in the 1950s to reverse economic and demographic decline by reducing direct taxation and encouraging off-shore banking. The impact of this policy is also examined. The character of the tax system before these changes is assessed C H Tolley *Incomes Taxes in the Channel Islands and the Isle of Man* Tolley 1950.

7809 Angela Kneale *Against Birching: Judicial Corporal Punishment in the Isle of Man* National Council of Civil Liberties 1973. An assessment of the arguments for and against the judicial use of birching, which was retained on the Isle of Man as a punishment after it was abolished on the mainland in 1948. The author is a critic of its use. She illustrates her argument with quotes from the Manx press and Tynwald and with a table of incidents 1952–72.

7810 *Annual Report of the Isle of Man Board of Education* 1863–. This publication has appeared under various titles. Twentieth century educational developments are examined in J W Cowley 'Progress in Education in the 20th Century in the Island' *Isle of Man Natural History and Antiquarian Society Proceedings* 7 1971 pp 281–91. See also J E G Jenkins 'The Introduction of Secondary Education in the Isle of Man' Hull MEd Thesis 1976.

## (2) Channel Islands

7811 *Who's Who in the Channel Islands* Channel Islands Publishing 1967–. An annual collection of potted biographies of the leading citizens of the islands.

7812 Raoul Lempriere *History of the Channel Islands* Hale 1980. A history of the islands up to the present day. Of more use for the post-war period is his *Portrait of the Channel Islands* 3rd ed, Hale 1979. This guide to the islands contains some reflections on post-war developments. Victor Coysh (ed) *The Channel Islands: A New Study* David and Charles 1977 surveys the history, agriculture, architecture, transport, way of life and importance of tourism to the islands. Another survey is Wilfrid D Hooke *The Channel Islands* Hale 1953.

7813 F de L Bois 'Parliamentary Supremacy in the Channel Islands' *Public Law* 1983 pp 385–93. A study of the constitutional relationship between the Channel Islands and the United Kingdom.

7814 J Robilliard 'Outlines of the Administration of Criminal Justice in the Channel Islands' *Criminal Law Review* 1979 pp 566–81.

7815 J Crozier (ed) *Catholicism in the Channel Islands: A Symposium Compiled on the Occasion of the Centenary of the Dedication of the Church of St Joseph's, Guernsey 1951* privately printed 1951.

7816 *Report of the Committee of the Privy Council on the Island of Alderney* Cmnd 7805, *Parliamentary Papers* xi 1948–49. An inquiry chaired by James Chuter Ede into the state of the island, its government, its economic prospects and its finances in the light of the problems of reconstruction after its occupation (along with the rest of the Channel Islands) by the Germans during the war. The story of the Alderney islanders from their evacuation in 1940 to Guernsey and Great Britain to their return after the war is told in Michael St J Packe and Maurice Dreyfus *The Alderney Story 1939–49: From Personal Accounts and Contemporary Documents* Alderney Society 1971. A more general study of the island is Victor Coysh *Alderney* David and Charles 1974.

7817 *Orders in Council and Other Matters of General Interest Registered on the Records of the Isle of Guernsey* Guernsey Herald 1803–. This is usually published biennially or triennially.

7818 Victor Coysh (ed) *The Bailiwick of Guernsey: The Jubilee Years 1952–1977* Brian J Duquemin 1977. A journalistic survey of the changes in the Bailiwick, which also includes the islands of Alderney, Sark, Herm and Jethou, during the first twenty-five years of the reign of Queen Elizabeth II. The autobiography of this Guernsey historian and journalist, *Call of the Island: Guernsey Remembered* Guernsey Press 1986 reflects on post-war changes in Guernsey and elsewhere in the Bailiwick of Guernsey.

7819 Alan Barber *100 Years: The Story of Lloyds Bank in Guernsey* Bailiwick 1987.

7820 Jenny Wood *Herm: Our Island Home* 2nd ed, Linton 1986. The autobiography of the wife of the Tenant who has held the island of Herm since 1949. It traces the post-war history of Herm.

7821 *Regulations and Orders* Bigwoods, St Helier 1939–. An annual guide to Jersey legislation.

7822 *Report on the Establishment and Work of the States' Police Force* States of Jersey 1965–. An annual report. Other useful reports are *Annual Report of the Medical Officer of Health* States of Jersey 1946–, *Report of the Public Health Committee* States of Jersey 1963– and *Agricultural Statistics (Jersey)* States of Jersey 1946–.

7823 Pierre Dalido *Jersey: Ile Agricole* Anglo-Normande Etude de Sociographie Inprimerie A Chaumeron, Vannes 1951. This examines the climate, demography, economy, society, law, religion and culture of the island.

7824 Marguerite Syvret and Joan Stevens *Balleine's History of Jersey* Phillimore 1981. The last chapter of this general history examines the post-war period.

7825 F de L Bois *A Constitutional History of Jersey* States of Jersey 1972. This was Jersey's submission to the Kilbrandon Royal Commission on the Constitution [273]. It reflects Jersey's constitutional position in relation to the United Kingdom in 1971 with a detailed historical background. The appendices fill in the position of Jersey in international law. Also useful is R G Le Hérissier *The Development of the Government of Jersey 1771–1972* States of Jersey 1974. On Jersey's constitution see also C W Duret Aubin 'Recent Constitutional Changes in Jersey' *International and Comparative Law Quarterly* 1 1952 pp 491–503.

7826 René Lemesurier *Le Droit de l'île de Jersey: La loi, le coutume et l'idéologie dans l'île de Jersey* Institute de Droit Comparé, Université de Paris 1956. See also P Le Geyt *Privilèges loix et coustumes de l'île de Jersey avec un essay pour des reglemens politiques* Bigwoods, St Helier 1953.

7827 *Report and Recommendations of the States of Jersey appointed to consult with Her Majesty's Government of the United Kingdom on all matters relating to the Government's application to join the European Economic Community* States of Jersey 1967. Jersey's response to the second attempt at entry to the European Community.

7828 G C Powell *Economic Survey of Jersey* States of Jersey 1971. Another piece of work undertaken as a result of the Kilbrandon Royal Commission. It provides a valuable study of the contemporary position. The principle factors in Jersey's economic growth since the war, and especially of the importance of tax breaks and the resulting development of offshore banking, are surveyed in Ward Rutherford 'Jersey's Micro-Miracle' *World Today* 40 1984 pp 79–84.

7829 R A Rumfitt (ed) *The Evening Post 1890–1965* Evening Post, St Helier 1965. A commemorative issue of the biggest selling newspaper in the Channel Islands (now the *Jersey Evening Post*). It however has little on the post-war period.

7830 Michael Ginns *Transport in Jersey: An Historical Survey of Transport Facilities 1788–1961* Transport World 1961.

7831 L J Hawkley *The Story of the Jersey Electricity Company Ltd* Jersey Electricity Company Ltd 1983. An extensive business history. Much briefer is Roger Long (comp) *Gas in Jersey 1831–1981: A Brief History of the Jersey Gas Company* Jersey Gas Company Ltd 1981.

7832 St A Robilliard *Jersey's Housing Control Law: A Study* the author 1984. A study of the housing controls used to restrict immigration and control land use on the island.

7833 Gerald Durrell *Menagerie Manor* Penguin 1979. Both this and his *The Stationary Ark* Collins 1978 deal with the development of Jersey zoo.

7834 Victor Coysh *Sark: The Last Stronghold of Feudalism* Toucan 1982. A short study of Sark and Sark society. See also S M Toyne *Sark: A Feudal Survival* Shakespeare Head Press 1959. The then feudal head of Sark society records her memoirs in Sibyl Mary Hathaway *Dame of Sark: An Autobiography* Heinemann 1961. Dame Sibyl died in 1974.

# 13 WALES

## A. GENERAL

### (1) General

**7835** *Bibliotheca Celtica: A Register of Publications Relating to Wales and the Celtic Peoples and Languages* National Library of Wales 1910–. An irregular publication. Both this and *Subject Index to Welsh Periodicals* 1934– Swansea and Monmouthshire Branch, Library Association 1933–64, have been replaced by the annual *Bibliography of Wales* National Library of Wales 1964–.

**7836** *Handlist of Manuscripts in the National Library of Wales* National Library of Wales, annual supplements 1943–. A guide to recent additions to the library's manuscript collection, which is the main depository for the archives of leading figures in Welsh politics, life and society.

**7837** *Board of Celtic Studies Bulletin* 1959–. This carries an annual bibliography. There has also been an annual checklist of relevant articles published in *Welsh History Review* since 1960. This latter journal additionally regularly carries a list of recent theses on Welsh history. *Llafur* 1972– carries regular and valuable bibliographies on Welsh labour history.

**7838** Graham Day and Gareth Rees (eds) *Contemporary Wales: An Annual Review of Economic and Social Research* University of Wales 1987–. An analysis of current research into the state of contemporary Wales.

**7839** *A Reader's Guide to Wales: A Selected Bibliography* National Book League 1973. There are about 1,500 unannotated entries in this bibliography. It is classified but its value is much reduced by the lack of an index.

**7840** *Digest of Welsh Statistics* HMSO 1955–. A comprehensive annual collection of statistics.

**7841** *Welsh Office Atlas/Atlas y Swyddfa Gyrmeig* HMSO 1972–75. An atlas of planning maps based on the Ordnance Survey series. It covers the environment, ad-

ministrative and political boundaries, agriculture and forestry, transport, population, energy and other matters. Since 1981 it has been gradually being superseded by the National Atlas of Wales.

**7842** Kenneth O Morgan *Rebirth of a Nation: Wales 1880–1980* Clarendon 1981. An excellent general history of the Welsh political, economic, cultural and social experience up to the end of the 1970s. It also contains a good bibliography. See also Prys Morgan and David Thomas *Wales: The Shaping of a Nation* David and Charles 1984.

**7843** Gareth Elwyn Jones *People, Protest and Politics: Case Studies in Twentieth Century Wales* Gomer 1987. A book designed as a teaching resource for schools. It provides a chronology and useful case studies on Plaid Cmyru and the devolution debate.

**7844** Alan Road *Newspaper Dragon* C Davies 1977. A collection of extracts from newspapers covering three decades of Welsh life.

**7845** David Thomas (ed) *Wales: A New Study* David and Charles 1979. A good geographical study of land use, climate, agriculture, industry, settlement patterns, transport and tourism in modern Wales.

**7846** Kenneth O Morgan 'Post War Reconstruction in Wales 1918 and 1945' in Jay Winter (ed) *The Working Class in Modern British History: Essays in Honour of Henry Pelling* Cambridge University Press 1983 pp 82–98.

**7847** John Davies 'Wales in the Nineteen Sixties' *Llafur* 4/4 1987 pp 78–88.

### (2) Welsh Language and Culture

**7848** Clive Betts *Culture in Crisis: The Future of the Welsh Language* Ffynnon Press 1976. This charts the decline of the language in the face of Anglicization and the development of a mass and nationally based media, despite the best efforts of activists and governments to strengthen it. It examines the place of the language in government, education and the media and suggests policies to assist its survival. On the decline of the language see also Colin H Williams 'Language Contact and Language Change in Wales 1901–1971: A Study in Historical Geolinguistics' *Welsh History Review* 10 1980 pp 207–38 and Colin H Williams 'Public Gain and Private Grief: The Rate of Language Loss among Welsh Speakers between 1921 and 1981' *Transactions of the Honourable Society of Cymmorodorion* 1985 pp 27–48.

**7849** J Aitchison and H Carter *The Welsh Language 1961–1981: An Interpretative Atlas* University of Wales Press 1985. This illustrates the changing distribution of Welsh speakers and their gradual decline. The distribution in the 1971 census is analysed in E G Bowen and H Carter 'Distribution of the Welsh Language in 1971: An Analysis' *Geography* 60 1975 pp 1–15.

**7850** Gwennant Davies *The Story of the Urdd: The Welsh League of Youth 1922–1972* Cwmni Urdd Gobaith Cymru 1973. This was an apolitical movement founded to minister to and inspire the Welsh-speaking young. It promoted Welsh language and culture and urged the greater use of the language in education and broadcasting. A more overt pressure group for the language was Undeb Cymru Fydd (the New Wales Union). Its history and development from a political organization into an educational charity by the end of the 1960s is traced in Richard Gerallt Jones *A Bid for Unity: The Story of Undeb Cymru Fydd 1946–1966* Undeb Cymru Fydd 1971. This includes an epilogue on 1966–70. It is also a biography of its founder, T I Ellis

**7851** Colin H Williams 'Non-Violence and the Development of the Welsh Language Society 1962–c1974' *Welsh History Review* 8 1977 pp 426–55. Cymdeithas yr Iaith Gymraeg, the Welsh Language Society, was founded to fight to protect and preserve the language at a Plaid Cymru summer school in 1962. Its vigorous campaign of sit-ins and disruption, its defacing of signposts and pressure contributed to such triumphs as the Welsh Language Act 1967, which gave Welsh equal validity with English in the Principality.

**7852** *Council for Wales and Monmouthshire Report on the Welsh Language Today* Cmnd 2198, *Parliamentary Papers* xx 1963–64. This report by the group chaired by R I Aaron pressed for Welsh broadcasting and led to the Welsh Education Office initiative in April 1964 to create a national agency to promote the teaching of Welsh. This development is described in E Evans 'The Establishment and Early Development of the National Language Unit in Wales' Wales PhD Thesis 1985.

**7853** *Legal Status of the Welsh Language* Cmnd 2785, *Parliamentary Papers* xxiii 1964–65. The committee chaired by Sir David Hughes Parry argued that the status of Welsh should be raised and clarified and recommended that the priniciple of the equal validity of Welsh should be embodied in statute, as was indeed done in the Welsh Language Act 1967.

**7854** S M Williams 'The Politics of Language Policy in Wales: The Case of Language Broadcasting and the Issue of the Fourth Television Channel' Manchester MA (Econ) Thesis 1983. A study of the struggle for a Welsh language television channel as the key to the survival of the language from 1970 up to the decision to go ahead with S4C. The history of the BBC in Wales, including an account of the struggle to improve the status of the Welsh language on television and radio, is told in Rowland Lucas *The Voice of a Nation? A Concise Account of the BBC in Wales 1923–1973* Gomer 1981.

### (3) Political History

#### (a) General

**7855** Denis Balsom and Martin Burch *A Political and Electoral Handbook for Wales* Gower 1980. A reference book on Welsh central and local administration, political parties, MPs and interest groups. It also gives full social, economic and linguistic profiles of the contemporary parliamentary constituencies.

**7856** Jane Morgan (comp) *A Breviate of Parliamentary Papers Relating to Wales 1868 1964* Board of Celtic Studies, Cardiff 1975.

**7857** Beti Jones *Parliamentary Elections in Wales 1900–1975* Y Lolfa 1977. A statistical guide with biographical details.

**7858** Kenneth O Morgan 'The Welsh in English Politics 1868–1982' in R R Davies, Ralph A Griffiths, Ieuan Gwynedd Jones and Kenneth O Morgan (eds) *Welsh Society and Nationhood: Historical Essays Presented to Glanmor Williams* University of Wales Press 1984 pp 232–50. This concentrates on Labour in the twentieth century.

**7859** P J Randall 'The Development of Adminstrative Decentralisation for Wales from the Establishment of the Welsh Department of Education in 1907 to the Creation of the Post of Secretary of State for Wales in October 1964' Wales MSc (Econ) Thesis 1968–9. The first innovation in adminstration in Wales of the post-war period was the creation of the Council for Wales and Monmouthshire in 1948. This was designed to assist the government in developing policies for Wales, but little more. Its history is traced in E L Gibson 'A Study of the Council for Wales and Monmouthshire 1948–1966'

Wales MA Thesis 1968–9. The establishment of the Welsh Office as a distinctive, policy-making department of state in 1964 by the incoming Wilson government is described in Edward Rowlands 'The Politics of Regional Administration: The Establishment of the Welsh Office' *Public Administration* 50 1972 pp 333–52. See also Ian C Thomas *The Creation of the Welsh Office: Conflicting Purposes in Institutional Change* Centre for the Study of Public Policy 91, University of Strathclyde 1981. The record of the Welsh Office is examined in A I C Thomas 'The Role of the Welsh Office in British Government in Wales' Strathclyde PhD Thesis 1984. He argues that it has not fostered Welsh particularism or indeed greatly altered the impact of central British government in Wales or slowed the rate of language decline.

**7860** Arnold J James and John E Thomas *Wales at Westminster: A History of the Parliamentary Representation of Wales 1800–1979* Gomer 1981. A reference guide to constituencies, MPs, franchise changes and electoral results. It supplies biographical details of Welsh MPs and an analysis of their social composition. It also supplies information on Welsh voting in the European elections, the referendum of 1975, the devolution referendum and the Sunday opening referenda of 1961, 1968 and 1975. On Welsh select committees see [536].

**7861** John Osmond (ed) *The National Question Again: Welsh Political Identity in the 1980s* Gomer 1985. A good collection of essays which in some ways offer a political history of Wales in the twentieth century. There are some autobiographical contributions by Welsh politicians.

**7862** Ian McAllister 'The Labour Party in Wales: The Dynamics of One-Partyism' *Llafur* 3 1981 pp 79–89. A study of the party and its electoral dominance in the post-war era. The political traditions in the party of nationalism, as represented by James Griffiths, and Marxism, as represented by Aneurin Bevan, are contrasted in the short paper, Kenneth O Morgan *The Red Dragon and the Red Flag* National Library of Wales 1989.

**7863** Denis Balsom 'An Analysis of Recent Voting Behaviour in Wales, with Particular Reference to Socio-Economic Factors derived from the Census' Wales PhD Thesis 1984. This argues that electoral behaviour in Wales has been distinctive. Denis Balsom, Peter J Madgwick and Denis Van Mechelen 'The Red and the Green: Patterns of Partisan Choice in Wales' *British Journal of Political Science* 14 1984 pp 483–508 is a good study of the basis of partisanship in Wales.

## (b) Nationalism

**7864** A A S Butt Philip *The Welsh Question: Nationalism in Welsh Politics 1945–70* University of Wales Press 1975. A well regarded, if now somewhat dated study. R Mears 'A Sociological Analysis of Welsh Nationalism' Leicester PhD Thesis 1986 is a useful attempt to explore the historical and social bases of the nationalist appeal. The importance of language decline to the rise of nationalism is examined in C Williams 'Language Decline and Nationalist Resurgence in Wales' Wales PhD Thesis 1978.

**7865** Denis Balsom *The Nature and Distribution of Support for Plaid Cymru* Centre for the Study of Public Policy 36, University of Strathclyde 1979. On support for the nationalist cause in Wales see also James M Lutz 'The Spread of the Plaid Cymru: The Spatial Impress' *Western Political Quarterly* 34 1981 pp 310–30.

**7866** Gwynfor Evans *Welsh Nationalist Aims* Plaid Cymru 1967. A statement by the then leader of Plaid Cymru. On Gwynfor Evans see also Pennar Davies *Gwynfor Evans: Golwg ar ei waith a'i feddwl* Ty John Penry 1976 and *Gwynfor Evans e Breizh* Hor Yezh 1986.

**7867** Ned Thomas *The Welsh Extremist: A Culture in Crisis* Gollancz 1971. An attempt to explain the growing nationalism in Wales in the context of decline of the language.

## (c) Devolution

**7868** D Foulkes, J Barry Jones and R A Wilford (eds) *The Welsh Veto: The Welsh Act of 1978 and the Referendum* University of Wales Press 1983. A collection of essays examining the devolution debate in the 1970s and the defeat of devolution in the 1979 referendum. On the devolution debate see also John Osmond *Creative Conflict: The Politics of Welsh Devolution* Gomer 1977 and J Barry Jones and R A Wilford *The Welsh Veto: The Politics of the Devolution Campaign* Centre for the Study of Public Policy 39, University of Strathclyde 1979.

## (4) Legal History

**7869** J A Andrews (ed) *Welsh Studies in Public Law* University of Wales Press 1970. A useful collection of essays.

## (5) Religion

**7870** Peter Brierley (ed) *Prospects for Wales: Report of the 1982 Census of the Churches* Bible Society 1983. A good statistical study of the state of the churches.

**7871** Vivian Jones (ed) *The Church in a Mobile Society: A Survey of the Zone of Industrial South West Wales* Christopher Davies 1969. A study of the presence and social role of the churches in the Swansea area.

**7872** Geraint D Fielder *'Excuse Me Mr Davies – Hallelujah!': Evangelical Student Witness in Wales 1923–83* Evangelical Press of Wales/Inter-Varsity Press 1983. A history of the Inter-Varsity Fellowship (the Evangelical student Christian movement) in Wales.

**7873** David Walker 'Disestablishment and Independence' in David Walker (ed) *A History of the Church in Wales* Church in Wales Publications 1976 pp 164–87. A history of the Anglican Church in Wales in the twentieth century. The history of the Church's ministry to young people since the Provincial Youth Council was started in 1943 is told in J G Keane (ed) *Coming of Age* Provincial Youth Council of the Church in Wales 1964. On the training of clergymen see D T W Price 'The Contribution of St David's College, Lampeter to the Church in Wales 1920–71' *Journal of Welsh Ecclesiastical History* 1 1984 pp 63–83.

**7874** Edward Lewis *John Bangor, the People's Bishop: The Life and Work of John Charles Jones, Bishop of Bangor 1949–56* SPCK 1962. The life of another prominent Church of Wales clergyman is told in Daniel Richards' autobiography, *Honest to Self* Christopher Davies 1971.

**7875** John S Peart-Binns 'Argywydd Archesgob Cymru: Alfred Edwin Morris – Election and Aftermath' *Journal of Welsh Ecclesiastical History* 2 1985 pp 55–86. A study of the controversy surrounding the archepiscopal election of 1957.

**7876** Brynley Roberts 'Welsh Nonconformist Archives' *Journal of Welsh Ecclesiastical History* 3 1986 pp 61–72. A guide.

**7877** D Ben Rees *Chapels in the Valley: A Study in the Sociology of Welsh Nonconformity* Ffynnon Press 1975. A useful sociological study based on interviews and questionnaires conducted by a local Calvinistic Methodist minister in the Aberdare valley in South Wales.

**7878** M M Lynch 'Hanes Methodistiaeth Galfinaidd yn Nwyrwain Meirionnydd 1900–1975' Wales MA Thesis 1983. A history of the Calvinistic Methodist

Church (now more usually known as the Presbyterian Church of Wales) in Merionedd.

**7879** D M Himbury *The South Wales Baptist College 1807–1957* South Wales Baptist College 1957.

**7880** Barrie Naylor *Quakers in the Rhondda 1926–1986* Maes-yr-Haf Educational Trust 1986. A history of Quaker social work in the depressed areas of South Wales.

## (6) Economic History

### (a) General

**7881** Graham Lloyd Rees *Survey of the Welsh Economy* HMSO 1973. A study conducted for the Kilbrandon Royal Commission on the Constitution. The performance of the Welsh economy since 1945 is assessed in Brinley Thomas (ed) *The Welsh Economy: Studies in Expansion* University of Wales Press 1962. This includes essays on various Welsh industries, population and consumption. See also Edward Nevin, A R Roe and J I Round *The Structure of the Welsh Economy* Welsh Economic Studies 4, University of Wales Press 1966 and Edward Nevin (ed) *The Social Accounts of the Welsh Economy 1948–1956* Welsh Economic Studies 2, University of Wales Press 1957.

**7882** *Welsh Economic Trends* HMSO 1974–. A biennial publication.

**7883** David Thomas (ed) *Wales: A New Study* David and Charles 1977. A study of the industrial geography of Wales.

**7884** Graham Humphreys *South Wales* David and Charles 1972. A study of the industrial geography of the region. See also his 'Economic Change in Industrial South Wales: Post-War Patterns and Developments' Wales PhD Thesis 1967–8. Gerald Manners (ed) *South Wales in the Sixties: Studies in Industrial Geography* Pergamon 1964 is another useful study of the changing economic character of the region.

**7885** K Morgan 'State Policy and Regional Development in Britain: The Case of Wales' Sussex DPhil Thesis 1982. Wales has been a target of regional development policies since their origins with the Special Areas Act 1934. State-led attempts to restructure the Welsh economy in the 1970s and 1980s in the face of the continuing decline of traditional heavy industry are examined in J L Morris 'The State and Industrial Restructuring: Government Policies in Industrial Wales' *Environment and Planning D* 5 1987 pp 195–213. The main agency of regional policy in Wales in this period has been the Welsh Development Agency. The development and policy of this body since its was set up in 1975 is analysed in J H Williams 'The Politics of the Welsh Development Agency' London MPhil Thesis 1984.

**7886** P Cooke and G Rees 'The Industrial Restructuring of South Wales: The Career of a State Managed Region' *Policy Studies Journal* 10 1981 pp 284–96. Regional development policy has particularly focused on the industrial economy of South Wales, which has been hit since the inter-war period by the decline of former staple industries such as coal and iron and steel. See also Philip Cooke and Gareth Rees 'The Social Democratic State in a Radical Region: Development Agencies, Industrial Change and Class Relations in South Wales' in Ivan Szelenyi (ed) *Cities in Recession: Critical Responses to the Urban Policies of the New Right* Sage 1984 pp 162–91. One of the tactics of regional policy, the creation of low-rent and rates industrial estates, is examined in J R Bale 'The Development of Industrial Estates, with Special Reference to South Wales 1936–1969' London MPhil Thesis 1971–72.

**7887** Timothy O'Sullivan *Julian Hodge: A Biography* Routledge and Kegan Paul 1981. A biography of the Chairman of the Commercial Bank of Wales. Hodge was an eminent Welsh Roman Catholic and businessman and the friend of James Callaghan and other leading Labour politicians in Wales.

**7888** John Benson and Robert G Neville 'A Bibliography of the Coal Industry in Wales' *Llafur* 2/4 1979 pp 78–91. An unannotated bibliography. Hywel Francis and Kim Howells 'The Politics of Coal in South Wales 1945–48' *Llafur* 3 1981 pp 74–85 traces the run-up in South Wales to the nationalization of the coal industry. On the coalfield and mining society see also Kim Howells 'A View from Below: Tradition, Experience and Nationalisation in the South Wales Coalfield 1937–1957' Warwick PhD Thesis 1979 and W G Thomas 'The Dulais Valley: Developments and Closures in the Coalmining Industry 1958–1977' Wales MSc (Econ) Thesis 1979.

**7889** T Mervyn Jones *Going Public* D Brown and Sons 1987. The autobiography of a Welsh businessman. It is particularly useful on the Welsh Gas Board and the Welsh Tourist Board.

**7890** G Clayton and J H Rees *The Economic Problems of Rural Transport* University of Wales Press 1967. An early assessment of the effects of the 1963 Beeching cuts of the rural railway network in Wales. It draws attention to the danger of declining general services. See also G W Jones 'The Development and Decline of Public Transport Services in Mid-Wales 1861–1966 and the Effects Thereof' London MA Thesis 1967–8.

**7891** T G Shaddon *History of Cambrian Airways: The Welsh Airline from 1935–1976* Airline Publications 1979.

**7892** W T Rees-Pryce 'The Location and Growth of Holiday Caravan Camps in Wales' *Transactions of the Institute of British Geographers* 42 1968 pp 127–53. A study of an aspect of the growth of tourism in Wales.

(b) Agriculture, Fisheries and Food

**7893** *Welsh Agricultural Statistics* HMSO 1979–. An annual statistical guide to the state of the industry.

**7894** J Aitchison 'The Agricultural Landscape of Wales' *Cambria* 7 1980 pp 43–68.

**7895** I R Bowler 'Spatial and Temporal Variations in the Relationship between Governments and Agriculture in England and Wales 1945–1967, with Special Reference to Livestock Farming in Central Wales' Liverpool PhD Thesis 1972–3.

**7896** E A Attwood and H G Evans *The Economics of Hill Farming* University of Wales Press 1961. A study of the economic problems of and government support for hill farming in Wales, especially in the light of the Hill Farming Act 1946.

**7897** Derek Rees *Rings and Rosettes: The History of the Pembrokeshire Agricultural Society 1784–1977* Gomer 1977.

**7898** C B E Ryle 'Forestry in the Economic Development of Wales' *Quarterly Journal of Forestry* 55 1961 pp 197–205. On forestry in Wales see also F C Best and J A Hampson 'Forestry in West Central Wales' *Forestry* 34 1961 pp 1–43 and W A Cadman 'Forestry and Silviculture in North Wales' *Forestry* 26 1953 pp 65–80.

**7899** R J Dean 'The South Wales Fishery 1945–83' Wales MSc Thesis 1983. A study of the industry's decline due to over-exploitation and increasing competition in its traditional waters off Ireland and the difficulties of subsequent adaptation.

(c) Labour

**7900** G Clare Wenger *Mid-Wales: Deprivation or Development: A Study of Patterns of Employment in Selected Communities* Social Science Monographs 5, University of Wales Press 1980.

**7901** Hywel Francis and David Smith *The Fed: A History of the South Wales Miners in the Twentieth*

*Century* Lawrence and Wishart 1980. An excellent history of the South Wales Miners Federation (which in 1945 became the South Wales region of the National Union of Mineworkers) from its foundation in 1898. It is in some ways a social history of the South Wales coalfield as well. This social history is very much reflected in the large oral archive held at the South Wales Miners Library, 50 Skethy Road, Uplands, Swansea, West Galmorgan SA2 0LG. This collection covers all matters relating to the coalfield. Along with touching on work, trade unionism, pit closures and mining in general the interviews also carry material of interest on education, customs, social life and Communism in the valleys. Almost all of the interviews have been transcribed. Another useful memoir of the coalfield is William Paget *Man of the Valleys: The Recollections of a South Wales Miner* Sutton 1985. For biographies of Welsh miners' leaders see [4796 and 4800].

**7902**  David Ingli Gidwell 'Philosophy and Geology in Conflict: The Evolution of Wages Structures in the South Wales Coalfields 1926–74' *Llafur* 1/4 1975 pp 44–57.

**7903**  Hywel Francis and Gareth Rees 'No Surrender in the Valleys: The 1984–5 Miners' Strike in South Wales' *Llafur* 5/2 1988 pp 41–71. See also Gareth Rees 'Regional Restructuring, Class Change and Political Action: Preliminary Comments on the 1984 85 Miners' Strike in South Wales' *Environment and Planning D: Society and Space* 3 1985 pp 389–406.

**7904**  Stephen W Town *After The Mines: Changing Employment Opportunities in a South Wales Valley* University of Wales Press 1978. A sociological study of the impact of the decline of mining in the former mining district of the Ammon valley 1948–74.

**7905**  Gwyn Edwards 'Mudiad y Di-waith Dyffrn Nantlle 1956–1960' *Llafur* 5/1 1987 pp 29–36. A study of the unemployment movement in the slate-quarrying Nantlle valley, Gywnedd.

**7906**  Gwyn A Williams 'Women Workers in Wales 1968–82' *Welsh History Review* 11 1983 pp 530–48. An assessment of the impact of sex discrimination and equal pay legislation in Wales.

## (7) Environment

**7907**  Gwyn Williams 'The Welsh National Parks: Their Achievements and Problems' *Cambria* 2 1975 pp 34–40. An account of the development of the national parks designated in Snowdonia in 1951, Pembroke in 1952 and Brecon Beacons in 1957.

**7908**  *Report of the Tribunal Appointed to Inquire into the Disaster at Aberfan on October 21st 1966* Cmnd 553, *Parliamentary Papers* xxi 1966–67. A report by the committee, chaired by Sir Herbert Davies, into the disaster at Aberfan when a coal tip suddenly subsided and engulfed over a hundred schoolchildren. This placed responsibility for the disaster on the National Coal Board and recommended a National Tip Safety Committee and greater supervision by the Mines Inspectorate. Tony Austin *Aberfan* Hutchinson 1967 is a useful instant history of the disaster and its aftermath.

**7909**  Irene M Hall *Community Action versus Pollution: A Study of a Residents' Group in a Welsh Urban Area* Social Science Monographs 2, University of Wales Press 1976. A study of responses to pollution in Swansea.

**7910**  Philip Riden *Rebuilding a Valley: A History of Cwmbran Development Corporation* Cwmbran Development Corporation 1988. A good official history of the only New Town in Wales, which was designated in 1949. It draws on both the files of the Development Corporation and of the Welsh Office (the latter made specially available).

**7911**  Clough Williams-Ellis *Portmeirion: The Place and its Meaning* Faber 1963. An autobiographical account by the creator of the foundation, growth and development of the unique pastiche community in Wales.

## (8) Social History

**7912**  *Welsh Social Trends* HMSO 1977–. An annual guide to Welsh social and environmental trends with supporting statistics.

**7913**  Welsh Folk Museum, St Fagan's, Cardiff CF5 6XB. This features an oral archive with over 10,000 tapes covering agriculture, rural crafts, folklore and rural customs.

**7914**  Paul H Ballard and Erastus Jones (eds) *The Valleys Call: A Self-Examination by People of the South Wales Valleys during the Year of the Valleys 1974* Ron Jones Publications 1975. Oral accounts of life in the valleys.

**7915**  H Carter and J G Thomas 'The Referendum on the Sunday Opening of Licensed Premises in Wales as a Criterion of a Cultural Region' *Regional Studies* 3 1969 pp 61–71. The Welsh Sunday Closing Act of 1881 was the first distinctively Welsh piece of legislation and was a response to the temperance demands of Welsh Nonconformity. Under the 1960 Licensing Act local referenda have to be held every seven years on whether or not to maintain Sunday closing. The referenda are here used to reveal the changing cultural and social character of the Principality. On the 1975 referendum see H Carter 'Y Fro Gymraeg and the 1975 Referendum on Sunday Opening of Public Houses in Wales' *Cambria* 3 1976 pp 89–101. This examines the referendum in Welsh-speaking Wales.

**7916**  S L Edwards and B J M Wilson *Migration Into, Out of and Within Wales in the 1966–71 Period* Welsh Office Occasional Paper 4, n.d. (1975?). This examines migration in Wales with maps and statistics.

**7917**  *Health and Personal Social Services Statistics for Wales* Welsh Office 1974–. An annual publication. See also *Health Service Wales: Report of the Chief Medical Officer* Welsh Office 1975–.

**7918**  R M Pill 'Education and Social Mobility in Wales 1938–1968' Wales PhD Thesis 1970–1.

**7919**  Gareth Rees and Teresa L Rees (eds) *Poverty and Social Inequality in Wales* Croom Helm 1980. A collection of empirical and theoretical essays on the situation in the 1970s. See also P Wilding *Poverty in Wales* Child Poverty Action Group 1977.

**7920**  David Smith and Gareth Williams *Fields of Praise: The Official History of the Welsh Rugby Union 1881–1981* University of Wales Press 1981. See also Alun Richards *A Touch of Glory: 100 Years of Welsh Rugby* Michael Joseph 1981, John Brinley George Thomas *The Illustrated History of Welsh Rugby* Pelham Books 1980 and John Brinley George Thomas and Rowe Harding (eds) *Rugby in Wales* C Davies 1970. Gareth Edwards *The Golden Years of Welsh Rugby* Harrap 1982 looks at Welsh rugby in the 1960s and 1970s. Welsh rugby in the 1970s is examined in Clem Thomas *Welsh Rugby* Collins 1980 and John Taylor *Decade of the Dragon* Hodder and Stoughton 1980. The story of the international side is told in John Brinley George Thomas *The Men in Scarlet: The Story of Welsh Rugby Football* Pelham 1972 and John Billot *History of Welsh International Rugby* Ron Jones Publications 1970. Phil Bennett *Everywhere for Wales* Stanley Paul 1981 is the autobiography of a great Welsh rugby union player as is Gareth Edwards *Gareth* Stanley Paul 1978. Other biographies and autobiographies of leading players are Lewis Jones *King of Rugger* Stanley Paul 1958, Bleddyn Williams *Rugger: My Life* Stanley Paul 1956, Barry John *The Barry John Story* Collins 1974, Gerald Davies *Gerald Davies* Allen and Unwin 1979, Mervyn Davies *Number 8* Pelham 1977, Graham Price *Price of Wales* Willow 1984 and J P R Williams *JPR* Collins 1979. Jonathan Davies with Peter Corrigan *Jonathan* Stanley Paul 1989 is the autobiography of the Welsh rugby captain who switched to rugby league in January 1989. On the history

of particular Welsh clubs see Danny Ellis Davies *Cardiff Rugby Club* 2nd ed, Starling Press 1976 and Jack Davies *One Hundred Years of Newport Rugby* Starling Press 1974.

**7921**  Wally Barnes *Captain of Wales* Stanley Paul 1953. The autobiography of a footballer. For other footballing autobiographies see William John Charles *The Gentle Giant* Stanley Paul 1962, Ian Rush *Rush* Barker 1985 and John Toshack *Tosh* Barker 1982. The history of a particular club is told in David Farmer *Swansea City 1912–1982* Pelham 1982.

**7922**  Wilfrid Wooler *Glamorgan* Barker 1971. A history of the county cricket club. Another history is John Hinds Morgan *Glamorgan County Cricket* Convoy Publications 1952.

**7923**  Lynn Davies *Winner Stakes All: Lynn Davies Face to Face with Peter Williams* Pelham 1970. Reminiscences of the winner of the long jump gold medal at the 1964 Olympics.

**7924**  *Welsh Housing Statistics* HMSO 1981–. An annual guide to construction and types of housing tenure.

**7925**  Chris Bollom *Attitudes and Second Homes in Rural Wales* Social Science Monographs, University of Wales Press 1978. A study of an inflammatory subject. The development of holiday cottages and retirement homes in rural Wales has been accompanied by nationalist resentment and by terrorist firebombs.

**7926**  Walter W Hunt *'To Guard My People': An Account of the Origins and History of the Swansea Police* Swansea Constabulary 1957.

**7927**  David Thomas *Seek Out The Guilty* John Long 1969. A police memoir of the cases he dealt with as a detective with Monmouthshire police.

### (9) Education

#### (a) General

**7928**  *Statistics of Education in Wales* HMSO 1976–. An annual guide.

**7929**  P J Randell 'Origins and Development of the Welsh Department of Education' *Welsh History Review* 7 1974 pp 450–71. A history of the development of the Welsh Education Department and its establishment in 1907.

**7930**  R B Howells 'A Study of the Emergence after 1945 of the Comprehensive Principle and Secondary School Organisation in Anglesey, Montgomeryshire, Denbighshire and Camarthenshire' Swansea MA Thesis 1965–6. The early development of comprehensive education in Anglesey, an area which then still contained a large number of monoglot Welsh speakers, by 1953, is traced in O A Williams 'Anglesey: Towards Comprehensive Education 1926–1953' Wales MEd Thesis 1985.

**7931**  H M Williams 'A Study of Secondary Education in Breconshire Since 1950' Wales PhD Thesis 1974–6.

**7932**  A G Geen 'Decision-Making in Relation to Secondary Education in the Cardiff Education Authority 1944–1970' Wales PhD Thesis 1979. Geen has published articles derived from this research on 'Educational Policy Making in Cardiff 1944–70' *Public Administration* 59 1981 pp 313–29 and 'A Resistance to Change: Attempts to Reorganise Cardiff's Elementary Schools 1918–1951' *Journal of Educational Administration and History* 18 1986 pp 62–74. See also J J Marsden 'An Evaluation of the Development of Further Education Provision within the City of Cardiff between 1916 and 1976' Wales PhD Thesis 1978.

**7933**  R D Jones 'The Development of Primary and Secondary Education in Gwynedd Since 1944: A Case Study in Educational Policy-Making in Rural Wales' Wales PhD Thesis 1985. A good study of policy-making in a heavily Welsh-speaking area.

**7934**  J A Davies *Education in a Welsh Rural County 1870–1973* University of Wales Press 1973. A study of education provision and policy in Montgomeryshire. See also C H Williams 'The Development of Secondary Education in Montgomeryshire Since 1889' Wales MA Thesis 1962–3. Williams has also published 'The Changing Pattern of Secondary Education in Montgomeryshire Since 1945' *Journal of Education Administration and History* 3 1971 pp 25–41.

**7935**  R S Griffiths 'The Development of Secondary Education in Radnorshire 1889–1963' Wales MA Thesis 1964–5.

**7936**  D G Williams 'Bilingual Education in Cardiganshire 1904–1974' Open University PhD Thesis 1984. This looks not only at bilingual education and measures to pass on Welsh linguistic heritage but also at the special problems of small rural schools and the effects of anglicization.

**7937**  R W Bevan 'The Development of Special Educational Treatment in Wales Since the Education Act of 1944' Wales MA Thesis 1973–4. A study of special education in Wales.

**7938**  E J Thomas 'The History of Physical Education in Wales up to 1970' Manchester MEd Thesis 1979.

**7939**  John Fletcher *A Technical Triumph: One Hundred Years of Public Further Education in Merthyr Tydfil 1873–1973* Methyr Tydfil Corporation 1974.

**7940**  *Coleg Technagal Rhydaman 1927–1977 = Ammanford Technical College 1927–1977* Ammanford Technical College 1977. A short history.

**7941**  D G Lewis *The University of Wales and the Colleges of Education in Wales 1925–78* University of Wales Press 1980. On teacher training see also T R Jenkins 'Teacher Training in Colleges of Education in Wales 1960–1970: A Study of Expansion in an Area Training Organisation' Wales PhD Thesis 1972–3.

**7942**  W T R Pryce 'The Open University in Wales' *Cambria* 1 1974 pp 12–16.

**7943**  Peter Stead *Coleg Harlech: The First Fifty Years* University of Wales Press 1977. A well regarded history of the adult education college established as a residential college for Welsh working men in Harlech in 1927.

**7944**  D G Griffith 'Aspects of the Provision of Local Authority and "Responsible Body" Adult Education in Flintshire 1925–1975' Liverpool MEd Thesis 1980.

**7945**  E L Ellis *The University College of Wales, Aberystwyth 1872–1972* University of Wales Press 1972. A good official history. For other college histories see Gwyn Jones and Michael Quinn *Fountains Of Praise: University College, Cardiff 1883–1983* University College, Cardiff 1983 and H K Archdall *St David's College, Lampeter: Its Past, Present and Future* St David's College, Lampeter 1952.

### (b) Libraries and Museums

**7946**  J Roe 'The Public Library in Wales: Its History and Development in the Context of Local Government' Queens, Belfast MA Thesis 1970. A history 1862–1970.

**7947**  *National Museum of Wales 1927–1977* National Museum of Wales 1977. A brief history. See also R T Jenkins *National Museum of Wales 1907–57: The Jubilee Lecture* National Museum of Wales 1957.

### (10) Cultural History

**7948**  Tony Curtis (ed) *Wales: The Imagined Nation: Essays in Cultural and National Identity* Poetry Wales Press 1986. An examination of all types of Welsh art and culture and their interrelationship with Welsh nationalism. M Stephens (ed) *The Arts in Wales 1950–1975* Welsh Arts Council 1979 is an illustrated survey of the literary, visual and musical arts in Wales, with specific reference to the encouragement given to the arts by the Welsh Arts Council.

**7949** K B Dunthorne *Artists Exhibited in Wales 1945–1974* Welsh Arts Council 1976. A directory with potted biographies of the artists and details of the exhibitions.

**7950** N E Werner 'Twentieth Century Musical Composition in Wales and its Relationship with Traditional Welsh Music' Wales MA Thesis 1978. On Welsh music see also K Adams 'Welsh Orchestral Music 1945–1970' Wales PhD Thesis 1981 and D E Thomas 'A Survey of Choral Composition in Wales 1945–1970' Wales MA Thesis 1969–70.

**7951** Richard Fawkes *Welsh National Opera* Julia McRae 1986. A good history of the opera company founded in 1946.

**7952** Sir Geraint Evans with Noel Godwin *Sir Geraint Evans: A Knight at the Opera* Michael Joseph 1984. The memoirs of the most celebrated Welsh opera singer of the post-war years.

**7953** Brymor Jones *A Bibliography of Anglo-Welsh Literature 1900–1965* Wales and Monmouthshire Branch, Library Association 1970. This has been updated by the series published by the Welsh Arts Council Literature Department since 1968.

**7954** Dannie Abse *A Poet in the Family* Hutchinson 1974. This poet's autobiography is supplemented by his *A Strong Dose of Myself* Hutchinson 1983.

**7955** Penelope Hughes *Richard Hughes: Author, Father* Sutton 1984. A biography of the novelist.

**7956** Richard Perceval Graves *The Brothers Powys* Routledge and Kegan Paul 1983. A study of the Welsh literary family. The short chapter on 1940–63 concentrates on John Cooper Powys (died 1963) and Theodore Powys (died 1953). H Coombes *T F Powys* Barrie and Rockliff 1960 adds some useful biographical material on Theodore Powys. See also John Cooper Powys *Autobiography* Macdonald 1967.

**7957** R Maud and A Glover *Dylan Thomas in Print: A Bibliographical History* Dent 1970. This lists everything the celebrated poet published, as well as the most important critical and biographical works. The best biography is Paul Ferris *Dylan Thomas* Hodder and Stoughton 1977. Constantine Fitzgibbon *The Life of Dylan Thomas* Dent 1965 is a useful memoir by a friend. So is Daniel Jones *My Friend Dylan Thomas* Dent 1977.

Gwen Watkins *Portrait of a Friend* Gomer 1983 is a memoir of Dylan Thomas by the wife of another great Welsh poet, Vernon Watkins. It is also useful on Watkins' life. Andrew Sinclair *Dylan Thomas: Poet of his People* Michael Joseph 1975 is an illustrated biography with some useful material on Dylan Thomas and his circle. The life of Dylan Thomas' wife is well told in her autobiography by Caitlin Thomas with George Tremlett *Caitlin: Life with Dylan Thomas* Secker and Warburg 1986, which reveals much of the poet's life and character that did not emerge in earlier works. Thomas' alcoholic excesses, decline and death in November 1953 in New York are detailed in John Malcolm Brinnin *Dylan Thomas in America* Dent 1976. The poet's letters right up to his death are collected in Paul Ferris (ed) *The Collected Letters of Dylan Thomas* Dent 1985.

**7958** K T A Clements 'The Theatre in Wales 1939–1980' Birmingham PhD Thesis 1982–3.

**7959** Melvyn Bragg *Rich: The Life of Richard Burton* Hodder and Stoughton 1988. A good biography of the Welsh actor who became an internationally respected star. See also Graham Jenkins with Barry Turner *Richard Burton My Brother* Michael Joseph 1988.

**7960** Quentin Falk *Anthony Hopkins: Too Good to Waste* Columbus 1989. A good biography of the distinguished Welsh actor.

## (11) Local History

**7961** *Welsh Local Government Financial Statistics* HMSO 1977–. An annual publication.

**7962** David Foulkes 'The Work of the Local Commissioner for Wales' *Public Law* 1978 pp 264–89. An account of the work of the ombudsman appointed to investigate local government administration in Wales.

**7963** Elwyn Davies and Alwyn D Rees (eds) *Welsh Rural Communities* University of Wales Press 1960. A good collection of sociological studies of Aber-porth and Tregaron in Ceredigion, Aberdaron on the Llyn peninsula, and Glan-Llyn in Merionedd.

**7964** D O Jones *Anglesey: A Bibliography* Gwynedd County Library Service 1979. An extensive, unannotated bibliography of material on the island with supporting maps. M Richards (ed) *An Atlas of Anglesey* Anglesey Community Council 1972 is a collection of physical and thematic maps.

**7965** Peter Ellis Jones *Bangor 1883–1983: A Study in Municipal Government* University of Wales Press 1986. A history of local government in the North Wales town.

**7966** *The Cardiff Region: A Survey Prepared for the Meeting of the British Association held in Cardiff 31 August to 7 September 1960* University of Wales Press 1960. A collection of essays on the climate, industry and agriculture of the region surrounding the capital of Wales prepared for the meeting of the British Association for the Advancement of Science. The history of the local authority up to local government reorganization is told in S Lloyd Jones (ed) *Cardiff 1889–1974: The Story of the County Borough* Corporation of Cardiff 1974.

**7967** Peter J Madgwick with Nan Griffiths and Valerie Walker *The Politics of Rural Wales: A Study of Cardiganshire* Hutchinson 1973. A good study of local and parliamentary politics in Cardiganshire from 1921 to the 1970s. The development of the Labour Party in the county over this period in an area which the Liberals have usually been able to continue to dominate, is usefully told in Howard C Jones 'The Labour Party in Cardiganshire 1918–66' *Ceredigion* 9 1982 pp 150–61. Social change in Cardiganshire as a result of changes in agriculture, population drift, rural services and the impact of tourism is analysed in J Geraint Jenkins 'Technological Improvement and Social Change in South Cardiganshire' *Agricultural History Review* 13 1965 pp 94–105. On social change in Cardiganshire see also C F A B J Le Vay 'The Social and Economic Changes Affecting the Farming Communities in Two Contrasting Cardiganshire Parishes 1961–1971' Wales Msc (Econ) Thesis 1972–3.

**7968** Clwyd County Library, County Civic Centre, Mold, Clwyd, CH7 6NW. This has an oral history archive on local agriculture, industry, education, religion and culture. On the history of the county council see [7669].

**7969** W Geraint Morgan 'Denbighshire Members of Parliament in the Twentieth Century' *Denbighshire Historical Society Transactions* 20 1971 pp 217–37. A guide to the county's parliamentary representatives and its parliamentary politics.

**7970** John Sewel *Colliery Closure and Social Change: A Study of a South Wales Mining Valley* Social Science Monographs 1, University of Wales Press 1975. A detailed and valuable sociological study of the impact of the decline of coalmining in the Dulais valley.

**7971** P T J Morgan (ed) *Glamorgan Society 1780–1980* University of Wales Press 1988. A collection of essays on society and politics in the county. Parliamentary representation and politics in the county are examined R Grant *The Parliamentary History of Glamorgan 1542–1976* Christopher Davies 1978. The vital role of central government regional development policy in the economic history of Glamorgan since 1945 is emphasized in Colin Beber and Jeffrey Demant 'Modern Glamorgan: Economic Development after 1945' in Arthur H John and Glanmor Williams (eds) *Glamorgan County History 5: Industrial Glamorgan from 1700 to 1970* Glamorgan County History Trust 1980 pp 581–658. Urban pressure on the rural hinterland in the Vale of Glamorgan is examined in M A Mason 'Residential Development and Social Change in the Vale of Glamorgan, South Wales c1960–1978' Wales MSc Thesis 1983.

**7972** H J Dickman *Haverfordwest Rural District Council: History of the Council 1894–1974* the author 1976.

**7973** Alwyn D Rees *Life in a Welsh Countryside: A Social Study of Llanfihangel yng Ngwynfa* 2nd ed, University of Wales Press 1951. A useful sociological study of a village in Montgomeryshire.

**7974** Ronald Frankenberg *Village on the Border: A Social Study of Religion, Politics and Football in a North Wales Community* Cohen and West 1957. A sociological study which usefully reflects social and political developments of the 1950s. The names of people and places have been disguised by pseudonyms, though it can be revealed that the identity of the village is Llansaintffraid Glyncoiriog in Denbighshire.

**7975** Isabel Emmett *A North Wales Village: A Social Anthropological Study* Routledge and Kegan Paul 1963. A useful study of contemporary rural society. It analyses a rural community somewhere in Merionedd whose name, as have all names in the study, has been disguised.

**7976** G P Ambrose (edited by G Prior) *Monmouthshire County Council 1888–1974* Gwent County Council 1974. A history of the authority, its politics and its activities up to local government reorganization.

**7977** W G V Balchin (ed) *Swansea and Its Region* University College of Swansea 1971. A good collection of essays on climate, the environment, agriculture and forestry, mining, industry, transport, society, urban growth, education and the university in Swansea and its hinterland. Colin Rosser and Christopher Harris *The Family and Social Change: A Study of Family and Kinship in a South Wales Town* Routledge and Kegan Paul 1965 is a detailed sociological study of Swansea. Swansea is the centre of the region being studied in Tom Brennan, E W Cooney and Harold Pollins *Social Change in South West Wales* Watts and Co 1954. This is a very useful study of social and political change in the region.

# 14 SCOTLAND

## A. GENERAL

### (1) Reference Works

**7978**  *List of Gifts and Deposits in the Scottish Record Office* HMSO 1972–. An annually updated guide to archives held. Other guides to Scottish archives are *Report* National Register of Archives (Scotland) 1946– and *National Library of Scotland: Catalogue of Manuscripts Acquired Since 1925* National Library of Scotland 1938–.

**7979**  *Scottish Abstract of Statistics* HMSO 1971–. An annual general statistical guide. This replaced the *Digest of Scottish Statistics* which appeared twice annually 1953–71.

**7980**  John Knox and E Wilson (eds) *Scotland 78: The Scots Yearbook* Wilson and Knox 1978. This was supposed to be the first of a series of yearbooks assessing the state of Scottish politics, administration, the economy, society, education, religion and sport and leisure. It includes a considerable amount of statistical information and ends with a chronology.

**7981**  *Bibliography of Scotland* HMSO 1978–. An annual catalogue of books published in Scotland and of books published elsewhere of relevance to Scotland, prepared from the accessions of the National Library of Scotland. It also includes a listing of articles. A bibliography of works on Scotland published 1916–50 is Philip D Hancock *A Bibliography of Works Relating to Scotland 1916–1950* 2v, Edinburgh University Press 1959–60.

**7982**  Eric G Grant *Scotland* Clio Press 1982. An excellent annotated bibliography organized in classified sections. It is basically confined to books, focusing on those published after 1960. D M Lloyd (ed) *Reader's Guide to Scotland: A Bibliography* National Book League 1968 is classified but unannotated.

**7983**  *British Humanities Index: Regional Lists: Scotland* Library Association 1954–68. An index of periodical articles relating to Scotland.

**7984**  *Scottish Historical Review* 1960–. This annually features a list of recent articles on Scottish history.

**7985**  *Scottish Economic and Social History* 1981–. This features an annual bibliography on Scottish economic and social history and also an annual review of current research.

**7986**  *Scottish Geographical Magazine* 1973–. Since 1973 this journal has carried an annual bibliography of recent literature relating to the geography and historical geography of Scotland.

**7987**  Joan Primrose Scott Ferguson (ed) *Scottish Newspapers held in Scottish Libraries* Scottish Central Library 1956. A guide and finding list. See also National Library of Scotland *A Select List of Scottish Periodicals* British Council 1963. See also [8134].

**7988**  *The Scotsman Index* Unit for the Study of Government in Scotland 1984–. An annual index to a leading Scottish daily newspaper.

**7989**  Gordon Donaldson and Robert S Morpeth *A Dictionary of Scottish History* Donald 1977. This unfortunately contains little of value for post-war historians.

### (2) General Histories

**7990**  Christopher Harvie *No Gods and Precious Few Heroes: Scotland 1914–1980* Arnold 1981. This general history of Scotland by a prominent nationalist historian is particularly strong on the links between Scotland's economic performance and the demand for independence. Harvie has also written *Scotland and Nationalism: Scottish Society and Politics 1707–1977* Allen and Unwin 1977, an examination of Scotland's sense of nationhood since the Act of Union, which contains many reflections on the growth of nationalism since 1945. Another valuable study of the modern history of Scotland is James G Kellas *Modern Scotland: The Nation Since 1870* 2nd ed, Allen and Unwin 1980. William Ferguson *Scotland 1689 to the Present* 2nd ed, Oliver and Boyd 1978, the fourth volume of the Edingburgh History of Scotland, has one chapter on the Second World War and after. See also R H Campbell *Scotland Since 1707* 2nd ed, John Donald 1984.

**7991** R F Mackenzie *A Search for Scotland* Collins 1989. An evocation of Scotland in the late twentieth century. It presents a somewhat severe picture

**7992** Tom Steel *Scotland's Story: A New Perspective* Collins 1984. A well-illustrated general history. The last two chapters cover 1939 onwards. See also Geoffrey D Credland and George T Murray *Scotland: A New Look* Scottish Television 1969.

**7993** David Turnock *The Historical Geography of Scotland Since 1707: Geographical Aspects of Modernisation* Cambridge University Press 1982. A useful study. A contemporary study of Scottish society and geography is Chalmers M Clapperton (ed) *Scotland: A New Study* David and Charles 1983. K J Lea with George Gordon and I R Bowler *A Geography of Scotland* David and Charles 1977 examines the natural environment, demography, planning, administration, transport, energy, water supply, rural life, industry and urban structure of the country.

**7994** Karl Miller (ed) *Memoirs of a Modern Scotland* Faber 1970. A collection of essays on Scottish politics and culture, especially on Scottish nationalism, by Scottish historians and leading literary figures.

**7995** Ron Parsler (ed) *Capitalism, Class and Politics in Scotland* Gower 1980. A collection of articles reprinted from the *Scottish Journal of Sociology*. Subjects covered include occupational mobility, Scottish industry, Scottish elites, nationalism, and the handling of the February 1974 general election in the Scottish media.

**7996** John Mercer *Scotland: The Devolution of Power* Calder 1978. A study of the economic, political and social characteristics of Scotland in the light of the on-going devolution debate of the 1970s. It ends by arguing that Scotland's social and economic problems are unlikely to be solved by devolution.

**7997** Gordon Brown (ed) *The Red Paper on Scotland* Edinburgh University Students Publishing Bureau 1975. A socialist contribution to the debate on Scotland's future. It features essays on such subjects as oil, economic instability, nationalism, devolution, social neglect, regional policy, the Highlands, housing, social work, public health and education.

# B. POLITICAL HISTORY

## (1) General

**7998** Henry M Drucker and Michael G Clarke (eds) *The Scottish Government Yearbook 1978–* Paul Harris 1977–. An annual collection of papers on subjects such as the Scottish Office, local government, the Scottish Development Agency or on topical issues. It also features a useful annual bibliography on Scottish government. It was first published as *Our Changing Scotland: A Yearbook of Scottish Government 1976–77*.

**7999** *Scotland's Regions: Incorporating the County and Municipal Yearbook for Scotland* W Culross 1974/75–. An annual information guide to local government in Scotland, mainly in tabular form. It is the successor to *County and Municipal Yearbook for Scotland*. W Culross 1940/41–1973/74.

**8000** James G Kellas 'Review Article: Political Science and Scottish Politics' *British Journal of Political Science* 10 1980 pp 365–79. A useful bibliographical essay on Scottish politics and government.

**8001** James G Kellas *The Scottish Political System* 4th ed, Cambridge University Press 1989. This has been updated to take account of the 1987 general election. It is the standard political textbook on politics and administration in Scotland. The Scottish political system is also assessed in Michael Keating and Arthur F Midwinter *The Government of Scotland* Humanities Press 1983.

**8002** Michael Fry *Patronage and Principle: A Political History of Modern Scotland* Aberdeen University Press 1987. A study of Scotland's distinctive political history from 1832 to the 1980s.

**8003** Colin Maclean (ed) *The Crown and the Thistle: The Nature of Nationhood* Scottish Academic Press 1979. A reader which includes essays on the constitution, the EC, the economy and the Scots language.

**8004** *Royal Commission on Scottish Affairs 1952–1954* Cmnd 9212, *Parliamentary Papers* xix 1953–54. This commission, chaired by the Earl of Balfour, produced little new in the way of recommendations, but does contain some interesting reflections on dissatisfaction in Scotland and the importance of the recognition of Scotland's national status.

**8005** Robert Mulholland *Scotland's Freedom Struggle: Political, Social and Cultural Aspects of the 1970s* Crann Tara 1978. A collection of articles from the *Irish Democrat* 1971–77, covering the links between nationalism and socialism, Ireland and Scotland, the language, Celtic Marxism and republicanism.

**8006**   John S Gibson *The Thistle and the Crown: A History of the Scottish Office* HMSO 1985. A useful official centenary history of the Scottish Office. David Milne *The Scottish Office and Other Scottish Departments* Allen and Unwin 1957 is an account of the scope and variety of the work undertaken by Scottish government departments.

**8007**   George Pottinger *The Secretaries of State for Scotland 1926–1976* Scottish Academic Press 1979. A collection of biographies of all the holders of this office which also reflects on the growth of the department and major political events. On the work of the Secretary of State see also J M Ross *The Secretary of State for Scotland and the Scottish Office* Centre for the Study of Public Policy 87, University of Strathclyde 1981.

**8008**   A W Coats 'The Changing Role of Economists in Scottish Government Since 1960' *Public Administration* 56 1978 pp 399–424.

**8009**   Brian W Hogwood *The Tartan Fringe: Quangos and Other Assorted Animals in Scotland* Centre for the Study of Public Policy 34, University of Strathclyde 1979. An examination of the work and role of quangos and other bodies such as administrative tribunals in Scottish administration.

**8010**   Clive Archer and John Main (ed) *Scotland's Voice in International Affairs: The Overseas Representation of Scottish Interests with Special Reference to the European Economic Community* Christopher Hurst 1980.

## (2) Scottish Nationalism and the Devolution Debate

**8011**   Gordon Bryan (ed) *Scottish Nationalism and Cultural Identity in the Twentieth Century: An Annotated Bibliography of Secondary Sources* Greenwood 1984. A well annotated, classified bibliography. Kenneth C Fraser *A Bibliography of the Scottish National Movement 1844–1973* Douglas S Mack 1976 is a mimeographed publication. It lists 539 classified entries with some brief annotations. It is particularly good on poetry and fiction.

**8012**   Keith Webb *The Growth of Nationalism in Scotland* Molendinar Press 1978. This is a carefully researched and impartial history of nationalism in Scotland since before the Act of Union in 1707 which concentrates on developments in the twentieth century. The important influence of the country's distinctive religious

and cultural history is brought out well. Another impressive general history of the development of nationalism in Scotland, in this case since the late nineteenth century, is H J Hanham *Scottish Nationalism* Faber 1969. Nationalism since the establishment of the Scottish National Party in 1928 is examined in the context of economic, social and political developments in Jack Brand *The National Movement in Scotland* Routledge and Kegan Paul 1978. The peak of the SNP's electoral support and the devolution debate of the 1970s are the particular themes of Henry M Drucker and Gordon Brown *The Politics of Nationalism and Devolution* Longman 1980. The search for devolution 1964–76 is traced in John Pitcairn Mackintosh 'The Problems of Devolution – The Scottish Case' in J A G Griffith (ed) *From Policy to Administration: Essays in Honour of William A Robson* Allen and Unwin 1976 pp 99–114.

**8013**   Neil MacCormick (ed) *The Scottish Debate: Essays on Scottish Nationalism* Oxford University Press 1970. A collection of articles on the history of nationalism, SNP policy, and critiques of nationalism.

**8014**   J N Wolfe (ed) *Government and Nationalism in Scotland: An Enquiry by Members of the University of Edinburgh* Edinburgh University Press 1969. Essays on subjects such as home rule, voting behaviour, defence, nationalism in Scottish literature or the financial problems of independence edited by the then leader of the SNP.

**8015**   Herbert J Paton *The Claim of Scotland* Allen and Unwin 1968. This considers the arguments for and against the case for independence and chronicles the history of the debate. It concludes that the balance of benefits, for the rest of the UK as well as for Scotland, is in favour of Scottish home rule. Hugh MacDiarmid considered that the lack of an English response to this book was final proof that only by militant action would Scotland achieve independence. In contrast Tam Dalyell *Devolution: The End of Britain?* Cape 1977 is a powerful argument against Scottish home rule by a Scottish Labour MP in the face of the devolution debate of the 1970s. It examines the history of the handling of the devolution issue in detail.

**8016**   Gavin Kennedy (ed) *The Radical Approach: Papers on an Independent Scotland* Palingenesis Press 1976. Socialist interpretations of the likely impact of Scottish independence.

**8017**   Michael Keating and David Bleiman *Labour and Scottish Nationalism* Macmillan 1979. A study of party attitudes and responses to nationalism. Since 1959 Labour's increasing electoral dominance in Scotland has inclined them to play the nationalist card, especially in the 1970s in order to contain the growth of the nationalist vote that was seen in 1967–74. This, it is argued, forms the background to the introduction of devolution measures by the Labour governments of 1974–79.

**8018** H M Begg and J M Stewart 'The Nationalist Movement in Scotland' *Journal of Contemporary History* 6 1971 pp 135–52. This particularly focuses on the wartime development of the SNP and the growth of the party 1945–70, not least at the municipal level. The general growth of the party in this early period is also examined in Iain McLean 'The Rise and Fall of the Scottish National Party' *Political Studies* 18 1970 pp 357–72 and S A Burrell 'The Scottish Separatist Movement: A Present Assessment' *Political Science Quarterly* 70 1955 pp 358–67. The ideology and aims of the SNP are assessed in J M Elder 'The Ideology of the Scottish National Party' Glasgow MLitt Thesis 1979. Its aims and attitudes are reflected through the eyes of the then chairman of the party in J N Wolfe *Scotland Lives* (The Quest for Independence) Reprographia 1974, which traces the growth and strategy of the party from the important West Lothian by-election of 1962 to 1973. It is also in some ways a political autobiography. On developments in this period see also R M Crawford 'The Scottish National Party 1960–74: An Investigation into its Organisation and Power Structure' Glasgow PhD Thesis 1982. Changing popular attitudes in this period are examined in D Bain 'The Scottish National Party from 1966 to the 1970 General Election: A Study of Electoral Polarisation in British General Elections' Strathclyde MSc Thesis 1972–3. Social change in Scotland is examined as the basis of the SNP surge in support peaking in 1974 in S W Kendrick 'Social Change and Nationalism in Modern Scotland' Edinburgh PhD Thesis 1983. The policy process as the SNP sought to respond to the devolution issue in the 1970s is studied in Roger Levy 'The Search for a Rational Strategy: The Scottish National Party and Devolution 1974–79' *Political Studies* 34 1986 pp 236–48. This issue led to divisions in the SNP over whether to press for full independence, which are analysed in Henry M Drucker 'Crying Wolfe: Recent Divisions in the SNP' *Political Quarterly* 50 1979 pp 503–8.

**8019** Ian R Hamilton *No Stone Unturned* Gollancz 1952. An account of the stealing of the Stone of Scone, used in coronations, from Westminster Abbey in 1950.

**8020** D Heald and Michael Keating 'The Impact of the Devolution Commitment on the Scottish Body Politic' *Australian Journal of Politics and History* 26 1980 pp 386–402. The failure of the Scotland Act and devolution in the 1979 referendum which failed to deliver a sufficiently strong vote for the devolution option is examined in Dougie Bain 'Doing It Ourselves' *Bulletin of Scottish Politics* Autumn 1980 pp 40–6. The referendum campaign itself is studied in detail in John Bochel, David Denver and Allan MacCartney *The Referendum Experience: Scotland 1979* Aberdeen University Press 1981.

This also has a chapter examining the contrasts with the contemporaneous referendum in Wales which decisively rejected devolution. Party attitudes played an important part in the result in Scotland according to Jack Brand 'Political Parties and the Referendum on National Sovereignty: The 1979 Scottish Referendum on Devolution' *Canadian Review of Studies in Nationalism* 13 1986 pp 31–47.

**8021** Roy Gronneberg (ed) *Island Futures: Scottish Devolution and Shetland's Constitutional Alternatives* Thuleprint 1978. A collection of short articles on the likely impact of Scottish devolution on the Shetland Islands which also looks at the impact of the development of oil facilities at Sullom Voe and calls for greater autonomy for the islands.

**8022** J A Agnew 'Political Regionalism and Scottish Nationalism in Gaelic Scotland' *Canadian Review of Studies in Nationalism* 8 1981 pp 115–29.

**8023** John M MacCormick *The Flag in the Wind: The Story of the National Movement in Scotland* Gollancz 1955. The autobiography of a nationalist covering the development of the SNP from the 1920s.

**8024** Wendy Wood *Yours sincerely for Scotland: The Autobiography of a Patriot* Barker 1970. A memoir of Scottish nationalism since 1916.

### (3) Other Political Parties

**8025** John Bochel 'The Values, Attitudes and Partisanships of Scottish Parliamentary Candidates at the 1979 General Election' Strathclyde MSc Thesis 1983. This study argues that background was most important in the partisanship of Labour and Liberal candidates and that values were most important for Conservative and SNP candidates.

**8026** Ian MacDougall (ed) *A Catalogue of Some Labour Records in Scotland and Some Scots Records Outside in Scotland* Scottish Labour History Society 1978. A well organized guide to archives of friendly societies, the co-operative movement, Christian Socialism, the Communist Party, working class education and propaganda, Fabians, the ILP, the Labour Party, the trade unions and trade councils and other organizations and the labour press. It has some details of the archives and also features a large bibliography.

**8027** William Knox (ed) *Scottish Labour Leaders 1918–1939: A Biographical Dictionary* Mainstream 1984. This has a valuable introduction. Some of the figures whose biographies appear here remained active after 1945.

**8028** J C Gordon 'The Temperance of the Labour Party in Glasgow 1920–1976' Newcastle MA Thesis 1983. This charts the lingering influence of the temperance movement in the Glasgow labour movement despite its national decline since the Second World War.

**8029** Henry M Drucker *Breakaway: The Scottish Labour Party* Edinburgh University Students Publications Bureau 1978. An account of the creation and history of the Scottish Labour Party, which was founded in 1976 by a couple of rebellious Scottish Labour MPs, dissatisfied with the Labour government's devolution proposals. It sought to combine socialism and nationalism but suffered, as this detailed account based on minutes and interviews shows, from Trotskyite entryism which contributed to the collapse of the party.

**8030** Derek W Urwin 'Scottish Conservatism: A Party Organisation in Transition' *Political Studies* 14 1966 pp 145–62. An examination of the restructuring of the party in 1965 in historical context.

### (4) Electoral History

**8031** Ian Budge and Derek W Urwin *Scottish Political Behaviour: A Case Study in British Homogeneity* Longman 1966. A study of social attitudes and electoral behaviour since 1707. It argues that Scotland is a distinctive political region with distinctive political attitudes.

**8032** William L Miller *The End of British Politics? Scots and English Political Behaviour in the Seventies* Clarendon 1981. An analysis of divergent political behaviour placed in a statistically based social and religious context. Jack Brand, Duncan McLean and William L Miller 'The Birth and Death of a Three-Party System: Scotland in the Seventies' *British Journal of Political Science* 13 1983 pp 463–88 is an attempt to explain the SNP surge in 1974 and its decline in 1979. It argues that the choice of the SNP had little to do with nationalism and more to do with alternatives to failing traditional parties at a time of economic distress.

**8033** William L Miller, Jack Brand and Maggie Jordan *Oil and the Scottish Voter 1974–1979* Social Science Research Council 1980. This study of the impact of the development of North Sea oil resources on nationalism and voting patterns explains the decline of nationalist voting at the end of the decade as being the result of a Scottish preparedness to share the benefits on a UK-wide basis.

**8034** Denis Van Mechelen 'The Growth of Third Party Support in Britain: A Comparative Study of the Electoral Bases for the Liberal and Scottish National Parties' Successes during the 1970s' London PhD Thesis 1983.

This argues that the SNP's growth was as a third party and not as a result of nationalism. A similar case is argued in William L Miller with Bo Sarvik, Ivor Crewe and James E Alt 'The Connection between SNP Voting and the Demand for Self-Government' *European Journal of Political Research* 5 1977 pp 83–102.

**8035** John Bochel and D T Denver 'Religion and Voting: A Critical Review and a New Analysis' *Political Studies* 18 1970 pp 204–19. A study based on research in Dundee.

### C. LAW

**8036** L F Maxwell and W H Maxwell (comps) *A Legal Bibliography of the British Commonwealth Vol 5: Scottish Law to 1956* Sweet and Maxwell 1957.

**8037** *The Laws of Scotland: Stair Memorial Encylopaedia* 25v, The Law Society of Scotland/Butterworths 1987–88. A comprehensive guide to Scottish law and the Scottish legal system.

**8038** *Scottish Current Law Year Book* 1948– Green 1949. The annual cumulation of the monthly *Current Law* Green 1948–. This is a digest of recent developments in the law with a bibliography section, notes on current bills, legislation and cases.

**8039** *The Edinburgh Gazette* HMSO 1680–. The official channel for communicating to the public changes in the law and official appointments. It appears twice weekly.

**8040** *The Scottish Law Directory* Hodge 1892–. A annual guide to Scottish lawyers and legal firms.

**8041** William Murray Gloag and R Candlish Henderson (edited by A B Wilkinson and W A Wilson) *Introduction to the Laws of Scotland* 9th ed, Green 1987. The latest edition of a major guide to Scots law which was first published in 1927. A good introductory textbook on Scottish law for the general reader is David M Walker *The Scottish Legal System: An Introduction to the Study of Scots Law* 5th ed, Green 1981. See also E A Marshall *General Principles of Scots Law* 4th ed, Green 1982.

**8042** J D B Marshall *Constitutional Law* 2nd ed, Green 1968. This is the only general study of British constitutional law which emphasizes the different texture of Scottish constitutional law.

**8043** John M Halliday *Conveyancing Law and Practice in Scotland* 3v, Green 1985–7.

**8044** G H Gordon *Criminal Law of Scotland* 2nd ed, Green 1978. The standard textbook. Supplements have been issued since 1984. The authoritative study of criminal procedure is R W Renton and H H Brown *Criminal Procedure According to the Law of Scotland* 3rd ed, Green 1983. This is a looseleaf publication.

**8045** David M Walker *Principle of Scottish Private Law* 4v, 3rd ed, Oxford University Press 1982–83. A guide to Scots law on persons, obligations, property, trusts, succession, civil remedies, diligence and insolvency.

**8046** A G Walker and N M L Walker *Law of Evidence in Scotland* Hodge 1964. A study of the admissibility and use of evidence in Scotland.

**8047** *The Sheriff Court: Report by the Committee Appointed by the Secretary of State for Scotland* Cmnd 3248, *Parliamentary Papers* xlviii 1966–67. A major report into how to deal with the pressures resulting from the growth of work transacted by the Sheriff Courts by the committee chaired by Lord Grant. W J Dobie *Law and Practice of the Sheriff Courts in Scotland* Hodge 1948 is now an outdated guide to the work of the Sheriff Courts.

**8048** *Committee on Children and Young Persons (Scotland) Report* Cmnd 2306, *Parliamentary Papers* ix 1963–64. This report by the committee chaired by Lord Kilbrandon contributed to the introduction of the system of children's hearings in 1968. F M Martin and K Murray (eds) *The Scottish Juvenile Justice System* Scottish Academic Press 1983 is a collection of studies of the growth and implementation of this system. The background to their introduction under Part III of the Social Work (Scotland) Act 1968 is investigated in Allison Morris 'Scottish Juvenile Justice: A Critique' in Roger Hood (ed) *Crime, Criminology and Public Policy: Essays in Honour of Sir Leon Radzinowicz* Heinemann 1974 pp 347–74. Nigel Bruce and John Spencer *Face to Face with Families: A Report on the Children's Panels in Scotland* Macdonald 1976 is a report on the first five years of the new system.

**8049** *Legal Aid and Legal Advice in Scotland: Report of the Committee* Cmnd 6925, *Parliamentary Papers* xiii 1945–46. The report of this committee chaired by John Cameron led to the setting up of a legal aid system in Scotland. C N Stoddart *Law and Practice of Legal Aid in Scotland* Green 1979 is a concise and comprehensive exposition of the law and practice of legal aid designed as a user's guide.

**8050** *Criminal Appeals in Scotland: First Report by the Committee* Cmnd 5038, *Parliamentary Papers* xx 1971–72. Further reports by this committee under the chairmanship of Lord Thomson were *Second Report* Cmnd 6218, *Parliamentary Papers* xv 1974–75 and *Third Report* Cmnd 7005, *Parliamentary Papers* 1977–

78. It led to a reduction in the police role in prosecution procedures.

**8051** *Royal Commission on Legal Services in Scotland* 2v, Cmnd 7846, *Parliamentary Papers* 1979–80. This major report made various recommendations on how to improve the legal services and legal aid. Chaired by Lord Hughes of Hawkhill it was the parallel to the Benson Royal Commission held concurrently in England and Wales.[2530]

**8052** Thomas Mackay Cooper *Selected Papers 1922–54* Oliver and Boyd 1957. Lord Cooper of Kinross was Lord Advocate of Scotland 1935–41, Lord Justice Clerk 1941–46 and Lord Justice General of Scotland and Lord President of the Court of Session 1947–54. He died in 1955.

**8053** Nicholas Fairbairn *A Life is Too Short: Autobiography 1* Quartet 1987. An account of his life as a leading Scottish defence advocate until his entry to parliament as a Conservative MP in 1974.

**8054** John, Lord Wheatley *One Man's Judgement* Butterworths 1987. The autobiography of an eminent Scottish judge who chaired the Royal Commission into Scottish local government 1966–69.

## D. RELIGIOUS HISTORY

### (1) General

**8055** Peter Brierley (ed) *Prospects for Scotland: Report of the 1984 Census of the Churches* MARC Europe 1985. A social study of the structure of the Scottish churches based on a head count of church attenders.

**8056** Callum Brown *The Social History of Religion in Scotland Since 1730* Methuen 1987. A useful social history, though it has little material on the post-war period.

**8056A** C A Piggott 'A Geography of Religion in Scotland' Edinburgh PhD Thesis 1979.

**8057** John Highet *The Scottish Churches: A Review of their State 400 Years after the Reformation* Skeffington 1960. After a good general introduction to the contemporary state of religion in Scotland this concentrates on studying some thirty congregations in detail. Highet also looks at the attitudes of laymen and ministers to social, moral and political issues. John Highet *The Churches in Scotland Today: A Survey of their Principles, Strengths, Work and Statements* Jackson 1950 is an earlier survey.

**8058** M Small *Growing Together: Some Aspects of the Ecumenical Movement in Scotland 1924–1964* Scottish Churches Council 1975. Ecumenism in Scotland is attacked in Ian Henderson *Power without Glory: A Study of Ecumenical Politics* Hutchinson 1967.

**8059** Tom Gallagher *Glasgow – The Uneasy Peace: Religious Tension in Modern Scotland* Manchester University Press 1988. A study of sectarian tension in Glasgow between Catholics and Protestants over the past two hundred years, which includes reflections on its political implications and the reactions of the media.

**8060** G P Morgan 'Church Life in the Rural Lowlands of Scotland: An Analytic Study 1952–1954' Edinburgh PhD Thesis 1957–8. A field study.

**8061** Ron Ferguson *Chasing the Wild Goose* Fount 1988. A history of the Iona Community, which was established on the site of St Columba's monastery on the island off the West coast by the Christian Socialist Church of Scotland minister, George MacLeod, as an ecumenical community witnessing for peace and social justice. It was published to mark the fiftieth anniversary of the foundation of the community.

**8062** Richard O'Brien, David Donnison, Duncan Forrester *et al Faith in the Scottish City: The Scottish Relevance of the Report of the Archbishop's Commission on Urban Priority Areas* Occasional Papers of the Department of Christian Ethics and Practical Theology 8, Centre for Theology and Public Issues, University of Edinburgh 1986. A study of the churches' problems and opportunities in inner city areas in Scotland.

## (2) Church of Scotland

**8063** *Church of Scotland Yearbook* Saint Andrew Press 1930–. An annual guide to the organization, decisions and ministers of the established church.

**8064** John Alexander Lamb (ed) *Fasti Ecclesiae Scotianae: The Succession of Ministers in the Church of Scotland Since the Reformation Vol 9: Ministers of the Church from the Union of the Church 2 October 1929 to 31 December 1954* Oliver and Boyd 1961.

**8065** James T Cox and D F M MacDonald *Practice and Procedure in the Church of Scotland* Church of Scotland 1976. A study of the organization and administration of the Church. Its structure, relationship with the state and Scottish society and its worship is examined in R Stuart Louden *The True Face of the Kirk: An Examination of the Ethos and Traditions of the Church of Scotland* Oxford University Press 1963. The Church of Scotland's pastoral role and stance on contemporary issues is assessed in Ian Henderson *Scotland: Kirk and People* Lutterworth 1969.

**8066** J N Wolfe and M Pickford *The Church of Scotland: An Economic Survey* Geoffrey Chapman 1980. A study of the Church's finances in the context of membership decline since 1956. It contains a number of tables, mainly on the 1970's, and also makes recommendations as to how the Church could deal with financial and structural problems.

**8067** L L L Cameron *The Challenge of Need: A History of Social Service by the Church of Scotland 1869–1969* Saint Andrew Press 1971.

**8068** Clive L Rawlins *William Barclay: The Authorized Biography* Paternoster/Eerdmans 1984. A good biography of the popular exegetical theologian with detailed appendices.

**8069** R H W Falconer *The Kilt Beneath My Cassock* Handsel Press 1978. The posthumous autobiography by the head of BBC religious broadcasting in Scotland for 26 years.

**8070** Augustus Muir *John White* Hodder and Stoughton 1958. White was the first Moderator of the Church of Scotland at reunion in 1929. He died in 1951.

**8071** Henry Charles Whitley *Laughter in Heaven* Hutchinson 1962. The autobiography of a leading Church of Scotland minister.

**8072** Ronald Selby Wright *Another Home* Blackwood 1980. The autobiography of a leading Church of Scotland minister.

## (3) Free Presbyterian Church of Scotland

This is the rump of a Presbyterian church which refused to reunite with the Church of Scotland in 1929.

**8073** *Handbook of the United Free Presbyterian Church of Scotland* Herald Press 1931–. A biennial or triennial guide to the church.

**8074** A MacPherson (ed) *History of the Free Presbyterian Church of Scotland* Vol 2: 1893–1970 Publications Committee, Free Presbyterian Church of Scotland 1975. A study of the survival of this strict Calvinist church which has strong adherence in the Highlands and Islands.

**8075** Andrew A Woolsey *Duncan Campbell: A Biography: The Sound of Battle* Hodder and Stoughton

1974. A biography of the great minister and evangelist who retired in 1963.

**8076** Iain H Murray (ed) *Diary of Kenneth A MacRae: A Record of Fifty Years in the Christian Ministry* Banner of Truth Trust 1980. MacRae died in 1964. His diary contains useful reflections on Scottish religion in the post-war years, Free Presbyterian Church policy and evangelism.

## (4) Other Churches

**8077** *Scottish Episcopal Church Yearbook* General Synod of the Scottish Episcopal Church 1892–. An annual guide to the administration and ministers of the church.

**8078** George Tibbatts *John How: Parish Priest, Cambridge Don and Scottish Primate* Becket Publications 1983. A short biography of How, who was Bishop of Glasgow and Galloway 1938–52.

**8079** *Catholic Directory for Scotland* Burns 1829–. A guide to the organization of the church, its dioceses, religious orders and priests.

**8080** David McRoberts (ed) *Modern Scottish Catholicism 1878–1978* Burns 1979. A comprehensive study of the Catholic community; its ecclesiatical organization, orders, educational work, politics, press and attitudes to ecumenism.

**8081** David W Bebbington (ed) *The Baptists in Scotland: A History* Baptist Union of Scotland 1988. A history up to the 1980s. It is a good study of the dynamics of church growth making good use of lots of maps, graphs and tables. It includes a series of area studies, which look at the problems of the churches since 1945. See also Derek B Murray *The First Hundred Years: The Baptist Union of Scotland* Baptist Union of Scotland 1969 and T W Moyes 'Scottish Baptist Relations with the Church of Scotland in the Twentieth Century' *Baptist Quarterly* 33 1989 pp 174–85.

**8082** Norman Adams *Goodbye Beloved Brethren* Impulse 1972. This traces the story of the Plymouth Brethren up to the 1970s. It particularly focuses on the series of scandals which rocked the Exclusive Brethren, who were very strong in North East Scotland, in the mid-1960s, and on their subsequent rapid decline.

**8083** Steve Bruce 'Ideology and Isolation: A Failed Scots Protestant Movement' *Archives de Sciences Sociales des Religions* 56 1983 pp 147–59. Alienated from Presbyterianism because of his attitude to infant baptism and from the Baptists because of his Calvinism Jack

Glass set up his Sovereign Grace Evangelical Baptist Union allied to Ian Paisley's Ulster Presbyterianism. However, the conditions which helped Paisley in Ulster were not present in Scotland.

**8084** F F Bruce *In Retrospect: Remembrance of Things Past* Pickering and Inglis 1980. The autobiography of a leader of the Brethren in Scotland, theologian and leading figure in British evangelical circles.

## (5) Pantheism

**8085** Eileen Caddy *Foundations of Findhorn* Findhorn Foundation 1978. An account of the somewhat esoteric, essentially pantheistic Findhorn community in Scotland, by one of its founders. See also Paul Hawken *The Magic of Findhorn* Souvenir Press 1975 and Jackson Spielvogel 'Findhorn: The Evolution of a Spiritual Utopian Community' *Journal of General Education* 37 1985 pp 231–45.

## E. ECONOMIC HISTORY

### (1) General

**8086** *Scottish Economic Bulletin* HMSO 1971–. A statistical guide published three times a year.

**8087** Charlotte Lythe and Madhari Majmudar *The Renaissance of the Scottish Economy* Allen and Unwin 1982. An appraisal of the Scottish economy since the 1950s. It concludes that the Scottish economy is inseparable from that of the rest of the UK, with all the implications this conclusion holds for nationalists. A similar conclusion is reached in Gavin McCrone *Scotland's Future: The Economics of Nationalism* Blackwell 1969. On the role of the British government in attempts to revive the Scottish economy see also Charlotte Lythe and Madhari Majmudar 'Government and Scottish Economic Performance 1952–1975' *Scottish Journal of Political Economy* 30 1983 pp 153–69. On the economy in this period see also Richard Saville (ed) *Economic Development of Modern Scotland 1950–1980* John Donald 1985.

**8088** Scottish Council (Research Institute) *Economic Development and Devolution* Scottish Council 1974. This argues that the central control of the economy by a British government based in London has failed to achieve a sufficiently rapid rate of economic development in Scotland and that therefore devolution is required in order to ensure growth and economic planning.

**8089** C G Miller 'The Scottish Economy and the Post-War British Governments 1945–1951' St Andrews MPhil Thesis 1982. A study of government attempts, especially through regional policy, to tackle housing, unemployment and structural problems in the Scottish economy in the aftermath of the Second World War.

**8090** Gavin McCrone *Scotland's Economic Progress 1951–1960: A Study in Regional Accounting* Allen and Unwin 1965. This assesses the differences of the Scottish economy as opposed to that of the rest of the UK and tries to explain why its rate of growth is so much slower. A well regarded contemporary study of the Scottish economy in the 1950s is Sir Alec Cairncross *The Scottish Economy: A Statistical Account of Scottish Life* Cambridge University Press 1954. This features essays on population, manpower, agriculture, mining, manufacturing, commerce, wages, local government, housing, health, crime, education, youth recruitment, trade unions and the churches.

**8091** T L Johnston, N K Buxton and D Mair *Structure and Growth of the Scottish Economy* Collins 1971. A useful examination of the contemporary Scottish economy. George T Murray *Scotland: The New Future* Scottish Television/Blackie 1973 is wide-ranging survey of the economy and consumption and of the expected impact of North Sea oil. This superseded the earlier studies, Geoffrey D Credland, George T Murray, B E Luby and Ian La Frenais *Scotland – The Vital Market: A Survey of Scotland's Economy* Scottish Television 1966.

**8092** Neil Hood and Stephen Young (eds) *Industry, Policy and the Scottish Economy* Edinburgh University Press 1984. A collection of studies of Scotland's response to and recovery from the oil crisis of 1973–74. It examines the Scottish economy and the impact of government sector by sector. The failure of engineering companies to capitalize on the opportunities presented by North Sea oil is indicted. A useful textbook which examines the Scottish economy in the 1970s and 1980s in a rather less detailed fashion is Keith Ingham and James Love (ed) *Understanding the Scottish Economy* Robertson 1983. Another study is J Scott and M Hughes *The Anatomy of Scottish Capitalism* Croom Helm 1980. See also Brian W Hogwood *The Primacy of Policy in the Economic Policy of Scottish Government* Centre for the Study of Public Policy 16, University of Strathclyde 1978.

**8093** Donald Iain Mackay *Geographical Mobility and the Brain Drain: A Case Study of Aberdeen University Graduates 1860–1960* Allen and Unwin 1969. This finds little change in the rate of skilled emigration from Scotland either overseas or to England and Wales over this period and concludes that Scotland's brain drain is a long-established phenomenon.

**8094** Anthony Slaven *The Development of the West of Scotland 1750–1960* Routledge and Kegan Paul 1975. A good study.

**8095** David Turnock *The New Scotland* David and Charles 1979. A study based on research conducted in 1971 into the introduction of manufacturing industries and tourism into the peripheral Highlands and Islands region which nevertheless remains dominated by agriculture, fishing and forestry. The final chapter looks at the likely impact of North Sea oil.

**8096** Iain H McNicoll *The Shetland Economy: An Empirical Study in Regional Input-Output Analysis* Fraser of Allander Institute, Glasgow 1976. This finds a suprising degree of inter- industry in the Shetland economy, which has since been affected by the impact of oil.

**8097** Christopher Carter 'Some Changes in the Post-War Geography of the Clydeside Conurbation' *Scottish Geography Magazine* 90 1974 pp 14–26.

## (2) Regional Development

**8098** R A Henderson 'Factors Determining the Location of Immigrant Industry within a UK Assisted Area: The Scottish Experience between 1945 and 1970' Glasgow MLitt Thesis 1977.

**8099** D I Trotman-Dickenson 'The Development of the Scottish Industrial Estates 1936–1952' Edinburgh PhD Thesis 1955–6. The creation of trading estates with rating incentives to firms to occupy them was an early feature of regional policy.

**8100** H M Begg, Charlotte Lythe, D R MacDonald and R Sotley *Special Regional Assistance in Scotland* Fraser of Allander Institute, Glasgow 1976. A short analysis of regional policy in Scotland 1960/61–1971/72.

**8101** Michael Cross *New Firm Foundations and Regional Development* Gower 1981. A detailed analysis of the literature on the subject 1968–77 using Scotland as a case study.

**8102** *Scottish Development Department: Annual Report* HMSO 1962–. The principal body guiding regional policy in Scotland was replaced in 1975 by the Scottish Development Agency. This was renamed Scottish Enterprise in 1990. This is annual survey of its work and achievements.

**8103** F X Kirwan *The Scottish Development Agency: Structures and Functions* Centre for the Study of Public Policy 81, University of Strathclyde 1981. A useful study. Originally set-up to further economic development and industrial efficiency in 1975 by the 1980s, as Urlan Wannop 'The Evolution and Roles of the Scottish Development Agency' *Town Planning Review* 55 1984 pp 313–21 argues, it was concentrating on urban renewal. The impact of the Scottish Development Agency on the built environ ment is assessed in S T McDonald 'The Scottish Development Agency and the Scottish Townscape' *Town Planning Review* 55 1984 pp 322–34. The range of economic development programmes is reflected in S Gulliver 'The Area Projects of the Scottish Devel opment Agency' *Town Planning Review* 55 1984 pp 322–34. The record of the agency in promoting new industry is examined in S Salmons 'Growing Pains for Scotland' *Management Today* July 1980 pp 35–41.

**8104** J W Findlay 'The Evolution of SDA Area Initiatives: Wigtown Rural Project' Strathclyde MSc Thesis 1985. By the 1980s the Scottish Development Agency was concentrating on self-help projects such as the development company established at Wigtown which is critically assessed in this case study.

**8105** J W J Moxon 'The Industrial Development Certificate System and Employment Creation' *Urban Studies* 9 1972 pp 229–33. This argues that IDCs had a limited impact in Scotland in the 1960s.

**8106** C P Aitken 'A Review of the Operation of the European Regional Development Fund (1975–1978) with Special Reference to the Central Region of Scotland' Strathclyde MSc Thesis 1979.

**8107** Michael Keating, Arthur F Midwinter and Peter Taylor *Enterprise Zones and Area Projects: Small Area Initiatives in Urban Economic Renewal in Scotland* Department of Administration, University of Strathclyde 1983. An interim study of the impact of the Thatcher government's innovation of enterprise zones in inner areas and their relationship with Scottish Development Agency policy.

**8108** Michael Keating and Robin Doyle *Remaking Urban Scotland: Strategies for Local Development* Edinburgh University Press 1986. In the 1970s and 1980s regional development increasingly concentrated on urban renewal. This is a good assessment of the work in this field of all the agencies, including the EC and local initiatives, and their impact on inner area economic revival, housing and urban policy.

**8109** William Lever and Chris Moore (eds) *The City in Transition: Policies and Agencies for the Economic Regeneration of Clydeside* Clarendon 1986. A study of the effect of regional policy in 1970s and 1980s. The Glasgow Eastern Area Renewal Scheme established in 1976 is critically assessed in S A S Booth, D C Pitt and W J Money 'Organisational Redundancy? A Critical

Appraisal of the GEAR Project' *Public Administration* 6 1982 pp 56–72.

**8110** P R Swinton 'Industry in West Central Scotland 1952–1975: An Analysis of Growth and Decline and its Implication for Regional Planning' Strathclyde MSc Thesis 1970–1.

**8111** David Turnock 'Regional Development in the Crofting Counties' *Transactions of the Institute of British Geographers* 48 1969 pp 189–204. A study of regional policy in the Highlands and Islands. See also A C O'Dell 'Highland and Islands Developments' *Scottish Geographical Magazine* 82 1966 pp 8–16, R S Forrest 'Regional Development and the Special Problem Area: A Case Study in the Highlands and Islands of Scotland' Birmingham MSocSci Thesis 1974–5 and P G Hutchinson 'Rural Growth Centre Policy: A Case Study of the Highlands and Islands of Scotland' Glasgow BPhil Thesis 1968–9.

**8112** David Simpson 'Investments, Employment and Government Expenditure in the Highlands 1951–1960' *Scottish Journal of Political Economy* 10 1963 pp 259–88.

**8113** *Annual Report* Highlands and Islands Development Board 1966–. The Highlands and Islands Development Board was established in 1965 to direct regional development in areas which are dominated by upland farming, forestry, fishing and some textile industries. The history of the Board is well told in Tony Mackay *The Highlands and Islands Development Board 1965–85* Edinburgh University Press 1985. Another useful study, written with some access to the Board's papers, is James Grassie *Highland Experiment: The Story of the Highlands and Islands Development Board* Aberdeen University Press 1983. The earlier development of the Board is assessed in I R Carter 'Six Years On: An Evaluative Study of the Highlands and Islands Development Board' *Aberdeen University Review* 45 1973 pp 55–78.

### (3) Industry

#### (a) General

**8114** *Scotland's Top 500 Companies* Jordan Dataquest 1977–. An annual guide to key statistics on Scotland's largest companies.

**8115** Anthony Slaven and Sydney G Checkland (eds) *Dictionary of Scottish Business Biography 1860–1960* 2v, Aberdeen University Press 1985–86. Each volume has a section on each industrial sector, with each section introduced by an essay placing the ensuing biographies in context.

**8116**   John Scott and Michael Hughes *The Anatomy of Scottish Capital: Scottish Companies and Scottish Capital 1900–1979* Croom Helm 1980. This traces Scottish corporations up to the impact of the oil crisis of 1973–74 and North Sea oil. The twentieth century has seen the Scottish economy change as a result of the decline of traditional heavy industry from being a separate economy to being a relatively autonomous sub-system of the UK economy in which companies are increasing London or overseas based. There has for instance been considerable US investment, encouraged by the UK government. The impact of this on domestic firms and on the Scottish economy and the reasons for this investment are examined in David J C Forsyth *US Investment in Scotland* Praeger 1972.

**8117**   Stephen Maxwell (ed) *Scotland's Multinationals and the Third World* Mainstream 1982. A polemical analysis of the role of multinational companies in Scotland. It argues that there was over-concentration on attracting foreign companies in the 1960s and 1970s rather than on developing native industry.

**8118**   John Scott *Multiple Directors in Top Scottish Companies* revised ed, the author 1983. A companion volume to [8116] which covers directors 1904–56.

**8119**   C A Oakley *Scottish Industry: An Account of What Scotland Makes and Where She Makes It* Scottish Council (Development and Industry) 1953. An illustrated survey of the contemporary state of Scottish industry.

**8120**   J B Collins 'The Development of Commercial Education in Scotland 1930–1975' Stirling MEd Thesis 1982. A study of business education in Scotland.

(b) Textiles

**8121**   J B Simpson 'The Development of the Knitwear Industry in the Scottish Borders Region Since 1960' Leeds MPhil Thesis 1979.

**8122**   *Planning for Progress: Shetland Woollen Industry* Highlands and Islands Development Board 1970. A report into the state of a declining industry suffering from a lack of skilled labour, fragmented plant and apathetic management. It recommended increases in capacity, the nationalization of uneconomic units and an improvement in marketing.

**8123**   Francis Thompson *Harris Tweed: The Story of a Hebridean Industry* David and Charles 1969. A conventional history concentrating on developments in the twentieth century, not least attempts to protect quality. See also H A Moisley 'Harris Tweed: A Growing Highland Industry' *Economic Geography* 37 1961 pp 353–70.

(c) Metals

**8124**   E Quinn 'The Ravenscraig Decision' Strathclyde PhD Thesis 1982. A study of the debate over the future of the Motherwell steel plant in which political and regional as well as industrial considerations played major parts.

**8125**   Peter L Payne *Colvilles and the Scottish Steel Industry* Oxford University Press 1979. A company history up to its nationalization in 1967.

**8126**   Augustus Muir *The Story of Shotts: A Short History of the Shotts Iron Company Limited* Shotts Iron Company 1954.

**8127**   John R Hume and Michael S Moss *Beardmore: The History of a Scottish Industrial Giant* Heinemann 1979. An illustrated business history of the giant engineering and steel-making concern which folded in 1975.

**8128**   G Gordon Drummond *The Invergordon Smelter: A Case Study in Management* Hutchinson 1977. An account of the £37m aluminium smelter in the North of Scotland from its announcement in 1968 to its first production in 1971/2. G A Mackay *A Study of the Economic Impact of the Invergordon Aluminium Smelter* Highlands and Islands Development Board 1978 is a detailed study of its effects.

(d) Shipbuilding and Engineering

**8129**   Fred M Walker *Song of the Clyde: A History of Clyde Shipbuilding* Patrick Stephens 1984. An illustrated history of shipbuilding on the Clyde since the eighteenth century. It includes a bibliography and details of each of the shipyards on the Clyde.

**8130**   J McGill *Crisis on the Clyde: The Story of Upper Clyde Shipbuilders* Davis Poynter 1973. Upper Clyde Shipbuilders was set up in the wake of the Geddes Report [3483] in 1968. It collapsed in 1971. A work-in by the employees with some government support followed in 1971–74. See also Robin Murray *UCS: Anatomy of a Bankruptcy* Spokesman 1972. A critical study of the history of UCS, and particularly of the role of the government in it, is Frank Broadway *Upper Clyde Shipbuilders: A Study of Government Intervention in Industry – The Way the Money Goes* Centre for Policy Studies

1976. A useful study of one of the yards that made up the Upper Clyde Shipbuilders is K J W Alexander and C L Jenkins *Fairfields: A Study of Industrial Change* Allen Lane 1970. Fairfields had gone into liquidation in 1965 but was rescued by Browns before becoming part of UCS. Most of this book is concerned with the efforts initiated at Fairfields in this period to try to improve industrial relations. See also F Herron 'Redundancy and Redeployment from UCS 1969–1971' *Scottish Journal of Political Economy* 19 1972 pp 231–51. On the work-in at UCS see [8214].

**8131** Michael S Moss and Iain Russell *Range and Vision: The First Hundred Years of Barr and Stroud* Mainstream 1988. A well illustrated centenary history of a Scottish engineering firm with traditional close ties with Glasgow University. In the post-war years it has particularly concentrated on optics. It was taken over by Pilkingtons in 1977.

**(e) The Media**

**8132** David Hutchinson (ed) *Headlines: The Media in Scotland* Edinburgh University Students Publications Bureau 1978. A collection of articles on the Scottish press, comics, publishing, advertising and public relations, broadcasting, ownership and control of the media, film and the impact of the media on nationalism.

**8133** System Three (Scotland) Ltd *Broadcasting in Scotland: A Survey of Attitudes* Famedram 1974. A survey conducted among almost 2,000 viewers and listeners for their opinions of news and coverage of current affairs on the broadcasting media in Scotland.

**8134** Joan Primrose Scott Ferguson *Directory of Scottish Newspapers* National Library of Scotland 1984. See also [7987].

**8135** George Fraser and Ken Peters *The Northern Lights* Hamilton 1978. A history of the Aberdeen newspapers, the *Press and Journal* and the *Evening Express* on the latter's centenary.

**8136** T Brotherstone 'The Suppression of The *Forward*' *Scottish Labour History Journal* 1 1969 pp 5–23. The *Forward* was the newspaper of the Glasgow Labour Movement. It ceased publication in the 1950s.

**8137** Alastair Philips *Glasgow's Herald 1783–1983* Richard Drew 1983. A full history of one of Scotland's two quality national newspapers.

**8138** *A Highland Newspaper: The First 150 Years of the Inverness Courier 1817–1967* Robert Carruthers 1969.

**8139** Donald Munro '175 Years of the *Montrose Review*: Scotland's Second Oldest Weekly Newspaper' *Journal of Newspaper and Periodical History* 2 1986 pp 14–21. This old Liberal newspaper was by 1970 the only weekly newspaper in the area. By 1986 it largely consisted of advertising using local news as a filler. A useful examination of the decline of the local press.

**8140** Magnus Magnusson *et al* (eds) *The Glorious Privilege: The History of The Scotsman* Nelson 1967. A history of one of the two quality national newspapers to celebrate the 150th anniversary of the founding of the newspaper. It remained independent until bought by the Canadian magnate Roy, later Lord, Thomson.

**8141** Ron McKay and Brian Barr *The Story of the Scottish Daily News* Canongate 1976. In March 1974 the production of the Scottish Daily Express was moved from Glasgow to Manchester. This is the story of the attempt to create a new newspaper by those who lost their jobs, to be controlled by the workers themselves. It analyses the part played by the government, the Beaverbrook organization, Robert Maxwell and the trade unions in the six month history of the new newspaper. On this workers' cooperative see also [8213]. The most in-depth study of this episode in Scottish media history is T Clarke 'Producer Co-operatives in Market Systems: A Case Study of the Scottish Daily News in the context of the Political Economy of the Press' Warwick PhD Thesis 1983. This is in three volumes. The first analyses the co-operative and the reasons for failure. The second examines the difficulties in launching a non-commercial newspaper committed to radical politics. The final volume reviews the historical development of workers' co-operatives in general in the context of case studies of two other co-operatives launched with Department of Industry support in 1975, KME and Triumph Meriden.

**8142** John Burrowes *Frontline Report: A Journalist's Notebook* Mainstream 1984. A collection of the notes Burrowes amassed in his journalistic career, which was mostly spent on Glasgow's *Daily Record*.

**8143** Alistair Dunnett *Among Friends: An Autobiography* Century Press 1984. Dunnett was editor of the *Daily Record* 1946–55 and of *The Scotsman* 1956–72.

**8144** Jack House *Pavement in the Sun* Hutchinson 1967. A biography reflecting on his life in broadcasting, as a writer, and as a Liberal candidate.

**8145** John Mackenzie *Country Editor: Relating Sixty-Seven Years with Weeklies on a Scottish Island and the Canadian Prarie 1901–1968* Bute Newspapers 1968. Mackenzie was the editor of *The Buteman*.

**8146** Jack Webster *A Grain of Truth: A Scottish Journalist Remembers* Paul Harris 1981. A memoir of his career on the *Scottish Daily Express* and *Scottish Sunday Express*. See also his *Another Grain of Truth* Collins 1988.

**8147** Fiona McAuslane *The Story of Radio Forth* Paul Harris 1985. The history of an independent radio station.

**8148** *Adam and Charles Black 1807–1957* A and C Black 1957. A commemorative in-house history of the publishing house.

**8149** F D Tredrey *The House of Blackwood 1804–1954* Blackwood 1954. This concentrates particularly on the recent history of the publishing house.

**8150** David Keir *The House of Collins: The Story of a Scottish Family of Publishers from 1789 to the Present Day* Collins 1952.

**8151** *Scottish Small Presses 1974: An Annotated Catalogue of Books in Print* National Book League 1974. There has been a considerable growth of small publishing houses in Scotland since 1945, and especially since 1960. This surveys these and lists all their publications up to 1974.

### (f) Brewing and Distilling

**8152** Ian L Donnachie *History of the Brewing Industry in Scotland* Donald 1979. A history of the industry up to the 1970s.

**8153** R J S McDowall *The Whiskies of Scotland* 2nd ed, Murray 1971. A general survey.

**8154** Michael S Moss and John R Hume *The Making of Scotch Whisky: A History of the Scotch Whisky Distilling Industry* James and James 1981. A well produced history with plenty of statistics on the state of Scotland's premier export industry. It concentrates on the production of the whisky. Another history of the industry since earliest times is David Daiches *Scotch Whisky: Its Past and Present* Deutsch 1978. This is quite useful on the growth of companies in the twentieth century, the impact of duties and the range of distilleries and brands. A further general history of Scotch whisky is Robert Bruce-Lockhart *Scotch: The Whisky of Scotland in Fact and Story* Putnam 1974.

**8155** Brian Spiller *The Chameleon's Eye: James Buchanan and Company Ltd 1884–1984* James Buchanan 1984. The official centenary history of a firm of whisky distillers.

### (g) Other Industry

**8156** Lorna Weatherill *One Hundred Years of Papermaking: An Illustrated History of the Guard Bridge Paper Company Ltd 1873–1973* the company 1973.

**8157** George Blake *'The Gourock'* Gourock Ropework Co Ltd 1963. A history of the great Glasgow family firm since 1736.

### (4) Energy

The most important sector of the Scottish energy industry since the 1970s has been North Sea oil and gas. Because of its importance to the whole of the British energy economy the literature on this subject has been located in the general section on energy [4005–17]. Other aspects of the Scottish energy industry have been relatively neglected. This includes for instance the development of hydro-electric power in the North of Scotland.

**8158** James McKechnie and Murray Macgregor *A Short History of the Scottish Coal Mining Industry* National Coal Board 1958. The nearest there is to a general history. A Conner *Coal in Decline* Maclellan 1962 is a critical study of the coal industry under public ownership.

**8159** John McNeil 'The Fife Coal Industry 1947–1967: A Study of Changing Trends and their Implications' *Scottish Geographical Magazine* 89 1973 pp 81–94, 163–79.

**8160** A Sellwood and M Sellwood *Black Avalanche* Muller 1960. An account of the Knockskinnoch Castle colliery disaster in Ayrshire in 1950.

**8161** Maxwell Gaskin and D I Mackay *The Economic Impact of North Sea Oil on Scotland* HMSO 1978 is a government survey of its general and regional impact on Scotland based on research conducted 1973–77. It also examines its impact on different sectors of the Scottish economy.

**8162** A Hutcheson and A Hogg *Scotland and Oil* Oliver and Boyd 1975. A survey of the oil's physical setting, its discovery and licensing and its economic and social impact. It includes case studies of areas affected by the oil. See also T M Lewis and I H McNicoll *North Sea Oil and Scotland's Economic Prospects* Croom Helm 1978.

**8163** G A Mackay and Anne C Moir *North Sea Oil and the Aberdeen Economy* Social Science Research Council 1980. Aberdeen benefited particularly from the oil in the

1970s. This examines the impact of the oil on the local economy.

8164　George Rosie *The Ludwig Initiative: A Cautionary Tale of North Sea Oil* Mainstream 1978. An analysis of the success of David K Ludwig and Cromarty Petroleum Co in winning permission for an oil refinery at Nigg Bay. It proved an expensive white elephant. This study is useful not just for its analysis of the planning procedure but also because it illustrates the relations between a multinational corporation and the British state. George Rosie *Cromarty – The Scramble for Oil* Canongate 1974 is a brief but lively survey of the oil boom in this area.

8165　Elizabeth Marshall *Shetland's Oil Era* Shetland Islands Council 1977. This and *Shetland's Oil Era: Phase 2* Shetland Islands Council 1978 cover the process of oil exploitation in the area of the islands since the discovery of the Brent field in 1972. It also looks at the development of facilities for the oil industry in Shetland, and particularly at the response of the planning authority. It includes maps and a bibliography. The development of the oil industry and its impact is examined in John Button (ed) *The Shetland Way of Oil: Reactions of a Small Community to Big Business* Thuleprint 1978. James R Nicolson *Shetland and Oil* William Luscombe 1975 laments the impact of the coming of the oil industry on the traditional life of the Shetlanders.

## (5) Financial Services

8166　Paul Draper *et al The Scottish Financial Sector* Edinburgh University Press 1988. A good general survey of banking, stockbroking and financial services in Scotland.

8167　Sydney G Checkland *Scottish Banking: A History 1695–1973* Collins 1975. The standard history. The final section covers developments in banking since 1945.

8168　Maxwell Gaskin *The Scottish Banks: A Modern Survey* Allen and Unwin 1965. This surveys the five large Scottish clearing banks as they were in 1964. The events leading up to the mergers of the 1960s are briefly reviewed as are their operation and their role in note-issuing, the sterling system and monetary policy.

8169　R N Forbes *The History of the Institute of Bankers in Scotland 1875–1975* the Institute 1975.

8170　Charles W Munn *Clydesdale Bank: The First 150 Years* Collins 1988. A history of the Scottish clearing bank.

8171　*The Royal Bank of Scotland 1727–1977* Royal Bank of Scotland 1977. A brief commemorative history.

8172　R B Weir *A History of the Scottish American Investment Company 1873–1973* Scottish American Investment Company 1973. A short history of the banking and finance company.

8173　Nario Tamaki *The Life Cycle of the Union Bank of Scotland 1830–1954* Aberdeen University Press 1983. A useful company history.

8174　C A Ingram *Four Score and Four: The Story of the Insurance and Actuarial Society of Glasgow* the Society 1967.

8175　Mamie Magnusson *A Length of Days: The Scottish Mutual Assurance Society Ltd* Melland 1983.

8176　Janet Pryce-Jones and R H Parker (eds) *Accounting in Scotland: A Historical Bibliography* Garland 1984. A bibliography with 323 annotated entries.

8177　E H V McDougall *Fifth Quarter Century: Some Chapters in the History of the Chartered Accountants of Scotland* Accountants' Publishing Co 1980.

## (6) Commerce and Tourism

8178　Michael Walter Flinn 'The Overseas Trade of Scottish Ports 1900–60' *Scottish Journal of Political Economy* 13 1966 pp 220–37.

8179　A J Mcldrum 'The Story of the Scottish Grocers' Federation 1918–1968' *Scottish Grocery Trade Handbook* 1969, section 3.

8180　*Glasgow: Report on Aspects of Future Shopping Provision* Gerald Eve and Company 1971. This report includes a review of retailing developments in Glasgow over the previous century in the light of the growing popularity of out-of-town shopping centres.

8181　Development Analysts/Edmund Kirkby and Sons *The Impact of a Town Centre Superstore: A Study of the Effects of the Asda Store in Coatbridge* HMSO 1978. A report commissioned to study the effects on shopping habits, spending patterns and trade levels of a town centre superstore. It found that the store had considerable impact on shopping patterns and on other retailers.

8182　James Kinloch and John Butt *History of the Scottish Co-operative Wholesale Society Limited* Co-operative Wholesale Society 1981. A sound, if rather dull, institutional history of the society up to 1973 when its impoverishment after uncharacteristic (and unwise) speculative adventures led to its merger with the CWS.

**8183**  M Brownrigg and M A Grieg *Tourism and Regional Development* University of Strathclyde, Glasgow 1976. This argues that the common belief that tourism contributes substantially to the economy of Scottish rural areas is mistaken and that its impact is superficial and mainly affects female labour. It contends that policy-makers should concentrate on a broader approach to rural development and allow market forces to develop tourism. The impact and nature of holidays in Scotland and their geographical spread is assessed in *Scottish Tourist and Recreation Study: Summary Report Tourism and Recreation* Research Unit, University of Edinburgh 1976, *Holidaymaking in Scotland* Tourism and Recreation Research Unit, University of Edinburgh 1976, *Patterns of Outdoor Recreation in Scotland* Tourism and Recreation Research Unit, University of Edinburgh 1977 and *The Economic Impact of Tourism: A Case Study of Greater Tayside* Tourism and Recreation Research Unit, University of Edinburgh 1975.

**8184**  Brian S Duffield *Tourism in the Highlands and Islands* Tourism and Recreation Research Unit, University of Edinburgh 1977. A study of the impact of tourism and leisure and of the nature of the holidays taken in the Highlands and Islands. The role of regional policy in the development of tourism in the region is assessed in A Williams 'The Highlands and Islands Development Board 1965–1970' Glasgow MLitt Thesis 1973–4.

## (7) Transport

**8185**  John R Turner *Scotland's Northern Gateway: Aberdeen Harbour 1136–1986* Aberdeen University Press 1986. A well illustrated history. It covers the impact of the post-war introduction of the dock labour scheme and the growth of the port as a centre of off-shore industry for supplying North Sea oil rigs in the 1970s and 1980s.

**8186**  R S McLellan *Anchor Line 1856–1956* Anchor Line 1956. A history of the Glasgow shipping line.

**8187**  Graeme Somner *From 70 North to 70 South: A History of the Christian Salvesen Fleet* Christian Salvesen 1984. A history of the shipping activities of the Edinburgh-based firm.

**8188**  George Blake *Gellatly's 1862–1962* Blackie 1962. A history of the shipping and international trading company.

**8189**  John Orbell with Edwin Green and Michael S Moss *From Cape to Cape: The History of Lyle Shipping*

*Company* Paul Harris 1978. A well illustrated history of a Scottish shipping firm 1791–1977 with detailed and informative appendices. In the 1970s it diversified into the off-shore industry.

**8190**  John R Hume and Michael S Moss *A Bed of Nails: The History of P MacCallum and Sons Ltd of Greenock 1781–1981* Lang and Fulton 1983. A well illustrated history of a shipping firm 1774–1982, with detailed and informative appendices. In the post-war period it diversified into property and engineering.

**8191**  D L G Hunter *From SMT to Eastern Scottish* John Donald 1987. In 1905 the Scottish Motor Traction Co was set up in Edinburgh. This history traces post-war nationalization, denationalization and 1980s deregulation.

**8192**  Valerie Stewart and Vivian Chadwick *Changing Trains: Messages for Management from the Scotrail Challenge* David and Charles 1987. An account of the successful turnround of the Scottish part of British Rail into the most successful part of the network in 1982–5.

## (8) Agriculture

**8193**  *Agriculture in Scotland* HMSO 1912–. An annual guide.

**8194**  Elgin Public Library, Grant Lodge, Elgin, Moray IV30 1HS. This contains a small oral archive on Scottish agriculture and fishing and life in the communities sustained by these industries.

**8195**  J T Coppock *An Agricultural Atlas of Scotland* Donald 1976. A collection of maps with a descriptive text based on the returns for the 1965 agricultural census. Themes include the physical geography, land use, crops, livestock and types of farm.

**8196**  J A Symons *Scottish Farming: Past and Present* Oliver and Boyd 1959. A history up to the 1950s.

**8197**  G Clark 'The Amalgamation of Agricultural Holdings in Scotland 1968–1973' Edinburgh PhD Thesis 1977. This attempt to explain the process has also produced his article 'Farm Amalgamation in Scotland' *Scottish Geographical Magazine* 95 1979 pp 93–107.

**8198**  G A Bright 'An Investigation of the Scottish Agricultural Labour Market 1950–1975' CNAA MPhil Thesis 1978. On the social changes resulting from the decline of agricultural labour in the post-war period see A H Rathore 'The Role of Agricultural Labour in the Depopulation Trends in Rural Scotland (1945–63)' Glasgow BLitt Thesis 1968–9.

**8199** O Rahman 'An Examination of Factors affecting the Profitability of Arable Farms in the Post-War Period, with Special Reference to the East of Scotland' Edinburgh MSc Thesis 1962–3.

**8200** John Gold and Margaret R Gold *The Crofting System: A Selected Bibliography* Oxford Polytechnic 1979. An alphabetically arranged unannotated listing of the literature on crofting in the Highlands and Islands excluding official reports and theses. The role of the Highlands and Islands Development Board in developing agriculture in the crofting areas is assessed in detail in John Bryden and George Houston *Agrarian Change in the Scottish Highlands: The Role of the Highlands and Islands Development Board in the Agricultural Economy of the Crofting Counties* Robertson 1976. Agriculture in the North of Scotland is assessed in W H Senior and W B Swan *Survey of Agriculture in Caithness, Orkney and Shetland* Highlands and Islands Development Board 1972. The state of agriculture in a crofting area under the impact of oil development is examined in John H Ormiston *Moray Firth: An Agricultural Study* Highlands and Islands Development Board 1973.

**8201** R Urquhart *History of the Scottish Milk Marketing Board* Scottish Milk Marketing Board 1979.

**8202** Mark L Anderson *A History of Scottish Forestry* Volume 2 Nelson 1967. The standard history. John Davies *The Scottish Forester* William Blackwood 1979 is a short, general popular history. These two volumes cover both the private and public sectors. On the public sector see Herbert L Edlin 'The Forestry Commission in Scotland 1919–69' *Scottish Geographical Magazine* 85 1969 pp 84–95. On forestry in Scotland see also R T Bradley 'Forestry in West Scotland' *Forestry* 48 1975 pp 33–50.

### (9) Fishing

**8203** *Scottish Sea Fisheries: Statistical Tables* HMSO 1939–. This has been published annually under various titles since 1872.

**8204** G T Sheven 'The Scottish Fishing Industry 1945–1979: An Economic Geography' Aberdeen PhD Thesis 1979.

**8205** William Russell *'In Great Waters': Report on the Study of the Economic and Social Impact of the Highlands and Islands Development Board's Investments in Fisheries* Highlands and Islands Development Board 1972. The Board was committed to expand, update and adequately equip the fishing fleet of the area. This report reviews progress.

### (10) Labour

**8206** W H Marwick *A Short History of Labour in Scotland* Chambers 1967. A useful short account.

**8207** G Payne *et al* 'Changes in Occupational Mobility in Scotland' *Scottish Journal of Sociology* 1 1976 pp 57–79. A study of changing labour mobility in line with the changing nature of industry in Scotland.

### (a) Industrial Relations

**8208** I P Miller *Industrial Law in Scotland* Green 1970. A useful, though increasingly outdated, textbook.

**8209** W Leslie *Industrial Tribunal Practice in Scotland* Green 1981. A detailed legal textbook which provides a guide to important cases and an account of the development of these tribunals, which were considerably expanded after the 1964 Industrial Training Act.

**8210** A E Thompson 'Industrial Relations in the Fuel and Power Industries, with Particular Reference to Selected Undertakings in Midlothian' Edinburgh PhD Thesis 1953. On the 1984–5 miners' strike in Scotland see C Levy *A Very Hard Year: The 1984–85 Miners' Strike in Mauchline* Workers' Educational Association 1985.

**8211** John W Leopold and P B Beaumont 'Personal Officers in the National Health Service in Scotland: Development and Change in the 1970s' *Public Administration* 63 1985 pp 219–27.

**8212** Thomas Clarke *Sit-In at Bendix Fisher* Institute for Workers Control, Nottingham, Pamphlet 42, 1974. In the early 1970s there were a number of well-publicized industrial sit-ins, one of which is briefly described here.

**8213** Keith Bradley and Alan Gelb 'The Political Economy of "Radical" Policy: An Analysis of the *Scottish Daily News* Worker Co-operative' *British Journal of Political Science* 9 1979 pp 1–20. An examination of government policy towards the *Scottish Daily News* workers cooperative. Funding policy is analysed in Keith Bradley 'Worker Control as a State Managerial Device: A Study of the *Scottish Daily News* Worker Cooperative' Essex PhD Thesis 1978.

**8214** R Hay and J McLauchlan 'The UCS Work-In: An Interim Catalogue' *Journal of the Scottish Labour History Society* 8 1974 pp 21–30. An early guide to the literature and sources on the most celebrated event in post-war Scottish industrial relations, the work-in at Upper Clyde Shipbuilders in 1971–72. The fullest account of this event is John Foster and Charles Woolfson *The Politics of the UCS Work-In: Class Alliances and the Right to Work* Lawrence and Wishart 1986. It is based on the records left by the taping of all the major meetings of the work-in and is a notable contribution to the study of industrial relations in an industry notorious for sectionalism which sets the work-in in the context of the downturn in international trade and the falling demand for ships and the impact of the work-in on domestic politics. The tapes of the work-in are deposited in Glasgow University Archives, Glasgow, G12 8QQ. More contemporary accounts are Alistair Buchan *The Right to Work: The Story of the Upper Clyde Confrontation* Calder and Boyers 1972 and Willie Thompson and Finlay Hunt *The UCS Work-In* Lawrence and Wishart 1972.

## (b) Trade Unions

**8215** *Scottish Trade Union Review* Trade Union Research Unit, Glasgow 1978–. A quarterly journal with articles on current trade union themes.

**8216** Angela Tuckett *The Scottish Trades Union Congress: The First 80 Years 1897–1977* Mainstream 1986. A useful institutional history, though it is not so good on the wider context. See also J M Craigen 'The Scottish Trades Union Congress (1897–1973) – A Study of a Pressure Group' Heriot-Watt MLitt Thesis 1974–6.

**8217** Sheila Lewenhak 'Women in the Leadership of the Scottish Trades Union 1897–1970' *Journal of the Scottish Labour History Society* 7 1973 pp 3–23.

**8218** P H Liddell 'The Role of the Trades Council in the Political and Industrial Life of Glasgow 1858–1976' Strathclyde MSc Thesis 1978. The importance of trades councils has declined in the post-war period and during this period the Glasgow council has been to the left of the Scottish TUC and has struggled to find a role in the post-war Labour Movement.

**8219** J T Ozga 'Teacher Contracts and Teacher "Professionalism": The Educational Institute of Scotland' in Martin Lewin (ed) *The Politics of Teacher Unionism: International Perspectives* Croom Helm 1985 pp 236–54. A study of teacher unionism in Scotland.

**8220** Angela Tuckett *The Scottish Carter: The History of the Scottish Horse and Motormen's Association 1898–1964* Allen and Unwin 1967. A model, well balanced trade union history.

**8221** Robin Page Arnot *A History of the Scottish Miners* Allen and Unwin 1955. A history up to the 1954 presidential election in the National Union of Mineworkers. It is useful on post-war nationalization and developments in fields such as industrial relations, wages and hours, health and safety and political influence. Alan B Campbell *The Lanarkshire Miners: A Social History of their Trade Unions 1775–1974* Donald 1979 is a detailed social history which concentrates more on the earlier years covered.

**8222** S C Gillespie *A Hundred Years of Progress: The Record of the Scottish Typographical Association 1853–1953* Heinemann 1953.

**8223** Abe Moffatt *My Life with the Miners* Lawrence and Wishart 1965. This autobiography by a miners' leader contains useful reflections on the post-war situation in the mining industry.

**8224** Jimmy Reid *Reflections of a Clyde-Built Man* Souvenir Press 1976. Reid was one of the principal leaders of the shipyard workers, and was heavily involved in the Upper Clyde Shipbuilders work-in and the Communist Party. This is a collection of speeches and articles 1966–76 with a short autobiographical section. See also B Cowe 'The Making of a Clydeside Communist' *Marxism Today* 17 1973 pp 112–6.

## (c) Training

**8225** *Manpower Shortages in Scottish Manufacturing Industry* Scottish Council Research Institute 1979. An important report. A survey of Scottish manufacturing industry revealed that despite higher rates of unemployment than most of the rest of the UK firms were experiencing recruitment difficulties because of shortages of skilled labour. It therefore calls for improved training and measures to correct the geographical mismatch of labour supply and demand in Scotland.

**8226** Alice Brown and John Fairey (eds) *The Manpower Services Commission in Scotland* Edinburgh University Press 1989. A reappraisal of the work of the Manpower Services Commission 1974–88 and its impact on employment, education and the churches from people who were closely involved with it.

**8227** R Mackie 'Training in Scottish Local Government 1960–1982: A Study of Policy Negotiation' Strathclyde MSc Thesis 1984. A study of the development of policy; it was not until 1980 that a national training body was set up.

## F. THE ENVIRONMENT

### (1) Water

**8228** A S Pitkethly 'Evolution of the Institutional Structure of Scottish Water Management 1929–1977' Edinburgh PhD Thesis 1980.

### (2) Town and Country Planning

#### (a) General

**8229** R C Henderson and D J Hogarth (eds) *Scottish Planning Sourcebook* Park Place Publishing 1984. A useful reference guide to sources of information and bibliography.

**8230** E Young *Law of Planning in Scotland* Hodge 1978. A legal textbook.

**8231** A W Burton and R Johnson *Public Participation in Planning: A Review of Experience in Scotland* Planning Exchange 1976. A review of the slow progress towards greater public involvement in planning in Scotland since the 1969 Skeffington Report [5056] with case studies.

**8232** John McEwen *Who Owns Scotland: A Study in Land Ownership* Edinburgh University Students Publications Bureau 1977. A study of land ownership and a call for reform.

**8233** *National Parks: A Scottish Survey: Report by the Scottish National Parks Survey Committee* Cmnd 6631, *Parliamentary Papers* v 1944–45. The report of the committee set up under Sir J Douglas Ramsey to recommend the designation of areas of Scotland as National Parks. In the event its recommendations were not acted upon and no National Parks have been designated in Scotland.

**8234** David N Skinner *A Situation Report on Green Belts in Scotland* Countryside Commission for Scotland 1976. A report on countryside conservation around towns and the development and operation of the green belts around Edinburgh, Aberdeen, Falkirk/Grangemouth, Dundee, Glasgow and Prestwick.

**8235** Roger Smith and Urlan Wannop (eds) *Strategic Planning in Action: The Impact of the Clyde Valley Regional Plan 1946–1982* Routledge and Kegan Paul 1985. A good analysis of the history of the strategic plan set up during and after the war for the Glasgow region. The mixed fortunes of population redistribution and

New Town planning in this region are assessed in Elspeth Farmer and Roger Smith *Glasgow Overspill 1943–71* Urban and Regional Studies Discussion Paper 6, University of Glasgow 1972. As R A Henderson 'Industrial Overspill from Glasgow 1958–1968' *Urban Studies* 11 1974 pp 61–79 comments, the policy of industrial relocation outside the city has not contributed towards and may even have hindered urban renewal. Planning and redevelopment in Glasgow, and especially Govan, after 1945 is examined in T Brennan *Reshaping a City* House of Grant 1959. In fact however this is as much a sociological study of Govan, though it does mention the Clyde Valley Regional Plan. The impact of comprehensive development areas (later action areas) on planning and redevelopment in Glasgow itself is considered in T Hart *The Comprehensive Development Area* Oliver and Boyd 1968. H Katz 'An Integrated Approach to Community Planning: A Case Study of Govanhill, Glasgow 1973–1978' Strathclyde PhD Thesis 1981 is a detailed study and critique of planning in Glasgow.

**8236** D Sim *Change in the City Centre* Gower 1982. A study of the operation of inner area renewal policy in Glasgow. The history of the major renewal project that developed as policy shifted away from decantation towards inner city policy in the 1970s is examined in David Donnison and Alan Middleton (eds) *Regenerating the Inner City: Glasgow's Experience* Routledge and Kegan Paul 1987. This concentrates on the Glasgow Eastern Area Renewal project. See also R Leclerc and D Draffan 'The Glasgow Eastern Area Renewal Project' *Town Planning Review* 55 1984 pp 335–51.

**8237** George Bruce *Some Practical Good: The Cockburn Association 1875–1975: A Hundred Year's Participation in Planning in Edinburgh* Cockburn Association 1975. This body was set up 'for the improvement of Edinburgh and the neighbourhood'.

#### (b) New Towns

**8238** Christopher J Carter *The Scottish New Towns: Their Contribution to Post-War Growth and Development in Central Scotland* School of Town and Regional Planning Occasional Paper 19, Duncan of Jordanstown College of Art, Dundee University 1984. The only general study of the economic impact of the Scottish New Towns. Social development and social planning in the New Towns of Glenrothes, East Kilbride and Livingstone is assessed in H M Wirz *Social Aspects of Planning in New Towns* Saxon House 1975.

**8239** Christopher J Carter *Innovation in Planning Thought and Practice at Cumbernauld New Town 1956–1962* School of Town and Regional Planning Occasional Paper 15, Duncan of Jordanstown College, Dundee

University 1983. The background to the designation of Cumbernauld under the 1957 Housing and Town Development (Scotland) Act as a response to Glasgow's overspill problem is examined in Roger Smith 'The Politics of an Overspill Policy: Glasgow, Cumbernauld and Housing and Town Development (Scotland) Act' *Public Administration* 55 1977 pp 79–94 and Michael Keating and Christopher J Carter 'Policy-Making and the Scottish Office: The Designation of Cumbernauld New Town' *Public Administration* 65 1987 pp 391–407.

**8240**  Roger Smith *East Kilbride: The Biography of a Scottish New Town 1947–1973* HMSO 1979. A good assessment of the success of East Kilbride in terms of dwellings built, jobs created, environment and relief of inner city congestion. Elizabeth B Mitchell *The Plan that Pleased* Town and Country Planning Association 1967 is the memoir of a planner closely involved in the early history of the Scottish New Towns, and especially East Kilbride.

**8241**  K Ferguson *Glenrothes: The First Twenty Five Years* K Ferguson 1974. A history of one the first New Towns designated in Scotland.

### (3) Urban History

**8242**  Ian H Adams *The Making of Urban Scotland* Croom Helm 1978. A history of Scottish cities since the turn of the century. George Gordon and Brian Dicks (eds) *Scottish Urban History* Aberdeen University Press 1983 and George Gordon (ed) *Perspectives of the Scottish City* Aberdeen University Press 1985 are useful collections of historical essays on the Scottish city in the twentieth century.

**8243**  R D P Smith 'The Changing Urban Hierarchy in Scotland' *Regional Studies* 12 1978 pp 331–51. An analysis of changes in urban ranking by population, facilities and the retail trade.

**8244**  Michael Keating *The City That Refused to Die: Glasgow: The Politics of Urban Regeneration* Aberdeen University Press 1988. A good study of attempts to regenerate Glasgow's economy and built environment.

**8245**  P J Bull 'The Spatial Components of Intra-Urban Manufacturing Change: Suburbanisation in Clydeside 1958–1968' *Transactions of the Institute of British Geographers* 3 1978 pp 91–100.

**8246**  David Donnison and Alan Middleton (eds) *Rejuvenating the Inner City: The Scottish Experience* Routledge and Kegan Paul 1987.

### G. SOCIAL HISTORY

### (1) General

**8247**  School of Scottish Studies, University of Edinburgh, 27 George Square, Edinburgh EH8 9LD. This holds a large oral archive recorded since 1951. This covers various aspects of Scottish life but concentrates on the Gaelic areas, culture, folklore and aspects of rural life. There is an oral archive of rural crafts and rural life in the Country Life Archive, National Museum of Antiques of Scotland, 1 Queen Street, Edinburgh, EH2 1JD.

**8248**  Ron Parsler and Dan Shapiro (eds) *The Social Impact of Oil on Scotland: A Contribution to the Sociology of Oil* Gower 1980. This collection of essays examines the impact of the oil economy in areas such as industrial relations, housing or Shetland society. See also Robert Moore *The Social Impact of Oil: The Case of Peterhead* Routledge and Kegan Paul 1982 and [8162, 8165].

**8249**  R M Callender 'Ghost Villages' *Scots Magazine* 118 1963 pp 564–72. An account of the decline of Scottish mining villages.

### (2) Population

**8250**  O Llewellyn Lloyd, F L R Williams, W G Berry and C du V Florey (eds) *An Atlas of Mortality in Scotland* Croom Helm 1987. An analysis of patterns of mortality since the 1960s. For the earlier period see Joyce Laker Harley and Catherine Amy Hytten (comp) *Death Rates by Site, Age and Sex 1911–60: Scotland* Chester Beatty Research Institute 1966.

**8251**  T H Hollingsworth *Migration: A Study based on Scottish Experience between 1939 and 1964* Oliver and Boyd 1970. See also Huw R Jones (ed) *Recent Migration in Northern Scotland: Pattern, Process, Impact* Social Science Research Council 1982 and H A Moisley 'Population Changes and the Highland Problem 1951–1961' *Scottish Studies* 6 1962 pp 194–200.

**8252**  E M Clive *Law of Husband and Wife in Scotland* 2nd ed, Green 1982. A legal textbook.

**8253**  J D Haldane *A Celebration of Marriage? Scotland 1931–1981: Implications of Marriage Counselling and Therapy* Aberdeen University Press 1982. A history of marriage guidance in Scotland.

## (3) Social Policy

**8254** J K Carnie 'Parliament and Scottish "Issues of Conscience" in the 1970s: Three Case Studies – Licensing, Divorce and Homosexuality' Edinburgh PhD Thesis 1983. An examination of developments in these three areas, exemplified by the 1976 Licensing (Scotland) Act, which introduced all-day drinking, the 1976 Divorce Act and the non-reform of the Scottish law on homosexuality, and the way these illustrate the legal and political differences between Scotland and England and Wales.

### (a) Social Services

**8255** John English (ed) *Social Services in Scotland* 3rd ed, Scottish Academic Press 1988. A good collection of essays on the various elements in the social services outlining the historical background to the contemporary situation with the aid of maps, statistics and other supporting details.

**8256** A E Campbell 'The Origin and Implementation of Section 12 of the Social Work (Scotland) Act 1968' Edinburgh PhD Thesis 1979. Section 12 of this Act was concerned with the promotion of social welfare by local authorities.

### (b) Health

**8257** *Health in Scotland* HMSO 1981–. The annual report by the Chief Medical Officer of the Scottish Home and Health Department. This succeeded *Health Services in Scotland* HMSO 1953–80. See also the annual *Scottish Health Statistics* HMSO 1959–.

**8258** Gordon McLachlan (ed) *Improving the Common Weal: Aspects of Scottish Health Services 1900–1984* Edinburgh University Press 1987. A good collection of essays on various aspects of health policy, administration and provision in the twentieth century.

**8259** D J Hunter *Coping With Uncertainty: Policy and Politics in the National Health Service* Research Studies Press 1980. The result of the findings of a two year project observing financial decisions in two Scottish health boards.

**8260** R V Segsworth 'Regional Variations in the Scottish Health Service 1951–1976: An Analysis of Public Policy' Stirling PhD Thesis 1981. An examination of the progress of the National Health Service towards its goal of regional equality in service provision.

**8261** Dorothy Bochel and Mary Maclaren *The Establishment and Development of Local Health Councils* Scottish Home and Health Department 1979. These councils were set up under the National Health Service (Scotland) Act 1972 to represent public interests to the NHS. This study finds that they have been constrained in function and far from well received.

**8262** H P Tait *A Doctor and Two Policemen: The History of Edinburgh Health Department 1862–1974* Edinburgh Health Department 1974. A useful institutional history.

**8263** Neil McFarlane 'Hospitals, Housing and Tuberculosis in Glasgow 1911–51' *Social History of Medicine* 2 1989 pp 59–86. A study of the way in which the appalling conditions in the Glasgow slums slowed the decline of tuberculosis in the twentieth century.

## (4) Class and Poverty

**8264** A Allan MacLaren *Social Class in Scotland: Past and Present* Donald 1975. The relevant essays in this collection are by James G Kellas and Peter Fotheringham 'The Political Behaviour of the Working Class' pp 143–66 (on the post-war decline of the Conservatives and the rise of the SNP) and by John Scott and Michael Hughes 'The Scottish Ruling Class: Problems of Analysis and Data' pp 166–88 (an attempt to define the Scottish elite).

**8265** Tony Dickson (ed) *Capital and Class in Scotland* Donald 1982. This collection includes essays on changes in working class organization in the militant area of the Vale of Leven, occupation and sexual stratification in work since 1945 and the reaction of the Labour Movement to the development of the oil industry.

**8266** Geoff Norris *Poverty: The Facts in Scotland* Child Poverty Action Group 1977. An estimate of the level of poverty and of its effect on groups such as the low paid, the unemployed, the sick and disabled, the orphaned and the old. See also Lee Soltow 'An Index of the Poor and Rich in Scotland 1861–1961' *Scottish Journal of Political Economy* 18 1971 pp 49–68.

**8267** A Grimes *Cold as Charity: Fuel Poverty in Scotland Today* Scottish Fuel Poverty Action Group 1979.

## (5) Women

**8268** Glasgow Women's Group *Uncharted Lives: Extracts from Scottish Women's Experiences 1850–1982* Pressgang 1983. A contribution to the understanding of Scottish working class history and culture through an oral history framework using women's life stories. See also P M Straw 'Times of their Lives: A Century of Working Class Women' Edinburgh PhD Thesis 1986.

## (6) Race Relations

8269  Robert Miles and Anne Dunlop 'The Reconciliation of Politics in Britain: Why Scotland is Different' *Patterns of Prejudice* 20 1986 pp 23–33. A rather theoretical attempt to explain the relative absence of racial conflict in Scotland. The operation of race relations legislation in Scotland is analysed in Martin MacEwen 'Race Relations in Scotland: Ignorance or Apathy' *New Community* 8 1980 pp 266–74.

## (7) Sport and Leisure

### (a) General

8270  J P Lawson *Hostels For Hikers: A Pictorial History of the Scottish Youth Hostels Association's First Fifty Years* Scottish Youth Hostel Association 1982.

8271  Adam Watson 'Paths and People in the Cairngorms' *Scottish Geographical Magazine* 100 1984 pp 151–60. An account of the development of walks and facilities for hikers since 1946.

### (b) Sport

8272  Bill Murray *The Old Firm: Sectarianism, Sport and Society in Scotland* Donald 1984. A good collection of reflections on the relationship between sport, religion and society in Scotland.

### (i) Football

8273  *The Scottish Football Annual* Stanley Paul 1984– . An annual guide.

8274  John Rafferty *One Hundred Years of Scottish Football* Pan 1973. A general history, as is Bob Crampsey *The Scottish Footballer* Blackwood 1978. The financial problems that faced the game in the 1970s are examined in Mike Aitken (ed) *When Will We See Your Like Again? The Changing Face of Scottish Football* Edinburgh University Students Publications Bureau 1977.

8275  Jack Webster *The Dons* Stanley Paul 1978. A history of Aberdeen FC.

8276  Jim Wilkie *Across the Great Divide: A History of Professional Football in Dundee* Mainstream 1984.

8277  Pat Wood and Tom Campbell *The Glory and the Dream: The Story of Celtic FC 1887–1986* Mainstream 1986. An extensive history of the Glasgow football club most associated with Catholicism. See also Gerald McNee *The Story of Celtic: An Official History 1888–1978* Stanley Paul 1978 and James Edmund Handley *The Celtic Story: A History of Celtic Football Club* Stanley Paul 1960.

8278  Stephen Halliday *Rangers: The Official Illustrated History* Barker 1989. A history of Glasgow Rangers. The two Glasgow clubs, Celtic and Rangers have traditionally been the most successful in Scotland. This history concentrates on the football rather than the social context of Protestantism. See also Ian Peebles *Growing with Glory* Rangers Football Club 1973, William Allison *Rangers: The New Era 1873–1966* Glasgow Rangers FC 1966 and John Fairgrieve *The Rangers: A Complete History of Scotland's Greatest Football Club* Hale 1964.

8279  Albert Mackie *The Hearts: The Story of Heart of Midlothian FC* Stanley Paul 1959.

8280  John Mackay *The Hibees: A History of Hibernian Football Club* Donald 1985. A history of the Edinburgh club most associated with Catholicism. See also Gerry Docherty and Phil Thomson *100 Years of Hibs 1875–1975* Donald 1975.

8281  R A Crampsey *The Game for the Game's Sake: The History of Queen's Park Football Club 1867–1967* Queen's Park FC 1967.

8282  Ian Archer *The Jags* Molendinar Press 1976. A history of Partick Thistle FC.

8283  Douglas Lamming *Who's Who of Scottish Internationalists 1872–1982* Association of Football Statisticians 1982–. A multi-volume biographical guide.

8284  Kenny Dalglish *King Kenny* revised ed, Panther 1984. An autobiography. Dalglish has since followed a remarkable international career with a noteworthy managerial career at Liverpool. Denis Law *Denis Law* Queen Anne Press 1979 is an autobiography by the great striker. Another useful footballing memoir is Bobby Lennox *A Million Miles for Celtic* Stanley Paul 1982. A career with Scotland and Liverpool is remembered in Billy Liddell *My Soccer Story* Stanley Paul 1960. Danny McGrain *In Sunshine or in Shadow* Donald 1987 is an autobiography. McGrain won 62 caps for Scotland, and also captained his country on a number of occasions. He was a star at Celtic for over twenty of the club's most successful years, ending his career in 1987. Ally McLeod *The Ally McLeod Story: An Autobiography*

Stanley Paul 1979 is a defence of his overshadowed stewardship by the man who captained Scotland during the 1978 World Cup campaign. Alan Rough *Rough at the Top* Donald 1988 is an autobiography at the end of a lengthy career in which Rough was capped 53 times as Scotland's goalkeeper. Graeme Souness with Bob Harris *No Half Measures* Willow 1985 is an autobiography by the Scotland midfield player. Bill Shankly *Shankly* Barker 1976 recalls a distinguished career in which an international career for Scotland was followed by a successful period as manager of Liverpool. Ken Gallagher *Jock Stein: The Authorised Biography* Stanley Paul 1987 is a biography of the man who became celebrated as the manager of Celtic who led them to the European Cup triumph of 1967. He also managed Scotland from 1982 until his death in 1986. Gordon Strachan with Jack Webster *Gordon Strachan* Stanley Paul 1984 is the autobiography of one of the leading Scottish players of the 1980s. Bob Wilson *Bob Wilson: An Autobiography* Pelham 1971 is the autobiography of the goalkeeper. Another football autobiography is George Young *Captain of Scotland* Stanley Paul 1951.

## (ii) Other

**8285**   William Carmichael and M McIntyre Hood (eds) *The Official History of the IXth British Commonwealth Games, Edinburgh, Scotland, 16–25 July 1970* Organising Committee of the IXth British Commonwealth Games 1971.

**8286**   Jim Watts with Norman Giller *Watts My Name: An Autobiography* Stanley Paul 1981. This recalls Watts' boxing career 1968–80, during which time he won the world lightweight championship.

**8287**   Pat Ward-Thomas *The Royal and Ancient* Scottish Academic Press 1980. A history of the Royal and Ancient Golf Club at St Andrews, Scotland's premier club. James Bell Salmond *The Story of the R and A* Macmillan 1956 is a history of the first two hundred years of the club.

**8288**   Doug Sanders *Come Swing With Me: An Autobiography* W H Allen 1974. A golfer's autobiography.

**8289**   *The Scottish Rugby Union* Collins 1985. A general history of the development and administration of the game in Scotland. See also Allan Massie *A Portrait of Scottish Rugby* Polygon 1984.

**8290**   Gordon Brown *Broon From Troon: An Autobiography* Stanley Paul 1979. The amateur code in rugby union tends to discourage the writing of autobiographies like this by the great Scottish lock forward. Another

rugby union autobiography is Ian McLauchlan *Mighty Mouse* Stanley Paul 1980.

**8291**   George Blake and Christopher Small *Cruise in Company: The History of the Royal Clyde Yacht Club 1856–1956* Royal Clyde Yacht Club 1959.

**8292**   Roger Hutchinson *Camenachd!* Mainstream 1989. A history of shinty.

**8293**   Peter Bilsborough *A Hundred Years of Scottish Swimming* Scottish Amateur Swimming Association 1989. A great Scottish swimmer recalls his career in Bobby McGregor and Athole Still *The Bobby McGregor Story* Eyre and Spottiswoode 1970. Another swimming memoir is David Wilkie *David Wilkie* Kemps 1976.

## (8) Drink

**8294**   Susan Moody *Drunken Offenders in Scotland: A Review of the Relevant Literature* HMSO 1979. A bibliographical study.

**8295**   *Report of the Department Committee on Scottish Licensing Law* Cmnd 5354, *Parliamentary Papers* xv 1972–73. The committee chaired by Christopher Clayson recommended in this report that Scotland should move to licensing hours of between 11am and 11pm and other important changes, most of which were subsequently embodied in the Licensing (Scotland) Act 1976.

## (9) Housing

**8296**   *Scottish Housing Statistics* HMSO 1978–. A quarterly bulletin.

**8297**   Richard Roger (ed) *Scottish Housing: Policy and Politics 1885–1985* Leicester University Press 1989. Relevant essays in this valuable collection are on the Scottish Special Housing Association, the politics of housing since 1945 and the decline of landlordism. There is also a good bibliography. See also Ronald Duncan Cramond *Housing Policy in Scotland 1919–64: A Study in State Assistance* Oliver and Boyd 1966. Housing policy in Scotland is critically assessed in Adela Adam Nevitt 'Housing in a Welfare State' *Urban Studies* 14 1977 pp 33–40.

**8298**   Douglas Niven *The Development of Housing in Scotland* Croom Helm 1979. A comparative study which encompasses a historical summary of housing development, an examination of the skewing of emphasis towards the public sector since 1918 and a discussion of the future of Scottish housing.

**8299** R G A Cochrane *The Law of Housing in Scotland* Hodge 1977. A legal textbook.

**8300** J Butt 'Working Class Housing in Scottish Cities 1900–1950' in George Gordon and Brian Dicks (eds) *Scottish Urban History* Aberdeen University Press 1983 pp 233–68.

**8301** J E Vlahostergios 'Post-World War II Housing Design and Development in Great Britain' Strathclyde MSc Thesis 1979. This looks particularly at housing standards and concentrates on housing in Scotland.

**8302** J B Cullingworth and C J Watson (eds) *Housing in Clydeside in 1970: A Report on a Household Survey and a House Condition Survey in the Central Clydeside Conurbation* HMSO 1971. A comprehensive survey of family size, living conditions, tenure, rent and housing conditions.

**8303** Valerie A Karn *East Kilbride Housing Survey: A Study of Housing in a New Town* Centre for Urban and Regional Studies 8, University of Birmingham 1970.

**8304** Frank Worsdall *The Tenements: A Way of Life: A Social, Historical and Architectural Study of Housing in Glasgow* Chambers 1979. A study focusing on the tenement blocks which form the traditional dwellings of much of Glasgow's working class population.

**8305** Pearl Jephcott *Homes in High Flats* Oliver and Boyd 1971. This is mainly based on research in Glasgow. It argues that high rise dwellings are costly, socially unsuitable, and unaesthetic and do not necessarily make better use of land.

**8306** Owen A Hartley 'Local Inquiries and Council House Rents in Scotland 1958–71' *Policy and Politics* 2 1973 pp 63–78. This particularly looks at the role of local administrative tribunals.

**8307** P Kemp *The Changing Ownership Structure of the Privately Rented Sector: A Case Study of Partick East 1964 to 1978* Centre for Urban and Regional Research, University of Glasgow 1980. This traces the changing pattern and the fate of property which left the sector.

**8308** T L Johnston, Lorna W Jackson, A Scott and P J Welham *The Demand for Private Houses in Scotland: A Report for the Scottish Housing Advisory Committee* HMSO 1972. This examines why demand seems less in Scotland than in England and Wales and the regional disparity in the cost of private housing. Movements in housing prices in Glasgow are studied in Moira Munro and Duncan MacLennan 'Intra-Urban Changes in Housing Prices: Glasgow 1972–83' *Housing Studies* 2 1987 pp 65–81. They demonstrate that a depressed labour market does not necessarily lead to a depressed housing market.

**8309** Tom Begg *50 Special Years: A Study in Scottish Housing* Scottish Special Housing Association 1988. A jubilee history of the association. See also *A Chronicle of Forty Years 1937–1977* Scottish Special Housing Association 1977. The development of the association and its relations with the Scottish Office are also examined in Husain Al-Qaddo and Richard Rodger 'The Implementation of Housing Policy: The Scottish Special Housing Association' *Public Administration* 65 1987 pp 313–29.

**8310** S J C Berry 'Managing by Ourselves: The Development of Housing Cooperatives in Scotland' *Housing Review* 30 1981 pp 116–19.

**8311** Sidney Jacobs *The Right to a Decent House* Routledge and Kegan Paul 1976. A highly critical account of local authority rehousing and of the fight against rehousing schemes in Glasgow based on primary and oral sources.

## (10) Crime and Policing

**8312** *Criminal Statistics, Scotland* HMSO 1930–. An annual statistical guide to occurrences and types of crime committed in the previous year.

**8313** Alison J E Arnott and Judith A Duncan *The Scottish Criminal* Edinburgh University Press 1970. A sociological study of contemporary male, female and juvenile offenders and the manner in which they are treated by the courts. It includes a study of the historical background since the turn of the century.

**8314** *Report of Her Majesty's Chief Inspector of Constabulary for Scotland* HMSO 1859–. A short annual statement.

**8315** Paul Gordon *Policing Scotland* 2nd ed, Scottish Council for Civil Liberties 1980. The first part of this study is a historical account of policing in Scotland. The second part is a critical study of contemporary policing. It includes a good bibliography.

**8316** Kenneth MacLeod *Dunbartonshire Constabulary 1858–1958* Dunbartonshire Joint Police Committee 1959.

## H. EDUCATION

### (1) General

**8317** James Craigie *A Bibliography of Scottish Education 1872–1972* University of London Press 1974. This unannotated bibliography covers all aspects of Scottish education. It is good on official publications. There is however a dearth of material generally on the post-war period.

**8318** *Scottish Educational Statistics* HMSO 1976–. An annual publication.

**8319** James Scotland *The History of Scottish Education Volume 2: From 1872 to the Present Day* University of London Press 1969. The standard history. See also his 'Scottish Education 1952–1982' *British Journal of Educational Studies* 30 1982 pp 122–35 and R Anderson 'Education and Society in Modern Scotland: A Comparative Perspective' *History of Education Quarterly* 25 1985 pp 459–81.

**8320** Andrew McPherson and Charles D Raab *Governing Education: A Sociology of Policy Since 1945* Edinburgh University Press 1988. An excellent and detailed study of post-war education policy in Scotland drawing on extensive interviewing.

**8321** Trevor Royle (ed) *Jock Tamson's Bairns: Essays on a Scots Childhood* Hamilton 1977. A collection of essays by Scottish writers and broadcasters on their education in Scotland in the 1950s.

**8322** Mary Mackintosh *Education in Scotland: Yesterday and Today* Gibson 1962. A lively appraisal of the then current Scottish education scene. On the Scottish education system in the 1960s see also G S Osborne *Change in Scottish Education* Longman 1968.

**8323** S Leslie Hunter *The Scottish Education System* Pergamon 2nd ed, 1972. A description of the contemporary situation.

**8324** Andrew McPherson 'An Angle on the Geist: Persistance and Change in the Scottish Educational Tradition' in Walter M Humes and Hamish M Paterson (eds) *Scottish Culture and Scottish Education 1800–1980* Donald 1983 pp 216–43. An appraisal of the relationship between national identity and education in recent years.

**8325** J Young 'The Advisory Council on Education in Scotland 1920–1961' Edinburgh PhD Thesis 1986. Although this was modelled on the English Consultative Committee to the Board of Education it did not have corresponding influence on the Scottish Education Department.

**8326** W B Dockrell (ed) *An Attitude of Mind: Twenty-Five Years of Educational Research* Scottish Council for Research in Education 1984. See also James Craigie *The Scottish Council for Research in Education 1928–1972* Scottish Council for Research in Education 1972.

**8327** A McLellan 'Education since Reorganisation' *Scottish Educational Studies* 8 1976 pp 75–83. A study of the impact of the local government reorganization of the early 1970s on the education system.

**8328** Scottish Education Department *Off the Beaten Track: Studies of Education in Rural Areas of Scotland* HMSO 1981. A report on the support for and the survival of small schools in rural Scotland.

**8329** D Thomson 'Education in Banffshire 1945–1970' Dundee MEd Thesis 1971–2.

**8330** A J C Kerr *Schools of Scotland* MacLellan 1962. A report which criticises excessive formalism, lack of imagination and lack of incentives for teachers and the lack of attention to the needs of the ablest and weakest pupils.

**8331** Alastair Macbeth 'Scottish School Councils: A New Initiative in School-Community Relations?' in George Baron (ed) *The Politics of School Government* Pergamon 1981 pp 105–30. These councils were introduced in 1973 and operating throughout Scotland by 1977. This examines the background to this innovation and its implementation.

**8332** C De Soyza 'The Post-Belt Era: A Critique on the Abolition of Corporal Punishment' Dundee MEd Thesis 1985. An evaluation of the debate over the abolition of corporal punishment in Scotland.

**8333** Thomas R Bone *School Inspection in Scotland 1840–1966* University of London Press 1969.

**8334** A L Stevenson 'The Development of Physical Education in the State Schools of Scotland 1900–1960' Aberdeen MLitt Thesis 1978.

**8335** Tom Conlon and Peter Cope (eds) *Computing in Scottish Education: The First Decade and Beyond* Edinburgh University Press 1989. In the course of the 1980s the number of school-based computers went from almost zero to over 10,000. This is the first work to assess the growing use of computers, their application and potential.

**8336** *Rising Standards in Scottish Primary Schools 1953–1963* University of London Press 1968. On policy-making for primary schools see F J McEnroe 'Freudianism, Bureaucracy and Scottish Primary Education' in Walter M Humes and Hamish M Paterson (eds) *Scottish Culture and Scottish Education 1800–1980* Donald 1983 pp 244–66, an analysis of the liberal 1965 Memorandum on Primary Education in Scotland.

**8337** David Hartley 'The Convergence of Learner-Centred Pedagogy in Primary and Further Education in Scotland 1965–1985' *British Journal of Educational Studies* 35 1987 pp 115–28.

**8338** Andrew McPherson and J Douglas Willms 'Equalisation and Improvement: Some Effects of Comprehensive Reorganisation in Scotland' *Sociology* 21 1987 pp 509–39. An assessment of the social effects of comprehensive education.

**8339** T A Fitzpatrick 'Catholic Secondary Education in South-West Scotland 1922–72: Its Contribution to the Educational, Religious, Cultural and Social Aspects of the Change in Status of the Catholic Community of the Area' Glasgow PhD Thesis 1982.

**8340** R F Mackenzie *The Unbowed Head: Events at Summerhill Academy 1968–1974* Edinburgh University Students Publications Bureau. This recounts his efforts to create a truly comprehensive school when headmaster at Summerhill in this period and the obstacles presented by parents and teachers. It also offers an interesting insight into the Scottish education system in the early 1970s. A biography of the leading founder of the school who also served as its director 1924–73 is Jonathan Croall *Neill of Summerhill: The Permanent Rebel* Routledge and Kegan Paul 1983. On Neill's educational ideas see Ray Hemmings *Fifty Years of Freedom: A Study of the Ideas of A S Neill* Allen and Unwin 1972.

**8341** Douglas Hutchison and Andrew McPherson 'Competing Inequalities: The Sex and Social Class Structure of the First Year Scottish University Student Population 1962–1972' *Sociology* 10 1976 pp 111–16.

**8342** Gordon Donaldson (ed) *Four Centuries: Edinburgh University Life 1583–1983* Edinburgh University Press 1983. On special aspects of the university's history see Ronald M Birse *Engineering at Edinburgh University: A Short History 1673–1983* School of Engineering, University of Edinburgh 1983 and Douglas Guthries *Extramural Medical Education in Edinburgh and the School of Medicine of the Royal Colleges* Livingstone 1965.

**8343** Sir Charles Illingworth *University Statesman: Sir Hector Hetherington* George Outram 1971. Hetherington was Principal and Vice-Chancellor of Glasgow University 1938–61. He chaired the Committee of Vice-Chancellors and Principals in 1943–7 and 1949–52.

**8344** Mabel Irvine *The Avenue of Years: Life of Sir James Irvine* Blackwood 1970. Irvine was Principal and Vice-Chancellor of Aberdeen University 1921–52.

**8345** J D Y Gray '"Why Should I Copy That? It's There Already": A Study of the Teaching of Art in Scotland from 1898 to 1980' Dundee MEd Thesis 1980.

**8346** Marjorie Cruikshank *A History of the Training of Teachers in Scotland* University of London Press 1970. The final section of this history deals with the post-war period. The history of a major teacher training college is told in John A Fairley *Jordanhill College of Education 1921–1971* History Department, Jordanhill College of Education, Glasgow 1974.

## (2) Libraries

**8347** *Scottish Libraries 1975–1977 Triennial Review* Scottish Library Association 1978. This review has appeared triennially since.

**8348** W R Aitken *A History of the Public Library Movement in Scotland to 1955* Scottish Library Association 1971. This published version of his thesis has had limited updating to cover the years to 1969. A good study with a useful bibliography. The later period is however perhaps better covered by W E Tyler 'The Development of Scottish Public Libraries' Strathclyde MA Thesis 1968, which stresses the difficulties in the development of the public library service.

**8349** C S Minto 'Sixteen Years On' *Scottish Library Association News* 66 1964 pp 3–16. A review of progress since the 1948 Minto Report on the distribution of library resources to poorly populated areas.

**8350** Kenneth J Cameron and Michael Roberts 'Amputation by Consent? Scottish University Library Finances Since Atkinson' *Library Review* 35 1986 pp 91–103. A review of developments since the mid-1960s.

**8351** A J Bunch *Hospital and Medical Libraries in Scotland: An Historical and Sociological Study* Scottish Library Association 1975.

**8352** William L Scott 'Argyll: Library Service to the Public before 1958' *Library Review* 34 1985 pp 195–213.

**8353** D C Soutter (ed) *The Mitchell Library, Glasgow 1877–1977* Glasgow District Libraries 1977.

## I. INTELLECTUAL AND CULTURAL HISTORY

### (1) General

**8354** David Daiches (ed) *A Companion to Scottish Culture* Arnold 1982. Illustrated articles on social customs, literature and the visual arts, putting them into their political and social context.

**8355** A J Aitken and Tom McArthur (eds) *Languages of Scotland* Chambers 1979. The most comprehensive collection of essays on the historical background and current usage of English, Scots and Gaelic in Scotland.

**8356** A J Aitken (ed) *Lowland Scots* Association for Scottish Literary Studies 1973. The only historical treatment of the language to have appeared this century. It also looks at modern literary Scots and the way in which the language is currently spoken.

**8357** Kenneth Mackinnon *Gaelic in Scotland 1971: Some Sociological and Demographic Considerations of the Census Report for Gaelic* Hatfield Polytechnic 1978. A detailed statistical survey of the state of the language. It finds that the number of Gaelic speakers rose between the censuses of 1961 and 1971. The arguments for the study and preservation of Gaelic are chronicled in Thomas Mackenzie Donn 'The Debate about the Gaelic Language of Scotland Since 1832' *Transactions of the Gaelic Society of Inverness* 49 1974 pp 26–52. The history of Gaelic's place in Scottish education is examined in Kenneth Mackinnon 'The School in Gaelic Scotland' *Transactions of the Gaelic Society of Inverness* 47 1971–72 pp 374–89. The decline of Gaelic in East Sutherland over a period of sixteen years is studied in Nancy C Dorion *Language Death: The Life Cycle of a Scottish Gaelic Dialect* University of Pennsylvania Press, Philadelphia, Pennsylvania 1981. This includes a lengthy bibliography.

### (2) Science and Intellectual Pursuits

**8358** Hermann A Bruck *The Story of Astronomy in Edinburgh from its Beginnings to 1975* Edinburgh University Press 1983. See also his *The Royal Observatory Edinburgh 1822–1972* Royal Observatory, Edinburgh 1972.

**8359** Harold R Fletcher and William H Brown *The Royal Botanic Garden, Edinburgh 1670–1970* HMSO 1970.

**8360** George Kereven 'Arguments within Scottish Marxism' *Bulletin of Scottish Politics* Spring 1981 pp 111–33. A review of the rich Marxist tradition in Scotland.

### (3) Medicine

**8361** William S Craig *History of the Royal College of Physicians of Edinburgh* Blackwell 1976. A history of the college 1681–1973 ending with a chapter on the contemporary state of the college and its national and international standing.

**8362** Sir John Boyd-Orr *As I Recall* MacGibbon and Kee 1968. Boyd-Orr was an important nutritionist and as such worked for UN commissions in the aftermath of the war. He was also an independent MP in 1945–6.

**8363** Gwyn Macfarlane *Alexander Fleming: The Man and the Myth* Chatto and Windus 1984. A reassessment of Fleming's career and of his role in the discovery and development of penicillin. It supersedes the hagiographical John Rowland *The Penicillin Man: The Story of Sir Alexander Fleming* Lutterworth 1957 and also L J Ludovici *Fleming: The Discoverer of Penicillin* Dakars 1952, Kathryn Surrey *Sir Alexander Fleming* Cassell 1959 and André Maurois *The Life of Sir Alexander Fleming: Discoverer of Penicillin* Cape 1959.

**8364** D K Henderson *The Evolution of Psychiatry in Scotland* Livingstone 1964. This is partly a history of the development of psychiatry in Scotland and partly an autobiography by the great Scottish psychiatrist. It covers the development of the Edinburgh School and its influence both elsewhere in the UK and on the continent.

**8365** R D Laing *Wisdom, Madness and Folly: The Making of a Psychiatrist* Macmillan 1985. A semi-autobiographical account of how the eminent Scottish psychiatrist came to write his controversial account of schizophrenia, *The Divided Self*, and a review of the current state of psychiatry. See also Richard I Evans *R D Laing: The Man and his Ideas* Dutton, New York 1976.

**8366** Leonard Mosley *Faces from the Fire: The Biography of Sir Archibald McIndoe* Weidenfeld and Nicolson 1962. McIndoe was an eminent plastic surgeon. See also Hugh McLeave *McIndoe: Plastic Surgeon* Muller 1961 and Ronald Seth *Sir Archibald McIndoe* Cassell 1962.

### (4) The Arts

**8367** George Bruce *Festival in the North: The Story of the Edinburgh Festival* Hale 1975. A history of Britain's largest and most celebrated arts festival.

**8368** George Bruce *'To Foster and Enrich': The First Fifty Years of the Saltire Society* Saltire Society 1986. This body was set up in 1936 'to foster and enrich the cultural heritage of Scotland'.

## (a) Visual Art

**8369** *The Vigorous Imagination: New Scottish Art* Scottish National Gallery of Modern Art 1987. An exhibition catalogue. Edward Gage *The Eye in the Wind: Scottish Painting Since 1945* Collins 1977 concentrates on 52 selected artists.

**8370** Esmé Gordon *The Royal Scottish Academy of Painting, Sculpture and Architecture 1826–1976* Skilton 1976. The official history.

**8371** William Buchanan *Joan Eardley* Edinburgh University Press 1976. A considerable painter Eardley was neglected after her death but there was a revival of interest in her work in the 1980s. This short biography incorporates a bibliography and chronology. Other biographies in this series are T Elder Dickson *W G Gillies* Edinburgh University Press 1974, David McClure *John Maxwell* Edinburgh University Press 1976, Maurice Lindsay *Robin Philipson* Edinburgh University Press 1976, George Bruce *Anne Redpath* Edinburgh University Press 1974 and Henry Harvey Wood *W MacTaggart* Edinburgh University Press 1974.

**8372** R Lewis *Sir William Flint 1880–1969* Skilton 1980. Flint was the President of the Royal Society of Painters in Watercolours 1936–56. Sir William Flint *In Pursuit* Medici Society 1969 is a beautifully produced autobiography well illustrated with his work.

**8373** G Cruikshank 'Scottish Pottery Today' *Scottish Art Review* 15 1977 pp 8–12.

## (b) Architecture

**8374** Fiona Sinclair *Scotstyle: 150 Years of Scottish Architecture* Royal Incorporation of Architects in Scotland 1984. The only modern general history. Peter Willis *New Architecture in Scotland* Lund Humphries 1977 gives brief illustrated descriptions of the 28 structures that best represent the architectural achievements of the 1960s and 1970s.

## (c) Music

**8375** Nöel Goodwin *A Ballet for Scotland: The First Ten Years of the Scottish Ballet* Canongate Publishing 1979. A well illustrated history of the ballet company.

**8376** Adam Sweeting *Simple Minds* Sidgwick and Jackson 1988. A study of the rock group.

**8377** Paul Nelson and Lester Bangs *Rod Stewart* Sidgwick and Jackson 1982. A critical biography from his blues days in the 1960s to his later solo career.

## (d) Literature

**8378** Roderic Watson *The Literature of Scotland* Macmillan 1984. A general history up to the twentieth century renaissance spawned by the likes of Hugh MacDiarmid, Neil Gunn and Edwin Muir. The last chapter of Maurice Lindsay *History of Scottish Literature* Hale 1977 examines the renaissance of Scottish literature in the twentieth century.

**8379** Alan Bold *Modern Scottish Literature* Longman 1983. A good critical study of twentieth century literature.

**8380** Maurice Lindsay (ed) *As I Remember: Ten Scottish Authors Recall How Writing Began For Them* Hale 1979. This includes contributions by George Mackay Brown, George Bruce, Robert Garioch, Maurice Lindsay, Norman MacCaig, Alexander Scott, Iain Crichton Smith, Derick Thomson, Sydney Tremayne and Fred Urquhart.

**8381** Terence Tobin *James Bridie (Osbourne Henry Mavor)* Twayne, Boston, Massachusetts 1980. A short biographical study of the life and work of the under-rated Scottish playwright who died in 1951. It includes a chronology and bibliography.

**8382** Neil M Gunn *The Atom of Delight* Faber 1956. The autobiography of the novelist and Scottish nationalist. See also J B Pick (ed) *Neil M Gunn: Selected Letters* Polygon 1987. Alexander Scott and Douglas Gifford (eds) *Neil M Gunn: The Man and the Writer* Blackwood 1973 is a tribute volume involving biographical material, critical essays and a bibliography.

**8383** Trevor Royle *James and Jim: A Biography of James Kennaway* Mainstream 1983. A biography of the writer and film scriptwriter. See also Susan Kennaway *The Kennaways* Cape 1981, which is based on his notebooks.

**8384** Maurice Lindsay *Thank You For Having Me: A Personal Memoir* Hale 1983. The autobiography of a Scottish poet and man of letters.

**8385** Alan Bold *MacDiarmid, Christopher Murray Grieve: A Critical Biography* Murray 1988. A good biography of the poet and Scottish nationalist (whose real name was Grieve but who wrote under the pseudonym of Hugh MacDiarmid). Kenneth Buthley *Hugh MacDiarmid* Oliver and Boyd 1964 is a well regarded biography which includes a good bibliography. There is also a good bibliography in the volume of critical studies, Duncan Glen (ed) *Hugh MacDiarmid: A Critical Survey* Scottish Academic Press 1972. Nancy K Gish *Hugh MacDiarmid: The Man and his Work* Macmillan 1984 is a biography and literary criticism. Gordon Wright *MacDiarmid: An Illustrated Biography* G Wright Publishing 1977 includes good photographs, a useful chronology and checklist of publications. MacDiarmid himself also wrote a collection of autobiographical essays, *The Company I've Kept* Hutchinson 1966. Also useful as a source is Alan Bold (ed) *The Letters of Hugh MacDiarmid* Hamilton 1984. This includes a chronology. The letters are not themselves arranged chronologically, but by addressee. This is an important collection because MacDiarmid was significant not just for his poetry. P H Scott and A C Davies *The Age of MacDiarmid: Essays on Hugh MacDiarmid and his Influence on Contemporary Scotland* Mainstream 1980 examines MacDiarmid's Left-Wing politics, nationalism, influence on Scottish language and literature and his international significance. On MacDiarmid's radicalism see also Christopher Harvie 'MacDiarmid the Socialist' *Journal of the Scottish Labour History Society* 16 1981 pp 4–11 and David Craig 'A Great Radical: Hugh MacDiarmid 1892–1978' *Marxism Today* 23 1979 pp 55–60. On MacDiarmid's place in twentieth century Scottish literature and in the revival that took place in the earlier part of the century see Duncan Glen *Hugh MacDiarmid: The Scottish Renaissance* Chambers 1964

**8386** David A Thomas and Joyce Thomas *Compton Mackenzie: A Bibliography* Mansell 1986. A guide to writings by and about the novelist. Andro Linklater *Compton Mackenzie: A Life* Chatto and Windus 1987 is a good biography of Mackenzie. Mackenzie also wrote the ten volume autobiography, *My Life and Times* Chatto and Windus 1963–71.

**8387** E W Mallown *Bibliography of the Writings of Edwin Muir* revised ed, Vana 1966. A guide to works by and about the poet. The most complete biography is P H Butter *Edwin Muir: Man and Poet* Oliver and Boyd 1966. See also Muir's *An Autobiography* Hogarth Press 1954 (this however does not really cover the post-war period). Willa Muir *Belonging: A Memoir* Hogarth Press 1968 is a memoir of her marriage to Muir and of literary life in Scotland. P H Butter (ed) *Selected Letters of Edwin Muir* Hogarth Press 1974 collects letters dating right up to shortly before Muir's death in 1959. It also features a chronology.

**8388** Allan Massie *Muriel Spark* Ramsay Head Press 1979. A study of the novelist and her work. See also

*Muriel Spark: A Biography and Critical Study* Centaur Press 1963, which includes a good bibliography. A useful short study which incorporates a bibliography and chronology is Velma Bourgeois Richmond *Muriel Spark* Ungar 1984. For a comprehensive bibliography on Spark see [7272].

(e) Theatre and Cinema

**8389** *The Theatre-Goer in Scotland* Tourism and Recreation Research Unit, University of Edinburgh 1977. A useful survey.

**8390** David Hutchinson *The Modern Scottish Theatre* Molendinar Press 1977. This examines both developments in writing for the theatre in Scotland and in the theatrical profession, as the century has seen the decline of the commercial theatre and the rise of subsidized arts theatre. See also A Cording 'Twentieth Century Scottish Drama' Glasgow PhD Thesis 1974–6.

**8391** Christopher D Innes *Edward Gordon Craig* Cambridge University Press 1983. A biography of the Scottish theatre set-designer and typographer.

**8392** Janet McBain *Pictures Past: Recollections of Scottish Cinema and Cinema-Going* Mootfoot 1985. A study of the social impact of the cinema.

**8393** Kenneth Passingham *Sean Connery: A Biography* Sidgwick and Jackson 1983. See also Michael Feeney Callan *Sean Connery: His Life and Films* W H Allen 1983. Concentrating particularly on his most famous role is Andrew Rissik *The James Bond Man: The Films of Sean Connery* Elm Tree 1983.

# J. LOCAL HISTORY

**8394** David Moody *Scottish Local History: An Introductory Guide* Batsford 1986. A guide to sources, writing and publishing on Scottish local history.

## (1) Local Government and Local Politics

**8395** *Scottish Local Government Financial Statistics* HMSO 1958/59–.

**8396** *Royal Commission on Local Government in Scotland 1966–1969* Cmnd 4150, *Parliamentary Papers* xxxix 1968–69. This report by the Royal Commission under Lord Wheatley laid the foundations of the local government reorganization of 1974–5. On the Royal Commission see also John Pitcairn Mackintosh 'The Royal Commission on Local Government in Scotland

1966–1969' *Public Administration* 48 1970 pp 49–56. On the thinking behind the reorganization see Andrew H Dawson 'The Idea of the Region: The Reorganisation of Scottish Local Government' *Public Administration* 59 1981 pp 279–94.

**8397** *The New Scottish Local Authorities: Organisation and Management Structures* HMSO 1973. An outline of how the new authoirites should operate. Ronald G Young *The Search for Democracy: A Guide to and Polemic about Local Government in Scotland* Heatherbank Books 1977 is an analysis of the public response to the new local authorities set up as a result of the local government reorganization of the early 1970s and of their decision making processes. It ends with a discussion of recent innovation, policy evaluation in future and the role of voluntary organizations in local government. The new system is assessed and contrasted with the previous system in Edward C Page and Arthur F Midwinter *Remote Bureaucracy or Administrative Efficiency? Scotland's New Local Government System* Centre for the Study of Public Policy 38, University of Strathclyde 1979. The development of corporate management after reorganization is examined in Arthur F Midwinter 'Management Reform in Scottish Local Government: An Analysis of Developments in the Post-Reorganisation Period' Aberdeen PhD Thesis 1981.

**8398** *Committee of Inquiry into Local Government in Scotland: Report* Cmnd 8115, *Parliamentary Papers* 1980–81. A review of the new system chaired by Anthony Stodart.

**8399** *Committee of Inquiry into the Functions and Powers of the Islands Councils of Scotland* Cmnd 9216, *Parliamentary Papers* 1983–84. This committee chaired by Sir David Montgomery reviewed the impact of oil and the 1975 reorganization on the islands councils. It called for the consolidation, development and extension of their powers.

**8400** Arthur F Midwinter *The Politics of Local Spending* Mainstream 1984. A study of relations between central and local government in Scotland.

**8401** John Bochel and David T Denver *The Scottish Local Government Elections 1974: Results and Statistics* Scottish Academic Press 1975. A useful survey which has since been repeated at each subsequent round of local elections.

**8402** Brian Elliott, David McCrone and Valerie Skelton 'Property and Political Power: Edinburgh 1875–1975' in John Garrard *et al* (eds) *The Middle Class in Politics* Saxon House 1978 pp 92–132. A useful analysis of local politics in the city.

**8403** R R Ballantine 'The "Save Fife" Campaign: A Case Study of a County's Fight against Local Government Reform Proposals' Dundee BPhil Thesis 1975. A study of the response in Fife to the local government reform proposals.

**8404** Ian Budge, Jack Brand, Michael Margolis and A L M Smith *Political Stratification and Democracy* Macmillan 1972. A study of contemporary politics in Glasgow. See also F W S Craig (ed) *City and Royal Burgh of Glasgow: Municipal Election Results 1948–73* Parliamentary Research Services 1984.

**8405** Frank Bealey and John Sewel *The Politics of Independence: A Study of a Scottish Town* Aberdeen University Press 1981. A case study of politics and the local political system in Peterhead.

**8406** *Report of HM Inspector of Fire Services for Scotland* HMSO 1950–. An annual Command Paper.

## (2) Local History

**8407** *The Third Statistical Account of Scotland* Oliver and Boyd 1951–53. Since 1958 most of the volumes in this series have been published by Collins. It aims to provide a comprehensive county-by-county survey of modern Scotland in its physical, political, social, religious and economic features. Within this framework most of the volumes offer well-illustrated guides to each parish written in most cases by local ministers or schoolmasters. Work on the series began in 1946 and the first volume appeared in 1951. Many of them, even those published in the 1980s, consist largely of essays written in the 1950s and 1960s which are already mainly of historical interest. In the more recent publications in the series cutbacks have meant that the extensive introductions that featured in the early volumes have had to be foregone. The volumes so far produced are John Strawhorn and William Boyd *Ayrshire* Oliver and Boyd 1951, Alexander Smith *The County of Fife* Oliver and Boyd 1952, Catherine P Snodgrass *The County of East Lothian* Oliver and Boyd 1953, Hugh Mackenzie *The City of Aberdeen* Oliver and Boyd 1953, J Cunnison and J B S Gilfillan (eds) *The City of Glasgow* Collins 1958, Margaret S Dilke and A A Templeton (eds) *The County of Dunbarton* Collins 1959, Henry Hamilton (ed) *The County of Aberdeen* Collins 1960, George Thomson (ed) *The County of Lanark* Collins 1960, Colin M MacDonald (ed) *The County of Argyll* Collins 1961, Henry Hamilton (ed) *The County of Banff* Collins 1961, H A Moisley and A G Thain (eds) *The County of Renfrew and the County of Bute* Collins 1962, George Houston (ed) *The County of Dumfries* Collins 1962, Alexander S Mather (ed) *The County of Ross and Cromarty* Scottish Academic Press 1987, John Laird and D G Ramsay (ed)

*The Stewartry of Kirkcudbright and the County of Wigtown* Collins 1965, David Keir (ed) *The City of Edinburgh* Collins 1966, Henry Hamilton (ed) *The Counties of Moray and Nairn* Collins 1965, R C Rennie and T Crouther Gordon (eds) *The County of Stirling, the County of Clackmannan* Collins 1966, John S Smith (ed) *The County of Caithness* Scottish Academic Press 1988, John S Smith (ed) *The County of Sutherland* Scottish Academic Press 1988, Hilary Kirkland (ed) *Midlothian* Scottish Academic Press 1985, J P B Bulloch and J M Urquhart (eds) *The County of Peebles and the County of Selkirk* Collins 1964, J M Jackson (ed) *The City of Dundee* Herald Press 1979, William Allen Illsley (ed) *The County of Angus* Herald Press 1977, David B Taylor (ed) *The Counties of Perth and Kinross* Culross 1979, Dennis Smith (ed) *The County of Kincardine* Scottish Academic Press 1988, James R Coull (ed) *The County of Shetland* Scottish Academic Press 1985, Ronald Miller (ed) *The County of Orkney* Scottish Academic Press 1985, and Hugh Barron (ed) *The County of Inverness* Scottish Academic Press 1985. At the time of going to press the volumes on Roxburgh, West Lothian and Berwick had still to appear.

**8408**   John Moore *Doon Valley Diary: The Critical Decade 1963–72* Cumnock and Doon Valley District Council 1980. A diary and chronology of industrial decline, and the effects of the Beeching railway cuts and colliery closures on an Ayrshire valley.

**8409·**  Jack House *Dunoon 1868–1968* Dunoon Town Council 1968. A centenary history of the burgh.

**8410**   S J Jones (ed) *Dundee and District* Dundee Local Executive Committee for the British Association for the Advancement of Science 1968. A collection of essays on the climate, agriculture, forestry, hydro-electric power, settlements and population, water supply, architecture, employment and economy, libraries, museums and education system of the region.

**8411**   J A Romanes (ed) *Centenary Souvenir 1859–1959: One Hundred Years of News in Dunfermline and West Fife* Dunfermline Press 1959. A history illustrated by extracts from the *Dunfermline Press*.

**8412**   Edinburgh Branch of the Geographical Association *An Atlas of Edinburgh City* Litho Co 1964. A well-produced atlas mapping a range of social data. J B Barclay (ed) *Looking at Lothian: Monographs on the Economy, Industry, Government, Culture and Services in Edinburgh and Lothian* Royal Scottish Geographical Society 1979 is a good collection of essays produced for the British Association for the Advancement of Science.

**8413**   Sydney G Checkland *The Upas Tree: Glasgow 1875–1975: and after 1975–80* 2nd ed, University of Glasgow Press 1981. A well-regarded history of the city.

See also [8244]. There are essays examining the local climate, economy, demography, urban system and culture in Ronald Miller and Joy Tivy (eds) *The Glasgow Region: A General Survey* Glasgow Local Executive Committee for the British Association for the Advancement of Science 1958. For an impressionistic portrait see Maurice Lindsay *Glasgow* 3rd ed, Hale 1989. The history of a Glasgow suburb is presented in Derek Dow and Michael S Moss *Glasgow's Gain: The Anderston Story* Parthenon Publishing 1986.

**8414**   Colin Milne *The Story of Gourock 1858–1958* Gourock Town Council 1958.

**8415**   Kenneth Mackinnon *Language, Education and Social Processes in a Gaelic Community* Routledge and Kegan Paul 1977. A scholarly sociological study based on field work in Harris in 1972–4. It examines island life, education and language use and language conservation.

**8416**   H Nivet 'Some Hawick Changes Since the Second World War' *Transactions of the Hawick Archaeological Society* 1985 pp 10–25.

**8417**   Derick Thomson and Ian Grimble (eds) *The Future of the Highlands* Routledge and Kegan Paul 1968. A collection of essays on subjects such as land use, language, the economy, literature and administration. Frank Fraser Darling *West Highland Survey: An Essay in Human Ecology* Oxford University Press 1955 is a survey tracing man's response to and influence on the environment. This survey was conducted in 1944–50 and looks at population change, land use, agriculture and society in the region.

**8418**   *The North-East of Scotland: A Survey Prepared for the Aberdeen Meeting of the British Association for the Advancement of Science 1963* Central Press 1963. Essays on climate, the economy, population, administration and education in the region.

**8419**   Tom Steel *The Life and Death of St Kilda: The Moving Story of a Vanished Island Community* revised ed, Fontana 1988. The native population of this remote archipelago were evacuated in 1930. This story does not however end there. It examines the treatment of St Kildans since 1930, the ownership of the islands by the National Trust for Scotland since 1957 and its life as an Ministry of Defence base over the same period.

**8420**   Gordon Donaldson *Isles of Home: Sixty Years of Shetland* Paul Harris 1983. A travelogue and recollection of visits over sixty years. It affectionately records changes to the islands, though rather glosses over the impact of oil.

**8421**   Alan G Oglivie *et al* (eds) *Scientific Survey of South and Eastern Scotland* Edinburgh Local Executive

Committee for the British Association for the Advancement of Science 1951. Essays on climate, the economy, population, transport, and education in the region.

**8422** Duncan Timms (ed) *The Stirling Region* University of Stirling 1974. A collection of essays on climate, the economy, population and education in the region. A local history of social change in Stirling is Tom Lennon *Stirling's Road to Mass Culture: A Local History of Social Change* the author 1979.

**8423** John Butt and George Gordon (eds) *Strathclyde: Changing Horizons* Scottish Academic Press 1985. A collection of essays on local government, new towns, the economy, the quality of life and higher education in the region.

# 15 NORTHERN IRELAND

The literature on Northern Ireland, whatever the overt subject, seems to almost always have a common theme derived from the sectarian conflict that afflicts the Province. This is true not only of the vast literature that this conflict itself has spawned, particularly since the Derry Riots of 1968, but of all other works relating to Northern Ireland in the post-war period. All in some sense are addressing either the root causes, the nature, or ways of managing and attempting to solve the conflict. This makes the task of classifying the literature for bibliographical purposes doubly difficult, particularly in the areas affected by the peculiarly interwoven relationship between religion and politics in the Province. Broadly speaking however precedence has been given to the latter; biographical material on the Rev Ian Paisley for instance thus appears in the section on Unionist biographies.

## A. GENERAL

### (1) Reference Works

**8424** *Social and Economic Trends* HMSO 1975–80. A useful annual guide and selection of statistics.

**8425** *Ulster Year Book* HMSO 1926–38, 1947–. An annual set of essays on the land and people, administration, security, economy and society of Northern Ireland. These are rather bland, if well illustrated, and less palatable aspects of Northern Ireland, such as sectarian conflict and terrorism, are played down. Each volume includes a bibliography.

**8426** Alan Eager *Guide to Irish Bibliographical Material: A Bibliography of Irish Bibliographies and Sources of Information* 2nd ed, Library Association 1980. The most comprehensive modern Irish bibliography is Michael Owen Shannon (ed) *Modern Ireland: A Bibliography on Politics, Planning, Research and Development* Greenwood, Westport, Connecticut 1981. This annotated bibliography concentrates on the Republic but also has a fair coverage of Northern Ireland. The best bibliography on Northern Ireland is Richard R Deutsch

*Northern Ireland: A Select Bibliography* Garland 1975. This has about 1,000 annotated entries and includes a large section on fiction. Bill Rolston *et al* (comps) *A Social Science Bibliography of Northern Ireland 1945–1983: Material Published Since 1945 Relating to Northern Ireland Since 1921* Queens University, Belfast 1987 is extensive but unannotated.

**8427** R J Collett *Northern Ireland Statistics: A Guide to Principal Sources* Department of Library and Information Studies, Queens University, Belfast 1979. A well annotated guide to the publications and the issuing bodies. The main statistical series is the twice yearly *Digest of Statistics, Northern Ireland* HMSO 1954–.

**8428** Richard R Deutsch and Vivian Magowan *Northern Ireland 1968–1974: A Chronology of Events* 3v, Blackstaff 1973–75. The first volume covers 1968–71, the second 1972–73 and the final volume 1974. This is a day-to-day account of events compiled from press reports, radio and television bulletins and other sources which provides an invaluable reference work. See also Pauline M Chakeres *Developments in Northern Ireland 1968–1976* Congressional Research Services, Library of Congress, Washington DC 1976.

**8429** *Who's Who, What's What and Where in Ireland* Geoffrey Chapman 1973. A guide to leading figures, groups, institutions and places in both the North and the South.

**8430** *Northern Ireland Statutes* HMSO 1922–. An annual publication of the details of all the legislation recently brought into force in Northern Ireland. After the suspension of the Stormont parliament in 1972 the laws issued in 1972–3 were Orders in Council which had the effect of Northern Ireland legislation under the Northern Ireland (Temporary Provisions) Act 1972. In 1974 this publication lists the measures of the Northern Ireland Assembly. Since then legislation for Northern Ireland has again been by Orders in Council under Schedule 1 of the Northern Ireland Act 1974. For a general guide to Northern Ireland legislation see *Chronological Table of the Statutes: Northern Ireland* 19th ed, HMSO 1987. This covers the legislation of Irish parliaments from

1310 to the law as it was in effect at 31st December 1986. This guide is complemented by *Index to the Statutes: Northern Ireland Covering the Legislation to 31 December 1984* 18th ed, HMSO 1986.

**8431**   *Index to the Statutory Rules and Orders of Northern Ireland in Force on 31st December 1982 Showing the Statutory Powers under which they are made* 16th ed, HMSO 1983. The latest issue published.

**8432**   *Northern Ireland Parliamentary Publications* Trans- Media Publishing Co, Oceana Group 1975. This consists of 86 reels of microfilm covering papers of the Northern Ireland Commons and Senate, Command Papers, Commons and Senate journals, and Commons and Senate debates 1922–72. The standard published guide to the Northern Ireland official publications of all kinds is *Consolidated List of Publications 1st January 1938 to 31st December 1947* HMSO 1948, continued by *Supplementary List of Publications* 1948–60, *Government of Northern Ireland Publications* 1961–65 and *Annual List of Publications* 1966–.

**8433**   Arthur Maltby *The Government of Northern Ireland 1922–72: A Catalogue and Breviate of Parliamentary Papers* Irish University Press, Dublin 1979. A well annotated guide. It also lists serial publications.

### (2) General Histories

**8434**   D G Boyce *The Irish Question and British Politics 1868–1986* Macmillan 1988. A good study of continuity and change in a major political issue over a long historical perspective. Patrick Buckland *The Northern Ireland Question 1886–1986* Historical Association 1987 is a good short textbook.

**8435**   T W Moody *The Ulster Question 1603–1973* Mercier Press, Cork 1974. A concise summary concentrating on the 1970s. Liam De Paor *Divided Ulster* 2nd ed, Penguin is a good short history of the Province since the seventeenth century.

**8436**   J J Lee *Ireland 1912–1985: Politics and Society* Cambridge University Press 1985. The standard history of Ireland in the twentieth century. Frank Gallagher *The Indivisible Island: The History of the Partition of Ireland* Gollancz 1957. An Irish journalist's history of the partition of Ireland from 1921 to the 1950s. Another study of the experience of partition is Richard W Mansbach *Northern Ireland: Half a Century of Partition* Facts on File, New York 1973.

**8437**   Tom Wilson *Ulster, Conflict and Consent* Blackwell 1989. The best general history of Northern Ireland. See also Patrick Buckland *History of Northern Ireland*

Gill and Macmillan, Dublin 1981 and David Harkness *Northern Ireland Since 1920* Helicon, Dublin 1983. Hugh Shearman *Northern Ireland 1921–1971* HMSO 1971 is an offical illustrated history. Martin Wallace *Northern Ireland: Fifty Years of Self-Government* David and Charles 1971 concentrates on the experience of devolution. John Biggs-Davidson *The Hand is Red* Johnson 1973 is an interpretation of Northern Ireland's history and contemporary situation by a Catholic who was a Conservative MP in England and played a prominent part in the debates on the future of Northern Ireland in the early 1970s, favouring the total integration of the Province into the United Kingdom. Gary MacEoin *Northern Ireland: Captive of History* Holt, Rinehart and Watson, New York 1974 examines the historical background to the situation in Northern Ireland but concentrates on the events of 1968–73.

**8438**   Thomas Wilson (ed) *Ulster Under Home Rule: A Study of the Political and Economic Problems of Northern Ireland* Oxford University Press 1955. A collection of essays assessing the experience of Northern Ireland in law and constitution, political parties, defence, the economy, public finance, partition and devolution.

**8439**   Geoffrey Bell *The British in Ireland* Pluto 1984. A Left-Wing critique covering the period from the foundation of the government of Northern Ireland as part of the United Kingdom in 1921 to the 1980s.

**8440**   Paul Arthur and Keith Jeffery *Northern Ireland Since 1968* Blackwell 1988. The best short account of the recent troubled history of Northern Ireland, dealing with the issues such as the social and economic background, nationalist and unionist politics, security and American involvement in a thematic fashion. It includes an outline chronology. Michael Farrell (ed) *Twenty Years On* Brandon 1988 is a series of reflections on the 'Troubles', largely from a Republican perspective.

**8441**   Charles Townsend (ed) *Consensus in Ireland: Approaches and Recessions* Clarendon 1988. A major survey of the nature of the Irish problem, particularly in the context of the 'Troubles' since 1968. Essays examine the varying interpretations of the problem, the responses of the Catholic and Protestant communities and the policy options available. Most writing on the problem focuses on the sectarian and military dimension. Paul Teague (ed) *Beyond the Rhetoric: Politics, the Economy and Social Policy in Northern Ireland* Lawrence and Wishart 1987 attempts to look instead at the underlying social and economic conditions that help to fuel it in a weak economy and a society which has some of the worst poverty in Europe. See also Paul Bew, Peter Gibbon and Henry Patterson *The State in Northern Ireland 1921–1972: Political Forces and Social Classes* Manchester University Press 1979. Alan J Ward (ed) *Northern Ireland: Living with the Crisis* Praeger, New

York 1987 looks more at the impact of the 'Troubles' on the economy, the churches, the legal system, the electorate and on literature. Denis P Barritt and Charles F Carter *The Northern Ireland Problem: A Study of Group Relations* 2nd ed, Oxford University Press 1972, long the standard work on society and politics in Northern Ireland, also remains a useful interpretative study.

## B. POLITICAL HISTORY

### (1) General

**8442** William D Flackes *Northern Ireland: A Political Directory 1968–1983* BBC 1983. A concise alphabetically arranged guide to political and quasi-political, paramilitary and politico- religious organizations, their activities and the persons associated with them. It also includes a chronology, and a guide to election results and security arrangements as well as an extensive range of statistics.

**8443** *Northern Ireland Political Literature 1968–1975* Irish Microforms n.d. (1976?). A microfiche catalogue.

**8444** Paul Arthur *Government and Politics of Northern Ireland* Longman 1980. The best general survey.

**8445** P O'Malley *The Uncivil Wars: Ireland Today* Blackstaff 1983. A collection of interviews with Irish politicians of all shades of opinion.

**8446** Liam O'Dowd, Bill Rolston and Mike Tomlinson 'From Labour to the Tories: The Ideology of Containment in Northern Ireland' *Capital and Class* 18 1982 72–90. This argues that there is a bipartisan consensus on Northern Ireland with both the major British parties agreed on the need to contain terrorism within certain bounds and to seek political solutions. Labour policy on Ireland is critically assessed in a committed study by a supporter of Irish unification in Geoffrey Bell *Troublesome Business: The Labour Party and the Irish Question* Pluto 1982. A perspective on Labour's attitude to Ireland earlier in the century is offered in B Stubbs 'The Attitude of the British Labour Party to the "Irish Question" 1906–51' London MPhil Thesis 1974.

### (2) Administrative History

#### (a) General

**8447** Derek Birrell and Alan Murie *Policy and Government in Northern Ireland: Lessons of Devolution* Gill and Macmillan, Dublin 1980. A useful study of the evolution of Northern Ireland administration since devolution with a good bibliography.

**8448** Reginald J Lawrence *The Government of Northern Ireland: Public Finance and Public Services 1921–1964* Clarendon 1965. A study of the administration of all aspects of Northern Ireland government under devolution. Local government, law-making, parliament and government in Northern Ireland are examined in Edwin Rhodes (ed) *Public Administration and Northern Ireland* Magee University College 1967.

**8449** Paul Bew and Henry Patterson *The British State and the Ulster Crisis: From Wilson to Thatcher* Verso 1986. An examination of the handling of the conflict in Northern Ireland and attempts to contain or defuse it by successive British governments since the 1960s. British management of the Irish situation over a longer perspective since partition and devolution is examined in outline in Martin Wallace *British Government in Northern Ireland: From Devolution to Direct Rule* David and Charles 1982. Liam O'Dowd, Bill Rolston and Mike Tomlinson *Northern Ireland: Between Civil Rights and Civil War* CSE Books 1980 is a Left-Wing critique of Britain's role and policy in the province. See also Bob Rowthorn and Naomi Wayne *Northern Ireland: The Political Economy of Conflict* Polity 1988 and Brian Crozier 'Ulster: Politics and Terrorism' *Conflict Studies* 36 1978 pp 1–20.

**8450** Paul Arthur 'Devolution as Administrative Convenience: A Case Study of Northern Ireland' *Parliamentary Affairs* 30 1977 pp 97–106. An appraisal of devolution as a means of managing Northern Ireland. The financial relationship between Stormont and London is also assessed in A J Green *Devolution and Public Finance: Stormont from 1926 to 1971* Centre for the Study of Public Policy 48, University of Strathclyde 1979. See also C E B Brett 'The Lessons of Devolution in Northern Ireland' *Political Quarterly* 41 1970 pp 261–80.

**8451** Derek Birrell 'The Stormont-Westminster Relationship' *Parliamentary Affairs* 26 1972–73 pp 471–91. On the representation of Northern Ireland at Westminster see R J Lawrence 'Northern Ireland at Westminster' *Parliamentary Affairs* 20 1966–67 pp 90–6.

**8452** D C Watt (ed) *The Constitution of Northern Ireland* Heinemann 1981. A useful collection of essays on Northern Ireland and its constitutional relations with the United Kingdom.

**8453** Richard Rose *Governing Without Consensus: An Irish Perspective* Faber 1971. A good and detailed analysis of the failings of policy and political management in the 1960s. James Callaghan *A House Divided: The Dilemma of Northern Ireland* Collins 1973 is an autobiographical account of the problem of managing the situation in Northern Ireland as Home Secretary at the end of the 1960s as the Unionist dominated Stormont lost control of the situation and the decision was taken, in 1969, to send the troops in. It is indispensable to those seeking to understand the initial British response to and handling of the 'Troubles'.

**8454** *A Record of Constructive Change* HMSO 1971. The record of progress as viewed by the Northern Ireland government since the beginning of the tentative reform under the Premiership of Terence O'Neill.

**8455** Henry Kelly *How Stormont Fell* Gill and Macmillan, Dublin 1972. A vivid instant history of the end of the Stormont parliament and the imposition of direct rule in March 1972.

**8456** D R S Gallagher 'The Failure of Attempts to Solve the Northern Ireland Problem 1972–80' Queen's University, Belfast PhD Thesis 1984. A review of efforts since the suspension of Stormont and the creation of the Northern Ireland Office to build consensus under successive Secretaries of State, based on extensive interviewing. The failure of these initiatives is seen as the result of the lack of willingness to compromise in Ulster. The failure of the first initiative after the setting up of the Northern Ireland Office under William Whitelaw is assessed in V Rajan 'A Critique of the Concept of Mediation in Political Conflict with Particular Reference to the 'Whitelaw Period' of the Northern Ireland Crisis 1972–73' London PhD Thesis 1976. The subsequent failure of the power-sharing executive that had been established is assessed in Ian McAllister 'The Legitimacy of Opposition: The Collapse of the 1974 Northern Ireland Executive' *Eire-Ireland* 12 1977 pp 25–42. The strike by the Ulster Workers' Council that brought the executive's demise and the resumption of direct rule in May 1974 is examined in the extravagantly and misleadingly titled book by Robert Fisk, *The Point of No Return: The Strike which broke the British in Ulster* Times Books 1975. By then Labour had come to power in February 1974 and Merlyn Rees became Northern Ireland Secretary (and from 1976–9 Home Secretary). He reflects on his period of responsibility in his *Northern Ireland: A Personal Perspective* Methuen 1985. For his views on taking up the seals of office see his 'Northern Ireland 1974' *Contemporary Review* 224 1974 pp 57–63.

(b) Civil Service

**8457** Derek Birrell 'The Northern Ireland Civil Service: From Devolution to Direct Rule' *Public Administration* 56 1978 pp 305–19. A general history from the creation of Northern Ireland in 1921.

**8458** John A Oliver *Working at Stormont* Institute of Public Administration, Dublin 1978. A memoir of his work as a Northern Ireland civil servant, in which he rose to be Permanent Secretary of the Ministry of Development 1971–4.

### (3) Political Parties

**8459** Ian McAllister and Sarah Nelson 'The Modern Development of the Northern Party System' *Parliamentary Affairs* 30 1979 pp 271–316. See also Ian McAllister *Territorial Differences and Party Development in Northern Ireland* Centre for the Study of Public Policy 66, University of Strathclyde 1980.

(a) Unionists

**8460** Frank Wright 'Protestant Ideology and Politics in Ulster' *European Journal of Sociology* 14 1973 pp 213–80. The most complete study of the political vehicle of Ulster Protestantism is John F Harbinson *The Ulster Unionist Party 1882–1973: Its Development and Organisation* Blackstaff 1973. The fragmentation of the Unionists since the 1960s is examined in Michael Distin *The Development of a Party Competition among Unionists in Ulster 1966–82* Centre for the Study of Public Policy, University of Strathclyde 1984.

**8461** John Whyte 'Intra-Unionist Disputes in the Northern Ireland House of Commons 1921–1972' *Economic and Social Review* 5 1974 pp 99–104.

**8462** Norah Bradford *A Sword Bathed in Heaven: The Life, Faith and Cruel Death of Rev Robert Bradford BTh MP* Pickering and Inglis 1984. A biography by his wife of the Methodist minister who was Unionist MP for South Belfast 1974–81 until his assassination.

**8463** David Bleakley *Faulkner: Conflict and Consent in Irish Politics* Mowbrays 1974. A generally sympathetic portrait by a political colleague of the last Prime Minister of Northern Ireland 1971–2, who also served as the only Chief Executive of the Northern Ireland Assembly in January–May 1974. It includes several speeches in the appendix. Andrew Boyd *Faulkner and the Crisis of Ulster Unionism* Anvil Books, Tralee 1972 is a critical biography. John Houston has also edited Brian Faulkner's memoirs which were published posthumously as *Memoir of a Statesman* Weidenfeld and Nicolson 1978.

**8464** Terence O'Neill *The Autobiography of Terence O'Neill: Prime Minster of Northern Ireland 1963–1969* Hart-Davis 1972. See also the volume of speeches from the years 1964–9, Terence O'Neill *Ulster at the Crossroads* Faber 1969.

**8465** Steve Bruce *God Save Ulster: The Religion and Politics of Paisleyism* Oxford University Press 1986. The first part of this valuable book examines the career of Ian Paisley, from being the minister of a breakaway Presbyterian church reacting against ecumenism and secularism in the 1950s to the leadership of the Democratic Unionist Party he founded in the 1970s. The second part is a sociological analysis of the Free Presbyterian Church he founded. On Paisleyism see also Roy Wallis, Steve Bruce and David Taylor 'Ethnicity and Evangelicalism: Ian Paisley and Protestant Politics in Ulster' *Comparative Studies in Society and History* 29 1987 pp 293–313. The links between Paisley's Protestantism and the DUP are further explored in David Taylor 'The Lord's Battle: An Ethnographic and Social Study of Paisleyism in Northern Ireland' Queen's University, Belfast PhD Thesis 1983 and A C Smith 'The Ulster Democratic Unionist Party: A Case Study in Political and Religious Convergence' Queen's University, Belfast PhD Thesis 1984.

**8466** Clifford Smyth *Ian Paisley: Voice of Protestant Ulster* Scottish Academic Press 1988. Paisley, founded his own Free Presbyterian Church in the 1950s and his own Democratic Unionist Party twenty years later. He has been an MP since 1970, which he has more recently combined with membership of the European Parliament (he was also an MP at Stormont 1970–2). This biographical study by a former member of the DUP has useful insights on Paisley's attitudes and character. Another useful study is E Moloney and A Pollak *Paisley* Poolbeg Press 1986. Patrick Morrison *Paisley: Man of Wrath* Anvil Books, Tralee 1973 is a critical biography by an Ulster Catholic. There are some interesting insights in Owen Dudley Edwards 'A Look at the Reverend Ian Paisley' *Nusight* May 1970 pp 11–16.

### (b) Nationalists

**8467** Clive Hedges 'Problems in Combining Labour and Nationalist Politics: Irish Nationalists in Northern Ireland' in R J Johnston, David B Knight and Eleonore Kofman (eds) *Nationalism, Self-Determination and Political Geography* Croom Helm 1988 pp 102–15. In contrast to its rather Right-Wing character in the interwar years Nationalism in the post-war period has increasingly identified itself with socialist perspectives.

**8468** J T Greene 'The Comparative Development of the SDLP and Sinn Fein 1972–85' Queen's University, Belfast MSSc Thesis 1986. A study of the competition between constitutional and revolutionary nationalists for the support of the Catholic communities.

**8469** Ian McAllister *The Northern Ireland Social Democratic and Labour Party: Political Opposition in a Divided Society* Macmillan 1977. A study of the constitutional nationalist party founded in the 1970s. McAllister has also examined its precursor in his 'Political Opposition in Northern Ireland: The National Democratic Party 1965–70' *Economic and Social Review* 6 1975 pp 353–66.

**8470** Bernadette Devlin *The Price of My Soul* Pan 1969. A leader in the Civil Rights Movement of the late 1960s Devlin won the Mid-Ulster by-election to the British parliament in 1969. This autobiographical essay reflects many of the concerns about discrimination against and the denial of civil rights to the Catholics. See also Claudia Dreifus 'St Joan of the Bogside: An Interview with Bernadette Devlin' *Evergreen Review* 15 1971 pp 25–9, 50–2. G W Target *Bernadette: The Story of Bernadette Devlin* Hodder and Stoughton 1975 is an unsympathetic and partisan biography.

**8471** Barry White *John Hume: Statesman of the Troubles* Blackstaff 1984. A biography of the leader of the SDLP since 1979. Hume was a Northern Ireland MP 1969–73 and has been a member of all the successor bodies to the Stormont parliament. He has been an MP in the UK parliament since 1983.

### (c) Other

**8472** Ian McAllister and Brian Wilson 'Bi-Confessionalism in a Confessional Party System: The Northern Ireland Alliance Party' *Economic and Social Review* 9 1978 pp 207–25. The Alliance Party studied here is the only party in Northern Ireland which is not in a sense also the political representation of either the Protestant or Catholic communities and is consciously non-sectarian.

**8473** G S Walker 'The Commonwealth Labour Party in Northern Ireland 1942–7' *Irish Historical Studies* 24 1984 pp 69–91. The Commonwealth Labour Party was formed by a split from the Northern Ireland Labour Party. Walker has also written a biographical study of the architect of this split, *The Politics of Frustration: Harry Midgeley and the Failure of Labour in Northern Ireland* Manchester University Press 1985. Midgeley became leader of the Northern Ireland Labour Party in the 1930s. In 1938–42 he was faced with increasing opposition from the party and in 1942 left to form the Commonwealth Labour Party, serving in Brookeborough's wartime coalition. In 1947 he joined the Unionists and served as Minister of Education 1950–7. This good study uses political biography to cast light upon the nature of Northern Irish politics in this period.

**8474** John F Harbinson 'A History of the Northern Ireland Labour Party 1891–1949' Queen's University,

Belfast MSc Thesis 1966. The history of the party is continued in J A V Graham 'The Consensus-Forming Strategy of the Northern Ireland Labour Party 1949–68' Queen's University, Belfast 1972. See also G F Rutan 'The Labour Party in Ulster: Opposition by Cartel' *Review of Politics* 29 1967 pp 526–31.

### (4) Electoral History

**8475**  Sydney Elliott *Northern Ireland Parliamentary Election Results 1921–1972* Political Reference Publications 1979. A valuable reference guide to results constituency-by-constituency.

**8476**  Sydney Elliott 'The Electoral System in Northern Ireland Since 1920' Queen's University, Belfast PhD Thesis 1971–2. Electoral sociology and geography in Northern Ireland is also analysed in R D Osborne 'The Political System, Voting Patterns and Voting Behaviour in Northern Ireland 1921–1974' Queen's University, Belfast PhD Thesis 1977.

**8477**  A D Blackburn 'Northern Ireland Electoral Law 1921–1972: The Question of Discrimination' Queen's University, Belfast LLM Thesis 1981. A study of whether or not the Stormont electoral system was weighted in favour of Protestants.

**8478**  L E Dutter 'The Structure of Vote Preferences: The 1921, 1925, 1973 and 1975 Northern Irish Parliamentary Elections' *Comparative Political Studies* 14 1982 pp 517–42. A study of continuity and change in the Northern Ireland electoral system.

**8479**  F W Boal and R H Buchanan 'The 1969 Northern Ireland Election' *Irish Geography* 6 1969 pp 78–84. A study of an important election held at the height of the Civil Rights Movement.

**8480**  Roger Scott 'The 1970 British General Election in Ulster' *Parliamentary Affairs* 24 1970–71 pp 16–32.

**8481**  M J Laver 'On Introducing STV and Interpreting the Results: The Case of Northern Ireland 1973–1975' *Parliamentary Affairs* 29 1976 pp 211–29. The single transferable vote was introduced in the Province in 1973 for the elections for the Northern Ireland Assembly. This article assesses its impact on the entrenched voting system in Ulster.

**8482**  R J Lawrence and Sydney Elliott *The Northern Ireland Border Poll 1973* Cmnd 5875, *Parliamentary Papers* xxviii 1974–75. A study of the border plebiscite which resulted in a vote in favour of continued membership of the United Kingdom.

**8483**  Reginald J Lawrence, Sydney Elliott and M J Laver *The Northern Ireland General Election of 1973* Cmnd 5851, *Parliamentary Papers* xxviii 1974–75. A study of the elections for the Northern Ireland Assembly and their political background. See also James Knight *Northern Ireland: The Elections of 1973* Arthur McDougall Fund 1974.

**8484**  Ian McAllister *The 1975 Northern Ireland General Election* Survey Research Centre Occasional Paper 14, University of Strathclyde 1975. A study of the election held for the Constitutional Convention held in May 1975. See also James Knight *Northern Ireland: The Election of the Constitutional Convention* Arthur McDougall Fund 1975.

**8485**  Sydney Elliott and R A Wilford *The 1982 Northern Ireland Assembly Election* Centre for the Study of Public Policy 119, University of Strathclyde 1983. A study of the election for the restored Northern Ireland Assembly.

**8486**  Michael Distin 'Official or Democratic? The Battle for Unionist Votes in Northern Ireland' Strathclyde PhD Thesis 1986. This study concludes that the competition for unionist votes that has developed since the early 1970s reflects profound cleavages in an embattled Protestant community over the importance and use of politics in securing the goals of that community.

### (5) Parliaments and Assemblies

**8487**  *Parliamentary Debates: House of Commons Official Report* 54v, HMSO 1921–72. The volumes of the debates of the Northern Ireland Commons. The debates of the Northern Ireland upper house are contained in *Parliamentary Debates: The Senate Official Report* 56v, HMSO 1921–72.

**8488**  *Official Report of the Debates: Northern Ireland Assembly* 4v, HMSO 1973–86. Volumes 1 to 3 cover the original assembly of 1973–74. The final volume covers the assembly of 1982–86.

**8489**  *Report of the Debates: Northern Ireland Constitutional Convention* HMSO 1975. The report of the debates held at the Convention between 8 May and 7 November 1975.

**8490**  P F McGill 'The Senate in Northern Ireland' Queen's University, Belfast PhD Thesis 1965. A study of the upper house in the Northern Ireland parliament.

**8491**  Cornelius O'Leary, Sydney Elliott and R A Wilford *The Northern Ireland Assembly 1982–1986: A Constitutional Experiment* Christopher Hurst 1988. A study of the background, establishment, operation and eventual breakdown over the Anglo-Irish Agreement of the Assembly. See also P D H Smyth 'The Northern Ireland Assembly 1982–86: The Failure of an Experiment' *Parliamentary Affairs* 40 1987 pp 482–500. The work of the Assembly committees set up to scrutinize the operation of the Northern Ireland government is assessed in Alan J Greer 'The Northern Ireland Assembly and Accountability of Government: The Statutory Committees 1982–1986' *Parliamentary Affairs* 40 1987 pp 98–113.

## C. SECTARIAN CONFLICT

### (1) General

**8492** Myron J Smith Jr *The Secret Wars: A Guide to Sources in English Vol 3: International Terrorism 1968–1980* ABC- Clio 1980. An unannotated bibliography with a useful chronology. Although international in flavour it contains plenty of material on Northern Ireland.

**8493** Robert A Friedlander *Terrorism: Documents of International and Local Control* 4v, Oceana Publications, New York 1979–84. An international collection. Volume one contains a number of United Nations reports and international anti-terrorist agreements and documents on Northern Ireland. The third volume contains documents on the Prevention of Terrorism Acts, other anti-terrorist legislation and judgments of the European Court of Human Rights in Northern Ireland cases.

**8494** John Magee *Northern Ireland: Crisis and Conflict* Routledge and Kegan Paul 1974. A collection of documents on the subject from the plantation in the seventeenth century to the 'Troubles', concentrating on the most recent period.

**8495** Charles Carlton (ed) *Bigotry and Blood: Documents on the Ulster Troubles* Nelson-Hall, Chicago 1977. A collection of contemporary documents, incorporating the views on the situation of several principal actors. A more general collection of documents is A C Hepburn (ed) *The Conflict of Nationality in Modern Ireland* Arnold 1980.

**8496** William H Van Voris *Violence in Ulster: An Oral Documentary* University of Massachusetts Press, Amherst 1975. This presents the views of hundreds of people, including leading politicians, protagonists and ordinary people on both sides of the conflict. The excerpts are arranged chronologically over the period 1943–72. There is also a good bibliography. Another collection of oral accounts of the conflict is Alf McGeary *Survivors: A Documentary Account of the Victims of Northern Ireland* Beekman Books 1977.

**8497** John P Darby *Conflict in Northern Ireland: The Development of a Polarised Community* Gill and Macmillan, Dublin 1976. A comprehensive study of the factors that have contributed to sectarian polarization, especially demographic trends, housing, education and unemployment, in the course of the twentieth century. The background to the 'Troubles' is also examined in John P Darby (ed) *Northern Ireland: The Background to the Conflict* Appletree 1983. Andrew Boyd *Holy War in Belfast: A History of the Troubles in Northern Ireland* 2nd ed, Anvil Books, Tralee 1970 is a general history of sectarian violence in the Province since the nineteenth century. An even longer perspective, since the settlement of Protestants in the seventeenth century, is used in A T Q Stewart *The Narrow Ground: The Roots of Conflict in Ulster* 2nd ed, Faber 1989. See also Donald P Doumitt *Conflict in Northern Ireland: The History, the Problems and the Challenge* Peter Lang 1985 and A Milnor *Politics, Violence and Social Change in Northern Ireland* Cornell University Press, Albany, New York 1976. The ideology of sectarianism is examined in P S Chartkow 'Orangeism and Republicanism 1948–1972: A Study of Two Ideologically Opposed Movements in Irish Politics' London PhD Thesis 1974–6. The religious dimension is analysed in John Hickey *Religion and the Northern Ireland Problem* Gill and Macmillan, Dublin 1984, Gary Easthope 'The IRA and the Changing Tactics of Terrorism' *Political Quarterly* 47 1976 pp 425–37 and Paul Bew and Henry Patterson 'The Protestant-Catholic Conflict in Ulster' *Journal of International Affairs* 36 1982–83 pp 223–34.

**8498** Kevin Kelley *The Longest War: Northern Ireland and the IRA* Zed Books 1982. This account by an American journalist makes little attempt at presenting a balanced view of the sectarian conflict in the Province. It is however useful on the IRA and their tactics. A Protestant view of the defence of the Province against republican violence in the period 1921–66 by a former member of the Ulster Special Constabulary (the B-Specials) is Wallace Clark *Guns in Ulster* Northern Whig 1967. This includes a foreword by the former Northern Ireland Prime Minister Lord Brookeborough.

**8499** Keith Jeffery (ed) *The Divided Province: The Troubles in Northern Ireland 1969–1985* Orbis 1985. A useful collection of essays on political violence in Northern Ireland since the start of the 'Troubles'. See also Taylor Downing (ed) *The Troubles* 2nd ed, Thames/Macdonald Futura 1982. Jack Holland *Too Long a Sacrifice: Life and Death in Northern Ireland Since 1969* Dodd Mead 1981 is an overview of the history of the 'Troubles'. Peter Jenke *Ulster: A Decade of Violence* Institute for the Study of Conflict, London 1979 is a short paper on the 'Troubles' since the troops were sent in to the Province in 1969.

**8500** F W Boal and J H N Douglas (eds) *Integration and Division: Geographical Perspectives and the Northern Ireland Problem* Academic Press 1982. Perspectives on the spatial, and social polarization between the Catholic and Protestant communities and the geography of political violence 1969–77, in the context of studies of demography, political geography, regional policy, housing, unemployment, religion and political violence.

**8501** Peter Jenke and D L Price *Ulster: Consensus and Coercion* Conflict Studies 50, Institute for the Study of Conflict 1974. The first part of this paper examines the failure of the power-sharing executive and the return to direct rule. The second examines the pressure the security forces were bringing to bear, in the early 1970s, on the Provisional IRA's urban network.

**8502** Kenneth Heskin *Northern Ireland: A Psychological Analysis* Gill and Macmillan, Dublin 1980. A study of the interrelation of the communities in Northern Ireland, the psychological barriers in the way of integration and the psychological effects of a decade of civil conflict.

**8503** Yonah Alexander and Alan O'Day (eds) *Terrorism in Ireland* Croom Helm 1983. A collection of essays examining its roots, its effect on women, political assassination, the international dimension and the role of North American support for terrorism in Ireland, and the psychology of terrorism.

**8504** Richard B Finnegan 'The United Kingdom's Security Policy and IRA Terrorism in Ulster' *Eire-Ireland* 23 1988 pp 87–110. A study of the management and course of the conflict. It is particularly useful on developments in the strategy of the authorities and the IRA since the 1960s. Paul Wilkinson (ed) *British Perspectives on Terrorism* Allen and Unwin 1981 is a good collection of essays mainly devoted to terrorism in Northern Ireland and its containment. It includes essays on the politics and propaganda of the IRA, public attitudes to the IRA, the management of terrorism by British police and the risks of kidnapping. The dynamics of terrorism 1968–80 and the efforts to control insurgency are examined in A McLung Lee *Terrorism in Northern Ireland* General Hall 1983. The different Catholic and Protestant views of security forces policy in Northern Ireland are examined in Ronald Weitzer 'Contested Order: The Struggle over British Security Policy in Northern Ireland' *Comparative Politics* 19 1987 pp 281–98.

**8505** New Ireland Forum *The Cost of Violence Arising from the Northern Ireland Crisis Since 1969* Stationery Office, Dublin 1983. An Irish government analysis of the costs incurred by the UK as a result of the 'Troubles'.

**8506** J McGarrity *Resistance: The Story of the Struggle in British Occupied Ireland* Irish Freedom Press 1957. A partisan view of sectarian struggle in Northern Ireland.

**8507** A J Barker *Bloody Ulster* Ballantine 1973. A journalistic account of the beginnings of the 'Troubles' and their background. Another useful journalistic account is the Sunday Times Insight Team *Ulster* 3rd ed, Penguin 1972. See also Simon Winchester *In Holy Terror* Faber 1974.

**8508** Ian Budge and Cornelius O'Leary *Belfast: Approach to Crisis – A Study of Belfast Politics 1613–1970* Macmillan 1973. A study of the historical background and immediate context of the beginnings of the 'Troubles' in Ulster's capital.

**8509** Eamonn MacCann *War and an Irish Town* Penguin 1974. A review of the Civil Rights Movement (by a leading participant) and the origins of the 'Troubles' in Londonderry from a Marxist and Republican perspective. Russell Stetler *The Battle of Bogside: The Politics of Violence in Northern Ireland* Sheed and Ward 1970 is a brief social and economic background to the 'Troubles', especially in Londonderry. Seamus Brady *Arms and the Men: Ireland in Turmoil* Seamus Brady, Wicklow 1972 is a personal account of the origins of the 'Troubles' in Londonderry. G W Target *Unholy Smoke* Hodder and Stoughton 1969 is a Protestant view of the August 1969 riots in Londonderry. Clive Limpkin *The Battle of the Bogside* Penguin 1972 is a photographic record of Derry life 1969–72.

**8510** Martin Dillon and Denis Lehane *Political Murder in Northern Ireland* Penguin 1973. A controversial account of political assassinations 1972–3. The changing pattern of terrorist murders in the Province in 1969–84 is reviewed in R M Pockrass 'Terroristic Murder in Northern Ireland: Who is Killed and Why?' *Terrorism: An International Journal* 9 1987 pp 341–59. See also Russell Murray 'Killings of Local Security Forces in Northern Ireland 1969–1981' *Terrorism* 7 1984 pp 11–52 and Richard N Lebow 'The Origins of Sectarian Assassination: The Case of Belfast' *Journal of International Affairs* 7 1978 pp 43–62.

**8511** Brian Gibson *The Birmingham Bombs* Rose 1976. An instant history of the Birmingham pub bombings of 1974.

**8512** B Loftus 'Images in Conflict: Visual Imagery and the Troubles in Northern Ireland (1968–1981)' Keele PhD Thesis 1982. A study of the imagery and art which the conflict has spawned, from the murals produced by both communities to the art of the official posters designed to help combat terrorism or to help recruit for the security forces.

## (2) Official Reports

**8513** *Report of the Enquiry into Allegations Against the Security Forces of Physical Brutality in Northern Ireland Arising out of Events on the 9th August 1971* Cmnd 4823, *Parliamentary Papers* xxxii 1971–72. A report by Sir Edmund Compton which argues that the security forces used physical ill treatment but not brutality.

**8514** *Report of the Tribunal Appointed to Inquire into the Events of Sunday 30th January 1972 which led to Loss of Life in Connection with the Procession in Londonderry on that Day* HC Paper 220, *Parliamentary Papers* xxxii 1971–72. An inquiry conducted by Lord Widgery into the circumstances that led to thirteen people being killed by the army on what became known as Bloody Sunday. Widgery found that the event was inevitable in the circumstances in which the army was attacked first and argued that therefore standing orders on when to open fire could not be changed without risking soldiers' lives.

**8515** *Report of an Inquiry by HM Chief Inspector of Prisons into the Security Arrangements at HM Prison, Maze Relative to the Escape on Sunday Sept 25 1983 including Relevant Recommendations for the Improvement of Security at HM Prison Maze* HC Paper 203, *Parliamentary Papers* 1983–84. A report into the security implications of a break-out of convicted terrorists from the Maze.

## (3) The American Connection

**8516** Jack Holland *The American Connection: United States Guns, Money and Influence in Northern Ireland* Viking 1987. An impressive study of the importance of supporters and sympathizers with the republican cause in the USA to the struggle in Northern Ireland, their links with republican organizations in the Province and their various activities. These organizations and their influence upon the American government are also analysed in Dennis Clark *Irish Blood, Northern Ireland and American Conscience* Kennikat, Port Washington 1977. On American public response to the Northern Ireland situation see also Francis M Carroll *American Opinion and the Irish Question* Gill and Macmillan, Dublin 1978 and Joseph E Thompson 'United States- Northern Ireland Relations' *World Affairs* 146 1984 pp 318–39.

## (4) The Civil Rights Movement

**8517** Max Hastings *Ulster 1969: The Fight for Civil Rights in Northern Ireland* Gollancz 1970. A journalist's account of the Civil Rights Movement in Ulster 1963–9.

The background to the Civil Rights Movement is examined in Mary Turner 'Social Democrats and Northern Ireland 1964–1970: The Origins of the Present Struggle' *Monthly Review* 30 1978 pp 30–45.

**8518** *We Shall Overcome: The History of the Struggle for Civil Rights in Northern Ireland 1968–78* Northern Ireland Civil Rights Association n.d. (1978?).

**8519** M M Morgan 'The Civil Rights Movement: A Reinterpretation' Queens' University, Belfast MSSc Thesis 1984. A study of the Civil Rights Movement 1968–70. It argues that the conventional view that it was highly structured, had a clearly defined base, a strong sense of discipline and was led by identifiable Catholic elites is almost completely the opposite of the truth.

**8520** Paul Arthur *The People's Democracy 1968–1973* Blackstaff 1974. People's Democracy was a Left-Wing students' movement, espousing the tactics pursued elsewhere during a time of international student unrest. Arthur was a participant and here describes the progress of its political aims which derived from the Civil Rights Movement. See also J Comerford 'The Dynamics of a Radical Movement in Northern Ireland Politics: The People's Democracy' Strathclyde MSc Thesis 1972–3.

## (5) The Catholic Community

**8521** Christopher Hewitt 'Catholic Grievances, Catholic Nationalism and Violence in Northern Ireland During the Civil Rights Period' *British Journal of Sociology* 32 1981 pp 362–80.

**8522** E Fairweather, R McDonough and H McFadyean *Only the Rivers Run Free: Northern Ireland: The Women's War* Pluto 1984. An insight into the experience of women in Catholic communities on the basis of interviews.

**8523** Frank Burton *The Politics of Legitimacy: Struggles in a Belfast Community* Henley 1978. A first-hand account of the Belfast Catholic community in 1972–3. Another useful account of life in Catholic Belfast is John Conroy *War As A Way Of Life: A Belfast Diary* Heinemann 1988. This is a journal by an American journalist sympathetic to the republican cause covering the years 1980–5.

## (6) The Protestant Community

**8524** David W Miller *Queen's Rebels: Ulster Loyalism in Historical Perspective* Harper and Row 1979. The best historical study. A political science analysis of Protestant factions in the 1970s is Sarah Nelson *Ulster's*

*UncertainDefenders: Protestant Political, Paramilitary and Community Groups and the Northern Ireland Conflict* Appletree Press 1984. See also R G Crawford *Loyal to King Billy: A Portrait of Ulster Protestants* Christopher Hurst 1988 and B M Probert 'The Northern Ireland Crisis: A Study in Political Economy of Protestant Social Formations' Lancaster PhD Thesis 1974–6.

**8525** Tony Gray *The Orange Order* The Bodley Head 1972. A history of the international Orange Order 1795–1970. Another general history is M W Dewer, John Brown and J E Long *Orangeism: A New Historical Appreciation* 2nd ed, Grand Lodge of Ireland 1969. On Orangcism in Ireland see D A Roberts 'The Orange Order in Ireland: A Religious Institution?' *British Journal of Sociology* 22 1971 pp 269–82.

## (7) Terrorism and Political Violence

### (a) The Irish Republican Army and Other Republican Factions

**8526** J Bowyer Bell *The Secret Army: The IRA 1916–1979* revised ed, Academy Press 1979. The standard history. A detailed study of the IRA and its military campaigns drawing on extensive interviewing. It contains a full bibliography. Tim Pat Coogan *The IRA* Fontana 1971 is a history up to 1970. See also Eamonn O'Doherty *An Illustrated History of the IRA* Mercier, Cork 1985. There is also a limited amount on the postwar history of the IRA in Sean O'Callaghan *The Easter Lily: The Story of the IRA* 2nd ed, Four Square Books 1967. The IRA's own account of its history is *Provisional Irish Republican Army Freedom Struggle* Irish Republican Publicity Bureau 1973.

**8527** Patrick Bishop and Eamonn Mellie *The Provisional IRA* Heinemann 1987. A study of the objectives and structure of the Provisionals over the twenty years since the 'Troubles' started and they split from the official IRA in 1969. See also J Bowyer Bell 'The Escalation of Insurgency: The Provisional Irish Republican Army's Experience 1969–1971' *The Review of Politics* 35 1973 pp 398–411. A journalistic insight into the world of the Provisionals is provided in Maria McGuire *To Take Arms: My Year with the Provisional IRA* Viking 1973 and in Roger Faligot *La Resistance Irlandaise 1916–1976* François Maspero, Paris 1977, a sympathetic French account.

**8528** Tom Bowden 'The IRA and the Changing Tactics of Terrorism' *Political Quarterly* 47 1976 pp 425–37. On the tactics of intimidation see Richard Clutterbuck 'Intimidation of Witnesses and Juries' *Army Quarterly* 104 1974 pp 285–94.

**8529** R W Barton 'Terrorist Activities in the United Kingdom' *Police College Magazine* 14 1975 pp 12–20. An account of terrorist activities and the problems they pose for the police.

**8530** P C F M Beresford 'The Official IRA and Republican Clubs in Northern Ireland 1968–1974, and their Relations with Other Political and Paramilitary Groups' Exeter PhD Thesis 1979. The split between the official and provisional wings of the IRA and the impact of far left ideas on the IRA since the 1960s are examined in E P Rooney 'From Opposition to Legitimacy? A Sociological Analysis of the Official Republican Movement' Queen's University, Belfast PhD Thesis 1985. This points to the shift, by the mid 1970s, towards a new willingness to recognize state institutions and the validity of elections, which was to have a growing impact on republican policy.

**8531** Paul Beresford *Ten Dead Men: The Story of the 1981 Irish Hunger Strike* Grafton 1987. An account of the IRA Hunger Strike of prisoners in the Maze in support of their campaign to be treated as political prisoners. The ideology and organization of the protest is examined in Paul Wilkinson 'The Provisional IRA: An Assessment in the Wake of the 1981 Hunger Strike' *Government and Opposition* 7 1982 pp 140–56. On a previous protest to try and gain political category status see Tim Pat Coogan *On The Blanket: The H Block Story* Ward River Press, Dublin 1979. This also examines prison conditions, trial procedures and torture as experienced by IRA terrorists. See also L Clarke *Broadening the Battlefield: The H Blocks and the Rise of Sinn Fein* Gill and Macmillan, Dublin 1987.

**8532** P Michael O'Sullivan *Patriot Graves: Resistance in Ireland* Folliott Publishing, Chicago 1972. A collection of interviews with IRA leaders.

**8533** Roger Faligot *Nous avons tué Mountbatten: L'IRA parle* Editions Jean Picollec, Paris 1981. Interviews with an IRA commander covering his role in the assassination of Earl Mountbatten in 1979, and also the 1981 Hunger Strikes, the IRA's international links and its strategy.

**8534** Jack Dowling 'Interview with Cathal Goulding: Chief of Staff of the IRA' *New Left Review* 64 1970 pp 50–61. Goulding was responsible for taking the Official IRA in a more socialist direction. This interview reviews developments since the unsuccessful border campaign of 1956–62.

**8535** Sean MacStiofain *Memoirs of a Revolutionary* Gordon Cremonesi 1975. The well-written memoirs of an IRA leader who first became active in the struggle in the 1950s. It deals particularly with the years 1969–72 and his imprisonment 1972–5.

**8536** Bobby Sands *One Day in My Life* Mercier, Cork 1983. A prison journal by the leader of the 1981 IRA hunger strike in the Maze Prison. John M Feehan *Bobby Sands and the Tragedy of Ireland* Mercier, Cork 1983 is a sympathetic biography and critique of British policy in Northern Ireland.

**(b) Loyalist Paramilitaries**

**8537** Arthur Aughey and Colin McIlherney 'Law before Violence? The Protestant Paramilitaries in Ulster Politics' *Eire-Ireland* 19 1984 pp 55–74.

**8538** David Boulton *The UVF (Ulster Volunteer Force) 1966– 1973: An Anatomy of Loyalist Rebellion* Gill and Macmillan, Dublin 1973. A study of the Protestant group that was banned 1966–74 and the origins of Protestant extremism. It also touches on the development of the unbanned Ulster Defence Association.

**(8) The Security Forces**

**(a) The Royal Ulster Constabulary**

**8539** Chris Ryder *The RUC: A Force Under Fire* Methuen 1989. A good analysis of the RUC during the 'Troubles'. Changing tactics and policy in this period are also examined in Ronald Weitzer 'Policing a Divided Society: Obstacles to Normalisation in Northern Ireland' *Social Problems* 33 1985 pp 41–55. See also 'Northern Ireland' in John D Brewer *et al The Police, Public Order and the State* Macmillan 1988 pp 47–84 and Paul Arthur 'Policing and Crisis Politics: Northern Ireland as a Case Study' *Parliamentary Affairs* 39 1986 pp 341–53.

**8540** R M Pockrass 'Police Response to Terrorism: The Royal Ulster Constabulary' *Police Journal* 59 1986 pp 143–57. A study of the history and contemporary organization of the RUC to combat terrorism.

**8541** Sir Arthur Hezlet *The 'B' Specials: A History of the Ulster Special Constabulary* 2nd ed, Pan 1973. A history of this exclusively Protestant special force from its inception until it was stood down in 1970. The history of the operation of this force in republican Fermanagh is examined in Mervyn Dane *The Fermanagh 'B' Specials* The Impartial Reporter 1970.

**8542** *Police Interrogation Procedure in Northern Ireland: Report of a Committee of Inquiry March 1979* Cmnd 7497, *Parliamentary Papers* 1978–79. An examination conducted under the chairmanship of H G Bennett.

**8543** Ronald Weitzer 'Accountability and Complaints against the Police in Northern Ireland' *Police Studies* 9 1986 pp 99– 109. A study of the deficiencies of the complaints procedure.

**8544** Russell Murray 'Police Officer Deaths in Northern Ireland 1969–1982' *Police Chief* 50 1983 pp 41–7.

**8545** B Loftus 'Images for Sale: Government and Security Advertising in Northern Ireland 1968–1978' *Oxford Art Journal* 3 1980 pp 70–80. A study of government leaflets and posters against terrorism and to recruit for the RUC. These become increasingly sophisticated after 1972 but are here seen as losing touch with their potential audience.

**8546** John Stalker *Stalker* Harrap 1988. The account by the former Deputy Chief Constable of Greater Manchester of his inquiry into whether the RUC were pursuing a shoot-to-kill policy in 1982 and the reasons for his eventual removal from the inquiry. The account of the affair and its ramifications by Stalker's close friend, Peter Taylor *Stalker: The Search for Truth* Faber 1987, is also useful. See also Frank Doherty *The Stalker Affair* Mercier, Cork 1986.

**(b) The British Army in Northern Ireland Since 1969**

**8547** David Barzilay *The British Army in Ulster* 4v, Century Services 1973–81. An in-depth study of military operations and weapons on both sides of the conflict since the army was sent in to aid the civil power in maintaining public order in the face of Protestant attacks on Catholic civil rights marches in 1969. The problems of the army in maintaining a peace-keeping role in the divided communities of the Province is examined in Desmond Hamill *Pig in the Middle: The Army in Northern Ireland 1969–1984* Methuen 1985. See also Michael Dewar *The British Army in Northern Ireland* Arms and Armour Press 1985, J Brian Garrett 'Ten Years of British Troops in Northern Ireland' *International Security* 4 1979–80 pp 80– 104 and G Sheffield 'The Army in Aid of the Civil Power: Northern Ireland 1969–1976' Aberdeen MLitt Thesis 1980. The workings of the army in Ulster are studied in A F N Clarke *Contact* Secker and Warburg 1983.

**8548** Max Arthur *Northern Ireland – Soldiers Talking: 1969 to Today* Sidgwick and Jackson 1988. An oral history of the experiences of the army in Ulster since 1969. It includes useful maps, a glossary and chronology and full appendices. On the army's experience in a frustrating peace-keeping role see also James B Deerin 'Northern Ireland's "Twilight War": Frustrating Duty for British Troops' *Army* 26 Dec 1976 pp 14–21.

**8549** Kenneth Lindsay *Ambush at Tully West: The British Intelligence Services in Action* Dunrod Press 1979. This alleges that the military intelligence services have been involved in election tampering and other illegal activities.

**8550** David Barzilay and Michael Murray *Four Months in Winter* Second Battalion, Royal Regiment of Fusiliers 1972. An account of a tour of duty by the regiment in Ulster.

**8551** Roger Faligot *Britain's Military Strategy in Ireland: The Kitson Experiment* Zed Press 1983. A study of the theory and practice of the low-intensity operations developed in Northern Ireland by Frank Kitson and their effects on the state more generally in institutionalizing counter-terrorism into the system.

**8552** Frank Kitson *Low-Intensity Operations: Subversion, Insurgency and Peacekeeping* Faber 1971. A first-hand account of anti-guerrilla tactics in Northern Ireland. Another personal account of counter-terrorist operations in Ulster is Showell G Styles *Bombs Have No Pity: My War Against Terrorism* Luscombe 1975. See also Elisha T Mealing *Ulster: Some Causes and Effects of Low Intensity Operations 1969–1972* Carlisle Barracks, Army War College 1972.

**8553** David A Charters 'Intelligence and Psychological Warfare Operations in Northern Ireland' *Journal of the Royal United Services Institution for Defence Studies* 122 1977 pp 22–7.

### (9) Imprisonment of Terrorists

**8554** John MacGuffin *Internment* Anvil Books, Tralee 1973. A history of the policy of internment without trial pursued between August 1971 and the imposition of direct rule in 1972 by one of its sufferers. See also his book *The Guinea Pigs* Penguin 1974 on the internees.

**8555** D R Lowry 'Draconian Powers: The New British Approach to Pretrial Detention of Suspected Terrorists' *Columbian Human Rights Law Review* 9 1977 pp 185–222. A study of the detention powers provided to the security forces under the Prevention of Terrorism (Temporary Provisions) Acts.

### (10) Peace Movement

**8556** E Eveson 'Northern Ireland's Peace Movement: Some Early Reactions' *Community Development Journal* 12 1977 pp 108– 11. An account of the peace movement that began among working class women in August 1976 after the failure of the Ulster Convention.

Eveson sees it as suffering from a lack of clear ideas or a strong central organization. On the women who led the movement and their objectives see Richard R Deutsch *Mairead Corrigan, Betty Williams: Two Women who Ignored Danger in Campaigning for Peace in Northern Ireland* Barrons, Woodbury, New York 1977.

## D. LAW

### (1) General

**8557** *The Belfast Gazette* HMSO 1927–. The weekly official channel for communicating to the public changes in the law and official appointments.

**8558** P O'Higgins *A Bibliography of Periodicial Literature Relating to Irish Law* Northern Ireland Legal Quarterly 1966. A classified bibliography with over 4,000 entries. Leslie F Maxwell and W Harold Maxwell (comps) *A Legal Bibliography of the British Commonwealth of Nations Vol 4: Irish Law to 1956* 2nd ed, Sweet and Maxwell 1957 is an alphabetically arranged unannotated bibliography.

**8559** *Northern Ireland Law Reports* Incorporated Council of Law Reporting for Northern Ireland 1925–. Reference guide to developments in Northern Ireland statute and case law. On case law see also *Index to Cases Decided in the Courts of Northern Ireland* Incorporated Council of Law Reporting for Northern Ireland 1975. This has subsequently been updated by periodic supplements.

**8560** Harry Greenall Calvert *Constitutional Law in Northern Ireland: A Study in Regional Government* Stevens 1968.

**8561** J C W Wylie *Irish Land Law* Professional Books 1975. A major textbook since supplemented. It covers land law in the whole of Ireland.

**8562** Barry Valentine *County Court Procedure in Northern Ireland* SLS Legal Publications 1985.

### (2) Anti-Terrorist Legislation and Legal Devices

**8563** Kevin Boyle, Tom Hadden and Paddy Hillyard *Law and State: The Case of Northern Ireland* Robertson 1975. A critical review of the nature and operation of law in Northern Ireland, especially in the context of the 'Troubles'. It outlines the decline of civil rights in the face of the terrorist threat and the consequent development of emergency powers and internment. The authors are perhaps too ready to invoke colonialism in their analysis even though they recognize that it 'cannot be directly applied'.

**8564** Kevin Boyle, Tom Hadden and Paddy Hillyard *Ten Years On in Northern Ireland: The Legal Control of Political Violence* Cobden Trust 1980. A study of the erosion of civil liberties and the rise of emergency legislation since the beginning of the 'Troubles'. They also note the increasingly evenhanded treatment of loyalist and republican offenders by the army, police and courts.

**8565** J W Bishop 'Law in the Control of Terrorism and Insurrection: The British Laboratory Experience' *Law and Contemporary Problems* 42 1978 pp 140–201. A study of the problems of applying the rule of law in a situation of political violence and the resulting development of emergency legislation. On emergency legislation see also Dermot Walsh *The Use and Abuse of Emergency Legislation in Northern Ireland* Cobden Trust 1983.

**8566** J E Finn 'Public Support for Emergency/Anti-Terrorist Legislation in Northern Ireland: A Preliminary Analysis' *Terrorism: An International Journal* 10 1987 pp 113–24. This argues that confidence in the legal system declined in both communities in the face of internment and recovered after internment was ended.

**8567** *Report of a Committee to Consider, in the Context of Civil Liberties and Human Rights, Measures to deal with Terrorism in Northern Ireland* Cmnd 5874, *Parliamentary Papers* xxviii 1974–75. A consideration by a committee chaired by Lord Gardiner of the working of the Prevention of Terrorism Act 1973. It recommends the need to apply the Van Straubenzee recommendations on ending discrimination in employment, and improving housing and community relations and to consider a Bill of Rights. It also argued that there was a need for improved powers of arrest, the ending of special categories of prisoner and detention and improvements in prison facilities. The operation of prevention of terrorism legislation is also reviewed by Lord Shackleton in *Review of the Operation of the Prevention of Terrorism (Temporary Provisions) Acts 1974 and 1976* Cmnd 7324, *Parliamentary Papers* xxiii 1977–78. Shackleton's recommendations had only been patchily implemented by the time of the next review. *Review of the Operation of the Prevention of Terrorism (Temporary Provisions) Act 1976* Cmnd 8803, *Parliamentary Papers* 1982–83, conducted by Earl Jellicoe, led to the 1984 Prevention of Terrorism Act. On the 1974 and 1976 Acts see also Catherine Scorer 'The United Kingdom Prevention of Terrorism Acts 1974 and 1976' *International Journal of Politics* 10 1980 pp 105–11.

**8568** *Report of the Commission to Consider Legal Procedures to Deal with Terrorist Activities in Northern Ireland* Cmnd 5185, *Parliamentary Papers* xxvi 1972–

73. This Commission was set up after the imposition of direct rule. Concerned about intimidation of judges and jurors the Commission, under the chairmanship of Lord Diplock, recommended the establishment of non-jury courts for the duration of the 'Troubles'. It also led to changes in the law of evidence and the law as applied to juveniles in a less liberal direction.

**8569** Tony Gifford *Supergrasses: The Use of Accomplice Evidence in Northern Ireland: A Report* Cobden Trust 1984. A critical study of the use of IRA informers to secure convictions. This policy is also examined in the context of the career of one of the most important informers in Geoff Robertson *Reluctant Judas: The Life and Death of the Special Branch Informer, Kenneth Lennon* Temple Smith 1976. This study of the use of IRA informers by the security forces highlights the legal questions raised by this policy and its impact on the effort to contain terrorism.

## E. RELATIONS BETWEEN THE UNITED KINGDOM AND THE REPUBLIC OF IRELAND

**8570** P J Drudy (ed) *Ireland and Britain Since 1922* Cambridge University Press 1986. Studies in relations between the two islands since the partition of Ireland. An Irish perspective on the relationship is presented in Patrick O'Farrell *Ireland's English Question: Anglo-Irish Relations 1934–70* Batsford 1977. Jack Lynch 'The Anglo-Irish Problem' *Foreign Affairs* 50 1972 pp 601–17 is an overview of relations by the then Irish Taioseach.

**8571** Trevor C Salmon *Unneutral Ireland: An Ambivalent and Unique Security Policy* Clarendon 1989. A political science analysis of Irish foreign and defence policy. It includes reflections on Anglo-Irish relations. On the Irish government's attitudes to and policy towards reunification of Ireland see W Harvey Cox 'The Politics of Irish Unification in the Irish Republic' *Parliamentary Affairs* 38 1985 pp 437–54.

**8572** G Boyce 'From War to Neutrality: Anglo-Irish Relations 1921–1950' *British Journal of International Studies* 5 1979 pp 15–36. Belfast's relations with the South in this period from the partition of Ireland to the transition of the Irish Free State from dominion to republic and departure from the Commonwealth are examined in D Kennedy 'Northern Attitudes to the Independent Irish State 1919–1949' Trinity College, Dublin PhD Thesis 1984–5. A contemporary view of the events of 1948–9 is Hugh Shearman 'Recent Developments in Anglo-Irish Relations' *World Affairs* 45 1949 pp 152–63. Ireland's departure from the Commonwealth is reconsidered in Ronan Fanning 'The Response of the London and Belfast Governments to the Declaration of the Republic of Ireland 1948–49' *International Affairs* 58 1981–82 pp 95–114. The reasons for Dublin's decision in September 1948 to repeal the External Relations Act which severed its relations with the Commonwealth and the Crown and the reactions of the Commonwealth and Belfast are examined in John O'Brien 'Ireland's Departure from the British Commonwealth' *Round Table* 306 1988 pp 179–94.

**8573** James E Downey *Us and Them: Britain, Ireland and the Northern Ireland Question 1969–1982* Ward River Press, Dublin 1983. Anglo-Irish relations since the beginning of the 'Troubles' are also examined in Paul Arthur 'Anglo-Irish Relations Since 1968: A "Fever-Chart" Interpretation' *Government and Opposition* 18 1983 pp 157–74. Aspects of Dublin's relations with Belfast and London are considered in B Arnold *What Kind of Country? Modern Irish Politics 1968–1983* Cape 1984.

**8574** Paul F Power 'The Sunningdale Strategy and the Northern Majority Consent Doctrine in Anglo-Irish Relations' *Eire- Ireland* 12 1977 pp 35–67. The Sunningdale conference of British, Irish and Northern Irish representatives of 1973 agreed a basis for the abortive attempt at power-sharing of the following year and recognized the constitutional status of Northern Ireland could only change with the agreement of the Protestant majority. See also Donal Barrington 'After Sunningdale' *Administration* 24 1976 pp 235–61.

**8575** Anthony Kenny *The Road to Hillsborough: The Shaping of the Anglo-Irish Agreement* Pergamon 1986. An examination of the significance of the Agreement signed by Mrs Thatcher and the Irish Taoiseach, Garret Fitzgerald in November 1985 which for the first time, and to the horror of unionists, gave Dublin a consultative role in the politics of the North. The full text is presented with a commentary in T Hadden and K Boyle *The Anglo-Irish Agreement: Commentary, Text and Official Review* Sweet and Maxwell 1987. The forging of the Agreement is examined in W Harvey Cox 'Managing Northern Ireland Intergovernmentally: An Appraisal of the Anglo-Irish Agreement' *Parliamentary Affairs* 40 1987 pp 80–97. See also Brendan O'Leary 'The Anglo-Irish Agreement: Statecraft or Folly?' *West European Politics* 10 1987 pp 5–32. The progress of the agreement is assessed in his 'The Limits to Coercive Consocialization in Northern Ireland' *Political Studies* 37 1989 pp 562–88. The prospects for it developing into a successful experiment in power-sharing are pessimistically reviewed in the context of the fate of other such initiatives since Sunningdale in John McGarry 'The Anglo-Irish Agreement and Unlikely Prospects for Power-Sharing in Northern Ireland' *Eire-Ireland* 23 1988 pp 111–28. The subsequent history of the Agreement in the context of the determination of unionists to rid themselves of it is traced in the collection of articles, David McKitterick

*Despatches from Belfast* Blackstaff 1989. On the reaction of the Unionists see also Arthur Aughey *Ulster Unionism and the Anglo-Irish Agreement* Hurst 1989. A Coughlan *Fooled Again? The Anglo-Irish Agreement and After* Mercier, Cork 1986 is an Irish view of the Agreement.

**8576** Michael O'Doyle 'Torture and Emergency Powers under the European Convention of Human Rights: Ireland Versus the United Kingdom' *American Journal of International Law* 71 1977 pp 674–706. The European Court of Human Rights did not find in favour of the Irish case that there had been incidents of torture by the British authorities in Northern Ireland. It did however find that the treatment of prisoners inhumane and degrading and criticized the sophisticated and disorientating interrogation methods used by the security forces. See also Pierre-Marie Martin 'A propos de L'Article 3 de la Convention européene des droits de l'homme: l'arrêt de la Cour européene des droits de l'homme dans l'affaire Irelande v Royaumi-Uni' *Revue generale de Droit international public* 83 1979 pp 104–25.

**8577** Conor O'Cleary 'The Effects of the European Monetary System on Anglo-Irish Relations' *Political Quarterly* 50 1979 pp 182–91. Until the 1970s the Irish pound was tied at parity to the pound sterling. This parity ended and the Irish floated their currency when they joined the EMS and the British did not at the end of the 1970s.

**8578** John Bowman *De Valera and the Ulster Question 1917–1973* Clarendon 1982. Eamonn de Valera was Taoiseach 1937–48, 1951–4 and 1957–9 and President of the Republic 1959–73. This study of De Valera's attitudes towards Northern Ireland argues that his rhetoric was more radical than his intentions. On De Valera's attitudes towards Britain and his manoeuvring to assert Irish independence see T Ryle Dwyer *De Valera's Finest Hour: In Search of National Independence 1932–1959* Mercier, Cork 1959. The best biography of De Valera, which was written with its subject's help and access to his papers, is Frank Pakenham, Earl of Longford and Thomas P O'Neill *Eamonn de Valera* Arrow 1974. Owen Dudley Edwards *Eamon de Valera* University of Wales Press 1988 is a short biography which is rather thin on the post-war period. See also Mary Bromage *De Valera and the March of the Nation* Hutchinson 1956.

**8579** John Peck *Dublin from Downing Street* Gill and Macmillan, Dublin 1978. Memoirs of the British ambassador to Dublin 1970–3 and of the principal events of the period, including the burning down of the Chancery of the embassy during three days of rioting.

## F. RELIGION

**8580** Eric Gallagher and Stanley Worrall *Christians in Ulster 1969–1980* Oxford University Press 1982. A study of the impact of and response to the 'Troubles' of the churches in the Province. Attempts to promote ecumenism in the face of sectarian conflict are examined in James McEvoy 'Ecumenism in Northern Ireland' *The Month* 264 1984 pp 227–34.

**8581** D J Roche, Derek Birrell and J I Greer 'A Socio-Political Opinion Profile of Clergymen in Northern Ireland' *Social Studies* 4 1975 pp 143–51.

**8582** Paul A Compton and John P Power 'Estimates of the Religious Composition of Northern Ireland Local Government Districts in 1981 and Change in the Geographical Pattern of Religious Composition between 1971 and 1981' *Economic and Social Review* 17 1986 pp 87–195.

**8583** *Irish Catholic Directory and Almanac* J Duffy, Dublin 1880–. An annual guide to the organization, administration, priests and monastic communities of the church. Des Wilson *This Turbulent Priest* Mercier, Cork 1985 is a study of the role of the Catholic church in Ulster politics since the beginning of the 'Troubles'. Patrick Cahy 'Some Political Behaviour Patterns and Attitudes of Roman Catholic Priests in a Rural Part of Northern Ireland' *Economic and Social Review* 3 1971 pp 1–23 is a useful sociological study.

**8584** *The Irish Church Directory and Year Book* Church of Ireland Printing and Publishing Co 1862–. An annual guide to the organization and administration of the Church of Ireland (part of the Anglican communion) and the deployment of its clergy throughout Ireland. A general history of the church since its disestablishment is R B McDowell *The Church of Ireland 1869–1969* Routledge and Kegan Paul 1975. See also M Harley (ed) *Irish Anglicanism 1869–1969* Figgis 1970.

**8585** Peter Brooke *Ulster Presbyterianism: The Historical Perspective 1610–1970* Gill and Macmillan, Dublin 1987. On Rev Ian Paisley and the Free Presbyterian Church which he founded see [8465–6].

## G. ECONOMIC HISTORY

**8586** K Isles *Economic Survey of Northern Ireland* HMSO 1957. See also R Davies, M A McGurnaghan and K I Sams 'The Northern Ireland Economy: Progress (1968–75) and Prospects' *Regional Studies* 11 1977 pp 297–307.

**8587** R T Harrison 'Industrial Development Policy and the Restructuring of the Northern Ireland Economy' *Economic and Planning C: Government and Policy* 4 1986 pp 53–70. An analysis of Northern Ireland's regional economic problems and unemployment and of the impact of industrial development programmes on employment change since the war. See also Alan S Murie, W Derek Birrell, P A R Hillyard and D J D Roche *Regional Policy and the Attraction of Manufacturing Industry to Northern Ireland* Centre for Environmental Studies, London 1974. A particular experiment in regional policy is reviewed in Liam O'Dowd and Bill Rolston 'Bringing Hong Kong to Belfast? The Case of an Enterprise Zone' *International Journal of Urban and Regional Research* 9 1985 pp 218–32. This examines the development of the enterprise zone created in Belfast in 1981.

**8588** G P F Steed 'Internal Organisation, Firm Integration and Locational Change: The Northern Ireland Complex 1954–1964' *Economic Geography* 47 1971 pp 371–83. The decline of linen and the growth of man-made fibres in the textile industry over the post-war period is examined in T G Taylor 'Changes in the Northern Ireland Textile Industry 1945–1975' Wales MA Thesis 1980.

**8589** J S Moore 'The Engineering History of the Motor Industry in Northern Ireland' Queen's University, Belfast MSc Thesis 1978. A history and industrial archaeology of the Northern Irish motor industry.

**8590** Michael S Moss and John R Hume *Shipbuilders to the World: 125 Years of Harland and Wolff, Belfast 1861–1986* Blackstaff 1986. A history of the Belfast shipbuilding firm.

**8591** J R R Adams *Northern Ireland Newspapers: Checklist and Locations* Library Association 1979. A finding list.

**8592** Rex Cathcart *The Most Contrary Region: The BBC in Northern Ireland 1924–1984* Blackstaff 1984. A good general history, especially on the problems involved in broadcasting the 'Troubles'. It is an important institution in the Province and its problems over its role in Northern Irish society are well covered here.

**8593** Noel Simpson *The Belfast Bank 1827–1970: 150 Years of Banking in Ireland* Blackstaff 1975. This bank is now known as Northern Bank. Another banking history is W J Knox *Decades of the Ulster Bank 1836–1964* Ulster Bank 1965.

**8594** Stephen Brown 'Crisis – Response and Retail Change in Belfast City Centre' *Irish Geography* 19 1986 pp 83–91. A study of the success of the response of the stores to terrorist bombings 1970–84 and the development of counter-terrorist security activities in stores.

**8595** P E Greer (ed) *Road Versus Rail: Documents on the History of Public Transport in Northern Ireland 1921–48* Public Record Office of Northern Ireland 1982.

**8596** *General Report of Northern Ireland Agriculture* Department of Agriculture, Northern Ireland 1942–. An annual report. Agricultural statistics are annually presented in *Statistical Review of Northern Ireland Agriculture* Department of Agriculture, Northern Ireland 1966–. Since the war artificial drainage has greatly increased the usable area of Northern Ireland. The improvement to the land and resulting land use changes are discussed, as is the potential environmental damage, in D N Wilson 'Post-War Land Drainage, Fertilizer Use and Environmental Impact in Northern Ireland' *Journal of Environmental Management* 8 1979 pp 137–49. On an aspect of horticulture in Ireland see D Willis 'The Daffodil in Ireland 1879–1979: With Special Reference to the Work of Guy L Wilson' New University of Ulster DPhil Thesis 1980.

**8597** Claire and Michael Jackson *A History of the Vaughan Charity* William Trimble 1985. An official history. Originally set up as an educational charity this now provides financial aid for the development of agriculture in County Fermanagh.

**8598** *The Encyclopaedia of Northern Ireland Labour Law and Practice* 3v, Labour Relations Agency 1983. A good comprehensive guide to legislation up to that introduced in 1982.

**8599** Boyd Black 'Collaboration or Conflict? Strike Activity in Northern Ireland' *Industrial Relations Journal* 18 1987 pp 14–25. This argues that Northern Ireland is relatively strike prone.

**8600** Andrew Boyd *The Rise of the Irish Trade Unions 1729–1970* Anvil Books, Tralee 1972. A short history. Despite trade union contraction elsewhere in the UK in the 1980s they continued to grow in Northern Ireland. This development is examined in Boyd Black 'Against the Trend: Trade Union Growth in Northern Ireland' *Industrial Relations Journal* 17 1986 pp 71–80. On government's role in industrial relations in the Province see K I Sams 'Government and Trade Unions: The Situation in Northern Ireland' *British Journal of Industrial Relations* 2 1964 pp 254–70. On the history of a particular civil service union from its formation in 1919 to 1976 see E T Donnelly 'The History of the Northern Ireland Public Service Alliance' Queen's University, Belfast MA Thesis 1981.

**8601** *Report of the Equal Opportunities Commission for Northern Ireland* HMSO 1977–. A useful annual report covering the incidence of sectarian discrimination at work. See also the useful survey, David Smith *Equality and Inequality in Northern Ireland* Policy Studies Institute 1987.

**8602** M De Frinse 'Sex Differentials in the Northern Ireland Economy 1963–1978' Ulster Polytechnic MPhil Thesis 1985. This study of discrimination against women at work argues that this discrimination in Northern Ireland is much worse than in most advanced societies because of the weakness of the economy.

**8603** M O McCullagh 'State Responses to Unemployment in Northern Ireland Since 1922: A Sociological Analysis' Queen's University, Belfast MSSc Thesis 1985. This focuses on the provision of unemployment insurance, employment creation and youth training and its consequences.

**8604** I G Henderson 'Industrial Training in Northern Ireland – The Effects of the 1964 Industrial Training Act' Queens M.Sc Thesis 1976.

## H. THE ENVIRONMENT

**8605** Neville Presho 'A Dying Lake' *Geographical Magazine* 48 Oct 1975 pp 8–14. An account of the eutrophication of Lough Neagh and the growth of algal bloom on the surface of the lake. See also R B Wood and C E Gibson 'Eutrophication and Lough Neagh' *Water Research* 7 1973 pp 173–87.

**8606** John Hendry 'Conservation in Northern Ireland' *Town Planning Review* 48 1977 pp 373–88. A study of the development of conservation legislation and practice in the Province and of the differences in housing, planning and conservation policy with the rest of the UK.

**8607** Alan S Murie 'Planning in Northern Ireland: A Survey' *Town Planning Review* 44 1973 pp 337–58. An outline history of planning in the Province since 1931. See also C F S Newman 'A Short History of Planning in Northern Ireland' *Journal of the Northern Ireland Institute* 51 1965 pp 47–53. The impact of the 'Troubles' on planning policy in Northern Ireland is examined in Dale Singleton 'Planning and Sectarianism in Northern Ireland' *Planner* 63 1977 pp 17–19.

**8608** Ron Weiner *The Rape and Plunder of the Shankill in Belfast: People and Planning* Notaems Press 1976. A study of the impact of economic decline since the turn of the century on Protestant power in this loyalist stronghold and the responses of the community to attempts by planners to plan for urban renewal and to try and reduce sectarian housing segregation. T Blackman 'The Politics of Place in Northern Ireland: Perspectives on a Case Study' *International Journal of Urban and Regional Research* 10 1976 pp 541–62 is a study of defensive reactions by working class communities against urban restructuring, looking particularly at the Shankill district. See also G M Dawson 'Defensive Planning in Belfast' *Irish Geographer* 17 1984 pp 27–41, which is a study of town planning in Belfast since the start of the 'Troubles'.

**8609** M McGurnaghan 'Integrated Operations and Urban Renewal: The Belfast Experience 1981–1985' *Administration* 34 1986 pp 505–26. An assessment of the success of the EC-inspired experiment in urban renewal in Belfast begun in 1981.

**8610** L T Symons *Land Use in Northern Ireland* University of London Press 1969.

## I. SOCIAL HISTORY

### (1) General

**8611** Paul A Compton *Northern Ireland: A Census Atlas* Gill and Macmillan, Dublin 1978. This maps the results of the 1971 census.

**8612** Paul A Compton (ed) *The Contemporary Population of Northern Ireland and Population-Related Issues* Institute of Irish Studies, Queen's University, Belfast 1981. After reviewing demographic trends over the previous 150 years this concentrates on contemporary issues such as the fertility of Catholics, demographic effects on housing, residential segregation and mixing in the midst of sectarian conflict, and the implications of demographic trends for planning and unemployment.

### (2) Social Policy and Social Problems

**8613** John Ditch *Social Policy in Northern Ireland between 1939–1950* Avebury 1988. The first detailed study of this subject explodes some former views and pictures the development of a Welfare State in Northern Ireland in this period as a policy to fend off an increasingly vociferous Labour Party.

**8614** *Health and Personal Social Services Statistics for Northern Ireland* HMSO 1974–. An annual statistical guide.

**8615** John Darby and Arthur Williamson *Violence and the Social Services in Northern Ireland* Heinemann Educational 1978. A study of the effect of the 'Troubles' on the health, education, personal social, housing, police and prison services. The direct relationship between paramilitary action and neighbourhood groups is also explored.

**8616** D J MacRandal 'Youth Clubs in Northern Ireland' Queen's University, Belfast MSc Thesis 1986. A historical survey of the development of the Youth Service and the implementation of the Youth Welfare (Northern Ireland) Act 1944. The 'Troubles' have increased the urgency of socializing disaffected youth.

**8617** E M McShane 'Day Nursery Provision 1942–1955: A Case Study of Women and Social Policy in Northern Ireland' Queen's University, Belfast PhD Thesis 1984. A study of the impact of nursery provision on women's lives. The transfer of responsibility to local authorities in 1950 led to major closures.

**8618** R J Lawrence 'The Health Service in Northern Ireland' *Public Administration* 34 1956 pp 289–308.

**8619** S Johnson (comp) *Poverty and Inequality in Northern Ireland: A Preliminary Bibliography* Policy Studies Institute 1980. An unannotated bibliography. The incidence of poverty in the poorest region of the kingdom and policy to alleviate it is examined in John Ditch, Mike Morrissey, Pat McGinn and Richard Steele *Low Pay and Family Poverty in Northern Ireland* Macmillan 1989. A useful local study is E Evason *Ends That Won't Meet: A Study of Poverty in Belfast* Child Poverty Action Group 1980. See also John Ditch 'The Perception of Poverty in Northern Ireland' *Policy and Politics* 12 1984 pp 167–82.

**8620** R Jenkins *Lads, Citizens and Ordinary Kids: Working Class Youth Life-Styles in Belfast* Routledge and Kegan Paul 1983. A study describing the transition from school to work of those who provide the prime constituency for the paramilitaries on both sides of the sectarian divide.

### (3) Sport

**8621** John Sugden and Alan Bairner 'Northern Ireland: Sport in a Divided Society' in Lincoln Allison (ed) *The Politics of Sport* Manchester University Press 1986 pp 90–117. An excellent essay. Its authors point out that in a divided society choices over which sport to play or to support have political implications. Gaelic Football is for instance associated with nationalism. They therefore offer little comfort that sport will provide a way of transcending the barriers in the Province.

**8622** Malcolm Brodie *100 Years of Irish Football* Blackstaff 1980. A general history. The best biography of the most talented, not to mention self-destructive, footballer to have been produced by Northern Ireland in the post-war period is Michael Parkinson *Best: An Intimate Biography* Hutchinson 1975. George Best has also written two autobiographical accounts; *Where Do I Go*

*From Here?* Queen Anne Press 1981 and *Best of Both Worlds* Trans-World Publishers 1968. Robert Allen *Billy: A Biography of Billy Bingham* Viking 1986 is a portrait of the manager of the national football team. See also the memoir of his playing career, Billy Bingham *Soccer with the Stars* Stanley Paul 1962. Danny Blanchflower in *The Double and Before: The Autobiography of Danny Blanchflower* Nicholas Kaye 1961 recalls his distinguished career with Northern Ireland and Tottenham Hotspur. Pat Jennings *Pat Jennings* Willow 1983 is the autobiography of the much capped Northern Ireland goalkeeper. See also Reg Drury *Pat Jennings* Collins 1983.

**8623**  Edmund Van Esbeck *One Hundred Years of Irish Rugby: The Official History of Irish Rugby Football Union* Gill and Macmillan, Dublin 1974. See also Sean Diffley *The Men in Green: The Story of Irish Rugby* Pelham 1973.

**8624**  Con Short *The Ulster GAA* Ulster County Board GAA 1984. A history of hurling in the Province. On hurling in Armagh see Con Short, Peter Murray and Jimmy Smith *Ard Mhacha 1884–1984: A Century of GAA Progress* Armagh County Board GAA 1985.

**8625**  Mary Peters with Ian Wooldridge *Mary P: Autobiography* Stanley Paul 1974. Peters won the women's pentathlon gold medal at the 1972 Olympics.

**8626**  Jim Sheridan *Leave the Fighting to McGuigan: The Official Biography of Barry McGuigan* Viking 1985. A biography of the former boxing world champion. See also Frank Mulligan *Me and McGuigan: The Making of a Champion* R&S Printers 1986.

**8627**  Jeff Clew *Sammy Miller: The Will to Win* Haynes 1976. A biography of the trials motorcycle rider.

### (4) Housing

**8628**  *Northern Ireland Housing Statistics* HMSO 1979–. An annual statistical guide, which was formerly published as *Digest of Housing Statistics for Northern Ireland* and before that as *Housing Return for Northern Ireland.*

**8629**  Tom B Hadden and W David Trimble *Housing Law in Northern Ireland* SLS Legal Publications 1984. A legal textbook guide to the law, institutions and regulation of Northern Ireland housing and housing policy.

**8630**  W Derek Birrell, P A R Hillyard, Alan Murie and D J D Roche *Housing in Northern Ireland* Centre for Environmental Studies 1971. A general study. J L Russell *Housing Amidst Civil Unrest* Centre for Environ-

mental Studies 1980 is an analysis of the impact of the 'Troubles' on housing in Northern Ireland and of attempts to use housing policy to alleviate sectarianism. The impact of housing policy on the spatial distribution of the Protestant and Catholic communities is examined in M C Keane 'Ethnic Residential Change in Belfast 1969–1977: The Impact of Public Housing Policy in a Plural Society' Queen's University, Belfast PhD Thesis 1986.

**8631**  M C Fleming and J G Nellis 'The Inflation of House Prices in Northern Ireland in the 1970s' *Economic and Social Review* 13 1981 pp 1–19.

## J. EDUCATION

**8632**  *Northern Ireland Education Statistics* 2v, HMSO 1965–. An annual statistical guide to schools, further and higher education in Northern Ireland.

**8633**  Margaret B Sutherland 'Progress and Problems in Education in Northern Ireland 1952–1982' *British Journal of Educational Studies* 30 1982 pp 136–49. See also J E Holmes 'Public Opinion and Educational Reform in the North of Ireland 1900–54' Queen's University, Belfast MA Thesis 1968–9 and S B G Lau 'The Economics of Education in Northern Ireland from 1959/60–1968/69' Queen's University, Belfast MSc Thesis 1972–3.

**8634**  Donald Akenson *Education and Enmity: The Control of Schooling in Northern Ireland 1920–1950* David and Charles 1973. A study of the persistence of segregated schooling, which is blamed on extremists on both sides who have resisted attempts to create a non-denominational schools system.

**8635**  T P Donaghy 'A Study of the Secondary School System in Northern Ireland 1947–1969, with Particular Reference to Developments of a Quasi-Comprehensive Nature' Queen's University, Belfast MA Thesis 1969–70.

**8636**  W R Spence 'The Growth and Development of the Secondary Intermediate School in Northern Ireland Since the Education Act of 1947' Queen's University, Belfast MA Thesis 1958–9.

**8637**  T W Moody and J C Beckett *Queen's Belfast 1845–1959: The History of a University* 2v, Faber 1959. A history of the oldest university in the Province.

**8638**  Norman McNeilly *Exactly Fifty Years: The Belfast Education Authority and its Work 1923–1973* Blackstaff 1974.

## K. CULTURAL HISTORY

**8639**  John Hewitt and M Catto *Art in Ulster: Paintings, Drawings, Prints and Sculpture for the Last 400 Years to 1957* 2v, Blackstaff 1977. A historical survey of the visual arts in Northern Ireland, incorporating potted biographies of artists. Visual art in the Province since the partition of Ireland and the extent to which it reflects the political and social conditions in which it is created is examined in M Catto 'Making Sense of Ulster' *Art and Artists* 14 1980 pp 8–13.

**8640**  Blake Morrison *Seamus Heaney* Methuen 1982. A short study of the poet's life and work. Neil Corcoran *Seamus Heaney* Faber 1986 is an account of the poet's life and a literary criticism of his work.

## L. LOCAL HISTORY

**8641**  Michael Connolly (ed) 'Local Government in Northern Ireland' *Local Government Studies* 12 1986 pp 13–60. A collection of papers on central/local relations, the effect of the political environment on local government, the legal protests of unionist councils and councillors against the rise of Sinn Fein in local government and against the Anglo-Irish Agreement and conflicts over such issues as leisure provision. On local government in Northern Ireland see also W Derek Birrell *Local Government Councillors in Northern Ireland* Centre for the Study of Public Policy 83, University of Strathclyde 1981.

**8642**  Brendan Sharkie *Antrim 1971–1982* B R Sharkie 1984. A classified bibliography of publications relating to County Antrim to have appeared in this period.

**8643**  E Estyn Evans *et al* (eds) *Belfast in its Regional Setting: A Scientific Study* Belfast Local Executive Committee for the British Association for the Advancement of Science 1952. A useful collection of essays on the local climate, agriculture, industry, land use, demographic trends, education and social services. Emrys Jones *A Social Geography of Belfast* Oxford University Press 1960 is a useful study which illuminates the geographically discrete nature of the sectarian communities in Belfast. Social life and living conditions in the heavily Protestant Shankill Road area of Belfast are examined in Paul Hamilton *Up the Shankhill* Blackstaff 1979.

**8644**  Pender Livingstone *The Fermanagh Story* Cumuan Seanchas Chlochair, St Michael's College 1969. A general history of Fermanagh. It is particularly useful on the IRA's border raids across into Fermanagh in the 1950s.

# AUTHOR INDEX

Baron Stanley Wade 286
Barooah D P 1276
Barr Brian 8141
Barr Charles 7388, 7405
Barr J 5086
Barr Keith 6658
Barraclough F 6379
Barratt Sir C 7600
Barrett Anthony 2419
Barrett Donald L 2462
Barrett F A 1798
Barrett J A 4428
Barrett Michael 3775
Barrich J 5028
Barrier Norman Gerald 1204
Barrington Donal 8574
Barrington Jonah 5942
Barrington Ken 5844
Barrington R C 6264
Barritt Denis P 8441
Barron Hugh 8407
Barrow Kenneth 7490
Barrows B M 5470
Barry E Eldon 3101
Barry Frank Russell 2714, 2728
Barry Sir Gerald 3283
Barry John 6072–6073
Barry Michael 6606
Barry Norman P 905
Barry Sir P K 6314
Barry Sir P R 6334
Bartholomew B J 546
Bartlett Christopher J 176, 1944, 2181
Bartlett Percy 2837
Bartlett Vernon 1336, 3639
Bartley Jeff 7635
Barton Bob 5856
Barton L 6530
Barton R W 8529
Barton T C 4758
Bartram Peter 883
Bartrip P W J 4844
Barty-King Hugh 433, 3238, 3491, 3532, 3841,
   3905, 3930, 4083, 4283, 5122, 5510, 6605
Barwick Sandra 3319
Barzilay David 8547, 8550
Baseley G 7380
Bass Elven E 7253
Bass Howard 4442
Bassett D K 1323
Bassett David K 6778
Bassett K A 6081, 6087, 6127
Bassett Keith 2959
Bassett P 7579
Bassett Philip 4544
Bassett Philippa 5003
Batchelor Mary 2832
Bates Herbert Ernest 7209
Bates John H 4997
Bates Julian Darrell 1182, 1618

Bates R W 4047
Bates Robert H 2459
Bather Leslie 319
Batkin A 2992
Batley Richard 5134, 5136, 6485
Batstone Eric 4535, 4554, 4586, 4641, 7734
Battersby Jean 7454
Bauer Carlos Garcia 1806
Baugh G C 7684
Baughan P E 4366
Baumhogger Goswin 1722
Bax A 106
Baxter C B 2790
Baxter Christine 7316
Baxter David 2247
Baxter J L 4855
Baxter John 7429
Baxter R J 7704
Bayley S 3270
Baylis John 2179, 2184, 2196, 2207, 2214
Bayliss B T 4316
Bayliss F J 4829
Bayliss-Smith T P 1887
Bayne Nicholas 2007
Baynes John 2310
Baynes Kate 3281, 3300, 4187
Beachey Veronica 5587
Beadle G C 3776
Beadle Gordon B 7275
Bealey Frank 914, 982, 4775, 7706, 8405
Bealey M E 3079
Beamish D R 499
Bean J M W 803, 989
Bean P 5296
Bean Philip 6012, 6014
Bean R 4601, 4750
Beard Geoffrey 4953
Beard M K 2831
Beardwell I J 4615
Bearman S 7337
Bearshaw Brian 5832
Beasant John 1893
Beasley J C 4189
Beaton Cecil 6967
Beaton Danny 3005
Beaton Leonard 2185
Beattie Alan 552
Beattie Geoffrey 7784
Beaufré André 2413
Beaumont Bill 5876
Beaumont Joan 2044
Beaumont P B 4701, 4828, 4848, 4912, 8211
Beaumont Roger 2236
Beaver Sir Hugh 4986
Beaver Patrick 3928, 3971, 3975
Bebbington A C 5412
Bebbington David W 549, 2619, 8081
Beber Colin 7971
Bechofer Frank 5540
Beck Ann 1568

de Crespigny Anthony  903
De Gaulle Charles  2139
De Graft Johnson E V C  1652
de Jouvenal Bertrand  293
de la Noy Michael  282
De La Rue P E G  6256
De Manio Jack  3781
de Moubray Guy  4064
De Mowbray Jocelyn  5892
de Sailly Jean  3023
de Smith Stanley  2532
de Sousa E  5666
de Valois Ninette  7072, 7075
De Vitis A A  7218
De Witt John  5724
De'Ath Wilfrid  691
Deacon Alan  5356, 5372
Deacon Richard  2353, 2357, 6575
Deakin D  5129
Deakin Nicholas  269, 1013, 1020, 1026, 5134, 5136,
  5145, 5244, 5254, 5293, 5626, 7606
Deakin Stephen  5244, 5679
Dean A J H  4826
Dean Andrew  3182
Dean Basil  7418
Dean C G T  2310
Dean D W  5252, 6384
Dean R J  7899
Deane Herbert Andrew  930
Deane Marjorie  3816
Deane Phyllis  2942
Deane-Drummond A J  2470
Dear Geoffrey  6229
Dearden Ann  1487
Dearden R F  6378
Dearlove John  267, 7571, 7646
Debenham F  1744
Debrapriya Ghosh  6145
Dee B D  1423
Deegan H M  1432
Deem Rosemary  6402
Deerin James B  8548
Dei-Anang Michael  1648
Deighton Anne  2029, 2097
Deitrich Richard F  7319
Dekel Efraim  2443
Dekker George  7229
Delafons J  395
Delamont Sara  6556
DeLancey Mark W  1630, 1698
Delderfield Ronald Frederick  7373
Delf George  1576
Dell Edmund  374, 3078
Dell S  6315
Dellar Geoffrey  681
Demant Jeffrey  7971
Dempster D D  3469
Dench Geoff  5762
Deng Francis M  1418
Denham D R  5074

Denis A B  6620
Denison G M  3632
Denison William Neil  1616
Denness Mike  5844
Dennett Laurie  2562, 4115
Denning Lord  288, 2569, 2599
Dennis I  2595
Dennis Norman  916, 5057, 6086, 7732
Dennis Peter  1186
Dennis Richard  5188
Dennis Robert  4923
Dennison S R  3114
Dennison W F  6452
Denny Barbara  2693
Dent Alan  7471
Dent Harold Collett  6373, 6381, 6384, 6476, 6607
Denver David T  597, 968, 1037, 8020, 8035, 8401
Deosaran Ramesh  1844
Derber M  4665
Derbyshire Ian  258
Derbyshire J Denis  258, 4553
Derdak Thomas  3194
Derrick Deborah  5997
Derrick E F  6087
Derrington Arnold P  6393
Derry John  6722
Desai R  5722
Deutsch Richard R  8426, 8428, 8556
Deutsch S J  425
Deutscher Tamara  6723
Devereux William A  6647
Devine P J  5563
Devlin Bernadette  8470
Devlin Lord  4401
Devlin Patrick  2559
Devon Stanley  3654
Devons E  2895
Devons Ely  4823
Dewar M  2436
Dewar Michael  8547
Dewdney John C  7751
Dewer M W  8525
Dewitt David B  1900
DeWitt Howard A  7117
Dexter Edward  5844
Deyong Moss  5929
Di Roma Edward  133
Diamond John  2998
Diamond Lord  5555
Dick Bernard F  7245
Dick Kay  7224
Dicken P  3215
Dickens Linda  4556, 4565, 4785
Dickens Peter  2481
Dickey A F  5684
Dickie John  827
Dickinson D M  7399
Dickinson G C  5086
Dickinson Leo  5923
Dickinson M  4675

Gold Margaret R 8200
Goldberg Alfred 2220
Golden James R 2211
Goldenberg Susan 3599
Goldfarb A 4606
Goldie Grace Wyndham 3747
Golding J 4775
Golding Lewis 7542
Golding Peter 3535, 3575
Goldman A R 7708
Goldman Sir Samuel 2998
Goldsmith John 7294
Goldsmith M 3123, 7621
Goldsmith Maurice 6800
Goldstein Joseph 4781
Goldstein-Jackson K 2559
Goldston Robin S 282
Goldsworthy David 485, 1122, 1596
Goldthorpe J H 5540, 5548
Golesworthy Maurice 5854
Gollan J 639
Gollan John 263
Gollancz Victor 2094, 3864
Golland R 6211
Golley John 3475
Gonje Suzanne 1688
Gooch G P 6730
Gooch Graham 5844
Gooch John 2180, 2201
Good R G 1952
Good Robert 1720
Goodair Christine M 81
Goodall Brian 4433
Goodall Francis 3202
Goodchild B 6065
Goodchild R 3526
Gooden Susanna 4199
Goodenough S 5595
Goodger B C 5940
Goodhart Charles 2946, 3009, 4060
Goodhart David 3620
Goodhart Philip 620, 971, 1071, 2461
Goodin R E 5303
Goodlad J S R 7324
Goodman Albert 7117
Goodman F B 4552
Goodman Geoffrey 4626, 4789
Goodman J 3368
Goodman J F B 4584, 4601
Goodman Jean 6940, 6942
Goodman Jonathan 6181, 6184
Goodman Michael J 4565
Goodman Nancy 6199
Goodman Neville 444
Goodrich P S 2116
Goodwin A J 7378
Goodwin C D W 1137
Goodwin Geoffrey Lawrence 2000
Goodwin H J 3295
Goodwin John 7334, 7336

Goodwin Nöel 8375
Goodwin P A T 6092
Goodwin Tim 7336
Goodwin Trevor W 6845
Goold-Adams Richard 2067
Goonetilleke L P 2019
Goorney Howard 7341
Gopal Ram 1229
Gopal Sarvepalli 1240, 1240
Gordon Alan 4863
Gordon Andrew 2256
Gordon Anne Wolridge 2626
Gordon B 4052
Gordon Colin 2210
Gordon D F 1570
Gordon D J 4366
Gordon David F 1575
Gordon Esmé 8370
Gordon G H 8044
Gordon Garnet H 1799
Gordon George 5093, 7993, 8242, 8423
Gordon Sir Home Seton Charles Montagu 5838
Gordon Ian 7635
Gordon J C 8028
Gordon Lyndall 7238
Gordon M C 6588
Gordon M R 1948
Gordon P 2582, 5251
Gordon Paul 3562, 5610, 5669, 5691–5692, 6227, 8315
Gordon Peter 6370–6372, 6377–6378, 6441, 6479–6480, 6716
Gordon Strathearn 466
Gordon T Crouther 8407
Gordon-Brown A D 6257
Gore-Booth Paul 1976
Gore-Brown P 1949
Gorer Geoffrey 5192, 5200, 5270
Gorham M 3724
Goritsas C 408
Gormly James L 2221
Gormley Joe 4793
Gorny Joseph 1432
Gorst Anthony 2188, 2207, 2398
Gosden Peter 6372, 6415, 6450, 6580
Goslin R J 6270
Gosnell Harold F 2072
Goss Anthony 3142
Goss Sue 7648
Gossip Andrew 5533
Gott Richard 2220
Gottfried Heidi 3504
Gotthold Donald W 1306
Gotthold Julia J 1306
Gottlieb Vera 7327
Gottschalk A W 4525
Gottschalk H 6693
Gough C L 4931
Gough Jamie 5977
Gough-Yates Kevin 7425

729

Marks John 6630
Marks P 4926
Marks S 6627
Markwell Donald J 1864
Marland Simon 5862
Marlowe John 1392, 1406, 1431, 1507
Marmor Theodore R 4646
Marmot M G 5221
Marnham Patrick 3614
Marowitz Charles 7323
Marples Morris 5849
Marquand David 269, 931, 1072
Marquis Frederick J 874
Marriott Oliver 3493
Marriott Stuart 6638
Marsack C C 1895
Marsden David 4655
Marsden J J 7932
Marsden K A 3942
Marsden Philip 514
Marsden W E 220
Marsh Arthur 4520, 4526, 4664, 4690, 4707, 4720
Marsh David 493, 1055, 3081, 3235, 3815, 4175,
    4704, 5185, 5293, 5298, 5971
Marsh Marcus 5903
Marsh Norman S 332
Marsh P 6231
Marsh Q R H 664
Marsh Sir Richard 737, 3074
Marsh Terry 4968
Marshall Arthur 6523
Marshall Barbara 2089–2090
Marshall David 1372
Marshall E A 8041
Marshall Elizabeth 8165
Marshall G P 2998, 3005
Marshall Geoffrey 319, 389, 6255
Marshall Gordon 5530
Marshall J D B 8042
Marshall J N 2909
Marshall John D 7679
Marshall John Norman 5838
Marshall Percy 5861, 7064
Marshall S L A 2388
Marshall T H 5298
Marshall Tilly 6938
Marshall W A L 4959
Marshallsay Diana 131
Marshment M A 7184
Martell Edward 3610
Marten Neil 1834
Martin A F 7781
Martin Ann 5931
Martin Colin 599
Martin D H 3469
Martin David 1721, 2613, 2648, 6627
Martin Derek 3498
Martin Dick 599
Martin E W 7780
Martin Edwin W 2156

Martin F 4142
Martin F M 5492, 8048
Martin Fenton S 466
Martin Geoffrey Howard 7540
Martin George 3897
Martin George M Thomson 3851
Martin J E 2956
Martin J P 6242, 6347, 6352
Martin J Purdon 6875
Martin John 4240, 5472, 5778
Martin Kingsley 212, 344, 728, 3682
Martin L W 2181, 2185
Martin M 6099
Martin Nancy 3899, 4384
Martin Pierre-Marie 8576
Martin Roderick 3583, 4672
Martin Ron 2937
Martin Ross M 4716
Martin T A 2310
Martin Werner 6693
Martin-Jenkins Christopher 5827
Marwick Arthur John Brereton 174, 5183, 5302,
    5545, 6622, 7394
Marwick W H 8206
Marx Roland 180, 5191
Masefield G B 2017
Maser Werner 2088
Masheter Martin 7462, 7477
Masheter Philip 7462, 7477
Maskell Eric 3632
Mason C M 3083, 5152, 7785
Mason Frank K 3473
Mason James 7474
Mason Keith 3683, 4511
Mason M A 7971
Mason Martin W 1720
Mason Michael 1324
Mason Oliver 150
Mason P C 7329
Mason Philip 1704
Mason R A 2426, 2439
Mason Ronald 5844
Mason Roy 2193
Mason Stan 4056
Mason Stewart C 6447
Mason Tim 5642
Mason Tony 5804, 7746
Mason Ursula Stuart 2276
Massareene and Ferrard Viscount 498
Massey A 4035
Massey Doreen 2906, 3488, 4863
Massey Sir Harrie 3138
Massey K A 6908
Massey R D 2840
Massie Allan 8289, 8388
Masterman Sir J C 410
Masters Brian 187
Matatko John 4102
Mather A R 2638
Mather Alexander S 8407

Neasom Mike 5861
Neate Jill 5921
Neate Simon 5168
Neave Airey 2088
Needham Leslie William 3692
Needleman L 3142
Neeld P 3415
Neeson J M 4514
Neff Donald 2401
Neff Terry Ann 6954
Negrine Ralph 3543, 3566, 3732
Neil McEwan 7179
Neill J D H 1341
Neill S 2661
Neillands Robin 2302
Neilson June 2121
Nellis J 6044
Nellis J G 3017, 6129, 8631
Nelson Elizabeth 6003
Nelson G K 2864
Nelson Paul 8377
Nelson Sarah 8459, 8524
Nemenzo F 1292
Netherton D E 2708
Nettleford Rex 1828
Netton Ian Richard 1389
Neu John 6784
Neufeld W J 5453
Neuss R F 2683
Neustadt Richard E 2057
Neustatter Angela 5598
Neve Brian 971
Nevett Terry R 3908
Nevile Sir Sydney Oswald 3943
Nevill P B 6001
Neville Robert G 3990, 4768, 7888
Nevin Edward 4101, 7881
Nevin Michael 183, 2988
Nevitt A A 6088
Nevitt Adela Adam 8297
New William H 7264
Newbery R G 3293
Newbigin Lesslie 2668
Newby Eric 3310
Newby Howard 5170, 5530
Newcombe R 6023
Newell David 4518
Newell Roy Norman 2817
Newlands David 4824
Newman Aubrey 2866–2867
Newman B R 2293
Newman Barbara 7086
Newman Bernard 4746
Newman C F S 8607
Newman D 5739
Newman George 4758
Newman I 5147
Newman John Robert 4759
Newman Karin 3904
Newman M 6647

Newman Michael 768
Newman R J 7624
Newsam Sir Frank 423
Newson Elizabeth 6000
Newson John 6000
Newson Sir John 6434
Newson M D 4972
Newson Tony 6036, 6039
Newton Gary 5894
Newton John Anthony 2825
Newton Kenneth 641, 7587, 7607, 7652, 7693
Newton R F 2675
Newton Scott 2060, 2107, 2928, 3026–3028
Newton-Norton Seraphim 2845
Ng Kwee Choo 5746
Ng Ting Fun 1386
Niall Ian 4464
Nicholas H G 2053
Nicholas Herbert G 992
Nicholls C S 107
Nicholls D 2686
Nicholson B 4401
Nicholson Bill 5861
Nicholson David 787
Nicholson J H B 6244
Nicholson Mary 6458
Nicholson Max 193
Nicholson Nigel 674, 4644
Nicholson R J 4286
Nickell Stephen 4508, 4851, 4902
Nicol Andrew G L 3541
Nicol Jean 3693
Nicoll Jane Vere 5931
Nicolson I F 287, 1661
Nicolson James R 8165
Nicolson Nigel 674, 785, 848, 4644, 7285
Nicolson R J 3211
Nicolson Robert 1894
Nield Robert 398
Nielsen Jorgen 2869
Nijjar Bakhshish S 1199
Nilsson R 3356
Niner Pat 6071, 6089
Nish Ian 2157, 2168
Nissel Muriel 421
Niven Alastair 1154
Niven C R 1666
Niven David 7482
Niven Douglas 8298
Niven M M 4566
Niven Sir Rex 1676
Nivet H 8416
Nixon J 534
Nixon N 534
Nixon St J C 3448
Njama Karari 2462
Nkomo Joshua 1729
Nkrumah Kwame 1659
Noakes Bob 3767
Nobay A R 2902

Nobes Christopher 3038
Noble D J 6078
Noble P 5498
Noble R W 7220
Noble Sheila 5407
Noble T 204, 5183
Noble Trevor 4835
Noble W C 6861
Nock Oswald Stevens 4352, 4356, 4820
Nockolds Harold 3437
Noel Gerard Eyre 302
Noor H S 1252
Nordlinger Eric A 982
Nordman C R 1638
Norkett Paul 3192
Norman Dorothy 1240
Norman Edward 2610, 2648
Norman Peter 6086
Norman Philip 3811, 7117, 7133
Norpoth Helmut 1055
Norrie Ian 3821
Norrington Arthur L P 3824
Norris Christopher 7275
Norris Geoff 8266
Norris Pippa 976, 1066
Norris W 105
North D 3148
North Rex 4432
North Richard 5011
Northam Garry 6213
Northcott Jim 3262, 3266
Northcott P 6586
Northedge Frederick Samuel 1944, 2039, 2185
Northfield Lord 499
Northouse Cameron 7066, 7363
Norton Alan 7589
Norton Augustus 2210
Norton G G 2305
Norton Nichael 6036
Norton Philip 267, 327, 474, 479, 493, 506–507, 512, 538–539, 610, 615, 5256, 6166
Norton-Taylor Richard 331, 411
Nossiter Bernard 199
Nott John 2197
Nott-Bower Sir Guy 3997
Nottage Raymond 6771
Nottingham John 2456
Nowell Denis 293
Nowell-Smith Simon 3829, 3846
Noyce John Leonard 3593
Noyce Wilfrid 5982
Nugent Neill 611, 667, 1081, 7595
Nulty Geoffrey 3625
Nunn G W A 162
Nunnerley David 2063
Nurcombe Valerie J 125
Nuttall M W 4734
Nutting Sir Harold Anthony 1397, 2111, 2400, 2488
Nwanwane Omorogbe 1669
Nyagah S 1569

Nye Doug 3431, 5913
Nyeko Balam 1770, 1772
Nyerere Julius K 1624
O'Ballance Edgar 2446
O'Brien Dennis Patrick 6708
O'Brien J 977
O'Brien John 8572
O'Brien Lord 4487
O'Brien Lucy 7137
O'Brien Oswald 6485
O'Brien Sir Richard 2646
O'Brien Richard 8062
O'Brien S 5222
O'Callaghan Sean 6013, 8526
O'Cleary Conor 8577
O'Connor Alan 6759
O'Connor Garry 7062, 7483, 7487
O'Connor Kevin 5749
O'Connor Terry 5920
O'Day Alan 8503
O'Dell A C 8111
O'Doherty Eamonn 8526
O'Donnell D-M 4004
O'Donovan John 7367
O'Donovan K 5585
O'Dowd Liam 8446, 8449, 8587
O'Doyle Michael 8576
O'Farrell Patrick 8570
O'Flinn Paul 7275
O'Gorman Frank 933
O'Hear Anthony 904
O'Herlihy C St J 6145
O'Higgins P 4513, 4731, 8558
O'Higgins Paul 3542, 4514, 5355
O'Keefe D J 6385
O'Leary Brendan 7634, 8575
O'Leary C 503
O'Leary Cornelius 8491, 8508
O'Malley J 5070
O'Malley P 8445
O'Maolian Ciaran 660
O'Neill Michael P 1138–1139
O'Neill Robert 1863
O'Neill Terence 8464
O'Neill Thomas P 8578
O'Prey Paul 7246
O'Riordan Timothy 4042
O'Sullivan P Michael 8532
O'Sullivan Sue 5599
O'Sullivan Timothy 7887
Oakeley Sir Atholl 5946
Oakes P 7527
Oakeshott J J 4870
Oakeshott Michael 906
Oakey Robin 3263
Oakley Ann 5589, 5608
Oakley C A 8119
Oakley Charles 7388
Oakley P A 4679
Oakley R E 5760

# SUBJECT INDEX

Mortimer John 7271
Morton A L 6732
Morton Sundour Fabrics 3311
Moscow 1968, 1980
Mosley Diana 899
Mosley Sir Oswald 237, 661–662, 899
Moss Bros 3312
Moss Pat 5913
Moss Side 5405, 5695, 6222
Moss Side riots 1981 6222
Moss Stirling 226, 5911, 5913
Mothers Union 2704
Motherwell 8124
motor car 4267, 4283, 4296
motor industry 2924, 3080, 3103, 3206, 3404–3449,
    4589, 4655–4659, 8589
motorsport 5904–5913, 8627
motorways 4283, 4288–4293, 5157
Mott Sir Nevill 6810
Mott-Radclyffe Sir Charles 846
mountaineering 5921–5923, 5982
Mountbatten of Burma Earl 233, 1186, 1211, 1236,
    1256, 1258, 1262, 1288, 2285, 2321, 8533
mourning 5200
Movement for Colonial Freedom 1706
Movement the 7175, 7244
Mugabe Robert 1722, 1728
Muggeridge Malcolm 222, 225, 230, 236, 3615, 3690
mugging 6190
Muir Edwin 8387
Muldowney Dominic 7031
Mullany Tommy 4799
multinational companies 3080, 3215, 3409, 4546,
    4713, 8116–8117, 8164
Munich air disaster 1958 5861
Municipal Mutual Insurance Ltd 4149
Munnings Sir Alfred 6940
murder 6173–6178
Murdoch Iris 675, 7272
Murdoch Peter 3956
Murdoch Rupert 3562, 3585, 3617, 3691
Murray Gilbert 6774
Murray William Staite 7006
Murrill Herbert 7027
Murry John Middleton 7273
Museum of London 6679
museums 6649, 6679, 6880, 7947, 8410
Musgrave Thea 7029–7030
music 2675–2678, 2709, 5709, 7012–7165,
    7950–7951, 8375–8377
music hall 7502–7504, 7506–7507, 7509, 7511,
    7513–7516
music teaching 6471, 6547
musicals 7372–7375
Musicians' Union 7018
Muslim League 1233
Muslims 6438, 6465
Mussaddiq Muhammed 1522
Mutesa Sir Edward 1608
mutiny 1253
Myer's 3959

Nabarro Sir Gerald 847
Naipaul V S 7181
Nairnshire 8407
Namier Lewis 1454, 6733
Nankeville Bill 5920
Napiorkowska Denka 7003
Nash E J N 2742
Nassau agreement 1962 2225
Nasser Gamel Abdel 1414, 1414
Nathan Lord 746
National and Grindlay's Bank 4120
National Art-Collections Fund 6909
National Assistance Board 5296
National Association of Colliery Overmen, Deputies
    and Shotfirers 4757
National Association of Journalists 3573
National Association of Local Goverment Officers
    4758
National Association of Operative Plasterers 4759
National Association of Probation Officers 6346
National Association of Schoolmasters 4760
National Audit Act 1983 3005
National Board for Prices and Incomes 833
National Book League 3821
National British Women's Total Abstinence Union
    6031
National Co-operative Development Agency 4613
National Coal Board 673, 3989, 3992, 3994, 3997,
    3999, 4628, 4633, 7908
National Council for Civil Liberties 340
National Council for One-Parent Families 5342
National Council for Technical Awards 6594
National Council of Labour Colleges 6639
National Council of Social Service 5333
National Council of Women of Great Britain 5592
National Democratic Party 8469
National Economic Development Office 447, 452,
    3061
National Education Association 6393
National Enterprise Board 3082
National Farmers' Union 2113, 4452–4453, 4467,
    4486
National Federation of Business and Professional
    Women 5593, 5604
National Federation of Young Farmers' Clubs 4468
National Freight Corporation 4316, 4318
National Front 662, 664, 984, 1036, 5627, 5644,
    6216, 6220, 7115
National Girobank 4102, 4121
National Graphical Association 4675
National Health Service 824, 4585, 4645–4650,
    4749, 5295, 5423, 5516, 8211, 8259–8260, 8618
National Housewives League 6326
National Housewives' Register 5594
National Hunt racing 5894
National Incomes Commission 3181
National Industrial Relations Court 4556
national insurance 5361
National Insurance Commission 5361
National Land Fund 5024
National Museum of Wales 7947